T0365736

5 Dictionaries in 1

5 in 1

No it easy

The bee's knees

Global

Double Native speaker's

Advanced materials for speaking

Extraordinarily

Part A

English

Chinese Cantonese

Dictionary

英粵辭典

Two formulas

○ Multiple 3 options Romanized &
● Chinese Cantonese tones English
○ it makes 5 to 125 times faster

(40689 words & phrases, pages 1096)

Words & Phrases
40689

Equivalent 5 dictionaries in one, such as:

(1) English Cantonese dictionary,

(2) English Cantonese dictionary (Yale Romanized American based),

(3) English Cantonese dictionary (Jyutping Romanized be used computer input method), it tones number and suitable for non-Chinese students of Hong Kong School as well as,

(4) English Cantonese (plain Romanized) and

(5) Cantonese tones English dictionary (first printed dictionary)

	ABBREVIATIONS 簡稱		gáan chīng	gaan2 cing1	kaan chheng
a/adj	adjective	形容詞	yìhng yùhng chìh	jing4 jung4 ci4	yehng yuhng chhih
abbr	abbreviation	簡稱	gáan chīng	gaan2 cing1	kaan chheng
adv	adverb	副詞	fu chìh	fu3 ci4	fu chhih
aux	auxiliary	輔助	fuh jòh	fu6 zo6	fuh choh
bt	British	英國	yìng gwók	jing4 gwok2	yeng kwok
Cant	Cantonese	粵語	yuht yúh	jyut6 jyu5	yuht yuh
coll¹	colloquial	慣用語	gwaan yuhng yúh	gwaan3 jung6 jyu5	kwaan yuhng yuh
coll²	real /native Cantonese	粵語獨有嘅話	yuht yúh duhk yáuhge wá	jyut6 jyu5 duk6 jau5 ge3 waa2	yuht yuh tuhk yauhke wa
conj	conjunction	連接	lìhn jip	ling4 zip3	lihn chip
de	direct English tone	英語拼音	yìng yúh peng yàm	jing4 jyu5 peng3 jam4	yeng yuh pheng yam
dw	dirty /foul /obscene words	粗言穢語	chòu yìhn wai yúh	cou4 jin4 wai3 jyu5	chhou yihn wai yuh
exlm	exclaimation	感嘆號!	gám taan houh	gam2 taan3 hou6	kam thaan houh
i /intr	intransitive	不及物	bāt kahp maht	bat1 kap6 mat6	pat khahp maht
IDM	idioms n/abbr	成語	sèhng yúh	seng4 jyu5	sehng sèhng yúh
int/interj	interjection	感嘆詞!	gám taan chìh	gam2 taan3 ci4	kam thaan chhih
n	noun	名詞	mèhng /mìhng chìh	meng4/ming4 ci4	mehng chhih
ph	phrases	短詞	dyún chìh	dyun2 ci4	tyun chyu
pre/pref	prefix	前綴	chìhn jeui	cin4 zeoi3	chhihn choi
prep	preposition	介系詞	gaai haih chìh	gaai3 hai6 ci4	kaai haih chhih
pron	pronoun	代名詞	doih mèhng chìh	doi6 meng4 ci4	toih mehng chhih
re	real /native english	英語獨有嘅話	yìng yúh duhk yáuhge wá	jing4 jyu5 duk6 jau5 ge3 waa2	yeng yuh tuhk yauhke wa
sl	slang informal	俗語	juhk yúh	zuk6 jyu5	chuhk yuh
text	text-writing/text-book	教科書	gaau fō syù	gaau3 fo1 syu4	kaau fo syu
us	America	美國	Méih gwok	mei5 gwok3	Meih Kwok
v	verb	動詞	duhng chìh	dung6 ci4	tuhng chhih
vdw	very dirty words / obscene language **(to be able to recognize ...)**	粗言穢語	chòu yìhn wai yúh	cou4 jin4 wai3 jyu5	chhou yihn wai yuh
vi	verb-intransitive	不及物動詞	bāt kahp maht duhng chìh	bat1 kap6 mat6 dung6 ci4	pat khahp maht tuhng chih
vt	verb-transitive	及物動詞	kahp maht duhngchìh	kap6 mat6 dung6ci4	khahp maht tohng chhih
wr	written/writing	書寫	syù sē	syu4 se1	syu se

5 in 1

No 1 Easy

The bee's knees
Global
Double Native speaker's
Advanced materials for speaking

Extraordinarily

Part A

English
Chinese Cantonese
Dictionary

英粵辭典

Two formulas

*Special addition
advanced Chinese
English Chinese
versions*

- Multiple 3 options Romanized &
- Chinese Cantonese tones English
- it makes 5 to 125 times faster

(40689 words & phrases, pages 1096)

Compiled by, UP Numlake

 www.traffordpublishing.com.sg

Singapore
toll-free: 800 101 2656 (Singapore)
Fax: 800 101 2656 (Singapore)

Preface

This dictionary book is effortless and unique, advanced materials based on self access for double speakers designed titled: **"Global Double Native Speaker's (part A) English Chinese Cantonese Dictionary,** yet it's larger English Cantonese dictionary readable Chinese characters by English *(non-Chinese)* speakers, to lookup met the needs of learners for essentially real colloquially English Cantonese various words and phrases used in the native real spoken languages, **and (part B) Chinese Cantonese tones English Dictionary"** Both English or Cantonese readers will get unexpected easy, even who have nothing either English or Cantonese, to lookup the English headwords and phrases through Cantonese tones, it is contained the large number of native speakers used in English and Chinese naturally daily real-speaking materials, It provides lot of more common words, phrases, idioms, slangs, colloquials, synonyms, definitions, direct English tone words, shorter sentences or phrases words as well as part of speech, the readers able to recognize over **40689** words and phrases including total **1096** pages. You will get along with comparative multiple **3 options** romanized systems all over the book based on six tones pronunciations in Cantonese. The most all-inclusive solution available here. yet so much incredible benefits, it is super powerful methods in over a century. *This new dictionary, a product of over eighteen years labored with researchers of new methods.*

I created the aim of this larger dictionary is to help learn affortless real native English or Chinese Cantonese languages together at the same time by both native speakers. If lot of time spent year or decades with Cantonese book or might have taken class that but didn't helped to real speak well. It will be great chance to teach yourself as their second language for all levels, it is to familiarizes with the use of basic to advance native words and phrases, to speak quickly, easily, automatically and better grammar through phrases.

I remain gratefully acknowledge for the help which I have received for compiling this dictionary from the volumes and also Chinese Cantonese native real spoken language of the Hong Kong et cetera.

Of course, I have deliberately taken much more prevent over my achievement, however, I believe that is a lot of potential for improvement on it, i hope that with the help of my knowledgeable users, I can make lot of new improvement in the quality of this volume.

Finally!, I would like to thank my wife Laxmi Maya Limbu & son Dilli for her/his understanding, patience, support and encouraging me to finish this book.

Have a wonderful studies!!!

UP Numlake

Introductions:

01) Achievements (**first two unique methods**)
   i)   **3 options Romanized**,
   ii) **Cantonese tones English,**
02) User's guidelines,
03) Native speakers speaks,
04) Shorter sentences or phrases,
05) Cantonese language,
06) Chinese characters,
07) Cantonese Romanized and their six tones,
08) Doubts romanizes in Cantonese,
09) Comparative chart; different tone same characters different meaning,
10) Comparative chart; same tones different characters different meaning,
11) Part A, Sample words and phrases ,
12) Part B, Sample Cantonese tones English,
13) Comparatived of initials romanized chart,
14) Compared with **Y**ale / **J**yutping and **R**oman,
15) Contents, and **Initials** (consonants)
16) **Appendix**, available only '**part B**'
   i) Numbers,
   ii) Drill in Cantonese 1 to 6 tones
   iii) Easy effortless grammar,
   iv) Useful phrases and greetings,

* Special unique features,

1, Multiple 3 options romanized systems (one instead of from the others)
2, Lookup English words & phrases through Chinese Cantonese tones,
3, Both non-Chinese and Chinese readers can similarly be benefited,
4, Larger English Cantonese dictionary readable Chinese characters by non-
   Chinese (English) speakers,
5, Equivalent **5 dictionaries** in one, such as **(i)** English Cantonese dictionary
   (ii) English Cantonese dictionary (Yale romanized) **(iii)** English Cantonese
   dictionary (Jyutping romanized) **(iv)** English Cantonese (plain romanized)
   & **(v)** Cantonese tones English dictionary (it is first printed dictionary book)

*Lookup instantly;

words phrases, colloquials, definitions, direct English tones, grammar (effortless),
greetings, idioms (common), part of speech, shorter sentences, slangs, synonyms, sex &
obscene words (to be able to recognizing)

01) Achievements (**first two unique methods**)

I have created the advanced affortless learning new two methods, these are unique super powerful features of this dictionary, it's called.

i) **3 options Romanized**,
'it makes **25** times faster to learn Cantonese for non-chinese native speakers'

ii) **Cantonese tones English**,
'it makes **125** times faster for both speakers to learn English or Cantonese'

- **i)** There are so many different kind of Romanized used in Cantonese language books, such as *(Yale/Jyutping/Sidney Lau/Meyer-wempe/Guang dond/Penk yamp/Yut yut etc),* among them used on it, as well as *(1)* **Yale** *(2)* **Jyutping** and *(3)* plain **Roman**, with optionally romanized, you have multiple 3 options based on six tones pronunciations in Cantonese with comparative tones, just select one instead of from the others multiple options romanized, as you feeling, more manageable, Than this will be helpful to find easy way, instantly able to reproduce self accurate right pronunciations without helps. These romanized broughts to you quick right tones. So, this feature will totally support your learning of Chinese Cantonese pronunciation greatly, it makes 25 times faster for the English speakers to speak and learn in Cantonese language.

Part B, **Cantonese tones English,**

- **ii)** Lookup English headwords via Cantonese tones:
Cantonese tones roman are listed in alphabetically tones order. Both speakers easily self access well, even who have nothing either English or Cantonese, to be able to lookup the English meanings, head-words or phrases via '**Cantonese tones English dictionary**', Let's imagine!, just similar to any of Cantonese tones, it doesn't matter what's meaning of these, as example tones, *mahng /meng /mihng /mohng /muhng /nan /ou /paai /saai /sai /sau /gau /se /tai /waai etc,* and users can also self-able to comparative analysis through 6 tones, it's makes different tone same character different meaning, same tone different characters different meaning. it's in a funnie and easier intelligent unique method.

02) User's guidelines:

English words are listed in alphabetically order. If same head words more than one, marked by small number on the right up side '1 /2 / 3' and similarly placed down side for the other words; and customary words up right side (coll) by bracket with small letters; synonyms words instantly placed on the right down side with small letters separated by slanting; there are also the part of speech is given, as well as difinitions of the different shades of meaning.

03) Native speakers speaks,

Native speakers use casual English or Chinese, that full of idioms, phrases, slang and colloquial to communicate with real native speakers, most of the languages are similarly ways, so you must not rely on text-book, you must learn casual English or Chinese speaking materials, if you are really want to learn second languages.

04) Shorter sentences or phrases,

The shorter or phrases sentences is more easily remembered and it makes easier for you, when you are speaking, Why is good to talk short *(phrases)* sentences? When you found very long sentences, they become complicated and you may find it a challenges to manage them use properly to talk, it makes much slower understand or speak slow because you do not have time to thinks about grammar rules, when you are speaking, but shorter sentences *(phrases)* are easier to remembered and quickly deal, also they are clear pictures and straight to points the meanings. When you study phrases, you are actually learning grammar too. You're getting free grammar, even though you might not know that.

05) Cantonese language,

Cantonese is spoken by at least 72 million people mainly in the south east of China, particularly in Hong Kong, Macau, Guangdong, Guangxi and Hainan. It is also spoken in London, America, Australia, Canada, Malaysia, Indonesia, Thailand, Singapore, Philippines, Nepal and among Overseas Chinese communities in many other countries as well.

06) Chinese characters,

It also gives you related Chinese characters *(called traditional big5)* along with all over the book. if you are interested in the Chinese characters best to look for book, it getting help to deeply advance studies, analysis of theirs tones, meaning or structure of characters and on the other hand, if you ever want to consult with a native speaker, you will needs the characters for quick deal, to progress listening practice or others manageable. You can instantly understand. There's no thinking. It just comes out easily. you will automatically improve grammar as well and speak fluent. Take advantages of this unique dictionary and get so many unimagined benefits.

07) Cantonese Romanized and their Six Tones:

Chinese is a tonal language; and Cantonese has even more tones than Mandarin. It is extremely important to use the correct tones in pronouncing each syllable. Cantonese romanizations systems are so many different kind of Romanized used in language books such as *(Yale/Jyutping/Sidney Lau/Meyer-wempe/Guang dond/Penk yamp/Yut yut etc),* but among them widely used **Yale** and **Jyutping**, **Yale** is **I**nternational **P**honetic **A**lphabet based on American English created by Yale University on 1943; **Jyutping** Cantonese based on tonal mark created by Linguistic Society of Hong Kong on 1993. It can also be used as a computer input method. Used **Yale/Jyutping** and plain **Roman** in this book, Jyutping is 6 tones pronunciation, such as;

the 1st tone is indicated by a horizontal tone mark; 1 / H.F/H.L.   (à /ā) high falling /high level1 (high flat)

the 2nd tone is indicated by a rising tone mark;   2 / M.R.   (á)   middle rising2

the 3rd tone does not carry a tone mark;   3 / M.L.   (a)   middle level3

the 4th tone is indicated by a falling tone mark along with the letter 'h' placed at the end of the vowel or group of vowels;   4 / L.L   (àh) low falling4

the 5th tone indicated by a rising tone mark along with the letter 'h' placed at the end of the vowel or group of vowels;   5 / L.R.   (áh) low rising 5

the 6th tone is indicated by the letter 'h' placed at the end of the vowel or group of vowels.   6 / L.L.   (ah) low level 6

If you get the pronunciation wrong from the beginning, it will be a lot harder to correct later.

08) Doubts romanized in Cantonese ;

There are also several systems of Romanization for Cantonese, it's difficult enough for learner to deal with that romanization systems for English Speakers. The most common being, **Yale**, **Jyutping**, and **Sydney Lau's** system in Hong Kong. The words same pronounced but used different books different Romanized systems. For example comparative romanized! (Yale[1] /Yale[2] /Jyutping and **R**oman) the sounds are exactly the same but Romanized are not the same.

English words	n	Chinese	Yale (i)	Yale (ii)	Jyutping	Roman
pig	n	豬	dzeu	jyù	zyu4	chyu
meat	n	肉	yook	yuhk	juk6	yuhk
money	n	錢	tsín	chín	cin2	chhin
thank	n	謝	dzè	jeh	ze6	cheh
six	n	六	look	luhk	luk6	luhk
seat		座	tsǒ	chóh	co5	chhoh
center	n	中	dzōōng	jùng	zung4	chung
seven	n	七	tsāt	chat /càt	cat1	chhat
long *thin items*	n	條	tiu	tìuh	tiu4	thiuh
orange	n	橙	tsaáng	cháang	caang2	chhaang
please	v	請	tséng	chéng /chíng	ceng2 /cing2	chheng
small thing	n	子	dzí	jí	zi2	chi
five	n	五	nǧ	ngh	ng5	nggh
meal	n	餐	tsāān	chāan	caan1	chhaan

09)

Comparative chart; **different tone same character different meaning,**

The characters exactly the same but romanized and meanings not the same.

CHINESE Trad B5		YALE US based	JYUTPING HK	ROMAN plain based	ENGLISH
長[1]	adj	chèuhng	coeng4	chheuhng	long /length
長[2]	n	jéung	zoeng2	cheung	head /chief
方[1]	n	fōng	fong1	fong	square
方[2]	n	fòng	fong4	fong	direction
行[1]	n	hàhng	hang4	hahng	behavior
行[2]	v	hàahng	haang4	haahng	walk
行[3]	n	hòhng	hong4	hohng	relating co
男[1]	v	nàahm	naam4	naahm	male /man
男[2]	v	làahm	laam4	laahm	male /man
女[1]	n	léuih	leoi5	lowih	girl/femal/woman /daughter
女[2]	n	néuih	neoi5	nowih	girl/femal/woman

10) Comparative chart; same tones different character different meaning,

YALE US based	JYUTPING HK	ROMAN plain based	CHINESE Trad B5		ENGLISH
cheung	coeng3	chheung	唱	v	sing
cheung	coeng3	chheung	暢	n	smoothly joyful
chyùhn	cyun4	chhyuhn	泉	n	spring fountain
chyùhn	cyun4	chhyuhn	存	v	store deposit
dím	dim2	tim	點	n	little /bit
dím	dim2	tim	店	n	shop /store/hotel
fan	fan3	fan	糞	n	stool shit
fan	fan3	fan	瞓	n	sleep
héi	hei2	hei	氣	v	anger
héi	hei2	hei	起	v	raise/rise/up/get up/build/ construct
héung	hoeng2	heung	享		benefit /enjoy
héung	hoeng2	heung	響		noise/make a noise
hòh	ho4	hoh	何		why? /how?
hòh	ho4	hoh	河	n	river, stream
hòh	ho4	hoh	荷	n	lotus
hòuh	hou4	houh	毫	n	cent/coin/unit
hòuh	hou4	houh	蠔	n	oyster
hùhng	hung4	huhng	熊	n	bear (animal)
hùhng	hung4	huhng	熊	n	male (human /animal /bird)
jaahp	zaap6	chaahp	閘	n	lock/brake
jaahp	zaap6	chaahp	集	v	gather/assemble/collected
jaahp	zaap6	chaahp	雜	n	internal organs/entrails
jaahp	zaap6	chaahp	襲	n	attack/raid/inherit/assault
jaahp	zaap6	chaahp	習	n	study/practice
jaahp	zaap6	chaahp	褶	n	crease
jāk	zak1	chak	側	n	side /one side
jāk	zak1	chak	則	n	rules
kyùhn	kyun4	khyuhn	鬈	n	curls /curled
kyùhn	kyun4	khyuhn	權	n	power /authority
sāt	sat1	sat	失	v	lost /lose
sāt	sat1	sat	室	n	chamber/small room
sāt	sat1	sat	膝	v	knee
tái	tai2	thai	睇	v	see/watch/look
tái	tai2	thai	體	v	form/style
wàih	wai4	waih	位	n	seat/location/space/place
wàih	wai4	waih	胃	n	stomach/tummy
wàih	wai4	waih	圍	n	round/all around/surround

The sounds is exactly the same but characters and meanings are not the same.

11) Part A, Sample words and phrases ,

how?[1] /what? (coll)	adv	點/嚟?	dím?	dim2?	tim?
how?[2]	adv	怎	jám	zam2	cham
how?[3]	adv	怎麼	jám mò	zam2 mo4	cham mo
how?[4]	adv	怎樣	jám yeuhng	zam2 joeng3	cham yeuhng
how are you?[1] (wr) (text)		你好嗎?	léih hóu má?	lei5 hou2 maa2?	leih hou ma?
how are you?[2] (coll)		點呀?	dīm àa /aa?	dim1 aa4 /aa3?	tim aa?
how are you?[3] /Hi what up? (us) /alright mate? (bt) /what are you doing? (re)		你點呀?	léih dīm aa?	lei5 dim1 aa3?	leih tim aa?
how are you?[4] /are you well? /how's going on? (re)		你好嗎?	léih hóu má?	lei5 hou2 maa2?	leih hou ma?
how are you?[5]		幾好嗎?	geih hóu má?	gei6 hou2 maa5	keih hou ma?
how big?		幾大呀?	gei daaih àa /aa?	gei3 daai6 aa3 /aa4?	kei taaih aa?
how can i get in touch with you?		點樣可以搵到你?	dím yéung hó yíh wán dou léih /néih?	dim2 joeng2 ho2 ji5 wan2 dou3 lei5 /nei5?	tim yeung ho yih wan tou leih /neih ?
how do?		點樣做?	dím yéung jouh?	dim2 joeng2 zou6?	tim yeung chouh?
how does it works?		怎樣做呢份工作?	jám yeuhng jouh lī fàn gùng jok?	zam2 joeng3 zou6 li1 fan4 gung4 zok3?	cham yeuhng chouh lih fan kung chok?
how get there?	n	點去?	dím heui ?	dim2 heoi3?	tim hoi?
how it works?		怎樣工作?	jám yeuhng gùng jok?	zam2 joeng3 gung4 zok3?	cham yeuhng kung chok?
how long?[1]	n	幾耐?	gei loi /noi?	gei3 loi3 /noi3?	kei loi /noi?
how long?[2]	n	有多久?	yáuh dò gáu?	jau5 do4 gau2?	yauh to kau?
how many?[1]	n	幾多個?	géi dō gó?	gei2 do1 go2?	kei toh ko?
how many?[2]	n	多少數?	dò síu sou?	doh1 siu2 so3?	toh siu sou?
how much?[1] /how many?	n	多少?	dò síu?	do4 siu2?	to siu?
how much?[2] /how?	n	幾?	géi?	gei2?	kei?
how much?[3]	n	點賣?	dím maaih?	dim2 maai6?	tim maaih?
how much?[4] /how many?	n	幾多?	géi dō?	gei2 do1?	kei toh?
how much?[5]	n	幾多呀?	géi do àa /aa?	gei2 do aa4 /aa3?	kei to aa?
how much?[6]	n	幾多錢呀?	géi do chín aa?	gei2 do cin aa3?	kei to chhin aa?
how much is this?		呢幾多錢?	lī /nī...géi dō chín?	li1 /ni1..gei2 do1 cin2?	li /ni gei doh chhin?
how much price?[1] /how much?	n	點賣呀?	dím maaih aa?	dim2 maai6 aa3?	tim maaih aa?
how much price?[2]	n	點賣呢?	dím maaih nè?	dim2 maai6 ne4?	tim maaih ne?
how old?	n	幾多歲呀?	geih dò seui aa?	gei6 do4 seoi3 aa3?	keih to swoi aa?
how old are you?		你幾歲呀?	léih géi seui aa?	lei5 gei2 seoi3 aa3?	leih kei swoi aa?
how's it going?[1] (coll)		點呀?	dím àa /aa?	dim2 aa4 /aa3?	tim aa?
how's it going?[2]	adv	事情進展如向?	sih chìhng jeun jín yùh heung?	si6 cing4 zeon3 zin2 jyu4 hoeng3?	sih chhihng cheun chin yuh heung?

12) Part B, Sample Cantonese tones English words,

gan	gan3	kan	斤	n	catty 0.5 kg
gán	gan2	kan	緊	n	present/continuing/_ing
gán	gan2	kan	緊	adj	near
gán	gan2	kan	緊	v	tight /tighten
gàn	gan4	kan	跟	v	follow
gàn	gan4	kan	根	n	root
gán àak	gan2 aak4	kan aak	緊握	v	grip hold tightly
gān bún	gan1 bun2	kan pun	根源	n	fact cause
gān bún	gan1 bun2	kan pun	根本	adj	primary/basic/basis
gàn bún seuhng	gan4 bun2 soeng6	kan pun seuhng	根本上	adj	basically /fundamentally /basic
gàn cheui	gan4 ceoi3	kan chheui	跟隨	v	follow
gàn cheui	gan4 ceoi3	kan chheui	跟隨	n	join on
gàn chèuih	gan4 ceoi4	kan chheuih	根除	v	eradicate
gán chí yìh yíh	gan2 ci2 ji6 ji5	kan chhi yih yih	僅此而已	adv	beyond
gán dīk	gan2 dik1	kan tik	緊的	adj	tight
gán gán	gan2 gan2	kan kan	緊緊	adj	tight
gán gán deih	gan2 gan2 dei6	kan kan teih	緊緊地	adv	tightly
gán gāp	gan2 gap1	kan kap	緊急	adj/n	urgent/hot /emergency
gán gāp chihng fong	gan2 gap1 cing4 fong3	kan kap chhehng fong	緊急情況	n	emergency
gán gāp deih	gan2 gap1 dei6	kan kap teih	緊急地	adv	urgently
gán gāp johng taai	gan2 gap1 zong6 taai3	kan kap chohng thaai	緊急狀態	n	emergency /state of emergency
gán gāp kàuh gau	gan2 gap1 kau4 gau3	kan kap khauh kau	緊急求救	n	urgent rescue/ emergency rescue
gán gāp sih gihn	gan2 gap1 si6 gin6	kan kap sih kihn	緊急事件	n	emergency
gán gāp sih gu chyú léih	gan2 gap1 si6 gu3 cyu2 lei5	kan kap sih ku chhyu leih	緊急事故處理		handling of emergencies
gán gāp wàih sàu	gan2 gap1 wai4 sau4	kan kap waih sau	緊急維修		emergency maintenance
gán gāp wúi yíh	gan2 gap1 wui2 ji5	kan kap wui yih	緊急會議	n	emergency meeting
gán gāp yiht sin	gan2 gap1 jit6 sin3	kan kap yiht sin	緊急熱線		urgent hotline
gán gei	gan2 gei3	kan kei	緊記	n	urgent remember
gàn geui	gan4 geoi3	kan kwoi	根據	prep/v	according/according to
gán jáau	gan2 zaau2	kan chaau	緊抓	v	grip/hold tightly
gàn jeun	gan4 zeon3	kan jeun	跟進	v	follow/follow up
gán jèung	gan2 zoeng4	kan cheung	緊張	adj	nervous /tension/excite
gán jèung bat òn /ngòn	gan2 zoeng4 bat1 on4 /ngon4	kan cheung pat on /ngon	緊張不安	adj	nervous
gán jèung guhk sai	gan2 zoeng4 guk6 sai3	kan cheung kuhk sai	緊張局勢	n	tensity/nervous situation
gàn jyuh	gan4 zyu6	kan chyuh	跟住	v	follow /follow closely
gān jyuh	gan1 zyu6	kan chyuh	跟住	conj	and / then
gàn jyuh góng	gan4 zyu6 gong2	kan chyuh kong	跟住講	v	repeat /speak again
gàn jyuh jouh	gan4 zyu6 zou6	kan chyuh chouh	跟住做	v	carry on
gàn jyuh jyún jó	gan4 zyu6 jyun2 zo2	kan chyuh chyun cho	跟住轉左		then turn left
gàn jyuh lái	gan4 zyu6 lai2	kan chyuh lai	跟住嚟	adv	subsequently/then
gān jyuh le /ne	gan1 zyu6 le1 /ne1	kan chyuh le /ne	跟住呢?	conj	and then? question
gán kái	gan2 kai2	kan khai	謹啓	n	your sincerely

13) Comparatived of initials romanized chart among (**Yale /IPA & Roman**) Used instead of from the next others two romanized systems and the sound is exactly the same.

(Yale, IPA, Roman) **(IPA)** *International Phonetics Alphabet*

(1)

● Yale	IPA	Roman
b	p	p
ch	tʃ	ch
ch	ts	ch
d	t	t
g	k	k
gw	Kw	kw
j	tʃ	ch
k	k	kh
kw	k'w	khw
p	p	ph
t	t	th
y	j	y

(2)

● IPA	Roman	Yale
j	y	y
k	k	g
k	kh	k
kw	kw	gw
K'w	khw	kw
p	p	b
p	ph	p
t	th	t
t	t	d
ts	ch	ch
tʃ	ch	ch
tʃ	ch	j

(3)

●Roman	Yale	IPA
ch	ch	tʃ
ch	ch	ts
ch	j	tʃ
k	g	k
kh	k	k
khw	kw	k'w
kw	gw	kw
p	b	p
ph	p	p
t	d	t
th	t	t
y	y	j

Note: n *(pronunciation also becomes)* l

14) Compared 6 tones among **Yale / Jyutping** and **Roman**,

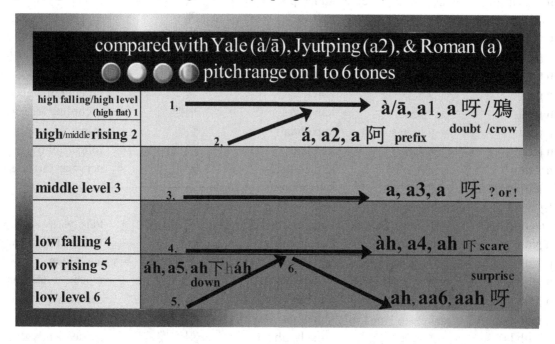

15) CONTENTS, and

Note:

*As you know, the textbooks is not real conversational. Textbook is very
   formal, and most useful for writing method only.

*Repetition: Repetition is the mother of skill. Please repetit as much as you can.
   It gets stored deeply in your brain. You'll never, never, never forget it,
   You will get the best results.

*Language: 60% all humans communication non-verbal or body language,
             30% your tones and
             10% coming out from your mouth.

Initials (consonants)
Aspirated

	Yale	IPA	Chinese	Yale	Sidney Lau	English
01,	ch	ch	叉	chā	caa[1]	fork
	ts	ch	尖	tsim	zim[1]	sharp
	za	ch	搾	ja	zaa[3]	press, extract
	dzá	ch	揸	já	zaa[2]	handful, (Cantonese) to take, carry
02,	k	kh, k	卡	ká	kaa[2]	card
03,	kw	kw	誇	kwā	kwaa[1]	praise
04,	p	ph	趴	pā	paa[1]	lying prone
05,	t	th	他	tā	taa[1]	he, him

Non-aspirated stops

	Yale	IPA	Chinese	Yale	Sidney Lau	English
06,	b	p	巴	bā	baa[1]	hope for
07,	d	t	打	dá	daa[2]	beat, hit
08,	g	k	加	gā	gaa[1]	add, plus
09,	gw	kw	瓜	gwā	gwaa[1]	melon
10,	j/ch	y	渣	jā/dza	zaa[1]	dregs
	z	ch	渣	za	zaa[1]	dregs
	dz	ch	渣	dza	zaa[1]	dregs

Nasals

	Yale	IPA	Chinese	Yale	Sidney Lau	English
11,	m	m	唔	m̀	m[4]/ng[4]	not
	m	m	媽	má	maa[2]	mamma
12,	n	n	能	nàhng	nang[4]	can, able
13,	ng	ŋ	五	ńgh	ngh[5]	five, 5

Fricatives/ Continuants

	Yale	IPA	Chinese	Yale	Sidney Lau	English
14,	f	f	花	fā	faa[1]	flower
15,	h	h	蝦	hā	haa[1]	shrimp
16,	l	l	啦	lā	laa[1]	auxiliary
17,	s	sh	沙	sā	saa[1]	sand

Semi+vowels

	Yale	IPA	Chinese	Yale	Sidney Lau	English
18,	w	w	蛙	wáh	waa[5]	frog
19,	y	j	也	yáh	yaa[5]	too / also
	j	y	一	yāt /jāt	yat[1]	one / 1

Thanks for sharing the introductions of this new dictionary.

Global Double Native Speaker's
English Chinese Cantonese Dictionary Part

It makes 25 times faster by this new methods to learn easy Cantonese

ENGLISH		CHINESE [1]	YALE US based	JYUTPING HK	ROMAN plain based
a /an/ one	n	一	yāt /yat/jat	jat1 /jat3	yat /yāt
a /an /one /single	adj	一個	yāt go	jat1 go3	yat ko
a book	n	一本書	yāt būn syù	jat1 bun2 syu4	yat pun syu
a box	n	一個盒	yāt go háap	jat1 go3 haap2	yat ko haap
a cloth (shirt)	n	一件衫	yāt gihn sāam	jat1 gin6 saam1	yat kihn saam
a day[1] /whole day	n	全日	chyùhn yaht	cyun4 jat6	chhyuhn yaht
a day[2] /24 hours	n	成日	sèhng yaht	seng4 jat6	sehng yaht
a dozen	n	一打	yāt dā	jat1 daa1	yat ta
a /an egg	n	一隻蛋	yāt jek dáan	jat1 zek3 daan2	yat chek taan
a key	n	一把鎖	yāt bá só	jat1 ba2 so2	yat pa so
a lamp	n	一盞燈	yāt jāan dàng	jat1 zaan2 dang1	yat chaan tang
a lot	adv	一批	yāt pài	jat1 pai4	yat phai
a man	n	一個人	yāt go yàhn	jat1 go3 jan4	yat ko yahn
a packet cigarette	n	一包煙	yāt bàau yìn	jat1 baau1 jin1	yat paau yin
a pair shoe	n	一對鞋	yāt deui hàai	jat1 deoi3 haai4	yat toei haai
a pair sock	n	一對襪	yāt deui màaht	jat1 deoi3 maat6	yat toei maaht
a pen	n	一支筆	yāt jī bat	jat1 zi1 bat1	yat chi pat
a purse	n	一個錢包	yāt go chīn bàau	jat1 go3 cin2 baau1	yat ko chhin paau
a river	n	一條河	yāt tìuh hòh	jat1 tiu4 ho6	yat thiuh hoh
a road	n	一條路	yāt tìuh louh	jat1tiu4 lou6	yat thiuh hoh
a sheet table		一張枱	yāt jèung tòih	jat1 zoeng1 toi4	yat cheung thoih
a stick	n	一支杖	yāt jī jeuhng	jat1 zi1 zoeng6	yat chi cheuhng
a teapot	n	一個茶壺	yāt gó cha wú	jat1 go3 caa4 wu2	yat ko chha wu
a trouser	n	一條褲	yāt tìuh fu	jat1 tiu4 fu3	yat thiuh fu
a /an umbrella	n	一把遮	yāt bāa jè	jat1 baa1 ze4	yat paa che
a vehicle /a car	n	一架車	yāt gá chè	jat1 gaa2 ce1	yat ka chhe
a. m. /morning	n	上晝	seuhng jau	soeng6 zau3	seuhng chau
abacus	n	算盤	syun pùhn	syun3 pun4	syun phuhn
abalone	n	鮑魚	baau yùh	baau1 jyu4	paau yuh
abalone dried	n	乾鮑	gòn baau	gon4 baau1	kon paau
abandonment[1] /give up/waive/surrender	v	放棄	fong hei	fong3 hei3	fong hei
abandonment[2] /leave	n/v	遺棄	wàih hei	wai4 hei3	waih hei
abase /obscene talk	v	說髒話	syút jōng wá	syut2 zong1 waa2	syut chong wa
abbreviation[1]	n	簡稱	gáan chīng	gaan2 cing1	kaan chheng
abbreviation[2]	n	縮寫字	sūk sé jih	suk1 se2 zi6	suk se chih
abdomen /stomach	n	肚	tóuh	tou5	thouh
abduct	v	綁票	bóng piu	bong2 piu3	pong phiu
abhorrent /hateful	adj	可惡	hó ok /ngok	ho2 ok3 /ngok3	ho ok /ngok

abide /overstay	v	逗留	dauh làuh	dau6 lau4	tauh lauh
abide by the rules		守規矩	sáu kwài géui	sau2 kwai4 geoi2	sau khwai kwoi
ability[1] /capability /might/competence/facult	n	能力	làhng /nàhng lihk	lang4 /nang4 lik6	lahng /nahng lehk
ability[2] /talent	n	才	choih	coi4	chhoih
ability[3] (of person)	n	質量	jāt leuhng	zat1 loeng6	chat leuhng
ablaze	adj	閃耀	sím yiuh	sim2 yiu6	sim yiuh
able[1]	adj	可	hó	ho2	ho
able[2]	adj	可能	hó làhng /nàhng	ho2 lang4 /nang4	ho lahng /nahng
able[3] /possible/able to	adj	可以	hó yíh	ho2 ji5	ho yih
able bodied man	adj	壯健	jong gihn	zong3 gin6	chong kihn
able to say		睇得出	tái dāk chēut	tai2 dak1 ceot1	thai tak chhot
ablution[1] /take a shower	n	乾淨嘅水	gòn jehng ge séui	gon1 zeng6 ge3 seoi2	kon chehng ke swoi
ablution[2] /bathing	n	洗澡	sái chou	sai2 cou3	sai chhou
abnegate/emotion-control	adj	克制	hàak jai	haak4 zai3	haak chai
abnegate	adj	放棄	fong hei	fong3 hei3	fong hei
abnormal[1]	adj	變態	bin taai	bin3 taai3	pin thaai
abnormal[2]	adj	異常	yih sèuhng	ji6 soeng4	yih seuhng
abnormal[3]	adj	畸形	kèi yìhng	kei4 jing4	khei yehng
abnormal[4]	adj	唔正常	m̀ jeng sèuhng	m4 zeng3 soeng4	mh cheng seuhng
abnormal[5]	adj	不正常	bāt jéng sèuhng	bat1 zeng3 soeng4	pat cheng seuhng
aboard /mount/to climb on	adv	登上	dàng séuhng	dang4 soeng5	tang seuhng
aboard on plane	adv	喺飛機上邊	hái fèi gèi seuhng bihn	hai2 fei4 gei4 soeng6 bin6	hai fei kei seuhng pihn
aboard on ship	adv	喺船上邊	hái syùhn seuhng bihn	hai2 syun4 soeng6 bin4	hai syuhn seuhng pihn
aboard on the ship	adv	船上	syùhn séuhng	syun4 soeng5	syuhn seuhng
abolish[1] /annulled	v	廢止	fai jí	fai3 zi2	fai chi
abolish[2] /end a law	v	廢除	fai chèuih	fai3 ceoi4	fai chhoih
aborigines	n	原住民	yùhn jyuh màhn	jyun4 zyu6 man4	yuhn chyuh mahn
abort /abortion/miscarry	v	小產	síu cháan	siu2 caan2	siu chhaan
abortion[1]	n	流產	làuh cháan	lau4 caan2	lauh chhaan
abortion[2]	n	人工流產	yàhn gùng làuh cháan	jan4 gung4 lau4 caan2	yahn kung lauh chhaan
abortion[3]	n	堕胎	doh tòi	do6 toi4	toh thoi
abound[1]	v	有好多	yáuh hóu dò	jau5 hou2 do4	yauh hou to
abound[2]	v	有好豐富	yáuh hóu fùng fu	jau5 hou2 fung4 fu3	yauh hou fung fu
about[1] /regarding	prep	關於	gwàan yù	gwaan4 jyu4	kwaan yu
about[2] /around/or rather/or	adv	大約	daaih yeuk	daai6 joek3	taaih yeuk
about[3] /approximately/ around	adv	左右	jó yáu	zo2 jau6	cho yau
about to[1] /close to/nearly	adv	將近	jèung gahn	zoeng4 gan6	cheung kahn
about to[2]/at once arriving	adv	就來	jauh lòih	zau6 loi4	chauh loih
about to[3]	adv	即將	jīk jèung	zik1 zoeng4	chek cheung
above[1] /up	adv	上	séuhng	soeng6	seuhng

English	POS	中文	Yale (diacritics)	Jyutping	Romanization
above[2] /above mentioned	adv	上面	séuhng mìhn	soeng6 min6	seuhng mihn
above[3]	adv	上便	seuhng bihn	soeng6 bin6	seuhng pihn
above[4]	adv	上頭	séuhng tàuh	soeng5 tau4	seuhng thauh
above mentioned[1]	adv	以上	yíh seuhng	ji5 soeng6	yih seuhng
above mentioned[2]	adv	上述	seuhng seuht	soeng seot6	seuhng seuht
abrasion[1] /damage	n	損	syún	suun2	syun
abrasion[2] /bark rub skin	n	擦傷	cháat sèung	caat3 soeng4	chhaat seung
abroad[1]	adj	喺外國	hái oih /ngoih gwok	hai2 oi6 /ngoi6 gwok3	hai oih /ngoih gwok
abroad[2]	adj	在國外	joih gwok oih /ngoih	zoi6 gwok3 oi6 /ngoi6	choih kwok oih /ngoih
abroad student	adv	留學生	làuh hohk sāang	lau4 hok6 saang1	lauh hohk saang
abruptly /all of sudden	adj	突然地	daht yihn dèih	dat6 jin4 dei6	taht yihn teih
absent[1] /absence	adj/n	缺	kyut	kyut3	khyut
absent[2] /not present	adj	缺席	kyut jihk	kyut3 zik6	khyut chehk
absent[3]	adj	缺勤	kyut kàhn	kyut3 kan4	khyut khahn
absentee[1]	n	缺席者	kyut jihk jé	kyut3 zik6 ze2	khyut chehk che
absentee[2]	n	缺勤者	kyut kàhn jé	kyut3 kan4 ze2	khyut khahn che
absentee[3]	n	缺課者	kyut fo jé	kyut3 fo3 ze2	khyut fo che
absolutism	n	專制	jyūn jai	zyun1 zai3	chyun chai
absorb[1] /attract	v	吸	kāp	kap1	khap
absorb[2] /suck/soak	v	吸收	kāp sàu	kap1 sau4	khap sau
absorber device	n	吸收器	kāp sàu hei	kap1 sau4 hei3	khap sau hei
abstain/stay far from meat /wine	v	齋	jāai	zaai1	chaai
abundant /ample/plenty	adj	大量的	daaih leuhng dìk	daai6 loeng6 dik4	taaih leuhng dek
abuse[1]	n	濫	láahm	laam6	laahm
abuse[2]	n	罵 / 罵	mah	maa6	mah
abuse[3] /bad word/obscene	n	粗口	chòu háu	cou4 hau2	chhou hau
abuse[4]	n	責罰	jaak faht	zaak3 fat6	chaak faht
abuser	n	濫用者	láahm yuhng jé	laam6 jung6 ze2	laahm yuhng che
abusive word	adj	辱罵	yuhk mah	juk6 maa6	yuhk mah
academic	adj	學術	hohk seuht	hok6 seot6	hohk swoht
educational /academic	adj	學歷	hohk lihk	hok6 lik6	hohk lehk
academic	adj	學院嘅	hohk yuhn ge	hok6 jyun6 ge3	hohk yuhn ke
academy/college/institute	n	學院	hohk yuhn	hok6 jyun6	hohk yuhn
accelerate	n	加快	gà faai	gaa4 faai3	ka faai
accelerator[1] /gas pedal	n	油門	yáu mùhn	jau2 mun4	yau muhn
accelerator[2]	n	加速器	gà chūk hei	gaa4 cuk1 hei3	ka chhuk hei
accent/spoken/pronounce	n	口音	háu yām	hau2 jam1	hau yam
accept/take over/got /receive/take in	v	收	sàu	sau4	sau
accept /undertake /receive/take in/come in for	v	接受	jip sauh	zip3 sau6	chip sauh
accept as /consider as	v	以	yíh / yǐ/ íh	ji5	yih
accept contract	v	承辦	sìhng bàahn	sing4 baan6	sehng paahn
accept or not?		收唔收呀!	sāu m̀ sāu àa?	sau1 m4 sau1 aa2	sau mh sau aa?

acceptability /to acknowledge	n	承認	sing yihng	sing3 jing6	seng yehng
acceptance	n	接受	jip sauh	zip3 sau6	chip sauh
acceptance /adopt	n	採納	chòih nàahp	coi4 naap6	chhoih naahp
accepting thanks /thanks	n	謝謝	jèh jèh	ze6 ze6	cheh cheh
access[1] /entrance/inlet /gate	n	入口	yahp háu	jap6 hau2	yahp hau
access[2] /enter/go into /ingress	v	進入	jeun yahp	zeon3 jap6	cheun yahp
access[3] reaching	n	接近	jip gahn	zip3 gan6	chip kahn
access[4] enter	n	接駁	jip bok	zip3 bok3	chip pok
access control	adj	訪客管制	fóng haak gùn jai	fong2 haak3 gun4 zai3	fong haak kun chai
accessory	adj	輔助部件	fuh jòh bòuh gìhn	fu6 zo6 bou6 gin6	fuh choh pouh kihn
accident[1]	n	意外	yi òih /ngoih	ji3 oi6 /ngoi6	yi oih /ngoih
accident[2] /die in accident /wreck	n	失事	sāt sih	sat1 si6	sat sih
accident[3]	n	事故	sih gu	si6 gu3	sih ku
accident[4]	n	偶然嘅事	ngáuh yìhn ge sih	ngau5 jin4 ge3 si6	ngauh yihn ke sih
accident place		意外地點	yi òih /ngoih deih dím	ji3 oi6 /ngoi6 dei6 dim2	yi oih /ngoih teih tim
accident report		意外報告	yi òih /ngoih bou gou	ji3 oi6 /ngoi6 bou3 gou3	yi oih /ngoih pou kou
accidentally	adv	偶然咁	ngáuh yìhn gám	ngau5 jin4 gam2	ngauh yihn kam
acclaim /praise/exaggerate	v	稱讚	chìng jaan	cing4 zaan3	chheng chaan
acclamation[1]	n	讚賞	jaan séung	zaan3 soeng2	chaan seung
acclamation[2] /cheer /acclaim/ hail	n	歡呼	fùn fù	fun4 fu4	fun fu
accommodate[1] /give shelter for charity	v	收容	sāu yùhng	sau1 jung4	sau yuhng
accommodate[2]	v	能提供	làhng /nàhng tàih gùng	lang4 /nang4 tai4 gung4	lahng /nahng thaih kung
accommodation /dwelling	n	寓所	yuh só	jyu6 so2	yuh so
accompanied / make friends /mix with persons	v	結交	git gàau	git3 gaau4	kit kaau
accompany[1] to assist/go with	v	陪	pùih	pui4	phuih
accompany[2]	v	陪同	pùih tùhng	pui4 tung4	phuih thuhng
accompany[3]	v	陪伴	pùih bùhn	pui4 bun6	phuih puhn
accompany[4]	v	伴隨	bùhn cheui	pui4 ceoi4	puhn chhoi
accomplished/proficient	adj	熟練	suhk lihn	suk6 lin6	suhk lehn
accomplishment / achievement	n	成就	sèhng jauh	seng4 zau6	sehng chauh
accord[1] /offer	v	給予	kāp yùh	kap1 jyu4	khap yuh
accord[2] /bargain price	v	協議	hip yíh	hip3 ji5	hip yih
accordance	n	依照	yì jíu	ji4 ziu2	yi chiu
according[1]	prep	據	geui	geoi3	kwoi
according[2] /according to	prep/v	根據	gàn geui	gan4 geoi3	kan kwoi
according[3]	v	相應	sèung yìng	soeng4 jing4	seung yeng

English	POS	Chinese	Romanization 1	Romanization 2	Romanization 3
according to[1]	v	照	jiu	ziu3	chiu
according to[2]	v	按照	on /ngòn jiu	on3 /ngon4 ziu3	on /ngon chiu
according to[3]	v	依照	yī jiu	ji1 ziu3	yi chiu
accordingly[1]	v	相應地	sèung yìng dèih	soeng4 jing4 dei6	seung yeng teih
accordingly[2]	ad	照著	jiu jeuk	ziu3 zoek3	chiu cheuk
accordion /music instrument	n	手風琴	sáu fūng kàhm	sau2 fung1 kam4	sau fung khahm
account[1] /debt	n	帳	jeung	zoeng3	cheung
account[2] bank	n	戶口	wuh háu	wu6 hau2	wuh hau
account[3]	n	帳目	jeung muhk	zoeng3 muk6	cheung muhk
account[4] /deem/think	v	認為	yìhng wàih	jing6 wai4	yehng waih
account balance	n	戶口結餘	wuh háu git yùh	wu6 hau2 git3 jyu4	wuh hau kit yuh
account book	n	簿	bouh	bou6	pouh
account no	n	戶口號碼	wuh háu houh máh	wu6 hau2 hou6 maa5	wuh hau houh mah
accountant[1]	n	會計	wuih gái	wui6 gai2	wuih kai
accountant[2]	n	會計師	wuih gái sì	wui6 gai2 si6	wuih kai sih
accumulate[1] /to store	v	積	jīk	zik1	chek
accumulate[2]	v	累積	leuih jīk	leoi6 zik1	lowih chek
accumulated	v	累積嘅	leuih jīk ge	leoi6 zik1 ge3	lowih chek ke
accumulator[1]	n	積聚者	jīk jeuih jé	zik1 zeoi6 ze2	chek cheuih che
accumulator[2]	n	聚財者	jeuih chòih jé	zeoi6 coi4 ze2	cheuih chhoih che
accumulator[3]	n	蓄能器	chūk làhng /nàhng hei	cuk1 lang4 /nang4 hei3	chhuk lahng /nahng hei
accuracy	n	準確性	jéun kok sing	zeon2 kok3 sing3	cheun khok seng
accurate[1]	adj	正	jeng	zeng3	cheng
accurate[2]	adj	準	jéun	zeon2	cheun
accurate[3]	adj	準绳	jéun sìhng	zeon2 sing4	cheun sehng
accurate[4] /exact	adj	準確	jéun kok	zeon2 kok3	cheun khok
accurately /correct	adv	精確	jēng kok	zeng1 kok3	cheng khok
accuse[1] /blame/charge	v	控	hung	hung3	hung
accuse[2]	v	指控	jí hung	zi2 hung3	chi hung
accused /alleged/charged /sue	v	控告	hung gou	hung3 gou3	hung kou
accustomed	adj	通常嘅	tùng seung ge	tung4 soeng3 ge3	thung seung ke
accustomed to /make a practice	n	習慣於	jaahp gwaan yū /yùh	zaap6 gwaan3 jyu1 /jyu4	chaahp kwaan yu /yuh
ache[1] /sore/pain/sorrow /grief	adj/v	痛	tung	tung3	thung
ache[2] /painful/tenderness	v	疼痛	dūng tung	dung1 tung3	tung thung
achieve[1] /carry out /work completed/finalize/	v	完成	yùhn sèhng	jyun4 seng4	yuhn sehng
achieve[2] /to reach	v	達成	daaht sèhng	daat6 seng4	taaht sehng
achieve[3]	v	達到	daaht dou	daat6 dou3	taaht tou
achieve one's aim		達到目標	daaht dou muhk bīu	daat6 dou3 nuk6 biu1	taaht tou muhk piu
achievement/to succeed	n	成	sèhng	seng4	sehng

aching	v	心痛	sàm tung	sam4 tung3	sam thung
acid /sour/sore/ache	adj/n	酸	syùn	syun4	syun
acid rain	n	酸雨	syùn yúh	syun4 jyu5	syun yuh
acidity	n	酸性	syùn sing	syun4 sing3	syun seng
acknowledgement /thanks/thankful	v	感謝	gám jeh	gam2 ze6	kam cheh
acquaintance[1]	n	熟人	suhk yàhn	suk6 jan4	suhk yahn
acquaintance[2] /to get to know each other	n	相識	sèung sīk	soeng4 sik1	seung sek
acquaintance[3]	n	了解	líuh gáai	liu5 gaai2	liuh kaai
acquainted[1]	adj	認悉	yihng sīk	jing6 sik1	yehng sek
acquainted[2]	adj	熟知	sùhk jī	suk6 zi1	suhk chi
acquainted[3]	adj	瞭解	líuh gàai	liu5 gaai6	liuh kaai
acquainted with /know /recognize	adj/v	識	sīk	sik1	sek
acquiescent	adj	默認	mahk yìhng	mak6 jing6	mahk yehng
acquire[1] /receiving skill	vt	學道	hohk dóu	hohk6 dou2	hohk tou
acquire[2] /to receive	vt	獲得	wohk dāk	wok6 dak1	wohk tak
acrid[1]	adj	辣嘅	laaht ge	laat6 ge3	laaht ke
acrid[2]	adj	攻鼻	gùng beih	gung4 bei6	kung peih
acrid[3]	adj	苦嘅	fú ge	fu2 ge3	fu ke
across[1]	prep	行過	hàahng gwo	haang4 gwo3	haahng kwo
across[2]	prep	橫過	wàahng gwo	waang4 gwo3	waahng kwo
across[3] /go through /pass through	prep	穿過	chyùn gwo	cyun4 gwo3	chhyun kwo
across by land /overland/route by across	adj	經由陸路	gìng yàuh luhk louh	ging4 jau4 luk6 lou6	keng yauh luhk louh
acrylic	adj	丙烯酸	bíhng hèi syùn	bing5 hei4 syun4	pehng hei syun
act[1] act as play	v	幕	mohk	mok6	mohk
act[2] act as play	v	扮演	baan yíhn	baan3 jin5	paan yihn
act[3] govern post /hold office job	v	擔任	dàam yahm	daam4 jam6	taam yahm
act[4] law	n	法案	faat on /ngon	faat3 on3 /ngon3	faat on /ngon
act as do	v	做戲	jouh hei	zou6 hei3	chouh hei
act of allowing /allow/permission	n/v	許可	héui hó	heoi2 ho2	hoi ho
act of increasing /expansion	n	擴充	kwong chùng	kwong3 cung4	khwong chhung
acting[1] /act on behalf	adj	代理	doih léih	doi6 lei5	toih leih
acting[2] /take over post	adj	接替者	jip tai jé	zip3 tai3 ze2	chip thai che
acting[3]	n	演戲	yín hei	jin2 hei3	yin hei
action /activity	n	活動	wuht duhng	wut6 dung6	wuht tohng
active[1] /clever/smart /acute/wise/clever & smart/ activeness	adj	聰明	chùng mìhng	cung4 ming4	chhung mehng
active[2] /lively	adj	活潑	wuht put	wut6 put3	wuht phut
active[3]	adj	活躍	wuht yéuk	wut6 joek2	wuht yeuk

English	Type	中文			
active children	n	活潑嘅細蚊仔	wuht put ge sai màn jái	wut6 put3 ge3 sai3 man4 zai2	wuht phut ke sai man chai
active service	n	現役	yihn yihk	jin6 yik6	yihn yehk
actively[1] /bustling	n	活躍地	wuht yéuk dèih	wut6 joek2 dei6	wuht yeuk dèih
actively[2]	n	有效地	yáuh hàauh dèih	jau5 haau6 dei6	yauh haauh teih
activist /activism	n	激進主義分子	gihk jeun jyú yih fàn jí	gik1 zeon3 zyu2 ji6 fan4 zi2	kehk cheun chyu yih fan chi
actor	n	男演員	làahm yíhn yùhn	laam4 jin5 jyun4	laahm yihn yuhn
actress	n	女演員	léuih yín yùhn	leui5 jin2 jyun4	lowih yin yuhn
actual	adj	實在	saht joih	sat6 zoi6	saht choih
actual-location	n	現場	yihn chèuhng	jin6 coeng4	yihn chheuhng
actually[1] /in fact/really	adv	其實	kèih saht	kei4 sat6	kheih saht
actually[2] /virtual	adv	實際上	saht jai seuhng	sat6 zai3 soeng6	saht chai seuhng
acuity	n	敏銳	máhn yeuih	man5 jeoi6	mahn yeuih
acupuncture	n	針灸	jàm gau	zam4 gau3	cham kau
acute[1] /sharp	adj	尖銳	jìm yeuih	zim4 jeoi6	chim yeuih
acute[2] /ardent/intense /fierce (in attack way)	adj	激烈	gīk liht	gik1 lit6	kek liht
acute disease	n	急症	gāp jing	gap1 zing3	kap cheng
acute mind	n	刺激心臟	chi gīk sàm jòhng	ci3 gik1 sam4 zong4	chhi kek sam chohng
acute toxicity	n	急性中毒	gāp sing jung duhk	gap1 sing3 zung3 duk6	kap seng chung tuhk
adam (de)	n	亞當	áa dòng	aa2 dong4	aa tong
adaptability	adj	適應力	sīk ying lihk	sik1 jing3 lik6	sek ying lehk
adaptation (environment)	n	適應	sīk ying	sik1 jing3	sek yeng
adapted (environmented)	n	適應咗	sīk ying jó	sik1 jing3 zo2	sek yeng cho
adapter[1] (electric device)	n	轉接器	jyún jip hei	zyun2 zip3 hei3	chyun chip hei
adaptor[2] (electric device)	n	電氣插座	dihn hei chaap joh	dim6 hei3 caap3 zo6	tihn hei chhaap choh
adaptor[3] /adaptor socket /electric device	n	萬能插蘇	maahn nàhng chaap sōu	maan6 nang4 caap3 sou1	maahn lahng chhaap sou
adaptor[4] man	n	改寫者	gói sé jé	goi2 se2 ze2	koi se che
add	v	附加嘅	fuh gà ge	fuh3 gaa1 ge3	fuh ka ke
add on /plus/to add/top of	v	加上	gā séuhng	gaa1 soeng5	ka seuhng
add up /to count	v	統計	túng gái	tung2 gai2	thung kai
adder	n	加者	gà jé	ga4 ze2	ka che
adding water /dilute	v	稀釋	hèi sīk	hei4 sik1	hei sek
addition[1]	n	加法	gā faat	gaa1 faat3	ka faat
addition[2] /annex	n/adj	附加	fuh gà	fuh3 gaa1	fuh ka
additional[1]	adj	又	yauh	jau6	yauh
additional[2] /second	adj	再	joi	joi3	choi
additional[3] /extra	adj	外加	oih /ngòih ga	oi6 /ngoi6 gaa1	oih /ngoih ka
additional[4] /extra	adj	額外	aahk /ngaahk òih	aak6 /ngaak6 oi6	aahk /ngaahk oih
address[1] /name/title to call/call by name	n	稱	chìng	cing4	chheng
address[2] /call named	n	名稱	méng chìng	meng2 cing4	meng chheng
address[3] call by title/rank	n	稱呼	chìng fù	cing4 fu4	chheng fù

address book	ph	通訊錄	tùng seun luhk	tung4 seon3 luk6	thung swon luhk
addressed	n	演講	yíhn gōng	jin5 gong4	yihn kong
adequate[1] /sufficient	adj	足夠	jūk gau	juk1 gau3	chuk kau
adequate[2] /contented /satisfied	adj	滿足	múhn jūk	mun5 zuk1	muhn chuk
adequately	adj	充分地	chùng fàn dèih	cung4 fan4 dei6	chhung fan teih
adhere[1] /stick/glue	v	黐	chì	ci4	chhi
adhere[2]	v	黏附	lim /nim fuh	lim3 /nim3 fu6	lim /nim fuh
adhesive	n/adj	膠黏劑	gàau lìm /nìm jāi	gaau4 lim4 /nim4 zai1	kaau lim /nim chai
adjacent /nearest	adj	鄰近	lèuhn káhn	leon4 kan5	leuhn khahn
adjective	n	形容詞	yìhng yùhng chìh	jing4 jung4 ci4	yehng yuhng chhih
adjourm[1] /make delay /procrastinate/spend time /don't want do it/timepass/ delay/to kill time	v	消磨時間	sìu mòh sìh gaan	siu4 mo6 si4 gaan3	siu moh sih kaan
adjourm[2] /delay/stall /procrastinate/don't want do it/make delay	v	拖延	tò yìhn	to4 jing4	thoh yihn
adjourned /to stoped	v	休會	yàu wùih	jau4 wui4	yau wuih
adjournment	n	休會	yàu wùih	jau4 wui4	yau wuih
adjust[1]	v	調	tìuh	tiu4	thiuh
adjust[2]	v	調校	tìuh gáau	tiu4 gaau2	thiuh kaau
adjust[3] /calibrate	v	校準	gaau jéun	gaau3 zeon2	kaau cheun
adjust[4]	v	已適應	yíh sīk ying	ji5 sik1 jing3	yih sek yeng
adjustable	adj	可調節	hó tìuh jit	ho2 tiu4 zit3	ho thiuh chit
adjusted focus /focus	n	焦距	jìu kéuih	ziu4 keoi5	chiu khoih
adjustment	n	調整	tìuh jíng	tiu4 zing2	thiuh cheng
administration[1]	n	行政	hàhng jing	hang4 zing3	hahng cheng
administration[2] /manager	n	經理	gìng léih	ging4 lei5	keng leih
administration[3] /control/direction/management	n	管理	gún léih	gun2 lei5	kun leih
administrator[1]	n	行政人員	hàhng jing yàhn yùhn	hang4 zing3 jan4 jyun4	hahng cheng yahn yuhn
administrator[2]	n	管理人	gún léih yàhn	gun2 lei5 jan4	kun leih yahn
admiral	n	海軍上將	hói gwàn seuhng jèung	hoi2 gwan4 soeng6 zoeng4	hoi kwan seuhng cheung
admiralty[1]	n	海事法庭	hói sih faat tìhng	hou2 si6 faat3 ting4	hoi sih faat thehng
Admiralty[2] place of HK	n	金鐘	gahm jùng	gam6 zung4	kahm chung
admire[1] /exaggerate /complimentary	v	讚美	jaan méih	zaan3 mei5	chaan meih
admire[2]	v	佩服	pui fuhk	pui3 fuk6	phui fuhk
admire[3]	v	欽佩	yàm pui	jam4 pui3	yam phui
admire[4] /appreciate	v	欣賞	yàn séung	jan4 soeng2	yan seung
admire[5]	v	讚美詞	jaan méih chìh	zaan3 mei5 ci4	chaan meih chhih
admission	n	許可	héui hó	heoi2 ho2	hoi ho

admit[1]	v	接納	jip laahp	zip3 laap6	chip laahp
admit[2]	v	准許進入	jáun héui jeun yahp	zeon2 heoi2 zeon3 jap6	chaun hoi cheun yahp
admit3 /recognize	v	承認	sìhng yihng	sing4 jing6	sehng yehng
adopt	v	收養	sàu yéuhng	sau4 joeng5	sau yeuhng
adopted	adj	被收養	bèih sāu yéuhng	bei6 sau1 joeng5	peih sau yeuhng
adored	v	敬重	geng juhng	geng3 zung6	keng chuhng
adorn /to decorate	v	打扮	dá baan	daa2 baan3	ta paan
adult	adj	成年人	sèhng lihn /nihn yàhn	seng4 lin4 /nin4 jan4	sehng lihn /nihn yahn
adult education	n	成人教育	sèhng yàhn gaau yuhk	seng4 jan4 gaau3 juk6	sehng yahn kaau yuhk
adultery /sex between other husband or wife	n	通姦	tūng gāan	tung1 gaan1	thung kaan
advance[1]	adj	進	jeun	zeon3	cheun
advance[2] /before	v	事前	sih chìhn	si6 cin4	sih chhihn
advance[3] /go forward /progress	v	前進	chìhn jeun	cin4 zeon3	chhihn cheun
advance[4] /earlier date	v	提前	tàih chìhn	tai4 cin4	thaih chhihn
advance[5] /pay in advance	a	預先嘅	yuh sìn ge	jyu6 sin4 ge3	yuh sin ke
advance expense	v	預繳費用	yuh gíu fái yuhng	jyu6 giu2 fai2 jung6	yuh kiu fai yuhng
advance paid[1]	v	上期	seuhng kèih	soeng6 kei4	seuhng kheih
advance paid[2] rent	v	上期租	seuhng kèih jòu	soeng6 kei4 zou1	seuhng kheih chou
advanced[1] technology	adj	先進	sìn jeun	sin4 zeon3	sin cheun
advanced[2]	adj	進階	jeun gāai	zeon3 gaai1	cheun kaai
advantage[1] /profit/benefit /interest of loan	n	利	leih	lei6	leih
advantage[2] /profit/benefi	n/v	益	yīk	jik1	yek
advantage[3] (of money) /interest/benefits	n/v	利益	leih yīk	lei6 jik1	leih yek
advantage[4] /interest	n	有利	yáuh lèih	jau5 lei6	yauh leih
advantage[5] /benefit	n	好處	hóu chyu	hou2 chyu3	hou chyu
advantage[6] /good points /merits/vantage	n	優點	yàu dīm	jau4 dim1	yau tim
advantage[7] /favorable /favorable situation	v	有利條件	yáuh lèih tìuh gihn	jau5 lei6 tiu4 gin6	yauh leih thiuh kihn
adventure /risky	adj	冒險	mouh hím	mou6 him2	mouh him
adverb	n	副詞	fu chìh	fu3 ci4	fu chhih
adverb particle	n	副詞小詞	fu chìh síu chìh	fu3 ci4 siu2 ci4	fu chhih siu chhih
adverse /backwards /reverse direction	adj	逆向	ngaahk heung	ngaak6 hoeng3	ngaahk heung
adversely[1]	adv	唔好	m̀ hóu	m4 hou2	mh hou
adversely[2]	adv	敵對	dihk deui	dik6 deoi3	tehk toei
adversity	n	患難	waahn naahn	waan6 naan4	waahn naahn
advertise[1]	v	做廣告	jouh gwóng gou	zou6 gwong2 gou3	chouh kwong kou
advertise[2]	n	登廣告	dàng gwóng gou	dang1 gwong2 gou3	tang kwong kou
advertisement	n	告白	gou baahk	gou3 baak6	kou paahk
advertising[1]	n	廣告	gwóng gou	gwong2 gou3	kwong kou

English		Chinese	Romanization	Jyutping	Yale
advertising[2]	n	廣告業	gwóng gou yihp	gwong2 gou3 jip6	kwong kou yihp
advertising agency	n	廣告公司	gwóng gou gūng sī	gwong2 gou3 gung1 s	kwong kou kung si
advice[1]	n	忠告	jùng gūk	zung4 guk1	chung kuk
advice[2] /idea/opinion /suggestion/objection/complaint/discuss/criticized	n	意見	yi gin	ji3 gin3	yi kin
advice[3]	n	指點	jí dím	zi2 dim2	chi tim
advice[4] /idea/opinion /suggestion//recommended by/proposition	n	建議	gin yi	gin3 ji3	kin yi
advisable	adj	明智	mìhng ji	ming4 zi3	mehng chi
advise[1] /persuade at quarrel	v	勸	hyun	hyun3	hyun
advise[2] at quarrel	v	勸交	hyun gāau	hyun3 gaau1	hyun kaau
advise[3] at quarrel	v	勸告	hyun gou	hyun3 gou3	hyun kou
advise[4] at quarrel	v	勸喻	hyun yuh	hyun3 jyu6	hyun yuh
advisor[1]	n	忠告者	jùng gūk jé	zung4 guk1 ze2	chung kuk che
advisor[2]	n	提供意見者	tàih gùng yi gin jé	tai4 gung4 ji3 gin3 ze2	thaih kung yi kin che
advocate[1] /suggest	n	主張	jyú jèung	zyu2 zoeng4	chyu cheung
advocate[2]	v	擁護	yúng wuh	jung2 wu6	yung wuh
adze[1]	n	扁斧	bín fú	bin2 fu2	pin fu
adze[2] /adz (cutter tool)	n	手斧	sáu fú	sau2 fu2	sau fu
aeon[1] /eon 1000 of years	n	萬古	maahn gú	maan6 gu2	maahn ku
aeon[2] /forever	n	永遠	wíhng yúhn	wing5 jyun5	wehng yuhn
aerial /antenna	n	天線	tìn sin	tin4 sin3	thin si
aerogram[1]	n	郵簡	yàuh gáan	jau4 gaan2	yauh kaan
aerogram[2]	n	航空郵簡	hòhng hùng yàuh gáan	hong4 hung4 jau4 gaan2	hohng hung yauh kaan
aeroplane /airplane /plane/air	n	飛機	fèi gèi	fei4 gei4	fei kei
affable[1] /kindly	adj	好相與	hóu sèung yúh	hou2 soeng4 jyu5	hou seung yuh
affable[2] /kindly	adj	好人事	hóu yàhn sí	hou2 jan4 si2	hou yahn si
affable[3] /kind/kindly /merciful	adj	和藹	wòh ói /ngói	wo4 oi2 /ngoi2	woh oi /ngoi
affair[1] /matter/event	n	事情	sih chìhng	si6 cing4	sih chhihng
affair[2]	n	事件	sih gìhn	si6 gin6	sih kihn
affair[3]	n	事幹	sih gon	si6 gon3	sih kon
affair[4] /job/task	n	務	mouh	mou6	mouh
affect[1]	v	感	gám	gam2	kam
affect[2] /interact/impact /disturb	v	影響	yéng héung	jeng2 hoeng2	yeng heung
affected	adj	受影響	sauh yéng héung	sau6 jeng2 hoeng2	sauh yeng héung
affectionate[1] /loved /deep love/devoted friend	adj	深情	sàm chìhng	sam4 cing4	sam chhehng
affectionate[2]	adj	感情	gám chìng	gam2 cing4	kam chheng
affectionate[3]	adj	富感情	fù gám chìng	fu4 gam2 cing4	fu kam chheng

affiliate to join	v	加入	gà yahp	gaa4 jap6	ka yahp
afford /provide/award	v	給予	kāp yùh	kap1 jyu4	khap yuh
afraid[1] /be scared /be frightened	adj	驚	gèng	geng4	keng
afraid[2] /be afraid/fear /be fear	adj/n	怕	pa	paa3	phaa
afraid[3] /scared/frightened	adj	嚇親	háak chān	haak2 can1	haak chhan
afraid[4]	adj	驚怕	gèng pa	geng4 paa3	keng phaa
afraid[5] /fear	adj	害怕	hoih pa	hoi6 paa3	hoih phaa
Africa	n	非洲	fèi jàu	fei4 zau4	fei chau
after[1]	prep	然后	yìhn hauh	jim4 hau6	yìhn hauh
after[2] /sometimes/someday	prep	日後	yaht háu	jat6 hau2	yaht hau
after[3]	prep	以後	yíh hauh	ji5 hau6	yih hauh
after all[1]	conj	到底	dou dái	dou3 dai2	tou tai
after all[2]	conj	究到	gau dou	gau3 dou3	kau tou
after all[3]	conj	畢竟	bāt gíng	bat1 ging2	pat keng
after dinner	adv	晚餐後	máahn chāan hauh	maan2 caan1 hau6	maahn chhaan hauh
after midnight /01:00-05:00 hrs	adv	凌晨	lìhng sàhn	ling4 san4	lehng sahn
after that[1] /later	adv	其後	kèih háu	kei4 hau2	kheih hau
after that?[2] question	adv	之後呢?	jì háu nē?	zi4 hau2 ne1?	chi hau ne?
after that?[3] question	adv	然後呢?	yìhn hauh lē /nē?	jin4 hau6 le /ne1?	yihn hauh le /ne?
after the birth /occurred (not innate) /postnatal/unnatural	adv	後天	hauh tìn	hau6 tin4	hauh thin
after the event	adv	事後	sih háu	si6 hau2	sih hau
after while[1]	adv	晏啲	aan dì	aan3 di4	aan ti
after while[2]	adv	遲啲	chìh dì	ci4 di4	chhih ti
after while[3]	adv	稍後	sáau hauh	saau2 hau6	saau hauh
after you	n	請先	chéng /chíng sìn	ceng2 /cing2 sin4	chheng sin
afternoon[1]	n	下午	hah ńgh	haa6 ng5	hah ngh
afternoon[2]	n	宴晝	yín jáu	jin2 zau2	yin chau
afterwards[1] /thereafter /hereafter/in the future/ later on	adv	以後	yíh hauh	ji5 hau6	yih hauh
afterwards[2]	adv	後來	hàuh lòih	hou6 loi4	hauh loih
afterword	n	後記	hauh gei	hau6 gei3	hauh kei
again[1] /once more /re.../ then/another	adv	再	joi	zoi3	choi
again[2]	adv	回	wùih	wui4	wuih
again[3] /double/repeat	adv	重	chúhng	cung5	chhuhng
again[4]	adv	再次	joi chi	zoi3 ci3	choi chi
again[5] /re...	adv	重新	chùhng sàn	cung4 san4	chhuhng san
against	prep	同對立	tùhng...deui lahp	tung4 deoi3 lap6	thuhng...toei lahp
against time	prep	分秒必爭	fàn míuh bīt jàang	fan6 miu5 bit1 zaang4	fan miuh pit chaang
age[1] (person's)	n	歲	seui	seoi3	swoi

age[2] (of the year)	n	齡	lìhng	ling4	lehng
age[3] /life of person	adj	世	sai	sai3	sai
age[4] old age person	n	年齡	lìhn lìhng	lin4 ling4	lihn lehng
age[5]	v	年紀	lìhn géi	lin4 gei2	lihn kei
age[6]	v	時代	sìh doih	si4 doi6	sih toih
aged /oldness/old age	adj	年老	lìhn lóuh	lin4 lou5	lihn louh
agency[1] /an agent	n	代辦處	doih baahn chyu	doi6 baan6 cyu3	toih paahn chhyu
agency[2] /company/firm /business/corporation	n	公司	gūng sī	gung1 si1	kung si
agenda[1]	n	程	chìhng	cing4	chhehng
agenda[2]	n	議程	yíh chìhng	ji5 cing4	yih chhehng
agent[1] /act on commission	n	代理	doih léih	doi6 lei5	toih leih
agent[2] /representative /next head/deputy	n	代理人	doih léih yàhn	doi6 lei5 jan4	toih leih yahn
agglutination /by chance	n	偶然	ngáuh yìhn	ngau5 jin4	ngauh yihn
aggressive	adj	霸道	ba douh	baa3 dou6	pa touh
aggressively	adv	侵略	chàm leuhk	cam4 loek6	chham leuhk
aggressor	n	侵略者	chàm leuhk jé	cam4 loek6 ze2	chham leuhk che
agitated[1]	v	鼓動	gú duhng	gu2 dung6	ku tohng
agitated[2] /incite/instigate	v	煽動	sín duhng	sin2 dung6	sin tohng
agitation /churn	n/v	攪動	gáau duhng	gaau2 dung6	kaau tuhng
agitator[1]	n	鼓動者	gú duhng jé	gu2 dung6 ze2	ku tohng che
agitator[2] /instigator	n	煽動者	sín dùhng jé	sin2 dung6 ze2	sin tohng che
ago[1] /before/prior /previous/ex	adv	之前	jì chìhn	zi4 cin4	chi chhihn
ago[2] /before/former/formerly /previous/previously	adv	以前	yíh chìhn	ji5 cin4	yih chhihn
agree[1] /endorse/concur /approve	v	贊成	jaan sìhng	zaan3 sing4	chaan sehng
agree[2] /approve/consent /grant/okay!	v	同意	tùhng yi	tung4 ji3	thuhng yi
agree[3]	v	意見一致	yi gin yāt ji	ji3 gin3 jat1 zi3	yi kin yat chi
agree on /stipulate /conclude a bargain	v	規定	kwài dehng	kwai4 deng6	khwai tehng
agreeable	adj	適意嘅	sīk yi ge	sik1 ji3 ge	sek yi ke
agreement[1]	n	契約	kai yeuk	kai3 joek3	khai yeuk
agreement[2]	n	協定	hip dehng /dìhng	hip3 deng6 /ding6	hip tehng
agreement[3]	n	協議	hip yíh	hip3 ji5	hip yih
agriculture /farming	n	農業	lùhng /nùhng yihp	lung4 /nung4 jip6	luhng /nuhng yihp
aha!	int/a	啊哈	àa hā	aa4 ha1	aa haa
ahead[1] /in front of/front	adj	前面	chìhn mìhn	cin4 min4	chhihn mihn
ahead[2]	adv	在前	joih chìhn	zoi6 cin4	choih chhihn
ahead[3] /forward/onward /move forward	adv	向前	heung chìhn	hoeng3 cin4	heung chhihn
ahead[4]	adv	係前邊	hái chìhn bihn	hai2 cin4 bin6	hai chhihn pihn
aid[1] /help/save/rescue	n	救	gau	gau3	kau

aid[2] /help/assistance	n	協助	hip joh	hip3 zo6	hip choh
aid[3] /help/assistance	n	援助	wùhn joh	wun4 zo6	wuhn choh
aider /helper/assistant /right hand man	n	助手	joh sáu	zo6 sau2	choh sau
aids[1] /helps	n	幫助	bòng joh	bong1 zo6	pong choh
aids[2] disease	n	愛滋病	oi /ngoi ji behng	oi3 /ngoi zi3 beng6	oi /ngoi chi pehng
aim at	n	志在	ji joih	zi3 zoi6	chi choih
aim at /target/point at	n	對準	deui jéun	deoi3 zeon2	toei cheun
aimless	adj	沒目標	muht muhk bīu	mut6 muk6 biu1	muht muhk piu
air /breath/gas/steam /vapor/spirit	n	氣	hei	hei3	hei
air bag[1] life safety device	n	氣袋	hei dòih	hei3 doi6	hei toih
air bag[2] for life safety device	n	安全氣袋	òn /ngòn chyun héi dòih	on4 /ngon4 cyun4 hei3 doi6	on /ngon chhyun hei toih
air bus[1] /mini bus	n	空中巴士	hùng jùng bà sí	hung4 zung4 baa4 si2	hung chung pa si
air bus[2]	n	大型客機	daaih yìhng haak gèi	daai6 jing4 haak3 gei4	taaih yehng haak kei
air condition	n	冷氣	láahng hei	laang5 hei3	laahng hei
air conditioner	n	冷氣機	láahng hei gèi	laang5 hei3 gei4	laahng hei kei
air gun	n	氣槍	hei chèung	hei3 coeng4	hei chheung
air hostess /flight attendant	n	空中小姐	hùng jùng síu jé	hung4 zung4 siu2 ze2	hung chung siu che
air hunger	v	空氣飢餓	hùng hei gèi ngoh	hung4 hei3 gei4 ngo6	hung hei kei ngoh
air leak	v	流氣	làuh hei	lau4 hei3	lauh hei
air line co	n	航空公司	hòhng hùng gūng sī	hong4 hung4 gung2 si1	hohng hung kung si
air pollutant	n	空氣污染物	hùng hei wù yíhm maht	hung4 hei3 wu4 jim5 mat6	hung hei wu yihm maht
air pollution	n	空氣污染	hùng hei wù yíhm	hung4 hei3 wu4 jim5	hung hei wu yihm
air raid /attack from air	n	空襲	hùng jaahp	hung4 zaap6	hung chaahp
airport /airfield	n	機場	gèi chèuhng	gei4 coeng4	kei chheuhng
airforce	n	空軍	hùng gwān	hung4 gwan1	hung kwan
airmail[1] letter	n	航空信	hòhng hùng seun	hong4 hung4 seon3	hohng hung swon
airmail[2]	n	空郵	hùng yàuh	hung4 jau4	hung yauh
airplane		飛機	fèi gèi	fei4 gei4	fei kei
airport express	n	機場快車	gèi chèuhng faai chè	gei4 coeng4 faai3 ce1	kei chheuhng faai chhe
airport tax	n	機場稅	gèi chèuhng seui	gei4 coeng4 seoi3	kei chheuhng swoi
akin[1] /like/same as	adj	如同	yùh tùhng	jyu4 tung4	yuh thuhng
akin[2] /blood relations	adj	血族	hyut juhk	hyut3 zuk6	hyut chohk
akin[3] /blood-related	adj	關係	gwàan haih	gwaan1 hai6	kwaan haih
alarmed /fear/afraid/panic	n	驚	gèng	geng4	keng
alarm[1] /siren/alertness signal	n	警報	gíng bou	ging2 bou3	keng pou
alarm[2] warning bell	n	警鐘	gíng jùng	ging2 zung4	keng chung
alas![1]	int	唉	āi /āai	ai1 /aai1	ai /aai
alas![2] /my god!	n	死咯	séi lo!	sei2 lo3	sei lo!
album[1]	n	相簿	sèung bouh	soeng4 bou6	seung pouh
album[2]	n	唱片集	cheung pín jaahp	coeng3 pin2 zaap6	chheung phin chaahp

English		Chinese	Yale	Jyutping	
albumen	n	白蛋白	baahk dáan báahk	baak6 daan2 baak6	paahk taan paahk
alcohol[1] /wine	n	酒	jáu	zau2	chau
alcohol[2]	n	火酒	fó jáu	fo2 zau2	fo chau
alcohol[3]	n	酒精	jáu jèng /jīng	zau2 zeng1 /zing1	chau cheng
alcoholic beverage /gin	n	酒類	jáu leuih	zau2 leoi6	chau lowih
alcoholometer	n	酒精計	jáu jèng gei	zau2 zeng1 gei3	chau cheng kei
alert[1]	n	警示	gíng sih	ging2 si6	keng sih
alert[2]	n	警覺地	gíng gok dèih	ging2 gok3 dei6	keng kok teih
alert affair /of the police	n	警務	gíng mouh	ging2 mou6	keng mouh
alertness /vigilance	n	警覺	gíng gok	ging2 gok3	keng kok
algebra[1]	n	代數	doih sou	doi6 sou3	toih sou
algebra[2]	n	代數學	doih sou hohk	doi6 sou3 hok6	toih sou hohk
alias /another name	adv	別名	biht méng	bit6 meng4	piht meng
alienor	n	讓渡人	yeuhng douh yàhn	joeng6 dou6 jan4	yeuhng touh yahn
alight[1] from the car/bus, get down from the bus/car	v	落車	lohk chè	lok6 ce1	lohk chhe
alight[2] get down, come down	v	下來	hah lòih	haa6 loi4	hah loih
alike /similar	adj	相似	seung chíh	soeng3 ci5	seung chhih
alive /live	adj	活著	wuht jeuk	wut6 zoek3	wuht cheuk
alkaline	adj	鹼性	gáan sing	gaan2 sing3	kaan seng
all[1] /whole/overall/totally /grand total/gross	pron adj	全	chyùhn	cyun4	chhyuhn
all[2]	pron	均	gwàn	gwan4	kwan
all[3]	pron	皆	gàai	gaai4	kaai
all[4] /whole/overall/totally /grand total/gross	adj	全部	chyùhn bouh	cyun4 bou6	chhyuhn pouh
all[5] everything	pron	一切	yāt chai	jat1 cai3	yat chhai
all[6] /whole	adj	全縣	chyùhn yùhn	cyun4 jyun4	chhyuhn yuhn
all[7] /all of	pron	所有	só yáuh	so2 jau6	so yauh
all[8]	adj	通通	tùng tùng	tung4 tung4	thung thung
all about /almost/hardly	adv	幾乎	gèi fùh	gei4 fu4	kei fuh
all along (IDM)	IDM	一貫	yāt gun	jat1 gun3	yat kun
all are okay		均可	gwàn hó	gwan4 ho2	kwan ho
all around /surrounding	adj	四圍	sei wàih	sei3 wai4	sei waih
all arrived	adj	返晒啦	fáan saai lā	faan2 saai3 laa1	faan saai la
all categories	adj	各類	gok leuih	gok3 leoi6	kok lowih
all gone[1] /sold		冇晒啦	móuh saai lā	mou5 saai3 laa1	mouh saai la
all gone[2] /sold		一D都冇啦	yāt dī dou móuh laak	jat1 di1 dou3 mou5 laa1	yat ti tou mouh laak
all in one[1]	adj	全體一致	chyùhn tái yāt ji	cyun4 tai2 jat1 zi3	chhyuhn thai yat chi
all in one[2]	adj	娛樂中心	yuh lohk jùng sàm	jyu6 lik6 zung4 sam4	yuh lohk chung sam
all kinds of		各種	gok júng	gok3 zung2	kok chung
all life/ till die (sl) [1314], whole lifetime	adj	一生一世	yāt sāng yāt sai	jat1 sang1 jat1 sai3	yat sang yat sai
all of sudden	adj	突然間	daht yìhn gāan	dat6 jin4 gaan1	taht yihn kaan

all of this		呢啲全部	lī /nī dī chyùhn bouh	li1 /ni1 di1 cyun4 bou6	li /ni ti chhyuhn pouh
all over	adj	完晒	yùhn saai	jyun4 saai3	yuhn saai
all people	adj	全體	chyhùn tái	cyun4 tai2	chhyhun thai
all right[1] /allow/okay /suitable	v	得	dāk	dak1	tak
all right[2] /good/alright /exactly right/extremely right/spot on	adj	啱晒	ngāam saai	ngaam1 saai3	ngaam saai
all right[3] /well/fine/good /exceeds standard	adj	良好	lèuhng hou	loeng4 hou3	leuhng hou
all right[4] /good/positive /no problem/no trouble at all	adj	冇問題	móuh mahn tàih	mou5 man6 tai4	mouh mahn thaih
all round[1] /total/overall /comprehensive	adj	全面	chyùhn mihn	cyun4 min6	chhyuhn mihn
all round[2] /everywhere /all four sides	adj	四周圍	sei jāu wàih	sei3 zau1 wai4	sei chau waih
all round[3] /talented /know all/multi talented	adj	多才多藝	dò chòih dò ngaih	do4 coi4 do4 ngai6	to chhoih to ngaih
all the same[1]	adj	完全一樣	yùhn chyùhn yāt yeuhng	jyun4 cyun4 jat1 joeng6	yuhn chhyuhn yat yeuhng
all the same[2]	adj	都係一樣	dōu haih yāt yeuhng	dou1 hai6 jat1 joeng6	tou haih yat yeuhng
all the time[1]	adj	周時	jàu sìh	zau4 si4	chau sih
all the time[2]		成日都	sèhng yaht dōu	seng4 jat6 dou1	sehng yaht tou
all the time[3] /always		一直	yāt jihk	jat1 zik6	yat chehk
all the way		一路咁	yāt louh gám	jat1 lou6 gam2	yat louh kam
all together		一切	yāt chai	jat1 cai3	yat chhai
all type of fire		一切類型火災	yāt chái lèuih yingfō jòi	jat1 cai3 leoi6 jing4 fo2 zoi1	yat chhai lowih yeng fo choi
alleged[1] state/to explain	v	辯解	bìhn gáai	bin6 gaai2	pihn kaai
alleged[2] /stated	v	申述	sàn sèuht	san4 seot6	san swoht
alleged[3] to state	v	聲稱	sèing /sìng chíng	seng4 /sing4 cing2	seing chheng
alleged[4] suspected crime /suspect	adj/v	涉嫌	sip yìhm	sip3 jim4	sip yihm
allegiance	n	忠貞	jùng jīng	zung4 zing1	chung cheng
allergic	adj	敏感	máhn gám	man5 gam2	mahn kam
allergy	n	敏感	máhn gám	man5 gam2	mahn kam
alley[1]	n	咁少	gám síu	gam2 siu2	kam siu
alley[2] /byroad/footway /sideway	n	小徑	síu gíng	siu2 ging2	siu keng
alliance[1] /league/union /organisation	n	同盟	tùhng màhng	tung4 mang4	thuhng mahng
alliance[2]	n	聯姻	lyùhn yān	lyun4 jan1	lyuhn yaan
allocate[1] /wiper/push aside	v	撥	buht	but6	puht
allocate[2] /distribute/assign	v	分配	fàn pui	fan4 pui3	fan phui
allocate[3] /to provide	v	配備	púi bèih	pui2 bei6	phui peih
allocate[4]	v	分派	fàn paai	fan6 paai3	fan phaai
allow[1] /come in	v	准	jéun	zeon2	cheun

allow[2]	v	等	dáng	dang2	tang
allow[3] /permit	v	許	héui	heoi2	hoi
allow[4] /permit	v	允	wáhn	wan5	wahn
allow[5] /let/permit /give away (do somethings)	v	讓	yeuhng	joeng6	yeuhng
allow[6]	v	准許	jáun héui	zeon2 heoi2	chaun hoi
allow[7] /let/let's/grant /permit	v	允許	wáhn hēui	wan5 heoi1	wahn hoi
allowable[1]	adj	可准許	hó jéuhn héui	ho2 zeon2 heoi2	ho cheuhn hoi
allowable[2]	adj	可允許	hó wáhn héui	ho2 wan5 heoi2	ho wahn hoi
allowance[1]	n	津貼	jèun tip	zeon4 tip3	cheun thip
allowance[2] /pocket money	n	零用錢	lìhng yuhng chín	ling4 jung6 cin2	lehng yuhng chhin
allowedly	ad	公認地	gūng yihng deih	gung1 jing6 dei6	kung yehng teih
allure /attract/interest /to attract	n	吸引	kāp yáhn	kap1 jan5	khap yahn
allusion[1] indirect say	n	暗指	am jí	am3 zi2	am chi
allusion[2] /indirect say /hint	n	典故	dín gu	din2 gu3	tin ku
allusion[3] /indirect say /indirect idea/hint	n	示意	sih yi	si6 ji3	sih yi
allusion[4] /indirect say /hint	n	提示	tàih sih	tai4 si6	thaih sih
Alma Mater	n	母校	móuh haauh	mou5 haau6	mouh haauh
almond	n	杏仁	hahng yàhn	hang6 jan4	hahng yahn
almost[1]/nearly/just about	adv	差唔多	chà m̀ dò	caa1 m4 do4	chha mh to
almost[2]/nearly/just about	adv	差不多	chā bāt dò	caa1 bat1 do4	chha bat to
almost[3] /soon	adv	就嚟	jauh làih	zau6 lai4	chauh laih
almost not /only just /hardly enough/scarcely	adv	幾乎沒有	gèi fùh muht yáuh	gei4 fu6 mut6 jau5	kei fuh muht yauh
alms[1] give money	n	救濟金	gau jai gàm	gau3 jai3 gam4	kau chai kam
alms[2] give things	n	救濟品	gau jai bán	gau3 zai3 ban2	kau chai pan
alms bowl	n	鉢	but	but3	put
aloevera	n	蘆薈	lòuh wuih	lou4 wui6	louh wuih
alone[1]	adv	一個人	yāt go yàhn	jat1 go3 jan4	yat ko yahn
alone[2] /own/personally	adv	自己	jih géi	zi6 gei2	chih kei
alone[3] /by oneself	adv	單獨	dāan dùhk	daan1 duk6	taan tohk
alone[4]	adv	獨自	duhk jih	duk6 zi6	tuhk chih
along[1] /following	adv	沿	yùhn	jyun4	yuhn
along[2]	adv	沿著	yùhn jyuh	jyun4 zyu4	yuhn chyuh
along with /together with	adv	連同	lìhn tùhng	lin4 tung4	lihn thuhng
alongside[1]	prep	拍住	paak jyuh	paak3 zyu6	phaak chyuh
alongside[2]	prep	拍埋	paak màaih	paak maai4	phaak maaih
aloudly shout /cry	adv	大聲	daaih sèng	daai6 seng4	taaih seng
alphabet (English)	n	英文字母	yìng màhn jih móuh	jing4 man4 zi6 mou5	yeng mahn chih mouh

alphabetical	adj	按字母表	on /ngòn jih móuh bíu	on3 /ngon4 zi6 mou5 biu2	on /ngon chih mouh piu
alphabetical order	adj	按字母表順序	on /ngòn jih móuh bíu seuhn jeuih	on3 /ngon4 zi6 mou5 biu2 seon6 zeoi6	on /ngon chih mouh piu seuhn choih
alpine	adj	高山	gòu sàan	gou4 saan4	kou saan
already[1] /bygone/finish	adv	咗	jó	zo2	cho
already[2] /done	adv	都	dōu	dou1	tou
already[3]		嘟咗	dōu jó	dou1 zo2	tou cho
already[4]	adv	已	yíh	ji5	yih
already[5] /have been /before	adv	已經	yíh gìng	ji5 ging4	yih keng
already[6] /have been /previous/sign of past /former	adv	曾經	chàhng gīng	cang4 ging1	chhahng keng
already arrived	v	返咗啦	fáan jó lā	faan2 zo2 lā a	faan cho la
already eat /eaten	v	食喎	sihk wóh	sik6 wo5	sehk woh
already came /arrived	v	嚟過	làih gwo	lai4 gwo3	laih kwo
already done /gone /done/previous/yester	adj	過去	gwo heui	gwo3 heoi3	kwo hoi
already enter /entered	adj	入咗去	yàhp jó heui	jap6 zo2 heoi3	yahp cho hoi
already joined	v	報咗名	bou jó mèhng	bou3 zo2 meng4	pou cho mehng
already open /opened	adj	開咗啦	hòi jó lā	hoi4 zo2 laa1	hoi cho la
already received	v	收咗啦	sàu jó lā	sau4 zo2 laa1	sau cho la
already sold		無嘢賣	mòuh yéh maaih	mou4 ye5 maai6	mouh yeh maaih
already told[1] /told	v	叫咗	giu jó	giu3 zo2	kiu cho
already told[2]	v	已經講咗	yíh gìng góng jó	ji5 ging4 gong2 zo2	yih keng kong cho
already used /used up /were already using		用完未	yuhng yùhn meih	jung6 jyun4 mei6	yuhng yuhn meih
alright mate? (coll) (BT)		點呀?	dīm àa /aa?	dim1 aa4 /aa3?	tim aa?
also[1] /too/even/as well	adv	都	dōu	dou1	tou
also[2]	adv	亦	yihk	jik6	yehk
also[3] (wr) too/as well/besides	adv	也	yáh /jáh	jaa5	yah
also[4] /and	adv	並	bing	bing3	peng
also[5] /again/once/too/as well	conj	又	yàuh	jau6	yauh
also has		都有	dōu yáuh	dou1 jau5	tou yauh
also okay /this also-okey		都得	dōu dāk	dou1 dak1	tou tak
altar[1] (sl)	n	祭品	jai bán	zai3 ban2	chai pan
altar[2] (sl)	n	生果	sàhn gwó	saang4 gwo2	sahn kwo
altar[3]	n	祭壇	jai tàahn	zai3 taan4	chai thaahn
alter[1] /change	v	改	gói	goi2	koi
alter[2] /modify/revision /amend/correction	v	修改	sàu gói	asu4 goi2	sau koi
alteration /change/shift	n	變動	bín dùhng	bin2 dung6	pin tuhng
alternate[1] /separate /apart/ next/another	adj	隔	gaak	gaak3	kaak
alternate[2] /alternation	adj	交替	gàau tai	gaau4 tai3	kaau thai

English		漢字	Yale	Jyutping	
alternate day	adj	隔日	gaak yaht	gaak 3 jat6	kaak yaht
alternative /choose /chose/option/opted/to select	adj	選擇	syún jaahk	syun2 zaak6	syun chaahk
although[1]	adv	不過	bāt go	bat1 gwo3	pat ko
although[2] /even though	adv	雖然	sèui yihn	seoi4 jin4	swoi yihn
altogether[1]	adv	一共	yāt guhng	jat1 gung6	yat kuhng
altogether[2]	adv	冚唪唥	hahm fúng laahng	ham6 fung2 laang6	hahm fung laahng
altruistic[1]	adj	為人	waih yàhn	wai6 jan4	waih yahn
altruistic[2]	adj	愛他	oi /ngoi tà	oi3 /ngoi ta4	oi /ngoi tha
aluminum /tin	n	鋁	léuih	leoi5	lowih
aluminum pot	n	鍟煲	tāi bōu	tai1 bou1	thai pou
alumni /ex-student	n	男校友	làahm haauh yáuh	laam4 haau6 jau5	laahm haauh yauh
always[1]	adv	常	sèuhng	soeng4	seuhng
always[2]	adv	總	júng	zung2	chung
always[3]	adv	成日	sèhng yaht	soeng4 jat6	sehng yaht
always[4]	adv	總是	júng sih	zung2 si6	chung sih
always[5] /constantly/often /frequently/again &	adv	時時都	sìh sìh dōu	si4 si4 dou1	sih sih tou
always new problem[(sl)]	adv	鑊鑊新鮮	wohk wohk sàn sìn	wok6 wok6 san4 sin4	wohk wohk san sin
always noise	adv	成晚鬧	sèhng máahn laauh /naauh	seng4 maan5 laau6/ naau6	sehng maahn laauh/ naauh
am /are [(wr)]	v	是	sih	si6	sih
amateur	n	業餘	yihp yùh	jip6 jyu4	yihp yuh
amaze /marvel/surprise	n	驚奇	gèng kèih	geng4 kei4	keng kheih
amber /yellow	n	黃色	wòhng sīk	wong4 sik1	wohng sek
amber red	n	紅雨	hùhng yúh	hung4 jyu5	huhng yuh
ambient /to surround	adj	環繞的	wàahn yuh dìk	waan4 jiu3 dik4	waahn yuh tik
ambition[1]	n	雄心	hùhng sàm	hung4 sam4	huhng sam
ambition[2] /inner intention	n	野心	yéh sàm	je5 sam4	yeh sam
ambition[3] /spirit	n	志氣	ji hei	zi3 hei3	chi hei
ambition[4] /aspiration /inner intention	n	抱負	póuh fuh	pou5 fu6	phouh fuh
ambitious	adj	有雄心	yáuh hùhng sàm	jau5 hung4 sam4	yauh huhng sam
ambulance[1]	n	救護車	gau wuh chè	gau3 wu6 ce4	kau wuh chhe
ambulance[2]	n	十字車	sahp jih chè	sap6 zi6 ce1	sahp chih chhe
ambulance[3]	n	白車	baahk chè	baak6 ce4	paahk che
ambulance[4]	n	救傷車	gau sēung chè	gau3 soeng1 ce1	kau seung chhe
ambulance corps	n	救傷隊	gau sēung déui	gau3 soeng deoi6	kau seung toei
ambush[1] /trap	n	埋伏	màaih fuhk	maai4 fuk6	maaih fuhk
ambush[2] /pitfall/trap	n	陷阱	hahm jihng	ham6 zing6	hahm chehng
ambush[3] /trap/trick	n	圈套	hyūn tou	hyun1 tou3	hyun thou
ambush[4] /trap/pitfall	n	設陷井	chit hahm jehng	cit3 ham6 zeng4	chhit hahm chehng
amen[1 (de)] /amun	n	阿門	á mùhn	aa2 mun4	a muhn

amen² (de) /amun	n	阿孟	á maahng	aa2 maang6	a maahng
amen³	n	祈禱的結束語	kèih tóu dìk git chūk yùh	kei4 tou2 dik4 git3 cuk1 jyu6	kheih thou tik kit chhuk yuh
amend¹	v	更改	gáng gói	gang2 goi2	kang koi
amend² /revision/revise	v	修訂	sau dehng	sau3 deng3	sau tehng
amendment /to revise	n	修正	sàu jeng	sau4 zeng3	sau cheng
America /U.S.A.	n	美國	Méih gwok	mei5 gwok3	Meih Kwok
amid /amidst	prep	在...之間	joih...jì gàan	zoi6 ··· zi4 gaan4	choih ... chi kaan
ammeter /amperemeter (de)	n	安培計	òn /ngòn pùih gai	on4 /ngon4 pui4 gai3	on /ngon phuih kai
ammonia (NH3)	n	氨	òn /ngòn	on4 /ngon4	on /ngon
among¹ /between	prep	際	jai	zai3	chai
among² /between/inter	prep	之間	jì gàan	zi4 gaan4	chi kaan
among³	prep	中間	jùng gàan	zung4 gaan4	chung kaan
among⁴	prep	其中	kèih jùng	kei4 zung4	kheih chung
amount¹ /measure/rate /quantity/qty/volume	n	量	lèuhng	loeng4	leuhng
amount² /quantity/qty	n	數量	sōu lèuhng	sou1 loeng6	sou leuhng
amount³ /total/sum /quantity	n	金額	gahm ngaahk	gam4 ngaak6	kahm ngaahk
amount⁴ /number /quantity/qty	n	數目	sou muhk	sou3 muk6	sou muhk
amount⁵	n	額	aahk /ngaahk	aak6 /ngaak6	aahk /ngaahk
amount⁶	v	總數	júng sou	zung2 sou3	chung sou
amount⁷	n	總額	júng aahk /ngaahk	zung2 aak6 /ngaak6	chung aahk /ngaahk
ample¹ /plenty/sufficient	adj	充足	chùng jūk	cung4 zuk1	chhung chuk
ample² /plenty	adj	充裕	chùng yùh	cung4 jyu6	chhung yuh
amuse	v	逗...高興	dauh gòu hing	dau6 gou4 hing3	tauh kou heng
amusement /fun /enjoyment/pleasure	n	樂趣	lohk cheui	lok6 ceoi3	lohk chhoi
amusing¹ /enjoyable /very fond/to do fun	adj	好玩	hóu wáan	hou2 waan2	hou waan
amusing² /laughable /comical/funny/ridiculous	adj	滑稽	waaht kài	waat6 kai4	waaht khai
amusing³ /funny /fascinating	adj	有趣	yáuh chéui	jau5 ceoi2	yauh chheui
an item	n	一項	yāt hohng	jat1 hong6	yat hohng
anaemia	n	貧血	pàhn hyut	pan4 hyut3	phahn hyut
anaesthetic	n	麻醉藥	màh jeui yeuhk	maa4 zeoi3 joek6	màh jeui yeuhk
anaesthetist	n	麻醉師	màh jeui sī	maa4 zeoi3 si1	mah cheui si
analgesic /pain killer	n	止痛劑	jí tung jāi	zi2 tung3 zai1	chi thung chai
analyser	n	分析家	fàn sīk gà	fan6 sik1 ga4	fan sek ka
analysis /analyze	n	分析	fàn sīk	fan6 sik1	fan sek
anatomy¹	n	解剖	gáai fáu	gaai2 fau2	kaai fau
anatomy²	n	解剖學	gáai fáu hohk	gaai2 fau2 hok6	kaai fau hohk
ancestor	n	宗	jung	zung3	chung
ancestral	adj	祖傳嘅	jóu chyùhn ge	zou2 cyun4 ge3	chou chhyuhn ke

English		Chinese	Yale	Jyutping	
ancestral hall	n	祠堂	chìh tóng	ci4 tong4	chhih thohng
ancient[1]	adj	古	gú	gu2	ku
ancient[2]	adj	古代嘅	gú doih ge	gu2 doi6 ge3	ku toih ke
ancient[3] /far back	adj	久遠	gáu yúhn	gau2 jyun5	kau yuhn
ancient thing /curio /antique	n	玩	wún	wun2	wun
ancient times /old time /prehistory/previous history	n/adv	古時	gú sìh	gu2 si4	ku sih
and[1] /or	conj	及	gahp	gap6	kahp
and[2] (coll)	conj	同	tùhng	tung4	thuhng
and[3] (wr)	conj	和	wòh	wo4	woh
and[4]	conj	與	yùh	jyu4	yuh
and[5]	conj	而	yìh	ji4	yih
and[6] (coll)	conj	同埋	tùhng màaih	tung4 maai4	thuhng maaih
and[7]	conj	以及	yíh kahp	ji5 kap6	yih khahp
and[8]	conj	及其	gahp kèih	gap6 kei4	kahp kheih
and[9]	conj	跟住	gān jyuh	gan1 zyu6	kan chyuh
and...?[10] what about...?/ question? /how about? if placed end of the sentence turn it into question	conj	呢?	lē /nē?	le1 /ne1?	le /ne?
and then[1]	conj	然后	yìhn hauh	jin4 hau6	yihn hauh
and then?[2] question	conj	跟住呢?	gān jyuh le /ne	gan1 zyu6 le1 /ne1	kan chyuh le /ne
and you? /about you?	conj	你呢?	léih lè, néih nè	lei5 le4, nei5 ne4	leih le, neih ne
angel	n	天使	tìn si	tin4 si3	thin si
anger[1]	v	氣	héi	hei2	hei
anger[2]	v	發怒者	faat louh jé	faat3 lou6 ze2	faat louh che
anger violence	v	突發	daht faat	dat6 faat3	taht faat
angle[1] /corner	n	角	gok	gok3	kok
angle[2] /point of view	n	角度	gok douh	gok3 dou6	kok touh
angry[1] /showing anger /indignant	adj	怒	louh	lou6	louh
angry[2]	adj	嬲	làu /nàu	lau4 /nau4	lau /nau
angry[3]	v	洩憤	sit fahn	sit3 fan5	sit fahn
angry[4]	adj	發怒	faat louh	faat3 lou6	faat louh
angry[5] /rage/violent anger	adj	大怒	daaih louh	daai6 lou6	taaih louh
angry[6] argument/wrangle	adj/n	口角	háu gok	hau2 gok3	hau kok
angry expression / frown/knit the brows/to scowl	v	皺眉頭	jau mèih tàuh	zau3 mei4 tau4	chau meih thauh
angry mood /bad blood /hatred	n	仇恨	sàuh hahn	sau4 han6	sauh hahn
angry say	adv	不耐煩地	bāt loih/noih fàahn deih	bat1 loi6 /noi6 faan4 dei6	pat loih /noih faahn teih
anguish /mental suffering/woe/annoy	n	苦惱	fú lóuh /nóuh	fu2 lou5/nou5	fu louh /nouh
animal	n	動物	duhng maht	dung6 mat6	tuhng maht

English	Part	Chinese	Reading 1	Jyutping	Reading 2
annalist	n	編年史	pīn lihn/nihn sí	pin1 lin4 /nin4 si2	phin lihn /nihn si
announce[1]	v	通告	tùng gou	tung4 gou3	thung kou
announce[2] /declare /promulgated	v	宣佈	syùn bou	syun4 bou3	syun pou
announce[3]	v	公佈	gūng bou	gung1 bou3	kung pou
announcement[1]	n	啓示	kái sih	kai2 si6	khai sih
announcement[2] /inform	n	佈告	bou gou	bou3 gou3	pou kou
announcer[1] /spokesperson	n	報告員	bo gou yùhn	bou3 gou3 jyun4	po kou yuhn
announcer[2]	n	宣告者	bou gou jé	bou3 gou3 ze2	pou kou che
announcer[3]	n	報音員告	bo yàm yùhn gou	bou3 jam4 jyun4 gou3	po yam yuhn kou
annoy /harass /invade & harass	v	侵擾	chàm yíu	cam4 jiu2	chham yiu
annoying[1] /harass/vex /bother	adj	煩	fàahn	faan4	faahn
annoying[2]	adj	猛憎	máng jáng	maang5 zang2	mang chang
annoying[3] /obnoxious	adj	討厭的	tōu yìm dìk	tou1 jim4 dik4	thou yim tek
annoying way	adj	厚臉皮	háuh líhm pèih	hau5 lim5 pei4	hauh lihm pheih
annual[1]	v	周年	jàu nìhn	zau4 nin4	chau nihn
annual[2]	v	一年	yāt nìhn	jat1 nim4	yat nihn
annual party /annual ball /dance party	n	週年舞會	jàu nìhn móuh wúi	jau4 nin4 mou5 wui2	chau nihn mouh wui
annual leave	n	放大假	fong daaih ga	fong3 daai6 gaa3	fong taaih ka
annual meeting[1]	n	年會	lihn wúih	lin4 wui5	lihn wuih
annual meeting[2]	n	週年大會	jàu nìhn daaih wúi	jau4 nin4 daai6 wui2	chau nihn taaih wui
anomalous	adj	異常	yih sèuhng	ji6 soeng4	yih seuhng
anomalous verb[1]	n	唔規則	m̀ kwài jāk	m4 kwai4 jak1	mh khwai chak
anomalous verb[2]	n	異常嘅	yih sèuhng ge	ji6 soeng4 ge3	yih seuhng ke
anonymity	n	匿名	nìk mèhng	nik4 meng4	nek mehng
anonymously	adv	匿名	nìk mèhng	nik4 meng4	nek mehng
another[1] /other	pron	另一	lihng yāt	ling6 jat1	lehng yat
another[2]	pron	另外	lihng oih /ngoih	ling6 oi6 /ngoi6	lehng oih /ngoih
another[3]	pron	又一	yàuh yāt	jau6 jat1	yauh yat
another one		另外一個	lihng oih /ngoih yāt go	ling6 oi6 /ngoi6 jat1 go	lehng oih/ngoih yat ko
another story		另一回事	lihng yāt wùih sih	ling6 jat1 wui4 si6	lehng yat wuih sih
answer[1] /reply/return	n	答	daap	daap3	taap
answer[2]	n	應	yíng	jing2	yeng
answer[3] /solution	n	答案	daap on /ngon	daap3 on3 /ngon3	taap on /ngon
answer[4]	n	答錄	daap luhk	daap3 luk6	taap luhk
answer back[1] with angry	v	駁嘴	bok jéui	bok3 zeoi2	pok choi
answer back[2] with angry	v	回嘴	wùih jéui	wui4 zeoi2	wuih choi
answer back[3] with angry	v	頂嘴	déng jéui	deng2 zeoi2	teng choi
answer machine	n	電話答錄機	dihn wá daap luhk gèi	din6 waa2 daap3 luk6 gei4	tihn wa taap luhk kei
answering back	n	厚臉皮	háuh líhm pèih	hau5 lim5 pei4	hauh lihm pheih

answering song /duet song/antiphonal answer/ two singers	n	對唱	deui cheung	deoi3 coeng3	toei cheung
ant	n	蟻	ngáih	ngai5	ngaih
antarctic	n	南極	làahm gihk	laam4 gih6	laahm kehk
anthropology	n	人類學	yàhn lèuih hohk	jan4 leoi6 hok6	yahn lowih hohk
anti[1] /against/contrary /opposite	prep	反	fáan	faan2	faan
anti[2] fight	prep	擾亂	yíu lyuhn	jiu2 lyun6	yiu lyuhn
anti[3] /to fight/to defy	adj	抗	kong	kong3	khong
anti[4] /negative/against /objection/opposition party	adj/n	反對	fáan deui	faan2 deoi3	faan toei
anti aircraft[1]	adj	防空	fòhng hùng	fong4 hung4	fohng hung
anti aircraft[2]	adj	對付飛機	deui fuh fèi gèi	deoi3 fu6 fei4 gei4	toei fuh fei kei
anti body	n	抗體	kong tái	kong3 tai2	khong thai
anti communist	adj	反共	fáan guhng	faan2 gung6	faan kuhng
antibiotic	n	抗生素	kong sàang sou	kong3 saang4 sou3	khong saang sou
anticipation /expectation	n	預料	yùh līu	jyu6 liu2	yuh liu
antimony	n	銻	tāi	tai1	thai
antipole	n	反對極	fáan deui gihk	faan2 deoi3 gik6	faan toei kehk
antiseptic	adj	消毒	sìu duhk	siu4 duk6	siu tuhk
antisocial	adj	擾亂社會	yíu lyuhn séh wúi	jiu2 lyun6 ce5 wui2	yiu lyuhn seh wui
antonym[1] /opposite meaning	n	反義字	fáan yìh jih	faan2 ji6 zi6	faan yih chih
antonym[2]	n	反義詞	fáan yìh chìh	faan2 ji6 ci4	faan yih chhih
anus[1]	n	肛門	gòng mùhn	gong4 mun4	kong muhn
anus[2]	n	屎忽	sí fāt	si2 fat1	si fat
anxiety[1] (wr) /worry	n	憂慮	yau leuih	jau3 leoi6	yau lowih
anxiety[2] /suffering	n	自忖道	jih chyún dou	zi6 cyun2 dou3	chih chhyun tou
anxiety[3]	n	焦慮	jìu làuih	ziu4 leoi6	chiu lowih
anxious[1] /to get caught	adj	掛住	gwa jyuh	gwaa3 zyu6	kwa chyuh
anxious[2] /hurried /impatient/be anxious	adj	心急	sàm gāp	sam4 gap1	sam kap
anxious[3]	adj	焦慮嘅	jìu leuih ge	ziu4 leoi6 ge3	chiu leuih ke
any[1] /whatever/whatsoever	pron	任何	yahm hòh	jam6 ho4	yahm hoh
any[2] /each/every	adj	每一	múih yāt	mui5 jat1	muih yat
any as you like / as one wishes		隨便	chèuih bihn	ceoi4 bin6	chheuih pihn
any body[1] /whoever /any one	pron	任何人	yahm hòh yàhn	jam6 ho4 jan4	yahm hoh yahn
any body[2] /whoever	pron	無論邊個	mouh leuhn bīn go	mou4 leon6 bin1 go3	mouh leuhn pin ko
any more?	adv	仲有呢?	juhng yáuh lè /nè?	zung6 jau5 le1 /ne1?	chuhng yauh le /ne?
any one[1] /no matter which/whichever	pron	無論哪個	móuh leuhn láh /náh go	mou4 leon6 la5 /na5 go3	mouh leuhn lah /nah ko
any one[2] (for things)	pron	任一	yahm yāt	jam6 jat1	yahm yat
any one person	pron	誰人	sèuih yàhn?	seoi4 yan4?	swoih yahn?

any thing /any matter	pron	什麼事	sahm mō sih	sam6 mo1 si6	sahm mo sih
any time /any moment	adv	隨時	chèuih sìh	ceoi4 si4	chheuih sih
anyhow[1] /anyway	adv	橫掂	wàahng dihm	waang4 dim6	waahng tihm
anyhow[2] /anyway /however	adj	無論如何	móuh leuhn yùh hòh	mou5 leon6 jyu4 ho4	mouh leuhn yuh hoh
anything	pron	任何事情	yahm hòh sih chìhng	jam4 ho4 si6 cing4	yahm hoh sih chhehng
anyway /however/only	adv	不過	bat gwo	bat1 gwo3	pat kwo
anywhere[1]	adv	隨處	chèuih syu	ceoi4 syu3	chheuih syu
anywhere[2]	adv	往任何地方	wóhng yahm hòh deih fōng	wong5 jam4 ho4 dei6 fong1	wohng yahm hoh teih fong
apart /separate/compart /partition/to part from	adv	分隔	fàn gaak	fan4 gaak3	fan kaak
apart from	prep	除...之外	chèuih jī oih /ngoih	ceoi4 zi1 oi6 /ngoi6	chheuih chi oih /ngoih
apart from this	prep	除此之外	chèuih chí jī òih	ceoi4 ci2 zi1 oi6	chheuih chhi chi oih
apartment[1]	n	公寓	gūng yuh	gung1 ju6	kung yuh
apartment[2]	n	公寓房間	gūng yuh fóng gàan	gung1 ju6 fong2 gaan4	kung yuh fong kaan
apartment building[1] /mansion/large building	n	大廈	daaih hah	daai6 haa6	taaih hah
apartment building[2]	n	公寓大樓	gūng yuh daaih làuh	gung1 ju6 daai6 lau4	kung yuh taaih lauh
apartment house	n	村屋	chyūn ùk	cyun1 uk1	chhyun uk
apathetic /insensible /unconcerned/numb/lose to feel/unconcerned	adj	冷淡	láahng daahm	laang5 daam6	laahng taahm
aperture /hole/hollow	n	孔	hung	hung3	hung
apex[1] /hump/peak/top	n	峰	fùng	fung2	fung
apex[2] /peak/top	n	頂	déng	deng2	teng
aphorism /proverb /common saying	n	俗話	juhk wá	zuk6 waa2	chuhk wa
apologize	v	道歉	douh hip	dou6 hip3	touh hip
apology	n	陪罪	pùih jeuih	pui4 zeoi6	phuih choih
apparently /visibly /obviously	adv	顯然地	hín yin dèih	hin2 jin4 dei6	hin yin teih
appeal[1] /beg/petition /pray/request/plea request	v	請求	chéng /chíng kàuh	ceng2 /cing2 kau4	chheng khauh
appeal[2] law	v	上訴	seuhng sou	soeng6 sou3	seuhng sou
appeal[3] /case appeal /lodged /call on	n/v	呼籲	fù yèuhk	fu4 joek6	fu yeuhk
appeal[4] /invoke/pray for /beg	v	懇求	hán kàuh	han2 kau4	han khauh
appear[1] /arise/emerge	v	出現	chēut yihn	ceot1 jin6	chhot yihn
appear[2] /arise	v	似性	chíh sing	ci5 sing3	chhih seng
appearance[1] /figure	n	象	jeuhng	zoeng6	cheuhng
appearance[2] /currently appear/phenomenon	n	現象	yihn jeuhng	jin5 zoeng6	yihn cheuhng
appearance[3] /profile	n	外貌	oih /ngoih maauh	oi6 /ngoi6 maau6	oih /ngoih maauh

appearance[4] /seems /looks	n	儀表	yìh bíu	ji4 biu2	yih piu
appellant (for law)	n	上訴人	sèuhng sóu yàhn	soeng6 sou3 jan4	seuhng sou yahn
append /add	v	添加	tīm gà	tim1 gaa1	thim ka
appendicitis	n	盲腸炎	màahng chéung yìhm	maang4 coeng4 jim4	maahng chheung yihm
appendix[1] anatomy	n	小腸	síu cheung	sio2 coeng4	siu chheung
appendix[2] anatomy	n	闌尾	làahn méih	laan4 mei5	laahn meih
appendix[3] /add	n	附加物	fuh gà maht	fuh3 gaa1 mat6	fuh ka maht
appendix of book /addendum/annex	n	附錄	fuh luhk	fu6 luk6	fuh luhk
appetite[1]	n	維口	waih háu	wai6 hau2	waih hau
appetite[2]	n	食慾!	sihk yuhk	sik6 juk6	sehk yuhk
appetite[3] /desire/lust	n	慾望	yuhk mohng	juk6 mong6	yuhk mohng
appetizing (to make favorite food)	adj	令人喜愛	ling yàhn héi ói/ ngoi	ling3 jan4 hei2 oi3 /ngoi3	leng yahn hei oi /ngoi
applaud[1] /clapping	v	拍手	paak sáu	paak3 sau2	phaak sau
applaud[2] /clapping	n/v	鼓掌	gú jéung	gu2 zoeng2	ku cheung
apple	n	蘋果	pìhng gwō	pan4 gwo1	phehng kwo
apple juice	n	蘋果汁	pìhng gwō jàp	pan4 gwo1 zap4	phehng kwo chap
appliances /instrument /implement/tool	n	器具	hei geuih	hei3 geui6	hei kwoih
applicant	n	申請人	sàn chíng yàhn	san4 ceng2 jan4	san chheng yahn
application[1]	n	申請	sàn chéng	san4 ceng2	san chheng
application[2] /use	n	用途	yuhng tòuh	jung6 tou4	yuhng thouh
application[3]	n	報考詳情	bou háau chèuhng chìhng	bou3 haau2 coeng4 cing4	pou haau chheuhng chhehng
application form	n	申請表	sàn chéng bīu	san4 ceng2 biu1	san chheng piu
apply[1] use/employ	v	用	yùhng	jung6	yuhng
apply[2]	v	應用	yìng yùhng	jing4 jung6	yeng yuhng
apply[3]	v	申請	sàn chéng	san4 ceng2	san chheng
apply lipstick	v	搽唇膏	chàh sèuhn gòu	caa4 seon4 gou4	chhah seuhn gou
apply powder	v	搽粉	chàh fán	caa4 fan2	chhah fan
apply put on[1] bandage /plaster/ointment/powder etc	v	敷	fū	fu1	fuh
apply put on[2] powder, ointment	v	搽	chàh	caa4	chhah
appoint[1] designate/ prescribe/destined	v	指定	jí dehng	zi2 deng6	chi tehng
appoint[2] /to command /to direct	v	指揮	jí paai	zi2 faai3	chi phaai
appoint[3] /nominate/to assign	v	任	yahm	jam4	yahm
appoint & nominate	v	任命	yam mehng /mihng	jam3 meng6 /ming6	yam mehng
appoint time[1]	v	時間	sìh gaan	si4 gaan3	sih kaan
appoint time[2]	v	約個	yeuk go	joek3 go3	yeuk ko
appointment	n	約會	yeuk wuih	joek3 wui6	yeuk wuih

English	Type	Chinese	Romanization	Jyutping	Pronunciation
appraisal	n	評估	pìhng gū	ping4 gu1	phehng ku
appraiser	n	評估人	pìhng gū yàhn	ping4 gu1 jan4	phehng ku yahn
appreciate	v	賞識	séung sīk	soeng2 sik1	seung sek
apprentice[1] /disciple	n	徒	tòuh	tou4	thouh
apprentice[2] /learner	n	徒弟	tòuh dái	tou4 dai2	thouh tai
approach[1]	v	來近	lòih káhn	loi4 kan4	loih khahn
approach[2]	v	將近到	jèung gahn dou	zoeng4 gan6 dou3	cheung kahn tou
approach[3]	v	接近	jip gahn	zip3 gan6	chip kahn
appropriate[1] /proper /suitable/fitting	adj	適當	sīk dong	sik1 dong3	sek tong
appropriate[2]	adj	適當的	sīk dong dìk	sik1 dong3 dik4	sek tong tek
appropriate[3]	adj	合宜嘅	hahp yìh ge	hap6 ji4 ge3	hahp yih ke
appropriate[4] /right/suit /proper/suitable/fitting	adj	適合	sīk hahp	sik1 hap6	sek hahp
appropriately	adj	適當地	sīk dong deih	sik1 dong3 dei6	sek tong teih
approve /sanction /acknowledgment	v	認可	yihng hó	jing6 ho2	yehng ho
approve by		批核	pài haht	pai4 hat6	phai haht
approximately[1] /near /close to	adv	近	káhn	kan5	khahn
approximately[2] /close to /about to arrive/very near /approach	adv	好近	hou káhn	hou3 kan5	hou khahn
approximately[3] /about	adv	約莫	yeuk mók	joek3 mok2	yeuk mok
approximately[4]	adv	乎	fùh	fu4	fuh
approximately[5] /close to	adv	近乎	káhn fùh	kan5 fu4	khahn fuh
apricot[1]	n	杏	hahng	hang6	hahng
apricot[2]	n	杏子	hahng jí	hang6 zi2	hahng chi
April	n	四月	sei yùht	sei3 jyut6	sei yuht
apron	n	圍裙	wàih kwán	wai4 kwan2	waih khwan
aquarium	n	水族	séui juhk	seoi2 zuk6	swoi chohk
aquarius	n	寶瓶座	bóu pèhng joh	bou2 peng4 zo6	pou phehng choh
aquatic	adj	水生嘅	séui sàang ge	seoi2 saang4 ge3	swoi saang ke
aqueous /hydro/water	adj	水	séui	seoi2	swoi
arabic language	n	阿拉伯文	áa lai ba màhn	aa2 lai3 baa3 man4	aa lai pa mahn
arable /suit for cultivate	n	適合耕種	sīk hahp gàang jung	sik1 hap6 gaang4 zung3	sek hahp kaang chung
arbiter[1] /judgement /judgment/umpire/referee	n	裁判	chòih pun	coi4 pun3	chhoih phun
arbiter[2]	n	決定者	kyut dehng jé	kyut3 deng6 ze2	khyut tehng che
arbitrator	n	公仲人	gùng juhng yàhn	gung4 zung6 jan4	kung chuhng yahn
arbour /shelter /pavilion	n	涼亭	lèuhng tíng	loeng4 ting2	leuhng theng
arcade	n	拱廊	gúng lòhng	gung2 long4	kung lohng
arch[1] /curve/crooked /dome	n	弧形	wu yihng	wu3 jing4	wu yehng
arch[2]	n	弓形	gúng yìhng	gung2 jing4	kung yehng
archer[1]	n	射手	sèh sáu	se6 sau2	seh sau

English		Chinese	Yale	Jyutping	Hakka
archer[2]	n	弓箭手	gùng jin sáu	gung4 zin3 sau2	kung jin sau
architect[1] /architecture	n	建築師	gin jūk sī	gin3 zuk1 si1	kin chuk si
architect[2(coll)] designer /stylist	n	設計師	chit gai sī	cit3 gai3 si1	chhit kai sih
architecture[1(coll)] architect	n	畫則師	waahk jīk sī	waak6 jik1 si1	waahk chek si
architecture[2]	n	建築式樣	gin jūk sīk yeuhng	gin3 zuk1 sik1 joeng6	kin chuk sek yeuhng
archive[1] /dossier/filed /record	n	檔案	dong on	dong3 on3	tong on
archive[2] /data book	n	資料館	jì líu gún	zi4 liu2 gun2	chi liu kun
are[1 (coll)]	vi	有	yáuh	jau5	yauh
are[2 (wr)]	v	是	sih	si6	sih
are you scared?		你驚唔驚呀?	néih gèng m̀ gèng áa?	nei5 geng4 m4 geng4 aa2	neih keng mh keng aa?
area[1] /district/zone	n	區	kèui	keoi4	khoi
area[2] region	n	區域	kèui wihk	keoi4 wik6	khoi wehk
area[3] /room/space /point of place/local/territory	n	地方	deih fòng	dei6 fong4	teih fong
area[4] /district/location /region/zone	n	地區	deih kèui	dei6 keoi4	teih khoi
area[5] /surface /surface area /dimension	n	面積	mihn jīk	min6 zik1	mihn chek
area code[1]	n	區號	kèui hòuh	keoi4 hou6	khoi houh
area code[2]	n	區域號碼	kèui wihk houh máh	keoi4 wik6 hou6 maa5	khoi wehk houh mah
area control center /district control center	n	區域管制中心	kèui wihk gún jai jùng sàm	keoi4 wik6 gun2 zai3 zung4 sam4	khoi wehk kun chai chung sam
argue[1] /quarrel	v	嗌交 / 咬	aai /ngaai gàau	aai3 /ngaai3 gaau4	aai /ngaai kaau
argue[2]	v	拗頸	áau /ngaau géng	aau2 /ngaau3 geng2	aau /ngaau keng
argue[3] /wrangle/debate	v	爭吵	jàang cháau	zang4 caau2	chaang chhaau
argue over /debate /dispute/quarrel	v	辯論	bihn leuhn	bin6 leong6	pihn lowhn
argument[1]	n	調	tìuh	tiu4	thiuh
argument[2] /cause /reason/sake	n	理由	léih yàuh	lei5 jau4	leih yauh
argument[3]	n	論據	leuhn geui	leon6 geoi3	leuhn kwoi
argument[4]	n	爭執	jàang jāp	zang4 zap1	chaang chap
arise[1] /raise/hoist/ascend	v	升	sìng	sing4	seng
arise[2] /go up	v	上升	séuhng sìng	soeng5 sing4	seuhng seng
arithmetic	n	算術	syun seuht	syun3 seot6	syun swoht
arm[1] of the body part	n	手臂	sáu béi	sau2 bei2	sau pei
arm[2] /military	n	兵種	bīng jung	bing1 zung3	peng chung
arm in arm		臂挽臂地	béi wáahn béi deih	bei2 waan5 bei2 dei6	pei waahn pei teih
armed-forces	n	服兵役	fuhk bīng yihk	fuk6 bing1 jik6	fuhk peng yihk
armor /armour	n	盔甲	kwài gaap	kwai4 gaap3	khwai kaap
armpit[1]	n	腋下	yiht hah	jit6 haa6	yiht hah
armpit[2]	n	咯肋底	gaak lāak dái	gaak3 kaak1 dai2	kaak laak tai
arms[1]	n	武	móuh	mou5	mouh

arms[2] /weapon/weaponry	n	武器	móuh hei	mou5 hei3	mouh hei
army[1] /arm/military/soldier	n	兵	bīng	bing1	peng
army[2] /military/soldiers /troop/arms/corps	n	軍	gwàn	gwan4	kwan
army[3] /military/soldiers /troop/arms/corps	n	軍隊	gwàn déui	gwan4 deui2	kwan toei
army[4]	n	陸軍	luhk gwàn	luk6 gwan4	luhk kwan
aroma	n	香氣	hèung hei	hoeng4 hei3	heung hei
around[1] /surrounding	adv	四周	sei jàu	sei4 zau4	sei chau
around[2] /right and left /on every side/here & there /everywhere	adv	到處	dou chyu	dou3 syu3	tou chyu
around[3] /probably /approximately	adj	大概	daaih kói	daai6 koi2	taaih khoi
around of district	adv	郊區	gàau kèui	gaau4 keoi4	kaau khoi
around the corner	adj	在附近	joih fuh gahn	zoi6 fu6 gan6	choih fuh kahn
around the world	adj	世界一周	sai gaai yāt jāu	sai3 gaai3 jat3 zau1	sai kaai yat chau
arouse[1] /excite/irritate	v	激	gīk	gik1	kek
arouse[2]	v	喚起	wuhn héi	wun6 hei2	wuhn hei
arouse[3] /make excited /make hot/make provoked	v	感動	gám duhng	gam2 dung6	kam tohng
arrange[1] /organize	v	編	pīn	pin1	phin
arrange[2] /fix	v	攪掂	gáau dihm	gaau2 dim6	kaau tihm
arrange for	v	為…作安排	waih jok òn /ngòn pàaih	wai6 zok3 on4 /ngon4 paai4	waih chok on /ngon phaaih
arrangement /arranged	n	安排	òn /ngòn paai	on4 /ngon4 paai3	on /ngon paai
arranger	n	編排人	pīn pàaih yàhn	pin1 paai4 jan4	phin phaaih yahn
arrest[1] (by police) /drag /pull/draw/pluck	v	拉	làai	laai4	laai
arrest[2] /catch/seize	v	逮	daih	dai6	taih
arrest[3]	v	逮捕	daih bouh	dai6 bou6	taih pouh
arrest him (by police)	v	拘捕他	kèui bouh tā	keoi4 bou6 ta1	khoi pouh tha
arrested (by police)	v	被捕	bèih bouh	bei6 bou6	peih pouh
arrester	n	逮捕者	daih bouh jé	dai6 bou6 ze2	taih pouh che
arresting	adj	逮捕人	daih bouh yàhn	dai6 bou6 jan4	taih pouh yahn
arrival[1]	n	到達	dou daaht	dou3 daat6	tou taaht
arrival[2]	n	到廠	dou chóng	dou3 con2	tou chhong
arrival & departure	n	到港同離港	dou góng tùhng lèih góng	dou3 gong2 tung4 lei4 gong2	tou kong thuhng leih kong
arrival time	n	到廠時間	dou chóng sìh gaan	dou3 cong2 si4 gaan3	tou chhong sih kaan
arrive[1] /reach	v	到	dou	dou3	tou
arrive[2] /reach/attain	v	達	daaht	daat6	taaht
arrive[3] /reach /get to a place	v	抵達	dái daaht	dai2 daat6	tai taaht
arrived[1] /came /already came		嚟咗	làih jó	lai4 zo2	laih cho

arrived[2]	v	到咗	dou jó	dou3 jo2	tou cho
arrived[3]	v	到咗㗎啦	dou jó gá lā	dou3 zo2 ga2 laa1	tou cho ka la
arrived there[1] /arriving soon		到架喇	dou ga la	dou3 gaa3 laa3	tou ka la
arrived there[2]		到那裏	dou lah /nah léuih	dou3 laa6 /naa6 leoi5	tou lah /nah leoih
arrogance /egoism	n	自大	jih daaih	zi6 daai6	chih taaih
arrogant[1]	adj	傲慢	ouh /ngouh maahn	ou6 /ngou6 maan6	ouh /ngouh maahn
arrogant[2] /very proud /too proud/big headed	n	傲慢的	ngouh maahn dìk	ngou6 maan6 dik4	ngouh maahn tek
arrow[1]	n	箭	jin	jin3	chin
arrow[2]	n	箭嘴	jin jéui	jin3 zeoi2	chin choi
arrow head	n	箭頭	jin tàuh	zin3 tau4	chin thauh
arrow-shirt [(de)]	n	鴉佬恤	ā lóu sēut	aa1 lou2 seot1	a lou seut
arsenic[1]	n	砒	pēi	pei1	phei
arsenic[2]	n	砒霜	pēi sèung	pei1 soeng4	phei seung
arson	n	縱火	jùng fó	zung4 fo2	chung fo
arsonist	n	放火犯	fong fó faahn	fong3 fo2 faan6	fong fo faahn
art[1] /skill/method/skill	n	術	seuht	seot6	swoht
art[2] /skill	n	藝術	aih /ngaih seuht	ai6 /ngai6 seot6	aih /ngaih swoht
art[3]	n	美術/美朮	méih seuht	mei5 seot6	meih swoht
art[4] subject of study	n	文學士	màhn hohk sih	man4 hok6 si6	mahn hohk sih
artery	n	動脈	duhng mahk	dung6 mak6	tuhng mahk
artful /crafty/bad clever /ridiculous/silly	adj	荒謬	fòng mauh	fong4 mau6	fong mauh
arthritis /gout (disease)	n	關節炎	gwaàn jit yìhm	gwaan4 zit3 jim4	kwaan chit yihm
article[1] /goods/thing	n	品	bán	ban2	pan
article[2] /clause of law	n	條	tìuh	tiu4	thiuh
article[3] grammar a /an	n	冠詞	gun chìh	gun3 ci4	kun chhih
articles /goods/object /matter/thing/	n	物品	maht bán	mat6 ban2	maht pan
articulate[1] (pronounce) /pronunciation/pronounce /utterance	adj/v	發音	faat yām	faat3 jam1	faat yam
articulate[2] /join/attach /connect/link	v	連接	lìhn jip	lin4 zip3	lihn chip
articulated lorry	v	鉸接式卡車	gáau jip sīk kāat chè	gaau2 zip3 sik1 kaat1 ce1	kaau chip sek khaat chhe
articulation	n	清晰發音	chēng /chīng sīk faat yām	ceng1 /cing1 sik1 faat3 jam1	chheng sek faat yam
artifice /clever	n	巧妙	háau miuh	haau2 miu6	haau miuh
artificial[1]	adj	人為	yàhn wai	jan4 wai3	yahn wai
artificial[2] /unnatural	adj	不自然	bāt jih yìhn	bat1 zi6 jin4	pat chi yihn
artificial[3] /item/thing /article	adj/n	項目	hohng muhk	hong6 muk6	hohng muhk
artificial fertilized /artificial insemination	n	人工受孕	yàhn gùng sauh yahn	jan4 gung1 sau6 jan6	yahn kung sauh yahn

artificial fiber /synthetic fiber	n	人造纖維	yàhn jouh chīm wàih	jan4 zou6 cim1 wai4	yahn chouh chhim waih
artiful design[1]	adj	陰謀	yàm màuh	jam4 mau4	yam mauh
artiful design[2] /crafty /cunning/dishonest/sly	adj	狡猾	gáau waaht	gaau2 waat6	kaau waaht
artist[1]	n	藝術家	ngaih seuht gā	ngai6 seot6 gaa1	ngaih swoht ka
artist[2] /sketcher /draftsman/drawer	n	製圖者	jai tòuh jé	zai3 tou4 ze2	chai thouh che
artless	adj	天真嘅	tìn jàn ge	tin4 zan4 ge3	thin chan ke
arts & crafts / hand-art /handicraft	n	手工藝	sáu gùng ngaih	sau2 gung4 ngai6	sau kung ngaih
arts college	n	文學院	màhn hohk yún	man4 hok6 jyun2	mahn hohk yun
as[1]	conj	如	yùh	jyu4	yuh
as[2]	conj	如同	yùh tùhng	jyu4 tung4	yuh thuhng
as[3]	conj	依照	yī jiu	ji1 ziu3	yi chiu
as[4] /same	adv	一樣地	yāt yeuhng deih	jat1 joeng6 dei6	yat yeuhng teih
as a result[1] /produce	v	結果	git gwó	git3 gwo2	kit gwo
as a result[2] /result/so that	v	因此	yàn chí	jan4 ci2	yan chhi
as a result[3] /thereby /thereon	adv	於是	yù sih	jyu4 si6	yu sih
as far as		遠到	yúhn dou	jyun5 dou3	yuhn tou
as for /as regards /concerning	v	至於	ji yù	zi3 jyu4	chi yu
as if[1]	v	仿	fóng	fong2	fong
as if[2] /as though/seems	conj	似乎	chíh fùh	ci5 fu4	chhih fuh
as if[3]	conj	猶如	yàuh yùh	jau4 jyu4	yauh yuh
as mad		若狂	yeuhk kòhng	joek6 kong4	yeuhk khohng
as much		同樣多	tùhng yèuhng dò	tung4 joeng6 do4	thuhng yeuhng toh
as much as		盡量	jeuhn leuhng	zeong6 loeng6	cheuhn leuhng
as one man	ad	一致地	yāt ji deih	jat1 zi3 dei6	yat chi teih
as regards /due to/ for /owing to/because	adj	因為	yàn waih	jan4 wai6	yan waih
as soon as[1]	n	盡快	jeuhn faai	zeon6 faai3	cheuhn faai
as soon as[2]	n	一經	yāt gìng	jat1 ging4	yat keng
as soon as possible		有咁快得 咁快	yáuh gam faai dāk gam faai	jau5 gam3 faai3 dak1 gam3 faai3	yauh kam faai tak kam faai
as to /with regard to /connection/connexion /relating to	n	關於	gwàan yù	gwaan4 jyu4	kwaan yu
as usual[1] /normal/usual/ ordinary/regular	adj	正常	jeng séuhng	zeng3 soeng6	cheng seuhng
as usual[2]		照常	jiu sèuhng	ziu3 soeng4	chiu seuhng
as usual[3]		照例	jiu laih	ziu3 lai6	chiu laih
as well		同樣地	tùhng yèuhng dèih	tung4 joeng6 dei6	thuhng yeuhng teih
as well as[1]	pr	也一樣	yáh yāt yeuhng	jaa5 jat1 joeng6	yah yat yeuhng
as well as[2]		又有	yauh yauh	jau6 jau6	yauh yauh

English		Chinese	Cantonese (diacritic)	Cantonese (romanized)	Cantonese (alt)
as well as[3] /besides / not only...but also/moreover furthermore	adv	而且	yìh ché	ji5 ce2	yih chhe
as yet /yet	adv	迄今為止	aht /ngaht gām waih jí	at6 /ngat6 gam1 wai6 zi2	aht /ngaht kam waih chi
as you wish /optional	a	隨意	cheui yi	ceoi4 ji3	chheui yi
ascend	v	登高	dàng gòu	dang4 gou4	tang kou
ascertain	v	查明	cha ming	cha3 ming3	chha meng
ascetic[1] /holy man/saint/sage	n	聖徒	sing tòuh	sing3 tou4	seng thouh
ascetic[2] /holy man/saint/sage	n	聖人	sing yàhn	sing3 jan4	seng yahn
ascetic[3]	adj	苦行	fú hàhng	fu2 hang4	fu hahng
ascetic person	n	苦行者	fú hàhng jé	fu2 hang4 ze2	fu hahng che
asexual	adj	無性器官	móuh sing hei gùn	mou4 sing3 hei3 gun4	mouh seng hei kun
asexual reproduction /clone	n	無性繁殖系	mòuh sing fàahn jihk haih	mou4 sing3 faan4 zik6 hai6	mouh seng faahn chehk haih
ash	n	灰	fùi	fui4	fui
ashamed[1] /be shy	adj	醜	cháu	cau2	chhau
ashamed[2] /be shame	adj	羞恥	sàu chí	sau4 ci2	sau chhi
ashtray[1]	n	烟灰碟	yīn fùi díp	jin1 fui4 dip2	yin fui tip
ashtray[2]	n	煙灰缸	yìn fùi gòng	jin1 fui4 gong4	yin fui kong
ashtray[3]	n	個煙灰缸	gó yìn fùi gòng	go2 jin4 fui4 gong4	ko yin fui kong
Asia	n	亞洲	áa jàu	aa2 zau4	aa chau
Asian	n	亞洲人	áa jàu yàhn	aa2 zau4 jan4	aa chau yahn
ask[1] /question/inquiry	v	問	mahn	man6	mahn
ask[2] /tell/call/request	v	叫	giu	giu3	kiu
ask advice /seek advice	v	請敎	chéng gaau	ceng2 gaau3	chheng kaau
ask after /give respects /greetings/send greetings/ send regards to	v	問候	mahn hauh	man6 hau6	mahn hauh
ask for /demand	n	討	tóu	tou2	thou
ask for trouble		找麻煩	jáau màh fàahn	zaau2 maa4 faan4	chaau mah faahn
ask intruction		請示	chéng /chíng sih	ceng2 /cing2 si6	chheng sih
ask leave[1] /apply leave		請假	chéng /chíng ga	ceng2 /cing2 gaa3	chheng ka
ask leave[2]		告假	gou ga	gou3 gaa3	kou ka
ask sick leave		請病假	chéng /chíng behng ga	ceng2 /cing2 beng6 gaa3	chheng pehng ka
ask way /ask directions	v	問路	mahn louh	man6 lou6	mahn louh
askance	adv	眼厲厲	ngáahn laih laih	ngaan5 lai6 lai6	ngaahn laih laih
askew1 /crooked/angle	adj	歪	mé	me2	me
askew[2] /not straight	adj	歪斜	mé che	me2 ce3	me chhe
asking price	n	問價	mahn ga	man6 ga3	mahn ka
asleep	adj	瞓著	fan jeuhk	fan3 zoek6	fan cheuhk
asparagus	n	蘆筍	lòuh séun	lou4 seon2	louh swon
aspect[1]	n	外觀	oih /ngoih gun	oi6 /ngoi6 gun3	oih /ngoih kun
aspect[2] /side/field side	n	方面	fòng mihn	fong4 min6	fong mihn

asphalt /thick black sticky substance used on roads surface	n	以瀝青鋪路	yíh lihk chèng pòu louh	ji5 lik6 ceng4 pou4 lou6	yih lehk chheng phou louh
aspirate	n	送氣音	sung hei yàm	sung3 hei3 jam4	sung hei yam
aspire /desire/thirst /get craving	v	渴望	hot mohng	hot3 mong6	hot mohng
aspirin	n	亞士匹靈	áa sī pāt lìhng	aa2 si1 pat1 ling4	aa sih phat lehng
aspro	n	亞士匹羅	áa sī pāt lòh	aa2 si1 pat1 lo4	aa sih phat loh
ass[1] (a animal)	n	驢仔	lèuih jái	leoi4 zai2	lowih chai
ass[2 (coll)] hateful word for man & woman	n	廢柴	fai chàaih	fai3 caai4	fai chhaaih
ass[3 (coll)] hateful word for man & woman	n	笨蛋	bahn dáan	ban6 daan2	pahn taan
assault[1]	n	毆	áu	au2	au
assault[2]	n	襲擊	jaahp gīk	zaap6 gik1	chaahp kek
assault & battery[1]	v	故意傷害	gu yi sèung hoih	gu3 ji3 soeng4 hoi6	ku yi seung hoih
assault & battery[2]	v	企圖傷害和毆打	kéih tòuh sèung hoih wòh áu dá	kei5 tou4 soeng4 hoi6 wo4 au2 daa2	kheih thouh seung hoih woh au ta
assault course	n	襲擊過程	jaahp gīk gwo chìhng	zaap6 gik1 gwo3 cing4	chaahp kek kwo chhehng
assemble[1] /gather /collected	v	集	jaahp	zaap6	chaahp
assemble[2]	v	會	wúi	wui2	wui
assemble[3] /gather	v	組合	jóu hahp	zou2 hap6	chou hahp
assemble[4] /gather	v	集合	jaahp hahp	zaap6 hap6	chaahp hahp
assemble[5] /install/fitting	v	裝配	jòng pui	zong4 pui3	chong phui
assembly	n	與會者	yùh wúih jé	jyu4 wui5 ze2	yuh wuih che
assess /evaluate	v	評估	pìhng gū	ping4 gu1	phehng ku
assessed	v	估計	gú gai	gu2 gai3	ku kai
assessing	v	估價	gú ga	gu2 gaa3	ku ka
assets	n	資產	jì cháan	zi4 caan2	chi chhaan
assets /belonging/ fortune/possession	n	財產	chòih cháan	coi4 caan2	chhoih chaan
assignment[1] /job/task/ work/worker/labour	n	工作	gùng jok	gung4 zok3	kung chok
assignment[2]	n	指派	jí paai	zi2 paai3	chi phaai
assignment[3] /mission /task/role	n	任務	yam mòuh	jam3 mou6	yam mouh
assist /help	v	助	joh	zo6	choh
assistant[1] /helper	n	幫手	bòng sáu	bong4 sau2	pong sau
assistant[2] /partner	n	夥	fo	fo3	fo
associate[1]	v	聯想	lyùhn séung	lyun4 soeng2	lyuhn seung
associate[2] /partner /comrade	n	夥伴	fó buhn	fo2 bun6	fo puhn
associated	adj	結交	git gàau	git3 gaau4	kit kaau
association /committee/ commission	n	委員會	wái yùhn wúi	wai2 jyun4 wui2	wai yuhn wui
assort /classification	n/v	分級	fàn kāp	fan6 kap1	fan khap
assorted	adj	什錦	sahm gám	sam6 gam2	sahm kam

assorted barbecued	adj	燒味拼盆	sīu meih ping pùhn	siu1 mei6 ping3 pun4	siu meih pheng phuhn
assorted fruit	adj	雜果	jaahp gwó	zaap6 gwo2	chaahp kwo
assume /hypothesis/ pretence/ suppose that	n/v	假設	gá chit	gaa2 cit3	ka chhit
assume that /supposed /assumption/so-called	v	假定	gá dehng	gaa2 deng6	ka tehng
assumption /pretend /underlying	n/v	假裝	gá jòng	gaa2 zong4	ka chong
astigmatism	n	散光	sáan gwòng	saan2 gwong4	saan kwong
astonish	v	驚訝	gèng ngah	geng4 ngaa6	keng ngah
astronomer /foreteller /astrologer/diviner	n	占卜家	jīm būk gā	zim1 buk1 ga1	chim buk ka
astrologer /foreteller /astronomer	n	天文學家	tìn man hohk gā	tin4 man3 hok6 gaa1	thin man hohk ka
astronaut /spaceman	n	太空人	taai hùng yàhn	taai3 hung4 jan4	thaai hung yahn
astronomy[1]	n	天文	tìn man	tin4 man3	thin man
astronomy[2]	n	天文學	tìn man hohk	tin4 man3 hok6	thin man hohk
astute	adj	精明嘅	jēng mìhng ge	zeng1 ming4	cheng mehng ke
asylum[1] /to shelter	n	收容所	sàu yùhng só	sau4 jung3 so2	sau yuhng so
asylum[2] /shelter/refuge	n	避難所	beih laahn /naahn só	bei6 laan6 /naan6 so2	peih laahn /naahn so
at[1] /in/on/be at (coll)	prep	喺	hái	hai2	hai
at[2] /in/on/be at (wr)	prep	在	joih	zoi6	choih
at[3] /site/place/spot place /venue/pick up point /location	prep	地點	deih dím	dei6 dim2	teih tim
at[4] /in	prep	於/于	yū / yùh	jyu1 / jyu6	yuh / yu
at[5] /in	prep	于/於	yùh / yū	jyu6 / jyu1	yu / yuh
at a time /times /counting time	n	次	chi	ci3	chhi
at any place	n	在任何	joih yahm hòh	zoi6 jam4 ho4	choih yahm hoh
at any time	n	在任何時候	joih yahm hòh sìh hauh	zoi6 jam4 ho4 si6 hau6	choih yahm hoh sih hauh
at dark /evening/dark	n	天黑	tìn hàak	tin4 haak4	thin haak
at discount	prep	打折扣	dā jit kau	daa1 zit3 kau3	ta chit khau
at first /originally	adv	本來	bún lòih	bun2 loi6	pun loih
at home		在家	joih gà	zoi6 gaa4	choih ka
at least		至少	ji síu	zi3 siu2	chi siu
at once /instant/ now/ immediate/right now/in a minute/in a moment	adj	立刻	lahp hāak	lap6 haak1	lahp haak
at once victorious /once a won		一擊即中	yāt gīk jīk jùng	jat1 gik1 zik1 zung4	yat kek chek chung
at premium		以高價	yíh gòu ga	ji5 gou4 ga3	yih kou ka
at that time[1] /then /just at the moment of	adv	嗰陣時	gó jahn sí	go2 zan6 si2	ko chahn si
at that time[2] /while	n	當時	dòng sìh	dong4 si4	tong sih
at that time[3] /by that time	prep	到時	dou sìh	dou3 si4	tou sih
at that time[4]		在那時	joih là /láh sìh	zoi6 laa6 /laa5 si6	choih lah sih

English	Type	漢字			
at the back	adj	後面	hauh mìhn	hau6 min6	hauh mihn
ate[1] /eaten/have eaten /already eat	v	食咗	sihk jó	sik6 zo2	sehk cho
ate[2]	v&i	進食	jeun sihk	zeon3 sik6	cheun sehk
ate[3] already	v	食飽喇	sihk báau la	sik6 baau2 la3	sehk paau la
ate[4] /eaten/eat already	v	食咗喇	sihk jó la	sik6 zo2 la3	sehk cho la
athlete	n	運動員	wahn duhng yùhn	wan6 dung6 jyun4	wahn tohng yuhn
atlas	n	地圖集	deih tòuh jaahp	dei6 tou4 zaap6	teih thouh chaahp
ATM machine	n	提款機	tàih fún gèi	tai4 fun2 gei4	thaih fun kei
atmosphere[1] /mood /feeling	n	氣氛	hei fān	hei3 fan1	hei fan
atmosphere[2] /air surrounds the earth	n	空氣	hùng hei	hung4 hei3	hung hei
atom	n	原子	yùhn jí	jyun4 zi2	yuhn chi
atomic[1]	adj	原子	yùhn jí	jyun4 zi2	yuhn chi
atomic[2] /atom	adj/n	分子	fàn jí	fan4 zi2	fan chi
atrophy	v	萎縮	wāi sūk	wai1 suk1	wai suk
attach /to attach/to adhere	v	依附	yí fuh	ji2 fu6	yi fuh
attack[1] /beat/fight/hit/bit	v	擊	gīk	gik1	kek
attack[2] /raid/inherit/assault	n	襲	jaahp	zaap6	chaahp
attack[3] /hit/beat/blew /to fight/to shoot/stroke	v	打	dá	daa2	ta
attack[4]	v	攻	gūng	gung1	kung
attack[5] /invade	v	征	jìng	zing4	cheng
attack[6] assault	v	進攻	jeun gūng	zeon3 gung1	cheun kung
attack[7] /rush attack /surprise attack/violence	v	襲擊	jaahp gīk	zaap6 gik1	chaahp kek
attack[8] /charge/hit	v	猛衝	máahng chùng	maang5 cung4	maahng chhung
attack by group	v	毆打	áu dá	au2 daa2	au ta
attack by verbally /verbally attack	v	抨擊	pèhng gīk	peng4 gik1	phehng kek
attacker[1] violence	n	猛攻者	máahng gūng jé	maang5 gung1 ze2	maahng kung che
attacker[2] offensive way	n	進攻者	jeun gūng jé	zeon3 gung1 ze2	cheun kung jé
attacker[3] /aggressor (violence)	n	攻擊者	gùng gīk jé	gung4 gik1 ze2	kung kek che
attain /reach	v	達到	daaht dou	daat6 dou3	taaht tou
attempt[1] /test/exam/try	n/v	試	si	si3	si
attempt[2] /try/to endeavour	v	企圖	kéih tòuh	kei5 tou4	kheih thouh
attempt[3] /to try	v	試圖	si tòuh	si3 tou4	si thouh
attempt firmly	n	試吓做	si háh jouh	si3 haa2 zou6	si hah chouh
attempt to do /do best /endeavour	n	盡力	jeuhn lihk	zeon6 lik6	cheuhn lehk
attend /presence/present	v	出席	cheut jihk	ceot1 zik6	chhot chehk
attendance[1]	n	到場	dou chèuhng	dou3 coeng4	tou chheuhng
attendance[2]	n	出席人數	chēut sihk yàhn sóu	ceot1 sik6 jan4 sou2	chhot sehk yahn sou

English		Chinese	Yale	Jyutping	Romanization
attendant[1] /servant	n	隨行嘅人	chèuih hàhng ge yàhn	ceoi4 hang4 ge3 jan4	chheuih hahng ke yahn
attendant[2] /servant	n	服務員	fuhk mouh yùhn	fuk6 mou6 jyun4	fuhk mouh yuhn
attention[1]	n	專心	jyùn sàm	zyun1 sam4	chyun sam
attention[2] /regard /take care/take note of	n	注意	jyu yi	zyu3 yi3	chyu yi
attentive	adj	注意嘅	jyu yi ge	zyu3 yi3 ge3	chyu yi ke
attitude[1] /manner/habit /conduct/character	n	態	taai	taai3	thaai
attitude[2]	n	態度	taai douh	taai3 dou6	thaai touh
attorney /solicitor /lawyer/advocate	n	律師	leuht sī	leot6 si1	lwoht si
attorney general[1]	n	檢察長	gím chaat jéung	gim2 caat3 zoeng2	kim chhaat cheung
attorney general[2]	n	司法部長	sī faat bouh jéung	si1 faat3 bou6 zoeng2	si faat pouh cheung
attorney general[3]	n	司法首長	sī faat sáu jéung	si1 faat3 sau2 zoeng2	si faat sau cheung
attract /to pull/draw out	v	引	yáhn	jan5	yahn
attract attention /to provoke	v	討	tóu	tou2	thou
attracted person	n	吸引人	kāp yáhn yàhn	kap1 jan5 jan4	khap yahn yahn
attraction[1] /sex appeal	n	引力	yáhn lehk	jan5 lek6	yahn lehk
attraction[2] /sex appeal	n	吸引力	kāp yáhn lihk	kap1 jan5 lik6	khap yahn lehk
attractive[1] /attraction /force	n	吸力	kāp lihk	kap1 lik6	khap lehk
attractive[2] /becoming attract /attraction power	adj	有吸引力	yáuh kāp yáhn lihk	jau5 kap1 jan5 lik6	yauh khap yahn lehk
atypical	adj	不合規則	bāt hahp kwài jāk	bat1 hap6 kwai4 zak1	pat hahp khwai chak
auction	n	拍賣	páak màaih	paak2 maai6	phaak maaih
audible	adj	聽得見	tèng dàk gín	teng4 dak4 gin2	theng tak kin
audience[1] /hearing	n	聽	tèng	teng4	theng
audience[2] /spectator	n	觀眾	gùn jung	gun4 zung3	kun chung
audience[3] /listener	n	聽眾	tèng jung	teng4 zung3	theng chung
audience[4]	n	愛好者	oi /ngoi hóu jé	oi3 /ngoi3 hou2 ze2	oi /ngoi hou che
audio	adj	聽覺嘅錄音	tèng gok ge luhk yām	teng4 gok3 ge3 luk6 jam1	theng kok ke luhk yam
audio tape	n	錄音帶	luhk yām dáai	luk6 jam1 daai2	luhk yam taai
audit[1]	n	查帳	chàh jeung	caa4 zong3	chhah cheung
audit[2]	n	稽查	kāi chàh	kai1 caa4	khai chhah
auditing	v	審計	sám gái	sam2 gai2	sam kai
auditor[1]	n	審計員	sám gái yùhn	sam2 gai2 jyun4	sam kai yuhn
auditor[2]	n	稽查員	kāi chàh yùhn	kai1 caa4 jyun4	khai chhah yuhn
auditorium /hall	n	會堂	wuih tòhng	wui6 tong4	wuih tohng
August month	n	八月	baat yuht	baat3 jyut6	paat yuht
August 27th	n	八月二十七	baat yùht yìh sàhp chāt	baat3 jyut6 ji6 sap6 cat1	paat yuht yih sahp chhat
aunt	n	姑	gù	gu4	ku
auspicious[1]	adj	吉利嘅	gāt leih ge	gat1 lei6 ge3	kat leih ke

auspicious[2]	adj	好意頭	hóu yi tàuh	hou2 ji3 tau4	hou yi thauh
auspicious begin	adj	好嘅開始	hóu ge hòi chí	hou2 ge3 hoi4 ci2	hou ke hoi chhi
auspicious sign[1]	adj	有跡可尋	yáuh jek hó chàhm	jau5 zek3 ho2 cam4	yauh chek ho chhahm
auspicious sign[2]	adj	好運嘅先兆	hóu wahn ge sin siuh	hou2 wan6 ge3 sin3 siu6	hou wahn ke sin siuh
Australia	n	澳洲	óu jàu	ou2 zau4	ou chau
authentic /believable	adj	可信	hó séun	ho2 seon2	ho swon
authenticity /reality	n	真實性	jàn saht sing	zan1 sat6 sing3	chan saht seng
author /writer	n	作者	jok jé	zok3 ze2	chok che
authority[1]	n	權	kyùhn	kyun4	khyuhn
authority[2]	n	權威	kyùhn wài	kyun4 wai4	khyuhn wai
authorization letter		授權書	sauh kyùhn syù	sau6 kyun4 syu4	sauh khyuhn syu
authorize /empower	v	授權	sauh kyùhn	sau6 kyun4	sauh khyuhn
autobiography / self propagating	n	自傳	jih jyún	zi6 zyun6	chih chyun
autocratic	adj	專制	jyūn jai	zyun1 zai3	chyun chai
autograph /signature /initial/sign/endorsed by		簽名	chìm méng	cim4 meng2	chhim meng
automatic /self acting	adj	自動	jih duhng	zi6 dung6	chih tuhng
automobile /car/auto/ vapor engine	n	汽車	hei chè	hei3 ce1	hei chhe
autonomous	adj	自治	jih jih	zi6 zi6	chih chih
autotoll[1]		快易通	faai yìh tùng	faai3 ji6 tung4	faai yih thung
autotoll[2]	v	駕易通	ga yìh tùng	gaa3 ji6 tung4	ka yih thung
autumn[1] /fall	n	秋季	chàw gwai	cau4 gwai3	chhaw kwai
autumn[2] /fall	n	秋天	chāu /chàw tìn	cau1 tin1	chhau thin
auxiliary /supporter	adj	輔助	fuh jòh	fu6 zo6	fuh choh
auxiliary machinery	adj	輔助機器	fuh jòh gèi hei	fu6 zo6 gei4 hei3	fuh choh kei hei
avail /useful/helpful	v	有用	yáuh yuhng	jau5 jung6	yauh yuhng
avail oneself of /utilize/employ/exploit/make -use of/take advantage	v	利用	leih yuhng	lei6 jung6	leih yuhng
available[1]	adj	有效	yáuh haauh	jau5 haau6	yauh haauh
available[2]	adj	可以搵得到	hó yíh wán dāk dóu	ho2 ji5 wan3 dak1 dou2	ho yih wan tak tou
available[3]	n	得閒	dāk hàahn	dak1 gaan4	tak haahn
avaricious[1] /extreme desire/greedy	n	婪	làahm	laam6	laahm
avaricious[2] /greedy	n	貪婪	tāam làahm	taam1 laam6	thaam laahm
average	adj	平均	pèhng gwàn	peng4 gwan4	phehng kwan
average grade	adj	平均分	pèhng gwàn fàn	peng4 gwan4 fan4	phehng kwan fan
aviation[1] /flight	n	飛行	fèi hàhng	fei4 hang4	fei hahng
aviation[2]	n	航空	hòhng hùng	hong4 hung4	hohng hung
avocado	n	牛油果	ngàuh yàuh gwó	ngau4 jau4 gwo2	ngauh yauh kwo
avoid[1] /exempt	n/v	免	míhn	min5	mihn
avoid[2] /to prevent	v	避免	beih míhn	bei6 min5	peih mihn
avoid[3] /keep away from	v	避開	bèih hòi	bei6 hoi4	peih hoi

English	Part	漢字	Yale	Jyutping	Romanization
avoid[4] /try not to do something	v	迴避	wùih bèih	wui4 bei6	wuih peih
avoid by all means	adj	切忌	chit geih	cit3 gei6	chhit keih
avoidable	adj	可以避免	hó yíh beih míhn	ho2 ji5 bei6 min5	ho yih peih mihn
awake[1] /wake up	v	叫醒	giu séng	giu3 seng2	kiu seng
awake[2]	v	喚醒	fun séng	fun3 seng2	fun seng
awaken[1]	v	醒	séng	seng2	seng
awaken[2]	v	覺醒	gaau séng	gaau3 seng2	kaau seng
awakened (by noised)	v	嘈醒	chòuh séng	cou4 seng2	chhouh seng
award /prize	n	獎	jéung	zoeng2	cheung
aware	adj	意識到	yi sìk dóu	ii3 sik4 dou2	yi sek tou
awareness	n	了悟	líuh ngh	liu5 ng6	liuh ngh
away	adv	離開	lèih hòi	lei4 hoi4	leih hoi
awful /dreadful/terrible! /terrifying/frightening/very bad	adj	得人驚	dāk yàhn gèng	dak1 jan4 geng4	tak yahn keng
awkward[1]	adj	唔熟練	m̀ suhk lihn	m4 suk6 lin6	mh suhk lihn
awkward[2] /embarrass	adj/v	尷尬	gaam gaai	gaam3 gaai3	kaam kaai
awkward[3] /inexpert	adj	不熟練	bāt sùhk lìhn	bat1 suk6 lin6	pat suhk lihn
awning	n	遮篷	jē pùhng	ze1 pung4	che phuhng
ax /axe/hatchet	n	斧頭	fú táu	fu2 tau2	fu thau
axe	n	長柄斧	chèuhng beng fú	coeng4 beng3 fu2	chhèuhng peng fu
axis /imaginary line	n	軸	juhk	zuk6	chuhk
axle (of vehicle)	n	車軸	chè juhk	ce4 zuk6	chhe chuhk
azalea (flower)	n	杜鵑花	douh gyūn fā	dou6 gyun1 faa1	touh kyun fa

English		Chinese	Romanization 1	Jyutping	Romanization 2
B /roman 'II'	n	乙	yut	jyut3	yut
B.A.	n	學士	hohk sih	hok6 si6	hohk sih
B.C. before Christ years	n	紀元前	géi yùhn chìhn	gei jyun4 cin4	kei yuhn chhihn
B.S.	n	學士	hohk sih	hok6 si6	hohk sih
baby[1](coll) (de) under 9 months	n	啤啤	bìh bī	bi4 bi1	pih pi
baby[2](coll) (de) under 9 months	n	啤啤仔/BB仔	bìh bī jái	bi4 bi4 zai2	pih pi chai
baby[3] /kid/child/infant 3-12 years	n	細蚊仔	sai mān jái	sai3 man1 zai2	sai man chai
baby[4] /kid (wr) 3-12 years	n	小孩	síu hàaih	siu2 haai4	siu haaih
baby[5] /child (wr) 3-12 years	n	孩子	hàaih jí	haai4 zi2	haaih chi
baby[6] (wr) under 9 months	n	嬰兒	yìng yìh	jing4 ji4	yeng yih
baby car /prams/buggy	n	嬰兒車	yìng yìh chè	jing4 ji4 ce1	yeng yih chhe
baby suit[1]	n	嬰兒嘅衫	yìng yìh ge sàam	jing4 ji4 ge3 saam4	yeng yih ke saam
baby suit[2]	n	嬰孩衣服	yìng hàaih yī fuhk	jing1 haai4 ji1 fuk6	yeng haaih yi fuhk
bachelor	n	青頭仔	chēng tàuh jái	ceng1 tau4 zai2	chheng thauh chai
back[1] /rear	n	後	hauh	hau6	hauh
back[2] backside of the body	n	背	bui	bui3	pui
back[3] spinal cord/vertebra	n	脊	jek	zek3	chek
back[4] of human	n	背脊	bui jek	bui3 zek3	pui chek
back door	n	後門	hauh mún	hau6 mun2	hauh mun
back page	n	背頁	bui yihp	bui3 jip6	pui yihp
back side[1] /on the back /in back of	n	後便	hauh bihn	hau6 bin6	hauh pihn
back side[2]	n	背面	bui mihn	bui3 min6	pui mihn
back side[3] /rear/back /in back of	n	後面	hauh mihn	hau6 min6	hauh mihn
back up[1] /reinforce	n	增援	jàng wùhn	zang4 wun4	chang wuhn
back up[2]	n	褪後	toi hauh	toi3 hau6	thoi hauh
back up[3]	n	備份	beih fān	bei6 fan1	peih fahn
backache	n	背疼	bui tung	bui3 tung3	pui thong
backbite	v	中傷	jùng sèung	zung4 soeng4	chung seung
backbiter[1]	n	喺背後中傷人	hái bui hauh jung sèung yàhn	hai2 bui3 hau6 zung3 soeng4 jan4	hai pui hauh chung seung yahn
backbiter[2]	n	誹謗者	féi póhng jé	fei2 pong5 ze2	fei phohng che
backbiting /libel/slander/defamation	n	誹謗	féi póhng	fei2 pong2	fei phohng
background[1]	n	底	dái	dai2	tai
background[2]	n	背景	bui gíng	bui3 ging2	pui geng
backhoe /large vehicle	n	反鏟挖土機	fáan cháan waat tóu gèi	faan2 caan2 waat3 tou2 gei4	faan chhaan waat thou kei
backstroke lie on back to swimming	n	仰游	yéuhng yàuh	joeng5 jau4	yeuhng yauh
backwards less progress	adj	向後	heung hauh	hoeng3 hau6	heung hauh
bacon	n	煙肉	yīn yuhk	jin1 juk6	yin yuhk
bacteria	n	細菌	sai kwán	sai3 kwan2	sai khwan

bacteria killer liquid /disinfect liquid	v	消毒水	sīu duhk séui	siu1 duk6 seoi2	siu tuhk swoi
bad boy	n	壞孩子	waaih hàaih jí	wai6 haai4 zi2	waaih haaih chi
bad debt	n	爛賬	laahn jeung	laan6 zoeng3	laahn cheung
bad faith	n	奸詐	gàan ja	gaan4 za3	kaan cha
bad feeling	n	反感	fáan gám	faan2 gam2	faan kam
bad habit	n	壞習慣	wàaih jaahp gwaan	waai6 zaap6 gwaan3	waaih chaahp kwaan
bad luck/evil omen/evil euspicious/bad luck time /have bad luck	adj	倒霉嘅時候	dou mùih ge sìh hauh	dou3 mui4 ge3 si4 hau6	tou muih ke sih hauh
bad man[1]	n	衰人	sèui yàhn	seoi4 jan4	swoi yahn
bad man[2] /evil-doer/ malefactor/villain	n	壞人	waaih yàhn	waai6 jan4	waaih yahn
bad man[3] (sl) /evil man/ morally bad/violent man/ gangster/hooligan/mobster /ruffian/wickeder	n	公仔人	gùng jái yàhn	gung4 zai2 jan4	kung chai yahn
bad might happen /phobia	n	恐懼	húng geuih	hung4 geoi6	hung kwoih
bad people /morally bad	n	惡人	ok /ngok yàhn	ok3 /ngok3 jan4	ok /ngok yahn
bad reputation	n	壞名聲	waaih mèhng sèng	waai6 meng4 seng4	waaih mehng seng
bad temper	adj	唔好脾氣	m̀ hóu pèih hei	m4 hou2 pei6 hei3	mh hou pheih hei
bad temper /irascible /irritable/showing anger/ crabby	adj	暴躁	bouh chou	bou6 cou4	pouh chhou
bad-tempered woman /vixen woman/shrew/witch	n	母夜叉	móuh yeh chā	mou5 je6 caa1	mouh yeh chha
bad thing happened		不雨則已	bāt yúh jāk yíh	bat1 jyu5 zak1 ji5	pat yuh chak yih
bad trick /dishonest /dirty trick	n	卑鄙的行為	bēi péi dīk hàahng wàih	bei1 pei2 dik1 haang4 wai4	pei phei tek haahng waih
bad weather	n	天氣唔好	tìn hei m̀ hóu	tin4 hei3 m4 hou2	thin hei mh hou
badge[1]	n	襟章	kàm jèung	kam4 zoeng4	kham cheung
badge[2] /rank/post/logo	n	徽章	fài jèung	fai4 zoeng4	fai cheung
badge[3]	n	證章	jing jèung	zing3 zoeng4	cheng cheung
badly	adv	拙劣地	jyuht lyut deih	zyut6 lyut3 dei6	chyuht lyut teih
bag[1] /sack/pocket	n	袋	dói /doih	doi2 /doi6	toi /toih
bag[2] (hand bag)	n	手抽	sáu chàu	sau2 cau4	sau chhau
baggage /luggage	n	行李	hàhng léih	hang4 lei5	hahng leih
laggage van /baggage carts	n	手推車	sáu tèui chè	sau2 teoi4 ce1	sau thoi chhe
baggage room	n	行李寄放處	hàhng léih gei fong syu	hang4 lei5 gei3 fong3 syu3	hahng leih kei fong syu
bail[1] /guarantee	n	擔保	dàam bóu	daam4 bou2	taam pou
bail[2]	n	保釋金	bóu sik gàm	bou2 sik3 gam4	pou sek kam
bait /food/pastry	n	餌	leih	lei6	leih
bake[1]	v	燒	sìu	siu4	siu
bake[2] /roast/heat by fire	v	烘	hong	hong3	hong
baked	n	焗	guhk	guk6	kuhk

English		Chinese	Cantonese	Jyutping	Romanization
bakery shop[1]	n	麵包鋪	mihn bàau póu	min6 baau4 pou2	mihn paau phou
bakery shop[2]	n	麵包店	mihn bàau dim	min6 baau4 dim3	mihn paau tim
balance[1] cash	n	結餘	git yùh	git3 jyu4	kit yuh
balance[2] equilibrium	n	平衡	pèhng hang	peng6 hang3	phehng hang
balance diet	n	全營養食品	chyùhn yìhng yéuhng sihk bán	cyun4 jing4 joeng5 sik6 ban2	chhyuhn yehng yeuhng sehk pan
balcony[1]	n	騎樓	kèh láu	ke6 lau2	kheh lau
balcony[2]	n	露臺/露台	lauh tòih	lau6 toi4	lauh thoih
baldness /bald head	n	禿頭	tūk tàuh	tuk1 tau4	thuk thauh
ball[1]	n	球	kàuh	kau4	khauh
ball[2] (de) football/handball	n	波	bō	bo1	po
ball bearing	n	滾珠	gwán jyú	gwan2 jyu2	kwan chyu
ball pen	n	原子筆	yùhn jí bāt	jyun4 zi2 bat1	yuhn chi pat
ball pepper	n	青椒	chèng jìu	ceng4 ziu4	chheng chiu
ballet	n	芭蕾舞	bā lèuih móuh	ba1 leoi5 mou5	pa lowih mouh
balloon	n	氣球	hei kàuh	hei3 kau4	hei khauh
ballroom[1] /theatre/stage of theatre	n	舞聽	móuh tèng	mou5 teng4	mouh theng
ballroom[2] /dancing hall	n	跳舞的大廳	tiu móuh dīk daaih tèng	tiu3 mou5 dik1 daai6 teng4	thiu mouh tik taaih theng
balsam cream for face	n	香脂	hèung jì	hoeng4 zi4	heung chi
bamboo	n	竹	jūk	zuk1	chuk
bamboo feedbox /crib/feedbox for cattle/ wooden feedbox	n	秣槽	mut chòuh	mut3 cou4	mut chhouh
bamboo pipe	n	竹筒	jūk tùhng	zuk1 tung4	chuk thuhng
bamboo scaffolding	n	竹棚	jūk pàahng	zuk1 paang4	chuk phaahng
bamboo stems /stems	n	竹節	jūk jit	zuk zit3	chuk chit
ban /prohibition/restriction /not allowed	n	禁令	gam lihng	gam3 ling6	kam lehng
banana[1] fruit	n	蕉	jìu	ziu4	chiu
banana[2] fruit	n	香蕉	hèung jìu	hoeng4 ziu4	heung chiu
banana[3] (sl) penis	n	蕉	jìu	ziu4	chiu
band[1] /tie/bind	v	捆	kwán	kwan2	khwan
band[2] (de) tie	n	縛	bong	bong3	pong
band[3] of music	n	樂隊	ngohk déui	ngok6 deoi2	ngohk toei
band[4] music	n	樂團	lohk tyùhn	lok6 tyun4	lohk thyuhn
band[5] (de) group	v	縛	bang	bang1	pang
bandage[1]	n	繃帶	bàng dáai	bang4 daai2	pang taai
bandage[2]	n	包紮	bāau jaat	baau1 zaat3	paau chaat
bang /knock	v	敲	hāau	haau1	haau
bangle	n	手鈪	sáu ngáak	sau2 ngaak2	sau ngaak
banishment	n	流放	làuh fong	lou4 fong3	lauh fong
bank[1] /for money	n	銀行	ngàhn hòhng	ngan4 hong4	ngahn hohng
bank[2] /beach/shore	n	岸	ngòhn	ngon6	ngohn
bank[3] /pile/heap	n	堆	dèui	deoi4	toei

English		Chinese	Yale	Jyutping	Alt. romanization
bank balance	n	銀行存款	ngàhn hòhng chyùhn fún	ngan4 hong4 cyun4 fun2	ngahn hohng chhyuhn fun
bank card	n	銀行卡片	ngàhn hòhng kāt pín	ngan4 hong4 kaat1 pin2	ngahn hohng khat phin
bank draft	n	銀行匯票	ngàhn hòhng wuih piu	ngan4 hong4 wui6 piu3	ngahn hohng wuih phiu
bank holiday	n	銀行休假期	ngàhn hòhng yāu ga kèih	ngan4 hong4 jau1 gaa3 kei4	ngahn hohng yau ka kheih
bank note[1]	n	銀紙	ngàhn jí	ngan4 zi2	ngahn chi
bank note[2]	n	鈔票	chaau piu	caau3 piu3	chhaau phiu
Bank of China	n	中國銀行	jùng gwok ngàhn hòhng	zung4 gwok3 ngan4 nong4	chung kwok ngahn hohng
bank statement	n	銀行對帳單	ngàhn hòhng deui jeung dāan	ngan4 hong4 deoi3 zoeng3 daan1	ngahn hohng toei cheung taan
banker[1] (bank owner)	n	銀行家	ngàhn hòhng gā	ngan4 hong4 ga1	ngahn hohng ka
banker[2] large gambling	n	莊家	jōng gā	zong1 ga1	chong ka
banking	n	銀行業務	ngàhn hòhng yihp mouh	ngan4 hong4 jip6 mou6	ngahn hohng yihp mouh
bankrupt	adj	破產	po cháan	po3 caan2	pho chhaan
banner	n	旗幟	kèih chi	kei4 ci6	kheih chhi
banns /to marry announce	n	結婚嘅公告	git fàn ge gùng gou	git3 fan4 ge3 gung4 gou3	kit fan ke kung kou
banquet[1] /formal dinner /dinner party	n	酒席	jáu jihk	zau2 zik6	chau chehk
banquet[2] /supper /dinner party/ formal dinner	n	宴會	yin wuih	jin3 wui6	yin wuih
banquet[3] /dinner /dinner party	n	晚宴	máahn yin	maan5 jin3	maahn yin
banter /joke/laugh/smile	v	笑	siu	siu3	siu
baptism	n	洗禮	sái láih	sai2 lai5	sai laih
baptismal certificate	n	洗禮證明	sái láih jíng meng /ming	sai2 lai5 zing2 meng3 /ming3	sai laih cheng meng
baptist mission	n	浸信會	jam seun wúi	zam3 seon3 wui2	cham swon wui
baptize	v	受洗成為	sàuh sái sèhng wàih	sau6 sai2 seng4 wai6	sauh sai sehng waih
bar[1]	n	棒	páahng	paang5	phaahng
bar[2] /beam/stick/pole	n	根木	gān muhk	gan1 muk6	kan muhk
bar[3] /fence/parapet /railing /banister	n	欄杆	làahn gòn	laan4 gon4	laahn kon
bar code[1]	n	條碼	tíuh máh	tiu5 ma5	thiuh mah
bar code[2]	n	流水碼	làuh séui máh	lau4 seoi2 ma5	lauh swoi mah
bar code[3]	n	電腦條碼	dihn nóuh tíuh máh	din6 nou5 tiu5 ma5	tihn nouh thiuh mah
barbecued /BBQ	n	燒嘢食	sìu yéh sìhk	siu4 je5 sik6	siu yeh sehk
barbecued pork	n	叉燒	chā sìu	caa1 siu4	chha siu
barbecued pork rice	n	叉燒飯	chā sīu faahn	caa1 siu1 faan6	chha siu faahn
barber /hairdresser/ahaver	n	理髮師	léih faat sī	lei5 faat3 si1	leih faat si
barber	n	飛髮佬	fēi faat lóu	fei1 faat3 lou2	fei faat lou
barber shop	n	飛髮鋪	fēi faat póu	fei1 faat3 pou2	fei faat phou

barber's shop / hairdresser's	n	理髮店	léih faat dim	lei5 faat3 dim3	leih faat tim
bargain (for price)	v	講價	góng ga	gong2 gaa3	kong ka
bargirl[1]	n	吧女	bā léoih /néoih	baa1 leui5 /neui5	pa lowih /nowih
bargirl[2]	n	酒吧女	jáu bà léoih /néoih	zau2 baa4 leoi5 /neoi5	chau pa lowih /nowih
bark[1] loud sound	v	吠	faih	fai6	faih
bark[2] loud sound	v	吠叫	faih giu	fai6 giu3	faih kiu
bark[3] outer cover of tree	n	樹皮	syuh pèih	syu6 pei4	syuh pheih
barn /stable	n	馬廄	máh gau	maa5 gau3	mah kau
barn owl	n	倉鴞	chōng hīu	cong1 hiu3	chhong hiu
barracks /cantonment/ camp	n	兵營	bīng yìhng	bing1 jing4	peng yihng
barrel[1] /tank/bin/bucket	n	桶	túng	tung2	thung
barrel[2]	n	大桶	daaih túng	daai6 tung2	taaih thung
barrel[3] like a tube	n	鎗管	chēung gún	coeng1 gun2	chheung kun
barren /unproductive/ unfertile/unproduce	adj	無得生	móuh dāk sàng	mou5 dak1 sang4	mouh tak sang
barrier[1] of gate	n	閘杆	jaahp gōn	zaap6 gon1	chaahp kon
barrier[2] /barricate road-blocker	n	路障	louh jeung	lou6 zoeng3	louh cheung
base[1]	n	座	joh	zo6	choh
base[2] /lowest part	n	基本	gèi bún	gei4 bun2	kei pun
base[3]	a	卑鄙	bèi pēi	bei4 pei1	pei phei
baseball	n	棒球	páahng kau	paang5 kau3	phaahng khau
baseball cap	n	棒球帽	páahng kau mòuh	paang kau3 mou6	phaahng khau mouh
based[1]	adj	基地	gèi deih	gei4 dei6	kei teih
based[2] /based on upon	adj	根據	gàn geui	gan4 geoi3	kan kwoi
basement /UG/F	n	地下室	deih há sāt	dei6 haa2 sat1	teih ha sat
basic[1]	adj	底	dái	dai2	tai
basic[2] /fundamental/main	adj	基本	gèi bún	gei4 bun2	kei pun
basic[3]	adj	基礎	gèi chó	gei4 co2	kei chho
basic salary		底薪	dái sān	dai2 san1	tai san
basic vocabulary		基本詞彙	gēi bún chìh wuih	gei1 bun2 ci4 wui6	kei pun chhih wuih
basic word dictionary		简单词典	gáan dàan chi dín	gaan2 daan4 ci4 din2	kaan taan chhi tin
basically[1] /fundamentally /basic	adj	根本上	gàn bún seuhng	gan4 bun2 soeng6	kan pun seuhng
basically[2]	adj	在根本上	joih gān bún seuhng	zoi6 gan1 bun2 soeng6	choih kan pun seuhng
basically[3] /in substance /on the whole	adj	基本上	gèi bún seuhng	gei4 bun2 soeng6	kei pun seuhng
basis[1] /foundation/root	n	本	bún	bun2	pun
basis[2]	n	根本	gàn bún	gan4 pun2	kan pun
basket[1]	n	籃	làham	laam4	laham
basket[2]	n	籃桶	làahm túng	laam4 tung2	laahm thung
basket[3] for baby sleep in /crib/baby's basket	n	小兒床	síu yìh chòhng	siu2 ji4 cong4	siu yih chhohng
basket for waste paper	n	字紙簍	jih jí lō	zi6 zi2 lo1	chih chi loh

basketball	n	藍球	làahm kàuh	laam4 kau6	laahm khauh
bass[1] lowest tone	n	低音	dài yām	dai4 jam1	tai yam
bass[2] male tone	n	男低音	làahm dāiyām	laam4 dai1 jam1	laahm tai yam
bastard[1] (sl) (vdw)	n	混蛋	wahn dáan	wan6 daan2	wahn taahn
bastard[2]	n	爛仔	laahn jái	laan6 zai2	laahn chai
bat[1] an animal	n	蝙蝠	pìn fùk	pin4 fuk4	phin fuk
bat[2] /racket games stick	n	球拍	kàuh páak	kau4 paak2	khauh phaak
bat[3] eyes quickly open close	v	眨	jáma	zaam2	chama
batch /a group	n	批處理	pāi chyú léih	pai1 cyu2 lei5	phai chhyu leih
bath[1] /wash	v	浴	yuhk	juk6	yuhk
bath[2]	v	浴缸	yuhk gòng	juk6 gong4	yuhk kong
bath jar /vat	n	缸浴	gòng yuhk	gong4 juk6	kong yuhk
bath towel	n	浴巾	yuhk gàn	juk6 gan4	yuhk kan
bath water	n	沖涼水	chùng lèung séui	cung4 loeng4 seoi2	chhung leong swoi
bathe /to rinse	n	浸洗	jam sái	zam3 sai2	cham sai
bathing /swimming	n	游水	yauh séui	jau6 seoi2	yauh swoi
bathing suit	n	沐浴衣服	muhk yuhk yī fuhk	muk6 juk6 ji1 fuk6	muhk yuhk yī fuhk
bathrobe[1]	n	浴袍	yuhk pòuh	juk6 pou6	yuhk phuh
bathrobe[2]	n	浴衣	yuhk yī	juk6 ji1	yuhk yi
bathroom[1]	n	浴室	yuhk sāt	juk6 sat1	yuhk sāt
bathroom[2] /shower room	n	沖涼房	chùng lèung fóng	cung4 loeng4 fong2	chhung leong fong
bathtub	n	浴缸	yuhk gòng	juk6 gong4	yuhk kong
baton[1] /police-stick/ police-truncheon/ light stick of police	n	警棍	gíng gwan	ging2 gwan3	keng kwan
baton[2] light stick of police	n	警棒	gíng páahng	ging2 paang5	keng phaahng
baton frog[1]	n	警棍袋	gíng gwan dói	ging2 gwan3 doi2	keng kwan toi
baton frog[2]	n	警棒青蛙	gíng páahng chìng wā	ging2 paang5 cing4 wa1	keng phaahng chheng wa
batta /trip money/extra pay/expense on trip	n	出差費	cheut chāai fai	ceot1 caai1 fai3	chhot chhaai fai
battalion	n	大隊	daaih deuih	daai6 deui6	taaih twoih
batter	v	打爛	dá laahn	daa2 laan6	ta laahn
battery[1]	n	電池	dihn chìh	din6 ci4	tihn chhih
battery[2]	n	電蕊	dihn sām	din6 sam1	tihn sam
battle /struggle/wrangle /dispute/friction	n	爭	jàang	zaang4	chaang
battle-field	n	打野戰	dá yéh jin	daa2 je5 zin3	ta yeh chin
battle-fight /make war /go to war	n	打仗	dá jeung	daa2 zoeng3	ta cheung
bay[1] /gulf/curve/bend	n	灣	wāan	waan1	waan
bay[2] /gulf/sea bend	n	海彎	hói wāan	hoi2 waan1	hoi waan
bayonet /sword	n	刺刀	chi dōu	ci3 dou1	chhi tou
be	v/aux	進行時態	jeun hàhng sìh taai	zeon3 hang4 si4 taai3	cheun hahng sih thaai
be able /ability/may/can /able	vt	能	làhng /nàhng	lang4 /nang4	lahng /nahng

be apart /at a distance	n	喵距	mēo kéuih	meo1 keoi5	meo khoih
be applicable at		適用於	sīk yuhng yū	sik1 jung6 jyu1	sek yuhng yu
be at Hong Kong		在港	joih góng	zoi6 gong2	choih kong
be at work /on duty /go to work/ report for duty	v	上班	séuhng bàan	soeng5 baan4	seuhng paan
be born /birth	n	出生	chēut sāng	ceot1 sang1	chhot sang
be known as /called by /be called	n	叫做	giu jouh	giu3 zou6	kiu chouh
be careful![1] /beware	v	小心	síu sàm	siu2 sam4	siu sam
be careful![2]		嘻小心!	hēi síu sàm!	hei1 siu2 sam4!	hei siu sam!
be concerned /worry /think		慮	leuih	leoi6	lowih
be crooked /get cramp	v	抽筋	chàu gàn	cau4 gan4	chhau gan
be easy damage		好花學	hóu fā hohk	hou2 faa1 hok6	hou fa hohk
be elected /election		當選	dòng syún	dong4 syun2	tong syun
be exiled /banishment /exile	v	流亡	làuh mòhng	lau4 mong4	lauh mohng
be fond of[1] /happiness /likes/enjoy/feel pleased	n/v	喜	héi	hei2	hei
be fond of[2] /fond/fondly	adv	鍾意	jùng yi	zung4 ji3	chung yi
be free of /rid something	v	擺脫	báai tyut	baai2 tyut3	paai thyut
be grieved /feel sorry	v	難過	làahn gwò	laan4 gwo4	laahn kwo
be happy		歡喜到	fùn héi dóu	foon1 hei2 dou3	fun hei tou
be healed /get well /heal/ get recover		痊癒	chyùhn yuh	cyun4 jyu6	chhyuhn yuh
be in a coma /senseless /unconscious/coma	adj	昏迷	fān màih	fan1 mai4	fan maih
be in charge	adj	負責	fuh jaak	fu6 zaak3	fuh chaak
be in heat /be irritated	v	性感	sing gám	sing3 gam2	seng kam
be involved /involved	v	捲入	gyún yahp	gyun2 jap6	kyun yahp
be joined /connected /join/linking/conjoint/join together	v	相連	sèung lìhn	soeng4 lin4	seung lihn
be killed		遇難	yuh làahn /nàahn	jyu6 laan4 /naan4	yuh laahn /naahn
be late	adv	遲到啦!	chìh dou la!	ci4 dou3 laa1	chhih tou la!
be loosen[1]	v	變鬆	bin sùng	bin3 sung4	pin sung
be loosen[2] /recited soft	v	軟唸唸	yúhn lihm lihm, yúhn nihm nihm	jyun5 lim6 lim6, jyun5 nim6 nim6	yuhn lihm lihm, yuhn nihm nihm
be lustful /sex appeal	v	性感	seng gám	seng3 gam2	seng kam
be not /no/not	adv	唔係	m̀ haih	m4 hai6	mh haih
be put in /be inserted me	v	插入我	chaap yahp ngóh	caap3 jap6 ngo5	chhaap yahp ngoh
be set in	n	依	yì	ji4	yi
be sold[1] /sell out	adj/v	賣晒	maaih saai	maai6 saai3	maaih saai
be sold[2] /sold out /no more available	adj	銷售一空	sīu sauh yāt hùng	siu1 sau6 jat1 hung4	siu sauh yat hung
be sorry /regret	v	遺憾	wàih hahm	wai4 ham6	waih hahm
be sure /by all means	adj	千祈	chìn kèih	cin1 kei4	chhin kheih
be sure of himself		有自信	yáuh jih seun	jau5 zi6 seon3	yauh chih swon

be sure to /be sure	adj	至緊	ji gan	zi3 gan3	chi kan
be surprised[1] /surprise	adj	訝	ngah	ngaa6	ngah
be surprised[2] /amazing	adj	驚喜	gèng héi	geng1 hei2	keng hei
be united[1] /harmonize /suit well	adj	調	tìuh	tiu4	thiuh
be united[2] /cooperate	n/v	協	hip	hip3	hip
be united[3] /cooperate /coordination	n/v	協調	hip tìuh	hip3 tiu4	hip thiuh
be upset	adj	使心煩意亂	sái sām fàahn yi lyuhn	sai2 sam1 faan4 ji3 lyun6	sai sam faahn yi lyuhn
be used for		用來	yuhng lòih	jung6 loi4	yuhng loih
be very hungry[1] /fasting /starve	v	好肚餓	hóu tóuh ngoh	hou2 tou5 ngo6	hou thouh ngoh
be very hungry[2] /starve	v	無嘢食	móuh yéh sihk	mou5 je5 sik6	mouh yeh sehk
BEA bank	n	東亞銀行	dùng ā ngàhn hòhng	dung4 aa1 ngan4 hong4	tung a ngahn hohng
beach[1] /seaside	n	沙灘	sà tāan	sa4 taan1	sa thaan
beach[2] /seaside	n	海灘	hói tāan	hou2 taan1	hoi thaan
beak (of the bird)	n	鳥嘴	líuh /níuh jéui	liu5 /niu5 zeoi2	liuh /niuh cheui
beam /crossbeam	n	橫樑	wàahng lèuhng	waang4 loeng4	waahng leuhng
bean	n	豆	dáu	dau2	tau
bean curd /tofu	n	豆腐	dáu fū	dau2 fu1	tau fu
bean sprouts	n	牙菜	ngàh choi	ngaa4 coi3	ngàh choi
beano	n	盛宴	sìhng yin	sing4 yin3	sehng yin
bear[1] /animal	n	熊	hùhng	hung4	huhng
bear[1] /tolerate/suffer	v	忍	yán	jan2	yan
bear[2] /endure/suffer	v	受	sauh	sau6	sauh
bear[3] /endure/suffer/abide	v	忍受	yán sauh	jan2 sau6	yan sauh
bear[4] /endure/tolerate	v	容忍	yùhng yán	jung4 jan2	yuhng yan
bear[5] /endure	v	寬容	fùn yung	fun4 jung3	fun yung
bearable	adj	可忍受	hó yán sauh	ho2 jan2 sau6	ho yan sauh
beard	n	鬍鬚	wu sòu	wu3 sou4	wu sou
bearer[1] /endure	n	持票人	chìh bìu yàhn	ci4 biu4 jan4	chhih piu yahn
bearer[2] /endure	n	帶信人	dáai seun yàhn	daai2 seon3 jan4	taai swon yahn
bearer[3] /holder	adj	持有人	chìh yáuh yàhn	ci4 jau5 jan4	chhih yauh yahn
bearing[1] /manner	n	儀表	yìh píu	ji4 piu2	yih phiu
bearing[2] /manner /comport	n/v	舉止	géui jí	geoi2 zi2	kwoi chi
bearing[3] roller balls	n	軸承	juhk sìhng	zuk6 sing4	chuhk sehng
bearl	n	珠	jyú	jyu2	chyu
beast	n	獸	sau	sau3	sau
beast /wild animals	n	野性	yéh sing	je5 sing3	yeh seng
beaten by hammer	adj	錘平	chèuih pèhng	ceoi4 peng4	chheuih phehng
beating /fight/rout /exchange of blows	n	潰敗	kúi baaih	kui2 baaih	khui paaih

beautiful[1] /attractive /handsome/pretty/good looking	adj	靚	leng	leng3	leng
beautiful[2] /beauty	n	美	méih	mei5	meih
beautiful[3] /pretty	adv	麗	laih	lai6	laih
beautiful[4] /pretty /nice looking/good looks /cute/ attractive/peach/smart	adj	漂亮	piu leuhng	piu3 loeng6	phiu leuhng
beautiful[5]	adj	美麗	méih laih	mei5 lai6	meih laih
beauty salon	n	美容院	méih yùhng yún	mei5 jung4 jyun2	meih yuhng yun
beaver a kind of animal	n	海狸	hói lèih	hoi2 lei4	hoi leih
became /turn into	adj	變成	bin sèhng	bin3 seng4	pin sehng
because	adv	既然	gei yìhn	gei3 jin4	kei yihn
because of[1] /due to/ there upon	adv	由於	yàuh yù	jau4 jyu4	yauh yu
because of[2] /in order to	adv	為咗	waih jó	wai6 zo2	waih cho
because of..reason / due to	adv	因為...嘅 關係	yàn waih..ge gwaan haih	jan6 wai6 ge3 gwaan3 hai6	yan waih...ke kwaan haih
beckon /indicates idea	v	示意	sìh yí	si6 ji2	sih yi
become[1]	adj	成	sèhng	seng4	sehng
become[2]	adj	成為	sèhng wàih	seng4 wai6	sehng waih
become citizen /naturalize/as a citizen/ become naturalized	adj/v	入籍	yahp jihk	jap6 jik6	yahp chehk
become conscious again /new life/resuscitation/start	n	急救進	gāp gau jeun	gap1 gau3 zeon3	kap kau cheun
become different[1]	adj	變咗	bīn jó	bin1 zo2	pin cho
become different[2] /turn into	adj	使變成	sái bin sèhng	sai2 bin3 seng4	sai pin sehng
become fat	adj	使肥	sí fèih	si2 fei4	sí feih
become good	adj	變得好	bín dāk hóu	bin2 dak1 hou2	pin tak hou
become of	adj	發生於	faat sàng yū	faat3 sang4 jyu1	faat sang yu/yuh
become pregnant /pregnant	adj	大肚	daaih tóuh	taai6 tou5	taaih thouh
become rich /get rich /make a fortune	adj	發達	faat daaht	faat3 daat6	faat taaht
become your turn	adj	輪到…	lèuhn dou...	leon4 dou3…	leuhn tou...
becoming[1]	adj	適宜	sīk yìh	sik1 ji4	sek yi
becoming[2]	adj	好看	hóu hòn	hou2 hon4	hou hon
becoming[3] well fitting	adj	合身	hahp sān	hap6 san1	hahp san
bed	n	床	chòhng	cong4	chhohng
bed room[1]	n	睡房	seuih fóng	seoi6 fong2	swoih fong
bed room[2]	n	臥室	ngoh sāt	ngo6 sat1	ngoh sat
bed spread[1]	n	床冚	chòhng kám	cong4 kam2	chhohng kham
bed spread[2]/sheet of bed	n	床單	chòhng dāan	cong4 daan1	chhohng taan
bed time	n	就寢時間	jauh chám sìh gaan	zau6 cam2 si4 gaan3	chauh chham sih kaan
bedeck /decorate/deck	vt	裝飾	jòng sīk	zong4 sik1	chong sek

English		Chinese	Cantonese	Jyutping	Romanization
bedstead	n	床架	chòhng gá	cong4 ga2	chhohng ka
bee	n	蜜蜂	maht fùng	mat6 fung4	maht fung
bee's knees[IDM] excellent person or thing /high standard	adj	非常好	fèi sèuhng hóu	fei4 soeng4 hou2	fei seuhng hou
beef meat	n	牛肉	ngàuh yuhk	ngau4 juk6	ngauh yuhk
beef noodles	n	牛肉麵	ngàuh yuhk mihn	ngau4 juk6 min6	ngauh yuhk mihn
beer	n	啤酒	bē jáu	be1 zau2	pe chau
beetles	v	用槌打	yùhng cheui dà	jung6 ceoi4 daa4	yuhng chhoi ta
befall /suffer/encounter	v	遭遇	jōu yuh	zou1 jyu6	chou yuh
before[1] /first/prior/advance	adj	先	sin	sin3	sin
before[2] /prior/advance	adv	前來	chìhn laih	cin4 lai4	chhihn laih
before[3] /not until	adv	先至	sìn ji	sin4 zi3	sin chi
before birth	adj	先天嘅	sìn tìn ge	sin4 tin4 ge3	sin thin ke
before day	adv	天亮前	tìn leuhng chìhn	tin4 loeng6 cin4	thin leuhng chhihn
before time /former /once upon/formerly	adv	從前	chùhng chìhn	cung4 cin4	chhuhng chhihn
beforehand[1]	adj	事先	sih sìn	si6 sin4	sih sin
beforehand[2] /prior	adj	預先	yuh sìn	jyu6 sin4	yuh sin
beg[1] /invoke/pursue/seek /pray for	v	求	kàuh	kau4	khauh
beg[2] /beggar	v	乞討	hāt tóu	hat1 tou2	hat thou
beg your pardon	v	請原諒	chéng /chíng yun lèuhng	ceng2 /cing2 jyun3 loeng6	chheng yun lowhng
beggar[1]	n	乞兒	hāt yī	hat1 zi1	hat yi
beggar[2]	n	乞丐	hāt koi	hat1 koi3	hat khoi
begin[1] /start/initial	v	始	chí	ci2	chhi
begin[2] /start/commence /commencement	v	起首	héi sáu	hei2 sau2	hei sau
begin[3] /initiate	v	發起	faat héi	faat3 hei2	faat hei
begin work at facrory	v	開工	hòi gùng	hoi4 gung4	hoi kung
beginner /novice /learner	n	初學者	chò hohk jé	co4 hok6 ze2	chho hohk che
beginning period /initial stage/elementary/ primary/begun	v	初期	chò kèih	co4 kei4	chho kheih
beginning study		開始學習	hòi chí hohk jaahp	hoi4 ci2 hok6 zaap6	hoi chhi hohk chaahp
begone /get out/go away /go out/go somewhere else	v	走開	jáu hòi	zau2 hoi4	chau hoi
behave /behavior/activity	n/v	行為	hahng wàih	hang6 wai4	hahng waih
behavior	n	品行	bán hahng	ban2 hang6	pan hahng
behaviour[1]	n	為人	waih yàhn	wai6 jan4	waih yahn
behaviour[2] /action/activity	n	舉動	géui duhng	geoi2 dung6	kwoi tuhng
behaviour[3] /manner/ attitude/posture	n	態度	taai douh	taai3 dou6	thaai touh
behead[1] cut head	v	杀	saat	saat3	saat
behead[2] cut head	v	杀頭	saat tàuh	saat3 tau4	saat thauh

English	POS	Chinese	Yale	Jyutping	Other
behead[3] cut head	v	斬頭	jáam táu	zaam2 tau2	chaam thau
behead[4] cut head	v	被砍頭	bèih hám tàuh	bei6 ham2 tau4	peih ham thauh
beheaded ghost	n	無頭鬼	mòuh tàuh gwái	mou4 tau4 gwai2	mouh thauh kwai
beheld /behold/look/see	v	睇見	tái gin	taai2 gin3	thai kin
behind the story /inside story/internal story	adv/n	內幕	loih /noih mohk	loi6 /noi6 mok6	loih /noih mohk
beige[1]	adj	米色	máih sīk	mai5 sik1	maih sek
beige[2]	adj	原色	yùhn sīk	jyun4 sik1	yuhn sek
being /exist/present	n	存在	chyùhn joih	cyun4 zoi6	chhuhn choih
being sex[(dw)] /having sex /physical activity of sex/sex moving act/coitus copulate /coition	v xy	性交(與某人)	sing gàau (yùh máuh yàhn)	sing3 gaau3 (jyu4 mau5 jan4)	seng kaau (yuh mauh yahn)
belch[1]	v	打嗝	dā gaak	daa1 gaak3	ta kaak
belch[2] /eructate	v	噴出	pan chèut	pan3 ceot4	phan chhot
belch[3]	v	打思噎	dá sì yīk	daa2 si4 jit1	ta si yek
belie /lied/cover up fault /conceal/hidden a	v	掩飾	yím sīk	jim2 sik1	yim sek
belief[1] /believe/trust /truthful	n	信	séun	seon2	swon
belief[2] /faith/reliance/trust	n/v	賴	laaih	laai6	laaih
belief[3] /believe	n	相信	sèung séun	soeng4 seon2	seung swon
believe religion	adj	信教	seun gaau	seon3 gaau3	swon kaau
believable /conceivable /can be believed/it is believable/deduce	v	可想而知	hó séung yìh jì	ho2 soeng2 ji4 zi4	ho seung yih chi
believable	adj	可信嘅	hó seun ge	ho2 seon3 ge3	ho swon ke
believe	n	被認為	bèih yihng waih	bei6 jing6 wai6	peih yehng waih
believed firmly	v	堅信	gīn seun	gin1 seon3	kin swon
believer /follower	n	信仰的人	seun yéuhng dìk yàhn	seon3 joeng5 dik4 jan4	swon yeuhng tik yahn
belived it or not		信不信由你	seun bāt seun yàuh léih /néih	seon3 bat1 seon3 jau4 lei5 /nei5	swon pat swon yauh léih /neih
bell[1] /small bell	n	鈴	lìhng	ling4	lehng
bell[2] /hour/clock/time	n	鐘	jùng	zung4	chung
bell beater /ringer	n	敲鐘人	hàau jùng yàhn	haau4 zung4 jan4	haau chung yahn
belong to[1]	n	屬	suhk	suk6	suhk
belong to[2]	n	屬於	suhk yù	suk6 jyu4	suhk yu
belonging[1] /property	n	財物	chòih maht	coi4 mat6	chhoih maht
belonging[2]	n	隸屬	daih suhk	dai6 suk6	taih suhk
beloved[1] /darling/dear/ affectionate/my dear/my dear/loved	adj	親愛	chan oi /ngoi	can3 oi3 /ngoi3	chhan oi /ngoi
beloved[2] /deep loved	adj	心愛	sàm oi /ngoi	sam4 oi3 /ngoi3	sam oi /ngoi
below[1] /down/under /underneath/on the down	adv	下便	hah bihn	haa6 bin6	hah pihn
below[2]	adv	以下	yíh hah	ji5 haa6	yih hah

English		Chinese	Romanization	Jyutping	Alt. Romanization
below standard/ not good enough		欠佳	jàang gāai	zaang4 gaai1	chaang kaai
belt	n	帶	daai	daai3	taai
bench	n	長凳	chèuhng dang	coeng4 dang3	chheuhng tang
bend[1] /fold	v	摺	jip	zip3	chip
bend[2]	v	折彎	jit wāan	zit3 waan1	chit waan
bend[3] /bent	v	彎曲	wàan kùk	waan4 kuk4	waan khuk
bend down/hang down /droop/dangle	v	垂	sèuih	seoi4	swoih
bender (man)	n	扭彎嘅人	láu wāan ge yàhn	lau2 waan1 ge3 jan4	lau waan ke yahn
beneficial[1] /profitable /helpful/wholesome	adj	有益	yáuh yīk	jau5 jik1	yauh yek
beneficial[2]	adj	有益處	yáuh yīk chyu	jau5 jik1 cyu3	yauh yek chhyu
benefit /enjoy	v	享	héung	hoeng2	heung
bequeath	v	遺贈	wàih jahng	wai4 zang6	waih chahng
bequest /legacy /willed document before die	v	遺產	wàih cháan	wai4 caan2	waih chhaan
bereave /take by force	v	使喪失	sái sòng sāt	sai2 song4 sat1	sai song sat
berely enough	adj	勉強	míhn kéuhng	min5 koeng5	mihn kheuhng
beret	n	貝雷帽	búi leui mòuh	bui2 leoi4 mou6	pui lowi mouh
beside[1] /closely/near/other	prep	旁	pòhng	pong4	phohng
beside[2] /next to	pren	旁邊	pòhng bīn	pong4 bin1	phohng pin
beside[3]	prep	近旁	gahn pòhng	gan6 pong4	kahn phohng
beside[4]	prep	隔離	gáak lèih	gaak2 lei4	kaak leih
besides	prep	另外	lihng oih /ngoih	ling6 oi6 /ngoi6	lehng oih /ngoih
best man[1]	adj	儐	bān	ban1	pan
best man[2]	adj	伴郎	buhn lóng	bun6 long2	puhn long
best of all[1]	adj	最抵	jeui daaih	zeoi3 daai6	cheui taaih
best of all[2] /paramount/ supreme	adj	至高無上	ji gou mouh seuhng	zi3 gou3 mou6 soeng6	chi kou mouh seuhng
best seller	n	暢銷書	cheung sīu syū	coeng3 siu1 syu1	chheung siu syu
bet[1]	v	輸賭	syù dóu	syu4 dou2	syu tou
bet[2] /to make bet/wager	v	打賭	dá dóu	daa2 dou2	ta tou
betray	v	背叛	bui buhn	bui3 bun6	pui buhn
betrayer /traitor	n	背叛者	bui buhn jé	bui3 bun6 ze2	pui buhn che
better[1]	adj	好過	hóu gwo	hou2 gwo3	hou kwo
better[2]	adj	好的	hóu dì	hou2 di4	hou ti
better[3] /comparatively good	adj	較佳	gaau gāai	gaau3 gaai1	kaau kaai
better-half /wife	n	老婆	lóuh pòh	lou5 po4	louh phoh
between ourselves	prep	我倆之間	ngóh léuhng jì gàan	ngo5 loeng5 zi4 gaan4	ngoh leuhng chi kaan
between two fires/ attract by two side	prep	腹背受敵	fùk bui sauh dihk	fuk4 bui3 sau6 dik6	fuk pui sauh tehk
beverage /drinks	n	飲料	yám liuh	jam2 liu6	yam liuh
beware of /mind/take care	v	當心	dong sàm	dong3 sam4	tong sam
bewilder /puzzle /be confuse	v	迷惑	màih waahk	mai4 waak6	maih waahk

beyond[1] /distant	adv	個邊	go bihn	go3 bin6	ko pihn
beyond[2] /distant place	adv	遠處	yúhn chyū	jyun5 cyu1	yuhn chhyu
beyond[3]	adv	再往後	joi wóohng hauh	zoi3 wong5 hau6	choi woohng hauh
beyond[4]	adv	僅此而已	gán chí yìh yíh	gan2 ci2 ji6 ji5	kan chhi yih yih
bib /tucker	n	領布	léhng /líhng bou	leng5 /ling5 bou3	lehng pou
Bible	n	聖經	Sing gìng	sing3 ging4	Seng keng
bicycle[1] /cycle	n	單車	dāan chē	daan1 ce1	taan chhe
bicycle[2]	n	自行車	jih hàhng chē	zi6 hang6 ce1	chih hahng chhe
bid[1]	v	出價	chēut ga	ceot1 gaa3	chhot ka
bid[2]	v	喊價	haam ga	haam3 gaa3	haam ka
bidder	n	出價者	chēut ga jé	ceot1 gaa3 ze2	chhot ka che
bidding[1] /tender	n	投標	tàuh bīu	tau4 biu1	thauh piu
bidding[2]	n	出賣	cheut maaih	ceot maai6	chhot maaih
big /hige/large/great/majo	adj	大	daaih	daai6	taaih
big coach	n	大巴	daaih bā	daai6 ba1	taaih pa
big community /metropolitan	n	大都會	daaih dou wúi	daai6 dou3 wui2	taaih tou wui
big explode /explode	v	大爆炸	gaaih baau ja	daai6 baau3 jaa3	taaih paau cha
big eyes	n	大眼	daaih ngáahn	daai6 ngaan5	taaih ngaahn
big game /hunt big animal	n	大獵物	daaih lihp maht	daai6 lip6 mat6	taaih lihp maht
big head	n	自大的人	jih daaih dìk yàhn	zi6 daai6 dik4 jan4	chih taaih tik yahn
big headed	n	自負的	jih fuh dìk	zi6 fu6 dik4	chih fuh tek
big hearted	adj	寬宏大量	fùn wàhng daaih lèuhng	hun4 wang4 daai6 loeng6	fun wahng taaih leuhng
big prize	n	大獎	daaih jéung	daai6 zoeng2	taaih cheung
big sale /big discount	n	大減價	daaih gáam ga	daai6 gaam2 ga3	taaih kaam ka
big sum	n	大錢	daaih chín	daai6 cin2	taaih chhin
bigot	n	頑固者	wàahn gu jé	waan4 gu3 ze2	waahn ku che
bilateral /two-sided	adj	有兩邊	yáuh léuhng bīn	jau5 loeng5 bin1	yauh leuhng pin
bilingual[1] Chinese English linguist	adj	中英對照	jùng ying deui jiu	zung4 jing3 deoi3 ziu3	chung yihn toei chiu
bilingual[2] /linguist	adj	兩種語言	léuhng jung yúh yìhn	loeng5 jung3 jya5 jin4	leuhng chung yuh yihn
bilingual[3] /linguist	adj	能講兩種語言	làhng /nàhng góng léuhng júng yúh yìhn	lang4 /nang4 gong2 loeng5 zung2 jyu5 jin4	lahng /nahng kong leuhng chung yuh yihn
bilirubin	n	膽紅素	dáam hùhng sou	daam2 hung4 sou3	taam huhng sou
bill[1] /list	n	單	dāan	daan1	taan
bill[2]	n	賬單	jeung dāan	zoeng3 daan1	cheung taan
bill[3] /chit	n	帳單	jeung dāan	zoeng3 daan1	cheung taan
bill[4]	n	票據	piu geui	piu3 geoi3	phiu kwoi
bill payment /pay the bill	n	埋單	màaih dāan	maai4 daan1	maaih taan
bimetallic	adj	複本位制	fūk bún wàih jai	fuk1 bun2 wai4 zai3	fuk pun waih chai
bind[1]	v	係	haih	hai6	haih
bind[2] /fasten/tie	v	紮住	jaat jyuh	zaat3 zyu6	chaat chyuh
bind[3] /knot/bond/tie	n/v	結	git	git3	kit
bind by hoops /hoop	n	箍	kū	ku1	khu
binder	n	包紮者	bāau jaat jé	baau1 zaat3 ze2	paau chaat che

English		Chinese	Yale	Jyutping	Romanization
binocular	n	雙筒望遠鏡	sèung tùhng mohng yúhn geng	soeng4 tung4 mong6 jyun5 geng3	seung thuhng mohng yuhn keng
biochemistry	n	生化	sàng fa	sang4 faa3	sang fa
biographical notes/ curriculum vitae/ curricula vitae/CV	n	生活簡歷	sàng wùht gāan lìhk	sang4 wut6 gaan1 lik6	sang wuht kaan lehk
biography[1]	n	傳	jyuhn	zyung6	chyuhn
biography[2] /life story	n	傳記	jyuhn gei	zyung6 gei3	chyuhn kei
biology /biological	adj/n	生物學	sàng maht hohk	sang4 mat6 hok6	sang maht hohk
bioscope	n	舊式電影放映機	gauh sīk din yéng fong yíng gèi	gau6 sik1 din3 jeng2 fong3 jing gei4	kauh sek tin yeng fong yeng kei
bird[1] long tail	n	鳥	líuh /níuh	liu5 /niu5	liuh /niuh
bird[2] yellow tail	n	黃尾鳳	wòhng méih fuhng	wong4 mei5 fung6	wohng meih fuhng
bird[3]	n	雀	jéuk /zóek	zoek2	cheuk
bird[4] (small)	n	雀仔	jéuk jái	zoek2 zai2	cheuk chai
bird's-eye	n	鳥瞰圖	líuh /níuh haahm tòuh	liu5 /niu5 ham6 tou6	liuh /niuh haahm thouh
bird's-house[1] /bird's-nest /nestle	n	雀巢	jeuk chàauh	zoek3 caau6	cheuk chhaauh
bird's-house[2] /inhabitation/perch of birds	n	棲息	chai sīk	cai1 sik1	chhai sek
bird's-nest[1]	n	雀竇	jeuk dau	zoek3 dau3	cheuk tau
bird's-nest[2]	n	燕窩	yin wō	jin3 wo1	yin wo
birth[1]	n	生	sàang	saang4	saang
birth[2] /born	n	出世	chēut sai	ceot1 sai3	chhot sai
birth anniversary	n	生紀念日	sàng géi nihm yaht	sang4 gei2 nim6 jat6	sang kei nihm yaht
birth certificate[1]	n	出世紙	chēut sai jí	ceot1 sai3 zi2	chhot sai chi
birth certificate[2]	n	出生證明書	chēut sàng jing mìhng syū	ceot1 sang1 zing3 ming4 syu1	chhot sang cheng mehng syu
birth control[1]	n	避孕	beih yahn	bei6 jan6	peih yahn
birth control[2]	n	生育控制	sàng yuhk hung jai	saang4 juk6 hung3 zai3	saang yuhk hung chai
birth control[3]	n	節育	jit yuhk	zit3 juk6	chit yuhk
birth flower	n	生根	sāng gān	sang1 gan1	sang kan
birth mother	n	親生母	chān sàang móuh	can1 saang4 mou5	chhan saang mouh
birth place/place of birth	n	出生地點	chēut sàng deih dím	ceot1 sang1 dei6 dim2	chhot sang teih tim
birthday	n	生日	sàang yaht	saang4 jat6	saang yaht
birthday card	n	生日咭	sàang yaht kaat	saang4 jat6 kaat3	saang yaht khaat
birthday gift	n	生日禮物	sàang yàht láih maht	saang4 jat4 lai2 mat6	saang yaht laih maht
birthday is on	n	係生日	hái sàang yàht	hai2 saang4 jat4	hai saang yaht
birthday party	n	生日會	sàang yaht wuih	saang4 jat6 wui6	saang yaht wuih
biscuit /crackers/cookie	n	餅乾	béng gōn	beng2 gon1	peng kon
bisexuality/gay sex /bisexual	n	雙性戀	sèung sing lyúhn	soeng4 sing3 lyun5	seung seng lyuhn
bit[1]	n	一的的	yāt dī dī	jat1 di1 di1	yat ti ti
bit[2] /drill bit	n	鑽頭	jyun tàuh	zyun3 tau4	chyun thauh
bit[3]	n	小片	síu pin	siu2 pin3	siu phin

bit part	n	小角色	síu gok sīk	siu2 gok3 sik1	siu kok sek
bite[1]	v	咬	áauh /ngáauh	aau5 /ngaau5	aauh /ngaauh
bite[2] /gnaw/snap	v	齧	ngaaht	ngaat6	ngaaht
bite by mouth		咬一啖	áauh yāt daahm	aau5 jat1 daan6	aauh yat taahm
bite off		咬掉	áauh diuh	aau5 diu6	aauh tiuh
biting[1]	adj	卡緊	ká gán	kaa2 gan2	kha kan
biting[2]	adj	刺痛	chek tung	cek3 tung3	chhek thung
biting person	n	尖銳刺人	jìm yeuih chi yàhn	zim4 jeoi6 ci3 jan4	chim yeuih chhi yahn
bitter[1]	adj	苦	fú	fu2	fu
bitter[2]	adj	苦處	fú chyu	fu2 cyu3	fu chhyu
bitter speaking		講壞話	góng waaih wá	gong2 waai6 waa2	kong waaih wa
bitter tea	n	壽眉茶	sauh mèih chàh	sau6 mei4 caa4	sauh meih chhah
black	n	黑	hāk /hāak	hak1 /haak1	hak /haak
black & white[1]	n	黑白	hāk baahk	hak1 baak6	hak paahk
black & white[2]	n	寫在紙上	sé joih jí seuhng	se2 zoi6 zi2 soeng6	se choih chi seuhng
black board	n	黑板	hāk báan	hak1 baan2	hak paan
black box[1] of airplane	n	黑盒	hāk háap	hak1 haap2	hak haap
black box[2] of airplane	n	黑匣子	hāk haahp jí	hak1 haap6 zi2	hak haahp chi
black coffee[1]	n	黑啡	hāk fē	hak1 fe1	hak feh
black coffee[2]	n	齋啡	jāai fē	zaai1 fe1	chaai fe
black flag	n	海盜旗	hói douh kèih	hoi2 dou6 kei4	hoi touh kheih
black heart	n	黑心	hāk sàm	hak1 sam4	hak sam
black hole in astronomy	n	黑洞	hāk duhng	hak1 dung6	hak tuhng
black list	n	黑名單	hāk mìhng dāan	hak1 meng4 daan1	hak mehng taan
black mail[1]	n	勒索	laahk sok	laak6 sok3	laahk sok
black mail[2]	n	打單	dá dāan	daa2 daan1	ta taan
black rain-storm		黑雨警告	hāk yúh gíng gou	hak1 jyu5 ging2 gou3	hak yuh king kou
black spot /traffic dangerous place	n	交通黑點	gāau tùng hāk dím	gaau1 tung4 hak1 dim2	kaau thung hak tim
bladder	n	膀胱	pòhng gwòng	pong4 gwong4	phohng kwong
blade	n	刀片	dōu pin	dou1 pin3	tou phin
blamable /dyslogistic	adj	責難	jaak làahn	zaak3 laan4	chaak laahn
blame[1] /charge/find fault	v	怪	gwaai	gwaai3	kwaai
blame[2] /to complain	v	怨	yun	jyun3	yun
blame[3] /complain	v	埋怨	màaih yun	maai4 jyun3	maaih yun
blame[4]	v	責任	jaak yahm	zaak3 jam6	chaak yahm
blame[5] /criticize/chide/ rebuke/reprove/scold/ condemn/speak angrily	v	責備	jaak beih	zaak3 bei6	chaak peih
blameless	adj	無可責備	mòuh hó jaak beih	mou5 ho2 zaak3 bei6	mouh ho chaak peih
blank space /vacant	a/n	空白	hùng baahk	hung4 baak6	hung paahk
blank space	n	空位	hùng wái	hung4 wai2	hung wai
blanket[1] /felt	n	氈	jīn	zin1	chin
blanket[2]	n	被	béih	pei5	peih
blanket[3]	n	毯	táan	taan2	thaan

blanket[4] /rug	n	毛毯	mòuh táan	mou6 taan2	mouh thaan
blanket[5] /extinguish felt	n	滅火氈	miht fó jīn	mit6 fo2 zin1	miht fo chin
blast[1] /burst/explode /explosion	n	爆炸	baau ja	baau3 jaa3	paau cha
blast[2]	n	氣浪	hei lohng	hei3 long6	hei lohng
blast[3] of air	n	陣風	jahn fùng	zan6 fung4	chahn fung
blast[4] of air	n	疾風	jaht fùng	zat6 fung4	chaht fung
blazer	n	運動上衣	wahn duhng seuhng yī	wan6 dung6 soeng6 ji1	wahn tohng seuhng yi
blazing /flame/inferno	adj	火焰	fó yihm	fo2 jim6	fo yihm
bleach[1]	n	漂白	piu baahk	piu3 baak6	phiu paahk
bleach[2]	n	漂白水	piu baahk séui	piu baak6 seoi2	phiu paahk swoi
bleeding[1]	n	流血	làuh hyut	lau4 hyut3	lauh hyut
bleeding[2]	n	出血	chēut hyut	ceot1 hyut3	chhot hyut
blemish[1] /disgrace	n	玷	dim	dim	tim
blemish[2] /disgrace/stain	n	玷污	dim wù	dim wu4	tim wu
bless	v	祝佑	jūk yauh	zuk1 jau6	chuk yauh
blessing[1] /bless & protect	v	保佑	bóu yauh	bou2 jau6	pou yauh
blessing[2]/thanks /fine thanks	v	有心	yáuh sàm	jau5 sam4	yauh sam
blessing[3]	v	祝福	jūk fūk	zuk1 fuk1	chuk fuk
blessings /happiness /blessed	n/v	幸福	hahng fūk	hang6 fuk1	hahng fuk
blind[1] eye /short-sighted	adj	盲	màahng	maang4	maahng
blind[2] eyeless	adj	盲眼	màahng ngáahn	maang4 ngaan5	maahng ngaahn
blind[3] cover window	n	防盜欄	fòhng douh gaan	fong4 dou6 gaan3	fohng touh kaan
blind spot	n	盲點	màahng dím	maang4 dim2	maahng tim
blindfold	v	蒙住眼睛	mùhng jyuh ngáahn jìng	mung4 zyu6 ngaan5 zing4	muhng chyuh ngaahn cheng
blindness /aimless	adj	盲目	màahng muhk	maang4 muk6	maahng muhk
blink /wink/winkle	v	眨	jáam	zaam2	chaam
blink eye /blinking eye	v	眨眼睛	jáam ngáahn jìng	zaam2 ngaan5 zing4	chaam ngaahn cheng
blister /bubble	n	水泡	séui póuh	seoi2 pou5	swoi phuh
block[1] /hinder/hold up /obstruct	v	阻	jó	zo2	cho
block[2] obstruct	n	障	jeung	zoeng3	cheung
block[3] /hinder/prevent /stunt/turn back	adj/v	阻止	jó jí	zo2 zi2	cho chi
block[4]/stop/obstruction /hinder	v	阻礙	jó ngoih	zo2 ngoi6	cho ngoih
block[5] /stop	v	攔住	làahn jyuh	laan4 zyu6	laahn chyuh
block A series	n	A 座	A jo / A cho	a zo	a cho
block letters (A/B/C)	vi	座	joh	zo6	choh
block up	v	塞住	sāk jyuh	sak1 zyu6	sak chyuh
blockade[1]	v	封鎖	fùng só	fung4 so2	fung so
blockade[2]	v	道塞	dóu sāk	dou2 sak1	tou sak

blocked stool /stoped stool/stoped feces /constipated of feces	v	大便不通	daaih pihn bāt tùng	daai6 pin4 bat1 tung4	taaih pihn pat thung
blocked urine	v	排尿阻滯	bai liuh /niuh jó jaih	baai3 liu6 /niu6 zo2 zai6	pai liuh/niuh cho chaih
blocker[1] of volleball or tennis	v	攔網人	làahn móhng yàhn	laan4 mong5 jan4	laahn mohng yahn
blocker[2] /barrier	n	障礙	jeung ngoih	zoeng3 ngoi6	cheung ngoih
blog /website loanword	n	博客	bok haak	bok3 haak	pok haak
blood[1]	n	血	hyut	hyut3	hyut
blood[2]	n	鮮血	sìn hyut	sin4 hyut3	sin hyut
blood brothers	n	親兄弟	chàn hìng daih	can4 hing4 dai6	chhan heng taih
blood clot	n	血塊	hyut faai	hyut3 faai3	hyut faai
blood pressure[1]	n	血壓	hyut ngaat	hyut3 ngaat3	hyut ngaat
blood pressure[2] high	n	高血壓	gòu hyut ngaat	gou4 hyut3 ngaat3	kou hyut ngaat
blood relation	n	有血緣關係	yáuh hyut yùhn gwàan haih	jau5 hyut3 jyun4 gwaan4 hai6	yauh hyut yuhn kwaan haih
blood stain	n	血蹟	hyut jīk	hyut3 zik1	hyut chek
blood sugar /glucose	n	血糖	hyut tòhng	hyut3 tong4	hyut thohng
blood test	n	驗血	yihm hyut	jim6 hyut3	yihm hyut
blood transfusion	n	輸血	syù hyut	syu4 hyut3	syu hyut
bloodstream	n	血循環	hyut cheun waan	hyut3 ceon4 waan3	hyut chheun waan
bloody	adj	血腥嘅	hyut sèng ge	hyut3 seng4 ge3	hyut seng ke
bloom	v	開花	hòi fā	hoi4 faa1	hoi fa
blotting-paper	n	吸墨紙	kāp mahk jí	kap1 mak6 ji2	khap mahk chi
blouse[1]	n	上衣	séuhng yì	soeng5 ji4	seuhng yi
blouse[2]	n	女裝	léuih jòng	leui5 zong4	lowih chong
blow by breathe	v	吹	cheui	ceoi3	chheui
blow flame	v	吹熄	cheui sīk	ceoi3 sik1	chheui sek
blow flute /play pipe	v	吹簫	cheui sīu	ceoi3 siu1	chheui siu
blow job[(sl)] oral sex	v	吹簫	cheui sīu	ceoi3 siu1	chheui siu
blows /fight /come to blows	v	打架	dá gá	daa2 gaa2	ta ka
blue	n	藍	làahm	laam4	laahm
blue blood	n	貴族血統	gwai juhk hyut túng	gwai3 zuk6 hyut3 tung2	kwai chuhk hyut thung
blue chip	adj	藍籌	làahm chauh	laam4 cau6	laahm chhauh
blueberry	n	藍莓	làahm mùih	laam4 mui4	laahm muih
blur /less clea	v	模糊	mou wu	mou3 wu3	mou wu
board[1] /plate	n	牌	faai	faai3	faai
board[2] /plate/plank	n	板	báan	baan2	paan
board[3] /commission /league	n	會	wúi	wui2	wui
board[1] get ship	v	係船	hái syùhn	hai2 syun4	hai syuhn
board[2] get plane	v	係飛機	hái fèi gèi	hai2 fei4 gei4	hai fei kei
board[3] get vehicle	v	係車	hái chè	hai2 ce1	hai chhe
board of directors	n	董事會	dúng sih wúi	dung2 si6 wui2	tung sih wui

boarder /boarding student	n	寄宿生	gei sūk sāng	gei3 suk1 sang1	kei suk sang
boarding get vehicle /get in car/get on bus	v	上車	séuhng chè	soeng5 ce1	seuhng chhe
boarding card	n	乘客證	sing haak jing	sing3 haak3 zing3	seng haak cheng
boarding for plane	v	上飛機	séuhng fèi gèi	soeng5 fei4 gei4	seuhng fei kei
boarding gate	n	登機門	dàng gei mun	dang4 gei3 mun3	tang kei mun
boarding pass	n	登機證	dàng gei jíng	dang4 gei3 zing3	tang kei cheng
boarding school[1]	n	寄宿學校	géi sūk hohk haauh	gei2 suk1 hok6 haau6	kei suuk hohk haauh
boarding school[2]	n	寄宿之學校	géi sūk jī hohk haauh	gei2 suk1 zi1 hok6 haau6	kei suuk chi hohk haauh
boast[1] /shout	v	自誇	jih kwā	zi6 kwaa1	chih khwa
boast[2] /proud way	n	誇口	kwā háu	kwaa1 hau2	khwa hau
boaster[1]	n	自誇人	jih kwā yàhn	zi6 kwaa1 jan4	chih khwa yahn
boaster[2] /shouter	n	誇口人	kwā háu yàhn	kwaa1 hau2 jan4	khwa hau yahn
boasting /proudly talk /brag/disapproving talk	v	吹噓	cheui hēui	ceoi3 heoi4	chheui hoi
boat /sampan	n	小船	síu syùhn	siu2 syun4	siu syuhn
boat people	n	艇家	tíhng gà	ting5 ga4	thehng ka
bob /thief/steal	n	盜	douh	dou6	touh
body[1]	n	身	sàn	san4	san
body[2] /human body/health	n	身體	sàn tái	san4 tai2	san thai
body itchy	v	身痕	sàn hàhn /hán	san4 han4 /han2	san hahn /han
body language	n	身體語言	sàn tái yúh yìhn	san4 tai2 jyu5 jin4	san thai yuh yehn
body lotion /lotion /moisturing	n	潤膚露	yeuhn fū louh	jeon6 fu1 lou6	yeuhn fu louh
body warmers	n	身體取暖衣	sàn tái chēui nyúhn yì	san4 tai2 ceoi1 nyun5 ji4	san thai chhoui nyuhnyi
body weight		體重	tái chúhng	tai2 cung5	thai chhuhng
bodyguard	n	保鏢	bóu bīu	bou2 biu1	pou biu
boil[1]	v	滾	gwán	gwan2	kwan
boil[2]	v	煮沸	jyú fai	zyu2 fai3	chyu fai
boil of skin	n	瘡	chōng	cong1	chhong
boil water	v	滾水	gwán séui	gwan2 seoi2	kwan swoi
boiled	v	煲	bòu	bou4	pou
boiler /cauldron /uprightcooking-	n	鑊	wohk	wok6	wohk
boiling	adj	滾燙	gwán tong	gwan2 tong3	kwan thong
boldness /fearless/daring	adj	大膽	daaih dáam	daai6 daam2	taaih taam
bolt nut & bolts	n	螺栓	lòh sàan	lo4 saan4	loh saan
bolt of cloth	n	包裝	bāau jòng	baau1 zong4	paau chong
bomb threat	n	炸彈威脅	ja táan wái hip	zaa3 taan2 wai2 hip3	cha thaan wai hip
bombard	v	轟炸	gwàng ja	gwang4 zaa3	kwang cha
Bombay duck	n	九肚魚	gáu tóuh yù	gau2 tou5 jyu4	kau thouh yu
bond[1]	n	債券	jaai gyun	zaai3 gyun3	chaai kyun
bond[2]	n	聯繫	lyùhn haih	lyun4 hai6	lyuhn haih
bonds /ticket	n	券	gyun	gyun3	kyun

English		Chinese	Romanization	Jyutping	Pronunciation
bone[1]	n	骨	gwāt	gwat1	kwat
bone[2] human bone	n	骨頭	gwāt tàuh	gwat1 dau4	kwat thauh
bones /skeleton	n	骨骼	gwāt gaak	gwat1 gaak3	kwat kaak
bones structure/skeleton	n	骷髏骨	fū lòuh gwāt	fu1 lou4 gwat1	fu louh kwat
bonnet cover /shade	n	罩	jaau	zaau3	chaau
bonus	n	獎金	jéung gām	zoeng2 gam1	cheung kam
book[1] printed/document/ letter/writing	n	書	syù	syu4	syu
book[2] /order/reserve/ subscribe	v	訂	dehng /dihng	deng6 /ding6	tehng
book binder	n	裝訂商	jòng dehng /dihng sèung	zong4 deng6 /ding6 soeng4	chong tehng seung
book-case /bookshelf	n	書架	syù gá	syu4 gaa2	syu ka
book cover	n	書皮	syù pèih	syu4 pei4	syu pheih
book cutter /guillotine /paper cutter	n	切紙機	chit jí gèi	cit3 zi2 gei4	chhit chi kei
book keeper	n	簿記員	bouh gei yùhn	bou6 gei3 jyun4	pouh kei yuhn
book-let	n	書仔	syù jái	syu4 zai2	syu chai
book-let /pamphlet /brochures	n	小冊子	síu cháak jī	siu2 caak2 zi1	siu chhaak chi
book-lover	n	喜歡讀書 嘅人	héi fūn duhk syù ge yàhn	hou2 fun1 duk6 syu4 ge3 jan4	hei fun tuhk syu ke yahn
book-maker	n	著作者	jyu jok jé	zyu3 zok3 ze2	chyu chok che
book-mark	n	書簽	syù chìm	syu4 cim4	syu chhim
book-seller	n	書商	syū sēung	syu1 soeng1	syu seung
bookshelf	n	書櫃	syù gwaih	syu4 gwai6	syu kwaih
bookshop[1] /bookstore	n	書舖	syù póu	syu4 pou2	syu phou
bookshop[2]	n	書局	syù gùhk	syu4 guk6	syu kuhk
bookstore	n	書店	syù dim	syu4 dim3	syu tim
boom sound of explosion	v	轟鳴	gwàng ming	gwang4 ming3	kwang meng
boot[1]	n	靴	hèu	hoe4	heu /heo
boot[2] long	n	長靴	chèuhng hèu	coeng4 hoe4	chheuhng heu
boot[3] long	n	長boot	chèuhng boot	coeng4 boot3	chheuhng poot
boot[4] short boot	n	短boot	dyún boot	dyun2 boot3	tyun poot
booth	n	攤	tàan	taan4	thaan
boots shoes	n	皮靴	pèih hèu /hoe	pei4 hoe4	pheih heu /heo
border /boundary/frontier	n	邊界	bìn gaai	bin4 gaai3	pin kaai
bore[1]	v	厭	yim	jim3	yim
bore[2] /tedious	v	無聊	mòuh lìuh	mou4 liu4	mouh liuh
bore[3] hole /pipe of gun	n	口徑	háu ging	hau2 ging3	hau keng
boring[1] /bore/dull	v	悶	muhn	mun6	muhn
boring[2] /feel tired /monotonous	adj	單調嘅	dàan diuh ge	daan4 diu6 ge3	taan tiuh ke
boring[3] /hole/cavity	n	洞	duhng	dung6	tuhng
boring[4] /dig hole	n	挖洞	waat duhng	waat3 dung6	waat tohng
born[1] same parents	v	胞	bāau	baau1	paau

born[2]	v	出世	chēut sai	ceot1 sai3	chhot sai
born[3] noble family/well born	v	出身高貴	chēut sān gōu gwai	ceot1 san1 gou1 gwai3	chhot san kou kwai
borrow[1] /lend	v	借	je	ze3	che
borrow[2] /lend	v	貸	taai	taai3	thaai
borrow[3]	v	借入	je yahp	ze3 jap6	che yahp
bortsch /beetroot soup	n	羅宋湯	lòh sung tòng	lo4 sung3 tong4	loh sung thong
bosom[1] /mind	n	懷	wàaih	waai6	waaih
bosom[2] /breast/chest /soul/mind	n	心口	sàm háu	sam4 hau2	sam hau
bosom[3] /chest	n	胸口	hùng háu	hung4 hau2	hung hau
boss[1] (de)	n	波士	bō sí	bo1 si2	po si
boss[2] /employer	n	事頭	sih táu	si6 tau2	sih thau
boss[3] /employer /proprietor/shopkeeper	n	老板/老闆	lóuh báan	lou5 baan2	louh paan
botanical /plant	n	植物	jihk maht	zik6 mat6	chehk maht
botany	n	植物學	jihk maht hohk	zik6 mat6 hok6	chehk maht hohk
botch	n	拙劣嘅修補	jyuht lyut ge sāu bóu	zyut6 lyut3 ge3 sau1 bou2	chyuht lyut ke sau pou
both[1] /all	pron	都	dōu	dou1	tou
both[2]	pron	兩個	léuhng go	loeng5 go3	leuhng ko
both legs /legs	n	雙腿	sèung téui	soeng4 teoi2	seung thoi
both side	pron	兩者	léuhng jé	loeng5 ze2	leuhng che
both sides	adj	雙方	sèung fòng	soeng4 fong4	seung fong
bother	v	煩擾	fàahn yíu	faan4 jiu2	faahn yiu
bothersome[1] /too much trouble	adj	費事	fai sih	fai3 si6	fai sih
bothersome[2] /troublesome	adj	傷腦筋	sèung lóuh gān	soeng4 lou5 gan1	seung louh kan
bottle[1]	n	樽	jèun /zèun	zeon4	cheun
bottle[2]	n	瓶子	pèhng jí	peng4 zi2	phehng chi
bottom[1] /lowest part /under	n	下	háh	haa5	hah
bottom[2] /lowest part	n	底部	dái bouh	dai2 bou6	tai pouh
bottom of vehicle	n	車底	chè dái	ce1 dai2	chhe tai
bought /buy/purchase /to buy	v	買	máaih	maai5	maaih
bounce /jump up	v	彈起	tàahn héi	taan4 hei2	thaahn hei
bouncing	v	跳躍嘅	tiu yéuk ge	tiu3 joek2 ge3	thiu yeuk ke
bound[1] limit	n	限	haahn	haan6	haahn
bound[2] /jump/skip/leap /vault/jump up	v	跳躍	tiu yéuk	tiu3 joek2	thiu yeuk
bound[3] /to go ahead	adj	前往	chìhn wóhng	cin4 wong5	chhihn wohng
bound[4] /run long steps	v	跳躍着跑	tiu yéuk jeuk fáau	tiu3 joek2 zoek3 faau2	thiu yeuk cheuk faau
boundary	n	界	gaai	gaai3	kaai
boundary area /precinct /domain area	n	界域	gaai wìhk	gaai wik6	kaai wihk
boutique /fashion shop	n	時裝店	sìh jòng dím	si4 zong4 dim2	sih chong tim

English	pos	漢字	Yale	Jyutping	Romanization
bow[1] weapon /arch	n	弓	gúng	gung2	kung
bow[2] salute	v	拱	gúng	gung2	kung
bow of a ship	n	船頭	syùhn tàuh	syun4 tau4	syuhn thauh
bow tie man's tie	n	煲呔	bōu tāai	bou1 taai1	pou thaai
bowl[1]	n	碗	wún	wun2	wun
bowl[2] /cup/glass	n	三碗細	sàam wún sai	saam1 woon2 sai3	saam wun sai
bowling (de)	n	保齡球	bóu lìhng kàuh	bou2 ling4 kau4	pou lehng khauh
box[1] /case /small box	n	盒	háap	haap6	haap
box[2] /case/tank/trunk	n	箱	sèung	soeng4	seung
box[3] hit by fist	v	擊打	gīk dá	gik1 daa2	kek ta
box junction	n	交叉口黃線區	gāau chā hāu wong sín kèui	gaau1 caa1 hau1 wong3 sin2 keoi4	kaau chha hau wong sin khoi
boxer[1] /boxing	n	拳擊	kyùhn gīk	kyun4 gik1	khyuhn kek
boxer[2]	n	拳擊手	kyùhn gīk sáu	kyun4 gik1 sau2	khyuhn kek sau
boxer short	n	拳擊手短褲	kyùhn gīk sáu dyún fu	kyun4 gik1 sau2 dyun2 fu3	khyuhn kek sau tyun fu
boxing[1] (de)	n	扑繩	bōk síng	bok1 sing2	pok sing
boxing[2]	n	拳術	kyùhn seuht	kyun4 seot6	khyuhn swoht
boy[1]	n	男仔	làahm jāi	laam4 zai1	laahm chai
boy[2] /guy/male/man	n	佬	lóu	lou2	lou
boycott[1]	v	抵制	dái jai	dai2 jai3	tai chai
boycott[2] (de)	v	杯葛	bùi got	bui4 got3	pui got
boyfriend	n	男朋友	làahm pang yáuh	laam4 pang3 jau5	laahm phang yauh
bra /brassiere /women's undewear	n	胸圍	hùng wàih	hung4 wai4	hung waih
brace[1] /scaffold	n	支架	jì gá	zi4 gaa2	chi ka
brace[2]	n	繃緊	bàng gán	bang4 gan2	pang kan
bracelet	n	鈪	ngáak	ngaak2	ngaak
bracket ( )	n	括號	wùh houh	wu4 hou6	wuh houh
bracket sign	n	括弧	kwut wùh	kwut3 wu4	khwut wuh
bragging /proudly talk	v	自吹自播	jih cheui jih lèuih	zi6 ceoi3 zi6 leoi5	chih chheui chih lowih
braid[1]	n	辮	bīn	bin1	pin
braid[2]	n	側辮	jāk bīn	zak1 bin1	chak pin
braid[3]	n	辮子	bīn jí	bin1 zi2	pin chi
brain	n	腦	lóuh /nóuh	lou5 /nou5	louh /nouh
brain-dead	adj	腦死亡	lóuh /nóuh séi mòhng	lou5 /nou5 sei2 mong4	louh /nouh sei mohng
brain drain /talent worker	n	人才流失	yàhn chòih làuh sāt	jan4 coi4 lau4 sat1	yahn chhoih lauh sat
brain fever	n	腦膜炎	nóuh mók yìhm	nou5 mok2 jim4	nouh mok yihm
brainpower/intelligence /witted	adj	智力	ji lihk	zi lik6	chi lehk
brainstorm	n	腦猝病	lóuh /nóuh shyut behng	lou5 /nou5 syut6 beng6	louh /nouh shyut pehng
brainteaser /brilliant idea	n	有趣嘅難題	yáuh cheui ge làahn /nàahn tàih	jau5 ceoi3 ge3 laan4 /naan4 tai4	yauh chheui ke laahn /naahn thaih
brainwash	v	洗腦	sái lóuh /nóuh	sai2 lou5 /nou5	sai louh /nouh

brake[1] /pull	v	掣	jai	zai3	chai
brake[2] /braking car	n	煞車	saat chè	saat3 ce1	saat chhe
brake[3] of the car	n	煞車掣	saat chè jai	saat3 ce1 zai3	saat chhe chai
brake[4] of the vehicle	n	煞停架車	saat tìhng ga chè	saat3 ting4 gaa3 ce1	saat thihng ka chhe
brake light /stop light	n	制動燈	jai duhng dāng	zai3 dung6 dang1	chai tohng tang
branch[1] part	v	分支	fahn jī	fan6 zi1	fahn chi
branch[2] part	v	分開	fahn hòi	fan6 hoi4	fahn hoi
branch office[1]	n	分行	fàn hóng	fan4 hong2	fan hong
branch office[1]	n	分公司	fān gūng sì	fan4 gung1 si4	fan kung si
brand[1] /tag/trademark /brand name	n	牌子	pàaih jí	paai4 zi2	phaaih chi
brand[2] /logo/brand name	n	商標	sèung bīu	soeng4 biu1	seung piu
brand name	n	商標名稱	sèung bīu mèhng chīng	soeng4 biu1meng4 cing1	seung piu mehng chheng
brandy[1]	n	白蘭地	baahk lāan déi	baak6 laan1 dei2	paahk laan tei
brandy[2]	n	白蘭地酒	baahk lāan déi jáu	baak6 laan1 dei2 zau2	paahk laan tei chau
brass	n	黃銅	wòhng tùhng	wong4 tung4	wohng thuhng
brassiere[1] /underwear	n	胸罩	hùng jaau	hung4 zaau3	hung chaau
brassiere[2] /bra	n	乳罩	yúh jaau	jyu5 zaau3	yuh chaau
brave[1]	n	勇	yúhng	jung5	yuhng
brave[2] /chivalrous	adj	勇敢	yúhng gám	jung5 gam2	yuhng kam
brave[3] /facing	adj	勇敢地面對	yúhng gám deih mihn deui	jung5 gam2 dei6 min6 deoi3	yuhng kam teih mihn toei
bravery	n	勇敢人	yúhng gám yàhn	jung5 gam2 jan4	yuhng kam yahn
brazen	v	厚臉皮	háuh líhm pèih	hau5 lim5 pei4	hauh lihm pheih
bread[1]	n	包	bàau	baau4	paau
bread[2] /bakery	n	麵包	mihn bàau	min6 baau4	mihn paau
breadth /width	n	闊度	fut douh	fut3 dou6	fut touh
break[1] /crack glass	v	碎	seui	seoi3	swoi
break[2] glass/shatter/smash	v	打碎	dá seui	daa2 seoi	ta swoi
break[3] /cut off	v	斷	tyúhn	tyun5	thyuhn
break[4] /suddenly stop	v	折斷	jit tyúhn	zit3 tyun5	chit thyuhn
break[5] /discontinue /interrupt	v	中斷	jùng tyúhn	zung4 tyun5	chung thyuhn
break[6] /broke	v	砸破	jaap po	zaap po	chaap pho
break[7] by hit/smash	v	打爛	dá laahn	daa2 laan6	ta laahn
break[8] by fall	v	整爛	jíng laahn	zing2 laan6	cheng laahn
break[9] by fingers	v	搣爛	mìt laahn	mit4 laan6	mit laahn
break[10] by fall down	v	跌爛	dit laahn	dit3 laan6	tit laahn
break apart	v	析	chaak	caak3	chhaak
break appointment		失約	sāt yeuk	sat1 joek3	sat yeuk
break by hand /to break	v	折	jit	zit3	chit
break contract[1]		毀約	wái yeuk	wai2 joek	wai yeuk
break contract[2]		違反協定	wàih fáan hip dehng	wai4 faan2 hip3	waih faan hip tehng

break down[1] /damage /badness/broken/out of order	n	壞	waaih	waai6	waaih
break down[2] by force	n	打破	dá po	daa2 po3	ta pho
break down[3]	n	粉碎	fán seui	fan2 seoi3	fan swoi
break down[4]	n	毀掉	wái diuh	wai2 diu6	wai tiuh
break down[5]	v	壞掉	waaih diuh	waai6 diu6	waaih tiuh
break fast	n	早餐	jóu chāan	zou2 caan1	chou chhaan
break in /interrupt	n	打斷	dá tyúhn	daa2 tyun5	ta thyuhn
break into pieces /shatter/come apart	v	破碎	po seui	po3 seoi3	poh swoi
break off /stop cease	adj	中止	jùng jí	zung4 zi2	chung chi
break out /sudden painful attack/ flare-up	n	發作	faat jok	faat3 zok3	faat chok
break record[1]	v	打破	dá po	daa2 po3	ta pho
break record[2]	v	打破記錄	dá po géi luhk	daa2 po3 gei2 luk6	ta pho kei luhk
break record[3]	v	破記錄	po géi luhk	po3 gei2 luk6	pho kei luhk
break the car	v	剎掣	saat jai	caat3 zai3	saat chai
breaker[1]	n	打破者	dá po jé	daa2 po3 ze2	ta pho che
breaker[2] /large wave	n	碎浪	seui lohng	seoi3 long6	swoi lohng
breast[1] milk/of woman	n	奶	láaih /náaih	laai5 /naai5	laaih /naaih
breast[2] /chest	n	胸	hùng	hung4	hung
breast[3] suck nipple	v	食人奶	sihk yàhn láaih /náaih	sik6 jan4 laai5 /naai5	sehk yahn laaih /naaih
breast[4] (sl) of woman	n	波菜	bō lòih	bo1 loi4	po loih
breast[5] (sl) touch gently by hand	n	揸波	já bō	zaa2 bo1	cha poh
breath[1]	n	唞氣	táu hei	tau2 hei3	thau hei
breath[2] /respire	n/v	呼吸	fù kāp	fu4 kap1	fu khap
breath out /exhale	v	呼	fù	fu4	fu
breathe deeply	v	使喘氣	si chyún hei	si3 cyun5 hei3	si chhyun hei
breathe in /suck in/ inhale/taking air/absorb	n	吸	kāp	kap1	khap
breathe quickly	v	喘氣	chyún hei	cyun5 hei3	chhyun hei
breechcloth /shorts/ briefs/underpants/half pant/short pants/short trouser	n	短褲	dyún fu	dyun2 fu3	tyun fu
breed /give birth /to givebirth	v	生育	sàang yuhk	saang4 juk6	saang yuhk
breeding season	n	發情期	faat chìhng kèih	faat3 cing4 kei4	faat chehng kheih
breeze /light wind	n	和風	wòh fùng	wo4 fung3	woh fung
brewery	n	啤酒廠	bē jáu chóng	be1 zau2 cong2	pe chau chong
bribe /bribery	n	賄賂	kúi louh	kui2 lou6	khui louh
bribe	v	洗黑錢	sái hāk chín	sai2 hak1 cin2	sai hak chhin
brick[1]	n	磚	jyūn	zyun1	chyun
brick[2]	n	磚塊	jyūn faai	zyun1 faai3	chyun faai

bricklayer[1] /stone worker /mason	n	泥水師傅	làih séui sī fuh	lai4 seoi2 si1 fu6	laih swoi si fuh
bricklayer[2]	n	泥水佬	làih séui lóu	lai4 seoi2 lou2	laih swoi lou
bride	n	新娘	sàn léung /néung	san4 loeng2 /noeng2	san leong /neong
bride's family	n	女家	léuih gā	leui5 gaa1	lowih ka
bridegroom	n	新郎哥	sàn lòhng gō	san4 long4 go1	san lohng ko
bridegroom necklace/ auspicious necklace	n	吉利嘅頸鍊	gāt leih ge géng lihn	gat1 lei6 ge3 geng2 lin6	kat leih ke keng lihn
bridegroom's family	n	男家	làahm gā	laam4 ga1	laahm ka
bridesmaid[1] /best girl bride's	n	伴娘	buhn léung/néung	bun6 loeng2/noeng2	puhn leong/neong
bridesmaid[2]	n	女儐相	léuih bān sèung	leui5 ban1 soeng4	lowih pahn seung
bridge	n	橋	kìuh	kiu4	khiuh
brief[1] /instruction	adj	簡短	gáan dyún	gaan2 dyun2	kaan tyun
brief[2]	adj	短暫	dyún jàahm	dyun2 zaam4	tyun chaahm
brief case	n	公事包	gùng sih bàau	gung4 si6 baau4	kung sih paau
briefing[1] /training	n	上堂	séuhng tòhng	soeng5 tong4	seuhng thohng
briefing[2]	n	簡報	gáan bou	gaan2 bou3	kaan pou
briefly	adv	簡短地	gáan dyún deih	gaan2 dyun2 dei6	kaan tyun teih
brigade of army	n	旅	léuih	leoi5	lowih
brigadier	n	旅長	léuih jéung	leoi5 zoeng2	lowih cheung
bright[1] /brilliant/light	adj	亮	leuhng	loeng6	leuhng
bright[2]	adj	明	mìhng	ming4	mehng
bright[3]	adj	明亮的	mìhng lèuhng dìk	ming4 loeng6 dik4	mehng leuhng tik
bright & clean	adj	光潔	gwòng git	gwong4 git3	kwong kit
bright color /colorful /variety	adj	彩	chói	coi2	chhoi
bright light[1]	adj	光彩奪目	gwòng chói dyuht muhk	gwong4 coi2 dyut6 muk6	kwong chhoi tyuht muhk
bright light[2]	adj	光	gwòng	gwong4	kwong
bright light[3]	adj	光猛	gwòng máahng	gwong4 maang5	kwong maahng
brightly	adj	閃亮地	sīm lèuhng deih	sim1 loeng6 dei6	sim leuhng teih
brilliant	adj	輝煌	fāi wòhng	fai1 wong4	fai wohng
bring[1]	v	取來	chéui loìh	ceoi2 loi4	chheui loih
bring[2]	v	拿來	lāh /nāh loìh	laa1 /naa1 loi4	lah /nah loih
bring by hand /take by hand	v	帶	daai	daai3	taai
bring it back	v	帶香嚟	daai heung lái	daai3 hoeng lai2	taai heung lai
bring up[1] take care/baby/kid	v	湊	chau	cau3	chhau
bring up[2] /support/rear/ keeping/raise support	v	養	yéuhng	joeng5	yeuhng
bring up[3] animals/childrens /support animal & child/ keep animal & child	v	馴養	sèuhn yéuhng	seon4 joeng5	swohn yeuhng
bring up an idea	v	提議	tàih yíh	tai4 ji5	thaih yih
bringing		攞緊	ló gán	lo2 gan2	lo kan

English	Part	Chinese	Romanization 1	Jyutping	Romanization 2
brisk /quickly/speedy	adj	迅速地	seun chùk dèih	seon3 cuk4 dei6	swon chhuk teih
British /England/Great Britain	n	英國	yìng gwók	jing4 gwok2	yeng kwok
broad /wide	adj	寬闊	fùn fút	fun4 fut2	fun fut
broad locust /cicada	n	蟬	sìhm	sim4	sihm
broad shoulders	n	闊肩	fut gìn	fut3 gin4	fut kin
broadcast	v	廣播	gwóng bo	gwong2 bo3	kwong po
broadcasting station /studio/tower	n	臺	tòih	toi4	thoi
broadway	n	百老匯	baak lóuh wuih	baak3 lou5 wui6	paak lowuh wuih
broccoli	n	西蘭花	sài làahn fā	sai3 laan4 faa1	sai laahn fa
broil¹ /roast	v	炙	jek	zek3	chek
broil² /burn/inflame	n	燒	sìu	siu4	siu
broke	v	砸	jaap	zaap	chaap
broken¹ /damaged /worn out/teared	adj	爛咗	laahn jó	laan6 zo2	laahn cho
broken² not continuous	adj	斷	tyúhn	tyun5	thyuhn
broken³ /crack	adj	破	po	po3	pho
broken bones /fracture	n/adj	骨折	gwāt jit	gwat1 zit3	kwat chit
broken down	adj	向下	heung hah	hoeng ha6	heung hah
broken language	adj	語言拙劣	yúh yin jyut lyut	jyu5 jin3 zyut3 lyut3	yuh yin chyut lyut
broken limb	adj	肢解	ji gāai	zi3 gaai1	chi kaai
broker¹	n	經紀	gìng géi	ging4 gei2	keng kei
broker² /middle-man	n	經紀人	gìng géi yàhn	ging4 gei2 jan4	keng kei yahn
brokerage /commission	n	佣金	yúng gām	jung2 gam1	yung kam
bronchi	n	支氣管	jì hei gún	zi4 hei3 gun2	chi hei kun
bronchitis	n	支氣管炎	jì hei gún yìhm	zi4 hei3 gun2 jim4	chi hei kun yihm
bronze /copper	n	銅	tùhng	tung4	thuhng
bronze statue	n	銅像	tùhng jeuhng	tung4 zoeng6	thuhng cheuhng
bronze	n	青銅	chèng tùhng	ceng4 tung4	chheng thuhng
brooch	n	女用胸針	léuih yuhng hùng jām	leui5 jung6 hung4 zam1	lowih yuhng hung cham
broom¹ /brush	n	掃把	sou bá	sou3 baa2	sou pa
broom² /brush	n	掃帚	sou jáu	sou3 zau2	sou chau
broth¹ /gravy	n	滷	lóuh	lou5	louh
broth² /fluid/juice	n	漿	jēung	zeung1	cheung
brothel¹	n	妓寨	geih jaaih	gei6 zaai6	keih chaaih
brothel² /prostitutes house	n	妓院	geih yún	gei6 jyun2	keih yun
brothel³ (sl) /house of prostitution	n	雞竇	gài dau	gai4 dau3	kai tau
brothel⁴ (sl)	n	架步	ga bouh	gaa3 bou6	ka pouh
brotherhood¹	n	手足之情	sáu jūk jí chìhng	sau2 zuk1 zi2 cing4	sau chuk chi chhehng
brotherhood²	n	兄弟關係	hìng daih gwàan haih	hing4 dai6 gwaan4 hai6	hing taih kwaan haih
brothers	n	兄弟	hìng daih	hing4 dai6	hing taih
brought /bring	adj	帶來	daai làih	daai3 lai4	taai laih
brought away	adj	帶咗去	daai jó heui	daai3 zo2 heoi3	taai cho hoi

brown	n	啡色	fē sīk	fe1 sik1	fe sek
brown sugar	n	黃糖	wòhng tòhng	wong4 tong4	wohng thohng
browse[1]	v	瀏覽	làuh láahm	lau4 laam5	lauh laahm
browse[2]	v	隨便看看	chèuih bihn hòn hòn	ceoi4 bin6 hon4 hon	chheuih pihn hon hon
browse[3] /eats grass eats grass by cow/goats	v	吃草	hek chóu	hek3 cou2	hek chhou
bruise[1] mark/blue mark/ hematoma/on the skin by bruised blood clot	n	瘀	yú	jyu1	yu
bruise[2] blue mark on the skin	n	瘀傷	yú sèung	jyu1 soeng4	yu seung
brush[1]	n	擦	cháat	caat3	chhaat
brush[2] for paint	v	刷	cháat	caat2	chhaat
brush teeth	v	擦牙	chaat ngàh	caat3 ngaa4	chhaat ngah
brutal	adj	野蠻嘅	yéh màahn ge	je5 maan4 ge3	yeh maahn ke
bubble	n	氣泡	hei póuh	hei3 pou5	hei phouh
bubble mirrors /fish eye mirror	n	魚眼鏡	yú ngáahn géng	jyu4 ngaan5 geng2	yu ngaahn keng
bucket	n	水桶	séui túng	seoi2 tung2	swoi thung
buckle[1]	n	搭扣	daap kau	daap3 kau3	taap khau
buckle[2]	n	帶鈕	daai kau	daai3 kau3	taai khau
buckles /fasten/tie	v	扣緊	kau gán	kau3 gan2	khau kan
buckram	n	硬棉布	ngaahng mìhn bou	ngaang6 min4 bou3	ngaahng mihn pou
Buddha bron in Nepal on BC 2557 years ago		Buddha係 二五五七 年前係尼 泊爾出世	**Buddha** haih yih ngh ngh chāt lihn /nihn chìhn haih nèih bòhk yíh chēut sai	Buddha hai6 ji6 ng5 ng5 cat1 lin4 /nin4 cin4 hai6 nei4 bok6 ji5 ceot1 sai3	**Buddha** haih yih nggh nggh chhat lihn /nihn chhihn haih neih pohk yih chhot sai
Buddhism /Buddhist	n	佛教	faht gaau	fat1 gaau3	faht kaau
Buddhist	n	佛教徒	faht gaau tòuh	fat1 gaau3 tou4	faht kaau thouh
budget	n	預算	yuh syun	jyu6 syun3	yuh syun
buffalo	n	水牛	séui ngàuh	seoi2 ngau4	swoi ngauh
buffer	n	緩衝器	wun chùng hei	maan6 cung4 hei3	wun chhung hei
buffet[1] meal	n	自助餐	jih joh chāan	zi6 zo6 caan1	chih choh chhaan
buffet[2] roughly knock	v	打擊	dá gīk	daa2 gik1	ta kek
bugle	n	軍號	gwàn houh	gwan4 hou6	kwan houh
build[1] /to construct	v	築	jùk	zuk4	chuk
build[2] make	v	起造	héi jouh	hei2 zou6	hei chouh
build[3] /construct	v	建造	gín jouh	gin3 zou6	kin chouh
build[4] /establish/set up /found	v	建立	gin lahp	gin3 lap6	kin lahp
build[5] /construct	v	建築	gin jūk	gin3 zuk1	kin chuk
builders	n	建造者	gín jouh jē	gin2 zou6 ze1	kin chouh che
building[1]	n	建築	gin jūk	gin3 zuk1	kin chuk
building[2]	n	建築物	gin jūk maht	gin3 zuk1 mat6	kin chuk maht
building[3] /house/housing	n	房屋	fóng ūk /ngūk	fong2 uk1 /nguk1	fong uk /nguk

building name	n	大廈名稱	daaih hah mèhng chìng	daai6 haa6 meng4 cing4	taaih hah mehng cheng
building's room	n	房	fóng	fong2	fong
bulb	n	電燈泡	dihn dāng póuh	din6 dang1 pou5	tihn tang phouh
bulk /chunk/large quantity	n	大塊	daaih pài	daai6 pai4	taaih phai
bulldozer	n	推土機	teui tóu gèi	teoi3 tou2 gei4	thoi thou kei
bullet[1]	n	彈	dáan	daan2	taan
bullet[2] /cartridge/pellet	n	子彈	jí dáan	zi2 daan2	chi taan
bullet[3]	n	槍彈	chèung dáan	coeng4 daan2	chheung taan
bulletin	n	公報	gùng bou	gung4 bou3	kung pou
bullseye /centre target /hit target	n/v	擊中	gīk jùng	gik1 zung4	kek chung
bullshit[1]	n	亂講	lyuhn góng	lyun6 gong2	lyuhn kong
bullshit[2] /horseshit	v	胡說	wùh syut	wu4 syut3	wuh syut
bullshit[3] (sl)	n	吹牛	cheui ngàuh	ceoi3 ngau4	chheui ngauh
bullshit me[1]	n	氹我	táhm ngóh	tam5 ngo5	thahm ngoh
bullshit me[2]	n	哄我	húng ngóh	hung2 ngo5	hung ngoh
bully[1] /gangster/ruffian/ big brother/hooligan/ mobster	n	欺凌	hei lihng	hei3 ling4	hei lehng
bully[2] /evil man/bully boy	n	惡霸	ok /ngok ba	ok3 /ngok3 baa3	ok /ngok pa
bully[3] /gangster/big brother	v	欺侮人	hēi móuh yàhn	hei1 mou5 jan4	hei mouh yahn
bump[1] /collide/to hit/touch /crash/impact/knock	v	碰	pung	pung3	phung
bump[2] /strike/collides/ knock/crash/hit/impact	v	撞	johng	zong6	chohng
bump[3] /impact/collide/to strike	n	碰撞	púng johng	pung2 zong6	phung chohng
bump into	n	無意中遇到	móuh yi jùng yuh dóu	mou5 ji3 zung4 jyu6 dou2	mouh yi chung yuh tou
bumper /special large	n	特大	dahk daaih	dak6 daai6	tahk taaih
bun /roll	n	髻	gai	gai3	kai
bunch[1] /bundle	n	扎	jaat	zaat3	chaat
bunch[2]	n	抽	chàu	cau4	chhau
bunch[3]	n	束	chūk	cuk1	chhuk
bundle	n	捆	kwán	kwan2	khwan
bungalow	n	平房	pèhng fóng	peng4 fong2	phehng fong
burden[1]	n	重負	chúhng fuh	cung5 fu6	chhuhng fuh
burden[2] /hard work/ difficulty work	n/adj	負擔	fuh dàam	fu6 daam4	fuh taam
bureau[1] /office/department	n	署	chyúh	cyu5	chhyuh
bureau[2]	n	辦公署	baahn gūng chyúh	baan6 gung1 cyu5	paahn kung chyuh
bureau[3]	n	事務處	sih mouh chyúh	si6 mou6 cyu5	sih mouh chhyuh
bureau chief	n	局長	gúk jéung	guk2 zoeng2	kuk cheung
burglar[1] /thief/robber	n	盜賊	dou chaahk	dou3 caak6	tou chhaahk
burglar[2] /thief	n	竊賊	sit chaahk	sit3 caak6	sit chaahk

burglar[3]	n	盜竊賊	dou sit chaahk	dou3 sit3 caak6	tou sit chhaahk
burglar alarm	n	防盜警鐘	fòhng douh gíng jùng	fong4 dou6 ging2 zung4	fohng touh geng chung
burglar alarmed	n	防盜警鐘響起	fòhng douh gíng jùng héung héi	fong4 dou6 ging2 zung4 hoeng2 hei2	fohng touh geng chung heung hei
burglary[1]	n	夜盜	yèh dòuh	je6 dou6	yeh touh
burglary[2]	n	盜竊罪行	dou sit jeuih hahng	dou3 sit3 zeoi6 hang4	tou sit cheuih hahng
burial	n	葬體	jong tái	jong3 tai2	chong thai
burial ground[1]	n	墓地	mouh deih	mou6 dei6	mouh teih
burial ground[2]	n	墳地	fàhn deih	fan4 dei6	fahn teih
burn[1]	v	燒灼	sìu cheuk	siu4 ceok	siu chheuk
burn[2] injury	n	燒傷	sìu sèung	siu4 soeng4	siu seung
burned	v	燶咗	lùng /nùng jó	lung4 /nung4 zo2	lung /nung cho
burner	n	燃燒器	yìhn sìu hei	jin4 siu4 hei3	yihn siu hei
burning smell	adj	燃燒氣味	yìhn sìu hei meih	jin4 siu4 hei3 mei6	yihn siu hei meih
burnish	v	擦亮	cháat leuhng	caat3 loeng6	chhaat leuhng
burnt /overcook	adj	煮燶	jyú/zyú lūng /lūng	zyu2 lung1/nung1	chyu lung /lung
burnted	adj	燒焦	sìu jīu	siu4 ziu1	siu chiu
burnt perfume	n	點香	dím hèung	dim2 hoeng4	tim heung
burst	v	噗	pok	pok3	phok
bury	v	埋藏	màaih chòhng	maai4 cong4	maaih chhohng
bus /coach	n	巴士	bā sí	baa1 si2	pa si
bus lane[1]	n	巴士專線	bā sí jyūn sin	baa1 si2 zyun1 sin3	pa si chyun sin
bus lane[2]	n	公車車道	gùng chè chè douh	gung4 ce1 ce1 dou6	kung chhe chhe touh
bus stop /rail stop	n	停車站	tìhng chè jaahm	ting4 ce4 zaam6	thehng chhe chaahm
bus station[1]	n	巴士站	bā sí jaahm	baa1 si2 zaam6	pa si chaahm
bus station[2]	n	公車站	gùng chè jaahm	gung4 ce1 zaam6	kung chhe chaahm
bus stop	n	車站	chè jaahm	ce1 zaam6	chhe chaahm
busy /very busy/busily/hectic/full of activity	adv	忙碌	mòhng lūk	mong4 luk1	mohng luk
business[1] /commerce	n	商業	sèung yihp	soeng4 jip6	seung yihp
business[2] /trade	n	營業	yìhng yihp	jing4 jip6	yehng yihp
business[3] /transaction	n	業務	yihp mouh	jip6 mou6	yihp mouh
business[4] /trade	n	生意	sàang yi	saang4 ji3	saang yi
business administer		工商管理	gùng sèung gún léih	gung3 soeng4 gun2 lei5	kung seung kun leih
business card[(de)] visiting card/name card	n	名片	kāat pín	kaat1 pin2	khaat phin
business class[1]	n	商務位	sèung mòuh wàih	soeng4 mou6 wai6	seung mouh waih
business class[2]	n	商務艙	sèung mòuh chōng	soeng4 mou6 cong1	seung mouh chhong
business deal /transaction/trading/buy and sell/deal	n	交易	gàau yihk	gaau4 jik6	kaau yehk
business hours	n	營業時間	yìhng yihp sìh gaan	jing4 jip6 si4 gaan3	yehng yihp sih kaan
business man /dealer/mercantile/trader/merchant	adj/n	商人	sèung yàhn	soeng4 jan4	seung yahn

business tel service	n	商業電話服務	sèung yihp dihn wá fuhk mouh	soeng4 jip6 din6 waa2 fuk6 mou6	seung yihp tihn wa fuhk mouh
business transaction /buy & sell activity/trading/ deal for business/buy & sell /do business	v	營業	yìhng yìhp	jing4 jip6	yehng yihp
busser restaurant worker	n	餐館工	chāan gún gùng	caan1 gun2 gung4	chhaan kun kung
bustling[1]	n	熱鬧	yiht laauh /naauh	jit6 laau6 /naau6	yiht laauh /naauh
bustling[2]	adv	活躍	wuht yéuk	wut6 joek2	wuht yeuk
busy[1] /complicated	adv	繁	fàan	faan4	faan
busy[2]	adv	繁忙	fàan mòhng	faan4 mong6	faan mohng
busy[3]	adv	熱鬧	yiht laauh /naauh	jit6 laau6 /naau6	yiht laauh /naauh
busy[4]	adv	唔得閑	m̀ dāk hàahn	m4 dak1 haan4	mh tak haahn
busy as a bee /very busy	adj	好忙	hóu mòhng	hou2 mong4	hou mohng
but[1]	conj	但	daahn	daan6	taahn
but[2] /however/still/yet	conj	但係	daahn haih	daan6 hai6	taahn haih
but[3]	conj	但是	daahn sih	daan6 si6	taahn sih
but[4] /also	conj	而且	yìh ché	ji4 ce2	yih chhe
but limit	conj	只限	yí haahn	zi2 haan6	yi haahn
butcher	n	豬肉鋪	jyù yuhk póu	zyu4 juk6 pou2	chyu yuhk phou
butt[1] /stem of fruit	n	蒂	dai	dai3	tai
butt[2]	n	槍柄	chèung beng	coeng4 beng3	chheung peng
butt stink	n	大俾	daaih pei	daai6 pei3	taaih phei
butter /ghee	n	牛油	ngàuh yàuh	ngau4 jau4	ngauh yauh
buttered pineapple bun		菠蘿油	bō lo yàuh	bo1 lo3 jau4	po lo yauh
butterfly	n	蝴蝶	wu dìhp	wu3 dip6	wu tihp
buttock out straight /stretch buttock/thighs out extend/wided buttock/ extended buttock	v	嘑大	la daaih	laa3 daai6	la taaih
buttocks[1] /butt	n	臀	tyùhn	tyun4	thyuhn
buttocks[2] /rump/hip	n	臀部	tyùhn bouh	tyun4 bou6	thyuhn pouh
button[1] /tache	n	扣 / 鈕	kau	kau3	khau
button[2]	n	鈕	láu	lau2	lau
button[3]	n	鈕扣	láu kau	lau2 kau3	lau kau
button[4]	n	釘鈕	dēng láu	deng1 lau2	teng lau
button[5]	n	衫鈕	sàam láu	saam4 lau2	saam lau
button up	n	扣鈕	kau láu	kau3 lau2	khau lau
buttonhole[1]	n	扣眼	kau ngáahn	kau3 ngaan5	khau ngaahn
buttonhole[2]	n	鈕孔	láu húng	lau2 hung2	lau hung
buy and sell[1] (illegal)	v	進行交易 (非法)	jeun hàhng gāau yihk (fèi faat)	zeon3 hang4 gaau1 jik6 (fei4 faat3)	cheun hahng kaau yehk (fei faat)
buy and sell[2] (illegal)	v	做買賣 (非法)	jouh máaih maaih (fèi faat)	zou6 maai5 maai6 (fei4 faat3)	chouh maaih maaih (fei faat)
buy crabs	v	買蟹	máaih hàaih	maai5 haai6	maaih haaih
buy eggs	v	買蛋	máaih dāan	maai5 daan1	maaih taan
buy for you		買俾你	máaih béi léih /néih	maai5 bei2 lei5 /nei5	maaih pei leih /neih

English	POS	中文	Romanization	Jyutping	Romanization 2
buy groceries	v	買餸	máaih sung	maai5 sung3	maaih sung
buy shares	v	股票投資	gú piu tàuh jī	gu2 piu3 tau4 zi1	ku phiu thauh chi
buy shoes	v	買鞋	máaih hàaih	maai5 haai4	maaih haaih
buyable	adj	可買嘅	hó máaih ge	ho2 maai5 ge3	ho maaih ke
buyer[1] /client	n	買家	máaih gà	maai5 gaa4	maaih ka
buyer[2]	n	買主	máaih jyú	maai5 zyu2	maaih chyu
buying[1]	v	購	kau	kau3	khau
buying[2]	v	購物	kau maht	kau3 mat6	khau maht
buying goods /shopping goods	v	買嘢	máaih yéh	maai5 je5	maaih yeh
buzzer	n	蜂音器	fùng yàm hei	fung4 jam4 hei3	fung yam hei
by[1]	prep	於	yū	jyu1	yu
by[2]	prep	在旁	joih pòhng	zoi6 pong4	choih phohng
by[3]	prep	被	bèih	bei6	peih
by accident	adj	偶然地	ngáuh yìhn deih	ngau5 jin4 dei6	ngauh yihn teih
by all means /surely /certainly/fixed	adj	一定	yāt dihng	jat1 ding6	yat tehng
by and by[(IDM)] shortly/no long	adv IDM	一陣	yāt jahn	jat1 zan6	yat chahn
by bus traveller	n	搭乘公車	daap sìhng gùng chè	daap3 sing4 gung4 ce1	taap sehng kung chhe
by chance /coincidental	adj	碰巧	púng háau	pung2 haau2	phung haau
by election	n	後補選舉	hauh bóu syún géui	hau6 bou2 syun geoi2	hauh pou syun kwoi
by no means	n	切勿	chit maht	cit3 mat6	chhit maht
by the day	prep	按日	on /ngòn yaht	on3 /ngon4 jat6	on /ngon yaht
by the way[1]	adv	講起上嚟	góng héi séuhng làih	gong2 hei2 soeng5 lai4	kong hei seuhng laih
by the way[2]	adv	講開就講	góng hòi chau góng	gong2 hoi4 zau6 gong2	kong hoi chhau kong
by the way[3]	adv	順便說說	seuhn bihn syut syut	seon6 bin6 syut3 syut3	swohn pihn syut syut
bye bye[(de)]	int	拜拜	báai báai	baai2 baai2	paai paai
bygone[1]	adj	過去嘅	gwo heui ge	gwo3 heoi3 ge3	kwo hoi ke
bygone[2]	adj	以往嘅	yíh wóhng ge	ji5 wong5 ge3	yih wohng ke
bygone[3]	adj	已往嘅	yíh wóhng ge	ji5 wong5 ge3	yih wohng ke
byname /full name/ name& surname/name	n	姓名	seng méng	seng3 meng2	seng meng
bypass[1]	n	旁路	pòhng louh	pong4 lou6	phohng louh
bypass[2] /overtake	n	旁道	pòhng dou	pong4 dou3	phohng tou
bypass[2] /triage	n	分流	fàn làuh	fan6 lau4	fan lauh
bypass[3] /pass by/transit/ through/via	n/adj	經過	gìng gwo	ging4 gwo3	keng gwo

C.D. label	n	彩色數碼	chói sīk sou máh	coi2 sik1 sou3 maa5	chhoi sek sou mah
c/o /care of	prep	轉交	jyun gāau	zyun3 gaau1	chyun kaau
Cab (wr) /taxi	n	計程車	gai chìhng chè	gai3 cing4 ce1	kai chhehng chhe
cabbage[1]	n	椰菜	yèh chói	je4 coi2	yeh chhoi
cabbage[2] white	n	白菜	baahk chói	baak6 coi2	paahk choi
cabbage[3] flowering	n	菜心	chói sàm	coi2 sam4	chhoi sam
cabin[1] of ship	n	船艙	syùhn chòng	syun4 cong4	syuhn chhong
cabin[2] /small room on a bus or ship	n	客艙	haak chōng	haak3 cong1	haak chhong
cabin class /second class seat	n	二等艙	daih yih chòng	dai6 ji6 cong4	taih yih chhong
cabinet[1] /wardrobe	n	櫥	chyùh	cyu4	chhyuh
cabinet[2] /cupboard/ wardrobe	n	櫥櫃	chyùh gwaih	cyu4 gwai6	chhyuh kwaih
cabinet[3] /cupboard	n	碗櫃 / 柜	wún gwaih	wun2 gwai6	wun kwaih
cabinet[4] /cupboard	n	檔案櫃	dong on gwaih	dong3 on3 gwai6	tong on kwaih
cabinet[5] of government	n	內閣	loih / noih gok	loi6 / noi6 gok3	loih / noih kok
cable[1] /line/thread/cord /string/wire/route		線	sin	sin3	sin
cable[2] /large rope	n	索	sok	sok3	sok
cable[3] /wire/metal string	n	鋼索	gong sok	gong3 sok3	kong sok
cable car /crane/hoist	n	吊車	diu chè	diu3 ce1	tiu chhe
cadence /rhythm	n	節奏	jit jau	zit3 zau3	chit chau
cadre /member	n	幹部	gon bouh	gon3 bou6	kon pouh
cadres	n	骨幹	gwāt gon	gwat1 gon3	kwat kon
café room	n	咖啡廳	ga fē tèng	gaa3 fe1 teng4	ka fe theng
café shop	n	咖啡館	ga fèi gūn	gaa3 fei4 gun1	ka fe kun
caffeine (de)	n	咖啡因	ga fē yān	gaa3 fe1 jan1	ka fe yan
cage (of the bird)	n	鳥籠	líuh /níuh lùhng	liu5 /niu5 lung4	liuh /niuh luhng
cajole child /persuade child	v	探細佬仔	tam sái lóu jāi	taam3 sai2 lou2 zai1	tham sai lou chai
cajole girl /persuade girl	v	探女仔	tam léoih /néoih jāi	taam3 leoi5 /neoi5 zai1	tham lowih /nowih chai
cake[1]	n	糕	gōu	gou1	kou
cake[2]	n	蛋糕	daahn gōu	daan6 gou1	taahn kou
cake[3] /pastry cake	n	西餅	sài béng	sai4 beng2	sai peng
cake shop	n	西餅店	sài béng dim	sai4 beng2 dim3	sai peng tim
calcium	n	鈣	koi	koi3	khoi
calculate[1] /count /figure out	v	計	gai	gai3	kai
calculate[2] (regard as)	v	算	syun	syun3	syun
calculate[3] /count	v	計算	gai syun	gai3 syun3	kai syun
calculate wrongly		計錯數	gai cho sóu	gai3 co3 sou2	kai chho sou
calculator[1]	n	計數機	gai sou gèi	gai3 sou3 gei4	kai sou kei
calculator[2]	n	計算機	gai syun gèi	gai3 syun3 gei4	kai syun kei
calendar[1]	n	曆	lihk	lik6	lehk
calendar[2] monthly	n	月曆	yuht lihk	jyut6 lik6	yuht lehk

calendar[3] /solar month	n	新曆	sàn lihk	san4 lik6	san lehk
calendar[4] year	n	日曆	yaht lihk	jat6 lik6	yaht lehk
calf of the leg	n	小腿	síu téui	siu2 teoi2	siu thoi
calibrate /check exam	v	校	gaau	gaau3	kaau
calibration	n	標定	bīu dehng	biu1 deng6	piu tehng
caliper	n	卡鉗	ká kìhm	kaa2 kim6	kha khihm
call[1]	v	喚	wuhn	wun6	wuhn
call[2] /express/opinion	v	表	bíu	biu2	piu
call[3] /summon	n	召	jiuh	ziu6	chiuh
call a strike	v	號召罷工	houh jiuh bah gùng	hou6 ziu6 baa6 gung4	houh chiuh pah kung
call back[1]	v	叫返嚟	giu…fàan làih	giu3…faan4 lai4	kiu…faan laih
call back[2]	v	覆電話	fūk dihn wá	fuk1 din6 waa2	fuk tihn wa
call back[2]	v	回電	wùih dihn	wui4 din6	wuih tihn
called behind	v	後面叫喊	hauh mìhn giu haam	hau6 min6 giu3 haam3	hauh mihn kiu haam
call for /demand /necessary/necessity/in need of	n	需要	sèui yiu	seoi4 jiu3	swoi yiu
call for help!	n	要人幫手	yiu yàhn bòng sáu	jiu3 jan4 bong4 sau2	yiu yahn pong sau
call girl[1] /prostitute	n/v	妓女	geih léuih /néuih	gei6 leoi5 /neoi5	keih lowih /nowih
call girl[2]	v	應召女郎	ying jiuh léuih /néuih lòhng	jing3 ziu6 leoi6 /neoi6 long4	yeng chiuh lowih /nowih lohng
call into quesion	v	對…表示懷疑	deui bíu sih wàaih yih	deoi3 biu2 si6 waai6 ji6	toei piu sih waaih yih
call off /cancel/delete /revoke	v	取消	chéui sìu	ceoi2 siu4	chheui siu
call on[1] /request	n	請求	chéng /chíng kàuh	ceng2 /cing2 kau4	chheng khauh
call on[2] /formal visit	n	拜訪	baai fóng	baai3 fong2	paai fong
call taxi	n	叫架的士	giu gá dìk sih	giu3 gaa2 dik1 si6	kiu ka tek sih
call the police!	n	叫警察!	giu gíng chaat	giu3 ging2 caat3	kiu keng chhaat
called	n	叫咗	giu jó	giu3 zo2	kiu cho
called behind	v	後面叫喊	hauh mìhn giu haam	hau6 min6 giu3 haam3	hauh mihn kiu haam
caller	n	呼叫者	fù giu jé	fu4 giu3 ze2	fu kiu che
calligraphy /handwriting	n	書法	syù faat	syu4 faat3	syu faat
calling[1] /invitation/invite	n	邀請	yìu chéng	jiu4 ceng2	yiu chheng
calling[2]	n	召喚	jiuh jaahp	ziu6 zaap6	chiuh chaahp
calm[1] /peaceful	v	平靜	pèhng jèhng	peng4 zing4	phehng chehng
calm[2] /quiet/silence/hush /peaceful	adj/v	安靜	òn /ngòn jìhng	on4 /ngon4 zing6	on /ngon chehng
calm[3] /undisturbed	adj	啖定	daahm dehng	daam6 deng6	taahm tehng
calm[4] /undisturbed	a/v	鎮定/鎮定	jan dehng /dìhng	zan3 deng6 /ding6	chan tehng
calm[5]	adj	鎮靜	jan jihng	zan3 zing6	chan chehng
calm down[1]	v	平靜下來	pèhng jèhng hàh lòih	peng4 zing6 haa5 loi4	phehng chehng hah loih
calm down[2] /cool down	v	鎮靜下來	jan jihng háh lòih	zan3 zing6 haa5 loi4	chan chehng hah loih
calming pitch /flowery speech	v	花言巧語	fā yìhn háau yuh	faa1 jing4 haau2 jyu6	fa yihn haau yuh

came[1] /arrived /already came	v	來咗	lòih jó	loi4 zo2	loih cho
came[2] /were	v	的過去式	dìk gwo heui sīk	dik4 gwo3 heoi3 sik1	tek kwo hoi sek
came out an idea	v	想出	séung chēut	soeng2 ceot1	seung chhot
came from	v	嚟㗎	lái gá	lai2 gaa2	lai ka
camera[1]	n	影相機	yéng sèung gèi	jeng2 soeng4 gei4	yeng seung kei
camera[2]	n	照相機	jiu sèung gèi	ziu3 soeng4 gei4	chiu seuhng kei
camera[3]	n	録影機	lohk yíng gèi	lok6 jing2 gei4	lohk ying kei
camp[1] /tent	n	營	yìhng	jing4	yehng
camp[2] /tent	n	營幕	yìhng mohk	jing4 mok6	yehng mohk
camp[3] /tent	n	帳篷	jeung pùhng	zoeng3 pung4	cheung phuhng
camp[4] (army)	n	軍營	gwàn yìhng	gwan4 jing4	kwan yehng
campaign[1] in social /commercial /political	n	運動	wahn duhng	wan6 dung6	wahn tohng
campaign[2] a war	n	戰役	jin yihk	zin3 jik6	chin yehk
campaigner /social worker	n	從事社會 運動嘅人	chùhng sih séh wúi wahn duhng ge yàhn	cung4 si6 ce5 wui2 wan6 dung6 ge3 jan4	chhuhng sih seh wui wahn tuhng ke yahn
camping site	n	營地	yìhng deih	jing4 dei6	yehng teih
campus	n	校園	haauh yùhn	haau6 jyun4	haauh yuhn
camshaft of vehicle	n	凸輪軸	daht lèuhn juhk	dat leon4 juk6	taht lowhn chuhk
can[1] /may	v/aux	可	hó	ho2	ho
can[2] /possible/be able to /know how to	v/aux	會	wúih	wui5	wuih
can[3] /agree/yes/may/ might/should/could	v/aux	可以	hó yíh	ho2 ji5	ho yih
can[4] (de) tin can	n	聽	tèng	teng4	theng
can ask!		問吓啦	mahn háh lā	man6 haa5 laa1	mahn hah la!
can control		可操縱	hó chòu jung	ho2 cou4 zung3	ho chhou chung
can get		攞到	ló dóu	lo2 dou2	lo tou
can i ask! /excuse me! /may i ask	v	請問	chéng /chíng mahn	ceng2 /cing2 man6	chheng mahn
can i help you?[1]		我有乜嘢 可以幫你?	ngóh yauh màt yéh hó yíh bòng léih /néih?	ngo5 jau5 mat4 je5 ho2 ji5 pong4 lei5/ nei5?	ngoh yauh mat yeh ho yih pong leih /neih?
can i help you?[2]		我可唔可 以幫你?	ngóh hó m̀ hó yíh bòng léih /néih?	ngo5 ho2 m4 ho2 ji5 bong1 lei5 /nei5?	ngoh ho mh ho yih pong leih /neih?
can not /is not/can not/ is not/negative	aux/v	莫	mohk	mok6	mohk
can not believe	adj	唔相信	m̀ sēung seun	m4 soeng1 seon3	mh seung seun
can opener[1] /tin opener	n	罐頭刀	gun táu dōu	gun3 tau2 dou1	kun thau tou
can opener[2] /tin opener	n	開罐器	hòi gun hei	hoi4 gun3 hei3	hoi kun hei
can operate /manageable	adj	操縱	chòu jung	cou4 zung3	chhou chung
can punish if lazy		懶會罰	láahn wúih faht	laan5 wui5 fat6	laahn wuih faht
can't[1 (coll)] /can not/may not	v	唔得	m̀ dāk	m4 dak1	mh tak
can't[2 (wr)] /must not/may not	v	不得	bāt dāk	bat1 dak1	pat tak
can't get		攞唔到	ló m̀ dóu	lo2 m4 dou2	lo mh tou
can't hear		聽唔到	tèng m̀ dóu	teng4 m4 dou2	theng mh tou

English		Chinese	Romanization 1	Jyutping	Romanization 2
can't help but		忍唔住	yán m̀ jyuh	jan2 m4 zyu6	yan m chyuh
can't trust[1]	n	信唔過	seun m̀ gwo	seon3 m4 gwo3	swon mh kwo
can't trust[2]	n	唔信得過	m̀ seun dāk gwo	m4 seon3 dak1 gwo3	mh swon tak kwo
can you do it?[1]		你可唔可以做?	léih hó m̀ hó yíh jouh?	lei5 ho2 m4 ho2 ji5 zou6?	leih ho mh ho yih chouh?
can you do it?[2]		請問你可唔可以做?	chéng mahn léih hó m̀ hó yíh jouh?	ceng2 man6 lei5 ho2 m4 ho2 ji5 zou6?	chheng mahn leih ho mh ho yih chouh?
can you help me?[1]		你可唔可以幫幫我?	léih hó m̀ hó yíh bòng bòng ngóh?	lei5 ho2 m4 ho2 ji5 bong1 bong1 ngo5?	leih ho mh ho yih pong pong ngoh?
can you help me?[2]		你可唔可以救我?	léih hó m̀ hó yíh gau ngóh?	lei5 ho2 m4 ho2 ji5 gau3 ngo5?	leih ho mh ho yih kau ngoh?
can you say it again?		唔該再講!?	m̀ gòi joi góng!?	m4 goi1 zoi3 gong2!?	mh koi choi kong!?
can you speak slowly?		唔該慢慢講!	m̀ gòi maahn máan góng!	m4 goi1 maan6 maan2 gong2!	mh koi maahn maan kong!
Canada	n	加拿大	ga na daaih	gaa3 na3 daai6	ka na taaih
canal[1] /stream/drain	n	渠	kèuih	keoi4	khoih
canal[2] /water canal /stream	n	運河	wahn hòh	wan6 ho4	wahn hoh
cancel /delete	v	刪除	sāan chèuih	saan1 ceoi4	saan chhoih
cancer[1] (de)	n	**	kèn sá	kan4 sa2	khen sa
cancer[2]	n	癌	ngàahm	ngaam4	ngaahm
cancer[3]	n	癌症	ngàahm jing	ngaam4 zing3	ngaahm cheng
cancer[4]	n	生癌	sàang ngàahm	saan4 ngaan4	saang ngaahm
candidate[1] exam	n	考生	háau sàng	haau2 sang4	haau sang
candidate[2] election	n	候選人	hauh syún yàhn	hau6 syun2 jan4	hauh syun yahn
candle	n	蠟燭	laahp jūk	laap6 zuk1	laahp chuk
candlestick	n	燭台	jūk tòih	zuk1 toi4	chuk thoih
candy	n	糖	tòhng	tong4	thohng
canned	adj	罐頭嘅	gun táu ge	gun3 tau2 ge3	kun thau ke
canned drinks /foods	n	罐頭	gun táu	gun3 fau2	kun thau
cannon	n	炮	pāau	paau1	phaau
cannot be touched /untouchable	adj	達唔到	daaht m̀ dou	daat6 m4 dou3	taaht mh tou
cannot handle		應付唔嚟	ying fuh m̀ làih	jing3 fu6 m4 lai4	yeng fuh mh laih
cannot help		忍不住	yán bāt jyuh	jan2 bat1 zyu6	yan pat chyuh
canoe /wooden boat	n	獨木舟	duhk muhk jāu	duk6 muk6 zau1	tuhk muhk chau
cantaloupe	n	哈蜜瓜	hà maht gwà	haa4 mat6 gwa4	ha maht kwa
canteen /dining hall /restaurant	n	餐廳	chāan tēng	caan1 teng1	chhaan theng
Cantonese language[1]	n	廣東話	gwóng dùng wá	gwong2 dung4 waa2	kwong tung wa
Cantonese language[2]	n	廣州話	gwóng jàu wá	gwong2 zau4 waa2	kwong chau wa
Cantonese language[3]	n	粵語	yuht yúh	jyut6 jyu5	yuht yuh
Cantonese traditional dance /Cantonese opera	n	大戲	daaih hei	daai6 hei3	taaih hei
Cantonese spring /egg roll	n	春卷	chèun kyun	ceon4 kyun3	chhon khyun

English		Chinese	Romanization 1	Jyutping	Romanization 2
Cantonese opera / Cantonese traditional dance	n	粵劇	yuht kehk	jyut6 kek6	yuht khehk
cantonment	n	駐紮	jyu jaat	zyu3 zaat3	chyu chaat
canvas[1]	n	布畫	bou wá	bou3 waa2	pou wa
canvas[2] /oil painting	n	油畫	yàuh wá	jau4 waa2	yauh wa
canvas bag	n	帆布袋	fàahn bou dói /doih	faan4 bou2 doi2 /doi6	faahn pou toi /toih
canvas belt	n	帆布帶	fàahn bou dáai	faan4 bou2 daai2	faahn pou taai
cap /hat/bonnet	n	帽	móu	mou2	mou
cap of bottle (wr) lid/cover	n/v	蓋	goi	goi3	koi
cap in hand		恭敬地	gùng ging deih	gung4 ging3 dei6	kung geng teih
capable[1] /ability	adj	本事	bún sih	bun2 si6	pun sih
capable[2] /have ability	adj	有本事	yáuh bún sih	jau5 bun2 si6	yauh pun sih
capable[3] /competent/ having enough skill	adj	能幹	làhng /nàhng gón	lang4 /nang4 gon2	lahng / nahng kon
capacity	n	容量	yùhng leuhng	jung4 loeng6	yuhng leuhng
cape garment	n	斗蓬	dáu pùhng	dau2 pung4	tau phuhng
capital[1] money	n	資本	jī bún	zi1 bun2	chi pun
capital[2] money	n	本錢	bún chìhn	bun2 cin4	pun chhihn
capital[3] money /principal	n	本金	bún gām	bun2 gam1	pun kam
capital[4] town	n	首都	sáu dōu	sau2 dou1	sau tou
capital[5] by death penalty	adj	死刑	séi yìhng	sei2 jing4	sei yehng
capital letters / block letters	n	大楷	daaih gàai	daai6 gaai4	taaih kaai
capital market	ph	資本市場	jì bún síh chèuhng	zi4 bun2 si5 coeng4	chi pun sih chheuhng
capital sum /funds	n	資金	jì gàm	zi4 gam4	chi kam
capital town /kingdom	n	王國	wòhng gwok	wong4 gwok3	wohng kwok
capitalism	n	資本主義	jì bún jyú yih	zi4 bun2 zyu2 ji6	chi pun chyu yih
capitalist	n	資本家	jì bún gā	zi4 bun2 ga1	chi pun ka
capsule/small container /vessel/bin	n	容器	yung héi	jung3 hei2	yung hei
captain[1] /leader /team leader/head of the team	n	隊長	deuih jéung	deoi6 zoeng2	toeih cheung
captain[2] /boss/chief/head	n	首領	sáu léhng /líhng	sau2 leng5 /ling5	sau lehng
captain[3] of army /colonel	n	上校	seuhng gaau	soeng6 gaau3	seuhng kaau
captain[4] of army	n	上尉	seuhng wai	soeng6 wai3	seuhng wai
captain of ship[1]	n	船長	syun jéung	syun4 zoeng2	syun cheung
captain of ship[2] /commander of ship	n	艦長	laahm jéung	laam6 zoeng2	laahm cheung
caption[1] /heading /title/headline	n	標題	bìu tàih	biu4 tai4	piu thaih
caption[2] /subtitle	n	字幕	jih mohk	zi6 mok6	chih mohk
captivity	n	囚禁	chàuh gam	cau4 gam3	chhauh kam
capture[1]	v	拘	kēui	keoi1	khoi
capture[2] /obtain/catch	v	獲	wohk	wok6	wohk

English		Chinese	Pronunciation 1	Jyutping	Pronunciation 2
capture[3] /catch	v	捉	jūk	zuk1	chuk
capture[4] /catch	v	捕獲	bóu wohk	bou2 wok6	pou wohk
car[1] /vehicle/carrier /chariot/transportation	n	車	chè	ce1	chhe
car[2]	n	四個轆	sei go lūk	sei3 go3 luk1	sei ko luk
car accident /car crash/ traffic accident/ vehicle accident		交通意外	gāau tùng yi oih /ngoih	gaau1 tung4 ji3 oi6 /ngoi6	kaau thung yi oih/ ngoih
car bomb	n	汽車炸彈	hei chè ja táan	hei3 ce1 zaa3 taan2	hei chhe cha thaan
car keys	n	車匙	chè sìh	ce1 si4	chhè sìh
car park /parking/ parking lot	n	停車場	tìhng chè chèuhng	ting4 ce1 coeng4	thehng chhe chheuhng
carboard box /paper box/carton	n	紙盒	jí háp	zi2 hap6	chi hap
carbon dioxide CO_2	n	二氧化碳	yih yéuhng fa taan	ji6 joeng5 faa3 taan3	yih yeuhng fa thaan
carbon monoxide CO	n	一氧化碳	yāt yéuhng fa taan	jat1 joeng5 faa3 taan3	yat yéuhng fa thaan
carbonate	n	碳酸鹽	taan syūn yìhm	taan3 syun1 jim4	thaan syun yihm
carburetor /carburettor	n	化油器	fa yàuh héi	faa3 jau4 hei2	fa yauh hei
carcass /dead body/ corpse	n	屍體	sì tái	si4 tai2	si thai
card[1] (coll)	n	咭	kāat	kaat1	khaat
card[2] (wr)	n	卡	ká	kaa2	kha
card expired		卡已過期	ká yíh gwo kèih	kaa2 ji5 kei4	kha yih kwo kheih
card retained		此卡暫扣	chí kāat jaahm kau	ci2 kaat1 zaam6 kau3	chhi kaat chaahm khau
card telephone	n	磁卡電話	chih ká dihn wá	ci4 kaa2 din6 waa2	chhih kha tihn wa
cardboard	n	硬紙板	ngaahng jí báan	ngaang6 zi2 baan2	ngaahng chi paan
cards /playing card	n	紙牌	jí pàaih	zi2 paai4	chi phaaih
care about /feel unhappy/feel objection	v	介意	gaai yi	gaai3 ji3	kaai yi
care for		計較	gai gaau	gai3 gaau3	kai kaau
care of	prep	轉交	jyun gāau	zyun3 gaau1	chyun kaau
career[1] /occupation /enterprise	n	事業	sìh yìhp	si6 jip6	sih yihp
career[2]	n	經歷	gìng lihk	ging4 lik6	keng lehk
carefree[1] /unanxiety /thoughtless/no worries	adj	唔擔心	m̀ dàam sàm	m4 daan4 sam4	mh taam sam
carefree[2] /unanxiety /thoughtless	adj	不憂慮	bāt yau làuih	bat1 jau3 leoi6	pat yau lowih
carefree relaxed / spirit pleased/refreshment	n	心曠神怡	sàm kwong sàn yìh	sam4 kwong3 san4 ji5	sam khwong san yih
careful[1] /thoughtful /scrupulous	adj	細心	sai sàm	sai3 sam4	sai sam
careful[2] /thorough	adj	周到	jàu dou	zau4 dou3	chau tou
careful[3] /cautious/wary/ scrupulous/watch out/ careful when dealing	adj	小心	síu sàm	siu2 sam4	siu sam
carefully[1] /maneuver	n	小心的	síu sàm dì	siu2 sam4 di4	siu sam ti
carefully[2] /in detail	adj	仔細	jí sai	zi2 sai3	chi sai

carefully planned /tactics/tactfully	n	策略	chaak leuhk	caak3 loek6	chhaak leuhk
careless[1]	adj	胡亂	wùh lyuhn	wu4 lyun6	wuh lyuhn
careless[2]	adj	不小心	bāt síu sàm	bat1 siu2 sam4	pat siu sam
careless[3] /negligently	adj	粗心	chòu sàm	cou4 sam4	chhou sam
careless[4] (sl)/mad-man /crazy person/extremely stupid/lunatic/ insane	adj	十吓十吓	sahp há sahp há	sap6 haa2 sap6 haa2	sahp ha sahp ha
careless[5]	adj	無了賴	móuh líuh laaih	no4 liu5 laai6	mouh liuh laaih
carelessness /negligence	n	疏忽	sò fàt	so4 fat4	so fat
caress (in a sexual way) fondle/fondle touch	v	愛撫	oi /ngoi fú	oi3 /ngoi3 fu2	oi /ngoi fu
caretaker	n	照顧者	jiu gu jé	ziu3 gu3 ze2	chiu ku che
caretaker government	n	臨時政府	làhm sìh jing fú	lam4 si4 zing3 fu2	lahm sih cheng fu
cargo	n	貨運	fo wahn	fo3 wan6	fo wahn
cargo ship /freighter	n	貨船	fo syùhn	fo3 syun4	fo syuhn
caricature[1]	n	漫畫	maahn wá	maan6 waa2	maahn wa
caricature[2]	n	諷刺模仿	fung chi mòuh fóng	fung3 ci3 mou4 fong2	fung chhi mouh fong
carline /old woman	n	老太婆	lóuh taai pòh	lou5 taai3 po4	louh thaai phoh
carnation (flower)	n	康乃馨	hōng náaih hèng	hong1 naai5 heng4	hong naaih heng
carol song	n	歡樂之歌	fùn lohk jī gō	fun4 lohk zi1 go1	fun lohk chi ko
carp fish	n	鯉魚	léih yú	lei5 jyu2	leih yu
carpenter[1]	n	木工	mùhk gùng	muk6 gung4	muhk kung
carpenter[2]	n	鬥木師傅	dau muhk sì fú	dau3 muk6 si4 fu2	tau muhk si fu
carpenter[3]	n	鬥木佬	dau muhk lóuh	dau3 muk6 lou5	tau muhk louh
carpentry[1]	n	鬥木	dau muhk	dau3 muk6	tau muhk
carpentry[2]	n	木匠業	muhk jeuhng yihp	muk6 zoeng6 jip6	muhk cheuhng yihp
carpet[1] /mat/rug	n	地氈	deih jīn	dei6 zin1	teih chin
carpet[2]	n	地毯	deih táan	dei6 taan2	teih thaan
carriage /baby buggy	n	四輪馬車	sei lèuhn máh chè	sei3 leon4 maa5 ce4	sei leuhn mah chhe
carriageway	n	行車路	hàhng chè louh	hang4 ce1 lou6	hahng chhe louh
carrier man /porter /remover	n	搬運工人	bùn wahn gùng yàhn	bun4 wan6 gung4 jan4	pun wahn kung yahn
carrier bag	n	購物袋	kau maht dói /doih	kau3 mat6 doi2 /doi6	khau maht toi /toih
carrot[1] red color	n	紅蘿蔔	hùhng lòh baahk	hung4 lo4 baak6	huhng loh paahk
carrot[2]	n	蘿卜	lòh būk	lo4 buk1	loh puk
carrot[3]	n	甘筍	gàm séun	gam4 seun2	kam swon
carry[1] /withdraw/bring out/hold by hand	v	提	tàih	tai4	thaih
carry[2] /grasping/pick up with fingers/take/to	v	揸	já /záa	zaa2	cha
carry[3] by persons	v	抬	tòih	toi4	thoih
carry[4] by vehicle/transport	v	載	joi	zoi3	choi
carry[5] /carrying	v	運送	wahn sung	wan6 sung	wahn sung
carry[6]	v	運載	wahn joi	wan6 zoi3	wahn choi
carry and give	v	轉交	jyun gāau	zyun3 gaau1	chyun kaau

carry away[1]	v	運走	wahn jáu	wan6 zau2	wahn chau
carry away[2]	v	拿走	lāh /nāh jáu	laa1 /naa1 zau2	lah /nah chau
carry back	v	拿回	lāh /nāh wùih	laa1 /naa1 wui4	lah /nah wuih
carry by hand	v	攜帶	kwàih daai	kwai4 daai3	khwaih taai
carry forward[1] a/c	v	結轉	git jyun	git3 zyun3	kit chyun
carry forward[2]	v	發揚	faat yèuhng	faat3 joeng4	faat yeuhng
carry in arm /embrace/ armful/hold in arm	v	抱	póuh	pou5	phouh
carry in arms	v	挑	téuh	tiu5	thiuh
carry in hand	v	拎	lìng /ning	ling3 /ning3	leng /neng
carry in pocket	v	袋住	doih jyuh	doi6 zyu6	toih chyuh
carry in pole	v	擔 / 担	dàam	daam4	taam
carry on[1] /underway/ carry out/progress/in progress	v	進行	jeun hàhng	zeon3 hang4	cheun hahng
carry on[2] /continue /keep on/go forwarding	v	繼續	gai juhk	gai3 zuk6	kai chuhk
carry on[3]	v	跟住做	gàn jyuh jouh	gan4 zyu6 zou6	kan chyuh chouh
carry on[4] /continue doing	v	繼續做	gai juhk jouh	gai3 zuk6 zou6	kai chuhk chouh
carry on back /load	n/v	負	fuh	fu6	fuh
carry on head	v	頂住	deng /díng jyuh	deng2 /ding2 zyu6	teng chyuh
carry out[1] /take away/ carry away/take out	v	帶走	daai jáu /záu	daai3 zau2	taai chau
carry out[2]	v	展開	jín hòi	zin2 hoi4	chin hoi
carry out[3] /acomplished /execute/performed/fulfill /completed a task	v	履行	léih hàhng	lei5 hang4	leih hahng
carry out[4] /execute/do an activity/execution/practice /practise	n/v	實行	sàht hàhng	sat6 hang4	saht hahng
carry out[5]	v	採取	chói chéui	coi2 ceoi2	chhoi chheui
carry out[6] /do	v	施	sì	si4	si
carry out death penalty	v	執行死刑	jāp hàhng séi yìhng	zap1 hang4 sei2 jing4	chap haang sei yehng
carry out order	v	執行命令	jāp hàhng mehng /mìhng lihng	zap1 hang4 meng6 /ming6 ling4	chap haang mehng lehng
carry out task/ execution of a task	v	執行工作	jāp hàhng gùng jok	zap1 hang4 gung4 zok3	chap haang kung chok
carry over	v	繼續存在	gai juhk chyùhn joih	gai zuk6 cyun4 zoi6	kai chuhk chhyuhn choih
carry under arm	v	挾	gihp	kip6	kehp
carry with one	v	一個人送	yāt go yàhn sung	jat1 go3 jan4 sung3	yat ko yahn sung
cart /kart/small buggy	n	小馬車	síu máh chè	siu2 maa5 cè	siu mah chhe
cartage /fare/freight fee	n	運費	wahn fai	wan6 fai3	wahn fai
cartel group of companies	n	企業聯合	kéih yihp lyùhn hahp	kei5 jip6 lyun4 hap6	kheih yihp lyuhn hahp
cartilage	n	軟骨	yúhn gwāt	jyun5 gwat1	yuhn kwat
carton	n	紙板盒	ji báan háap	zi3 baan2 haap2	chi paan haap
cartoon[1] (de)	n	卡通	kà tùng	kaa4 tung4	kha thung

English		Chinese	Yale	Jyutping	Romanization
cartoon[2]	n	卡通影片	kà tùng yéng /yíng pin	kaa4 tung4 jeng2 / jing2 pin3	kha thung yeng phin
cartoonist	n	漫畫家	maahn wá gā	maan6 waa2 ga3	maahn wa ka
cartoons movies	n	漫畫節	maahn wá jit	maan6 waa2 zit3	maahn wa chit
cartridge[1] /bullet/bomb	n	炸彈	ja /záa dáan	zaa3 /zaa2 daan2	cha taan
cartridge[2] cassette tape	n	卡式帶	ká sīk dáai	kaa2 sik1 daai2	kha sek taai
cartridge ink	n	墨水筒	mahk séui tùhng	mak6 seoi2 tung4	mahk swoi thuhng
carve	v	雕刻	dìu hak	diu4 hak3	tiu hak
case[1] small box	n	盒仔	háap jái	haap2 zai2	haap chai
case[2] box	n	柜	gwaih	gwai6	kwaih
case[3] of incident	n	個案	go ngon	go3 ngon3	ko ngon
case[4] law /law case	n	訴訟	sou juhng	sou3 zung6	sou chuhng
case[5] legal	n	案	on /ngon	on3 /ngon3	on /ngon
cash[1] /funds	n	款	fún	fun2	fun
cash[2]	n	現錢	yihn chín	jin6 cin2	yihn chhin
cash[3] /ready money	n	現款	yihn fún	jin6 fun2	yihn fun
cash[4] /ready money	n	現金	yihn gàam	jin6 gaam4	yihn kaam
cash[5]	n	兌	deui	deui3	toei
cash box	n	錢箱	chín sèung	cin2 soeng4	chhin seung
cash card	n	現金支取卡	yihn gàam jì chéui kāat	jin6 gaam4 zi4 ceoi2 kaat1	yihn kaam chi chheui khaat
cash coupon	n	現金券	yihn gām gyun	jin6 gam1 gyun3	yihn kam kyun
cash discount card	n	現金折扣	yihn gàam jit kau	jin6 gaam4 zit3 kau3	yihn kaam chit khau
cash dispenser	n	自動提款機	jih duhng tàih fún gèi	zi6 dung6 tai4 fun2 gei4	chih tuhng thaih fun kei
cash drawer	n	現金抽屜	yihn gàam chàu tai	jin6 gaam4 cau4 tai3	yihn kaam chhau thai
cash flow	n	現金流轉	yihn gàam làuh jyun	jin6 gaam4 lau6 zyun3	yihn kaam lauh chyun
cash register	n	收款機	sàu fún gèi	sau4 fun2 gei4	sau fun kei
cash register counter /till service	n	交款處	gāau fún chyu	gaau1 fun2 cyu3	kaau fun chhyu
cash tendered /payment receipt	n	收訖	sàu ngaht	sau4 ngat6	sau ngaht
cashier[1]	n	出納員	chēut naahp yùhn	ceot1 naap6 jyun4	chhot naahp yuhn
cashier[2]	n	收銀員	sàu ngán yùhn	sau4 ngan2 jyun4	sau ngan yuhn
cashier[3]	n	出納	chēut naahp	ceot1 naap6	chhot naahp
cashmere[(de)]	n	茄士咩	kè sih mē	ke4 si6 me1	khe sih me
casino[1] /gambling	n	賭場	dóu chèuhng	dou2 coeng4	tou chheuhng
casino[2]	n	賭館	dóu gún	dou2 gun2	tou kun
casket[1] /coffin	n	棺材	gùn chòih	gun4 coi4	kun chhoih
casket[2] /coffin	n	棺木	gùun muhk	gun4 muk6	kun muhk
cassette	n	卡式磁帶	ká sīk chìh dáai	kaa2 sik1 ci4 daai2	kha sek chhih taai
cassette player	n	錄音放音機	luhk yām fong yām gèi	lok6 jam1 fong3 jam1 gei4	luhk yam fong yam kei
cassette recorder /tape recorder/recorder	n	錄音機	luhk yām gēi	lok6 jam1 gei1	luhk yam kei

English		Chinese	Yale	Jyutping	Other
cast[1] /throw down /discard/throwing	n	扰	dám	dam2	tam
cast[2] (throwing)	n	抛	paau	paau3	phaau
cast[3] throwing/change/drop/fall/reduce/throw/missing/to lose	n/v	掉	diuh	diu6	tiuh
cast[4] throwing /throw /abandon	n	廢棄	fai hei	fai3 hei3	fai hei
cast[5] (mould)	n	金屬製模	gàm suhk jai móuh	gam4 suk6 zai3 mou4	kam suhk chai mouh
caste /surname/last name/family name	n	姓	seng /sing	seng3 /sing3	seng
casting[1] (mould)	n	鑄件	jyu gihn	zyu3 gin6	chyu kihn
casting[2] (mould)	n	鑄做	jyu jouh	zyu3 zou6	chyu chouh
castle /walls	n	城堡	sèhng bóu	seng4 bou2	sehng pou
castrate /remove testicles	v	割去睪丸	got heui gòu yún	got3 heoi3 gou4 jyun2	kot hoi kou yun
castration	n	閹割	yìm got	jim4 got3	yim kot
casual	adj	偶然嘅	ngáuh yin ge	ngau5 jin3 ge3	ngauh yuhk yin ke
casual acquaintance / common friend	adj	普通朋友	póu tùng pàhng yáuh	pou2 tung4 pang4 jau5	phou thung phahng yauh
casually[1]	adj	求其	kàuh kèih	kau4 kei4	khauh kheih
casualty[2]	n	傷亡	sèung mong	soeng4 mong3	seung mong
casualty[3] /fatal accident	n	死傷嘅人	séi sèung ge yàhn	sei2 soeng4 ge3 jan4	sei seung ke yahn
cat	n	貓	māau	maau1	maau
cat feed	n	貓飼料	māau jih líu	maau1 zi6 liu2	maau chih liu
catalogue	n	目	muhk	muk6	muhk
catapult	n	弩	lóuh /nóuh	lou5 /nou5	louh /nouh
cataract[1] of eye	n	白內障	baahk noih jeung	baak6 noi6 zoeng3	paahk noih cheung
cataract[2] /water fall	n	大瀑布	daaih buhk bou	daai6 buk6 bou3	taaih puhk pou
catch[1] /meet/receive/get /connect phone	v	接	jip	zip3	chip
catch[2] /hold/wrap around	v	擁	yúng	jung2	yung
catch[3] /hold	v	抓	jáau	zaau2	chaau
catch[4] /holding	n/v	接住	jip jyuh	zip3 zyu6	chip chyuh
catch[5] /hold	v	捉到	jūk dóu	zuk1 dou2	chuk tou
catch[6]	v	逮住	daih jyuh	dai6 zyu6	taih chyuh
catch cold[1]	v	冷親	láahng chàn	laang5 can4	laahng chhan
catch cold[2] /have a cold	v	發冷	faat láahng	faat3 laang5	faat laahng
catch fire[1] /fire-outbreak /firing/fired	v	火災	fó jòi	fo2 zoi4	fo choi
catch fire[2]	v	著火	jeuk fó	zoek3 fo2	cheuk fo
catch it /received blame	v	受責挨罵	sauh jaak āai mah	sau6 zaak3 aai1 ma6	sauh chaak aai mah
catcher	n	捕捉者	bóu jūk jé	bou2 juk1 ze2	pou chuk che
catching fish /fishing	n	釣魚	diu yú	diu3 jyu2	tiu yu
category[1] /categorized/ classification/classified	n	類別	lèuih bìht	leoi6 bit6	lowih piht
category[2] /class/type /kind/sort/species	n	類	leuih	leoi6	lowih

English	Part	Chinese	Romanization 1	Romanization 2	Romanization 3
category[3]	n	屬	suhk	suk6	suhk
category[4]	n	範疇	faahn chàuh	faan6 cau4	faahn chhauh
category[5] /class	n	疇	chàuh	cau4	chhauh
cater /food services	v	承辦宴席	sing bàahn yín jìhk	sing3 baan6 jin3 zik6	seng paahn yin chehk
catering /food & drink	n	餐飲	chāan yám	caan1 jam2	chhaan yam
caterpillar	n	履帶車	léih daai chè	lei5 daai3 ce4	leih taai chhe
Catholic /Catholicism	n	天主教	Tìn jyú gaau	tin1 zyu2 gaau3	Thin chyu kaau
Catholic (Roman)	n	天主教徒	Tìn jyú gaau tòuh	Tin1 zyu2 gaau3 tou4	Thin chyu kaau thouh
catsup	n	茄汁	ké jāp	ke2 zap1	khe chap
cattle /beef/cow	n	牛	ngàuh	ngau4	ngauh
catty 0.5 kg	n	斤	gan	gan3	kan
caught /clutch/grab /grasp/snatching/hold on	v&i	抓住	jaau jyuh	zaau3 zyu6	chaau chyuh
cauldron[1] /frying pan /sauce pan	n	平底鑊	pèhng dái wohk	peng4 dai2 wok6	phehng tai wohk
cauldron[2] /tea pot/kettle	n	茶壺	chàh wùh	caa4 wu4	chhah wuh
cauliflower	n	椰菜花	yèh chói fà	je4 coi2 faa4	yeh chhoi fa
causal /cause & effect	adj/v	因果關係	yàn gwó gwáan haih	jan4 gwo2 gwaan2 hai6	yan kwo kwaan haih
cause[1] /reason	n	故	gu	gu3	ku
cause[2] /reason	n	原	yùhn	jyun4	yuhn
cause[3] /reason	n	緣故	yùhn gu	jyun4 gu3	yuhn kuu
cause[4] a reason	n	成因	seng yān	seng3 jan1	seng yan
cause[5] /reason /fact cause /main cause/origin/root of cause/root of problem	n	起因	héi yàn	hei2 jan4	hei yan
cause[6] /to create	v	導致	douh ji	dou6 zi3	touh chi
cause of accident	v	肇事	siuh sih	siu6 si6	siuh sih
cause trouble /harm /damage/do harm	n/v	害	hoih	hoi6	hoih
caused /happened/ create	n	令	lihng	ling4	lehng
causeless	adj	無理由	mòuh léih yàuh	mou4 lei5 jau4	mouh leih yauh
causer	n	肇因者	siuh yān jé	siu6 jan1 ze2	siuh yan che
causeway	n	堤道	tàih dou	tai4 dou3	thaih tou
caustic[1]	adj	腐蝕性	fuh sihk sing	fu6 sik6 sing3	fuh sehk seng
caustic[2]	adj	打火	dā fō	daa1 fo2	ta fo
caustic soda	n	腐蝕劑	fuh sihk jàih	fu6 sik6 zai6	fuh sehk chai
cauterize /burning	v	灼	cheuk	ceok	chheuk
caution[1] /take care/care	n	小心	síu sàm	siu2 sam4	siu sam
caution[2] /warning /admonish	n/v	警告	gíng gou	ging2 gou3	keng kou
cave[1] /grotto/hole/den	n	穴/*	yuht	jyut6	yuht
cave[2]	n	山洞	sàan duhng	saan4 dung6	saan tohng
cave[3] /trap/pitfall	n/v	陷	hahm	ham6	hahm
cave[4] /hole	n	窟	dau	dau3	tau
cavity /dental cavities	n	蛀牙	jyu ngàh	zyu3 ngaa4	chyu ngah

CCTV	n	閉路電視	bai louh dihn sih	bai3 lou6 din6 si6	pai louh tihn sih
CD shop[1]	n	影音舖	yéng yām pou	jeng2 jam1 pou3	yeng yam phou
CD shop[2]	n	唱片舖	cheung pin pou	coeng3 pin3 pou3	chheung phin phou
cease /terminate	v	終止	jūng jí	jung1 zi2	chung chi
ceasefire[1] /stop fighting	n	停戰	tíhng jin	ting5 zin3	thehng chin
ceasefire[2] /stop fighting	n	停火	tíhng fó	ting5 fo2	thehng fo
ceaselessly[1] /not stopping	adj	唔停嚟	m̀ tìhng gam	m4 ting4 gam3	mh thehng kam
ceaselessly[2]	adj	不停嚟	bāt tìhng gam	bat1 ting4 gam3	pat thehng kam
cecum	n	盲腸	màahng chéung	maang4 coeng2	maahng chheung
ceiling[1]	n	天花	tìn fà	tin4 faa4	thin fah
ceiling[2]	n	天花板	tìn fà báan	tin4 faa4 baan2	thin fah paan
celebrate[1]	v	慶祝	hing jūk	hing3 zuk1	hing chuk
celebrate[2] /festival	v	做節	jouh jit	zou6 zit3	chouh chit
celebrate[3] new year	v	過年	gwo nìhn	gwo3 nin4	kwo nihn
celebrate a wedding	v	舉行婚禮	geui hahng fān láih	geoi2 hang4 fan1 lai5	kwoi hahng fan laih
celebrated[1] after new year	adj	春茗	chēun méng /mìng	ceon1 meng2 /ming4	chhon meng
celebrated[2] /famous/well-known/noted	adj	著名嘅	jyu mèhng /mìhng ge	zyu3 meng4 /ming4 ge3	chyu mehng ke
celebration /lustre/luster/radiance	n	光彩	gwòng chói	gwong4 coi2	kwong chhoi
celery	n	芹菜	kàhn chói	kan4 coi2	khahn chhoi
cell[1] of plants or animals	n	細胞	sai bāau	sai3 baau1	sai paau
cell[2] /room	n	牢房	lòuh fòhng	lou4 fong4	louh fohng
cell[3] /room	n	密室	maht sāt	mat6 sat1	maht sat
cell[4] /single room	n	單人牢房	dāan yàhn lòuh fòhng	daan1 jan4 lou4 fong4	daan yahn louh fohng
cellar /underground floor	n	地窖	deih gaau	dei6 gaau3	teih kaau
basement / UG/F/cellar/underground floor	n	地牢	deih lòuh	dei6 lou4	teih louh
cellular[1] skin's hole	adj	細胞	sai bāau	sai3 baau1	sai paau
cellular[2] skin's hole	adj	細胞組成	sai bāau jóu sèhng	sai3 baau1 zou2 seng4	sai paau chou sehng
cellular phone	n	移動電話	yìh dúhng dihn wá	ji4 dung5 din6 waa2	yih tuhng tihn wa
celsius 0-100°c	n	攝氏	síp sih	sip2 si6	sip sih
cement	n	水泥	séui làih /nàih	seoi2 lai4 /nai4	swoi laih /naih
cement (sl)	n	紅毛泥	hùhng mòuh làih /nàih	hung4 mou4 lai4 /nai4	huhng mouh laih /naih
censor[1]	v	刪剪	sāan jín	saan1 zin2	saan chin
censor[2]	n	審查員	sām chàh yùhn	sam1 caa4 jyun4	sam chhah yuhn
censure[1] /misbehaviour	n	責備	jaak beih	zaak3 bei6	chaak peih
censure[2]	n	責難	jaak làahn	zaak3 laan4	chaak laahn
censure[3]	n	斥責	chīk jaak	cik1 zaak3	chhek chaak
census[1]	n	普查	póu chàh	pou2 caa4	phou chhah
census[2]	n	人口普查	yàhn háu póu chàh	jan4 hau2 pou2 caa4	yahn hau phu chhah
cent[1] /coin/unit	n	毫	hòuh	hou4	houh
cent[2] /coin	n	仙	sīn	sin1	sin

cent[3] /coin/dime	n	毫子	hòuh jí	hou4 zi2	houh chi
cent[4] /coin	n	硬幣	ngaahng baih	ngaang6 bai6	ngaahng paih
centenary 100 years	n	百年紀念	baak nìhn géi nihm	baak nin4 gei2 nim6	paak nihn kei nihm
center[1] /centre/middle	n	中	jùng /joong	zung4	chung
center[2] /centre/center point	n	中心	jùng sàm	zung4 sam4	chung sam
center[3] /centre/mid	n	中央	jùng yèung	zung4 joeng4	chung yeung
center[4]	n	正中	jeng jùng	zeng zung4	cheng chung
centigrade 0-100°c	n	攝氏度	síp sih douh	sip2 si6 dou6	sip sih touh
centipede	n	蜈蚣	ngh gūng	ng4 gung1	ngh kung
central	n	中環	jùng wàahn	zung4 waan4	chung waahn
center /focus/central point	n	中心點	jùng sàm dím	zung4 sam4 dim2	chung sam tim
centralize /focus/concentrate	v	集中	jaahp jùng	zaap6 zung4	chaahp chung
centre of interest/ focal point	n	重點	juhng dīm	zung6 dim1	chuhng tim
century /hundred years	n	世紀	sai géi	sai3 gei2	sai kei
cereal	n	穀類植物	gūk leuih jihk maht	guk1 leoi6 zik6 mat6	kuk lowih chehk maht
ceremonial entry[1] newly house	n	新屋入居	sàn ūk yahp gēui	san4 uk1 jap6 geoi1	san uk yahp kwoi
ceremonial entry[2] newly house	n	新居入伙	sàn gèui yahp fó	san4 geoi4 jap6 fo2	san kwoi yahp fo
ceremony[1]	n	禮儀	láih yìh	lai5 ji4	laih yih
ceremony[2]	n	儀式	yìh sīk	jip4 sik1	yih sek
certain[1] /true/right/real	adj	確	kok	kok3	khok
certain[2]/sured/determined	adj	確定	kok dehng	kok3 deng6	khok tehng
certain[3]	adj	必然	bīt yìhn	bit1 jin4	pit yihn
certain[4] /doubtless/no doubt	adj	無疑	mòuh yìh	mou4 ji4	mouh yih
certainly[1] /sure/of course	adv	固	gu	gu3	ku
certainly[2] /indeed/really	adv	眞/真係	jàn haih	zan4 hai6	chan haih
certainly[3] /sure/definitely	adv	一定	yāt dehing	jat1 deng6	yat yāt dihng
certainly[4] (sl) definitely	adv	梗	gáng	gang2	kang
certainly[5] /must be	adv	梗係…啦	gáng haih…lā	gang2 hap6 laa1	kang haih…la
certainly[6]	adv	冇問題	móuh mahn tàih	mou5 man6 tai4	mouh mahn thaih
certainly[7]	adv	無疑地	móuh yì deih	mou5 ji4 dei6	mouh yi teih
certainty[8] /reliability	n	確實	kok saht	kok3 sat6	khok saht
certainty[9]	n	確實無疑	kok saht mòuh yìh	kok3 sat6 mou5 ji4	khok saht mouh yih
certificate[1]	n	文憑	màhn pàhng	man4 pang4	mahn phahng
certificate[2]	n	證書	jìng syù	zing3 syu4	cheng syu
certificate[3] of stock market /stock document	n	股票	gú piu	gu2 piu3	ku phiu
certificate[4] give	n	證書頒發	jing syù bāan faat	zing3 syu4 baan1 faat3	cheng syu paan faat
certificate[5] give	n	頒發證書	bāan faat jing syù	baan1 faat3 zing3 syu4	paan faat cheng syu
certificate[6] (de)	n	沙紙	sà jí	saa4 zi2	sa chi

certificate[7]	n	證明書	jing mìhng syù	zing3 ming4 syu4	cheng mehng syu
certificate check	n	檢查支票	gím chàh jì piu	gim2 caa4 zi4 piu3	kim chhah chi phiu
certifier	n	保證書	bóu jing syù	bou2 zing3 syu4	pou cheng syu
cervix uteri	n	子宮頸	jí gùng géng	zi2 gung4 geng2	chi kung keng
chain	n	鏈	lín	lin2	lin
chair[1] (coll) stool/bench	n	櫈/凳	dang	dang3	tang
chair[2]	n	椅	yí	ji2	yi
chair[3]	n	椅子	yí jí	ji2 zi2	yi chi
chairman[1] of the board	n	董事長	dúng sih jéung	dung2 si6 zoeng2	tung sih cheung
chairman[2] of legislative assembly (speaker)	n	議長	yíh jéung	ji5 zoeng2	yih cheung
chairmanship	n	主席嘅職位	jyú jihk ge jīk waih	zyu2 zik6 ge3 zik1 wai6	chyu chehk ke chek waih
chalk	n	粉筆	fán bāt	fan2 bat1	fan pat
challenge /threat	n	挑戰	tìu jin	tiu4 zing3	thiu chin
challenging	adj	挑戰性	tìu jin sing	tiu4 zin3 sing3	thiu chin seng
chamber[1] /small room	n	室	sāt	sat1	sat
chamber[2]	n	房間	fóng gàan	fong2 gaan4	fong kaan
champagne wine	n	香檳酒	hèung bān jáu	hoeng4 ban1 zau2	heung pan chau
champion[1]	n	冠軍	gun gwān	gun3 gwan1	kun kwan
champion[2]	n	第一名	daih yāt mèhng	dai6 jat1 meng4	taih yat mehng
championship contest	n	錦標賽	gám bīu choi	gam2 biu1 coi3	kam piu chhoi
chance[1] /opportunity	n	機	gèi	gei4	kei
chance[2] /opportunity/ occasion/scope/probability	n	機會	gèi wuih	gei4 wui6	kei wuih
chance[3] /contingency	n	偶然性	ngáuh yìhn sing	ngau5 jin4 sing3	ngauh yihn seng
chance[4] /luck/lottery	n	運氣	wahn hei	wan6 hei3	wahn hei
chance event /random accident/contingency		偶然事件	ngáuh yìhn sih gihn	ngau5 jin4 si6 gin6	ngauh yihn sih kihn
chancellor[1]	n	大臣	daaih sàhn	daai6 san4	taaih sahn
chancellor[2] vice chancellor	n	名譽校長	mèhng /mìhng yuh gaau jéung	meng4 /ming4 jyu6 gaau3 zeong2	mehng yuh kaau cheung
change[1]	v	變	bin	bin3	pin
change[2]	n	变	bìn	bin4	pin
change[3]	v	更	gáng	gang2	kang
change[4] /to exchange	v	易	yìhk	jik6	yehk
change[5] /move/remove/ shift	v	移	yìh	ji4	yih
change[6] /posting	v	調	deuh	deu6	teuh
change[7] /shift/diversions /convert/transform	n	轉換	jyún wuhn	zyun2 wun6	chyun wuhn
change[8] /alter/transform	v	改變	gói bín	goi2 bin2	koi pin
changeable /variable	adj	易變	yihk bin	jik6 bin3	yehk pin
change address		改地址	gói deih jí	goi2 dei6 zi2	koi teih chi
change bus /transfer bus/train/plane	v	轉車	jyun chè	zyun3 ce1	chyun chhe
change cloths	v	換衫	wuhn sāam	wun6 saam1	wuhn saam

English		Chinese	Cantonese	Jyutping	Romanization
change date /rain check	n	改期	gói kèih	goi2 kei4	koi kheih
change down		放慢車速	fong maahn chè chūk	fong3 maan6 ce4 cuk1	fong maahn chhe chhuk
change for /trains or buses		轉車到...去	jyun chè dou...heui	zyun3 ce4 dou3 heoi3	chyun chhe tou...hoi
change gear		改變方法	gói bín fòng faat	goi2 bin2 fong4 faat3	koi pin fong faat
change hands		易手	yìh sáu	ji6 sau2	yih sau
change of heart	n	改變心意	gói bín sàm yi	goi2 bin2 sam4 ji3	koi pin sam yi
change one time	n	為了改變一下	waih líuh gói bin yàt hah	wai6 liu5 goi2 bin3 jat4 ha6	waih liuh koi pin yat hah
change over	n	改變	gói bin	goi2 bin3	koi pin
change position	n	郁	yūk	juk1	yuk
change station /on the bus/train	v	換車站	wuhn chè jaahm	wun6 ce4 zaam6	wuhn chhe chaahm
change subject		改變話題	gói bín wah tàih	goi2 bin2 waa6 tai4	koi pin wah thaih
change track by vehicles /shunting	v	轉向	jyún heung	zyun2 hoeng3	chyun heung
changed bad[1] /decay/ spoil food	v	爛	laahn	laan6	laahn
changed bad[2] /decay /rotten/spoil food	n/v	腐	fùh	fu4	fuh
changeless /enernal/ unchangeable	adj	永恒	wíhng hàhng	wing5 hang6	wehng hahng
changer (by man)	n	改變者	gói bin jē	goi2 bin3 ze2	koi pin che
changing room /locker room/dressing room	n	更衣室	gáng yī sāt	gang2 ji1 sat1	kang yi sat
channel[1] of radio	n	頻道	pàhn douh	pan4 dou6	phahn touh
channel[2] /way	n	途徑	tóuh ging	tou5 ging3	thouh keng
chaos /turmoil/disorder	n	混亂	wahn lyuhn	wan6 lyun6	wahn lyuhn
Catholics church /Catholics chapel/Temple sacred	n	聖堂	sing tóhng	sing3 tong4	seng thohng
chapel	n	禮拜堂	láih baai tòhng	lai5 baai3 tong4	laih paai thohng
charter/chapter of book	n	章	jèung	zoeng4	cheung
chapter one[1]	n	第一課	daih yāt fo	daai6 jat1 fo3	taih yat fo
chapter one[2]	n	第一章	daih yāt jēung	daai6 jat1 zoeng1	taih yat cheung
character[1] /word/letters /symbol	n	字	jih /zih	zi6	chih
character[2] calligraphic style	n	字體	jih tái	zi6 tai2	chih thai
character[3] of person	n	性格	sing gaak	sing3 gaak3	seng kaak
character[4] /natureof person	n	性質	sing jāt	sing3 zat1	seng chat
character[5] of person	n	特性	dahk sing	dak6 sing	tahk seng
characteristic[1] /special	adj	特點	dahk dím	dak6 dim2	tahk tim
characteristic[2]	adj	表示特性	bíu sih dahk sing	biu2 si6 dak6 sing	piu sih tahk seng
characteristics	adj	獨特的	duhk dahk dìk	duk6 dak6 dik4	tuhk tahk tek
charcoal[1]/coal/carbon/ burned wood/ember	n	炭	taan	taan3	thaan
charcoal[2] /wood coal	n	木炭	muhk taan	muk6 taan3	muhk thaan
charge[1] /price	v	索價	sok ga	sok3 ga3	sok ka

charge[2] /fee	n	收費	sàu fai	sau4 fai3	sau fai
charge[3] /beat	v	猛攻	máahng gùng	maang5 gung4	maahng kung
charge account	n	記帳戶口	gei jeung wuh háu	gei3 jeung wu6 hau2	kei cheung wuh hau
credit card /charge card	n	信用卡/咭	seun yuhng kāat	seon3 jung6 kaat1	swon yuhng khaat
charge meter	n	收費器	sàu fai hei	sau4 fai3 hei3	sau fai hei
charitable	adj	寬容	fùn yung	fun4 jung3	fun yung
charity[1]	n	慈善	chìh sihn	ci4 sin6	chhih sihn
charity[2] /compassionate/ kindly/mercy	n	慈悲	chìh bèi	ci4 bei4	chhih pei
charity[3]	n	仁愛	yàhn ói /ngoi	jan4 oi3 /ngoi3	yahn oi /ngoi
charlie[(de)]Chaplin	n	差利	chā léi	caa1 lei2	chha lei
chart[1] /table/list/register	n	譜	póu	pou2	phou
chart[2] /diagram/drawing /map/picture	n	圖	tòuh	tou4	thouh
chart[3] /diagram/figure /graph	n	圖表	tòuh bíu	tou4 biu2	thouh piu
chart[4]	n	製圖	jai tòuh	zai3 tou4	chai thouh
chart[5]	n	製圖表	jai tòuh bíu	zai3 tou4 biu2	chai thouh piu
chart[6] map/map/atlas	n	地圖	deih tòuh	dei6 tou4	teih thouh
charter[1] hiring	v	包租	bàau jòu	baau4 zou4	paau chou
charter[2] /hire/rent	v	租賃	jòu yahm	zou4 jam6	chou yahm
charter[3] /statement	n	特許狀	dahk héui johng	dak6 heoi2 zong6	tahk hoi chohng
charter flight /hiring		包機	bàau gèi	baau4 gei4	paau kei
chartered accountant	n	特許會計師	dahk héui wuih gai sī	dak6 heoi2 wai6 gai3 si1	tahk hoi wuih kai si
chase[1] /follow/pursuit	v	追	jèui	zeoi4	cheui
chase[2]	v	追逐	jèui juhk	zeoi4 zuk6	cheui chohk
chase away /catch up	v	趕	gón	gon2	kon
chassis (of the car)	n	底盤	dái pún	dai2 pun2	tai phun
chaste[1]/virginity of women	adj	貞節	jìng jit	zing4 zit3	cheng chit
chaste[2] /chastity	adj	貞潔	jìng git	zing4 git3	cheng kit
chat[1] /converse/dialogue	v	傾偈	kìng gái	king4 gai2	khing kai
chat[2] /converse/talk	v	交談	gàau taam	gaau4 taam3	kaau taam
cheap[1] /low price/ inexpensive	adj	平	pèhng /pìhng	peng4 /ping4	phehng
cheap[2]	adj	平啲	pèhng dì	peng4 di4	phehng ti
cheap[3]	adj	便宜	bihn yìh	bin6 ji4	pihn yih
cheap dishes	adj	小菜	síu choi	siu2 coi3	siu choi
cheap sell and buy		平買賣	pèhng máaih maaih	peng4 maai5 maai6	phehng maeih maaih
cheaper please!	adj	平啲啦!	pèhng dì lā!	peng4 di4 laa1	phehng ti la!
cheat[1] (coll)	v	呃	àak /ngàak	aak4 /ngaak4	aak /ngaak
cheat[2] /pretence/pretend /pretense	v	詐	ja	zaa3	cha
cheat[3] (wr) trick	v	騙	pin	pin3	phin
cheat[4] (wr) deceive/dupe/deceive	v	欺騙	hèi pin	hei4 pin3	hei phin

English	Part	Chinese	Romanization 1	Romanization 2	Romanization 3
cheat[5] /deceive/fake	v	欺詐	hèi ja	hei4 zaa3	hei cha
cheat[6] /trick	v	騙取	pin chéui	pin3 ceoi2	phin chhoi
cheat[7]	v	作弊	jok baih	zok3 bai6	chok paih
cheater /swindler/ruse/ dishonest person	n	騙子	pin jí	pin3 zi2	phin chi
cheater	n	作弊者	jok baih jé	zok3 bai6 ze2	chok paih che
cheating[1]	v	白撞	baahk johng	baak6 zong6	paahk chohng
cheating[2]	v	行騙	hahng pin	hang6 pin3	hahng phin
cheating[3]	v	呀詐	ah /ngah ja	aa6 /ngaa6 zaa3	ah /ngah cha
check[1] (de)	v	*	chēk	zek1	chhek
check[2] /test/search	n/v	檢	gím	gim2	kim
check[3] /search /investigation	v	查	chàh	caa4	chhah
check[4] /exam/inspect	v	鑒	gaam	gaam3	kaam
check[5] /examine	v	考	háau	haau2	haau
check[6] /stop/restrict	n/v	制止	jai jí	zai3 zi2	chai chi
check in counter (plane)	n	登機臺	dàng gei tòih	dang4 gei3 toi4	tang kei thoih
check in plane /get in plane	n	登機	dàng gei	dang4 gei3	tang kei
check out[1] from hotel	n	退房	teui fóng	teoi3 fong2	thoi fong
check out[2] from hotel	n	退房	teui fóng	teoi3 fong2	thoi fong
check out[3] hotal	n	結數	git sóu	git3 sou2	kit sou
check out counter	n	付款處	fu fún chyu	fu3 fun2 cyu3	fu fun chhyu
check out from hotal /settlement account	n	結帳	git jeung	git3 zong3	kit cheung
check temperature	n	探熱	taam yiht	taam3 jit6	thaam yiht
checked	v	查核	chah haht	caa4 hat6	chhah haht
checked already	v	檢查咗	gím chàh jó	gim2 caa4 zo2	kim chhah cho
checker /examiner /looker/inspector	n	檢查員	gím chàh yùhn	gim2 caa4 jyun4	kim chhah yuhn
checker in volleball or tennis	n	攔網人	làan móhng yàhn	laan4 mong5 jan4	laan mohng yahn
cheek[1]	n	頰	haap	haap3	haap
cheek[2] /face	n	面	mihn	min6	mihn
cheek[3]	n	面頰	mihn haap	min6 haap3	mihn haap
cheer[1] gladness	v	喜悅	héi yuht	hei2 jyut6	hei yuht
cheer[2] /shout of joy	n	喝采	hot chói	hot3 coi2	hot chhoi
cheer[3]	v	加油	gà yàuh	gaa4 jau4	ka yauh
cheerful[1] /enjoyable/ happy/pleasure	adj	快樂	faai lohk	faai3 lok6	faai lohk
cheerful[2] /happy/glad/ pleased/willing/delighted	adj	高興	gou hīng	gou3 hing1	kou heng
cheerful[3] /comfortable /pleasance/pleasant	adj	愉快	yùh faai	jyu4 faai3	yuh faai
cheerful[4]	adj	興高采烈	hìng gòu chói liht	hing4 gou4 coi2 lit6	hing kou chhoi liht
cheerful mind	adj	精神	jìng sàhn	zing4 san4	cheng sahn
cheerless[1]	adj	不快活	bāt faai wùht	bat1 faa3 wut6	pat faai wuht

cheerless[2]	adj	不暢快	bāt cheung faai	bat1 coeng3 faai3	pat cheung faai
cheers[1] soft drinking	adj	飲杯	yám bùi	jam2 but4	yam pui
cheers[2] wine drinking	adj	敬酒	ging jáu	ging3 zau2	keng chau
cheers[3] wine drinking	adj	飲勝	yám sīng	jam2 sing1	yam seng
cheers[4] at drinking	adj	幹杯	gon būi	gon3 bui1	kon pui
cheese[1(de)]	n	芝士	chī sí, jì sí	zi1 si2, zi4 si2	chhi si, chi si
cheese[2]	n	奶酪	láaih /náaih lok	laai5 /naai5 lok3	laaih /naaih lok
chef cook[1] /cook	n	廚師	chyùh sì	cyu4 si4	chhyuh si
chef cook[2] /head cook	n	大廚	daaih chyù	daai6 cyu4	taaih chhyu
chemical	n	化學品	fa hohk bán	faa3 hok6 ban2	fa hohk pan
chemical engineer	n	化學工程師	fa hohk gùng ching sì	faa3 hok6 gung4 cing4 si4	fa hohk kung chhing si
chemist	n	化學家	fa hohk gà	faa3 hok6 ga4	fa hohk ka
chemistry[1]	n	化學	fa hohk	faa3 hok6	fa hohk
chemistry[2]	n	化學性質	fa hohk sing jāt	faa3 hok6 sing3 zat1	fa hohk seng chat
cheque[1 (de)]	n	仄	chēk	zak1	chhek
cheque[2]	n	支票	jì piu	zi4 piu3	chi phiu
cheque[3]	n	核對	haht deui	hat6 deoi3	haht toei
cheque book	n	支票簿	jì piu bouh	zi4 piu3 bou6	chi phiu pouh
cherry	n	車厘子	chè lèih jí	ce1 lei4 zi2	chhe leih chi
chess player /checker	n	捉棋	jūk kéi	zuk1 kei4	chuk khei
chevrons (v shape)	n	V 型記號	V ying géi hou	V jing3 gei2 hou3	V yeng kei hou
chew[1]	v	嚼	jeuhk	zeuk6	cheuhk
chew[2]	v	咬嚼	ngáauh jeuhk	ngaau5 zeuk6	ngaauh cheuhk
chicken[1] /fowl/bird /poultry	n	雞	gài	gai4	kai
chicken[2]	n	雞肉	gài yuhk	gai4 juk6	kai yuhk
chicken breast	n	雞胸肉	gài hūng yuhk	gai4 hung1 juk6	kai hung yuhk
chicken bundle	n	雞扎	gài jáat	gai4 zaat2	kai chaat
chicken dish	n	雞炒菜	gài cháau choi	gai1 chaau2 choi3	kai chhaau chhoi
chicken leg /chicken drumsticks	n	雞脾	gài pèih	gai4 pei4	kai peih
chicken egg	n	雞蛋	gài dàahn	gai4 daan6	kai taahn
chicken feed	n	雞飼料	gài jih líu	gai4 zi6 liu2	kai chih liu
chicken feet[1]	n	鳳爪	fuhng jāau	fung6 zaau2	fuhng chau
chicken feet[2]	n	雞腳	gài geuk	gai4 goek3	kai keuk
chicken kidney	n	雞腎	gài sahn	gai4 san6	kai sahn
chicken porridge	n	雞粥	gài jūk	gai4 zuk1	kai chuk
chicken's internal organs/entrails	n	雞雜	gài jaahp	gai4 zaap6	kai chaahp
chicken steak	n	雞扒	gài pá	gai4 paa2	kai pha
chicken stock	n	雞粉	gài fān	gai4 fan1	kai fan
chicken wing	n	雞翼	gài yihk	gai4 jik6	kai yehk
chicken-hearted/ timid/cowardly	adj	懦	loh /noh	lo6 /no6	loh /noh

chide[1] /scold/speak angrily/criticize	v	鬧	laauh /naauh	laau6 /naau6	laauh /naauh
chide[2] /rebuke/speak angrily/scold/lambast	v	怪責	gwaai jaak	gwaai3 zaak3	kwaai chaak
chief[1] head man/head	n	總	júng	zung2	chung
chief[2] /leader/head	n	首	sáu	sau2	sau
chief[3] /leader	n	領袖	léhng /líhng jauh	leng5 /ling5 zau6	lehng chauh
chief executive	n	行政長官	hàhng jing jéung gùn	hang4 zing3 zoeng2 gun4	hahng cheng cheung kun
chief guide /leader of an expedition	n	探險隊嘅 領隊	taam hím déui ge líhng déui	taam3 him2 deoi6 ge3 ling5 deoi2	thaam him toei ke lehng toei
chief person	n	阿頭	áa táu	aa2 tau2	aa thau
child[1] (coll) /infant/below one month	n	蘇蝦仔	sòu hā jái	sou4 haa1 zai2	sou ha chai
child[2] (wr)	n	孩	hàaih	haai4	haaih
child[3] /children/baby 6-10 years	n	兒童	yi tung	ji3 tung3	yi thung
child[4] below 12 years	n	細佬哥	sai lóu gō	sai3 lou2 go1	sai lou ko
child[5] /baby (coll) 3-12 years	n	細路仔	sai louh jái	sai3 lou6 zai2	sai louh chai
child asylum /orphanage	n	孤兒院	gù yìh yún	gu4 ji4 jyun2	ku yih yun
child in the womb /embryo/womb/fetus/foetus	n	胎	tòi	toi4	thoi
childbearing[1]	n	生細路	sàang sai louh	saang4 sai3 lou6	saang sai louh
childbearing[2] /childbirth	n	生孩子	sàang hàaih jí	saang4 haai4 zi2	saang haaih chi
childhood[1]	n	稚	jih	zi6	chih
childhood[2]	n	童年	tùhng nìhn	tung4 nin4	thuhng nihn
childhood[3]	n	幼年	yau nìhn	jau3 nin4	yau nihn
childhood[4]	n	童年時代	tùhng nìhn sìh doih	tung4 nin4 si4 doi6	thuhng nihn sih toih
childless[1] /no childs/ heirless	adj/n	無繼承人	mòuh gai sìhng yàhn	mou4 gai3 sing4 jan4	mouh kai sehng yahn
childless[2]	adj	無子女	mòuh jí léui /néui	mou4 zi2 leui 5 /neui5	mouh chi lowi /nowih
children[1] /offspring	n	子女	jái léui /néui	zai2 leui5 /neui5	chai lowi /nowi
children[2] /offspring	n	孩子	haai jí	haai3 zi2	haai chi
children[3] /kids/little children	n	小朋友	síu pang yáuh	siu2 pang3 jau5	siu phang yauh
children[4]	n	細路	sai louh	sai3 lou6	sai louh
children[5]	n	小童	síu tùhng	siu2 tung4	siu thuhng
chili	n	辣椒	laaht jìu	laat6 ziu4	laaht chiu
chili sauce /hot sauce	n	辣椒醬	laaht jìu jeung	laat6 ziu4 zoeng3	laaht chiu cheung
chill[1]	n	發冷	faat láahng	faat3 laang5	faat laahng
chill[2] /cold	n	寒冷	hòhn láahng	hong4 laang5	hohn laahng
chill[3]	v	打冷震	dá láahng jan	daa2 laang5 zan3	ta laahng chan
chimney	n	煙囪	yīn chēung	jin1 coeng1	yin chheung
chimpanzee	n	黑猩猩	hāk sīng sīng	hak1 sing1 sing1	hak seng seng
chin /jaw	n	下巴	hah pàh	haa6 paa4	hah phah
China[1]	n	華	wàh	waa4	wah

English		Chinese	Yale	Jyutping	Other
China[2]	n	中國	jùng gwók	zung4 gwok2	chung kwok
China mainland	n	大陸	daaih luhk	daai6 luk6	taaih luhk
China gas	n	中華煤氣	jùng wah mùih hei	zung4 waa6 mui4 hei3	chung wah muih hei
China light power /CLP	n	中華電力	jùng wah dihn lihk	zung4 waa6 din6 lik6	chung wah tihn lehk
China town[1]	n	唐人街	tòhng yàhn gāai	tong4 jan4 gaai1	thohng yahn kaai
China town[2]	n	中國城	jùng gwok sèhng	zung4 gwok3 seng4	chung kwok sehng
Chinese /Chinese man	n	中國人	jùng gwok yàhn	zung4 gwok3 jan4	chung kwok yahn
Chinese calendar	n	農曆	lùhng /nùhng lihk	lung4 /nung4 lik6	luhng /nuhng lehk
Chinese characters	n	中國字	jùng gwok jih	zung4 gwok3 zi6	chung kwok chih
Chinese costume	n	唐裝	tòhng jòng	tong4 zong4	thohng chong
Chinese doctor /physician	n	中醫	jùng yì	zung4 ji4	chung yi
Chinese dragon	n	龍	lùhng	lung4	luhng /loon
Chinese dress	n	唐裝	tòhng jòng	tong4 zong4	thohng chong
Chinese food[1] /Chinese cuisine	n	中菜	jùng choi	zung4 coi3	chung chhoi
Chinese food[2]	n	唐餐	tòhng chāan	tong4 caan1	thohng chhaan
Chinese herbal tea	n	涼茶	lèuhng chàh	loeng4 caa4	leuhng chhah
Chinese HK Hakka (family name)	n	客家	haak gā	haak3 gaa1	haak ka
Chinese language	n	中文	jùng màhn	zung4 man4	chung mahn
Chinese man	n	阿燦	áa chaan	aa2 caan3	aa chhaan
Chinese medicine	n	中藥	jūng yeuhk	zung1 joek6	chung yeuhk
Chinese mushroom	n	冬菇	dūng gù	dung1 gu4	tung ku
Chinese new year's Eve[1]	n	年三十晚	lìhn sāam sahp máahn	lin4 saam1 sap6 maan5	lihn saam sahp maahn
Chinese new year's Eve[2]	n	年卅晚	lìhn sāa máahn	lin4 saa1 maan5	lihn saa maahn
Chinese people	n	唐人	tòhng yàhn	tong4 jan4	thohng
Chinese style dish	n	中國菜	jùng gwok choi	zung4 gwok3 coi3	chung kwok chhoi
Chinese style dress	n	長衫	chèuhng sāam	coeng4 saam1	chheuhng saam
Chinese style ladies	n	旗袍	kèih póu	kei4 pou2	kheih phou
Chinese tea	n	中國茶	jùng gwok chàh	zung4 gwok3 caa4	chung kwok chhah
Chinese woman	n	中國女人	jùng gwok léoih / néoih yàhn	zung4 gwok3 leoi5 /neoi5 jan4	chung kwok lowih / nowih yahn
chin-up /pull up physical exercise	n	引體向上	yáhn tái heung seuhng	jan5 tai2 hoeng3 soeng6	yahn thai heung seuhng
Chio /Jhau family name of HK Chinese	n	潮州	chìuh jāu	ciu4 zau1	chhiuh chau
chip[1]	n	碎片	seui pín	seoi3 pin2	swoi phin
chip[2]	n	屑片	sit pin	sit3 pin3	sit pin
chippings /gravel	n	碎石	seui sèhk	seoi3 sek6	swoi sehk
chitchat /chat	n/v	閒談	hàahn tàahm	haan4 taam4	haahn thaahm
chlorination	n	加氯消毒	gà luhk sīu duhk	ga4 luk6 siu1 duk4	ka luhk siu tuhk
chlorine (chemistry)	n	氯	luhk	luk6	luhk
chocolate[1] (de)(coll)		朱古力	jyū gù līk, zyù gū lìhk	zyu1 gu4 lik1, zyu4 gu1 lik6	chyu ku lehk
chocolate[2] (wr)	n	巧克力	háau hāk lìhk	haau2 hak1 lik6	haau hak lehk

English		Chinese	Yale	Jyutping	Romanization
choice /pick/selection /preference	n	選擇	syún jaahk	syun2 zaak6	syun chaahk
choice yourself /one's choice/select yourself	v	自己揀	jih géi gáan	zi6 gei2 gaan2	chih kei kaan
choir	n	聖樂團	sing lohk tyùhn	sing3 lok6 tyun4	seng lohk thyuhn
choke[1] /hiccup/hiccough	n	噎	yit	jit	yit
choke[2] breathing	v	窒氣	jaht hei	zat6 hei3	chaht hei
choke[3] breathing	v	阻氣門	jó hei mùhn	zo2 hei3 mun4	cho hei muhn
choke[4] /air hunger/stuffybreathing	v	窒息	jaht sīk	zat6 sik1	chaht sek
choked with silt / silted up	v	淤塞	yu sāk	jyu3 sak1	yu sak
cholera	n	霍亂	fok lyuhn	fok3 lyun6	fok lyuhn
cholesterol	n	膽固醇	dáam gu sèuhn	daam2 gu3 seon4	taam ku seuhn
choose[1] /select/pick up	v	擇	jaahk	zaak6	chaahk
choose[2] /pick/select	v	挑	tìu	tiu4	thiu
choose[3] /pick up/select	v	揀	gáan	gaan2	kaan
choose[4] /select	v	挑選	tìu syún	tiu4 syun2	thiu syun
chop[1]	n	蓋	koi	koi3	khoi
chop[2] /stamp	n	蓋印	koi yan	koi3 jan3	khoi yan
chop[3] /seal/stamp	n	圖章	tòuh jēung	tou4 zoeng1	thouh cheung
chop[4] /cut	v	斬	jáam	zaam2	chaam
chop[5] /cut/slash	v	砍	hám	ham2	ham
chopper /kitchen knife/vegetable knife	n	菜刀	choi dōu	coi3 dou1	chhoi tou
chopping block/ cutting board	n	砧板	jām báan	zam1 baan2	cham paan
chopsticks	n	筷子	faai jí	faai3 zi2	faai chi
chorus[1] /group dance	n	合唱團	hahp cheung tùhn	hap6 coeng3 tyun4	hahp cheung thyuhn
chorus[2]	n	合唱隊	hahp cheung deuih	hap6 coeng3 deoi6	hahp cheung twoih
chorus[3]	n	合唱曲	hahp cheung kūk	hap6 coeng3 kuk1	hahp cheung khuk
Christ[1] /Jesus/Yesus	n	耶穌	yèh sōu	je4 sou1	yeh sou
Christ[2]	n	基督	gēi dūk	gei1 duk1	kei tuk
Christian	n	基督徒	gēi dūk tòuh	gei1 duk1 tou4	kei tuk thouh
Christmas	n	聖誕	síng dáan	sing2 daan2	seng taan
Christmas cake	n	聖誕蛋糕	sing daan daahn gōu	sing3 daan3 daan6 gou1	seng taan taahn kou
Christmas card[1]	n	聖誕咭	síng dáan kàt	sing2 daan2 kat4	seng taan khat
Christmas card[2]	n	聖誕賀卡	sing daan hoh kāat	sing3 daan3 ho6 kaat1	seng taan hoh khaat
Christmas carol[1]	n	報佳音	bou gāai yām	bou3 gaai1 jam1	pou kaai yam
Christmas carol[2]	n	聖誕歌	síng dáan gō	sing2 daan2 go1	seng taan koh
Christmas decorations	n	聖誕裝飾	síng dáan jòng sìk	sing2 daan2 zong4 sik4	seng taan chong sek
Christmas Eve[1]	n	平安夜	pèhng òn /ngòn yèh	peng4 on3 /ngon3 je6	phehng on /ngon yeh
Christmas Eve[2]	n	聖誕夜	síng dáan yèh	sing2 daan2 je6	seng taan yeh
Christmas present	n	聖誕禮物	síng dáan láih màht	sing2 daan2 lai5 mat4	seng taan laih maht
Christmas pudding	n	聖誕布丁	síng dáan bou dīng	sing2 daan2 bou3 ding3	seng taan pou teng
Christmas tree[1]	n	聖誕樹	síng dáan syùh	sing2 daan2 syu6	seng taan syuh

English		Chinese	Romanization	Jyutping	Reading
Christmas tree[2]	n	耶誕樹	yèh daan syuh	je4 daan3 syu6	yeh taan syuh
chronic[1] /old disease/ previous disease/slow & patient	n	慢性	maahn sing	maan6 sing3	maahn seng
chronic[2] disease	adj	慢性嘅	maahn sing ge	maan6 sing3ge3	maahn seng ke
chronic illness	adj	慢性病	maahn sing behng	maan6 sing3 beng6	maahn seng pehng
chronograph	n	記時法	gei sìh faat	gei3 si4 faat3	kei sih faat
chronological	adj	順序时間	seuhn jèuih sìh gàan	seon6 zeoi6 si4 gaan1	swohn choih sih kaan
chrysanthemum	n	菊花	gūk fà	guk1 faa4	kuk fa
chum /friend/close friend	n	好友	hóu yáuh	hou2 jau5	hou yauh
chunk	n	厚塊	háuh faai	hau5 faai3	hauh faai
church large /chapel	n	教堂	gaau tòhng	gaau3 tong4	kaau thohng
churn[1] /stir	v	攪拌	gáau buhn	gaau2 bun6	kaau puhn
churn[2]	n	攪乳器	gáau yúh hei	gaau2 jyu5 hei3	kaau yuh hei
CID[1]	n	型事偵緝處	yìhng sih jīng chāp chyú	jing4 si6 zing1 cap1 cyu2	yehng sih cheng chhap chhyu
CID[2]	n	刑事調查部	yìhng sih diuh chàh bouh	jing4 si6 diu6 caa4 bou6	yehng sih tiuh chhah pouh
cigar[(de)]	n	雪茄	syut gā	syut3 gaa1	syut ka
cigars /a mouth smoke	n	口	háu	hau2	hau
cigarette[1] /smoke/tobacco	n	烟	yīn	jin1	yin
cigarette[2]	n	烟仔	yīn jái	jin1 zai2	yin chai
cigarette[3]	n	香煙	hèung yīn	hoeng4 jin1	heung yin
cigarette ashes	n	烟灰	yīn fūi	jin1 fui1	yin fui
cigarette butt /butts/ end of a cigarette/remains piece of cigarette/ short piece	n	烟頭	yīn táu	jin1 tau2	yin thau
cinema[1] /theatre	n	戲院	hei yún	hei3 jyun2	hei yun
cinema[2]	n	電影院	dihn yíng yūn	din6 jeng2 jyun1	tihn yeng yun
cinnamon	n	肉桂皮	yuhk gwai pèih	juk6 gwai3 pei4	yuhk kwai pheih
circle[1]	n	回	wùih	wui4	wuih
circle[2]	n	圓圈	yùhn hyūn	jyun4 hyun1	yuhn hyun
circles of group /group	n	界	gaai	gaai3	kaai
circuit[1] /electric rote	n	電路	dihn louh	din6 lou6	tihn louh
circuit[2] /wiring electric	n	線路	sin louh	sin3 lou6	sin louh
circuitous[1]	adj	迂回	yù wùih	jyu4 wui4	yu wuih
circuitous[2] /indirect	adj	間接	gaan jip	gaan3 zip3	kaan chip
circular[1] /society/group	n	團	tyùhn	tyun4	thyuhn
circular[2] /round	adj	圓的	yùhn dìk	jyun4 dik4	yuhn tek
circular[3] /round	a	圓形	yùhn yìhng	jyun4 jing4	yuhn yehng
circular[4] /notification /notice	n	通告	tùng gou	tung4 gou3	thung kou
circulate[1] /pass on spread/ transfer/transmit	v	傳	chyùhn	cyun4	chhyuhn
circulate[2]	v	行	hòhng	hong4	hohng

circulate[3]	v	循環	chèuhn wàahn	ceon4 waan4	chheuhn waahn
circulate[4]	n	流通	làuh tùng	lau4 tung4	lauh thung
circulation	n	流轉	làuh jyún	lau4 zyun2	lauh chyun
circumcise /foreskin remove	v	割包皮	got bàau pèih	got3 baau4 pei4	kot paau pheih
circumstances[1] /condition/situation/position	n	情形	chìhng yìhng	cing4 jing4	chhehng yehng
circumstances[2] /posture/condition/situation	n	情況	chìhng fong	cing4 fong3	chhehng fong
circus[1]	n	馬戲	máh hei	maa5 hei3	mah hei
circus[2]	n	馬戲團	máh hei tyùhn	maa5 hei3 tyun4	mah hei thyuhn
citation /list	n	列舉	liht géui	lit6 geoi2	liht kwoi
Citibank	n	花旗銀行	fā kèih ngàhn hòhng	faa1 kei4 ngan4 hong4	fa kheih ngahn hohng
citizen/civic/people/ nationality	n	民	màhn	man4	mahn
citizenship /nationality	n	國籍	gwok jihk	gwok3 zik6	kwok chehk
citrus	n	柑橘	gàm gwāt	gam4 gwat1	kam kwat
city[1] /town	n	城市	sèhng síh	seng4 si5	sehng sih
city[2] /metropolis	n	都市	dōu síh	dou1 si5	tou sih
city area /town/city center/ downtown/urban dustrict	n	市區	síh kēui	si5 keoi1	sih khoi
city center /downtown	adv	市政中心	síh jing jùng sàm	si5 zing3 zung4 sam4	sih cheng chung sam
city hall[1] /municipality	n	市政府	síh jing fú	si5 zing3 fu2	sih cheng fu
city hall[2] /town hall	n	市政廳	síh jing tèng	si5 zing3 teng4	sih cheng theng
city hall[3]	n	大會堂	daaih wúi tòhng	daai6 wui2 tong4	taaih wui thohng
civil[1] /citizen/civic	n/adj	公民	gùng màhn	gung4 man4	kung mahn
civil[2]	adj	民用	màhn yuhng	man4 jung6	mahn yuhng
civil[3]	adj	市民	síh màhn	si5 man4	sih mahn
civil law	n	民法	màhn faat	man4 faat3	mahn faat
civil rights	n	公民權	gùng màhn kyùhn	gung4 man4 kyun4	kung mahn khyuhn
civil transport	n	民運	màhn wahn	man4 wan6	mahn wahn
civil war	n	內戰	loih /noih jin	loi6 /noi6 zin3	loih /noih chin
civilian	n	平民	pèhng màhn	peng4 man4	phehng mahn
civilization	n	文明	màhn mìhng	man4 ming4	mahn mehng
civilized[1]	adj	文明	màhn mìhng	man4 ming4	mahn mehng
civilized[2]	adj	教化	gaau fa	gaau3 fa3	kaau fa
civilized person /gentleman/refined person/elegant man	n	斯文	sì màhn	si4 man4	si mahn
claim money[1] /demand/ask for	n	要求	yìu kàuh	jiu4 kau4	yiu khauh
claim money[2]	v	認領	yihng léhng	jing6 leng5	yehng lehng
claim right /legal right	n	權利	kyùhn leih	kyun4 lei6	khyuhn leih
claimant	n	原告	yùhn gou	jyun4 gou3	yuhn kou
clam[1] /oysters	n	蚌	póhng	pong5	phohng
clam[2] /shellfish/oysters	n	蜆	hín	hin2	hin

English	Part	Chinese	Romanization	Jyutping	Yale
clam[3] /silence	n	唔開口	m̀ hòi háu	m4 hoi4 hau2	mh hoi hau
clam[4] /silence	n	不開口	bāt hòi háu	bat1 hoi4 hau2	pat hoi hau
clamber[1]	v	爬上人	pàh séuhng yàhn	paa4 soeng5 jan4.	phah seuhng yahn
clamber[2]	v	攀登人	pāan dāng yàhn	paan1 dang1 jan4	phaan tang yahn
clamp[1] /pliers	v	拑	kím	kim2	khim
clamp[2]	v	夾	gáap	gaap2	kaap
clamp[3] /clip	v	夾住	gip jyuh	gip zyu6	kep chyuh
clamp[4] of wood /splint	n	夾板	gáap baan	gaap2 baan3	kaap paan
clamp[5]	n	夾鉗	gip kìhm	gip kim6	kep khihm
clamp place	v	鉗位	kím wái	kim2 wai2	khim wai
clan[1] /caste/race/tribe/ nationality/ethnicity/social group	n	族	juhk	zuk6	chuhk
clan[2] /race	n	宗族	jung jùhk	zung3 zuk6	chung chuhk
clap[1] /slap/slightly hit/pat /gentle hit/give clap on/give pat on	vt	拍	paak	paak3	phaak
clap[2] /thundering/clap of thunder	adj	霆	tìhng	ting4	thehng
clap of thunder	n	霹靂	pihk lihk	pik1 lik1	phehk lehk
clapper	n	鈴鎚	lìhng chèuih	ling4 ceoi4	lehng chheuih
clarifier	n	淨化物	jehng fa maht	zeng6 faa3 mat6	chehng fa maht
clarify	v	澄清	chèng chèng	ceng4 ceng4	chheng chheng
clash /collide/collision	v	碰撞聲	púng johng sèng	pung2 zong6 seng4	phung chohng seng
clasp[1] /armful	v	抱緊	póuh gán	pou5 gan2	phouh kan
clasp[2] /cling/grasp	v	抓緊	jáau gán	zaau2 gan2	chaau kan
clasp[3] by force	v	扣住	kau jyuh	kau3 zyu6	khau chyuh
class[1] /course/lesson/ subject/classwork	n	課	fo	fo3	fo
class[2] /teach	n/v	教	gaau	gaau3	kaau
class[3] /category/kind/ genus/type/sortspecies/race /variety	n	種類	júng leuih	zung2 leoi6	chung lowih
class[4] /degree/grade/rank	n	等級	dáng kāp	dang2 kap1	tang khap
class is over /class finished (a day class)	n	落堂	lohk tòhng	lok6 tong4	lohk thohng
classic	adj	最優秀	jeui yàu sau	zeoi3 jau4 sau3	cheui yau sau
classic music[1]	n	古典音樂	gú dín yàm ngohk	gu2 din2 jam4 ngok6	ku tin yam ngohk
classic music[2]	n	古典樂	gú dín lohk	gu2 din2 loh6	ku tin lohk
classical	adj	古典	gú dín	gu2 din2	ku tin
classifier	n	計算者	gai syun jé	gai3 syun3 ze2	kai syun che
classifier for long thin, a fish/key/rope/road/string /thread tie/pant/ ribbon/ trouser/necklace	n	條	tìuh	tiu4	thiuh
classifier for paper/ beds/money/blades/chairs /knifes/tables/records	n	張	jēung /jèung	zoeng1 /zeung4	cheung

classifier for books	n	本	bún	bun2	pun
classifier for bun/ clock/nations/oranges/ persons/as round-shape	n	個	go	go3	ko
classifier for clothes piece or items	n	件	gihn	gin6	kihn
classifier for flowers	n	朵	dó	do2	to
classifier for pens /pencils/sticks/long round shape objects	n	枝	jī	zi1	chi
classifier for plays on the stage	n	齣 / 出	chēut	ceot1	chhot
classifier for scissors /locks/knives & umbrellas	n	把	pá	pa2	pa
classifier for story /layer/floor/flats/storeys (of building)	n	層	chàhng	cang4	chhahng
classifier for trees	n	棵	pō	po1	pho
classifier for vehicle /aircraft/machine/TV	n	架	ga	gaa3	ka
classifier of vehicles	n	輛	léung	loeng2	leung
classifiered /birds/ boats/hands/legs/utensils (not humans)	n	隻	jek	zek3	chek
classify[1]	v	別	bìht	bit6	piht
classify[2]	v	分等級	fàn dáng kāp	fan6 dang2 kap1	fàn tang khap
classless	adj	無階級	mòuh gāai kāp	mou4 gaai1 kap1	mouh kaai khap
classmate	n	同班同學	tùhng bāan tùhng hohk	tung4 baan1 tung4 hok6	thuhng paan thuhng hohk
classroom[1]	n	教室	gaau sāt	gaau3 sat1	kaau sat
classroom[2]	n	班房	bàan fóng	baan4 fong2	paan fong
classroom[3]	n	課室	fo sāt	fo3 sat1	fo sat
classroom[4]	n	課堂	fo tòhng	fo3 tong4	fo thohng
clause (of law) terms/agreement	n	條款	tìuh fún	tiu4 fun2	thiuh fun
claw /nail	n	爪	jāau	zaau2	chaau
clay[1] potter's	n	陶土	tòuh tóu	tou4 tou2	thouh thou
clay[2]	n	黏土	lim /nim tóu	lim3 /nim3 tou2	lim /nim thou
clean[1] /rinse/wash	v	洗	sái	sai2	sai
clean[2]	v	乾淨	gòn jehng	gon4 zeng6	kon chehng
clean[3] /cleaning/sweep	v	打掃	dá sou	daa2 sou3	ta sou
clean[4]	adj	清潔	chēng git /chīng git	ceng1 /cing1 git3	chheng kit
clean & neat /neat & clean	adj	乾淨企理	gòn jehng kéih léih	gon4 zeng6 kei5 lei5	kon chehng kheih leih
clean living	n	生活嚴謹	sàng wuht yìhm gán	sang4 wut6 jim4 gan2	sang wuht yehm kan
cleaner	n	清潔人	chēng /chīng git yàhn	cing1 /ceng1 git3 jan4	chheng kit yahn
cleaner	n	清潔工	chēng /chīng git gùng	cing1 /ceng1 git3 gung4	chheng kit kung

cleanning in	n	清潔進	chēng /chīng git jeun	ceng1 /cing1 git3 zeon3	chheng kit cheun
clear[1] /bright	adj	朗	lóhng	long5	lohng
clear[2] /pure/distinct	adj	清	chèng /chìng	ceng4 /cing4	chheng
clear[3]	adj	潔淨	git jehng /jihng	git3 zeng6 /zing6	kit chehng
clear understand	adj	清楚明白	chèng /chìng chó mìhng baahk	ceng4 /cing4 co2 ming4 baak6	chheng chho mehng paahk
clear & bright of weather	adj	爽朗	sóng lóhng	song2 long5	song lohng
clear cut[1]	adj	清晰	chèng /chìng sīk	ceng4 /cing4 sik1	chheng sek
clear cut[2] /specific/ definite/explicit/to clarify	adj	明確	mìhng kok	ming4 kok3	mehng khok
clear garbage	v	倒垃圾	dóu laahp saap	dou2 laap6 saap3	tou laahp saap
clear understand		清楚晒	chìng chó saai	ching1 choh2 saai3	chheng chhoh saai
clear water[1]	n	清水	chèng /chìng séui	ceng4 /cing4 seoi2	chheng swoi
clear water[2] /drinking water	n	食水	sihk séui	sik6 seoi2	sehk swoi
clearance	n	清除	cheng /chìng chèuih	ceng4 /cing4 ceoi4	chheng chhoih
clerk[1]	n	書記	syù gei	syu4 gei3	syu kei
clerk[2]	n	文員	màhn yùhn	man4 jyun4	mahn yuhn
clever[1] /skillful	adj	巧	háau	haau2	haau
clever[2] (bad) /not sincere	adj	唔誠懇	m̀ sìhng hán	m4 sing4 han2	mh sehng han
clever & smart	adj	聰明伶俐	chùng mìhng lìhng leih	cung4 ming4 ling4 lei6	chhung mehng lehng leih
click card sound	n	卡嗒聲	ká dāp sèng	kaa2 dap1 seng4	kha tap seng
clicking fingers	v	打響指	dá héung jí	daa2 hoeng2 zi2	ta heung chi
client[1]	n	主顧	jyú gu	zyu2 gu3	chyu ku
client[2] /customer	n	客戶	haak wuh	haak3 wu6	haak wuh
client[3] /customer	n	顧客	gu haak	gu3 haak3	ku haak
client service /customer service/room service	n/adj	客戶服務	haak wuh fuhk mouh	haak3 wu6 fuk6 mou6	haak wuh fuhk mouh
cliff[1]	n	懸崖	yun ngaai	jyun4 ngaai3	yun ngaai
cliff[2] /hard stone	n	峭壁	chiu bīk	ciu3 bik1	chhiu pek
climacteric	n	轉變期	jyun bin kèih	zyun3 bin3 kei4	chyun pin kheih
climate[1] /environment	n	水土	séui tóu	seoi2 tou2	swoi thou
climate[2]	n	氣候	hei hauh	hei3 hau6	hei hauh
climax /high tide/orgasm	n	高潮	gòu chìuh	gou4 ciu4	kou chhiuh
climax of sex[1] /most exciting of sex/hypertension of lust/come sex	v	性慾亢進	sing yuhk gōng jeun	sing3 juk6 gong1 zeon3	seng yuhk kong cheun
climax of sex[2](sl) have an orgasm/come sex	v	達到性高潮	daaht dou sing gòu chìuh	daat6 dou3 sing3 gou4 ciu4	taaht tou seng kou chhiuh
climb[1] /creep/get up/ to crawl	v	爬	pàh	paa4	phah
climb[2] /mount/go up	v	登	dāng	dang1	tang
climb[3] /climb up/mount/go up on/to get	v	爬上	pàh séuhng	paa4 soeng5	phah seuhng
climber[1]	n	爬上者	pàh séuhng jé	paa4 soeng5 ze2	phah seuhng che

climber[2] mountain	n	爬山人	pàh sàan yàhn	paa4 saan4 jan4	phah saan yahn
climber[3] mountain	n	攀登者	pāan dāng jé	paan1 dang1 ze2	phaan tang che
cling /adhesive	v	黏著	lim /nim jeuk	lim3 /nim3 zoek3	lim /nim cheuk
clinic[1]	n	診所	chán só	can2 so2	chhan so
clinic[2]	n	醫療所	yī liuh só	ji1 liu6 so2	yi liuh so
clinic[3]	n	診療所	chán liuh só	can2 liu6 so2	chhan liuh so
clip[1]	v	夾	gip	gip	kep
clip[2]	v	翦	jín	zin2	chin
clip[3]	v	別住	biht jyuh	bit6 zyu6	piht chyuh
clip[4] /hair cut	v	修剪	sau jín	sau3 zin2	sau chin
clipped[1]	v	翦斷	jín dyún	zin2 dyun2	chin tyun
clipped[2]	v	打窿	dá lūng	daa2 lung1	ta lung
clit /clitoris [dw]	n	小穴的陰道	síu yuht dìk yàm douh	siu2 jyut6 dik4 yam4 dou6	siu yuht tek yam touh
clitoris[1] [dw]	n	陰蒂	yàm tai	yam4 dai3	yam thai
clitoris[2] [dw]	n	陰核	yàm haht	yam4 hat6	yam haht
clitoris[3] [sl][dw]	n	G點	g dím	g dim2	gi tim
clitoris[4] [sl][dw]	n	刺激點	chi gīk dím	ci3 gik1 dim2	chhi kek tim
clock /time/hour	n	時鐘	sìh jùng	si4 zung4	sih chung
clock bell	n	鬧鐘	naauh jùng	naau6 zung4	naauh chung
clock radio	n	自動收音機	jih duhng sāu yāmgèi	zi6 dung6 sau4 jam4 gei4	chih tuhng sau yam kei
clog /clogged/to stop/obstruct/block up/block	v	阻塞	jó sàk	zo2 sak4	cho sak
clogged	v	塞滿	sàk múhn	sak4 mun5	sak muhn
clone[1] /produced artificially exactly same from the cells	n	克隆	hāak lùhng	haak1 lung4	haak luhng
clone[2] exact copy men by cells	n	複製人	fūk jai yàhn	fuk1 zai3 jan4	fuk chai yahn
clone[3] exact copy things	n	複製品	fūk jai bán	fuk1 zai3 ban2	fuk chai pan
close[1(wr)] shut (door/window)	v	關	gwaan	gwaan3	kwaan
close[2] /closest/closer/near	adv	接近	jip gahn	zip3 gan6	chip kahn
close[3] /next/near/to/next to	adv	近住	gahn jyuh	gan6 zyu6	kahn chyuh
close[4] /stop/shut	v	截止	jiht jí	zit6 zi2	cheht chi
close business /shut business/close down business/stop job	v	停業	tíhng yihp	ting5 jip6	thehng yihp
close business /shut business	v	停止營業	tíhng jí yìhng yihp	ting5 zi2 jing4 jip6	thehng chi yehng yihp
close by	adv	在旁邊	joih pòhng bīn	zoi6 pong4 bin1	choih phohng pin
close door[1]	v	關門	gwàan mùhn	gwaan4 mun4	kwaan muhn
close door[2] /shut door	v	關上	gwàan seuhng	gwaan4 soeng6	kwaan seuhng
close eye	v	閉眼	bai ngáahn	bai3 ngaan5	pai ngaahn
close friend[1] /best friend	adj	好朋友	hóu pàhng yáuh	hou2 pang4 jau5	hou phahng yauh
close friend[2] /best friend	adj	密友	maht yáuh	mat6 jau5	maht yauh
close gate	v	落閘	lohk jaahp	lok6 zaap6	lohk chaahp

close on ending	v	漸漸趕上	jihm jím gón séuhng	zim1 zim2 gon2 soeng5	chihm chim kon seuhng
close related/intimate/ most intimate relative	n	亲	chàn	can4	chhan
close relation[1]	adj	密	maht	mat6	maht
close relation[2]	adj	密切	maht chit	mat6 cit3	maht chhit
close relation[3] /intimate/familiar	adv	親密	chàn maht	can4 mat6	chhan maht
close to[1]	adv	接近嘅	jip gahn ge	jip3 gan3 ge3	chip kahn ke
close to[2]	adj	切	chit	cit3	chhit
close up[1] /sealed	adj	封口	fùng háu	fung4 hau2	fung hau
close up[2] blockage	v	堵塞	dóu sāk	dou2 sak1	tou sak
closely[1]	adv	近	gahn	gan6	kahn
closely[2]	adv	接近地	jip gahn deih	jip3 gan3 dei6	chip kahn teih
closely[3] intimate	adv	緊密地	gán maht deih	gan2 mat6 dei6	kan maht teih
close relation	adv	近親	gahn chān	gan6 can1	kahn chhan
closing time[1]	n	收市	sàu síh	sau4 si5	sau sih
closing time[2]	n	打烊時間	dā yèuhng sìh gaan	daa1 joeng4 si4 gaan3	ta yeuhng sih kaan
clot liquid	n	凝結咗	yìhng git jó	jing4 git3 zo2	yehng kit cho
cloth[1]	n	布	bou	bou3	pou
cloth[2]	n	衣料	yī líu	ji1 liu2	yi liu
clothes[1] /dress/garment	n	衫	sāam	saam1	saam
clothes[2] /dress	n	服	fuhk	fuk6	fuhk
clothes[3]/clothing/garment	n	衣服	yī fuhk	ji1 fuk6	yi fuhk
clothes[4]	n	衣著	yī jeuk	ji1 zoek3	yi cheuk
clothes[5]/dressing/wearing	n	穿著	chyùn jeuk	cyun4 zoek3	chhyun cheuk
clothes[6 (wr)] dressing	n	穿衣	chyùn yī	cyun4 ji1	chhyun yi
clothing[1]/costume/dress/a role	n	裝	jòng	zong4	chong
clothing[2 (coll)] wearing	adj	著衫	jeuk sàam	zoek3 saam4	cheuk saam
clothing[3] /attire	v	服裝	fuhk jòng	fuk4 zong4	fuhk chong
cloths rack/ cloths hanger	n	衣架	yī gá	yi1 ga2	yi ka
cloud	n	雲	wàhn	wan4	wahn
clouded	v&i	多雲	dò wàhn	do4 wan4	to wahn
cloudy[1]	adj	陰	yām	jam1	yam
cloudy[2]	adj	天陰	tìn yām	tin4 jam1	thin yam
cloudy[3]	adj	密雲	maht wàhn	mat6 wan4	maht wàhn
clown	n	小丑	síu cháu	siu2 cau2	siu chhau
clown role in opera/joker		丑角	cháu gok	cau2 gok3	chhau kok
club[(de)]	n	俱樂部	kèui lohk bouh	geoi4 lok6 bou6	khoi lohk bouh
clues of crime /based of story/story of a crime/ thread of crime	n	線索	sin sok	sin3 sok3	sin sok
clumsy[1 (sl)] /unskilled/ awkward/lack of skill	adj	倫盡	leuhn jeuhn	leon6 zeon6	leuhn cheuhn
clumsy[2]	adj	拙劣	jyut lyut	zyut3 lyut3	chyut lyut

clutch[1] /pedal	v	踏板	daahp báan	daap6 baan2	taahp paan
clutch[2]	n	離合器	lèih hahp hei	lei4 hap6 hei3	leih hahng hei
clutch[3]	v	掐住	haap jyuh	haap3 zyu6	haap chyuh
co-education	n	男女同校	làahm leuih tùhng gaau	laam4 leoi6 tung4 gaau3	laahm lowih thuhng kaau
co ordinating[1]	adj	同等	tùhng dáng	tung4 dang2	thuhng tang
co ordinating[2]	adj	同格	tùhng gaak	tung4 gaak3	thuhng kaak
co ordinating[3]	adj	對等	deui dáng	deoi3 dang2	toei tang
co ordination /harmonize	adj	協調	hip tìuh	hip3 tiu4	hip thiuh
co-wife[1] /wives/rival wife/ concubine	n	妾	chip	cip3	chhip
co-wife[2] /rival wife/ junior wife/concubine	n	小老婆	síu lóuh pòh	siu2 lou5 po4	siu louh phoh
co-wife[3] /concubine/ rival wife	n	姨太太	yìh taai taai	ji4 taai3 taai3	yih thaai thaai
coach[1] /trainer/instructor/ training	n	教練	gaau lihn	gaau3 lin6	kaau lihn
coach[2] bus	n	公車	gùng chè	gung4 ce1	kung chhe
coach[3] /long distance bus/ bus	n	長途客車	chèuhng touh haak chè	coeng4 tou6 haak3 ce1	chheuhng thouh haak chhe
coaching /training	n	當教練	dong gaau lihn	dong3 gaau3 lin6	tong kaau lihn
coagulate	v	凝結	yìhng git	jing4 git3	yehng kit
coal[1]	n	煤	mùih	mui4	muih
coal[2] /charcoal/ember/ cinders/carbon/burned wood	n	燒燶	sìu lūng /nūng	siu4 lung1 /nung1	siu lung /nung
coalition[1] /combination	n	聯合	lyùhn hahp	lyun4 hap6	lyuhn hahp
coalition[2] /alliance	n	聯盟	lyùhn màhng	lyun4 mang4	lyuhn mahng
coarse[1] /thick	adj	粗	chòu	cou4	chhou
coarse[2]	adj	粗糙	chòu chou	cou4 cou3	chhou chhou
coast of ocean	n	海岸	hói ngòhn	hou2 ngon6	hoi ngohn
coastal	adj	沿海	yùhn hói	jyun4 hoi2	yuhn hoi
coastal area /near a coast	adj	沿海嘅	yùhn hói ge	jyun4 hoi2 ge3	yuhn hoi ke
coaster /cup cushion	n	杯墊	bùi jín	bui4 zin2	pùi chin
coat	n	褸	lāu	lau1	lau
overcoat	n	大褸	daaih lāu	daai6 lau1	taaih lau
coax[1] for child	v	氹細佬仔	táhm sái lóu zāi	tam5 sai2 lou2 zai1	thahm sai lou chai
coax[2] for girl	v	氹女仔	táhm léuih /néuih jāi	tam5 leoi5 /neoi5 zai1	thahm lowih /nowih chai
cobweb /spider web/web	n	蜘蛛網	jì jyū móhng	zi4 zyu1 mong5	chi chyu mohng
coca-cola[1] /coke	n	可樂	hó lohk	ho2 lok6	ho lohk
coca-cola[2]	n	可口	hó háu	ho2 hau2	ho hau
cock male	n	雞公	gāi gūng	gai1 gung1	kai kung
cockpit[1] driver sits	n	駕駛座	ga sái chóh	ga3 sai2 co5	ka sai chhoh
cockpit[2] driver sits	n	駕駛艙	ga sái chòng	ga3 sai2 cong4	ka sai chhong
cockpit-drill	v	駕駛操練	ga sái chóu lìhn	ga3 sai2 cou2 lin4	ka sai chhou lihn

cockroach[1] (coll)	v	甲由	gaahk jáat	gaak6 zaat2	kaahk chaat
cockroach[2] (wr)	v	蟑螂	jèung lòhng	zoeng4 long4	cheung lohng
cocktail[1]	n	酒會	jáu wúi	zau2 wui2	chau wui
cocktail[2] (de)	n	鷄尾酒	gài méih jáu	gai4 mei5 zau2	kai meih chau
cocktail[3]	n	開胃品	hòi waih bán	hoi4 wai6 ban2	hoi waih pan
cocoa (de)	n	唂咕	gūk gú	guk1 gu2	kuk ku
coconut	n	椰子	yèh jí	je4 zi2	yeh chi
code no	n	代號	dòih hòuh	dou6 hou6	toih houh
code of laws	n	法典	faat dín	faat3 din2	faat tin
code number	n	密碼	maht máah	mat6 maa5	maht maah
coexisting[1] /same category	n	共存	guhng chyùhn	gung1 cyun4	kuhng chhyuhn
coexisting[2] /contemporary	adj/n	同時存在	tùhng sìh chyùhn joih	tung4 si4 cyun4 zoi6	thuhng sih chhyuhn choih
coffee (de)	n	咖啡	ga fē	gaa3 fe1	ka fe
coffee color /brown	n	咖啡色	ga fē sīk	gaa3 fe1 sik1	ka fe sek
coffee shop	n	咖啡鋪	ga fē póu	gaa3 fe1 pou2	ka fe pou
coffee table /tea table	n	茶几	chàh gèi	caa4 gei4	chhah kei
coffin	n	靈柩	lehng /lìhng gauh	leng4 /ling4 gau6	lehng kauh
cog	n	輪齒	lèuhn chí	leon4 ci2	leuhn chhi
cognitive	adj	認知	yàhn jì	jan6 zi4	yahn chi
cogwheel	n	鈍齒輪	deuhn chī lèuhn	deon6 ci1 leon4	tuhn chhi lowhn
cohabit[1]	v	同居	tùhng gèui	tung4 geoi4	thuhng kwoi
cohabit[2]	v	住埋	jyuh màaih	zyu6 maai4	chyuh maaih
coil[1] /roll up	v	捲	gyún	gyun2	kyun
coil[2]	v	盤圈	pùhn hyùn	pun4 hyun4	phuhn hyun
coil around /twist together/entangle/tangle	n	纏結	chìhn git	cin4 git3	chhihn kit
coin	n	碎銀	seui ngàhn	seoi3 ngan4	swoi ngahn
coincidence /same time	n	巧合	háau hahp	haau2 hap6	haau hahp
coincidence by chance! /well done!	adj	眞係啱嘞!	jàn haih ngāam la!	zan4 hai6 ngaam4 lak3	chan haih ngaam la!
coincidencetally	adv	巧合地	háau hahp deih	haau2 hap6 dei6	haau hahp teih
coins	n	幣	baih	bai6	paih
coir	n	椰子殼之 纖維	yèh jí hok jī chīm wàih	je4 zi2 hok3 zi1 cim1 wai4	yeh chi hok chi chhim waih
coitus cut /sexual interrupt	n xy	性交中斷	sing gaau jùng tyúhn	sing3 gaau3 zung4 tyun5	seng kaau chung thyuhn
cold[1] /freeze	adj/n	凍	dung	dung3	tung
cold[2] for weather	n	冷	láahng	laang5	laahng
cold[3]	n	寒	hòhn	hon4	hohn
cold[4]	n	寒凍	hòhn dung	hong4 dung3	hohn tong
cold again! /returned cold		凍返啦!	dung fàan lā!	dung3 faan4 la1!	tung faan la!
cold cream for skin /face cream	n	雪花膏	syut fā gōu	syut3 faa1 gou1	syut fa kou
cold dish	n	冷盤	láahng pún	laang5 pun4	laahng phun

cold meat /frozen meat	n	凍肉	dung yuhk	dung3 juk6	tung yuhk
cold storage food /frozen food	n	冷藏食物	láahng chòhng sihk maht	laang5 cong4 sik6 mat6	laahng chhohng sehk maht
cold store	n	冷藏庫	láahng chòhng fu	laang5 cong4 fu3	laahng chhohng fu
cold water	n	凍水	dung séui	dung3 seoi2	tung swoi
collapse[1]	n	崩	bāng	bang1	pang
collapse[2] /fall	n	倒	dóu	dou2	tou
collapse[3]	v	倒下	dóu hah	dou2 haa6	tou hah
collapse[4]	v	瓦解	ngáh gáai	ngaa5 gaai2	ngah kaai
collapse[5] of building parts	v	倒塌	dóu taap	dou2 taap3	tou thaap
collapse[6] of building parts	v	樓宇部分 結構倒塌	làuh yúh bouh fān gít kau dóu taap	lou4 jyu5 bou6 fan1 git2 kau3 dou2 taap3	lauh yuh pouh fan kit khau tou thaap
collar[1]	n	領	lehng /lihng	leng3 /ling3	lehng
collar[2]	n	衣領	yī léhng	ji1 leng5	yi lehng
collar pin	n	領針	lehng /líhng jām	leng3 /ling5 zam1	lehng cham
collect[1] /pick	v	採	chói	coi2	chhoi
collect[2] /store	v	藏	chòhng	cong4	chhohng
collect[3] /gather	v	收集	sau jàahp	sau3 zaap6	sau chaahp
collection[1] /store	n	藏品	chòhng bán	cong4 ban2	chhohng pan
collection[2] keep	n	收藏品	sàu chòhng bán	sau4 cong4 ban2	sau chhohng pan
collective	adj	集體嘅	jaahp tái ge	zaap6 tai2 ge3	chaahp thai ke
collector[1]	n	收稅員	sàu seui yùhn	sau4 seui3 jyun4	sau soi yuhn
collector[2]	n	收藏家	sàu chòhng gā	sau4 cong4 gaa1	sau chhohng ka
collector[3]	n	收集者	sau jàahp jé	sau3 zaap6 ze2	sau chaahp che
college /university	n	大學	daaih hohk	daai6 hok6	taaih hohk
collide head	v	碰頭	pung tàuh	pung3 tau4	phung thauh
contention /quarrel/ strife/collided opinion	v	衝突	chùng daht	cung4 dat6	chhung taht
collision /crash/knock	v	碰撞	púng johng	pung2 zong6	phung chohng
colloquial usage /idiom/ commonly used phrase	n	慣用語	gwaan yuhng yúh	gwaan3 jung6 jyu5	kwaan yuhng yuh
colloquially	adv	口語	háu yúh	hau2 jyu5	hau yuh
colony	n	殖民地	jihk màhn deih	zik6 man4 dei6	chehk mahn teih
color[1] /colour /sex	n	色	sīk	sik1	sek
color[2]	n	顏色	aan /ngaan sīk	aan3 /ngaan3 sik1	aan /ngaan sek
color chalk /crayon	n	顏色粉筆	aan /ngaan sīk fán bāt	aan3 /ngaan3 sik1 fan2 bat1	aan /ngaan sek fan pat
colour blindness	adj	色盲	sīk màahng	sik1 maang4	sek maahng
colour picture	n	彩色相	chói sīk séung	coi2 sik1 soeng2	chhoi sek seung
colourful /multi colour/gaudy	adj	五顏六色	ngh ngaan luhk sīk	ng5 ngaan3 luk6 sik1	ngh ngaan luhk sek
colt /horse baby	n	馬仔	máh jái	maa5 zai2	mah chai
column[1] /pillar/pole/post	n	柱	chyúh	cyu5	chhyuh
column[2] newspaper	n	欄	làhn	laan4	laahn
column[3] newspaper	n	專欄	jyūn làhn	zyun1 laan4	chyun laahn

column⁴ /cylinder	n	圓柱	yùhn chyúh	jyun4 cyu5	yuhn chhyuh
coma /faint /shock	n	休克	yàu hāak	jau4 haak1	yau haak
comb¹	n	梳	sò	so4	so
comb²	n	毛刷	mòuh cháat	mou4 caat2	mouh chhaat
comb hair	v	梳頭	sò tàuh	so4 tau4	so thauh
combat	n	戰鬥	jin dau	zin3 dau3	chin tau
combatant	n	戰鬥員	jin dau yùhn	zin3 dau3 jyun4	chin tau yuhn
combination /coalition /integration/come together	n	結合	git hahp	git3 hap6	kit hahp
combine¹	v	合埋	hahp màaih	hap6 mai4	hahp maaih
combine² /conjoint/join together	v	結合	git hahp	git3 hap6	kit hahp
combine³ /merge/annex	v	併吞	pihng tàn	ping1 tan4	phehng than
combine⁴ /join together	v	銜接	hàahm jip	haam4 zip3	haahm chip
combine⁵ /unite/join	v	聯合	lyùhn hahp	lyun4 hap6	lyuhn hahp
combined	v	使結合	sai git hahp	sai3 git3 hap6	sai kit hahp
combined letters /articulating letters	n/v	連接字	lìhn jip jih	lin4 zip3 zi6	lihn chip chih
combustion /to burn	n	燃燒	yìhn sìu	jin4 siu4	yihn siu
come (coll) /arrive	v	嚟	lái	lai2	lai
come again	v	再嚟	joi lái	zoi3 lai2	choi lai
come along /arriving together	v	一起來	yāt héi loìh	jat1 hei2 loi4	yat hei loih
come and go	v	來來去去	loìh loìh heui heui	loi4/lai4 heoi3 heoi3	loih loih hoi hoi
come back¹	v	返嚟	fàan lái	faan4 lai2	faan lai
come back² (sl) return back	v	番嚟	fàan lái	faan4 lai2	faan lai
come back³	v	返來	fàan loìh	faan4 loi4	faan loih
come back⁴ /return back	v	回來	wùih lòih	wui4 loi4	wuih loih
come down /descend/ get down	v	落嚟	lohk lái	lok6 lai2	lohk lai
come here¹	v	過嚟	gwo lái	gwo3 lai2	kwo lai
come here² /walk to here	v	行過嚟	hàahng gwo lái	haang4 gwo3 lai2	haahng kwo lai
come in¹	v	進來	jeun loìh	zeon3 loi4	cheun loih
come in²	v	入嚟	yahp lái	jap6 lai2	yahp lai
come now	v	而家嚟喇	yìh gà lái la	ji4 ga4 lai2 laa3	yih ka lai la
come or go back /get back/go back/rejoin/ return	v	返回	fáan wùih	faan2 wui4	faan wuih
come to nothing¹ /nothing/doesn't matter	pron	無嘢/冇嘢	móuh yéh	mou5 je5	mouh yeh
come to nothing²	v	成為泡影	sèhng wàih paau yíng	seng4 wai4 paau3 jing2	sehng waih phaau yeng
come together	n	集合	jàahp hahp	zaap6 hap6	chaahp hahp
come up¹	v	上來	séuhng loìh	soeng5 loi4	seuhng loih
come up² (sl)	v	上嚟	séuhng lái	soeng5 lai2	seuhng lai
come up³ /to suggest	v	提出	tàih chēut	tai4 ceot1	thaih chhot
come up⁴	v	走過來	jáu gow lòih	zau2 gow3 loi4	chau kow loih

come with me!		跟我嚟!	gān ngóh lái!	gan1 ngo5 lai2!	kahn ngoh lai
comedian	n	喜劇演員	héi kehk yín yùhn	hei2 kek6 jin2 jyun4	hei kehk yin yuhn
comer a person	n	來嘅人	loìh ge yàhn	loi4 ge jan4	loih ke yahn
comet	n	衛星	waih sīng	wai6 sing	waih seng
comfort[1] /to relax	n	舒	syù	syu4	syu
comfort[2] /ease/to relax	n	舒適	syù sīk	syu4 sik1	syu sek
comfort[3] /consolation	n	安慰	òn /ngòn wai	on4 /ngon4 wai3	on /ngon wai
comfortable[1]	adj	舒服	syù fuhk	syu4 fuk6	syu fuhk
comfortable[2]	adj	舒適	syù sīk	syu4 sik1	syu sek
comics[1]	adj	漫畫	maahn wá	maan6 waa2	maahn wa
comics[2]	adj	喜劇漫畫	héi kehk maahn wá	hei2 kek6 maan6 waa2	hei kehk maahn wa
comics book[1]	n	漫畫書	maahn wá syù	maan6 waa2 syu4	maahn wa syu
comics book[2]	n	公仔書	gùng jái syù	gung4 zai2 syu4	kung chai syu
coming[1] (coll)	n	嚟	làai	laai4	laai
coming[2] (wr) /arrive/return	n/v	來	loìh	loi4	loih
coming[3]	n	來到	loìh dou	loi4 dou3	loih tou
coming here (coll)	n	嚟緊	làai gán	laai4 gan2	laai kan
coming out[1]	n	出來	chēut loìh	ceot1 loi4	chhot loih
coming out[2]	n	出緊	chēut gan	ceot1 gan3	chhot kan
coming out[3]	n	來緊	loìh gan	loi4 gan3	loih kan
coming third day /day after tomorrow/the day after tomorrow	adv	後日	hauh yaht	hau3 jat6	hauh yaht
coming to deliver	v	送貨嚟㗎	sung fo lái gá	sung3 fo3 lai2 gaa2	sung fo lai ka
comma /punct (,)	n	逗號	dauh houh	dau6 hou6	tauh houh
command[1] /leading site	n	勒	láhk	lak5	lahk
command[2] /order	n	令	lihng	ling4	lehng
command[3]	n	指揮	jí paai	zi2 pai3	chi phaai
command[4] /instruction/ order/tell	n	吩咐	fàn fu	fan4 fu3	fan fu
command by force[1]	n	迫令	bīk lihng	bik1 ling4	pek lehng
command by force[2] /compel/order by force/press/ order by pressured	n	強迫	kèuhng bīk	koeng4 bik1	kheuhng pek
commander	n	指揮官	jí fāi gùn	zi2 fai1 gun4	chi fai kun
commando	n	突擊隊員	daht gīk deuih yùhn	dat6 gik1 deoi6 jyun4	taht kek twoih yuhn
commemorate	v	紀念	géi lihm /nihm	gei2 lim6 /nim6	kei lihm /nihm
commencement	v	畢業典禮	bāt yíhp din láih	bat1 jip6 din3 lai5	pat yihp tin laih
comment[1]	n	註解	jyu gáai	zyu3 gaai2	chyu kaai
comment[2] /point out/ input/remark/commentary	n	留言	làuh yìhn	lau4 jin4	lauh yihn
comment[3] /commentary	n	評論	pìhng leuhn	ping4 leong6	phehng leuhn
comment[4]	n	註釋	jyu gáai	zyu3 gaai2	chyu kaai
comment[5]	n	評話	pìhng wá	ping4 wa2	phehng wa
commentary	n	註釋	jyu sīk	zyu3 sik1	chyu sek

commerce /business/ trade	n	商	sèung	soeng4	seung
commercial port	n	商埠	sèung fauh	soeng4 fau6	seung fauh
commission[1]	n	委任	wái yahm	wai2 jam4	wai yahm
commission[2]	n	調查委員會	tìuh chah wái yùhn wúi	tiu4 caa4 wai2 jyun4 wui2	thiuh chhah wai yuhn wui
commission[3] official	n	正式委託	jeng sīk wái tok	zeng3 sik1 wai2 tok3	cheng sek wai thok
commissioner /governor/sir/senior officer	n	長官	jéung gún	zoeng2 gun2	cheung kun
commissioner of police	n	警察的委員	gíng chaat dìk wái yùhn	ging2 caat dik4 wai2 jyun4	keng chhaat tek wai yuhn
commit[1]	v	犯事	faahn sìh	faan6 si6	faahn sih
commit[2] /sin /break law	v	犯罪	faahn jeuih	faan6 zeoi6	faahn cheuih
commit[3]	v	交給	gàau kāp	gaau4 kap1	kaau khap
commit suicide /kill oneself/self killed/suicide	ad/v	自殺	jih saat	zi6 saat3	chih saat
commitment	n	承諾	sìhng nohk	sing4 mok6	sehng nohk
commodity /merchandise/goods	n	商品	sèung bán	soeng4 ban2	seung pan
common[1] /general/ ordinary	adj	普通	póu tùng	pou2 tung4	phou thung
common[2] /normal/ ordinary/usual/usually	adj	平常	pèhng sèuhng	peng4 soeng4	phehng seuhng
common[3] /general	adj	普遍	póu pin	pou2 pin3	phou phin
common[4] /commonly seen	adj	常見	sèuhng gin	soeng4 gin3	seuhng kin
common boundary	n	交界	gàau gaai	gaau4 gaai3	kaau kaai
common ground /public opinion	n	共同點	guhng tùhng dím	gung6 tung4 dim2	kuhng thuhng tim
common land	n	公地	gùng deih	gung4 dei6	kung teih
common law	n	普通法	póu tùng faat	pou2 tung4 faat3	phou thung faat
common noun	n	普通名詞	pōu tùng mehng	pou1 tung4 meng6	phou thung mehng
common people /people/public people	n	人民	yàhn màhn	jan4 man4	yahn mahn
common phrases	n	常用短語	sèuhng yuhng dyún yúh	soeng4 jung6 dyun2 jyu5	seuhng yuhng tyun yuh
common sense	n	常識	sèuhng sīk	soeng4 sik1	seuhng sek
common usage	n	常用	sèuhng yuhng	soeng4 jung6	seuhng yuhng
common use[1] /public use	n	公共	gùng guhng	gung4 gung6	kung guhng
common use[2]	adj	通俗	tùng jùhk	tung4 zuk6	thung chuhk
commonly /commonly/ roughly/in general/usually	adv	大致上	daaih ji seuhng	daai6 zi3 soeng6	taaih chi seuhng
commonwealth /federation	n	聯邦	lyùhn bōng	lyun4 bong1	lyuhn pong
communicate[1]	v	溝通	kàu tùng	kau4 tung4	khau thung
communicate[2]	v	傳達	chyùhn daaht	cyun4 daat6	chhyuhn taaht
communications	n	通訊	tùng seun	tung4 seon3	thung swon

English	POS	中文	Yale	Jyutping	Romanization
communism	n	共產主義	guhng cháan jyú yih	gung1 caan2 zyu2 ji6	kuhng chhaan chyu yih
communist	n	共產黨員	guhng cháan dóng yùhn	gung1 caan2 dong2 jyun4	kuhng chhaan tong yuhn
communist party	n	共產黨	guhng cháan dóng	gung1 caan2 dong2	kuhng chhaan tong
community[1]	n	社區	séh kèui	se5 keoi4	seh khoi
community[2] /big society	n	社會	séh wúi	se5 wui2	seh wui
community[3]	n	公眾	gùng jung	gung4 jung3	kung chung
community[4] /collection/ team/group of people	n	團體	tyùhn tái	tyun4 tai2	thyuhn thai
community small	n	社群	séh kwàhn	se5 kwan4	seh khwahn
community centre	n	社區中心	séh kèui jùng sàm	se5 keoi4 zung3 sam4	seh khoi chung sam
community hall	n	社區大堂	séh kèui daaih tòhng	se5 keoi4 daai6 tong4	seh khoi taaih thohng
community service /social service	n	社會服務	séh wúi fuhk mouh	se5 wui2 fuk6 mou6	seh wui fuhk mouh
compact disc	n	光碟機	gwòng dihp gèi	gwong4 dip6 gei4	kwong tihp kei
companion /mate/ partner/friendship	n	伴侶	buhn léuih	bun6 leoi5	puhn lowih
companionship /friendship	n	友情	yáuh chìhng	jau5 cing4	yauh chhehng
company[1] /enterprise/ venture/firm business	n	企業	kéih yihp	kei5 jip6	kheih yihp
company[2] /professional	n	行	hóng	hong2	hong
company[3] /firm/business	n	商行	sèung hóng	soeng4 hong2	seung hong
company bus	n	廠車	chóng chè	cong2 ce1	chhong chhe
company law	ph	公司法	gūng sī faat	gung1 si1 faat3	kung si faat
compare[1] /contest/than	v	比	béi	bei2	pei
compare[2] /contrast	v	比較	béi gaau	bei2 gaau3	pei kaau
compared to /comparison/contrast	v	相比	sèung béi	soeng4 bei2	seung pei
compass[1]	n	指南針	jí nàahm jām	zi2 naam4 zam1	chi naahm cham
compass[2]	n	羅盤	lòh pùhn	lo4 pun4	loh phuhn
compass[3] drafting	n	圓規	yùhn kwāi	jyun4 kwai1	yuhn khwai
compassion /sympathy	n	同情	tùhng chìhng	tung4 cing4	thuhng chhehng
compassionate	adj	唔忍心	m̀ yán sàm	m4 jan2 sam4	mh yan sam
compel[1]	v	迫	bīk	bik1	pek
compel[2]	v	迫使	bīk sí	bik1 si2	pek si
compel[3] /order by force/ command by force	n/v	迫令	bīk lihng	bik1 ling4	pek lehng
command by force /compel/order by force/ order by pressured	n/v	監住	gàam jyuh	gaam4 zyu6	kaam chyuh
compensation[1]	v	賠償	pùih sèuhng	pui4 soeng4	phuih seuhng
compensation[2]	v	補償	bóu sèuhng	bou2 soeng4	pou seuhng
compensator	n	補償者	bóu sèuhng jé	bou2 soeng4 ze2	pou seuhng che
compete[1] /struggle/fight	v	鬥	dau	dau3	tau

compete[2]	v	競	gihng	ging6	kehng
competent[1]	adj	勝任	síng yam	sing2 jam3	seng yam
competent[2]	adj	有能力的	yáuh nang lìhk dìk	jau5 nang3 lik6 dik6	yauh nang lehk tek
competition[1] /match/ contest/race	n	比賽	béi choi	bei2 coi3	pei chhoi
competition[2] /rival	n	競爭	gihng jāang	ging6 zaang1	kehng chaang
competitive	adj	競爭嘅	gihng jāang ge	ging6 zaang1 ge3	kehng chaang ke
competitor[1]	n	競爭嘅人	gihng jàng ge yàhn	ging6 zang3 ge3 jan4	kehng chaang ke yahn
competitor[2]	n	競爭嘅者	gihng jāang ge jé	ging6 zaang1 ge3 ze2	kehng chaang ke che
competitor[3]	n	對手	deui sáu	deoi3 sau2	toei sau
competitor[4]	n	競爭者	gihng jāang jé	ging6 zaang1 ze2	kehng chaang che
complain /sue/lawsuit	v	訴	sou	sou3	sou
complaint/suit/sue /lawcourt/have a law suit	v	打官司	dá gùn sì	daa2 gun4 si4	ta kun si
complementary	n	補是物	bóu sih maht	bou2 si6 mat6	pou sih maht
complete[1] /finish	adj	成	sèhng	seng4	sehng
complete[2] /absolute/ whole/utter	adj	完全	yùhn chyùhn	jyun4 cyun4	yuhn chhyuhn
complete[3]	adj	齊備	chàih beih	cai4 bei6	chhaih peih
complete[4]	adj	齊全	chàih chyùhn	cai4 cyun4	chhaih chhyuhn
complete[5]	adj	完備	yùhn beih	jyun4 bei6	yuhn peih
complete[6]	adj	完整嘅	yùhn jíng ge	jyun4 zing2 ge3	yuhn cheng ke
completed[1] /finished	adj	清	chèng	ceng4	chheng
completed[2]	adj	全部	chyùhn bouh	cyun4 bou6	chhyuhn pouh
completed task /finished task	adj	完成咗	yùhn sèhng jó	jyun4 seng4 zo2	yuhn sehng cho
completely[1]	adv	十分	sahp fān	sap6 fan1	sahp fan
completely[2] /absolutely	adv	完全地	yùhn chyùhn dèih	jyun4 cyun4 dei6	yuhn chhyuhn teih
completely new /all new/brand new	adj	全新	chyùhn sān	cyun4 san1	chhyuhn san
complex[1] (not simple)	n	複	fūk	fuk1	fuk
complex[2]	n	複合	fū hahp	fu1 hap6	fu hahp
complex[3]	n	合成	hahp sehng	hap6 seng4	hahp sehng
complex[4]/difficult /hard/complicated	v/adj	複雜(嘅)	fūk jaahp (ge)	fuk1 zaap6 ge3	fuk chaahp (ke)
complex company	n	聯合企業	lyùhn hahp kéih yihp	lyun4 hap6 kei5 jip6	lyuhn hahp kheih yihp
complexion	n	面色	mihn sīk	min6 sik1	mihn sek
compliance	n	順從	seuhn chùhng	seon6 cung4	swohn chhuhng
complicate	v	使複雜化	sai fūk jaahp fa	sai3 fuk1 zaap6 faa3	sai fuk chaahp fa
complicated /difficult to deal/hard to understand		疑難	yih làahn /nàahn	ji6 laan4 /naan4	yih laahn /naahn
comply with /obey	v	依從	yi chùhng	ji3 cung4	yi chhuhng
components	n	成分	sèhng fahn	seng4 fan6	sehng fahn
compose[1]	v	撰	syún	syun2	syun
compose[2] /write	v	寫	sé	se2	se

English		Chinese	Yale	Jyutping	
compose[3] /write/make/ do/works	v	作	jok	zok3	chok
compose[4]	v	作詩	jok sì	zok3 si4	chok si
compose[5] /constitute	v	組成	jóu sìhng	zou2 sing4	chou sehng
composer[1] /songwriter	n	作曲家	jok kūk gā	zok3 kuk1 gaa1	chok khuk ka
composer[2] /songwriter	n	作曲者	jok kūk jé	zok3 kuk1 ze2	chok khuk che
composing	n	排字	paaih jih	paai6 zi6	phaaih chih
composite	adj	合成	hahp sèhng	hap6 seng4	hahp sehng
composition[1]	n	寫作	sé jok	se2 zok3	se chok
composition[2] /structure	n	構造	kau jouh	kau3 zou6	khau chouh
compound[1] /wall around area	n	有圍牆	yáuh wàih cheuhng	jau5 wai4 coeng6	yauh waih chheuhng
compound[2] /mixture/ compost	n	混合物	wahn hahp maht	wan6 hap6 mat6	wahn hahp maht
comprehensive[1]	adj	詳盡	chèuhng jeuhn	coeng4 zeong6	chheuhng cheuhn
comprehensive[2]	adj	理解	leih gaai	lei5 gaai3	leih kaai
comprehensive[3]	adj	理解嘅	leih gaai ge	lei5 gaai3 ge3	leih kaai ke
compress[1]	v	壓	áat	aat2	aat
compress[2]	v	壓縮	áat sùk	aat2 suk4	aat suk
compress[3]	v	加壓	gá ngaat	gaa2 ngaat3	ka ngaat
compress[4]	v	壓柞	áat ja	aat2 za3	aat cha
compressor	n	壓縮機	áat sùk gèi	aat2 suk4 gei4	aat suk kei
comprise /include/ involve/inclusive	v	包括	bàau kwut	baau4 kwut3	paau khwut
compromise /to reach terms	n	妥協	tóh hip	to5 hip3	thoh hip
compulsive	adj	強迫嘅	kèuhng bīk ge	koeng4 bik1 ge3	kheuhng pek ke
compulsorily[1]	adj	夾硬	gaap ngáang	gaap3 ngaang2	kaap ngaang
compulsorily[2]	adj	強迫地	kèuhng bīk deih	koeng4 bik1 dei6	kheuhng pek teih
compulsory[1]	adj	必修	bīt sàu	bit1 sau4	pit sau
compulsory[2]	adj	必須做的	bìt sèui jòuh dìk	bit4 seoi4 zou6 dik4	pit swoi chouh tek
computer	n	電腦	dihn nóuh	din6 nou5	tihn nouh
computer pattern	n	電腦程式	dihn lóuh /nóuh chìhng sīk	din6 lou5 /nou5 cing4 sik1	tihn louh /nouh chehng sek
computer structure /computer program	n	電腦程式	dihn nóuh chìhng sīk	din6 nou5 cing4 sik1	tihn nouh chehng sek
concave[1] /hollow/valley	n	凹	lāp /nāp	lap1 /nap1	lap /nap
concave[2]	n	凹	āau	aau1	aau
conceal[1] /hide/cover up	n/v	隱藏	yán chòhng	jan2 cong4	yan chhohng
conceal[2] /hide/put aside	v	收埋	sàu màaih	sau4 maai4	sau maaih
conceal[3]	v	隱瞞	yán mùhn	jan2 mun4	yan muhn
conceal room	n	藏室	chòhng sāt	cong4 sat1	chhohng sat
concede /acknowledge	v	承認	sìhng yihng	sing4 jing6	sehng yehng
conceivable	adj	可想到	hó séung dou	ho2 soeng2 dou3	ho seung tou
concentrate[1]	v	中心	jùng sàm	zung4 sam4	chung sam
concentrate[2]	v	全心	chyùhn sàm	cyun4 sam4	chhyuhn sam

concentrate[3] /condense/condensation	n/v	濃縮	lùhng /nùhng sūk	lung4 /nung4 suk1	luhng /nuhng suk
concepts[1] /conception/ construct/opinion/idea	n	概念	koi lihm /nihm	koi3 lim6 /nim6	khoi lihm /nihm
concepts[2] /views /thought/ideology/conceptual	n	觀念	gùn lihm /nihm	gun4 lim6 /nim6	kun lihm /nihm
concern[1] /related/relevant	v	有關	yáuh gwàan	jau5 gwaan4	yauh kwaan
concern[2] /regard/to care/ pay attention/care about	n	關心	gwàan sàm	gwaan4 sam4	kwaan sam
concern[3]	v	掛住	gwa jyuh	gwa3 zyu6	kwa chyuh
concern[4]	v	關懷	gwàan wàaih	gwaan4 waai4	kwaang waaih
concert	n	音樂會	yàm ngòhk wúi	jam4 ngok6 wui2	yam ngohk wui
concert hall	n	音樂廳	yàm ngòhk tèng	jam4 ngok6 teng4	yam ngohk theng
concession /discount	n	讓步	yeuhng bouh	joeng6 bou6	yeuhng pouh
conch[1]	n	貝殼	bui hok	bui3 hok3	pui hok
conch[2]	n	海螺殼	hói lòh hok	hoi2 lo4 hok3	hoi loh hok
conclude	v	斷定	tyúhn dehng /dihng	tyun5 deng6 /ding6	thyuhn tehng
conclude a bargain /agree	v	約定	yeuk dehng /dihng	joek3 deng6 /ding6	yeuk tehng
conclusion[1] /result/in the end/outcome/effect	n	結果	git gwó	git3 gwo2	kit gwo
conclusion[2]	n	終結	jūng git	jung1 git3	chung kit
concord[1]	n	和睦	wòh muhk	wo4 muk6	woh muhk
concord[2]	n	協和	hip wòh	hip3 wo4	hip woh
concrete	n	混凝土	wahn yihng tóu	wan6 jing4 tou2	wahn yehng thou
concrete layer[1]	v	石屎師傅	sehk sí sī fuh	sek6 si2 si1 fu6	sehk si si fuh
concrete layer[2]	v	石屎佬	sehk sí lóu	sek6 si2 lou2	sehk si lou
concrete mixer	n	混凝土攪拌機	wahn yihng tóu gáau buhn gèi	wan6 jing4 tou2 gaau2 bun6 gei4	wahn yehng thou kaau puhn kei
concubine	n	妾侍	chip sih	cip3 si6	chhip sih
concur	v	一致	yāt ji	jat1 zi3	yat chi
concussion[1] /to shake	n	震蕩	jan dohng	zan3 dong6	chan tohng
concussion[2]	n	腦震蕩	lóuh /nóuh jan dohng	lou5 /nou5 zan3 dong6	louh /nouh chan tohng
concussion[3]	n	腦震盪	lóuh /nóuh jan dohng	lou5 /nou5 zan3 dong6	louh /nouh chan tohng
condemn[1] /criticize/ misbehaviour	v	懲戒	chìhng gaai	cing4 gaai3	chhehng kaai
condemn[2]	v	判處	pun chyú	pun3 cyu2	phun chhyu
condemn[3] /to criticize	v	譴責	hín jaak	hin2 zaak3	hin chaak
condemnation[1] /censure	n	譴責	hín jaak	hin2 zaak3	hin chaak
condemnation[2]	n	非難	fēi làahn	fei1 laan4	fei laahn
condemnation[3]	n	非難的理由	fēi làahn dīk léih yàuh	fei1 laan4 dik1 lei5 jau4	fei laahn tek leih yauh
condenser	n	壓縮器	áat sùk hei	aat2 suk4 hei3	aat suk hei

English	POS	中文	Yale	Jyutping	
condition of marital/ marital status	n	狀況	johng fong	zong6 fong3	chohng fong
conditional	adj	有條件	yáuh tìuh gín	jau5 tiu4 gin2	yauh thiuh kin
conditions	n	細則	sái jāk	sai2 zak1	sai chak
condolence[1]	n	吊慰	diu wai	diu3 wai3	tiu wai
condolence[2]	n	弔辭	gúng chìh	gung2 ci4	kung chhih
condolent	n	弔慰	gúng wai	gung2 wai3	kung wai
condom[1] (coll)	n	雨褸	yúh lāu	jyu5 lau1	yuh lau
condom[2]	n	避孕套	beih yahn tou	bei6 jan6 tou3	peih yahn thou
condom[3]	n	陰莖套	yàm gíng tou	jam4 ging2 tou3	yam keng
conduct[1] /manner/port	n	端	dyūn	dyun1	tyun
conduct[2] carry out		行為操守	hàhng wàih chòu sáu	hang4 wai4 cou4 sau2	hahng waih chhou sau
conduct[3] command	v	指揮	jí fāi	zi2 fai1	chi fai
conductor[1] /order/ commanding	n	指揮	jí fāi	zi2 fai1	chi fai
conductor[2] command/ captain of ship	n	領導者	léhng /líhng douh jé	leng5 /ling5 dou6 ze2	lehng touh che
conductor[3] of bus	n	售票員	sauh piu yùhn	sau6 piu3 jyun4	sauh phiu yuhn
cone[1]	n	圓錐體	yùhn jèui tái	jyun4 zeoi4 tai2	yuhn choi thai
cone[2] /traffic cone	n	雪糕筒	syut gòu túng	syut3 gou4 tung2	syut kou thung
cone of icecream /ice-cream cone	n	甜筒	tìhm túng	tim4 tung2	thihm tung
confederation	n	聯合體	lyùhn hahp tái	lyun4 hap6 tai2	lyuhn hahp thai
conference /convention/ congress/council/meeting	n	會議	wuih yíh	wui6 ji5	wuih yih
conferred[1]	vt&i	商議	sèung yi	soeng4 ji3	seung yi
conferred[2]	vt&i	協商	hip sèung	hip3 soeng4	hip seung
confidant	n	知己	jì géi	zi4 gei2	chi kei
confidence[1]	n	自信	jih seun	zi6 seon3	chih swon
confidence[1] /faith/ have a faith in	n	信任	seun yahm	seon3 jam4	swon yahm
confident[1]	adj	把握	bá ngāak	baa2 aak1/ak1	pa ngaak
confident[2] /sure	adj	確信	kok seun	kok3 seon3	khok swon
confidential	adj	密件	maht gihn	mat6 gin6	maht kihn
confidential in /trustful	adj	信任	seun yahm	seon3 jam4	swon yahm
configuration	n	形態	yìhng táai	jing4 taai2	yehng thaai
confirm[1] /ensure	v	確	kok	kok3	khok
confirm[2] /sure/be sure/ certain/positive	adj	肯定	háng dehing /dìhng	hang2 deng6 /ding6	hang tehing
confirm[3]/verify	v	證實	jing saht	zing3 sat6	cheng saht
confirm[4] /reconfirm/ identify/reconfirm	v	確認	kok yihng	kok3 jing3	khok yehng
confiscate /seize/ forfeiture	v	沒收	muht sau	mut6 sau3	muht sau
confiscation /forfeiture	n	充公	chùng gùng	cung4 gung4	chhung kung
conform[1]	v	遵照	jèun jiu	zeon4 ziu3	cheun jiu

English	POS	Chinese	Yale	Jyutping	Romanization
conform[2] respect agreement/abide	v	遵守	jèun sáu	zeon4 sau2	cheun sau
confront[1]	v	迎面	ying mìhn	jing3 min6	yeng mihn
confront[2]/face to face/facing	v	面對	mihn deui	min6 deoi3	mihn toei
Confucianism Chinese	n	孔教	húng gaau	hung2 gaau3	hung kaau
Confucius[1] Chinese a person	n	孔子	húng jí	hung2 zi2	hung chi
Confucius[2]/Sadhu Chinese religion	n	中國聖人	jùng gwók sing yàhn	zung4 gwok2 sing3 jan4	chung kwok seng yahn
Confucius[3]	n	尼泊爾聖人	nèih bòhk yíh sing yàhn	nei4 bok6 ji5 sing3 jan4	neih pohk yih seng yahn
confused[1]	adj	混	wahn	wan6	wahn
confused[2]	adj	淆	ngàauh	ngaau6	ngàauh
confused[3]	adj	迷	màih	mai4	maih
confused[4]/confusion	adj	混亂	wahn lyuhn	wan6 lyun6	wahn lyuhn
confused[5]	adj	混淆	wahn ngàauh	wan6 ngaau6	wahn ngaauh
confused[6]	adj	困惑	kwan waahk	kwan3 waak6	khwan waahk
confused[7]/doubtful/indecisive/uncertain	adj	心大心細	sàm daaih sàm sai	sam4 daai6 sam4 sai3	sam taaih sam sai
confusing /be confused	adj	令人困惑	ling yàhn kwan waahk	ling3 jan4 kwan3 waak6	leng yahn khwan waahk
confusion	n	混淆	wahn ngàauh	wan6 ngaau6	wahn ngaauh
congeal /freeze	v	凝	yìhng	jing4	yehng
congee[1]/gruel/porridge/rice gruel	n	粥	jūk	zuk1	chuk
congee[2] /leave/depart bye bye	n	告別	gou bìht	gou3 bit6	kou piht
congenital /natural/inborn/before birth	adj	先天	sìn tìn	sin4 tin4	sin thin
conger-pike eel[1]	n	海鰻	hói màahn	hoi2 maan4	hoi maahn
conger-pike eel[2]	n	門鱔	mùhn síhn	mun4 sin5	muhn sihn
congest /jams/crowd/gathering/congestion	adj	塞	sāk	sak1	sak
congested[1] /crowd	adj	迫	bīk	bik1	pek
congested[2]	adj	擁塞	yúng sāk	jung2 sak1	yung sak
congestion[1]	adj	擠擁	jāi yúng	zai1 jung2	chai yung
congestion[2] /very/very much/impletion/full of	adj	充滿	chùng múhn	cung4 mun5	chhung muhn
congestion[3] /blood congestion/hyperemia	adj	充血	chùng hyut	cung4 hyut3	chhung hyut
congratulated	v	預祝	yuh jūk	jyu6 zuk1	yuh chuk
congratulate /congratulation	n/v	祝賀	jūk hoh	zuk1 ho6	chuk hoh
congratulation[1]	n	恭喜	gùng hēi	gung4 hei1	kung hei
congratulation[2]	n	慶賀	hing hoh	hing3 ho6	heng hoh
congratulation[3]	n	祝詞	jūk chìh	zuk1 ci4	chuk chhih

congratulation[4]	n	賀詞	hoh chìh	ho6 ci4	hoh chhih
congratulation[5]	n	祝福	jūk fūk	zuk1 fuk1	chuk fuk
congratulations	n	慶祝	hing jūk	hing3 zuk1	heng chuk
congratulator[1]	n	賀詞人	hoh chìh yàhn	ho6 ci4 jan4	hoh chhih yahn
congratulator[2]	n	慶賀者	hing hoh jé	hing3 ho6 ze2	heng hoh che
congratulator[3]	n	慶賀嘅人	hing hoh ge yàhn	hing3 ho6 ge3 jan4	heng hoh ge yahn
congratulator[4]	n	祝賀嘅人	jūk hoh ge yàhn	zuk1 ho6 ge3 jan4	chuk hoh ke yahn
congratulator[5]	n	道賀者	dou hoh jé	dou3 ho6 ze2	tou hoh che
congress[1] /diet / parliament	n	國會	gwok wúi	gwak3 wui2	kwok wui
congress[2] /parliament/ general assembly/lower house/house of parliament/ legislative assembly	n	議會	yíh wúi	ji5 wui2	yih wui
conjecture /guessing/ speculative	v	推測	tèui chàak	teoi4 caak4	thoi chhaak
conjugation[1] grammar	n	詞形變化	chìh yìhng bin fa	ci4 jing4 bin3 fa3	chhih yihng pin fa
conjunction[2]	n	連接詞	lìhn jip chìh	lin4 zip3 ci4	lihn chip chhih
connabis sativa /hashish/hemp/marijuana	n	大麻	daaih màh	daai6 maa4	taaih mah
connection[1] /relation	n	係	haih	hai6	haih
connection[2] /link	n	關係	gwàan haih	gwaan4 hai6	kwaan haih
connection[3]	n	聯絡	lyùhn lok	lyun4 lok3	lyuhn lok
connection linked /connexion/linkages/related	n	關聯	gwàan lyùhn	gwaan4 lyun4	kwaan lyuhn
connection rod	n	活塞桿	wuht sàk gòn	wut6 sak6 gon4	wuht sak kon
connector	n	連結者	lìhn git jé	lin4 git3 ze2	lihn kit che
conquer capture/by force	v	攻克	gói hāak	goi2 haak1	koi haak
conscience /discerning	n	良心	lèuhng sàm	loeng4 sam4	leuhng sam
conscienceless[1]	adj	冇良心	móuh lèuhng sām	mou5 loeng4 sam1	mouh leuhng sam
conscienceless[2]	adj	沒良心	muht lèuhng sàm	mut6 loeng4 sam4	muht leuhng sam
conscientious	adj	有良心	yáuh lèuhng sām	jau5 loeng4 sam1	yauh leuhng sam
conscious	adj	有知覺	yáuh jì gok	jau5 zi4 gok3	yauh chi kok
consciousless /in a coma/passed out	adj	不省人事	bāt síng yàhn sih	bat1 sing2 jan4 si6	pat sing yahn sih
consciousness	n	有知覺	yáuh jì gok	jau5 zi4 gok3	yauh chi kok
consecutive	adj	連續不斷	lìhn juhk bāt dyún	lin4 zuk6 bat1 dyun2	lihn chuhk pat tyun
consensus	n	輿論	yùh leuhn	jyu4 leon6	yuh leuhn
consequence[1] (sl) /event	n	結果	git gwó	git3 gwo2	kit gwo
consequence[2] /in the end/ conclusion	n	因此	yàn chí	jan4 ci2	yan chhi
consequence[3] /as a result	n/v	後果	hauh gwó	hau6 gwo2	hauh kwo
consequence of sin /sin	n	孽	yihp	jip6	yihp
conservative	adj	保守	bóu sáu	bou2 sau2	pou sau

consider /considerable /regard	adj/v	考慮	háau leuih	haau2 leoi6	haau lowih
considerable /great value	adj	相當大	sèung dòng daaih	soeng4 dong4 daai6	seung tong taaih
considerate[1]	adj	審慎	sām sàhn	sam1 san6	sam sahn
considerate[2]	adj	有心	yáuh sàm	jau5 sam4	yauh sam
consideration[1]	n	體諒	tái leuhng	tai2 loeng6	thai leuhng
consideration[2] /thought/think about/think of/think over	n	考慮	háau leuih	haau2 leoi6	haau lowih
consideration[3]	n	報酬	pou chàuh	pou3 cau4	phou chhauh
considering /with an eye to	prep	考慮到	háau leuih dou	haau2 leoi6 dou3	haau lowih tou
consignor /issued by	n	發貨人	faat fo yàhn	faat3 fo3 yan4	faat fo yahn
consistency	n	一致	yāt ji	jat1 zi3	yat chi
consistently /start to finish	adv	一貫	yāt gun	jat1 gun3	yat kun
consists	v	組成	jóu sèhng /sìhng	zou2 seng4 /sing4	chou sehng
consolation prize	n	安慰獎	òn /ngòn wai jéung	on4 /ngon4 wai3 zoeng2	on /ngon wai cheung
console[1] /fondle rub/ softly rub	v	撫	fú	fu2	fu
console[2]/give sympathy	v	安慰	òn /ngòn wai	on4 /ngon4 wai3	on /ngon wai
consolidate[1]	v	鞏固	gúng gu	gung2 gu3	kung gu
consolidate[2]	v	使聯合	sái lyùhn gap	sai2 lyun4 gap3	sai lyuhn kap
consolidate[3] /merge	v	合併	hahp peng	hap6 peng3	hahp pheng
consonant[1] /alphabet /letter	n	字母	jih móuh	zi6 mou5	chih mouh
consonant[2]	n	子音	jí yām	zi2 jam1	chi yam
consonant[3]	n	輔音	fuh yām	fu6 jam1	fuh yam
conspirator /plotter	n	陰謀嘅人	yàm màuh ge yàhn	jam4 mau4 ge3 jan4	yam mauh ke yahn
constant	adj	固定的	gu dehng dìk	gu3 deng6 dik4	ku tehng tek
constantly /often/again & again/frequently/time & again/repeatedly	adv	時常地	sìh seung dèih	si4 soeng3 dei6	sih sìh seung dèih
constellation	n	星座	sèng chóh	seng4 co5	seng chhoh
constipated	adj	便秘	bihn bei	bin6 bei3	pihn pei
constipated of urine	n	排尿阻滯	pàaih liuh /niuh jó jaih	paai4 liu6 /niu6 zo2 zai6	phaaih liuh /niuh cho chaih
constituent	n	組成	jóu sìhng	zou2 seng4	chou sehng
constituent assembly	n	國民代表 大會	gwok màhn doih bíu daaih wúi	gwok3 man4 doi6 biu2 daai6 wui2	kwok mahn toih piu taaih wui
constitute[1]	v	制定	jai dìhng	zai3 ding6	chai tehng
constitute[2]	v	構成	kau sìhng	kau3 sing4	khau sehng
constitute[3]	v	合法	hahp faat	hap6 faat3	hahp faat
constitution[1] of a country	n	憲	hin	hin3	hin
constitution[2] of a country	n	憲法	hin faat	hin3 faat3	hin faat
constitution[3] /rule of law	n	法規	faat kwài	faat3 kwai4	faat khwai

English		Chinese	Yale	Jyutping	Other
constitutor	n	構成者	kau sìhng jé	kau3 sing4 ze2	khau sehng che
construct[1] /raise/rise /up/get up/build	v	起	héi	hei2	hei
construct[2] build	v	構成	kau sìhng	kau3 sing4	khau sehng
contractor (work)	n	承辦商	sìhng bàahn sēung	sing4 baan6 soeng1	sehng paahn seung
construction[1]	n	建造	gin jouh	gin3 zou6	kin chouh
construction[2]	n	建造術	gin jouh seuht	gin3 zou6 seot6	kin chouh swoht
construction co	n	建築公司	gin jūk gùng sì	gin3 zuk1 gung4 si4	kin chuk kung si
construction site	n	工地	gùng deih	gung4 dei6	kung teih
construction work/ engineer work/engineering /project engineering	n	工程	gùng chìhng	gung4 cing4	kung chhehng
consul /consul general	n	領事	léhng /líhng sí	leng5 /ling5 si2	lehng si
consul general	n	總領事	júng léhng sí	zung2 leng5 si2	chung lehng si
consular	n	領事嘅	léhng /líhng sí ge	leng5 /ling5 si2 ge3	lehng si ke
consulate /embassy	n	領事館	léhng /líhng sí gún	leng5 /ling5 si2 gun2	lehng si kun
consulate general	n	總領事館	júng léhng /líhng sí gún	zung2 leng5 /ling5 si2 gun2	chung lehng si kun
consult	v	諮詢	jì sèun	zi4 seon4	chi swon
consult a dictionary	v	查字典	chàh jih dín	caa4 zi6 din2	chhah chih tin
consult with /discuss	v	商量	sèung lèuhng	soeng4 loeng4	seung leuhng
consult with	v	交換意見	gàau wuhn yi gin	gaau4 wun6 ji3 gin3	kaau wuhn yi kin
consultant /advisor	n	顧問	gu mahn	gu3 man6	ku mahn
consultation[1]	n	會診	wuih chán	wui6 can2	wuih chhan
consultation[2]	n	諮詢	jì sèun	zi4 seon4	chi swon
consume/to used/to use up	v	消耗	sìu hou	siu4 hou3	siu hou
consumer	n	消費者	sìu fai jé	siu4 fai3 ze2	siu fai che
consumer council	n	消委會	sìu wái wuih	siu4 wai2 wui6	siu wai wuih
consuming /consumption	adj	消耗	sìu hou	siu4 hou3	siu hou
contact /touch	n	接觸	jip jūk	zip3 zuk1	chip chuk
contact lenses	n	隱形眼鏡	yán yìhng ngáahn	jan2 jing4 ngaan5 geng2	yan yihng ngaahn keng
contagious[1] by bacteria /epidemical	adj	感菌	gám kwán	gam2 kwan2	kam khwan
contagious[2]	adj	傳染性	chyùhn yíhm sing	cyun4 jim5 sing3	chhyuhn yihm seng
contagious disease /epidemic disease	adj	傳染病	chyùhn yíhm behng	cyun4 jim5 beng6	chhyuhn yihm pehng
contain[1]/incorporate	v	包含	bàau ham	baau4 ham3	paau ham
contain[2]	v	容忍	yung yān	jung3 jan1	yung yan
containable /accommodate	v	容納	yùhng laahp /naahp	jung4 laap6 /naap6	yuhng laahp /naahp
container[1] /cupboard/ closet	n	櫃	gwaih	gwai6	kwaih
container[2] for goods	n	貨櫃	fo gwaih	fo3 gwai6	fo kwaih
contaminate	v	沾染	jīm yíhm	zim1 jim5	chim yihm

contamination /pollution/environment dirty /making environment dirty	n	污染	wù yíhm	wu4 jim5	wu yihm
contemplate /think	v	惗	lám /nám	lam2 /nam2	lam /nam
contemporary[1] /person of same age	n	同齡人	tùhng lìhng yàhn	tung4 ling4 jan4	thuhng lehng yahn
contemporary[2]	n	當代	dong doih	dong3 doi6	tong toih
contempt[1] /disgrace/ dishonour	n	恥辱	chí yuhk	ci2 juk6	chhi yuhk
contempt[2] /hates/insult /no respect	n	藐視	míuh sih	miu5 si6	miuh sih
contempt[3]	n	輕視	hìng sih	heng4/hing4 si6	hing sih
contemptuous	adj	輕蔑	hēng miht	heng1 mit6	heng miht
content	n	內容	loih /noih yùhng	loi6 /noi6 jung4	loih /noih yuhng
contented[1]	adj	知足	jì jūk	zi3 zuk1	chi chuk
contented[2]	adj	安心	òn /ngòn sàm	on4 /ngon4 sam4	on /ngon sam
contention /dispute	n	爭吵	jàng cháau	zang3 caau2	chang chhaau
contents /list/table/ catalog/catalogue	n	目錄	muhk luhk	muk6 luk6	muhk luhk
contest wrangle	n	爭辯	jàng bihn	zang4 bin6	chang pihn
context[1]	n	上下文	seuhng hah màhn	soeng6 haa6 man6	seuhng hah mahn
context[2] /sequence of event		來龍去脈	lòih lùhng heui mahk	loi4 lung4 heoi3 mak6	loih luhng hoi mahk
continence[1]/self-control	n	克制	hàak jai	haak6 zai3	haak chai
continence[2]/wish control	n	節欲	jit yuhk	zit3 juk6	chit yuhk
continence[3] sex control /control of feelings		節制	jit jai	zit3 zai3	chit chai
continence[4]/control of feelings/self sex control[(sl)]	n	自制	jih jai	zi6 zai3	chih chai
contingency[1]	n	意外情況	yí òih /ngoih ching fóng	ji2 oi6 /ngoi6 cing4 fong2	yi oih /ngoih chheng fong
contingency[2]	n	意外事故	yí òih /ngoih sih gu	ji2 oi6 /ngoin si6 gu3	yi oih /ngoih sih ku
contingent /delegation /mission	n	代表團	doih bíu tyùhn	dou6 biu2 tyun4	toih piu thyuhn
continually /again & again/time to time/thick and fast/ repeatedly/ frequently	adv	頻頻	pàhn pàhn	pan4 pan4	phahn phahn
continuants	v	連續音	lìhn juhk yām	ling4 zuk6 jam1	lihn chuhk yam
continue[1] /extend/ prolong/stretch out	v	延長	yìhn chèuhng	jin4 coeng4	yihn chheuhng
continue[2] /hold back/ reservation/keeping	v	保留	bóu lau	bou2 lau3	pou lau
continue upholding	adj	堅持	gīn chìh	gin1 ci4	kin chhih
continued	adj	未續約	meih juhk yeuk	mei6 zuk6 joek3	meih chuhk yeuk
continuing[1] /_ing	n	緊	gán	gan2	kan
continuing[2] /having	v	持續	chìh juhk	ci4 juk6	chhih chohk
continuous	adj	連續的	lìhn juhk dīk	lin4 zuk6 dik1	lihn chuhk tik

continuously[1]	adv	不斷地	bāt dyún dèih	bat1 dyun2 dei6	pat tyun teih
continuously[2]	adv	連續不斷地	lìhn juhk bāt dyún deih	lin4 zuk6 bat1 dyun2 dei6	lihn chuhk pat tyun teih
contortionist	n	作柔體表演者	jok yau tái bíu yín jé	zok3 yau3 tai2 biu2 jin2 ze2	chok yau thai piu yin che
contraception /preventing from pregnant	n	避孕	beih yan	bei6 jan3	peih yan
contract[1]	n	合同	hahp tùhng	hap6 tung4	hahp thuhng
contract[2] /treaty	n	合約	hahp yeuk	hap6 joek3	hahp yeuk
contract out	v	退出合約	teui chēut hahp yeuk	teoi3 ceot1 hap6 joek3	thoi chhot hahp yeuk
contract period	n	合約期	hahp yeuk kèih	hap6 joek3 kei4	hahp yeuk kheih
contractor[1] (a person)	n	承包人	sìhng bàau yàhn	sing4 baau4 jan4	sehng paau yahn
contractor[2]	n	承造人	sìhng jouh yàhn	sing4 zou6 jan4	sehng chou yahn
contractor[3] (a person)	n	承辦人	sìhng baahn yàhn	sing4 baan6 jan4	sehng paahn yahn
contractor[4] (work)	n	承包商	sìhng bàau sèung	sing4 baau4 soeng4	sehng paau seung
contractor[5]	n	承判商	sìhng pun sèung	sing4 pun3 soeng4	sehng phun seung
contractor[6]	n	承建商	sìhng gín sèung	sing4 gin2 soeng4	sehng kin seung
contractor[7]	n	立契約人	lahp kai yeuk yàhn	lap6 kai3 joek3 jan4	lahp khai yeuk yahn
contradiction	n	矛盾	màauh téuhn	maau4 teen5	maauh thohn
contradictory	adj	唔一致	m̀ yāt ji	m4 jat1 zi3	mh yat chi
contraflow	n	公路上一雙側向行駛	gùng louh séuhng yāt sēung jāk heung hàhng sāi	gung4 lou6 soeng5 jat1 soeng1 zak1 hoeng3 hang4 sai1	kung louh seuhng yat seung chak heung hahng sai
contrapuntal	adj	對位元法 (音樂)	deui wái yùhn faat (yàm ngohk)	deoi3 wai2 jyun4 faat3 (jam4 ngok6)	toei wai yuhn faat (yam ngohk)
contrary[1]	adj	對立	deui lahp	deoi3 lap6	toei lahp
contrary[2]	adj	相反	seung fáan	soeng3 faan2	seung faan
contrary[3] /counter	adj	相反地	sèung fáan deih	soeng4 faan2 dei6	seung faan teih
contribute /offer	v	貢獻	gung hin	gung3 hin3	kung hin
contribution/donation	n	投稿	tàuh góu	tau4 gou2	thauh kou
contributor[1]	n	貢獻嘅人	gung hin ge yàhn	gung3 hin3 ge3 jan4	kung hin ke yahn
contributor[2]	n	投稿嘅人	tàuh góu ge yàhn	tau4 gou2 ge3 jan4	thauh kou ke yahn
contributor[3] /donor	n	捐贈者	gyùn jahng jé	gyun4 zang6 ze2	kyun chahng che
control[1]	n	控	hung	hung3	hung
control[2]	n	持	chi	ci3	chhi
control[3] /to manage	n	治	jih	zi6	chih
control[4] /domination	n	控制	hung jai	hung3 zai3	hung chai
control[5]	n	克服	hāak fuhk	haak1 fuk6	haak fuhk
control[6] /handling /deal with/manageable/treat/ transact	n	處理	chyú léih	cyu2 lei5	chhyu leih
control room	n	控制室	hung jai sāt	hung3 zai3 sat1	hung chai sat
controllable /manageable	adj	可管理	hó gún léih	ho2 gun2 lei5	ho kun leih
controlled[1]	adj	受鎮壓	sauh jan aat /ngaat	sau6 zan3 aat3 /ngaat3	sauh chan aat/ngaat
controlled[2]	adj	受控制	sauh hung jai	sau6 hung3 zai3	sauh hung chai
controller[1]/manager	n	管理員	gùn léih yùhn	gun4 lei5 jyun4	kun leih yuhn

controller[2]	n	管制者	gùn jai jé	gun4 zai3 ze2	kun chai che
controller[3]/manipulator	n	控制者	hung jai jé	hung3 zai3 ze2	hung chai che
controversial[1]	adj	引起爭論	yáhn héi jàng leuhn	jan5 hei2 zang4 leon6	yahn hei chang leuhn
controversial[2]	adj	有爭議	yáuh jàng yih	jau5 zang4 ji6	yauh chang yih
convene /gather	v	召集	jiuh jàahp	ziu6 zaap6	chiuh chaahp
convenient	adj	方便	fòng bìhn	fong4 bin6	fong pihn
conversant /acquainting	adj	熟悉的	sùhk sìk dìk	suk6 sik4 dik4	suhk sek tek
conversation[1]/dialog/ dialogue/talk	n	對話	deui wah	deoi3 waa6	toei wah
conversation[2]	n	會話	wuih wá	wui6 waa2	wuih wa
conversation[3]	n	會談	wuih tàahm	wui6 taam4	wuih thaahm
conversation plot /ploy/tactics	v	會話策略	wuih wá chaak leuhk	wui6 waa2 caak3 loek6	wuih wa chhaak leuhk
converse	v	交話	gàau wah	gaau4 wa6	kaau wah
convert[1] /change/to transform	v	化	fa	fa3	fa
convert[2]	v	轉化	jyún fa	zyun2 faa3	chyun fa
convert[3]	v	轉變	jyún bin	zyun2 bin3	chyun pin
converter[1]	n	轉化者	jyún fa jé	zyun2 faa3 ze2	chyun fa che
converter[2]/transformer	n	轉換器	jyún wuhn hei	zyun2 wun6 hei3	chyun wuhn hei
convex[1]	adj	凸	daht	dat6	taht
convex[2]	adj	凸面	daht mín	dat6 min2	taht min
convey[1] /transport/ delivery goods	v	運送	wahn sung	wan6 sung3	wahn sung
convey[1]	v	轉讓	jyun yeuhng	zyun2 joeng6	chyun yeuhng
convey[2] /relay /receive & send	v	轉達	jyun daaht	zyun2 daat6	chyun taaht
convey[3] /transmit	v	傳送	chyùhn sung	cyun4 sung3	chhyuhn sung
convict[1]	v	過失	gwo sāt	gwo3 sat1	kwo sat
convict[2]	v	搶劫罪	chéung gip jeuih	coeng2 gip3 zeoi6	chheung kip choih
convict killed people	v	謀殺罪	màuh saat jeuih	mau4 saat3 zeoi6	mauh saat choih
convict of crime /conviction	n	定罪	dehng /dihng jeuih	deng6 /ding6 zeoi6	tehng choih
conviction	n	判罪	pun jeuih	pun3 zeoi6	phun choih
convinced	v	使信服	sái seun fuhk	sai2 seon3 fuk6	sai swon fuhk
convolvulus flower	n	牽牛花等	hīn ngàuh fā dáng	hin1 ngau4 fa1 dang2	hin ngauh fa tang
convulsions /faint from fear	n	驚厥	gèng kyut	geng4 kyut3	keng khyut
cook[1]	v	烹調	pāang tìuh	paang1 tiu4	phaang thiuh
cook[2]	n	炊事員	chèui sih yùhn	ceoi4 si6 jyun4	chheui sih yuhn
cook rice	v	煮飯	jyú faahn	zyu2 faan6	chyu faahn
cooked[1] /ripe food/ripe fruit/skilled	adj	熟	suhk	suk6	suhk
cooked[2]	adj	燒熟	sìu suhk	siu4 suk6	siu suhk
cooked[3] meal/rice	n	飯	faahn	faan6	faahn
cooker[1] /cooking pot	n	廚灶	chyuh jou	cyu5 zou	chhyuh chou

cooker[2] pot	n	電灶	dihn jou	din6 zou	tihn chou
cookie [(de)]	n	曲奇	kùk kèih	kuk4 kei4	khuk kheih
cooking[1]	n	煮熟	jyú suhk	zyu2 suk6	chyu suhk
cooking[2]	n	烹飪	pāang yáhm	paang1 jaam5	phaang yahm
cooking oil[1]	n	菜油	chòih yàuh	coi4 jau4	chhoih yauh
cooking oil[2]	n	食油	sihk yàuh	sik6 jau4	sehk yauh
cool[1]	adj	涼	lèuhng	loeng4	leuhng
cool[2]	adj	涼爽	lèuhng sóng	loeng4 song2	leuhng song
cool[3]	adj	涼快	lèuhng faai ge	loeng4 faai3 ge3	leuhng faai ke
cool down /quench	v	冷卻	láahng keuk	laang5 koek3	laahng kheuk
coolant	n	冷卻劑	láahng keuk jāi	laang5 koek3 zai1	laahng keuk chai
cooler /radiator /cooling device	n	冷卻器	láahng keuk hei	laang5 koek3 hei3	laahng kheuk hei
coolie[1] [(sl)(de)] porter	n	苦力	gū lēi	gu1 lei1	ku lei
coolie[2] /hard labor/toil	n	苦工	fú gùng	fu2 gung4	fu kung
cooperate	v	合作	hahp jok	hap6 zok3	hahp chok
cooperation /friendship	n	合作	hahp jok	hap6 zok3	hahp chok
cooperatively[(sl)]	adv	夾手夾脚	gaap sáu gaap geuk	gaap3 sau2 gaap3 goek3	kaap sau kaap keuk
cooperator /co-operator	n	合作者	hahp jok jé	hap6 zok3 ze2	hahp chok che
coordinate[1] equal	a	同等的	tùhng dáng dìk	tung4 dang2 dik4	thuhng tang tik
coordinate[2] /harmonize	v	使協調	sái hip tiu	sai2 hip3 tiu3	sai hip thiu
coordinated /harmonized	v	使相配合	sái sèung pui hahp	sai2 soeng4 pui3 hap6	sai seung phui hahp
coordinator	n	協調者	hip tiu jé	hip3 tiu3 ze2	hip thiuh che
copier /copyist	n	抄寫員	chaau sé yùhn	caau3 se2 jyun4	chhaau se yuhn
copper wire	n	銅線	tùhng sín	tung4 sin2	thuhng sin
copse small tree or bushes /brushwood/coppice	n	矮林	áai /ái /ngái làhm	aai2 /ai2 /ngai2 lam4	aai /ai/ngai lahm
copulate	v	交尾	gāau méih	gaau1 mei5	kaau meih
copy[1]	v	抄	chàau	caau4	chhaau
copy[2] /duplicate	n	複	fūk	fuk1	fuk
copy[3] /imitate	v	仿	fóng	fong2	fong
copy[4] /photo copy	v	影印	yéng yan	jeng2 jan3	yeng yan
copy[5] /duplicate	adj	副本	fu bún	fu3 bun2	fu pun
copy[6]/imitate/mock/ emulate/simulate	v	模仿	mòuh fóng	mou4 fong2	mouh fong
copy paper	n	影印紙	yéng yan jí	jeng2 jan3 zi2	yeng yan chi
copyist /imitator /simulator	n	模仿者	mòuh fóng jé	mou4 fong2 ze2	mouh fong che
copyright[1]	adj	版權	báan kyùhn	baan2 kyun4	paan khyuhn
copyright[2]	n	著作權	jyu jok kyùhn	zyu3 zok3 kyun4	chyu chok khyuhn
coquetry[1(sl)]/prickteaser /intended to attract men	n	五三五四/ 5354	ńgh sàam ńgh sei	ng5 saam4 ng5 sei3	ngh saam ngh sei
coquetry[2] /prickteaser /intended to attract men	n	發姣	faat haau	faat3 haau3	faat haau

coquetry[3] /prickteaser /intended to attract men	n	賣俏	maaih chiu	maai6 ciu3	maaih chhiu
coquetry[4] /prickteaser /intended to attract men	n	賣弄風情	maaih luhng fùng chìhng	maai6 lung6 fung4 cing4	maaih luhng fung chhehng
cor[1] be wonder	interj	啊呀	ā ah	a1 a6	a ah
cor[2] look at that!/be wonder	interj	天哪	tīn náh	tin1 na5	thin nah
cor[3] /be wonder	interj	驚奇	gèng kèih	geng4 kei4	keng kheih
coral	n	珊瑚	sàan wùh	saan4 wu4	saan wuh
cord[1] /string/rope	n	細繩	sai síng	sai3 sing2	sai seng
cord[2] /ligament	n	韌帶	ngàhn dáai	ngan6 daai2	ngahn taai
cordial[1] /enthusiastic	adj	熱誠	yiht sìhng	jit6 sing4	yiht sehng
cordial[2]	adj	有誠意	yauh sìhng yi	jit6 sing4 ji3	yauh sehng yi
core[1]	n	果核	gwó haht	gwo2 hat6	kwo haht
core[2] /kernel/nuclear	n	核心	haht sàm	hat6 sam4	haht sam
corelation	n	交互作用	gàau wuh jok yuhng	gaau4 wu6 zok3 jung6	kaau wuh chok yuhng
coriander	n	玉桂	yùhk gwái	juk6 gwai2	yuhk kwai
cork /bottle cork	n	瓶塞	pèhng sāk	peng4 sak1	phehng sak
corkscrew	n	拔塞鑽	baht sāk jyun	bat6 sak1 zyun3	paht sak chyun
corn[1] /maize	n	粟米	sūk máih	suk1 mai5	suk maih
corn[2] /maize	n	玉米	yuhk máih	juk6 mai5	yuhk maih
corn[3] wheat	n	小麥	síu mahk	siu2 mak6	siu mahk
corn[4] cereal	n	穀物	gūk maht	guk1 mat6	kuk maht
corn oil	n	粟米油	sūk máih yàuh	suk1 mai5 jau4	suk maih yauh
corn soup	n	粟米羹	sūk máih gāng	suk1 mai5 gang1	suk maih kang
corner	n	角落頭	gok lòhk tau	gok3 lok6 tau3	kok lohk thau
corolla	n	花冠	fā gùn	faa1 gun4	fa kun
coronary /heart disease	n	冠心病	gun sàm pehng	gun3 sam4 peng6	kun sam pehng
corporate	adj	法團	faat tyùhn	faat3 tyun4	faat thyuhn
corporate business	n	股份生意	gú fán sāan yi	gu2 fan2 saan1 ji3	ku fan saan yi
corporation[1]	n	法人團體	faat yàhn tyùhn tái	faat3 jan4 tyun4 tai2	faat yahn thyuhn thai
corporation[2]	n	社團	séh tyùhn	se5 tyun4	seh thyuhn
correct[1] (coll) fit/proper /right/alright/right for/exactly right/extremely right	adj	啱	ngāam	ngaam1	ngaam
correct[2]	adj	正	jing	zing3	cheng
correct[3] /right/proper/ correctly	adj	正確	jeng kok	zeng3 kok3	cheng khok
correct answer (wr) reply	adj	對	deui	deoi3	toei
correction	n	改	gói	goi2	koi
correspond	v	通信	tùng seun	tung4 seon3	thung swon
correspondent[1] /reporter/journalist	n	記者	gei jé	gei3 ze2	kei che
correspondent[2]	n	通訊者	tùng seun jé	tung4 seon3 ze2	thung swon che
correspondent[3]	n	特派員	dahk paaih yùhn	dak6 paai6 jyun4	tahk phaaih yuhn
corresponding[1]	adj	符合	fùh hahp	fu4 hap6	fuh hahp
corresponding[2]	adj	相關	séung gwāan	soeng2 gwaan1	seung kwaan

corresponding[3]/like that/same as	adj	相應	séung yìng	soeng2 jing4	seung yeng
corresponding[4]	adj	對應	deui yíng	deoi3 jing2	toei yíng
corridor	n	廊	lòhng	long4	lohng
corridor seat /aisle seat	n	走廊位	jáu lòhng wái	zau2 long4 wai2	chau lohng wai
corrosive[1]	adj	腐蝕物	fuh sihk maht	fu6 sik6 mat6	fuh sehk maht
corrosive[2]	adj	腐蝕劑	fuh sihk jāi	fu6 sik6 zai1	fuh sehk chai
corrosive[3]	adj	腐蝕性	fuh sihk síng	fu6 sik6 sing2	fuh sehk seng
corruption[1] in political	n	貪污	tàam wù	taam4 wu4	thaam wu
corruption[2]	n	腐敗	fuh baaih	fu6 baai6	fuh paaih
corsage	n/v	襟頭花	kàm tàuh fā	kam4 tau4 faa1	kham thauh fa
cortex	n	表皮	bīu pèih	biu1 pei4	piu pheih
cosmetic shop	n	化妝品店	fa jōng bán dim	faa3 zong1 ban2 dim3	fa chong pan tim
cosmetics[1] /make-up article	n	化妝品	fa jōng bán	faa3 zong1 ban2	fa chong pan
cosmetics[2]	n	美容品	méih yùhng bán	mei5 jung4 ban2	meih yuhng pan
cost /expense/spend/ fee/batta/extra pay	n	費	fai	fai3	fai
cost free /no charge/ free of charge	adj	免費	míhn fai	min5 fai3	mihn fai
cost go up /price rise/ price up/value up/soar	adj	漲	jeung	zoeng3	cheung
cost of living[1]	n	生活消費	sàng wuht sìu fai	sang4 wut6 siu4 fai3	sang wuht siu fai
cost of living[2]	n	生活費用	sàng wuht fai yuhng	sang4 wut6 fai3 jung6	sang wuht fai yuhng
costly/expensive/valuable	adj	貴	gwai	gwai3	kwai
costs	n	成本	sèhng bún	seng4 bun2	sehng pun
costume	n	服裝	fuhk jòng	fuk4 zong4	fuhk chong
cottage /hut/dwelling/ adode/house	n	舍	se	se3	se
cottager	n	住在鄉下房子嘅人	jyuh joih hèung hah fòhng jí ge yàhn	zyu6 zoi6 hoeng4 ha6 fong4 zi2 ge3 jan4	chyuh choih heung hah fohng chi ke yahn
cotton[1]	n	綿/棉	mìhn	min4	mihn
cotton[2]	n	棉花	mìhn fà	min4 faa4	mihn fa
cotton[3]	n	棉質	mìhn jāt	min4 zat1	mihn chat
cotton[4]	n	棉布	mìhn bou	min4 bou3	mihn pou
cotton[5]	n	布類	bou leuih	bou3 leoi6	pou lowih
cough[1]	n	咳	kāt	kat1	khat
cough[2]	n	咳嗽	kāt sau	kat1 sau3	khat sau
could /may/might /should be	v/axu	可能	hó làng /nàng	ho2 lang4 /nang4	ho lang /nang
could it be that...?	v	抑或?	yīk waahk?	jik1 waak6?	yek waahk?
could you do it?		請問可唔可以幫做?	chéng mahn hó m̀ hó yíh bòng jouh?	ceng2 man6 ho2 m4 ho2 ji5 bong4 zou6?	chheng mahn ho mh ho yih pong chouh?
couldn't removing /unmoving/nonmoving	adj	唔郁	m̀ yùk	m4 juk1	mh yuk
couldn't see him		唔見到佢	m̀ gin dou kéuih	m4 gin3 dou3 keoi5	mh kin tou khoih
couldn't understand		唔明白	m̀ mìhng baahk	m4 ming4 baak6	mh mehng paahk

council[1]	n	區議	kèui yih	keoi4 ji6	khoi yih
council[2]	n	理事會	léih sih wúi	lei5 si6 wui2	leih sih wui
count[1]	v	數	sou	sou3	sou
count[2]	v	數計	sou gai	sou3 gai3	sou kai
count by abacus	n	會打算盤	wúih dá syun pùhn	wui5 daa2 syun3 pun4	wuih ta syun phuhn
countdown	n	倒數	dóu sóu	dou2 sou2	tou sou
counter[1] /table/till	n	柜面	gwaih mín	gwai6 min2	kwaih min
counter[2] /service table	n	籌碼	chàuh máh	cau4 maa5	chhauh mah
counter[3] /service desk	n	反櫃台	fáan gwaih tòih	faan2 gwai6 toi4	faan kwaih thoih
counter[4] device	n	計數器	gai sou hei	gai3 sou3 hei3	kai sou hei
counter[5] count by person	n	計算者	gai syun jé	gai3 syun3 ze2	kai syun che
counter feit[1]	adj	行騙	hahng pin	hang4 pin3	hahng phin
counter feit[2]	adj	冒牌	mouh pàaih	mou6 paai4	mouh phaaih
counter feit[3]/fake as a genuine	adj	假冒	gá mouh	gaa2 mou6	ka mouh
counter sign[1]	v	副署	fu chyúh	fu3 cyu5	fu chhyu
counter sign[2] secret talk of army	n	軍事口令	gwàn sih háu lihng	gwan3 si6 hau2 ling4	kwan sih hau lehng
counter sign[3] secret number	n	暗號	ngam houh	am3 hou6	ngam houh
counter sign[4] /countersignature	v	附署	fu chyúh	fu3 cyu5	fu chhyu
counter sign[5] /countersignature	v	聯署	lyùhn chyúh	lyun4 cyu5	lyuhn chhyuh
countersignature[1] /counter sign	v	加簽	gà chīm	gaa4 cim1	ka chhim
countersignature[2] /counter sign	v	連署	lìhn chyúh	lin4 cyu5	lihn chhyuh
counterpart same class/level	n	對方	deui fōng	deoi3 fong1	toei fong
counting men	n	人數計	yàhn sou gei	jan4 sou3 gei3	yahn sou kei
country[1] /national/state /nation	n	國家	gwok gà	gwok3 gaa4	kwok ka
country[2] /village	n	村	chyùn	cyun4	chhyun
country dance	n	土風舞	tóu fùng móuh	tou2 fung4 mou5	thou fung mouh
country folk /folksong	n	鄉村民歌	hèung chyùn màhn gō	hoeng4 cyun4 man4 go1	heung chhyun mahn koh
country man[1]	n	鄉下人	hèung há yàhn	hoeng4 ha2 jan4	heung ha yahn
country man[2]	n	鄉村嘅居民	hèung chyūn ge gèui màhn	hoeng4 cyun1 ge3 geoi4 man4	heung chhyun ke kwoi mahn
country wide	adj	全國性地	chyùhn gwok sing deih	cyun4 gwok3 sing3 dei6	chhyuhn kwok seng teih
country woman	n	村姑	chyūn gù	cyun1 gu4	chhyun ku
countryside[1] /village/rustic	n	鄉村	hēung chyùn /tsùen	hoeng1 cyun4	heung chhyun
countryside[2] /villageside	n	鄉村地方	hèung chyùn deih fòng	hoeng4 cyun4 dei6 fong4	heung chhyun teih fong
coup[1]	n	突然一擊	daht yìhn yāt gīk	dat6 jin4 jat1 gik1	taht yihn yat kek

coup[2] gov changed by force	n	政變	jing bin	zing3 bin3	cheng bin
couple[1] /pair/both/two	n/pron	兩	léuhng	loeng5	leuhng
couple[2] /pair/twin	n	對	deui	deoi3	toei
couple[3]	n	兩人	léuhng yàhn	loeng5 jan4	leuhng yahn
couple[4] /pair/twain/one	n	一對	yāt deui	jat1 deui3	yat toei
couple[5] /husband & wife/ married couple/spouse	n	兩夫婦	léuhng fù fúh	loeng5 fu4 fu5	leuhng fu fuh
couple[6] /husband & wife/ married couple/spouse	n	兩夫妻	léuhng fù chài	loeng5 fu4 cai4	leuhng fu chhai
couple[7] /spouse/husband & wife	n	兩公婆	léuhng gùng pó	loeng5 gung4 po2	leuhng kung pho
couple days later	v	過兩日	gwo léuhng yaht	gwo3 loeng5 jat6	kwo leuhng yaht
coupon[1] of money	n	禮卷	láih gyun	lai5 gyun3	laih kyun
coupon[2] of gift	n	贈卷	jahng gyun	zang6 gyun3	chahng kyun
courage[1]	n	勇氣	yúhng hei	jung5 hei3	yuhng hei
courage[2]	n	勇敢	yúhng gám	jung5 gam2	yuhng kam
courier[1] /post-man	n	速遞人	chūk daih yàhn	cuk1 dai6 jan4	chhuk taih yahn
courier[2] /post-man	n	速遞員	chūk daih yùhn	cuk1 dai6 jyun4	chhuk taih yuhn
courier[3] /postman/mailman	n	郵差	yàuh chāai	jau4 caai1	yauh chhaai
course[1] /study	n	修	sàu	sau4	sau
course[2] class/curriculum	n	課程	fo chìhng	fo3 cing4	fo chhehng
course[3] guideline	n	路線	louh sin	lou6 sin3	louh sin
course[4] /course of events/ process/process of events	n	過程	gwo chìhng	gwo3 cing4	kwo chhehng
course[5] /work/task	n	作業	jok yihp	zok3 jip6	chok yihp
course book text book	n	課本	fo bún	fo3 bun2	fo pun
course of action /work method/ manner	n	做法	jouh faat	zou6 faat3	chouh faat
court[1] law	n	法院	faat yūn	faat1 jyun1	faat yun
court[2] /courtyard of the house	n	庭院	tèhng yūn	ting4 jyun1	thehng yun
court[3] king's house	n	宮廷	gūng tìhng	gung1 ting4	kung tehng
court of tribunal of law	n	法庭	faat tìhng	faat1 ting4	faat thehng
court-dress	n	褶	jip	zip3	chip
courteous /polite	adj	有禮貌	yáuh láih màauh	jau5 lai5 maau6	yauh laih maauh
cousin /relative/kin	n	親戚	chān chīk	can1 cik1	chhan chhek
cove	n	小海灣	síu hói wāan	siu2 hoi2 waan1	siu hoi waan
covenant /promise	n	盟約	màhng yeuk	mang4 joek3	mahng yeuk
cover[1] (coll) /spread /to cover/cover	v	冚	kám	kam2	kham
cover[2]	v	蔽	bai	bai3	pai
cover[3] (wr) /to cover	v	套	tou	tou3	thou
cover[4] /lid/hood	n/v	蓋子	goi jí	goi3 zi2	koi chi
cover[5]	v	遮蓋	jē koi	ze1 koi3	che khoi
cover[6]	v	覆蓋	fūk koi	fuk1 koi3	fuuk khoi
cover[7]	v	遮掩	jē yím	ze1 jim2	che yim

English	POS	中文	Romanization 1	Jyutping	Romanization 2
cover letter	n	附信	fuh seun	fu6 seon3	fuh swon
cover up[1]	v	罩	jaau	jaau3	chaau
cover up[2] /shield	n	包庇	bāau bei	baau1 bei3	paau pei
cover up[3] /drape	n/	蓋住	goi jyuh	koi3 zyu6	koi chyuh
cover up[4]	n	掩蓋	yím goi	jim2 goi3	yim koi
covered all over the body	v	滿身	múhn sàn	mun5 san4	muhn san
cow		牛	ngàuh	ngau4	ngauh
cow's milk /milk	n	牛奶	ngàuh láaih /náaih	ngau4 laai /naai5	ngauh laaih /naaih
cow on the tree		牛上樹	ngàuh séuhng syuh	ngau4 seung5 sue6	ngauh seuhng syuh
coward	n	懦夫	loh fù, noh fùh	lo6 fu4, no6 fu6	loh fu, noh fuh
cowboy[1]	n	牛仔	ngàuh jái	ngau4 zai2	ngauh chai
cowboy[2]	n	牧牛人	muhk ngàuh yàhn	muk6 ngau4 jan4	muhk ngauh yahn
cowrie	n	瑪瑙貝	máh lóuh/nóuh bui	ma5 lou5 /nou5 bui3	mah louh /nouh pui
coy /shy/embarrassed	adj	害羞	hoih sàu	hoi6 sau4	hoih sau
crab	n	蟹	háaih	haai5	haaih
crab meat	n	蟹肉	háaih yuhk	haai5 juk6	haaih yuhk
crack[1] /burst	n	爆	baau	baau3	paau
crack[2] /burst	v	爆裂	baau liht	baau3 lit6	paau liht
crack[3] /break/rend/tear /to split	n	裂	liht	lit6	liht
crack[4]	n	罅	la	la	la
crack[5] /split/gap	n	隙	kwīk	kwik1	khwik
crack by steal		爆竊	baau sit	baau3 sit3	paau sit
crack of time	v	空隙	hùng kwīk	hung4 kwik1	hung khwik
cracked /break down	adj	破裂	po liht	po3 lit6	pho liht
craft	n	工藝	gùng ngaih	gung4 ngai6	kung ngaih
crafty[1] /cunning/sly/ dishonest	adj	狡	gáau	gaau2	kaau
crafty[2] /cunning	adj	招	jīu	ziu1	chiu
cramp /hoop/iron hoop		鐵箍	tit kū	tit3 ku1	thit khu
crane[1] bird	n	鶴	hohk /hók	hok6	hohk /hok
crane[2] an elevator	n	吊車	diu chè	diu3 ce4	tiu chhe
crank	n	曲軸	kūk juhk	kuk1 zuk6	khuk chuhk
crank handle	n	曲柄	kūk beng	kuk1 beng3	khuk peng
crankshaft	n	機軸	gèi juhk	gei4 zuk6	kei chuhk
crash[1]	v	巨響	geuih héung	geoi6 hoeng2	kwoih heung
crash[2]	v	墜落	jeuih lohk	zeoi6 lok6	cheuih lohk
crate	n	條板箱	tìuh báan sèung	tiu4 baan2 soeng4	thiuh paan seung
crater	n	火山口	fó sàan háu	fo2 saan4 hau2	fo saan hau
craving /very wishful/ like very much/extremely want	n/adj	極度渴望	gìhk douh hot mohng	gik6 dou6 hot3 mong6	kehk touh hot mohng
crawl /creep	vi	爬行	pàh hàhng	paa4 hang4	phah hahng
crazy[1] /insane	adj	黐線	chì sin	ci4 sin3	chhi sin

crazy[2]	adj	神經	sàhn gìng	san4 ging4	sahn keng
crazy[3]	adj	怪誕	gwaai daan	gwaai3 daan3	kwaai taan
crazy[4]	n/adj	瘋狂	fùng kong	fung3 kong3	fung khong
crazy person /mad-man	n	瘋子	fùng jí	fung3 zi2	fung chi
creak sound	n	嘎吱聲	gā jī sèng	ga1 zi1 seng1	ka chi seng
crunch /creak sound	n	嘎吱作響	gā jī jok héung	ga1 zi1 zok3 heung2	ka chi chok heung
cream[1] (de)	n	忌廉	geih līm	gei6 lim1	keih lim
cream[2]	n	奶油	náaih /láaih yàuh	naai5 /laai5 jau4	naaih /laaih yauh
cream of walnut	n	合桃露	hahp tou lòuh	hap6 tou3 lou6	hahp thou louh
cream soda (de)	n	忌廉梳打	geih lìm sō dá	gei6 lim4 so1 daa2	keih lim so ta
crease[1]	n	褶	jaahp	zaap6	chaahp
crease[2]	n	縐	chàauh	caau6	chhaauh
crease[3]	n	摺痕	jip hàhn	zip3 han4	chip hahn
crease[4]	v	整縐	jíng chàauh	zing2 caau6	cheng chhaauh
crease[5]	v	摺縫	jip fuhng	zip3 fung6	chip fuhng
crease[6]	v	變縐	bin chàauh	bin3 caau6	pin chhaauh
create[1] /invent/inventive /invention	adj/v	發明	faat mìhng	faat3 ming4	faat mehng
create[2] /make/produce	v	創造	chong jouh	cong3 zou6	chhong chouh
create[3]	v	創作	chong jók	cong3 zok2	chhong chok
create idea /new scheme/ hatch scheme/plot plan	v	策劃	chaak waahk	caak3 waak6	chhaak waahk
creatinine /muscle ache	v	肌酸酐	gèi syùn gōn	gei4 syun4 gon4	kei syun kon
creation /foundation	n	建立	gin lahp	gin3 lap6	kin lahp
credible	adj	相信	sèung séun	soeng4 seon2	seung swon
credit /trustworthiness /trust	n	信用	seun yuhng	seon3 jung6	swon yuhng
credited[1]	adj	貸記	taai gei	taai3 gei3	thaai kei
credited[2]	adj	計入	gai yahp	gai3 jap6	kai yahp
creditor	n	債主	jaai jyú	zaai3 zyu2	chaai chyu
creeping walk	v	爬行	pàh hàhng	paa4 hang4	phah hahng
creep /baby moving	v	卑鄙小人	bèi pēi síu yàhn	bei4 pei1 siu2 jan4	pei phei siu yahn
creeper[1]	n	爬	pàh	paa4	phah
creeper[2]	n	蔓	màahn	maan4	maahn
creeping	adj	遲緩的	chìh wun dìk	ci4 wun3 dik4	chhih wun tek
creeping plant	n	遍地蔓延嘅植物	pín deih màahn yìhn ge jihk maht	pin2 dei6 maan4 jing4 ge3 zik6 mat6	phin teih maahn yihn ke chehk maht
cremation	n	火葬	fó jong	fo2 zong3	fo chong
cremation dead body	n	火化	fó fa	fo2 faa3	fo fa
crescent /new moon	n	新月	sàn yuht	san4 jyut6	san yuht
crest	n	頂點	déng dím	deng2 dim2	teng tim
crew /ship staffs	n	全體人員	chyùhn tái yàhn yùhn	cyun4 tai2 jan4 jyun4	chhyuhn thai yahn yuhn
crew neck	n	圓領	yùhn léhng /líhng	jyun4 leng5 /ling5	yuhn lehng
cricket insect	n	蟋蟀	sīk sēut	sik1 seot1	sek swot

English		Chinese	Yale	Jyutping	Other
cricket player	n	板球隊員	báan kàuh deuih yùhn	baan2 kau4 deoi6 jyun4	paan khauh twoih yuhn
crime /vice	n	罪行	jeuih hahng	zeoi6 hang4	cheuih hahng
crimeless /innocent/ innocence	adj/n	無罪	mòuh jeuih	mou4 zeoi6	mouh choih
criminal[1] /violate	adj	犯	faahn	faan6	faahn
criminal[2]	adj	罪犯	jeuih faahn	zeoi6 faan6	cheuih faahn
criminal[3]	adj	犯罪嘅	faahn jeuih ge	faan6 zeoi6 ge3	faahn cheuih ke
criminal[4] /perpetrator	n	一犯罪者	yāt faahn jeuih jé	jat1 faan6 zeoi6 ze2	yat faahn choih che
criminal activities /criminal case	n	罪案	jeuih on	zeoi6 on3	cheuih on
criminal again /felon/ reviolate/recommit	adj	重犯	chùhng faahn	cung4 faan6	chhuhng faahn
criminal charge	n	罪名	jeuih mèhng	zeoi6 meng4	cheuih mehng
criminal law	n	刑法	yìhng faat	jing4 faat3	yehng faat
criminal suit[1] /unlawful /offence/law breaking	n	犯法	faahn faat	faan6 faat3	faahn faat
criminal suit[2]	n	涉及犯罪	sip kahp faahn jeuih	sip3 kap6 faan6 zeoi6	sip khahp faahn choih
criminate	v	告發	gou faat	gou3 faai3	kou faat
crinkle[1] /crepe	n	縐	jau	zau3	chau
crinkle[2] /wrinkle	n	縐紋	jau màhn	zau3 man4	chau mahn
crinkle[3]	n	令到縐	lihng dou jau	ling4 dou3 zau3	lehng tou chau
crinkle[4]	n	令到縮	lìhng dou sūk	ling4 dou3 suk1	lehng tou suk
crinkled	n	起皺的	héi jau dì	hei2 zau3 di4	hei chau ti
crisis /risk/danger/hazard		危機	ngàih gèi	ngai4 gei4	ngaih kei
crisp	adj	脆嘅	cheui ge	ceoi3 ge3	chheui ke
crispy	adj	脆	cheui	ceoi3	chheui
criss-cross[1]	adj	十字形	sahp jih yìhng	sap6 zi6 jing4	sahp chih yehng
criss-cross[2]	adj	交叉	gāau chā	gaau1 caa1	kaau chha
criteria[1]	n	判斷標準	pún dyún bìu jēun	pun2 dyun2 biu4 zeon1	phun tyun piu cheun
criteria[2]	n	判斷	pun dyun	pun3 dyun3	phun tyun
critical /serious/grievous	adj	嚴重	yìhm juhng	jim4 zung6	yihm chuhng
criticism	n	批評	pài pìhng	pai4 ping4	phai phehng
criticize[1] /chide/scold/ rebuke/speak angrily/ condemn	v	指責	jí jaak	zi2 zaak3	chi chaak
criticize[2]	v	批判	pài pun	pai4 pun3	phai phun
criticize[3]	v	挑剔	tìu tīk	tiu4 tik1	thiu thek
criticizing an event /fault finding/opinion on/ explaining	n/v	吹毛求疵	chèui mòuh kàuh chì	ceoi4 mou4 kau4 ci4	chheui mouh khauh chhi
crocodile	n	鱷魚	ngohk yùh	ngok6 jyu4	ngohk yuh
crooked[1] /curve/bent	n	曲	kūk	kuk1	khuk
crooked[2] /curved	adj	彎曲	wàan kùk	waan4 kuk4	waan khuk
crooked[3] /wiggle/cramp	adj/v	扭動	láu duhng	lau2 dung6	lau tong
crooked talk /devious/ not straight talk/noxious	adj	歪	wāai	waai1	waai

crop[1]	n	作物	jok maht	zok3 mat6	chok maht
crop[2] /grain	n	穀粒	gūk lāp	guk1 lap1	kuk lap
cross[1]	n	十字架	sahp jih gá	sap6 zi6 gaa2	sahp chih ka
cross[2]	n	十字形	sahp jih yìhng	sap6 zi6 jing4	sahp chih yehng
cross exam	n	盤問	pùhn mahn	pun4 man6	phuhn mahn
cross eye	adj	射喱眼	seh lēi ngáahn	se6 lei1 ngaan5	seh ngaahn
cross harbour-tunnel	adj	海底隧道	hói dái seuih douh	hoi2 dai2 seoi6 dou6	hoi tai swoih touh
cross legged[1]	adj	交叉脚	gāau chā geuk	gaau1 caa1 goek3	kaau chha keuk
cross legged[2]	adj	盤著腿	pun jeuk téui	pun3 zoek3 teoi2	phun cheuk thoi
cross mind /to think of	v	想起	séung héi	soeng2 hei2	seung hei
cross over /go across /go over	v	過	gwò	gwo4	kwo
cross road[1]	n	渡過	douh gwo	dou6 gwo3	touh kwo
cross road[2]	n	越過	yuht gwo	jyut6 gwo3	yuht kwo
cross road[3]	n	橫路	wàahng louh	waang4 lou6	waahng louh
cross road[4]	n	橫過	waahng gwo	waang6 gwo3	waahng kwo
cross road[5]	n	交叉路	gāau chā louh	gaau1 caa1 lou6	kaau chha louh
cross road[6] /junction /intersection/ crossroads		十字路口	sahp jih louh háu	sap6 zi6 lou6 hau2	sahp chih louh hau
cross roads	n	交界處	gàau gaai chyu	gaau4 gaai3 cyu3	kaau kaai chhyu
cross the road	n	過馬路	gwò máh louh	gwo4 maa5 lou6	kwo mah louh
crossed	v	過咗	gwò jó	gwo4 zo2	kwo cho
crossed over /already past	v	過咗去	gwò jó heui	gwo4 zo2 heoi3	kwo cho hoi
crossed the sea	v	過咗海	gwò jó hói	gwo4 zo2 hoi2	kwo cho hoi
crossing	n	橫渡	waahng douh	waang6 dou6	waahng touh
crossword	n	縱橫填字遊戲	jūng wàahng tìhn jih yàuh hei	zung1 waang4 tin4 zi6 jau4 hei3	chung waahng thihn chih yauh hei
crow /raven	n	烏鴉	wū ngā	wu1 ngaa1	wu nga
crowd[1]	n	人群	yàhn kwan	jan4 kwan3	yahn khwan
crowd[2] /masses	n	眾	jung	zung3	chung
crowd[3] /marsh/mass	n	群眾	kwàhn jung	kwan4 zung3	khwahn chung
crowd[4] /group/flock	n	群	kwàhn	kwan4	khwahn
crowd & noise /mass & noise/gathering & noise/ hustling & bustling/great noised	adj/v	熱鬧	yiht laauh /naauh	jit6 laau6 /naau6	yiht laauh /naauh
crowd control	n	人群聚集	yàhn kwan jèuih jàahp	jan4 kwan3 zeoi6 zaap6	yahn khwan cheuih chaahp
crucial[1] /extremely important	adj	極其重要	gìhk kèih juhng yiu	gik6 kei4 zung6 jiu3	kehk kheih chuhng yiu
crucial[2] /determined/ decisive/conclusive/fact decision	adj	決定性	kyut dehng /dihng sing	kyut deng6 /ding6 sing3	khyut tehng seng
crude oil	n	原油	yùhn yàuh	jyun4 jau4	yuhn yauh
cruel	adj	殘酷	chāan huhk	caan1 huk6	chhaan huhk

English		Chinese	Yale	Jyutping	Romanization
cruet	n	調味瓶	tìuh mèih pèhng /pihng	tiu4 mei6 peng4 /ping4	thiuh meih phehng
cruet stand	n	調味架	tìuh mèih gá	tiu4 mei6 gaa2	thiuh meih ka
cruising	n	巡航	chèuhn hòhng	ceon4 hong4	chheuhn hohng
crumb	n	屑	sit	sit3	sit
crumbs of bread[1]	n	麵包屑	mihn bàau sit	min6 baau4 sit3	mihn paau sit
crumbs of bread[2]	n	麵包碎	mihn bàau seui	min6 baau4 seoi3	mihn paau swoi
crumble	v	弄碎	luhng /nuhng seui	lung6 /nung6 seui3	luhng /nuhng swoi
crumpled	adj	皺巴巴肫	jau bā bā dì	zau3 baa1 baa1 di4	chau pa pa ti
crunch /creak sound	v	嘎吱作響 地咬嚼	gā jī jok héung deih ngáauh jeuhk	ga1 zi1 zok3 heung2 dei6 ngaau5 zeuk6	ka chi chok heung teih ngaauh cheuhk
crupper	n	後鞦	hauh chāu	hau6 cau1	hauh chhau
crush	v	壓壞	áat waaih	aat2 waai6	aat waaih
crutch[1](dw)/buttocks /leg's joins point/thighs crack part /thighs join part	n	股罅	gú la	gu2 la	ku la
crutch[2] /jointed point of two legs	n	陰部	yàm bouh	jam4 bou6	yam pouh
crutches /stick/walking stick	n	拐杖	gwáai jeuhng	gwaai2 zoeng6	kwaai cheuhng
cry[1] /weep	n	哭	hūk	huk4	huk
cry[2] /weep/high shout/loud sound	v	大叫	daaih giu	daai6 giu3	taaih kiu
cry[3] (of birds and animals) sound/make sound	v	鳴	mìhng	ming4	mehng
cry baby	n	愛哭嘅人	oi /ngoi hūk ge yàhn	oi3 /ngoi huk1 ge3 jan4	oi /ngoi huk ke yahn
cry for help![1] /help! help!/ call for help!	v	救命呀!	gau mèhng áa	gau3 neng6 aa2	kau mehng aa
cry for help![2]	v	求救!	kàuh gau!	kau4 gau3	khauh gau!
crying[1] /weep/tears	v	眼淚	ngáahn leuih	ngaan5 leoi6	ngaahn lowih
crying[2] /yell/loudly cry/ shout loudly	v	叫喊	giu haam	giu3 haam3	kiu haam
crying[3]/sobbing/weeping/ shouting & weeping/great sadness/disappointment/ lamentation/mourning/grief/ distress	n	泣	yāp	jap1	yap
crystal[1] natural	n	水晶	séui jīng	seoi2 zing1	swoi cheng
crystal[2]	n	結晶	git jīng	git3 zing1	kit cheng
crystal[3]	n	晶體	jīng tái	zing1 tai2	cheng thai
crystal[4] /crystallization	n	結晶體	git jīng tái	git3 zing1 tai2	kit cheng thai
crywolf	v	發假警報	faat gá gíng bou	faat3 ga2 ging2 bou3	faat ka keng pou
cube measure	n	立方體	lahp fòng tái	lap6 fong4 tai2	lahp fong thai
cubic measure	adj	立方形	lahp fōng yìhng	lap6 fong1 jing4	lahp fong yehng ke
cubicle /small bed room	n	小臥室	síu ngoh sāt	siu2 ngo6 sat1	siu ngoh sat
cuckoo[1] bird	n	杜鵑鳥	douh gyùn níuh	dou3 gyun4 niu5	touh kyun niuh
cuckoo[2] (coll) stupid man	adj	傻念頭	sòh lihm /nihm tàuh	so4 lim6 /nim6 tau4	soh lihm /nihm thauh
cucumber	n	青瓜	chèng gwà	ceng4 gwaa4	chheng kwa

cuff /slap	v	摑一巴	gwaak yāt bā	gwaak3 jat1 baa1	kwaak yat pa
cuffbutton /cufflinks	n	袖口鈕	jauh háu náu	zau6 hau2 nau2	chauh hau nau
cultivate[1] way of life	adj	栽培	jòi pùih	zoi4 pui4	choi phuih
cultivate[2] way of life	adj	建立結交	gín làahp gít gàau	gin2 laap6 git2 gaau4	kin laahp kit kaau
cultivation	v	耕作	loih /noih jok	loi6 /noi6 zok	loih /noih chok
cultivator	n	耕種嘅人	gàang jung ge yàhn	gaang4 zung3 ge3 jan4	kaang chung ke yahn
cultural programme /cultural activity/cultural party/dancing party/ball dance	n	舞會	móuh wúi	mou5 wui2	mouh wui
culture[1] /cultural way of life	n	文化	màhn fa	man4 faa3	mahn fa
culture[2] way of life	n	斯文	sì màhn	si4 man4	si mahn
cultured pearl	n	養珠	yéuhng jyù	joeng5 zyu4	yeuhng chyu
culvert	n	陰溝	yàm kàu	jam4 kau4	yam kahau
cunt [(vdw)] /vagina very offensive word	n	閪	hài	hai1	hai
cup[1] /glass	n	杯	bùi	bui4	pui
cup[2] /glass	n	杯子	bùi jái	bui4 zai2	pui chai
cup[3] hold action	v	使(手掌)成 杯狀	sái (sāu jōeng) seng bùi jòhng	sai2 (sau1 zoeng1) seng3 bui4 zong6	sai (sau choeng) seng pui chohng
cup[4] of game	n	獎杯	jéung bū	zoeng2 bui1	cheung pui
cupboard	n	杯櫃	būi gwaih	bui1 gwai6	pui gwaih
curb[1] /limit/time limit	n	限制	haahn jai	haan6 zai3	haahn chai
curb[2] /dominate/to control	n	控制	hung jai	hung3 zai3	hung chai
cure[1] /therapy/treatment	v	療	lìuh	liu4	liuh
cure[2] /doctor/medical/treat /treatment	v	醫	yī	ji1	yi
cure[3] as meat	v	醫好	yì hóu	ji4 hou2	yi hou
cure[4]	v	治癒	jih yuh	zi6 jyu6	chih yuh
cure a disease /remedy	n	治療法	jih lìuh faat	zi6 liu4 faat3	chih liuh faat
curfew	n	宵禁	sìu gam	siu4 gam3	siu kam
curio[1] /antique	n	古玩	gú wún	gu2 wun2	ku wun
curio[2] /antique	n	古董	gú dúng	gu2 dung2	ku tong
curio[3] /antique	n	古婉	gú wún	gu2 wun2	ku wun
curio[4] /antique	n	古蹟	gú jīk	gu2 zik1	ku chek
curiosity /interest in	n	好奇心	hou kèih sàm	hou3 kei4 sam4	hou kheih sam
curious /funny/odd	n	好奇	hou kèih	hou3 kei4	hou kheih
curled hair	n	鬈髮	kyùhn faat	kyun4 faat3	khyuhn faat
curls	n	鬈	kyùhn	kyun4	khyuhn
curly	adj	捲曲	gyún kūk	gyun2 kuk1	kyun khuk
currency[1] /money	n	金錢	gām chìhn	gam1 cin4	kam chhihn
currency[2] /money	n	貨幣	fo baih	fo3 bai6	fo paih
currency exchange /money exchange	n	貨幣兌換 商	fo baih deui wuhn sèung	fo3 bai6 deui3 wun6 soeng4	fo paih toei wuhn seung
current[1] /now/today	n/prep	今	gàm	gam4	kam

current[2] /now/present/existing	adj	現	yihn	jin6	yihn
current[3] /existing	adj	現時	yihn sìh	jin6 si4	yihn sih
current[4] /present	adj	當前	dòng chìhn	dong4 cin4	tong chihn
current age	adj	現年	yihn nìhn	jin6 nin4	yihn nihn
current situation /quo	adj	現狀	yihn johng	jin6 zong6	yihn chohng
currently /presently/present time/present/now	adv	目前	muhk chìhn	muk6 cin4	muhk chhihn
currently existing	adv	現有	yihn yáuh	jin6 jau5	yihn yauh
currently until /now	adv	目前為止	muhk chìhn wàih jí	muk6 cin4 wai4 zi2	muhk chhihn waih chi
curry (de)	n	咖喱	gā lēi	gaa1 lei1	ka lei
curry chicken	n	咖哩雞	gā léih gài	gaa1 lei1 gai4	ka leih kai
curt /brief	adj	簡要	gáan giu	gaan2 jiu	kaan kiu
curtain[1] /tent/screen	n	幕	mohk	mok6	mohk
curtain[2]	n	簾	lìhm	lìhm	lihm
curtain for window	n	窗簾	chēung lím	coeng1 lim2	chhēung lim
curve line	n	弓	gúng	gung2	kung
curve	n	曲線	kùk sin	kuk4 sin3	khuk sin
cushion[1] (de)	n	咕*	gū séun	gu1 seun2	ku swon
cushion[2] /pad/mat	n	墊	jín	zin2	chin
cushion[3]	n	椅墊	yí jín	ji2 zin2	yi chin
cushion[4]	n	靠墊	kaau jín	kaau3 zin2	khaau chin
custard	n	蛋奶凍	dáan láaih/náaih dung	daan2 laai5 /naai5 dung3	taan laaih/naaih tung
custard apple	n	番鬼荔枝	fāan gwái laih jī	faan1 gwai2 lai6 zi1	faan kwai laih chi
custard tart (de) egg tart	n	蛋撻	dáan táat	daan2 taat2	taan thaat
custody[1]	n	捕管	bóu gún	bou2 gun2	pou kun
custody[2]	n	監護	gaam wuh	gam3 wu6	kaam wuh
social custom	n	俗	juhk	zuk6	chuhk
custom[1] social	n	習俗	jaahp juhk	zaap6 zuk6	chaahp chohk
custom[2] social manners	n	風俗	fùng juhk	fung4 zuk6	fung chuhk
custom[3] /manners/style	n	風格	fùng gaak	fung4 gaak3	fung kaak
custom[4] /as usual /daily	n	習慣	jaahp kwaan	zaap6 gwaan3	chaahp kwaan
custom office /custom house (of the government)	n	海關	hói gwàan	hoi2 gwaan4	hoi kwaan
customer[1] /guest/visitor	n	客	haak	haak3	haak
customer[2] /patron	n	客仔	haak jái	haak3 zai2	haak chai
customer[3] /guest	n	客人	haak yàhn	haak3 jan4	haak yahn
customer complaints	n	顧客投訴	gu haak tàuh sou	gu3 haak3 tau4 sou3	ku haak thauh sou
customers services[1]	n	好客	hóu haak	hou2 haak3	hou haak
customers services[2]	n	款待	fún doih	fun2 dii6	fun toih
customer service hotline	n	客戶服務熱線	haak wuh fuhk mouh yiht sin	haak3 wu6 fuk6 mou6 jit6 sin3	haak wuh fuhk mouh yiht sin
customs /revenue/tariff/tax	n	關稅	gwàan seui	gwaan4 seoi3	kwaan swoi
cut[1] (de) divide/partition	n/v	割	got	got3	kot

cut[2] by knife	v	切	chit	cit3	chhit
cut[3] by scissors	v	剪	jín	zin2	chin
cut[4] /wound	n	傷口	sèung háu	soeng4 hau2	seung hau
cut apart	v	切開	chit hòi	cit3 hoi4	chhit hoi
cut electric /short circuit		短路	dyún louh	dyun2 lou6	tyun louh
cut grain /harvest crop	n	收穫	sàu wohk	sau4 wok6	sau wohk
cut off /disconnect/ supply cut	n	切斷	chit tyúhn	cit3 tyun5	chhit thyuhn
cut one's throat	n	自刎	jih máhn	zi6 man5	chih mahn
cut out /removal/remove	n	切除	chit chèuih	cit3 ceoi4	chhit chhoih
cut piece	n	切塊	chit faai	cit3 faai3	chit faai
cut throat	v	刎	máhn	man5	mahn
cut tree[1(coll)] hew/cut down	v	斬樹	jáam syuh	zaam2 syu6	chaam syuh
cut tree[2 (text)] /fell by cut/ hew/cut down tree	v	砍伐	hám faht	ham2 fat6	ham faht
cute[1] /attractive	adj	得意	dāk yi	dak1 ji3	tak yi
cute[2] /attractive	adj	趣緻	cheui ji	ceoi3 zi3	chheui chi
cutlery	n	餐具	chāan gèuih	caan1 geoi6	chhaan kwoih
cutter machine	n	剪機	jín gèi	zin2 gei4	chin kei
cuttle fish	n	墨魚	mahk yùh	mak6 jyu4	mahk yuh
cyber[1] /network/internet	n	聯網	lyùhn móhng	lyun4 mong5	lyuhn mohng
cyber[2] internet shop	n	電腦網路	dihn nóuh móhng louh	din6 nou5 mong5 lou6	tihn nouh mohng louh
cyber café	n	網路咖啡館	móhng lohk ga fèi gūn	mong5 lok6 gaa3 fei4 gun1	mohng lohk ga fèi gūn
cycle[1] /motorcycle	n	兩個轆	léuhng go lūk	loeng5 go3 luk1	leuhng ko lowk
cycle[2] /motorcycle	n	兩個輪	léuhng go léuhn	loeng5 go3 loen5	leuhng ko leuhn
cycle[3] /circle	n	循環	chèuhn wàahn	ceon4 waan4	chheuhn waahn
cycle[4] /bike	n	摩托車	mō dá chè	mo1 daa2 ce4	mo ta chhe
cyclist	n	騎腳踏車嘅人	kèh geuk daahp chē ge yàhn	ke4 goek3 daap6 ce1 ge3 jan4	kheh keuk taahp chhe ke yahn
cyclone[1] measured	n	氣旋	hei syùhn	hei3 syun4	hei syuhn
cyclone[2] /whirlwind	n	旋風	syùhn fùng	syun4 fung4	syuhn fung
cylinder[1] /pipe/tube	n	筒	tùhng	tung4	thuhng
cylinder[2]	n	圓筒容器	yun tung yung héi	jyun3 tung3 jung3 hei2	yun thung yung hei
cymbal	n	鐃鈸	nàauh baht	naau4 bat6	naauh paht
cymbidium /orchid	n	蘭花	làahn fā	laan4 faa1	laahn fa
cypress	n	柏	paak	paak3	phaak

D roman 'IV'		丁	dīng	ding1	teng
D.N.A.[1] (coll) Deoxyribo Nucleic Acid	abbr	遺傳因子	waih chyùhn yàn jí	wai6 cyun4 jan4 zi2	waih chhuhn yan chi
D.N.A.[2] (text) Deoxyribo Nucleic Acid	abbr	脫氧核糖核酸	tyut yéuhng haht tòhng haht syūn	tyut3 joeng5 hat6 tong4 hat6 syun1	thyut yeuhng haht tohng haht syun
daddy[1] (de)	n	爹哋	dè dìh	de4 di4	te tih
daddy[2] /dad	n	爸爸	bàh bā	baa4 baa1	pah pa
daffodil flower /narcissus	n	水仙花	séui sīn fā	seoi2 sin1 faa1	swoi sin fa
dagger	n	短劍	dyún gim	dyun2 gim3	tyun kim
dagger hidden in smiles (sl) smile face tiger /maked trap with smile/ entraped with smiles	v	笑裡藏刀	siu léuih chòhng dōu	siu3 leoi5 cong4 dou1	siu lowih chhohng tou
Dah Sing Bank	n	大新銀行	daaih sān ngàhn hòhng	daai6 san1 ngan4 hong4	taaih san ngahn hohng
dail wrong number		打錯	dá cho	daa2 co3	ta chho
daily[1] (coll) every day	adv	日日	yaht yaht	jat6 jat6	yaht yaht
daily[2] (wr) /each day/every day	adv	每日	múih yaht	mui5 jat6	muih yaht
daily[3] (wr) every day	adv	每天	múih tìn	mui5 tin4	muih thin
daily[4] (wr)	adj	周時	jàu sìh	zau4 si4	chau sih
daily[5] (wr)	adj	日常	yaht sèuhng	jat6 soeng4	yaht seuhng
daily[6] (wr) /every day/ constantly/day-to-day	adv	經常	gìng sèuhng	ging4 soeng4	keng seuhng
daily basis[1] /day-wages/ daily work	n	日散	yaht sáan	jat6 saan2	yaht saan
daily basis[2] /daily work	n	按日嘅	on yaht ge	on3 jat6 ge3	on yaht ke
daily help[1]	n	僕人	buhk yàhn	buk6 jan4.	puhk yahn
daily help[2]	n	打雜嘅佣人	dá jaahp ge yuhng yàhn	daa2 zaap6 ge3 jung6 jan4	ta chaahp ke yuhng yahn
daily update	v	更新日誌	gāng sàn yaht ji	gang1 san4 jat4 zi3	kang san yaht chi
dairy milk kept	n	製酪場	jai lok chèuhng	zai3 lok3 coeng4	chaijai lok chèuhng
dairy farm	n	牛奶公司	ngàuh láaih/náaih gūng sī	ngau4 laai5 /naai5 gung1 si1	ngauh laaih /naaih kung si
daisy wild flower	n	雛菊	chō gùk	co1 guk4	chho kuk
dam[1]	n	壩	ba	baa3	pa
dam[2] /dike	n	水壩	séui ba	seoi2 baa3	swoi pa
damage[1]	n	爛	laahn	laan6	laahn
damage[2] /disadvantage	n/v	損害	syún hoih	syun2 hoi6	syun hoih
damage[3]	v	傷害	sèung hoih	soeng4 hoi6	seung hoih
damage[4]	v	損壞	syún wàaih	syun2 waai6	syun waaih
damage[5]	v	受損	sauh syún	sau6 syun2	sauh syun
damage[6] /waste/destroy	v	毀壞	wái wàaih	wai2 waai6	wai waaih
damage loss	n	損失	syún sāt	syun2 sat1	syun sat
damage to property	v	財物損壞	chòih màht syún waaih	coi4 mat6 syun2 waai6	chhoih maht syun waaih

English	Part	Chinese	Romanization 1	Romanization 2	Romanization 3
damp /humid/moist	n	潮濕	chìuh sap	ciu4 sap3	chhiuh sap
dance[1]	n	舞	móuh	mou5	mouh
dance[2]	n	舞蹈	móuh douh	mou5 dou6	mouh touh
dance[3]	n	跳舞	tiu móuh	tiu3 mou5	thiu mouh
dancer	n	舞蹈家	móuh douh gà	mou5 dou6 ga4	mouh touh ka
dancing house	n	跳舞嘅大廳	tiu móuh ge daaih tèng	tiu3 mou5 ge3 daai6 teng4	thiu mouh ke taaih theng
dandruff /scalp/scurf	n	頭皮	tàuh pèih	tau4 pei4	thauh pheih
dare[1] /presume	v.aux	敢	gám	gam2	kam
dare[2]	v	勇敢	yúhng gám	jung5 gam2	yuhng kam
dark	n	黑暗	haak am /ngam	haak3 am3 /ngam3	haak am /ngam
dark age	n	黑暗時代	hāk am /ngam sìh doih	hak1 am3 /ngam3 si4 doi6	hak am /ngam sih toih
dark color[1]/deep color	adj	深	sàm	sam4	sam
dark color[2]/deep color	adj	深色	sàm sīk	sam4 sik1	sam sek
dark glasses /sun glasses	n	太陽鏡	taai yèuhng géng	taai3 joeng4 geng2	thaai yeuhng keng
dark green[1]	n	菜青	chói chèng	coi2 ceng4	chhoi chheng
dark green[2]	n	深綠色	sàm luhk sīk	sam4 luk6 sik1	sam luhk sek
darken	v	使變黑	sái bin haak	sai2 bin3 haak3	sai pin haak
darkly	adv	黑暗	hāk am /ngam	hak1 am3 /ngam3	hak ngam
darkness /lack of light	n	黑忟忟	hāak máng máng	haak1 mang2 mang2	haak mang mang
darling[1] (de)	n	打令	dā líng	daa1 ling2	ta ling
darning[2] /to darn	n	織補	jīk bóu	zik1 bou2	chek pou
dash[1] /move forward	v	突	daht	dat6	taht
dash[2]	v	猛撞	máahng johng	maang5 zong6	maahng chohng
dash[3] race in	n	短跑	dyún pàauh	dyun2 paau4	tyun phaauh
dash[4] symbol	n	符號 (一)	fuh houh	fu6 hou6	fuh houh
dashboard	n	儀錶板	yi bìu bāan	ji3 biu4 baan1	yi piu paan
data /information	n	資料	jì líu	zi4 liu2	chi liu
database /data bank	n	資料庫	jì líu fu	zi4 liu2 fu3	chi liu fu
date	n	日期	yaht kei	jat6 kei4	yaht khei
date and time	n	日期及時間	yaht kei gahp jahn gāan	jat6 kei4 gap6 zang6 gaan1	yaht khei kahp chahn kaan
date joined	n	入職日期	yahp jīk yaht kei	jap6 zik1 jat6 kei4	yahp chek yaht khei
date of birth	n	出生日期	chēut sāng yaht kèih	ceot1 sang1 jat6 kei4	chhot sang yaht kheih
daughter	n	女兒	léuih yì	leui5 ji4	lowih yih
daughter's husband /son in law	n	女婿	léuih sai	leui5 sai3	lowih sai
dawn[1]	n	天濛光	tìn mūng gwòng	tin4 mung1 gwong4	thin mung kwong
dawn[2]	n	曉	híu	hiu2	hiu
dawn[3]	n	拂曉	fāt híu	fat1 hiu2	fat hiu
day[1] /date	n	日	yaht	jat6	yaht
day[2]	n	天	tìn	tin4	thin
day[3]	n	一日	yāt yaht	jat1 jat6	yat yaht

English		Chinese	Yale	Jyutping	Other
day[4]	n	一天	yāt tìn	jat1 tin4	yat thin
day after day[1]	n	一日又一日	yāt yaht yahu yāt yaht	jat1 yat6 yau6 jat1 yat6	yat yaht yahu yat yaht
day after day[2]	n	一天又一天	yāt tīn yahu yāt tīn	jat1 tin1 yau6 jat1 tin1	yat thin yahu yat thin
day after today[1] (coll) tomorrow	n	聽日	tèng yàht	teng4 jat6	theng yaht
day after today[2] (wr) tomorrow	n	明天	mìhng tīn	ming4 tin1	mehng thin
day and night	n	日日夜夜	yaht yaht yeh yeh	jat6 jat6 je6 je6	yaht yaht yeh yeh
day before yesterday	n	前日	chìhn yaht	cin4 jat6	chhihn yaht
day dream /delusion/ fantasy/phantasy/illusion	n	幻想	waahn séung	waan6 soeng2	waahn seung
day light /sunlight	n	日光	yaht gwōng	jat6 gwong1	yaht kwong
day of the month /date	n	號	houh	hou6	houh
day shift	n	日更	yaht gāng	jat6 gang1	yaht kang
daybreak[1]	n	天光	tìn gwòng	tin4 gwong4	thin kwong
daybreak[2]	n	黎明	làih mìhng	lai4 ming4	laih mehng
daytime[1]	n	晝	jau	zau3	chau
daytime[2]	n	白晝	baahk jau	baak6 zau3	paahk chau
daytime[3]/sunshine/sun	n	日頭	yaht táu	jat6 tau2	yaht thau
daytime[4]	n	日間	yaht gāan	jat6 gaan1	yaht kaan
dazzle[1] /giddiness /blurred/not clear	v	眼花	ngáahn fà	ngaan5 faa4	ngaahn fa
dazzle[2] /make unclear vision	v	使眼花	sái ngáahn fà	sai2 ngaan5 faa4	sai ngaahn fa
DBS bank	n	星展銀行	sèng jín ngàhn hòhng	seng4 zin2 ngan4 hong4	seng chin ngahn hohng
dead[1] /late/die/deceased	adj	死	séi	sei2	sei
dead[2] /dying/late/no longer alive/gone to heaven	adj	死嘅	séi ge	sei2 ge3	sei ke
dead body[1]	n	拉柴	lāai chàaih	laai1 caai4	laai chhaaih
dead body[2] cover with cloth		布遮掩	bou jē yím	bou3 ze1 jim2	pou che yim
dead body check /post mortem/postmortem exam	n	死後的檢查	sēi hàuh dì gīm cha	sei1 hau6 di4 gim1 caa4	sei hauh ti kim chha
dead body wear cloths /burial clothes	n	壽衣	sauh yī	sau6 ji1	sauh yi
dead person	n	死人	séi yàhn	sei2 jan4	sei yahn
deadline	n	最後限期	jeui hauh haahn kèih	zeoi3 hau6 haan6 kei4	cheui hauh haahn kheih
deadly[1] /sleep to die/to die	adj/n	死亡	séi mòhng	sei2 mong4	sei mohng
deadly[2] /fatal	adj	致命	ji mihng	zi3 ming6	chi mehng
deaf[1] /deafness	adj	聾	lùhng	lung4	luhng
deaf[2]	n	聾啞人	lùhng āh yàhn	lung4 ah6 jan4	luhng ah yahn
deal[1]	n	易	yihk	jik6	yehk
deal[2] /pine wood	n	松木	chùhng muhk	cung4 muk6	chhuhng muhk
deal in cash /negotiable	adj	可兌現	ho deui yihn	ho2 deui3 jin6	ho toei yihn
deal with[1] /to treat	v	待	doih	doi6	toih
deal with[2] cope with /a tough problem/ person	v	對付	deui fuh	deoi3 fu6	toei fuh

dealing /intercourse/ contacts	n	往來	wóhng lòih	wong5 loi4	wohng loih
dealt /reach a deal	n	成交	seng gàau	seng3 gaau4	seng kaau
dean (of the university)	n	教務長	gaau mouh jéung	gaau3 mou6 zoeng2	kaau mouh cheung
dear friend	n	親愛嘅人	chàn oi /ngoi ge yàhn	can3 oi3 /ngoi3 ge3 jan4	chhan oi /ngoi ke yahn
dear customer	n	親愛嘅客戶	chàn oi /ngoi ge haak wuh	can3 oi3 /ngoi3 ge3 haak3 wu6	chhan oi /ngoi ke haak wuh
dearly /deep love	adv	充滿深情地	chùng múhn sàm chìhng deih	cung4 mun5 sam4 cing4 dei6	chhung muhn sam chehng teih
death[1]	n	死	séi	sei2	sei
death[2] (coll)	n	去咗	heui jó	heoi3 zo2	hoi cho
death penalty /death punishment	adj	死刑嘅	séi yìhng ge	sei2 jing4 ge3	sei yehng ke
death roll /number of killed people	n	死亡人數	séi mòhng yàhn sou	sei2 mong4 jan4 sou3	sei mohng yahn sou
debit /debtor	n	借方	je fòng	ze3 fong4	che fong
debt[1]	n	債	jaai	zaai3	chaai
debt[2] /loan money	n	借款	je fún	ze3 fun2	che fun
debtor	n	債務人	jaai mouh yàhn	zaai3 mou6 jan4	chaai mouh yahn
decade /decennium/ 10 years	n	十年	sahp lihn /nihn	sap6 lin4 /nin4	sahp lihn /nihn
decapitation /murder	n	杀頭	saat tàuh	saat3 tau4	saat thauh
decapitation /behead/ cut head	n	斬首	jáam sáu	zaam2 sau2	chaam sau
decay of food /rotten/ spoilage	v/adj	腐爛	fuh laahn	fu6 laan6	fuh laahn
deceased /late/die	adj	死	séi	sei2	sei
deceit mark /tricky sign /fake sign/fraud sign	n	行跡	hahng jīk	hang6 zik1	hahng chek
deceive (coll)	v	呃	àak /ngàak	ak4 /aak4	aak /ngaak
decelerate /reduce speed /slow down	v	減速	gáam chùk	gaam2 cuk4	kaam chhuk
December	n	十二月	sàhp yìh yùht	sap6 ji6 jyut6	sahp yih yuht
December 28th	n	十二月二十八	sàhp yìh yùht yìh sàhp báat	sap6 ji6 jyut6 ji6 sap6 baat2	sahp yih yuht yih sahp paat
decentralization	n	地方分權	deih fòng fàn kyuhn	dei6 fong4 fan4 kyun4	teih fong fan khyuhn
deception	n	欺騙	hei pin	hei3 pin3	hei phin
decide[1]	v	決	kyut	kyut3	khyut
decide[2]	v	選定	syún dehng /dihng	syun2 deng6 /ding6	syun tehng
decide[3] /resolve/settle/ solution/solve	n/v	解決	gáai kyut	gaai2 kyut3	kaai khyut
decimal[1]	adj	十進位	sahp jeun wàih	sap6 zeon3 wai4	sahp cheun waih
decimal[2] (.)	n	小數	síu sou	siu2 sou3	siu sou
decision[1] /decide /resolve casting choosing	n/v	決定	kyut dehng /dihng	kyut3 deng6 /ding6	khyut tehng
decision[2] /put out	n	作出	jok chēut	zok3 ceot1	chok chhot
deck	n	甲板	gaap báan	gaap3 baan2	kaap paan

English		Chinese	Yale	Jyutping	Romanization
decker	n	層板	chang báan	cang3 baan2	chhang paan
declaration /statement	n	聲明	sèng mìhng	seng4 ming4	seng mehng
declared	v	聲明	sèng mìhng	seng4 ming4	seng mehng
decline[1] /postpone	v	退遲	tèui chìh	teoi4 ci4	thoi chhih
decline[2] /go down	n	減退	gáam tèui	gaam2 teoi4	kaam thoi
decorator	n	裝飾者	jòng sīk jé	zong4 sik1 ze2	chong sek che
decrease[1] /subtract /minus/subtract/reduce	n/v	減	gáam	gaam2	kaam
decrease[2] /reduce	n/v	貶	pín	pin2	phin
decrease[3] /reduce/ lessen/weaken	v	減少	gáam síu	gaam2 siu2	kaam siu
dedicate	n	受奉獻	sauh fuhng hin	sau6 fung6 hin3	sauh fuhng hin
dedicatee	n	受奉獻者	sauh fuhng hin jé	sau6 fung6 hin3 ze2	sauh fuhng hin che
deduct /subtract	v	扣除	kau chèuih	kau3 ceoi4	khau chheuih
deducted monthly	v	扣除月份	kau chèuih yuht fahn	kau3 ceoi4 jyut6 fan6	khau chheuih yuht fahn
deed /action/operation/ proceeding	n	行動	hàhng duhng	hang4 dung6	hahng tohng
deed poll[1]	n	單務契約	dāan mouh kai yeuk	daan1 mou6 kai3 joek3	daan mouh khai yeuk
deed poll[2]	n	單方執行 的契約	dāan fòng jāp hàhng dìk kai yeuk	daan1 fong4 zap1 hang4 dik4 kai3 joek3	taan fong chap hahng tek khai yeuk
deem /see as	v	視為	sìh wai	si6 wai3	sih wai
deep /deeply/very deep	adj	深深	sàm sām	sam4 sam1	sam sam
deep breath		深呼吸	sàm fù kàp	sam4 fu4 kap4	sam fu khap
deep fried	v	炸	ja	zaa3 /zaa2	cha
deep fry /fried	vt	油炸	yàuh ja	jau4 za3	yauh cha
deep emotion /deep expression/deep feeling/deep mood	n	深情	sàm chìhng	sam4 cing4	sam chhehng
deep love		大慈愛	daaih chìh oi	daai6 ci4 oi3	taaih chhih oi
deep sad /sadden/distress /grieved/painfully sad/ srrowful	vt	悲痛	bēi tung	bei1 tung3	pei thung
deep sorrow /grieved	v	悲痛咗	bēi tung jó	pei1 tung3 zo2	pei thung cho
deep stick oil measure	n	機油尺	gèi yàuh chek	gei4 jau4 cek3	kei yauh chhek
deep track[1] of wheel /track/rut	n	轍	chit	cit6	chhit
deep track[2] /rut/wheel track	n	車轍	chè chit	ce4 cit6	chhe chhit
deep water	n	深水	sàm séui	sam3 seoi2	sam swoi
deeply search	v	修整過	sàu jéng gwo	sau1 jeng2 gwoh3	sau cheng gwo
deer	n	鹿	lúk	luk5	luk
defamation[1] /slander	n	詆譭	dái wái	dai2 wai2	tai wai
defamation[2]	n	譭謗人格	wái pong yàhn gaak	wai2 pong3 jan4 gaak3	wai phong yahn kaak
default	n	不履行	bāt léih hàhng	bat1 lei5 hang4	pat leih hahng
defeat /loss/fail	n	敗	baaih	baai6	paaih
defeated[1]	v	打敗	dá baaih	daa2 baai6	ta paaih
defeated[2]	v	敗北	baaih bāk	baai6 bak1	paaih pak

defect[1] /fault/demerit /shortcoming/weak point	n	缺點	kyut dím	kyut3 dim2	khyut tim
defect[2]	n	缺陷	kyut haahm	kyut3 haam6	khyut haahm
defect[3]	n	故障	gu jeung	gu3 zoeng3	ku cheung
defence[1] /prevention	n	預防	yuh fòhng	jyu6 fong4	yuh fohng
defence[2]	n	防護	fòhng wùh	fong4 wu6	fohng wuh
defend[1] /guard/protect	v	衛	waih	wai6	waih
defend[2]	v/i	防禦	fòhng yùh	fong4 jyu6	fohng wuh
defend[3] /preserve/shield /defense/protection/secure	v	保護	bóu wùh	bou2 wu6	pou wuh
defendant	n	被告	bèih gou	bei6 gou3	peih kou
defender /guardian	n	保護者	bóu wuh jé	bou2 wu6 ze2	pou wuh che
defense /security	n	保衛	bóu waih	bou2 wai6	pou waih
defensive[1]	adj	防衛	fòhng waih	fong4 wai6	foohng waih
defensive[2]	adj	防禦物	fòhng yùh maht	fong4 jyu6 mat6	fohng yuh maht
defensive[3]	adj	防禦的	fòhng yùh dìk	fong4 jyu6 dik4	fohng yuh tek
deficient[1] /scarcity	adj	不足	bāt jūk	bat1 juk1	pat chuk
deficient[2]	adj	有缺陷	yáuh kyút hàhm	jau5 kyut2 ham6	yauh khyut hahm
deficit	n	不足額	bāt jūk ngaahk	bat1 zuk1 ngaak6	pat chuk ngaahk
definitely[1] /surely	adv	一於	yāt yù	jat1 jyu4	yat yu
definitely[2]	adv	明確地	mìhng kok dèih	ming4 kok3 dei6	mehng khok teih
definition[1] /description/ explanation/interpretation	n	解釋	gáai sīk	gaai2 sik1	kaai sek
definition[2] /define	v	定議	dehng /dihng yih	deng6 /ding6 ji6	tehng yih
defogger (device)	n	除霧器	chèuih mòuh héi	ceoi4 mou6 hei2	chheuih mouh hei
deformed /ill-looking/ ugly/unshapely	adj	難看	làhn /nàhn hòn	laan4 /naan6 hon4	lahn /nahn hon
defragment	v	进行碎片 整理	jeun hàahng seui pin jíng léih	zeon3 haang4 seoi3 pin3 zing2 lei5	cheun haahng swoi phin cheng leih
defragmenter	n	整理碎片	jíng léih seui pin	zing2 lei5 seoi3 pin3	cheng leih swoi phin
defrost	v	除霜	chèuih sèung	ceoi4 soeng4	chheuih seung
defuse	v	拆除雷管	cháak chyù leui gūn	caak2 cyu4 leoi3 gun1	chhaak chhyu lowi kun
defy[1]	v	違抗	wàih kong	wai4 kong3	waih khong
defy[2] /not obey	v	唔服從	m̀ fuhk chùhng	m4 fuk6 cung4	mh fuhk chhuhng
degradation /sacked	n/v	革職	gaak jīk	gaak3 zik1	kaak chek
degrade[1] /demotion/ degradation	n	降級	gong kāp	gong3 kap1	kong khap
degrade[2]	v	貶低	bīn dài	bin1 dai4	pin tai
degree[1] /level/standard /manner	n	度	douh	dou6	touh
degree[2]	n	學位	hohk wái	hok6 wai2	hohk wai
degree[3] /angle	n	度數	douh sōu	dou6 sou1	touh sou
degrees /level	n	程度	ching dòuh	cing3 dou4	chheng touh
deity /god	n	神	sàhn	san4	sahn
delay[1] /postpone	v	延遲	yìhn chìh	jing4 ci4	yihn chhih
delay[2]	v	耽擱	dàam gók	daam4 gok2	taam kok

delay[3] /slow	v	阻遲	jó chìh	zo2 ci4	cho chhih
delay[4] /hold up/postpone	v	延誤	yìhn ngh	jin2 ng6	yihn ngh
delayed[1]	adj	遲	chìh	ci4	chhih
delayed[2]	adj	延遲	yìhn chìh	jing4 ci4	yihn chhih
delegate /represent/ representative/deputy/on behalf	n	代表	doih bíu	doi6 biu2	toih piu
deliberate[1]	v	慎重考慮	sahn juhng háau leuih	san6 zung6 haau2 leoi6	sahn chuhng haau lowih
deliberate[2] /knowingly/ consciously/wilfully	adj	深思熟慮	sām sī suhk leuih	sam1 si1 suk6 leoi6	sam si suhk lowih
deliberate violation	v	明知故犯	mìhng jì gu faahn	ming4 zi4 gu3 faan6	mehng chi ku faahn
deliberation	n	慎重嘅	sahn juhng ge	san6 zung6 ge3	sahn chuhng ke
delicate[1]	adj	清香嘅	seun doih	seon4 doi6	swon toih
delicate[2]	adj	細緻優雅	sai ji yāu ngáh	sai3 zi3 jau1 nga5	sai chi yau ngah
delicious[1] /tasty/very tasty	adj	好食	hóu sihk	hou2 sik6	hou sehk
delicious[2] /very delicious	adj	好好食	hóu hóu sihk	hou2 hou2 sik6	hou hou sehk
delicious[3] /tasty	adj	好味道	hóu meih douh	hou2 mei6 dou6	hou meih touh
delicious[4] /tasty	adj	美味	méih meih	mei5 mei6	meih meih
delicious[5]	adj	妙嘅	miuh ge	miu6 ge3	miuh ke
delicious food /very tasty/good test/tasty foods	adj	齒頰留香	chí gaap làuh hèung	ci2 gaap3 lau4 hoeng4	chhi kaap lauh heung
delighted	adj	喜事	héi sih	hei2 si6	hei sih
deliver[1] /send/give present	v	送	sung	sung3	sung
deliver[2]	v	致	ji	zi3	chi
deliver[3] /send/to send	v	派	paai	paai3	phaai
deliver[4] /hand over	v	交付	gāau fuh	gaau1 fu6	kaau fuh
deliver[5] give baby	v	接生兒	jip sāang yìh	zip saang1 ji4	chip saang yi
deliver child /giving birth/childbirth/childbearing /parturition	v	分娩	fahn míhn	fan6 min5	fahn mihn
delivery man	n	送貨人	sung fo yàhn	sung3 fo3 jan4	sung fo yahn
demand[1]	n	要	yiu	jiu3	yiu
demand[2] /pray/request	n	求	kàuh	kau4	khauh
demand[3]	n	需求	sèui kau	seoi4 kau3	swoi khau
demand[4]	n	所需之物	só sēui jī maht	so2 seoi1 zi1 mat6	so sēui chi maht
demander /claimant	n/v	要求者	yìu kàuh jé	jiu4 kau4 ze2	yiu khauh che
demean (sl)	v	踩	cháai	caai2	chhaai
dementia	n	癡呆	chī òih	ci1 oi4	chhi oih
demerit /weak point/ shortcoming/fault in character	n	短處	dyún chyu	dyun2 cyu3	tyun chyu
demo /demonstration/ protest	n	遊行示威	yàuh hàhng sìh wāi	jau4 hang4 si6 wai1	yauh hahng sih wai
democracy	n	民主	màhn jyú	man4 zyu2	mahn chyu

democratic[1]	adj	民主嘅	màhn jyú ge	man4 zyu2 ge3	mahn chyu ke
democratic[2]	adj	民主國家	màhn jyú gwok gà	man4 zyu2 gwok3 gaa4	mahn chyu kwok ka
demon	n	惡魔	ok /ngok mò	ok3 /ngok3 mo4	ok /ngok mo
demonstrate[1]	v	證明	jing mìhng	zing3 ming4	cheng mehng
demonstrate[2] /display/ exhibit	v	發揮	faat fāi	faat3 fai1	faat fai
demonstrate[3] /display/ show/let see	v	顯示	hín sih	hin2 si6	hin sih
demonstration[1]	n	示範	sih faahn	si6 faan6	sih faahn
demonstration[2] /procession	n	遊行	yàuh hàhng	jau4 hang4	yauh hahng
demonstration[3]	n	示威	sìh wāi	si6 wai1	sih wai
demonstration room	n	示範室	sih faahn sāt	si6 faan6 sat1	sih faahn sat
demonstrative	adj	感情外露嘅人	gám chìhng oih /ngoih louh ge yàhn	gam2 cing4 oi6 /ngoi6 lou6 ge3 jan4	kam chhehng oih /ngoih louh ke yahn
demonstrator /protester	n	示威者	sìh wāi jé	si6 wai1 ze2	sih wai che
denaturation /transsexual	n	變性者	bin sing jé	bin3 sing3 ze2	pin seng che
Denmark	n		dāan màhk	daan1 mak6	taan mahk
denote[1] /to notice	v	預示	yuh sih	jyu6 si6	yuh sih
denote[2] /indicate	v	指示	jí sih	zi2 si6	chi sih
dense	adj	密集	maht jaahp	mat6 zaap6	maht chaahp
density	n	密度	maht douh	mat6 dou6	maht touh
dental	adj	牙齒嘅	ngàh chī ge	ngaa4 ci1 ge3	ngah chhi ke
dentist	n	牙醫	ngàh yī	ngaa4 ji1	ngah yi
dentistry[1]	n	牙科	ngàh fō	ngaa4 fo1	ngah fo
dentistry[2]	n	牙科醫學	ngàh fō yī hohk	ngaa4 fo1 ji1 hok6	ngah fo yi hohk
deny /no/not/reject	adv/v	否	fáu	fau2	fau
denying /refuse/reject answer/opposing/not agree/ not decide/deny answer/ negative answer	adj/v	否定	fáu dihng	fau2 ding6	fau dehng
depart[1] /leave/go/went	v	去	heui	heoi3	hoi
depart[2] /go towards	v	往	wóhng	wong5	wohng
depart[3] (time)	v	逝	saih	sai6	saih
depart[4] /go out	v	開出	hòi chēut	hoi4 ceot1	hoi chhot
depart[5] /leave/quit	v	離開	lèih hòi	lei4 hoi4	leih hoi
depart[6]	v	背離	bui lèih	bui3 lei4	pui leih
depart[7] /pass away/die/late	adj/v	去世	héui sai	heoi2 sai3	hoi sai
departed[1] died/dead person	n	死者	séi jé	sei2 ze2	sei che
departed[2] (wr) /died	n	去世者	héui sai jé	heoi2 sai3 ze2	hoi sai che
department[1] /section/ division	n	部	bouh	bou6	pouh
department[2] bureau/ classifier of government office	n	局	gúk	guk2	kuk

department[3] /office/bureau	n	處	chyu	cyu3	chhyu
department[4] /division/sector	n	部門	bouh mùhn	bou6 mun4	pouh muhn
department store	n	百貨公司	baak fó gūng sì	baak3 fo2 gung1 si4	paak fo kung si
departure /leaving	n	離開	lèih hòi	lei4 hoi4	leih hoi
depend on self	adj	靠自己	kaau jih géi	kaau3 zi6 gei2	khaau chih kei
depends on /depend upon	n	靠	kaau	kaau3	khaau
dependable /reliable	adj	靠得住	kaau dāk jyuh	kaau3 dak1 zyu6	khaau tak chyuh
dependence /recourse/be dependent on	n	依賴	yì laaih	ji4 laai6	yi laaih
dependant[1] family	adj	卷屬	gyun suhk	gyun3 suk6	kyun suhk
dependant[2]	n	受撫養者	sauh fú yéuhng jé	sau6 fu2 joeng5 ze2	sauh fu yeuhng che
dependent on each other		彼此依賴	béi chí yì laaih	bei2 ci2 ji4 laai6	pei chhi yi laaih
depends on	v	睇	tái	tai2	thai
depends on you	n	你決定	léih kyut dehng /dihng	lei5 kyut3 deng6 /ding6	leih khyut tehng
deplete[1] /consume/eat up/ use up	v	耗盡	hou jeuhn	hou3 zeon6	hou cheuhn
deplete[2] /use up completely	v	用盡	yuhng jeuhn	jung6 zeon6	yuhng cheuhn
deploy	v	配置	pui ji	piu3 zi3	phui chi
deport[1] /expel/repel/pushes away/banishment	v	驅逐	kèui juhk	keoi4 zuk6	khoi chuhk
deport[2]	v	驅逐出境	kèui juhk chēut gìng	keoi4 zuk6 ceot1 ging4	khoi chuhk chhot keng
deposit[1] /balance/store	v	存	chyùhn	cyun4	chhyuhn
deposit[2]	v	寄存	gei chyùhn	gei3 cyun4	kei chhyuhn
deposit[3]	v	存儲	chyùhn chyúh	cyun4 cyu5	chhyuhn chhyuh
deposit[4] /advance payment/trust money	n	定金	dehng /dihng gām	deng6 /ding6 gam1	tehng kam
depositor	n	存款人	chyùhn fún yàhn	cyun4 fun2 jan4	chhyuhn fun yahn
deposits[1] mineral	n	礦床	kwong chòhng	kwong3 cong4	khwong chhohng
deposits[2] gold	n	金礦	gām chòhng	gam1 cong4	kam chhohng
depot /stored	n	儲藏	chyúh chòhng	cyu5 cong4	chhyuh chhohng
deprave[1]	v	使墮落	sái doh lohk	sai2 do6 lok6	sai toh lohk
deprave[2]	v	使腐化	sái fú fa	sai2 fu2 faa3	sai fu fa
depraved /morally bad	adj	墮落嘅	doh lohk ge	do6 lok6 ge3	toh lohk ke
depressed[1] /anxious	v	怫	fai	fai3	fai
depressed[2]	v	憂鬱	yàu wāt	jau4 wat1	yau wat
depressed[3]	v	壓低的	áat dài dìk	aat2 dai4 dik4	aat tai tek
depth[1]	n	深度	sàm dòuh	sam4 dou6	sam touh
depth[2] of water	n	水深	séui sām	seoi2 sam1	swoi sam
desalination	n	去鹽作用	heui yìhm jok yuhng	heoi3 jim4 zok jung6	hoi yihm chok yuhng
descent[1] /get down/drop /alight/to fall/leave/go down out/dismount/get off/go out	n/v	落	lohk	lok6	lohk

descent[2] downfall	n	降落	gong lohk	gong3 lok6	kong lohk
descent[3] /downfall	n	倒台	dou tòih	dou3 toi4	tou thoih
descent[4] family origins	n	血統	hyut túng	hyut3 tung2	hyut thong
descent[5] family origins	n	遺傳	wàih chyùhn	wai4 cyun4	waih chhyuhn
description[1]	n	描寫	mìuh sé	miu4 se2	miuh se
description[2] /details	adj	內容	loih /noih yung	loi6 /noi6 jung3	loih /noih yung
description[3]	n	形容	yìhng yùhng	jing4 jung4	yehng yuhng
desert[1]	n	沙漠	sà mohk	saa4 mok6	sa mohk
desert[2]	v	離棄	leih hei	lei4 hei3	leih hei
deserted area /remote area	n	偏僻	pīn pìk	pin1 pik4	phin phek
deserves /it is right	v	該得	gòi dāk	goi4 dak1	koi tak
design /layout/outline /outline/sketch	v	設計	chit gai	cit3 gai3	chhit kai
designate	v	標明	bīu mìhng	biu1 ming4	piu mihng
designer[coll] /stylist /architect	n	設計者	chit gai jé	cit3 gai3 ze2	chhit kai che
desire[1] /intention/wish/ to think/idea/thought/ to expect	n	意	yi	ji3	yi
desire[2] /wish/aspire /wish to become/would	v/aux	願望	yuhn mòhng	jyun6 mong6	yuhn mohng
desire[3] /thirst	v	欲望	yuhk mohng	juk6 mong6	yuhk mohng
desire[4] /wish/intention /motive	v	動機	duhng gèi	dung6 gei4	tuhng kei
desirous /wishful	adj	渴望	hot mohng	hot3 mong6	hot mohng
desk	n	書桌	syù chéuk	syu4 coek2	syu chheuk
despair[1] /frustration/ lose hope	n	失望	sāt mohng	sat1 mong6	sat mohng
despair[2] /hopeless /desperation	adj/n	絕望	jyuht mohng	zyut6 mong6	chyuht mohng
despatch[1]	v	派遣	paaih hín	paai6 hin2	phaaih hin
despatch[2]	v	快遞	faai daih	faai3 dai6	faai taih
despatch[3]	v	迅速了結	seun chùk líuh git	seon3 cuk4 liu5 git3	swon chhuk liuh kit
desperate person[coll] uncivilized/uncultured/awolf man	n	狼	lòhng	long4	lohng
despise	v	藐	míuh	miu5	miuh
despite	n	惡意	ok /ngok yi	ok3 /ngok3 ji3	ok /ngok yi
dessert[1] /sweet	n	甜品	tìhm bán	tim4 ban2	thihm pan
dessert[2]	n	餐後甜點	chāan hauh tìhm dím	caan1 hau6 tim4 dim2	chhaan hauh thihm tim
destination	n	目的地	mùhk dìk dèih	muk6 dik4 dei6	muhk tek teih
destined	adj	整定	jíng dehng /dihng	zing2 deng6 /ding6	cheng tehng
destroy[1] /damage/undo	v	破壞	po waaih	po3 waai6	pho waaih
destroy[2]	v	毀掉	wái diuh	wai2 diu6	wai tiuh
destroyer	n	驅逐艦	kèui juhk laahm	keoi1 zuk6 laam6	khoi chuhk laahm

destruction[1] /violence /fierce	adj	兇殘	hung chàahn	hung1 caan4	hung chhaahn
destruction[2]	n	破壞	po waaih	po3 waai6	pho waaih
detached	adj	分離嘅	fàn lèih ge	fan4 lei4 ge3	fan leih ke
details /particulars details	n	細節	sai jit	sai3 zit3	sai chit
detailed[1]	adj	詳	chèuhng	coeng4	chheuhng
detailed[2] /in detail/history	adj	詳細	chèuhng sai	coeng4 sai3	chheuhng sai
detailed[3] /describe	adj/v	描述	mìuh seuht	miu4 seot6	miuh swoht
detain /detention /retention/arrest	n/v	扣留	kau làuh	kau3 lau4	khau lauh
detain & question	v	扣查	kau chàh	kau3 caa4	khau chhah
detect[1]	v	偵查	jìng chàh	kau3 caa4	cheng chah
detect[2]	v	察覺	chàai gok	caat3 gok3	chhaai kok
detective /spy	n	偵探	jìng taam	zing4 taam3	cheng thaam
detector[1]	n	探測器	tàam chàak héi	taam4 caak4 hei2	thaam chhaak hei
detector[2] /finder	n	發現者	faat yihng jé	faat3 jin6 ze2	faat yihng che
detention[1] /imprisonment	n	監禁	gàam gam	gaam4 gam3	kaam kam
detention[2]	n	扣押	kau aat	kau3 aat3	khau aat
deterge	v	洗淨	sái jehng	sai2 zeng6	sai chehng
detergent[1]	n	洗潔精	sái git jeng /jìng	sai2 git3 zeng4 /zing4	sai kit cheng
detergent[2]	n	去垢劑	heui gau jāi	heoi3 gau3 zai1	hoi kau chai
determinately	adj	果斷	gwó túhn	gwo2 tyun5	kwo thuhn
determined	adj	決心	kyut sàm	kyut sam4	khyut sam
detest hate	v	猛憎	máhng jàng	maang5 zang4	mahng chang
devaluated	v	貶值	pín jihk	pin2 zik6	phin chehk
develop[1] /evolution /expand	v	發展	faat jín	faat3 zin2	faat chin
develop[2]	v	演變	yín bin	jin2 bin3	yin pin
develop[3]	v	使發達	si faat daaht	si3 faat3 daat6	si faat taaht
developed	adj	發達嘅	faat daaht ge	faat3 daat6 ge3	faat taaht ke
developing /development	adj/n	開發	hòi faat	hoi4 faat3	hoi faat
development	n	成長	sèhng jéung	seng4 zoeng2	sehng cheung
deviate	v	脫離	tyut lèih	tyut3 lei4	thyut leih
deviation /error	n	誤差	ngh chā	ng6 ca1	ngh chha
device[1] /equipment	n	設備	chít bèih	cit2 bei6	chhit peih
device[2]	n	設計	chit gai	cit3 gai3	chhit kai
devil[1] /demon/satan/giant/ ghose/evil spirit/fiend/goblin	n	魔鬼	mò gwái	mo4 gwai2	mo kwai
devil[2] /sprite/monster	n	妖怪	yìu gwáai	jiu4 gwaai2	yiu kwaai
devil mind	n	心魔	sàm mo	sam4 mo3	sam mo
devote /dedication	n	奉獻	fuhng hin	fung6 hin3	fuhng hin
devoted	adj	專心	jyùn sàm	zyun1 sam4	chyun sam
devotee /devoted	n/adj	好心機	hóu sām gèi	hou2 sam1 gei4	hou sam kei
devotion[1] /worship	n	拜	baai	baai3	paai

devotion[2]	n	熱誠	yiht sìhng	jit6 sing4	yiht sehng
devotional	adj	虔誠嘅	kìhn sìhng ge	kin4 sing4 ge3	khihn sehng ke
devour	v	狼吞虎嚥	lòhng tàn fú yin	long4 tan4 fu2 jin3	lohng than fu yin
devout[1] /reverent	adj	虔誠	kìhn sìhng	kin4 sing4	khihn sehng
devout[2] /reverent	adj	虔敬	kìhn ging	kin4 ging3	khihn keng
devouter[1]	n	虔誠人	kìhn sìhng yàhn	kin4 sing4 jan4	khihn sehng yahn
devouter[2]	n	虔誠者	kìhn sìhng jé	king4 sing4 ze2	khihn sehng che
dew[1]	n	露	lauh	lau6	lauh
dew[2]	n	露水	lauh séui	lau6 seoi2	lauh swoi
dexterity /skillful-hand	n	手巧	sáu hāau	sau2 haau1	sau haau
diabetes	n	糖尿病	tòhng niuh behng /bihng	tong4 niu6 beng6 /bing6	thohng niuh pehng
diagnose[1]	v	診症	chán jing	can2 zing3	chhan cheng
diagnose[2]	v	睇症	tái jing	tai2 zing3	thai cheng
diagnose[3] /diagnosis	v	診斷	chán dyuhn	can2 dyun6	chhan tyuhn
diagonal[1] /slash	adj	斜線	chèh sin	ce4 sin3	chheh sin
diagonal[2] /a straight line	adj	對角線	deui gok sin	deoi3 gok3 sin3	toei kok sin
diagonally	adj	斜地	che deih	ce3 dei6	chhe teih
diagonally opposite	adj	斜對面	chèh deui mihn	ce4 deui3 min6	chheh twoi mihn
dial telephone	v	撥號	buht hòuh	but6 hou4	puht houh
dial of watch	n	錶面	bīu mín	biu1 min2	piu min
dial phone /give ring/ ring phone/make phone call/telephone dial/ring up	v	打電話	dá dihn wá	daa2 din6 waa2	ta tihn wa
dialect	n	方言	fòng yìhn	fong4 jin4	fong yihn
diameter[1] /narrow road /path	n	徑	ging	ging3	keng
diameter[2]	n	直徑	jihk ging	zik6 ging3	chehk keng
diamond	n	鑽石	jyun sehk	zyun3 sek6	chyun sehk
diaphram	n	橫隔膜	wàahng gaak mók	waang4 gaak3 mok2	waahng kaak mok
diarrhea[1]	n	肚疴	tóuh ngò	tou5 o1	thouh ngo
diarrhea[2]	n	肚瀉	tóuh sē	tou5 se1	thouh se
diarrhoea & vomiting /cholera	n	水土不服	séui tōu bāt fuhk	seoi2 tou1 bat1 fuk6	swoi thou pat fuhk
diary	n	日記	yaht gei	jat6 gei3	yaht kei
dice western. game	n	骰仔	sīk jái	sik1 zai3	sek chai
diced of foot/meat /cubes	n	丁	dīng	ding1	teng
diced beef	n	牛肉粒	ngàuh yuhk lap /nap	ngau juk6 lap3 /nap3	ngauh yuhk lap /nap
diced chicken[1]	n	雞丁	gài dīng	gai4 ding1	kai teng
diced chicken[2]	n	雞粒	gài lap /nap	gai4 lap3 /nap3	kai lap /nap
diced meat	n	肉粒	yuhk lap /nap	juk6 lap3 /nap3	yuhk lap /nap
diced pork	n	豬肉丁	jyù yuhk dīng	zyu4 juk6 ding1	chyu yuhk teng
dictation	n	聽寫	tèng sé	teng4 se2	theng se
dictator	n	獨裁者	duhk chòih jé	duk6 coi4 ze2	tuhk chhoih che
dictionary[1]	n	字典	jih dín	zi6 din2	chih tin
dictionary[2]	n	辭典/词典	chìh dín	ci4 din2	chhih tin

dictionary³	n	詞彙表	chìh wuih bíu	ci4 wui6 biu2	chhih wuih piu
did	aux	幹	gon	gon3	kon
did he say?		佢有冇話	kéuih yauh móuh wá?	keoi5 jau6 mou5 waa2?	khoih yauh mouh wa?
did i hurt you?		我有冇傷害到你？	ngóh yáuh móuh sèung hoih dou léih /néih?	ngo5 jau5 mou5 soeng4 hoi6 dou3 lei5 /nei5?	ngoh yauh mouh seung hoih tou leih /neih?
did not expect /not expected	adj	估唔到	gú m̀ dou	gu2 m4 dou3	ku mh tou
did not match		唔親	m̀ chàn	m4 can4	mh chhan
did reserved time?	v	有冇預約	yáuh móuh yuh yeuk	jau5 mou5 jyu6 joek3	yauh mouh yuh yeuk
did they mind?		佢哋唔介意吧？	kéuih deih m̀ gaai yi bā?	keoi5 dei6 m4 gaai3 ji3 baa1?	khoih teih mh kaai yi pa?
did you see? /do you see?		有冇見到？	yáuh móuh gin dou?	jau5 mou5 gin3 dou3?	yauh mouh kin tou?
die¹	v	死	séi	sei2	sei
die² /late/pass away	adj/v	過身	gwo sàn	gwo3 san4	kwo san
die³ old man	v	仙遊	sìn yàuh	sin4 jau4	sin yauh
die⁴ /pass away	v	逝世	saih sai	sai6 sai3	saih sai
die by sick	v	病死	behng /bihng séi	beng6 /bing6 sei2	pehng sei
die by vehicle	v	車死	chè séi	ce1 sei4	chhe sei
died (sl)	v	走咗	jáu jó	zau2 zo2	chau cho
diesel oil	n	柴油	chàaih yàuh	caai4 jau4	chhaaih yauh
difference¹	n	分別	fàn biht	fan4 bit6	fan piht
difference² /contrast	n	差別	chāai biht	caai1 bit6	chhaai piht
difference³ of opinion /position	n	分歧	fàn kèih	fan6 kei4	fan kheih
different¹ /other/separate	adj	異	yih	ji6	yih
different² /varied/unlike/ dissimilar/differs	adj/v	唔同	m̀ tùhng	m4 tung4	mh thuhng
different³ /dissimilar /differs	adj	不同	bāt tùhng	bat1 tung4	pat thuhng
different⁴	adj	再嚟	joi làih	zoi3 lai4	choi laih
different caste /not same caste	n	異族	yih juhk	ji6 zuk6	yih chuhk
different road /not same road/unsuitable road	adj	唔啱路	m̀ ngāam louh	m4 ngaam1 lou6	mh ngaam louh
different sex	n	異性	yih sing	ji6 sing3	yih seng
differential gear	n	差動齒輪	chà dùhng chí leun	caa4 dung6 ci2 leon3	chha tohng chhi leun
difficult¹	adj	難	làahn /nàahn	laan4 /naan4	laahn /naahn
difficult²	adj	難深	làahn sām	laan4 sam1	laahn sam
difficult question¹ /puzzle question/riddle	n	粗篩	chòu sài	cou4 sai4	chhou sai
difficult question² /riddle/confusing question	n	出謎	chēut màih	ceot1 mai4	chhot maih
difficult situation	adj	身處	sàn chyú	san4 cyu2	san chhyu
difficult to explain /mysterious/weirdness	adj	神秘	sàhn bei	san4 bei3	sahn pei

difficult to learn		難 學	làahn hohk	laan4 hok6	laahn hohk
difficult to reach area /far from the city	adj	偏僻	pīn pìk	pin1 pik4	phin phek
difficult to study /complicate to study		難以學	làahn yíh hohk	laan4 yi5 hok6	laahn yih hohk
difficulty[1]	n	難關	làahn gwàan	laan4 gwaan4	laahn kwaan
difficulty[2]	n	困難	kwan làahn /nàahn	kwan3 laan4 /naan4	khwan laahn /naahn
difficulty work /hard work	n	重負	chúhng fuh	cung5 fu6	chhuhng fuh
diffusion	n	擴散	kwong saan	kwong3 saan3	khwong saan
dig[1]	v	掘	gwaht	gwat6	kwaat
dig[2]	v	挖	waat	waat3	waat
dig up	v	掘起	gwaht héi	gwat6 hei2	kwaat hei
digest	v	消化	sìu fa	siu4 faa3	siu fa
digestive /digestion	adj/n	消化	sìu fa	siu4 faa3	siu fa
digital (electronics) /number/figure/digit/ numerals/amount	n	數字	sou jih	sou3 zi6	sou chih
digital camera	n	數碼相機	sōu máh sèung gèi	sou1 ma5 soeng4 gei4	sou mah seung kei
digital video	n	數碼錄影機	sōu máh lùhk yīng gèi	sou1 ma5 luk6 jing1 gei4	sou mah lùhk ying kei
dignified[1]	adj	有尊嚴	yáuh jyùn yìhm	jau5 zeon4 jim4	yauh chyun yihm
dignified[2]	adj	威嚴	wāi yìhm	wai1 jim4	wai yihm
dignity[1] honor	n	尊嚴	jyùn yìhm	zyun4 jim4	chyun yihm
dignity[2] /honesty	n	誠實	sing sàht	sing3 sat6	seng saht
dignity[3] /proud/arrogant /egoist/pride	n	得意	dāk yi	dak1 ji3	tak yi
dike[1] /dam /dyke	n	堤	tàih	tai4	thaih
dike[2] /pond	n	塘	tòhng	tong4	thohng
diligent[1] /hardworking/ laborious/industrious/hard labour	adj	勤力	kàhn lihk	kan4 lik6	khahn lehk
diligent[2]	adj	勤奮	kàhn fáhn	kan4 fan5	khahn fahn
diligent[3] /hardworking	adj	勤勞	kàhn lòuh	kan4 lou4	khahn louh
dim[1] /dark/gloomy	adj	陰暗	yām am /ngam	jam1 am3 /ngam3	yam am /ngam
dim[2] /gloomy	adj	暗淡	am /ngam táahm	am3 /ngam3 taam6	am /ngam thaahm
dim[3] /dark	adj	蒙查查	muhng chàh chàh	mung4 caa4 caa4	muhng chhah chhah
dimension[1] /size	n	尺寸	chek chyun	cek3 cyun3	chhek chhyun
dimension[2]	n	範圍	faahn wai	faan6 wai3	faahn wai
dimensional	n	尺寸的	chek chyún dìk	cek3 cyun3 dik4	chhek chhyun tek
dimsum	n	點心	dím sām	dim2 sam1	tim sam
dining	n	進餐	jeun chāan	zeon3 caan1	cheun chhaan
dining room	n	飯廳	faahn tēng	faan6 teng1	faahn teng
dining table	n	餐桌	chāan chéuk	caan1 coek3	chhaan cheuk
dinner /supper	n	晚餐	máahn chāan	maan2 caan1	maahn chhaan
dinner 18:00-20:00 /supper	n	晚飯	máahn faahn	máan5 faan6	maahn faahn

English		Chinese	Romanization	Jyutping	Alt
dinner dance	n	舞宴	móuh yin	mou5 jin3	mouh yin
dinner party	n	餐會	chāan wuih	caan1 wui6	chhaan wuih
dinosaur	n	恐龍	húng lùhng	hung2 lung4	hung luhng
dip[1] /to soak/to immerse	v	浸	jam	zam3	cham
dip[2] fall down	v	下降	hah hòhng	ha6 hong4	hah hohng
diploma	n	學位證書	hohk wái jing syù	hok6 wai2 zing3 syu4	hohk wai cheng syu
diplomacy /foreign affairs	n	外交	oih /ngoih gāau	oi6 /ngoi6 gaau1	oih /ngoih kaau
diplomat	n	外交官	oih /ngoih gāau gùn	oi6 /ngoi6 gaau1 gun4	oih /ngoih kaau kun
diplomatic	adj	外交	oih /ngoih gāau	oi6 /ngoi6 gaau1	oih /ngoih kaau
diplomatic bag	n	外交信袋	oih /ngoih gāau seun dói	oi6 /ngoi6 gaau1 seon3 doi2	oih /ngoih kaau swon toi
dire[1] /fearful/awful/terrible! /horrendous/frightful	adj	可怕	hó pa	ho2 paa3	ho pha
dire[2] /sorrowful/tragic	adj	悲慘	bèi cháam	bei4 caam2	pei chhaam
direct	adj	指揮	jí paai	zi2 paai3	chi phaai
direct say/directly speak /straight speak/frank speaking	adv	直言	jihk yìhn	zik6 jin4	chehk yihn
direct travel	adj	直通	jihk tùng	zik6 tung4	chehk thung
direction[1]	n	方	fòng	fong4	fong
direction[2]	n	方向	fòng heung	fong4 hoeng3	fong heung
direction[3] /the face/to side	n	向	heung	hoeng3	heung
directly	adv	直接地	jihk jip deih	zik6 zip3 dei6	chehk chip teih
directly road[1]	n	近路	káhn louh	kan5 lou6	khahn louh
directly road[2]	n	捷徑	jit gíng	zit3 ging2	chit keng
director[1] /major/head /in charge/supervisor	n	主任	jyú yahm	zyu2 jam6	chyu yahm
director[2] /in charge	n	主管	jyú gún	zyu2 gun2	chyu kun
director general	n	總裁	júng chòih	zung2 coi4	chung chhoih
directory[1] /guide book	n	指南	jí nàahm	zi2 naam4	chi naahm
directory[2]	n	姓名住址簿	seng méng jyuh jí bouh	seng3 meng2 jyu6 zi2 bou6	seng meng chyuh chi pouh
directress	n	女主管	léuih jyú gún	leui5 zyu2 gun2	lowih chyu kun
dirt thing	n	污物	wū maht	wu1 mat6	wu maht
dirty[1]	adj	污	wù	wu4	wu
dirty[2] /foul	adj	髒	jōng	zong1	chong
dirty[3] /foul/filthy/nasty	adj	骯	ōng /ngōng	ong1 /ngong1	ong /ngong
dirty[4] /waste	adj	污糟	wù jòu	wu4 zou4	wu chou
dirty[5]	adj	污穢	wū wai	wu1 wai3	wu wai
dirty[6] /litter/rubbish/waste /garbage/trash/refuse/waste	n/adj	垃圾	laahp saap	laap6 saap3	laahp saap
dirty[7]	adj	髒嘅	jōng ge	zong1 ge3	chong ke
dirty[8]	adj	不潔	bāt git	bat1 git3	pat kit
dirty[9]	adj	邋遢	laaht taat	laat6 taat3	laaht thaat
dirty face /bad thinking	adj	臭臉	chau líhm	cau3 lim5	chhau lihm

dirty look	adj	醜樣	cháu yéung	cau2 joeng2	chhau yeung
dirty minded /horny bastard		成晚混	sìhng máahn wahn	sing3 maan5 wan6	sehng maahn wahn
dirty money	n	黑錢	hāk chìhn	hak1 cin4	hak chhihn
dirty water	adj	污濁	wū juhk	wu1 zuk6	wu chuhk
dirty word /bad language	adj	髒話	jōng wá	zong1 waa2	chong wa
dirty work	adj	不法行為	bāt faat hàahng wàih	bat1 faat3 haang4 wai4	pat faat haahng waih
disabled[1]	adj	功能失效	gùng nàhng sāt haauh	gung4 nang4 sat1 haau6	kung nahng sat haauh
disabled[2]	adj	有缺陷的	yáuh kyút hàhm dìk	jau5 kyut2 ham6 dik4	yauh khyut hahm tek
disabled person[1]	n	殘疾人	chàahn jaht yàhn	caan4 zaht jan4	chhaahn chaht yahn
disabled person[2]	n	傷殘者	sèung chàahn jé	soeng4 caan4 ze2	seung chhaahn che
disadvantage	n	不利	bāt leih	bat1 lei6	pat leih
disadvantaged	adj	不利嘅	bāt leih ge	bat1 lei6 ge3	pat leih ke
disagree[1]	v	唔同意	m̀ tùhng yi	m4 tung4 ji3	mh thuhng yi
disagree[2]	v	意見不合	yi gin bāt hahp	ji3 gin3 bat1 hap6	yi kin pat hahp
disappear /vanish/pass	v	消失	sìu sàt	siu4 sat4	siu sat
disappointed[1]	adj	失望	sāt mohng	sat1 mong6	sat mohng
disappointed[2]	adj	使失望	sái sāt mohng	sai2 sat1 mong6	sai sat mohng
disapprove	v	不贊成	bāt jaan sìhng	bat1 zaan seng4	pat chaan sehng
disarmed /disarmament /unarmed/not carrying weapon	n/adj	解除武裝	gaai chèuih móuh jòng	gaai3 ceoi4 mou5 zong1	kaai chheuih mouh chong
disorder[1] /disarrangement	n	冇秩序	móuh diht jeuih	mou2 dit6 zeoi6	mouh tiht choih
disorder[2] /disarrangement	n	雜亂	jaahp lyuhn	zaap6 lyun6	chaahp lyuhn
disaster[1]	n	災害	jòi hot	zoi4 hot3	choi hot
disaster[2] /mishap/agony /misfortune/distress	n	災禍	jòi wóh	zoi4 wo5	choi woh
disaster[3]	n	災難	jòi naahn	zoi4 maan6	choi naahn
disaster-area	n	災區	jòi kèui	zoi4 keoi4	choi khoi
disbelief[1] /unbelief	n	唔相信	m̀ sēung seun	m4 soeng1 seon3	mh seung seun
disbelief[2]	n	好難相信	hóu nàahn sēung seun	hou2 naan4 soeng1 seon3	hou naahn seung swon
disbelieve /discredit/ suspect/doubt/suspicion	v	懷疑	wàaih yìh	waai4 ji4	waaih yih
disc[1] /CD	n	片	pin	pin3	phin
disc[2] /CD	n	盤狀物	pun jòhng màht	pun3 zong4 mat4	phun chohng maht
disc[3] /CD	n	磁盤	chìh pùhn	ci4 pun4	chhih phuhn
disk /disc /CD	n	圓盤	yùhn pun	jyun4 pun3	yuhn phun
discharge[1] of liquid /drip liquid /leak out liquid	n	洩	sit	sit3	sit
discharge[2] /expelled	v	排出	paai chèut	paai3 ceot4	phaai chhot

English		Chinese	Yale	Jyutping	Romanization
discharge[3] /dismiss job/ fire-a person/terminate/sack /turn away	v	解僱	gáai gu	gaai2 gu3	kaai ku
discharge[4] (from hospital) /leave hospital	v	出院	chēut yún	ceot1 jyun2	chhot yun
discharge[5] /releasing	v	履行	léih hàhng	lei5 hang4	leih hahng
discharge from nose /snivel/nasal mucus	n	鼻涕	beih tai	bei6 tai3	peih thai
discharge semen[1] (sl)	n	九淺一深	gáu chín yāt sàm	gau2 cin2 jat1 sam4	kau chhin yat sam
discharge semen[2] (sl) /ejaculation/semen rush discharged	n	射精	sèh jēng	se6 zeng1	seh cheng
discharge warring	v	再充電指示燈	joi chūng dihn jí sih dāng	zoi3 cung1 din6 zi2 si6 dang1	choi chhung tihn chi sih tang
disciple /follower	n	門徒	mùhn tòuh	mun4 tou4	muhn thouh
discipline[1]	n	紀律	géi leuht	gei2 leot6	kei leuht
discipline[2]	n	訓練	fan lihn	fan3 lin6	fan lihn
disclosed secret /leak a secret/secret leak out/leak water/ooze	v	洩漏	sit lauh	sit3 lau6	sit lauh
disclosure	n	披露	pēi louh	pei1 lou6	phei louh
disco[1]	n	的士高	dīk sih gōu	dik1 si6 gou1	tik sih kou
disco[2]	n	舞廳	móuh tèng	mou5 teng4	mouh theng
disconnect /disengage	v	使分離	sí fàn lèih	si2 fan4 lei4	si fan leih
discontente oneself /gloomy	adj	欸	hām	ham1	ham
discontinue[1] /bring to halt/stop doing	v	斷	túhn	tyun5	thuhn
discontinue[2] /stop doing	v	冇延長	móuh yìhn chèuhng	mou5 jin4 coeng4	mouh yihn chheuhng
discount[1]	n	折	jit	zit3	chit
discount[2]	n	折扣	jit kau	zit3 kau3	chit khau
discount[3]	n	優待	yàu doih	jau4 doi6	yau toih
discouraged	adj	令到...灰	lihng dou...fùi sàm	ling4 dou3...fui4 sam4	lehng tou ... fui sam
discouragement	n	灰心	fùi sàm	fui4 sam4	fui sam
discourteous	adj	粗魯	chòu lóuh	cou4 lou5	chhou louh
discover[1]	v	看出	hōn chēut	hon1 ceot1	hon chhot
discover[2] /find/find out/finding	v	發現	faat yihn	faat3 jim6	faat yihn
discover[3] /found/to find	v	找到	jáau dou	zaau2 dou3	chaau tou
discovery /find	n/v	發覺	faat gok	faat3 gok3	faat kok
discretionary /unconditional	adj	無條件	móuh tìuh gín	mou5 tiu4 gin2	mouh thiuh kin
discriminate[1]	v	歧視	kèih sih	kei4 si6	kheih sih
discriminate[2]	v	辨別	baahn biht	baan6 bit6	paahn piht
discrimination	n	區別	kèui biht	keoi4 bit6	khoi piht
discrown	v	使退位	sai teui wàih	sai3 teui3 wai4	sai teoi waih
discus athletics event	n	鐵餅	tit béng	tit3 beng2	thit peng

discuss[1] problems	v	探討	tàam tóu	taam4 fou2	thaam thou
discuss[2] /speak/converse /chat	v	談	tàahm	taam4	thaahm
discuss[3]	v	談吐	tàahm tóu	taam4 tou2	thaahm thou
discuss[4] /debate	v	論	leun	leon3	leun
discussion /treat/discus	n	討論	tóu leuhn	tou2 leon6	thou leuhn
disdain /look down on /to despise	v	輕視	hèng sih	heng4 si6	heng sih
disease[1]	n	疾病	jaht behng	zat6 beng6	chaht pehng
disease[2] of penis	n	椰菜花	yèh choi fā	je4 coi3 faa1	yeh chhoi fa
disease venereal/VD/ sexually transmitted disease /S.T.D.infected by sex		性病	sing behng	sing3 beng6	seng pehng
diseased /sick man	adj	有病嘅	yáuh behng ge	jau5 beng6 ge3	yauh pehng ke
disembarkation	v	使上岸	sái séuhng ngòhn	sai2 soeng5 ngon6	sai seuhng ngohn
disgrace[1] /dishonor/ hates/insult/ridicule	n	侮	móuh	mou5	mouh
disgrace[2] /dishonour/ contempt/dishonor/indignity	n	侮辱	móuh yuhk	mou5 juk6	mouh yuhk
disgrace[3]	v	丟...嘅架	dīu ge ... ge gá	diu1 ...ge3 gaa2	tiu ... ke ka
disguise[1]	v	裝扮	jòng baan	zong4 baan3	chong paan
disguise[2] /to fake/livingunder a false	n	偽裝	ngàih jòng	ngai6 zong4	ngaih chong
disguise[3]	n	假扮	gá baan	gaa2 baan3	ka paan
disgust[1]	n	傾吓	kìng háh	king4 haa5	khing hah
disgust[2]	n	商量	sèung lèuhng	soeng4 loeng4	seung leuhng
disgust[3] /nuisance/ nausea/bothersome	v	令人討厭	lihng yàhn tóu yim	ling4 jan4 tou2 jim3	lehng yahn thou yim
disgusting /nasty	adj	鶻突	waaht daht	waat6 tat6	waaht taht
dish /plate/saucer	n	瓦碟	ngáh dip	ngaa5 dip3	ngah tip
dish of food[1]	n	一樣餸	yāt yeuhng sung	jat1 joeng6 sung3	yat yeuhng sung
dish of food[2]	n	一碟餸	yāt díp/dihp sung	jat1 dip2 /dip6 sung3	yat tip /tihp sung
dish of food[3]	n	一道菜	yāt douh choi	jat1 dou6 coi3	yat lihn chhoi
dish of food[4] /variety of food	n	餸	sung	sung3	sung
dish washer man	n	洗碗人	sái wún yàhn	sai2 wun2 jan4	sai wun kei yahn
dish washer machine	n	洗碗機	sái wún gèi	sai2 wun2 gei4	sai wun kei
dish water[1] /sewage	n	污水	wū séui	wu1 seoi2	wu swoi
dish water[2]	n	泔水	gām séui	gam1 seoi2	kam swoi
dishes order[1]	n	叫餸	giu sung	giu3 sung3	kiu sung
dishes order[2]	n	落單	lohk dāan	lok6 daan1	lohk taan
dishonest[1]	adj	唔誠實	m̀ sìhng saht	m4 sing4 sat6	mh sehng saht
dishonest[2]	adj	不誠實	bāt sìhng saht	bat1 sing4 sat6	pat sehng saht
dishonest[3] /cunning/sly	adj	鬼	gwái	gwai2	kwai
dishonest plan to get money /scam	n	詐財騙局	ja chòih pin guhk	za3 coi6 pin3 guk6	cha chhoih phin kuhk
dishonest trick /dodge	n	躲避	dó beih	do2 bei6	to peih

English		Chinese	Romanization	Jyutping	Yale
dishonorable[1]/improper	adj	唔端	m̀ dyūn	m4 dyun1	mh tyun
dishonorable[2]/improper	adj	不端	bāt dyūn	bat1dyun1	pat tyun
dishonour	n	不名譽	bāt mèhng /mìhngyù	bat1 meng4 /ming4 jyu6	pat mehng yu
disk /wheel/round objects	n	輪	lèuhn	leon4	leuhn
dislike[1]	v	嫌	yìhm	jim4	yihm
dislike[2] strongly does not like	v	反感	fáan gám	faan2 gam2	faan kam
dislike[3] /hates/mislike	v	厭惡	yim wu	jim3 wu3	yim wu
dislike[4]	v	不喜愛	bāt héi oi /ngoi	bat1 hei2 oi3 /ngoi3	pat hei oi /ngoi
disliked	v	不喜歡	bāt héi fùn	bat1 hei2 fun4	pat hei fun
disloyal	adj	不忠誠	bāt jùng sìhng	bat1 zung4 sing4	pat chung sehng
dismiss[1]/remove/expel from office	v	革	gaak	gaak3	kaak
dismiss[2]	v	炒解僱	cháau gáai gu	caau2 gaai2 gu3	chhaau kaai ku
dismiss a person /fire-a person	v	炒人	cháau yàhn	caau2 jan4	chhaau yahn
dismissal[1] from the job	n	炒魷魚	cháau yàuh yú	caau jan4 jyu4	chhaau yauh yu
dismissal[2]/sack/expel/ forceful dismiss	n/v	開除	hòi chèuih	hoi4 ceoi4	hoi chhoih
disobedient[1]/disobey	adj	不服從	bāt fuhk chùhng	bat1 fuk6 cung4	pat fuhk chhuhng
disobedient[2]	adj	不聽命	bāt tèng mehng	bat1 teng4 meng6	pat theng mehng
disobey[1]	v	違	wai	wai3	wai
disobey[2]	v	唔聽話	m̀ tèng wah	m4 teng4 waa6	mh theng wah
disobey person /does not obey (the law)	n	違法者	wai faat jé	wai3 faat3 ze2	wai faat che
disorder[1] /mixed/ inter-mixing	n	淆	ngàauh	ngaau6	ngaauh
disorder[2] /little sick	n	小病	síu behng /bihng	siu2 beng6 /bing6	siu pehng
disorderly[1] /in disorder	adj	亂	lyuhn	lyun6	lyuhn
disorderly[2]	adj	有秩序	móuh diht jeuih	mou5 dit6 zeoi6	mouh tiht choih
dispart	v	分離	fàn lèih	fan4 lei4	fan leih
dispatch[1]/issue/send out	v	發	faat	faat3	faat
dispatch[2]/send by radio	v	發送	faat sung	faat3 sung3	faat sung
dispatch[3]	n	派遣	paaih hín	paai6 hin2	phaaih hin
dispatch[4]	n	差遣	chāai hín	caai1 hin2	chhaai hin
dispatch[5] /despatch	n	快使者	paai... si jé	paai3...si3 ze2	phaai... si che
dispatch[6]	v	迅速處理	seun chūk chyu léih	seon3 cuk1 cyu3 lei5	swon chhuk chhyu leih
dispatch box /dispatch case	n	公文遞送箱	gùng màhn daih sung sēung	gung4 man4 dai6 sung3 soeng1	kung mahn taih sung seung
dispatcher	n	調度員	diuh douh yùhn	diu6 dou6 jyun4	tiuh touh yuhn
dispenser /pharmacist	n	藥劑師	yeuhk jāi sì	joek6 zai1 si4	yeuhk chai si
dispenser box	n	液機	yihk gèi	jik6 gei4	yehk kei
displace[1] /displacement	v	代替	doih tai	doi6 tai3	toih thai
displace[2] /displacement/replace	v	取代	cheui doih	ceoi3 doi6	chheui toih
display[1]	v	擺	báai	baai2	paai
display[2]	v	凸顯	daht hín	dat6 hin2	taht hin

display[3] /exhibition/put on for sale/people to look	n	展覽	jín láahm	zin2 laam5	chin laahm
displeasure /tedious/ feeling vexed/talk	n/v	乏味	faht meih	fat6 mei6	faht meih
disport	v	娛樂	yuh lohk	jyu6 lik6	yuh lohk
disposable /use & throw	adj	可任意處理	hó yahm yi chyú léih	ho2 jam6 ji3 cyu2 lei5	ho yahm yi chhyu leih
disposition /nature	n	性情	sing chìhng	sing3 cing4	seng chhehng
dispute[1] /argue/haggle	v	爭論	jàng leuhn	zang4 leon6	chang lowhn
dispute[2]	v	辯駁	bihn bok	bin6 bok3	pihn pok
disqualify[1]	v	便唔合格	bihn m̀ hahp gaak	bin6 m4 hap6 gaak3	pihn mh hahp kaak
disqualify[2]	v	便唔適合	bihn m̀ sīk hahp	bin6 m4 sik1 hap6	pihn mh sek hahp
disqualify[3]	v	便不適合	bihn bāt sīk hahp	bin6 bat1 sik1 hap6	pihn pat sek hahp
disqualify[4]	v	便不合格	bihn bāt hahp gaak	bin6 bat1 hap6 gaak3	pihn pat hahp kaak
disqualify[5]	v	取消資格	chéui sìu jì gaak	ceoi2 siu4 zi4 gaak3	chheui siu chi kaak
disregard[1]	v	唔 尊重	m̀ jyūn juhng	m4 zeon1 zung6	mh chyun chuhng
disregard[2]	v	不尊重	bāt jyūn juhng	bat1 zeon1 zung6	pat chyun chuhng
disrepair	n	失修	sāt sāu	sat1 sau1	sat sau
disrespect[1]	n	唔尊敬	m̀ jyùn ging	m4 zyun4 ging3	mh chyun keng
disrespect[2]	n	無禮藐	móuh láih míuh	mou5 lai5 miu5	mouh laih miuh
disseminate /publicity/propaganda	n	宣傳	syùn chyùhn	syun4 cyun4	syun chhuhn
dissident[1]	n	唔同意	m̀ tùhng yi	m4 tung4 ji3	mh thuhng yi
dissident[2]	n	持不政見	yi bāt jing gin	ji3 bat1 zing3 gin3	yi pat cheng kin
dissident[3] in political	n	持不同政見者	chìh bāt tùhng jing gin jé	ci4 bat1 tung4 zing3 gin3 ze2	chhih pat thuhng cheng kin che
dissolute	adj	放縱嘅	fong jùng ge	fong3 zung4 ge3	fong chung ke
dissolve[1] /soluble/melt	adj/v	溶	yùhng	jung4	yuhng
dissolve[2] /melt	v	溶解	yùhng gáai	jung4 gaai2	yuhng kaai
distance[1]	n	距	kéuih	keoi5	khoih
distance[2] /distant/range/ be apart	n	距離	kéuih lèih	keoi5 lei4	khoih leih
distance[3]	n	隔開一	gaak hòi yāt	gaak3 hoi4 jat1	kaak hoi yat
distant[1] /far/remote	adj	遠地	yúhn deih	jyun5 dei6	yuhn teih
distant[2] /remote	adj	遙遠	yìuh yúhn	jiu4 jyun5	yiuh yuhn
distill	v	餾	lauh	lau6	lauh
distillate	n	餾液	lauh yihk	lau6 jik6	lauh yehk
distillation	n	蒸餾	jìng lauh	zing4 lau6	cheng lauh
distilled /purification	adj/n	淨化	jehng fa	zeng6 faa3	chehng fa
distilled water	n	蒸餾水	jìng làuh séui	zing4 lau4 seoi2	cheng lauh swoi
distinct[1]	adj	有區別	yáuh kèui biht	jau5 keoi4 bit6	yauh khoi piht
distinct[2] /recognized/ clear understood/explicit/ plain	adj	清楚	chèng /chìng chó	ceng4 /cing4 co2	chheng chho
distinguish[1]	v	分得出	fān dāk chēut	fan1 dak1 ceot1	fan tak chhot
distinguish[2]	v	鑒別	gaam bìht	gaam3 bit6	kaam piht

distinguish³ /identify	v	識別	sīk bìht	sik1 bit6	sek piht
distinguished guest /honored guest/special guest /first class guest/VIP guest	n	貴賓	gwai bān	gwai3 ban1	kwai pan
distinguished meeting /flourish party	n	盛會	sìhng wúih	sing4 wui5	sehng wuih
distort /making untrue/ warp true	v	歪曲	wāai kūk	waai1 kuk1	waai kuk
distract	v	分散	fàn sàan	fan4 saan4	fan saan
distress¹ /suffering /tingling	n	痛苦	tung fú	tung3 fu2	thung fu
distress²	n	令到痛苦	lihng dou tung fú	ling4 dou3 tung3 fu2	lehng tou thung fu
distressed¹	adj	厄	āk /àak	ak1 /aak1	ak /aak
distressed² /pitiable condition/be pity on	adj	令人憐憫	ling yàhn lèuhn máhn	ling3 jan4 leon4 man5	leng yahn leuhn mahn
distribute /issue/emit	v	散發	sáan faat	saan2 faat3	saan faat
distributer	n	分發者	fàn faat jé	fan6 faat3 ze2	fan faat che
district council	n	區議會	kèui yih wúi	keoi4 ji6 wui2	khoi yih wui
district council member /councillor	n	區議員	kèui yih yùhn	keoi4 ji6 jyun4	khoi yih yuhn
distrustful	adj	唔信任	m̀ seun yàhm	m4 seon3 jam4	mh swon yahm
disturb¹	v	擾	yíu	jiu2	yiu
disturb² /annoy/harass/ trouble/vex	v	騷擾	sòu yíu	sou4 jiu2	sou yiu
disturb³ /intrude/upset	v	打擾	dá yíu	daa2 jiu2	ta yiu
disturb	v	攪擾	gáau yíu	gaau2 jiu2	kaau yiu
disturbance /riot/ violent protest	n	騷亂	sōu lyuhn	soi1 lyun6	sou lyuhn
ditch /furrow/gutter/ groove	n	溝	kàu	kau4	khau
dive¹ /diving	v	跳水	tiu séui	tiu3 seoi2	thiu swoi
dive² /diving	v	潛水	chìhm séui	cim4 seoi2	chhihm swoi
diver¹	n	跳水人	tiu séui ge yàhn	tiu3 seoi2 ge3 jan4	thiu swoi ke yahn
diver² /frogman	n	潛水員	chìhm séui yùhn	cim4 seoi2 jyun4	chhihm swoi yùhn
divergent	n	歧	kèih	kei4	kheih
diverging	n	分叉	fàn chà	fan4 caa4	fan chha
diversify /variety	v	多樣化	dò yeuhng fa	do4 joeng6 faa3	to yeuhng fa
diversions¹ /distract	n/v	分心	fàn sàm	fa4 sam4	fan saam
diversions² /turning road	n	轉向	jyun heung	zyun3 hoeng3	chyun heung
divert		使轉向	sái jyún heung	sai2 zyun2 hoeng3	sai chyun heung
divide	v	劃分	wàahk fān	waak6 fan1	waahk fan
divide equally	v	平分	pèhng fàn	peng4 fan4	phehng fan
divide into	v	分成	fàn sèhng	fan4 seng4	fan sehng
dividing¹	adj	區分	kèui fàn	keoi4 fan4	khoi fan
dividing²	adj	劃分作用	wàahk fàn jok yuhng	waak6 fan4 zok3 jung6	waahk fan chok yuhng
divine /observe omen	v	占	jīm	zim1	chim

division[1] /fraction/part of/portion/section/share	n	部分	bouh fahn	bou6 fan6	pouh fahn
division[2]	n	分部	fàn bouh	fan4 bou6	fan pouh
division[3] /separation /split/ to divide	n	分開	fàn hòi	fan4 hoi4	fan hoi
division[4]	n	波段	bō dyuhn	po1 dyun6	po tyuhn
divorced[1]	n	離婚	lèih fàn	lei4 fan4	leih fan
divorced[2]	n	同離婚	tùhng...lèih fān	tung4...lei4 fan1	thuhng...leih fan
divulger	n	透露人	tau louh yàhn	tau3 lou6 jan4	thau louh yahn
dizzy[1] /faint	adj	暈	wàhn	wan4	wahn
dizzy[2] /faint	adj	頭暈	tau wàhn	tau3 wan4	thau wahn
do[1] /be/make/act as do	v	做	jouh	zou6	chouh
do[2] /handle/manage	v	弄	luhng	lung6	luhng
do as role /to act as/ play role of	n	充當	chùng dòng	cung4 dong4	chhung tong
do as wishes		自便	jih bín	zi6 bin2	chih pin
do business	n	做生意	jouh sāang yi	zou6 saang1 ji3	chouh saang yi
do easily /work easily/ don't worry!/take it easy!	v	唔駛咁緊引	m̀ sái gam gán jèung	m4 sai2 gam3 gan2 zoeng4	mh sai kam kan cheung
do finish		作成	jok sèhng	zok3 seng4	chok sehng
do fix	n	作弄	jok luhng	zok3 lung6	chok luhng
do like this		咪得囉	máih dāk ló	mai5 dak1 lo2	maaih tak lo
do mistake		弊嘞	baih laa!	bai6 laa!	paih laa!
do momework		做功課	jouh gùng fo	zou6 gung4 fo3	chouh kung fo
do my best /wholeheartedly	adv	盡心盡力	jeuhn sàm jeuhn lihk	zeon6 sam4 zeon6 lik6	cheuhn sam cheuhn lehk
do not[1]	aux v	別	biht	bit6	piht
do not[2]	aux v	唔准	m̀ jéun	m4 zeon2	mh cheun
do not[3] /not good/not	aux	唔好	m̀ hóu	m4 hou2	mh hou
do not[4]	aux v	不應	bāt yìng	bat1 jing4	pat ying
do not do it		唔係咁做	m̀ haih gam jouh	m4 hai6 gam3 zou6	mh haih kam chouh
do not like /hates/undesired	adj	唔鍾意	m̀ jùng yi	m4 zung4 ji3	mh chung yi
do not press me! /don't hold me!/ leave me alone!		唔好搞我!	m̀ hóu gáau ngóh!	m4 hou2 gaau2 ngo5	mh hou kaau ngóh!
do not use		勿用	maht yuhng	mat6 jung6	maht yuhng
do overpress		大力	daaih lihk	daai6 lik6	taaih lehk
do so		皆可以	gāai hó yíh	gaai1 ho2 ji5	kaai ho yih
do sports /take exercise	n	做運動	jouh wahn duhng	zou6 wan6 dung6	chouh wahn tohng
do well	n	成功	sèhng gūng	seng4 gung1	sehng kung
do you know?[1]		識唔識?	sīk m̀ sīk?	sik1 m4 sik1?	sek mh sek?
do you know?[2]		你知唔知呀?	léih jì m̀ jì àa?	lei5 zi4 m4 zi4 aa4?	leih chi mh chi aa?
do you like it? (coll)		你鍾唔鍾意?	léih jùng m̀ jùng yi?	lei5 zung1 m4 zung1 ji3?	leih chung mh chung yi?
do you need?		你要用啊?	léih yiu yuhng ā?	lei5 jiu3 jung6 aa1?	leih yiu yuhng aa?

do you remember me?		記得我嗎?	gei dāk ngóh mā?	gei3 dak1 ngo5 maa1?	kei tak ngoh ma?
do you speak?[1]		你會講?	léih wúih góng?	lei5 wui5 gong2?	leih wuih kong?
do you speak?[2]		你識唔識講?	léih sīk m̀ sīkgóng!?	lei5 sik1 m4 sik1 gong2?	leih sek mh sek kong!?
dock /shipyard	n	船塢	syùhn wú	syun4 wu2	syuhn wu
doctor /physician/ practitioner	n	醫生	yī sāng	ji1 sang1	yi sang
doctor of philosophy	n	博士學位	bok sih hohk wái	bok3 si6 hok6 wai2	pok sih hohk wai
doctor's fee		診金	chán gàm	can2 gam4	chhan kam
doctor's private office /clinic	n	醫務所	yī mouh só	ji1 mou6 so2	yi mouh so
doctrine /teachings	n	教義	gaau yih	gaau3 ji6	kaau yih
document /file	n	文件	màhn gín	man4 gin2	mahn kin
dodge	v	閃避	sím beih	sim2 bei6	sim peih
does /to put out	v	做出	jouh chēut	zou6 ceot1	chouh chhot
does not[1]	aux/v	否定句	fáu dihng geui	fau2 ding6 geoi3	fau dehng kwoi
does not[2]	aux v	嘟唔到呀	dōu m̀ dou a	dou1 m4 dou3 aa3	tou mh tou a
does she?	aux v	對吧?	deui bā?	deoi3 ba1?	toei pa?
doesn't help		無幫助	mòuh bòng joh	mou5 bong1 zo6	mouh pong choh
doesn't matter /it's nothing/never mind/no matter/nothing	v	沒什麼	muht sahm mò	mut6 sam6 mo4	muht sahm mo
dog[1]	n	狗	gáu	gau2	kau
dog[2]	n	犬	hyún	hyun2	hyun
dog feed	n	狗飼料	gáu jih líu	gau2 zi6 liu2	kau chih liu
dogma[1] /theory/thesis /principle	n	論點	leuhn dím	leon4 dim2	leuhn tim
dogma[2]	n	信條	seun tìuh	seon3 tiu4	swon thiuh
doll[1]	n	公仔	gùng jái	gung4 zai2	kung chai
doll[2]	n	洋娃娃	yèuhng wā wā	joeng waa1 waa1	yeuhng wa wa
doll[3] /toy/puppet	n	玩偶	wáan ngáuh	waan2 ngau5	waan ngauh
dollar[1] /$/rupee (coll)	n	蚊/文	mān	man1	man
dollar[2]	n	元	yùhn	jyun4	yuhn
dollar[3] /money (coll)	n	錢幣	chín baih	cin2 bai6	chhin paih
dollar[4] (HK)	n	港元	góng yùhn	gong2 jyun4	kong yuhn
dolphin	n	海豚	hói tyùhn	hoi2 tyun4	hoi thyuhn
domain[1] /territory	n	領土	léhng /líhng tóu	leng5 /ling5 tou2	lehng thou
domain[2] /field/area	n	領域	léhng /líhng wihk	leng5 /ling5 wik6	lehng wehk
domain[3]	n	地盤	deih pùhn	dei6 pun4	teih phuhn
domestic fowl /poultry	n	家禽	gā kàhm	gaa1 kam4	ka khahm
domestic life		家庭生活	gā tèhng /tìhng	gaa1 teng4 /ting4	ka thehng sang wuht
domesticate /tame/raise and train	ad/v	馴養	sèuhn yéuhng	seon4 joeng5	swohn yeuhng
dominate	v	支配	jī pui	zi1 pui3	chi phui
dominion /sovereignty	n	統治權	túng jih kyùhn	tung3 zi6 kyun4	thung chih khyuhn
don't![1]		咪	máih	mai5	maih

English		Chinese	Pronunciation	Jyutping	Yale
don't² /no need/must not	aux v	唔使	m̀ sái	m4 sai2	mh sai
don't³ /must not	aux v	不要	bāt yiu	bat1 jiu3	pat yiu
don't⁴ /must not	aux v	切莫	chit mohk	cit6 mok6	chhit mohk
don't⁵ /do not	aux v	休想	yàu séung	jau4 soeng2	yau seung
don't afraid /don't be scared/don't panic	adv	唔好驚	m̀ hóu gèng	m4 hou2 geng4	mh hou keng
don't answer		別回嘴	biht wùih jéui	bit6 wui4 zeoi2	piht wuih choi
don't blame me	v	別怪我	biht gwaai ngóh	bit6 gwaai3 ngo5	piht kwaai ngoh
don't bullshit me!	v	休想哄我	yàu séung húng ngóh	jau4 soeng2 hung2 ngo5	yau seung hung ngoh
don't care /no matter how /no matter what/no take care		冇管	móuh gún	mou5 gun2	mouh kun
don't crying		唔喊	m̀ haam	m4 haam3	mh haam
don't fool me		唔好呃我	m̀ hóu ngāak ngóh	m4 hou2 aak1 ngo5	mh hou ngaak ngoh
don't know¹		唔識	m̀ sīk	m4 sik1	mh sek
don't know² /ignorance	n	無知啦	móuh jì lā	mou5 zi4 laa1	mouh chi la
don't let free hand		不放手	bāt fong sáu	bat1 fong3 sau2	pat fong sau
don't talk /stop talking/ shut up!/hush/don't noisv/ don't make noise	v	唔好嘈	m̀ hóu chòuh	m4 hou2 cou4	mh hou chhouh
don't mention it¹		唔使客氣	m̀ sái haak hei	m4 sai2 haak3 hei3	mh sai haak hei
don't mention it²	v	別客氣	bìht háak héi	bit6 haak2 hei2	piht haak hei
don't overpress		冇大力	móuh daaih lihk	mou5 daai6 lik6	mouh taaih lehk
don't panic¹/don't scare	adv	唔使驚慌	m̀ sai gèng fòng	m4 sai3 geng4 fong4	mh sai keng fong
don't panic¹	adv	不要驚慌	bāt sai gèng fòng	bat1 sai3 geng4 fong4	pat sai keng fong
don't speak		唔會講	m̀ wúih góng	m4 wui5 gong2	mh wuih kong
don't take		唔攞	m̀ ló	m4 lo2	mh lo
don't talk	v	唔好出聲	m̀ hóu chēut sèng	m4 hou2 ceot1 seng4	mh hou chhot seng
don't tell¹	v	唔使講	m̀ sái góng	m4 sai2 gong2	mh sai kong
don't tell²	v	唔使出聲	m̀ sái chēut sèng	m4 sai2 ceot1 seng4	mh sai chhot seng
don't worried	adv	別急	biht gāp	bit6 gap1	piht kap
don't worry!¹ /never mind!	adj	唔駛担心	m̀ sai dàam sàm!	m4 sai3 daam4 sam4	mh sai taam sam!
don't worry!²		唔好擔心	m̀ hou dàam sàm!	m4 hou3 daam4 sam4!	mh hou taam sam!
don't worry!³		放心	fong sām!	fong3 sam1!	fong sahm!
don't you?¹/isn't it?	aux v	唔係嗎?	m̀ haih mā ?	m4 hai6 ma1?	mh haih ma?
don't you?²	aux v	不是嗎?	bāt sih mā ?	bat1 si6 ma1?	pat sih ma ?
don't you?³	aux v	唔是嗎?	m̀ sih mā ?	m4 si6 ma1?	mh sih ma ?
donate /contribute	v	捐	gyùn	gyun4	kyun
donate money¹	v	捐錢	gyùn chín	gyun4 cin2	kyun chhin
donate money² /contribution/subscription	n/v	捐款	gyùn fún	gyun4 fun2	kyun fun
donate box¹	n	捐款箱	gyún fun seung	gyun2 fun3 soeng3	kyun fun seung
donate box²	n	功德箱	gùng dāk seung	gung4 dak1 soeng3	kung tak seung
done¹	adj	做	jouh	zou6	chouh
done²	adj	完了	yùhn líuh	jyun4 liu5	yuhn liuh

done quickly /in a hurry/ hasty/hurried	n	匆忙	chùng mòhng	cung4 mong4	chhung mohng
door[1] /gate/gateway	n	門	mùhn	mun4	muhn
door[2] /entrance/gate/entry	n	門口	mùhn háu	mun4 hau2	muhn hau
door[3]	n	戶	wuh	wu6	wuh
door[4] /in and out/gate	n	出入	chēut yahp	ceot1 jap6	chhot yahp
door[5]	n	門戶	mùhn wuh	mun4 wu6	muhn wuh
door keeper /watchman	n	看更	hōn gàang	hon1 gaang4	hon kaang
door key	n	門匙	mùhn sìh	mun4 si4	muhn sih
door knob	n	球形門拉手	kàuh yìhng mùhn lāai sáu	kau4 jing4 mun4 laai1 sau2	khauh yehng muhn laai sau
door lock		門鎖	mùhn só	mun4 so2	muhn so
door lock key	n	門金肖	mùhn gām chiu	mun4 gam1 ciu3	muhn kam chhiu
door man	n	看門人	hon mùhn yàhn	hon3 mun4 jan4	hon muhn yahn
door mat	n	門口地墊	mùhn háu deih jīn	mun4 hau2 dei6 zin1	muhn hau teih chin
doorbell[1]	n	門鐘	mùhn jùng	mun4 zung4	muhn chung
doorbell[2]	n	門鈴	mùhn líhng	mun4 ling5	muhn lehng
dormitory /big badroom	n	大寢室	daaih chám sāt	daai6 cam2 sat1	taaih chham sat
dose[1] /dosage/amount	n	劑	jāi	zai1	chai
dose[2]	n	一劑	yāt jāi	jat1 zai1	yat chai
dossier /file	n	卷宗	gyun jūng	gyun3 zung1	kyun chung
dot[1] /limit point	n	點	dím	dim2	tim
dot[2] /spot/point	n	小點	síu dím	siu2 dim2	siu tim
dotted	adj	有點的	yáuh dím dìk	jau5 dim2 dik4	yauh tim tek
double[1] /dual/having two parts	adj	雙重	sèung chúhng	soeng4 cung5	seung chhohng
double[2]	v	加倍	gā púih	gaa1 pui5	ka phuih
double[3]	adj	兩倍	léuhng púih	loeng5 pui5	leuhng phuih
double bed	n	雙人床	sèung yàhn chòhng	soeng4 jan4 cong4	seung yahn chhohng
double extra large size /xxx	n	加加大碼	gà gà daaih máh	gaa4 gaa4 daai6 maa5	ka ka taaih mah
double registered		雙掛號	sèung gwa houh	soeng4 gwa3 hou6	seung kwa houh
double room[1] living+dining room		兩廳	léuhng tèng	loeng5 teng4	leuhng theng
double room[2]	n	雙人房	sèung yàhn fóng	soeng4 jan4 fong2	seung yahn fong
doubling	n	加倍	gā púih	gaa1 pui5	ka phuih
doubt[1] /suspect/question	n/v	疑	yih	ji6	yih
doubt[2] /confused	n	惑	waahk	waak6	waahk
doubt[3] /question	n	乎	fù	fu4	fu
doubt[4] /suspect	n	思疑	sì yìh	si4 ji4	si yih
doubt[5] /suspicion	n	可疑	hó yìh	ho2 ji4	ho yih
doubt[6]	n	疑義	yìh yìh	ji4 ji6	yih yih
doubtful	adj	可想像嘅	hó séung jèuhng	ho2 soeng2 zoeng6	ho seung cheuhng
dough /uncooked pastry /mixtured flour with	n	生麵糰	sàang mìhn tyùhn	saang4 min6 tyun6	saang mihn thyuhn

douse /put out fire by hand/to extinguish by	v	弄熄	luhng sīk	lung6 sik1	luhng sek
dove /pigeon	n	白鴿	baahk gáp	baak6 gap2	paahk kap
dove eyed	n	眼神柔和	ngáahn sàhn yàuh wòh	ngaan5 san4 jau4 wo4	ngaahn sahn yauh woh
down[1]	adv	下	háh	haa5	hah
down[2]	adv	垂	sèuih	seoi4	swoih
down[3] /lower	adv	低	dài	dai4	tai
down[4] bird/s fur /nap	n	絨毛	yúng mòuh	jung2 mou4	yung mouh
down stairs /ground floor	n	樓下	làuh hah	lau4 haa6	lauh hah
downcast[1] /no thinking	adj	冇心机/機	móuh sām gèi	mou5 sam1 gei4	mouh sam kei
downcast[2] /downward	adj	向下	heung hah	hoeng ha6	heung hah
downhill[1]	n	下山	hah sàan	haa6 saan4	hah saan
downhill[2]	n	下坡	hah pò	haa6 po4	hah pho
download computing	v	下載	hah jói	haa6 zoi2	hah choi
downstairs /underneath	n	下面	hah mihn	haa6 min6	hah mihn
downtown	n	商業區	sèung yihp kèui	soeng jip6 keoi4	seung yihp khoi
dowry[1]	n	嫁妝	ga jòng	gaa3 zong4	ka chong
dowry[2]	n	陪嫁	pui gá	pui4 gaa2	phui ka
doxology[1] /song of praise /hymn	n	聖詩	sing sī	sing3 si1	seng si
doxology[2] /hymn/psalm/ song of praise	n	讚美詩	jaan méih sī	zaan mei5 si1	chaan meih si
doze[1] /sleepy	n	眼瞓	náahn fan	ngaan5 fan3	naahn fan
doze[2] /be sleepy	n	令人睏倦	lihng yàhn kwan gyuhn	ling6 jan4 kwan3 gyun6	lehng yahn khwan kyuhn
doze[3] /fall asleep	n/v	瞌睡	hahp seuih	hap6 seoi6	hahp swoih
dozen (de)	n	打	dā	daa1	ta
Dr[1] doctor	abbr	醫生	yī sāng	ji1 sang1	yi sang
Dr[2] of Philosophy	n	博士	bok sih	bok3 si6	pok sih
draft /draught/cheque	n	匯票	wùih piu	wui6 piu3	wuih phiu
drafts of document		草稿	chóu góu	cou2 gou2	chhou kou
drag /tow/towing/pull/ dragging	v	拖	tò	to4	thoh
dragger[1]	n	拖人	tò yàhn	to4 jan4	thoh yahn
dragger[2]	n	拖曳之人 或物	tò yáih jī yàhn waahk maht	to4 jai5 zi1 jan4 waak6 mat6	thoh yaih chi yahn waahk maht
dragon well tea	n	龍井	lùhng jéng	lung4 zeng2	luhng cheng
dragonfly	n	蜻蜓	ching tíhng	cing6 ting5	chhing tehng
drain[1]	n	渠	kèuih	keoi4	khoih
drain[2]	n	水渠	séui kèuih	seoi2 keoi4	swoi kheuih
drain[3] /drainage	n	排水	pàaih séui	paai4 seoi2	phaaih swoi
drain[4]	n	排水管	pàaih séui gūn	paai4 seoi2 gun1	phaaih swoi kun
drain[5]	n	排出	paai chèut	paai3 ceot4	phaai chhot
drain[6] /make empty	v	枯竭	fù kít	fu4 kit3	fu khit

English		Chinese	Romanization 1	Jyutping	Romanization 2
drain[7] /make empty	v	喝乾	hot gòn	hot3 gon4	hot kon
drain service depart	n	渠務署	kèuih mouh chyúh	keoi4 mou6 cyu5	khoih mouh chhyuh
drama[1] /show/play	n	戲	hei	hei3	hei
drama[2]	n	劇本	kehk bún	kek6 bun2	khehk pun
drank[1]	v	飲咗	yám jó	jam2 zo2	yam cho
drank[2]	v	乾杯	gòn bùi	gon4 bui4	kon pui
drape[1] /cover	v	冚住	kám jyuh	kam2 zyu6	kham chyuh
drape[2]	v	罩住	jaau jyuh	zaau3 zyu6	chaau chyuh
drape[3] /to cover	v	覆蓋	fūk goi	fuk1 goi3	fuuk koi
draught /draft/rough sketch	n	草圖	chóu tòuh	cou2 tou4	chhou thouh
draw[1] /pull	n	扠	pāan	paan1	phaan
drew[2] /draw pictures	v	畫	wá	waa2	wa
draw[3] /paint	n	繪	kúi	kui2	khui
draw a line	n	劃線	waahk sín	waak6 sin2	waahk sin
draw game	v	平手	pèhng sāu	peng4 sau1	phehng sau
drawer[1]	n	櫃筒	gwaih tùhng	gwai6 tung4	kwaih thuhng
drawer[2] /tray/tier	n	厔	tai	tai3	thai
drawer[3]	n	抽屜	chàu	cau4	chhau
drawing	n	畫圖	waahk tòuh	waak6 tou4	waahk thouh
drawing paper	n	圖畫紙	tòuh wá jí	tou4 waa2 zi2	thouh wa chi
drawing room /living room	n	客廳	haak tēng	haak3 teng1	haak theng
drawn /drew	v	劃畫	waahk wá	waak4 waa2	waahk wa
drawstring[1]	n	褲頭帶	fu tàuh daai	fu3 tau4 daai3	fu thauh taai
drawstring[2]	n	拉繩	lāai sìhng	laai1 sing4	laai sehng
dream[1]	n	夢	muhng	mung6	muhng
dream[2] (good)	n	好夢	hóu muhng	hou2 mung6	hou muhng
dream[3] (good)	n	發好夢	faat hóu muhng	faat3 hou2 mung6	faat hou muhng
dream[4] /ideal/desirable	n	理想	leih séung	lei5 soeng2	leih seung
dream of	n	夢見	muhng gin	mung6 gin3	muhng kin
dreamer /visionary	n	夢想家	muhng séung gā	mung6 soeng2 ga1	muhng seung ka
dregs	n/v	渣	jā /dza	zaa1	cha
dress (skirt)	n	衫裙	sàam kwan	saam4 kwan3	saam khwan
dress light green	n	青衣	chèng yì	ceng4 ji1	chheng yi
dress uniform /formal dress/gown	n	禮服	láih fuhk	lai5 fuk6	laih fuhk
dress up /make up	v	扮	baan	baan3	paan
dressed	adj	穿衣服	chyùn yī fuhk	cyun4 ji1 fuk6	chhyun yi fuhk
dressed up man	n	油頭粉面	yàuh tàuh fán mihn	jau4 tau4 fan2 min6	yauh thauh fan mihn
dresser	n	服裝員	fuhk jòng yùhn	fuk4 zong4 jyun4	fuhk chong yuhn
dressing	n	敷藥	sóu yeuhk	sou2 joek6	sou yeuhk
dried /dry	adj/v	乾	gòn	gon4	kon
dried goods	n	乾貨	gòn fo	gon4 fo3	kon fo
drill[1] /training /coach/train	n/v	訓練	fan lihn	fan3 lin6	fan lihn

drill[2] /training/exercise/ practice/rehearsal	n	練習	lihn jaahp	lin6 zaap6	lihn chaahp
drill[3] /to bore	v	鑽窿	jyun lūng	zyun3 lung1	chyun lung
drill[4] /a hole	v	鑽	jyun	zyun3	chyun
drill[5] /hole by plow	n	播種犁	bo júng làih /nàih	bo3 zung2 lai4 /nai4	po chung laih /naih
drink[1]	v	飲	yám	jam2	yam
drink[2]	v	喝	hot	hot3	hot
drink driving	n	酒後開車	jáu hauh hòi che	zau2 hau6 hoi4 ce4	chau hauh hoi chhe
drink tea	v	飲茶	yám chàh	jam2 caa4	yam chhah
drink to excess /get drunk	v	酗酒	yu jáu	ju zau	yu chau
drinker[1]	n	酒徒	jáu tòuh	zau2 tou4	chau thouh
drinker[2]	n	飲酒者	yám jáu jé	jam2 zau2 ze2	yam chau che
drinking-fountain[1]	n	飲用噴泉	yám yuhng pan chyùhn	jam2 jung6 pan3 cyun4	yam yuhng phan chhyuhn
drinking-fountain[2]	n	自動飲水器	jih duhng yám séui hei	zi6 dung6 jam2 seoi2 hei3	chih tuhng yam swoi hei
drinking pipe	n	飲筒	yám túng	jam2 tung2	yam thung
drinking straw	n	飲筒	yám túng	jam2 tung2	yam thung
drinking water[1] /water fountain	n	飲水	yám séui	jam2 seoi2	yam swoi
drinking water[2] /water fountain	n	飲用水	yám yuhng séui	jam2 jung6 seoi2	yam yuhng swoi
drinks /beverage	n	飲品	yám bán	jam2 ban2	yam pan
dripping water	v	滴水	dihk séui	dik5 seoi2	tehk swoi
drive[1]	v	駕	ga	gaa3	ka
drive[2] (wr) vehicle	v	開車	hòi chè	hoi4 ce4	hoi chhe
drive[3] driving car	v	駛車	sái chè	sai2 ce4	sai chhe
drive back	v	趕回去	gón wùih heui	gon2 wui4 heoi3	kon wuih hoi
driver	n	司機	sì gèi, sī gēi	si4 gei4, si1 gei1	si kei
driving /drive car/vehicle	v	駕駛	ga sái	gaa3 sai2	ka sai
driving license[1] /driving plate	n	車牌	chè pàaih	ce4 paai6	chhe phaaih
driving license[2]	n	駕駛許可證	ga sái héui hó jing	ga3 sai2 heoi2 ho2 zing3	ka sai hoi ho jeng
drizzle rain /lightly raining	v	下毛毛雨	hah mòuh mòuh yúh	haa6 mou4 mou4 jyu5	hah mouh mouh yuh
drizzling rain /light rain/ raining lightly/ spit light rain	v	毛毛雨	mòuh mòuh yúh	mou4 mou4 jyu5	mouh mouh yuh
drop[1] /fall/dip into	v	點	dím	dim2	tim
drop[2] /go down/fall	n/v	降	gong	gong3	kong
drop[3] /fall/fallen	adj/v	落下	lòhk hah	lok6 haa6	lohk hah
drop[4] /passing	v	順便	seuhn bihn	seon6 bin6	swohn pihn
drop[5] /spot	n	滴	dihk	dik6	tehk
drop dead! /go to hell!/ get out of the way!/fuck you! (sl)	adv dw	仆街	puk gāai	puk3 gaai1	phuk kaai

drop down	v	掉下	diuh hah	diu6 haa6	tiuh hah
drop into	v	墜入	jeuih yahp	zeoi6 jap6	cheuih yahp
drop of liquid /spray	n	浪花	lohng fā	long6 fa1	lohng fa
drop off[1] /separated /divided	v	甩咗	lāt jó	lat1 zo2	lat cho
drop off[2] /to fall asleep /asleep	adj	睡著	seuih jeuk	seoi6 zoek3	swoih cheuk
drop off[3] /get down from car	v	讓...下車	yeuhng hah chè	joeng6 ha6 ce1	yeuhng hah chhe
droped	v	跌咗	dit jó	dit3 zo2	tit cho
dropping[1] /by car or plane /to carry	n	運送	wahn sung	wan6 sung3	wahn sung
dropping[2] /leak water	n	滴下	dihk hah	dik6 ha6	tehk hah
drought /dry/arid	n	乾旱	gòn hóhn	gon4 hon5	kon hohn
drove /gang/group/flock	n	一群	yāt kwàhn	jat1 kwan4	yat khwahn
drowned die in the water	v	淹死	jam séi	zam3 séi2	cham sei
drowse[1] (sl) /sleepy	v	釣魚	diu yú	diu3 jyu2	tiu yu
drowse[2]	v	椿眼瞓	jùng ngáahn fan	zong4 ngaan5 fan3	chung ngaahn fan
drowse[3] /fall asleep	v	打瞌睡	dá hahp seuih	daa2 hap6 seoi6	ta hahp swoih
drowsiness /sleepiness	n	睡意	seuih yi	seoi6 ji3	swoih yi
drug /medicine	n	藥	yeuhk	joek6	yeuhk
drug factory /medicine factory/pharmacy factory	n	藥廠	yeuhk chóng	joek6 cong2	yeuhk chhong
drugpusher[1] /pushing drugs	n	販毒	faan duhk	faan3 duk6	faan duhk
drugpusher[2]	n	賣毒品嘅人	maaih duhk bán ge yàhn	maai6 duk6 ban2 ge3 jan4	maaih tuhk pan ke yahn
drugpusher[3]	n	毒品販子	duhk bán faan jé	duk6 ban2 faan3 ze2	tuhk pan faan che
drugpusher[4]	n	販毒者	faan duhk jé	faan3 duk6 ze2	faan duhk che
drugs	n	毒品	duhk bán	duk6 ban2	tuhk pan
drum[1]	n	鼓狀物	gú johng maht	gu2 zong6 mat6	ku chohng maht
drum[2] /barrel	n	打鼓	dá gú	daa2 gu2	ta ku
drum[3]	n	圓桶	yùhn túng	jyun4 tung2	yuhn thung
drum[4] beat	v	打鼓	dá gú	daa2 gu2	ta ku
drum stick	n	鼓	gú	gu2	ku
drunk[1] /intoxicated	v	醉	jeui	zeoi3	cheui
drunk[2]	a	喝醉酒	hot jeui jáu	hot3 zeoi3 zau2	hot cheui chau
drunkard[1]	n	醉鬼	jeui gwái	zeoi3 gwai2	cheui kwai
drunkard[2]	n	醉漢	jeui hon	zeoi3 hon3	cheui hon
drunkard[3]	v	死酒鬼	séi jáu gwái	sei2 zau2 gwai2	sei chau kwai
drunkard[4]	n	醉漢者	jeui hon jé	zeoi3 hon3 ze2	cheui hon che
drunkard[5]	n	醉鬼人	jeui gwái yàhn	zeoi3 gwai2 jan4	cheui kwai yahn
dry battery	n	乾電池	gòn dihn chìh	gon4 din6 ci4	kon tihn chhih
dry clean	v	乾洗	gòn sái	gon4 sai2	kon sai
dry-eyed /not weeping	adj	無哭	móuh hùk	mou5 huk4	mouh huk
dry fish	n	魚乾	yú gòn	jyu2 gon4	yu kon

English		Chinese	Cantonese	Jyutping	Romanization
dry fried rice with beef meat	n	乾炒牛飯	gòn cháau ngàuh faahn	gon4 caau2 ngau4 faan6	kon chhaau ngauh faahn
dry ice solid carbon-dioxide	n	乾冰	gòn bìng	gon4 bing4	kon peng
dry in the air /hang to dry	v	晾	lohng	long6	lohng
dry powder	n	乾粉	gòn fán	gon4 fan2	kon fan
dry steering /to steer completely full	v	淨操舵	jehng chou tóh	zeng6 cou4 to5	chehng chhou thoh
dual carriageway	n	雙向分隔行駛公路	sèung héung fàn gáak hang sāi gùng lòuh	soeng4 hoeng2 fan4 gaak2 hang3 sai1 gung4 lou6	seung heung fan kaak hang sai kung louh
dubbing /dubs	v	配音	pui yàm	pui3 jam4	phui yam
dubious[1]	adj	可疑嘅	hó yìh ge	ho2 ji4 ge3	ho yih ke
dubious[2]	adj	無把握	móuh bá àak /àk	mou5 baa2 aak4 /ak4	mouh pa aak
dubious[3] /indecision	adj	猶豫不決	yàuh yuh bāt kyut	jau4 jyu6 bat1 kyut3	yauh yuh pat khyut
duck[1]	n	鴨	áap /ngáap	aap2 /ngaap2	aap /ngaap
duct[2] /pipe	n	輸送管	syù sung gún	syu4 sung gun2	syu sung kun
duck[1]	n	鴨	áap /ngáap	aap2 /ngaap2	aap /ngaap
duck[2] (coll) /polite	v	低下頭	dài hah tàuh	dai4 ha6 tau4	tai hah thauh
duck breast	n	鴨胸	áap /ngáap hùng	aap2 /ngaap2 hung4	aap /ngaap hung
duck feet	n	鴨腳	áap /ngáap geuk	aap2 /ngaap2 goek3	aap /ngaap keuk
due	adj	應	yíng	jing2	yeng
due to	adj	由	yàuh	jau4	yauh
duet love-song /question answer song	n	二重奏唱曲	yih chúhng jau cheung kūk	ji6 cung5 zau3 coeng3 kuk1	yih chhuhng chau chheung khuk
duet song	n	二重唱	yih chúhng cheung	ji6 cung5 coeng3	yih chhuhng chheung
dull[1] person /foolish	adj	傻	sòh	so4	soh
dull[2] /clouds	adj	晦暗	fùi ám	fui4 am2	fui am
dull[3] /boring	adj	單調	dàan diuh	daan4 diu6	taan tiuh
dull[4] little know	adj	不明顯	bāt mìhng hín	bat1 ming4 hin2	pat mihng hin
dull person[1] stupid /blunt /foolish	adj	鈍	deuhn	deon6	tuhn
dull person[2] /awkward/clumsy	adj	拙	jyut	zyut3	chyut
dull sky /cloudy	adj	陰天	yàm tìn	jam4 tin4	yam thin
duly	adv	適當	sīk dong	sik1 dong3	sek tong
dumb[1] /dumbness	adj	啞	ngá /āa /áa	nga2 /aa1/aa2	nga /aa
dumb[2] /foolish	adj	獃	òih /ngòih	oi4 /ngoi4	oih /ngoih
dump area	n	垃圾場	laahp saap chèuhng	laap6 saap3 coeng4	laahp saap chheuhng
dumper truck	n	翻斗車	fāan dáu chè	faan1 dau2 ce4	faan tau chhe
dumpling[1]	n	餃	gáau	gaau2	kaau
dumpling[2]	n	餃子	gáau jí	gaau2 zi2	kaau chi
duodenum /intestine small	n	十二指腸	sàhp yìh jī cheung	sap6 ji6 zi1 coeng4	sahp yih chi chheung
duplex /double/twofold	adj	雙倍	sèung púih	soeng4 pui5	seung phuih
durable[1]	adj	冚	kàm	kam4	kham
durable[2] /lasting	adj	冚晒	kàm sái	kam4 sai2	kham sai

English	PoS	漢字	Yale	Jyutping	Romanization
durable[3]	adj	耐用	loih /noih yuhng	loi6 /noi6 jung6	loih /noih yuhng
duration[1]	n	長短	chèuhng dyún	coeng4 dyun2	chheuhng tyun
duration[2]	n	持續期間	chìh juhk kèih gáan	ci4 zuk6 kei4 gaan2	chhih chohk kheih kaan
duration of course		修業期限	sàu yihp kèih haahn	sau4 jip6 kei4 haan6	sau yihp kheih haahn
durian fruit	n	榴蓮	làuh lihn	lau4 lin4	lauh lihn
during[1]	prep	之際	jì jai	zi4 zai3	chi chai
during[2]	prep	個陣時	gó jahn sí	go2 zan6 si2	ko chahn si
during[3] /period of time	prep	在這個時間	joih jé go sí gáan	zoi6 ze2 go3 si2 gaan2	choih che ko si kaan
during[4]	prep	在...嘅整個期間	joih ge jíng go sìh gaan	zoi6 ge3 zing2 go3 si4 gaan3	choih ke cheng ko sih kaan
during one's life		生前	sàang chìhn	saan4 cin4	saang chhihn
dusk /evening/night fall	n	黃昏	wòhng fàn	wong4 fan4	wohng fan
dust[1]	n	塵	chàhn	can4	chhahn
dust[2]	n	灰塵	fùi chàhn	fui4 can4	fui chhahn
dust cover	n	防塵罩	fòhng chàhn jaau	fong4 can4 zaau3	fohng chhahn chaau
dust remover roller	n	除塵轆	chèuih chàhn lùk	ceoi4 can4 luk4	chheuih chahn lok
dustbin /garbage can/ litter-bin/rubbish bin	n	垃圾箱	laahp saap sèung	laap6 saap3 soeng4	laahp saap seung
duster[1]	n	雞毛掃	gái mòuh sòu	gai2 mou4 sou4	kai mouh sou
duster[2]	n	撒粉器	saat fán hei	saat3 fan2 hei3	saat fan hei
dusty	adj	滿是灰塵	múhn sih fūi chàhn	mun5 si6 fui1 can4	muhn sih fui chhahn
Dutch language	n	荷蘭話	ho làahn wá	ho3 laan4 waa2	ho laahn wa
duty[1] /job/career	n	職	jīk	zik1	chek
duty[2] /function/ responsibility	n	職責	jīk jaak	zik1 zaak3	chek chaak
duty[3]	n	當值	dong jihk	dong3 zik6	tong jehk
duty[4] /responsibility	n	任	yahm	jam4	yahm
duty[5] /responsibility	n	任務	yahm mòuh	jam4 mou6	yahm mouh
duty[6] /liability/obligation	n	責任	jaak yahm	zaak3 jam6	chaak yahm
duty off[1] /off duty/stop work	n	收工	sàu gùng	sau4 gung4	sau kung
duty off[2]	n	走去	jáu heui	zau2 heoi3	chau hoi
duty on[1] /report duty	n	報到	bou dou	bou3 dou3	pou tou
duty on[2] /report for duty /report duty	n/v	喺當值	hái dong jihk	hai2 dong3 zik6	hai tong chehk
duty roster[1]	n	更表	gāng bíu	gang1 biu2	kang piu
duty roster[2] /time table	n	間表	gaan bíu	gaan3 biu2	kaan piu
duty shift /work shift	n	更份	gāng fahn	gang1 fan6	kang fahn
dwarf[1]	n	矮人	ngái yan	ngai2 jan4	ngai yan
dwarf[2]	n	侏儒	jyù yùh	zyu4 jyu4	chyu yuh
dwell /inhabit/live/stay/ reside	v	住	jyuh	zyu6	chyuh
dye	n	染色	yíhm sīk	jin5 sik1	yihm sek
dyer	n	染房工	yíhm fóng gùng	jin5 fong2 gung4	yihm fong kung
dying[1]	adj	奄奄一息	yīm yīm yāt sīk	jim1 jim1 jat1 sik1	yim yim yat sek

dying[2]	adj	結束	git chùk	git3 cuk4	kit chhuk
dynamic[1] /moving	n	動態	duhng taai	dung6 taai3	tuhng thaai
dynamic[2] /momentum	adj	動力	duhng lihk	dung6 lik6	tuhng lehk
dynamo /generator	n	發電機	faat dihn gēi	faat3 din6 gei1	faat tihn kei
dynasty[1]	n	朝	chìuh	ciu4	chhiuh
dynasty[2]	n	朝代	chìuh doih	ciu4 doi6	chhiuh toih
dynasty[3]	n	王朝	wòhng chìuh	wong4 ciu4	wohng chhiuh
dysentery[1]	n	痢疾	leih jaht	lei6 zat6	leih chaht
dysentery[2]	n	赤紅痢	chek hùhng leih	cek3 hung4 lei6	chhek hohng leih

E	n	茂	mauh	mau6	mauh
each[1] /every	adj	各	gok	gok3	kok
each[2]	adj	各自	gok jih	gok3 zi6	kok chih
each[3] /every/per	adj	每	múih	mui5	muih
each day /day after day	n	日復一日	yaht fuhk yāt yhat	jat6 fuk6 jat1 jat6	yaht fuhk yat yhat
each other[1]/one another	pron	相	sèung	soeng4	seung
each other[2] /interact	pron	互相	wuh sèung	wu6 soeng4	wuh seung
each other[3]/one another	pron	彼此	béi chí	bei2 ci2	pei chhi
each other[4]	pron	彼此間	béi chí gāan /gaan	bei2 ci2 gaan1 /gaan3	pei chhi kaan
each other talk	v	換句話講	wuhn geui wah góng	wun6 geoi3 waa3 gong2	wuhn kwoi wah kong
eager[1]	adj	好想	hóu séung	hou2 soeng2	hou seung
eager[2]	adj	熱切	yiht chit	jit6 cit3 ge3	yiht chhit
eagle[1]	n	鷹	ying	jing3	yeng
eagle[2]	n	禿鷹	tūk ying	tuk1 jing3	thuk yeng
ear[1]	n	耳仔	yíh jāi	ji5 zai1	yih chai
ear[2]	n	耳朵	yíh dō	ji5 do1	yih to
ear ache	n	耳痛	yíh tung	ji5 tung3	yih thung
ear lobe[1]	n	耳垂	yíh seui	ji5 seoi4	yih swoi
ear lobe[2]	n	耳珠	yíh jyù	ji5 zyu4	yih chyu
ear nose-throat department		耳鼻喉科	yíh beih hàuh fō	ji5 bei6 hau4 fo1	yih peih hauh fo
ear ring	n	耳環	yíh wáan	ji5 waan2	yih waan
ear wax	n	耳屎	yíh sí	ji5 si2	yih si
earless	n	聽覺不佳	tèng gok bāt gāai	teng4 gok3 bat1gaai1	theng kok pat kaai
earlier[1]	adj	早期	jóu kèih	zou2 kei4	chou kheih
earlier[2]	adj	喺早期	hái jóu kèih	hai2 zou2 kei4	hai chou kheih
earlier[3]	adj	早先的	jóu sin dìk	zou2 sin3 dik4	chou sin tik
earliest	n	最早	jeui jóu	zeoi3 zou2	cheui chou
early[1] /fast	adj	早啲	jóu di	zou2 di3	chou ti
early[2] /earlier/earliness	adj	早	jóu	zou2	chou
early[3]	adj	晨早	sàhn jóu	san4 zou2	sahn chou
early morning[1]	adj	清晨	chèng /chìng sàhn	ceng4 /cing4 san4	chheng sahn
early morning[2]	adj	天光	tìn gwòng	tin4 gwong4	thin kwong
earn[1] /make a profit /earnings	v	賺	jaahn	zaan6	chaahn
earn[2]	v	賺得	jaahn dāk	zaan6 dak1	chaahn tak
earn lot of money /large profit/money much making/scoop large sum	v	賺錢多的	jaahn chín dò dì	zaan6 cin2 do4 di4	chaahn chhin toh tih
earn money /make money/make profit	v	賺錢	jaahn chín	zaan6 cin2	chaahn chhin
earner	n	賺錢的人	jaahn chín dīk yàhn	zaan6 cin2 dik1 jan4	chaahn chhin tik yahn
earnest /serious	adj	認真	yihng jàn	jing6 zan4	yehng chan
earnings[1] /income	n	收入	sàu yahp	sau4 jap6	sau yahp
earnings[2] /profit	n	收益	sàu yīk	sau4 jik1	sau yek

earphone /headphone/ receiver	n	聽筒	tèng túng	teng4 tung2	theng tung
earth[1] /ground/land/soil/ dust/clay	n	土	tóu	tou2	thou
earth[2] /globe/world/planet	n	地球	deih kàuh	dei6 kau4	deih khauh
earth-quake	n	地震	deih jan	dei6 zan3	teih chan
earthworm	n	蚯蚓	yāu yáhn	jau1 jan5	yau yahn
ease[1]	n	容易	yung yìh	jung3 ji6	yung yih
ease[2] /lessen/lighten/relax/ relief	n/v	減輕	gáam hèng	gaam2 heng4	kaam heng
easiest	v	容易的	yung yìh dìk	jung3 ji6 dik4	yung yih tik
easily	adv	容易	yung yìh	jung3 ji6	yung yih
easily hurt /vulnerable /easy to hurt	adj	易受傷	yìh sàuh sèung	ji6 sau6 soeng4	yih sauh seung
East	n	東	dùng	dung4	tung
East Rail (HK)	n	東鐵(港)	dùng tit (góng)	dung4 tit3 (gong2)	tung thit (kong)
East Rail line (HK)	n	東鐵線(港)	dùng tit sin (góng)	dung4 tit3 sin3 (gong2)	tung thit sin (kong)
Easter festival on Sunday Mar/Apr	n	復活節	Fuhk wuht jit	fuk6 wut6 zit	Fuhk wuht jit
eastern[1] /orient/oriental	adj	東方	dùng fòng	dung4 fong4	tung fong
eastern[2]	adj	東部	dùng bouh	dung4 bou6	tung pouh
easterner /oriental	n	東方人	dùng fòng yàhn	dung4 fong4 jan4	tung fong yahn
eastwards /facing east	n	向東	heung dùng	hoeng3 dung4	heung tung
easy[1] /easy to/fragile	adj	易	yih	ji6	yih
easy[2] /likely	adj	容易	yùhng yih	jung4 ji6	yuhng yih
easy[3] /comfortable /contented	adj	安樂	òn /ngòn lohk	on4 /ngon4 lok6	on /ngon lohk
easy[4] /simple	adj	簡易	gáan yih	gaan2 ji6	kaan yih
easy[5] /simply/simple/not	adj	簡單	gáan dàan	gaan2 daan4	kaan taan
easy[6]	adj	方便嘅	fòng bihn ge	fong4 bin6 ge3	fong pihn ke
easy come easy go	adv	來得容易 去得快	lòih dāk yùhng yih heui dāk faai	loi4 dak1 jung4 ji6 heui3 dak1 faai3	loih tak yuhng yih hoi tak faai
easy go	adv	去得快	heui dāk faai	heui3 dak1 faai3	hoi tak faai
easy to learn		易學	yih hohk	ji6 hok6	yih hohk
easily seen /conspicuous/ noticeable/easy to see	adj	顯眼處	hín ngáahn chyú	hin2 ngaan5 cyu2	hin ngaahn chhyu
eat[1]	v	食	sihk	sik6	sehk
eat[2]	v	吃	hek	hek3	hek
eat of smoke /mouthful/puff	v	啖	daahm	daam6	taahm
eat in total		共食幾多	guhng sihk géi dō?	gung6 sik6 gei2 do1?	kuhng sehk kei toh?
eat later		遲啲食	chìh dì sihk	ci4 di4 sik6	chhih ti sehk
eat more! /eat somemore	v	食多啲啦!	sihk dò dì lā!	sik6 do4 di4 la1	sehk toh ti la!
eat outdoors /picnic	n	野餐	yéh chàan	je5 caan4	yeh chhaan
eat rice	v	吃飯	hek faahn	hek3 faan6	hek faahn

eat till full	v	飽	báau	baau2	paau
eatable /foods /use as food	adj	食用	sihk yuhng	sik6 jung6	sehk yuhng
eater[1]	n	食嘅人	sihk ge yàhn	sik6 ge jan4	sehk ke yahn
eater[2]	n	吃嘅人	hek ge yàhn	hek3 ge jan4	hek ke yahn
eating[1]	n	食緊	sihk gan	sik6 gan3	sehk kan
eating[2]	n	吃飲食	hek yám sihk	hek3 jam2 sik6	hek yam sehk
eating breakfast		食早餐	sihk jóu chāan	sik6 zou2 caan1	sehk chou chhaan
eating dinner /have dinner		食晚飯	sihk máahn faahn	sik6 maan2 faan6	sehk maahn faahn
eating lunch		食晏	sihk aan	sik6 aan3	sehk aan
eaves[1] of house	n	屋檐	ūk /ngūk yìhm	uk1 /nguk1 jim4	uk /nguk yihm
eaves[2] of house	n	屋簷	ùk /ngūk yìhm	uk1 /nguk1 jim4	uk /nguk yihm
eaves[3] /corridor/hallway /passageway (of the house)	n	走廊	jáu lòhng	zau2 long4	chau lohng
ebb /flows/go out	n	退潮	tèui chìuh	teoi4 ciu4	thoi chhiuh
ebb and flow /tide	n	潮水	chìuh séui	ciu4 seoi2	chhiuh swoi
echo[1]	n	回音	wùih yām	wui4 jam1	wuih yam
echo[2]	n	反響	fáan héung	faan2 hoeng2	faan heung
eclipse[1]	n	蝕	siht	sit6	siht
eclipse[2] of moon	n	月蝕	yuht sihk	jyut6 sik6	yuht sehk
eclipse[3] (sun)/solar eclipse	n	日蝕	yaht sihk	jat6 sik6	yaht sehk
ecology	n	生態學	sàang taai hohk	saang4 taai3 hok6	saang thaai hohk
economy /economic /saving	n/adj	經濟	gìng jai	ging4 zai3	keng chai
economic[1] saving	adj	經濟上	gìng jai séuhng	ging4 zai3 soeng5	keng chai seuhng
economic[2]	adj	經濟嘅	gìng jai ge	ging4 zai3 ge3	keng chai ke
economics	n	經濟學	gìng jai hohk	ging4 zai3 hok6	keng chai hohk
economize[1] /saving /save/scrimp	v	節省	jit sáang	zit3 saang2	chit saang
economize[2] /saving/economy	v	節約	jit yeuk	zit3 joek3	chit yeuk
economize on expenditure /safe on spending	v	開源節流	hòi yùhn jit lauh	hoi4 jyun4 zit3 lau6	hoi yuhn chit lauh
economy /greedy/stingy /thrifty	n/adj	慳	hàan	haan4	haan
economy class	n	普通位	pōu tùng wāi	pou1 tung4 wai1	phou thung wai
ecosystem	n	生態系統	sàang taai haih túng	saang4 taai3 hai6 tung2	saang thaai haih thung
eczema[1] /rash/heat rash	n	皮疹	pèih chán	pei4 can2	pheih chhan
eczema[2] /heat rash	n	濕疹	sāp chán	sap1 can2	sap chhan
...ed past/done/completed action marker	adj	咗 / 了	jó / líuh	zo2 / liu5	cho / liuh
edge /margin/side/border /frontier	n	邊	bìn	bin4	pin
edify /to educate/enlighten		陶冶	tòuh yéh	tou4 je5	thouh yeh
edit	v	主編	jyú pìn	zyu2 pin4	chyu phin
edition[1] /version	n	版	báan	baan2	paan

English		Chinese	Yale	Jyutping	
edition[2]	n	版本	báan bún	baan2 bun2	paan pun
editor[1] /editorial	n	編輯	pìn chàp	pin4 cap4	phin chhap
editor[2]	n	主筆	jyú bāt	zyu2 bat1	chyu pat
editor-in-chief[1]	n	主編	jyú pīn	zyu2 pin1	chyu phin
editor-in-chief[2] /chief editor	n	總編輯	júng pìn chàp	jung2 pin4 cap4	chung phìn chhap
editorial	adj	社論	séh leuhn	se5 leong6	seh lowhn
educate /inculcate/to teach	v	教育	gaau yuhk	gaau3 juk6	kaau yuhk
educated[1]	adj	知識淵學	jì sìk yūn hohk	zi4 sik4 jyun1 hok6	chi sek yun hohk
educated[2] /lettered	adj	受過高等教育	sauh gwo gòu dang gaau yuhk	sau6 gwo3 gou4 dang2 gaau3 juk6	sauh kwo kou tang kaau yuhk
education	n	教育	gaau yuhk	gaau3 juk6	kaau yuhk
education allowance		教育津貼	gaau yuhk jèun tip	gaau3 juk6 zeon4 tip3	kaau yuhk cheun thip
education bureau	n	教育局	gaau yuhk gúk	gaau3 juk6 guk2	kaau yuhk kuk
education level		教育程度	gaau yuhk chìhng douh	gaau3 juk6 cing4 dou6	kaau yuhk chhehng touh
educational	adj	教育嘅	gaau yuhk ge	gaau3 juk6 ge3	kaau yuhk ke
eel /fish	n	鰻魚	maahn yú	maan4 jyu2	maahn yu
eels[1] /fish	n	鱔	síhn	sin5	sihn
eels[2] /dry fish	n	門鱔乾	mùhn síhn gòn	mun4 sin5 gon4	muhn sihn kon
effect /result	n	效果	haauh gwó	haau6 gwo2	haauh kwo
effective[1] /show results	adj	奏效	jau haauh	zau3 haau6	chau haauh
effective[2]	adj	生效	sàang haauh	saang4 haau6	saang haauh
effective[3]	adj	有效嘅	yáuh haauh ge	jau5 haau6 ge3	yauh haauh ke
effective[4]	adj	有力嘅	yáuh lihk ge	jau5 lik6 ge3	yauh lehk ke
effectively	n	有效地	yauh hàauh dèih	jau5 haau6 dei6	yauh haauh teih
effects	v	動產	duhng cháan	dung6 caan2	tuhng chhaan
efficiency	n	效率	haauh leuht	haau6 leot6	haauh lwoht
efficient[1] /effective	adj	有效	yauh hàauh	jau5 haau6	yauh haauh
efficient[2]	adj	有效率	yáuh haauh léuht	jau5 haau6 leot6	yauh haauh lwoht
efficiently[1]	adv	高效率地	gòu haauh leuht dèih	gou4 haau6 leot6 dei6	kou haauh lowht teih
efficiently[2]	adv	效率高地	haauh leuht gōu deih	haau6 leot6 gou1 dei6	haauh lwoht kou teih
effort /attempt/exert /strive	n	努力	lóuh /nóuh lìhk	lou5 /nou5 lik6	louh /nouh lehk
effortless /no effort	adj	無努力	mòuh lóuh/nóuh lìhk	mou4 lou5 /nou5 lik6	mouh louh /nouh lehk
egg	n	蛋	dáan	daan2	taan
egg & ham sandwich	n	腿蛋治	tēui dāan chi	teoi1 daan1 ci4	thoi taan chi
egg beater	n	打蛋機	dá dáan gēi	daa2 daan2 gei1	ta taan kei
egg of pigeon	n	鴿蛋	gáap dāan	gaap2 daan1	kaap taan
egg sandwich	n	蛋治	dáan jih	daan2 zi6	taan chih
egg white	n	蛋白	dāan baahk	daan1 baak6	taan paahk
egg yolk	n	蛋黃	dāan wóng	daan1 wong2	taan wong
ego	n	自尊	jih jeun	zi6 zeon3	chih cheon
egoist	n	自高自大者	jih gōu jih daaih jé	zi6 gou1 daai6 ze2	chih kou chih taaih che
egotism[1]	n	自我主義	jih ngóh jyú yih	zi6 ngo5 zyu2 ji6	chih ngoh chyu yih

English		Chinese	Yale	Jyutping	Other
egotism[2]	n	利己主義	leih géi jyú yih	lei6 gei2 zyu2 ji6	leih kei chyu yih
egress[1] /go out/exodus	n/v	外出	oih /ngoih chēut	oi6 /ngoi6 ceot1	oih /ngoih chhot
egress[2] /exit-way/out-way	n	出路	chēut louh	ceot1 lou6	chhot louh
eight	n	八	baat	baat3	paat
eighteen	n	十八	sahp baat	sap6 baat3	sahp paat
eightfold	adj	八倍	baat púih	baat3 pui5	paat púih
eighty	n	八十	baat sàhp	baat3 sap6	paat sàhp
either[1]	n	或者	waahk jé	waak6 ze2	waahk che
either[2]	adj	兩者之中	léuhng jé jí jùng	loeng5 ze2 zi2 zung4	leuhng che chi chung
either side[1]	adj	一邊	yāt bīn	jat1 bin1	yat pin
either side[2] /both sides	adj	兩邊	léuhng bīn	loeng5 bin1	leuhng pin
ejaculatory duct	n	射出管	sèh chēut gún	se6 ceot1 gun2	seh chhot kun
eject /evict/to expel	v	逐出	juhk chēut	zuk6 ceot1	chuhk chhot
ejection /exclude	n	排斥	paaih chīk	paai6 cik1	phaaih chhik
ejector	n	推出器	tèui chēut hei	teoi4 ceot1 hei3	thoi chhot hei
elaborate	adj	精心製作	jēng sàm jai jok	zeng1 sam4 zai3 zok3	cheng sam chai chok
elaboration	n	精巧	jēng háau	zeng1 haau2	cheng haau
elapse[1] /go over/in the past	v	過去	gwo heui	gwo3 heoi3	kwo hoi
elapse[2] in the past	v	消逝(時間)	sīu saih (sìh gaan)	siu1 sai6 (si4 gaan3)	siu saih (sih kaan)
elastic /flexible	adj	有彈性	yáuh daahn sing	jau5 daan6 sing3	yauh taahn seng
elasticity /returned original shape	n	彈性	dàahn sing	daan4 sing3	taahn seng
elbow[1]	n	肘	jaau	zaau3	chaau
elbow[2]	n	手踭	sáu jàang	sau2 zang4	sau chaang
elbow[3]	n	手肘	sáu jáau	sau2 zaau2	sau chaau
elbow patch		肘子補丁	jaau jí bóu dīng	zaau3 zi2 bou2 ding1	chaau chi pou teng
elder	adj	年齡較大	lìhn lìhng gaau daaih	lin4 ling4 gaau3 daai6	lihn lehng kaau taaih
elder brother[1]	adj	哥	gō	go1	ko
elder brother[2]	adj	哥哥	gò gò	go4 go4	ko ko
elder brother[3]	adj	阿哥	áa gò	aa2 go4	aa ko
elder brother[4]	adj	大佬	daaih lóu	daai6 lou2	taaih lou
elderly	adj	上了年紀	séuhng líuh lihn /nihn géi	soeng5 liu5 lin4 /nin4 gei2	seuhng liuh lihn /nihn kei
eldest	adj	最年長	jeui lihn /nihn jéung	zeoi3 lin4 /nin4 zoeng2	cheui lihn /nihn cheung
election /public election /voting/ poll	n	選舉	syún géui	syun2 geoi2	syun kwoi
electric /electricity	n	電	dihn	din6	tihn
electric current	n	電流	dihn làuh	din6 lau4	tihn lauh
electric energy	n	電能	dihn nàhng	din6 nang4	tihn nahng
electric fan	n	電風扇	dihn fùng sin	ding6 fung4 sin3	tihn fung sin
electric fire	n	漏電火災	lauh dihn fó jòi	lau6 din6 fo2 zoi4	lauh tihn fo choi
electric iron	n	電熨斗	dihn tong dáu	din6 tong3 dau2	tihn thong tau
electric light	n	電燈	dihn dāng	din6 dang1	tihn tang
electric multi-plug /multi plug of electric		萬能插蘇	maahn làhng chaap sōu	maan6 lang4 caap3 sou1	maahn lahng chhaap sou
electric oil /gasoline	n	電油	dihn yàuh	din6 jau4	tihn yauh

English		Chinese	Cantonese	Jyutping	Romanization
electric plug[1]	n	插蘇	chaap sōu	caap3 sou1	chhaap sou
electric plug[2]	n	電插頭	dihn chaap tàuh	din6 caap3 tau4	tihn chhaap thauh
electric power	n	電源	dihn yùhn	din6 jyun4	tihn yuhn
electric stove	n	電爐	dihn lòuh	din6 lou4	tihn louh
electric wire	n	電線	dihn sín	din6 sin2	tihn sin
electrical	a	電氣	dihn hei	din6 hei3	tihn hei
electrical appliances store /electrical goods store	n	電器鋪	dihn hei pou	din6 hei3 pou3	tihn hei phou
electrical device	n	電器	dihn hei	din6 hei3	tihn hei
electrical engineer	n	電學工程師	dihn hòhk gùng chìhng sī	din6 hok6 gung4 cing4 si1	tihn hohk kung chhehng sih
electrical power	n	電力	dihn lihk	din6 lik6	tihn lehk
electrician[1]	n	電工	dihn gùng	din6 gung4	tihn kung
electrician[2]	n	電氣佬	dihn hei lóu	din6 hei3 lou2	tihn hei lou
electrician[3]	n	電氣師傅	dihn hei sī fuh	din6 hei3 si1 fu6	tihn hei si fuh
electricity failure		電力故障	dihn lihk gu jeung	din6 lik6 gu3 zoeng3	tihn lehk ku cheung
electricity supply		供電	gùng dihn	gung4 din6	kung tihn
electrification	n	電氣化	dihn hei fa	din6 hei3 fa3	tihn hei fa
electrolytes	n	電解質	dihn gáai jāt	din6 gaai2 zat1	tihn kaai chat
electronics	n	電子	dihn jí	din6 zi2	tihn chi
elegant[1] (sl) man or female /dignified/generous	n	大方	daaih fòng	daai6 fong4	taaih fong
elegant[2] (sl) man/female	n	闊佬	fut lóu	fut3 lou2	fut lou
elegant female/highness	n	高貴	gòu wai	gou4 wai3	kou wai
element	n	元素	yùhn sou	jyun4 sou3	yuhn sou
elemental	adj	自然力	jih yìhn lihk	zi6 jin4 lik6	chih yihn lehk
elephant[1]	n	象	jeuhng	zoeng6	cheuhng
elephant[2]	n	大笨象	daaih bahn jeuhng	daai6 ban6 zoeng6	taaih pahn cheuhng
elevate	n	抬起	tòih héi	toi6 hei2	thoih hei
elevator[1] /lift	n	升降機	sìng gong gēi	sing4 gong3 gei1	seng kong kei
elevator[2] /escalator/lift	n	電梯	dihn tài	din6 tai4	tihn thai
elevator door	n	電梯門	dihn tài mùhn	din6 tai4 mun4	tihn thai muhn
elevator's holder	n	扶手把 (自動電梯)	fùh sāu bá (jih duhng dihn tài)	fu4 sau1 ba2 (zi6 dung6 din6 tai4)	fuh sau pa (chih tuhng tihn thai)
eleven	adj	十一	sàhp yāt	sap6 jat1	sahp yat
elf /devil/sprite	n	小精靈	síu jèng lèhng	siu2 zeng4 leng6	siu cheng lehng
eligibility	n	合格	hahp gaak	hap6 gaak3	hahp kaak
eligible[1]	adj	合格嘅	hahp gaak ge	hap6 gaak3 ge3	hahp kaak ke
eligible[2]	adj	合資格	hahp jī gaak	hap6 zi1 gaak3	hahp chi kaak
eligible person	n	合資格人士	hahp jī gaak yàhn sih	hap6 zi1 gaak3 jan4 si6	hahp chi kaak yahn sih
eligibly	ad	合適地	hahp sīk deih	hap6 sik1 dei6	hahp sek teih
eliminate[1] /remove/ eradicate	v	消除	sìu cheui	siu4 ceoi4	siu chhoi
eliminate[2] /pare	v	消滅	sìu miht	siu4 mit6	siu miht
eliminator	n	排除者	paai cheui jé	paai3 ceoi4 ze2	phaai chhoih che

else[1] /might/may be/either /possibly	adv	或	waahk	waak6	waahk
else[2] /others/miscellaneous	adv	其他	kèih tà	kei4 taa4	kheih tha
else[3]	adv	別的	bìht dìk	bit6 dik4	piht dek
else[4] /others/second	adv	第二的	daih yih dì	dai6 ji6 dik4	taih yih tek
else[5] /other/different	adv	其他	gèih tà	gei4 taa4	keih tha
else[6] /otherwise	adv	若唔係	yeuhk m̀ haih	joek6 m4 hai6	yeuhk mh haih
elsewhere[1]	adv	係第二處	haih daih yih syu	hai6 dai6 ji6 syu3	haih taih yih syu
elsewhere[2]	adv	在別處	joih bìht syu	zoi6 bit6 syu3	choih piht syu
elsewhere[3]	adv	別處	bìht syu	bit6 syu3	piht syu
elude /escape	v	逃出	tòuh chēut	tou4 ceot1	thouh chhot
email	n	電郵	dihn yàuh	din6 jau4	tihn yauh
embark[1] /as a passenger	v	搭乘	daap sìhng	daap3 sing4	taap sehng
embark[2] /take plane	v	搭飛機	dáap fèi gèi	daap2 fei4 gei4	taap fei kei
embarkation /to transport	n	搭載	dáap jói	daap2 zoi2	taap choi
embarrassed	adj	窘嘅	dau ge	dau3 ge3	tau ke
embarrassing[1]	adj	令人難堪	lihng yàhn nàahn hàm	ling4 jan4 naan4 ham4	lehng yahn naahn ham
embarrassing[2] /trying /hard to take	adj	難堪	làahn hām	laan4 ham1	laahn ham
embassy	n	大使館	daaih si gún	daai6 si3 gun2	taaih si gun
embrace /cling	v	緊抱	gán póuh	gan2 pou5	kan phouh
embroider /weave /knit/sew/embroidery	v	織	jīk	zik1	chek
embroider /embellish	v	繡	sau	sau3	sau
embroidered	v	綉花	sau fā	sau3 faa1	sau fa
embryo	n	胚胎	pūi tōi	pui1 tui1	phui thoi
embryo of animal	n	胚胎動物	pūi tōi duhng maht	pui1 tui1 dung6 mat6	phui thoi tohng maht
embryo plant	n	胚芽	pūi ngàh	pui1 ngaa4	phui ngah
emendator	n	校訂者	gaau dìng jé	gaau3 ding ze2	kaau deng che
emerald	n	綠寶石	luhk bóu sehk	luk6 bou2 sek6	luhk pou sehk
emergency[1]	n	緊急事件	gán gāp sih gihn	gan2 gap1 si6 gin6	kan kap sih kihn
emergency[2]	n	緊急情況	gán gāp chihng fong	gan2 gap1 cing4 fong3	kan kap chhehng fong
emergency case	n	急诊病例	gāp chān bèhng làih	gap1 can1 beng6 lai6	kap chhan pehng laih
emergency door	n	太平門	táai pèhng /pìhng mùhn	taai2 peng4 /ping4 mun4	thaai phehng muhn
emergency maintenance		緊急維修	gán gāp wàih sàu	gan2 gap1 wai4 sau4	kan kap waih sau
emergency meeting	n	緊急會議	gán gāp wúi yíh	gan2 gap1 wui2 ji5	kan kap wui yih
emergency room[1]	n	急症室	gāp jing sāt	gap1 zing3 sat1	kap cheng sat
emergency room[2]	n	急診室	gāp chān sāt	gap1 can1 sat1	kap chhan sat
emergency sick	n	急診病人	gāp chān bèhng yàhn	gap1 can1 beng6 jan4	kap chhan pehng yahn
emergency treatment /first aid	n	急救	gāp gau	gap1 gau3	kap kau
emergency treatment		急診	gāp chān	gap1 can1	kap chhan
emigrant	adj	移民	yìh màhn	ji4 man4	yih mahn

English		Chinese	Yale	Jyutping	
emigrate	v	移居外國	yìh gèui oih /ngoih gwok	ji4 geoi4 oi6 /ngoi6 gwok3	yih kwoi oih /ngoih kwok
emit /noised	v	發吵	faat cháau	faat3 caau2	faat chhaau
emotion /excitement/ agitation	n	激動	gīk duhng	gik1 dung6	kek tohng
emotion /passion/ feeling/willing	n	情	chìhng	cing4	chhehng
emotional	adj	情感	chìhng gám	cing4 gam2	chhehng kam
emotionally	adv	情緒上	chìhng séuih séuhng	cing4 seoi5 soeng5	chhehng swoih seuhng
emperor	n	皇帝	wòhng dai	wong4 dai3	wohng tai
emphasis[1]	n	重點	chúhng dīm	cung5 dim1	chhuhng tim
emphasis[2]	n	強調	kèuhng diuh	koeng4 diu6	kheuhng tiuh
emphasis[3] /forceful tone	n	加強語氣	gà kèuhng yúh hei	gaa4 koeng4 jyu5 hei3	ka kheuhng yuh hei
emphasize[1] /pay attention	v	注重	jyu juhng	zyu3 zung6	chyu chuhng
emphasize[2] (a statement) /highlighted	v	強調	kèuhng diuh	koeng4 diu6	kheuhng tiuh
employ[1] /hire/to hire	v	雇	gu	gu3	ku
employ[2] /hiring worker	v	聘用	ping yuhng	ping3 jung6	pheng yuhng
employ[3] /engage	v	雇用	gu yuhng	gu3 jung6	ku yuhng
employee[1] /member /person/staff	n	員	yùhn	jyun4	yuhn
employee[2] /staff/clerk/ staff member/office staff /office worker	n	職員	jīk yùhn	zik1 jyun4	chek yuhn
employee[3] /staff	n	員工	yùhn gùng	jyun4 gung4	yuhn kung
employee[4] /employment	n	僱員	gu yùhn	gu3 jyun4	ku yuhn
employee[5]	n	雇工	gu gùng	gu3 gung4	ku kung
employee[6] /hire worker /helper	n	佣人	yuhng yàhn	jung6 jan4	yuhng yahn
employee[7]	n	受雇者	sauh gu jé	sau6 gu ze2	sauh ku che
employer	n	僱主	gu jyú	gu3 zyu2	ku chyu
employment /giving job	n	聘任	ping yàm	ping3 jam4	pheng yam
employment	n	就業	jauh yihp	zau6 jip6	chauh yihp
emporium /town centre	n	商業中心	sèung yihp jùng sàm	soeng4 jip6 zung4 sam4	seung yihp chung sam
empress /ruling queen /queen	n	女皇	léuih wòhng	leui5 wong4	lowih wohng
empty /vacancy	adj	空	hùng	hung4	hung
empty bag /hollow bag	adj	清袋	chèng dói /doih	ceng4 doi2 /doi6	chheng toi /toih
empty stomach[(sl)] /not eat/ fasting	adj	空腹	hùng fùk	hung4 fuk4	hung fuk
enable /can/capable	v/aux	能夠	làhng /nàhng gáu	lang4 /nang4 gau2	lahng /nahng kau
encase[1]	v	裝入	jōng yahp	zong1 jap6	chong yahp
encase[2]	v	包住	bāau jyuh	baau1 zyu6	pāau chyuh
encase[3]	v	包裝	bāau jòng	baau1 zong4	paau chong
encephalitis /brain fever	n	腦炎	nóuh yìhm	nou5 jim4	nouh yihm
enchant /magic	v	魔法	mò faat	mo4 faat3	mo faat

enclose /surround	v	圍住	wàih jyuh	wai4 zyu6	waih chyuh
enclosure[1]	n	包圍	bàau wàih	baau4 wai4	paau waih
enclosure[2]	n	圍場	wàih chèuhng	wai4 coeng4	waih chheuhng
encounter[1] occur /occurrence	n	發生	faat sàng	faat3 sang4	faat sang
encounter[2] /coming upon	v	遇到	yuh dóu	jyu6 dou2	yuh tou
encourage[1] /give support	v	鼓勵	gú laih	gu2 lai6	ku laih
encourage[2] /support assist	v	支持	jì chìh	zi4 ci4	chi chhih
encouragement[1]	n	鼓勵	gú laih	gu2 lai6	ku laih
encouragement[2]	n	獎勵	jéung laih	zoeng2 lai6	cheung laih
encouragement[3] /support/assist	n	贊助	jaan joh	zaan3 zo6	chaan choh
encroachment[1]	n	侵佔	chàm jim	cam4 zim3	chham chim
encroachment[2] /invade/invasion	n	侵犯	chàm faahn	cam4 faan6	chham faahn
encyclopedia	n	百科全書	baak fō chyùhn syù	baak3 fo1 cyun4 syu4	paak fo chhyuhn syu
end[1] /finish	n/v	完	yùhn	jyun4	yuhn
end[2] /finish/in the end	n	終	jūng	jung1	chung
end[3] /final/last/final stage	n	末	muht	mut6	muht
end[4] /head/nob/top	n	頭	tàuh	tau4	thauh
end[5] /finish/stop/termination	n	終止	jūng jí	jung1 zi2	chung chi
end[6] side or edge /finish /conclude	v	結束	git chùk	git3 cuk4	kit chhuk
end[7] /die	v	收皮	sāu pèih	sau1 pei4	sau pheih
end[8] /finish/complete	v	完畢	yùhn bāt	jyun4 bat1	yuhn pat
end of the letter	v	結尾	git méih	git3 mei5	kit meih
end of the month	v	月尾	yuht méih	jyut6 mei5	yuht meih
end of the street[1]	v	街口	gāai háu	gaai1 hau2	kaai hau
end of the street[2]	v	街尾	gāai méih	gaai1 mei5	kaai meih
end of the year[1]	v	年尾	lìhn méih	lin4 mei5	lihn meih
end of the year[2]	v	在今年年底	joih gām nìhn nìhn dái	zoi6 gam1 nin4 nin4 dai2	choih kam nihn nihn tai
end of time /finish time	v	够鐘	gau jūng	gau3 zung1	kau chung
endangering	v	危及	ngàih kàhp	ngai4 kap6	ngaih khahp
ended	v	完全地	yùhn chyùhn deih	jyun4 cyun4 dei6	yuhn chhyuhn teih
ending[1]	n	結尾	git méih	git3 mei5	kit meih
ending[2] /outcome	n	結局	git guhk	git3 guk6	kit kuhk
endorsed by[1]	n	背書	bui syù	bui3 syu4	pui syu
endorsed by[2] /verification	n	確認	kok yihng	kok3 jing3	khok yehng
endow[1] /grant	v	賜	chi	ci3	chhi
endow[2]	v	捐予	gyùn yúh	gyun4 jyu5	kyun yuh
endow[3]	v	賦與	fu yúh	fu3 jyu5	fu yuh
endurance[1] /patience /fortitude	n	忍耐力	yán loih /noih lihk	jan2 loi6 /noi6 lik6	yan loih /noih kehk
endurance[2] /patience	n	耐性	loih /noih sing	loi6 /noi6 sing3	loih /noih seng

endure /suffer/vex/annoy /harass/persecute	v	捱	ngàaih	ngaai4	ngaaih
enemy /foe/hostile	n	敵人	dihk yàhn	dik6 jan4	tehk yahn
energetic[1]	adj	有活力	yáuh wuht lihk	jan5 wut6 lik6	yauh wuht lehk
energetic[2]	adj	精神飽滿	jèng sàhn báau múhn	zeng4 san4 baau2 mun5	cheng sahn paau muhn
energy[1] /vigour	n	精力	jeng lihk	zeng3 lik6	cheng lehk
energy[2]	n	幹勁	gon gihng	gon3 ging6	kon kehng
energy[3]	n	能量	làhng /nàhng lèuhng	lang4 /nang4 loeng6	lahng /nahng leuhng
energy[4]	n	熱量	yiht lèuhng	jit6 loeng6	yiht leuhng
energy converter	n	能量轉換器	làhng /nàhng lèuhng jyún wuhn hei	lang4 /nang4 loeng6 zyun2 wun6 hei3	lahng /nahng leuhng chyun wuhn hei
enforce[1] /carry out/fulfill/ commence/execute/conduct/ perform/to implement	v	執行	jāp hàang	zap1 hang4	chap haang
enforce[2] /carry out	v	實施	saht sì	sat6 si4	saht si
enforce[3] /enforcement	n/v	強制	kéuhng jai	koeng5 zai3	kheuhng chai
enforcing[1]	n	強制執行	kéuhng jai jāp hàhang	koeng5 zai3 zap1 hang4	kheuhng chai chap hahang
enforcing[2] /impose	n	聽話執行	tèng wā jàp hang	teng4 waa1 zap4 hang3	theng wa chap hang
engage	v	吸引	kāp yáhn	kap1 jan5	khap yahn
engine	n	發動機	faat duhng gèi	faat3 dung6 gei4	faat tuhng kei
engine stop		熄匙	sīk sìh	sik1 si4	sek sih
engineer	n	工程師	gùng chìhng sī	gung4 cing4 si1	kung chhehng si
engineering college	n	工學院	gùng hohk yún	gung4 hok6 jyun2	kung hohk yun
engineering depart	n	工程部	gùng chìhng bouh	gung4 cing4 bou6	kung chhehng pouh
England [(de)]	n	英格蘭	yìng gaak laan	jing4 gaak3 laan3	yeng kaak laan
English[1]	n	英文	yìng màhn	jing man4	yeng mahn
english[2]	adj	英語	yìng yúh	jing4 jyu5	yeng yuh
english man[1]	n	英國人	yìng gwók yàhn	jing4 gwok2 jan4	yeng kwok yahn
english man[2] /westerner	n	西人	sài yàhn	sai4 jan4	sai yahn
english man[3] /foreigner /westerner no polite called	n	鬼佬	gwái lóu	gwai2 lou2	kwai lou
english sentence	n	英文句	yīng màhn geui	ying1 man4 gui3	yehng mahn kwoi
english tea	n	西茶	sài chàh	sai4 caa4	sai chhah
english woman[1]	n	外國女人	oih /ngoih gwok léuih /néuih yàhn	oi6 /ngoi6 gwok3 leoi5 /neoi5 jan4	oih /ngoih kwok lowih /nowih yahn
english woman[2] /caucasian woman/foreigner woman/caucasian woman (no polite called for …)	n	鬼婆	gwái pòh	gwai2 po4	kwai phoh
engrave[1]	v	銘	mìhng	ming4	mehng
engrave[2] /carve	v	雕	dīu	diu1	tiu
engraver	n	雕刻師	dìu hak sī	diu4 hak3 si1	tiu hak si
enhancement /pick up	n	改進	gói jeun	goi2 zeon3	koi cheun
enjoy /enjoyment	n/v	享受	héung sauh	hoeng2 sau6	heung sauh
enjoy little time /spree/enjoy short time	n	作樂	jok lohk	zok3 lok6	chok lohk

English	Part	Chinese	Romanization 1	Jyutping	Romanization 2
enjoyable	adj	玩	wáan	waan2	waan
enlarge[1]	v	擴	kwong	kwong3	khwong
enlarge[2] /magnify	v	放大	fong daaih	fong3 daai6	fong taaih
enlarger machine	n	放大機	fong daaih gèi	fong3 daai6 gei4	fong taaih kei
enlighten[1]	v	啓蒙	kái muhng	kai2 mung4	khai mohng
enlighten[2]	v	啓發	kái faat	kai2 faat3	khai faat
enlists	v	從軍	chùhng gwàn	cung4 gwan4	chhuhng kwan
enough[1] /have enough /adequate	adv	夠	gau	gau3	kau
enough[2]	pron	足夠	jūk gau	zuk1 gau3	chuk kau
enough[3] /many/lot of/ plenty	pron	好多	hóu dò	hou2 do4	hou toh
enough[4]	pron	夠啦!	gau la	gau3 laa	kau la
enough[5] /full eat	pron	飽啦!	báau la	baau2 laa	paau la
enough great & mighty		夠偉大	gau wáih daaih	gau3 wai5 daai6	kau waih taaih
enquirer	n	詢問者	sēun mahn jé	seon1 man6 ze2	swon mahn che
enquiries	n	查詢	chàh sèun	caa4 seon4	chhah swon
enquiry desk /information desk	n	詢問處	sēun mahn chyu	seon1 man6 cyu3	swon mahn chhyu
enraged[1]	v	激嬲	gīk làu /nàu	gik1 lau4 /nau4	kek lau /nau
enraged[2] /angry/incense angry	v	憤怒	fahn louh /nouh	fan5 lou6 /nou6	fahn louh /nouh
enrol[1]	v	入讀	yahp duhk	jap6 duk6	yahp tuhk
enrol[2] /enlist /registery /registration	v	登記	dàng gei	dang4 gei3	tang kei
enrolment	n	入學	yahp hohk	jap6 hok6	yahp hohk
ensign /flag/national flag	n	掛旗	gwa kèih	gwaa3 kei4	kwa kheih
ensure[1] /confirm/decide /confirm/positive talk	v	確定	kok dehng /dihng	kok3 deng6 /ding6	khok tehng
ensure[2]	v	保障	bóu jeung	bou2 zoeng3	pou cheung
ensure[3] /pledge/promise/ assure/guarantee	v	保證	bóu jing	bou2 zing3	pou cheng
enter[1]	v	入	yahp	jap6	yahp
enter[2]	v	臻	jēun	zeon1	cheun
enter[3]	v	入來	yahp lòih	jap6 loi4	yahp loih
enter a house (by force)	v	破門入屋	po mùhn yahp ūk /ngūk	po3 mun4 jap6 uk1 /nguk1	pho muhn yahp uk /nguk
entertain[1] /treat reception	v	招待	jìu doih	ziu4 doi6	chiu toih
entertain[2]	v	使歡樂	sái fún lohk	sai2 fun2 lok6	sai fun lohk
enthusiast	n	熱心者	yiht sām jé	jit6 sam1 ze2	yiht sam che
enthusiastic[1] /zealous /lot of excitement/cordial	adj	熱心	yiht sām	jit6 sam1	yiht sam
enthusiastic[2]	adj	落力	lohk lihk	lok6 lik6	lohk lehk
entire[1] /whole/total	ad	整個	jing go	zing3 go3	cheng ko
entire[2]	adj	全部	chyùhn bouh	cyun4 bou6	chhyuhn pouh
entirely /completely	adv	完全	yùhn chyùhn	jyun4 cyun4	yuhn chhyuhn

entitle[1]	v	給權	káp kyùhn	kap2 kyun4	khap khyuhn
entitle[2]	v	給權力	káp kyùhn lihk	kap2 kyun4 lik6	khap khyuhn lehk
entitle[3]	v	有資格	yáuh jì gáak	jau5 zi4 gaak2	yauh chi kaak
entrails /internal organs /mixed internal	n	雜	jaahp	zaap6	chaahp
entrails of animals /offal/internal parts/viscera/internal	n	內臟	loih /noih johng	loi6 /noi6 zong6	loih /noih chohng
entrance /gate	n	大門	daaih mun	daai6 mun3	taaih mun
entrap	v	打龍通	dá lùhng tùng	daa2 lung4 tung4	ta luhng thung
entrée	n	頭盤	tàuh pun	tau4 pun3	thauh phun
entries dictionary words	n	詞條	chìh tíuh	ci4 tiu5	chhih thiuh
entrust /support by hand /hold in hand/lift by hand		託	tok	tok3	thok
entrust[1] /request	v	拜託	baai tok	baai3 tok3	paai thok
entrust[2]	v	信託	seun tok	seon3 tok3	swon thok
entrust[3] /to trust	v	委託	wái tok	wai2 tok3	wai thok
entry	n	進入	jeun yahp	zeon3 jap6	cheun yahp
envelope[1]	n	信封	seun fūng	seon3 fung1	swon fung
envelope[2]	v	掩蓋	yím koi	jim2 koi3	yim koi
envious[1] /envy/jealous	adj	妒忌	douh geih	dou6 gei6	touh keih
envious[2]	adj	妒忌嘅	douh geih ge	dou6 gei6 ge3	touh keih ke
environment[1]	n	環境	wàahn gíng	waan4 ging2	waahn keng
environment[2]	n	自然環境	jih yìhn wàahn gíng	zi6 jin4 waan4 ging2	chih yihn waahn keng
environment dirty /pollution/contamination / making environment	n	污穢	wù wai	wu4 wai3	wu wai
environmental	adj	環保	wàahn bóu	waan4 bou2	waahn pou
envisage	v	設想	chit séung	cit3 soeng2	chhit seung
envoy	n	使者	si jé	si3 ze2	si che
envy	n	羨慕	sihn mouh	sin6 mou6	sihn mouh
epaulet /epaulette/ shoulder-seal	n	肩章	gīn jèung	gin1 zoeng4	kin cheung
epicentre	n	震央	jan yèung	zan3 joeng4	chan yeung
epidemic	n	流行性	làuh hàhng sing	lau4 hang4 sing3	lauh hahng seng
epidemic disease /spread disease/pandemic	n	流行病	làuh hàhng behng /bihng	lau4 hang4 beng6 /bing6	lauh hahng pehng
epididymis	n	附睾	fu gòu	fu gou4	fu kou
episodes /circumstances	n	情節	chìhng jit	cing4 zit3	chhehng chit
epistaxis	n	鼻出血	beih chēut hyut	bei6 ceot1 hyut3	peih chhot hyut
equal[1] /equality	n/v	平等	pèhng dáng	peng4 dang2	phehng tang
equal[2] /equality	n/v	相等	sèung dáng	soeng4 dang2	seung tang
equal[3] /equals (=)	v	等於	dáng yù	dang2 jyu4	tang yu
equal to		能勝任	làhng /nàhng sing yahm	lang4 /nang4 sing3 yam6	lahng /nahng seng yahm
equalized	v	使相等	sai sèung dáng	sai3 soeng4 dang2	sai seung tang
equally	adv	相同地	sèung tung dèih	soeng4 tung3 dei6	seung tung teih

English	POS	Chinese	Jyutping (diacritic)	Jyutping (numbered)	Romanization
equator	n	赤道	chek douh	cek3 dou6	chhek touh
equilateral triangle	n	等邊三角形	dáng bīn sàam gok yihng	dang2 bin1 saam4 gok3 jing4	tang pin saam kok yehng
equipment[1]	n	器材	hei chòih	hei3 coi4	hei chhoih
equipment[2] /device	n	裝置	jòng ji	zong4 zi3	chong chi
equipment[3]	n	器械	hei haaih	hei3 haai6	hei haaih
equipp	v	配備着	púi bèih jeuk	pui2 bei6 zoek6	phui peih cheuk
equitable[1]/even handed /fair/fairly/justice	adj	公平	gùng pèhng /pìhng	gung4 peng4 /ping4	kung phehng
equitable[2] /fair	adj	公正嘅	gùng jing ge	gung4 zing3 ge3	kung cheng ke
equivalent	adj	相等的	sèung dáng dīk	soeng4 dang2 dik1	seung tang tik
era[1] /age/period/time	n	時代	sìh doih	si6 dou6	sih toih
era[2] age/period	n	年代	lihn doih	lin4 doi6	lihn toih
era[3] beginning of era	n	紀元	géi yùhn	gei2 jyun4	kei yuhn
eradicate	v	根除	gàn chèuih	gan4 ceoi4	kan chheuih
eradicateable	adj	可根除	hó gàn chèuih	ho2 gan4 ceoi4	ho kan chheuih
erase	v	擦掉	cháat diuh	caat3 diu6	chhaat tiuh
eraser[1]	n	擦膠	chaat gāau	caat3 gaau1	chhaat kaau
eraser[2]	n	擦紙膠	chaat jí gàau	caat3 zi2 gaau4	chhaat chi kaau
eraser[3]	n	擦除器	cháat chèuih hei	caat3 ceoi4 hei3	chhaat chhoih hei
erect[1] of penis/nipples	adj	豎挺	syuh tíhng	syu6 ting5	syuh thehng
erect[2] /vertical	v	直立	jihk lahp	zik6 lap6	chehk lahp
erect[3]	v	垂直	seui jìhk	seoi4 zik6	swoi chehk
erect[4] /vertical	v	豎直	syuh jihk	syu6 zik6	syuh chehk
erect[5] /hold up	v	豎起	syuh héi	syu6 hei2	syuh hei
erect nipples	adj	乳暈	yúh waan	jyu5 waan3	yuh waan
erected of penis	adj	起頭	héi tàuh	hei2 tau4	hei thauh
erection[1] of penis	n	鳩硬	gáu ngaahng	gau2 ngaang6	kau ngaahng
erection[2] /install/to mount/get an erection	v	安裝	òn /ngòn jong	on4 /ngon4 zong4	on /ngon chong
erection[3]/set up/built	v	建立	gin lahp	gin3 lap6	kin lahp
erection[4] /built/found/ set up/establishment	v	設立	chit lahp	cit3 lap6	chhit lahp
erection[5] /built	v	豎立	syuh lahp	syu6 lap6	syuh lahp
erection[6] /built	v	架設	gá chit	ga2 cit3	ka chhit
erotic /intended to sex	adj	性愛	sìng oi /ngoi	sing3 oi3 /ngoi3	seng oi /ngoi
err /be mistake	v	做錯	jouh cho	zou6 co3	chouh cho
error[1]/fault/mistake/wrong	n	錯	cho	co3	chho
error[2] /miss/mistake	n	誤	ngh /ng	ng6	ngh /ng
error[3] /mistake/slip-up	n	錯誤	cho ngh	co3 ng6	chho ngh
error[4] /fault	n	過失	gwo sāt	gwo3 sat1	kwo sat
escalator	n	自動樓梯	jih duhng làuh tài	zi6 dung6 tai4 tai4	chih tuhng lauh thai
escape[1]	v	走甩	jáu lāt	zau2 lat1	chau lat
escape[2] /run away	v	逃脫	tòuh tyut	tou4 tyut3	thouh tyut

189

escape[3] /flee/fly/take flight v	逃走	tòuh jáu	tou4 zau2	thouh chau
escape[4] /run away /get away v	逃跑	tòuh fáau	tou4 faau2	thouh faau
escape[5] /flee v	逃	tòuh	tou4	thouh
escape[6] n	退去	teui héui	teoi3 heoi2	thoi hoi
escape[7] /retreat/move away n	退避	teui beih	teoi3 bei6	thoi peih
escape[8] /flee v	走難	jáu naahn	zau2 naan4	chau naahn
escaped v	走甩咗	jáu lāt jó	zau2 lat1 zo2	chau lat cho
escaped by force [sl] run away v	走鬼	jáu gwái	zau2 gwai2	chau kwai
escort[1] /guarding v	帶去	daai heui	daai3 heoi3	taai hoi
escort[2] /guard v	護衛	wuh waih	wu6 wai6	wuh waih
escort[3] /bodyguard/ accompaniment v	護送	wuh sung	wu6 sung3	wuh sung
escort[4] v	伴遊	buhn yàuh	bun6 jau4	puhn yauh
esophagus/oesophagus/ gullet n	食道	sihk douh	sik6 dou6	sehk touh
especial package /package n	特別包裝	dahk biht bāau jōng	dak6 bit6 baau1 zong1	tahk piht paau chong
especially[1] adv	尤其	yàuh kèih	jau4 kei4	yauh kheih
especially[2] adv	尤其是	yàuh kèih sih	jau4 kei4 si6	yauh kheih sih
especially in /particular v	特別	dahk biht	dak6 bit6	tahk piht
esperanto n	世界語	sai gaai yúh	sai3 gaai3 jyu5	sai kaai yuh
essay[1] n	雜文	jaahp màhn	zaap6 man4	chaahp mahn
essay[2] n	文章	màhn jèung	man4 zoeng4	mahn cheung
essential[1] adj	必需	bìt sēui	bit4 seoi1	pit swoi
essential[2] /necessity/ require adj	必要	bìt yìu	bit4 jiu4	pit yiu
essential[3] adj	必要的	bìt yìu dìk	bit4 jiu4 dik4	pit yiu tek
essential[4] /fundamental /basic adj	根本	gáan būn	gaan2 bun1	kaan pun
essential points /main point n	綱要	gòng yìu	gong4 jiu4	kong yiu
establish[1] v	徹立	chit lahp	cit3 lap6	chhit lahp
establish[2] /found v	創立	chong lahp	cong1 lap6	chhong lahp
establish[3] /set up v	成立	sèhng laahp	seng4 laap6	sehng laahp
establish[4] (by community/government) v	公立	gùng lahp	gung4 lap6	kung lahp
establish[5] /found v	創辦	chong baahn	cong3 baan6	chhong paahn
estate n	屋村	ngūk /ùk chyùn	nguk1 /uk1 cyun4	nguk /uk chhyun
esteemed[1] n	榮幸	wìhng hàhng	wing4 hang6	wehng hahng
esteemed[2] /honor /deeply respect/ respect/ distinguished person n	尊重	jyùn juhng	zyun4 zung6	chyun chuhng
esteemed[3] /deeply respect n	敬重	geng juhng	geng3 zung6	keng chuhng

English		Chinese	Yale	Jyutping	Romanization
estimate[1] /guess/thinks	v	估	gú	gu2	ku
estimate[2] /assessment/ calculation	n	估計	gú gai	gu2 gai3	ku kai
estimated time of arrival /ETA	n	估計到廠時間	gú gai dou chóng sìh gaan	gu2 gai3 dou3 cong2 si4 gaan3	ku kai tou chhong sih kaan
estimated time of depart /ETD	n	估計離開時間	gú gai lèih hòi sìh gaan	gu2 gai3 lei4 hoi4 si4 gaan3	ku kai leih hoi sih kaan
estrogen /oestrogen	n	雌激素	chī gīk sou	ci1 gik1 sou3	chhi kek sou
eternity	n	永	wíhng	wing5	wehng
ethics	n	倫理	leuhn léih	leon4 lei5	leuhn leih
ethnic	adj	人種	yàhn chīng	jan4 cing1	yahn chheng
ethnic minority	n	少數民族	síu sou màhn juhk	siu2 sou3 man4 juk6	siu sou mahn chohk
etiology	n	病原學	behng /bihng yùhn hohk	beng6 /bing6 jyun4 hok6	pehng yuhn hohk
etiquette /formality /propriety/ritual/etiquette/ polite behaviour	n	禮節	láih jit	lai5 zit3	laih chit
eunuch /ladyboy /shemale/neuter person	n	人妖	yàhn yīu	jan4 jiu1	yahn yiu
eunuch worker (ancient royal palace's in China)	n	公公	gùng gùng	gung4 gung4	kung kung
Europe	n	歐洲	àu zàu	au1 zau1	au chau
Europe & America	n	歐美	àu méih	au4 mei5	au meih
evacuate[1]	v	疏散	sò saan	so4 saan3	so saan
evacuate[2] /withdraw from	v	撤離	chit lèih	cit3 lei4	chhit leih
evaluated	v	評估咗	pìhng gū jó	ping4 gu1zo2	phehng ku cho
evangelist /missionary	n	傳道人	chyùhn douh yàhn	cyun4 dou6 jan4	chhyuhn touh yahn
evaporate	n	蒸發	jìng faat	zing4 faat3	cheng faat
evaporation	n	蒸發作用	jìng faat jok yuhng	zing4 faat3 zok3 jung6	cheng faat chok yuhng
evasion /shirk avoid	v	逃避	tou bèih	tou3 bei6	thou peih
evasive[1]	adj	逃避	tou bèih	tou3 bei6	thou peih
evasive[2]	adj	逃避	tòuh beih ge	tou4 bei6	thouh peih ke
evasive[3]	adj	推諉	tèui wái	teoi4 wai2	thoi wai
eve[1] /evening/at dusk	n	傍晚	pohng máahn	pong6 maan5	phohng maahn
Eve[2] (31 Dec)	n	前夜	chìhn yeh	cin4 je6	chhihn yeh
Eve[3] /story woman/first woman	n	夏娃	hah wā	ha6 wa1	hah wa
Eve[4] /first story man	n	故事人物	gu sìh yàhn maht	gu3 si6 jan4 mat6	ku sih yahn maht
even[1] /flat/level/equal	adj	平	pèhng /pìhng	peng4 /ping4	phehng
even[2] /level/evenly/equal	adj/v	勻	wàhn	wan4	wahn
even[3] /yet/still	conj	尚	seuhng	soeng6	seuhng
even[4] /yet	adv	甚至	sahm ji	sam6 zi3	sahm chi
even[5] /yet	adv	連都	lìhn…dōu	lin4...dou1	lihn... tou
even[6] /yet	adv	平坦的	pèhng táan dìk	peng4 taan2 dik4	phehng thaan tek
even as timely /just same time	adv	正當	jeng dong	zeng3 dong3	cheng tong
even if	adv	即使…都	jīk sí…dōu	zik1 si2...dou1	chek si...tou

even minded	adj	公平嘅	gùng pìhng ge	gung4 ping4 ge3	kung phehng ke
even number[1] (pair)	n	雙數	sèung sou	soeng4 sou3	seung sou
even number[2] (pair)	n	偶數	ngáuh sou	ngau5 sou3	ngauh sou
even one		一啲都	yāt di dōu	jat1 di4 dou1	yat ti tou
even then	adv	儘管如此	jéun gún yùh chí	zeon2 gun2 jyu4 ci2	cheun kun yuh chhi
even though[1]/even if	adv	就算	jauh syun	zau6 syun3	chauh syun
even though[2]/even if	adv	都算	dòu /dzu syun	dou4 syun3	tou syun
even though[3] /even so/ even if	adv	即使	jīk sí	zik1 si2	chek si
even though[4]/even if	adv	縱然	jùng yìhn	zung4 jin4	chung yihn
evening[1] /night fall /night time	n	晚上	máahn sèuhng	maan5 soeng5	maahn seuhng
evening[2] /night/late at night	n	夜晚	yeh máahn	je6 maan5	yeh maahn
evening[3]	n	下午黃昏	hah ngh wòhng fán	haa6 ng5 wong4 fan2	hah ngh wohng fan
evening class[1]	n	夜課	yèh po	je6 po3	yeh pho
evening dress[2]	n	晚禮服	máahn láih fuhk	maan5 lai5 fuk6	maahn laih fuhk
evening school /night school	n	夜校	yeh haauh	je6 haau6	yeh haauh
evening snack	n	宵夜	sīu yé	siu1 je5	siu ye
evenly	adv	均衡地	gwàn hang dèih	gwan4 hang3 dei6	kwan hang teih
event[1] /major event	n	大事	daaih sih	daai6 si6	taaih sih
event[2] public program	n	社交活動	séh gàau wuht duhng	se5 gaau4 wut6 dung6	seh kaau wuht tohng
event by /organisation/ organization/organize	n	組織	jóu jīk	zou2 zik1	chou chek
events recording book /memo book	n	記事簿	gei sih bouh	gei3 si6 bou6	kei sih pouh
eventual	adj	結果嘅	git gwó ge	git3 gwo2 ge3	kit gwo ke
eventually[1]/final/finally /last/at the end/lastly	adj	最後	jeui hauh	zeoi3 hau6	cheui hauh
eventually[2] /finally/at last/in the end	adj	終於	jùng yū	zung4 jyu1	chung yu
ever[1] /forever	adv	永	wíhng	wing5	wehng
ever[2]	adv	從來	chùhng lòih	cung4 loi4	chhuhng loih
ever[3]/never/never before /never seen	adv	從來未	chùhng lòih meih	cung4 loi4 mei6	chhuhng loih meih
ever after		從此以後	chùhng chí yíh hauh	cung4 ci2 ji5 hau6	chhuhng chhi yih hauh
ever so /exceptionally /extreme/extremely/so unusual	adv	非常	fèi sèuhng	fei4 soeng4	fei seuhng
Everest /Sagarmatha[1] the world highest mountain 8.848 m /29.028 ft (in Nepal)	n	珠穆朗瑪峰	jyú muhk lóhng máh fùng	zyu2 muk6 long5 maa5 fung4	chyu muhk lohng mah fung
Everest /Sagarmatha[2] the world highest mountain 8.848 m /29.028 ft (in Nepal)	n	世界最高峰	sai gaai jeui gòu fùng	sai3 gaai3 zeoi3 gou4 fung4	sai kaai choi kou fung
evergreen	adj	常青嘅	sèuhng chèng ge	soeng4 ceng4 ge3	seuhng chheng ke
evermore /ever/forever /never/eternal	adj	永遠	wíhng yúhn	wing5 jyun5	wehng yuhn

every body	pron	各位	gok waih	gok3 wai6	kok waih
everyone /every body	n/pron	各人	gok yàhn	gok3 jan4	kok yahn
every day use	adj	通俗嘅	tung jùhk ge	tung3 zuk6 ge3	thung chuhk ke
every month /monthly	adj	每月	múih yuht	mui5 jyut6	muih yuht
every night	n	晚晚	máahn máahn	maan5 maan5	maahn maahn
every sunday	n	逢星期日	fòng sèng kèih yaht	fung4 seng4 kei4 jat6	fong seng kheih yaht
every week	n	每星期	múih sèng/sìng kèih	mui5 seng4 /sing kei4	muih seng kheih
everyone[1] /perhead /every body	n/pron	人人	yàhn yàhn	jan4 jan4	yahn yahn
everyone[2]	pron	眾人	jung yàhn	zung3 jan4	chung yahn
everyone[3]	pron	每個	múih go	mui5 go3	muih ko
everyone[4]	pron	個人	go yàhn	go3 jan4	ko yahn
everyone[5]	pron	每人	múih yàhn	mui5 jan4	muih yahn
everything	pron	一切事物	yāt chai sih maht	jat1 cai3 si6 mat6	yat chhai sih maht
everywhere[1]	adv	普	póu	pou2	phou
everywhere[2] /here & there	adv	處處	chyu chyu	cyu3 cyu3	chhyu chhyu
evictor	n	逐出者	juhk chēut jé	zuk6 ceot1 ze2	chuhk chhot che
evidence[1] /verification /proof	n	證明	jing mìhng	zing3 ming4	cheng mehng
evidence[2] /proof /testimony	n	證據	jing geui	zing3 geoi3	cheng kwoi
evidence[3] /witness	n	見證人	gin jing yàhn	gin3 zing3 jan4	kin cheng yahn
evidence[4] /eyewitness /witness	n	目擊證人	muhk gīk jing yàhn	muk6 gik1 zing3 jan4	muhk kek cheng yahn
evidently /distinctly /clearly	adv	明顯地	juhk mìhng hín deih	zuk6 ming4 hin2 dei6	chuhk mehng hin teih
evil[1] /wicked	adj	邪	chèh	ce4	chheh
evil[2] /wicked/bad/foul	adj	惡	ok /ngok	ok3 /ngok3	ok /ngok
evil[3] /wicked/morally bad	n	邪惡	chèh ngok	ce6 ngok3	chheh ngok
evil[4] /sin/crime	n	罪惡	jeuih ngok	zeoi6 ngok3	cheuih ngok
evil man	n	祟人	seuih yàhn	seoi6 jan4	swoih yahn
ex (former)	pref	免除	míhn chèuih	min5 ceoi4	mihn chhoih
ex-smoker /presmoker	n	之前食煙人	jī chìhn sihk yīn yàhn	zi1 cin4 sik6 jin1 jan4	chi chhihn sehk yin yahn
exacerbate	v	使惡化	sái ngok fa	sai2 ngok3 fa3	sai ngok fa
exact	adj	確切	kok chit	kok3 cit3	khok chhit
exactly[1]	adv	依靠	yi kaau	ji3 kaau3	yi khaau
exactly[2]	adv	精密	jing maht	zing3 mat6	cheng maht
exactly[3]	adv	確切地	kok chit deih	kok3 cit3 dei6	khok chhit teih
exactly[4] /like same	adv	就是	jauh sih	zau6 si6	chauh sih
extremely right[1] /exactly right	adj	完全正確	yùhn chyùhn jeng kok	jyun4 cyun4 zeng3 kok3	yuhn chhyuhn cheng khok
extremely right[2] (wr) /all right/spot on/alexactly right	adj	對極了	deui gihk líuh	deoi3 gik6 liu5	toei gehk liuh
exactly three o'clock		三點正	sàam dīm jéng	saam4 dim1 zeng2	saam tim cheng

English	Part	Chinese	Romanization 1	Jyutping	Romanization 2
exaggerate[1]	v	誇張	kwà jèung	kwaa4 zoeng4	khwa cheung
exaggerate[2]	v	對言過其實	deui… yìhn gwo kèih saht	deoi3… jin4 gwo3 kei4 sat6	toei… yihn kwo kheih saht
exaggerator[1]	n	誇張人	kwà jèung	kwaa4 zoeng4	khwa cheung
exaggerator[2]	n	讚美人	jaan méih yàhn	zaan3 mei5 jan4	chaan meih yahn
exaggerator[3]	n	稱讚人	chìng jaan yàhn	cing4 zaan3 jan4	chheng chaan yahn
exam[1] /test	n	考	háau	haau2	haau
exam[2] /test/examination	n	考試	háau síh	haau2 si5	haau seuhn sih
exam paper /test paper	n	試卷	síh gyún	si5 gyun2	sih kyun
examination room[1]	n	診症室	chán jing sāt	can2 jing3 sat1	chhan cheng sat
examination room[2] /laboratory room/lab testing room	n	化驗室	fa yihm sāt	faa3 jim6 sat1	fa yihm sat
examine[1] /test	n	驗	yihm	jim6	yihm
examine[2]/check/exam/ see over	v	檢查	gím chàh	gim2 caa4	kim chhah
examine[3] /view/exam	v	審查	sám chàh	saam2 caa4	sam chhah
examiner[1]	n	主考人	jyú háau yàhn	zyu2 haa2 jan4	chyu haau yahn
examiner[2] /lab technician	n	化驗師	fa yihm sī	faa3 jim6 si1	fa yihm si
example[1]/model/pattern	n	範	faahn	faan6	faahn
example[2]	n	例	laih	lai6	laih
example[3] /instance /if suppose/model-example/ such as	n/pron	例如	laih yùh	lai6 jyu4	laih yuh
example[4] /instance	n	例子	laih jí	lai6 zi2	laih chi
example[5] /for instance/ instance/if suppose/model	n	譬如	pei yùh	pei3 jyu4	phei yuh
example[6] /model	n	榜樣	bóng yeuhng	bong2 joeng6	pong yeuhng
excavator	n	挖掘機	waat gwaht gèi	waat3 gwat6 gei4	waat kwaht kei
exceed[1] /over	v	超	chìu	ciu4	chhiu
exceed[2] /over	v	超出	chìu chēut	ciu4 ceot1	chhiu chhot
exceed[3]	v	超過	chìu gwo	ciu4 gwo3	chhiu kwo
exceeding[1] /so much	v	咁鬼多	gam gwái dò	gam3 gwai2 do4	kam kwai to
exceeding[2]	v	極度	gìhk douh	gik6 dou6	kehk touh
exceedingly	adv	非常地	fèi sèuhng deih	fei4 soeng4 dei6	fei seuhng teih
excel	v	勝過	sing gwo	sing3 gwo3	seng kwo
excellence[1] /goodness /morality & conduct	n	美德	méih dāk	mei5 dak1	meih tak
excellence[2] /outstanding	n	優秀	yàu sau	jau4 sau3	yau sau
excellency[1] /sir	n	閣下	gok hah	gok3 haa6	kok hah
excellency[2] /adult	n	大人	daaih yàhn	daai6 jan4	taaih yahn
excellent[1]	adj	好到極	hou dou gihk	hou3 dou3 gik6	hou tou kehk
excellent[2]	adj	出色	chēut sìk	ceot sik4	chhot sìk
excellent[3]	adj	極優	gihk yāu	gik6 jau1	kehk yau
except[1] /besides/separate/ remove/extra	prep	除	chèuih	ceoi4	chheuih

except[2] /only if	conj	除非	cheui fèi	ceoi3 fei4	chheui fei
exception	n	例外	laih oih	lai6 oi6	laih oih
exceptions /exclude/ exclusive	adv	除外	chèuih òih /ngòih	ceoi4 oi6 /ngoi6	chheuih oih /ngoih
excess[1] /over	n/adv	過度	gwo douh	gwo3 dou6	kwo touh
excess[2] /surplus	n	過剩	gwo sihng	gwo3 sing6	kwo sehng
excess[3] /exceed	n	超過	chìu gwo	ciu4 gwo3	chhiu kwo
excess[4] /surpass	n	多過	dò gwo	do4 gwo3	to kwo
excessive[1] /superfluous more then is needed or wanted	adj	過多	gwo dò	gwo3 do4	kwo to
excessive[2]/over/undue /too much/ overdo	adj/v	過份	gwo fahn	gwo3 fan6	kwo fahn
excessively[1] /extreme /much/too/very	adv	太	taai	taai3	thaai
excessively[2]	adv	太...喇	taai là	taai3 laa4	thaai la
excessively[3]	adv	過分地	gwo fàn dèih	gwo3 fan4 dei6	kwo fan teih
exchange[1] /substitute /change/renew	v	換	wuhn	wun6	wuhn
exchange[2]	v	換過	wuhn gwo	wun6 gwo3	wuhn kwo
exchange[3] cash	v	兌換	deui wuhn	deoi3 wun6	toei wuhn
exchange[4] /replacement	n	交換	gàau wuhn	gaau4 wun6	kaau wuhn
exchange cash		匯	wùih	wui6	wuih
exchange intercourse	n	交流	gàau làuh	gaau4 lau4	kaau lauh
exchange of sex[(sl)]	v	打野戰	dá yéh jin	daa2 je5 zin3	ta yeh chin
exchange rate[1]	v	滙率	wùih léut	wui6 leot2	wuih lowt
exchange rate[2]	v	外匯率	oih /ngòih wùih léut	oi6 /ngoi6 wui6 leot2	oih /ngoih wuih lowt
excite[1]	v	滋	jì	zi4	chi
excite[2]	v	緊張	gán jèung	gan2 zoeng4	kan cheung
excite[3] /make/make agitate/make thrill	v	使激動	sai gīk duhng	sai gik1 dung6	sai kek tohng
excited of feeling		興奮嘅	hìng fáhn ge	hing4 fan5 ge3	hing fahn ge
excited of sex /fall in love/passionate/on heat of animal	v/intr	動情	duhng chìhng	dung6 cing4	tuhng chhehng
excitement[1 (sl)]	n	刺激	chi gīk	ci3 gik1	chhi kek
excitement[2] /thrill /tingle/ an exciting	n	興奮	hìng fáhn	hing4 fan5	hing fahn
exciter[1]	n	興奮者	hìng fáhn jé	hing4 fan5 ze2	hing fahn che
exciter[2]	n	興奮人	hìng fáhn yàhn	hing4 fan5 jan4	hing fahn yahn
exciting (happy) /happy feeling	adj	令人激動	lihng yàhn gīk duhng	ling4 jan4 gik1 dung6	lehng yahn kam tohng
exclaim[1]	v	大叫講	daaih giu góng	daai6 giu3 gong2	taaih kiu kong
exclaim[2]	v	大聲嗌	daaih seng aai	daai6 seng3 aai3	taaih seng aai
exclaim[3]	v	呼喊	fù haam	fu4 haam3	fu haam
exclamation![1] /interjection!	n	感嘆詞!	gám taan chìh	gam2 taan3 ci4	kam thaan chhih
exclamation![2]	n	感嘆號!	gám taan houh	gam2 taan3 hou6	kam thaan houh

exclamation!³	n	喇	lāh /nāh	laa1 /naa1	lah /nah
exclamation!⁴	n	驚叫	gèng giu	geng4 giu3	keng kan kiu
exclude¹ /not count	v	唔計	m̀ gai	m4 gai3	mh kai
exclude²	v	不包括	bāt bāau kut	bat1 baau1 kut3	pat paau khut
exclusively¹	adv	專門	jyūn mún /mùhn	zyun1 mun2 /mun4	chyun mun /muhn
exclusively² /thorough	adj	完全	yùhn chyun	jyun4 cyun4	yuhn chhyun
excrement /waste	n	排泄物	pàaih sit maht	paai4 sit3 mat6	phaaih sit maht
excrete /stool /feces	n	大便	daaih bihn	daai6 bin6	taaih pihn
excuse /forgive/remit	v	寬恕	fùn syu	fun4 syu3	fun syu
excuse me!¹ reason	v	理由	léih yàuh	lei5 jau4	leih yauh
excuse me!² /sorry!	v	抱歉	póuh híp	pou5 hip2	phouh hip
excuse me!³ i must leave	v	失陪	sàt pùih	sat4 pui4	sat phuih
excuse me!⁴	v	請原諒	chéng yun lèuhng	ceng2 jyun3 loeng6	chheng yun lowhng
excuse oneself	v	要求得到原諒	yìu kàuh dāk dóu yùhn leuhng	jiu4 kau4 dak1dou2 ivun4 loeng6	yiu khauh tak tou yuhn leuhng
execute	v	執	jāp	zap1	chap
executer /executioner	n	劊子手	kúi jí sáu	kui2 zi2 sau2	khui chi sau
execution	n	施行	si hang	si3 hang3	si hang
execution of a task	n	完成了	yùhn sèhng líuh	jyun4 seng4 liu5	yuhn sehng liuh
executioner¹	n	行刑者	hàhng yìhng jé	hang4 jing4 ze2	hahng yehng che
executioner²	n	死刑執行者	séi yìhng jāp hàhng jé	sei2 jing4 zap1 hang4 ze2	sei yehng chap hahng che
executive¹	n	執行委員	jāp hàhng wúi yùhn	zap1 hang4 wui2 jyun4	chap haang wui yuhn
executive²	n	主管人員	jyú gún yan yùhn	zyu2 gun2 jan3 jyun4	chyu kun yan yuhn
exempt (from free)	n	豁	kut	kut3	khut
exempted	n	豁免	kut míhn	kut3 min2	khut mihn
exemption /to excuse /forgiveness	n	免除	míhn chèuih	min5 ceoi4	mihn chhoih
exercise book¹	n	本子	bún zí	bun2 zi2	pun chi
exercise book² /work book	n	練習簿	lihn jaahp bóu	lin6 zaap6 bou2	lihn chaahp pou
exercise book³	n	練習本	lihn jaahp bún	lin6 zaap6 bun2	lihn chaahp pun
exerciser	n	做練習嘅人	jouh lihn jaahp ge yàhn	zou6 lin6 zaap6 ge3 jan4	chouh lihn chaahp ke yahn
exert /to use	v	運用	wahn yuhng	wan6 jung6	wahn yuhng
exert oneself	v	出力	cheut lihk	ceot1 lik6	chhot lehk
exhaust	v	排氣	paai héi	paai3 hei2	phaai hei
exhaust gas	n	廢氣	fai héi	fai3 hei2	fai hei
exhaust pipe /exhaust manifold	n	排氣管	paai héi gūn	paai3 hei2 gun1	phaai hei kun
exhausted /tired /tiredness	adj	劼 / 瘤	guih	gui6	kuih
exhausting¹	adj	索氣	sok héi	sok3 hei3	sok hei
exhausting²	adj	使耗盡	sái hou jeuhn	sai2 hou3 zeon6	sai hou cheuhn
exhaustion	n	精疲力竭	jēng pèih lihk kit	zeng1 pei4 lik6 kit3	cheng pheih lehk khit
exhibit /unfold/to show	v	展示	jín sih	zín2 si6	chin sih

English	POS	Chinese	Romanization 1	Jyutping	Romanization 2
exhibition /show things	n	展覽會	jín láahm wúi	zin2 laam5 wui2	chin laahm wui
exhibitor[1]	n	展出者	jín chēut jé	zín2 ceot1 ze2	chin chhot che
exhibitor[2]	n	參展者	chàam jín jé	caam4 zin2 ze2	chhaam chin che
exile[1] /remove	v	退	teui	teoi3	thoi
exile[2]	v	放逐	fong juhk	fong3 zuk6	fong chuhk
exile[3]	v	流放	làuh fong	lau4 fong3	lauh fong
exist[1] /survive	v	存	chyùhn	cyun4	chhyuhn
exist[2] /live/survive/presen	v	生存	sàng chyùhn	sang4 cyun4	sang chhyuhn
exist from previously[1] /pre-exist	v	以前已經有	yíh chìhn yíh gīng yáuh	ji5 cin4 ji5 ging1 jau5	yih chhihn yih keng yauh
exist from previously[2] /pre-exist	v	早先存在	jóu sin chyùhn joih	zou2 sin3 cyun4 zoi6	chou sin chhyuhn choih
existing /have being	adj	現有	yihn yáuh	jin6 jau5	yihn yauh
exit[1] /go out/issue/come out/happen/occur/rise	n	出	chēut	ceot1	chhot
exit[2] /outlets/door	n	出口	chēut háu	ceot1 hau2	chhot hau
expand /swell	v	膨脹	pàahng jeung	paang4 zoeng3	phaahng cheung
expatriate[1] /exile	adj	唔同國藉嘅人	m̀ tùhng gwok jihk ge yàhn	m4 tung6 gwok3 zik6 ge3 jan4	mh thuhng kwok chehk ke yahn
expatriate[2]	adj	不同國藉嘅人	bāt tùhng gwok jihk ge yàhn	bat1 tung6 gwok3 zik6 ge3 jan4	pat thuhng kwok chehk ke yahn
expect[1] /think/like/think /wish	v	意	yi	ji3	yi
expect[2] /guess/anticipate	v	料	líu	liu2	liu
expect[3] /desire/wish/hope	v	希望	hèi mohng	hei4 mong6	hei mohng
expect[4]	v	預期	yùh keih	jyu6 kei4	yùh kheih
expectation[1]	n	滿足	múhn jūk	mun5 zuk1	muhn chuk
expectation[2]	n	期待	keih doih	kei4 doi6	kheih toih
expected	n	估到	gú dou	gu2 dou3	ku tou
expected date of birth		預產期	yuh cháan kèih	jyu6 caan2 kei4	yuh chhaan kheih
expedite[1] /quicken	v	加快	gà faai	ga4 faai3	ka faai
expedite[2] /speed	v	速度	chūk douh	cuk1 dou6	chhuk touh
expel[1] /push/shove	v	推	tèui	teoi4	thoi
expel[2] /drive out /drive away	v	趕走	gón jáu	gon2 zau2	kon chau
expend /to spend/ expenditure/outlay	v	花費	fā fai	faa1 fai3	fa fai
expenditure /expense	n	支出	jì chēut	zi4 ceot1	chi chhot
expenses on incidental	n	零用	lìhng yuhng	ling4 jung6	lehng yuhng
expensive[1] /costly /worthy valuable	adj	值錢	jihk chín	zik6 cin2	chehk chhin
expensive[2]	adj	昂貴	ngòhng gwai	ngong6 gwai	ngohng kwai
expensive house	n	貴屋	gwai ùk	gwai3 uk4	kwai uk
experience[1]	n	經驗	gìng yihm	ging4 jim6	keng yihm
experience[2]	n	體驗	tái yihm	tai2 jim6	thai yihm
experience[3] feel	n	感受	gám sauh	gam2 sau6	kam sauh

English		Chinese	Yale	Jyutping	Other
experienced	n	有經驗	yáuh gìng yihm	jau5 ging4 jim6	yauh keng yihm
experiment	n	實驗	saht yihm	sat6 jim6	saht yihm
expert[1] /specialist	n	專家	jyūn gā	zyun1 gaa1	chyun ka
expert[2] /proficient/skilful	adj	在行	joih hòhng	zoi6 hong4	choih hohng
expert[3] /perfect/proficient/skilful/good at	adj	精通	jèng tùng	zing4 tung4	cheng thung
expert phone service whole over the China	n	中國通	jùng gwok tùng	zung4 gwok3 tung4	chung kwok thung
expire[1]	v	過期	gwo kèih	gwo3 kei4	kwo kheih
expire[2]	v	呼氣	fù hei	fu4 hei3	fu hei
expire[3] /stop breathing /die	v	斷氣	tyúhn hei	tyun5 hei3	thyuhn hei
expire[4]	v	屆期	wāt kèih	wat1 kei4	wat kheih
expiry	n	期滿	keih múhn	kei4 mun5	kheih muhn
explain[1]	n	講嘢	góng yéh	gong2 je5	kong yeh
explain[2]	v	講解	góng gáai	gong2 gaai2	kong kaai
explain[3]	v	解	gáai	gaai2	kaai
explain[4] /make clear /to brief	v	交代	gàau doih	gaau4 doi6	kaau toih
explain[5] /say something /speak	v	說說	syut syut	syut3 syut	syut syut
explain[6] /formulate	v	說明	syut mèhng /mìhng	syut3 meng4 /ming4	syut mehng
explainable	adj	可解釋	hó chūk sīk	ho2 cuk1 sik1	ho chhuk sek
explanation /statement	n	說明	syut mèhng /mìhng	syut3 meng4 /ming4	syut mehng
explode	v	爆	baau	baau3	paau
exploit[1]	v	榨取	ja chéui	zaa3 ceoi2	cha chhoi
exploit[2]	v	剝削	mōk seuk	mok1 soek3	mok swok
explore[1] /research /study/investigation	n/v	研究	yìhn gau	jin4 gau3	yihn kau
explore[2] /investigate	v	探討	taam tóu	taam3 fou2	thaam thou
explore[3]	v	勘探	ham taam	ham3 taam4	ham thaam
explore[4]	v	探測	tàam chàak	taam4 caak4	thaam tàam chàak
explorer[1]	n	考察者	háau chaat jé	haau2 caat3 ze2	haau chhaat che
explorer[2]	n	探險家	taam hīm gā	taam3 him1 ga1	thaam him ka
explorer[3]	n	探測者	tàam chàak jé	taam4 caak4 ze2	thaam chhaak che
explosion sound	n	炮仗聲	paau jéung sèng	paau3 zoeng2 seng4	phaau cheung seng
explosive[1]/fire-cracker	n	炮仗	paau jéung	paau3 zoeng2	phaau cheung
explosive[2]	n	已爆炸	jih baau ja	zi6 baau3 zaa3	chih paau cha
export[1]	n	運出口	wahn chēut háu	wan6 ceot1 hau2	wahn chhot hau
export[2]	v	輸出	syù chēut	syu4 ceot1	syu chhot
export & import	v	出入口	chēut yahp háu	ceot1 jap6 hau2	chhot yahp hau
exports /export goods	n	出口貨	chēut háu fó	ceot1 hau2 fo2	chhot hau fo
exportable	a	可出口	hó chēut háu	ho2 ceot1 hau2	ho chhot hau
exportation	n	輸出	syù chēut	syu4 ceot1	syu chhot
exporter	n	出口商	chēut háu sēung	ceot1 hau2 soeng1	chhot hau seung

expose[1]	n	揭穿	kit chyùn	kit3 cyun4	khit chhyun
expose[2]	n	揭發	kit faat	kit3 faat3	khit faat
expose[3]	n	晒菲林	saai féi làhm	saai3 fei2 lam4	saai fei lahm
expose[4]	n	暴露	bouh louh	bou6 lou6	pouh louh
expose[5] /disclose	n	揭露	kit louh	kit3 lou6	khit louh
expose oneself [(sl)] shows little pravite parts		走光	jáu gwòng	zau2 gwong4	chau kwong
exposed	adj	外露	oih /ngoih louh	oi6 /ngoi6 lou6	oih /ngoih louh
express[1] /state/chat	v	敘	jeuih	zeoi6	cheuih
express[2] /quick	adv	快運	faai wahn	faai3 wan6	faai wahn
express[3] /say	v	表達	bíu daaht	biu2 daat6	piu taaht
express[4] /non stop /direct travel	n	直通	jihk tùng	zik6 tung4	chehk thung
express bus	n	快車	faai chè	faai3 ce4	faai chhe
express letter	adv	快信	faai seun	faai3 seon3	faai swon
express thanks /owe/appreciate	v	感激	gám gīk	gam2 gik1	kam kek
expressing sadness /sigh/suspire/heave a sigh	v	嘆氣	taan hei	taan3 hei3	thaan hei
expression[1] /words	n	詞	chìn	cin4	chhin
expression[2] /facial expression	n	表情	bíu chìhng	biu2 cing4	piu chehng
expression[3]	n	無法子表達	mòuh faat jí bíu daaht	mou4 faat3 zi2 biu2 daat6	mouh faat chi piu taaht
expressway	n	高速公路	gòu chūk gùng louh	gou4 cuk1 gung4 lou6	kou chhuk kung louh
exquisite[1] /fine	adj/n	精緻	jèng ji	zeng4 zi3	cheng chi
exquisite[2] [(sl)]	adj	骨子	gwāt jí	gwat1 zi2	kwat chi
extend[1] /stretch/stick out/stretch out	v	伸	sàn	san4	san
extend[2] /widen	v	擴大	kwong daaih	kwong3 daai6	khwong taaih
extended buttock /buttock out straight/ stretch buttock/thighs out extend/wided buttock/to extended buttock	v	張開大髀	jèung hòi daaih béi	zoeng4 hoi4 daai6 bei2	cheung hoi taaih pei
extension[1]	n	延長	yìhn chèuhng	jin4 coeng4	yihn chheuhng
extension[2] telephone lines	n	內線	loih /noih sin	loi6 /noi6 sin3	loih /noih sin
extensive /comprehensive	adj	廣泛	gwong faan	gwong3 faan3	kwong faan
exterior	n	外部	oih /ngoih bòuh	oi6 /ngoi6 bou6	oih /ngoih pouh
external[1]	adj	外部	oih /ngoih bòuh	oi6 /ngoi6 bou6	oih /ngoih pouh
external[2] /outside	adj	外面	oih /ngoih mìhn	oi6 /ngoi6 min6	oih /ngoih mihn
extinguish[1] /wipe out/ off	v	熄	sīk	sik1	sek
extinguish[2] /quench /of fire/stop burning	v	熄滅	sìk mìht	sik4 mit6	sek miht
extinguish[3] /eradicate	v	撲滅	pok mìht	pok3 mit6	phok miht

extinguish foam	n	泡沫滅火筒	póuh mut miht fó túng	pou5 mut3 mit6 fo2 tung2	phouh mut miht fo thung
extinguisher	n	滅火筒	miht fó túng	mit6 fo2 tung2	miht fo thung
extra /remain/surplus	adv	餘	yùh	jyu6	yuh
extra large (XL)	n	加大碼	gà daaih máh	gaa4 daai6 maa5	ka taaih mah
extracted[1]	n	猛出嚟	màng chēut làih	mang4 ceot1 lai4	mang chhot laih
extracted[2] /main theme	n	擇錄	jaahk luhk	zaak6 luk6	chaahk luhk
extracted[3]	n	輯錄	chāp luhk	cap1 luk6	chhap luhk
extraordinary /fantastic	adj	了不起	líuh bāt héi	liu5 bat1 hei2	liuh paht hei
extravagant /luxury /ascivious	adj	奢侈	chè chí	ce4 ci2	chhe chhi
extreme[1] /depth	adv	深	sàm	sam4	sam
extreme[2] /extremely/ultra	n/adj	極端	gìhk dyūn	gik6 dyun1	kehk tyun
extreme[3] /extremely	adv	極	gihk	gik6	kehk
extremely[1]	adv	唔知幾	m̀ jì géi	m4 zi4 gei2	mh chi kei
extremely[2]	adv	不知幾	bāt jì géi	bat1 zi4 gei2	pat chi kei
extremely heavy rain	adj	太大雨	táai daaih yúh	taai2 daai6 jyu5	thaai taaih yuh
extremely want/very wishful/like very much/craving/strong desire	adj	非常想	fèi sèuhng séung	fei4 soeng4 soeng2	fei seuhng seung
extremism	n	激進主義	gihk jeun jyú yih	gik6 zeon3 zyu2 ji6	kehk cheun chyu yih
extremist /man of iron /orthodox	n	意志堅強嘅人	yí ji gīn kèuhng ge yàhn	ji2 zi gin1 koeng4 ge3 jan4	yi chi kin kheuhng ke yahn
eye[1]	n	眼	ngáahn	ngaan5	ngaahn
eye[2]	n	眼睛	ngáahn jìng	ngaan5 zing4	ngaahn cheng
eye[3] /look/see listed	n	目	muhk	muk6	muhk
eye drops /eye lotion	n	眼藥水	ngáahn yeuhk séui	ngaan5 joek6 seoi2	ngaahn yeuhk swoi
eye patch	n	眼罩	ngáahn jaau	ngaan5 zaau3	ngaahn chaau
eye's pencil	n	眉筆	mèih bāt	mei4 bat1	meih pat
eye shadow	n	眼蓋膏	ngáahn koi gōu	ngaan5 koi3 gou1	ngaahn khoi kou
eye signal to /wink signal to	n	眨眼示意	jáam ngáahn sìh yí	zaam2 ngaan5 si6 ji2	chaam ngaahn sih yi
eyebrow[1]	n	眉毛	mèih mouh	mei4 mou3	meih mouh
eyebrow[2]	n	眼眉	ngáahn mèih	ngaan5 mei4	ngaahn meih
eyelashes	n	眼睫毛	ngáahn jìht mou	ngaan5 zit6 mou3	ngaahn chiht mou
eyeliner	n	眼線筆	ngáahn sín bàt	ngaan5 sin2 bat4	ngaahn sin pat
eyesight /strength of vision	n	眼力	ngáahn lihk	ngaan5 lik6	ngaahn lehk
eyesore	n	礙眼	ngoih ngáahn	ngoi6 ngaan5	ngoih ngaahn
eyewitness /witness	n	目擊者	muhk gīk jé	muk6 gik1 ze2	muhk kek che

F, 6th	n	己	yíh	ji5	yih
fable[1]	n	寓言	yuh yìhn	jyu6 jin4	yuh yihn
fable[2] /legend/legendary /piece of story/rumour	n	傳說	chyùhn syut	cyun4 syut3	chhyuhn syut
fabri /weave cloth	n	織物	jīk maht	zik1 mat6	chek maht
face[1]	n	臉	líhm	lim5	lihm
face[2]	n	面	mihn	min6	mihn
face[3]	n	面孔	mihn húng	min6 hung2	mihn hung
face[4] /of the face /front	n	面向	mihn heung	min6 heung3	mihn heung
face right-side	n	向右	heung yauh	hoeng3 jau6	heung yauh
face to face /facing	n	當面	dòng mín	dong4 min2	tong min
face to face /mutual looking	n	面對面	mihn deui mihn	min6 deoi3 min6	mihn toei mihn
face wash		洗面膏	sái mìhn góu	sai2 min6 gou2	sai mihn kou
faces /facing problem/ meet a contingency/deal with incident		應變	yìng bin	jing4 bin3	yeng pin
facial	adj	面部	mihn bouh	min6 bou6	mihn pouh
facilitate[1]	v	利便	leih bihn	lei6 bin6	leih pihn
facilitate[2]	v	使容易	sái yùhng yíh	sai2 jung4 ji5	sai sái yùhng yíh
facilitate[3]	v	使便利	sái bihn leih	sai2 bin6 lei6	sai pihn leih
facilities[1]	n	設備	chit beih	cit3 bei6	chhit peih
facilities[2]	n	設施	chit yih	cit3 ji6	chhit yih
facing /opposite (side)	n/v	對	deui	deoi3	toei
facing downwards	v	拜倒在地下	bāai dóu joih deih há	baai1 dou2 zoi6 dei6 haa5	paai tou choih teih ha
facsimile /fax	n	傳真	chyùhn jàn	cyun4 zan4	chhyuhn chan
fact[1]	n	事實	sih saht	si6 sat6	sih saht
fact[2] /actually/in fact/fact matter/as a matter of fact	adv	事實上	sih saht seuhng	si6 sat6 soeng6	sih saht seuhng
fact cause	n	根源	gān bún	gan1 bun2	kan pun
faction	n	內訌	loih /noih hùhng	loi6 /noi6 hung4	loih /noih huhng
factor[1]	n	因素	yàn sóu	jan1 sou2	yan sou
factor[2]	n	因子	yàn jí	jan1 zi2	yan chi
factory[1] /mill/workhouse	n	廠	chóng	cong2	chhong
factory[2] /plant	n	工廠	gùng chóng	gung4 cong2	kung chhong
factual	adj	事實嘅	sih saht ge	si6 sat6 ge3	sih saht ge
faculty /subject group of university	n	系	haih	hai6	haih
faffle (sl)	v	黐脷根	chì leih gān	ci4 lei6 gan1	chhi leih kan
fag /tired	adj/n	苦差事	fú chàai si	fu2 caai4 si3	fu chhaai si
fag male(sl) /impassable male /uncrossable male	n	死基佬	séi gēi lóu	sei2 gei1 lou2	sei kei lou
fahrenheit	adj	華氏	wah sih	waa6 si6	wah sih
fail[1] (de)	v	肥佬	fèih lóu	fei4 lou2	feih lou
fail[2]	n	不及格	bāt kahp gaak	bat1 kap6 gaak	pat khahp kaak
fail to catch for train	v	搭唔到	daap m̀ dóu	daap3 m4 dou2	taap mh tou

English	POS	中文	Romanization	Jyutping	Romanization 2
fail to hear[1] /mishear	v	聽錯	tèng cho	teng4 co3	theng cho
fail to hear[2] /mishear	v	誤聽	ngh tèng	ng6 teng4	ngh theng
fail to hit	v	打唔中	dá m̀ jung	daa2 m4 zung3	ta mh chung
fail to meet	v	接唔到	jip m̀ dóu	zip3 m4 dou2	chip mh tou
fail to see	v	睇唔到	tái m̀ dóu	tai2 m4 dou2	thai mh tou
failure[1]	n	故障	gu jeung	gu3 zoeng3	ku cheung
failure[2]	n	失敗	sāt baaih	sat1 baai6	sat paaih
failure[3] parts of the body	n	衰竭	sēui kit	seoi1 kit3	swoi khit
faint /thin weak	adj	微弱	mèih yeuhk	mei4 joek6	meih yeuhk
fair[1] /reasonable	adj	合理	hahp léih	hap6 lei5	hahp leih
fair[2] /market/marketplace	n	市場	síh chèuhng	si5 coeng4	sih chheuhng
fair[3] /market	n	集市	jaahp síh	zaap6 si5	chaahp sih
fair & reasonable /reasonable	adj	通情達理	tùng chìhng daaht léih	tung4 cing4 daat6 lei5	thung chhehng taaht leih
fairly[1] /few/quite/rather /some	adj	幾	géi	gei2	kei
fairly[2] /fully/totally	adv	完全地	yùhn chyun dèih	jyun4 cyun4 dei6	yuhn chhyun teih
fairy[1] /immortal	n	神仙	sàhn sìn	san4 sin4	sahn sin
fairy[2]	n	仙女	sìn léoih /néoih	sin4 leoi5 /neoi5	sin lowih /nowih
fairy[3] imaginary flying person /small person with wings/small flying person	n	小仙子	síu sīn jí	siu2 sin1 zi2	siu sin chi
faith[1] /belief	n	信心	seun sàm	seon3 sam4	swon sam
faith[2] /belief	n	信念	seun nihm	seon3 nim6	swon nihm
faithful[1] /loyal/loyalty/ faithfulness	adj/n	忠	jùng	zung4	chung
faithful[2] /loyal	adj	忠實	jùng saht	zung4 sat6	chung saht
faithfully	adv	忠實地	jùng saht deih	zung4 sat6 dei6	chung saht teih
fake[1]	n	鍛	dyun	dyun3	tyun
fake[2] /false/forged	adj	偽	ngàih	ngai6	ngaih
fall[1] /drop	n/v	墜	jeuih	zeoi6	cheuih
fall[2] /autumn	n	秋	chāu	cau1	chhau
fall away	v	疏遠	sò yúhn	so4 jyun5	so yuhn
fall down[1]	v	下墮	hah doh	haa6 do6	hah toh
fall down[2]	v	噠低	daat dài	daat3 dai4	taat tai
fall down[3] /slip down/ stumble/get stumble	v	摔倒	sèui dóu	seoi4 dou2	swoi tou
fall down on	v	跌落	dit lohk ...	dit3 lok6···	tit lohk ...
fall in with[1]	adj	偶然遇到	ngáuh yìhn yuh dóu	ngau5 jin4 jyu6 dou2	ngauh yihn yuh tou
fall in with[2]		贊同	jaan tùhng	zaan3 tung4	chaan thuhng
fall into difficulty		陷入困境	haahm yahp kwan gíng	haam6 jap6 kwan3 ging2	haahm yahp khwan keng
fallen	adj	倒坍嘅	dóu tāan ge	dou2 taan1 ge3	tou thaan ke
falling[1] /drop	n	跌倒	dit dóu	dit3 dou2	tit tou
falling[2] /dropping	n	跌下	dit hah	dit3 haa6	tit hah
falling object	n	高空擲物	gòu hung jaahk maht	gou4 hung3 zaak6 mat6	kou hung chaahk maht

English		Chinese	Yale	Jyutping	Romanization
fallopian tube	n	輸卵	syū léuhn	syu1 leon5	syu leuhn
false[1] /artificial/fake/ untrue/pseudo	adj	假	gá	gaa2	ka
false[2] /fraud/fake/forged /full of tricks/untrue/foul means	n/adj	鍛	dyun	dyun3	tyun
false[3] /untrue/untruthful/ unreal	adj	唔正確	m̀ jéng kok	m4 zeng2 kok3	mh cheng khok
false[4] /incorrect/ inaccurate/ improperly	adj	不正確	bāt jéng kok	bat1 zeng2 kok3	pat cheng khok
false[5] /unreal/untruthful	adj	不真實	bāt jàn saht	bat1 zan4 sat6	pat chan saht
false alarm	n	假警報	gá gíng bou	gaa2 ging2 bou3	ka keng pou
false arrest	n	非法拘留	fèi faat kēui làuh	fei4 faat3 keoi1 lau4	fei faat khoi lauh
false teeth	n	假牙	gá ngàh	gaa2 ngaa4	ka ngah
falsely	ad	不正確地	bāt jéng kok deih	bat1 zeng2 kok3 dei6	pat cheng khok teih
fame /reputation	n	聲譽	sèing /sìng yuh	seng4 /sing4 yu6	seing yuh
familiar[1] /acquainted	adj	熟悉	suhk sīk	suk6 sik1	suhk sek
familiar[2]	adj	熟友	suhk yáuh	suk6 jau5	suhk yauh
familiar[3] /famous /noted/notable	adj	著名	jyu mèhng /mìhng	zyu3 meng4 /ming4	chyu mehng
familiar with		熟	suhk	suk6	suhk
family[1] /one family/family members/household	n	家人	gā yàhn	gaa1 jan4	ka yahn
family[2] /home/household	n/adj	家庭	gà tèhng	gaa4 ting4	ka thehng
family[3] /household	n	戶	wuh	wu6	wuh
family background		出身	chēut sān	ceot1 san1	chhot san
family clan /household	n	家族	gā juhk	gaa1 zuk6	ka chuhk
family doctor	n	家庭醫生	gà tèhng /tìhng yī sāng	gaa4 teng4 /ting4 ji1 sang1	ka thehng yi sang
family members[1]	n	家卷	gà gyun	gaa4 gyun3	ka kyun
family members[2]	n	家庭成員	gà tèhng /tìhng sèhng yùhn	gaa1 teng4 /ting4 seng4 jyun4	ka thehng sehng yuhn
family planning	n	家庭計劃	gà tèhng /tìhng gai waahk	gaa1 teng4 /ting4 gai3 waak6	ka thehng kai waahk
famine[1] scarcity of food	n	肌荒	gèi fòng	gei4 fong4	kei fong
famine[2] scarcity of food	n	饑荒	gèi fòng	gei4 fong4	kei fong
famous /known/well know/reputed /renowned	adj	出名	chēut méng	ceot1 meng2	chhot meng
famous brand	n	名牌	míhng /méhng pàaih	ming2 /meng2 paai4	mehng phaaih
famous person[1]	n	名人	mèhng /mìhng yàhn	meng4 /ming4 jan4	mehng yahn
famous person[2]	n	容貌	yùhng maauh	jung4 maau6	yuhng maauh
famous singer	n	歌星	gō sēng /sīng	go1 seng1 /sing1	ko seng
famously	adv	著名地	jyu mèhng /mìhng deih	zyu3 meng4 /ming4 dei6	chyu mehng teih
fan[1] (for air)	n	扇	sin	sin3	sin
fan[2] (electric fan)	n	風扇	fùng sin	fung4 sin3	fung sin

English	POS	Chinese	Reading 1	Jyutping	Reading 2
fan³ (air fan)	n	扇子	sin jí	sin3 zi2	sin chi
fan⁴ (lover)	n	仰慕者	yéuhng mouh jé	joeng5 mou6 ze2	yeuhng mouh che
fanciful¹ /humorous	n/adj	滑稽有趣	gaaht kái yáuh chéui	gwat6 kai2 jau5 ceoi2	kaaht khai yauh chheui
fanciful² /fashioner/ humorous	adj	洋晚服	yèuhng máahn fuhk	yeung4 maan5 fuk6	yeuhng maahn fuhk
fancy¹	n	喜愛	héi ói /ngoi	hei2 oi3 /ngoi3	hei oi /ngoi
fancy²	adj	別緻	bìht ji	bit6 zi	piht chi
fang	n	毒牙	duhk ngàh	duk6 ngaa4	tuhk ngah
fanta crush	n	芬達	fàn daaht /taat	fan4 daat6 /taat3	fan taaht
fantastic¹ /excellent	adj	極好	gihk hóu	gik6 hou2	kehk hou
fantastic² /unexpected /previously unimagined	adj	意想不到	yí sēung bàt dóu	ji2 soeng1 bat4 dou2	yi seung pat tou
fantasy¹ /magic	n	幻	wàahn	waan6	waahn
fantasy² /phantasy	n	想像	séung jèuhng	soeng2 zoeng6	seung cheuhng
far¹ /remote	adv	好遠	hou yúhn	hou3 jyun5	hou yuhn
far²	adv	遠方	yúhn fòng	jyun5 fong4	yuhn fong
far east	n	遠東	yúhn dùng	jyun5 dung4	yuhn tung
faraway /remotely	adj	遙遠地	yìuh yúhn deih	jiu4 jyun5 dei6	yiuh yuhn teih
fare /price of ticket	n	票價	piu ga	piu3 gaa3	phiu ka
farewell /meet again	int	再會	joi wúih	zoi3 wui5	choi wuih
farewell party /seeing off	n	歡送會	fùn sung wúi	fun4 sung3 wui2	fun sung wui
farm	n	農場	lùhng /nùhng chèuhng	lung4 /nung4 coeng4	luhng /nuhng chèuhng
farmhouse /cottage	n	農舍	lùhng /nùhng se	lung4 /nung4 se3	luhng /nuhng se
farmland /field/land /rice field	n	田	tìhn	tin4	thihn
farsighted /farsightedness	adj	遠視	yúhn sih	jyun5 si6	yuhn sih
farsighted	adj	有遠見嘅	yáuh yúhn gin ge	jau5 jyun5 gin3 ge3	yauh yuhn kin ke
fart /break wind	v	放屁	fong pei	fong3 pei3	fong phei
farther	adj	更遠地	gāng yúhn deih	gang1 jyun5 dei6	kang yuhn teih
fascinate /enamour	vt	吸引	kāp yáhn	kap1 jan5	khap yahn
fashion¹	n	時裝	sìh jòng	si4 zong4	sih chong
fashion² /style	n	時尚	sìh seuhng	si6 soeng6	sih seuhng
fashionable¹	adj	時髦嘅	sìh mōu ge	si4 mou1 ge3	sih mou ke
fashionable² /prevailing	adj	流行	làuh hàhng	lau4 hang4	lauh hahng
fashionable man¹	n	時髦人	sìh mōu yàhn	si4 mou1 jan4	sih mou yahn
fashionable man²	n	重要人士	chùhng yìu yàhn sih	cung4 jiu4 jan4 si6	chhuhng yiu yahn sih
fashionable man³ /interested in clothes/fop/ swinger /much	n	時髦活躍 嘅人物	sìh mòuh wuht yéuk ge yàhn maht	sih4 mou6 wut6 joek2 ge3 jan4 mat6	sih mouh wuht yeuk ke yahn maht
fashionable woman	n	時髦女	sìh mōu léoih /néoih	si4 mou1 leoi5 /neoi5	sih mou lowih /nowih
fast¹ /quick/rapid/rush /hurry/soon/speed/express /swift/haste	adj/n	快	faai	faai3	faai
fast² /quick	adj	快趣	faai cheui	faai3 ceoi3	faai chhoi
fast³ /rapid/quick	adj	速	chūk	cuk1	chhuk

fast[4] /speedy/rapid/quick	adj	迅速	seun chùk	seon3 cuk4	swon chhuk
fasting[1] /not eat	n	齋	jāi	zai1	chai
fasting[2] /not eat/fast	n	禁食	gam sihk	gam3 sik6	kam sehk
fast food /buffet meal	n	快餐	faai chāan	faai3 caan1	faai chhaan
fast food shop /restaurant	n	快餐店	faai chāan dim	faai3 caan1 dim3	faai chhaan tim
fasten[1] /buckles/tie	v	扣好	kau hóu	kau3 hou2	khau hou
fasten[2] /tie	v	綁住	bóng jyuh	bong2 jyu6	pong chyuh
fasten[3] /tie/bind	v	紮牢	jaat lòuh	zaat3 lou5	chaat louh
fasten[4] button	n	鈕	kau	kau3	khau
fasten door's /hasp	n	搭扣	dap kau	dap3 kau3	tap khau
fastening clothes /velcro/fastening tape	n	維可牢搭扣	wàih hó lòuh daap kau	wai4 ho2 lou4 daap3 kau3	waih ho louh taap khau
fat[1]	adj	肥	fèih	fei4	feih
fat[2] /fatness/obesity	adj	肥胖	fèih buhn	fei4 bun6	feih puhn
fat body	adj	脂肪質	jī fóng ji	zi1 fong2 zi3	chi fong chi
fat and short		肥肥矮矮	fèih fèih ngái ngái	fei4 fei4 ngai2 ngai2	feih feih ngai ngai
fat man (sl)	n	豬人	jyù yàhn	zyu4 jan4	chyu yahn
fate[1] /luck/fortune	n	運	wahn	wan6	wahn
fate[2] /fortune/luck/life	n	命	mehng /mihng	meng6 /ming6	mehng
fate[3] /fortune/luck/destiny	n	命運	mehng /mihng wahn	ming6 /meng6 wan6	mehng wahn
father[1]	n	父	fuh	fu6	fuh
father[2] /pop address to father	n	父親	fuh chàn	fu6 can4	fuh chhan
father[3]	n	爸	baa	baa3	paa
father[4]	n	爸爸	baa bàa	baa3 baa4	paa paa
father[5] (sl)	n	老豆	lóuh dauh	lou5 dau6	louh tauh
father[6] husband's	n	老爺	lóuh yèh	lou5 je4	louh yeh
father[7] wife's	n	外父	oih /ngoih fú	oi6 /ngoi6 fu2	oih /ngoih fu
father Christmas /Santa Claus	n	聖誕老人	sing daan lóuh yàhn	sing3 daan3 lou5 jan4	seng taan louh yahn
father land /mother country	n	祖國	jóu gwok	zou2 gwok3	chou kwok
father's day	n	父親節	fuh chàn jít	fu6 can4 zit2	fuh chhan chit
father's elder brother	n	大伯	daaih ba	daai6 baa3	taaih pa
father's elder sister	n	姑媽	gu mā	gu3 ma1	ku ma
father's younger sister	n	故姐	gu jé	gu3 ze2	ku che
fatigue	n	疲勞	pèih lòuh	pei4 lou4	pheih louh
faucet[1] /tap (of water)	n	水喉	séui hàuh	seoi2 hau4	swoi hauh
faucet[2] /tap (of water)	n	水龍頭	séui lùhng tàuh	seoi2 lung4 tau4	swoi luhng thauh
fault /crime/offence /guilt/sin	n	罪	jeuih	zeoi6	cheuih
fault finder	n	吹毛求疵者	chèui mòuh kàuh chì jé	ceoi4 mou4 kau4 ci4 ze2	chheui mouh khauh chhi che
faultless	adj	無缺點	mòuh kyut dím	mou4 kyut3 dim2	mouh khyut tim
favor	n	贊成	jaan sìhng	zaan3 cing4	chaan sehng

favorable	adj	優惠	yàu waih	jau4 wai6	yau waih
favourite[1]	adj	嗜好	si hou	si3 hou3	si hou
favourite[2]	adj	特別喜愛	dahk biht héi oi /ngoi	dak6 bit6 hei2 oi3 /ngoi3	tahk piht hei oi /ngoi
favourite[3]	adj	受寵	sauh chúng	sau6 cung2	sauh chhong
fax hotline		傳真熱線	chyùhn jàn yiht sin	cyun4 zan4 jit6 sin3	chhyuhn chan yiht sin
fax incidents		傳真打擾	chyùhn jàn dā yīu	cyun4 zan4 daa1 jiu1	chhyuhn chan ta yiu
fear /afraid	n	恐	húng	hung2	hung
fearism /anxious/worried /to worry/to be anxious	v	擔/担心	dàam sàm	daam4 sam4	taam sam
fearless	adj	輸得起	syù dāk héi	syu4 dak1 hei2	syu tak hei
feast	n	盛宴	sìhng yin	sing4 jin3	sehng yin
feat	n	技藝	geih ngaih	gei6 ngai6	keih ngaih
feather	n	羽毛	yúh mou	jyu5 mou3	yuh mou
features /characteristic	n	特徵	dahk jìng	dak6 zing4	tahk cheng
February	n	二月	yìh yùht	ji6 jyut6	yih yuht
February 1st	n	二月一日	yìh yùht yāt yàht	ji6 jyut6 jat1 jat6	yih yuht yat yaht
fee[1] (to pay)	adj	交費	gàau fai	gaau4 fai3	kaau fai
fee[2]	n	酬金	chàuh gām	cau4 gam1	chhauh kam
feeble[1] (sl) /flimsy	adj	科學怪人	fò hohk gwaai yàhn	fo4 hok6 gwaai3 jan4	fo hohk kwaai yahn
feeble[2]	adj	身體弱	sàn tái yeuhk	san4 tai2 joek6	san thai yeuhk
feed[1]	v	餵	wai	wai3	wai
feed[2] /to feed for animal	v	料	líu	liu2	liu
feed[3] for birds & animals	n	飼料	jih líu	zi6 liu2	chih liu
feed for animal	n	秣	mut	mut3	mut
feedback	n	反饋	fáan gwaih	faan2 gwai6	faan kwaih
feedbox (for cattle food) trough/wood box	n	飼料槽	jih líu chòuh	zi6 liu2 cou4	chih liu chhouh
feeder[1]	n	進食嘅人	jeun sihk ge yàhn	zeon3 sik6 ge3 jan4	cheun sehk ke yahn
feeder[2]	n	飼養者	jih yéuhng Jé	zi6 joeng5 ze2	chih yeuhng che
feel[1] /thinking/aware/ conscious	adj	覺	gok	gok3	kok
feel[2]	v	感	gám	gam2	kam
feel[3] /sense	n/v	覺得	gok dāk	gok3 dak1	kok tak
feel cold	v	覺得凍	gok dāk dung	gok3 dak1 dung3	kok tak tung
feel criminal /feel offense	v	觸犯罪行	chūk faahn jeuih hahng	cuk1 faan6 zeoi6 hang6	chhuk faahn choih hahng
feel humble /disgrace /shame/loss respect/lose face	v	丟架	dìu gá	diu4 gaa2	tiu ka
feel nervous /feel uncertain /hesitate	v	猶豫	yàuh yuh	jau4 jyu6	yauh yuh
feel pity /pitiable	adj	憫	máhn	man5	mahn
feel pulse	v	把脈	bá mahk	baa2 mak6	pa mahk
feel relieved	v	安心	òn /ngòn sàm	on4 /ngon4 sam4	on /ngon sam
feel small	v	覺得好渺小	gok dāk hóu míuh síu	gok3 dak1 hou2 miu5 siu2	kok tak hou miuh siu
feel sorry /regret/repent	v	懺悔	chaam fui	caam3 fui3	chhaam fui

feel strong emotion /excite	v	興奮	hìng fáhn	hing4 fan5	hing fahn
feel very sad /grieve	v	傷心	sèung sàm	soeng4 sam4	seung sam
feel with hand	n	摸	mó	mo2	mo
feeling /felt/sense	n/v	感覺	gám gok	gam2 gok3	kam kok
feeling agitated	n	情緒激動	chìhng séuih gīk duhng	cing4 seoi5 gik1 dung6	chhehng swoih kek tohng
feeling angry[1]	adj	好嬲	hou làu /nàu	hou3 lau4 /nau4	hou lau /nau
feeling angry[2]	adj	憤慨	fáhn kói	fan5 koi2	fáhn khoi
feeling bitter	adj	忿恨嘅	fāt hahn ge	fat1 han6 ge3	fat hahn ke
feeling happy[1] /glee /joy/happiness/pleasure	n	快樂	faai lohk	faai3 lok6	faai lohk
feeling happy[2] /self happy	n	自尊心	jih jyūn sàm	zi6 zeon1 sam4	chih chyun sam
feeling ill	n	心神不安	sàm sàn bàt òn	sam4 san4 bat4 on4	sam san pat on
feeling strong shock	adj	傷心嘅	sèung sàm ge	soeng4 sam4 ge3	seung sam ke
feeling surprise	n	覺得出奇	gok dāk chēut kèih	gok3 dak1 ceot1 kei4	kok tak chhot kheih
feeling unwell /get irritated /uneasy	n/v	唔舒服	m̀ syù fùhk	m4 syu4 fuk4	mh syu fuhk
feeling well	n	舒服	syù fùhk	syu4 fuk4	syu fuhk
feet /foot/leg (of foot)	n	足	jūk	zuk1	chuk
feller machine	n	伐木機	faht muhk gèi	fat6 muk6 gei4	faht muhk kei
fellow /classmate/same school/ school's friend/ schoolmate	n	同學	tùhng hohk	tung4 hok6	thuhng hohk
felt	n	毛氈	mòuh jīn	mou4 zin1	mouh chin
female[1] /daughter/lady/ woman	n	女	léuih /néuih	leoi5 /neoi5	lowih /nowih
female[2] (sl)	n	嫲	lá /ná	laa2 /naa2	la /na
female[3]	n	雌	chī	ci1	chhi
female[4] /mother	n	母	móuh	mou5	mouh
female friend /girlfriend	n	女朋友	léuih pang yáuh	leui5 pang3 jau5	lowih phang yauh
female private parts	n	女性陰部	léuih sing yàm bouh	leui5 jam4 bou6	lowih seng yam pouh
female's breast (sl)	n	波波	bō bō	bo1 bo1	po po
female servant	n	工人女	gùng yàhn léoih /néoih	gung4 jan4 leoi5 /neoi5	kung yahn lowih/nowih
female sex[1] /feminine	adj	女性	léuih sing	leui5 sing3	lowih seng
female sex[2]	adj	陰性	yàm sing	jam4 sing3	yam seng
female sex imagined (coll)		金魚	gàm yú	gam4 jyu2	kam yu
female sex intercourse (sl)		木魚	muhk yú	muk6 jyu2	muhk yu
female sexual way (coll) like dead body	v/xy	死魚	séi yú	sei2 jyu2	sei yu
female toilet /lady toilet/ woman toilet	n	女廁	léoih /néuih chi	leoi5 /neoi5 chi3	lowih /nowih chhi
feminine	adj	陰性	yàm síng	jam4 sing3	yam seng
fence[1] /railing	n	欄	làhn	laan4	laahn

fence[2] /railings	n	圍欄	wàih làahn	wai4 laan4	waih laahn
fence[3] bamboo/wood	n	籬笆	lèih bā	lei4 ba1	leih pa
fencing sport game	n	劍擊	gím gìk	gim2 gik4	kim kek
fermentation sugar is converted into alcohol	v	激動	gīk duhng	gik1 dung6	kek tohng
fern plant	n	羊齒植物	yèuhng chí jihk maht	joeng4 ci2 zik6 mat6	yeuhng chhi chehk maht
ferry[1]	n	小輪	síu lèuhn	siu2 leon4	siu leuhn
ferry[2]	n	渡輪	douh lèuhn	dou6 leon4	touh lowhn
ferryboat[1]	n	過海船	gwo hói syùn	gwo3 hoi2 syun4	kwo hoi syun
ferryboat[2]	n	渡船	douh syùhn	dou6 syun4	touh syuhn
fertile[1]	adj	肥沃	fèih yūk	fei4 juk1	feih yuk
fertile[1] /prolific	adj	多產	dò cháan	do4 caan2	to chhaan
fertilisation[1]	n	已受精	yíh sauh jèng /jìng	ji5 sau6 zeng4 /zing4	yih sauh cheng
fertilisation[2]	n	使受精	saí sauh jèng	sai2 sau6 zeng4	sai sauh cheng
fertilisation[3]	n	施肥於	sì fèih yū	si4 fei4 jyu1	si feih yu
fertilisation[4]	n	使肥沃	sí fèih yūk	si2 fei4 juk1	si feih yuk
fertilisation[5]	n	施肥令到肥沃	sì fèih lihng dou fèih yūk	si4 fei4 ling4 dou3 fei4 juk1	si feih lehng tou feih yuk
festival[1]	n	節	jit	zit3	chit
festival[2] /holiday	n	節日	jit yaht	jit3 jat6	chit yaht
festival[3]	n	節日嘅	jit yaht ge	zit3 jat6 ge3	chit yaht ke
fetuse /embryo/unborn child	n	胎兒	tòi yìh	toi4 ji4	thoi yih
feudal[1]	adj	封地	fùng deih	fung4 dei6	fung teih
feudal[2]	adj	封建	fùng gin	fung4 gin3	fung kin
feudal society	n	封建社會	fùng gin séh wúi	fung4 gin3 ce5 wui2	fung kin seh wui
feudalism	n	封建制度	fùng gin jai douh	fung4 gin3 zai3 dou6	fung kin chai touh
fever /have a fever	n	發燒	faat sìu	faat3 siu4	faat siu
few[1] /little bit/slight	adj	少量	síu lèuhng	siu2 loeng4	siu leuhng
few[2] /small amount	adj	少數	síu sou	siu2 sou3	siu sou
few[3] /some	adj	有些	yáuh sè	jau5 se4	yauh se
few days ago		日前	yaht chìhn	jat6 cin4	yaht chhihn
few days later		過幾日	gwo geih yaht	gwo3 gei6 jat6	kwo keih yaht
few understand		小小明白	síu síu mìhng baahk	siu2 siu2 ming4 baak6	siu siu mehng paahk
fiance	n	未婚夫	meih fān fù	mei6 fan1 fu4	meih fan fu
fiancee	n	未婚妻	meih fān chài	mei6 fan1 cai4	meih fan chhai
fiber /fibre	n	纖維	chìm wàih	cim4 wai4	chhim waih
fiction /novel	n	小說	síu syut	siu2 syut3	siu syut
field[1] /place/area/space /an open space	n	場	chèuhng	coeng4	chheuhng
field[2] /area/place/open space/jungle	n	野	yéh	je5	yeh
field[3] /subject/principle /course subject	n	科目	fò muhk	fo4 muk6	fo muhk
field[4] /land	n	田地	tìhn deih	tin4 dei6	thihn teih
fierce[1]	adj	盲烈	màahng liht	maang4 lit6	maahng liht

fierce[2] /raging	adj	猛烈	máahng liht	maang2 lit6	maahng liht
fierce[3]	adj	凶惡	hūng ok /ngok	hung1 ok3 /ngok3	hung ok /ngok
fiercest /unkind person	adj	凶惡者	hūng ok /ngok jé	hung1 ok3 /ngok3 ze2	hungok /ngok che
fifteenth	n	第十五個	daih sahp ńgh go	dai6 sap6 ng5 go3	taih sahp ngh ko
fifth	n	第五嘅	daih ńgh ge	dai6 ng5 ge3	taih ngh ke
fifty	n	五十	ńgh sahp	ng5 sap6	ngh sahp
fifty % discount	v	對半	deui bun	deoi3 bun3	toei pun
fig	n	無花果	mòuh fa gwó	mou4 faa3 gwo2	mouh fa kwo
fight[1] (sl)	n	搯	haap	haap3	haap
fight[2]	n	戰	jin	zin3	chin
fight[3]	n	打交	dá gāau	daa2 gaau1	ta kaau
fight[4]	n	打鬥	dá dau	daa2 dau3	ta tau
fight for /strive	v	爭	jàang	zaang4	chaang
fight the fire /try to put off fire	v	救火	gau fó	gau3 fo2	kau fo
fighter /warrior	n	戰士	jin sih	zin3 si6	chin sih
fighting	adj	戰爭	jin jàang	zin3 zaang4	chin chaang
figurative	adj	比喻	béi yuh	bei2 jyu6	pei yuh
figure[1] /image/portrait /shape/statue	n	像	jeuhng	zoeng6	cheuhng
figure[2] /model	n	塑	sou	sou3	sou
figure[3] /picture	n	影像	yéng jeuhng	jeng2 zoeng6	yeng cheuhng
filament	n	細線	sai sin	sai3 sin3	sai sin
filch /steal	v	偷	tàu	tau4	thau
file[1] (de) paper holder	n	快勞	fàai lóu	faai4 lou2	faai lou
file[2] paper holder	n	文件夾	màhn gín gip	man4 gin2 gip3	mahn kin kip
file[3] a steel hand tool	n	銼刀	cho dòu	co3 dou4	chho tou
file record	v	檔	dong	dong3	tong
filing	n	文件歸檔	màhn gín gwài dong	man4 gin2 gwai4 dong3	mahn kin kwai tong
fill[1] /fulfill/sufficient	v	充	chùng	cung4	chhung
fill[2] /stuff/stop up /something with tightlt	v	塞	sāk	sak1	sak
fill a form		填表	tìhn bíu	tin4 biu2	thihn piu
fill a gap		填補空白	tìhn bóu hùng baahk	tin4 bou2 hung4 baak6	thihn pou hung baahk
fill hole		補窿	bóu lùng	bou2 lung4	pou lung
fill in a blank		填補	tìhn bóu	tin4 bou2	thihn pou
fill tooth	v	補牙	bóu ngàh	bou2 ngaa4	pou ngah
fill vacancy		補缺	bóu kyut	bou2 kyut3	pou khyut
filled /surplus	v	盈	yìhng	jing4	yehng
filler thing	n	注入器	jyu yahp hei	zyu3 jap6 hei3	chyu yahp hei
film[1]	n	片	pin	pin3	phin
film[2] (de) cartridge	n	菲林	fēi lám	fei1 lam2	fei lam
film[3] /video	n	影碟	yéng díp	jeng2 dip2	yeng tip
film[4] /movie	n	影片	yéng pin	jeng2 pin3	yeng phin
film rolled	n	膠捲	gàau gyún	gaau4 gyun2	kaau kyun

filmy	adj	似薄膜	chíh bohk mók	ci5 bok6 mok2	chhih pohk mok
filter	n	過濾器	gwo leuih hei	gwo3 leoi6 he3	kwo lowih hei
filters	v	濾	leuih	leoi6	lowih
filthy word	adj	多能餘	dò làhng /nàhng yùh	do4 lang4 /nang4 jyu4	toh lahng /nahng yuh
filtrate	n	濾液	leuih yihk	leoi6 yik6	lowih yehk
filtration	n	過濾法	gwo leuih faat	gwo3 leoi6 faat3	kwo lowih faat
fin /wing	n	翅	chi	ci3	chhi
final of match	n	決賽	kyut choi	kyut3 coi3	khyut chhoi
finally[1]	adv	終	jūng	zung1	chung
finally[2]	adj	結果	git gwo	git3 gwo3	kit gwo
finally[3]	adj	卒之	jēut jì	zeot1 zi4	cheut chi
finance provided	v	供給經費	gùng kāp gìng fai	gung4 kap1 ging4 fai3	kung khap geng fai
financial[1]	adj	金融	gàm yùhng	gam4 jung4	kam yuhng
financial[2] /world of finance	adj	金融界	gàm yùhng gaai	gam4 jung4 gaai3	kam yuhng kaai
financial difficulty /money problem/no money /stiff/pitfall	n	困難	kwan làahn /nàahn	kwan3 laan4 /naan4	khwan laahn /naahn
financial market	n	金融市場	gàm yùhng síh chèuhng	gam4 jung4 si5 coeng4	kam yuhng sih chheuhng
financial supporter /sponsor	n	贊助者	jaan joh jé	zaan3 zo6 ze2	chaan choh che
financier	n	金融家	gàm yùhng gā	gam4 jung4 ga1	kam yuhng kah
find[1] /check/see/seek/ search	v	搵	wán	wan2	wan
find[2] /find out/finding	n	發現	faat yihn	faat3 jin6	faat yihn
find[3]	v	查到	chàh dóu	caa4 dou2	chhah tou
find[4]	v	找	jáau	zaau2	chaau
find[5] /found /to find	v	搵到	wán dóu	wan2 dou2	wan tou
find a day		搵日	wán yaht	wan2 jat6	wan yaht
find fault /fault finding	v	找岔子	jáau chà jí	zaau2 caa4 zi2	chaau chha chi
find out /realize /understand	v	了解	líuh gáai	liu5 gaai2	liuh kaai
findable	adj	可發現	hó yìh yihn	ho2 ji4 jin6	ho yih yihn
finder[1]	n	發現嘅人	faat yihng ge yàhn	faat3 jin6 ge3 jan4	faat yihng ke yahn
finder[2]	n	搵到嘅人	wán dóu ge yàhn	wan2 dou2 ge3 jan4	wan tou ke yahn
fine[1] /thanks/very good /very well/good/nicely	adj	好好	hóu hóu	hou2 hou2	hou hou
fine[2] /well/nice	adj	美好	méih hóu	mei5 hou2	meih hou
fine[3] /well/good	adj	緻	ji	zi	chi
fine[4] /thin/small /minute /thin and small	adj	幼細	yau sai	jau3 sai3	yau sai
fine[5] /sunshine	adj	陽光	yeung gwòng	joeng3 gwong4	yeung kwong
fine[6] /punish/penalty /penalize	n	罰	faht	fat6	faht
fine[7] /punish/penalty /penalize	n	罰款	faht fún	fat6 fun2	faht fun

English	POS	Chinese	Romanization 1	Jyutping	Romanization 2
fine art	adj	美術作品	méih seuht jok bán	mei5 seot6 jok3 ban2	meih swoht chok pan
fine-food	adj	美食	méih sihk	mei5 sik6	meih sehk
fine-horse /excellent horse/spirited horse/steed (best horse)	n	駿馬	jeun máh	zeon3 maa5	cheun mah
finger[1]	n	指	jí	zi2	chi
finger[2]	n	手指	sáu jī	sau2 zi1	sau chi
finger language	n	手話	sáu wá	sau2 waa2	sau wa
finger print[1]	n	指紋	jí màhn	zi2 man4	chi mahn
finger print[2]	n	指模	jí mòuh	zi2 mou4	chi mouh
finger print[3]	n	指印	jí yan	zi2 jan4	chi yan
fingernails[1]	n	指甲	jī gáap	zi1 gaap2	chi kaap
fingernails[2] /nail	n	手指甲	sáu jī gáap	sau2 ji1 gaap2	sau chi kaap
finish work/task	v	做完	jouh yùhn	zou6 jyun4	chouh yuhn
finish work /get off work	v	下班	hah bāan	haa6 baan1	hah paan
finished /completed	adj	結束了	git chùk líuh	git3 cuk4 liu5	kit chhuk liuh
finisher[1]	n	完工者	yùhn gùng jé	jyun4 gung4 ze2	yuhn kung che
finisher[2]	n	完成嘅人	yùhn sèhng ge yàhn	jyun4 seng4 ge3 jan4	yuhn sehng ke yahn
fire[1]	n	火	fó	fo2	fo
fire[2] /have a fire	n	火燭	fó jūk	fo2 zuk1	fo chuk
fire[3]	n	火擊	fó gīk	fo2 gik1	fo gīk
fire![4] /burn!	n	火燭呀!	fó jūk ā !	fo2 zuk1 aa1 /aa3!	fo chuk a !
fire-alarm[1] /fire-outbreak	n	火警	fó gíng	fo2 ging2	fo geng
fire-alarm[2]	n	火災警報器	fó jòi gíng bou hei	fo2 zoi4 ging2 bou3 hei3	fo choi geng pou hei
fire-alarm[3]	n	防火警報器	fòhng fó gīng bóu héi	fong4 fo2 ging1 bou2 hei2	fohng fo geng pou hei
fire-blanket	n	防火氈	fòhng fó jìn	fong4 fo2 zin4	fohng fo chin
fire-break	n	防火地帶	fòhng fó dèih dāai	fong4 fo2 dei6 daai1	fohng fo teih taai
fire-control[1]	n	消防	sìu fong	siu4 fong3	siu fong
fire-control[2]	n	消防控制	sìu fong húng jái	siu4 fong3 hung2 zai2	siu fong hung chai
fire-cracker	n	爆竹	baau jūk	paau3 zuk1	paau chuk
fire-service /fire-services department/fire-depart	n	消防署	sìu fong chyúh	siu4 fong3 cyu5	siu fong chhyuh
fire-door	n	防火安全門	fòhng fó òn chyun mùhn	fong4 fo2 on4 cyun4 mun4	fohng fo on chhyun muhn
fire-drills[1]	n	防火演習	fòhng fó yíhn jàahp	fong4 fo2 jin5 zaap6	fohng fo yihn chaahp
fire-drills[2]	n	消防演習	sìu fong yíhn jàahp	siu4 fong4 jin5 zaap6	siu fong yihn chaahp
fire-drills[3]	n	混亂局面	wàhn lyùhn gùhk mìhn	wan6 lyun6 guk6 min6	wahn lyuhn kuhk mihn
fire-engine /fire truck	n	消防車	sìu fong chè	siu4 fong3 ce4	siu fong chhe
fire-escape[1]	n	雲梯	wan tài	wan3 tai4	wan thai
fire-escape[2]	n	太平梯	táai pèhng /pìhng tài	taai2 peng4 /ping4 tai4	thaai phehng thai
fire-exit[1]	n	火災出口	fó jòi chēut háu	fo2 zoi4 ceot1 hau2	fo choi chhot hau
fire-exit[2]	n	火警出路	fó gíng chēut louh	fo2 ging2 ceot1 lou6	fo geng chhot louh

fire-extinguisher	n	滅火器	mìht fó hei	mit6 fo2 hei3	miht fo hei
fire-extinguisher equipments	n	滅火器材	mìht fó hei chòih	mit6 fo2 hei3 coi4	miht fo hei chhoih
fire-man /fire-fighter	n	消防員	sìu fong yùhn	siu4 fong3 jyun4	siu fong yuhn
fire-fighter /fire-man	n	消防隊員	sìu fong deuih yùhn	siu4 fong3 deoi6 jyun4	siu fong toeih yuhn
fire-fighting	n	撲救	pok gau	pok3 gau3	phok kau
fire-fly	n	螢火蟲	yèhng fó chùhng	jeng fo2 cung4	yehng fo chhuhng
fire-hose pipe	n	消防水龍頭	sìu fong sēui lung tau	siu4 fong3 seoi2 lung3 tau3	siu fong swoi lung thau
fire-hose reel	n	消防喉捲軸	sìu fong hau gyūn jùhk	siu4 fong3 hau3 gyun1 zuk6	siu fong hau kyun chohk
fire-hydrant /hydrant	n	消防龍頭	sìu fong lung tau	siu4 fong3 lung3 tau3	siu fong lung thau
fire-insurance	n	火災保險	fó jòi bóu hím	fo2 zoi4 bou2 him2	fo choi pou him
fire-place[1] /furnace /oven		爐	lòuh	lou4	louh
fire-place[2]	n	火場	fó chèuhng	fo2 coeng4	fo chheuhng
fire-place[3]	n	壁爐	bék lou	bek2 lou3	pek lowu
fire-prevention	adj	防火須知	fòhng fó sèui jí	fong4 fo2 seoi2 zi2	fohng fo swoi chi
fire-proof[1] /protect-against fire	adj	防火	fòhng fó	fong4 fo2	fohng fo
fire-proof[2]	adj	耐火	loih /noih fó	loi6 /noi6 fo2	loih /noih fo
fire-sprinkle inlet	n	消防入水閥	sìu fong yàhp sēui fàht	siu4 fong3 jap6 seoi1 fat6	siu fong yahp swoi faht
fire-station[1]	n	消防局	sìu fong gùhk	siu4 fong3 guk6	siu fong kuhk
fire-station[2]	n	消防站	sìu fong jàahm	siu4 fong3 zaam6	siu fong chaahm
fire-truck	n	救火車	gau fō chè	gau3 fo1 ce4	kau fo chhe
fire-water	n	烈酒	liht jáu	lit6 zau2	liht chau
fire-water reserve tank	n	消防用水	sìu fong yùhng sēui	siu4 fong3 jung6 seoi1	siu fong yuhng swoi
fire-wood[1]	n	柴	chàaih	caai4	chhaaih
fire-wood[2]	n	木柴	muhk chàaih	muk6 caai4	muhk chhaaih
fire-words	n	火災用語	fó jòi yùhng yùh	fo2 zoi4 jung6 jyu6	fo choi yuhng yuh
fireworks[1]	n	烟花	yīn fā	jin1 faa1	yin fa
fireworks[2]	n	煙火大會	yīn fó taaih wùih	jin1 fo2 daai6 wui4	yin fo thaaih wuih
firing	n	燒毀	sìu wāi	siu4 wai1	siu wai
firm[1] /solid	adj	實	saht	sat6	saht
firm[2] /solid	adj	確	kok	kok	khok
firm[3] /solid/strong	adj	堅	gìn	gin4	kin
firm[4] /steady /uncompromising	adj	堅定	gìn dehng	gin4 deng6/ding6	kin tehng
firm[5] /steady/safe	adj	穩陣	wán jahn	wan2 zan6	wan chahn
firm[6] /stable	adj	穩固	wān gú	wan1 gu2	wan ku
firm & upright	adj	堅挺	gìn tíhng	gin4 ting5	kin thehng
firmly /steadily	adv	堅定地	gìn dèhng dèih	gin4 deng6 dei6	kin tehng teih
first[1] / A/ roman I	n	甲	gaap	gaap3	kaap
first[2] /primary	n	元	yùhn	jyun4	yuhn
first[3]	n	上	seuhng	soeng3	seuhng

English	Part	Chinese	Romanization	Jyutping	Romanization 2
first & foremost[1] /first-time/1st	n	第一	daih yāt	dai6 jat1	taih yat
first & foremost[2] /first of all /for first one	adv	首先	sáu sìn	sau2 sin4	sau sin
first aider /rescuer	n	救護員	gau wuh yùhn	gau3 wu6 jyun4	kau wuh yuhn
first best /first choose /one of the best/very best	adj	數一數二	sóu yāt sóu yih	sou2 jat1 sou2 ji6	sou yat sou yih
first cause /main cause	n	根源	gáan yùhn	gaan2 jyun4	kaan yuhn
first class[1]	adj	一級	yāt kāp	jat1 kap1	yat khap
first class[2] /best of all /best/top class	adj	最好	jeui hóu	jeoi3 hou2	cheui hou
first come	adv	先來先接待	sīn lòih sīn jip doih	sin1 loi4 sin1 zip3 doi6	sin loih sin chip toih
first hand /new	adj	第一手	daih yāt sáu	dai6 jat1 sau2	taih yat sau
first home /native place	n	故鄉	gu hèung	gu3 hoeng4	ku heung
first served	adv	先到先供應	sīn dou sīn gùng ying	sin1 dou3 sin1 gung4 jing3	sin tou sin kung yeng
first times	adj	初次	chò chi	co1 ci3	chho chhi
firstly /the first	adv	其一	kèih yāt	kei4 jat1	kheih yat
fiscal /finance/financial /public money	adj	財政	chòih jíng	coi4 zing2	chhoih jeng
fish	n	魚	yú	jyu2	yu
fish farm	n	養魚場	yéuhng yú chèuhng	joeng5 jyu2 coeng4	yeuhng yu chheuhng
fish head	n	魚頭	yùh tàuh	jyu4 tau4	yuh thauh
fish market	n	魚市場	yú síh chèuhng	jyu2 si5 coeng4	yu sih chheuhng
fish maw	n	魚肚	yú tóuh	jyu2 tou5	yu thouh
fisher[1]	n	魚翁	yùh yūng	jyu4 jung1	yuh yung
fisher[2]	n	魚夫	yùh fù	jyu4 fu4	yuh fu
fisher man	n	魚人	yùh yàhn	jyu4 jan4	yuh yahn
fishhook[1]	n	釣	diu	diu3	tiu
fishhook[2]	n	魚釣	yùh diu	jyu4 diu3	yuh tiu
fishing rod	n	釣竿	diu gòn	diu3 gon4	tiu kon
fishy /similar fish	adj	像魚	jeuhng yú	zoeng6 jyu2	cheuhng yu
fishy smell[1]	adj	腥	sèng	seng4	seng
fishy smell[2]	adj	魚腥味	yùh sèng mēih	jyu4 seng4 mei6	yuh seng meih
fist[1] /boxing	n	拳	kyùhn	kyun4	khyuhn
fist[2] /boxing	n	拳頭	kyùhn tàuh	kyun4 tau4	khyuhn thauh
fistula	n	瘺管	lauh gún	lauh gun2	lauh kun
fit[1] /suit/suitable/proper/well	adj/n	適	sīk	sik1	sek
fit[2]	adj	啱嘅	ngāam ge	ngaam1 ge3	ngaam ke
fit[3]	n	適合	sīk hahp	sik1 hap6	sek hahp
fit[4] cloth	n	合身	hahp sān	hap6 san1	hahp san
fit as		非常健康	fèi sèuhng gihn hòng	fei4 soeng4 gin6 hong4	fei seuhng kihn hong
fited /suitable/useful	adj	適宜嘅	sīk yìh ge	sik1 ji4 ge3	sek yi ke
fitted /suitable/becoming /fitting	adj	合適	hahp sīk	hap6 sik1	hahp sek
fitting /installations /fixture /setting	adj	設備	chit beih	cit3 bei6	chhit peih

fitting room	n	試衣室	si yì sāt	si3 ji4 sat1	si yi sat
five	n	五	ńgh /ng	ng5	nggh /ng
five past one¹ /one five hrs	n	一點一	yāt dím yàt	jat1 dim2 jat4	yat tim yat
five past one² /one five hrs	n	一點零五分	yāt dím ling ńgh fàn	jat1 dim2 ling3 ng5 fan4	yat tim leng ngh fan
five senses /sense of organ	n	感覺器官	gám gok hei gūn	gam2 gok3 hei3 gun1	kam kok hei kun
five star hotel	n	五星級	ńgh sèng /sìng kāp	ng5 seng4 /sing4 kap1	ngh seng khap
fix¹ /decide	v	定	dehng /dihng	deng6 /ding6	tehng
fix² make/renovate/orderly act	v	整	jíng	zing2	cheng
fix³ /install/setting /installation	n	安裝	òn /ngòn jòng	on4 /ngon4 zong4	on /ngon chong
fixed¹	v	使固定	sai gu dehng /dihng	sai3 gu3 deng6 /ding6	sai ku tehng
fixed² /immobile/regular	adj	固定	gu dehng /dihng	gu3 deng6 /ding6	ku tehng
fixed³	adj	確定	kok dehng /dihng	kok3 deng6 /ding6	khok tehng
fixed deposit	adj	定期存款	dehng /dihng kèih chyùhn fún	deng6 /ding6 kei4 cyun4 fun2	tehng kheih chhyuhn fun
fixer	n	固定器	gu dehng /dihng hei	gu3 deng6 /ding6 hei3	ku tehng hei
flag /ensign	n	旗	kèih	kei4	kheih
flaking /loose	adj	鬆脫	sùng dìk	sung4 dik4	sung tek
flaming	v	灼熱	cheuk yiht	ceok jit6	chheuk yiht
flammable	adj	易燃的	yìh yin dìk	ji6 jin3 dik4	yih yin tek
flare by sick	v	突然加劇	daht yihn gā kehk	dat6 jin4 gaa1 kek6	taht yihn ka khehk
flash /gleam	v	閃	sím	sim2	sim
flashing¹ /blink of light	v	閃光	sīm gwóng	sim1 gwong2	sim kwong
flashing² of light	v	眨眨	jáma jáma	zaam2 zaam2	chama chama
flashlight¹	n	電光	dihn gwòng	din6 gwong4	tihn kwong
flashlight² of camera	n	閃光燈	sím gwóng dàng	sim2 gwong2 dang4	sim kwong tang
flashlight³ /torch light	n	手電筒	sáu dihn túng	sai2 din6 tung2	sau tihn thung
flat¹ /smooth	adj	坦	táan	taan2	thaan
flat²	adj	平嘅	pèhng ge	peng4 ge3	phehng ke
flat³ /smooth/level/even	adj	平坦	pèhng táan	peng4 taan2	phehng thaan
flat⁴ (rooms)	n	樓房	làuh fóng	tai4 fong2	lauh fong
flat⁵ /ground land	n	土地	tóu deih	tou2 dei6	thou teih
flat tyre /tyre burst	adj	爆呔	baau tāai	baau3 taai1	paau thaai
flatbed truck	n	平析車	pèhng sīk chè	peng4 sik1 ce4	phehng sek chhe
flatter¹ (sl) flattery	n/v	托大脚	tok daaih geuk	tok3 daai6 goek3	thok taaih keuk
flatter² (sl)	v	托大脚嘅	tok daaih geuk ge	tok3 daai6 goek3 ge3	thok taaih keuk ke
flatter³ (sl)	v	拍馬屁	paak máh pei	paak3 maa5 pei3	phaak mah pei
flatter⁴ (sl) flattery	v	托大脚嘅人	tok daaih geuk ge yàhn	tok3 daai6 goek3 ge3 jan4	thok taaih keuk ke yahn
flattering	adj	恭維	gùng wàih	gung4 wai4	kung waih
flatus	n	屁	pei	pei3	phei
flavor¹ /taste	n	味	meih	mei6	meih

flavor[2] /taste	n	味道	meih douh	mei6 dou6	meih touh
flavoring[1]	n	調味品	tìuh meih bán	tiu4 mei6 ban2	thiuh meih pan
flavoring[2] /sauce/spices /seasonings/flavour/dressing	n	調味料	tìuh mèih lìuh	tiu4 mei6 ban2 liu6	thiuh meih liuh
flavorless /no taste	adj	無滋味	mòuh jì meih	mou4 zi4 mei6	mouh chi meih
flea[1]	n	虱	sāt	sat1	sat
flea[2]	n	蚤	jou	zou3	chou
flead[1] without repay		著草	jyu chóu	zyu3 cou2	chyu chhou
flead[2] run away without repay		走路	jáu lóu	zau2 lou2	chau lou
fledge	v	長翅嘅	chèuhng chi ge	coeng4 ci3 ge3	chheuhng chhi ke
flee /ran/hurry walk /leave in hurry	v	跑	pāau	paau1	phaau
fleece	n	抓毛	jàau mòu	zaau4 mou4	chaau mou
flesh[1] /pulp	n	果肉	gwó yuhk	gwo2 juk6	kwo yuhk
flesh[2]	n	瓜子	gwà jí	gwaa4 zi2	kwa chi
flesh[3] /muscle	n	肌肉	gèi yuhk	gei4 juk6	kei yuhk
flew /flying	v	飛行	fèi hàhng	fei4 hang4	fei hahng
flex /wire	n	皮線	pèih sin	pei4 sin3	pheih sin
flexibility	n	靈活性	lìhng wuht sing	leng4 wut6 sing3	lehng wuht seng
flexible[1] of attitude	adj	靈活嘅	lìhng wuht ge	leng4 wut6 ge3	lehng wuht ke
flexible[2] of wire/tube	adj	易屈嘅	yih wāt ge	ji6 wat1 ge3	yih wat ke
flight	n	板機	báan gèi	baan2 gei4	paan kei
flight attendant /air hostess	n	空姐	hùng jé	hung4 ze2	hung che
flimsy	adj	單薄	dāan bohk	daan1 bok6	taan pohk
flint	n	打火石	dā fō sehk	daa1 fo2 sek6	ta fo sehk
flip-flops /slipper	n	拖鞋	tō haai	to1 haai3	thoh haai
float	n	浮	fàuh	fau4	fauh
floating	adj	漂浮嘅	piu fàuh ge	piu3 fau4 ge	phiu fauh ke
floating restaurant	n	海鮮舫	hói sīn fóng	hoi2 sin1 fong2	hoi sin fong
floating voter[1]	n	散票者	saan piu jé	saan3 piu3 ze2	saan phiu che
floating voter[2]	n	流動票者	làuh duhng piu jé	lau4 dung6 piu3 ze2	lauh tohng phiu che
flood[1]	n	洪水	hùhng séui	hung4 seoi2	huhng swoi
flood[2] /infinity	n	水災	séui jòi	seoi2 zoi4	swoi choi
flooding	n	水浸	séui jám	seoi2 zam2	swoi cham
floor[1] /story	n	樓	làuh	lau4	lauh
floor[2] /ground/story /storey	n	地下	deih há	dei6 haa6	teih ha
floor[3] /story	n	地板	deih báan	dei6 baan2	teih paan
floor[4] platform	n	地台	deih tòih	dei6 toi4	teih thoih
floor[5] /story/storey	n	樓層	làuh chàhng	tai4 cang4	lauh chhahng
floor lamp /standard lamp	n	落地燈	lohk deih dāng	lok6 dei6 dang1	lohk teih tang
floor plan	n	平面圖	pèhng mín tòuh	peng4 min2 tou4	phehng min thouh
florist	n	種花者	júng fā jé	zung2 fa1 ze2	chung fa che

English	POS	中文	Yale	Jyutping	Romanization
flour	n	麵粉	mihn fán	min6 fan2	mihn fan
flourish /prosper	v	茂盛	mauh sihng	mau6 sing6	mauh sehng
flourishing[1]/prosperous	v	旺	wohng	wong6	wohng
flourishing[2]/prosper /prosperous	adj/v	繁榮	fàahn wìhng	faan4 wing4	faahn wehng
flow[1] /shed/ flow out	v	流出	làuh chēut	lau4 ceot1	lauh chhot
flow[2]	v	都流	dòu làuh	dou4 lau4	tou lauh
flow[3]	v	流動	làuh dùhng	lau4 dung6	lauh tohng
flow of water /watertap	n	喉嘴	hàuh jéui	hau4 zeoi2	hauh choi
flower[1] /blossom	n	花	fā	faa1	fa
flower[2]	n	聞花	màhn fā	man4 faa1	mahn fa
flower[3]	n	花卉	fā wái	faa1 wai2	fa wai
flower arranging	n	插花藝術	chaap fā ngaih seuht	caap3 fa1 ngai6 seot6	chhaap fa ngaih swoht
flower garden /garden	n	花園	fā yún	faa1 jyun2	fa yun
flower market	n	花市	fā síh	faa1 si5	fa sih
flower pot[1] /vase	n	花瓶	fā pèhng /pìhng	faa1 peng4 /ping4	fa phehng
flower pot[2] /vase	n	花樽	fā jēun	faa1 zeon1	fa cheun
flower pot[3]/plant pot	n	花盆	fā pùhn	faa1 pun4	fa phuhn
flower show	n	花展	fā jín	faa1 zin2	fa chin
flown /air transport	n	空運	hùng wahn	hung4 wan6	hung wahn
flu[1] (coll) influenza	n	流感	làuh gám	lau4 gam2	lauh kam
flu[2] influenza	n	流行性感冒	làuh hàhng sing gám mouh	lau4 hang4 sing3 gam2 mou6	lauh hahng seng kam mouh
flu vaccine /influenza vaccine	n	流感針	làuh gám jám	lau4 gam2 zam2	lauh kam cham
fluency /freely/joyful /smoothly	n	暢	cheung	cong3	chheung
fluent /fluency/smooth and easy (of speech)	adj/n	流暢	làuh cheung	lau4 cong3	lauh chheung
fluid[1] /juice/liquid	n	液	yihk	jik6	yehk
fluid[2] /liquid	n	液體	yihk tái	jik6 tai2	yehk thai
fluid[3]	n	流體	lauh tái	lau4 tai2	lauh thai
fluid flow /flowing	n	流動	làuh dùhng	lau4 dung6	lauh tohng
fluorescent[1]	adj	發亮	faat lèuhng	faat3 loeng6	faat leuhng
fluorescent[2]	adj	螢光燈	yíhng gwòng dāng	jing5 gwong4 dang1	yehng kwong tang
fluorescent[3]	adj	發出螢光	faat cheut yíhng gwòng	faat3 ceot1 jing5 gwong4	faat chhot yehng kwong
fluoridation	n	加氟作用	gà fāt jok yuhng	ga4 fat1 zik3 jung6	ka fat chok yuhng
fluoride	n	氟化物	fāt fa maht	fat1 fa mat6	fat fa maht
flush[1] /rinse	v	沖	chùng	cung4	chhung
flush[2] /rinse	v	用水沖洗	yùhng séui chùngsái	jung6 seoi2 cung4 sai2	yuhng swoi chhung sai
flushing toilet	v	沖廁所	chùng chi só	cung4 ci3 so2	chhung chhi so
fly[1] /flew	v	飛	fèi	fei4	fei
fly[2] insect	n	蠅	ying	jing3	yeng
fly[3] insect	n	烏蠅	wù ying	wu4 jing3	wu yeng

flying horse /spirited horse	n	飛馬	fèi máh	fei4 maa5	fei mah
flying saucer	n	飛碟	fèi dihp	fei4 dip6	fei tihp
flying-time	v	飛行時間	fèi hàahng sìh gaan	fei4 haang4 si4 gaan3	fei haahng sih kaan
flyover	n	立交橋	lahp gàau kìuh	lap6 gaau4 kiu4	lahp kaau khiuh
foam[1] liquid /bubble	n/v	泡泡	póuh póuh	pou5 pou5	phouh phouh
foam[2] liquid	n	泡沫	póuh mut	pou5 mut3	phouh mut
foam[3] rubber	n	海綿	hói mìhn	hoi2 min4	hoi mihn
focus	v	焦點	jìu dím	ziu4 dim2	chiu tim
fodder	n	草料	chóu liuh	cou2 liu6	chhou liuh
foe[1] /hazard/harm	n	危害	ngàih hoih	ngai4 hoi6	ngaih hoih
foe[2] /enemy/rival	n	敵	dihk	dik6	tehk
foetus (home of the embryo)	n	兒胎	yi tòi	ji toi4	yi thoi
fog /mist	n	霧	mòuh	mou6	mouh
foggy	adj	大霧	daaih mòuh	daai6 mou6	taaih mouh
fold[1] /multiple	n	倍	púih	pui5	phuih
fold[2] /bend/to fold in two	v	對摺	deui jip	deoi3 zip3	toei chip
fold[3] /sheep cage	n	羊欄	yèuhng làahn	joeng4 laan4	yeuhng laahn
folded	n	摺叠肑	jaap dihp dì	zaap3 dip6 di4	chaap tihp ti
folding door	n	摺門	jip mùhn	zip3 mun4	chip muhn
folk	n	民眾	màhn jung	man4 jung3	mahn chung
folk custom	n	民俗	màhn juhk	man4 zuk6	mahn chuhk
folk dance	n	民族舞	màhn juhk móuh	man4 zuk6 mou5	mahn chuhk mouh
folklore	n	民間傳說	màhn gaan chyùhn syut	man4 gaan3 cyun4 syut3	mahn kaan chhyuhn syut
folksong[1] /mountain song/question answer song	n	山歌	sàan gō	saan4 go1	saan koh
folksong[2]	n	民歌	màhn gō	man4 go1	mahn ko
folksong[3]	n	民謠	màhn yìuh	man4 jiu4	mahn yiuh
follow[1]	v	跟	gàn	gan4	kan
follow[2] /keep up /walk along	v	由	yàuh	jau4	yauh
follow[3] /follow closely	v	跟住	gàn jyuh	gan4 zyu6	kan chyuh
follow[4]	v	依循	yī chèuhn	ji1 ceon4	yi chheuhn
follow[5]	v	跟隨	gàn cheui	gan4 ceoi3	kan chheui
follow[6] /follow up	v	跟進	gàn jeun	gan4 zeon3	kan jeun
follow on[1]	v	尾隨	méih chèuih	mei5 ceoi4	meih chhoih
follow on[2]	v	由...而起	yàuh yìh héi	jau4 ji4 hei2	yauh yih hei
follow rules	v	照辦	jiu baahn	ziu3 baan6	chiu paahn
follow up	v	在...之後採 取進一步 行動	joih jī hauh chói chéui jeun yāt bouh hàhng duhng	zoi6 zi1 hau6 coi2 ceoi2 zeon3 jat1 bou6 hang4 dung6	choih chi hauh chhoi chheui cheun yat pouh hahng tuhng
follower[1] /disciple	n	弟子	daih jí	dai6 zi2	taih chi
follower[2]	n	追隨者	jèui chèuih jé	zeoi4 ceoi4 ze2	cheui chheuih che
follower[3] /believer	n	信徒	seun tòuh	seon3 tou4	swon thouh

following[1]	adj	下列	hah liht	haa6 lit6	hah liht
following[2]	adj	其次嘅	kèih chi ge	kei4 ci3 ge3	kheih chhi ke
following detailed	adj	下述詳	hah seuht chèuhng	haa6 seot6 coeng4	hah swoht chheuhng
folly /foolish /stupid /brainless/silly	adj	愚蠢	yu chéun	jyu3 ceon2	yu chhon
fond	adj	愛好的	oi /ngoi hóu dīk	oi3 /ngoi3 hou2 dik1	oi /ngoi hou tik
fondly touch[1]	adj	喜歡	héi fūn	hei2 fun1	hei fun
fondly touch[2] /gently stroke/gently touch	v	輕挪	hehng lòh /nòh	heng6 lo4 /no4	hehng loh /noh
fondly touch[3] /gently stroke/gently touch	v	輕觸	hehng jùk	heng4 zuk4	hehng chuk
fondly touch[4] /touch gently	v	温情摩摩	wān chìhng mō mō	wan1 cing4 mo1 mo1	wan chhehng moh moh
font	n	一副鉛字	yāt fu yùhn jih	jat1 fu3 jyun4 zi6	yat fu yuhn chih
food[1] /meal	n	食	sihk	sik6	sehk
food[2] /foodstuff	n	食品	sìhk pán	sik6 pan2	sehk pan
food[3] /meal/sustenance	n	食物	sihk maht	sik6 mat6	sehk maht
food[4]/type of dish/ food type/vegetable	n	菜	choi	coi3	chhoi
food & drink /diet	n	飲食	yam sihk	jam3 sik6	yam sehk
food bureau[1] /food & environmental hygiene department	n	食環署	sihk wàahn chyú	sik6 waan4 cyu5	sehk waahn chhyu
food bureau[2]	n	食物安全環境處	sihk maht òn/ngòn chyùhn wàahn gíng chyú	sik6 mat6 on4/ngon4 cyun4 waan4 ging2 cyu2	sehk maht on /ngon chhyuhn waahn keng chhyu
food of animals	n	草料	chóu liuh	cou2 liu6	chhou liuh
fool[1] /stupid/foolish/idiot	n	蠢材	chéun chòih	ceon2 coi4	chhon choih
fool[2]	n	傻瓜	sòh gwā	so4 gwaa1	soh kwa
fool boy	n	傻仔	sòh jái	so4 zai2	soh chai
fool girl	n	傻女	sòh léui /néui	so4 leoi5 /neoi5	soh lowih /nowih
fool man	n	傻佬	sòh lóu	so4 lou5	soh lou
fool woman	n	傻婆	sòh pó	so4 po2	soh pho
foolish[1] /stupid/clumsy	adj	笨拙	bàhn jyuht	ban4 zyut6	pahn chyuht
foolish[2] /stupid/fool/idio	adj	蠢	chéun	ceon2	chhon
foot[1] /ruler/measure	n	尺	chek	cek3	chhek
foot[2] /feet 0.3048 m	n	英尺	yìng chek	jing4 cek3	yeng chhek
foot race /walking race	n	競走	gihng jáu	ging6 zau2	kehng chau
football /goal	n	足球	jūk kàuh	zuk1 kau4	chuk khauh
footbrake	n	腳掣	geuk jai	goek3 zai3	keuk chai
footbridge[1] /overhead bridge	n	行人天橋	hàahng yàhn tīn kiu	hang4 jan4 tin1 kiu3	haahng yahn thin khiu
footbridge[2]	n	人行橋	yàhn hàahng kiu	jan4 hang4 kiu3	yahn haahng khiu
footprint[1]	n	蹤	jùng	zung3	chung
footprint[2]/mark/sign/ trace/track/scar mark	n	跡	jīk	zik1	chek

English	Part	漢字	Romanization	Jyutping	Alt. Romanization
for[1] /to /become/by /because of	prep	為	waih	wai6	waih
for[2] /to /to direction	prep	對	deui	deoi3	toei
for[3] for replace	prep	替	tai	tai3	thai
for[4]	prep	為了	waih líuh	wai6 liu5	waih liuh
for[5]	conj	因為	yàn waih	jan4 wai6	yan waih
for all same /uniformly	adj	一律	yāt leuht	jat1 leot6	yat lwoht
for first time		首次	sáu chi	sau2 ci3	sau chhi
for our /give us	v	比我地	beih ngóh deih	bei6 ngo6 dei6	peih ngoh teih
for pleasure		為了消遣	waih líuh sīu hín	wai6 liu5 siu1 hin2	waih liuh siu hin
for rent[1] /let	n	出租	chēut jòu	ceot1 zou4	chhot chou
for rent[2]		為了租	waih líuh jòu	wai6 liu5 zou4	waih liuh chou
for well		為...好	waih...hóu	wai6...hou2	waih...hou
forbid /prohibit	v	禁	gam	gam3	kam
force[1] /power/strength	n	力	lihk	lik6	lehk
force[2] /might/power /strength	n	力量	lihk lèuhng	lik6 loeng6	lehk leuhng
force[3] /power/strength	n	迫	bīk	bik1	pek
force self control /willpower/strength self-control	n	自制力	jih jai lihk	zi6 zai3 lik6	chih chai lehk
forced labor[1] /servitude	n	苦役	fú yihk	fu2 jik6	fu yehk
forced labor[2] /servitude	n	勞役	lóuh yihk	lou5 jik6	louh yehk
forcibly	adv	強制	kéuhng jai	koeng5 zai3	kheuhng chai
fore part	n	前部	chìhn bouh	cin4 bou6	chhihn pouh
fore finger /index finger	n	食指	sihk jí	sik6 zi2	sehk chi
forearm	n	前臂	chìhn bei	cin4 bei3	chhihn pei
forecast[1] /predict/say future	v	預告	yuh gou	jyu6 gou3	yuh kou
forecast[2] /predict/say future	v	預測	yuh chāk	jyu6 caak1	yuh chhak
forefather[1] /ancestor /grandparents	n	祖	jóu	zou2	chou
forefather[2] /ancestor	n	祖宗	jóu jùng	zou2 zung4	chou chung
forefather[3] /ancestor /ancestry	n	祖先	jóu sìn	zou2 sin4	chou sin
forehead[1]	n	額	aahk /ngaahk	aak6 /ngaak6	aahk /ngaahk
forehead[2]	n	額頭	aahk /ngaahk tàuh	aak6 /ngaak6 tau4	aahk /ngaahk thauh
foreign	adj	外國	oih /ngoih gwok	oi6 /ngoi6 gwok3	oih /ngoih kwok
foreign affairs	n	外交事務	oih /ngoih gāau sih mòuh	oi6 /ngoi6 gwok3 si6 mou6	oih /ngoih kaau sih mouh
foreign country	n	外國	oih /ngoih gwok	oi6 /ngoi6 gwok3	oih /ngoih kwok
foreign currency	n	外匯	oih /ngòih wùih	oi6 /ngoi6 wui6	oih /ngòih wuih
foreign dialect	n	外話	oih /ngoih wá	oi6 /ngoi6 waa2	oih /ngoih wa
foreign lands	n	外地	oih /ngoih deih	oi6 /ngoi6 dei6	oih /ngoih teih
foreign minister	n	外交部長	oih /ngoih gāau bouh jéung	oi6 /ngoi6 gwok3 bou6 zoeng2	oih /ngoih kaau pouh cheung

foreigner[1]	n	外人	oih /ngoih yàhn	oi6 /ngoi6 jan4	oih /ngoih yahn
foreigner[2]	n	外國人	oih /ngoih gwok yàhn	oi6 /ngoi6 gwok3 jan4	oih /ngoih kwok yahn
foreigner[3] no polite	n	番鬼佬	fàan gwái lóu	faan4 gwai2 lou2	faan kwai lou
foreigner woman /westerner woman	n	外國女人	oih /ngoih gwok léuih /néuih yàhn	oi6 /ngoi6 gwok3 leoi5 /neoi5 jan4	oih /ngoih kwok lowih /nowih yahn
foreman[1] /overseer	n	工頭	gùng táu	gung4 tau2	kung thau
foreman[2] (de)	n	科文	fò mán	fo4 man2	fo man
forerunner /pioneer	n	先驅	sìn kēui	sin4 keoi1	sin khoi
foreskin /prepuce	n	包皮	baau pèih /péi	baau3 pei4 /pei2	paau pheih
foreskin pull back	v	捲起包皮	gyún héi bàau pèih	gyun2 hei2 baau4 pei4	kyun hei paau pheih
foreskin remove /circumcise	v	行割禮	hàhng got láih	hang4 got3 lai5	hahng kot laih
forest[1]	n	林	làhm	lam4	lahm
forest[2] /woodland/jungle /woods	n	森林	sàm làhm	sam4 lam4	sam lahm
forest[3] /woods/jungles /trees/woods	n	樹林	syuh làhm	syu6 lam4	syuh lahm
foretell[1] /fortune-teller	n	卜	būk	buk1	puk
foretell[2] /predict /say future	v	預言	yuh yìhn	jyu6 jin4	yuh yihn
foreteller	n	預言家	yuh yìhn gā	jyu6 jin4 ga1	yuh yihn ka
forewarning	n	預先警告	yuh sìn gíng gou	jyu6 sin4 ging2 gou3	yuh sin keng kou
forgery	n	偽造	ngàih chóu	ngai6 cou2	ngaih chhou
forget[1]	v	唔記得	m̀ gei dāk	m4 gei3 dak1	mh kei tak
forget[2] /forgot	v	忘記	mòhng gei	mong4 gei3	mohng kei
forget to see		忘形	mòhng yìhng	mong4 jing4	mohng yehng
forging	n	鍛造	dyun jouh	dyun3 zou6	tyun chouh
forgive /excused	v	原諒	yùhn leuhng	jyun4 loeng6	yuhn leuhng
forgive a sin	v	赦罪	se jeuih	se3 zeoi6	se choih
forgiving[1]	adj	大諒	daaih leuhng	daai6 loeng6	taaih leuhng
forgiving[2]	adj	寬大	fùn daaih	fun4 daai6	fun taaih
forgotten /to forget	adj	遺忘	wàih mòhng	wai4 mong4	waih mohng
fork	n	叉	chā	caa1	chha
fork lift truck	n	叉車	chā chè	caa1 ce4	chha chhe
form[1] /shape/figure	n	表	bíu	biu2	piu
form[2] /shape/model /pattern/to appear	n	形	yìhng	jing4	yehng
form[3] /style	n	體	tái	tai2	thai
form[4] forge	v	結成	git sìhng	git3 sing4	kit sehng
form[5] /style	n	形式	yìhng sīk	jing4 sik1	yehng sek
form[6] /shape	n	形狀	yìhng johng	jing4 zong6	yehng chohng
formal /official /officially	adj	正式	jeng sīk	zeng3 sik1	cheng sek
formal dinner	n	酒席	jáu jihk	zau2 zik6	chau chehk
formality /procedure /order/sequence	n	程序	chìhng jeuih	cing4 zeoi6	chhehng choih

English	POS	Chinese	Yale	Jyutping	Other
formalities /process /procedure	n	手續	sáu juhk	sau2 zuk6	sau chohk
formation[1]/make-up	n	構成	kau sìhng	kau3 sing4	khau sehng
formation[2]/format	n	形成	yìhng sìhng	jing4 sing4	yehng sehng
former	adj	原	yùhn	jyun4	yuhn
former husband	n	前夫	chìhn fùh	cin4 fu4	chhihn fuh
formerly /previously /olden days/old/not new	adj	舊時	gauh sìh	gau6 si4	kauh sih
formula[1]	n	程式	chìhng sīk	cing4 sik1	chhehng sek
formula[2]	n	公式	gùng sīk	gung4 sik1	kung sek
formula[3]	n	方程式	fòng chìhng sīk	cing4 sik1	fong chihehng sek
formula[4]	n	慣用語句	gwaan yuhng yùh geui	gwaan3 jung6 jyu6 geoi3	kwaang yuhng yuh kwoi
fornicate[1]	v	私通	sī tùng	si1 tung4	si thung
fornicate[2] sex before married	v	同居先搞	tùhng gèui sing gaau	tung4 geoi4 sing3 gaau3	thuhng kwoi seng kaau
fort	n	堡壘	bóu léuih	bou2 leoi5	pou lowih
forth /next	ad	來	loìh	loi4	loih
forth-coming	adj	到來	dou làih	dou3 lai4	tou laih
fortnight	n	兩星期	léuhng sèng kèih	loeng5 seng4 kei4	leuhng seng kheih
fortunate /lucky /good luck!	adj	好運	hóu wahn	hou2 wan6	hou wahn
fortune-telling	n	算命	syun mehng /mihng	syun3 ming6 /meng6	syun mehng
forty /fortieth		卌	se	se	se
forum[1]	n	論壇	leuhn tàahn	leon4 taan4	leuhn thaahn
forum[2]	n	廣場	gwóng chèuhng	gwong2 coeng4	kwong chheuhng
forum[3]	n	討論會	tóu leuhn wúi	tou2 leon6 wui2	thou leuhn wui
forum[4]	n	公開討論嘅場所	gùng hòi tóu leun ge chèuhng só	gung4 hoi4 tou2 leon3 ge3 coeng4 so2	kung hoi thou leun ke chheuhng so
forward a letter	v	轉	jyún	zyun2	chyun
further /forward/to promote (an idea)	adv	促進	chūk jeun	cuk1 zeon3	chhuk cheun
forward message	v	轉寄	jyún gei	zyun2 gei3	chyun kei
fossil	n	化石	fa sehk	faa3 sek6	fa sehk
fossil fuel	n	化石燃料	fa sehk yin lìuh	faa3 sek6 jin liu6	fa sehk yin liuh
foul /dirty	adj	骯髒	ōng /ngōng jōng	ong1 /ngong1 jong1	ong /ngong chong
foul violated rule	adj	違反規則	wai fāan kwài jāk	wai3 faan1 kwai4 zak1	wai faan khwai chak
found to get	v	尋得	cham dāk	cam4 dak1	chham tak
found property		財物發現	chòih màht faat yihn	coi4 mat6 faat3 jing6	chhoih maht faat yihn
foundation	n	基礎	gèi chó	gei4 co2	kei chho
founder[1]	n	創辦人	chong baahn yàhn	cong3 baan6 jan4	chhong paahn yahn
founder[2]	n	創立者	chong lahp jé	cong3 lap6 ze2	chhong lahp che
fountain[1] /spring	n	泉	chyùhn	cyun4	chhyuhn
fountain[2] /spring water	n	泉水	chyùhn séui	cyun4 seoi2	chhyuhn swoi
fountain[1]/spring/source	n	噴泉	pan chyùhn	pan3 cyun4	phan chhyuhn
fountain[2]	n	噴水池	pan séui chìh	pan3 seoi2 ci4	phan swoi chhih

English		Chinese	Cantonese	Jyutping	Romanization
fountain[3] /water spring	n	源泉	yùhn chyùhn	jyun4 cyun4	yuhn chhyuhn
fountain pen /pen /ink pan	n	墨水筆	mahk séui bāt	mak6 seoi2 bat1	mahk swoi pat
fountain pen	n	自來水筆	jih loìh séui bāt	zi6 loi4 seoi2 bat1	chih loih swoi pat
four	n	四	sei /sey	sei3	sei /sey
four o'clock	n	四點	sei dīm	sei3 dim1	sei tim
four pair of glasses	n	四副眼镜	sei fú ngáahn géng	sei3 fu2 ngaan5 geng3	sei fu ngaahn keng
fourfooted /cattle	n	家畜	gā chūk	ga1 cuk1	ka chhuk
fourth	n	第四	daih sei	dai6 sei3	taih sei
fox	n	狐狸	wùh léi	wu4 lei4	wuh lei
fraction[1] /score	n	分數	fān sou	fan1 sou3	fan sou
fraction[2]	n	小部分	síu bouh fahn	siu2 bou6 fan6	siu pouh fahn
fracture /snap	n	折斷	jit tyúhn	zit3 tyun5	chit thyuhn
fragile	adj	易碎	yìh seui	ji6 seoi3	yih swoi
fragrant[1]	adj	芳	fòng	fong4	fong
fragrant[2] /smells good	adj	香	hèung	hoeng4	heung
fragrant[3]	adj	芳香	fòng hèung	fong4 hoeng4	fong heung
frail /weak	adj	脆弱	cheui yeuhk	ceoi3 joek6	chheui yeuhk
frame	n	架	gá	gaa2	ka
frame of car	n	車架	chè ga	ce4 gaa3	chhe ka
France	n	法國	faat gwók	faat3 gwok2	faat kwok
franchised bus (as HK) particular privileged buses: KMB, City bus, NWFB, Long Win, NLB etc	n	特權專利 巴士	dahk kyùhn jyūn lèih bā sí	dak6 kyun4 zyun1 lei6 baa1 si2	tahk khyuhn chyun leih pa si
frankly speaking /honestly speaking		老實說	louh saht syut	lou5 sat6 syut3	louh saht syut
fraud /scam/dishonest plan	n	欺詐	hēi ja	hei1 za	hei cha
fraudster	n	欺詐者	hēi ja jé	hei1 zaa3 ze2	hei cha che
freak /strong interest	v	怪物	gwaai maht	gwaai3 mat6	kwaai maht
free[1]	v	漫	maahn	maan6	maahn
free[2]	adv	放	fong	fong3	fong
free from duty /duty off /let go/dismiss duty/free from duty	v	放工	fong gùng	fong3 gung4	fong kung
free hand /let hand	adj	放手	fong sáu	fong3 sau2	fong sau
free of charge	adv	加送	ga sung	gaa3 sung3	ka sung
free port	n	自由港	jih yàuh góng	zi6 jau4 gong2	chih yauh kong
free-spoken[1] /frank /plainspoken	adj	率	sēut	seot1	swut
free-spoken[2] /without trickery/frankly	adv	坦白	táan baahk	taan2 baak6	thaan paahk
free time /unoccupied	adj	閒	hàahn	haan4	haahn
freedom /liberty	n	自由	jih yàuh	zi6 jau4	chih yauh
freely	adv	自由地	jih yàuh deih	zi6 jau4 dei6	chih yauh teih
freeze /frozen	v/adj	結冰	git bìng	git3 bing4	kit peng
freezer[1]	n	冰櫃	bìng gwàih	bing4 gwai6	peng kwaih
freezer[2]	n	冰格	bìng gaak	bing4 gaak3	peng kaak

freezer[3]	n	製冷工	jai láahng gùng	zai3 laang5 gung4	chai laahng kung
freezing	adj	凝固	yìhng gu	jing4 gu3	yehng ku
freezing point	n	凝固點	yìhng gu dím	jing4 gu3 dim2	yehng ku tim
freighter	n	承運人	sìhng wahn yàhn	sing4 wan6 jan4	sehng wahn yahn
French language	adj	法文	faat màhn	faat3 man4	faat mahn
french toast	n	四多士	sei dò sìh	sei3 do4 si6	sei toh sih
french-style dish	n	法國菜	faat gwók chói	faat3 kwok2 coi2	faat kwok chhoi
frequency of radio	n	頻率	pàhn léut	pan4 leot2	phahn lowt
frequent /often /again & again	adj	屢	léuih	leoi5	lowih
frequent	adj	屢次	léuih chi	leoi5 ci6	lowih chhi
frequently[1] /often/daily /constantly/again and again/ time and again/repeatedly	adv	時時	sìh sìh	si6 si6	sih sih
frequently[2]	adv	不時	bāt sìh	bat1 si6	pat sih
frequently[3]	adv	頻繁地	pàhn faan dèih	pan4 faan3 dei6	phahn faan teih
fresh	adj	新鮮	sàn sìn	san4 sin4	san sin
fresh fruit plate	n	生果盤	sàang gwó pun	saang4 gwo2 pun3	saang kwo phun
fresh water[1]	adj	食水	sihk séui	sik6 seoi2	sehk swoi
fresh water[2]	adj	淡水	táahm séui	taam5 seoi2	thaahm swoi
fricative[1] same phonetics tone	n	摩擦	mòh chaat	mo4 caat3	moh chhaat
fricative[2] same phonetics tone	n	摩擦音	mòh chaat yām	mo4 caat3 jam1	moh chhaat yam
Friday[1]	n	禮拜五	láih baai ńg	lai5 baai3 ng2	laih paai ng
Friday[2]	n	星期五	sèng kèih ńg	seng4 kei4 ng2	seng kheih ng
fridge[1] /refrigerator	n	雪櫃	syut gwàih	syut3 gwai6	syut kwaih
fridge[2] /refrigerator	n	電冰箱	dihn bìng sèung	din6 bing4 soeng4	tihn peng seung
fried chicken	n	炸子雞	ja jí gāi	zaa3 zi2 gai1	cha chi kai
fried chicken wings	n	炸雞翼	ja gāi yihk	zaa3 gai1 jik6	cha kai yehk
fried noodles	n	炒麵	cháau mihn	caau2 min6	chhaau mihn
fried rice	n	炒飯	cháau faahn	caau2 faan6	chhaau faahn
friend	n	朋友	pàhng yáuh	faan4 jau5	phahng yauh
friend life		朋友命	pàhng yáuh mehng	pang4 yau5 meng6	phahng yauh mehng
friendless	adj	沒有朋友	muht yáuh pàhng yáuh	mut6 jau5 faan4 jau5	muht yauh phahng yauh
friendly[1] /nice	adj	友善	yáuh sihn	jau5 sing6	yauh sihn
friendly[2]	adj	友好	yáuh hóu	jau5 hou2	yauh hou
friendly[3]	adj	藹	ói /ngói	oi2 /ngoi3	oi /ngoi
friends & relatives		親友	chàn yáuh	can4 jau5	chhan yauh
friendship[1]	n	友誼	yáuh yìh	jau5 ji4	yauh yih
friendship[2]	n	友愛	yáuh oi /ngoi	jau5 oi3 /ngoi3	yauh oi /ngoi
friendship[3] /companion	n	同伴	tùhng buhn	tung4 bun6	thuhng puhn
frighten[1] /scare/terrify	v	駭	háaih	haai5	haaih
frighten[2] /get frightend	v	嚇	haak	haak3	haak

frighten[3]	v	嚇唬	haak fú	haak3 fu2	haak fu
frighten[4]	v	驚恐	gèng húng	geng4 hung2	keng hung
frighten[5]	v	受驚	sauh gèng	sau6 geng4	sauh keng
frighten to death /scared to death	adj	驚死	gèng séi	geng4/ging4 sei2	keng sei
fringe[1] /edge/verge	n	邊緣	bīn yùhn	bin1 jyun4	pin yuhn
fringe[2]	n	緣飾	yùhn sīk	jyun4 sik1	yuhn sek
frog[1]	n	蛙	wáh	waa5	wah
frog[2]	n	青蛙	chèng wā	ceng4 waa5	chheng wa
frog[3]	n	田雞	tìhn gài	tin4 gai4	thihn kai
from[1] /via /passing through	prep	從	chùhng	cung4	chhuhng
from[2]	prep	由	yàuh	jau4	yauh
from[3]	prep	喺	hái	hai2	hai
from[4] /via/through	prep	來自	loìh jih	loi4 zi6	loih chih
from a far		離遠	lèih yúhn	lei4 jyun5	lèih yuhn
from A to Z		從頭至尾	chùhng tàuh ji méih	cung4 tau4 zi3 mei5	chhuhng thauh chi meih
from beginning to end		從頭到尾	chùhng tàuh dou méih	cung4 tau4 dou3 mei5	chhuhng thauh tou meih
from dawn till dusk		從早到晚	chùhng jóu dou	cung4 zou2 dou3 maan5	chhuhng chou tou maahn
from day to day	adv	天天	tìn tìn	tin4 tin4	thin thin
from door to door		每家每戶地	múih gā múih wuh deih	mui5 ga1 mui5 wu6 dei6	muih ka muih wuh teih
from here? (coll)		呢度呢?	lì /nì dòuh lē/nē?	li4 /ni4 dou6 le1/ne1?	li /ni touh le /ne?
from head /from A /from the start		從頭	chùhng tàuh	cung4 tau4	chhuhng thauh
from here[1]		喺呢度	hái li /ni dou	hai2 li3 /ni3 dou3	hai li /ni tou
from here[2]		離呢度	lèih lī, nī douh	lei4 li1, ni1 dou6	leih li, ni touh
from morning till night		從早到晚	chùhng jóu dou máahn	cung4 zou2 dou3 maan5	chhuhng chou tou maahn
from now on[1] /henceforth		從今以後	chùhng gām yíh hauh	cung4 gam1 ji5 hau6	chhuhng kam yih hauh
from now on[2]		從現在開始	chùhng yihn joih hòi chí	cung4 jin6 zoi6 hoi4 ci2	chhuhng yihn choih hoi chhi
from start to finish		自始至終	jih chí ji jùng	zi6 ci2 zi3 jung4	chih chhi chi chung
from time to time[1]		久唔久	gáu m̀ gáu	gau2 m4 gau2	kau mh kau
from time to time[2]		耐不耐	loìh /noih bāt nói	loi6 /noi6 bat1 noi2	loih /noih pat noi
front[1] /ago/before/fore /in front of	adj/n	前	chìhn /cheen	cin4	chhihn /chheen
front[2] /fore/in front of	n	前便	chìhn bihn	cin4 bin6	chhihn pihn
front door	n	前門	chìhn mùhn	cin4 mun4	chhihn muhn
front line	n	前線	chìhn sin	cin4 sin3	chhihn sin
front man	n	負責人	fuh jaak yàhn	fu6 zaak3 jan4	fuh chaak yahn
frontier	n	邊疆	bīn gèung	bin1 goeng4	pin keung
frost	n	霜	sèung	soeng4	seung
frown[1] /scowl /knit the brows	v	眉頭	mèih tàuh	mei4 tau4	meih thauh

English	Part	Chinese	Pronunciation	Jyutping	Romanization
frown[2] /scowl /knit the brows	v	皺起眉頭	jau héi mèih tàuh	zau3 hei2 mei4 tau4	chau hei meih thauh
frown[3]	v	皺眉	jau mèih	zau3 mei4	chau meih
frozen[1]	adj	結咗冰	git jó bìng	git3 zo2 bing4	kit cho peng
frozen[2]	adj	冰凍	bìng dung	bing4 dung3	peng tung
frozen food[1]	n	急凍食物	gāp dung sihk maht	gao1 dung3 sik6 mat6	kap tung sehk maht
frozen food[2]	n	凍結食物	dung git sihk maht	dung3 git3 sik6 mat6	tung kit sehk maht
frozen food[3]	n	冰凍食品	bìng dung sìhk bán	bing4 dung3 sik6 ban2	peng tung sehk pan
frugal[1]	adj	儉	gihm	gim6	kihm
frugal[2]	adj	儉樸	gihm pok	gim6 pok3	kihm phok
fruit[1]	n	果	gwó	gwo2	kwo
fruit[2]	n	生果	sàang gwó	saang4 gwo2	saang kwo
fruit[3]	n	水果	séui gwó	seoi2 gwo2	swoi kwo
fruit juice /juice	n	果汁	gwó jāp	gwo2 zap1	kwo chap
fruit shop	n	生果店	sàang gwō dim	saang1 gwoh2 dim3	saang gwo tim
fruity	adj	水果嘅	séui gwó ge	seoi2 gwo2 ge3	swoi kwo ke
frustrated[1]	adj	谷氣	gūk hei	guk1 hei3	kuk hei
frustrated[2]	adj	沮喪	jēui song	zeoi1 song3	cheui song
frustrating	adj	令人沮喪	lihng yàhn jēui song	ling4 jan4 zoei1 song3	lehng yahn choi song
frustration[1]	n	失敗	sāt baaih	sat1 baai6	sat paaih
frustration[2] feeling	n	受挫感	sauh cho gám	sau6 co3 gam2	sauh cho kam
frustration[3]	n	受折	sauh jit	sau6 zit3	sauh chit
fry[1]	v	炒	cháau	caau2	chhaau
fry[2] with oil/shallow fried	v	煎	jìn /zìn	zin4	chin
fry egg	n	煎蛋	jìn dáan	zin4 daan2	chin taan
Fubon Bank	n	富邦銀行	fu bōng ngàhn hòhng	fu3 bong1 ngan4 hong4	fu pong ngahn hohng
fuck (de) (dw)	n	扑嘢	pok yéh	pok3 je5	phok yeh
fuck you![1] (sl) (dw)	n/dw	嗱	làh /nàh	la4 /na4	lah /nah
fuck you![2] (sl) (vdw) mother-fucker	n	仆街	fuk gàai	fuk3 gaai4	fuk kaai
fuck you![3] (sl) (dw)	n/dw	閪佬	hài lóu	hai4 lou2	hai lou
fucking (dw)	n	屌閪	díu hài	diu2 hai4	tiu hai
fuel	n	燃料	yin lìuh	jin liu6	yin liuh
fuel gauge	n	燃料測量器	yin lìuh chàak lèuhng héi	jin3 liu6 caak4 loeng4 hei2	yin liuh chaak leuhng hei
fulfill (for promise)	v	實踐	saht chín	sat6 cin5	saht chhin
fulfill one's duty		盡責任	jeuhn jaak yahm	zeon6 jaak3 jam6	cheuhn chaak yahm
fulfillment	n	履行	léih hàhng	lei5 hang4	leih hahng
fulfilment	n	滿額	múhn ngàahk	mun5 ngaak6	muhn ngaahk
full[1]	adj	盈	yìhng	jing4	yehng
full[2] /fill	adj/v	裝滿	jòng múhn	zong4 mun5	chong muhn
full[3] /fulled/packed /quite/reach the limit /contented	adj	滿	múhn	mun5	muhn

full house[1] /full seat /no place	n	滿座	múhn joh	mun5 zo6	muhn joh
full house[2]	n	客滿	haak múhn	haak3 mun5	haak muhn
full marks /integer /whole number	n	整數	jing sou	zing3 sou3	cheng sou
full moon	n	望	mohng	mong6	mohng
full of life		生猛	sāang máahng	saang1 maang5	saang maahng
full pay		全薪	chyùhn sān	cyun4 san1	chhyuhn san
full stop[1]	n	句號	geui houh	geoi3 hou6	kwoi houh
full stop[2]	n	句點	geui dím	geoi3 din2	kwoi tim
full stop[3]	n	給...加標	kāp gā biu dím	kap1 ga1 biu3 dim2	khap ka piu tim
full time[1]	adj	長工	chèuhng gùng	coeng4 gung3	chheuhng kung
full time[2]	adj	正職	jeng jīk	zeng4 zik1	cheng jīk
full time[3]	adj	全賃	chyùhn yahm	cyun4 jam6	chhyuhn yahm
full time[4]	adj	全職	chyùhn jīk	cyun4 zik1	chhyuhn jīk
fumble /grope	v	摸索	mó sók	mo2 sok2	mo sok
fun /play/sport/toy /sexual enjoyment	n	玩	wáan	waan2	waan
function[1] /celebration /ceremony	n	典禮	dín láih	din2 lai5	tin laih
function[2] /effect	n	作用	jok yuhng	zok3 jung6	chok yuhng
function[3]	n	功能	gùng làhng /nàhng	gung4 lang4 /nang4	kung lahng /nahng
function[4]	n	職務	jīk mouh	zik1 mou6	chek mouh
function[5]	n	盛大嘅集會	sihng daaih ge jaahp wúi	sing6 daai6 ge3 zaap6 wui2	sehng taaih ke chaahp wui
functional	adj	機能	gèi nàhng	gei4 nang4	kei nahng
fund /funds	n	基金	gèi gàm	gei4 gam4	kei kam
fundamental /main point	adj	綱要	gòng yìu	gong4 jiu4	kong yiu
funds	n	經費	gìng fai	ging4 fai3	keng fai
funeral[1] /rites /funeral rites	n	喪禮	sòng láih	song4 lai5	song laih
funeral[2]	n	葬禮	jong láih	zong3 lai5	chong laih
funeral[3]	n	喪葬	sòng jong	song4 zong3	song chong
funeral home	n	殯儀館	bán yi gūn	ban2 ji3 gun1	pan yi kun
funeral procession	n	出殯	chēut ban	ceot1 ban3	chhot pan
funeral pyre /incinerator	n	焚化爐	fàhn fa lòuh	fan4 faa3 lou4	fahn fa louh
funnel for liquid	n	漏斗	lauh dáu	lau6 dau2	lauh tau
funny[1] /laughable /ridiculous	adj	好笑	hóu siu	hou2 siu3	hou siu
funny[2]	adj	灰諧	fùi hàaih	fui4 haai4	fui haaih
funny[3]	adj	滑稽嘅	gaaht kái ge	gwat6 kai2 ge3	kaaht khai ke
fur[1]	n	皮草	pèih chóu	pei4 cou2	pheih chhou
fur[2]	n	軟毛	yúhn mòuh	jyun5 mou6	yuhn mouh
furnace /oven	n	焗爐	guhk lòuh	guk6 lou4	kuhk louh
furnish /provide	v	供給	gùng kāp	gung4 kap1	kung khap

furnishings shop	n	傢俬店	gā sì dim	gaa1 si4 dim3	ka si tim
furniture[1]	n	傢俱	gā gēui	gaa1 geoi1	ka kwoi
furniture[2]	n	傢俬	gā sì	gaa1 si4	ka si
furrow[1] make by plough	n	犁溝	làih kàu	lai4/nai4 kau4	laih / naih khau
furrow[2] by plough	n	耕地	gàang deih	gaang3 dei6	kaang teih
further	adj	促進	chūk jeun	cuk1 zeon3	chhuk cheun
furthermore /beside	adv	此外	chí oih /ngoih	ci2 oi6 /ngoi6	chhi oih /ngoih
fury[1] /get anger	n	惱	lóuh /nóuh	lou6 /nou6	louh /nouh
fury[2] /get anger	n	狂怒	kòhng louh	kwong4 lou6	khohng louh
fuse /fuze	n	保險絲	bóu hím sī	bou2 him2 si1	pou him si
fusion	n	融合	yùhng hahp	jung4 hap1	yuhng hap
fussy	adj	大驚小怪	daaih gèng síu gwaai	daai6 geng4 siu2 gwaai3	taaih keng siu kwaai
futile /meaningless	adj	徒勞嘅	tòuh lòuh ge	tou4 lou4 ge3	thouh louh ke
future	n	將來	jèung lòih	zoeng4 loi4	cheung loih
future prospect /prospect	n	前途	chìhn tòuh	cin4 tou4	chhihn thouh
future tense[1]	n	將來式	jèung lòih sīk	zoeng4 loi4 sik1	cheung loih sek
future tense[2]	n	將來時	jèung lòih sìh	zoeng4 loi4 si4	cheung loih sih
future tense[3]	n	未來式	meih lòih sīk	mei6 loi4 sik1	meih loih sek

gable /peak of house	n	山牆	sàan chèuhng	saan4 coeng4	saan chheuhng
gadget	n	小機件	síu gèi gihn	siu2 gei4 gin6	siu kei kihn
gagger	n	塞嘴	sāk jéui	sak1 zeoi2	sak choi
gain profit	n	牟利	màuh leih	mau4 lei6	mauh leih
gained	v	獲取	wàih chēui	waai4 ceoi1	waih chhoi
galaxy /milky way	n	銀河	ngàhn hòh	ngan4 ho4	ngahn hoh
gale	n	強風	kèuhng fùng	koeng4 fung4	kheuhng fung
gall bladder	n	膽囊	dáam lòhng /nòhng	daam2 long4 /nong4	taam lohng /nohng
gallery	n	美術館	méih seuht gún	mei5 seot6 gun2	meih swoht kun
gallon (de)	n	加侖	gā léun	ga1 leon2	ka leon
gallstone	n	膽石	dáam sehk	daam2 sek6	taam sehk
galvanize /zinc galvanize	v	鍍鋅	douh sān	dou6 san1	touh san
gamble[1] /to bet money	v	賭錢	dóu chín	dou2 cin2	tou chin
gamble[2] /wager	v	賭博	dóu bok	dou2 bok3	tou pok
gambler[1]	n	賭徒	dóu tòuh	dou2 tou4	tou thouh
gambler[2]	n	爛賭鬼	laahn dóu gwái	laan6 dou2 gwai2	laahn tou kwai
gambler[3]	n	賭客	dóu haak	dou2 haak3	tou haak
gambling lost		輸唔切	syu m̀ chit	syu3 m4 cit1	syu mh chhit
game /recreation	n	遊戲	yàuh hei	jau4 hei3	yauh hei
game hall /indoor sports centre	n	室內運動場	sāt loih /noih wahn duhng chèuhng	sat loi6 /noi6 wan6 dung6 coeng4	sat loih /noih wahn tohng chheuhng
game hide & seek /play hide & seek	n	伏呢呢	fuhk lēi lēi, fuhk nēi nēi	fuk6 lei1 lei1, fuk6 nei1 nei1	fuhk lei lei, fuhk nei nei
gang[1] /group	n	幫	bòng	bong4	pong
gang[2] /group/party	n	一幫	yāt bòng	jat1 bong1	yat pong
gangster[1]	n	匪徒	féi tòuh	fei2 tou4	fei thouh
gangster[2] with gun	n	歹徒	dáai tòuh	daai2 tou4	taai thouh
gangster[3] girl	n	捉黃腳雞	juk wòng geuk gāi	zuk3 wong4 goek3 gai1	chuk wong keuk kai
gangster[4] boy/bad boy	n	古惑仔	gú waahk jái	gu2 waak6 zai2	ku waahk chai
gangster boy /hoodlum /hooligan/punk	n	小流氓	síu làuh màhn	siu2 lau4 man4	siu lauh mahn
gap[1]	n	缺口	kyut háu	kyut3 hau2	khyut hau
gap[2] /hiatus	n	空隙	hùng kwīk	hung4 kwik1	hung khwik
gaping /cave	adj/n	洞穴	duhng yuht	dung6 jyut6	tuhng yuht
garage[1]	n	車房	chè fòhng	ce4 fong4	chhe fohng
garage[2]	n	汽車間	hei chè gaan	hei3 ce4 gaan3	hei chhe kaan
garbage can	n	垃圾桶	laahp saap túng	laap6 saap3 tung2	laahp saap thung
garbage collector /janitor/sweeper	n	清潔工	chēng /chīng git gùng	cing1 /ceng1 git3 gung4	chheng kit kung
garden party	n	園遊會	yùhn yàuh wúi	jyun2 jau4 wui2	yuhn yauh wui
gardener[1]	n	花王	fā wong	faa1 wong3	fa wong
gardener[2]	n	園丁	yùhn dīng	jyun4 ding1	yuhn teng
gargle[1] /mouth rinse /mouthwash	n	嗽口/漱口	sau háu	sau3 hau2	sau hau
gargle[2]	v	漱口水	sau háu séui	sau3 hau2 seoi2	sau hau swoi

garland	n	花環	fā wàahn	faa1 waan4	fa waahn
garland for dead body /holly wreath	n	冬青花環	dūng chèng fā wàahn	dung1 ceng4 faa1 waan4	tung chheng fa waahn
garlic[1] /scallion /spring onion	n	葱	chūng	cung1	chhung
garlic[2]	n	大葱	daaih chūng	daai6 cung1	taaih chhung
garlic[3] white color	n	蒜頭	syun tàuh	syun3 tau4	syun thauh
garlic[4]	n	蒜	syún	syun2	syun
garlic[5] red colored	n	乾葱頭	gòn chūng tàuh	gon4 cung1 tau4	kon chhung thauh
gas[1] /gasoline/petrol/oil	n	汽油	hei yàuh	hei jau4	hei yauh
gas[2]	n	氣體	hei tāi	hei3 tai1	hei thai
gas fire[1]	adj	氣體火災	hei tāi fó jòi	hei3 tai1 fo2 zoi4	hei thai fo choi
gas fire[2]	adj	取暖爐	cheui lyúhn lòuh	ceoi3 lyun5 lou4	chheui lyuhn louh
gas leakage	n	氣體洩漏	hei tāi sit lauh	hei3 tai1 sit3 lau6	hei thai sit lauh
gas pressure		氣壓	hei aat /ngaat	hei3 aat3 /ngaat	hei aat /ngaat
gas repair man	n	煤氣佬	mùih hei lóu	mui4 hei3 lou2	muih hei lou
gas station	n	油站	yàuh jaahm	jau4 zaam6	yauh chaahm
gas stove	n	煤氣爐	mùih hei lòuh	mui4 hei3 lou4	muih hei louh
gasket /washer/ring of rubber	n	墊圈	jin hyūn	zin3 hyun1	chin hyun
gasometer	n	氣體計量器	hei tāi gai lèuhng hei	hei3 tai1 gai2 loeng4 hei3	hei thai kai leuhng hei
gastrology	n	烹飪學	pāang yáhm hohk	paang1 jam5 hok6	phaang yahm hohk
gate[1]	n	門	mùhn	mun4	muhn
gate[2] /doorsill/threshold /door way	n	門口	mùhn háu	mun4 hau2	muhn hau
gate[3]	n	入口	yahp háu	jap6 hau2	yahp hau
gate[4]	n	大門	daaih mun	daai6 mun3	taaih mun
gate[5]	n	出入	chēut yahp	ceot1 lap6	chhot yahp
gate barrier /lock/brake	n	閘	jaahp	zaap6	chaahp
gate open	adj	開閘	hòi jaahp	hoi4 zaap6	hoi chaahp
gate pass	n	閘口紙	jaahp háu jí	zaap6 hau2 zi2	chaahp hau chi
gather /meeting	v	會	wúih	wui5	wuih
gather together[1] /round up assemble	n	聚集	jeuih jaahp	zeoi6 zaap6	cheuih chaahp
gather together[2] /round up	n	聚攏	jeuih lúhng	zeoi6 lung5	cheuih luhng
gather up things		執埋	jāp màaih	zap1 maai4	chap maaih
gather up again		重新繼續	chùhng sàn gai juhk	cung4 san4 gai3 zuk6	chhuhng san kai chohk
gathering	n	集會	jaahp wuih	zaap6 wui6	chaahp wuih
gathers /speed up /to accelerate	n	增速	jàng chūk	zang4 cuk1	chang chhuk
gauge[1]	n	量度器	lèuhng douh hei	loeng4 dou6 hei3	leuhng touh hei
gauge[2]	n	標準規格	bīu jéun kwāi gaak	biu1 zeon2 kwai1 gaak3	piu cheun khwai kaak
gave p.t. of give	v	給咗	kāp jó	kap1 zo2	khap cho
gay sex /bisexual	n	戀性	lyúhn sìng	lyun5 sing3	lyuhn seng

gay sex person /homo	n	同性戀者	tèung sing lyúhn jé	tung4 sing3 lyun5 ze2	thong seng lyuhn che
gaze[1]	n	凝視	yìhng sih	jing4 si6	yehng sih
gaze[2]	n	睇實	tái saht	tai1 sat6	thai saht
gear[1] /gearwheel	n	齒輪	chí lèuhn	ci2 leon4	chhi lowhn
gear[2] of vehicle/ripple	n	波	bō	bo1	po
gear[3] gear no two	n	二波	yih bō	ji6 bo1	yih po
gear[4] /put in gear		入波	yahp bō	jap6 po1	yahp po
gear[5] (of vehicle)	n	排檔	paaih dong	paai6 dong3	phaaih tong
gear shift		波棍	bō gwan	po1 gwan3	po kwan
gearbox /speed changer /transmission	n	變速器	bín chùk héi	bin3 cuk4 hei2	pin chuk hei
geared	n	傳動裝置	chyùhn duhng jōng ji	cyun4 dung6 zong4 zi3	chhyuhn touhng chong chi
female duck /geese	n	雌鵝	chhì ngòh	ci4 ngo6	chhi ngoh
geisha /japanese female entertainer	n	藝妓	aih /ngaih geih	ai6 /ngai6 gei6	aih /ngaih keih
gem /precious stone	n	玉	yuhk	juk6	yuhk
gender /sex	n	性	sing	sing3	seng
genealogical[1]	adj	宗譜	jung póu	zung3 pou2	chung phou
genealogical[2]	adj	族譜	juhk póu	zuk6 pou2	chuhk phou
genealogist	n	系譜學者	haih póu hohk jé	hai6 pou2 hok6 ze2	haih phou hohk che
general /in general	adj	一般	yāt bùn	jat1 bun4	yat pun
general condition of		大致嘅情形	daaih ji ge chìhng yìhng	daai6 zi3 ge3 cing4 jing4	taaih chi ke chehng yehng
general headquarters /headquarter	n	總部	júng bouh	zung2 bou6	chung pouh
general idea		大致嘅意思	daaih ji ge yi si	daai6 zi ge3 ji3 si3	taaih chi ke yi si
general manager /managing	n	總經理	júng gìng léih	zung2 ging4 lei5	chung keng leih
general meeting	n	大會	daaih wúi	daai6 wui2	taaih wui
general office	n	總署	júng chyúh	zung2 cyu5	chung chhyuh
general public	n	普通百姓	póu tùng báak sing	pou2 tung4 baak2 sing3	phou thung paak seng
general visitors	n	一般訪客	yāt bùn fóng haak	jat1 bun4 fong2 haak3	yat pun fong haak
generally /mainly /mostly	adv	主要地	jyú yiu deih	zyu2 jiu3 dei6	chyu yiu teih
generate /producing /yield	v	產生	cháan sàng	caan2 sang4	chhaan sang
generation	n	一代人	yāt doih yàhn	jat1 doi6 jan4	yat toih yahn
generous woman	adj	闊太	fut tài	fut3 taai3	fut thai
genetic	adj	起源的	héi yùhn dīk	hei2 jyun4 dik1	hei yuhn tik
genitals[1]/sexual organs /penis & vagina	n	性器官	sing hei gùn	sing3 hei3 gun4	seng hei kun
genitals[2]/sexual organs /reproductive organ/sexual organs	n	生殖器	sàng jihk hei	sang4 jik6 hei3	sang chehk hei
genius /talent/keen	n	天才	tìn chòih	tin4 coi4	thin chhoih
gentle[1]	adj	柔和	yàuh wòh	jau4 wo4	yauh woh

English	POS	中文	Romanization	Jyutping	Pronunciation
gentle[2]	adj	溫和	wān wòh	wan1 wo4	wan woh
gentle push /light knock/light push	n	輕推	hèng tèui	heng4 teoi4	heng thoi
gentleman /polite	adj/n	紳士	sān sí	san1 si2	san si
Mr /mister/gentleman /sir/respected sir/husband	n	先生	sìn sàang	sin4 sang4	sin saang
gentleman[1]	n	男士	làahm sih	laam4 si6	laahm sih
gentleman[2]	n	男界	làahm gaai	laam4 gaai3	laahm kaai
gentleman farmer	n	鄉紳	hèung sān	hoeng4 san1	heung san
gentlewoman /madam /young lady /Miss/lady/Ms /address for a woman	n	女士	léuih sih	leui5 si6	lowih sih
gently[1] /slowly/gradually	adv	逐漸	juhk jím	juk6 zim2	chuhk chim
gently[2] /softly	adv	溫柔地	wàn yau dèih	wan4 jau3 dei6	wan yau teih
gently[3] /slowly	adv	慢慢嚟	maahn máan làih	maan6 maan2 lai4	maahn maan laih
gently touch /fondle /feel with one's hand	adj/v	摸	mó /mō	mo2 /mo1	mo
genuine[1] /pure	adj	純	sèuhn	seon4	swohn
genuine[2]	adj	真正	jàn jing	zan4 zing3	chan cheng
genuine[3] /truly/sincerely	adv	真誠地	jàn sìhng dèih	zan4 sing4 dei6	chan sehng teih
geography[1]	n	地理	deih léih	dei6 lei5	teih leih
geography[2]	n	地理學	deih léih hohk	dei6 lei5 hok6	teih leih hohk
geologist	n	地質學家	deih jàt hohk gā	dei6 zat1 hok6 ga1	teih chat hohk ka
geology[1]	n	地質	deih jàt	dei6 zat1	teih chat
geology[2]	n	地質情況	deih jàt chìhng fong	dei6 zat1 cing4 fong3	teih chat chehng fong
geomancy /auspicious time/auspicious omen/ auspicious moment	n/adj	風水	fùng séui	fung4 seoi2	fung swoi
geometrically	ad	幾何圖形	géi hòh tòuh yìhng	gei2 ho4 tou4 jing4	kei hoh thouh yehng
geometry[1]	n	幾何	géi hòh	gei2 ho4	kei hoh
geometry[2]	n	幾何學	géi hòh hohk	gei2 ho4 hok6	kei hoh hohk
geothermal power	adj	地熱能	deih yiht làhng/nàhng	dei6 jit6 lang4 /nang4	teih yiht lahng /nahng
germ[1]	n	病菌	behng /bihng kwán	beng6 /bing6 kwan2	pehng khwan
germ[2] /origin	n	起源	héi yùhn	hei2 jyun4	hei yuhn
germ of plant	n	萌芽	màhng ngàh	mang4 ngaa4	mahng ngah
German language	n	德文	dāk màhn	dak1 man4	tak mahn
Germany	n	德國	dàk gwók	dak4 gwok2	tak kwok
gesture[1] /hand signal /motion of hand	n	手勢	sáu sai	sau2 sai3	sau sai
gesture[2] /attitude	n	姿態	jī taai	zi1 taai3	chi thaai
get[1] /obtain	v	得	dāk	dak1	tak
get[2] will/would/shall/future tense	v/aux	將	jéung	zoeng2	cheung
get[3] /take/receive	v	取	chéui	ceoi2	chheui
get[4] /receive/accept	v	受	sauh	sau6	sauh
get[5] /got/gotten/received	v	收到	sàu dóu	sau4 dou2	sau tou

get[6] receive	v	接到	jip dóu	zip3 dou2	chip tou
get[7] /arrive/came/arrive	v	到達	dou daaht	dou3 daat6	tou taaht
get across/overtake /pass/surpass/go over/pass through	v	超過	chìu gwo	ciu4 gwo3	chhiu kwo
get along	v	相處	sèung chyú	seng4 cyu2	seung chyu
get angry	v	生氣	sàang héi	saang4 hei2	saang hei
get away from /escape	v	脫	tyut	tyut3	thyut
get cry (in fear way)	v	得驚呼	dak gèng /gìng fū	dak3 geng4 /ging4 fu1	tak keng fu
get down[1]	v	落	lōk	lok1	lok
get down![2]	v	落嚟呀!	lohk làih ā	lok1 lai4 aa1/aa3	lohk laih aa
get frightend	v	嚇得	haak dāk	haak3 dak1	haak tak
get hold of /grope	v	搞	gáau	gaau2	kaau
get in[1] /let in /insert /thrust	v	插	chaap	caap3	chhaap
get in[2] /penetrate/pierce /pass through	v	透	tau	tau3	thau
get in bus /get in car /ride vehicle	v	踏車	daahp chè	daap6 ce4	taahp chhe
get in car /to take a car	n	搭車	daap chè	daap3 ce1	taap chhe
get involved for aid	v	介入協助	gaai yahp hip joh	gaai3 jap6 hip3 zo6	kaai yahp hip choh
get irritated	v	激怒	gīk làu /nàu	gik1 lau4 /nau4	kek lau /nau
get it	v	收穫	sāu wohk	sau1 wok6	sau wohk
get lost	v	滾	gwán	gwan2	kwan
get marriage /marry/wed	v	結婚	git fàn	git3 fan4	kit fan
get moist /get wet	v	濕哂	sāp saai	sap1 saai3	sap saai
get on boat /aboard	v	上船	seuhng syùhn	soeng5 syun4	seuhng syuhn
get on horse /to mount on horse	v	上馬	séuhng máh	soeng5 maa5	seuhng mah
get out[1]	v	出走	chēut jáu	ceot1 zau2	chhot chau
get out![2] disliked	v	死開	séi hòi	sei2 hoi4	sei hoi
get out from home /leave house	v	出門口	chēut mun háu	ceot1 mun3 hau2	chhot mun hau
get ready /ready /prepared	adj/v	備	beih	bei6	peih
get rice[1]	v	得米	dàk máih	dak4 mai5	tak maih
get rich[2] /wealth /prosperity	n	發財	faat chòih	faat3 coi4	faat chhoih
get rise up /raise/rise /increase	v	奮起	fáhn héi	fan5 hei2	fahn hei
get sex /climb up	v	爬爬	pàh pàh	paa4 paa4	phah phah
get sick[1]	v	病咗	behng /bihng jó	beng6 /bing6 zo2	pehng cho
get sick[2] /be sick	v	有病	yáuh behng	jau5 beng6	yauh pehng
get there	v	達到目	daaht dou muhk	daat6 dou3 muk6	taaht tou muhk
get up[1] /wake up /stand up /stop sleeping/rise	v	起身	héi sàn	hei2 san4	hei san
get up[2] /uprise	v	起床	héi chòhng	hei2 cong4	hei chhohng

English	PoS	Chinese	Romanization 1	Jyutping	Romanization 2
get well soon	v	快啲好番呀	faai dì hóu fàan ā	faai3 di4 hou2 faan4 aa1	faai ti hou faan a
go bad /get worse	v	變壞	bin waaih	bin3 waai6	pin waaih
get worse /gone bad	v	變壞左	bin waaih jó	bin3 waai6 zo2	pin waaih cho
gets	v	獲得	wohk dāk	wok6 dak1	wohk tak
getting anger	v	發脾氣	faat pèih hei	faat3 pei4 hei3	faat pheih hei
getting cold	v	好凍	hóu dung	hou2 dung3	hou tung
ghost[1] /wraith	n	鬼	gwái	gwai2	kwai
ghost[2] /wraith	n	幽靈	yàu lehng	jau4 leng4	yau lehng
ghost house	n	鬼屋	gwái ūk	gwai2 uk1	kwai uk
giant	n	巨人	geuih yàhn	geoi6 jan4	kwoih yahn
gift[1]	n	禮	láih	lai5	laih
gift[2] /present/giving	n	禮物	láih maht	lai5 mat6	laih maht
gift collection		收取禮品	sàu chéui láih bán	sau4 ceoi2 lai5 ban2	sau chhoi laih pan
gigs[1] GB computing/ Giga Byte	n	十億位組	sahp yīk wái jóu	sap6 jik1 wai2 zou2	sahp yik wai chou
gigs[2] GB computing/ Giga Byte	n	十億位元組	sahp yīk wái yùhn jóu	sap6 jik1 wai2 jyun4 zou2	sahp yik wai yuhn chou
gill[1] of fish	n	鰓	sōi	soi1	soi
gill[2]	n	魚鰓	yùh sōi	jyu4 soi1	yuh soi
gill[3] /cheek of man or animals	n	腮	sòi	soi4	soi
gin (de)	n	氈酒	jìn jáu	zin4 zau2	chin chau
ginger	n	薑	gèung	goeng4	keung
ginger tea	n	薑茶	goeng chàh	goeng4 caa6	koeng chhah
girdle /belt/cord fastened round the waist	n	腰帶	yìu dáai	jiu4 daai2	yiu taai
girl[1] /lady/maid	n	女仔	léuih jāi	leui5 zai1	lowih chai
girl[2] of 16 years	n	女兒	léoih /néoih yi	leui5 /neui5 ji3	lowih /nowih yi
girl[3]	n	瓦	ngáh	ngaa5	ngah
girl[4] /young lady	n	娘	lèuhng /nèuhng	loeng4 /noeng4	leuhng /neuhng
girl[5] /young lady /young woman	n	姑娘	gù lèuhng /nèuhng	gu4 loeng4 /noeng4	ku leuhng /neuhng
girl baby	n	女嬰	léoih /néoih yīng	leui5 /neui5 jing1	lowih /nowih yīng
girls and boys!	n	孩子們好	haai jí mùhn hóu	haai3 zi2 mun4 hou2	haai chi muhn hou
give[1] /deliver/pay /hand over	v	交	gàau	gaau4	kaau
give[2] (coll) let/allow	v	畀	béi	bei2	pei
give[3] (coll)	v	比	béi	bei2	pei
give[4] (wr) to give/allow	v	給	kāp	kap1	khap
give[5]	v	予	yùh	jyu4	yuh
give[6]	v	予以	yùh yíh	jyu4 ji5	yùh yih
give a dinner party /give a supper/invite dinner/ give a party	v	請客	chéng /chíng haak	ceng2 /cing2 haak3	chheng haak
give a name first	v	起名	héi méng /míng	hei2 meng2 /ming2	hei meng
give a second name	v	改名	gói méng /míng	goi2 meng2 /ming2	koi meng

give a speech	v	演講	yín góng	jin2 gong2	yin kong
give an example	v	舉例	géui laih	geui2 lai6	kwoi laih
give anger	v	洩憤	sit fahn	sit3 fan5	sit fahn
give away	v	贈送	jahng sung	zang6 sung	chahng sung
give back	v	俾/比返	béi fàan	bei2 faan4	pei faan
give care to younger	v	栽培	jòi pùih	zoi4 pui4	choi phuih
give for man	v	給人	kāp yàhn	kap1 jan4	khap yahn
give instruct /to teach	v	授	sauh	sau6	sauh
give me	v	交俾我	gàau béi ngóh	gaau4 bei2 ngo5	kaau pei ngoh
give me a call	v	俾電話我	béi dihn wá ngóh	bei2 din6 waa2 ngo5	pei tihn wa ngoh
give me a hand/help me	v	幫手	bòng sáu	bong4 sau2	pong sau
give me these	v	俾嗰的我啦	béi gó dī ngóh lā	bei2 go2 di1 ng5 laa1	pei ko ti ngoh la
give me this!		俾我!	béi ngóh!	bei2 ngo5!	pei ngoh!
give New Year's greetings	v	拜年	baai lìhn /nìhn	baai3 lin4 /nin4	paai lihn/nihn
give notice /notice /inform/notify	v	通知	tùng jì	tung4 zi4	thung chi
give present	n	贈	jahng	zang6	chahng
give respect /show respect (aged parents)	v	孝敬	haau ging	haau3 ging3	haau keng
give suck /inhale/intake/taking air	n/v	吸入	kāp yahp	kap1 jap6	khap yahp
give too much food /overfeed	v	給…餵過度	kāp wai gwo douh	kap1 wai3 gwo3 dou6	khap wai kwo touh
give up /stop doing /to give up	v	戒	gaai	gaai3	kaai
give vent to /anger /to show feeling	v	發	faat	faat3	faat
give vent to anger / lust	v	發洩	faat sit	faat3 sit3	faat sit
give way	v	讓步	yeuhng bouh	joeng4 bou6	yeuhng pouh
give you a portion /share with you		分俾你	fān béi léih /néih	fan1 bei2 lei5 /nei5	fan pei leih /neih
give you as a gift		送俾你	sung béi léih /néih	sung3 bei2 lei5 /nei5	sung pei leih /neih
givebirth[1] /birth	v	生	sàang	saang4	saang
givebirth[2] /delivery	v	分娩	fàn míhn	fan4 min5	fan mihn
given	adj	交咗	gàau jó	gaau4 zo2	kaau cho
given to lust /lewd/lustful	adj	好色	hou sīk	hou3 sik1	hou sek
giver[1]	n	俾嘢嘅人	béi yéh ge yàhn	bei2 je5 ge3 jan4	pei yeh ke yahn
giver[2]	n	贈予者	jahng yùh jé	zang6 jyu4 je2	chahng yuh che
giving intructions /go to class	v	上堂	séuhng tòhng	soeng5 tong4	seuhng thohng
glad[1] /happy	adj	喜	héi	hei2	hei
glad[2] /happy/joyful	adj	歡喜	fùn héi	fun4 hei2	fun hei
gladly	adv	高興地	gòu hing deih	gou4 hing3 dei6	kou heng teih
glamor[1]/magic power /spell	n	咒語	jau yúh	zau3 jyu5	chau yuh
glamor[2]/magic power /spell	n	符咒	fùh jau	fu4 zau3	fuh chau

glamor[3] /glamour/lure /charm/spell/magic power/fascination	n	魅力	meih lihk	mei6 lik6	meih lehk
glamor[3] /magic power /spell/spell glamour	n	魔力	mò lihk	mo4 lik6	mo lehk
glances	v	凹下	laap /aāu háh	lap1 /aau1 haa5	laap /aau hah
gland	n	腺	sín	sin2	sin
glass[1]	n	玻璃	bō lei	bo1 lei3	po lei
glass[2] /glasses/optical /spectacle	n	眼鏡	ngáahn géng	ngaan5 geng2	ngaahn keng
glass[3] /cup	n	玻璃杯	bō lei bùi	bo1 lei3 bui4	po lei pui
glass eye	n	假眼	gá ngáahn	gaa2 ngaan5	ka ngaahn
gleam	n	閃光	sīm gwóng	sim1 gwong2	sim kwong
glib /smooth & evasive /slick and sly	adj	圓滑	yùhn wàaht	jyun4 waat6	yuhn waaht
global /universal /worldwide/whole world	adj	全世界	chyùhn sai gaai	cyun4 sai3 gaai3	chhyuhn sai kaai
globe	n	地球儀	deih kàuh yìh	dei6 kau4 ji4	teih khauh yih
globulin	n	球蛋白	kàuh dáan bàahk	kau4 daan2 baak6	khauh taan paahk
gloom /dark	n	暗	am /ngam	am3 /ngam3	am /ngam
glorious /honourable	adj	光榮	gwóng wìhng	gwong2 wing4	kwong wehng
glossary	n	詞彙表	chìh wuih bíu	ci4 wui6 biu2	chhih wuih piu
gloves[1]	n	手套	sáu tou	sau2 tou3	sau thou
gloves[2]	n	手襪	sáu maht	sau2 mat6	sau maht
glow /feverish/emit heat	v	發熱	faat yiht	faat3 jit6	faat yiht
glue[1] /plastic	n	膠	gàau	gaau4	kaau
glue[2]	n	膠水	gàau séui	gaau4 seoi2	kaau swoi
glue[3]	n	黏	lim /nim	lim3 /nim3	lim /nim
glue[4]	n	黏合	lìm /nìm hahp	lim4 /nim4 hap6	lim /nim hahp
glue on	v	黏	lim /nim	lim3 /nim3	lim /nim
glutinous rice /sticky rice/dumplings rice	n	糯米	noh máih	no6 mai5	noh maih
glutton for eat	n	饞嘴	chàahm jéui	caam4 zeoi2	chhaahm choi
GMT UK, Greenwich Mean Time	n	世界時	sai gaai sìh	sai3 gaai3 si4	sai kaai sih
go[1]	v	走啦	jáu lā	zau2 laa1	chau la
go[2] for boy	v	企開	kéi hòi	kei2 hoi4	khei hoi
go[3] for girl	v	瓓開	laahn hòi	laan6 hoi4	laahn hoi
go[4] start to go	v	行開	hàahng hòi	haang4 hoi4	haahng hoi
go[5]	v	通行令	tùng hàahng lihng	tung4 haang4 ling4	thung haahng lehng
go aboard	v	在船上	joih syùhn seuhng	zoi6 syun4 soeng6	choih syuhn seuhng
go ahead	v	走前面	jáu chìhn mìhn	zau2 cin4 min4	chau chhihn mihn
go ahead til end		直去到尾	jihk heui dou méih	zik6 heoi3 dou3 mei5	chehk hoi tou meih
go back[1] /return back	v	回去	wùih heui	wui4 heoi3	wuih hoi
go back[2] /back to /return to back	v/n	返去	fàan heui	faan4 heoi3	faan hoi
go back[3]	v	倒後	dóu hauh	dou2 hau6	tou hauh

go back[4] (sl) move back	v	褪後	toi hauh	toi3 hau6	thoi hauh
go back[5] (sl)	v	退後	teui hauh	teoi3 hau6	thoi hauh
go down	v	落去	lohk heui	lok6 heoi3	lohk hoi
go for	v	從事	chùhng sih	cung4 si6	chhuhng sih
go for honeymoon /honeymoon	v	渡蜜月	douh maht yuht	dou6 mat6 jyut6	touh maht yuht
go for piss[1] (coll) have a wash-room	n	去洗手間	heui sái sáu gàan	heoi3 sai2 sau2 gaan4	hoi sai sau kaan
go for piss[2] (coll) urinating	n	去痾尿	heui ō liuh /niuh	heoi3 o1 liu6 /niu6	hoi o liuh /niuh
go for piss[3] (wr) urinating	n	去撒尿	heui saat liuh /niuh	heoi3 saat3 liu6 /niu6	hoi saat liuh /niuh
go for walk /stroll	v	散步	saan bouh	saan3 bou6	saan pouh
go forward[1]	v	上前	séuhng chìhn	soeng5 cin4	seuhng chhihn
go forward[2]	v	帶往	daai wóhng	daai3 wong5	taai wohng
go from bad to worse	v	越來越壞	yuht lòih yuht waaih	jyut6 loi4 jyut6 waai6	yuht loih yuht waaih
go often	v	常去	sèuhng heui	soeng4 heoi3	seuhng hoi
go on!	n	來呀!	lòih ah!	loi4 a6!	loih ah!
go on foot /go/go fast /leave/run/ walk	v	走	jáu /záu	zau2	chau
go on foot /walk	v	步行	bòuh hàahng	bou6 haang4	pouh haahng
go on strike /strike	v	罷工	bah gùng	baa6 gung4	pah kung
go out[1] /get out /step out/ walk out	v	出去	chēut heui	ceot1 heoi3	chhot hoi
go out[2]	v	出街	chēut gāai	ceot1 gaai1	chhot kaai
go quickly /swiftly /run/hurry	v	馳	chìh	ci4	chhih
go sight-seeing	v	遊覽	yàuh láahm	jau4 laam5	yauh laahm
go smok free		戒咗煙	gaai jó yīn	gaai3 zo2 jin1	kaai cho yin
go straight[1]	v	直行	jihk hàhng	jik6 hang4	chehk hahng
go straight[2]	v	直去	jihk heui	jik6 heoi3	chehk hoi
go straight again	v	再向前行	joi heung chìhn hàahng	zoi3 hoeng3 cin4 haang4	choi heung chhihn haahng
go there	v	去嗰度	heui gó dòuh	heoi3 go2 dou6	hoi ko touh
go through[1] /through/via adj/v		通	tùng	tung4	thung
go through[2] /via go /pass by	v	通行	tùng hàahng	tung4 haang4	thung haahng
go to bed[1] /sleep together	v	上床	séuhng chòhng	soeng5 cong4	seuhng chhohng
go to bed[2] (text) sleep	v	睡覺	seuih gaau	seoi6 gaau3	swoih kaau
go to bed[3] (sl) sleep	v	瞓覺	fan gaau	fan3 gaau3	fan kaau
go to bed[4]	v	就寢	jauh chám	zau6 cam2	chauh chham
go to house /return home	n/v	番屋企	fàan ùk kéi	faan4 uk4 kei2	faan uk khei
go to jail	v	入獄	yahp yuhk	jap6 juk6	yahp yuhk
go to school	v	番學	fàan hohk	faan4 hok6	faan hohk
go to see	v	去睇	heui tái	heoi3 tai2	hoi thai
go to work /on duty	v	番工	fàan gùng	faan4 gung4	faan kung
go up[1] /get on	v	上	séuhng	soeng5	seuhng

English	Part	Chinese	Romanization 1	Jyutping	Romanization 2
go up[2] /to go up	v	上去	séuhng heui	soeng5 heoi3	seuhng hoi
go up[3]	v	走上	jáu seuhng	zau2 soeng5	chau seuhng
go up high priced /inflation/high costly	v	通貨膨脹	tùng fo pàahng jeung	tung4 fo3 paang4 zoeng3	thung fo phaahng cheung
go upstairs	v	上樓去	séuhng lau heui	soeng5 lau3 heoi3	seuhng lau hoi
go walk	v	出去行吓	chēut heui hàahng háh	ceot1 heoi3 haang4 haa5	chhot hoi haahng hah
goal /aim/target/purpose /objective	n	目標	muhk bīu	muk6 biu1	muhk piu
goat[1]	n	山羊	sàan yèuhng	saan4 joeng4	saan yeuhng
goat[2]	n	羊咩	yèuhng mē	joeng4 me1	yeuhng me
goat[3] /lamb/sheep	n	羊	yèuhng	joeng4 me1	yeuhng
goblin /sprite/devil	n	小妖精	síu yìu jèng	siu2 jiu4 zeng4	siu yiu cheng
god[1]	n	天主	tìn jyū	tin4 zyu1	thin chyu
god[2] /lord	n	上帝	séuhng dái	soeng5 dai2	seuhng tai
god[3] Chinese's	n	關帝	gwaan dài	gwaan3 dai4	kwaan tai
god's statue /idol	n	神像	sàhn jeuhng	san4 zoeng6	sahn cheuhng
goes to /road leading to	v	通到	tùng dou	tung4 dou3	thung tou
go towards	n	往	wóhng	wong5	wohng
going	n	離去	leih heui	lei4 heoi3	leih hoi
going down	n	落嚟	lohk làih	lok6 lai4	lohk laih
going down-hill	n	落斜路	lohk che lóu	lok6 ce3 lou6	lohk chhe lou
going to /gonna/shall	n	將要	jéung yiu	zoeng2 jiu3	cheung yiu
gold	n	金	gām	gam1	kam
gold and silver	n	金銀	gām ngàhn	gam1 ngan4	kam ngahn
gold card	n	金卡	gām kāat	gam1 kaat1	kam khaat
gold chain	n	金鍊	gām lín	gam1 lin2	kam lin
gold coast	n	黃金海岸	wòhng gām hói ngòhn	wong4 gam1 hoi2 ngon6	wohng kam hoi ngohn
golden[1]	adj	金質	gām jāt	gam1 zat1	kam chat
golden[2] /golden color	n/adj	金色	gām sīk	gam1 sik1	kam sek
goldfish	n	金魚	gām yú	gam1 jyu2	kam yu
goldsmith[1] /ornamentalist	n	裝飾家	jōng sīk gā	zong1 sik1 gaa1	chong sek ka
goldsmith[2] /ornamentalist	n	飾物師父	sīk maht sì fú	sik1 mat6 si4 fu2	sek maht si fu
golf ball (de)	n	高爾夫球	gòu yíh fù kàuh	gou4 ji5 fu4 kau4	kou yih fu khauh
golf game	n	哥爾夫球	gō yíh fù kàuh	go1 ji5 fu4 kau4	ko yih fu khauh
gone missing	adj	不知去向	bāt jì heui heung	bat1 zi4 heoi3 hoeng3	pat chi hoi heung
gone up /went upstairs		上咗去	séuhng jó heui	soeng6 zo2 heoi3	seuhng cho hoi
gong	n	鑼	lòh	lo4	loh
gonorrhoea /syphilis	n	梅毒	mùih duhk	mui4 duk6	muih tuhk
good[1] /all right/well/nice/ fine/to be close	adj	好	hóu	hou2	hou
good[2] /very much	adj	良	lèuhng	loeng4	leuhng
good afternoon!	int	午安!	ngh òn	ng5 on4/ngon4	ngh on
good & honest /kind hearted	adj	善良	sihn lèuhng	sin6 loeng4	sihn leuhng

good buy	n	好抵	hóu dái	hou2 dai2	hou tai
good day[1] /auspicious day	n	好日子	hóu yaht jí	hou2 jat6 zi2	hou yaht chi
good day[2]	n	日安	yaht hóu	jat6 hou2	yaht hou
good example /model/pattern	adj/n	模範	mòuh faahn	mou4 faan6	mouh faahn
good faith	n	誠懇	sìhng háh	sing4 haa5	sehng hah
good for health[1]	adj	健康嘅	gihn hòng ge	gin6 hong4 ge3	kihn hong ke
good for health[2]	adj	有益嘅	yáuh yīk ge	jau5 jik1 ge3	yauh yek ke
good for health[3] /wholesome/hygiene	adj	衛生	waih sàng	wai6 sang1	waih sang
good health![1] /fitness	n	健康	gihn hòng	gin6 hong4	kihn hong
good health![2]	n	身體健康	sàn tái gìhn hòng	san4 fai2 gin6 hong4	san thai kihn hong
good health![3]	n	精神好好	jìng sàhn hóu hóu	zeng4 san4 hou2 hou2	cheng sahn hou hou
good health![4]	n	敬酒	ging jáu	ging3 zau2	keng chau
good health![5]	n	飲杯	yám bùi	jam2 bui4	yam pui
good health![6]	n	幹杯	gon būi	gon3 bui1	kon pui
good health![7]	n	飲勝	yám sing	jam2 sing3	yam seng
good hearted /kindly/ kindness /good intentions	adj	好心	hóu sàm	hou2 sam4	hou sam
good living standard		小康	síu hòng	siu2 hong4	siu hong
good looking[1] /beautiful/very pretty	adj	好靚	hóu léng	hou2 leng2	hou leng
good looking[2]	adj	好樣	hóu yèuhng	hou2 joeng6	hou yeuhng
good luck![1]	n	福	fùk	fuk4	fuk
good luck![2]		福氣	fūk hei	fuk1 hei3!	fuk hei!
good luck![3]		機緣!	gēi yùhn!	gei1 jyun4!	kei yuhn!
good luck![4]	n	祝你好運	jūk néih hóu wahn	zuk1 nei5 hou2 wan6	chuk neih hou wahn
good man	n	好人	hóu yàhn	hou2 jan4	hou yahn
good manners /well mannered/ritual/etiquette	adj/n	禮節	láih jit	lai5 zit3	laih chit
good morning! greetings for the morning express	int	早晨！	jóu sàhn, (jou san)	zou2 san4, (zou san3)	chou sahn
good natured /politeness/humble/modest /good conduct	adj	謙虛	hìm hèui	him4 heoi4	him hoi
good news	n	好消息	hóu sìu sīk	hou2 siu4 sik1	hou siu sek
good night![1] /good evening!	n	晚安！	máahn òn /ngòn	maan5 on4 /ngon4	maahn on /ngon
good night![2] /greetings	int	早抖！	jóu táu	zou2 tau2	chou thau
good point of view	n	好事成雙	hóu sih sìhng sèung	hou2 si6 sing4 soeng4	hou sih sìhng seung
good sense	n	正確的決...	jing kyut dìk chaak ...	zing3 kyut3 dik4 caak3 ...	cheng khyut tik chhaak ...
good time[1]	n	吉利嘅	gāt leih ge	gat1 lei6 ge3	kat leih ke
good time[2]	n	好意投嘅	hóu yi tàuh ge	hou2 ji3 tau4 ge3	hou yi thauh ke
good view /landscape /lovely scene/lovely view/ scene/scenery	n	風景	fùng gíng	fung4 ging2	fung keng

good weather		好天	hóu tīn	hou2 tin1	hou thin
good will /kindness	n	好意	hóu yi	hou2 ji3	hou yi
good wishes	n	好願望	hóu yuhn mohng	hou2 jyun6 mong6	hou yuhn mohng
goodness	n	善良	sihn lèuhng	sin6 loeng4	sihn leuhng
goods[1]	n	貨	fó	fo2	fo
goods[2] /ware	n	貨物	fo maht	fo3 mat6	fo maht
goose	n	鵝	ngó	ngo2	ngo
goose liver	n	鵝肝	ngó gòn	ngo2 gon4	ngo kon
gorgeous[1] /pompous show /showing more important	adj	架勢	ga sai	gaa3 sai3	ka sai
gorgeous[2] /luxurious	adj	豪華	hòuh wah	hou4 waa6	houh wah
gorilla[1]	n	猩猩	sīng sīng	sing1 sing1	seng seng
gorilla[2]	n	大猩猩	daaih sīng sīng	daai6 sing1 sing1	taaih seng seng
gospel book	n	福音	fūk yam	fuk1 jam3	fuk yam
gossip[1]	n	噏	āp /ngāp	ap1 /ngap1	ap /ngap
gossip[2]	n	是非	sih fēi	si6 fei1	sih fei
gossip[3]	n	講是非	góng sih fēi	gong2 si6 fei1	kong sih fei
gossip[4]	n	閒聊	hàahn lìuh	haan4 liu4	haahn liuh
got problem	v	賴野	laaih yéh	laai6 je5	laaih yeh
got success /success	v	成就	sèhng jauh	seng4 zau6	sehng chauh
got wet (by rain)	v	揉濕	dahp sāp	dap6 sap1	tahp sap
gout	n	痛風	tung fùng	tung3 fung4	thung fung
govern[1] /rule	n	治	jih	zi6	chih
govern[2]	n	治理	jih léih	zi6 lei5	chih leih
government	n	政府	jing fú	zing3 fu2	cheng fu
government branch	n	政府部門	jing fú bouh mùhn	zing3 fu2 bou6 mun4	cheng fu pouh muhn
government office	n	政府合署	jing fú haap chyu	zing3 fu2 hap6 cyu5	cheng fu haap chyu
governor	n	首長	sáu jeung	sau2 zoeng2	sau cheung
grab[1] /snatch	v	搶	chéung	coeng2	chheung
grab[2]	v	拉住	lá jyuh	la2 zyu6	la chyuh
grab[3]	v	攫取	fok chéui	fok3 ceoi2	fok chheui
grace	n	女仔名	léuih jái méng	leui5 zai2 meng2	lowih chai meng
graceful[1] /handsome /elegant/refined	adj	秀	sau	sau3	sau
graceful[2] /exquisite /elegant/fine/tasteful	adj	優美	yàu méih	jau4 mei5	yau meih
grade[1] /rank	v	等	dáng	dang2	tang
grade[2] /level/post/ramk	n/v	級	kāp	kap1	khap
gradually[1] /slowly /take one's time	adv	慢慢	maahn máan	maan6 maan2	maahn maan
gradually[2]	adv	漸漸	jihm jím	zim1 zim2	chihm chim
gradually bigger	v	漸盈	jihm yìhng	zim1 jing4	chihm yehng
like moon					
gradually weaker /wane/fall down/go down /drop down	v	衰落	sèui lohk	seoi4 lok6	swoi lohk

graduate	n	畢業	bāt yihp	bat1 jip6	pat yihp
graduate school	n	研究院	yìhn gau yún	jin6 gau3 jyun2	yihn kau yun
graft	v	移植	yìh jihk	ji4 zik6	yih chehk
grain /food/corn/stuff /material	n	料	líu	liu2	liu
gram /grm	n	克	hàak	haak4	haak
grammar	n	文法	màhn faat	man4 faat3	mahn faat
grammatical	adj	文法嘅	màhn faat ge	man4 faat3 ge3	mahn faat ke
grand person	n	偉大	wáih daaih	waih2 daai6	waih taaih
grand-daughter[1] daughter's	n	外孫	oih /ngoih syùn	oi6 /ngoi6 syun4	oih /ngoih syun
grand-daughter[2] son's	n	孫	syùn	syun4	syun
grand-father[1] husband's grand-father	n	太老爺	tài lóuh yèh	taai4 lou5 je4	thai louh yeh
grand-father[2] father's father	n	爺爺	ye ye	je4 je4	ye ye
grand-father[3] father's father	n	祖父	jóu fuh	zou2 fu6	chou fuh
grand-father[4] mother's father	n	公公	gùng gùng	gung4 gung4	kung kung
grand-father[5] mother's father	n	外公	oih /ngòih gùng	oi6 /ngoi6 gung4	oih /ngoih kung
grand-father[6] mother's father	n	外祖父	òih /ngòih jōu fùh	oi6 /ngoi6 zou1 fu6	oih /ngoih chou fuh
grand-father[7] mother's father	n	老爺	lóuh yèh	lou5 je4	louh yeh
grand-mother[1] /lady	n	婆	pòh	po4	phoh
grand-mother[2] father's mother	n	祖母	jóu móuh	zou2 mou5	chou mouh
grand-mother[3] mother's mother	n	外祖母	oih /ngoih jōu móuh	oi6 /ngoi6 zou1 mou5	oih /ngoih chou mouh
grand-mother[4] mother's mother	n	婆婆	pòh po	po4 po3	phoh pho
grand-mother[5] father's mother	n	嫲嫲	ma ma	maa3 maa3	ma ma
grand-mother[6] husband's grand-mother	n	太奶奶	tài lai lai	taai3 laai3 laai3	thai lai lai
grand-parents	n	祖父母	jóu fùh móuh	zou2 fu6 mou5	chou fuh mouh
grand-son /son's son	n	孫仔	syùn jái	syun4 zai2	syun chai
grant /approved	v	批准	pài jéun	pai4 zeon2	phai cheun
granulated sugar	n	沙糖	sà tòhng	saa4 tong4	sa thohng
grape[1]	n	提子	tai jī	tai3 zi1	thai chi
grape[2]	n	葡提子	pòuh tàih jí	pou4 tai4 zi2	phouh thaih chi
grape fruit[1] Chine pomelo	n	沙田柚	sà tìhn yáu	saa4 tin4 jau2	sa thihn yau
grape fruit[2]	n	西柚	sài yáu	sai4 jau2	sai yau
graphic	adj	圖解	tòuh gáai	tou4 gaai2	thouh kaai
grasp[1] /hold	v	持	chi	ci3	chhi
grasp[2] /to pick/to pluck	v	執	jàp	zap4	chap

grasp[3]/fluency/know well	v	掌握	jéung āak /ngāak	zoeng2 ak1 /aak1	cheung aak /ngaak
grasshopper	n	蚱蜢	ja máang	zaa3 maang5	cha maang
grate	n	鐵欄	tít laan	tit3 laan3	thit laan
grateful /thankful /obliged	adj	感激	gám gīk	gam2 gik1	kam kek
gratuity	n	小帳	síu jeung	siu2 zoeng3	siu síu jeung
grave /tomb	n	墳	fàhn	fan4	fahn
grave	n	墓穴	koi yuht	koi3 jyut6	khoi yuht
gravel[1]	n	鋪石仔	pòu sehk jái	pou4 sek6 zai2	phou sehk chai
gravel[2]	n	礫石	līk sehk	lik1 sek6	lek sehk
gravels /rock	n	石仔	sehk jái	sek6 zai2	sehk chai
gravitational energy	n	萬有引力	maahn yáuh yáhn lihk	maan6 jau5 yan5 lik6	maahn yauh yahn lehk
gravity[1]	n	地心吸力	deih sàm kap lihk	dei6 sam4 kap3 lik6	teih sam khap lehk
gravity[2] /gravitation	n	重力	chúhng lihk	cung5 lik6	chhuhng lehk
gravy /juice/sauce /liquid/ sap	n	汁	jāp	zap1	chap
gray /grey/ash color	adj	灰色	fūi sīk	fui1 sik1	fui sek
graze[1]	v	牧牛	muhk ngàuh	muk6 ngau4	muhk ngauh
graze[2]	v	食草	sihk chóu	sik6 cou2	sehk chhou
graze[3]	v	牧羊	muhk yèuhng	muk6 joeng4	muhk yeuhng
grazier[1] /shepherd	n	牧人	muhk yàhn	muk6 jan4	muhk yahn
grazier[2]	n	畜牧者	chūk muhk jé	cuk1 muk6 ze2	chhuk muhk che
grazing	n	食草	sihk chóu	sik6 cou2	sehk chhou
grease /lubricant oil	n	潤滑油	yeuhn waaht yàuh	jeon6 waat6 jau4	yeuhn waaht yauh
greasy[1]	adj	油膩	yàuh leih	jau4 lei6/nei6	yauh leih
greasy[2]	adj	油污嘅	yàuh wù ge	jau4 wu4 ge3	yauh wu ke
great desire /highly ambitious	v	夠志氣	gau ji hei	gau3 zi3 hei3	kau chi hei
great earthquake	n	大地震	daaih deih jan	daai6 dei6 zan3	taaih teih chan
great lakes	n	北美五大湖	bàak méih ńgh daaih wùh	baak4 mei5 ng5 dai6 wu4	paak meih ngh taaih wuh
great person	n	偉人	wáih yàhn	waih2 jan4	waih yahn
great respect[1] /honourable	adj	尊重	jyùn juhng	zyun4 zung6	chyun chuhng
great respect[2] /honourable	adj	敬重	ging juhng	ging3 zung6	keng chuhng
great respect[3]	adj	恭敬嘅	gùng ging ge	gung4 ging3 ge3	kung geng ke
great respect[4] /reverent	adj	非常尊敬	fèi sèuhng jyūn ging	fei4 soeng4 zyun1 ging3	fei seuhng chyun geng
great suffering /tribulation	n	磨難	mòh laahn /naahn	mo4 laan6 /naan6	moh laahn /naahn
great wall of China	n	長城	chèuhng sèhng	coeng4 seng4	chheuhng sehng
great war	n	大戰	daaih jin	daai6 zin3	taaih chin
greatest /biggest	adj	最大	jeui daaih	zeoi3 daai6	cheui taaih
greedier /luster	n	渴望者	hot mohng jé	hot3 mong6 ze2	hot mohng che
greedy[1]	adj	貪心	tàam sàm	taam4 sam4	thaam sam

greedy[2] for money	adj	貪錢	tàam chín	taam4 cin2	thaam chhin
greedy[3] for food/glutton	adj	為食	waih sihk	wai6 sik6	waih sehk
greedy[4]	adj	貪婪嘅	tàam làahm ge	taam4 laam6 ge3	thaam laahm ke
greedy for	adj	餓	ngoh	ngo6	ngoh
green	n	綠	luhk	luk6	luhk
green color	n	綠色	luhk sīk	luk6 sik6	luhk sek
green apple	adj	青蘋果	chèng pìhng gwó	ceng4 ping4 gwo2	chheng phihng kwo
green tea	adj	綠茶	luhk chàh	luk6 caa4	luhk chhah
greener	adj	青	chèng	ceng4	chheng
greenhouse effect	n	溫室效應	wān sāt haauh yīng	wan1 sat1 haau6 jing1	wan sat haauh yeng
greet /to pay respects to	v	致敬	ji ging	zi3 ging3	chi keng
greet /hello!	v	招呼	jiu fù	ziu1 fu4	chiu fu
greeting card	n	賀卡	hoh ká	ho6 kaa2	hoh kha
greetings![1]	v	迎接	yìhng jip	jing4 zip3	yehng chip
greetings[2]/welcome /welcoming/reception	v/adj	歡迎	fùn yìhng	fun4 jing4	fun yehng
grid /barrier	n	欄柵	laahn saan	laan4 saan3	laahn saan
grid lines	n	標線	bīu sin	biu1 sin3	piu sin
grief[1]	n	傷心事	sèung sàm sih	soeng4 sam4 si6	seung sam sih
grief[2]	n	悲	bèi	bei4	pei
grievance	n	不滿	bāt múhn	bat1 mun5	pat muhn
grieve[1]	v	悲哀	bèi òi	bei4 oi1	pei oi
grieve[2]/great sadness /condolence/mourn/great disappointment/lamentaion/ weeping in somebody death	n/v	哀悼	òi /ngòi douh	oi4 /ngoi4 dou6	oi /ngoi touh
grill[1] /barbecue	v	燒烤	sìu hàau	siu4 haau4	siu haau
grill[2] /fireplace	n	烤架	hàau gá	haau4 gaa2	haau ka
grill[3] /tortured questions	v	拷問	hāau mahn	haau1 man6	haau mahn
grill pork /roast pork	n	叉燒	chā sìu	caa4 siu4	chha siu
grind[1]	v	磨	mòh	mo4	moh
grind[2]	v	研	yìhn	jin4	yihn
grinder	n	研磨器	yìhn	jin4	yihn
grindstone	n	石磨	sehk mò	sek6 mo4	sehk mo
grip[1] /hold tightly	v	緊抓	gán jáau	gan2 zaau2	kan chaau
grip[2] hold tightly	v	緊握	gán àak	gan2 aak4	kan aak
grisly	adj	可怕嘅	hó pa ge	ho2 paa3 ge3	ho pha ke
groan[1] /moan/hum	n	吟	ngàhm	ngam4	ngahm
groan[2] /moan/hum make a long deep sound for suffering or sexual pleasure	n	呻	sān	san1	san
groan[3] /moan sounds	n	呻吟聲	sān ngàhm sèng	san1 ngam4 seng4	san ngahm seng
grocer	n	雜貨商	jaahp fo sèung	zaap6 fo3 soeng4	chaahp fo seung
groceries	n	雜貨	jaahp fo	zaap6 fo3	chaahp fo
groceries store	n	雜貨店	jaahp fo dim	zaap6 fo3 dim3	chaahp fo tim
groceries shop	n	雜貨舖	jaahp fo póu	zaap6 fo3 pou2	chaahp fo phou

groom /bridegroom	n	新郎	sàn lòhng	san4 long4	san lohng
groping sexually an act	v	猥褻	wúi sit	wui2 sit3	wui sit
gross[1] /total	n	總	júng	zung2	chung
gross[2] /totally/total	adv	總共	júng guhng	zung2 gung6	chung kuhng
gross[3] /total/overall amount	adv	總量	júng leuhng	zung2 loeng6	chung leuhng
gross[4] /144 pc	n	十二打	sàhp yìh dā	sap6 ji6 da1	sahp yih ta
ground[1] /field/land/earth /ground/place/floor/story/ surface	n	地	deih	dei6	teih
ground[2]	n	地面	deih mín	dei6 min2	teih min
ground[3] /based on	n	根據	gàan gèui	gaan4 geoi4	kaan kwoi
ground pepper /pepper	n	胡椒粉	wùh jìu fán	wu4 ziu4 fan2	wuh chiu fan
groundless	adj	毫無根據	hòuh mòuh gān geui	hou4 mou4 gan1 geoi3	houh mouh kan kwoi
group[1]	n	社	séh	se5	seh
group[2] /team	n	班	bàan	baan4	baan
group[3] /small group /faction	n	派	pàai	paai4	phaai
group[4]	n	會	wúih	wui5	wuih
group[5] /team	n	隊	déui	deui2	toei
group[6]	n	群體	gwàn tái	gwan4 tai2	kwan thai
group[7]	n	小組	síu jóu	siu2 zou2	siu chou
group of men /flock of men/collection	n	一群人	yāt kwàhn yàhn	jat1 kwan4 jan4	yat khwahn yahn
group work[1]	n	一班人	yāt bàan yàhn	jat1 baan4 jan4	yat paan yahn
group work[2] /teamwork	n	幫手做嘢	bòng sáu jouh yéh	bong4 sau2 zou6 je5	pong sau chouh yeh
group work[3] /teamwork	n	協同工作	hip tùhng gùng jok	hip3 tung4 gung4 zok3	hip thuhng kung chok
grow[1] plant	v	種	jéung	zung2	cheung
grow[2]	v	增長	jàng jéung	zang4 zoeng2	chang cheung
grow beard	v	留鬚	làuh sōu	lau4 sou1	lauh sou
grow fat /loose fitting	v	肥	fèih	fei4	feih
grow up[1] /rise	v	長大	jéung daaih	zoeng2 daai6	cheung taaih
grow up[2] /grew	v	成長	sèhng jéung	seng2 zoeng2	sehng cheung
growing up /keep on growing	v	生生不息	sàang sàang bāt sīk	saang4 sang4 bat1 sik1	saang sang pat sek
growl /to shout	n	咆哮	paau hāau	paau4 haau1	phaau haau
grown-up /adult of man	n	成人	sèhng yàhn	seng4 jan4	sehng yahn
growth[1] body, plant	n	生長	sàng jéung	sang4 zoeng2	sang cheung
growth[2] population /enhancement	n	增加	jàng gā	zang4 gaa1	chang ka
growth[3]	n	發育	faat yuhk	faat3 juk	faat yuhk
grumble[1] /murmur /humming	v	吟吟沈沈	ngàhm ngàhm chàhm chàhm	ngam4 ngam4 cam4 cam4	ngahm ngahm chhahm chhahm

grumble[2] /chattering /nag/idle talker/criticize continuous	v	囉嗦	lō sò	lo1 so4	lo so
grumble[3]	v	抱怨	póuh yun	pou5 jyun3	phouh yun
guarantee	n	確保	kok bóu	kok3 bou2	khok pou
guarantor /sponsor /bailor	n	保證人	bóu jing yàhn	bou2 zing3 jan4	pou cheng yahn
guarantor	n	擔保人	dàam bóu yàhn	daam4 bou2 jan4	taam pou yahn
guard[1] /security	n	保安員	bóu on yùhn	bou2 on3 jyun4	pou on yuhn
guard[2] /security	n	警衛員	gíng waih yùhn	ging2 wai6 jyun4	keng waih yuhn
guard[3]	v	把守	bāa sáu	baa1 sau2	paa sau
guard[4] /security	n	護衛員	wuh waih yùhn	wu6 wai6 jyun4	wuh waih yuhn
guard post /security post	n	警衛室	gíng waih sāt	ging2 wai6 sat1	keng waih sat
guardian (legal)	n	監護人	gaam wuh yàhn	gam3 wu6 jan4	kaam wuh yahn
guardless	adj	無人看管	móuh yàhn hōn gún	mou5 jan4 hon1 gun2	mouh yahn hon kun
guava	n	番石榴	fàan sehk làuh	faan4 sek6 lau4	faan sehk lauh
guava juice	n	番石榴汁	fàan sèhk lau jàp	faan4 sek6 lau4 zap4	faan sehk lau chap
guess	v	猜測	chàai chāak	caai4 caak1	chhaai chaak
guest[1] /visitor	n	賓	bān	ban1	pan
guest[2] /visitor /polite way	n	來賓	lòih bān	loi4 ban1	loih phan
guest[3] /visitor	n	人客	yàhn haak	jan4 haak3	yahn haak
guest room	n	款客室	fún haak sāt	fun2 haak3 sat1	fun haak sat
guest's opinion	n	客人嘅意見	haak yàhn ge yi gin	haak3 jan4 ge3 ji3 gin3	haak yahn ke yi gin
guest worker	n	款客工人	fún haak gùng yàhn	fun2 haak3 gung4 jan4	fun haak kung yahn
guesthouse	n	賓館	bān gún	ban1 gun2	pan kun
guidance	n	指導	jí douh	zi2 dou6	chi touh
guide[1]	n	指引	jí yáhn	zi2 jan5	chi yahn
guide[2] /lead	n	導	douh	dou6	touh
guide[3] for tourist	n	導遊	douh yàuh	dou6 jau4	touh yauh
guide[4]	n	嚮導	douh hèung	dou6 hoeng4	touh heung
guide book	n	旅行指南	léuih hàhng jí làahm /nàahm	leoi5 hang4 zi2 laam4 /naam4	lowih hahng chi laahm /naahm
guide dog	n	導盲犬	douh màahng hyún	dou6 maang4 hyun2	touh maahng hyun
guidelines book /booklet	n	指導方針	jí douh fōng jám	zi2 dou6 fong1 zam2	chi touh fong cham
guiding	adj	領導	léhng /líhng douh	leng5 /ling5 dou6	lehng touh
guiltless /innocent	n	無辜	móuh gū	mou5 gu1	mouh ku
guilty	adj	有罪	yáuh jeuih	jau5 zeoi6	yauh cheuih
guitar (de)	n	結他	git tā	git3 taa1	kit thah
gulf	n	分歧	fàn kèih	fan6 kei4	fan kheih
gum[1] /resin	n	樹脂	syuh jì	syu6 zi4	syuh chi
gum[2] /resin	n	松香	chùhng hèung	cung4 hoeng4	chhuhng heung
gum[3]	n	樹膠	syuh gàau	syu6 gaau4	syuh kaau
gum[4] of tooth	n	牙肉	ngàh yuhk	ngaa4 juk6	ngah yuhk

gun /rifle/pistol	n	槍	chèung	coeng4	chheung
gunner	n	槍手	chèung sáu	coeng4 sau2	chheung sau
gunpowder	n	火藥	fó yeuhk	fo2 joek6	fo yeuhk
gutter[1] for run dirty water /drain/drainpipe	n	坑渠	hāang kèuih	haang1 keoi4	haang khoih
gutter[2]	n	排水溝	pàaih séui kàu	paai4 seoi2 kau4	phaaih swoi khau
guy /lad/laddie/young boy	n	小伙子	síu fó jí	siu2 fo2 zi2	siu fo chi
gymnasium[1]	n	體育館	tái yùhk gūn	tai2 juk6 gun1	thai yùhk gūn
gymnasium[2]	n	健身房	gihn sàn fòhng	gin6 san4 fong4	kihn san fohng
gymnast	n	體操運動員	tái chòu wahn duhng yùhn	tai2 cou4 wan6 dung6 jyun4	thai chhou wahn tohng yuhn
gymnastics /sports /recreation	n	運動	wahn duhng	wan6 dung6	wahn tohng
gymnastics	n	體操	tái chòu	tai2 cou4	thai chhou
gynaeceum	n	婦女嘅房間	fúh léuih /néuih ge fóng gàan	fu5 leui5 /neui5 ge3 fong2 gaan4	fuh lowih /nowih ge fong kaan
gynecology[1] /gynaecology	n	婦科學	fúh fò hohk	fu5 fo4 hok6	fuh fo hohk
gynecology[2]	n	婦科	fúh fò	fu5 fo4	fuh fo

English	Part	漢字	Romanization 1	Jyutping	Romanization 2
ha! ha!	int	哈	hā	ha6	ha
habit[1] /perfecting /usual practice	n	習慣	jaahp gwaan	zaap6 gwaan3	chaahp kwaan
habit[2] /habitude/character /conduct/nature/behaviour	n	心經	sàm gíng	sam4 ging2	sam keng
habit[3] /accustomed	adj/n	習以為常	jaahp yíh wàih sèuhng	zaap6 ji5 wai4 soeng4	chaahp yih waih seuhng
habitant	n	居住者	gèui jyuh jé	geoi4 zyu6 ze2	kwoi chyuh che
habitat /inhabit	n	棲	chai	cai1	chhai
habitation[1] /abode/home	n	住所	jyuh só	zyu6 so2	chyuh so
habitation[2] /reside	n/v	居住	gèui jyuh	geoi4 zyu6	kwoi chyuh
habitual /current custom/ to be used	adj	習慣	jaahp gwaan	zaap6 gwaan3	chaahp kwaan
habitually	adv	習慣地	jaahp gwaan deih	zaap6 gwaan3 dei6	chaahp kwaan teih
habituated	adj	使習慣於	sai jaahp gwaan yū	sai3 zaap6 gwaan3 jyu1	sai chaahp kwaan yu
hack	v	文丐	màhn koi	man4 koi3	mahn khoi
hacker [(de)] computing data	n	黑客	hāak haak	haak1 haak3	haak haak
had /p.t. of have	v	已經	yíh gìng	ji5 ging4	yih keng
haemoglobin /hemoglobin	n	血色素	hyut sīk sou	hyut3 sik1 sou3	hyut sek sou
haemorrhage	v	大出血	daaih chēut hyut	daai6 ceot1 hyut3	taaih chhot hyut
hail /hailstone/ice balls	n	冰雹	bìng bòhk	bing4 bok6	peng pohk
hainan chicken rice	n	海南雞米	hōi naam gài máih	hoi1 naam3 gai4 mai5	hoi naam kai maih
hair[1] fine (wool)	n	毛	mòuh	mou4	mouh
hair[2] on the head	n	頭髮	tàuh fáat	tau4 faat2	thauh faat
hair[3]	n	毛髮	mòuh fáat	mou6 faat2	mouh faat
hair clip long size	n	髮鉗	faat kím	faat3 kim2	faat khim
hair of fingers	n	手毛	sáu mòuh	sau2 mou4	sau mouh
hair of nostrils	n	鼻毛	bèih mòuh	bei6 mou4	peih mouh
hair pin[1]	n	頂夾	déng gíp	deng2 gio2	teng kip
hair pin[2]/hair clip short	n	髮夾	faat gíp	faat3 gip2	faat kip
hair pin[3] /hair clip	n	束髮夾	chūk faat gip	cuk1 faat3 gip3	chhuk faat kip
hair salon[1]/salon shop	n	髮型屋	faat yìhng ùk	faat3 jing4 uk4	faat yehng uk
hair salon[2]	n	髮型鋪	faat yìhng pou	faat3 jing4 pou3	faat yehng phou
haircut[1] for man	n	飛髮	fēi faat	fei1 faat3	fei faat
haircut[2] for lady	n	剪頭髮	jín tàu faat	zin2 fau4 faat3	chin thau faat
haircut[3]	n	理髮	léih faat	lei5 faat3	leih faat
hairdresser	n	美髮師	méih faat sì	mei5 faat3 si4	meih faat si
hairdryer	n	吹風機	cheui fùng gèi	ceoi3 fung4 gei4	chheui fung kei
hairstyle	n	髮型	faat yìhng	faat3 jing4	faat yehng
hairstylist	n	髮型師	faat yìhng sī	faat3 jing4 si1	faat yehng si
Haka language	n	圍頭話	wàih tàuh wá	wai4 tau4 waa2	waih thauh wa
hale /healthy old person	adj	大隻	daaih jek	daai6 zek3	taaih chek
half[1] /semi	n	半	bun	bun3	pun
half[2] /one half	n	一半	yāt bun	jat1 bun3	yat pun
half day		半日	bun yaht	bun3 jat6	pun yaht

English		Chinese	Romanization	Jyutping	Alt
half hour[1]	n	半個鐘	bun gó jùng	bun3 go2 zung4	pun ko chung
half hour[2]	n	半小時	bun síu si	bun3 siu2 si3	pun siu si
half past three /three thirty		三點半	sàam dím bun	saam1 dim2 boon3	saam tim pun
half price[1]	adj	半價	bun ga	bun3 ga3	pun ka
half price[2]	adj	半票	bun píu	bun3 piu2	pun phiu
half-brain		真古怪	jān gú gwaai	jan1 gu2 gwaai3	chan ku kwaai
half-senseless /hypnotize	v	催眠	chèui mìhn	ceoi4 min4	chheui mihn
half-share	n	半股份	bun gú fán	bun3 gu2 fan2	pun ku fan
halfway[1]	adv	中間點	jùng gàan dím	zung4 gaan4 dim2	chung kaan tim
halfway[2]	adv	在嘅中間	joih ge jùng gàan	joi6 ge3 zung4 gaan4	choih ke chung kaan
half-yearly	adj	半年	bun lihn /nihn	bun3 lin4 /nin4	pun lihn /nihn
hall[1] /large room /big room	n	堂	tòhng	tong4	thohng
hall[2] /reception /sitting room	n	廳	tèng	teng4	theng
halloween (night of 31 oct)	n	萬聖節	maahn sing jit	maan6 sing3 zit3	maahn seng chit
halt[1] /stop	v	停下	tìhng hah	ting4 haa6	thehng hah
halt[2] /pause/to suspend		暫停	jaahm tìhng	zaam6 ting4	chaahm thehng
ham	n	火腿	fó téui	fo2 teoi2	fo thoi
hammer	n	鎚仔	chèuih jái	ceoi4 zai2	chheuih chai
hammock /cot/swing bed	n	吊床	diu chòhng	diu3 cong4	tiu chhohng
hand	n	手	sáu	sau2	sau
hand bag[1]	n	手袋	sáu dói	sau2 doi2	sau toi
hand bag[2]	n	手提包	sáu tàih bāau	sau2 tai4 baau1	sau thaih paau
hand baggage	n	手提行李	sáu tàih hàhng léih	sau2 tai4 hang4 lei5	sau thaih hahng leih
hand brake[1] of the vehicle	n	手掣	sáu jai	sau2 zai3	sau chai
hand brake[2]	n	手制動	sáu jai duhng	sau2 zai3 dung6	sau chai tohng
hand cuffs	n	手銬	sáu kaau	sau2 kaau3	sau khaau
hand in hand	n	手拉手	sáu lāai sáu	sau2 laai1 sau2	sau laai sau
hand luggage	n	旅行袋	léuih hàhng dói	leoi5 hang4 doi2	lowih hahng toi
hand over[1] /to give /to pass	n	遞	daih	dai6	taih
hand over[2]	n	交代	gàau doih	gaau4 doi6	kaau toih
hand over[3]	n	交俾	gàau béi	gaau4 bei2	kaau pei
hand over[4]	n	交出	gàau chēut	gaau4 ceot1	kaau chhot
hand rise	v	起手	héi sáu	hei2 sau2	hei sau
handed		有手	yáuh sāu	jau5 sau1	yauh sau
hand towel /handkerchief	n	手巾	sáu gàn	sau2 gan4	sau kan
handkerchief[1]	n	手巾仔	sáu gàn jái	sau2 gan4 zai2	sau kan chai
handkerchief[2]	n	手帕	sáu paak	sau2 paak3	sau phaak
handle[1] (coll) ear of the handle	n	耳	yíh	ji5	yih
handle[2] /shaft	n	柄	beng	beng3	peng

handle[3] of the railing /handrail	n	扶手	fùh sāu	fu6 sau1	fuh sau
handle[4] of elevator	n	升降機扶手	sìng gong gèi fùh sáu	sing4 gong3 gei4 fu6 sau2	seng kong kei fuh sau
handle[5] of elevator	n	電梯槽	dihn tài chòuh	din6 tai4 cou4	tihn thai chhouh
handle[6] /deal/cope with /deal with	v	應付	ying fuh	jing3 fu6	yeng fuh
handle knob[1] /lug	n	把手	bā sáu	ba1 sau2	pa sau
handle knob[2]	n	手抽	sáu chāu	sau2 cau1	sau chhau
handlebar	n	手把	sáu bá	sau2 ba2	sau pa
handling[1]	n	對待	deui dòih	deui3 doi6	toei toih
handling[2] /dealings /of debate	v	對付	deui fuh	deui3 fu6	toei fuh
handling of emergencies	n	緊急事故	gán gāp sih gu chyú	gan2 gap1 si6 gu3 cyu2	kan kap sih ku chhyu
handling office	n	辦公	baahn gūng	baan6 gung1	paahn kung
handmade	adj	手製	sáu jai	sau2 zai3	sau chai
handover /deliver/give /pay	n/v	付	fuh	fu6	fuh
handsaw	n	手鋸	sáu geui	sau2 geoi3	sau kwoi
handshake	n	握手	āk /āak sáu	ak1 /aak1 sau2	ak /aak sau
handsome	adj	英俊	yìng jeun	jing4 zeon3	yeng cheun
handsome boy!	n	靚仔!	leng jái	leng3 zai2	leng chai
handstand	n	倒立	dou lahp	dou3 lap6	tou lahp
handwork	n	手工嘅	sáu gùng ge	sau2 gung4 ge3	sau kung ke
handwriting	n	筆跡	bāt jīk	bat1 zik1	pat chek
handwritten /manuscript	adj	手寫	sáu sé	sau2 se2	sau se
handy /portable /hand carry	adj	手提	sáu tàih	sau2 tai4	sau thaih
hang[1] /suspend	v	吊	diu	diu3	tiu
hang[2] /to suspend	v	挂起	kwa héi	kwa3 hei2	khwa hei
hang[3] /suspend	v	懸掛	yùhn kwa	jyun4 kwaa3	yuhn khwa
hang[4] death by...	v	吊死	diu séi	diu3 sei2	tiu sei
hang glidingly	n	懸掛式滑翔運動	yùhn kwa sìk waaht chèuhng wahn duhng	jyun4 kwaa3 sik4 waat6 coeng4 wan6 dung6	yuhn khwa sek waaht chheuhng wahn tohng
hang off phone stop	v	掛斷	gwa túhn	gwaa3 tyun5	kwa thuhn
hang on /pull	v	攀	pāan	paan1	phaan
Hang Seng Bank	n	恒生銀行	hàhng sàng ngàhn hòhng	hang4 sang4 ngan4 hong4	hahng sang ngahn hohng
hang sex (sl)	v	龍舟掛鼓	lùhng jau kwa gú	lung4 zau3 gwaa3 gu2	luhng chau khwa gu
hang up[1]	v	吊下面	diu hah mihn	diu3 haa6 min6	tiu hah mihn
hang up[2]	v	挂起	gwa héi	gwaa3 hei2	kwa hei
hang up[3]	v	掛斷電話	gwa túhn dihn wá	gwaa3 tyun5 din6 waa2	kwa thuhn tihn wa
hanging[1]	v	掛著嘅	gwa jeuk ge	gwa3 zoek3 ge3	kwa cheuk ke
hanging[2] /execute	n	絞刑	gáau yìhng	gaau2 ying6	kaau yehng
hanging basket	v	吊花籃	diu fā làahm	diu3 faa1 laam4	tiu fa laahm

happen /occurred	v	發生	faat sàng	faat3 sang4	faat sang
happen at same time /synchronized/same time happen	v	同時發生	tùhng si fáat sàng	tung4 si3 faat2 sang4	thuhng si faat sang
happen soon	v	禍不單行	wóh bāt dāan hàhng	wo5 bat1 daan1 hang4	woh pat taan hahng
happening incident	n	事件	sih gín	si6 gin2	sih kin
happy[1]	adj	歡	fùn	fun4	fun
happy[2] /cheerful	adj	樂	lohk	lok6	lohk
happy[3] /glad	adj	開心	hòi sàm	hoi4 sam4	hoi sam
happy[4] /pleasant	adj	愉快	yu fáai	jyu3 faai2	yu faai
happy[5] /fortunate/lucky	adj	幸運	hahng wahn	hang6 wan6	hahng wahn
happy[6] /lucky	adj	有福氣	yáuh fūk hei	jau5 fuk1 hei3	yauh fuk hei
happy birthday!	adj	生日快樂!	sàang yàht fáai lohk	saang4 jat6 faai2 lok6	saang yaht faai lohk
Happy Easter Sunday	adj	復活節快樂	Fuhk wuht jit faai lohk	Fuk6 wut6 zit3 faai3 lok6	Fuhk wuht chit faai lohk
happy feeling /pleasure feeling/be touching	adj	令人感動	lihng yàhn gám duhng	ling4 jan4 gam2 dung6	lehng yahn kam tohng
happy journey	adj	旅途愉快	léuih tòuh yùh faai	leoi5 tou4 jyu4 faai3	lowih thouh yuh faai
Happy New Year![1] /happy anniversary	adj	新年快樂	sàn lìhn /nìhn faai lohk	san4 lin4 /nin4 faai3 lok6	san lihn /nihn faai lohk
Happy New Year![2]	adj	拜年	baai lìhn /nìhn	baai3 lin4 /nin4	paai lihn /nihn
Happy New Year![3] Chinese	adj	恭喜發財	gùng hēi faat chòih	gung4 hei1 faat3 coi4	kung hei faat chhoih
happy to /fain/glad to /pleasure to	adj	樂意	lohk yi	lok6 ji3	lohk yi
harass	v	不斷騷擾	bāt dyuhn sòu yíu	bat1 dyun6 sou4 jiu2	pat tyuhn sou yiu
harassment[1] by touching	n	非禮	fèi láih	fei4 lai5	fei laih
harassment[2]	n	騷擾	sòu yíu	sou4 jiu2	sou yiu
harbor city /port	n	港市	góng síh	gong2 si5	kong sih
harbour	n	海港	hói góng	hou2 gong2	hoi kong
hard[1] /strong/solid	adj	固	gu	gu3	ku
hard[2] /firmly	adj	堅固	gīn gu	gin1 gu3	kin ku
hard[3] /stiff/tough	adj	硬	ngaahng	ngaang6	ngaahng
hard[4] /tough/solid	adj	堅硬	gīn ngaahng	gin1 ngaang6	kin ngaahng
hard[5] /tough	adj	韌	ngàhn	ngan6	ngahn
hard[6] /try hard	adv	努力地	lóuh /nóuh lìhk deih	lou5 /nou5 lik6 dei6	louh /nouh lehk teih
hard & cruel /ruthless	adj	殘忍	chāan yán	caan1 jan2	chhaan yan
hard drink	adj	烈酒	liht jáu	lit6 zau2	liht chau
hard palate	n	上顎	séuhng ngòhk	soeng5 ngok6	seuhng ngohk
hard shoulder vehicles /stoping lane for emergency	n	路肩	louh gìn	lou6 gin4	louh kin
hard to	adj	難以	làahn yíh	laan4 ji5	laahn yih
hard working /strive /exert oneself	adj/v	奮	fáhn	fan5	fahn
hard working person (coll)	n	牛	ngàuh	ngau4	ngauh

English		Chinese	Yale	Jyutping	Pinyin-style
harden	v	使變得堅固	sái bin dāk gīn gu	sai2 bin3 dak1 gin1 gu3	sai pin tak kin ku
hardly /difficulty	adv	艱難地	gāan làahn /nàahn	gaan1 laan4 /naan4 dei6	kaan laahn /naahn teih
hardship[1] /to endure /to bear	n	忍受	yáhn sauh	jan5 sau6	yahn sauh
hardship[2]	n	受苦	sauh fú	sau6 fu2	sauh fu
hardship[3] /difficulty	n	艱難	gāan làahn /nàahn	gaan1 laan4 /naan4	kaan laahn /naahn
hardship[4]	n	艱苦	gāan fú	gaan1 fu2	kaan fu
hardware[1]	n	五金器具	ńgh gām hei geuih	ng5 gam1 hei3 geoi6	ngh kam hei kwoih
hardware[2] computer	n	硬體	ngaahng tái	ngaang6 tai2	ngaahng thai
hardworking	adj	努力工作	lóuh /nóuh lìhk gùng jok	lou5 /nou5 lik6 gung4 zok3	louh /nouh lehk kung chok
harm[1] /damage	n	害處	hoih chyu	hoi6 cyu3	hoih chyu
harm[2] /injured/wounded	v	損害	syún hoih	syun2 hoi6	syun hoih
harm[3] /injure	v	傷害	sèung hoih	soeng4 hoi6	seung hoih
harmful /injurious	adj	有害	yáuh hoih	jau5 hoi6	yauh hoih
harmless	adj	無害	mòuh hoih	mou4 hoi6	mouh hoih
harmonica	n	口琴	háu kàhm	hau2 kam4	hau khahm
harmonious[1]	adj	諧	hàaih	haai4	haaih
harmonious[2]	adj	和諧	wòh haai	wo4 haai3	woh haai
harmonious[3]	adj	和聲	wòh sèng	wo4 seng4	woh seng
harmony[1]	n	調和	tìuh wòh	tiu4 wo4	thiuh woh
harmony[2] music	n	和聲	woh sìng	wo6 sing4	woh seng
harmony[3] /co-ordination /combination	n	和諧	wòh haai	wo4 haai3	woh haai
harmony[4] persons	n	融洽	yùhng hahp	jung4 hap1	yuhng hap
harmony[5]	n	和	wòh	wo4	woh
harmony[6] /tranquility	n	安	òn /ngòn	on4 /ngon4	on /ngon
harp	n	豎琴	syuh kàhm	syu6 kam4	syuh khahm
harsh	adj	嚴酷	yìhm huhk	jim4 huk6	yihm huhk
harvest	n	穫	wohk	wok6	wohk
has /have/having	axu/v	有	yáuh	jau5	yauh
has gone out[1] /went out	n	出咗去	chēut jó heui	ceot1 zo2 heoi3	chhot cho hoi
has gone out[2] /went out		出咗去啦!	chēut jó heui lā!	ceot1 zo2 heoi3 la1!	chhot cho hoi la!
has lost /miss/lose anything	n/v	失去	sāt heui	sat1 heoi2	sat hoi
has won	adj	勝利嘅	sing leih ge	sing3 lei6 ge3	seng leih ke
hasn't /no/not/not be/do not have/not have/not any/ sans/haven't/without/un...	adv	冇 / 無	móuh	mou5	mouh
haven't /hasn't/without /not have /not be/doesn't exist [(coll)]	axu/v	沒有	muht yáuh	mut6 jau5	muht yauh
hasp /latch/hinge	n	門塞	mùhn sāk	mun4 sak1	muhn sak
haste[1]	n	急	gāp	gap1	kap
haste[2]	n	衝忙	chùng mòhng	cung4 mong4	chhung mohng

hasten /hurry/rush /promote	n	促	chūk	cuk1	chhuk
hasty /rash	adj	輕率	hèng sèut	heng4 seot4	heng swut
hat /cap	n	帽	mòuh	mou6	mouh
hatch[1] breeding	v	孵	fù	fu4	fu
hatch[2] breeding	v	孵化	fù fa	fu4 fa3	fu fa
hatch[3] draw a line	v	劃影線	wàahk yēng sín	waak6 jeng1 sin2	waahk yeng sin
hatchet /handy axe	n	短柄小斧	dyún beng /bing síu fú	dyun2 beng3 /bing3 siu2 fu2	tyun peng siu fu
hate[1] /drtest	v	憎	jàng	zang4	chang
hate[2]	v	低	dài	dai4	tai
hates[1] /scorn	v	睇低	tái dài	tai2 dai4	thai tai
hates[2]	v	睇唔起	tái m̀ héi	tai2 m4 hei2	thai mh hei
hates[3]	v	恨	hahn	han6	hahn
hateful	adj	可恨	hó hahn	ho2 han6	ho hahn
hateful boy (sl)	n	白鴿眼	baahk gáp ngáahn	baak6 gap2 ngaan5	paahk kap ngaahn
hated /hatred	n	猛憎	máng jáng	maang2 zang2	mang chang
hatred[1]	n	怨恨	yun hahn	jyun3 han6	yun hahn
hatred[2] /hates	n	恨怨	hahn yun	han6 jyun3	hahn yun
haulage vehicle	n	運輸	wahn syù	wan6 syu4	wahn syu
have	v/aux	擁有	yúng yáuh	jung2 jau5	yung yauh
have a chance		有機會	yáuh gèi wuih	jau5 gei4 wui6	yauh kei wuih
have a cold		傷風	sèung fùng	soeng4 fung4	seung fung
have a command of /to control/mastering	n	掌握	jéung āk	zoeng2 ak1	cheung ak
have a dream	n	發夢	faat muhng	faat3 mung6	faat muhng
have a fun	adj	玩得開心	waan dak hòi sàm	waan3 dak3 hoi4 sam4	waan tak hoi sam
have a good day[1]		玩得開心啲	waan dak hòi sàm dì	waan3 dak3 hoi4 sam4 di4	waan tak hoi sam te
have a good day[2]		開心嘅一日	hòi sàm ge yāt yaht	hoi4 sam4 ge3 jat1 jat6	hoi sam ke yat yaht
have a good holiday		節日愉快	jit yaht yu fáai	zit3 jat6 jyu3 faai2	chit yaht yu faai
have a good memory		好記性	hóu gei sing	hou2 gei3 sing3	hou kei seng
have a good night		睡得好	seuih dak hóu	seoi6 dak3 hou2	swoih tak hou
have a good time[1]		玩得好開心	waan dak hóu hòi sàm	waan3 dak3 hou2 hoi4 sam4	waan tak hou hoi sam
have a good time[2]		玩得高興	waan dak	waan3 dak3	waan tak
have a guess!	n	猜測看	chàai chāak hòn	caai4 caak1 hon4	chhaai chaak hon
have a look[1]		睇睇	tái tāi	tai2 tai1	thai thai
have a look[2]		看一看	hōn yāt hōn	hon1 jat1 hon1	hon yat hon
have a look![3] /let's see!	v	睇吓先	tái háa sin!	tai2 haa2 sin3!	thai haa sin!
have a meeting /hold meeting/sit meeting /start meeting	v	開會	hòi wúi	hoi4 wui2	hoi wui
have a picnic	n	舉行野餐	geui hàhng yéh chàan	geoi3 hang4 je5 caan4	kwoi hahng yeh chhaan
have a reunion[1]		團聚	tyùhn jeuih	tyun4 zeoi6	thyuhn choih

have a reunion[2] /reunion	n	重聚	chùhng jeuih	cung4 zeoi6	chhuhng choih
have a seat /sit down /take a seat!	n	坐下	chóh hah	co5 ha6	chhoh hah
have a shock /mentally shock		受刺激	sauh chi gīk	sau6 ci3 gik1	sauh chhi kek
have a stool		開大	hòi daaih	hoi4 daai6	hoi taaih
have altogether		共同擁有	guhng tùhng úng /yúng yáuh	gung1 tung4 ung2 /jung2 jau5	kuhng thuhng ung /yung yauh
have authority		有權	yáuh kyùhn	jau5 kyun4	yauh khyuhn
have been told		已被告知	yíh beih gou jī	ji5 bei6 gou3 zi1	yih peih kou chi
have erection of penis	v	勃起 (男人)	buht héi (làahm/nàahm yàhn)	but6 hei2 (laam4 /naam4 jan4)	puht hei (laahm/naahm yahn)
have free time /relaxation/leisure	n	得閒	dāk hàahn	dak1 gaan4	tak haahn
have goods		有貨	yáuh fo	jau5 fo3	yauh fo
have indigestion		食滯咗	sihk jaih jó	sik6 zai6 zo2	sehk chaih cho
have job		有嘢做	yáuh yéh jouh	jau5 je5 zou6	yauh yeh chouh
have little bit /has little bit	adv	一啲都有	yāt di dōu yáuh	jat1 di3 dou1 jau5	yat ti tou yauh
have not /no/not	n	沒	muht	mut6	muht
have nothing to do /it's nothing/never mind/ not important	v	沒事兒	muht sih yi	mut6 si6 ji3	muht sih yi
have or not?[1]		有冇?	yáuh móuh?	jau5 mou5?	yauh mouh?
have or not?[2]		有冇呀?	yáuh móuh aa?	jau5 mou5 aa3?	yauh mouh aa?
have problem[1]		有問題	yáuh mahn tàih	jau5 man6 tai4	yauh mahn thaih
have problem[2] (sl)		鑊鑊甘	wohk wohk gām	wok6 wok6 gam1	wohk wohk kam
have sex[1]		交媾	gāau kau	gaau1 kau3	kaau khau
have sex[2] (sl) /copulate	v xy	攪嘢	gáau yéh	gaa2 je5	kaau yeh
have to[1] /want/wanna /need/must/should	v/aux	要	yiu	jiu3	yiu
have to[2] /necessary /needs/shall/must	v/aux	必須	bìt sèui	bit4 seoi4	pit swoi
have to do[1]		有做	yáuh jouh	jau5 zou6	yauh chouh
have to go[2] /go there /must go	v	要過去	yiu gwo heui	jiu3 gwo3 heoi	yiu kwo hoi
have to see		有見	yáuh gin	jau5 gin3	yauh kin
have you eaten yet?		食咗飯未呀?	sihk jó faahn meih aa ?	sik6 zo2 faan6 mei6 aa3?	sehk cho faahn meih aa?
having	n	擁有	yúng yáuh	jung2 jau5	yung yauh
having fond	adj	享受	héung sauh	hoeng2 sau6	heung sauh
having register	v	登記緊	dàng gei gán	dang4 gei3 gan2	tang kei kan
hawker	n	叫賣小販	gíu maaih síu fáan	giu2 maai6 siu2 faan2	kiu maaih siu faan
hay	n	乾草	gòn chóu	gon4 cou2	kon chhou
hazard /risk	n	風險	fùng hím	fung4 him2	fung him
hazardous	adj	危險	ngàih hīm	ngai4 him1	ngaih him
he[1] /her /his /she (coll)	n/pron	佢	kéuih /héuih	keoi5 /heoi5	khoih /hoih

English		Chinese	Cantonese	Jyutping	Yale
he[2] /him (wr)	pron	他	tā	taa1	tha
he also[1]		佢都	kéuih dōu	keoi5 dou1	khoih tou
he also[2]		佢亦	kéuih yihk	keoi5 jik6	khoih yehk
he also[3]		他也	tā yá	taa1 jaa5	tha ya
he also fine		佢都好	kéuih dōu hóu	keoi5 dou1 hou2	khoih tou hou
he asked me		佢問我	kéuih mahn ngóh	keoi5 man6 ngo5	khoih mahn ngoh
he is not here		佢唔喺度	kéuih m̀ hái douh	keoi5 m4 hai2 dou6	khoih mh hai touh
he is very fast		佢好快	kéuih hou faai	keoi5 hou3 faai3	khoih hou faai
he is very sad		佢好傷心	kéuih hou séung sàm	keoi5 hou3 soeng2 sam4	khoih hou seung sam
he said		有佢話	yauh kéuih wá	jau5 keoi5 waa2	yauh khoih wa
head[1]	n	頭顱	tàuh lòuh	tau4 lou4	thauh louh
head[2]	n	頭部	tàuh bouh	tau4 bou6	thauh pouh
head[3] /leader/monitor	n	班長	bàan jéung	baan4 zoeng2	paan cheung
head district	n	總區	júng kèui	zung2 keoi4	chung khoi
head itchy /headache /head scar	n	頭痕	tàuh hàhn /hán	tau4 han4 /han2	thauh hahn /han
head light	n	頭燈	tàuh dàng	tau4 dang4	thauh tang
head of political party /party leader	n	党魁	dóng fùi	dong2 fui4	tong fui
head of the family /parent/guardian	n	家長	gā jéung	gaa1 zoeng2	ka cheung
head of the party	n	首腦	sáu lóuh /nóuh	sau2 lou5 /nou5	sau louh /nouh
head of turtle	n	龜頭	gwāi tàuh	gwai1 tau4	kwai thauh
head office	n	總公司	júng gūng sī	zung2 gung1 si1	chung kung si
head position	n	最高首長	jeui gōu sáu jéung	zeoi3 gou1 sau2 zoeng2	cheui kou sau cheung
headache	n	頭痛	tàuh tung	tau4 tung3	thauh tung
heading[1] /subject/topic	n	題	tàih	tai4	thaih
heading[2] /subject/title /topic	n	題目	tai mùhk	tai3 muk6	thai muhk
headline	n	頭條	tàuh tìuh	tau4 tiu4	thauh thiuh
headphone	n	頭戴式耳機	tàuh daai sīk yíh gèi	tau4 daai3 sik1 ji5 gei4	thauh taai sek yih kei
headrest	n	靠頭物	kaau tàuh maht	kaau3 tau4 mat6	khaau thauh maht
headroom	n	淨高	jehng gòu	zeng6 gou4	chehng kou
headscarf	n	頭巾	tàuh gān	tau4 gan1	thauh kan
headstrong[1] (sl)	adj	硬頸	ngaahng géng	ngaang6 geng2	ngaahng keng
headstrong[2] /obstinate /self-willed/willful	adj	難理掂	làahn léih dihm	laan4 lei5 dim6	laahn leih tihm
health & safety	n	職業安全	jīk yihp òn /ngòn	zik1 jip6 on4 /ngon4	chek yihp on /ngon
health center	n	保健處	bóu gihn chyu	bou2 gin6 cyu3	pou kihn chhyu
health check-up		體格檢查	tái gaak gím chàh	tai2 gaak3 gim2 caa4	thai kaak kim chhah
health dept	n	醫管局	yī gún guhk	ji1 gun2 guk6	yi kun kuhk
health department /hygiene department/ health bureau	n	衛生署	waih sàng chyúh	wai6 sang4 cyu5	waih sang chhyuh
health /healthy /wholesome	n/adj	健康	gihn hòng	gin6 hong4	kihn hong

heap[1] /pile/lot	n	疊	daahp	daap6	taahp
heap[2] /accumulate /pile up	n	褶	dihp	dip6	tihp
heap[3] /accumulate /pile up	n	堆積	dèui jīk	deoi4 zik1	toei chek
heap[4] /pile/lot/whole lot	n	一批啦	yāt pài lā	jat1 pai4 laa1	yat phai la
hear /listen	v	聽	tèng	teng4	theng
hear news /listen news	v	聽取	tèng chéui	teng4 ceoi2	theng chhoi
hearer /listener	n	聽者	tèng jé	teng4 ze2	theng che
hearing[1]	n	風聞	fùng màhn	fung4 man4	fung mahn
hearing[2] (in a court)	n	聽證會	tèng jing wúi	teng4 zing3 wui2	theng cheng wui
hearing power	n	聽力	tèng lihk	teng4 lik6	theng lehk
hearsay[1]	n	聽返嚟	tèng fàan làih	teng4 faan4 lai4	theng faan laih
hearsay[2] /much noise	n	吐霧	tou mouh	tou3 mou6	thou mouh
hearsay[3] /piece of story /rumour	n	傳聞	chyùhn màhn	cyun4 man4	chhyuhn mahn
heart[1] /mind	n	心	sàm	sam4	sam
heart[2]	n	心臟	sàm jòhng	sam4 zong6	sam chohng
heart attack /heart flare-up	n	心臟病發作	sàm jòhng bèhng faat jok	sam4 zong6 beng6 faat3 zok3	sam chohng pehng faat chok
heart beat	n	心跳	sàm tiu	sam4 tiu3	sam thiu
heart broken[1] /sad /poignant	adj	傷心	sèung sàm	soeng4 sam4	seung sam
heart broken[2]	adj	心碎	sàm seui	sam4 seoi3	sam swoi
heart disease[3]	n	心臟病	sàm jòhng bèhng	sam4 zong6 beng6	sam chohng pehng
heart disease patient	n	心臟病病人	sàm jòhng bèhng bèhng yan	sam4 zong6 beng6 beng6 jan3	sam chohng pehng pehng yan
heart valves	n	心瓣	sàm fàahn	sam4 faan6	sam faahn
heartless	adj	無情	móuh chìhng	mou5 cing4	mouh chhehng
heat /heating	n	加熱	gà yiht	ga4 jit6	ka yiht
heat wave	n	熱浪	yiht lohng	jit6 long6	yiht lohng
heater for water	n	熱水爐	yiht séui lòuh	jit6 seoi2 lou4	yiht swoi louh
heaters	n	加熱器	gà yiht hei	ga4 jit6 hei3	ka yiht hei
heaven[1] /God/God's home	n	天	tìn	tin4	thin
heaven[2] /paradise /God's home	n	天堂	tìn tòhng	tin4 tong4	thin thohng
heaven[3] /God's home	n	得道升仙	dāk douh sīng sīn	dak1 dou6 sing1 sin1	tak touh seng sin
heaven[4] /God's home	n	上天堂	seuhng tìn tòhng	soeng6 tin4 tong4	seuhng thin thohng
heaven[5]/God's home /kingdom of heaven	n	天國	tìn gwok	tin4 gwok3	thin kwok
heavier /weighty	adj	重的	chúhng dìk	cung5 dik4	chhuhng tek
heavy[1] /weight	adj	重	chúhng	cung5	chhuhng
heavy[2]	adj	重量	chúhng leuhng	cung5 loeng6	chhuhng lowhng
heavy[3] /large caliber	adj	重型	chúhng ying	cung5 jing4	chhuhng yeng
heavy drinking	adj	酗酒	yu jáu	ju zau	yu chau

heavy vehicles	n	重型車輛	chúhng ying chè leuhng	cung5 jing4 ce4 loeng6	chhuhng yeng chhe lowhng
heavy wheel /flywheel (of the engine)	n	飛輪	fèi lèuhn	fei4 leon4	fei lowhn
hedge	n	樹籬	syuh lèih	syu6 lei4	syuh leih
heel[1] of foot	n	腳後	geuk hauh	goek3 hau6	keuk hauh
heel[2] of foot/ankle	n	腳跟	geuk gàn	goek3 gan4	keuk kan
height[1] /altitude	n	高度	gòu douh	gou4 dou6	kou touh
height[2] /of person	n	身高	sàn gòu	san4 gou4	san kou
heighten	v	加高	gà gòu	ga4 gou4	ka kou
heinous	adj	可憎嘅	hó jāng ge	ho2 zang1 ge3	ho chang ke
heir /successor/legal right/right person	n	繼承人	gai sìhng yàhn	gai3 sing4 jan4	kai sehng yahn
held of hold	v	堅持	gīn chìh	gin1 ci4	kin chhih
helicopter[1]	n	直升機	jihk sìng gēi	zik6 sing4 gei1	chehk seng kei
helicopter[2]	n	直升飛機	jihk sìng fèi gēi	zik6 sing4 fei4 gei1	chehk seng fei kei
hell /underworld/infernal	n	地獄	deih yuhk	dei6 juk6	teih yuhk
hello![1] /hey! /hi! (de)	int	哈佬	hā lóuh	ha6 lou5	ha louh
hello![2] on the phone	int	喂!	wái	wai2	wai
helly down	n	危險狀態	ngàih hīm jòhng táai	ngai4 him2 zong6 taai3	ngaih him chohng thaai
helmet	n	頭盔	tàuh kwài	tau4 kwai4	thauh khwai
help /support/assist	n	幫	bòng	bong4	pong
help me[1]	n	幫我	bòng ngóh	bong4 ngo5	pong ngoh
help me![2]	n	救命!	gau mèhng!	gau3 meng3!	kau mehng!
helped	n	幫咗	bōng jó	bong1 zo2	pong cho
helpless[1] /miserable /pitiful/pitiable/wretched	adj	可憐	hó lìhn	ho2 lin6	ho lihn
helpless[2] /unaided	adj	無助	móuh jòh	mou5 zo6	mouh choh
helpless[3] a person	adj	孤弱者	gù yeuhk jé	gu4 joek6 ze2	ku yeuhk che
helplessness	n	無能為力	móuh làhng /nàhng waih lihk	mou5 lang4 /nang4 wai6 lik6	mouh lahng /nahng waih lehk
hem /folded edge /crease of cloth	n	褶邊	jip bīn	zip bin1	chip pin
hemisphere /semicircle	n	半球	bun kàuh	bun3 kau4	pun khauh
hemorrhoids /piles disease	n	痔瘡	jih chōng	zi6 cong1	chih chhong
hemp rope	n	麻繩	màh síng	maa4 sing2	mah seng
hen[1]	n	母雞	móuh gài	mou5 gai4	mouh kai
hen[2] /biddy	n	雞嫲	gài ná	gai4 haa2	kai na
hepatic	adj	治肝病	jih gòn behng	zi6 gon4 beng6	chih kon pehng
hepatitis [A]	n	肝炎	gòn yìhm	gon4 jim4	kon yehm
hepatitis [B]	n	乙型肝炎	yut yìhng gōn yìhm	jyut3 jing4 gon1 jim4	yut yehng kon yehm
heptagon /seven angles	n	七角形	chāt gok yìhng	cat1 gok3 jing4	chhat kok yehng
her /his	pron	佢嘅	kéuih /héuih ge	keoi5 /heoi5 ge3	khoih /hoih ke
herb	n	草本植物	chóu bún jihk maht	cou2 bun2 zik6 mat6	chhou pun chehk maht
herbal	n	草本	chóu bún	cou2 bun2	chhou pun

herbal tea	n	派茶	lœng chàh /tsa	loeng3 caa4	loeng chhah
herd	n	牧群	muhk kwàhn	muk6 kwan4	muhk khwahn
here[1] (coll)	adv	呢度	lì /nì dòuh	li4 /ni4 dou6	li /ni touh
here[2] /... is here	adv	喺度	hái douh	hai2 dou6	hai touh
here[3] (wr)	adv	這兒	jéh yìh	ze5 ji4	cheh yih
here[4] /a place	adv	到	dou	dou3	tou
here[5]	adv	這裡	jéh léuih	ze5 leoi5	cheh lowih
hereafter	adv	此後	chí hauh	ci2 hau6	chhi hauh
heritage /legacy/bequest /inheritance	n	遺產	wàih cháan	wai4 caan2	waih chhaan
hero[1]	n	傑	giht	git6	kiht
hero[2]	n	英雄	yìng hung	jing4 hung3	yeng hung
hero[3] of a play	n	主角	jyú gok	zyu2 gok3	chyu kok
heroin (de)	n	海洛英	hói lok yìng	hoi2 lok3 jing4	hoi lok yeng
heroine[1]	n	女主角	léuih jyū gók	leui5 zyu1 gok2	lowih chyu kok
heroine[2]	n	女傑	léuih giht	leui5 git6	lowih kiht
hesitancy /uncertain doing/uncertain saying	n	猶豫不決	yàuh yuh bāt kyut	jau4 jyu6 bat1 kyut3	yauh yuh pat khyut
hesitant /hesitating	adj	唔想	m̀ séung	m4 soeng2	mh seung
hesitate /hesitant /feel uncertain	v	遲疑	chìh yi	ci4 ji3	chhih yi
hexagon	n	六邊形	luhk bīn yìhng	luk6 bin1 ying4	luhk pihn yehng
hey![1]	int	嘿	hēi	hei1	hei
hey![2] /hello!/hi! infomal	int	你好	léih hōu	lei5 hou1	leih hou
hey![3] /hi! infomal	int	喂!	wái	wai2	wai
hi! What up? (coll) (US)		點呀?	dīm àa /aa?	dim1 aa4 /aa3?	tim aa?
hibernation	v	冬眠	dùng mìhn	dung4 min4	tung mihn
hiccup[1] (coll) /hiccough	n	呃	īk / àak/ ngàak	ik1 / ak1/ aak1	ik /aak / ngaak
hiccup[2] (coll) /hiccough	n	打思	dá sī	daa2 si1	ta sih
hickey (sl) love bited /bite with love/mouth marks/lips		咖哩雞	gā léih gài	gaa1 lei5 gai4	ka leih kai
hidden love /secret love/underground love	n	地下情	deih há chìhng	dei6 haa2 cing4	teih ha chhehng
hide[1] /conceal	v	藏	chòhng	cong4	chhohng
hide[2]	v	收	sàu	sau4	sau
hide[3]	v	呢	lēi /nēi	lei1 /nei1	lei /nei
hide[4]	v	呢埋	lēi màaih	lei1 maai4	lei1 màaih
hide and seek[1]	n	捉迷藏	jūk màih chòhng	zuk1 mai4 cong4	chuk maih chhohng
hide and seek[2]	n	伏呢呢	puhk lēi lēi	puk6 lei1 lei1	phuhk lei lei
high /tall	adj	高	gòu	gou4	kou
high altitude	adj	高空	gòu hung	gou4 hung3	kou hung
high authority	n	霸權	ba kyùhn	baa3 kyun4	pa khyuhn
high beams	n	遠光燈	yúhn gwòng dàng	jyun5 gwong4 dang4	yuhn kwong tang
high class /high level	adj	高層	gòu chàhng	gou4 cang4	kou chhahng
high cry[1] /shout	v	嗌	aai /ngaai	aai3 /ngaai3	aai /ngaai

English		Chinese	Yale	Jyutping	Romanization
high cry[2] /scream	v	尖叫	jìm giu	zim4 giu3	chim kiu
high density	adj	高密度	gòu maht douh	gou4 mat6 dou6	kou maht touh
high grade[1] /high rank /high level superior rank	adj	高級	gòu kāp	gou4 kap1	kou khap
high grade[2] /super	adj	超級	chìu kāp	ciu4 kap1	chhiu khap
high heel	n	高跟	gòu gàn	gou4 gan4	kou kan
high heel shoe /heel	n	高跟鞋	gòu gàn haaih	gou4 gan4 haai6	kou kan haaih
high jump	n	跳高	tiu gòu	tiu3 gou4	thiu kou
high opinion[1]	adj	高觀點	gòu gun dím	gou4 gun3 dim2	kou kun tim
high opinion[2]	adj	讚賞	jaan séung	zaan3 soeng2	chaan seung
high opinion[3]	adj	佩服	pui fuhk	pui3 fuk6	phui fuhk
high place	adj	高處	gòu syu	gou4 syu3	kou syu
high place there /there's the high place/gets high place there/arriving high place there		去到最高嗰道	heui dou jeui gòu gó dòuh	heoi3 dou3 zeoi3 gou4 go2 dou6	hoi tou cheui kou ko touh
high roller gambler (spends lot of money)	n	豪賭者	hòuh dóu jé	hou4 dou2 ze2	houh tou che
high speed	adj	高速	gòu chūk	gou4 cuk1	kou chhuk
high street /main street	n	大街	daaih gāai	daai6 gaai1	taaih kaai
high temperature	n	高溫	gòu wān	gou4 wan1	kou wan
higher authorities	adj	上級	seuhng kāp	soeng6 kap1	seuhng khap
higher direction	adj	向上級	heung seuhng kāp	hoeng3 soeng6 kap1	heung seuhng khap
highest post /top leader	adj	最高等級	jeui gou dáng kāp	zeoi3 gou3 dang2 kap1	cheui kou tang khap
highest quality /first class/superior class/ top quality	adj	上等	seuhng dáng	soeng6 dang2	seuhng tang
highland	n	高地	gòu deih	gou4 dei6	kou teih
highlighter pen[1]	n	螢光筆	yìhng gwōng bāt	jing4 gwong1 bat1	yehng gwōng bāt
highlighter pen[2]	n	亮光筆	leuhng gwōng bāt	loeng6 gwong1 bat1	leuhng kwong paht
highly	adj	高度地	gòu douh deih	gou4 dou6 dei6	kou touh teih
highway[1] /public road /road	n	公路	gùng louh	gung4 lou6	kung louh
highway[2]	n	幹道	gon douh	gon3 dou6	kon touh
hijack[1] /kidnap	v	拐	gwáai	gwaai2	kwaai
hijack[2]	v	劫持	gip chi	gip3 ci3	kip chhi
hijacker[1] /kidnapper	n	拐子佬	gwáai jí lóu	gwaai2 zi2 lou2	kwaai chi lou
hijacker[2]	n	劫盜	gip douh	gip3 dou6	kip touh
hike[1] /hiking/walk/tour	n	遠足	yúhn jūk	jyun5 zuk1	yuhn chuk
hike[2] /hiking	v	徒步旅行	tòuh bòuh léuih hàhng	tou4 bou6 leoi5 hang4	thouh pouh lowih hahng
hiker /walker	n	遠足者	yúhn jūk jé	jyun5 zuk1 ze2	yuhn chuk che
hiking	n	行山	hàhng sàan	hang4 saan4	hahng saan
hill[1] /mountain	n	山	sàan	saan4	saan
hill-side[1]	n	山邊	sàan bìn	saan4 bin4	saan pin
hill-side[2]	n	山側	sàan jāk	saan4 zak1	saan chak

hilly	adj	多山丘	dò sàan yàu	do4 saan4 jau4	to saan yau
himalaya (de)	n	喜馬拉雅山脈	héi máh lā ā sāan mahk	hei2 maa5 laa1 aa1 saan1 mak6	hei mah la a saan mahk
hinder /obstruct	v	格	gaak	gaak	kaak
hindered	n	受妨礙	sàuh fong ngòih	sau6 fong3 ngoi6	sauh fong ngoih
hindrance[1]	n	障礙	jeung ngoih	zoeng3 ngoi6	cheung ngoih
hindrance[2] /interfere	n	妨礙	fòhng ngoih	fong4 ngoi6	fohng ngoih
hindrance[3] /obstruct	n	阻擋	jó dong	zo2 dong3	cho tong
Hindu religion	n	印度教	yan dòuh gaau	jan3 dou6 gaau3	yan touh kaau
hinge of door	n	鉸鏈	gaau lín	gaau3 lin2	kaau lin
hint[1] indirect say	n	暗示	am sih	am3 si6	am sih
hint[2] indirect say	n	暗指	am jí	am3 zi2	am chi
hint[3] /allusion/indirect say	n	影射	yéng seh	jeng2 se6	yeng seh
hip	n	屁股	pèih gū	pei4 gu1	pheih ku
hip-hip-hurrah! / wash a long life/ victory cheer!	int	萬歲	maahn seui	maan6 seoi3	maahn swoi
hire[1] /rent/lease/charter	v	租	jòu	zou4	chou
hire[2] (a person)	v	聘請	ping chéng /chíng	ping3 ceng2 /cing2	pheng chheng
hire worker	n	雇請	gu chéng	gu3 ceng2	ku chheng
hiring lawer	v	聘請律師	ping chéng /chíng leuht sī	ping ceng2 /cing2 leot6 si1	pheng chheng lwoht si
his /her, its, theirs, that, such	pron	其	kèih	kei4	kheih
hiss[1]	n	噓	hēui	heoi1	hoi
hiss[2] sounds	n	嘶嘶聲	sìh sí sèng	si6 si2 seng4	sih si seng
historian	n	歷史學家	lihk sí hohk gā	lik6 si2 hok6 gaa1	lehk si hohk ka
historic[1]	adj	歷史上著名	lihk síh seuhng jyu mèhng	lik6 si2 soeng6 zyu3 meng4	lehk sih seuhng chyu mehng
historic[2]	adj	有歷史性	yáuh lihk síh sing	jau5 lik6 si3 sing3	yauh lehk sih seng
history[1]	n	史記	sí gei	si2 gei3	si kei
history[2]	n	歷史	lihk sí	lik6 si2	lehk si
hit a target	n	打中	dā jùng	daa1 zung4	ta chung
hit by natural calamity	v	受災	sàuh jòi	sau6 zoi4	sauh choi
hit oneself	v	打自己	dá jih géi	daa2 zi6 gei2	ta chih kei
hitter	n	打擊者	dá gīk jé	daa2 gik1 ze2	ta kek che
honey comb /hive of bees	n	蜂巢	fùng chàauh	fung4 caau6	fung chhaauh
HK Bank /HSBC	n	滙豐銀行	wuih fùng ngàhn hòhng	wui6 fung4 ngan4 hong4	wuih fung ngahn hohng
HK governor	n	港督	góng dūk	gong2 duk1	kong tuk
HK Macao	n	省港澳	sáang góng ou	saang2 gong2 ou3	saang kong ou
HK people	n	港燦	góng chaan	gong2 caan3	kong chhaan
HK telecom	n	香港電訊	hèung góng dihn seun	hoeng4 gong2 din6 seon3	heung kong tihn swon
hobby	n	嗜好	si hou	si3 hou3	si hou
hoc committee	n	特設委員會	dahk chit wái yùhn wúi	dak6 cit3 wai2 jyun4 wui2	tahk chhit wai yuhn wui

hockey[1]	n	曲棍球	kūk gwan kàuh	kuk1 gwan3 kau4	khuk kwan khauh
hockey[2] field on the ice	n	冰上曲棍球	bìng seuhng kūk gwan kàuh	bing4 soeng6 kuk1 gwan3 kau4	peng seuhng khuk kwan khauh
hoist[1] /raise/spread /scatter	v	揚	yèuhng	joeng4	yeuhng
hoist[2] /rise/arise	v	升起	sing hēi	sing3 hei1	seng hei
hoister	n	升起人	sing hēi yàhn	sing3 hei1 jan4	seng hei yahn
hold[1] /take/took/to take /fetch	v	拿	lāh /nāh	laa1 /naa1	lah /nah
hold[2]	v	把	bāa	baa1	paa
hold[3] /strangle/clutch	v	揢	haap	haap3	haap
hold[4]	v	握著	āk /āak jeuk	ak1 /aak1 zoek3	ak /aak cheuk
hold conversation /hold talking	v	通話	tùng wá	tung4 wa2	thung wa
hold in hand	v	拎住	līng /nīng jyuh	ling1 /ning1 zyu6	leng /neng chyuh
hold meeting	v	舉行	geui hàhng	geoi3 hang4	kwoi hahng
hold on please! /one moment please!/ a moment please!/ waiting on the phone		唔該等下!	m̀ gòi dáng háh!	m4 goi4 dang2 haa5!	mh koi tang hah!
hold passport	v	持有	chìh yáuh	ci4 jau5	chhih yauh
hold responsibility /respond/liable to/undertake respons/to undertake respons	v	承擔責任	sing dáam jaak yahm	sing3 daam2 zaak3 jam6	seng taam chaak yahm
hold tight!	adv	抓緊了	jáau gán líuh	zaau2 gan2 liu5	chaau kan liuh
hold up /hold in hand		手拎住	sáu līng jyuh	sau2 ling1 zyu6	sau leng chyuh
holder[1] /holding	n	持有者	chìh yáuh jé	ci4 jau5 ze2	chhih yauh che
holder[2] /rack	n	支架	jì gá	zi4 gaa2	chi ka
hole[1]	n	窿	lūng	lung1	lung
hole[2] /cave	n	陷	hahm	ham6	hahm
holiday[1] /vacation/day off	n	放假	fong ga	fong3 gaa1	fong ka
holiday[2]	n	假期	ga kèih	gaa1 kei4	ka kheih
holiday[3]	n	假日	gá yaht	gaa2 yat6	ka yaht
holiday[4] /weekend	n	週末	jàu muht	zau4 mut6	chau muht
hollow[1] /empty/space	adj	空嘅	hùng ge	hung4 ge3	hung ke
hollow[2] /valley /ravine deep valley	n	山谷	sàan gūk	saan4 guk1	saan kuk
holly wreath /garland for dead body /wreath garland for dead body	n	花圈	fā hyūn	faa1 hyun1	fa hyun
holy[1] /sacred	adj	聖	sing	sing3	seng
holy[2] /sacred	adj	神聖	sàhn sing	san4 sing3	sahn seng
homage[1] /respect	n	尊敬	jyùn ging	zeon4 ging3	chyun keng
homage[2]	n	效忠	haauh jùng	haau6 zung4	haauh chung
homage[3] /tribute	n	致敬	ji ging	zi3 ging3	chi keng
home[1] /house (coll)	n	屋企	ùk /ngùk kéi	uk4 /nguk4 kei2	uk /nguk khei
home[2] /house (wr)	n	家	gà	gaa4	ka

English	Part	Chinese	Yale	Jyutping	Romanization
home affairs depart	n	民政署	màhn jing chyu	man4 jing3 cyu5	mahn cheng chyu
home for aged	n	老人院	lóuh yàhn yún	lou5 jan4 jyun2	louh yahn yun
home page	n	主頁	jyú yihp	zyu2 jip6	chyu yihp
home sick	adj	掛住屋企	gwa jyuh ūk /ngūk kéi	gwaa3 zyu6 uk1 /nguk1 kei5	kwa chyuh uk /nguk khei
home tel service	n	家居電話服務	gā gèui dihn wá fuhk mouh	gaa1 geoi4 din6 wa2 fuk6 mou6	ka kwoi tihn wa fuhk mouh
home village /country/village	n	鄉下	hèung há	hoeng4 haa5	heung ha
home work[1]	n	功課	gùng fo	gung4 fo3	kung fo
home work[2]	prep/n	家庭作業	gà tèhng /tìhng jok yihp	gaa1 teng4 /ting4 zok3 jip6	ka thehng chok yihp
homeless[1]	adj	無家可歸	mòuh gā hó gwài	mou4 gaa1 ho2 gwai4	mouh ka ho kwai
homeless[2]	adj	無家	mòuh gā	mou4 gaa1	mouh ka
homeopathy	n	類似醫療論	leuih chíh yī lìuh leun	leoi6 ci5 ji1 liu4 leon3	lowih chhih yih liuh leun
homo-geneity	n	同種	tùhng júng	tung4 zung2	thuhng chung
homosexual /gay love	n	同性戀	tùhng sing lyúhn	tung4 sing3 lyun5	thuhng seng lyuhn
homosexual	n	同性戀者	tùhng sing lyúhn jé	tung4 sing3 lyun5 ze2	thuhng seng lyuhn che
honest[1] /sincere	adj	老實	lóuh saht	lou5 sat6	louh saht
honest[2]		實	saht	sat6	saht
honest[3]	adj	誠	sing	sing3	seng
honest[4]	adj	誠實	sing sàht	sing3 sat6	seng saht
honestly	adj	誠實地	sing sàht deih	sing3 sat6 dei6	seng saht teih
honey[1]	n	蜜糖	maht tòhng	mat6 tong4	maht thohng
honey[2]	n	蜂蜜	fùng maht	fung4 mat6	fung maht
honey comb	n	蜜蜂窟	maht fùng dau	mat6 fung4 dau3	maht fung tau
honeydew melon	n	蜜瓜	maht gwà	mat6 gwaa4	maht kwa
honeymoon	n	蜜月	maht yuht	mat6 jyut6	maht yuht
Hong Kong[1]	n	香港	hèung góng	hoeng4 gong2	heung kong
Hong Kong[2]	n	省港	sáang góng	saang2 gong2	saang kong
hong kong dollar[1]	n	港紙	góng jí	gong2 zi2	kong chi
hong kong dollar[2]	n	港幣	góng bàih	gong2 bai6	kong paih
hong kong girl	n	港女	góng léuih /néuih	gong2 leoi5 /neoi5	kong lowih /nowih
Hong Kong MTR	n	港鐵	góng tit	gong2 tit3	kong thit
hong kong people	n	香港人	hèung góng yàhn	hoeng4 gong2 jan4	heung kong yahn
honor[1] /respect deeply	n	敬重	ging juhng	ging3 zung6	keng chuhng
honor[2] /honour	n	榮譽	wìhng yùh	wing4 jyu6	wehng yuh
honorary[1]	adj	名譽上	mìhng yuh seuhng	meng4 jyu6 soeng6	mehng yuh seuhng
honorary[2]	adj	名譽上的	mìhng yuh seuhng dìk	meng4 jyu6 soeng6 dik4	mehng yuh seuhng tek
honored /honoured	v	榮幸	wìhng hàhng	wing4 hang6	wehng hahng
honored guest	n	嘉賓	gā bān	gaa1 ban1	ka pan
honour with one's presence[1]	v	俾面	bei mín	bei2 min2	pei min

honour with one's presence[2]	v	賞面	séung mín	soeng2 min2	seung min
honourable	adj	尊敬	jyùn gìng	zyun4 ging3	chyun keng
hood[1]	n	兜帽	dāu mouh	dau1 mou6	tau mouh
hood[2]	n	車蓋	chè goi	ce4 goi3	chhe koi
hoodlum[1(sl)] /punk/rude way boys	n	無賴	móuh laaih	mou5 laai6	mouh laaih
hoodlum[2 (sl)]	n	小流氓	síu làuh màhn	siu2 lau4 man4	siu lauh mahn
hoof[1] of animal	n	蹄	tàih	tai4	thaih
hoof[2] of men/leg/foot	n	腳	geuk	goek3	keuk
hook	n	鉤	àu /ngàu	au4 /ngau4	au /ngau
hooligan[1 (sl)]	n	飛仔	fèi jái	fei4 zai2	fei chai
hooligan[2 (sl)]	n	阿飛	áa fèi	aa2 fei4	aa fei
hooligan[3 (sl)]	n	小流氓	síu làuh màhn	siu2 lau4 man4	siu lauh mahn
hooligan[4(sl)] /ruffian /violent man	n	惡棍	ok /ngok gwan	ok3 /ngok3 kwan3	ok /ngok kwan
hoop	n	箍住	kū jyuh	ku1 zyu6	khu chyuh
hoover /vacuum cleaner	n	真空吸塵器	jàn hùng káp chàhn hei	zan4 hung4 kap2 can4 hei3	chan hung khap chhahn hei
hoover tube	n	真空管	jàn hùng gún	zan4 hung4 gun2	chan hung kun
hop /skip/jump/leap	v	跳	tiu	tiu3	thiu
hope /see/watch /expect/to look	v	望	mohng	mong6	mohng
hope for	v	巴	bā	baa1	pa
hopeful[1]	adj	有望	yáuh mohng	jau5 mong6	yauh mohng
hopeful[2]	adj	願全	yuhn chyùhn	jyun6 cyun4	yuhn chhyuhn
hopeful[3] /prospective /promising	adj	有希望	yáuh hèi mohng	jau5 nei4 mong6	yauh hei mohng
hopeful[4]	adj	有希望嘅	yáuh hèi mohng ge	jau5 nei4 mong6 ge3	yauh hei mohng ke
hopeful[5] /optimistic	adj	樂觀	lohk gùn	lok6 gun4	lohk kun
hopeless	adj	無希望	móuh hèi mohng	mou5 hei4 mong6	mouh hei mohng
hopeless person	n	悲觀論人	bēi gùn leuhn yàhn	bei1 gun4 leon6 jan4	pei kun lowhn yahn
horizon /sky-line	n	地平線	dèih pèhng sin	dei6 peng4 sin3	teih pehng sin
horizontal line[1]	n	橫線	wàahng sin	waang4 sin3	waahng sin
horizontal line[2]	n	水平線	séui pìhng sin	seoi2 ping4 sin3	swoi phehng sin
horn[1] of animal	n	角	gok	gok3	kok
horn[2] /trumpet/sharp sound	n	喇叭	la bā	laa3 baa1	la pa
hornless	adj	無角	móuh gok	mou5 gok3	mouh kok
horny bastard	n	鹹濕佬	hàahm sāp lóu	haam4 sap1 lou2	haahm sap lou
horoscope /astrology	n	占星術	jīm sìng seuht	zim1 sing4 seot6	chim sing swoht
horrible	adj	極討厭	gìhk tóu yim	gik6 tou2 jim3	kehk thou yim
horror /terrible!	a/n	恐怖	húng bou	hung2 bou3	hung pou
horse	n	馬	máh	maa5	mah
horse racing[1]	n	跑馬	páau máh	paau5 maa5	phaau mah

horse racing[2]/jockey	n	賽馬	choi máh	coi3 maa5	chhoi mah
horse-rider /jockey /horse-man	n	騎師	kèh sì	kei4 si4	kheh si
horse's shed /stable	n	馬棚	máh pàahng	maa5 paang4	mah phaahng
horticulture /gardening	n	園藝	yùhn ngaih	jyun2 ngai6	yuhn ngaih
hose (long pipe)	n	軟管	yúhn gùn	jyun5 gun4	yuhn kun
hospital	n	醫院	yī yún	ji1 jyun2	yi yun
hospital area		醫院處	yì yuhn chyu	yi1 yuen6 sue3	yi yuhn chhyu
hospital card	n	醫療咭	yī lìuh kāat	ji1 liu4 kaat1	yi liuh khaat
hospital fee	n	住院費	jyuh yún fai	zyu6 jyun2 fai3	chyuh yun fai
hospitality[1]	n	招待性行業	jìu doih sing hóng yihp	ziu4 doi6 sing3 hong2 jip6	chiu toih seng hong yih
hospitality[2]	n	好客	hóu haak	hou2 haak3	hou haak
hospitality[3]	n	款待	fún doih	fun2 dii6	fun toih
hospitalization	n	住院治療	jyuh yuhn jih lìuh	zyu6 jyun6 zi6 liu4	chyuh yuhn chih liuh
hospitalized[1]	v	住院	jyuh yuhn	zyu6 jyun6	chyuh yuhn
hospitalized[2]	v	入院	yahp yuhn	jap6 jyun6	yahp yuhn
host (official invitate)	n	東道主	dùng dou jyú	dung4 dou3 zyu2	tung tou chyu
host for event[1] /organizer	n	主辦	jyú baahn	zyu2 baan6	chyu paahn
host for event[2] /organizer	n	主持	jyú chìh	zyu2 ci4	chyu chhih
hostage /to pawn/pledge	n	質	ji	zi3	chi
hostage article	n	抵押品	dái aat bán	dai2 aat3 ban2	tai aat pan
hostel[1]	n	旅舍	léuih se	leoi5 se3	lowih se
hostel[2] living quarter/ dormitory	n	宿舍	sūk se /sūk séh	suk1 se3 /suk1 se5	suk se /suk seh
hostel[3]	n	招待所	jìu doih só	ziu4 doi6 so2	chiu toih so
hostess /mistress	n	女主人	léuih jyú yán	leui5 zyu2 jan2	lowih chyu yan
hot[1]	adj	熱	yiht	jit6	yiht
hot[2]	adj	辣	laaht	laat6	laaht
hot dish	n	熱前菜	yiht chìhn choi	jit6 cin4 coi3	yiht chhihn chhoi
hot dog (de)	n	熱狗	yiht gáu	jit6 gaau2	yiht kau
hot food /piping hot /warm food	n	熱辣辣	yiht laaht laaht	jit6 laat6 laat6	yiht laaht laaht
hot news	n	最新消息	jeui sàn sìu sīk	zeoi3 san4 siu4 sik1	cheui san suu sek
hot sauce	n	熱醬汁	yiht jeung jāp	jit6 zoeng3 zap1	yiht cheung chap
hot spring (of water)	n	溫泉	wān chyùhn	wan1 cyun4	wan chhyuhn
hot tempered[1]	n	暴怒	bouh louh/nouh	bou6 lou6/nou6	pouh louh/nouh
hot tempered[2]	n	易怒	yìh louh /nouh	ji6 lou6 /nou6	yih louh /nouh
hot water	n	熱水	yiht séui	jit6 seoi2	yiht swoi
hot water bottle	n	熱水袋	yiht séui doih	jit6 seoi2 doi6	yiht swoi toih
hotel[1]/shop/store/inn /pup	n	店	dím	dim2	tim
hotel[2] /hostel	n	旅館	léuih gún	leoi5 gun2	lowih kun

hotel[3]	n	酒店	jáu dim	zau2 dim3	chau tim
hotel accommodation	vi	住宿安排	jyuh sūk òn /ngòn paai	zyu6 suk1 on4 /ngon4 paai4	chyuh suuk on /ngon phaai
hotel industry	n	招待性行業	jìu doih sing hóng yihp	ziu4 doi6 sing3 hong2 jip6	chiu toih seng hong yihp
hotline	n	熱線	yiht sin	jit6 sin3	yiht sin
hound dog /hunter dog	n	獵犬	lihp hyún	lip6 hyun2	lihp hyun
hour[1]	n	小時	síu si	siu2 si3	siu si
hour[2] /hrs	n	鐘頭	jùng tau	zung4 tau3	chung thau
hour[3] /o'clock?	adv	點鐘?	dím jūng?	dim2 zung1?	tim chung?
hourly work		時散	sìh sáan	si4 saan2	sih saan
house[1] (coll) room	n	屋	ngūk /ùk	nguk1 /uk1	nguk /uk
house[2]	n	住宅	jyuh jáak	zyu6 zaak2	chyuh chaahk
house[3] (a family)	v	住在一起	jyuh joih yāt héi	zyu6 zoi6 jat1 hei2	chyuh choih yat hei
house[4] /front side sea & backside mountains /good view house	n	背山面海	buih sàan mihn hói	biu6 saan4 min6 hoi2	puih saan mihn hoi
house[5] /public building	n	館	gún	gun2	kun
house for rent	n	吉屋出租	gāt ùk /ngùk chēut jòu	gat1 uk4 /nguk4 ceot1 zou4	kat uk/nguk chhot chou
house of commons /lower house (UK)	n	下議院	háh yíh yún	haa5 ji5 jyun2	hah yih yun
house of representatives (US)	n	眾議院	jung yíh yún	zung3 ji5 jyun2	chung yih yun
house owner /landlord	n	房東	fòhng dūng	fong4 dung1	fohng tung
house rent	n	屋租	ùk /ngūk jòu	uk4 /nguk1 zou4	uk /nguk chou
household[1]	n	專戶	jyùn wuh	zyun4 wu6	chyun wuh
household[2]	n	家居	gā gèui	gaa1 geoi4	ka kwoi
household items	n	家居用品	gā gèui yuhng bán	gaa1 geoi4 jung6 ban2	ka kwoi yuhng pan
householder	n	住戶	jyuh wuh	zyu6 wu6	chyuh wuh
housewife[1]	n	主婦	jyú fúh	zyu2 fu5	chyu fuh
housewife[2]	n	家庭主婦	gà tèhng /tihng jyú fúh	gaa1 teng4 /ting4 zyu2 fu5	ka thehng chyu fuh
housework /household duties/housekeeping	n	家務	gà mouh	gaa1 mou6	ka mouh
housing depart	n	房屋署	fóng ūk /ngūk chyú	fong2 uk1 /nguk1 cyu5	fong uk /nguk chhyu
housing estate /residential area	n	住宅區	jyuh jáak kēui	zyu6 zaak2 keoi1	chyuh chaahk khoi
housing problem	n	住屋嘅問題	jyuh ùk ge màhn taih	zyu6 uk4 ge3 man6 tai6	chyuh uk ke mahn thaih
hover /to orbit	v	盤旋	pun syùhn	pun3 syun4	phun syuhn
how?[1] /what? (coll)	adv	點/嘅?	dím?	dim2?	tim?
how?[2]	adv	怎	jám	zam2	cham
how?[3]	adv	怎麼	jám mò	zam2 mo4	cham mo
how?[4]	adv	怎樣	jám yeuhng	zam2 joeng3	cham yeuhng
how?[5]	adv	何	hòh	ho4	hoh
how?[6] (wr)	adv	如何?	yùh hòh?	jyu4 ho6?	yuh hoh?
how are you?[1] (wr) (text)		你好嗎?	léih hóu má?	lei5 hou2 maa2?	leih hou ma?

how are you?[2] (coll)		點呀?	dīm àa /aa?	dim1 aa4 /aa3?	tim aa?
how are you?[3] /Hi what up?[us] /alright mate? [bt] /what are you doing? [re]		你點呀?	léih dīm aa?	lei5 dim1 aa3?	leih tim aa?
how are you?[4] /are you well? /how's going on? [re]		你好嗎?	léih hóu má?	lei5 hou2 maa2?	leih hou ma?
how are you?[5]		幾好嗎?	geih hóu má?	gei6 hou2 maa5	keih hou ma?
how big?		幾大呀?	gei daaih àa /aa?	gei3 daai6 aa3 /aa4?	kei taaih aa?
how can i get in touch with you?		點樣可以 搵到你?	dím yéung hó yíh wán dou léih /néih?	dim2 joeng2 ho2 ji5 wan2 dou3 lei5 /nei5?	tim yeung ho yih wan tou leih /neih ?
how do?[1]		怎樣做?	jám yeuhng jouh	zam2 joeng3 zou6?	cham yeuhng chouh?
how do?[2]		點樣做?	dím yéung jouh?	dim2 joeng2 zou6?	tim yeung chouh?
how does it works?		怎樣做呢 份工作?	jám yeuhng jouh lī fàn gùng jok?	zam2 joeng3 zou6 li1 fan4 gung4 zok3?	cham yeuhng chouh lih fan kung chok?
how get there?	n	點去？	dím heui ?	dim2 heoi3?	tim hoi?
how it works?		怎樣工作?	jám yeuhng gùng jok?	zam2 joeng3 gung4 zok3?	cham yeuhng kung chok?
how long?[1]	n	幾耐?	gei loi /noi?	gei3 loi3 /noi3?	kei loi /noi?
how long?[2]	n	有多久?	yáuh dò gáu?	jau5 do4 gau2?	yauh to kau?
how many?[1]	n	幾多個?	géi dō gó?	gei2 do1 go2?	kei toh ko?
how many?[2]		多少數?	dò síu sou?	doh1 siu2 so3?	toh siu sou?
how much?[1] /how many?	n	多少?	dò síu?	do4 siu2?	to siu?
how much?[2] /how?	n	幾?	géi?	gei2?	kei?
how much?[3]	n	點賣?	dím maaih?	dim2 maai6?	tim maaih?
how much?[4] /how many?	n	幾多?	géi dō?	gei2 do1?	kei toh?
how much?[5]	n	幾多呀?	géi do àa /aa?	gei2 do aa4 /aa3?	kei to aa?
how much?[6]	n	幾多錢呀?	géi do chín aa?	gei2 do cin aa3?	kei to chhin aa?
how much is this?		呢幾多錢?	lī /nī…géi dō chín?	li1 /ni1..gei2 do1 cin2?	li /ni gei doh chhin?
how much price?[1] /how much?	n	點賣呀?	dím maaih aa?	dim2 maai6 aa3?	tim maaih aa?
how much price?[2]	n	點賣呢?	dím maaih nè?	dim2 maai6 ne4?	tim maaih ne?
how old?	n	幾多歲呀?	geih dò seui aa?	gei6 do4 seoi3 aa3?	keih to swoi aa?
how old are you?		你幾歲呀?	léih géi seui aa?	lei5 gei2 seoi3 aa3?	leih kei swoi aa?
how's it going?[1] (coll)		點呀?	dím àa /aa?	dim2 aa4 /aa3?	tim aa?
how's it going?[2]	adv	事情進展 如向?	sih chìhng jeun jín yùh heung?	si6 cing4 zeon3 zin2 jyu4 hoeng3?	sih chhihng cheun chin yuh heung?
how's life?	n	生活得點 呀?	sàng wuht dāk dím aa?	sang4 wut6 dak1 dim2 aa3?	sang wuht tak tim aa?
how short?	n	幾短?	geih dyún?	gei6 dyun2?	keih tyun?
how to do?[1]	n	點做?	dím jouh?	dim2 zou6?	tim chouh?
how to do?[2]	n	點辦?	dím baahn?	dim2 baan6?	tim paahn?
how to do?[3]	n	怎麼辦?	ján mò baahn?	zan2 mo4 baan?	chan mo paahn?

how to go?	n	點去？	dím heui？	dim2 heoi3?	tim hoi?
how to go from here?		我點樣去呢度？	ngóh dím yéung heui lì /nì dòuh?	ngo5 dim2 joeng6 heoi3 li4/ni4 dou6?	ngoh tim yeung hoi li /ni touh?
how to go there? /how get there?		點去呀？	dím heui àa /aa?	dim2 heoi3 aa4 /aa3?	tim hoi aa?
how to pronunciation?		點讀呀？	dím duhk àa /aa？	dim2 duk6 aa4 /aa3?	tim tuhk aa?
how to say?[1]		點樣講？	dím yéung góng?	dim2 joeng6 gong2?	tim yeung kong?
how to say?[2]		點講呀？	dím góng àa /aa?	dim2 gong2 aa4 /aa3?	tim kong aa?
however[1]	adv	然而	yìhn yìh	jin4 ji4	yihn yih
however[2]	adv	可是	hó sih	ho2 si6	ho sih
howl /roar /noise	v	呼嘯	fù siu	fu4 siu3	fu siu
hubbub[1]	n	喧鬧	hyùn naauh	hyun4 naau6	hyun naauh
hubbub[2] /uproar	n	吵鬧聲	chòuh laauh/naauh sèng	caau4 laau6 /naau6 seng4	chhouh laauh /naauh seng
huddle[1] /to curl up	v	蜷縮	kyùhn sūk	kyun4 suk1	khyuhn suk
huddle[2]	v	縮埋一堆	sūk màaih yāt dèui	suk1 maai4 jat1 deoi4	suk maaih yat toei
huddle[3]	v	擠在一起	jāi joih yāt héi	zai1 zoi6 jat1 hei2	chai choih yat hei
hug[1] (coll) /to embrace	v	攬住	láam jyuh	laam2 zyu6	laam chyuh
hug[2] (text) /to embrace	v	擁抱	yúng póuh	jung2 pou5	yung phouh
huge /large/greater/big /titanic/enormous/extremely big	adj	巨大	geuih daaih	geoi6 daai6	kwoih taaih
huge problem(sl) /large problem/huge problem	n	大鑊	daaih wohk	daai6 wok6	taaih wohk
hull[1] /to peel/remove skin	v	去皮	heui pèih	heoi3 pei4	hoi pheih
hull[2]	v	去殼	heui hok	heoi3 hok3	hoi hok
hum sound of insect	v	嗡嗡聲	yūng yūng sèng	jung1 jung1 seng4	yung yung seng
human[1] /man/person	n	人	yàhn	jan4	yahn
human[2]	adj	人類	yàhn lèuih	jan4 leoi6	yahn lowih
human being /human race/mankind/species	n	人類	yàhn lèuih	jan4 leoi6	yahn lowih
human life	n	人命	yàhn mehng /mihng	jan4 meng6 /ming6	yahn mehng
human nature	n	人性	yàhn sing	jan4 sing3	yahn seng
human right	n	人權	yàhn kyùhn	jan4 kyun4	yahn khyuhn
humanity	n	人道	yàhn dou	jan4 dou3	yahn tou
humble[1] /low	adj	卑	bēi	bei1	pei
humble[2]	adj	謙恭	hìm gùng	him4 gung4	him kung
humid /moist	adj	潮濕	chìuh sap	ciu4 sap3	chhiuh sap
humidity /moisture	n	濕度	sāp dòuh	sap1 dou6	sap touh
humiliation /feel humble/ loss respect/loss of face	n	丟臉	dìu líhm	diu4 lim5	tiu lihm
humorous[1]	adj	風趣	fùng cheui	fung4 ceoi3	fung chhoi
humorous[2](de) /humour	adj	幽默	yàu mahk	jau4 mak6	yau mahk
hump[1]	n	駝背	tòh bui	to4 bui3	thoh pui
hump[2]	n	隆起	lùhng héi	lung4 hei2	luhng hei
hunch[1]	v	弓身	gùng sàn	gung1 san1	kung san

hunch[2]	n/v	背部隆起	bui bouh lùhng héi	bui3 bou6 lung4 hei2	pui pouh lowhng hei
hundred	n	百	baak	baak3	paak
hundred percent	n	十足	sahp jūk	sap6 zuk1	sahp chuk
hundred thousand	adj	十萬	sahp maahn	sap6 maan6	sahp maahn
hung /hang/suspend	adj/v	掛	gwa	gwa3	kwa
hunger	n	飢餓	gēi ngoh	gei1 ngo6	kei ngoh
hungry[1]	adj	餓	ngoh	ngo6	ngoh
hungry[2]	adj	肚餓	tóuh ngoh	tou5 ngo6	thouh ngoh
hungry[3]	adj	飢餓	gēi ngoh	gei1 ngo6	kei ngoh
hunt /search	v	獵取	lihp chéui	lip6 ceoi2	lihp chhoi
hunter /huntsman	n	獵人	lihp yàhn	lip6 jan4	lihp yahn
hunting	n	獵	lihp	lip6	lihp
hurdle for skip	v	跳欄	tiu làahn	tiu3 laan4	thiu laahn
hurrah! hurray!	n	表示歡喜	bíu sih fún héi	biu2 si6 fun2 hei2	piu sih fun hei
hurricane	n	龍捲風	lùhng gyún fùng	lung4 gyun2 fung4	luhng kyun fung
hurry[1] /quick/soon/speed		快啲	faai dī	faai3 di1	faai ti
hurry[2] /rush/run	n	奔	bàn	ban4	pan
hurry up![1]	v	快啲喇!	faai dī la!	faai3 di1 laa3	faai ti la!
hurry up![2]		快脆!	faai chèui!	faai3 ceoi3!	faai chheui
hurted	v	使受傷	saí sauh sèung	sai2 sau6 soeng4	sai sauh seung
husband[1] married	n	夫	fùh	fu4	fuh
husband[2] (sl)	n	老公	lóuh gùng	lou5 gung4	louh kung
husband[3]	n	丈夫	jeuhng fù	zoeng6 fu4	cheuhng fu
husband & wife[1] /pair	n	偶	áuh /ngáuh	au5 /ngau5	auh /ngauh
husband & wife[2] /spouse/couple	n	夫婦	fù fúh	fu4 fu5	fu fuh
husband's father	n	老爺	lóuh yèh	lou5 je4	louh yeh
husband's grand father	n	太老爺	tài lóuh yèh	tai4 lou5 je4	thai louh yeh
husband's grand mother	n	太奶奶	táai láaih láaih, táai náaih náaih	taai2 laai5 laai5, taai2 naai5 naai5	thaai laaih laaih
husband's mother	n	奶奶	láaih láaih, náaih náaih	laai5 laai5, naai5 naai5	laaih laaih, naaih naaih
hush /don't shout	v	別叫喊	biht giu haam	bit6 giu3 haam3	piht kiu haam
husk[1] /shell/case/box /casing	n	殼	hok	hok3	hok
husk[2] outer shell	n	外殼	oih /ngoih hok	oi6 /ngoi6 hok3	oih /ngoih hok
husk[3] outer of corn-cob	n	外表部分	oih /ngoih bíu bouh fàn	oi6 /ngoi6 biu2 bou6 fan4	oih /ngoih piu pouh fan
hustle /to urge	v	催促	chèui chūk	ceoi4 cuk1	chheui chhuk
hut /wood house	n	木屋	muhk ngūk	muk6 nguk1	muhk nguk
hydraulic power	adj	水力	séui lihk	seoi2 lik6	swoi lehk
hydraulic lift	n	水力升降機	séui lihk sìng gong gèi	seoi2 lik6 sing4 gong3 gei4	swoi lehk seng kong kei
hydraulic pump	n	液壓泵	yihk áat bām	jik6 aat2 bam1	yehk aat pam
hydroelectric power	n	水電	séui dihn	seoi2 din6	swoi tihn
hydrofoil boat	n	水翼船	séui yihk syùhn	seoi2 jik6 syun4	swoi yehk syuhn

hydrofoil ship	n	水上飛機	séui sèuhng fèi gèi	seoi2 soeng6 fei4 gei4	swoi seuhng fei kei
hydrogen[1]	n	氫	hīng	hing1	hing
hydrogen[2] gas	n	氫氣	hīng hei	hing1 hei3	hing hei
hygiene /sanitation	n	衛生	waih sàng	wai6 sang4	waih sang
hymn	n	聖歌	sing gō	sing3 go1	seng ko
hyper /hypertension	n	高血壓	gòu hyut aat /ngaat	gou4 hyut3 aat3 /ngaat3	kou hyut aat /ngaat
hyperopia /hypermetropia	n	遠視	yúhn sih	jyun5 si6	yuhn sih
hyphen (-)	n	連字號	lìhn jih houh	lin4 zi6 hou6	lihn chih houh
hypnotize /mesmerize	v	施催眠術	sì chèui mìhn seuht	si4 ceoi4 min4 seot6	si chhoi mihn swoht
hypothetical /suppose that	adj	假設嘅	gá chit ge	ga2 cit6 ge3	ka chhit ke
hysterectomy	n	子宮切除	jí gùng chit chèuih	zi2 gung4 cit3 ceoi4	chi kung chit chheuih
hysteria (de)	n	歇斯底里	hit sī dái léih	hit3 si1 dai2 lei5	hit si tai leih

i am not very happy	我唔係好開心	ngóh m̀ hàih hōu hòi sàm	ngo5 m4 hai4 hou1 hoi4 sam4	ngoh mh haih hou hoi sam
i arrived[1]	我嚟咗	ngóh làih jó	ngoh5 lai4 zo2	ngoh laih cho
i arrived[2]	我到咗啦	ngóh dou jó lā	ngoh5 dou3 zo2 laa1	ngoh tou cho la
i arrived[3]	嚟我度	làih ngóh douh	lai4 ngoh5 do6	laih ngoh touh
i ate already[1] v	我食咗喇	ngóh sihk jó la	ngo5 sik6 zo2 la3	ngoh sehk cho la
i ate already[2] v	我食喎	ngóh sihk wóh	ngo5 sik6 wo5	ngoh sehk woh
i beg to state /i wish to inform you /whom it may concern	敬啟者	ging kái jé	ging3 kai2 ze2	keng khai che
i did aux v	我贏咗	ngóh yèhng jó	ngo5 jeng4 zo2	ngoh yehng cho
i did so	我咁樣做	ngóh gam yeuhng jouh	ngo5 gam3 joeng6 zou6	ngoh kam yeuhng chouh
i didn't aux v	我無贏	ngóh mòuh yèhng	ngo5 mou4 jeng4	ngoh mouh yehng
i didn't told[1]	我無講	ngóh mòuh góng	ngo5 mou4 gong2	ngoh mouh kong
i didn't told[2]	我無叫	ngóh mòuh giu	ngo5 mou4 giu3	ngoh mouh kiu
i didn't told[3]	我無講喎	ngóh mòuh góng wóh	ngo5 mou4 gong2 wo5	ngoh mouh kong woh
i didn't told[4]	我無叫喎	ngóh mòuh giu wóh	ngo5 mou4 giu3 wo5	ngoh mouh kiu woh
i don't know! /i've no idea!	我唔知道!	ngóh m̀ jì douh!	ngo5 m4 zi4 dou6!	ngoh mh chi touh!
i don't said	我唔講	ngóh m̀ góng	ngo5 m4 gong2	ngoh mh kong
i don't speak	我唔識講	ngóh m̀ sīk góng	ngo5 m4 sik1 gong2	ngoh mh sek kong
i don't think so	不過我想	bāt gwo ngóh séung	bat1 gwo3 ngo5 soeng2	pat gwo ngoh seung
i don't understand!	我唔明!	ngóh m̀ mìhng!	ngo5 m4 ming4!	ngoh mh mehng!
i feel sick!	我唔舒服	ngóh m̀ syū fuhk	ngo5 m4 syu1 fuk6	ngoh mh syu fuhk
i go up the tower	我去上塔	ngóh hēui séuhng taap	ngo5 heoi1 soeng5 taap3	ngoh hoi seuhng thaap
I got excited	我很興奮	ngóh hān hìng fáhn	ngo5 han1 hing4 fan5	ngoh han hing fahn
i hope so	我希望	ngóh hèi mohng	ngo5 nei4 mong6	ngoh hei mohng
i know[1]	照我所知	jiu ngóh só jì	ziu3 ngo5 so2 zi4	chiu ngoh so chi
i know[2]	我識做	ngóh sīk jouh	ngo2 sik1 jou6	ngoh sek chouh
i like Cantonese	我鍾意廣東話	ngóh jùng yi gwóng dùng wá	ngo5 zung4 ji3 Gwong2 dung4 waa2	ngoh chung yi kwong tung wa
i live in …	我住喺...	ngóh jyuh haih ...	ngo5 zyu6 hai6 ...	ngoh chyuh haih ...
i love you	我愛你	ngóh ói léih /néih	ngo5 oi3 lei5 /nei5	ngoh oi leih /neih
i'm...years old	我...歲	ngóh... seui	ngo5... seoi3	ngoh...swoi
i'm fine[1]	我好好	ngóh hóu hóu	ngo5 hou2 hou2	ngoh hou hou
i'm fine[2]	我幾好	ngóh geih hóu	ngo5 gei4 hou2	ngoh keih hou
i'm fine too	我都幾好	ngóh dòu geih hóu	ngo5 dou4 gei4 hou2	ngoh tou keih hou
i'm from …	我來自...	ngóh loìh jih ...	ngo5 loi4 zi6 ...	ngoh loih chih ...
i'm hungry	我肚餓	ngóh tóuh ngoh	ngo5 tou5 ngo6	ngoh thouh ngoh
i'm lost…!	我唔見咗...!	ngóh m̀ gin jó ...!	ngo5 m4 gin3 zo2...!	ngoh mh kin cho
i'm thirsty	我頸渴	ngóh géng hot	ngo5 geng2 hot3	ngoh keng hot
i'm[1]	我係	ngóh haih	ngo5 hai6	ngoh haih
i'm[2]	我係呀	ngóh hai aa /āa	ngo5 hai3 aa3 /aa1	ngoh hai aa
i'm[3]	我係啦	ngóh hai la	ngo5 hai3 laa3	ngoh hai la
i may say /i might say	我可以講	ngóh hó yíh góng	ngo5 ho2 ji5 gong2	ngoh ho yih kong

English		Chinese	Romanization 1	Jyutping	Romanization 2
i mean		我是說	ngóh sih syut	ngo5 si6 syut3	ngoh sih syut
i need		我要	ngóh yiu	ngo5 jiu3	ngoh yiu
i need a doctor		我要睇醫生	ngóh yiu tái yì sāng	ngo5 jiu3 tai2 ji4 sang1	ngoh yiu thai yi sang
i order this		我要點這個	ngóh yiu dím je gó	ngo5 jiu3 dim2 ze3 go2	ngoh yiu tim che ko
i pays		由我付	yàuh ngóh fuh	yau4 ngoh5 foo6	yauh ngoh fuh
i really like it!		我真鍾意!	ngóh jān jùng yi!	ngo5 zan1 zung4 ji3!	ngoh chan chung yi!
i speak		我識講	ngóh sīk góng	ngo2 sik1 gong2	ngoh sek kong
i tell you		我叫你	ngóh giu léih /néih	ngo2 giu3 lei5 /nei5	ngoh kiu leih /neih
i told[1]	v	我講咗	ngóh góng jó	ngo5 gong2 zo2	ngoh kong cho
i told[2]	v	我叫咗	ngóh giu jó	ngo5 giu3 zo2	ngoh kiu cho
i think[1]		我諗係	ngóh lám hai	ngo5 lam2 hai6	ngoh lam hai
i think[2] /i feel		我覺得	ngóh gaau dāk	ngo5 gaau3 dak1	ngoh kaau tak
i've found!		我已經撳到啦!	ngóh yíh gìng wán dou lā!	ngo5 ji5 ging4 wan2 dou3 laa1!	ngoh yih keng wan tou la!
i've to go		我必須走	ngóh bīt sēui jáu	ngo5 bit1 seoi1 zau2	ngoh pit swoi chau
i wanna go		我走先	ngóh jáu sin	ngo5 zau2 sin3	ngoh chau sin
i want to /i wanna		我想	ngóh séung	ngo5 soeng2	ngoh seung
i want to buy		我想買	ngóh séung máaih	ngo5 soeng2 maai5	ngoh seung maaih
i was born in…		我生於…年	ngóh sàng yù…lìhn /nìhn	ngo5 sang4 jyu4 …lin4 /nin4	ngoh sang yu…lihn /nihn
i was so excited		我是如此興奮	ngóh yùh chí hìng fáhn	ngo5 jyu4 ch2 hing4 fan5	ngoh yuh chhi hing fahn
i watching	n	我睇住	ngóh tái jyuh	ngo5 tai2 zyu6	ngoh thai chyuh
i will be right back!		我即刻回來	ngóh jīk haak wùih loìh	ngo5 zik1 haak3 wui4 loi4!	ngoh chek haak wuih loih!
i will show you		我會話比	ngóh wúi wá béi	ngo5 wui2 waa2 bei2	ngoh wui wa pei leih
i would also like		我仲想	ngóh juhng séung	ngo5 zung6 soeng2	ngoh chuhng seung
i would never say		唔係咁識講	m̀ haih gam sīk góng	m4 hai6 gam3 sik1 gong2	mh haih kam sek kong
i would say		我想講	ngóh séung góng	ngo5 soeng2 gong2	ngoh seung kong
IC /electric parts /integration	n/abbr	集成電路	jaahp sehng /sihng din louh	zaap6 seng4 /sing4 din6 lou6	chaahp sehng tin louh
ICAC[1] Independent Commission Against Corruption hk	n/abbr	廉記	lìhm gei	lim4 gei3	lihm kei
ICAC[1] Independent Commission Against Corruption hk	n/abbr	廉政公署	lìhm jing gūng chyu	lim4 zing3 gung4 cyu	lihm cheng kung chyu
ice	n	冰	bìng	bing4	peng
ice-axe	n	冰鎬	bīng góu	bing1 gou2	peng kou
ice-berg	n	冰山	bìng sàan	bing4 saan4	peng saan
ice-cream	n	雪糕	syut gòu	syut3 gou4	syut kou
ice-skateboard (four wheels)	n	滾軸溜冰	gwán juhk làuh bīng	gwan2 zuk6 lau4 bing1	kwan chuhk lauh peng
icon /statue/effigy	n	塑像	sou jeuhng	sou3 zoeng6	sou cheuhng
ID /identity card	n/abbr	身份證	sàn fán jing	san4 fan2 zing3	san fan cheng
IDD international phone call /long-distance call	n/abbr	長途電話	chèuhng touh dihn wá	coeng4 tou4 din6 waa2	chheuhng thouh tihn wa
idea[1] /opinion	n	意思	yi sī, yi si	ji3 si1, ji3 si3	yi si

idea[2]/conception/ideology /opinion/thinking/thought /point of thinking	n	思想	sì séung	si4 soeng2	si seung
ideal	n	典範	dín faahn	din2 faan6	tin faahn
idealism	n	唯心主義	wàih sàm jyú yi	wai4 sam4 zyu2 ji6	waih sam chyu yi
ideally /theory	adv	理論	léih leuhn	lei5 leon6	léih leuhn
identical	adj	相同的	seung tùhng dīk	soeng3 tung4 dik1	seung thhng tek
identification	n	身分證明	sàn fán jing mìhng	san4 fan2 zing3 ming4	san fan cheng mehng
identify[1] /recognize	v	認出	yihng chēut	jing6 ceot1	yehng chhot
identity[2] /acquaintance	n	身份	sàn fàn	san4 fan2	san fan
ideographs	n	漢字	hon jih	hon3 zi6	hon chih
ideology system of thought	n	思想體系	sì sēung tāi hàih	si4 soeng1 tai1 hai6	si seung thai haih
idioms /IDM	n	成語	sèhng yúh	seng4 jyu5	sehng yuh
idle[1] /lazy	n	惰	dou	dou3	tou
idle[2]/lazy/loaf/laziness	adj/v	懶散	láahn sáan	laan5 saan2	laahn saan
idle[3]	adj	閒散	hàahn sáan	haan4 saan2	haahn saan
idle chit-chat /gab	v	空談	hùng tàahm	hung4 taam4	hung thaahm
idler[1] /lazy person	n	懶漢	láahn hon	laan5 hon3	laahn hon
idler[2]	n	懶惰者	láahn doh jé	laan5 do6 ze2	laahn toh che
idol /statue	n	偶像	ngáuh jeuhng	ngau5 zoeng6	ngauh cheuhng
if[1] /in case/would	conj/n	如果	yùh gwó	jyu4 gwo2	yuh kwo
if[2]	conj/n	若有	yeuhk yauh	joek6 jau6	yeuhk yauh
if[3]	conj/n	若喺	yeuhk hái	joek6 hai2	yeuhk hai
if any[1]		如有	yùh yáuh	jyu4 jau5	yuh yauh
if any[2]		若有的話	yeuhk yauh dīk wá	joek6 jau6 dik1 wa2	yeuhk yauh tik wa
if anything		如果有區別嘅話	yùh gwó yauh kèui bìht ge wá	jyu4 gwo2 jau6 keoi4 bit6 ge3 wa2	yuh kwo yauh khoi piht ke wa
if applicable		如適用	yùh sīk yuhng	jyu4 sik1 jung6	yuh sek yuhng
if discover		若發現	yeuhk faat yihn	joek6 faat3 jin6	yeuhk faat yihn
if i could help him!		可唔可以幫佢!	hó m̀ hó yíh bòng kéuih!	ho2 m4 ho2 ji5 bong4 keoi5!	ho mh ho yih pong khoih!
if i were you		如果我是你	yùh gwó ngóh sih léih /néih	jyu4 gwo2 ngo5 si6 lei5 /nei5	yuh kwo ngoh sih leih /neih
if necessary		如果必要嘅話	yùh gwó bìt yìu ge wá	jyu4 gwo2 bit4 jiu4 ge3 wa2	yuh kwo pit yiu ke wa
if needs?[1] /shall needs? /is necessary?		駛唔駛?	sái m̀ sāi?	sai2 m4 sai1?	sai mh sai?
if needs?[2] /shall need? /is necessary?		要唔要?	yiu m̀ yiu?	jiu3 m4 jiu3?	yiu mh yiu?
if needs?[3] /shall needs? /is necessary?		駛不駛?	sái bāt sāi?	sai2 bat1 sai1?	sai pat sai?
if needs?[4]		如需要	yùh sèui yiu	jyu4 seoi4 jiu3	yuh swoi yiu
if needs?[5] /shall need? /is necessary?		要不要？	yiu bāt yiu	jiu3 bat1 jiu3	yiu pat yiu
if only	conj	只要	yí yiu	ji2 jiu3	yi yiu
if possible	conj	如有可能	yùh yáuh hó nàhng	jyu4 jau5 ho2 ji4 nang4	yuh yauh ho nahng

if she is busy		佢休唔休閒	kéuih dāk m̀ dāk hàahn	keoi5 dak1 m4 dak1 haan4	khoih tak mh tak haahn
if so!¹		如果係咁	yùh gwó hái gam	jyu4 gwo2 hai2 gam3	yuh kwo hai kam
if so!²		如果係咁樣	yùh gwó hái gam yeuhng	jyu4 gwo2 hai2 gam3 joeng6	yuh kwo hai kam yeuhng
if so!³		如果是咁樣	yùh gwó sih gam yeuhng	jyu4 gwo2 si6 gam3 joeng6	yuh kwo sih kam yeuhng
if you like¹		如果你鍾意	yùh gwó léih /néih jùng yi	jyu4 gwo2 lei5 /nei5 zung4 ji3	yuh kwo leih /neih chung yi
if you like²		如果你喜歡	yùh gwó léih /néih héi fūn	jyu4 gwo2 lei5 /nei5 hei2 fun1	yuh kwo leih /neih hei fun
if you like³		如果你樂意	yùh gwó léih /néih lohk yi	jyu4 gwo2 lei5 /nei5 lok6 ji3	yuh kwo leih /neih lohkyi
ignition	n	點火	dím fō	dim2 fo1	tim fo
ignition point	n	燃點	yìhn dím	jin4 dim2	yihn tim
ignoble /unkind/mean	adj	黑薄	hāak bohk	haak1 bok6	haak pohk
ignorance	n	無知	mòuh jì	mou4 zi4	mouh chi
ignore¹	v	不合	bāt hahp	bat1 hap6	pat hahp
ignore² /neglect	v	唔理	m̀ léih	m4 lei5	mh leih
ignore³	v	唔睬	m̀ chói	m4 coi2	mh chhoi
ignore⁴ /neglect	v	忽視	fāt sih	fat1 si6	fat sih
ignore⁵	v	不顧	bāt gu	bat1 gu3	pat ku
ill	adj	唔精神	m̀ jèng sàhn	m4 zeng4 san4	mh cheng sahn
ill-look /evil sight	adj	立壞心腸	lahp wàaih sām chèuhng	lap6 waai6 sam1 coeng4	lahp waaih sam chheuhng
illegal¹ /lawlessly /illicit/against the law	adj	非法	fèi faat	fei4 faat3	fei faat
illegal²	adj	非法嘅	fèi faat ge	fei4 faat3 ge3	fei faat ke
illegal³ /unlawful	adj	唔合法	m̀ hahp faat	m4 hap6 faat1	mh hahp faat
illegal hunter /poacher for birds or	n	偷獵者	tàu lihp jé	tau4 lip6 ze2	thau lihp che
illegal secret plan /plot	n	密謀	maht màuh	mat6 mau4	maht mauh
illiberal¹	adj	不開明	bāt hòi mìhng	bat1 hoi4 ming4	pat hoi mehng
illiberal²	adj	思想偏狹	sì sèung pīn haahp	si4 soeng4 pin1 haap6	si seung phin haahp
illiterate	adj	文盲	màhn màahng	man4 maang4	mahn maahng
illness¹ /sick/ill	n	病	behng /bihng	beng6 /bing6	pehng
illness² /sickness	n	患病	waahn behng	waan6 beng6	waahn pehng
illuminatingly	adj	照耀地	jiu yiuh deih	ziu3 jiu6 dei6	chiu yiuh teih
illumination /lighting	n	照明	jiu mìhng	ziu3 ming4	chiu mehng
illustrious	n	華	wàh	waa4	wah
image¹ /portrait	n	肖像	chiu jeuhng	ciu3 zoeng6	chhiu cheuhng
image²	n	圖像	tòuh jeuhng	tou4 zoeng6	thouh cheuhng
image³	n	形象	yìhng jeuhng	jing4 zoeng6	yehng cheuhng
image⁴ /reflect/reflection	n/v	反映	fáan yíng	faan2 jing2	faan yeng
imaginary	adj	虛構的	hèui kau dìk	heoi4 kau3 dik4	hoi khau tek
imagination power	n	想像力	séung jéuhng lihk	soeng2 zoeng6 lik6	seung cheuhng lehk

imagination	n	心理作用	sàm leih jok yuhng	sam4 lei5 zok3 jung6	sam leih chok yuhng
imagine /visualize	v	想像	séung jèuhng	soeng2 zoeng6	seung cheuhng
imitable	adj	可模仿	hó mòuh fóng	ho2 mou4 fong2	ho mouh fong
imitative /imitation	adj/n	模仿	mòuh fóng	mou4 fong2	mouh fong
immature[1]	adj	未發育好	meih faat yuhk hóu	mei6 faat3 juk6 hou2	meih faat yuhk hou
immature[2] /unskill/young	adj	幼稚	yau jih	jau3 zi6	yau chih
immediate[1]	adj	即時	jīk sìh	zik1 si4	chek sih
immediate[2]	adj	直接	jihk jip	zik6 zip3	chehk chip
immediate[3] /instant /at once/now/right now /in a minute/in a moment	adj	立即	lahp jīk	lap6 zik1	lahp chek
immediate[4] /right away/at once	adj	馬上	máh seuhng	maa5 soeng3	mah seuhng
immediate die /suddenly die/easy damage		好化學	hóu fa hohk	hou2 faa3 hok6	hou fa hohk
immediately	adj	就嚟	jauh làih	zau6 lai4	chauh laih
immediately back! /right back!		即刻走	jīk haak jáu	zik1 haak3 zau2	chek haak chau
immersed[1] /go into water	v	入水裏便	yahp séui léuih bihn	jap6 seoi2 leoi5 bin6	yahp swoi lowih pihn
immersed[2] /think deeply /thoughtful/ponder/thought/ thinking	v	沉思	chàhm sì	cam4 si4	chhahm si
immigrant[1] /migration /settler	n	移民	yìh màhn	ji4 man4	yih mahn
immigrant[2]	n	外來	ngoih loìh	ngoi6 loi4	ngoih loih
immigrate[1]	v	遷入	chìn yahp	cin4 jin4	chhin yahp
immigrate[2] /migrate	v	移民	yìh màhn	ji4 man4	yih mahn
immigration department[1]	n	入境處	yahp gíng chyu	jap6 ging2 cyu3	yahp keng chhyu
immigration department[2]	n	入境事務處	yahp gíng sih mouh chyu	jap6 ging2 si6 mou6 cyu3	yahp keng sih mouh chhyu
immigration department[3]	n	人民入境事務處	yàhn màhn yahp gíng sih mouh chyu	jan4 man4 jap6 ging2 si6 mau6 cyu3	yahn mahn yahp keng sih mouh chhyu
immigration office[1]	n	移民局	yìh màhn gúk	ji4 man4 guk2	yih mahn kuk
immigration office[2]	n	移民屋	yìh màhn ùk	ji4 man4 uk4	yih mahn uk
immobilization	n	鉗製	kìhm jai	kim4 zai3	khihm chai
immoral[1]	adj	冇道德	móuh douh dāk	mou5 dou6 dak1	mouh touh tak
immoral[2]	adj	不道德	bāt douh dāk	bat1 dou6 dak1	pat touh tak
immortal[1] /forever /fairy/everlasting	adj/n	仙	sìn	sin4	sin
immortal[2] /everlasting	adj	唔朽	m̀ láu /náu	m4 lau2 /nau2	mh lau /nau
immortal[3]	adj	不朽	bāt láu /náu	bat1 lau2 /nau2	pat lau /nau
immune	adj	免疫	míhn yihk	min5 jak6	mihn yehk
immunity	n	免疫力	míhn yihk lihk	min5 jak6 lik6	mihn yehk lehk
immunization	n	免疫	míhn yihk	min5 jak6	mihn yehk
impact /collide/strike	n	撞擊	johng gīk	zong6 gik1	chohng kek
impair /weaken/worse	v	削弱	séuk yèuhk	soek2 joek6	swok yeuhk

impairment /disability	n	損傷	syún sèung	syun2 soeng4	syun seung
impartial	adj	公正的	gùng jeng dīk	gung4 zeng3 dik1	kung cheng tik
impassability[1] (coll) impassable/unpassable	adj	唔能通行	m̀ làhng /nàhng tùng hàahng	m4 lang4 /nang4 tung4 haang4	mh lahng /nahng thung haahng
impassability[2] (text)	adj	不能通行	bāt làhng /nàhng tùng hàahng	bat1 lang4 /nang4 tung4 haang4	pat lahng /nàhng thung haahng
impassioned	adj	激情	gīk chìhng	gik1cing4	kek chhehng
impatient[1]	adj	忟	máng	maang5	mang
impatient[2]	adj	唔耐煩	m̀ noih fàahn	m4 noi6 faan4	mh noih faahn
impatient[3]	adj	不耐煩	bāt loih/noih fàahn	bat1 loi6 /noi6 faan4	pat loih /noih faahn
impeachment /accuse of misconduct	n	彈劾	tàahn haht	taan4 hat6	thaahn haht
imperialism	n	帝國主義	dai gwok jyú yih	dai3 gwok3 zyu2 ji6	tai kwok chyu yih
imperialist	n	帝國主義者	dai gwok jyú yih jé	dai3 gwok3 zyu2 ji6 ze2	tai kwok chyu yih che
implant[1]	v	注入	jyu yahp	zyu3 jap6	chyu yahp
implant[2] /place into	v	置入	ji yahp	zi3 jap6	chi yahp
implant[3]	v	灌輸	gun syū	gun3 syu1	kun syu
implement /tool	n	工具	gùng geuih	gung4 geoi6	kung kwoih
implicate[1]	v	使牽連	saí hìn lìhn	sai2 hin4 lin4	sai hin lihn
implicate[2] (do bad) /involved in bad/ participate in	v	涉及	sip kahp	sip3 kap6	sip khahp
implicate[3]	v	使捲入	sai gyún yahp	sai3 gyun2 jap6	sai kyun yahp
implicated /involved	v	牽涉	hìn sip	hin4 sip3	hin sip
implicit /indirectly expressed/imply	adj	含蓄	hahm chūk	ham4 cuk1	hahm chuk
imply[1] /indirect suggestion	v	暗示	ngam sih	ngam3 si6	ngam sih
imply[2] /indirectly say	v	含有···嘅意思	hàhm yáuh…ge yi si	ham4 jau5 …ge3 ji3 si3	hahm yauh ... ke yi si
impolite[1] /rude	adj	無禮	móuh láih	mou5 lai5	mouh laih
impolite[2] /rude/not polite /lack of respect/unmannerly	adj	粗魯	chòu lóuh	cou4 lou5	chhou louh
impolite[3] /unmannerly /not polite/unpolite/offensive	adj	無禮貌	móuh láih maauh	mou5 lai5 maau6	mouh laih maauh
impolite[4]	adj	唔客氣	m̀ haak héi	m4 haak3 hei2	mh haak hei
impolite[5] /rude/unkind	adj	不客氣	bāt haak héi	bat1 haak3 hei2	pat haak hei
import[1] /carry forward	v	輸入	jyun yahp	zyun3 jap6	chyun yahp
import[2]	v	進口	jeun háu	zeon3 hau2	cheun hau
import[3]	v	運入口	wahn yahp háu	wan6 jap6 hau2	wahn yahp hau
import goods	n	入口貨	yahp háu fo	jap6 hau2 fo3	yahp hau fo
import taxes	n	入口稅	yahp háu seui	jap6 hau2 seoi3	yahp hau swoi
importance /value	n	重要性	juhng yiu sing	zung6 jiu3 sing3	chuhng yiu seng
important person[1] /famous person	n	要人	yìu yàhn	jiu4 jan4	yiu yahn
important person[2] /big shot VIP/worthy person/ great personage	n	大人物	daaih yàhn maht	daai6 jan4 mat6	taaih yahn maht

English		Chinese	Yale	Jyutping	Romanization
important person[3]	n	知名人士	jì mèhng /mìhng yàhn sih	zi4 meng4 /ming4 jan4 si6	chi mehng yahn sih
important[1] /vital	adj	要	yìu	jiu4	yiu
important[2] /serious	adj	緊要	gán yiu	gan2 jiu3	kan yiu
important[3] /significant/ major/value	adj/n	重要	juhng yiu	zung6 jiu3	chuhng yiu
importer	n	進口商	jeun háu sèung	zeon3 hau2 soeng4	cheun hau seung
importune /importunity	n/v	強求	keuhng kàuh	koeng4 kau4	kheuhng khauh
impose[1] /penalty	v	抽	chàu	cau4	chhau
impose[2] tax	v	抽稅	chàu seui	cau4 seoi3	chhau swoi
impose[3] /to force to do	v	勉強	míhn kéuhng	min5 koeng5	mihn kheuhng
impose[4]	v	強加	kéuhng ga	koeng5 gaa3	kheuhng ka
impose[5]	v	徵稅	jìng seui	zing4 seoi3	cheng swoi
imposing[1] /majestic /solemn/sacred	adj	莊嚴	jòng yìhm	zong4 jim4	chong yihm
imposing[2]	adj	雄偉	hùhng wáih	hung4 wai5	huhng waih
impossible[1]	adj	唔可能	m̀ hó làhng /nàhng	m4 ho2 lang4 /nang4	mh ho lahng /nahng
impossible[2]	adj	冇可能	móuh hó làhng/ nàhng	mou5 ho2 lang4 /nang4	mouh ho lahng /nahng
impossible[3]	adj	不可能	bāt hó làhng/nàhng	bat1 ho2 lang4/nang4	pat ho lahng/nahng
impotence /impotent of sexless	adv	陽痿	yèuhng wái	joeng4 wai2	yeuhng wai
impotent[1] /weak/inability /powerless/disability	adj/n	無能	móuh làhng/nàhng	mou2 lang4 /nang4	mouh lahng /nahng
impotent[2] /weak/frail /poor health/weakness	adj	虛弱	hèui yeuhk	heoi4 joek6	hoi yeuhk
impound[1]	v	扣押	kau aat	kau3 aat3	khau aat
impound[2] /intern	v	拘留	kèui làuh	keoi4 lau4	khoi lauh
impression[1]/impress	v	使銘記	sai mèhng gei	sai3 meng4 gei3	sai mehng kei
impression[2]/impress	v	印象	yan jeuhng	jan3 zoeng6	yan cheuhng
impression[3]	n	印象	yan jeuhng	jan3 zoeng6	yan cheuhng
impressive[1]	adj	感人	gám yàhn	gam2 jan4	kam yahn
impressive[2]	adj	令人難忘	lihng yàhn nàahn mòhng	ling6 jan4 naan4 mong4	lehng yahn naahn mohng
impressive[3]	adj	給人深刻 印象	kāp yàhn sàm hàak yan jeuhng	kap1 jan4 sam4 haak4 jan3 zoeng6	khap yahn sam haak yan cheuhng
impressive[4]	adj	深刻印象	sàm hàak yan jeuhng	sam4 haak4 jan3 zoeng6	sam haak yan cheuhng
imprison	v	關押	gwàan aat	gwaan4 aat3	kwaan aat
improper[1] /wrongful	adj	不正當	bāt jéng dóng	bat1 zeng2 dong2	pat cheng tong
improper[2] IDM 5354	adj	唔三唔四	m̀ saam m̀ sei	m4 saam3 m4 sei3	mh saam mh sei
improper[3] /unfit /inappropriate	adj	不適當	bāt sīk dong	bat1 sik1 dong3	pat sik tong
improper time		唔啱時間	m̀ ngāam sìh gaan	m4 ngaam1 si4 gaan3	mh ngaam sih kaan
improper use		不合適	bāt hahp sīk	bat1 hap6 sik1	pat hahp sek
improve[1]	v	改善	gói sihn	goi2 sin6	koi sihn
improve[2] /reform	v	改良	gói lèuhng	goi2 loeng4	koi lowhng

improve[3]	v	改進	gói jeun	goi2 zeon3	koi cheun
improve[4]	v	進步	jeun bouh	zeon3 bou6	cheun pouh
improve of space	n	進步嘅空間	jeun bouh ge hùng gàan	zeon3 bou6 ge3 hung4 gaan4	cheun pouh ke hung kaan
improved	adj	改進過	gói jeun gwò	goi2 zeon3 gwo4	koi cheun kwo
Improvement[1] /progress/progression	n	進步	jeun bouh	zeon3 bou6	cheun pouh
improvement[2]	n	有進步	yáuh jeun bouh	jau5 zeon3 bou6	yauh cheun pouh
impulse /pulse physics	n	脈衝	mahk chùng	mak6 cung4	mahk chhung
impurity	n	不純	bāt seun	bat1 seon3	pat swon
impurity food /remain food	n	食剩	sihk jihng	sik6 zing6	sehk chehng
impute[1]	v	歸咎	gwài gau	gwai4 gau3	kwai kau
impute[2]	v	推給	tèui kaap	teoi1 kap1	thoi khaap
in /inside	adv	進	jeun	zeon3	cheun
in a hurry /more quickly/ very quickly	n	趕促	gón chūk	gon2 cuk1	kon chhuk
in a hurry /speedily	n/adv	趕住	gón jyuh	gon2 zyu6	kon chyuh
in a moment /moment	n	一陣間	yāt jahn gāan	jat1 zang6 gaan1	yat chahn kaan
in a sense /in this context	n	就某種意義來說	jauh máuh júng yi yih lòih syut	zau6 mau5 zung2 ji3 ji6 loi4 syut3	chauh mauh chung yi yih loih syut
in a short time /short-term	n/adj	短期	dyún kèih	dyun2 gei4	tyun kheih
in a temper	n	在盛怒	joih sihng louh	zoi6 sing6 lou6	choih sehng louh
in a thorough /according to a system	adj	系統嘅	hàih tūng ge	hai6 tung2 ge3	haih thung ke
in a word[1]	n	從字	chùhng jì	cung4 zi4	chhuhng chi
in a word[2]/in summary /in brief/ in short/in one word/shortly	n	總之	júng jì	zung2 zi4	chung chi
in a word[3]	n	一言以蔽之	yāt yìhn yíh bai jī	jat1 jing4 ji5 bai3 zi1	yat yihn yih pai chi
in addition /beside	n	此外	chí ngoih	ci2 oi6	chhi ngoih
in advance[1] /pre /advance	adj	預	yuh	jyu6	yuh
in advance[2]	n	預先	yuh sìn	jyu6 sin4	yuh sin
in between	n	其間	kèih gaan	kei4 gaan3	kheih kaan
in brief /in one word		總而言之	júng yìh yìhn jì	zung2 ji4 jin4 zi4	chung yih yihn chi
in case[1] /just in case	conj	萬一	maahn yāt	maan6 jat1	maahn yat
in case[2] /if		假使	gá sìh	gaa2 si6	ka sih
in case happening /possibility happening /potential	n	潛在性	chìhm jòih sing	cim4 zoi6 sing3	chhihm choih seng
in detail	adj	詳情	chèuhng chìhng	coeng4 cing4	chheuhng chiehng
in dispute		在爭論中	joih jàng leuhn jùng	zoi6 zang3 leon6 zung4	choih chang leuhn chung
in good repair		良好維修	lèuhng hou wàih sàu	loeng4 hou3 wai4 sau4	leuhng hou waih sau
in good spirits		好精神	hóu jìng sàhn	hou2 zeng4 san4	hou cheng sahn
in hand		手頭	sáu tàuh	sau2 tau4	sau thauh

English	Chinese	Yale	Jyutping	Romanization
in my old age	我老嘅時候	ngóh lóuh ge sìh háuh	ngo5 lou5 ge3 si4 hau6	ngoh louh ke sih hauh
in order to /sake /in order (n)	為了	waih líuh	wai6 liu5	waih liuh
in other words	換言之	wuhn yìhn jì	wun6 jin4 zi4	wuhn yihn chi
in patient	住院病人	jyuh yuhn behng yàhn	zyu6 jyun4 beng6 jan4	chyuh yuhn pehng yahn
in person /personally	親自	chàn jih	can4 zi6	chhan chih
in progress	行中	hàhng jùng	hang4 zung4	hahng chung
in reserve /spare /reserve/back up (n)	備用	beih yuhng	bei6 jung6	peih yuhng
in room	間房	gaan fóng	gaan3 fong2	kaan fong
in safety /safe/secure (adj)	安全	òn /ngòn chyùhn	on4 /ngon4 cyun4	on /ngon chhyuhn
in style[1] /interest in	興	hìng	hing4	hing
in style[2]	有氣派地	yáuh hei pāai deih	jau5 hei3 paai1 dei6	yauh hei phaai teih
in substance (n)	事實上	sih saht seuhng	si6 sat6 soeng6	sih saht seuhng
in such way /then/thus (adv)	咁樣	gám yéung	ganm2 joeng2	kam yeung
in ten days	喺十日	hái sahp yaht	hai2 sap6 jat6	hai sahp yaht
in that case[1]	噉	gám	gam2	kam
in that case[2]	既然那樣	gei yìhn láh /náh yeuhng	gei3 jin4 la5 /na5 joeng4	kei yihn lah /nah yeuhng
in the center	當中	dong jùng	dong zung4	tong chung
in the meantime (n)	於此際	yu chí jai	jyu3 ci2 zai3	yu chhi chai
in the middle (n)	在...當中	joih...dòng jùng	zoi6...dong4 zung4	choih...tong chung
in the minority (n)	處於少數	chyu yù síu sou	cyu3 ju4 siu2 sou3	chhyu yu siu sou
in the past (n)	以往嘅	yíh wóhng ge	ji5 wong5 ge3	yih wohng ke
in the process (n)	在...過程中	joih gwo chìhng jùng	zoi6 gwo3 cing4 zong4	choih kwo chhehng chung
in the right (n)	有理	yáuh léih	jau5 lei5	yauh leih
in the same boat (sl) (n)	處境相同	chyú gíng sèung tùhng	cyu2 ging2 soeng4 tung4	chhyu king seung thohng
in the world (n)	世界上	sai gaai seuhng	sai3 gaai3 soeng6	sai kaai seuhng
in this context (n)	在上下文中	joih...seuhng hah màhn jùng	zoi6 soeng6 haa6 man6 zung4	choih...seuhng hah mahn chung
in this month (n)	在本月	joih bún yuht	zoi6 bun2 jyut6	choih pun yuht
in time[1] (n)	及時	kahp sìh	kap6 si4	khahp sih
in time[2] /not late (n)	來得及	lòih dāk kahp	loi4 dak1 kap6	loih tak khahp
in total cash /total cash	共銀	guhng ngàhn	gung6 ngan4	kuhng ngahn
in vogue fashionable (n)	時髦	sìh mōu	si4 mou1	sih mou
in writing /written (n)	書面	syu mín	syu3 min2	syu min
inability /coward (n)	無力	mòuh lihk	mou4 lik6	mouh lehk
inaccessible area[1] (adj)	唔入得	m̀ yahp dāk	m4 jap6 dak1	mh yahp tak
inaccessible area[2] (adj)	難去得度	nàahn heui dāk dou	naan4 heoi3 dak1 dou3	naahn hoi tak tou
inaccessible things (adj)	得唔度	dak m̀ dou	dak3 m4 dou3	tak mh tou
inaccessible[1] things (adj)	難以得度	làahn yíh dāk dou	laan4 ji5 dak1 dou3	laahn yih tak tou

inaccessible[2] /persons no entry	adj	難以接近	làahn yíh jip gahn	laan4 ji5 zip3 gan6	laahn yih chip kahn
inaccurate[1]	adj	冇精確	móuh jēng kok	mou5 jeng1 kok3	mouh cheng khok
inaccurate[2]	adj	不精確	bāt jēng kok	bat1 jeng1 kok3	pat cheng khok
inactive	adj	不活躍	bāt wùht yéuk	bat1 wut6 joek2	pat wuht yeuk
inadequate[1]	adj	不充足	bāt chùng jūk	bat1 cung4 zuk1	pat chhung chuk
Inadequate[2]	adj	不充分	bāt chùng fàn	bat1 cung4 fan4	pat chhung fan
inapplicable	adj	不適用	bāt sīk yuhng	bat1 sik1 jung6	pat sik yuhng
inaugural	adj	就職	jauh jīk	zau6 zik1	chauh chek
inaugurate	vt	為...舉行就職典禮	waih...géui hòhng jauh jīk dín láih	wai6 geoi2 hong4 zau6 zik din2 lai5	waih...kwoi hohng chauh chek tin laih
inauspicious[1]	adj	唔吉利	m̀ gāt leih	m4 gat1 lei6	mh kat leih
inauspicious[2]	adj	唔利是	m̀ laih sih	m4 lai6 si6	mh laih sih
inbron /congenital/innate /native/natural/be born with	adj	天生	tìn sàang	tin4 saang4	thin saang
incalculable /innumerable	adj	無數嘅	mòuh sou ge	mou4 sou3 ge3	mouh sou ke
incapable[1] /unable	adj	無法	mòuh faat	mou4 faat3	mouh faat
incapable[2] /unable/can not/must not/ should not	adj	不能	bāt làhng /nàhng	bat1 lang4 /nang4	pat lahng /nahng
incase		這時候	jéh sìh hauh	ze5 si4 hai6	cheh sih hauh
incense stick /joss-stick/incense smell	n	香	hèung	hoeng4	heung
incense-burner	n	香爐	hèung lòuh	hoeng4 lou4	heung louh
incessantly[1] /unending	adv	不斷	bāt dyuhn	bat1 dyun6	pat tyuhn
incessantly[2] /unending/uninterrupted	adv	不絕	bāt jyut	bat1 zyut3	pat chyut
inch	n	吋	chyun	cyun3	chhyun
incidence	n	影響範圍	yéng héung faahn wàih	jeng2 hoeng2 faan6 wai4	yeng heung faahn waih
incident	n	事變	sih bin	si6 bin3	sih pin
inclement	adj	天險惡劣	tìn hím ok /ngok lyut	tin4 him2 ok3 /ngok3 lyut3	thin him ok /ngok lyut
incline /slope/gradient	n	傾斜	kìng che	king4 ce3	khing chhe
include[1]	v	包埋	bāau màaih	baau1 maai4	paau maaih
include[2]	v	計埋	gai màaih	gai3 maai4	kai maaih
inclusion	n	列入	liht yahp	laat6 jap6	liht yahp
income	n	入息	yahp sīk	jap6 sik1	yahp sek
income tex	n	入息稅	yahp sīk seui	jap6 sik1 seoi3	yahp sek swoi
inconvenience	adj	不便	bāt bihn	bat1 bin6	pat pihn
incoordinate	adj	不協調	bāt hip tìuh	bat1 hip3 tiu4	pat hip thiuh
incorrect[1] /wrong /improper/not correct/not right/not suit	adj	唔啱	m̀ ngāam	m4 ngaam1	mh ngaam
incorrect[2] /mistake	adj	有錯	yáuh cho	sau5 co3	yauh cho
incorrect character		錯字	cho jih	co3 zi6	chho chih

incorrectly	adv	錯誤地	cho ngh deih	co3 ng6 dei6	chho ngh teih
incorrupt[1]	adv	廉正	lìhm jeng	lim4 zeng3	lihm cheng
incorrupt[2]	adv	不腐敗嘅	bāt fùh baaih ge	bat1 fu4 baai6 ge3	pāt fùh baaih ge
increase[1]/promotion /promote	n/v	晉	jeun	zeon3	cheun
increase[2]	n	添	tīm	tim1	thim
increase[3] /raise up/add to/multiply/multiplication	v	增加	jàng gà	zang4 gaa4	chang ka
increase[4] /to grow	v	增長	jàng chèuhng	zang4 coeng4	chang chheuhng
increase[5] /raise/elevate /enhancing	v	提高	tàih gòu	tai4 gou4	thaih kou
incredible[1] /fabulous /unbelievable/unbelieving	adj	唔相信	m̀ sēung seun	m4 soeng1 seon3	mh seung seun
incredible[2] /fabulous /unbelievable/unbelieving	adj	不相信	bāt sēung seun	bat1 soeng1 seon3	pat seung swon
incredible[3]	adj	不可信	bāt hó seun	bat1 ho2 seon3	pat ho swon
incredible[4] /fabulous /unbelievable	adj	難以置信	làahn yíh ji seun	laan4 ji5 zi3 seun3	laahn yih chi swon
incredible[5] /miraculous /unimaginable/inconceivable	adj	不可思議	bāt hó sì yíh	bat1 ho2 si4 ji5	pat ho si yih
incredible[6]	adj	不可相信	bāt hó sēung seun	bat1 ho2 soeng1 seon3	pat ho seung swon
incredible[7]	adj	未必可能	meih bīt hó làhng /nàhng	mei6 bit1 ho2 lang4 /nang4	meih pit ho lahng /nahng
incurred[1]	v	招惹	jìu yéh	ziu4 je5	chiu yeh
incurred[2]	v	招致	jìu jí	ziu4 zi2	chiu chi
indecisive	adj	不明確	bāt mìhng kok	bat1 ming4 kok3	pat mihng khok
indeed[1] /really/duly	adj	的確	dīk kok	dik1 kok3	tek kok
indeed[2] /surely	adv	確實	kok saht	kok3 sat6	khok saht
indeed[3]	adv	確係	kok haih	kok3 hai6	khok haih
indeed[4]	adv	確實地	kok saht deih	kok3 sat6 dei6	khok saht teih
indefiniteness	adv	無限期地	mouh haahn keih deih	mou6 haan6 kei6 dei6	mouh haahn kheih teih
indemnity	n	賠償	pùih sèuhng	pui4 soeng4	phuih seuhng
independent[1]	adj	獨立	duhk lahp	duk6 lap6	tuhk lahp
independent[2]	n	獨立派	duhk lahp pāai	duk6 lap6 paai1	tuhk lahp phaai
independently	adj	獨立地	duhk lahp deih	duk6 lap6 dei6	tuhk lahp teih
index[1]	n	指標	jí bīu	zi2 biu1	chi piu
index[2] of book	n	索引	sok yáhn	sok3 jan5	sok yahn
indian-style dish	n	印度菜	yan dòuh choi	jan3 dou6 coi3	yan touh chhoi
indian tea	n	印度茶	yan dòuh cha	jan3 dou6 caa4	yan touh chha
indicate	v	標	bīu	biu1	piu
indicated figure /index/statistical index /numerical index	n	指數	jí sou	zi2 sou	chi sou
indication /label/mark /sign/tag	n	標	bīu	biu1	piu
indicator device	n	指示器	jí sih hei	zi2 si6 hei3	chi sih hei

indicator	n	指示劑	jí sih jài	zi2 si6 zai4	chi sih chai
indicator by man	n	指示者	jí sih jé	zi2 si6 ze2	chi sih che
indicator object /pointer	n	指示物	jí sih maht	zi2 si6 mat6	chi sih maht
indigenous[1]	adj	土產	tōu chāan	tou1 caan1	thou chhaan
indigenous[2]	adj	本地的	sāt deih dìk	sat1 di6 dik4	sat teih tek
indigestable	adj	難消化	làhn /nàhn sìu fa	laan4 /naan4 siu4 faa3	lahn /naahn siu fa
indigestion[1]	n	唔消化	m̀ sìu fa	m4 siu4 faa3	mh siu fa
indigestion[2]	n	消化不良	sìu fa bāt lèuhng	siu4 faa3 bat1 loeng4	siu fa pat leuhng
indirect[1]	adj	間接嘅	gaan jip ge	gaan3 zip3 ge3	kaan chip ke
indirect[2]	adj	軟轉地	yúhn jyun deih	jyun5 zyun3 dei6	yuhn chyun teih
indispensable	adj	不可缺少	bāt hó kyut síu	bat1 ho2 kyut3 siu2	pat ho khyut siu
individual[1] /person	n	個人	go yàhn	go3 jan4	ko yahn
individual[2] /single person	n	個別	go biht	go3 bit6	ko piht
individual property /own property/private property/self property	n	私人財產	sī yàhn chòih cháan	si1 jan4 coi4 caan2	si yahn chhoih chhaan
individually	adv	逐個地	juhk go deih	zuk6 go3 dei6	chuhk ko teih
individually integrity /personal integrity	n	操守	chòu sáu	cou4 sau2	chhou sau
indolent /lazy mind	adj	無精神	móuh jìng sàhn	mou5 zing4 san4	mouh cheng sahn
indoor[1]	adj	室內	sāt loih /noih	sat1 loi6 /noi6	sat loih /noih
indoor[2]	adj	在室內	joih sāt loih /noih	zoi6 sat1 loi6 /noi6	choih sat loih /noih
indoor design /interior design		室內設計	sāt loih /noih chit gai	sat1 loi6 /noi6 cit3 gai3	sat loih /noih chhit kai
indoors /inside		入面	yahp mihn	jap6 min6	yahp mihn
industrial area	n	工業地區	gùng yihp deih kèui	gung4 jip6 dei6 keoi4	kung yihp teih khoi
industry	n	行業	hóng yihp	hong2 jip6	hong yihp
inefficient	adj	無效率	mòuh haauh leuht	mou4 haau6 leot6	mouh haauh lwoht
inertia	n	慣性	gwaan sing	gwaan3 sing3	kwaan seng
inevitable	adj	必然嘅	bīt yìhn ge	bit1 jin4 ge3	pit yihn ke
inexpensive /cheap	adj	低廉	dài lìhm	dai4 lim4	tai lihm
inexperienced /unskilled/awkward/little knowledge/not proficient	adj	唔熟練	m̀ suhk lihn	m4 suk6 lin6	mh suhk lihn
infant [wr] child below one month	n	幼兒	yau yìh	jau3 sai3 ji4	yau yih
infection	n	感染	gám yíhm	gam2 jim5	kam yihm
infection pain /inflammation	n	發炎	faat yìhm	faat3 jim4	faat yihm
infectious by bacteria /infected	adj	感菌嘅	gám kwán ge	gam2 kwan2 ge3	kam khwan ke
inferior /lower quality	adj	劣	lyut	lyut3	lyut
infinite /very big	adj	極大	gihk daaih	gik6 daai6	kehk taaih
infinity /countless/too many/so many	n	數不清	sóu bāt chèng /chìng	sou2 bat1 ceng4 /cing4	sou pat chheng
infirm[1] /sicked weak	adj	體弱	tái yeuhk	tai2 joek6	thai yeuhk
infirm[2]	adj	不堅定	bāt gìn dèhng	bat1 gin4 deng6	pat kin tehng

inflame /motivate/incite/excites	v	激起	gīk héi	gik1 hei2	kek héi
inflamed sore / hot	n	發炎嘅	faat yìhm ge	faat3 jim4 ge3	faat yihm ke
inflammation[1]	n	炎	yìhm	jim4	yihm
inflammation[2]	n	炎症	yìhm jing	jim4 zing3	yihm cheng
inflammationof lungs /pneumonia	n	肺炎	fai yìhm	fai3 jim4	fai yìhm
influence	n	影響	yéng héung	jeng2 hoeng2	yeng heung
influenza /catch cold /common cold/flu	n/v	感冒	gám mouh	gam2 mou6	kam mouh
inform /report/announce /say/tell	v	告	gou	gou3	kou
informal dress /casual wear	n	便服	bihn fuhk	bin6 fuk6	pihn fuhk
information[1] /asking/ inquire/inquiry/ask	n/v	詢問	sèun mahn	seon4 man6	swon mahn
information[2] /news /message	n	消息	sìu sīk	siu4 sik1	siu sek
information[3] /informative	n	信息	seun sīk	seon4 sik1	swon sek
information centre	n	信息中心	seun sīk jùng sàm	seon3 sik1 zung4 sam4	swon sek chung sam
informed	adj	消息靈通	sìu sīk lèhng tūng	siu4 sik1 leng4 tung1	siu sek lehng thung
informer /notifier	n	通知者	tùng jì jé	tung4 zi4 ze2	thung chi che
infrared	adj	紅外線嘅	hùhng oih sin ge	hung4 oi6 sin3 ge3	huhng oih sin ke
infringement /to infringe on	n	侵害	chàm hoih	cam4 hoi6	chham hoih
infuriated /provocation	v	觸怒	jùk louh /nouh	zuk4 lou6 /nou6	chuk louh /nouh
ingredient[1]	n	成分	sèhng fahn	seng4 fan6	sehng fahn
ingredient[2]	n	要素	yìu sóu	jiu4 sou2	yiu sou
ingredient[3] /to mix materials of foods	n	配料	pui líu	piu3 liu2	phui liu
ingredient[4]/items/thing /material/stuff/substance	n	材料	chòih líu	coi4 liu2	chhoih liu
inhabitable	adj	適於居住	sīk yū /yùh gèui jyuh	sik1 jyu1 /jyu4 geoi4 zyu6	sek yu /yuh kwoi chyuh
inhabitant /resident	n	居民	gèui màhn	geoi4 man4	kwoi mahn
inharminous	adj	唔和諧	m̀ wòh hàaih	m4 wo6 haai4	mh woh haaih
inherent	adj	固有(嘅)	gu yáuh (ge)	gu3 jau5 (ge3)	ku yauh (ke)
inherent quality /nature	n	本性	bún sing	bun2 sing3	pun seng
initial[1] /begin	adj	開始的	hòi chí dìk	hoi4 ci2 dik4	hoi chhi tek
initial[2] /first letter	n	第一嗰字母	daih yāt go jih móuh	dai6 jat1 go3 zi6 mou5	taih yat ko chih mouh
initial[3] first	adj	最初	jeui chò	zeoi3 co4	cheui chho
initial letters	n	首字母	sáu jih móuh	sau2 ji6 mou5	sau chi mouh
initiative	n	主動性	jyú duhng sing	zyu2 dung6 sing3	chyu tuhng seng
injection[1] /vaccine /needle/pin/inoculative	n	針	jám	zam2	cham
injection[2] /vaccine	n	打針	dá jám	daa2 zam2	ta cham
injection[3]	n	注射	jyu sèh	zyu3 se4	chyu seh
injure /injury /wound	n/v	傷	sèung	soeng4	seung

injure person /wounder/wounded person	n	傷人	seung yàhn	soeng4 jan4	seung yahn
injury /wound/hurt	n	傷害	sèung hoih	soeng4 hoi6	seung hoih
injustice[1]	n	唔 公平	m̀ gūng pèhng / pìhng	m4 gung1 peng4 /ping4	mh kung phehng
injustice[2]	n	唔 公正	m̀ gūng jeng	m4 gung1 zeng3	mh kung cheng
injustice[3] /unfair	n	不公正	bāt gūng jeng	bat1 gung1 zeng3	pat kung cheng
injustice[4] /wronged	n	冤枉	yūn wóng	jyun1 wong2	yun wong
ink[1]	n	墨	mahk	mak6	mahk
ink[2]	n	墨水	mahk séui	mak6 seoi2	mahk swoi
inland	adv	內地	loih /noih deih	loi6 /noi6 dei6	loih /noih teih
inland revenue department /tax bureau /revenue department	n	稅務局	seui mouh gúk	seui3 mou6 guk2	swoi mouh kuk
inn /wine shop/pup shop	n	小酒店	síu jáu dim	siu2 zau2 dim3	siu chau tim
innate after born	adj	與生俱來	yùh sàang kèui loìh	jyu4 sang4 keoi4 loi4	yuh saang khoi loih
inner /internal/inside	adj	內	loih /noih	loi6 /noi6	loih /noih
innocuous	adj	無惡意	mòuh ok /ngok yi	mou4 ok3 /ngok3 ji3	mouh ok /ngok yi
innovation /new ideas	n	創新	sèung sàn	soeng4 san4	seung san
input /enter	v	輸入	syù yahp	syu4 jap6	syu yahp
inquire[1]	n	查問	chàh mahn	caa4 man6	chhah mahn
inquire[2] /investigation /research/search	n	察	chaat	caat3	chhaat
inquirer	n	查問者	chàh mahn jé	caa4 man6 ze2	chhah mahn che
inquiry[1]	n	訊問	sèun mahn	seon4 man6	swon mahn
inquiry[2]	n	查詢	chàh sèun	caa4 seon4	chhah swon
inquiry[3]	n	調	diuh	diu6	tiuh
inquiry[4] /investigation	n	調查	tìuh chàh	tiu4 caa4	thiuh chhah
insane /madness	adj	心魔	sàm mò	sam4 mo4	sam mo
insect[1] /worms	n	蟲	chùhng	cung4	chhuhng
insect[2]	n	昆蟲	gwān chùhng	gwan1 cung4	kwan chhuhng
insecure /unsafe	adj	不安全	bat òn chyùhn	bat1 on4 cyun4	pat on chhyuhn
Insensible[1]/lose to feel /numb/shock	adj	刺激	chi gīk	ci3 gik1	chhi kek
insensible[2] /numb/ lose to feel	adj	麻悲	màh bei	maa4 bei3	mah pei
insensible[3] /numb /lose to feel	adj	打激	dá gīk	daa2 gik1	ta kek
insensible[4] /senseless /numb	adj	失去知覺	sāt heui jì gok	sat1 heoi3 zi4 gok3	sat hoi chi kok
insert /let in/penetrate /sink into	v	插入	chaap yahp	caap3 jap6	chhaap yahp
insert out insert	v	抽插	chàu chaap	cau4 caap3	chhau chaap
inserting act	v	插入做	chaap yahp jouh	caap3 jap6 zou6	chhaap yahp chouh
inside[1]	n	入便	yahp bihn	jap6 bin6	yahp pihn
inside[2] /into	n	裡面	léuih mihn	leoi5 min6	lowih mihn
inside[3]	n	內面	loih /noih mìhn	loi6 /noi6 min4	loih /noih mihn

inside[4] /interior	n	內部	loih /noih bòuh	loi6 /noi6 bou6	loih /noih pouh
inside[5]	n	之內	jí lòih /nòih	zi2 loi6 /noi6	chi loih /noih
inside book	n	冊內	chaak loih /noih	caak3 loi6 /noi6	chhaak loih /noih
inside car	n	車廂	chè sèung	ce4 soeng4	chhe seung
inside room	n	宇內	yúh loih /noih	jyu5 loi6 /noi6	yuh loih /noih
inside the closet		櫃入面	gwaih yahp mihn	gwai6 jap6 min6	kwaih yahp mihn
inside you		你入面	léih yahp mihn	lei5 jap6 min6	leih yahp mihn
insipid /no taste /tasteless/without taste	adj	淡	táahm	taam6	thaahm
insist[1] /persist/insistence /obstinacy	v	堅持	gìn chìh	gin4 ci4	kin chhih
insist[2]	v	係要	haih yiu	hai6 jiu3	haih yiu
insistently[1] /obstinant	adv	一味	yāt méi	jat1 mei2	yat mei
insistently[2] /persistently	adv	堅持地	gīn chìh deih	gin1 ci4 dei6	kin chhih teih
insomnia	n	失眠	sāt mìhn	sat1 min4	sat mihn
insouciance /unconcerned	n	無憂無慮	mòuh yàu mòuh leuih	mou4 jau4 mou4 leoi6	mouh yau mouh lowih
inspect	v	視察	sih chaat	si6 caat3	sih chhaat
inspection /exam/test		檢查	gím chàh	gim2 caa4	kim chhah
inspiration[1]	n	靈感	lìhng gám	leng4/ling4 gam2	lehng kam
inspiration[2]	n	啟發	kái faat	kai2 faat3	khai faat
inspiration[3]	n	啟示	kái sih	kai2 si6	khai sih
inspirator	n	呼吸器	fù kāp hei	fu4 kap1 hei3	fu khap hei
inspire[1]	v	吸氣	kāp hei	kap1 hei3	khap hei
inspire[2]	v	鼓舞	gú móuh	gu2 mou5	ku mouh
install[1]	v	較	gaau	gaau3	kaau
install[2] /to fix	v	裝	jòng	zong4	chong
instalment[1] /pay by instalement	n/v	分期付款	fàn kèih fuh fún	fan4 kei4 fu6 fun2	fan kheih fuh fun
instalment[2]	n	一部分	yāt bouh fahn	jat1 bou6 fan6	yat pouh fahn
instant[1] /rush/hurry /hurriedly	n/adj	趕緊	gón gán	gon2 gan2	kon kan
instant[2] /immediate	adj	即刻	jīk hāak	zik1 haak1	chek haak
instant[3] drink	n	即冲即飲	jīk chùng jīk yám	zik1 cung4 zik1 jam2	chek chhung chek yam
instant eat	n	即食	jīk sihk	zik1 sik6	chek sehk
instead[1] /to replace	adv	代	doih	doi6	toih
instead[2] /replace/change /replacement/substitute	adv	代替	doih tai	doi6 tai3	toih thai
instead[3]	adv	替代	tái dòih	tai3 doi6	thai toih
instep	n	腳背	geuk bui	goek3 bui3	keuk pui
instigate	v	慫恿	súng yúng	sung2 jung2	sung yung
instigator	n	慫恿者	súng yúng jé	sung2 jung2 ze2	sung yung che
institution of political /system/principle	n	制度	jai douh	zai3 dou6	chai touh
instruct[1] /tell	v	交帶	gàau daai	gaau4 daai3	kaau taai

instruct[2] /teach/taught /initiate	v	教導	gaau douh	gaau3 dou6	kaau touh
instruct[3] /direct/pointer	n	指示	jí sih	zi2 si6	chi sih
instruction[1] /advice /lesson/speech	n	講	góng	gong2	kong
instruction[2]	n	講授	góng sauh	gong2 sau6	kong sauh
instruction booklet /cover letter	n	說明書	syut mèhng /mìhng syù	syut3 meng4 /ming4 syu4	syut mehng syu
instructor[1]	n	教師	gaau sī	gaau3 si1	kaau sih
instructor[2] /teacher	n	教員	gaau yùhn	gaau3 jyun4	kaau yuhn
instructor[3] /conductor	n	指導者	jí douh jé	zi2 dou6 ze2	chi touh che
instrument[1]	n	儀器	yìh hei	jip4 hei3	yih hei
instrument[2] /device /tool/equipment /utensil	n	具	geuih	geoi6	kwoih
insufficient[1] /shortage /not enough/deficient	adj	唔夠	m̀ gau	m4 gau3	mh kau
insufficient[2]	adj	不夠	bāt gau	bat1 gau3	pat kau
insult /humiliate	v	侮辱	móuh yuhk	mou5 juk6	mouh yuhk
insurance[1]	n	保險	bóu hím	bou2 him2	pou him
insurance[2]	n	燕梳	yin sō	bou2 so1	yin sō
insurant	v	保險契約者	bóu hím kai yeuk jé	bou2 him2 kai3 joek3	pou him khai yeuk che
insurgent	a	叛亂者	buhn lyuhn jé	bun6 lyun6 ze2	puhn lyuhn che
intake[1]	n	引入	yáhn yahp	jan5 jap6	yahn yahp
intake[2] /pull into	n	引入口	yáhn yàhp hāu	jan5 jap6 hau1	yahn yahp hau
intake[3]	n	攝取	sip chéui	sip3 ceoi2	sip chhoi
integrated	adj	綜合嘅	jung hahp	jung3 hap6	chung hahp
integration[1]	n	混合	wahn hahp	wan6 hap6	wahn hahp
integration[2]	n	融合	yùhng hahp	jung4 hap1	yuhng hap
integration[3] /complex	n	綜合	jung hahp	zung3 hap6	chung hahp
intellectual	a	智力嘅	ji lihk ge	zi3 lik6 ge3	chi lehk ke
intelligent	adj	靈性	lìhng sing	leng4/ling4 sing3	lehng seng
intend[1]	v	有意	yáuh yi	jau5 ji3	yauh yi
intend[2] /plan/going to do	v	打算	dá syun	daa2 syun3	ta syun
intend[3] /plan/aim	adj	擬	yìh	ji4	yih
intended sexual desire /much sexual intercourse /lust/oversexed/desire sex /erotic	adj/v	性慾	sing yuhk	sing3 juk6	seng yuhk
intended to attract /entice/come-on/ sexually attract/presuade/sex into a trap/sexually attract	n	誘惑	yáuh waahk	jau5 waak6	yauh waahk
intended to attract men /coquetry	n	媚態	mouh taai	mou6 taai3	mouh thaai
intense[1] /ardent/passionate	adj	烈	liht	lit6	liht
intense[2] /zeal/raging /feel strongly	adj	熱情	yiht chìhng	jit6 cing4	yiht chhehng
intense[3]	adj	酷烈	huhk liht	huk6 lit6	huhk liht

intense[4] violently	adj	強烈	keuhng liht	koeng4 lit6	kheuhng liht
intensify[1] /increase	v	加強	gà kèuhng	gaa4 koeng4	ka kheuhng
intensify[2]	v	強化	kèuhng fa	koeng4 faa3	kheuhng fa
intention[1]	n	意圖	yi tòuh	ji3 tou4	yi thouh
intention[2] /mind/feel	n/v	心意	sàm yi	sam4 ji3	sam yi
intention[3] /purpose	n	用意	yuhng yi	jung6 ji3	yuhng yi
intentionally[1]	adv	特登	dahk dāng	dak6 dang1	tahk tang
intentionally[2] /on desire	adv	故意	gu yi	gu3 ji3	ku yi
intentionally[3]	adv	故意地	gu yi deih	gu3 ji3 dei6	ku yi teih
intently /single minded /only thinking one aim/with strained/eager attention(sl) IDM '1312'	adj IDM	一心一意	yāt sàm yāt yi	jat1 sam4 jat1 ji	yat sam yat yi
inter[1] /between	prefix	在間	joih gáan	zoi6 gaan2	choih kaan
inter[2] each other	prefix	相互	seung wuh	soeng3 wu6	seung wuh
inter[3] in middle	prefix	在...中	joih...jùng	zoi6 zung4	choih...chung
inter[4] /bury/to bury (dead body)	v	葬	jong	zong3	chong
inter[5] dead body	v	理葬	léih jong	lei5 zong3	leih chong
interact	v	交互式	gàau wuh sìk	gaau4 wu6 sik4	kaau wuh sek
interaction[1]	n	互相酉合	wuh sèung yáuh hahp	wu6 seung3 jau5 hap6	wuh seung yauh hahp
interaction[2]	n	互動	wuh duhng	wu6 dung6	wuh tohng
interactive	adj	互動	wuh duhng	wu6 dung6	wuh tohng
intercession	n	推薦	tèui jin	teoi4 zin3	thoi chin
interchange[1]	v	交換	gàau wuhn	gaau4 wun6	kaau wuhn
interchange[2]	v	互換	wuh wuhn	wu6 wun6	wuh wuhn
intercourse[1] /communicate	n	交際	gàau jai	gaau4 jai3	kaau chai
intercourse[2] to contact	n	交往	gàau wóhng	gaau4 wong5	kaau wohng
intercourse sex[1]	n	交媾	gāau gau	gaau1 gau3	kaau kau
intercourse sex[2] /sexual contact/sexual relations	n	性關係	sing gwāan haih	sing3 gwaan1 hai6	seng kwaan haih
interdependent	adj	互助	wuh joh	wu6 zo6	wuh choh
interest[1] /to concern	n	關係	gwàan haih	gwaan4 hai6	kwaan haih
interest[2]	n	興趣	hing cheui	hing3 ceoi3	hing chhoi
interest[3]	v	對…有興趣	deui...yáuh hing cheui	deui3 jau5 hing3 ceoi3	toei ...yauh hing chhoi
interest group /pressure group	n	利益集團	leih yīk jaahp tyùhn	lei6 jik1 zaap6 tyun4	leih yek chaahp thyuhn
interest of loan	n	利息	leih sīk	lei6 sik1	leih sek
interest rate	n	利率	leih léut	lei6 leot2	leih leut
interesting	adj	引起興趣	yáhn héi hing cheui	jan5 hei2 hing3 ceoi3	yahn hei heng chhoi
interface	n	分界面	fān gaai mihn	fan1 gaai3 min6	fan kaai mihn
interfere /to conflict	v	抵觸	dái jūk	dai2 zuk1	tai chuk
interference /intrude	n/v	干涉	gòn sip	gon4 sip3	kon sip

English	POS	Chinese	Yale	Jyutping	Romanization
intergrade	n	中間等級	jùng gàan dáng kāp	zung4 gaan4 dang2 kap1	chung kaan tang khap
interim period	adj	過渡期間	gwo douh kèih gaan	gwo3 dou6 kei4 gaan3	kwo touh kheih kaan
interior /lining/in /inside	n/prep	裡	léuih	leoi5	lowih
interior design	n	室內裝飾	sāt loih /noih jōng sīk	sat1 loi6 /noi6 zong1 sik1	sat loih /noih chong sek
intermarriage	n	異族結婚	yih juhk git fàn	ji6 zuk6 git3 fan4	yih chuhk kit fan
intermittent	adj	間歇	gaan hit (sing)	gaan3 hit3 (sing3)	kaan hit (sing)
intern doctor /inexperenced doctor	n	實習醫生	saht jaahp yī sāng	sat6 zaap6 ji1 sang1	saht chaahp yi sang
internal[1] /inner	adj	內部	loih /noih bouh	loi6 /noi6 bou6	loih /noih pouh
internal[2] /inside	adj/n	裡便	léuih bihn	lei5 bin6	lowih pihn
internal[3]	adj	入便	yahp bihn	jap6 bin6	yahp pihn
internal discussion (sl)	v	圍內討論	wàih loih /noih tóu lèuhn	wai4 loi6 /noi6 tou2 leong4	waih loih /noih thou leuhn
internal organs[1] /viscera	n	臟	johng	zong6	chohng
internal organs[2] /offal /entrails/internal parts of body	n	動物內臟	duhng maht loih /noih johng	dung6 mat6 loi6 /noi6 zong6	tuhng maht loih /noih chohng
internal parts of the body	n	身體嘅內部	sàn tái ge loih /noih bouh	san4 tai2 ge3 loi6 /noi6 bou6	san thai ke loih /noih pouh
international	adj	國際	gwok jai	gwok3 zai3	kwok chai
international law	adj	國際法	gwok jai faat	gwok3 zai3 faat3	kwok chai faat
international public law	adj	國際公法	gwok jai gùng faat	gwok3 zai3 gung4 faat3	kwok chai kung faat
international airport	n	國際機場	gwok jai gèi chèuhng	gwok3 zai3 gei4 coeng4	kwok chai kei chheuhng
internationalism	n	國際主義	gwok jai jú yih	gwok3 zai3 zyu2 ji6	kwok chai chu yih
internet[1] /web page/on the internet/be on the internet/surf the internet	n	上網	seuhng móhng	soeng6 mong5	seuhng mohng
internet[2] /web/network	n	網絡	móhng lohk	mong5 lok6	mohng lohk
internet[3]	n	互聯網	wu lyùhn móhng	wu3 lyun4 mong5	wu lyuhn mhng
internet address /web page/network	n	網頁	móhng yihp	mong5 jip6	mohng yihp
interpret[1] /translate	v	譯	yihk	jik6	yehk
interpret[2]	v	口譯	háu yihk	hau2 jik6	hau yehk
interpret[3] /translate /render	v	翻譯	fān yihk	faan1 jik6	fan yehk
interpreter[1]	n	口譯者	háu yihk jé	háu yihk ze2	hau yehk che
interpreter[2] /translator	n	傳譯員	chyùhn yihk yùhn	cyun4 jik6 jyun4	chhyuhn yehk yuhn
interrogative	adj	疑問嘅	yìh mahn	ji4 man6	yih mahn
interruption[1]	n	休止	yàu jí	jau4 zi2	yau chi
intersection[2]	n	橫斷	wàahng tyúhn	waang4 tyun5	waahng thyuhn
intersection[3] /junction	n	交叉點	gāau chā dīm	gaau1 ca1 dim1	kaau chha tim
interval[1]	n	間隙	gaan kwīk	gaan3 kwik1	kaan khwik
interval[2]	n	間隔	gaan gaak	gaan3 gaak3	kaan kaak
interval time	n	休息時間	yàu sīk sìh gaan	jau4 sik1 si4 gaan3	yau sek sih kaan
intervention	n	介入	gaai yahp	gaai3 jap6	kaai yahp

interview[1] focr job	n	見工	gin gùng	gin3 ging4	kin kung
interview[2] for job	n	面試	mihn síh	min6 si5	mihn sih
intestate not wish to write before die	adj	無遺囑嘅死亡者	móuh wàih jūk ge séi mòhng jé	mou5 wai4 zuk1 ge3 sei2 mong4 ze2	mouh waih chuk ke sei mohng che
intestine	n	腸	chéung	coeng2	chheung
intestine large	n	大腸	daaih chéung	daai6 coeng2	taaih chheung
into	prep	進入	jeun yahp	zeon3 jap6	cheun yahp
intoxication	n	使醉	sìh jeui	si6 zeoi3	sih choi
introduce /introduction	v	介紹	gaai siuh	gaai3 siu6	kaai siuh
introducer[1]	n	介紹人	gaai siuh yàhn	gaai3 siu6 jan4	kaai siuh yahn
introducer[2] /usher	n	引座員	yáhn joh yuhn	jan5 zo6 jyun4	yahn choh yuhn
introducer[3]	n	介紹…俾…識	gaai siuh…béi …sīk	gaai3 siu6…bei2…sik1	kaai siuh…pei…sek
introduction[1] /preface /forward (of book)	n	序	jeuih	zeoi6	cheuih
introduction[2] of book /forward of book	n	前言	chìhn yìhn	cin4 jin4	chhihn yihn
introduction[3]	n	引言	yáhn yìhn	jan5 jin4	yahn yihn
introduction[4]	n	課程簡介	fo chìhng gáan gaai	fo3 cing4 gaan2 gaai3	fo chhehng kaan kaai
invade[1] /attack/raid	v	侵	chàm	cam4	chham
invade[2]	v	入侵	yahp chàm	jap6 cam4	yahp chham
invalid	adj	無效	mòuh hàauh	mou4 haau6	mouh haauh
invest	v	投資	tàuh jī	tau4 zi1	thauh chi
invest money /lending money	v	出錢	chēut chín	ceot1 cin2	chhot chhin
investigate[1]	v	審	sám	sam2	sam
investigate[2]	v	究	gau	gau3	kau
investigator	n	調查者	tìuh chàh jé	tiu4 caa4 ze2	thiuh chhah che
investment	n	投資	tàuh jī	tau4 zi1	thauh chi
investor	n	投資者	tàuh jī jé	tau4 zi1 ze	thauh chi che
invidious	adj	易引起反感	yìh yáhn héi fáan gám	ji6 jan5 hei2 faan2 gam2	yih yahn hei faan kam
invisible[1] /invisibility	adj	看唔見	hōn m̀ gin	hon1 m4 gin3	hon mh kin
invisible[2] /invisibility	adj	看不見	hōn bāt gin	hon1 bat1 gin3	hon pat kin
invitation card	n	請帖	chéng /chíng tip	ceng2 /cing2 tip3	chheng thip
invite	v	邀	yìu	jiu4	yiu
invite you		邀您	yìu séung	jiu4 soeng2	yiu seung
invoice /receipt/bill	n	發票	faat piu	faat3 piu3	faat phiu
invoke /pray for	v	祈求	kèih kàuh	kei4 kau4	kheih khauh
involve[1]	v	波及	bō kahp	bo1 kap6	po khahp
involve[2]	v	有關	yáuh gwàan	jau5 gwaan4	yauh kwaan
involve others (into trouble)	v	拖累	tòh leuih	to6 leoi6	thoh lowih
involved into case	v	涉案	sip on /ngon	sip3 on3 /ngon3	sip on /ngon
involvement[1] /join in /participate in/ become member/take part in/mix into in	n/adj	加入	gà yahp	gaa4 jap6	ka yahp

English		Chinese	Yale	Jyutping	Romanization
involvement[2] in debate	n	插手	chaap sáu	caap3 sau2	chhaap sau
IPA, International Phonetic Alphabet	abbr	國際音標	gwok jai yām bīu	gwok3 zai3 jam1 biu1	kwok chai yam piu
irascible	adj	暴躁的	bouh chou dìk	bou6 cou3 dik4	pouh chhou dek
Ireland	n	愛爾蘭	ói /ngoi yíh laan	oi3 /ngoi3 ji5 laan3	oi /ngoi yih laan
iron[1] metal	n	鐵	tit	tit3	thit
iron[2] for clothes	n	熨斗	wai dáu	wai3 dau2	wai tau
iron gate	n	鐵閘	tit jaahp	tit3 zaap6	thit chaahp
iron nail /nail/peg	n	釘	dēng	deng1	teng
iron wire	n	鐵線	tit sín	tit3 sin2	thit sin
ironing (for cloths)	n	熨衣服	wai yī fuhk	wai3 ji1 fuk6	wai yi fuhk
ironing board[1]	n	熨衫板	wai sāam báan	wai3 saam1 baan2	wai paan
ironing board[2]	n	熨燙板	wai tong báan	wai3 tong3 baan2	wai thong paan
ironing cloth	n	熨衫	wai sāam	wai3 saam1	wai saam
irregular	adj	不規則的	bāt kwài jàk dìk	bat1 kwai4 zak4 dik4	pat khwai chak tek
irrelative	v	無關係	mòuh gwàan haih	mou4 gwaan4 hai6	mouh kwaan haih
irritate /angry	v	使惱怒	saí nóuh nouh	sai2 nou5 nou6	sai nouh nouh
irritated /unhappy /upset	adj	心煩	sàm fàahn	sam4 faan4	sam faahn
irritatingly	adj	使慣怒地	sai fahn louh /nouh deih	sai3 fan6 lou6 /nou6 dei6	sai fahn louh /nouh teih
irritation	adv	氣惱	hei lóuh /nóuh	hei3 lou6 /nou6	hei louh /nouh
is[1] /has/have/having (coll)	aux/v	有	yáuh	jau5	yauh
is[2] /are/be/to be (coll)	aux/v	係	haih /hai	hai6 /hai3	haih /haih
is[3] (wr)	aux/v	是	sih	si6	sih
is at home?		係屋企嗎?	hai ùk kéi má?	hai3 uk4 kei5 maa5?	hai uk khei ma?
is far?		遠唔遠呀?	yúhn m̀ yúhn aa?	jyun5 m4 jyun5 aa3?	yuhn mh yuhn aa?
is he coming?		佢來嗎?	kéuih /héuih loìh mā?	keoi5 /heoi5 loi5 maa1?	khoih /hoih loih ma?
is necessary? /needs?		要用啊?	yiu yuhng ā?	jiu3 jung6 aa1?	yiu yuhng ah?
is okay?		好唔好啊?	hóu m̀ hóu aa?	hou2 m4 hou2 aa3?	hou mh hou aa?
is or is not? a person		喺唔喺度?	hái m̀ hái dou?	hai2 m4 hai2 dou3?	hai mh hai tou?
is or isn't?[1]		有冇呀?	yáuh móuh àa /aa?	jau5 mou5 aa3 /aa4?	yauh mouh aa?
is or isn't?[2] /yes or no?		是不是?	sih bāt sih?	si6 bat1 si6?	sih pat sih?
is or isn't?[3] /whether? /whether or not	conj	是否?	sih fáu?	si6 fau2?	sih fau?
is there? person		係度嗎?	hai douh má?	hai3 dou6 maa2?	hai touh ma?
is took out?		攞咗未呀?	ló jó meih àa /aa?	lo2 zo2 mei6 aa4 /aa3?	lo cho meih aa ?
is where!		喺邊度!	hái bīn dou!	hai2 bin1 dou3!	hai pin tou!
Islam /Moslem	n	回教	wùih gaau	wui4 gaau3	wuih kaau
islamic	n	清真	chèng /chìng jān	ceng4 /cing4 zan1	chheng chan
island[1] /continent	n	洲	jāu	zau1	chau
island[2]	n	島	dóu	dou2	tou
island[3] traffic safety land	n	安全島	òn /ngòn chyun dōu	on4 /ngon4 cyun4 dou1	on /ngon chhyun tou
islander	n	島上居民	dóu séuhng gèui màhn	dou2 soeng5 geoi4 man4	tou seuhng kwoi mahn
isn't?		唔係呀?	m̀ haih a?	m4 hai6 a3?	mh haih a?

English		Chinese	Yale	Jyutping	Other
isn't it?	aux v	係咪	haih máih?	hai6 mai5?	haih maih?
isolate[1] /separate /to isolate	v	隔離	gaak lèih	gaak3 lei4	kaak leih
isolate[2]	v	孤立	gū lahp	gu1 lap6	ku lahp
isolate[3] for electric	v	絕缘	jyuht yùhn	zyut6 jyun4	chyuht yuhn
isolated[1] /solitary/lonely	adj	空虛	hūng hēui	hung1 heoi1	hung heui
isolated[2]	adj	隔绝	gáak jyùht	gaal2 zyut6	kaak chyuht
isolator	n	隔離掣	gaak lèih jai	gaak3 lei4 zai3	kaak leih chai
isosceles triangle	n	等腰三角形	dáng yiu sàam gok yìhng	dang2 jiu3 saam4 gok3 jing4	tang yiu saam kok yehng
issue[1]	v	流出	làuh chēut	lau4 ceot1	lauh chhot
issue[2]	v	頒發	bāan faat	baan1 faat3	paan faat
issue number		刊號	hòn houh	hon4 hou6	hon houh
issue quantity		發出數量	faat chēut sōu lèuhng	faat3 ceot1 sou1 loeng6	faat chhot sou leuhng
issued comments		發佈嘅留言	faat bou ge làuh yìhn	faat3 bou3 ge3 lau4 jin4	faat pou ke lauh yihn
issued order /send out	v	發出	faat chēut	faat3 ceot1	faat chhot
issued proof		發證	faat jing	faat3 zing3	faat cheng
it[1] /that	pron	嗰 / 個	gó	go2	ko
it[2] used for things	pron	它	tà	taa4	tha
it[3] for animal	pron	牠	tà	taa4	tha
it[4]		佢	kéuih	keoi5	khoih
it all depends...[1]		睇…嚟凑吖	tái...làih chau lā!	tai2...lai4 cau3 laa1	thai...laih chhau la!
it all depends...[2]		要看情況而定	yìu hòn chìhng fong yìh dehng	jiu4 hon4 cing4 fong3 ji4 deng6	yiu hon chhehng fong yih tehng
it can't be helped		實在沒辦法	saht joih muht baahn faat	sat6 zoi6 mut6 baan6 faat3	saht choih muht paahn faat
it doesn't matter		冇乜所謂	móuh māt só waih	mou5 mat1 so2 wai6	mouh mat so waih
it is a long story /not easy to express/difficult to say/hard to explain	adj	一言難盡	yāt yìhn làahn /nàahn jeuhn	jat1 jin4 laan4 /naan4 zeon6	yat yihn laahn /naahn cheuhn
it is better to		不如	bāt yùh	bat1 jyu4	pat yuh
it is reported that		據報道	geui bou douh	geoi3 bou3 dou6	kwoi pou touh
it is right /correct /sure/no wrong/no	adj	冇錯	móuh cho	mou5 co3	mouh chho
it's possible		有可能	yáuh hó nàhng	jau5 ho2 nang4	yauh ho nahng
it's your turn[1] /one's turn/your turn/ your times /your's rotation	n	輪到	lèuhn dou...	leon4 dou3	leuhn tou...
it's your turn[2]		到你啦	dou leih /neih lā	dou3 lei6 /nei6 laa1	tou leih /neih la
Italy	n	意大利	yí dàaih lèih	ji2 daai6 lei6	yi taaih leih
itch[1] /itchy	n/v	痕	hàhn /hán	han4 /han2	hahn /han
itch[2]	v	癢	yéuhng	joeng5	yeuhng
itchy	v	好痕	hóu hàhn	hou2 han4	hou hahn
itchying foot		香港腳	hèung góng geuk	heung1 gong2 geuk3	heung kong keuk
item[1] /thing	n	件	gihn	gin6	kihn
item[2] /matter/thing /work/ affair	n	事	sih	si6	sih

item³	n	目	muhk	muk6	muhk
item code	n	貨品代號	fo bán doih houh	fo3 ban2 doi6 hou6	fo pan toeih houh
itinerary /journey time	n	行程表	hàhng chìhng bíu	hang4 cing4 biu2	hahng chhehng piu
itself¹ /herself/himself	pron	它自己	tà jih géi	taa4 zi6 gei2	tha chih kei
itself² by animal/man	pron	本身	bún sàn	bun2 san4	pun san
itself³ by man/animal	pron	自身	jih sàn	zi6 san4	chih san
ivory elephant's teeth	n	象牙	jeuhng ngàh	zoeng6 ngaa4	cheuhng ngah
ivy creeping plant	n	長春籐	chèuhng chēun tàhng	coeng4 ceon1 tang4	chheuhng chheun thahng

English		Chinese	Pinyin	Jyutping	Romanization
jack[1] /weight lifting device/lifting	n	千斤頂	chìn gàn dēng	cin4 gan4 deng1	chhin kan teng
jack[2] of cards	n	傑克	giht hāak	git6 haak1	kiht haak
jack fruit	n	大樹菠蘿	daaih syuh bō lòh	daai6 syu6 bo1 lo4	taaih syuh po loh
jacket[1] /wrap/wears	n	外套	oih /ngoih tou	oi6 /ngoi6 tou3	oih /ngoih thou
jacket[2] /windbreaker	n	風褸	fùng làu	fung4 lau4	fung lau
jacket[3] /windbreaker	n	風衣	fùng yì	fung4 ji4	fung yi
jade[1]	n	玉	yúk	juk2	yuk
jade[2]	n	翡翠	féi cheui	fei2 ceoi3	fei chhoi
jail[1] /prison home	n	坐監	chóh gāam	co5 gaam1	chhoh kaam
jail[2] /prison/slammer [(sl)]	n	監獄	gāam yuhk	gaam1 juk6	kaam yuhk
jailer	n	監獄看守者	gāam yuhk hōn sáu jé	gaam1 juk6 hon1 sau2 ze2	kaam yuhk hon sau che
jam[1] [(de)] food	n	菓占	gwó jīm	gwo2 zim1	kwo chim
jam[2] /pulp/ food	n	果醬	gwó jeung	gwo2 zoeng3	kwo cheung
jam[3] /traffic jam	n	塞住	sāk jyuh	sak1 zyu6	sak chyuh
janitor[1]	n	工友	gùng yáuh	gung4 jau5	kung yauh
janitor[2] /caretaker	n	看門人	hōn mùhn yàhn	hon1 mun4 jan4	hon muhn yahn
January	n	一月	yāt yùht	jat1 jyut6	yat yuht
Japan	n	日本	yaht būn	jat6 bun1	yaht pun
japanese	n	日文	yāt màhn	jat1 man4	yat mahn
japanese tea	n	日本茶	yaht būn chàh	jat6 bun1 caa4	yaht pun chhah
japanese style dish	n	日本菜	yaht būn chói	jat6 bun1 coi2	yaht pun chhoi
jar /jug/can	n	大罐	daaih gun	daai6 gun3	taaih kun
jasmine tea	n	茉莉	muht leih	mut6 lei6	muht leih
javelin	n	標槍	bīu chèung	biu1 coeng4	piu chheung
jaw[1]	n	牙較	ngàh gáau	ngaa4 gaau2	ngah kaau
jaw[2]	n	下巴	hahp bā	hap6 baa1	hahp pa
jazz music[1] [(de)]	n	爵士音樂	jeuk sih yàm ngohk	zoek3 si6 jam4 ngok6	cheuk sih yam ngohk
jazz music[2]	n	爵士樂舞	jeuk sih lohk móuh	zoek3 si6 lok6 mou5	cheuk sih lohk mouh
jealous	adj	羨慕	sihn mouh	sin6 mou6	sihn mouh
jeep	n	吉普車	gāt póu chè	gat1 pou2 ce4	kat phou chhe
jeer /sneer/make fun /laugh at	v	嘲笑	jàau sìu	zaa4 sin4	chaau siu
jelly [(de)]	n	啫喱	jē léi	ze1 lei5	che lei
jerk[1] /to dash/jolt	n	衝	chùng	cung4	chhung
jerk[2]	v	猛推	máahng tèui	maang5 teoi4	maahng thoi
jerky[1] /shake/vibrate /trembling	adj/v	震	jan	zan3	chan
jerky[2] not smoothly moving as a vehicle	adj	顛簸嘅	dìn bó ge	din4 bo2 ge3	tin po ke
jest /joke	n	笑話	siu wá	siu3 waa2	siu wa
jet[1]	n	黑玉	hāk yuhk	hak1 juk6	hak yuhk
jet[2]	n	噴射	pan seh	pan3 se6	phan seh
jet engine	n	噴射引擎	pan seh yáhn kìhng	pan3 se6 jan5 king4	phan seh yahn khehng

English	POS	Chinese	Romanization 1	Romanization 2	Romanization 3
jet plane	n	噴射機	pan seh gēi	pan3 se6 gei1	phan seh kei
jetfoil /fly on boat		飛翔船	fèi chèuhng syùhn	fei4 coeng4 syun4	fei cheuhng syuhn
jew	n	猶太人	yàuh tài yàhn	jau4 tai4 jan4	yauh thai yahn
jewel[1] /gem	n	寶	bóu	bou2	pou
jewel[2] /jewelry	n	首飾	sáu sīk	sau2 sik1	sau sek
jewel case	n	珠寶盒	jyū bóu háap	zyu1 bou2 haap2	chyu pou haap
jewellery	n	珠寶	jyū bóu	zyu1 bou2	chyu pou
jewelry box	n	首飾箱	sáu sīk sēung	sau2 sik1 soeng1	sau sek seung
job /have job	n	做嘢	jouh yéh	zou6 je5	chouh yeh
job applicant /seeker	n	求職者	kàuh jīk jé	kau4 zik1 ze2	khauh chek che
job candidates	n	應徵人	ying jīng yàhn	jing3 zing1 jan4	yeng cheng yahn
job centre[1]	n	就業服務中心	jauh yihp fuhk mouh jùng sàm	zau6 jip6 fuk6 mou6 zung4 sam4	chauh yihp fuhk mouh chung sam
job centre[2]	n	就業中心	jauh yihp jùng sàm	zau6 jip6 zung4 sam4	chauh yihp chung sam
job knowledge		工作知識	gùng jok jì sìk	gung4 zik3 zi4 sik4	kung chok chi sek
job letter[1]	n	推薦信	tèui jin seun	teoi4 zin3 seon3	thoi chin swon
job letter[2]	n	理曆	léih līk	lei5 lik1	leih lek
job performance		工作表現	gùng jok bíu yín	gung4 zik3 biu2 jin2	kung chok piu yin
jobless[1]	adj	冇嘢做	móuh yéh jouh	mou5 je5 zou6	mouh yeh chouh
jobless[2] /unemployed /out of work	adj	失業	sāt yihp	sat1 jip6	sat yihp
Jockey Club (HK)	n	馬會	Máh wúi	maa5 wui2	Mah wui
jogging /walk quickly /racing/running	n	跑步	páau bouh	paau2 bou6	phaau pouh
join[1] /combine/gather /unite/agree	v	合	hahp	hap6	hahp
join[2]	v	連	lìhn	lin6	lihn
join[3] /connection/link	n/v	連結	lìhn git	lin4 git3	lihn kit
join forces /unite in common effort	v	協力	hip lìhk	hip3 lik4	hip lehk
join in / participate	v	參加	chàam gà	caam4 gaa4	chhaam ka
join on	n	跟隨	gàn cheui	gan4 ceoi3	kan chheui
join together[1]	v	拼	ping	ping3	pheng
join together[2]	v	合成	hahp sèhng	hap6 seng4	hahp sehng
joinable	adj	可連接	hó lìhn jip	ho2 lin6 zip3	ho lìhn jip
joined	adv	有關節	yáuh gwàan jit	jau5 gwaan4 zit3	yauh kwaan chit
joint[1]	n	節	jit	zit3	chit
joint[2]	n	關節	gwaàn jit	gwaan4 zit3	kwaan chit
joint[3] /together	n/adv	共	guhng	gung6	kuhng
joint[4]	n	共有	guhng yáuh	gung6 jau5	kuhng yauh
joint family /nuclear family		核心家庭	haht sàm gà tèhng	hat6 sam4 gaa4 ting4	haht sam ka thehng
jointly	adv	共同	guhng tùhng	gung6 tung4	kuhng thuhng
joints /knuckle of fingers	n	指關節	jí gwāan jit	zi2 gwaan1 zit3	chi kwaan chit
joke[1]	n	玩笑	wáan síu	waan2 siu2	waan siu
joke[2] /ridicule/mockery/fun	n	嘲笑	jàau sìu	zaau4 siu4	chaau siu

joker[1] man	n	愛開玩笑嘅人	oi /ngoi hòi wáan sìu ge yàhn	oi3 /ngoi3 hoi4 waan2 siu4 ge3 jan4	oi /ngoi hoi waan siu ke yahn
joker[2] card	n	丑角牌	cháu gok pàaih	cau2 gok3 paai4	chhau kok phaaih
joking	n	滑稽	waaht kài	waat6 kai4	waaht khai
jolly	adj	快活	faai wuht	faai3 wut6	faai wuht
jolt /to shake	v	顛簸	dìn bó	din4 bo2	tin po
JOSS (statue of Buddha)	n	佛像	faht jeuhng	fat1 zoeng6	faht cheuhng
joss-house	n	中國寺院	jùng gwok jí yūn	zung4 gwok3 zi2 jyun1	chung kwok chi yun
journal	n	日報	yaht bou	jat6 bou3	yaht pou
journalist	n	新聞記者	sàn màhn gei jé	san4 man4 gei3 ze2	san mahn kei che
journey /trip	n	程	chìhng	cing4	chhehng
joy	n	歡樂	fùn lohk	fun4 lok6	fun lohk
jubilee	n	慶典	hing dín	hing3 din2	hing tin
judge[1]	n	評	pìhng	ping4	phehng
judge[2] in a contest	n	評判	ping pún	ping3 pun2	pheng phun
judge[3]/magistrate/bench in a court	n	法官	faat gùn	faat3 gung4	faat kun
judgment[1] /evaluation /evaluate/judgement/appraise /valuation	n/v	評價	pìhng gá	ping4 ga2	phehng ka
judgment[2] /case decided	n	判斷	pun dyun	pun3 dyun3	phun tyun
judgement[1] /ability to judgement/judgment power	n	判斷力	pun dyun lihk	pun3 dyun3 lik6	phun tyun lehk
judgement[2]/judgment	n	判決	pun kyut	pun3 kyut3	phun khyut
judicial	adj	司法	sī faat	si1 faat3	si faat
jug[1] /pot/small water pot	n	壺	wú /wùh	wu2 /wu4	wu /wuh
jug[2]	n	罐	gun	gun3	kun
juggle[1] /hoodwink	v	玩把戲	wáan bá hei	waan2 baa2 hei3	waan pa hei
juggle[2] /beguile	v	玩雜耍	wáan jaahp sá	waan2 zaap6 sa2	waan chaahp sa
juicy	adj	多汁嘅	dò jāp ge	do4 zap1 ge3	to chap ke
juicy of bean /soya bean	n	豆汁	dáu jāp	dau2 zap1	tau chap
July month	n	七月	chāt yùht	cat1 jyut6	chhat yuht
jumbo	adj	巨型	geuih ying	geoi6 jing3	kwoih yeng
jumbo jet	n	噴氣式飛機	pan hei sīk fèi gèi	pan3 hei3 sik1 fei4 gei4	phan hei sek fei kei
jump	v	蹦	baahng	baang6	paahng
jump into[1] /plunge	v	投入	tàuh yahp	tau4 jap6	thauh yahp
jump into[2] /plunge	v	陷入	hahm yahp	ham6 jap6	hahm yahp
jump out	v	跳出	tiu chēut	tiu3 ceot1	thiu chhot
jump up	v	跳躍	tiu yéuk	tiu3 joek2	thiu yeuk
jumper[1] person	n	跳躍者	tiu yéuk jé	tiu3 joek2 ze2	thiu yeuk che
jumper[2] /muffler/scarf	n	套頭衫	tóu tau sàam	tou2 tau3 saam4	thou thau saam
junction[1]	n	聯合	lyùhn hahp	lyun4 hap6	lyuhn hahp
junction[2]	n	匯合點	wùih hàhp dīm	wui6 hap6 dim1	wuih hahp tim
junction[3]	n	接合點	jip hàhp dīm	zip3 hap6 dim1	chip hahp tim
junction-road	n	聯合道	lyùhn hahp douh	lyun4 hap6 gou6	lyuhn hahp douh

English		Chinese	Yale	Jyutping	Romanization
June month	n	六月	luhk yuht	luk6 jyut6	luhk yuht
jungle /forest	n	叢林	chùhng làhm	cung4 lam4	chhuhng lahm
junior	adj	資淺嘅	jì chín ge	zi4 cin2 ge3	chi chhin ke
junk[1] /sailboat/ship	n	帆船	fàahn syùhn	faan4 syun4	faahn syuhn
junk[2] /old rubbish	n	破爛物	po laahn maht	po3 laan6 mat6	pho laahn maht
junk[3] worn-out things	n	廢棄嘅舊物	fai hei ge gauh maht	fai3 hei3 ge3 gau6 ma	fai hei ke kauh maht
junk food	n	垃圾食物	laahp saap sihk maht	laap6 saap3 sik6 mat6	laahp saap sehk maht
junket /picnic/outing /field trip	n	郊遊	gāau yàuh	gaau1 jau4	kaau yauh
jurisdiction	n	管轄權	gún haht kyùhn	gun2 hat6 kyun4	kun haht khyuhn
jury in a court	n	陪審團	pùih sám tyùhn	pui4 sam2 tyun4	phuih sam thyuhn
just[1]	adv	公度	gùng douh	gung4 dou6	kung touh
just[2] /length of time/ duration of time	adv	久	gáu	gau2	kau
just right /duly/right time/just in time	adv	正好	jeng hóu	zeng3 hou2	cheng hou
just a moment ago	adv	正話	jeng wah, jing wah	zeng3 waa6, zing3 waa6	cheng wah
just a moment please /please wait	adv	請等一等	chéng /chíng dáng yāt dāng	ceng2 /cing2 dang2 jat1 dang1	chheng tang yat tang
just a while ago	adv	頭先	tàuh sìn	tau4 sin4	thauh sin
just about to	adv	正在要	jeng joih yiu	zeng3 zoi6 jiu3	cheng choih yiu
just arrived[1]		暗暗到咗	ngāam ngāam dou jó	ngam3 ngam3 dou3 jo2	ngaam ngaam tou cho
just arrived[2]		剛剛抵達	gōng gōng dái daaht	gong1 gong1 dai2 daat6	kong kong tai taaht
just at the moment of	adv	正在…嗰陣時	jing joih … gó jahn sí	zeng3 zoi6 go2 zan6 si2	cheng choih…ko chahn si
just gone	adv	啱啱行開咗	ngaam ngaam hàahng hòi jó	ngaam1 ngaam1 haang4 hoi4 zo2	ngaam ngaam haahng hoi cho
just left /just leaved	adv	啱啱離開咗	ngaam ngaam lèih hòi jó	ngaam1 ngaam1 lei4 hoi4 zo2	ngaam ngaam leih hoi cho
just let me say	adv	嗲兩句	dè léuhng geui	de4 loeng5 geoi3	te lowhng kwoi
just next /neighbor /next door	adv	隔離	gaak lèih	gaak3 lei4	kaak leih
just now[1(coll)] /just a moment ago	adv	啱啱	ngāam ngāam	ngaam1 ngaam1	ngaam ngaam
just now[2]	adv	剛才	gōng choih	gong1 coi4	kong chhoih
just now ready	adv	啱啱好吖	ngāam ngāam hóu ā	ngaam1 ngaam1 hou2 aa1	ngaam ngaam hou aa
just recently[(wr)] /just a while ago/just a moment ago/ just now	adv	剛剛	gōng gōng	gong1 gong1	kong kong
just seen	adv	啱啱睇咗	āam āam tái jó	aam1 aam1 tai2 zo2	aam aam thai cho
just so so /tolerable /not bad/not very good/ not very well	adj	麻麻地啦!	màh màh deih lā!	maa4 ma2 dei6 laa1	mah ma teih la!
just that's it /right place /approaching/that's it place	n	就係	jauh hai	zau6 hai3	chauh hai
justice	n	公正	gùng jing	gung4 jing3	kung cheng

justified[1] /legal	adj	合法	hahp faat	hap6 faat3	hahp faat
justified[2] /certify/justify	adj	證明	jing mìhng	zing3 ming4	cheng mehng
justified[3]	adj	理由	léih yàuh	lei5 jau4	leih yauh
justify	v	辯護	bihn wuh	bin6 wu6	pihn wuh
jute	n	黃麻	wòhng màh	wong4 maa4	wohng mah

karaoke	n	卡拉ok	ká lā ok	kaa2 laa1 ok	kha la ok
keen[1] /acute/sharp knowledge	adj	銳	yeuih	jeoi6	yeuih
keen[2] /acute	adj	敏捷嘅思考	máhn jit ge sì háau	man5 zit3 ge3 si4 haau2	mahn chit ke si haau
keen[3] brains	adj	頭腦	tàuh nóuh	tau4 nou5	thauh nouh
keen[4] interested	adj	感興趣	gám hìng cheui	gam2 hing4 ceoi3	kam heng chheui
keen[5] /sharp (of knife)	adj	鋒利	fùng leih	fung4 lei6	fung leih
keep[1]	v	留	làu	lau4	lau
keep[2] /save/reserve	v	留番	làuh fàan	lau4 faan4	lauh faan
keep away	v	不接近	bāt jip gahn	bat1 zip3 gan6	pat chip kahn
keep confidential	v	保密	bōu maht	bou1 mat6	pou maht
keep faith		守信	sáu seun	sau2 seon3	sau swon
keep good time /on time/punctual	n	準時	jéun sìh	zeon2 si4	cheun sih
keep guarantee	v	保管	bōu gún	bou1 gun2	pou kun
keep help in critical /help out	v	關照	gwàan jiu	gwaan4 zit3	kwaan chiu
keep here /place here		擠喺處	jāi hái chyu	jai1 hai2 sue3	chai hai chyu
keep in mind /remember	v	記住	gei jyuh	gei3 zyu6	kei chyuh
keep in mouth /contain (in mouth) /hold in mouth	v	含	hàhm	ham4	hahm
keep in record	v	紀錄	gei luhk	gei3 luk6	kei luhk
keep in touch with		與 保持聯絡	yùh bōu chìh lyùhn lok	jyu4 bou1 ci4 lyun4 lok3	yuh pou chhih lyuhn lok
keep listen[1] /listening /be heard	v	聽倒	tèng dou	teng4 dou3	theng tou
keep listen[2] /listening	v	聽緊	tèng gán	teng4 gan2	theng kan
keep lookout /alert /alertness/pay attention	v	留心	làuh sàm	lau4 sam4	lauh sam
keep on eye on /pay attention/look out/look sharp	v	注意	jyu yi	zyu3 yi3	chyu yi
keep quiet	v	保持安靜	bóu chìh òn/ngòn	bou2 ci4 on4 /ngon4	pou chhih on /ngon
keep secret /keep confidential	v	私語	sī yúh	si1 jyu5	si yuh
keep up /continuing	v	不停止	bāt tíhng jí	bat1 ting5 zi2	pat thehng chi
keeper[1] /supervisor /warden	n	管理人	gún léih yàhn	gun2 lei5 jan4	kun leih yahn
keeper[2] /caretaker	n	看管人	hōn gún yàhn	hon1 gun2 jan4	hon kun yahn
keeping /take care /watch over	n/v	看守	hōn sáu	hon1 sau2	hon sau
keg beer gas pressure	n	小桶	síu túng	siu2 tung2	siu thung
kept	v	保持過去	bóu chìh gwo heui	bou2 ci4 gwo3 heoi3	pou chhih kwo hoi
kerb mound	n	街道的路邊石	gāai douh dìk lòuh bìn sehk	gaai1 dou6 dik4 lou4 bin4 sek6	kaai touh tek louh pin sehk
kerosene[1] oil/paraffin	n	火水	fó séui	fo2 seoi2	fo swoi
kerosene[2]	n	煤油	mùih yàuh	mui4 jau4	muih yauh

English	Type	Chinese	Romanization 1	Romanization 2	Romanization 3
kettle /tea pot	n	茶煲	chàh bōu	caa4 bou1	chhah pou
key[1]	n	匙	sìh	si4	sih
key[2]	n	鎖匙	só sìh	so2 si4	so sih
key[3]	n	鑰	yeuhk	yeuhk	yeuhk
key[4]	n	鑰匙	yeuhk sìh	yeuhk si4	yeuhk sih
key in music /tone /tune/melody	n	調	tìuh	tiu4	thiuh
key-ring[1]	n	鎖匙圓	só sìh yùhn	so2 si4 jyun4	so sih yuhn
key-ring[2]	n	鑰匙環	yeuhk sìh wàahn	joek6 si4 waan4	yeuhk sih waahn
keyboard	n	鍵盤	gihn pùhn	gin6 pun4	kihn phuhn
kick	v	踢	tek	tek3	thek
kicker	n	踢者	tek jé	tek3 ze2	thek che
kidnap	v	綁架	bóng gá	bong2 ga2	pong ka
kidnapped	v	禁錮	gām gu	gam1 gu3	kam ku
kidnapped not releasing /kill a hostage even obtained money/usually held for ransom	v	撕票	sī piu	si1 piu3	si phiu
kidnapper	n	綁票者	bóng piu jé	bong2 piu3 ze2	pong phiu che
kidnapping	n	誘拐	yáuh gwáai	jau5 gwaai2	yauh kwaai
kidney[1]	n	腎	sáhn	san5	sahn
kidney[2] /waist	n	腰	yìu	jiu4	yiu
kidney failure /renal failure	n	腎衰竭	sáhn sēui kit	san5 seoi1 kit3	sahn swoi khit
kidney-function /renal function	n	腎功能	sáhn gùng làhng /nàhng	san5 gung4 lang4 /nang4	sahn kung lahng /nahng
kidney wash		洗腎	sái sáhn	sai2 san5	sai sahn
kill[1]	n	殺	saat	saat3	saat
kill[2]	n	殺死	saat séi	saat3 sei2	saat sei
kill man /life rob	n	奪命	dyuht mehng/mihng	dyut6 meng6 /ming6	tyuht mehng
killed man /men death	v	人死亡	yàhn séi mòhng	jan4 sei2 mong4	yahn sei mohng
killed oneself /stab oneself/commit suicide	v	自戕	jih chèuhng	zi6 coeng4	chih chheuhng
killer	n	殺人者	saat yàhn jé	saat3 jan4 ze2	saat yahn che
killing[1]	n	致命	ji mehng /mihng	zi3 meng6 /ming6	chi mehng
killing[2] /murder	n	謀殺	màuh saat	mau4 saat3	mauh saat
kilogram (kg)	n	公斤	gūng gan	gung1 gan3	kung kan
kilohertz (khz)	n	千赫茲	chìn hāk jī	cin4 hak1 zi1	chhin hak chi
kilometer (km)	n	公里	gūng léih	gung1 lei5	kung leih
kilowatt (KW)	n	千瓦	chìn ngán	cin4 ngan2	chhin ngan
kindly[1] /kind/humane /merciful	adj	仁慈	yàhn chìh	jan4 ci4	yahn chhih
kindly[2] /kind	adj	親切	chàn chit	can4 cit3	chhan chhit
kindergarten	n	幼稚園	yau jin yùhn	jau3 zi6 jyun4	yau chin yuhn
kindle /to burn /light up/ to light	vt	燃點	yìhn dím	jin4 dim2	yihn tim
kindly feeling	adv	軟化	yúhn fa	jyun5 faa3	yuhn fa
kindness[1]	n	仁慈	yàhn chìh	jan4 ci4	yahn chhih

kindness[2]	n	善心	sihn sām	sin6 sam1	sihn sam
king /royal	n	王	wòhng	wong4	wohng
kiosk[1] /booth small store	n	小亭	síu tìhng	siu2 ting4	siu thehng
kiosk[2] /booth small store	n	售貨亭	sauh fo tìhng	sau6 fo3 ting4	sauh fo thehng
kiss[1] (sl)	v	打茄輪	dá kèh lèuhn	daa2 ke4 leon4	ta kheh lowhn
kiss[2] (sl)	v	錫吓	sek háh	sek3 haa5	sek hah
kiss[3]	v	吻	máhn	man5	mahn
kiss[4]	v	接吻	jip máhn	zip3 man5	chip mahn
kiss[5]	v	親吻	chàn máhn	can4 man5	chhan mahn
kiss[6]	v	緋吻	fèi máhn	fei4 man5	fei mahn
kisser	n	接吻者	jip máhn jé	zip3 man5 ze2	chip mahn che
kitchen[1]	n	廚	chyùh	cyu4	chhyuh
kitchen[2]	n	廚房	chyùh fóng	cyu4 fong2	chhyuh fong
kite[1]	n	風箏	fùng jāng	fung4 zang1	fung chang
kite[2]	n	紙鳶	jí yíu	zi2 jyun1	chi yiu
kiwi[1]	n	奇異果	kèih yih gwó	kei4 ji6 gwo2	kheih yih kwo
kiwi[2]	n	獼猴桃	lèih hàuh tòuh	lei4 hau4 tou4	leih hauh thouh
kleenex /brand name	n	商標名	sèung bīu mèhng	soeng4 biu1 meng4	seung piu mehng
knead[1] /rub down	v	揉	yàuh	jau4	yauh
knead[2] /pinch/massage	v	捏	lihp /nihp	lip6 /nip6	lihp /nihp
knead[3]	v	揑做	nihp jouh	nip6 zou6	nihp chouh
knee	n	膝	sāt	sat1	sat
kneel /crouch	v	跪	gwaih	gwai6	kwaih
kneel down /crouch /knelt/kneel	n/v	跪低	gwaih dài	gwai6 dai4	kwaih tai
kneel & worship	v	跪拜	gwaih baai	gwai6 baai3	kwaih paai
kneeling	v	跪下	gwaih hah	gwai6 ha6	kwaih hah
kneen	n	膝頭	sāt tàu	sat1 tau4	sat thau
knife[1] /sword	n	刀	dōu	dou1	tou
knife[2]	n	小刀	síu dōu	siu2 dou1	siu tou
knife & fork	n	刀叉	dōu chā	dou1 caa1	tou chha
knight[1] /gentleman	n	士	sí	si2	si
knight[2]	n	騎士	kèh sih	ke4 si6	kheh sih
knight[3] /sir	v	武士	móuh sih	mou5 si6	mouh sih
knit /weave/woven	v	編織	pīn jīk	pin1 zik1	phin chehk
knob[1] of handle	n	圓形把手	yùhn yìhng bá sáu	jyun4 jing4 bag2 sau2	yuhn yehng pa sau
knob[2] of handle	n	按鈕	on láu, ngòn náu	on3 lau2, ngon4 nau2	on lau, ngon nau
knob[3] of handle	n	旋鈕	syun láu	syun3 lau2	syun lau
knock /strike	v	撽	chaau	caau3	chhaau
knock on the door[1]	v	拍門	paak mùhn	paak3 mun4	phaak muhn
knock on the door[2]	v	敲門	hāau mùhn	haau1 mun4	haau muhn
knoll[1] /mound /small /round hill	n	小丘	síu yàu	siu2 jau4	siu yau
knoll[2] small round hill	n	土墩	tóu dèun	tou2 deon4	thou tohn

knot	v	打結	dá git	daa2 git3	ta kit
knotty difficult to solve	adj	傷腦筋的	sèung lóuh gān dīk	soeng4 lou5 gan1 dik1	seung louh kan tek
know[1]	v	知	jì	zi4	chi
know[2] /understand	v	知道	jì douh	zi4 dou6	chi touh
know him	n	識佢	sīk kéuih	sik1 keoi5	sek khoih
know something well		熟識	suhk sīk	suk6 sik1	suhk sek
knowable	adj	能認知	làhng /nàhng yihng jì	lang4 /nang4 jing6 zi4	lahng /nahng yehng chi
knowing[1]	n	會意	wuih yi	wui6 ji3	wuih yi
knowing[2] /to understand	n	知曉	jì híu	zi4 hiu2	chi hiu
knowledge /wisdom	n	知識	jì sìk	zi4 sik4	chi sek
known /shown	adj	的過去分詞	dìk gwo heui fahn chìh	dik4 gwo3 heoi3 fan6 ci4	tek kwo hoi fahn chhih
Korea	n	韓國	hòn gwok	hon4 gwok3	hon kwok
korean language	n	韓文	hòn màhn	hon4 man4	hon mahn
kung fu	n	功夫	gùng fù	gung4 fu4	kung fu

English	POS	Chinese	Yale	Jyutping	Other
L.E.D. light emitting diode	abbr	發光二極管	faat gwòng yih gìhk gún	faat3 gwong4 yi6 gik6 gun2	faat kwong yih gehk kun
label list /sticker/tag	n	標籤	bīu chīm	biu1 cim1	piu chhim
labor /labourer/worker /servant/staff	n	工人	gùng yàhn	gung4 jan4	kung yahn
labors /labourers	n	勞工	lòuh gùng	lou4 gung4	louh kung
labour depart /labor department	n	勞工處	lòuh gùng chyú	lou4 gung4 cyu2	louh kung chhyu
laboratory	n	實驗室	saht yihm sāt	sat6 jim6 sat1	saht yihm sat
laboratory fee[1]	n	化驗費	fa yihm fai	faa3 jim6 fai3	fa yihm fai
laboratory fee[2]	n	實驗室費用	saht yihm sāt fai yuhng	sat6 jim6 sat1 fai3 jung6	saht yihm sat fai yuhng
lac /shellac	n	蟲膠	chùhng gàau	cung4 gaau4	chhuhng kaau
lace[1] /shoelace	n	鞋帶	hàaih dáai	haai4 daai2	haaih taai
lace[2]	n	花邊	fā bīn	faa1 bin1	fa pin
lacerate	v	割破	got po	got3 po3	kot pho
lack[1] /short of/poor	v	乏	faht	fat6	faht
lack[2]	v	缺乏	kyut faht	kyut3 fat6	khyut faht
lack of energy	adj	慣性	gwaan sing	gwaan3 sing3	kwaan seng
lacking /deficient /be short of	adj	缺乏	kyut faht	kyut3 fat6	khyut faht
lactometer	n	檢乳器	gím yúh hei	gim2 jyu5 hei3	kim yuh hei
lactose	n	乳糖	yúh tòhng	jyu5 tong4	yuh thohng
lad /young boy boy under 14 years	n	後生仔	hauh sàang jái	hau6 saang4 zai2	hauh saang chai
ladder[1] /stairs/lift	n	梯	tài	tai4	thai
ladder[2]	n	梯子	tài jí	tai4 zi2	thai chi
ladder holder	n	扶手梯	fùh sāu tài	fu4 sau1 tai4	fuh sau thai
laddie /boy	n	男孩	làahm hàaih	laam4 haai4	laahm haaih
ladle /spoon made by wooden	n	杓子	cheuk jí	coek3 zi2	chheuk chi
lady market	n	女人街	léuih yan gàai	leui5 jan3 gaai4	lowih yan kaai
laissez[1] /liberalism	n	自由主義	jih yàuh jyú yih	zi6 jau4 zyu2 ji6	chih yauh chyu yih
laissez[2] /liberalism	n	放任主義	fong yahm jyú yih	fong3 jam4 zyu2 ji6	fong yahm chyu yih
laissez[3] /liberalism	n	自由放任	jih yàuh fong yahm	zi6 jau4 fong3 jam4	chih yauh fong yahm
lake /pond/pool	n	湖	wùh	wu4	wuh
Lama (Tibetti)	n	喇嘛	lā ma	laa1 maa3	la ma
lamb steak	n	羊扒	yèuhng pá	joeng4 paa2	yeuhng pha
lame /lameness	n	跛	bài	bai4	pai
lamentable /thinkable /conceivable /questionable	adj	可想像	hó séung jèuhng	ho2 soeng2 zoeng6	ho seung cheuhng
lamente	adj	被悼念	bèih douh lìhm /nìhm	bei6 dou6 lim6 /nim6	peih touh lihm /nihm
lamp[1] /light	n	燈	dāng	dang1	tang
lamp[2] /lantern/light/lamp	n	射燈	seh dāng	se6 dang1	seh tang
lamp-black	n	燈黑	dāng hāk	dang1 hak1	tang hak
lamp-light	n	燈光	dāng gwòng	dang1 gwong4	tang kwong
lampshade	n	燈罩	dāng jaau	dang1 zaau3	tang chaau

lance[1]	n	矛	màauh	maau4	maauh
lance[2] /pike	n	長矛	chèuhng màauh	coeng4 maau4	chheuhng maauh
land[1]	a	陸	luhk	luk6	luhk
land[2]	n	陸地	luhk deih	luk6 dei6	luhk teih
land route	n	陸路	luhk louh	luk6 lou6	luhk louh
landlord /landholder /owner of land	n	地主	deih jyú	dei6 zyu2	teih chyu
landing[1] (aeroplane) /descent/downfall	n	降落	gong lohk	gong3 lok6	kong lohk
landing[2] plane	n	登陸艇	dàng luhk téhng	dang4 luk6 teng5	tang luhk thehng
landlady	n	女地主	léuih deih jyú	leui5 dei6 zyu2	lowih teih chyu
landless[1]	adj	無土地	mòuh tóu deih	mou4 tou2 dei6	mouh thou teih
landless[2]	adj	無田無地	móuh tìhn mòuh deih	mou5 tin4 mou4 dei6	mouh thihn mouh teih
landmark	n	地標	deih biu	dei6 biu3	teih piu
landmine	n	地雷	deih lèuih	dei6 leoi4	teih lowih
landscape /scene/vista	n	景色	gíng sīk	ging2 sik1	keng sek
landslide[1] /landfall /landslip	n	山泥傾瀉	sàan làih /nàih kìngse	saan4 lai4 /nai4 king4 se3	saan laih kheng se
landslide[2]	n	山崩	sàan bāng	saan4 bang1	saan pang
lane piece /small piece of land/plot of land	n	一塊地	yāt faai deih	jat1 faai3 dei6	yat faai teih
language[1] /dialect /tongue/message	n	話	wá	waa2	wa
language[2]	n	語言	yúh yin	jyu5 jin3	yuh yin
language[3] /speech	n	語	yúh	jyu5	yuh
language[4] instructor	n	語言導師	yúh yìhn douh sī	jyu5 jin4 dou6 si1	yuh yihn touh si
language skill		語言技巧	yúh yìhn geih háau	jyu5 jin4 gei6 haau2	yuh yihn keih haau
lantern	n	燈籠	dāng lùhng	dang1 lung4	tang luhng
lanyard[1]	n	繫索	haih sok	hai6 sok3	haih sok
lanyard[2]	n	短繩	dyún sing	dyun2 sing3	tyun seng
lap[1] /lick	v	舔食	lím sihk	lim5 sik6	lim sehk
lap[2] /cross-legged	n	大腿部	daaih téui bouh	daai6 teoi2 bou6	taaih thoi pouh
lap[3] /cross-legged	n	膝部	sāt bouh	sat1 bou6	sat pouh
laptop	n	手提電腦	sáu tai dìhn nóuh	sau2 tai3 din6 nou5	sau thai tihn nouh
large bag /sack	n	粗布袋	chòu bou dói /doih	cou4 bou3 doi2 /doi6	chhou pou toi /toih
large hearted	n	大心	daaih sàm	daai6 sam4	taaih sam
large qty /a lot/lot of /over	n	大量	daaih leuhng	daai6 loeng6	taaih leuhng
large size (L)	n	大碼	daaih máh	daai6 maa5	taaih mah
large spoon[1] /scoop	n	勺	seuk	soek3	swok
large spoon[2]	n	勺子	cheuk jai	coek3 zai3	chheuk chai
large spoon[3] /scoop	n	舀	yíuh	jiu5	yiuh
large wide	n	廣闊嘅	gwóng fut ge	gwong2 fut3 ge3	kwong fut ke
lark[1] (small bird)		百靈鳥	baak lèhng /lìhng níuh	baak3 leng4 /ling4 niu5	paak lehng niuh
lark[2]	n	雲雀	wàhn jéuk	wan4 zoek2	wahn cheuk
larva	n	幼體	yau tái	jau3 tai2	yau thai

larynx[1] anatomy	n	咽	yìn	jin4	yin
larynx[2] /canal/throat	n	喉嚨	hàuh lùhng	nau4 lung4	hauh luhng
laser	n	雷射	lèuih sèh	leoi4 se6	lowih seh
laser disc	n	雷射唱片	lèuih sèh cheung pin	leoi4 se6 coeng3 pin3	lowih seh chheung phin
laser printer	n	雷射打印機	lèuih sèh dā yan gèi	leoi4 se6 daa1 jan3 gei4	lowih seh ta yan kei
lass /maiden	n	少女	síu léoih /néoih	siu2 leoi5 /neoi5	siu lowih /nowih
last day of the month		月底	yuht dái	jyut6 dai2	yuht tai
last month	n	上月	seuhng yuht	soeng6 jyut6	seuhng yuht
last night[1]	n	嚟晚	kàhm máahn	kam6 maan5	khahm maahn
last night[2]	n	昨晚	jok máahn	zok3 maan5	chok maahn
last night[3]	n	尋晚夜	chàhm máahn yeh	cham4 maan5 je6	chhahm maahn yeh
last stage /critical /very serious/zero hour	n/adv	關鍵時刻	gwàan gihn sìh hāak	gwaan4 gin6 si4 haak1	kwaan kihn sih haak
last station[1] /terminus /of train/bus	n	總站	júng jaahm	zung2 zaam6	chung chaahm
last station[2] /terminus /final stop of train or bus	n	終點站	jūng dím jaahm	jung1 dim2 zaam6	chung tim chaahm
last time	adv	上次	seuhng chi	soeng6 ci3	seuhng chhi
last week	n	上個禮拜	seuhng go láih baai	soeng6 go3 lai5 baai3	seuhng ko laih paai
last year[1]	n	舊年	gauh lìhn /nìhn	gau6 lin4 /nin4	kauh lihn /nihn
last year[2]	n	去年	heui lìhn /nìhn	heoi3 lin4 /nin4	hoi lihn /nihn
lasting[1] /sustained	adj	持久	chìh gáu	ci4 gau2	chhih kau
lasting[2]	adj	耐久	loih /noih gáu	loi6 /noi6 gau2	loih /noih kau
lasting[3]	adj	冚使	kàm sái	kam2 sai2	kham sai
late[1] /slow	adv	遲	chìh	ci4	chhih
late[2] coming time/late time	adv	晏	aan	aan3	aan
late[3] /slow	adv	晚	maahn	maan5	maahn
late arrived	adv	遲到	chìh dou	ci4 dou3	chhih tou
late at night	n	深夜	sàm yeh	sam4 je6	sam yeh
late back /return back		遲啲走	chìh dì jáu	ci4 di4 zau2	chhih ti chau
lately /recently	adv	近來	gahn lòih	gan6 loi4	kahn loih
later[1] /after	adv	後	hauh	hau6	hauh
later[2] /after/behind	adv	後面	hauh mìhn	hau6 min6	hauh mihn
later on /afterwards /to finish	adv	收尾	sāu mēi	sau1 mei1	sau mei
latest	adv	最新	jeui sàn	zeoi3 san4	cheui san
latin language[1] /latin letters	n	拉丁文	lāai dīng màhn	laai1 ding1 man6	laai teng mahn
latin language[2]	adj	拉丁語	lāai dīng yúh	laai1 ding1 jyu5	laai teng yuh
latin literature	adj	拉丁文	lāai dīng màhn	laai1 ding1 man6	laai teng mahn
latitude	n	緯度	wáih douh	wai5 dou6	waih touh
latrine toilet	n	茅坑	màau hāang	maau4 haang1	maau haang
lattice[1]	n	格製	gaak jái	gaak3 zai3	kaak chai
lattice[2]	n	格子	gaak jái	gaak3 zai2	kaak chai
lattice[3] (pattern of squares)	n	打斜嘅格子	da che ge gaak jái	daa3 ce3 ge3 gaak3 zai2	ta chhe ke kaak chai
lattice[4]	n	格子木架	gaak jái muhk gá	gaak3 zai2 muk6 gaa2	kaak chai muhk ka

laughter	n	笑聲	siu sèng	siu3 seng4	siu seng
launch[1] /set in motion /get start	v	創辦	chong baahn	cong3 baan6	chhong paahn
launch[2] /get start	v	開辦	hòi baahn	hoi4 baan6	hoi paahn
launch[3] /start/get start	v	發動	faat duhng	faat3 dung6	faat tuhng
launch[4] /begin	v	開展	hòi jín	hoi4 zin2	hoi chin
launch[5] missile	n	放射	fong seh	fong3 se6	fong seh
launch[6] missile/firing/shoot fire	n	發射	faat seh	faat3 se6	faat seh
launching ceremony	n	下水禮	hah séui láih	haa6 seoi2 lai5	hah swoi laih
laundry /washhouse	n	洗衣店	sái yì dim	sai2 ji4 dim3	sai yi tim
lava	n	熔岩	yùhng ngàahm	jung4 ngaam4	yuhng ngaahm
lavatory[1] /rest room /toilet	n	廁	chi	ci3	chhi
lavatory[2]/washroom /toilet	n	廁所	chi só	ci3 so2	chhi so
lavender[1]	n	薰衣草	fàn yì chói	fan4 ji4 coi2	fan yi chhoi
lavender[2] /light purple /light violet	n	淡紫色	táahm jí sīk	taam5 zi2 sik1	thaahm chi sek
law[1]	n	律	leuht	leot6	lwoht
law[2]	n	法律	faat leuht	faat3 leot6	faat lwoht
law[3] /rule	n	規	kwài	kwai4	khwai
law breaker /offender	n	違法者	wai faat jé	wai3 faat3 ze2	wai faat che
law case /legal case	n	案件	on /ngon gín	on3 /ngon3 gin2	on /ngon kin
law college	n	法學院	faat hohk yún	faat3 hok6 jyun2	faat hohk yun
law rule	n	法例	faat laih	faat3 lai6	faat laih
lawmakers of government body /body of lawmakers /cabinet of government /lagislature of government	n	內閣	loih /noih gok	loi6 /noi6 gok3	loih /noih kok
lawn /field green grass	n	草坪	chóu pìhng	cou2 ping4	chhou phehng
lawn-mower[1]	n	剪草機	jín chóu gèi	zin2 cou2 gei4	chin chhou kei
lawn-mower[2]	n	割草機	got chóu gèi	got3 cou2 gei4	kot chhou kei
lawsuit /complaint	n	訴訟	sou juhng	sou3 zung6	sou chuhng
lawyer's office	n	律師樓	leuht sī làuh	leot6 si1 lau4	lwoht si lauh
lay off /stop work	n	停工	tíhng gùng	ting5 gung4	thehng kung
laydown[1] /put down	v	放下	fong hah	fong3 haa6	fong hah
laydown[2]	n	傾卸	kìng se	king4 se3	khing se
layer	n	階層	gaai chàhng	gaai3 cang4	kaai chhahng
lazy[1]	adj	懶	láahn	laan5	laahn
lazy[2]	adj	懶惰	láahn dou	laan5 dou3	laahn tou
lazy[3] /shiftless	adj	得過且過	dāk gwò ché gwò	dak1 gwo4 ce2 gwo4	tak kwo chhe kwo
lazy[4] /shiftless	adj	唔做得嘢	m̀ jouh dāk yéh	m4 zou6 dak1 je5	mh chouh tak yeh
lead[1] /leading/guide	v	帶	daai	daai3	taai
lead[2] /take lead/guide /leading	v	領導	léhng /líhng douh	leng5 /ling5 dou6	lehng touh
lead[3] of pencil	n	鉛	yùhn	jyun4	yuhn

leading /guiding	v	引導	yáhn douh	jan5 dou6	yahn tou
lead on command	v	率領	sēuht léhng /líhng	seot6 leng5 /ling5	swoht lehng
leader[1] /gangster/gang /big brother	n	首腦	sáu lóuh /nóuh	sau2 lou5 /nou5	sau louh /nouh
leader[2] /guide/leadership	n	領導	léhng /líhng douh	leng5 /ling5 dou6	lehng touh
leaderless /without leader	adj	無領導	móuh léhng /líhng douh	mou5 leng5 /ling5 dou6	mouh lehng touh
leading[1]	v	領導嘅	léhng /líhng douh ge	leng5 /ling5 dou6 ge3	lehng touh ke
leading[2] /show the way	v	帶路	daai louh	daai3 lou6	taai louh
leading action	v	帶著	daai jeuhk	daai3 zeok6	taai cheuhk
leads /wire of electrical	n	導線	douh sin	dou6 sin3	touh sin
leaf[1] /tree's leaf	n	葉	yìhp	jip4	yihp
leaf[2] /page	n	頁	yihp	jip6	yihp
leaf[3] /page	n	葉子	yìhp jí	jip6 zi2	yihp chi
leaflet /pamphlet	n	傳單	chyùhn dàan	cyun4 daan4	chhyuhn taan
leafy /lot of leaves	adj	多葉	dò yìhp	do4 jip6	to yihp
league[1]	n	同盟	tùhng màhng	tung4 mang4	thuhng mahng
league[2] /association	n	協會	hip wúi	hip3 wui2	hip wui
league[3] /confederation /union	n	聯盟	lyùhn màhng	lyun4 mang4	lyuhn mahng
leak /leak hole	n	漏洞	lauh duhng	lau6 dung6	lauh tohng
leak informations /let out secret/unbury	v	洩露	sit lauh	sit3 lau6	sit lauh
leak out[1]	v	漏出	lauh chēut	lau6 ceot1	lauh chhot
leak out[2] /discover /disclose/divulge/unfold	v	透露	tau louh	tau3 lau6	thau louh
leak out matter	v	告物	gou maht	gou3 mat6	kou maht
leakage water	v	漏洞	lauh duhng	lau6 dung6	lauh tohng
leaking water or electric	n	漏	lauh	lau6	lauh
lean[1] /thin/skinny	adj	瘦	sau	sau3	sau
lean[2] /slant/sloping /decline	v	傾斜	kìng chèh	king4 ce4	khing chheh
lean against	v	挨	àai /ngàai	aai4 /ngai4	aai /ngaai
lean on /rely/upon /depends on/rely upon	v	依靠	yi kaau	ji3 kaau3	yi khaau
lean on one side	v	側	jāk	zak1	chak
lean one side /one sided	v	偏	pīn	pin1	phin
lean out to bend one side	v	屈身後望	wàt sàn hàuh mòhng	wat4 san4 hau4 mong6	want san hauh mohng
leap over	v	跳過	tiu gwo	tiu3 gwo3	thiu kwo
learn[1] /learning	n/v	學習	hohk jaahp	hok6 jaap6	hohk jaahp
learn[2]	v	學會	hohk wúi	hok6 wui2	hohk wui
learned[1]	adj	有學問嘅	yáuh hohk mahn	jau5 hok6 man6	yauh hohk mahn
learned[2]	adj	受過高等 教育嘅	sauh gwo gòu dang gaau yuhk ge	sau6 gwo3 gou4 dang2 gaau3 juk6 ge3	sauh kwo kou tang kaau yuhk ke

English		Chinese	Yale	Jyutping	Other
learned woman	v	受過高等教育的女人	sauh gwo gòu dang gaau yuhk dìk neuih yàhn	sau6 gwo3 gou4 dang2 gaau3 juk6 dik4 leui6 jan4	sauh kwo kou tang kaau yuhk tek lowih yahn
learner	n	學習者	hohk jaahp jé	hok6 zaap6 ze2	hohk jaahp che
learning	n	學問	hohk mahn	hok6 man6	hohk mahn
lease	n	租約	jòu yeuk	zou4 joek3	chou yeuk
least /smallest	adv	最少	jeui síu	zeoi3 siu2	cheui siu
leather[1] /skin/skin	n	皮	pèih	pei4	pheih
leather[2]	n	真皮	jàn pèih	zan4 pei4	chan pheih
leather remove	n	皮革	pèih gaak	pei4 gaak3	pheih kaak
leather belt /strap	n	皮帶	pèih dáai	pei4 daai2	pheih taai
leather seat /saddle of horse	n	馬鞍	máh ōn /ngōn	maa5 on1 /ngon1	mah on /ngon
leather shoes	n	皮鞋	pèih hàaih	pei4 haai4	pheih haaih
leather strap /thong	n	皮條	pèih tìuh	pei4 tiu4	pheih thiuh
leave[1] /exit/go	v	離去	leih heui	lei4 heoi3	leih hoi
leave[2] /begin/start /depart	v	開	hòi	hoi4	hoi
leave[3] /vacation	n	假	ga	gaa3	ka
leave[4] /annual leave	n	年假	lihn ga	lin4 gaa3	lihn ka
leave[5] (in marry)	n	婚假	fān ga	fan1 gaa3	fan ka
leave[6] (in delivery child)	n	分娩假	fahn míhn ga	fan6 min5 ga3	fahn mihn ka
leave[7] (in injury)	n	工傷病假	gùng sèung behng /bìhng ga	gung4 soeng4 beng6 /bing6 gaa3	kung seung pehng ka
leave[8] (in winter) /winter vacation /summer holiday	n	寒假	hòhn ga	hon4 gaa3	hohn ka
leave[9] winter or summer long vacation	n	暑假	syū gá	syu1 gaa2	syu syu ka
leave[10] (else)	n	其他假	kèih tà ga	kei4 taa4 ga3	kheih tha ka
leave[11] (absence)	n	事假	sih ga	si6 ga3	sih ka
leave[12] (in funeral rites)	n	息恤假	sīk sēut ga	sik1 seot1 gaa3	sek swot ka
leave a note[1] /write a message	v	留紙	làuh jí	lau4 zi2	lauh chi
leave a note[2] /write a message	v	留字條	làuh jih tìuh	lau4 zi6 tiu4	lauh chih thiuh
leave application		假期申請	ga kèih sàn chéng	gaa1 kei4 san4 ceng2	ka kheih san chheng
leave early		早退	jóu teui	zou2 teoi3	chou thoi
leave home		離開屋企	lèih héui ùk kéi	lei4 heoi2 uk4 kei2	leih hoi uk khei
leave message[1]	v	留	làuh	lau4	lauh
leave message[2]		留口訊	làuh háu seun	lau4 hau2 seon3	lauh hau swon
leave message[3]	v	留言	làuh yìhn	lau4 jin4	lauh yihn
leave secretly		招招地	chíuh chíuh deih	ciu5 ciu5 dei6	chhiuh chhiuh teih
leave type	n	假期類別	ga kèih lèuih bìht	gaa1 kei4 leoi6 bit6	ka kheih lowih piht
leaved /lefted message	n	留咗	làuh jó	lau4 zo2	lauh cho
leaven quality	n	酵母	hàau móuh	haau4 mou5	haau mouh
lecher (for unwilled sex)	n	色狼	sīk lòhng	sik1 long4	sek lohng

lechery /obscene of female	n	淫蕩	yàhm dohng	jam4 dong6	yahm tohng
lecture[1] /speak/say /explain/talk/tell/utter	v	講	góng	gong2	kong
lecture[2] /professor	n	教授	gaau sauh	gaau3 sau6	kaau sauh
lecture[3]	n	講演	góng yín	gong2 jin2	kong yin
lecturer	n	講演者	góng yín jé	gong2 jin2 ze2	kong yin che
ledger	n	總帳	júng jeung	zung2 zong3	chung cheung
leech /worm of water	n	水蛭	séui jaht	seoi2 zat6	swoi chaht
leek	n	韭菜	gáu choi	gau2 coi3	kau chhoi
left[1] (side)	n	左	jó /jaw	zo2	cho
left[2] /be left/remains	n	剩	jihng	zing6	chehng
left[3] (direction)	n	左方	jó fōng	zo2 fong1	cho fong
left[4] /leftist (in political)	n	左派	jó paai	zo2 paai3	cho phaai
left and right	n	左右	jó yáu	zo2 jau2	cho yau
left face side		左便面	jó bihn mihn	zo2 bin6 min6	cho pihn mihn
left hand side		左手面	jó sáu mihn	zo2 sau2 min6	cho sau mihn
left over /remain /having	n	保持	bóu chi	bou2 ci3	pou chhi
left over food	n	食剩嘅食物	sihk jihng ge sihk maht	sik6 zing6 ge3 sik6 mat6	sehk chehng ke sehk maht
left side	n	左面	jó mihn	zo2 min6	cho mihn
lefted /departed		離開咗	lèih hòi jó	lei4 hoi4 zo2	leih hoi cho
leg	n	腿	téui	teoi2	thoi
leg room	n	伸腳空間	sàn geuk hùng gāan	san4 goek3 hung4 gaan1	san keuk hung kaan
legal /according to law	adj	依法	yi faat	ji3 faat3	yi faat
legal aid dept	n	法援署	faat wùhn chyu	faat3 wun4 cyu5	faat wuhn chyu
legality	n	合法	hahp faat	hap6 faat3	hahp faat
legally	adv	合法 (嘅)	hahp faat (ge)	hap6 faat3 (ge3)	hahp faat ke
legibility	n	清晰的	chíhng sik dìk	ceng5 sik1 dik4	chhihng sek tek
legible	adj	易讀	yìh dàuh	ji6 dau6	yih tauh
legislation	n	立法	lahp faat	lap6 faat3	lahp faat
leisure[1]	n	閒	hàahn	haan4	haahn
leisure[2]	n	休閒	dāk hàahn	dak1 haan6	tak haahn
leisure[3]	n	有閑	yàu haan	jau4 haan3	yau haan
leisure & cultural services dept	n	康樂處	hōng lohk chyu	hong1 lok6 cyu3	hong lohk chhyu
lemon [(de)]	n	檸檬	líng /níng mung	ling2 /ning2 mung3	líng /níng mung
lemon coke	n	檸樂	lìhng lohk	ling4 lok6	lehng lohk
lemon tea	n	檸茶	líng /níng chàh	ling2 /ning2 caa4	leng /neng chhah
lend[1] /borrow	v	借俾	je béi	ze3 bei2	che pei
lend[2]	v	借給	je kāp	ze3 kap1	che khap
lender money /borrower	n	放款人	fong fún yàhn	fong3 fun2 jan4	fong fun yahn
lending money	n	放款	fong fún	fong3 fun2	fong fun
length[1] /long	n	長	chèuhng	coeng4	chheuhng
length[2]	n	長度	chèuhng dòuh	coeng4 dou6	chheuhng touh

English		Chinese	Yale	Jyutping	Other
lens	n	鏡片	géng pin	geng2 pin3	keng phin
lens hood of camera	n	遮光罩	jē gwōng jaau	ze1 gwong1 zaau3	che kwong chaau
lens of camera /camera shot	n	鏡頭	géng tàuh	geng2 tau4	keng thauh
lent Christian's 40 days fasting	n	大齋期	daaih jāi kèih	daai6 zai1 kei4	taaih chai kheih
lesbian sexual /same sex/ unnatural sex	n	男女同性戀	làahm leuih tùhng sing lyúhn	laam4 leoi6 tung4 sing3 lyun5	laahm lowih thuhng seng lyuhn
less	adv	較小的	gaau síu dìk	gaau3 siu2 dik4	kaau siu tik
less active /slow down	v	減緩	gáam wùhn	gaam2 wun4	kaam wuhn
lessitude /weakness	n	軟弱	yúhn yeuhk	jyun5 joek6	yuhn yeuhk
lesson	n	堂	tòhng	tong4	thohng
lest / in order/so as not to!	conj	免得	míhn dāk	min5 dak1	mihn tak
let (de) /allow/give/pay	v	俾	béi	bei2	pei
let-down for hope /deceived/make hopeless	v	使失望	sái sāt mohng	sai2 sat1 mong6	sai sat mohng
let in	v	讓...進來	yeuhng...jeun loìh	joeng6...zeon3 loi4	yeuhng...cheon loih
let loose /put by hand /free by hand	v	放	fong	fong3	fong
let me see		等我睇吓	dáng ngóh tái háh	dang2 ngo5 tai2 haa5	tang ngoh thai hah
let me think!		等我想吓!	dáng ngóh séung háh!	dang2 ngo5 soeng2 haa5!	tang ngoh seung hah!
let out /release	v	放	fong	fong3	fong
let pass	v	放行	fong hàhng	fong3 hang4	fong hahng
let's[1] (coll) let us	v	讓我哋	yeuhng ngóh dèih	joeng6 ngo5 dei6	yeuhng ngoh teih
let's[2] (coll) let us	v	我們	ngóh mùhn	ngo5 mun4	ngoh muhn
let's[3] /let us (wr)	v	咱們	jā mùhn	za1 mun4	cha muhn
let's eat!	v	食飯!	sihk faahn	sik6 faan6	sehk faahn
let's listen!	v	傾吐	kīng tou	king1 tou3	khing thou
let's say[1]		比如話	béi yùh wá	bei2 jyu4 waa2	pei yuh wa
let's say[2]		比如講	béi yùh góng	bei2 jyu4 gong2	pei yuh kong
let's say[3]		比方說	béi fōng syút	bei2 fong1 syut2	pei fong syut
let's see!	v	去睇吓	heui tái háa	heoi3 tai2 haa2	hoi thai haa
let's try	v	試吓啦	si há lā	si3 haa2 laa1	si ha la
letter /mail	n	信	seun	seon3	swon
letter box[1] /mailbox /letter receiving box	n	信箱	seun sēung	seon3 soeng1	swon seung
letter box[2] receiving mailbox	n	郵箱	yàuh sēung	jau4 soeng1	yauh seung
lettered	n	傅學嘅	fuh hohk ge	fu6 hok6 ge3	fuh hohk ke
letting	n	允許	wáhn hēui	wan5 heoi1	wahn hoi
lettuce	n	生菜	sàang chói	saang4 coi2	saang chhoi
level[1] /surface/horizontal	adj	水平	séui pìhng	seoi2 ping4	swoi phehng
level[2] /ground	adj	平地	pèhng deih	peng4 dei6	phehng teih
level[3] /grade	n	級別	kāp biht	kap1 bit6	khap piht
level[4] /rank/position /status	n	地位	deih waih	dei6 wai6	teih waih
level[5] /horizon level	n	水準	séui jéun	seoi2 zeon2	swoi cheon

English		Chinese	Romanization	Jyutping	Yale
level crossing	n	平交道	pèhng gàau dóu	peng4 gaau4 dou2	phehng kaau tou
lever[1] /pole/as stick	n	桿	túng	tung2	thung
lever[2]	n	槓桿	góng gòn	gong2 gon4	kong kon
levi's pant /jeans	n	牛仔褲	ngàuh jāi fú	ngau4 zai1 fu2	ngauh chai fu
levy[1] /tax	v	稅	seui	seoi3	swoi
levy[2]	v	徵稅	jìng seui	zing4 seoi3	cheng swoi
levy[3]	v	徵收	jìng sāu	zing4 sau1	cheng sau
lewd[1] /of female/lustful	adj	淫蕩	yàhm dohng	jam4 dong6	yahm tohng
lewd[2] /sex offensive way	adj	猥褻	wúi sit	wui2 sit3	wui sit
lewd[3] /morality less	adj	下流	hah làuh	haa6 lau6	hah lauh
liability	n	惹麻煩嘅人	yéh màh fàahn ge yàhn	je maa4 faan4 ge3 jan4	yeh mah faahn ke yahn
liaise	v	取得聯絡	chēui dàk lyun lók	ceoi1 dak4 lyun3 lok2	chheui tak lyun lok
libel /charge/blame	n	毀謗	wái póhng	wai2 pong5	wai phohng
liberal[1] /generous	adj	慷慨	hong koi	hung3 koi3	hong khoi
liberal[2]	adj	寬宏	fùn wang	fun4 wang3	fun wang
liberation /liberate	n/v	解放	gáai fong	gaai2 fong3	kaai fong
library	n	圖書館	tòuh syù gún	tou4 syu4 gun2	thouh syu kun
library card	n	借書證	je syu jing	ze3 syu3 zing3	che syu cheng
license-plate /licence commercial	n	牌照	pàaih jiu	paai4 ziu3	phaaih chiu
license permit/commercial	n	執照	jāp jiu	zap1 ziu3	chap chiu
licentious[1]	adj	放肆	fong si	fong3 si3	fong si
licentious[2]	adj	放蕩	fong dohng	fong3 dong6	fong tohng
lick[1] /lap	n	舔	lím	lim2	lim
lick[2] /lap up	n	舐	láai	laai2	laai
lick[3] (vdw) penis or vagina	n/xy	啥能	ham làhng /nàhng	ham3 lang4 /nang4	ham lahng /nahng
lick-cunt (vdw)	n xy	食佢條閪	sihk héuih tìuh hài	sik6 heoi5 tiu4 hai4	sehk hoih thiuh hai
lie[1]	v	臥	ngoh	ngo6	ngoh
lie[2] /lying/untrue/deny	adj/v	否認	fáu yihng	fau2 jing6	fau yehng
lie[3] /lies/untrue	n	謊	fóng	fong2	fong
lie[4] /untrue/tell lies	v	撒謊	saat fóng	saat3 fong2	saat fong
lie down[1] /sleep	v	臥	oh	o6	oh
lie down[2] /sleep/rest	v	寢	chám	cam2	chham
lie down[3] (wr) /lean down /sleep/to lie down	v	躺下	tóng hah	fong2 haa6	thong hah
lie down[4] (coll) /fall down	v	瞓低	fan dài	fan3 dai4	fan tai
lie low /lie hidden/trap	n	伏	fuhk	fuk6	fuhk
life[1]	n	生命	sàng mehng /mihng	sang4 meng6 /ming6	sang mehng
life[2] /daily life/to live /livelihood	n	生活	sàng wuht	sang4 wut6	sang wuht
life[3] /alive/exist/lively /survive/live	adj	活	wuht	wut6	wuht
life[4] /surving	n	壽	sauh	sau6	sauh
life boat	n	救生艇	gau sàng tíhng	gau3 sang4 ting5	kau sang thehng

life guard	n	救生員	gau sàang yùhn	gau3 saang4 jyun4	kau saang yuhn
life insurance[1]	n	人壽保險	yàhn sauh bóu hím	jan4 sau6 bou2 him2	yahn sauh pou him
life insurance[2]	n	人壽燕梳	yàhn sauh yin sō	jan4 sau6 jin3 so1	yahn sauh yin so
life jacket	n	救生衣	gau sàng yī	gau3 sang4 ji1	kau sang yi
life member	n	終身會員	jūng sàn wúi yùhn	jung1 san4 wui2 jyun4	chung san wui yuhn
life rob	n	攞命	lō mehng /mihng	lo1 meng6 /ming6	loh mehng
life story	n	人生故事	yàhn sāang gu sih	jan4 saang1 gu3 si6	yahn saang ku sih
life support system	n	生命維持系統	sàng mehng waìh chìh haih túng	sang4 meng6 wai4 ci4 hai6 tung2	sang mehng waih chhih haih thung
lifedie /die of old age	a	壽終正寢	sauh jūng jeng chám	sau6 zung1 zeng3 cam2	sauh chung cheeng chham
lifeline	n	生命線	sàng mehng /mihng sin	sang4 meng6 /ming6 sin3	sang mehng sin
lift[1] (de)	n	*	līp	lip1	lip
lift[2] /hold up/to raise	v	舉	géui	geoi2	kwoi
lift failure	adj	電梯故障	dihn tài gú jéung	din6 tai4 gu2 zoeng2	tihn thai ku cheung
lifted	v	提高咗	tàih gòu jó	tai4 gou4 zo2	thaih kou cho
lifter[1] /crane	n	起重機	héi chúhng gèi	hei2 cung5 gei4	hei chhuhng kei
lifter[2] /lifter man	n	舉重者	géui chúhng jé	geoi2 cung5 ze2	kwoi chuhng che
light[1]	n	光	gwòng	gwong4	kwong
light[2] /ray	n	光線	gwòng sin	gwong4 sin3	kwong sin
light[3] /lamp	v	點	dím	dim2	tim
light[4] /tube-light	n	電光管	dihn gwòng gùn	din6 gwong4 gun4	tihn kwong kun
light[5] /shallow of weight/ sound/color	adj	淺	chín	cin2	chhin
light bulb[1]	n	燈胆	dāng dáam	dang1 daam2	tang taam
light bulb[2]	n	燈泡	dāng póuh	dang1 pou5	tang phouh
light colour	adj	淺色	chín sìk	cin2 sik4	chhin sek
light confections /tiffin/ refreshments	n	點心	dím sām	dim2 sam1	tim sam
light flashing[1]	n	閃一閃	sím yāt sím	sim2 jat1 sim2	sim yat sim
light flashing[2]	n	閃吓閃吓	sím hah sím hah	sim2 haa6 sim2 haa6	sim hah sim hah
light green	n	青	chèng	ceng4	chheng
light-house	n	燈塔	dāng taap	dang1 taap3	tang thaap
light problem /small problem		因小故	yàn síu gu	yan1 siu2 gwoo3	yan siu ku
light source	n	光源	gwòng yùhn	gwong4 jyun4	kwong yuhn
light switch[1]	n	燈掣	dāng jai	dang1 zai3	tang chai
light switch[2]	n	光線開關	gwòng sin hòi gwàan	gwong4 sin3 hoi4 gwaan4	kwong sin hoi kwaan
light up[1]		燃點	yìhn dím	jin4 dim2	yihn tim
light up[2]		照亮	jiu leuhng	ziu3 loeng6	chiu leuhng
lighten	v	變亮	bín lèuhng	bin2 loeng6	pin leuhng
lighter[1] /for cigarette	n	打火機	dá fó gèi	daa2 fo2 gei4	ta fo kei
lighter[2] /sea container /barge	n	駁船	bok syùhn	bok3 syun4	pok syuhn

lighthearted /light and graceful	a	輕盈	hèng yìhng	heng4 jing4	heng yehng
lightless	n	不發光	bāt faat gwòng	bat1 faat3 gwong4	pat faat kwong
lightly¹ /easy/soft/light of weight	adj	輕	hèng /hìng	heng4 /hing4	heng
lightly² /softly	adj	輕輕	hèng hèng, hìng hìng	heng4 heng4, hing4 hing4	heng heng
lightly³	adj	輕輕地	hèng hèng deih, hìng hìng deih	heng4 heng4 dei6, hing4 hing4 dei6	heng heng teih
lightning	n	閃電	sím dìhn	sim2 din6	sim tihn
lightning bug	n	螢火蟲	yìhng fó chùhng	jing4 fo2 cung4	yehng fo chhuhng
lightning rod	n	避雷針	beih lèuih jām	bei6 leoi4 zam1	peih lowih cham
lightweight	n	輕量級	hèng leuhng kāp	heng4 loeng6 kap1	heng leuhng khap
like¹ /love	v&i	愛	ói /ngói	oi2 /ngoi3	oi /ngoi
like² /wish	v	鍾意	jùng yi	zung4 ji3	chung yi
like³ /love	v	喜歡	héi fūn	hou2 fun1	hei fun
like⁴ /same/lok like/similar	adj	似	chíh	ci5	chhih
like⁵ /same as	conj	像…一樣	jeuhng…yāt yeuhng	zoeng6 jat1…joeng6	cheuhng…yat yeuhng
like same /similar	adj	好相似	hou seung chìh	hou3 soeng3 ci5	hou seung chhih
like that¹ /thus	adj	爾	yíh	ji5	yih
like that²	adj	像那樣	jeuhng láh /náh yeuhng	zoeng6 la5 /na5 joeng6	cheuhng lah /nah yeuhng
like this¹ (sl) in this way	adj	噉	gám	gam2	kam
like this² /thus	adj	這樣	jé yeuhng	ze2 joeng6	che yeuhng
likely	adj	很可能	hān hó làhng /nàhng	han1 ho2 lang4 /nang4	han ho lahng /nahng
likes¹ /loved	vt&i	好喜愛	hóu héi ói /ngói	hou2 hei2 oi2 /ngoi3	hou hei oi /ngoi
likes² /loved/very fond of	vt&i	好鍾意	hóu jùng yi	hou2 zung4 ji3	hou chung yi
lily	n	百合花	baak hahp fā	baak3 hap6 faa1	paak hahp fa
limbs /of the body parts	n	肢體	jì tái	zi4 tai2	chi thai
lime¹	n	青檸	chèng nìhng	ceng4 ling4	chheng nihng
lime²	n	石灰	sehk fùi	sek6 fui4	sehk fui
limited	n	有限	yáuh haahn	jau5 haan6	yauh haahn
limitless¹	adv	無限	mòuh haahn	mou4 haan6	mouh haahn
limitless² /unlimited	adv	無限制	mòuh haahn jai	mou4 haan6 zai3	mouh haahn chai
line¹ /row	n	行	hòhng	hong4	hohng
line²	n	繩	síng	sing2	seng
line³ /line up/row	n	排	pàaih	paai4	phaaih
line of sight	n	視線	sih sin	si6 sin3	sih sin
linen	n	麻質	màh jāt	maa4 zat1	mah chat
linguist¹ /bilingual	n	語言學家	yúh yìhn hohk gā	jyu5 jin4 hok6 gaa1	yuh yihn hohk ka
linguist²	n	語言學	yúh yin hohk	jyu5 jin3 hok6	yuh yin hohk
linguistics	n	語言學	yúh yìhn hohk	jyu5 jin4 hok6	yuh yihn hohk
link¹	v	連	lìhn	lin4	lihn
link²	v	聯繫	lyùhn haih	lyun4 hai6	lyuhn haih
link-up	n	銜接	hàahm jip	haam4 zip3	haahm chip

linkages /connection /links/joining	n	連接	lìhn jip	lin4 zip3	lihn chip
linseed	n	亞麻子	a màh jí	a3 ma6 zi2	aa mah chi
lion[1]	n	獅	sī /see	si1	si /see
lion[2]	n	獅子	sì jí	si1 zi2	si chi
lip[1]	n	唇	sèuhn	seon4	swohn
lip[2]	n	口唇	háu sèuhn	hau2 seon4	hau seuhn
lip[3]	n	嘴唇	jéui sèuhn	zeoi2 seon4	cheui seuhn
lipid /fat (in the blood)	n	血脂肪	hyut jī fòng	hyut3 zi1 fong4	hyut chi fong
lips mark /loved mark		唇印	sèuhn yan	seon4 jan3	swohn yan
lipstick[1]	n	唇膏	sèuhn gōu	seon4 gou1	swohn kou
lipstick[2]	n	口唇膏	háu sèuhn gōu	hau2 seon4 gou1	hau seuhn kou
lipstick[3]	n	口紅	háu hùhng	hau2 hung4	hau huhng
liquid fire /oil liquid fire		汽油火災	hei yàuh fó jòi	hei3 jau4 fo2 zoi4	hei yauh fo choi
list /topic/contents	n	目	muhk	muk6	muhk
list of items /wishlist	n	清單	chèng /chìng dāan	ceng4 /cing4 daan1	chheng taan
list of name /name list	n	名單	mèhng dāan	meng4 daan1	mehng taan
listen[1]	v	聆聽	lìhng tèng	ling4 teng4	lehng theng
listen[2] (with care)	v	留神	lauh sàhn	lau4 san4	lauh sahn
listening	n	聽	tèng	teng4	theng
listening music	n	聽音樂	tèng yàm ngòhk	teng4 jam4 ngok6	theng yam ngohk
listening pop music	n	聽流行乐	tèng lau hang ngòhk	teng4 lau3 hang3 ngok6	theng lau hang ngohk
listening radio	n	聽收音機	tèng sàu yàm gèi	teng4 sau4 jam4 gei4	theng sau yam kei
listening rock music	n	聽摇滚乐	tèng yiu kwān lòhk	teng4 jiu3 kwan1 lok6	theng yiu khwan lohk
litchi [(de)] fruit /lychee	n	荔枝	laih jī	lai6 zi1	laih chi
literate[1]	adj	識字	sīk jìh	sik1 zi6	sek chih
literate[2]	adj	有文化修養	yáuh màhn fá sàu yèuhng	jau5 man6 faa2 sau4 joeng6	yauh mahn fa sau yeuhng
literate[3]	adj	能讀寫	làhng /nàhng duhk sé	lang4 /nang4 duk6 se2	lahng /nahng tuhk se
literature	n	文學	màhn hohk	man4 hok6	mahn hohk
lithium	n	鋰	léih	lei5	leih
litre (1000 ml)	n	公升	gūng sìng	gung1 sing4	kung seng
litter-bin /rubbish bin	n	廢物箱	fai maht sēung	fai3 mat6 soeng1	fai maht seung
little[1] /small/few/young	adj	小	síu /seew	siu2	siu /seew
little[2] /few/lowering /petty	adj	小的	síu dìk	siu2 dik4	siu tek
little[3] /few	adj	一點	yāt dím	jat1 dim2	yat tim
little[4] /a bit/few [(coll)] qty	adj	一啲	yāt dī	jat1 di1	yat ti
little[5] /few/rather/some /quite/somewhat	adj	有啲	yáuh dī	jau5 di1	yauh ti
little[6] /few/some [(wr)] people/things/places	adj	一些	yāt sē	jat1 se1	yat se
little[7] /few/small qty	adj	少	síu	siu2	siu
little[8] /junior	adj	年少	lihn síu	lin4 siu2	lihn siu
little[9] /small size/age/area	adj	細	sai	sai3	sai

little[10]/short time/distance	adj	短	dyún	dyun2	tyun
little bit[1]/small amount	adv	些少	sē síu	se1 siu2	se siu
little bit[2]/bit	adv	啲咁多	dìk gam dō	dik4 kam3 do1	tek kam to
little bit[3]	adv	小小呀	síu síu āa /aa	siu2 siu2 aa1 /aa3	siu siu aa
little by little	adv	一啲一啲咁	yāt dī yāt dī gám	jat1 di1 jat1 di1 gam2	yat ti yat ti kam
little dizzy		暈暈地	wàhn wán déi	wan4 wan2 dei2	wahn wan tei
little dog /small dog /puppy	n	狗仔	gáu jái	gau2 zai2	kau chai
little far		幾遠啫	géi yúhn jē	gei2 jyun5 ze1	kei yuhn che
live /real/live scene /live show/on the spot	adj	現場	yihn chèuhng	jin6 coeng4	yihn chheuhng
livelihood[1]	n	生計	sàng gai	sang4 gai3	sang kai
livelihood[2]	n	謀生	màuh sàng	mau4 sang4	mauh sang
livelong	adj	漫長	maahn chèuhng	maan6 coeng4	maahn chheuhng
lively	adj	精力充沛	jeng lihk chùng pui	zeng3 lik6 cung4 pui3	cheng lehk chhung phui
liver	n	肝	gòn	gon4	kon
living[1] /live standards	adj	活嘅	wuht ge	wut6 ge3	wuht ke
living[2] /staying	n	住在	jyuh joih	zyu6 zoi6	chyuh choih
living standard[1]	n	生活水準	sàng wuht séui jéun	sang4 wut6 seoi2 zeon2	sang wuht swoi cheun
living standard[2]	n	生活水平	sàng wuht séui pèhng /pìhng	sang4 wut6 seoi2 peng4 /ping4	sang wuht swoi phehng
living thing	n	生物	sàng maht	sang4 mat6	sang maht
living together /not married/cohabitation	n	同居	tùhng gèui	tung4 geoi4	thuhng kwoi
lizard	n	鹽蛇	yìhm sé	jim4 se2	yihm se
load[1] /pack/fill	n	裝	jòng	zong4	chong
load[2]	n	裝載	jòng joi	zong4 zoi	chong choi
load[3]	n	負載	fuh joi	fu6 zoi3	fuh choi
load star /North pole star	n	北極星	bāk gihk sēng /sīng	bak1 gik6 seng1 /sing1	pak kehk seng
load stone	n	磁石	chih sehk	ci4 sek6	chhih sehk
loan[1]/lend on interest	n	貸	taai	taai3	thaai
loan[2] /borrow money	n	貸款	taai fún	taai3 fun2	thaai fun
loan-shark	n	放高利貸者	fong gōu leih taai jé	fong3 gou1 lei6 taai3 ze2	fong kou leih thaai che
loaner /creditor	n	債權人	jaai kyùhn yàhn	zaai3 kyun4 jan4	chaai khyuhn yahn
loath	adj	不願意	bāt yuhn yi	bat1 jyun6 ji3	pat yuhn yi
loathe	v	厭	yim	jim3	yim
lobby[1]	n	大堂	daaih tòhng	daai6 tong4	taaih thohng
lobby[2]	n	大廳	daaih tèng	daai6 teng4	taaih theng
lobes	n	波瓣	bō fàahn	bo1 faan6	po faahn
lobster	n	龍蝦	lùhng hā	lung4 haa1	luhng ha
local[1]	n	當地	dòng deih	dong4 dei6	tong teih
local[2]	adj	本地	bún dèih	bun2 dei6	pun teih
local-goods	n	本地貨	bún deih fo	bun2 dei6 fo3	pun teih fo
local-people[1]/native	n	當地人	dòng deih yàhn	dong4 dei6 jan4	tong teih yahn

local-people[2] /native people	n	本地人	bún deih yàhn	bun2 dei6 jan4	pun teih yahn
local-people[3]	n	土人	tóu yàhn	tou2 jan4	thou yahn
local-products	n	土產品	tóu cháan bán	tou2 caa2 ban2	thou chhaan pan
local telephone	n	本地電話	bún dèih dihn wá	bun2 dei6 din6 waa2	pun teih tihn wa
local time	n	地方時	deih fòng sìh	dei6 fong4 si4	teih fong sih
locality	n	場所	chèuhng só	coeng4 so2	chheuhng so
located[1] /situated	adv	在	joih	zoi6	choih
located[2]	adj	位於	wàih yù	wai6 jyu4	waih yu
location[1] /space/seat /place/position	n	位	wàih	wai4	waih
location[2] /place/seat	n	位置	wàih jí	wai6 zi2	waih chi
location[3] /site	n	址	jí	zi2	chi
location[4] /address /place/site	n	地址	deih jí	dei6 zi2	teih chi
location map	n	街道圖	gāai douh tòuh	gaai1 dou6 tou4	kaai touh touh
lock	v	鎖	só	so2	so
locked up	v	鎖咗	só jó	so2 zo2	so cho
locker[1]	n	衣物櫃	yī maht gwaih	ji1 mat6 gwai6	yi maht kwaih
locker[2]	n	有鎖存物櫃	yáuh só chùhn maht gwaih	jau5 so2 cyun4 mat6 gwai6	yauh so chhuhn maht kwaih
locket /jewellery	n	盒式項鏈墜	háap sīk hohng lihn jeuih	haap2 sik1 hong6 lin6 zeoi6	haap sek hohng lihn choih
locomotive[1] /train engine	n	火車頭	fó chè tàuh	fo2 ce4 tau4	fo chhe thauh
locomotive[2]	n	蒸汽火車頭	jìng hei fó chè tàuh	zing4 hei3 fo2 ce4 tau6	cheng hei fo chhe thauh
lodge[1]	n	宿	sūk	suk1	suk
lodge[2] /hut	n	小屋	síu ùk /ngùk	siu2 uk4 /nguk4	siu uk /nguk
lodge[3] /lodging/abode /resting place	n	門房	mùhn fóng	mun4 fong2	muhn fong
lodge[4]	n	宿容	sūk yùhng	suk1 jung4	suk yùhng
lodge[5] /welcome guest	n	迎賓館	ying bān gún	jing3 ban1 gun2	yeng pan kun
lodge[6] /sue/complaint	v	投訴	tàuh sou	tau4 sou3	thauh sou
lodge[7] /hostel/boarding /rented room	n	寄宿	géi sūk	gei2 suk1	kei suk
lodger[1]	n	寄宿人	gei sūk yàhn	gei3 suk1 jan4	kei suk yahn
lodger[2]	n	房客	fóhng haak	fong5 haak3	fohng haak
lodging	n	借宿	je sūk	ze3 suk1	che suk
log[1] (of wood)	n	木頭	muhk tàuh	muk6 tau4	muhk thauh
log[2]	n	日誌	yaht gei	jat6 gei3	yaht kei
log in[1] /on computing /go inside/entering inside	v	入去	yàhp heui	jap6 heoi3	yahp hoi
log in[2] /on computing	v	進入	jeun yahp	zeon3 jap6	cheun yahp
log off[1] /close/shut/out computing	v	關閉	gwàan bai	gwaan4 bai3	kwaan pai

log off[2]/out computing /quit	v	退出	teui chēut	teoi3 ceot1	thoi chhot
logic	n	道理	dou léih	dou3 lei5	tou leih
logical[1]	adj	邏輯	lòh chāp	lo4 cap1	loh chhap
logical[2] /right/correct	adj	有道理	yáuh douh léih	jau5 dou6 lei5	yauh touh leih
logical[3]	adj	合乎邏輯	hahp fùh lòh chāp	hap6 fu4 lo4 cap1	hahp fuh loh chhap
logical[4]	adj	按理	on /ngòn léih	on3 /ngon4 lei4	on /ngon leih
logically	adj	能推理地	làhng /nàhng tèui léih deih	lang4 /nang4 teoi4 lei4 dei6	lahng /nahng theui leih teih
logistics	n	後勤	hauh kàhn	hau6 kan4	hauh khahn
loiter[1]	v	流連	làuh lìhn	lau4 lin4	lauh lihn
loiter[2] /person loitering	v	遊蕩	yau dòhng	jau3 dong6	yau tohng
loiter[3]	v	蕩蕩吓	dohng dohng há	dong6 dong6 haa2	tohng tohng ha
London	n	倫敦	Lèuhn dēun	leon4 deon1	Leuhn tohn
lone[1] /single	adj	單	dāan	daan1	taan
lone[2] /lonely/single person	adj	孤單	gù dāan	gu4 daan1	ku taan
lonely /solitude/quiet /silent	adj/n	寂寞	jihk mohk	zik6 mok6	chehk mohk
long & tedious	adj	冗長	yúng chèuhng	jung2 coeng4	yung chheuhng
long angry speech /tirade/criticizing	n	激烈嘅發言	gīk liht ge faat yìhn	gik1 lit6 ge3 faat3 jing4	kek liht ke faat yihn
long distance[1]	adj	長途	chèuhng	coeng4	chheuhng
long distance[2]/distant /remote/far	adj	遠	yúhn	jyun5	yuhn
long hair[1]	n	長髮	chèuhng faat	coeng4 faat3	chheuhng faat
long hair[2]	n	長頭髮	chèuhng tàuh fáat	coeng4 tau4 faat2	chheuhng thauh faat
long hand	n	普通寫法	póu tùng sé faat jì	pou2 tung4 se2 faat3 zi2	phou thung se faat chi
long items /pens /stick/cigarettes/bottles	n	支			
long lasting relation	adj	持久的關係	chìh gáu dìk gwāan haih	ci4 gau2 dik1 gwaan1 hai6	chhih kau tik kwaan haih
long live	adj	萬歲	maahn seui	maan6 seoi3	maahn swoi
long lived[1]	adj	長命	chèuhng mehng	coeng4 memg6	chheuhng mehng
long lived[2]	adj	長命百歲	chèuhng mehng baak seui	coeng4 memg6 baak3 seoi3	chheuhng mehng paak swoi
long memorable[1]		長難望	chèuhng nàahn mòhng	coeng4 naan4 mong6	chheuhng naahn mohng
long memorable[2]		長值得紀念	chèuhng jihk dāk gei nihm	coeng4 zik6 dak1 gei3 nim6	chheuhng chehk tak kei nihm
long narrow way /passage/access enter	n	通路	tùng louh	tung4 lou6	thung louh
long period /long time	adj	好耐	hóu loih /noih	hou2 loi6 /noi6	hou loih /noih
long sleeved	n	長袖	chèuhng jauh	coeng4 zau6	chheuhng chauh
long sleeves shirt	n	長袖衫	chèuhng jauh sāam	coeng4 zau6 saam1	chheuhng chauh saam
long standing	adj	長時間	chèuhng sìh gáan	coeng4 si4 gaan2	chheuhng sih kaan
long suffering	adj	長受苦	chèuhng sauh fú	coeng4 sau6 fu2	chheuhng sauh fu

long term	adj	長線	chèuhng sin	coeng4 sin3	chheuhng sin
long time[1] (coll)	adj	耐	loih /noih	loi6 /noi6	loih /noih
long time[2] (wr)	adj	久	gáu	gau2	kau
long time[3]	adj	長期	chèuhng kèih	coeng4 kei4	chheuhng kheih
long vehicle	n	長車	chèuhng chè	coeng4 ce4	chheuhng chhe
long vision	n	遠見	yúhn gin	jyun5 gin3	yuhn kin
longan	n	龍眼	lùhng ngáahn	lung4 ngaan5	luhng ngaahn
longitudinal	n	長度的	chèuhng dòuh dìk	coeng4 dou6 dik4	chheuhng douh tek
look[1] (coll) /observe/read /see /watch	v	睇	tái	tai2	thai
look[2] (wr) /see/view/watch	v	看	hòn	hon4	hon
look[3] /sight	n/v	視	sih	si6	sih
look after[1] /take care	n	顧	gu	gu3	ku
look after[2] /care/tender	n	照料	jiu liuh	ziu3 liu6	chiu liuh
look after[3] /attend to /wait upon	n	服侍	fuhk sih	fuk6 si6	fuhk sih
look after[4]	n	照顧	jiu gu	ziu3 gu3	chiu ku
look askance /squint	v	斜眼	chèh ngáahn	ce4 ngaan5	chheh ngaahn
look at[1] /survey	v	睇嘢	tái yéh	tai je5	thai yeh
look at[2]	v	觀看	gùn hòn	gun4 hon4	kun hon
look downward[1]		嗒低個頭	dāp dài go tàuh	dap1 dai4 tau4	tap tai ko thauh
look downward[2]		向下望	heung hah mohng	hoeng3 haa6 mong6	heung hah mohng
look downward[3]		向下看	heung hah hōn	hoeng3 haa6 hon1	heung hah hon
look for[1] /to seek /to meet	adj	搵	wán	wan2	wan
look for[2] /to try to find	adj	找	jáau	zaau2	chaau
look for[3] /to search /search	v	搜尋	sáu cham	sau2 cam4	sau chham
look for[4] /seeking /to seek/sought/quest/find	adj	尋找	cham jáau	cam3 zaau2	chham chaau
look forward to	adj	盼望	paan mohng	paan3 mong6	phaan mohng
look it up /find out /to search out	v	找出	jáau chēut	zaau2 ceot1	chaau chhot
look like[1] /similar	adj	像	jeuhng	zoeng6	cheuhng
look like[2] /be like /same/ similar to	adj	好似	hou chíh	hou3 ci5	hou chhih
look like[3] /same/alike /same as/a kind of	adj	一樣	yāt yeuhng	jat joeng6	yat yeuhng
look out from tower /observation from high place	n	瞭望台	lìuh mohng tòih	liu4 mong6 toi4	liuh mohng thoih
look over[1] /watch over	n	覽	láahm	laam5	laahm
look over[2]	n	仔細檢查	jí sai gím chàh	zi2 sai3 gim2 caa4	chi sai kim chhah
look round[1] /look on all sides	v	四圍睇吓	sei wàih tái háh	sei3 wai4 tai2 haa5	sei waih thai hah
look round[2]	v	四週視察	sei jāu sih chaat	sei3 zau1 si6 caat3	sei caau sih chhaat
look round[3]	v	回頭看	wùih tàuh hòn	wui4 fau4 hon4	wùih thauh hon

look round[4]	v	參觀遊覽	chàam gùn yàuh láahm	caam4 gun4 jau4 laam5	chhaam kun yauh laahm
look round[5]	v	回頭望	wùih tàuh mohng	wui4 tau4 mong6	wùih thauh mohng
look sly /peep /secret look	v	偷睇	tàu tái	tau4 tai2	thau thai
look towards	adj	望	mohng	mong6	mohng
look up /lying on the back	adj	仰	yéuhng	joeng5	yeuhng
look up for you		搵俾你	wán béi léih /néih	wan2 bei2 lei5 /nei5	wan pei leih /neih
look up to /reverent	v	尊敬	jyùn ging	zyun4 ging3	chyun keng
look upward	adj	擔高個頭	dāam gòu go tàuh	daam1 gou4 go3 tau4	taam kou ko thauh
looker[1] /viewer	n	觀看者	gùn hòn jé	gun4 hon4 ze2	kun hon che
looker[2]	n	好看的女性	hóu hòn dìk leuih /neuih sing	hou2 hon4 dik4 leoi6 /neoi6 sing3	hou hon tek lowih /nowih seng
looking	n	看上去	hōn séuhng heui	hon1 soeng5 heoi3	hon seuhng hoi
looking attractived /presentable	adj	可上演	hó séuhng yín	ho2 soeng5 jin2	ho seuhng yin
looking down /upside down/down	adv	向下	heung hah	hoeng6 ha6	heung hah
looking downwards	v	拜倒	bāai dóu	baai1 dou2	paai tou
looking job /look for work	adj	搵工	wán gùng	wan2 gung4	wan kung
looks familiar		面善	mihn sihn	min6 sin6	mihn sihn
loop	n	環狀物	wàahn johng maht	waan4 zong6 mat6	waahn chohng maht
loose[1] /loosen/not tight /soft	adj	鬆	sùng	sung4	sung
loose[2]	adj	鬆的	sùng dìk	sung4 dik4	sung tek
loose[3] /loosen/not tight /soft	adj	鬆脫	sùng tyut	sung4 tyut3	sung thyut
loose[4] /soft/slack/not hard	adj	柔軟	yàuh yúhn	jau4 jyun5	yauh yuhn
loose[5] /scatter	v	散	sáan	saan2	saan
loose in morals	adj	墮落	doh lohk	do6 lok6	toh lohk
loosened[1]	v	疏鬆	sò sùng	so4 sung4	so sung
loosened[2] /relaxation /relax muscles	v	放鬆	fong sùng	fong3 sung4	fong sung
loosened[3] /untie	v	鬆開	sūng hòi	fong3 hoi4	sung hoi
looting /robbery /plunder/ rob/stolen/spoil	n	搶劫	chéung gip	coeng2 gip3	chheung kip
loot things	n	贓物	jōng maht	zong1 mat6	chong maht
looter[1] /robber	n	搶劫人	chéung gip yàhn	coeng2 gip3 jan4	chheung kip yahn
looter[2] /robber	n	搶劫者	chéung gip jé	coeng2 gip3 ze2	chheung kip che
loppy	adj	散垂	sàan sèuih	saan4 seoi4	saan swoih
loquat (fruit)	n	枇杷果	pèih pàh gwó	pei4 paa4 gwo2	pheih phah kwo
Lord /God/chief /chief owner/head man	n	主	jyú	zyu2	chyu
Lord's prayer[1]	n	主禱文	jyú tóu màhn	zyu2 tou2 man6	chyu thou mahn
Lord's prayer[2] /prayer to god	v	祈禱文	kèih tóu màhn	kei4 tou2 man6	kheih thou mahn

lorries /truck	n	貨車	fo chè	fo3 ce4	fo chhe
lorry /truck	n	十個轆	sàhp go lūk	sap6 go3 luk1	sahp ko luk
Los Angeles	n	羅省	Lòh sáang	lo4 saang2	Loh saang
lose[1] /to lose/lose game	v	輸	syù	syu4	syu
lose[2] (by death)	v	喪	sòng	song4	song
lose business	v	蝕本	siht bún	sit6 bun2	siht pun
lose color	n	失色	sāt sīk	sat1 sik1	sat sek
lose conscious	v	昏迷	fān màih	fan1 mai4	fan maih
lose control of	v	失去控制	sāt heui hung jai	sat1 heoi3 hung3 zai3	sat hoi hung chai
lose count of	v	不知道... 確切嘅數	bāt jì douh... kok chit ge sou muhk	bat1 zi4 dou6 kok3 cit3 ge3 sou3 muk6	pat chi touh khok chit ke sou muhk
lose in gambling	v	輸錢	syù chín	syu4 cin2	syu chhim
lose money[1]	v	失利	sāt leih	sat1 lei6	sat leih
lose money[2]	v	損失	syún sàt	syun2 sat4	syun sat
lose money[3]	v	丟失錢	dīu sāt chín	diu1 sat1 cin2	tiu sat chhin
lose way /lost way	n	迷路	màih louh	mai4 lou6	maih louh
loser (property)	n	失主	sāt jyú	sat2 zyu2	sat chyu
loser playing at sex[1] (sl) most of by man	v	馬上風	máh séuhng fùng	maa5 soeng6 fung4	mah seuhng fung
loser playing at sex[2] (sl) ejaculated semen by man	v	玩死	waahn séi	waan4 sei2	waahn sei
loss[1] /disappear/couldn't see/where missing/gonna missing	n	唔見咗	m̀ gin jó	m4 gin3 zo2	mh kin cho
loss[2]	n	遺失	wàih sàt	wai4 sat4	waih sat
loss[3]	n	喪失	sòng sāt	song4 sat1	song sat
lost[1] /lose	v	失	sāt	sat2	sat
lost[2]	adj	遺失	wàih sàt	wai4 sat4	waih sat
lost property[1]	n	遺失財物	wàih sàt choi màht	wai6 sat4 coi4 mat6	waih sat chhoi maht
lost property[2]	n	招領之失物	jìu léhng jí sāt maht	ziu4 leng5 zi2 sat1 mat6	chiu lehng chi sat maht
lost road[1]	adj	蕩失	dohng sāt	dong6 sat1	tohng sat
lost road[2] /road mistake /wrong road	n/v	行錯路	hàahng cho louh	haang4 co3 lou6	haahng chho louh
lost way /to miss road	n	蕩失路	dohng sàt louh	dong6 sat4 lou6	tohng sat louh
lot[1]	n	籤	chīm	cim1	chhim
lot[2] /many much	n	很多	hān dò	han1 do4	han to
lot of /many/much/more	adv	多	dò	do4	toh
lot of liquid	adj	多水汁	dò séui jāp	do4 seoi2 zap1	to swoi chap
lot of water & juice	adj	多水多汁	dò séui dò jāp	do4 seoi2 do4 zap1	to swoi to chap
lots of	n	大疊	daaih daahp	daai6 daap6	taaih taahp
lotter	n	蹣跚	pùhn sāan	pun4 saan1	phuhn saan
lottery[1]	n	彩票	chói piu	coi2 piu3	chhoi phiu
lottery[2]	n	獎券	jéung gyun	zoeng2 gyun3	cheung kyun
lotus[1]	n	荷	hòh	ho6	hoh
lotus[2]	n	荷花	hòh fā	ho6 faa1	hoh fa
lotus[3]	n	蓮花	lìhn fā	lin4 faa1	lihn fa

English	POS	Chinese	Reading 1	Reading 2	Reading 3
loud sound[1] /peal	n	鳴響	mìhng héung	ming4 hoeng2	mehng heung
loud sound[2] /peal	n	響亮	héung leuhng	hoeng2 loeng6	heung leuhng
loudly	adv	高聲	gòu sèng	gou4 seng4	kou seng
loudspeaker[1]	n	擴音機	kong yām gèi	kong3 jam1 gei4	khong yam kei
loudspeaker[2] /speaker	n	揚聲器	yèuhng sèng hei	joeng4 seng4 hai3	yeuhng seng hei
lounge[1]	v	閒蕩	hàahn dohng	haan4 dong6	haahn tohng
lounge[2]	v	候機室	hauh gēi sāt	hau6 gei1 sat1	hauh kei sat
louse	n	蝨	sāt	sat1	sat
lovable /lovely	adj	可愛	hó oi /ngoi	ho2 oi3 /ngoi3	ho oi /ngoi
love[1]	n	愛	ói /ngói	oi2 /ngoi3	oi /ngoi
love[2]	n	愛心	ói /ngoi sàm	oi3 /ngoi3 sam4	oi /ngoi sam
love[3] (male+female)	n	愛情	ói /ngói chìhng	oi3 /ngoi3 cing4	oi /ngoi chhehng
love child	n	愛兒	oi /ngoi yìh	oi3 /ngoi ji4	oi /ngoi yih
love-letter[1]	n	情信	chihng seun	cing4 seon3	chhehng seun
love-letter[2]	n	情書	chìhng syù	cing4 syu4	chhehng syu
love male+female /in love/romantic love		戀愛	lyún ói, nyún ngoi	lyun2 oi2, nyun2 ngoi3	lyuhn oi, nyun ngoi
love marriage	n	造愛結婚	jouh ói /ngoi git fàn	zou6 oi3 /ngoi3 git3 fan4	chouh oi /ngoi kit fan
love sick /sick with love	adj	害相思病	hoih seung si behng	hoi6 soeng3 si3 beng6	hoih seung si pehng
love-story[1]	n	愛情故事	ói /ngói chìhng gu sih	oi2 /ngoi3 cing4 gu3 si6	oi /ngoi chhehng gu sih
love-story[2]	n	戀愛故事	lyún ói gu sih, nyún ngoi gu sih	lyun2 oi2 gu3 si6, nyun2 ngoi3 gu3 si6	lyuhn oi ku sih, nyun ngoi ku sih
loveless	adj	無愛情	móuh ói /ngoi chìhng	mou5 oi3 /ngoi3 cing4	mouh oi /ngoi chhehng
lover[1]	n	戀人	cháam yàhn	caam2 jan4	chhaam yahn
lover[2] /spouse	n	愛人	oi /ngoi yàhn	oi3 /ngoi3 jan4	oi /ngoi yahn
lover[3] /lust	n	姦夫滛婦	gāan fùh yán fúh	gaan1 fu4 jan2 fu5	kaan fuh yan fuh
lover[4] passion man	n	姦夫	gāan fùh	gaan1 fu4	kaan fuh
lover[5] passion woman	n	滛婦	yán fúh	jan2 fu5	yan fuh
lover[6] passion woman	n	情婦	chìhng fúh	cing4 fu5	chhehng fuh
loves country /patriotic	adj	愛國	oi /ngoi gwok	oi3 /ngoi3 gwok3	oi /ngoi kwok
loving[1]	adj	鍾愛	jùng oi /ngoi	zung4 oi3 /ngoi3	chung oi /ngoi
loving[2]	adj	愛嘅	oi /ngoi ge	oi3 /ngoi3 ge3	oi /ngoi ke
low[1]	adv	低的	dài dīk	dai4 dik1	tai tik
low[2] /short	adv	矮的	áai /ái /ngái dìk	aai2 /ai2 /ngai2 dik4	aai /ai /ngai tek
low density	adj	低密度	dài maht douh	dai4 mat6 dou6	tai maht touh
low lying area	adj	低窪土地	dài wà tóu deih	dai4 waa4 tou2 dei6	tai wa thou teih
low risk	adj	低風險	dài fùng hím	dai4 fung4 him2	taii fung him
low season /off season	n	淡季	táahm gwai	taam6 gwai3	thaahm kwai
low voice /soft voice /small voice/sweet voice	adj/n	細聲	sai sēng	sai3 seng1	sai seng
lower[1]	v	降低	gong dài	gong3 dai4	kong tai
lower[2]	v	下級	hah kāp	haa6 kap1	hah khap
lower[3]	adj	較低嘅	gaau dài ge	gaau3 dai4 ge3	kaau tai ke
lower level	adj	低級	dài kāp	dai4 kap1	tai khap

lowest /minimum	n	最小	jeui síu	zeoi3 siu2	cheui siu
lowly	adj	謙卑嘅	hìm bēi ge	him4 bei1 ge3	him pei ge
loyal[1] /good faith /devotion	adj	忠心	jùng sàm	zung4 sam4	chung sam
loyal[2] /loving/true	adj	忠誠	jùng sìhng	zung4 sing4	chung sehng
loyalist	n	忠誠嘅人	jùng sìhng ge yàhn	zung4 sing4 ge3 jan4	chung sehng ke yahn
loyalty[1] (for husband) /real loved/true loved/ chaste/moral integrit	n	貞節	jìng jit	zing4 zit3	cheng chit
loyalty[2]	n	忠誠	jùng sìhng	zung4 sing4	chung sehng
luckily[3]	adj	有好運	yáuh hóu wahn	jau5 hou2 wan6	yauh hou wahn
lucky money[1] red-envelope in Chinese festival	n	利是	leih sih	lei6 si6	leih sih
lucky money[2] red-envelope in Chinese festival	n	幸運嘅錢	hahng wahn ge chín	hang6 wan6 ge3 cin2	hahng wahn ke chhin
luggage rack	n	行李架	hàhng léih gá	hang4 lei5 ga2	hahng leih ka
lump /piece/chunk	n	塊	faai	faai3	faai
lump sum	n	一次付款額	yāt chi fuh fún ngaahk	jat1 ci3 fu3 fun2 ngaak6	yat chhi fuh fun ngaahk
lump together	adv	一併	yāt ping	sat1 ping3	yat pheng
lunar	adj	月的	yuht dīk	jyut6 dik1	yuht tik
Lunar calendar[1] Chinese	n	舊曆	gauh lihk	gau6 lik6	kauh lehk
Lunar calendar[2] Chinese	n	農曆	lùhng /nùhng lihk	lung4 /nung4 lik6	luhng /nuhng lehk
Lunar calendar[3] English Western calendar	n	西曆	sài lihk	sai4 lik6	sai lehk
Lunar calendar[4] Chinese	n	陰曆	yàm lihk	jam4 lik6	yam lehk
lunch[1]	n	午飯	ńgh faahn	ng5 faan6	ngh faahn
lunch[2] (12:00-14:000)	n	晏晝	aan /ngaan jau	aan3 /ngaan3 zau3	aan /ngaan chau
lunch[3] (12:00-14:000)	n	晏晝飯	aan /ngaan jau faahn	aan3 /ngaan3 zau3 faan6	aan /ngaan chau faahn
lunch[4] (12:00-14:000)	n	中午飯	jūng ńgh faahn	zung1 ng5 faan6	chung ngh faahn
lunch box	n	飯盒	faahn háap	faan6 haap2	faahn haap
lunch break time	n	放晏晝	fong aan jau	fong3 aan3 zau3	fong aan chau
luncheon meat	n	午餐肉	ńgh chāan yuhk	ng5 caan1 juk6	ngh chhaan yuhk
lung	n	肺	fai	fai3	fai
attraction power /lure	n	誘惑力	yáuh waahk lihk	jau5 waak6 lik6	yauh waahk lehk
lure of sex	v	勸誘	hyun yáuh	hyun4 jau5	hyun yauh
lust[1] /wishful/yen	n	渴望	hot mohng	hot3 mong6	hot mohng
lust[2] /sexual desire	n	色欲	sīk yuhk	sik1 juk6	sek yuhk
lustre	n	光澤	gwòng jaahk	gwong4 zaak6	kwong chaahk
luxuriant	adj	茂盛	mauh sihng	mau6 sing6	mauh sehng
luxury	n	奢華	chè wàh	ce4 waa6	chhe wah
lying prone	v	趴	pā	paa1	pha
lymph colourless liquid containing white blood cells	n	淋巴	laam ba	laam3 ba3	laam pa
lynch	v	以私刑處死	yíh sì yìhng chyú séi	ji5 si4 jing4 cyu2 sei2	yih si yehng chhyu sei
lyricist[1]	n	抒情詩人	syù ching sì yàhn	syu4 cing4 si4 jan4	syu chheng si yahn

lyricist[2]	n	抒情歌手	syù ching gò sāu	syu4 cing4 go4 sau1	syu chheng koh sau
lysis[1] /patient improving	n	好番少少	hóu fàan síu síu	hou2 faan4 siu2 siu2	hou faan siu siu
lysis[2] /patient improving	n	病勢減退	behng /bihng sai gáam tèui	beng6 /bing6 sai3 gaam2 teoi4	pehng sai kaam thwoi

M.A.[1] /M.S.	abbr	碩士	sehk sih	sek6 si6	sehk sih
M.A.[2]	abbr	文學碩士	màhn hohk sehk sih	man4 hok6 sek6 si6	mahn hohk sehk sih
M.C.[1] master of ceremony	abbr	司儀	sì yìh	si4 ji4	si yih
M.C.[2]	abbr	典禮官	dín láih gún	din2 lai5 gun2	tin laih kun
M.S.	abbr	理科碩士	léih fō sehk sih	lei5 fo1 sek6 si6	leih fo sehk sih
Macao	n	澳門	óu mún	ou2 mun4	ou mun
macaroni	n	通心粉	tùng sàm fán	tung4 sam4 fan2	thung sam fan
machine[1]	n	機	gèi	gei4	kei
machine[2] /machinery	n	機器	gèi hei	gei4 hei3	kei hei
machine gun	n	機關槍	gèi gwàan chēung	gei4 gwaan4 coeng1	kei kwaan chheung
machinist	n	機械師	gèi haaih sī	gei4 haai6 si1	kei haaih sih
mad /wild	adj	猖	chēung	coeng1	chheung
madam	n	夫人	fùh yàhn	fu4 jan4	fuh yahn
made /make/manufacture	vt	製	jai	zai3	chai
made by man /artificial/man made	adj	人造	yàhn jouh	jan4 zou6	yahn chouh
madhouse /mental hospital	n	精神病院	jèng sàhn behng yuhn	zeng4 san4 beng6 jyun6	cheng sahn behng yuhn
mad-man[1]	n	瘋人	fùng yàhn	fung3 jan4	fung yahn
mad-man[2] /insane /madly/ as crazy	adj	發瘋	faat fùng	faat3 fung4	faat fung
magazine[1]	n	誌	ji	zi3	chi
magazine[2]	n	雜誌	jaahp ji	zaap6 zi3	chaahp chi
magazine[3]	n	彈盤	tàahn pùhn	taan4 pun4	thaahn phuhn
magazinist /journalist	n	新聞工作者	sàn màhn gùng jokjé	san4 man4 gung4 zok3 ze2	san mahn kung chok che
magi	n	東方三士	dùng fòng sàam sih	dung4 fong4 saam4 si6	tung fong saam sih
magic eye	n	電眼	dihn ngáahn	din6 ngaan5	tihn ngaahn
magical	adj	魔術嘅	mò seuht ge	mo4 seot6 ge	mo swoht ke
magician[1] /sorcerer /wizard	n	男巫	làahm mòuh	laam4 mou4	laahm mouh
magician[2]	n	魔術師	mò seuht sih	mo4 seot6 si4	mo swoht sih
magistrate	n	行政官	hàhng jing gùn	hang4 zing3 gun4	hahng cheng kun
magma /lava	n	岩漿	ngàahm jèung	ngaam4 zoeng4	ngaahm cheung
magnesia	n	鎂	méih	mei5	meih
magnet[1]	n	磁	chìh	ci4	chhih
magnet[2]	n	磁鐵	chìh tit	ci4 tit3	chhih thit
magnificent[1] /majestic	adj	壯麗	jong laih	zong3 lai6	chong laih
magnificent[2] /imposing	adj	宏偉	wàhng wái	wang4 wai5	wahng wai
magnificent[3]	adj	華麗嘅	wàh laih ge	waa4 lai6 ge3	wah laih ke
maid	n	女子	léuih jí	leui5 zi2	lowih chi
maid servant[1] /nurse	n	護士	wuh sih	wu6 si6	wuh sih
maid servant[2] /femal servant	n	女工人	léuih gùng yàhn	leui5 gung4 jan4	lowih kung yahn
mail[1] send	n	寄	gei	gei3	kei
mail[2]	n	郵遞	yàuh daih	jau4 dai6	yauh taih

English		Chinese	Yale	Jyutping	Romanization
mailbox sending /letter box	n	郵筒	yàuh túng	jau4 tung2	yauh thung
main dish		主菜	jyú choi	zyu2 coi3	chyu chhoi
main key /paramount	adj	最重要	jeui juhng yìu	zeoi3 zung6 jiu4	cheui chuhng yiu
main part[1] /substance /summary/ most	n	輯錄	chāp luhk	cap1 luk6	chhap luhk
main point[2] /outline	n	大綱	daaih gòng	daai6 gong4	taaih kong
mainland China	n	中國大陸	jùng gwok daaih luhk	zung4 gwok3 daai6 luk6	chung kwok taaih luhk
maintain[1] /uphold/upheld	v	維護	wàih wuh	wai4 wu6	waih wuh
maintain[2] /to maintain /to hold/to preserve/to keep /sustain	v	維持	waìh chìh	wai4 ci4	waih chhih
maintenance[1] /make a living/livelihood/subsistence to earning	n	揾食	wán sihk	wan2 sik6	wan sehk
maintenance[2] /repair/ maintain/protect & maintain	n	維修	wàih sàu	wai4 sau4	waih sau
maintenance[3] /support /to help living/to keep living	n	維持	waìh chìh	wai4 ci4	waih chhih
maize's cover	n	粟米包	sūk máih bao	suk1 mai5 bao3	suk maih pao
majesty	n	陛下	baih hah	bai6 hah	paih hah
major[1] /main	adj	專業	jyùn yihp	zyun4 jip6	chyun yihp
major[2] /principal/main /main part/staple	adj	主要	jyú yiu	zyu2 jiu3	chyu yiu
major[3] /large	adj	較大	gaau daaih	gaau3 daai6	kaau taaih
major[4] (of army)	n	陸軍少校	luhk gwān siu gaau	luk6 gwan1 siu3 gaau3	luhk kwan siu kaau
major road	n	主幹道	jyú gon douh	zyu2 gon3 dou6	chyu kon touh
major subject	n	主修	jyú sàu	zyu2 sau4	chyu sau
majority[1]	n	大數	daaih sou	daai6 sou3	taaih sou
majority[2]	n	大多數	daaih dò sou	daai6 do4 sou3	taaih toh sou
majority[3]	n	大多数人	daaih dò sou yàhn	daai6 do4 sou3 jan4	taaih toh sou yahn
majority[4]	n	多數派	dò sou paai	do4 sou3 paai3	to sou phaai
make[1] /build	v	造	jouh	zou6	chouh
make[2]	v	使	sái	sai2	sai
make[3] install	v	組裝	jóu jòng	zou2 zong4	chou chong
make a bed	v	鋪床	pòu chòhng	pou4 cong4	phou chhohng
make a face	v	做鬼臉	jouh gwái líhm	zou6 geai2 lim5	chouh kwai lihm
make a fortune	v	發跡	faat jīk	faat3 zik1	faat chek
make a joke	v	開玩笑	hòi wáan sìu	hoi4 waan2 siu4	hoi waan siu
make a knot /make a knob	v	打纈	dá kit	daa2 kit3	ta khit
make a noise	n	響	héung	hoeng2	heung
make a speech /lecture/statement	n	演講	yín góng	jin2 gong2	yin kong
make appointment /time settlement/arranged time		約	yeuk	joek3	yeuk
make arrange		事宜	sih yìh	si6 ji4	sih yih
make better	v	改善	gói sihn	goi2 sin6	koi sihn

English		Chinese	Yale	Jyutping	
make big /make large /make wide/make wider	v	使變大	sái bin daaih	sai2 bin3 daai6	sai pin taaih
make change /return ransom/ransom money/ return remaining balance	n	找贖	jáau juhk	zaau2 zuk6	chaau chuhk
make clear /manifest	v	表明	bíu mìhng	biu2 ming4	piu mihng
make coffee	v	冲咖啡	chùng ga fēi	cung4 gaa3 fei1	chhung ka fei
make contact with		與...聯繫	yùh lyùhn haih	jyu4 lyun4 hai6	yuh lyuhn haih
make decision	v	下決心	hah kyut sàm	haa6 kyut3 sam4	hah khyut sam
make easy /make convenient	v	使便利	sái bin leih	sai2 bin3 lei6	sai pin leih
make empty	v	搬空	bùn hùng	bun4 hung4	pun hong
make friends	v	交朋友	gàau pàhng yáuh	gaau4 pang4 jau5	kaau phahng yauh
make fun	v	拿…開心	làh /nàh...hòi sām	laa1 /naa1...hoi4 sam1	lah /nah ... hoi sam
make into	v	做成	jouh sèhng /sìhng	zou6 seng4 /sing4	chouh sehng
make money		搵錢	wan chín	wan3 cin2	wan chhin
make pack		包好	bàau hóu	baau1 hou2	paau hou
make peace /solution	n	排解	pàaih gáai	paai4 gaai2	phaaih kaai
make progress	v	進	jeun	zeon3	cheun
make shift	v	權宜之計	kyùhn yìh jì gai	kyun4 ji4 zi4 gai3	khyuhn yih chi kai
make sound	v	作響	jok héung	zok3 heung2	chok heung
make tea[1]	n	冲茶	chùng chàh	cung4 caa4	chhung chah
make tea[2]	n	泡茶	póuh chàh	pou5 caa4	phouh chhah
make turn		轉彎	jyun wāan	zyun3 waan1	chyun waan
make-up face[1]	n	靚	leng	leng3	leng
make-up face[2] /be dressed up/cosmetic /ornamented	n	化妝	fa jōng	faa3 zong1	fa chong
make-up (for study)	n	補習	bóu jaahp	bou2 zaap6	pou chaahp
make-use /use/usage	n	使用	sái yuhng	sai2 jung6	sai yuhng
make way		讓路	yeuhng louh	joeng6 lou6	yeuhng louh
maker[1] by man	n	製造人	jai jouh yàhn	zai3 zou6 jan4	chai chouh yahn
maker[2] by man	n	出票人	chēut piu yàhn	ceot1 piu3 jan4	chhot piu yahn
maker[3] by man	n	製造者	jai jouh jé	zai3 zou6 ze2	chai chouh che
maker[4] by man	n	製造員	jai jouh yùhn	zai3 zou6 jyun4	chai chouh yuhn
making /make	n/v	製作	jai jok	zai3 zok3	chai chok
maladministration	n	行政失當	hàhng jing sāt dòhng	hang4 zing3 sat1 dong4	hahng cheng sat tohng
malaria[1]	n	瘧疾	yeuhk jaht	joek6 zat6	yeuhk chaht
malaria[2]	n	瘴氣	jeung hei	zoeng3 hei3	cheung hei
Malaysia	n	馬來西亞	máh lai sài á	maa5 lai3 sai4 aa3	mah lai sai a
male[1] (man)	n	男	làahm /nàahm	laam4 /naam4	laahm /naahm
male[2] (animals)	n	公	gūng	gung1	kung
male[3] (men/adult/human)	n	丁	dīng	ding1	teng
male[4] (human/animal/bird)	n	雄	hùhng	hung4	huhng
male child /boy	n	男童	làahm tùhng	laam4 tung4	laahm thuhng

male sex	n	男性	làahm sing	laam4 sing3	laahm seng
mallet[1]	n	木槌	muhk chèuih	muk6 ceoi4	muhk chhoih
mallet[2]	n	木錘	muhk chèuih	muk6 ceoi4	muhk chhoih
malnutrition /deficiency disease/ undernourished	n	營養不良	yìhng yéuhng bāt lèuhng	jing4 joeng5 bat1 loeng4	yehng yeuhng pat leuhng
malodorous[1] /stink/bad smell	adj	臭	chau	cau3	chhau
malodorous[2]	adj	有惡臭	yáuh ok/ngok chau	jau5 ok3 /ngok3 cau3	yauh ok /ngok chhau
mammal	n	哺乳動物	bouh yúh duhng maht	bou6 jyu5 dung6 mat6	pouh yuh tohng maht
mammilla /nipple	n	乳頭	yúh tàuh	jyu5 tau4	yuh thauh
mammy [(de)]	n	嗎咪	mā mìh	maa1 mi4	ma mih
man[1] /fellow	n	男人	làahm yan	laam4 jan3	laahm yan
man[2]	n	男子	làahm jí	laam4 zi2	laahm chi
man & boy	n	從小到大	chùhng síu dou daaih	cung4 siu2 dou3 daai6	chhuhng siu tou taaih
man die [(sl)]		上咗去	séuhng jó heui	soeng6 zo2 heoi3	seuhng cho hoi
man go up & down		人上落	yàhn séuhng lohk	yan4 seung5 lok6	yahn seuhng lohk
man servant	n	工人男	gùng yàhn làahm /nàahm	gung4 jan4 laam4 /naam4	kung yahn naahm
man toilet	n	男廁	làahm chi	laam4 chi3	laahm chhi
manage[1]	v	辦	baahn	baan6	paahn
manage[2]	v	營	yìhng	jing4	yehng
manage[3]	v	管理	gún léih	gun2 lei5	kun leih
manageable[1]	adj	攪得掂	gàau dāk dihm	gaau4 dak1 dim6	kaau tak tihm
manageable[2]	adj	可以管理	hó yíh gún léih	ho2 ji5 gun2 lei5	ho yih kun leih
managing	adj	管理	gún léih	gun2 lei5	kun leih
mandarin[1]	n	官吏	gùn leih	gun4 lei6	kun leih
Mandarin[2]	n	中國嘅官言	jùng gwok ge gùn yìhn	zung4 gwok3 ge3 gun4 jin4	chung kwok ke kun yihn
Mandarin[3] Chinese national language	n	普通話 (中國)	póu tùng wá (jùng gwók)	pou2 tung4 waa2 (zung4 gwok3)	phou thung wa (chung kwok)
Mandarin[4] Chinese national language	n	北京話 (中國)	bāk gìng wá (jùng gwók)	baak1 ging4 waa2 (zung4 gwok3)	pak king wa (chung kwok)
Mandarin Chinese national language	n	國語中國	gwok yúh jùng gwók	gwok3 jyu5 zung4 gwok3	kwok yuh chung kwok
mandarin ducks	n	鴛鴦	yūn yēung	jyun1 joeng1	yun yeung
mandarin orange /tangerine	n	柑	gàm	gam4	kam
mandate /order /prescript/command	n/v	命令	mehng /mihng lihng	meng6 /ming6 ling4	mehng lehng
mandatory	adj	強制	kéuhng jai	koeng5 zai3	kheuhng chai
mane[1] (man's hair)	n	有長髮	yauh chèuhng faat	jau6 coeng4 faat3	yauh chheuhng faat
mane[2] (horse's hair)	n	鬃毛	jùng mòuh	zung4 mou6	chung mouh
mane[3] (horse's hair)	n	馬毛	máh mòuh	maa5 mou6	mah mouh
mane[4] /lion's hair	n	獅鬣	sì lihp	si4 lip6	si lihp

maneuver[1] /cautious	n	謹慎	gán sahn	gan2 san6	kan sahn
maneuver[2] /manoeuvre	n	熟巧操縱	sùhk hāau chóu júng	suk6 haau1 cou2 zung2	suhk haau chhou chung
manganese	n	錳	máahng	maang5	maahng
mango(de)	n	杧果	mòhng gwó	mong4 gwo2	mohng kwo
mango pudding	n	芒果布丁	mòhng gú bou dīng	mong4 gu2 bou3 ding1	mohng ku pou teng
manifold[1] /multi/variety /multifrom/veried	adj	多方面	dò fòng mihn	do4 fong4 min6	to fong mihn
manifold[2]	adj	多種用途	dò júng yuhng tòuh	do4 zung2 jung6 tou4	to chung yuhng thouh
manipulate	v	暗中控制	am /ngam jùng hung jai	am3 /ngam3 zung4 hung3 zai3	am /ngam chung hung chai
manner[1] /way/method	n	法	faat	fat3	faat
manner[2] (of speaking)	n	可以說	hó yíh syut	ho2 ji5 syut	ho yih syut
manner of life /way	n	方式	fòng sīk	fong4 sik1	fong sek
manners[1]/courtesy /good manners	n	禮貌	láih maauh	lai5 maau6	laih maauh
manners[2] (all kinds)	n	形形色色	yìhng yìhng sīk sīk	jing4 jin4 sik1 sik1	yehng yehng sek sek
manoeuvre /skill/ tactics/ tricks/technique	n	手法	sáu faat	sau2 faat3	sau faat
manpower	n	人力	yàhn lihk	jan4 lik6	yahn lehk
manslaughter /murderer	n	過失殺人	gwo sāt saat yàhn	gwo3 sat1 saat3 jan4	kwo sat saat yahn
mantis	n	螳螂	tòhng lòhng	tong4 long4	thohng lohng
manual (using by hand)	adj	手工	sáu gùng	sau2 gung4	sau kung
manual book /hand book	n	手冊	sáu chaak	sau2 caak3	sau chhaak
manufacture[1]	n	加工	gà gùng	gaa4 gung4	ka kung
manufacture[2] /made in/ make	v	製造	jai jouh	zai3 zou6	chai chouh
manufacturer	n	製造業者	jai jouh yihp jé	zai3 zou6 jip6 ze2	chai chouh yihp che
manufacturing co	n	製造商	jai jouh sèung	zai3 zou6 soeng4	chai chouh seung
manuscript[1]	n	手抄本	sáu chàau bún	sau2 caau4 bun2	sau chhaau pun
manuscript[2] /original copy	n	原稿	yùhn góu	jyun4 gou2	yuhn kou
many[1] /so/very	pron	好	hóu	hou2	hou
many[2] /pile of	pron	沓	daahp	daap6	taahp
many[3]	pron	咁多	gam dò	gam3 do4	kam toh
many[4]	pron	大多	daaih dò	daai6 do4	taaih toh
many[5]/more/voluminous	pron	多的	dò dì	do4 di4	toh ti
many[6]	pron	多個	dò go	do4 go3	toh ko
many[7] /much/numerous	pron	許多嘅	héui dò ge	heoi2 do4 ge3	hoi toh ke
many days		日久	yaht gáu	jat6 gau2	yaht kau
many people /more people/men	n	多的人	dò dì yàhn	dò dì yàhn	toh ti yahn
many times[1]		好多次	hóu dò chi	hou2 do4 ci3	hou toh chhi
many times[2]	adj	數次	sou chi	sou3 ci3	sou chi
marble	n	大理石	daaih léih sehk	daai6 lei5 sek6	taaih leih sehk

English		Chinese	Yale	Jyutping	Yale-style
March[1] (month)	n	三月	sàam yùht	saam4 jyut6	saam yuht
March[2] (parade)	v	遊行	yàuh hàhng	jau4 hang4	yauh hahng
March[3] (of army)	v	行軍	hàahng gwàn	haang4 gwan4	haahng kwan
March 19th	n	三月十九日	sàam yùht sàhp gáu yàht /jàht	saam4 jyut6 sap6 gau2 jat6	saam yuht sahp kau yaht
marcher	n	遊行示威者	yàuh hàhng sìh wāi jé	jau4 hang4 si6 wai1 ze2	yauh hahng sih wai che
margarine /artificial butter	n	人造黃油	yàhn jouh wòhng yàuh	jan4 zou6 wong4 jau4	yahn chouh wohng yauh
margin	n	白邊	baahk bīn	baak6 bin1	paahk pin
marginal	adj	頁邊嘅	yihp bīn ge	jip6 bin1 ge3	yihp pin ke
marginal notes	n	旁註	pòhng jyu	pong4 zyu3	phohng chyu
marine[1]	n	航海	hòhng hói	hong4 hoi2	hohng hoi
marine[2]	adj	海產嘅	hói cháan ge	hoi2 caan2 ge3	hoi chhaan ke
marital	adj	婚姻	fàn yàn	fan4 jan4	fan yan
marital status	n	婚姻狀況	fàn yàn johng fong	fan4 jan4 zong6 fong3	fan yan chohng fong
mark[1] /sign	n	記	gei	gei3	kei
mark[2] /stain/taint	n	污點	wù dím	wu4 dim2	wu tim
marking/grading /classification	v	打分	dá fān	daa2 fan1	ta fan
marker	n	界標	béi bīu	bei2 biu1	pei piu
marker pen	n	記號筆	gei houh bāt	gei3 hou6 bat1	kei houh pat
market /city /streetmarket (open area)	n	街市	gāai síh	gaai1 si5	kaai sih
market price	n	市場價	síh chèuhng ga	si5 coeng4 gaa3	sih chheuhng ka
marketable	adj	可銷售嘅	hó sīu sauh ge	ho2 siu1 sau6 ge3	ho siu sauh ke
marking /signs/signals /symbol	n	標誌	bīu jí	biu1 zi2	piu chi
marriage /wedding	n	結婚	git fàn	git3 fan4	kit fan
marriage procession	n/v	結婚遊行	git fàn yàuh hàhng	git3 fan4 jau4 hang4	kit fan yauh hahng
marriage propose /woo/proposal		求婚	kàuh fàn	kau4 fan4	khauh fan
marriaged relation		通過姻親關係	tùng gwo yān chān gwàan haih	tung4 gwo3 jan1 can1 gwaan4 hai6	thung kwo yan chhan kwaan haih
married[1] /wedded	adj	已婚	yíh fàn	ji5 fan4	yih fan
married[2]	adj	結咗婚	git jó fàn	git3 zo2 fan4	kit cho fan
married man[1]	n	夫	fùh	fu4	fuh
married man[2] have sex with others women/paramour husband/paramour man		有夫之婦	yáuh fùh jī fúh	jau5 fu4 zi1 fu5	yauh fuh chi fuh
married woman[1]	n	婦	fúh	fu5	fuh
married woman[2] have sex with others mens /paramour woman		有婦之夫	yáuh fúh jī fùh	jau5 fu5 zi1 fu4	yauh fuh chi fuh
marrow	n	骨髓	gwāt séuih	gwat1 seoi5	kwat swoi
marry agreement	n	訂婚	dihng fān	ding6 fan1	tihn fan
mars /spark	n	火星	fó sēng /sīng	fo2 seng1 /sing1	fo seng

English		Chinese	Yale	Jyutping	
marsh /wetlands/swamp /glade	n	沼澤	jíu jaahk	ziu2 zaak6	chiu chaahk
marshal	n	元帥	yùhn seui	jyun4 seoi3	yuhn swoi
martyr /sufferer	n	烈士	liht sih	lit6 si6	liht sih
martyry	n	受難者	sauh naahn jé	sau6 naan4	sauh naahn che
marvellously	adv	驚奇地	gèng kèih deih	geng4 kei4 dei6	keng kheih teih
mascara	n	眼睫毛膏	ngáahn jìht mou góu	ngaan5 zit6 mou3 gou2	ngaahn chiht mou kou
mask	n	面具	mihn geuih	min6 geoi6	mihn kwoih
mask surgical	n	口罩	háu jaau	hau2 zaau3	hau chaau
masker[1] /masked man /covered face	n	蒙面人	mùhng mihn yàhn	mung4 min6 jan4	muhng mihn yahn
masker[3] /masked man	n	戴面具嘅人	daai mihn geuih ge yàhn	daai3 min6 geoi6 ge3 jan4	taai mihn keuih ke yahn
mass /masses/crowd	n	大眾	daaih jung	daai6 zung3	taaih chung
massacre[1]	n	殘殺	chàahn saat	caan4 saat3	chhaahn saat
massacre[2] /carnage	v	大屠殺	daaih tòuh saat	daai6 tou4 saat3	taaih thouh saat
massacre[3]	v	屠殺	tòuh saat	tou4 saat3	thouh saat
massage	n	按摩	on /ngòn mò	on3 /ngon4 mo4	ɵn /ngon mo
massage chair	n	按摩椅	on /ngòn mò yí	on3 /ngon4 mo4 ji2	on /ngon mo yi
mast /antenna pole	n	天線杆	tìn sin gōn	tin4 sin3 gon1	thin sin kon
master[1] /teacher	n	師	sì	si4	si
master[2] /skilled worker	n	師傅/師父	sì fú	si4 fu2	si fu
master[3] holy man/lord	n	大師	daaih sì	daai6 si4	taaih si
master key	n	百合匙	baak hahp sìh	baak3 hap6 si4	paak hahp sih
master room /suite	n	套房	tou fóng	tou3 fong2	thou fong
master's degree	n	碩士	sehk sih	sek6 si6	sehk sih
mastered /verse	v	精通	jèng tùng	zeng4 tung4	cheng thung
mastermind[1] /policymaker	n	決策者	kyut chaak jé	kyut3 caak3 ze2	khyut chhaak che
mastermind[2]	n	出謀劃策者	chēut màuh waahk chaak jé	ceot1 mau4 waak6 caak3 ze2	chhot mauh waahk chaak che
masturbate(sl) by boy	v	濕鳩	sāp gàu	sap1 gau4	sap kau
masturbation[1] by man	v	自瀆	jih jók	zi6 zok2	chih chok
masturbation[2](sl) by man	v	打飛機	dā fèi gèi	daa1 fei4 gei4	ta fei kei
masturbation[3]	v	手淫	sáu yàhm	sau2 jam4	sau yahm
masturbation[4] by female	v	自淫	jih yàhm	zi6 jam4	chih yahm
mat (woven mat)	n	蓆	jehk	zek6	chehk
match[1] /game/race/cope /contest/compete/competion	n/v	競賽	gihng choi	ging6 coi3	kehng chhoi
match[2] /game	n	敵手	dihk sáu	dik6 sau2	tehk sau
match[3] /game	n	拍得住	paak dāk jyuh	paak3 dak1 zyu6	phaak tak chyuh
match[4] /fit	adj	配	pui	pui3	phui
match[5] of clothes/well suited/becoming match	adj	相配	séung pui	soeng2 pui3	seung phui
match[6] /firing/fire	n	火柴	fó chàaih	fo2 caai4	fo chhaaih

English		Chinese	Romanization 1	Jyutping	Romanization 2
match box	n	火柴盒	fó chàaih háap	fo2 caai4 haap6	fo chhaaih haap
match stick	n	火柴桿	fó chàaih gòn	fo2 caai4 gon4	fo chhaaih kon
matchless[1]	adj	無比	mòuh béi	mou4 bei2	mouh pei
matchless[2] /unequalled	adj	無敵	mòuh dihk	mou4 dik6	mouh tihk
matchless[3] /unmatchable	adj	無可比擬	mòuh hó béi yìh	mou5 ho2 bei2 ji4	mouh ho pei yih
matchmaker	n	媒人	mùih yán	mui4 jan2	muih yan
mate[1] /partner/companion	n	侶	léuih	leoi5	lowih
mate[2] /copulate /sex of birds/animals	v	交配	gāau pui	gaau1 pui3	kaau phui
mate of sex[1]/spouse /consort/sexual partner	n	配偶	pui ngáuh	pui3 ngau5	phui ngauh
mate of sex[2] /sexual partner	n	性伴侶	sing buhn léuih	sing3 bun6 leoi5	seng puhn lowih
material[1]	n	物料	maht líu	mat6 liu2	maht liu
material[2] /substance /real things	adj/n	物質	maht jāt	mat6 zat1	maht chat
material[3] /quality	n	質地	jāt déi	zat1 dei2	chat tei
materialism	n	唯物主義	wàih maht jyú yih	wai4 mat6 zyu2 ji6	waih maht chyu yih
materialist	n	唯物論者	wàih maht lèuhn jé	wai4 mat6 leon4 ze2	waih maht leuhn che
maternal	adj	母親嘅	móuh chàn ge	mou5 can4 ge3	mouh chhan ke
maternity[1]	n	婦產	fúh cháan	fu5 caan2	fuh chhaan
maternity[2]/obstetrics	n	產科	cháan fò	caan2 fo4	chhaan fo
maternity home[1]	n	婦產醫院	fúh cháan yī yún	fu5 caan2 ji1 jyun2	fuh chhaan yi yun
maternity home[2]	n	婦科病房	fúh fò behng fóng	fu5 fo4 beng6 fong2	fuh fo pehng fong
mathematics[1]	n	數學	sou hohk	sou3 hok6	sou hohk
mathematics[2] symbols	n	符號	fùh houh	fu4 hou6	fùh houh
mating season /sex season	n	交配季節	gāau pui gwai jit	gaau1 piu3 gwai3 zit3	kaau phui kwai chit
matricide[1] /kill mother	n	弒母	si móuh	si3 mou5	si mouh
matricide[2]/mother killer	n	弒母者	si móuh jé	si3 mou5 ze2	si mouh che
matriculate[1] /SLC	v	准許入學	jáun héui yahp hohk	zeon2 heoi2 jap6 hok6	chaun hoi yahp hohk
matriculate[2]	v	錄取入大學	luhk chéui yahp daaih hohk	luk6 ceoi2 jap6 daai6 hok6	luhk chhoi yahp taaih hohk
matriculation	n	大學預科	daaih hohk yuh fō	daai6 hok6 jyu6 fo1	taaih hohk yuh fo
matron	n	结婚婦女	git fàn fúh léuih / néuih	git3 fan4 fu5 leoi5 / neoi5	kit fan fuuh lowih / nowih
matter[1] /thing/object	n	物	maht	mat6	maht
matter[2]	n	材	chòih	coi4	chhoih
matter[3] /item	n	事項	sih hohng	si6 hong6	sih hohng
matter[4] /topic	n	問題	mahn tàih	man6 tai4	mahn thaih
mattress (for beds)	n	床墊	chòhng jín	cong4 zim2	chhohng chin
mature[1]	v	成熟	sèhng suhk	seng4 suk6	sehng suhk
mature[2]	v	到期	dou kèih	dou3 kei4	tou kheih
mature[3]	v	成人	seng yàhn	seng4 jan4	seng yahn
mature[4]	adj	成熟嘅	sèhng suhk ge	seng4 suk6 ge3	sehng suhk ge
maturity	n	成熟	sèhng suhk	seng4 suk6	sehng suhk

maund (40 kg = 1 man /unit of 40 kg weight)	n	重量單位	chúhng leuhng dāan wái	cung5 loeng6 daan1 wai2	chhuhng lowhng taan wai
maximize	v	最大限度	jeui daaih haahn douh	zeoi3 daai6 haan6 dou6	cheui taaih haahn touh
maximum	n	最大	jeui daaih	zeoi3 daai6	cheui taaih
maximum big	adj	極大嘅	gihk daaih ge	gik6 daai6 ge3	kehk taaih ke
may[1] /will/should/future	v/axu	將會	jèung wúih	zoeng4 wui5	cheung wuih
May[2] month	n	五月	ńgh yùht /jyùht	ng5 jyut6	ngh yuht
May 6th	n	五月六日	ńgh yùht lùhk yàht	ng5 jyut6 luk6 jat1	ngh yuht luhk yaht
may be /to do so/okay!	adv	可以	hó yíh	ho2 ji5	ho yih
may be not		未必	meih bīt	mei6 bit1	meih pit
may be punish	adj	會罰	wúih faht	wui5 fat6	wuih faht
may be trouble?		唔得掂?	m̀ dāk dihm	m4 dak1 dim6	mh tak tihm
may call me?		俾電話我呀?	béi dihn wá ngóh aa ?	bei2 din6 waa2 ngo5 aa3?	pei tihn wa ngoh aa?
may decay		眞可惡	jān hó wu	jan1 hoh2 woo3	chan hoh wu
may enough?		够唔够	gau m̀ gau	gau3 m4 gau3	kau mh kau
may i know ?		我知嗎?	ngóh jì mā?	ngo5 zi4 maa1?	ngoh chi ma?
what's your family? /may i know surname?		貴姓呀?	gwai seng aa?	gwai3 seng3 aa3?	kwai seng aa?
may not[1] /unable	adj	唔可以	m̀ hó yíh	m4 ho2 ji5	mh ho yih
may not[2]		不可以	bāt hó yíh	bat1 ho2 ji5	pat ho yih
may okey? /can i...? may i...?		可唔可以?	hó m̀ hó yíh?	ho2 m4 ho2 ji5?	ho mh ho yih?
may punish if late		遲會罰	chìh wúih faht	ci4 wui5 fat6	chhih wuih faht
may suspicious		如有可疑	yùh yáuh hó yìh	jyu4 jau5 ho2 ji4	yuh yauh ho yih
may understand?		明唔明	mìhng m̀ mìhng aa?	ming4 m4 ming4 aa3?	mehng mh mehng aa?
mayor[1]	n	市長	síh jéung	si5 zoeng2	sih cheung
mayor[2]	n	市長夫人	síh jéung fù yàhn	si5 zoeng2 fu4 jan4	sih cheung fu yahn
me[1] / i/ my	n/pron	我	ngóh /óh	ngo5 /o5	ngoh /oh
me[2] /mine/my (it's me/ that's mine/it's my)	n/pron	我嘅	ngóh ge	ngo5 ge3	ngoh ke
meal[1]		餐	chāan	caan1	chhaan
meal[2]	n	膳食	sihn sihk	sin6 ik6	sihn sehk
mean[1] /meaning	vt	意思	yi sī, yi si	ji3 si1, ji3 si3	yi si
mean[2] /unkind	adj	不善良	bāt sihn lèuhng	bat1 sing loeng4	pat sihn leuhng
mean[3] /center/centre/mid /middle/average/medium/ middle way	n	中間	jùng gàan	zung4 gaan4	chung kaan
meaning[1]	n	意	yi	ji3	yi
meaning[2] /significance	n	意義	yi yih	ji3 ji6	yi yih
meaning have		意思係	yi sī haih	ji3 si1 hai6	yi si haih
meaningful[1]	adj	有意思	yáuh yi sī	jau5 ji3 si1	yauh yi si
meaningful[2]	adj	意味深長	yi meih sàm chèuhng	ji3 mei6 sam4 coeng4	yi meih sam chheuhng
meanwhile[1] /meantime	adv	一時	yāt sìh	jat1 si4	yat sih

meanwhile[2]/same time/atthe same time/together/whilst/simultaneously	adv	同時	tùhng sìh	tung4 si4	thuhng sih
measure[1] /count	v	數量	sōu lèuhng	sou1 loeng4	sou leuhng
measure[2]	v	衡量	hàhng lèuhng	hang4 loeng4	hahng leuhng
measure[3] (for small objects)	n	粒	lāp /nāp	lap1 /nap1	lap /nap
measure[4] /estimate /survey	n	測	chàak	caak4	chhaak
measure[5]	v	措施	chou sih	cou3 si6	chhou sih
measure word (for building)		座	joh	zo6	choh
measurement /estimate	n	度	dohk	dok6	tohk
measurement[1]	n	量度	lèuhng douh	loeng4 dou6	leuhng touh
measurement[2]	n	測量	chàak lèuhng	caak4 loeng4	chhaak leuhng
measurement criteria		評核準則	ping haht jéun jāk	ping3 hat6 jeon2 zak1	pheng haht cheun chak
meat[1]	n	肉	yuhk	juk6	yuhk
meat[2]	n	瘦	sau	sau3	sau
meat[3] (red)	n	紅肉	hùhng yuhk	hung4 juk6	huhng yuhk
meat[4] (minced ball)	n	丸	yún	jyun2	yun
meat ball	n	肉丸	yuhk yún	juk6 jyun2	yuhk yun
meat category	n	肉類	yuhk leuih	juk6 leoi6	yuhk leuih
meat grinder	n	絞肉機	gáau yuhk gèi	gaau2 juk6 gei4	kaau yuhk kei
meat steak	n	扒	pàh	paa4	phah
mechanic[1] /technician	n	技工	geih gùng	gei6 gung4	keih kung
mechanic[2]	n	機械工	gèi haaih gūng	gei4 haai6 gung1	kei haaih kung
mechanic[3]	n	力學	lihk hohk	lik6 hok6	lehk hohk
mechanical	adj	機械嘅	gèi haaih ge	gei4 haai6 ge3	kei haaih ke
mechanical engineer	n	機械工程師	gèi haaih gūng chìhng sī	gei4 haai6 gung1 cing4 si1	kei haaih kung chhehng sih
mechanism /organisation/institution	n	機關	gēi gwāan	gei1 gwaan1	kei kwaan
medal	n	獎章	jéung jèung	zoeng2 zoeng4	cheung cheung
media[1]	n	傳媒	chyùhn mui	cyun4 mui3	chhyuhn mui
media[2] /medium	n	媒介	mùih gaai	mui4 gaai3	muih kaai
media[3] /medium	n	媒體	mùih tái	mui4 tai2	muih thai
media incident		傳媒事件	chyùhn mui sìh gìhn	cyun4 mui3 si6 gin6	chhyuhn mui sih kihn
mediation	n	調解	tìuh gáai	tiu4 gaai2	thiuh kaai
mediator /intermediator	n	調停者	teuh tíhng jé	teu6 ting5 ze2	thiuh thehng che
medical[1] /treatment /medical treatment	adj	醫療	yī lìuh	ji1 liu4	yi liuh
medical[2]	adj	醫藥	yī yeuhk	ji1 joek6	yi yeuhk
medical college	n	醫學院	yī hòhk yún	ji1 hok6 jyun2	yi hohk yun
medical exam	n	健康檢查	gihn hòng gím chàh	gin6 hong4 gim2 caa4	kihn hong kim chhah
medical examiner	n	體檢醫師	tái gím yī sī	tai2 gim2 ji1 si1	thai kim yi si
medical fee[1]		醫藥費	yī yeuhk fai	ji1 joek6 fai3	yi yeuhk fai
medical fee[2]		醫療酬金	yī liuh chàuh gām	ji1 liu6 cau4 gam1	yi liuh chhauh kam

medical history		病歷	behng /bihng lihk	beng6 /bing6 lik6	pehng lehk
medical insurance[1]		醫藥保險	yī yeuhk bóu hím	ji1 joek6 bou2 him2	yi yeuhk pou him
medical insurance[2]		醫療保險	yī lìuh bóu hím	ji1 liu4 bou2 him2	yi liuh pou him
medical officer	n	醫師	yī sī	ji1 si1	yi si
medical patient	n	內科病人	loih /noih fò bèhng yan	loi6 /noi6 fo4 beng6 jan4	loih /noih fo pehng yan
medical prescription	n	醫療處方	yī liuh chyú fōng	ji1 liu6 cyu2 fong1	yi liuh chhyu fong
medically	n	醫學上	yī hòhk séuhng	ji1 hok6 soeng5	yi hohk seuhng
medicine (take)		內服藥	loih /noih fuhk yeuhk	loi6 /noi6 fuk6 joek6	loih /noih fuhk yeuhk
medium	adj	中碼	jūng máh	zung1 maa5	chung mah
medium size	n	中等大小	jùng dáng daih síu	zung4 dang2 dai6 siu2	chung tang taih siu
meet[1]	v	碰見	púng gin	pung2 gin3	phung kin
meet[2] /sports meeting	v	遇到	yuh dóu	jyu6 dou2	yuh tou
meet[3]	v	會合	wuih hahp	wui6 hap6	wuih hahp
meet[4]	v	遇見	yuh gin	jyu6 gin3	yuh kin
meet relatives /see relatives	v	探親戚	taam chan chīk	taam3 can1 cik1	thaam chhan chhek
meet there		個度見	go douh gin	go3 dou6 gin3	ko touh kin
meeting	n	見客	gin haak	gin3 haak3	kin haak
meets standard /common/general	adj	常	sèuhng	soeng4	seuhng
megaphone	n	擴音器	kong yām hei	kong3 jam1 hei3	khong yam kei
melancholy /sorrow /woe/worry/suffering	n	愁	sau	sau3	sau
mellow	adj	甜美	tìhm méih	tim4 mei5	thihm meih
melodious	adj	旋律優美	syun leuht yāu méih	syun3 leot6 jat1 mei5	syun lwoht yau meih
melodist	n	作曲	jok kūk	zok3 kuk1	chok khuk
melody	n	旋律	syun leuht	syun3 leot6	syun lwoht
melon	n	瓜	gwà	gwaa4	kwa
melt[1] /gradually combine	v	續漸消失	juhk jím sìu sāt	zuk6 zim2 siu4 sat1	chuhk chim siu sat
melt[2] /combine	v	融化	yùhng fa	jung4 faa3	yuhng fa
melt[3] harmonious/to merge	v	融	yùhng	jung4	yuhng
member[1]	n	成員	seng yùhn	seng3 jyun4	seng yuhn
member[2] /membership	n	會員	wúi yùhn	wui2 jyun4	wui yuhn
member[3] (of the political)	n	黨員	dóng yùhn	dong2 jyun4	tong yuhn
member[4] (of council/ parliament) /councillor/ councilor	n	議員	yíh yùhn	ji5 jyun4	yih yuhn
member[5]	n	社員	séh yùhn	se5 jyun4	seh yuhn
member of a church[1]	n	教友	gaau yáuh	gaau3 jau5	kaau yauh
member of a church[2]	n	教徒	gaau tòuh	gaau3 tou4	kaau thouh
memberless	n	無會員	móuh wúi yùhn	mou5 wui2 jyun4	mouh wui yuhn
members of one's family		親人	chàn yàhn	can4 jan4	chhan yahn
membership	n	會員身份	wúi yùhn sàn fán	wui2 jyun4 saa4 fan2	wui yuhn san fan
memo[1] /memorandum	n	記錄	gei luhk	gei3 luk6	kei luhk

memo[2]/memorandum	n	備忘錄	beih mòhng lúk	bei6 mong4 luk2	peih mohng lowk
memorial	n	紀念	géi lihm /nihm	gei2 lim6 /nim6	kei lihm /nihm
memorial day /anniversary	n	紀念日	géi lihm /nihm yaht	gei2 lim6 /nim6 jat6	kei lihm /nihm yaht
memorize	v	記住品	gei jyuh bán	gei3 zyu6 ban2	kei chyuh pan
memory[1]	n	記性	gei sing	gei3 sing3	kei seng
memory[2]	n	記憶	gei yīk	gei3 jik1	kei yek
men	n	人嘅複數	yàhn ge fūk sou	jan4 ge3 fuk1 sou3	yahn ke fuk sou
menace /threat	n	威脅	wāi hip	wai1 hip3	wai hip
menage	n	家政	gà jing	gaa4 zing3	ka cheng
mend[1] /fixing/repair	v	修補	sau bóu	sau3 bou2	sau pou
mend[2] /to correct/rights	v	糾正	dáu jéng /jìng	dau2 zeng3 /zing3	tau cheng
menopause[1] female menstrual cycle ends	n	絕經期	jyuht ging kèih	zyut6 ging3 kei4	chyuht king kheih
menopause[2] female menstrual cycle ends	n	更年期	gāng lihn /nihn kèih	gang1 lin4 /nin4 kei4	kang lihn /nihn kheih
menses /menstruation	n	月經	yuht gìng	jyut6 ging4	yuht keng
menstrual	adj	經期	gìng kèih	ging4 kei4	keng kheih
mental	adj	心智	sàm ji	sam4 zi3	sam chi
mental disease	n	神經病	sàhn gìng behng	san4 ging4 beng6	sahn keng pehng
mental disorder	n	精神病	jèng sàhn behng	zeng4 san4 beng6	cheng sahn pehng
mental hospital /neuropathy hospital	n	神經病院	sàhn gìng behng yún	san4 ging4 beng6 jyun2	sahn keng behng yun
mentality disorder	n	癡呆	chī òih	ci1 oi4	chhi oih
mentally	adv	心理	sàm léih	sam4 lei5	sam leih
mention[1]	v	講及	góng kahp	gong2 kap6	kong khahp
mention[2] /isse	v	提	tàih	tai4	thaih
mention[3]	v	提及	tàih kahp	tai4 kap6	thaih khahp
mentioned[1]	v	講及咗	góng kahp jó	gong2 kap6 zo2	kong khahp cho
mentioned[2]	v	提及咗	tàih kahp jó	tai4 kap6 zo2	thaih khahp cho
mentioned[3]	v	說起咗	syut héi jó	syut3 hei2 zo2	syut hei cho
menu[1]	n	餐牌	chāan páai	caan1 paai2	chhaan phaai
menu[2] Chinese	n	菜牌	choi páai	coi3 paai2	chhoi phaai
menu[3]	n	菜單	choi dāan	coi3 daan1	chhoi taan
meow/miaow (cat's sound)	n	喵	mēo	meo1	meo
mercury /liquid/quicksilver	n	水銀	séui ngàhn	seoi2 ngan4	swoi ngahn
mercury star	n	水星	séui sèng /sìng	seoi2 seng4 /sing4	swoi seng
mercy /pity	n	憫	máhn	man5	mahn
merely	adv	只是	jí sih	zi2 si6	chi sih
merge	v	融合	yung hàhp	jung4 hap6	yung hahp
merino	n	毛紗	mòuh sā	mou4 sa1	mouh sa
merit /value/price/worth	n/adj	價值	ga jihk	gaa3 zik6	ka chehk
mermaid	n	美人魚	méih yàhn yú	mei5 jan4 jyu2	meih yahn yu
merry	adj	歡樂嘅	fùn lohk ge	fun4 lok6 ge3	fun lohk ke

Merry Christmas[1] /Happy christmas	adj	聖誕快樂	sing daan faai lohk	sing3 daan3 faai3 lok6	seng taan faai lohk
Merry Christmas[2]	adj	聖誕節	síng dáan jít /zít	sing3 daan2 zit2	seng taan chit
Merry Christmas & happy new year!	adj	聖誕節同 新年	síng dáan jít tùhng sàn lìhn /nìhn	sing3 daan2 zit2 tung4 san lihn /nihn	sing taan chit thuhng san lihn /nihn
merry-go-round[1] children's park (wood horse)	n	旋轉木馬	syun jyún muhk máh	syun3 zyun2 muk6 maa5	syun chyun muhk mah
merry-go-round[2]	n	一連串嘅 活動	yāt lìhn chyun ge wuht duhng	jat1 lin4 cyun3 ge3 wut6 dung6	yat lihn chhyun ke wuht tohng
mess[1] of meals/canteen	n	飯堂	faahn tòhng	faan6 tong4	faahn thohng
mess[2]	n	伙食	fó sihk	fo2 sik6	fo sehk
message[1] /saying /tongue/sentence	n	說話	syut wah	syut3 waa6	syut wah
message[2]	n	口信	háu seun	hau2 seon3	hau seun
message[3]	n	口訊	háu seun	hau2 seon3	hau seun
messenger	n	信差	seun chàai	seon4 caai4	swon chhaai
met /seen/watched /be looked/already saw	v	見咗	gin jó	gin3 zo2	kin cho
met you		見到你	gin dou léih /néih	gin3 dou3 lei5 /nei5	kin tou leih /neih
metal	n	金屬	gàm suhk	gam4 suk6	kam suhk
meter[1] (de)	n	米	máih	mai5	maih
meter[2]	v	公尺	gùng chek	gung4 cek3	kung chhek
meter[3]	n	儀錶	yi bìu	ji3 biu4	yi piu
meter[4] (of the taxi)	n	咪錶	māi bīu	mai1 biu1	mai piu
method[1] /path/road /street/way	n	道	douh	dou6	touh
method[2] /means /an action/way/mode/process/ manner/approaches	n	方法	fòng faat	fong4 faat3	fong faat
method[3]	n	辦法	baahn faat	baan6 faat3	paahn faat
method[4]	n	條理	tìuh léih	tiu4 lei5	thiuh leih
metropolis	n	都會	dōu wuih	dou1 wui6	tou wuih
Mexico	n	墨西哥	Mahk sāi gō	mak6 sai1 go1	Mahk sai ko
mica	n	雲母	wàhn móuh	wan4 mou5	wahn mouh
micro /small/tiny	adj	微	mèih	mei6	meih
microbe	n	微生物	mèih sāang maht	mei4 saang1 mat6	meih saang maht
microbiology	n	微生物學	mèih sāang maht hohk	mei4 saang4 mat6 hok6	meih saang maht hohk
microphone[1] (de)	n	咪	māi	mai1	mai
microphone[2] (de) mike	n	麥克風	mahk hāak fùng	mak6 haak1 fung4	mahk haak fung
microscope	n	顯微鏡	hín mèih geng	hin2 mei4 geng3	hin meih geng
microwave oven	n	微波爐	mèih bō lòuh	mei4 bo1 lou4	meih po louh
mid autumn festival	n	中秋節	jùng chāu jit	zung4 cau1 zit3	chung chhau chit
midday /noon	n	中午	jùng ńgh	zung4 ng5	chung ngh
middle level /intermediate	adj	中級	jùng kāp	zung4 kap1	chung khap
middle-man	n	中間人	jùng gàan yàhn	zung4 gaan4 jan4	chung kaan yahn

English		Chinese	Jyutping-style	Romanization	
middle-ranking	adj	中層	jùng chàhng	zung4 cang4	chung chhahng
middle-seat	n	中間位	jūng gāan wái	zung4 gaan1 wai2	chung kaan wai
midnight[1] (00:00) /nil	n	零晨	lìhng sàhn	ling4 san4	lehng sahn
midnight[2] (00:00)	n	午夜	ńgh yèh	ng5 je6	ngh yeh
midnight[3] (01:00)	n	子夜	jí yèh	zi2 je6	chi yeh
midnight[4] (03:00)	n	半夜	bun yèh	bun3 je6	pun yeh
midnight snack /evening snack	n	宵夜	sìu yé	siu4 je2	siu ye
midwife	n	助產士	joh cháan sih	zo6 caan2 si6	choh chhaan sih
might (p.t of may)	v	滿可以	múhn hó jíh	mun5 ho2 ji5	muhn ho chih
might as well		該...做	gōi jouh	goi1 zou6	koi chouh
mighty	adj	強大	kèuhng daaih	koeng4 daai6	kheuhng taaih
migrant[1] moves house /emigration/immigration	n	移居	yìh gèui	ji4 geoi4	yih kwoi
migrant[2] /moves place by men	n	移居嘅人	yìh gèui ge yàhn	ji4 geoi4 ge jan4	yih kwoi ke yahn
migrant (by birds)	n	候鳥	hauh níuh	hau6 niu5	hauh niuh
migrate /shifting/change residence/new settlement	v	徙	sáai	saai2	saai
migration[1]	n	遷徙	chìn sáai	cin4 saai2	chhin saai
migration[2] /migrate /migratory	adj	遷移	chìn yih	cin4 ji4	chhin yih
mildew	n	霉	mui	mui3	mui
mil (de)	n	咪	māi	mai1	mai
mile[1] /unit of distance	n	哩 / 里	léih	lei5	leih
mile[2]	n	英里	yìng léih	jing4 lei5	yeng leih
mileage 1.609 km	n	計數	gai sou	gai3 sou3	kai sou
militant	adj	好戰嘅	hou jin ge	hou3 zin3 ge3	hou chin ke
military	n	軍事	gwàn sih	gwan4 si6	kwan sih
military force /sword weapon	n	武力	móuh lihk	mou5 lik6	mouh lehk
military officer[1] /army officer	n	軍官	gwàn gùn	gwan4 gun4	kwan kun
military officer[2]	n	校	haauh	haau6	haauh
military vehicle (de) tank of war	n	坦克	táan hāak	taan2 haak1	thaan haak
military's student /cadet	n	軍校學生	gwàn haauh hohk sāang	gwan4 haau6 hok6 saang1	kwan haauh hohk saang
militia /volunteer army	n	義勇軍	yih yúhng gwān	ji6 jung5 gwan1	yih yuhng kwan
milk	n	乳汁	yúh jāp	jyu5 zap1	yuh chap
milk bottle	n	奶樽	láaih /náaih jēun	laai5 /naai5 zeon1	laaih /naaih cheun
milk selling		牛奶賣	ngàuh láaih/náaih maaih	ngau4 laai5 /naai5 maai6	ngauh laaih /naaih maaih
milk tea	n	奶茶	làaih /náaih chàh	laai5 /naai5 caa4	laaih /naaih chhah
milk tooth /baby tooth	n	乳牙	yúh ngàh	jyu5 ndaa4	yuh ngah
milkshake (de)	n	奶昔	làaih /náaih sīk	laai5 /naai5 sik1	laaih /naaih sek
mill	n	磨坊	mòh fòng	mo4 fong4	moh fong

millennium /100 years	n	千年期	chìn lihn /nihn kèih	cin4 lin4 /nin4 kei4	chhin lihn /nihn kheih
miller	n	磨坊主人	mòh fòng jyú yàhn	mo4 fong4 zyu2 jan4	moh fong chyu yahn
milli-gram	n	毫克	hòuh hàk	hou4 hak4	houh hak
milli-liter	n	毫升	hòuh sìng	hou4 sing4	houh seng
milli-meter	n	毫米	hòuh máih	hou4 mai5	houh maih
million	n	百萬	baak maahn	baak3 maan6	paak maahn
millionaire	n	百萬富翁	baak maahn fu yūng	baak3 maan6 fu3 jung1	paak maahn fu yung
minaret /steeple/spire /peak	n	尖塔	jīm taap	zim1 taap3	chim thaap
mince (of meat /to chop meat)	v	切碎	chít seui	cit2 seoi3	chhit swoi
minced¹ (de)	v	免治	míhn jih	min5 zi6	mihn chih
minced² /to cut/to chop	v	剁	deuk	doek3	tok
minced³ /to cut/to chop	v	剁碎	deuk seui	doek3 seoi3	tok swoi
minced beef	n	牛肉碎	ngàuh yuhk seui	ngau4 juk6 seoi3	ngauh yuhk swoi
minced meat¹	n	肉碎	yuhk seui	juk6 seoi3	yuhk swoi
minced meat²	v	剁肉	deuk yuhk	doek3 juk6	tok yuhk
minced pork	n	免治豬肉	míhn jih jyù yuhk	min5 zi6 zyu4 juk6	mihn chih chyu yuhk
mind¹ /care	n	介意	gaai yi	gaai3 ji3	kaai yi
mind² /spirit/thoughts	n	心靈	sàm lehng /lìhng	sam4 leng4 /ling4	sam lehng
mind³ /intelligent	n	智力	ji lihk	zi3 lik6	chi lehk
mine /ore	v	礦	kwong	kwong3	khwong
mineral	n	礦物	kwong maht	kwong3 mat6	khwong maht
mini (de)	n	迷你	màih néih	mai4 nei5	maih neih
minibus	n	小巴	síu bà	siu2 baa4	siu pa
minify/reduce/cut down	v	削減	séuk gáam	soek2 gaam2	swok kaam
minimal	adj	最小	jeui síu	zeoi3 siu2	cheui siu
minimum	n	最低限度	jeui dāi haahn douh	zeoi3 dai1 haan6 dou6	cheui tai haahn touh
minimum taxi fare	n	最低車費	jeui dài chè fai	zeoi3 dai4 ce4 fai3	cheui tai chhe fai
mining¹	n	採礦	chói kwong	coi2 kwong3	chhoi khwong
mining²	n	礦業	kwong yihp	kwong3 jip6	khwong yihp
minister	n	部長	bouh jéung	bou6 zoeng2	pouh cheung
ministry	n	內閣	loih /noih gok	loi6 /noi6 gok3	loih /noih kok
mink fur	n	貂皮	dìu péi	diu4 pei2	tiu phei
minor¹	adj	較小	gaau síu	gaau3 siu2	kaau siu
minor² /unimportant	adj	不重要	bāt chung yìu	bat1 cung4 jiu4	pat chhung yiu
minor injuries		輕傷	hèng sèung	heng4 soeng4	heng seung
minority /minorities	n	少數	síu sou	siu2 sou3	siu sou
mint¹	n	薄荷	bòhk ho	bok6 ho3	pohk ho
mint²	n	造幣廠	jouh baih chóng	zou6 bai6 cong2	chouh paih chhong
minus¹ (figure)	adj	負數	fuh sou	fu6 sou3	fuh sou
minus²	adj	失去	sāt heui	sat1 heoi3	sat hoi
minute¹ (of hour)	n	分鐘	fān jūng	fan1 zung1	fan chung
minute² /divide/grade /class/separate/fraction/mark	adj/v	分	fàn	fan4	fan

English		Chinese	Cantonese	Jyutping	Yale
minute[3]/extremely small	adj	微小	mèih síu	mei4 siu2	meih siu
minute[4]/while/a moment	n	一會兒	yāt wūi yi	jat1 wui1 ji3	yat wui yi
miracle[1]	n	神蹟	sàhn jīk	san4 zik1	sahn chek
miracle[2]	n	奇蹟	kèih jīk	kei4 zik1	kheih chek
miraculous /magical	adj	神奇	sàhn kèih	san4 kei4	sahn kheih
mirror[1]	n	鏡	géng	geng2	keng
mirror[2]	n	鏡子	géng jí	geng2 zi2	keng chi
misapply /misspend /misuse/wrong way	v	濫用	láahm yuhng	laam6 jung6	laahm yuhng
misappropriate	v	盜用	douh yuhng	dou6 jung6	touh yohng
misbehave[1]	v	行為唔好	hàhng wàih m̀ hóu	hang4 wai4 m4 hou2	hahng waih mh hou
misbehave[2]	v	行為不端	hàhng wàih bāt dyūn	hang4 wai4 bat1 dyun1	hahng waih pat tyun
misbehaved	v	唔規矩	m̀ kwài géui	m4 kwai4 geoi2	mh khwai kwoi
misbehaviour[1]	n	指責	jí jaak	zi2 zaak3	chi chaak
misbehaviour[2]	n	品行不端	bán hàhng bāt dyūn	ban2 hang4 bat1 dyun1	pan hahng pat tyun
misbelieve	v	不可信	bāt hó seun	bat1 ho2 seon3	pat ho swon
miscall	v	叫錯	giu cho	giu3 co3	kiu chho
miscellaneous[1]	adj	雜項	jaahp hohng	zaap6 hong6	chaahp hohng
miscellaneous[2](sl)	adj	濕濕碎碎	sāp sāp seui seui	sap1 sap1 seoi3 seoi3	sap sap swoi swoi
miscellaneous[3] /various/varied/all kinds of/all kinds and sorts	adj	各種各樣	gok júng gok yeuhng	gok3 zung2 gok3 jeong3	kok chung kok yeuhng
mischief /prank/joke by hand	n	惡作劇	ok /ngok jok kehk	ok3 /ngok3 zok3 kek6	ok /ngok chok khehk
mischievous /trick /mischievous act	adj	惡作劇	ok /ngok jok kehk	ok3 /ngok3 zok3 kek6	ok /ngok chok khehk
misconduct	n	不端行為	bāt dyūn hàhng wàih	bat1 dyun1 hang4 wai6	pat tyun hahng waih
miscount	v	數錯	sōu cho	sou1 co3	sou chho
miserable[1] /pitiable	adj	慘	cháam	caam2	chhaam
miserable[2]	adj	悽慘	chāi cháam	cai1 caam2	chhai chaam
misfire	v	打唔出	dá m̀ chēut	daa2 m4 ceot1	ta mh chhot
misfit	n	唔適合	m̀ sīk hahp	m4 sik1 hap6	mh sek hahp
misfortune/unlucky /unfortunate/ill-fated	n	不幸	bāt hahng	bat1 hang6	pat hahng
misgovernment	v	管理唔當	gún léih m̀ dòng	gun2 lei5 m4 dong4	kun leih mh tong
misguide /misdirection	adj	指導錯誤	ji douh cho ngh	zi3 dou6 co3 ng6	chi touh chho ngh
mishandle	v	虐待	fú /foo doih	fu2 doi6	fu /foo toih
mishap	n	不幸嘅事	bāt hahng ge sih	bat1 hang6 ge si6	pat hahng ke sih
misinform[1] /wrong information	v	報錯	bou cho	bou3 co3	pou cho
misinform[2]	v	誤傳	ngh chyùhn	ng6 cyun4	ngh chhyuhn
misinterpret[1]	v	詮錯	chyùhn cho	cyun4 co3	chhyuhn chho
misinterpret[2] /mistranslate	v	譯錯	yihk cho	jik6 co3	yehk chho

misinterpret[3] /mistake /misunderstand	v	誤解	ngh gáai	ng6 gaai2	ngh kaai
misjudge[1]	v	估計錯誤	gú gai cho ngh	gu2 gai3 co3 ng6	ku kai chho ngh
misjudge[2]	v	怪錯	gwaai cho	gwaai3 co3	kwaai chho
misjudge[3]	v	判斷錯誤	pun dyun cho ngh	pun3 dyun3 co3 ng6	phun tyun chho ngh
mislead[1]	v	誤引	ngh yáhn	ng6 jan5	ngh yahn
mislead[2]	v	誤導	ngh dou	ng6 dou3	ngh tou
mislead[3]	v	帶錯路	daai cho louh	daai3 co3 lou6	taai chho louh
misleading	adj	誤解的	ngh gāai dìk	ng6 gaai1 dik4	ngh kaai tek
mismanage	v	處理錯誤	chyú léih cho ngh	cyu2 lei5 co3 ng6	chhyu leih chho ngh
mismanagement	v	管理不善	gún léih bāt sihn	gun2 lei5 bat1 sin6	kun leih pat sihn
misname	v	叫錯名	giu cho méng	giu3 co3 meng2	kiu chho meng
misplace[1]	v	放錯	fong cho	fong3 co3	fong chho
misplace[2]	v	誤放	ngh fong	ng6 fong3	ngh fong
misplace[3]	v	錯愛	cho oi /ngoi	co3 oi3 /ngoi3	chho oi /ngoi
misplace[4] /unable to find/ put somewhere	v	誤置	ngh jí	ng6 zi2	ngh chi
misprint /mistake spelling	n	印錯	yan cho	jan3 co3	yan cho
mispronounce[1]	v	發錯音	faat cho yām	faat3 co3 jam1	faat chho yam
mispronounce[2]	v	讀錯音	duhk cho yām	duk6 co3 jam1	tuhk chho yam
misread	v	讀錯	duhk cho	duk6 co3	tuhk chho
miss[1] /fail/fall down/ defeated/miscarry	v	失敗	sāt baaih	sat1 baai6	sat paaih
miss[2] /lose	n	念	lihm	lim6	lihm
miss[3] /lose	n	想念	séung lihm /nihm	soeng2 lim6 /nim6	seung lihm /nihm
miss[4] (de) young lady	n	搣士	mīt sìh	mit1 si4	mit sih
miss[5] not married/bachelor /spinster	n	未婚	meih fàn	mei6 fan4	meih fan
miss world	n	世界小姐	sai gaai síu jé	sai3 gaai3 siu2 ze2	sai kaai siu che
missile[1] /flying weapon	n	飛彈	fèi dáan	fei4 daan2	fei taan
missile[2] /weapon	n	導彈	douh dáan	dou6 daan2	touh taan
missile[3] (as stones)	n	投射物	tàuh seh maht	tau4 se6 mat6	thauh seh maht
missile[4] antiballistic	n	反彈道導彈	fáan dáan dou douh dáan	faan2 daan2 dou3 dou6 daan2	faan taan tou touh taan
missing[1] /lost/not find	adj	失蹤	sāt jūng	sat1 zung1	sat chung
missing[2]	adj	缺掉	kyut diuh	kyut3 diu6	khyut tiuh
mission[1] /task	n	使命	si mehng /mihng	si3 meng6 /ming6	si mehng
mission[2]	n	使團	sih tyùhn	si6 tyun4	sih thyuhn
missionary[1]	n	傳教士	chyùhn gaau sih	cyun4 gaau3 si6	chhyuhn kaau sih
missionary[2]	n	傳教	chyùhn gaau	cyun4 gaau3	chhyuhn kaau
misspell	v	拼錯	ping cho	ping3 co3	pheng chho
missy/little girl/young lady	n	小姑娘	síu gù lèuhng / nèuhng	siu2 gu4 loeng4 /noeng4	siu ku leuhng
mistake	v	過錯	gwo cho	gwo3 co3	kwo cho

English		Chinese	Yale	Jyutping	
mistaked /wronged /faulted	v	錯咗	cho jó	co3 zo2	chho cho
mistaken[1]	adj	錯誤嘅	cho ngh ge	co3 ng6 ge3	chho ngh ke
mistaken[2]	adj	弄錯	luhng cho	lung6 co3	luhng chho
mistime	v	不合時宜	bāt hahp sìh yìh	bat1 hap6 si4 ji6	pat hahp sih yih
mistress	n	女教師	léuih gaau sī	leui5 gaau3 si1	lowih kaau si
misunderstand	v	誤會	ngh wuih	ng6 wui6	ngh wuih
mitigate	v	使緩和	sái wuhn wòh	sai2 wun6 wo4	sai wuhn woh
mix[1]	v	溝	kàu	kau4	khau
mix[2] /stir/whisk	v	攪	gáau	gaau2	kaau
mixed	v	使混和	sái wahn wòh	sai2 wan6 wo4	sai wahn woh
mixed drinking party /cocktail party	n	鷄尾酒會	gāi méih jáu wúi	gai1 mei5 zau2 wui2	kai meih chau wui
mixer[1] /blender machine	n	果汁機	gwó jāp gèi	gwo2 zap1 gei4	kwo chap gei
mixer[2] (by a person)	n	調酒師	tìuh jáu sì	tiu4 zau2 si4	thiuh chau si
mixer machine[1]	n	攪拌器	gáau buhn héi	gaau2 bun6 hei2	kaau puhn hei
mixer machine[2]	n	攪拌機	gáau buhn gei	gaau2 bun6 gei3	kaau puhn kei
mixing	n	混合	wahn hahp	wan6 hap6	wahn hahp
mobile /not fixed	adj	機動	gèi duhng	gei4 dung6	kei tuhng
mobile phone[1] /cell phone/cellular phone	n	手機	sáu gèi	sau2 gei4	sau kei
mobile phone[2]	n	手提電話	sáu tai dìhn wàh	sau2 tai3 din6 waa4	sau thai tihn wah
mode /method	n	模式	mòuh sìk	mou4 sik4	mouh sek
model[1] /pattern/cast	n/v	模	mòuh	mou4	mouh
model[2] /mold/pattern /shape/style	n	歀	fún	fun2	fun
model[3] /pattern	n	模型	mòuh yìhng	mou4 jing4	mouh yehng
model[4]	n	標準	bīu jéun	biu1 zeon2	piu cheun
model fashion(de)	n	模特兒	mòuh dahk yìh	mou4 dak6 ji4	mouh tahk yih
model number	n	型號	yìhng houh	jing4 hou6	yehng houh
modeling /mold-making	n	造型	jouh yihng	zou6 jing4	chouh yehng
modeller	n	造型者	jouh yihng jé	zou6 jing4 ze2	chouh yehng che
modern(de)	adj	摩登	mō dàng	mo1 dang4	mo tang
modern time	adj	現代	yihn doih	jin6 doi6	yihn toih
modernization	n	現代化	yihn doih fa	jin6 doi6 faa3	yihn toih fa
modernize /update	v	使現代化	sái yihn doih fa	sai2 jin6 doi6 faa3	sai yihn toih fa
module[1] /pattern no	n	模數	mòuh sou	mou4 sou3	mouh sou
module[2]	n	組件	jóu gín	zou2 gin2	chou kin
modulus	n	係數	hai sou	hai3 sou3	hai sou
moist[1]	adj	濕哂	sāp saai	sap1 saai3	sap saai
moist[2] /wet/humid	adj	潮	chìuh	ciu4	chhiuh
moisturing	n	保濕	bóu sap	bou2 sap3	pou sap
moisturizer	n	潤面霜	yèuh mìhn sèung	jeon6 min6 soeng4	yeuhn mihn seung
mold[1] /shape/type model	n	模	móu	mou2	mou
mold[2] /fungi	n	黴	mōu	mou1	mou

molecule	n	分子	fahn jí	fan6 zi2	fahn chi
short time /a moment	n	刻	hāk	hak1	hak
moment	n	片刻	pin hāk	pin3 hak1	phin hak
Mon to Sun	n	星期一至星期日	sèng kèih yāt jí sèng kèih yaht	seng4 kei4 jat1 zi2 seng4 kei4 jat6	seng kheih yat chi seng kheih yaht
monarch	n	君主	gwàn jyú	gwan4 zyu2	kwan chyu
monarchy[1]	n	君主政體	gwàn jyú jing tái	gwan4 zyu2 zing3 tai2	kwan chyu cheng thai
monarchy[2]	n	君主國	gwàn jyú gwok	gwan4 zyu2 gwok3	kwan chyu kwok
monastery	n	修道院	sau douh yún	sau3 dou6 jyun2	sau touh yun
Monday[1]	n	禮拜一	láih baai yāt	lai5 baai3 jat1	laih paai yat
Monday[2]	n	星期一	sèng kèih yāt	seng4 kei4 jat1	seng kheih yat
money[1]	n	錢	chín	cin2	chhin
money[2] /assets/wealth /property/capital/expense	n	資	jī	zi1	chi
money[3] (in small note)		散紙	sáan jí /zí	saan2 zi2	saan chi
money[4] /coin/small coins /small money	n	散銀	sáan ngaán	saan2 ngaan2	saan ngaan
money & valuables /treasure	n	財寶	chòih bóu	coi4 bou2	chhoih pou
money deposit /savings in the bank	v	存款	chyùhn fún	cyun4 fun2	chhyuhn fun
Mongolia	n	蒙古國	mùhng gú gwok	mung4 gu2 gwok3	muhng ku kwok
monitor /lookout/to spy on/oversee/surveillance /watch over	n	監視	gàam sih	gaam4 si6	kaam sih
monk (Buddist)	n	和尚	wòh séung	wo4 soeng2	woh seung
monkey (coll)	n	馬騮	máh lāu	maa5 lau1	mah lau
monkey hill	n	馬騮山	máh làuh sāan	maa5 lau4 saan1	mah lauh saan
monolingual /only one language	adj	單語	dāan yúh	daan1 jyu5	taan yuh
monopolizer	n	壟斷者	lúhng dyuhn jé	lung5 dyun6 ze2	luhng tyuhn che
monopoly[1] /patent	n	專利	jyùn leih	zyun4 lei6	chyun leih
monopoly[2]	n	專利品	jyùn leih bán	zyun4 lei6 ban2	chyun leih pan
monopoly[3]	n	壟斷	lúhng dyuhn	lung5 dyun6	luhng tyuhn
monotone /samely	n	單調	dàan diuh	daan4 diu6	taan tiuh
monoxide	n	一氧物	yāt yáuhng maht	jat1 joeng5 mat6	yat yauhng maht
monsoon[1]/rainy season	n	雨季	yúh gwai	jyu5 gwai3	yuh kwai
monsoon[2]	n	季風	gwai fùng	gwai3 fung4	kwai fung
monsoon[3]	n	季候風	gwai hauh fùng	gwai3 hau6 fung4	kwai hauh fung
monster[1] /demon	n	怪物	gwaai maht	gwaai3 mat6	kwaai maht
monster[2] (extremely huge man)	n	殘忍嘅人	chàahn yán ge yàhn	caan4 jan2 ge3 jan4	chhaahn yan ke yahn
month /moon/lunar	n	月	yuht	jyut6	yuht
monthly charged		按月計	on /ngòn yuht gai	on3 /ngon4 jyut6 gai3	on /ngon yuht kai
monthly ticket	n	月票	yuht piu	jyut6 piu3	yuht phiu
moon[1] /full moon	n	月球	yuht kàuh	jyut6 kau4	yuht khauh

moon[2] (coll) be absent-minded	v	出神獃看	chēut sàhn ngòih hòn	ceot1 san4 ngoi4 hon4	chhot sahn ngoih hon
mooncake	n	月餅	yuht béng	jyut6 beng2	yuht peng
moonlight	n	月光	yuht gwōng	jyut6 gwong1	yuht kwong
mop[1]	n	地拖	deih tō	dei6 to1	teih tho
mop[2]	n	拖把	tò bá	to4 ba2	thoh pa
mop up[1] /mopping	n	拖地	tō deih	to1 dei6	tho teih
mop up[2]	v	用拖把拖洗	yuhng tò bá tò sái	jung6 to4 ba2 to4 sai2	yuhng tho pa tho sai
moped	n	機器腳踏車	gèi hei geuk daahp chè	gei4 hei3 goek3 daap6 ce4	kei hei keuk taahp chhe
moral[1] /morality	adj	德	dāk	dak1	tak
moral[2]	adj	道德	douh dāk	dou6 dak1	touh tak
moral behavior /principle	n	原則	yùhn jāk	jyun4 zak1	yuhn chak
morality & conduct /behaviour/habit/manner /conduct/principle/moral /virtue	n	德行	dāk hahng	dak1 hang6	tak hahng
morality good /good behavior/good conduct	adj	好行為	hóu hahng wàih	hou2 hang6 wai6	hou hahng waih
morally bad[1] /bad people/violent man/ wickeder	n	黑心人	hāk sām yàhn	hak1 sam1 jan4	hak sam yahn
morally bad[2] /bad people	n	邪惡嘅人	chèh ok /ngok ge yàhn	ce6 ok3 /ngok3 ge3 jan4	chheh ok /ngok ke yahn
more[1]	adv	更	gāng	gang1	kang
more[2] /plural/some/few/ little	adv	啲	dī	di1	tī
more & more		越來越多	yuht lòih yuht dò	jyut6 loi4 jyut6 do4	yuht loih yuht toh
more manageable	adj	可以操縱	hó yíh chòu jung	ho2 ji5 cou4 zung3	ho yih chhou chung
more or less[1]	adj	多啲	dō dī	do1 di1	toh ti
more or less[2] /roughly /not exactly	adj	大致	daaih ji	daai6 zi3	taaih chi
more or less		多少有些	dò síu yáuh sè	do4 siu2 jau5 se4	toh siu yauh se
more slowly	n	慢小小	maahn síu síu	maan6 siu2 siu2	maahn siu siu
more than[1]	n	以上	yíh seuhng	ji5 soeng6	yih seuhng
more than[2]	n	多於	dò yù	do4 jyu4	toh yu
morning[1]	n	上早	sèuhng jōu	soeng6 zou1	seuhng chou
morning[2]	n	上午	sèuhng ngh	soeng6 ng6	seuhng ngh
morning[3]	n	早晨	jóu sàhn, (jou san)	zou2 san4, (zou san3)	chou sahn
morning[4] (early)	n	朝早	jìu jóu	ziu4 zou2	chiu chou
morning[5] (early)	n	朝頭早	jìu tàuh jóu	ziu4 tau4 zou2	chiu thauh chou
morning prayer	n	早禱	jóu tóu	zou2 tou2	chou thou
mortal /must die	adj	必死	bīt séi	bit1 sei2	pit sau
mortar	n	研缽	yìhn but	jin4 but3	yihn put
mortgagee[1]	n	押	aat	aat2	aat
mortgagee[2]	n	受抵押人	sauh dái aat /ngaat yàhn	sau6 dai2 aat2 /ngaat3 jan4	sauh tai aat /ngaat yahn

English	Part	Chinese	Romanization 1	Romanization 2	Romanization 3
mortgagee[3]	n	承受抵押人	sing sàuh dāi áa yan	sing3 sau6 dai1 aat3 jan4	seng sauh tai aa yan
mortgagor	n	抵押人	dái aat /ngaat yàhn	dai2 aat3 /ngaat3 jan4	tai aat /ngaat yahn
mortuary	n	停屍間	tíhng sì gàan	ting5 si4 gaan4	thehng si kaan
mosque[1]	n	清真寺	chēng /chīng jàn jih	ceng1 /cing1 zan1 zi6	chheng chan chih
mosque[2]	n	回教寺院	wùih gaau jih yūn	wui4 gaau3 zi6 jyun1	wuih kaau chih yun
mosquito	n	蚊	mān	man1	man
moss	n	苔蘚	tòih sín	toi4 sin2	thoih sin
most[1]	pron	最	jeui	zeoi3	cheui
most[2]	adv	最多	jeui dò	zeoi3 do4	cheui toh
most important	adj	主要嘅	jyú yiu ge	zyu2 jiu3 ge3	chyu yiu ke
most of		大部	daaih bouh	daai6 bou6	taaih pouh
most recent /recently	adj	最近	jeui gahn	zeoi3 gan6	cheui kahn
mote (piece of dust)	n	微粒	mèih lāp /nāp	mei4 lap1 /nap1	meih lap /nap
moth	n	蛾	ngòh	ngo6	ngoh
mother[1]	n	媽	mà	maa4	ma
mother[2]	n	媽媽	màh mā	maa4 maa1	mah ma
mother[3]	n	母親	móuh chàn	mou5 can4	mouh chhan
mother[4]	n	啊媽	àa mā	aa4 maa1	aa maa
mother[5] (husband's)	n	奶奶	lai lai	lai3 lai3	lai lai
mother daughter	n	母女	móuh léoih /néoih	mou5 leoi5 /neoi5	mouh lowih /nowih
mother father /parents	n	父母	fuh móuh	fu6 mou5	fuh mouh
maternal aunt /mother's brother's wife	n	舅母	káuh móuh	kau5 mou5	khauh mouh
Mother's Day may 2nd Sun	n	母親節	móuh chàn jit	mou5 can4 zit3	mouh chhan chit
mother's elder brother	n	大舅父	daaih káuh fuh	daai6 kau5 fuh	taaih khauh fuh
mother's elder sister	n	大姨媽	daaih yìh mā	daai6 ji4 ma1	taaih yih ma
mother's elder sister's husband		大姨丈	daaih yìh jeuhng	daai6 ji4 zoeng6	taai6 yih cheuhng
mother's home	n	娘家	lèuhng gā	loeng gaa1	leuhng ka
mother's young sister's husband		姨丈	yìh jeuhng	ji4 zoeng6	yih cheuhng
mother's younger brother	n	舅父	káuh fuh	kau5 fuh	khauh fuh
mother's younger sister (aunt)	n	姨媽	yìh mā	ji4 ma1	yih ma
mother tongue	n	母語	móuh yúh	mou5 jyu5	mouh yuh
mother-fucker[1] (vdw)	n	屌你老母閪	díu léih lóuh móuh hài	diu2 lei5 lou5 mou5 hai4	tiu leih louh mouh hai
mother-fucker[2] (vdw)	n	屌你老母臭閪	díu léih lóuh móuh chau hài	diu2 lei5 lou5 mou5 cau3 hai4	tiu leih louh mouh chhau hai
mother-fucker[3](sl) (vdw)	n	雜種	jaahp júng	zaap6 zung2	chaahp chung
mother-fucker[4](sl) (vdw)	n	渾蛋	wàhn daahn	wan4 daan6	wahn taahn
motherhood	n	母性	móuh sing	mou5 sing3	mouh seng
motherless	adj	無母親	móuh móuh chàn	mou5 mou5 can4	mouh mouh chhan
motion[1] /movement	n	運動	wahn duhng	wan6 dung6	wahn tohng

motion[2] /action	n	動作	duhng jok	dung6 zok3	tuhng chok
motion[3] /running/to run /moving	n	運行	wahn hahng	wan6 hang4	wahn hahng
motionless /not move /stationary	adj	不動	bāt duhng	bat1 dung6	pat tuhng
motivate[1]	v	激發	gīk faat	gik1 faat3	kek faat
motivate[2] /spur/stimulate	v	刺激	chi gīk	ci3 gik1	chhi kek
motiveless	adj	沒有動機	muht yáuh duhng gèi	mut6 jau5 dung6 gei4	muht yauh tohng kei
motor[1] (de)	n	摩打	mō dá	mo1 daa2	mo ta
motor[2] (de)	n	馬達	máh daaht	maa5 daat6	mah taaht
motorbike	n	電單車	dihn dàan chè	din6 daan4 ce4	tihn taan chhe
motorist	n	駕駛者	ga sái jé	gaa3 sai2 ze2	ka sai che
mould[1]	n	模具	mòuh geuih	mou4 geoi6	mouh kwoih
mould[2]	n	鑄模	jyu mòuh	zyu3 mou4	chyu mouh
moulding	n	模子	mòuh jí	mou4 zi2	mouh chi
mount[1] /ride	v	騎	kèh	ke4	kheh
mount[2] /ride/to climb	v	乘	sìhng	sing4	sehng
mount[3] to climb on	v	騎上	kèh séuhng	ke4 soeng5	kheh seuhng
mount[4] to mount on	v	乘騎	sìhng kèh	sing4 ke4	sehng kheh
mountain ridge	n	山嶺	saan léhng	saan3 leng5	saan lehng
mountain stream /ravine/stream	n	山澗	sàan gaan	saan4 gaan3	saan kaan
mountaineer[1] /climber mountain/expedition	n	登山家	dàng sàan gà	dang4 saan4 gaa4	tang saan ka
mountaineer[2]	n	爬山能手	pàh sàan làhng sáu	paa4 saan4 lang4 sau2	phah saan lahng sau
mountaineering[1] /hiking hill/climb	n	爬山	pàh sàan	paa4 saan4	phah saan
mountaineering[2]	n	登山	dàng sàan	dang4 saan4	tang saan
mounted		搭咗	daap jó	daap3 zo2	taap cho
mourn /woeful/ruth	v	悲哀	bèi òi	bei4 oi1	pei oi
mouse[1]	n	鼠	syú	syu2	syu
mouse[2] /rat	n	老鼠	lóuh syú	lou5 syu2	louh syu
mouse[3] (of computer)	n	滑鼠	waāt syú	waat1 syu2	waat syu
moustache /beard	n	鬚	sòu	sou4	sou
mouth[1]	n	口	háu	hau2	hau
mouth[2]	n	嘴	jéui	zeoi2	cheui
mouth[3]	n	嘴巴	jéui /zéoi bàa	zeoi2 baa4	cheui paa
mouth's liquid /saliva	n	口水	háu séui	hau2 seoi2	hau swoi
mouthful	n	一口	yāt háu	jat1 hau2	yat hau
move[1] /shift	v	遷	chìn	cin4	chhin
move[2] /remove	v	搬	bùn	bun4	pun
move[3] (wr)/to move/change	v	動	duhng	dung6	tuhng
move[4] (coll) to move	v	嘟	yūk	juk1	yuk
move[5] /to move (coll)	v	郁	yūk	juk1	yuk
move[6]	v	動傷	duhng sēung	dung6 soeng1	tuhng seung

move[7] /remove/mobile	v	移動	yìh dúhng	ji4 dung5	yih tuhng
move as snake	n	蜿	yūn	jyun1	yun
move away	n	移去	yi heui	ji3 heoi3	yi hoi
move forward /onwards	adv	進一步	jeun yāt bouh	zeon3 jat1 bou6	cheun yat pouh
move hand /wave hand	v	揮	fài	fai1	fài
move house /shifting house	v	搬屋	bùn ūk /ngūk	bun4 uk1 /nguk1	pun uk /nguk
moved already		搬左去	bùn jó heui	bun4 zo2 heoi3	pun cho hoi
mover	n	行動者	hàhng duhng jé	hang4 dung6 ze2	hahng tohng che
movie /film	n	電影	dihn yéng /yíng	din6 jeng2 /jing2	tihn yeng
movie star[1]	n	明星	mìhng séng /sìng	ming4 seng4 /sing4	mehng seng
movie star[2] /film star	n	電影明星	dihn yéng mìhng sèng /sìng	din6 jeng2 ming4 seng4 /sing4	tihn yeng mehng seng
movies /drama/theater /staging/comedy	n	戲劇	hei kehk	hei3 kek6	hei kehk
moving	adj	移動的	yìh dúhng dìk	ji4 dung5 dik4	yih tuhng tek
moving off[1]		搬走	bùn jáu	bun4 zau2	pun chau
moving off[2] /move off /to go		移離	yi lei	ji3 lei3	yi lei
Mrs[1] /wife/mistress married woman	n	太太	táai táai	taai2 taai2	thaai thaai
Mrs[2] married woman	n	婦人	fúh yàhn	fu5 jan4	fuh yahn
MTR/ HK rail	n	地鐵	dèih tit	dei6 tit3	teih thit
much more		更加	gāng gā	gang1 gaa1	kang ka
much pressure /overpress/undue pressure	v	過分壓力	gwo fàn aat /ngaat lihk	gwo3 fan4 aat3 /ngaat3 lihk	kwo fan aat /ngaat lehk
mucous membrane	n	黏膜	lìm /nìm mók	lim4 /nim4 mok	lim /nim mok
mud	n	泥	làih /nàih	lai4 /nai4	laih /naih
muddle	v	混亂	wahn lyuhn	wan6 lyun6	wahn lyuhn
muddled /dull person	n	糊塗	wùh tòuh	wu4 tou4	wuh thouh
muffler[1] /scarf/veil	n	頸巾	géng gān	geng2 gan1	keng kan
muffler[2] /scarf/shawl	n	圍巾	wàih gān	wai4 gan1	waih kan
muffler[3] /silencer	n	消音器	sìu yàm héi	siu4 jam4 hei3	siu yam hei
muffler[4] /silencer	n	無聲器	mòuh sèng /sìng hei	mou4 seng4 /sing4 hei3	mouh seng hei
mug /big cup	n	大杯	daaih būi	daai6 bui1	taaih pui
mule /self will	n	固執	gu jāp	gu3 zap1	ku chap
multi[1]	adj	多用	dò yeuhng	do4 jung6	toh yeuhng
multi[2]	adj	多種	dò júng	do4 zung2	to chung
multi purpose[1] /multi function	adj	多用途	dò yeuhng tòuh	do4 jung6 tou4	to yeuhng thouh
multi purpose[2] /multi function	adj	多功能	dò gùng nàhng	do4 gung4 nang4	to kung nàhng
multi lane RD	adj	多行車線	dò hàhng chè sin	do4 hang4 ce4 sin3	to hahng chhe sin
multicultural	adj	多元文化	dò yùhn màhn fa	do4 jyun4 man4 faa3	toh yuhn mahn fa
multimedia	adj	多媒體	dò mùih tái	do4 mui4 tai2	toh muih thai
multiple	adj	多樣	dò yeuhng	do4 joeng6	toh yeuhng

multiplication[1]	n	乘法	sìhng faat	sing4 faat3	sehng faat
multiplication[2]	n	數法	sou faat	sou3 faat3	sou faat
mumble /grumble	v	咕噥	gū lùhng /nùhng	gu1 lung4 /nung4	ku luhng /nuhng
municipality[1]	n	自治市	jih jih síh	zi6 zi6 si5	chih chih sih
municipality[2]	n	自治區	jih jih kèui	zi6 zi6 keoi4	chih chih khoi
municipality[3]	n	市政當局	síh jing dong gúk	si5 zing3 dong3 guk6	sih cheng tong kuk
municipality[4]	n	市政	síh jing	si5 zing3	sih cheng
murder[1] /killer	n	杀	saat	saat3	saat
murder[2] /man kill	n	殺人	saat yàhn	saat3 jan4	saat yahn
murder3 /slaughter	n	殺者	saat jé	saat3 ze2	saat che
murder[4] (wr)	n	弒	si	si3	si
murder[5] /slay	n	屠殺	tòuh saat	tou4 saat3	thouh saat
murder[6]	n	謀殺罪	màuh saat jeuih	mau4 saat3 zeoi6	mauh saat choih
murmur /whisper	n	私語	sī yúh	si1 jyu5	si yuh
muscular	adj	肌肉人	gèi yuhk yàhn	gei4 juk6 jan4	kei yuhk yahn
musculoskeletal		肌肉與骨骼	gèi yuhk yúh gwāt gaak	gei4 juk6 jyu5 gwat1 gaak3	kei yuhk yuh kwat kaak
museum[1]	n	博物館	bok maht gún	bok3 mat6 gun2	pok maht kun
museum[2]	n	博物院	bok maht yún	bok3 mat6 jyun2	pok maht yun
mushroom[1]	n	冬菇	dūng gū	dung1 gu1	tung ku
mushroom[2]	n	草菇	chóu gū	cou2 gu1	chhou ku
mushroom[3]	n	蘑菇	mòh gū	mo4 gu1	moh ku
music	n	音樂	yàm ngòhk	jam4 ngok6	yam ngohk
musician	n	音樂家	yàm ngòhk gà	jam4 ngok6 gaa4	yam ngohk ka
muslims temple	n	清真寺	chèng /chìng jān jih	ceng4 /cing4 zan1 zi6	chheng chan chih
mussel	n	淡菜	daahm choi	daam6 coi3	taahm chhoi
must[1]	v	須	sēui	seoi1	swoi
must[2] /should/compulsory	v/aux	必	bīt	bit1	pit
must[3] /demand must	v/aux	一定要	yāt dehng yiu	jat1 deng6 jiu3	yat tehng mh yiu
must be /sure	adj	必定	bìt dèhng /dihng	bit4 deng6 /ding6	pit tehng
must give		須予	sēui yùh	seoi1 jyu4	swoi yuh
must not[1]	v	唔駛	m̀ sai	m4 sai3	mh sai
must not[2] /no thanks/no	v	是嗎	sih mā	si6 ma1	sih ma
must not[3]	v	一定唔要	yāt dehng m̀ yiu	jat1 deng6 m4 jiu3	yat tehng mh yiu
mustard paste	n	芥辣	gaai laaht	gaai3 laat6	kaai laaht
mute[1] /silence/muteness	v	啞	ngá /āa/áa	nga2 /aa1/aa2	nga /aa
mute[2] /silent	adj	沈默	chàhm mahk	cam4 mak6	chhahm mahk
mutton /lamb meat of sheep	n	羊肉	yèuhng yuhk	joeng4 juk6	yeuhng yuhk
mutual	adj	彼此嘅	béi chí ge	bei2 ci2 ge3	pei chhi ke
mutually /reciprocal	adj	互相	wuh sèung	wu6 soeng4	wuh seung
my	pron	我個	ngóh gó	ngo5 go2	ngoh ko
my daughter	n	我嘅女	ngóh ge léoi /néoi	ngo5 ge3 leoi2 /neoi2	ngoh ke lowih /nowih
my friend	n	我嘅老友	ngóh ge lóuh yáuh	ngo5 ge3 lou5 jau5	ngoh ke louh yauh

my lord	n	我主	ngóh jyú	ngo5 zyu2	ngoh chyu
my name	n	我叫做	ngóh giu jouh	ngo5 giu3 zou6	ngoh kiu chouh
my name is...[1]	n	我嘅名叫做	ngóh ge méng giu jouh	ngo5 ge3 meng2 giu3 zou6	ngoh ke meng kiu chouh
my name is...[2]		我個名係.	ngóh go méng haaih...	ngo5 go3 meng2 haai6...	ngoh ko meng haaih...
my son	n	我嘅子	ngóh ge jái	ngo5 ge3 zai2	ngoh ke chai
myself	pron	我自己	ngóh ji géi	ngo5 zi3 gei2	ngoh chi kei
mysterious	adj	奧	ou	ou3	ou
mystery[1]	n	神秘嘅	sàhn bei ge	san4 bei3 ge3	sahn pei ke
mystery[2]	n	奧祕	ou bei	ou3 bei3	ou bei
mythical	adj	神話	sàhn wá	san4 waa2	sahn wa

nag[1] /make distressed	v	使煩惱	si fàhn lóuh /nóuh	si fan4 lou5 /nou5	si fahn louh /nouh
nag[2] /daily blaming daily worries, finding fault	v	老使人煩惱	lóuh si yàhn fàhn lóuh /nóuh	lou5 si jan4 fan4 lou5 /nou5	louh si yahn fahn louh /nouh
nail (of the finger)	n	釘	deng /ding	deng3 /ding3	teng
nail cutter /nail clippers	n	指甲鉗	jī gáap kím	zi1 gaap2 kim2	chi kaap khim
nail polish /nail varnish	n	指甲油	jī gáap yàuh	zi1 gaap2 jau4	chi kaap yauh
naked[1] /nude/bare/undress	adj	裸	ló	lo2	lo
naked[2] /nude/unclad/ unclothed	adj	裸體	ló tái	lo2 tai2	lo thai
naked[3] /bare/stark	adv	赤裸裸	chek ló ló	cek3 lo2 lo2	chhek lo lo
naked person	n	赤裸人士	chek ló yàhn sih	cek3 lo2 jan4 si6	chhek lo yahn sih
name	n	名	méng /míng	meng2 /ming2	meng
name in Chinese	n	中文姓名	jùng màhn seng méng	zung4 man4 seng3 meng2	chung mahn seng meng
name list (of send out goods)	n	開單	hòi dāan	hoi4 daan1	hoi taan
name plate	n	名牌	mèhng /mìhng pàaih	meng4 /ming4 paai4	mehng phaaih
named brand	n	名牌	méng pàaih	meng2 paai4	meng phaaih
nap /short sleep	n	覺	gaau	gaau3	kaau
napkin /towel	n	餐巾	chāan gàn	caan1 gan4	chhaan kan
narcotic (by drug)	adj	麻醉藥	màh jeui yeuhk	maa4 zeoi3 joek6	màh choi yeuhk
narrate /tell story	v	敘述	jeuih seuht	zeoi6 seot6	cheuih swoht
narrow[1] /tight	adj	窄	jaak	zaak3	chaak
narrow[2] /tight	adj	狹	haahp	haap6	haahp
narrow[3] /tight	adj	狹窄	haahp jaak	haap6 zaak3	haahp chaak
narrow[4]	v	變窄	bin jaak	bin3 zaak3	pin chaak
narrow minded	adj	氣量小	hei lèuhng síu	hei3 loeng4 siu2	hei leuhng síu
narrowing		缺隘	kyut aai	kyut3 aai3	khyut aai
NASA National Aeronautics and Space Administration	abbr	太空總署	taai hùng júng chyúh	taai3 hung4 zung2 cyu5	thaai hung chung chhyuh
nose /nasal	adj	鼻	beih	bei6	peih
nasal catarrh	adj	鼻黏膜炎	beih lìhm /nìhm mók yìhm	bei6 lim4 /nim4 mok2 jim4	peih lihm /nihm mok yihm
nasal congestion /blocked nose	adj	鼻塞	beih sāk	bei6 sak1	peih sak
nasal discharge	adj	鼻涕	beih tai	bei6 tai3	peih thai
nasal sound	adj	鼻音	beih yām	bei6 jam1	peih yam
nasty[1]	adj	污糟**	wù jòu laaht taat	wu4 zou4 laat6 taat3	wu chou laaht thaat
nasty[2]	adj	齷齪	āk /àak chūk	ak1 /aak1 cuk1	ak /aak chhuk
nation[1] /country/national	n	國	gwok	gwok3	kwok
nation[2]	n	國民	gwok màhn	gwok3 man6	kwok mahn
national song /national anthem	n	國歌	gwok gō	gwok3 go1	kwok koh
national language	n	國語	gwok wá	gwok3 waa2	kwok wa
nationalism	n	民族主義	màhn juhk jyú yih	man4 juk6 zyu2 ji6	mahn chuhk chyu yih
nationwide /whole country/nationally/ as a whole country	adv	在全國範圍內	joih chyùhn gwok faahn wàih loih /noih	zoi6 chyun4 gwok3 faan6 wai4 loi6 /noi6	choih chhyuhn kwok faahn waih loih /noih

native dialect	n	本地話	bún deih wá	bun2 dei6 waa2	pun teih wa
native language	n	母話使用	móuh wá sái yuhng	mou5 waa2 sai2 jung6	mouh wa sai yuhng
nativity	n	出生情況	chēut sāng chìhng fong	ceot1 sang1 cing4 fong3	chhot sang chhehng fong
natural	adj	自然	jih yìhn	zi6 jin4	chih yihn
natural gas	n	天然氣	tìn yìhn hei	tin4 ji4 hei3	thin yihn hei
natural science	n	自然科學	jih yìhn fō hohk	zi6 jin4 fo1 hok6	chih yihn fo hohk
naturalization	n	歸化	gwài fa	gwai4 faa3	kwai fa
naturalize	v	採納	chòih nàahp	coi4 naap4	chhoih naahp
naturally	adv	自然地	jih yìhn deih	zi6 jin4 dei6	chih yihn teih
nature[1] /quality	n	性	sing	sing3	seng
nature[2] /quality /character	n	質	jāt	zat1	chat
nature	n	自然	jih yìhn	zi6 jin4	chih yihn
naughty[1] /mischievous	adj	反斗	fáan dáu	faan2 dau2	faan tau
naughty[2]	adj	百厭	baak yim	baak3 jim3	paak yim
naughty[3]	adj	曳	yáih	jai5	yaih
naughty[4]	adj	頑皮的	wàahn pèih dīk	waan4 pei4 dik1	waahn pheih tik
naughty kid[(sl)]	adj	馬騮	máh lāu	maa5 lau1	mah lau
nausea[1]	n	嘔心	áu sām	au2 sam1	au sam
nausea[2] /feel vomit	n	噁心嘔吐	ok /ngok sām áu tóu	ok3 /ngok3 sam1 au2 tou2	ok /ngok sam au thou
nausea[3]	n	暈船	wàhn syùhn	wan4 syun4	wahn syuhn
nausea[4] /disgust	n	討厭	tóu yim	tou2 jim3	thou yim
navel /pit of the stomach	n	肚臍	tóuh chìh	tou5 ci4	thouh chhih
navigation[1]	n	導航	douh hòhng	dou6 hong4	touh hohng
navigation[2]	n	領航	léhng hòhng	leng5 hong4	lehng hohng
navigator[1]	n	航行者	hòhng hàhng jé	hong4 hang4 ze2	hohng hahng che
navigator[2]	n	領航員	léhng /líhng hòhng yùhn	leng5 /ling5 hong4 jyun4	lehng hohng yuhn
navy	n	海軍	hói gwàn	hoi2 gwan4	hoi kwan
near[1] /nearest/adjacent	adj	接近	jip gahn	zip3 gan6	chip kahn
near[2]	adj	隔離	gaak lèih	gaak3 lei4	kaak leih
near[3]	adj	緊	gán	gan2	kan
nearby[1] /close to/near area	adj	附近	fuh gahn	fu6 gan6	fuh kahn
nearby[2] /vicinity/adjacent	adv	左近	jó gán	zo2 gan2	cho kan
nearly afternoon		下午約	hah ngh yeuk	haa6 ng6 joek3	hah ngh yeuk
neat	adj	企理	kéih léih	kei5 lei5	kheih leih
neatly	adv	整潔地	jíng git dèih	zing2 git3 dei6	cheng kit teih
neatly & tidy[1] /neat	adj	整潔	jíng git	zing2 git3	cheng kit
neatly & tidy[2] /orderly	adj	整齊	jíng chàih	zing2 cai4	cheng chaih
neck /cervix	n	頸	géng	geng2	keng
necklace	n	頸鍊	géng lín	geng2 lin2	keng lin
necktie /tie (of the neck)	n	領呔	léhng /líhng tāai	leng5 /ling5 taai1	lehng thaai

necktie clip	n	呔夾	tāai gíp	taai1 gip2	thaai kip
necktie pin	n	呔針	tāai jām	taai1 zam1	thaai cham
need	v	需	sèui	seoi4	swoi
needle	n	麻	màh	maa4	mah
needle eye /small hole of needle	n	針眼	jām ngáahn	zam1 ngaan5	cham ngaahn
needlessly	adj	不必要地	bāt bìt yìu dèih	bat1 bit4 jiu4 dei6	pat pit yiu teih
needs[1]	adj	要呀	yiu aa /āa /àa	jiu3 aa3 /aa1 /aa4	yiu aa
needs[2]	adj	就要	jauh yīu	zau6 jiu1	chauh yiu
negation /refuse	n	唔	m̀	m4	mh
negative[1] (of the battery)	adj	負極	fuh gihk	fu6 gik6	fuh kehk
negative[2] (electric)	adj	陰電	yàm dihn	jam4 din6	yam tihn
negative[3] (photo)	n	相底	séung dái	soeng2 dai2	seung tai
negative[4] (math)	n	負嘅	fuh ge	fu6 ge3	fuh ke
neglect	v	忽略	fāt leuhk	fat1 loek6	fat leuhk
neglect duties	n	疏忽職守	sò fāt jīk sáu	so4 fat1 zik1 sau2	so fat chek sau
negotiable in business /deal in cash	adj	對現	deui yihn	deoi3 jin6	toei yihn
negotiate /discuss/treat	v	談判	tàahm pun	taam4 pun3	taahm phun
negotiation	n	協商	hip sèung	hip3 soeng4	hip seung
negotiator	n	談判人	tàahm pun yàhn	taam4 pun3 jan4	taahm phun yahn
negro /black man	n	黑人	hāk yàhn	hak1 jan4	hak yahn
neighbor[1] /neighborhood	n	街坊	gāai fōng	gaai1 fong1	kaai fong
neighbor[2] /next door	n	鄰居	lèuhn gèui	leon4 geoi4	lèuhn kwoi
neighborhood	n	鄰近地區	lèuhn káhn deih kèui	leon4 kan5 dei6 keoi4	leuhn khahn teih khoi
neighbour	n	鄰舍	lèuhn se	leon4 se3	leuhn se
neither	adv	兩者都不	léuhng jé dōu bāt	loeng5 ze2 dou1 bat1	leuhng che tou paht
neon	n	氖	láaih /náaih	laai5 /naai5	laaih /naaih
neon sign /of tube light box/light signs	n	光管招牌	gwòng gún jìu pàaih	gwong4 gun2 ziu4 paai4	kwong kun chiu phaaih
Nepal	n	尼泊爾	nèih bòhk yíh	nei4 bok6 ji5	neih pohk yih
Nepali baby	n	尼泊爾嬰兒	nèih bòhk yíh yìng yìh	nei4 bok6 ji5 jing4 ji4	neih pohk yih ying yih
Nepali boy	n	尼泊爾男仔	nèih bòhk yíh làahm /nàahm jāi	nei4 bok6 ji5 laam4 /naam4 zai1	neih pohk yih laahm chai
Nepali child	n	尼泊爾蘇蝦仔	nèih bòhk yíh sòu hā jái	nei4 bok6 ji5 sou4 haa1 zai2	neih pohk yih sou ha chai
Nepali confucius	n	尼泊爾教聖人	nèih bòhk yíh gaau sing yàhn	nei4 bok6 ji5 gaau3 sing3 jan4	neih pohk yih kaau seng yahn
Nepali dish	n	尼泊爾菜	nèih bòhk yíh chói	nei4 bok6 ji5 coi2	neih pohk yih chhoi
Nepali girl	n	尼泊爾女人	nèih bòhk yíh léoih /néoih yàhn	nei4 bok6 ji5 leoi5 /neoi5 jan4	neih pohk yih lowih /nowih yahn
Nepali man	n	尼泊爾男人	nèih bòhk yíh làahm yàhn	nei4 bok6 ji5 laam4 jan4	neih pohk yih laahm yahn
Nepali's house	n	尼泊爾嘅屋企	nèih bòhk yíh ge ùk kēi	nei4 bok6 ji5 ge3 uk4 kei1	neih pohk yih ke uk khei

English		Chinese	Yale	Jyutping	Romanization
Nepali tea	n	尼泊爾茶	nèih bòhk yíh chàh	nei4 bok6 ji5 caa4	neih pohk yih chhah
Nepali woman	n	尼泊爾婦人	nèih bòhk yíh fúh yàhn	nei4 bok6 ji5 fu5 jan4	neih pohk yih fuh yahn
nephew /sister's son	n	姪	ját	zat2	chat
neptune	n	海神	hói sàhn	hou2 san4	hoi sahn
nerve[1]	n	神經	sàhn gìng	san4 ging4	sahn keng
nerve[2]	n	膽量	dáam leuhng	daam2 loeng6	taam leuhng
nervous[1] /tension	adj	緊張	gán jèung	gan2 zoeng4	kan cheung
nervous[2]	adj	緊張不安	gán jèung bat òn /ngòn	gan2 zoeng4 bat1 on4 /ngon4	kan cheung pat on /ngon
nervous breakdown	n	神經衰弱	sàhn gìng sèui yeuhk	san4 ging4 seoi4 joek6	sahn keng swoi yeuhk
nervous system	n	神經系統	sàhn gìng haih túng	san4 ging4 hai6 tung2	sahn keng haih thung
nest[1]	n	窩	wò	wo4	wo
nest[2]	n	巢	chàauh	caau6	chhaauh
nestle	v	安臥	òn /ngòn oh	on4 /ngon4 o6	on /ngon oh
net[1]	n	絡	lohk	lok6	lohk
net[2] /network	n	網	móhng	mong5	mohng
net[3]	adj	淨值嘅	jehng jihk ge	zeng6 zik6 ge3	chehng chehk ke
nettle (plant' if touch sting)	n	蕁麻	chàhm màh	cam4 maa4	chhahm mah
neuter[1]/castrate /remove sex organs	v	閹	yìm	jim4	yim
neuter[2]/castrate /remove sex organs	v	閹割	yìm got	jim4 got3	yim kot
neutral	adj	中立	jùng lahp	zung4 lap6	chung lahp
never[1]	adj	從未	chùhng meih	cung4 mei6	chhuhng meih
never[2] /will never	adj	永不	wíhng bāt	wing5 bat1	wehng pat
never chatty		唔好傾	m̀ hóu kìng	m4 hou2 king4	mh hou khing
never had sex (female) /virgin female/hymen	n	處女	chyúh léuih /néuih	cyu5 leoi5 /neoi5	chhyuh lowih /nowih
never mind /take it easy!	v	唔緊要	m̀ gán yiu	m4 gan2 jiu3	mh kan yiu
never mind[1]	v	冇關係	móuh gwàan haih	mou5 gwaan4 hai6	mouh kwaan haih
never mind[2] /forget it	v	沒關係	muht gwàan haih	mut6 gwaan4 hai6	muht kwaan haih
never say		咁識講	gam sīk góng	gam3 sik1 gong2	kam sek kong
new[1] /fresh	adj	新	sàn	san4	san
new[2]	adj	新嘅	sàn ge	san4 ge3	san ke
new blood[1] (sl) new idea	adj	新血	sàn hyut	san4 hyut3	san hyut
new blood[2] (sl) new member	n	新成員	sàn sìk yùhn	san4 sik4 jyun4	san sek yuhn
new born baby (sl)	adj	蘇蝦仔	sōu hā jái	sou1 haa1 zai2	sou ha chai
new face /new man	n	新人	sàn yàhn	san4 jan4	san yahn
new leave of plants/bud /shoot/sprout	n	芽	ngàh	ngaa4	ngah
new model		新欵嘅	sàn fún ge	san1 foon2 ge3	san fun ke
new style[1] /new type /latest type	n	新式	sàn sìk	san4 sik4	san sek
new style[2] /new fashion	n	新歡	sàn fún	san4 fun2	san fun

English		Chinese	Yale	Jyutping	Romanization
New Territories	n	新界	sàn gaai	san4 gaai3	san kaai
new testament[1] bible	n	新約	sàn yeuk	san4 joek3	san yeuk
new testament[2] bible	abbr	新約聖經	sàn yeuk sing gìng	san4 joek3 sing3 ging4	san yeuk seng keng
new town	n	新城	sàn sèhng	san4 seng4	san sehng
New Year	n	新年	sàn lìhn /nìhn	san4 lin4 /nin4	san lihn /nihn
New Year's Day	n	元旦	yùhn daan	jyun4 daan3	yuhn taan
New Year's Eve[1] 31 Dec (00:00 hrs)	n	除夕	chèuih jihk	ceoi4 zik6	chheuih chehk
New Year's Eve[2] Chinese	n	年卅晚	lìhn sāah máahn	lin4 saa6 maan5	lihn saa maahn
New Year's Eve[3] Chinese	n	大除夕	daaih chèuih jihk	daai6 chèuih jihk	taaih chheuih chehk
New Year's Eve[4]	n	新年夜	sàn lìhn /nìhn yèh	san4 lin4 /nin4 je6	san lihn /nihn yeh
New York (de)	n	紐約	Náu yeuk	nau2 joek3	Nau yeuk
newcomer	n	受人	sauh yàhn	sau6 jan4	sauh yahn
newly /recently	adv	新近	sàn gahn	san4 gan6	san kahn
news	n	新聞	sàn màhn /mán	san4 man4 /man2	san mahn /man
news agency[1]	n	通訊社	tùng seun séh	tung4 seon3 se5	thung swon she
news agency[2]	n	新聞通訊社	sàn màhn tùng seun séh	san4 man4 tung4 seon3 se5	san mahn thung swon seh
news paper	n	報紙	bou jí	bou3 zi2	pou chi
news report		新聞報告	sàn màhn /mán bou gou	san4 man4 /man2 bou3 gow	san mahn /man pou kou
news script /press release	n	新聞稿	sàn màhn góu	san4 man4 gou2	san mahn kou
news stand	n	報攤	bóu tàan	bou2 taan4	pou thaan
newsagent	n	報紙攤	bou jí tàan	bou3 zi2 taan4	pou chi thaan
newspaper	n	報社	bou séh	bou3 se5	pou seh
newspaper press	n	報刊	bou hón	bou3 hon2	pou hon
newspaper office	n	辦報館	baahn bou gún	baan6 bou3 gun2	paahn pou gun
next[1]	pron	下	hah	haa6	hah
next[2]	pron	下一	hah yāt	haa6 jat1	hah yat
next[3]	pron	下個	hah go	haa6 go3	hah ko
next[4] under /below	adv	下面	hah mihn	haa6 min6	hah mihn
next[5] /then/afterwards /after that	adj	然後	yìhn háu	jin4 hau2	yihn hau
next[6]	adj	其後	kèih háu	kei4 hau2	kheih hau
next[7]	adj	跟住	gahn jyuh	gan4 zyu6	kahn chyuh
next[8]	adj	接下去	jip hah héui	zip3 haa6 heoi2	chip hah hoi
next door	adv	隔壁	gaak bek	gaak3 bek3	kaak pek
next excellent	adv	次優	chi yāu	ci3 jau1	chhi yau
next month	adj	下個月	hah go yuht	haa6 go3 jyut6	hah ko yuht
next time	adj	下次	hah chi	haa6 ci3	hah chhi
next in position /next to (proximity)	pron	隔籬	gaak lèih	gaak3 lei4	kaak leih
next week[1]	pron	下個禮拜	hah go láih baai	haa6 go3 lai5 baai3	hah ko laih paai
next week[2]	pron	下個星期	hah go sìng kèih	haa6 go3 seng4 kei4	hah ko sing kheih
next week[3]	pron	下週	hah jāu	haa6 zau1	hah chau

next world [coll] death	pron	另外地方	lihng òih /ngoih deih fòng	ling6 oi6 /ngoi6 dei6 fong4	lehng oih /ngoih teih fong
next year[1]	pron	出年	chēut lìhn /nìhn	ceot1 lin4 /nin4	chhot lihn /nihn
next year[2]	pron	明年	mìhng lìhn /nìhn	ming4 lin4 /nin4	mehng lihn /nihn
nib	n	鋼筆尖	gong bāt jìm	gong3 bat1 zim4	kong pat chim
nice /quite good	adj	幾好	géi hóu	gei2 hou2	kei hou
nice to meet you!		好高興認識你呀!	hóu gōu heng yihng sīk léih aa!	hou2 gou1 heng3 jing6 sik1 nei5 aa3!	hou kou heng yehng sek leih aa!
nickel (atomic no 28)	n	鎳	lihp /nihp	lip6 /nip6	lihp /nihp
nickname[1]	n	花名	fà méng	faa4 meng2/ming2	fa meng
nickname[2]	n	綽號	mìhn houh	min4 hou6	mihn houh
nicotiana	n	煙草屬	yìn chóu suhk	jin4 cou2 suk6	yin chhou suhk
nicotine [de]	n	尼古丁	nèih gú dèng	nei4 gu2 deng4	neih ku teng
nidify	v	築巢	jùk chàauh	zuk4 caau6	chuk chhaauh
niece[1] (sister's daughter)	n	外甥女	oih /ngoih sāng léui /néui	oi6 /ngoi6 sang1 leui2 /neui2	oih /ngoih sang lowi /nowi
niece[2] (brother's daughter)	n	侄女	jaht léui /néui	zat6 leui /neui2	chaht leui /neui
night[1]	n	夜	yeh	je6	yeh
night[2]	n	晚	máahn	maan5	maahn
night and day	n	日以繼夜	yaht yíh gai yeh	jat6 ji5 gai3 je6	yaht yih kai yeh
night club	n	夜總會	yeh júng wúi	je6 jung2 wui2	yeh chung wui
night dress /pajamas /pyjamas	n	睡衣	seuih yī	seoi6 ji1	swoih yi
night mare /bad dream	n	噩夢	ngohk muhng	ngok6 mung6	ngohk muhng
night shift	n	夜更	yeh gāng	je6 gang1	yeh kang
night time[1]	n	夜間	yèh gàan	je6 gaan4	yeh kaan
night time[2]	n	晚黑	máahn hāak	maan5 haak1	maahn haak
night time[3]	n	夜晚黑	yeh máahn hāak	je6 maan5 haak1	yeh maahn haak
night time[4]	n	晚頭黑	máahn tàuh hāak	maan5 tau4 haak1	maahn thauh haak
nightingale	n	夜鶯	yeh āng /ngāng	je6 ang1 /ngang1	yeh ang /ngang
nightmare bad dream /a frightening dream	n	惡夢	ok /ngok muhng	ok3 /ngok3 mung6	ok /ngok muhng
nine	adj	九	gáu	gau2	kau
nine die one live /very critical condition[sl] 9413		九死一生 9413	gáu séi yāt sāng	gau2 sei2 jat1 sang1	kau sei yat sang
nineteen seventy five	adj	一千九百七十五	yāt chìn gāu báak chàt sàhp ńgh	jat1 cin4 gau1 baak2 cat4 sap6 ng5	yat chhin kau paak chhat sahp ngh
no alternative		無辦法	móuh baahn faat	mou5 baan6 faat3	mouh paahn faat
no answer	n	無答案	móuh daap on/ ngon	mou5 daap3 on3 /ngon3	mouh taap on /ngon
no body came [coll]		放飛機	fong fèi gèi	fong3 fei4 gei4	fong fei kei
no both[1]		都冇	dōu móuh	dou1 mou5	tou mouh
no both[2]		都不	dōu bāt	dou1 bat1	tou pat
no childs	adj	無子女嘅	móuh jí léui /néui ge	mou4 zi2 leui5 /neui5	mouh chi lowi /nowih ke
no coming		唔來	m̀ loìh	m4 loi4	mh loih
no comment[1]		無可奉告	mòuh hó fuhng gou	mou5 ho2 fung6 gou3	mouh ho fuhng kou

no comment[2]	無評論	móuh pìhng leuhn	mou5 ping4 leon6	mouh phehng leuhn
no difference	無分別	móuh fàn biht	mou5 fan4 bit6	mouh fan piht
no entry[1]	唔進入	m̀ jéun yahp	m4 zeon2 jap6	mh cheun yahp
no entry[2]	不進駛入	bat jéun sái yahp	bat1 zeon2 sai2 jap6	pat cheun sai yahp
no expression /stupid adj	呆	òih /ngòih	oi4 /ngoi4	oih /ngoih
no goods	冇貨	móuh fo	mou5 fo3	mouh fo
might as well /no harm	不妨	bāt fòhng	bat1 fong4	pat fohng
no hot water	冇熱水	móuh yìht séui	mou5 jit6 seoi2	mouh yiht swoi
no job	無疑做	móuh yéh jouh	mou5 je5 zou6	mouh yeh chouh
no long[1] /shortly/by and by[(IDM)] adv IDM	一陣間	yāt jahn gāan	jat1 zan6 gaan1	yat chahn kaan
no long[2] /shortly /presently adv	不久	bāt gáu	bat1 gau2	pat kau
no longer adj	唔係啦	m̀ hái lā	m4 hai2 la1	mh hai la
no longer exists	而家都冇	yìh gā dōu móuh	ji4 gaa1 dou1 mou5	yih ka tou mouh
no longer needs	而家唔使	yìh gā m̀ sái	ji4 gaa1 m4 sai2	yih ka mh sai
no matter how	無論	móuh leuhn	mou5 leon6	mouh leuhn
no matter if	乜嘢	māt yéh	mat1 je5	mat yeh
no means	冇法子	móuh faat jí	mou5 faat3 zi2	mouh faat chi
no mistake	無錯無錯	móuh cho móuh cho	mou5 co3 mou5 co3	mouh chho mouh chho
no more	未有	meih yáuh	mei6 jau5	meih yauh
no more than /just/only adv	之係	jí haih	zi2 hai6	chi haih
no need[1]	何必	hòh bīt	ho4 bit1	hoh pit
no need[2]	無用/冇用	móuh yuhng	mou5 jung6	mouh yuhng
no need[3]	不用	bāt yuhng	bat1 jung6	pat yuhng
no need[4] /no thanks	駛乜	sái māt	sai2 mat1	sai mat
no needs let's go v	唔使找啦!	m̀ sái jáau lā!	m4 sai2 zaau2 laa1	mh sai chaau la!
no one /nobody n	無人	móuh yàhn	mou5 jan4	mouh yahn
no one came [(coll)]	放飛機	fong fèi gèi	fong3 fei4 gei4	fong fei kei
no parking [(coll)]	唔准停車	m̀ jéun tìhng chè	m4 zeon2 ting4 ce4	mh cheun thihng chhe
no pay /no salary	無薪	móuh sān	mou5 san1	mouh san
no rain	無雨	móuh yúh	mou5 jyu5	mouh yuh
no raise [(dw)]	不舉	bāt géui	bat1 geoi2	pat kwoi
no right adj	無權	móuh kyùhn	mou5 kyun4	mouh khyuhn
no see	冇見	móuh gin	mou5 gin3	mouh kin
no smoking	唔准食煙	m̀ jéun sihk yīn	m4 zeon2 sik6 jin1	mh cheun sehk yin
no stop /unending /incessantly/uninterrupted adj	唔停	m̀ tìhng	m4 ting4	mh thehng
no take care /don't care	不管	bāt gún	bat1 gun2	pat kun
no testament	無遺囑	móuh wàih jūk	mou5 wai4 zuk1	mouh waih chuk
no things	無嘢加	móuh yéh gà	mou5 je5 gaa4	mouh yeh ka
no treatment	不治	bāt jih	bat1 zi6	pat chi
no use[1] /useless/futile/vain adj	無用/冇用	móuh yuhng	mou5 jung6	mouh yuhng

no use[2]		沒用	muht yùhng	mut6 jung6	muht yuhng
no way /wayless	adj	無路嘅	móuh louh ge	mou5 lou6 ge3	mouh louh ke
no wonder		唔怪特	m̀ gwaai dāk	m4 gwaai3 dak1	mh kwaai tak
nob	n	球形把手	kàuh yìhng bá sáu	kau4 jing4 ba2 sau2	khauh yehng pa sau
noble family[1]	v	高貴	gōu gwai	gou1 gwai3	kou kwai
noble family[2]		貴族	gwai juhk	gwai3 zuk6	kwai chuhk
nod	v	點頭	dím táu	dim2 tau2	tim thau
node	n	節	jit	zit3	chit
noise[1]	n	嘈吵	chòuh cháau	cou4 caau2	chhouh chaau
noise[2] /make a noise	n	喧鬧聲	hyùn naauh sèng /sìng	hyun4 naau6 seng4 /sing4	hyun naauh seng
noiseful	adj	喧鬧嘅	hyùn naauh ge	hyun4 naau6 ge3	hyun naauh ke
noiseless /silence	adj	無聲	mòuh sèng /sìng	mou4 seng4 /sing4	mouh seng
noisy[1] /bustling	adj	嘈	chòuh	cou4	chhouh
noisy[2]	adj	吵鬧	chòuh laauh /naauh	caau4 laau6 /naau6	chhouh laauh /naauh
nominate	n	提名	tàih mèhng/mìhng	tai4 meng6 /ming6	thaih mehng
non[1] /no/not/un... (coll)	adv	唔	m̀	m4	mh
non[2] /not	adv	非	fèi	fei4	fei
non[3]	adv	在非	joih fèi	zoi6 fei4	choih fei
non aggression[1]	n	唔侵略	m̀ chàm leuhk	m4 cam4 loek6	mh chham leuhk
non aggression[2]	n	不侵略	bāt chàm leuhk	bat1 cam4 loek6	pat chham leuhk
non aggression[3]	n	唔侵犯	m̀ chàm faahn	m4 cam4 faan6	mh chham faahn
non aggression[4]	n	不侵犯	bāt chàm faahn	bat1 cam4 faan6	pat chham faahn
non alcoholic	adj	不含酒類	bāt hàhm jáu leuih	bat1 ham4 zau2 leoi6	pat hahm chau lowih
non co-operation	n	不合作	bāt hahp jok	bat1 hap6 zok3	pat hahp chok
non essential[1]	adj	唔重要	m̀ juhng yiu	m4 zung6 jiu3	mh chuhng yiu
non essential[2]	adj	唔必要	m̀ bit yiu	m4 bit3 jiu3	mh pit yiu
non member	n	非會員	fèi wúi yùhn	fei4 wui2 jyun4	fei wui yuhn
non smoker	n	唔食煙人	m̀ sihk yīn yàhn	m4 sik6 jin1 jan4	mh sehk yin yahn
non smoking area	n	非吸煙區	fèi kāp yīn kèui	fei4 kap1 jin1 keoi4	fei khap yin khoi
non stop /continue	adj	唔停止	m̀ tíhng jí	m4 ting5 zi2	mh thehng chi
non violence	n	非暴力政策	fèi bouh lihk jing chaak	fei4 bou6 lik6 zing3 caak3	fei pouh lehk cheng chhaak
none	adv	毫不	hòuh bāt	hou4 bat1	houh pat
nonexistent	adj	不存在	bāt chyun jòih	bat1 cyun4 zoi6	pat chhyun choih
nonnegotiable	adj	唔可談判解決	m̀ hó tàahm pun gáai kyut	m4 ho2 taam4 pun3 gaai2 kyut3	mh ho thaahm phun kaai khyut
nonoffice hours		非辦公時間	fèi baahn gūng sìh gaan	fei4 baan6 gung1 si4 gaan3	fei paahn kung sih kaan
nonprofit	adj	非牟利	fèi màuh leih	fei4 mau4 lei6	fei mauh leih
nonrefundable[1]	adj	無得退	móuh dāk tèui	mou5 dak1 teoi4	mouh tak thoi
nonrefundable[2]	adj	唔可退	m̀ hó tèui	m4 ho2 teoi4	mh ho thoi
nonsense[1]	n	胡	wùh	wu4	wuh
nonsense[2]	n	胡說	wùh syut	wu4 syut3	wuh syut
nonsense[3]	n	無聊	mòuh lìuh	mou4 liu4	mouh liuh

English	Part	Chinese	Yale	Jyutping	Romanization
nonsense talker	n	無惗嘢	móuh láhm yéh	mou5 lam5 je5	mouh lahm yeh
noodle[1]	n	麵	mihn	mon6	mihn
noodle[2]	n	腩麵	náahm mihn	naam5 min6	naahm mihn
nor[1] /or	conj	有唔	yauh m̀	jau6 m4	yauh mh
nor[2]	conj	唔係…又	m̀ haih…yauh	m4 hai6 jau6	mh haih…yauh
nor[3] /neither	conj	也不	yáh bāt	jaa5 bat1	yah pat
norm /fix rules	n	規範	kwài faahn	kwai4 faan6	khwai faahn
normal[1] (coll) usual	adj	平事	pèhng sìh	peng4 si6	phehng sih
normal[2]	adj	正常嘅	jeng séuhng ge	zeng3 soeng6 ge3	cheng seuhng ke
North	n	北	bàak	baak4	paak
northeast	n	東北	dùng bāk	dung4 bak1	tung pak
northern	adj	北方	bàak fòng	baak4 fonf4	paak fong
northwest	adj	西北	sài bàk	sai4 bak4	sai pak
Norway	n	挪威	no wài	no3 wai4	no wai
nose (coll)	n	鼻哥	beih gō	bei6 go1	peih ko
nose ring	n	鼻環	beih wàahn	bei6 waan4	peih wàahn
not[1] /not yet/have not		未	meih	mei6	meih
not[2] /no /nay	adv	不	bāt	bat1	pat
not[3] /non	adv	唔未	m̀ meih	m4 mei6	mh meih
not acclimatized		水土不服	séui tóu bāt fuhk	seoi2 tou2 bat1 fuk6	swoi thou pat fuhk
not afraid	adj	勇敢嘅	yúhng gám ge	jung5 gam2 ge3	yuhng kam ke
not alike /various	adj	不同的	bāt tung dìk	bat1 tung3 dik4	pat thung dek
not arrive[1]		未嚟	meih làih	mei6 lai4	meih laih
not arrive[2] /not come back		無返嚟	móuh fáan lái	mou5 faa2 lai2	mouh faan lai
not arrived[1] /not come back		冇嚟	móuh lái	mou5 lai2	mouh lai
not arrived[2]	adj	未到囉	meih dou ló	mei6 dou3 lo2	meih tou lo
not arrived yet		未抵達	meih dái daaht	mei6 dai2 daat6	meih tai daaht
not asking		唔會問	m̀ wúih mahn	m4 wooi5 man6	mh wuih mahn
not at all[1]		一啲都冇	yāt di dōu móuh	jat1 di4 dou1 mou5	yat ti tou mouh
not at all[2]		並不	bing bāt	bing3 bat1	peng pat
not at all[2] thanks	adv	謝謝	jèh jèh	ze6 ze6	cheh cheh
not bad[1]		唔錯	m̀ chó	m4 co3	mh chho
not bad[2]		唔壞	m̀ waaih	m4 waai6	mh waaih
not bad[3]		不壞	bāt waaih	bat1 waai6	pat waaih
not bad[4] /so so	adj	算係咁啦	syun haih gám lā	syun3 hai6 gam2 laa1	syun haih kam la
not bad[5] /not evil		唔會壞	m̀ wuih waaih	m4 wooi5 waai6	mh wuih waaih
not balance /unbalance	v	使唔平衡	sái m̀ pèhng hang	sai2 m4 peng6 hang3	sai mh phehng hang
not be in		不在	bāt joih	bat1 zoi6	pat choih
not busy /free time /not working	adj	休閒	yàu hàahn	jau1 haan4	yau haahn
not came out[1] /late coming		未出囉	meih chēut ló	mei6 ceot1 lo2	meih chhot lo
not came out[2] busy		唔出囉	m̀ chēut ló	m4 ceot1 lo2	mh chhot lo

not carrying weapon /radicalism/unarmed	n/adj	激進主義	gihk jeun jyú yih	gik1 zeon3 zyu2 ji6	kehk cheun chyu yih
not certain		唔一定	m̀ yāt dehng	m4 jat1 deng6	mh yat tehng
not crying	adj	不哭	bāt hùk	bat1 huk4	pat huk
not decay /not rotten		唔會爛	m̀ wúih laahn	m4 wooi5 laan6	mh wuih laahn
not delicious		唔好食	m̀ hóu sihk	m4 hou2 sik6	mh hou sehk
not die /survived	v	無死到	móuh séi dou	mou5 sei2 dou3	mouh sei tou
not easy[1]	adj	唔用易	m̀ yuhng yih	m4 jung6 ji6	mh yuhng yih
not easy[2]	adj	不用易	bāt yuhng yih	bat1 jung6 ji6	pat yuhng yih
not enough[1]/wanting /shortage of	adj	缺少	kyut síu	kyut3 siu2	khyut siu
not enough[2]	adj	不足夠	bāt jūk gau	bat1 zuk1 gau3	pat chuk kau
not feeling well /unwell feeling	adj	唔係幾精神	m̀ haih géi jèng sàhn	m4 hai6 gei2 zeng4 san4	mh haih kei cheng sahn
not find /got lost /not found/missed/to lose	v	失咗	sàt jó	sat4 zo2	sat cho
not for sale		非賣品	fèi maaih bán	fei4 maai6 ban2	fei maaih pan
not genuine[1] (coll)unreal	adj	假嘅	gá ge	gaa2 ge3	ka ke
not genuine[2]/pseudo	adj	冒充	mouh chùng	mou6 cung4	mouh chhung
not good		不好	bāt hóu	bat1 hou2	pat hou
not happy /heart beat	n	心病	sàm behng	sam4 beng6	sam pehng
not helpful		冇幫助	móuh bòng joh	mou5 bong4 zo6	mouh pong choh
not here		唔喺度	m̀ hái dou	m4/ng4 dou3	mh hai tou
not hurry /not so quick/ not so fast		無咁快	móuh gam faai	mou5 gam3 faai3	mouh kam faai
not hurry go		無咁快走	móuh gam faai jáu	mou5 gam3 faai3 zau2	mouh kam faai chau
not important /it's nothing /never mind/have nothing to do/doesn't matter	v	無事	mòuh sih	mou5 si6	mouh sih
not in used		唔慣	m̀ gwaan	m4/ng4 gwaan3	mh kwaan
not individual word		唔係單個的字	m̀ haih dāan go dìkjih	m4 hai6 daan1 go3 dik4 zi6	mh haih taan ko chih
not interested		冇興趣	móuh hing cheui	mou5 hing3 ceoi3	móuh hing chhoi
not interested in sex /asexual	adj	性冷淡	sing láahng daahm	sing3 laang5 daam6	seng laahng taahm
not know[1]		唔知道	m̀ jì douh	m4 zi4 dou6	mh chi touh
not know[2]		不知道	bāt jì douh	bat1 zi4 dou6	pat chi touh
not listen[1]		唔聽喎	m̀ tèng wóh	m4 teng4 wo5	mh theng woh
not listen[2]		未聽喎	meih tèng wóh	mei6 teng4 wo5	meih theng woh
not long /soon	adj	唔久	m̀ gáu	m4 gau2	mh kau
not me! /am not!	adv	唔係我!	m̀ haih ngóh!	m4 hai6 ngo5!	mh haih ngoh!
not much		無乜	móuh māt	mou5 mat1	mouh mat
not objection		無異議	mòuh yih yi	mou6 ji6 ji3	mouh yih yi
not often[1] /seldom	adv	好少	hóu síu	hou2 siu2	hou siu
not often[2] /seldom	adv	很少	hān sīu	han1 siu1	han siu
not only[1]		不但	bāt daahn	bat1 daan6	pat taahn
not only[2]		唔止	m̀ jí	m4 zi2	mh chi

English		Chinese	Romanization 1	Jyutping	Romanization 2
not paid /overdue /unpaid/pay not yet	adj	未付	meih fuh	mei6 fu6	meih fuh
not polite		失禮	sāt láih	sat1 lai5	sat laih
not preparation /unready	adj	未準備	meih jéun beih	mei6 zeon2 bei6	meih cheun peih
not pretty /unattractive	adj	唔靚	m̀ leng	m4 leng3	mh leng
not quite good		唔係幾好	m̀ haih géi hóu	m4 hai6 gei2 hou2	mh haih kei hou
not really		並非	bing fèi	bing3 fei4	peng fei
not recognised /i don't know/not understood/ can't recognized	v	唔清楚	m̀ chēng chó	m4 ceng1 co2	mh chheng chho
not remember	v	唔記得添	m̀ gei dāk tīm	m4 gei3 dak1 tim1	mh kei tak thim
not repaired		無維修	móuh wàih sàu	mou5 wai4 sau4	mouh waih sau
not return		未番來	meih fàan làih	meih fàan làih	meih faan laih
not seen[1] /didn't see	n	唔見喎	m̀ gin wóh	m4 gin3 wo5	mh kin woh
not seen[2]		未見喎	meih gin wóh	mei6 gin3 wo5	meih kin woh
not seen[3]		未睇喎	meih tái wóh	mei6 tai2 wo5	meih thai woh
not serious[1]		唔緊要啦	m̀ gán yiu lā	m4 gan2 jiu3 laa1	mh kan yiu lah
not serious[2]		唔緊要囉	m̀ gán yiu lòh	m4 gan2 jiu3 lo4	mh kan yiu loh
not spend /save	v	慳	hāan	haan1	haan
not taken		冇攞到	móuh ló dou	mou5 lo2 dou3	mouh lo dou
not taken yet		未攞	meih ló	mei6 lo2	meih lo
not tasted		全冇味	chyùhn móuh meih	chuen4 mou5 mei6	chhyuhn mouh meih
not tight pant /slack /loose pant	adj	鬆長褲	sùng cheung fú	sung4 coeng4 fu2	sung chheung fu
not too		唔係太	m̀ haih taai	m4 hai6 taai3	mh haih thaai
not too bad	adj	過得去	gwo dāk heui	gwo3 dak1 heoi3	kwo tak hoi
not trained /untrained	adj	未受訓練	meih sauh fan lìhn	mei6 sau6 fan3 lin6	meih sauh fan lihn
not use well /waste	v	浪費	lohng fai	long6 fai3	lohng fai
not very		唔係幾	m̀ haih géi	m4 hai6 gei2	mh haih kei
not very good at all!		唔係幾好呀!	m̀ haih gei hóu ā	m4 hai6 gei3 hou2 aa1	mh haih kei hou aa
not willing to do /loath/ reluctant	adj	唔捨得	m̀ sé dāk	m4 se2 dak1	mh se tak
not wish /unwilled /unintentionally	adj	非故意地	fèi gu yi deih	fei4 gu3 ji3 dei6	fei ku yi teih
not yet[1]		未到	meih dou	mei6 dou3	meih tou
not yet[2]		未經	meih gīng	mei6 ging1	meih keng
not yet[3]		有待	yáuh doih	jau5 doi6	yauh toih
not yet?[4]		未呀?	meih àa /aa?	mei6 aa4 /aa3?	meih aa?
not yet eaten /never eaten/not eaten yet/ haven't eaten yet	adj	未食個	meih sihk gwo	mei6 sik6 gwo3	meih sehk kwo
not yet to testify /unproved/uncertified	adj	尚未證實	seuhng meih jing saht	soeng6 mei6 zing3 sat6	seuhng meih cheng saht
notable[1] /marked	adj	顯著	hín jyu	hin2 zyu	hin chyu
notable[2] /noted		見稱	gin chìng	gin3 cing4	kin chheng
notable[3] /noted		聞名	màhn mèhng	man4 meng4	mahn mehng

note /write down	n	筆記	bāt gei	bat1 gei3	pat kei
note book[1]	n	簿	bóu	bou2	pou
note book[2]	n	筆記簿	bāt gei bóu	bat1 gei3 bou2	pat kei pou
note book[3]	n	筆記本	bāt gei bún	bat1 gei3 bun2	pat kei pun
noted[1]	adj	知名	jì mèhng /mìhng	zi4 meng4 /ming4	chi mehng
noted[2]	adj	記入	gei yahp	gei3 jap6	kei yahp
noted[3] /to record	n	記	gei	gei3	kei
nothing /questionless /no question	pron	無疑	móuh yì	mou5 ji4	mouh yi
notice[1]	v	通告於	tùng gou yù	tung4 gou3 jyu4	thung kou yu
notice[2]	v	通知書	tūng jī syù	tung1 zi1 syu4	thung chi syu
notice board[1] /bulletin	n	報告板	bou gou báan	bou3 gou3 baan2	pou kou paan
notice board[2]	n	佈告牌	bou gou pàaih	bou3 gou3 paai6	pou kou phaaih
noticed	v	通告咗	tùng gou jó	tung4 gou3 zo2	thung kou cho
notification /message /information	n	通知	tùng jì	tung4 zi4	thung chi
notified	v	報告咗	bou gou jó	bou3 gou3 zo2	pou kou cho
notify	v	傳呼	chyùhn fù	cyun4 fu4	chhyuhn fu
noun	n	名詞	mèhng /mìhng chìh	meng4 /ming4 ci4	mehng chhih
nourishing	adj	養育	yéuhng yuhk	joeng5 juk6	yeuhng yuhk
nourishment /nutrition	n	營養	yìhng yéuhng	jing4 joeng5	yehng yeuhng
novel /a new	adj	新奇	sān kēi	san1 kei1	san khei
novelist	n	小說家	síu syut gā	siu2 syut3 gaa1	siu syut ka
November	n	十一月	sàhp yāt yùht	sap6 jat1 jyut6	sahp yat yuht
November 9th	n	十一月九日	sàhp yàt yùht gāu yàht	sap6 jat1 jyut6 gaau1 jat6	sahp yat yuht kau yaht
novice /learner	n	新手	sàn sáu	san4 sau2	san sau
now[1] (coll) /present/this time	prep	而家	yìh gā	ji4 gaa1	yih ka
now[2] /at present/at this time	adv	依家	yìh gā	ji4 gaa1	yih ka
now[3]	conj	既然	gei yìhn	gei3 jin4	kei yìhn
now[4] /due	conj	由於	yàuh yù	jau4 jyu4	yauh yu
now[5] /at once/right now /forthwith	adv	即刻	jīk hāak	zik1 haak1	chek haak
now[6]	adv	此時	chí sìh	ci2 si4	chhi sih
now[7] (wr) /just now/at present	adv	現在	yihn joih	jin6 zoi6	yihn choih
now[8] /at this moment	adv	此時此刻	chí sìh chí hāak	ci2 si4 ci2 haak1	chhi sih chhi haak
now evaluate		即時評估	jīk sìh pìhng gū	zik1 si4 ping4 gu1	chek sih phehng ku
now go to hell!		正仆街	jeng puk gāai	zeng3 puk3 gaai1	cheng phuk kaai
now valuate		即時評價	jīk sìh pìhng gá	zik1 si4 ping4 ga2	chek sih phehng ka
nowhere[1]	adv	甚麼地方都沒有	sahm mò deih fòng dōu muht yáuh	sam6 mo4 dei6 fong4 dou1 mut6 jau5	sahm mo teih fong tou muht yauh
nowhere[2]	adv	任何地方都不	yahm hòh deih fòng dòu bāt	jam4 ho4 dei6 fong4 dou4 bat1	yahm hoh teih fong tou pat
nozzle	n	管嘴	gún jéui	gun2 zeoi2	kun choi

nub	n	結節	git jit	git3 zit3	kit jit
nuclear	n	核子嘅	haht jí ge	hat6 zi2 ge3	haht chi ke
nucleus[1]	n	核	haht	hat6	haht
nucleus[2]	n	細胞核	sai bāau haht	sai3 baau1 hat6	sai paau haht
nudist /naked person	n	裸體者	ló tái jé	lo2 tai2 ze2	lo thai che
nuisance /annoying	n	討厭	tóu yim	tou2 jim3	thou yim
number	n	號數	houh sou	hou6 sou3	houh sou
number of people	v	人數	yàhn sou	jan4 sou3	yahn sou
number plate	n	數字牌	sou jih pàaih	sou3 zi6 paai4	sou chih phaaih
Nun[1] /Lama (Buddhist)	n	師姑	sī gū	si1 gu1	si ku
Nun[2] /Lama (Buddhist religious)	n	尼姑	nèih gū	nei4 gu1	neih ku
Nun[3] (Buddhist)	n	老尼	lóuh nèih	lou5 nei4	louh neih
Nun[4] (Catholic)	n	修女	sau leui /neui	sau3 leoi3 /neoi3	sau lowi /nowi
nurse /nursing	n	看護	hōn wuh	hon1 wu6	hon wuh
nursery blow 3 years baby	n	托兒所	tok yìh só	tok3 ji4 so2	thok yih so
nursing home[1] for aged	n	護老院	wuh lóuh yún	wu6 lou5 jyun2	wuh louh yun
nursing home[2] for sicked	n	療養院	lìuh yéuhng yún	liu4 joeng5 jyun2	liuh yeuhng yun
nut[1] /bark/skin of fruit	n	堅果	gīn gwó	gin1 gwo2	kin kwo
nut[2] of fruits /flesh/kernel	n/v	果仁	gwó yàhn	gwo2 jan4	kwo yahn
nut of the screw	n	絲母	sì móuh	si4 mou5	si mouh
nutritious	adj	營養	yìhng yéuhng	jing4 joeng5	yehng yeuhng
nylon (de)	n	尼龍	nèih lùhng	nei4 lung4	neih luhng
nylon socks	n	絲襪	sī maht	si1 mat6	si maht
nymphc /goddess	n	女神	léuih sàhn	leoi5 san4	lowih sahn

O.T.[1] /overtime	n	加班	gà bàan	gaa4 baan4	ka paan
O.T.[2] /overtime	n	加班時間	gà bàan sìh gaan	gaa4 baan4 si4 gaan3	ka paan sih kaan
o'clock	adv	點	dím	dim2	tim
oar /paddle	n	槳	jéung	zoeng2	cheung
oasis (a tree in the desert area)	n	綠洲	luhk jāu	luk6 zai1	luhk chau
oat	n	燕麥	yin mahk	jin3 mak6	yin mahk
oath	n	誓	saih	sai6	saih
oaths[1] /oathed	n	誓約	saih yeuk	sai6 joek3	saih yeuk
oaths[2] (take/received oath)	n	宣誓	syùn saih	syun4 sai6	syun saih
oaths[3] /swear (make oaths)	n/v	發誓	faat saih	faat3 sai6	faat saih
oatmeal[1] /porridge	n	麥皮	mahk pèih	mak3 pei4	mahk pheih
oatmeal[2]	n	燕麥粉	yin mahk fán	jin3 mak6 fan2	yin mahk fan
obedient[1] /well behaved of child	adj	乖	gwàai	gwaai4	kwaai
obedient[2] (for adult)	adj	聽話	tèng wah	teng4 waa6	theng wah
obedient[3] /filial/filial piety (for parents)	adj/	孝順	haau seuhn	haau3 seon6	haau seuhn
obedient[4] (for superior)	adj	順從	seuhn chùhng	seon6 cung4	swohn chhuhng
obey[1]	v	聽	tèng	teng4	theng
obey[2]	v	遵從	jèun chùhng	zeon4 cung4	cheun chhuhng
obey[3] an order /comply /submit	v	使服從	sai fuhk chùhng	sai3 fuk6 sung4	sai fuhk chhohng
object[1] /things	n	件	gin	gin3	kin
object[2] /things	n	物體	maht tái	mat6 tai2	maht thai
object[3] against/protest /oppose	v	反對	fáan deui	faan2 deoi3	faan toei
objectionable	adj	會引起反對	wuih yáhn héi fáan deui	wui6 jan5 hei2 faan2 deoi3	wuih yahn hei faan toei
objective only facts	adj	客觀	haak gùn	haak3 gun4	haak kun
objector /enemy	n	反對者	fáan deui jé	faan2 deoi3 ze2	faan toei che
obligation[1] /liability	n	義務	yih mouh	ji6 mou6	yih mouh
obligation[2] /amount due/debt/liability	n	債務	jaai mouh	zaai3 mou6	chaai mouh
obligatory	adj	必須嘅	bìt sèui ge	bit4 seoi4 ge3	pit swoi ke
obliged	adj	感謝	gám jeh	gam2 ze6	kam cheh
oblique /slanting/slope	adj	斜	che	ce3	chhe
oboe /clarinet musical instrument	n	雙簧管	sèung wòhng gún	soeng4 wong4 gun2	seung wohng kun
obscene language[1]		穢語	wai yúh	wai3 jyu5	wai yuh
obscene language[2]		粗言穢語	chòu yìhn wai yúh	cou4 jin4 wai3 jyu5	chhou yihn wai yuh
obscure	adj	暗的	ám /ngam dìk	am2 /ngam3 dik4	am /ngam tik
observable	adj	可測	hó chàk	ho2 caak4	ho chhak
observation /observe	n	觀察	gùn chaat	gun4 caat3	kun chhaat
observatory[1]	n	天文台	tìn màhn tòih	tin4 man4 toi4	thin mahn thoih
observatory[2]	n	天文臺	tìn man tòih	tin4 man3 toi4	thin man thoih
observe[1] to obey rules	v	遵守	jèun sáu	zeon4 sau2	cheun sau

observe[2]	v	觀察到	gùn chaat dou	gun4 caat3 dou3	kun chhaat tou
observer	n	觀察員	gùn chaat yùhn	gun4 caat3 jyun4	kun chhaat yuhn
obstacle /barrier/snag	n	障礙/碍	jeung ngoih	zoeng3 ngoi6	cheung ngoih
obstetrical patient	n	產科病人	cháan fò bèhng yàhn	caan2 fo4 beng6 jan4	chhaan fo pehng yahn
obstinacy	n	執拗	jāp áau /ngaau	zap1 aau2 /ngaau3	chap aau /ngaau
obstinate /persistent /stiff-necked/stubborn /untoward	adj	倔強	gwaht kéuhng	gwat6 koeng5	kwaat kheuhng
obstruct[1]		擋住	dong jyuh	dong3 zyu6	tong chyuh
obstruct[2]	v	阻住	jó jyuh	zo2 zyu6	cho chyuh
obstruct[3]	v	阻撓	jó nàauh	zo2 naau4	cho naauh
obstruct[4] to block blow /block blow	v	擋	dong	dong3	tong
obstruct[5]	v	置障	ji jeung	zi3 zoeng3	chi cheung
obtain /available/receive /attain/get/gain/deserve	v	得到	dāk dóu	dak1 dou2	tak tou
obvious[1]	adj	明顯	mìhng hín	ming4 hin2	mehng hin
obvious[2] /obviously	adj	顯然	hín yin	hin2 jin3	hin yin
obviously	adv	明明	mìhng mìhng	ming4 ming4	mehng mehng
obviously know		明知	mìhng jì	ming4 zi4	mehng chi
opportunity /good luck/ chance/occasion/fortunate	n	時機	sìh gèi	si4 gei4	sih kei
occasion[1] /situation	n	場合	chèuhng hahp	coeng4 hap6	chheuhng hahp
occasion[2] (happy)	n	喜事	héi sih	hei2 si6	hei sih
occasionally[1] /time to time/sometimes	adv	時不時	sìh bāt sìh	si4 bat1 si4	sih pat sih
occasionally[2] /on occasion	adv	偶爾	ngáuh yíh	ngau5 ji5	ngauh yih
occupant	n	佔有人	jim yáuh yàhn	zim3 jau5 jan4	chim yauh yahn
occupation /business	n	業	yihp	jip6	yihp
occupied[1] /busy	adv	忙	mòhng	mong6	mohng
occupied[2]	adj	已佔有的	yíh jim yáuh dīk	ji5 zim3 jau5 dik1	yih chim yauh tik
occupier /holder	n	佔有者	jim yáuh je	zim3 jau5 ze2	chim yauh che
occupies	v	佔領	jim léhng /líhng	zim3 leng5 /ling5	chim lehng
occupy[1]	v	佔	jim	zim3	chim
occupy[2]	v	佔有	jim yáuh	zim3 jau5	chim yauh
occurrence[1] /record of incident	n	目誌	muhk ji	muk6 zi3	muhk chi
occurrence[2] /event /incident/happening	n	事件	sìh gìhn	si6 gin6	sih kihn
occurrence book[1]	n	流水簿	làuh séui bouh	lau4 seoi2 bou6	lauh swoi pouh
occurrence-book[2] /log book	n	日誌簿	yaht ji bouh	jat6 zi3 nou6	yaht chi pouh
occurrence-book[3]	n	事件簿	sìh gìhn bouh	si6 gin6 bou6	sih kihn pouh
ocean[1]	n	洋	yèuhng	joeng4	yeuhng
ocean[2]	n	海洋	hói yèuhng	hoi2 joeng4	hoi yeuhng
ocean[3]	n	大海	daaih hói	daai6 hoi2	taaih hoi

octo "8"	pref	表示 "八"	bíu sih "baat"	biu2 si6 "baat3"	piu sih "paat"
October	n	十月	sàhp yùht	sap6 jyut6	sahp yuht
October 30th	n	十月三十日	sàhp yùht sàam sàhp yàht	sap6 jyut4 saam4 sap6 jat6	sahp yuht saam sahp yaht
octopus	n	八爪魚	baat jáau yùh	baat3 zaau2 jyu4	paat chaau yuh
octopus card	n	八達通卡	baat daaht tùhng kāat	baat3 daat6 tung4 kaat1	paat taaht thuhng khaat
octopus dried	n	章魚	jèung yú	zoeng4 jyu2	cheung yu
odd[1]	adj	奇	kèih	kei4	kheih
odd[2]/strange/unusual /uneven	adj	怪	gwaai	gwaai3	kwaai
odd[3] /uneven/strange /unusual	adj	怪異	gwaai yih	gwaai3 ji6	kwaai yih
odd number /singular	adj	單數	dāan sou	daan1 sou3	taan san
odorous /perfume /fragrant	adj	芬芳	fān fòng	fan1 fong4	fan fong
of[1] /'s/ is (coll) noun	prep	嘅	ge	ge3	ke
of[2] /'s(wr) plural noun, aim, clear	prep	的 /D	dīk /dìk/de/ dì/D	dik1 /dik4 /de3 /di4 /d3	tik / te/ ti /tek
of[3] /him/her/it	prep	之	jī	zi1	chi
of course[1] /surely	adv	梗係	gáng haih	gang2 hai6	kang haih
of course[2]	adv	梗係啦	gáng haih lā	gang2 hai6 laa1	kang haih la
of course[3]	adv	當然	dòng yìhn	dong4 jin4	tong yihn
off[1] (shut off)	adj	關掉	gwāan deuh	gwaan4 deu6	kwaan teuh
off[2] /depart /went	adj	離開	lèih hòi	lei4 hoi4	leih hoi
off[3] /depart /went	adj	離距	leih kéuih	lei4 keoi5	leih khoih
off[4] (already) /turned off/ log off/log out/shut down door/tv/radio/tap/computing etc	adj	閂咗	sàan jó	saan4 zo2	saan cho
off duty	adj	走開	jáu hòi	zau2 hoi4	chau hoi
offend[1]	v	得罪	dāk jeuih	dak1 zeoi6	tak choih
offend[2]	v	觸犯	jùk faahn	zuk4 faan6	chuk faahn
offend[3] /provoke	v	衝撞	chùng johng	cung4 zong6	chhung chohng
offend[4]	v	冒犯	mouh faahn	mou6 faan6	mouh faahn
offend[5] /illegal	v	違法	wai faat	wai3 faat3	wai faat
offended /violated	v	犯嘅	faahn ge	faan6 ge3	faahn ke
offender[1]	n	違者	wai jé	wai3 ze2	wai che
offender[2] /prisoner /perpetrator	n	犯人	faahn yàhn	faan6 jan4	faahn yahn
offensive[1]	adj	採取攻勢	chói chéui gùng sai	coi2 ceoi2 gung4 sai3	chhoi chheui kung sai
offensive[2]	adj	討厭嘅	tóu yim ge	tou2 jim3 ge3	thou yim ke
offensive[3] try to do sex	adj	有攻擊性	yáuh gùng gīk seng	jau5 gung4 gik1 seng3	yauh kung kek seng
offensive angry		專講惡	jyūn góng ok /ngok	juen1 gong2 ok3 /ngok3	chyun kong ok /ngok
offer	v	獻	hin	hin3	hin
offer money	v	出錢	chēut chín	ceot1 cin2	chhot chhin
offering	n	提供	tàih gùng	tai4 gung4	thaih kung
office[1]	n	寫字樓	sé jih làuh	se2 zi6 lau4	se chih lauh

office[2]	n	辦公室	baahn gūng sāt	baan6 gung1 sat1	paahn kung sat
office assistant	n	辦公室助理	baahn gūng sāt joh léih	baan6 gung1 sat1 zo6 lei5	paahn kung sat choh leih
office block	n	辦公室大樓	baahn gūng sāt daaih láu	baan6 gung1 sat1 daai6 lau2	paahn kung sat taaih lau
office boy	n	後生	hauh sāang	hau6 saang1	hauh saang
office hours	n	辦公時間	baahn gūng sìh gaan	baan6 gung3 si4 gaan3	paahn kung sih kaan
official staff /public staff/government staff/ officer of government	n	官員	gùn yùhn	gun4 jyun4	kun yuhn
officer of government	n	差	chāai	caai1	chhaai
official[1]/of government /government body/public service	n	官	gùn	gun4	kun
official[2]	adj	官方的	gùn fòng dìk	gun4 fong4 dik4	kun fong tek
officially	adv	正式地	jeng sīk deih	zeng3 sik1 dei6	cheng sek teih
officiate /witness at wedding	n	證婚	jing fān	zing3 fan1	cheng fan
offset /reduce	v	抵銷	dái sìu	dai2 siu4	tai siu
offside of car	n	車外側	chè òih jàk	ce4 oi6/ngoi6 zak4	chhe oih chak
often[1] /constantly/again and again/ frequently/time and	adv	時常	sìh sèuhng	si4 soeng4	sih sèuhng
often[2]	adv	很多時	hān dò sìh	han1 do4 si4	han to sih
oh![1]	interj	唉呀!	āi /āai ah	ai1 /aai1 a6	ai /aai ah
oh![2]	interj	哦!/啊!/呀!	óh! /àh! /ah!	o5 /a4 /a6	oh! /ah! /ah!
oh! air conditioned		有冷氣嗎!	yáuh láahng hei mā!	jau5 laang5 hei3 maa1!	yauh laahng hei ma!
oh aye	interj	啊是嘅	àh sih ge	a4 si6 ge3	ah sih ke
oh god![1] /oh my god!	interj	死咯	séi lo!	sei2 lo3	sei lo!
oh god![2]	interj	弊啦	baih lo!	bai6 lo3	paih lo!
ohm	n	歐姆	àu móuh	au1 mou5	au mouh
oil	n	油	yàuh	jau4	yauh
oil and gas	n	石油氣	sehk yàuh hei	sel6 jau4 hei3	sehk yauh hei
oil bottle	n	油樽	yàuh jēun	jau4 zeon1	yauh cheun
oil man	n	石油工人	sehk yàuh gùng yàhn	sel6 jau4 gung4 jan4	sehk yauh kung yahn
oily	adj	油膩	yàuh leih	jau4 lei6/nei6	yauh leih
ointment[1]	n	藥膏	yeuhk gōu	joek6 gou1	yeuhk kou
ointment[2]	n	軟膏	yúhn gōu	jyun5 gou1	yuhn kou
okay!	adv	好喇	hóu lā!	hou2 laa1	hou la!
okay okay	adv	可以到	hó yih dou	ho2 ji6 dou3	ho yih tou
okay or not okay? /yes or not?	exlm	好唔好?	hóu m̀ hóu?	hou2 m4 hou2?	hou mh hou?
old	adj	故	gu	gu3	ku
old age[1] /old man	n	老	lóuh	lou5	louh
old age[2]	n	晚年	máahn lìhn /nìhn	maan5 lin4 /nin4	maahn lihn /nihn
old day	adj	昔日	sīk yaht	sik1 jat6	sek yaht
old fashion[1] /old style	adj	古老	gú lóuh	gu2 lou5	ku louh

English	POS	Chinese	Yale	Jyutping	Romanization
old fashion[2]	adj	舊欵	gauh fún	gau6 fun2	kauh fun
old fashioned	adj	古板嘅	gú báan ge	gu2 baan2 ge3	ku paan ke
old man[1]	n	伯爺公	baak yē gūng	baak3 je1 gung1	paak ye kung
old man[2] /old people	n	老人	lóuh yàhn	lou5 jan4	louh yahn
old man-woman /old person (polite way)	n	老人家	lóuh yàhn gā	lou5 jan4 gaa1	louh yahn ka
old style	adj	舊式	gauh sīk	gau6 sik	kauh sek
old testament	n	舊約	Gauh yeuk	gau6 joek3	Kauh yeuk
old thing /old object	n	舊物	gauh maht	gau6 mat6	kauh maht
old torn cloth	adj	衣衫蓝褸	yī sàam làahm láuh	ji1 saam4 laam4 lau5	yi saam laahm lauh
old woman	n	伯爺婆	baak yē pó	baak3 je1 po2	paak ye pho
oldest	n	大	daaih	daai6	taaih
olive (tree)	n	橄欖	gaam láahm	gaam3 laam5	kaam laahm
omega		希臘文的	hèi laahp màhn ge	hei4 laap6 man4 ge3	hei laahp mahn ke
	n	最後一個字母	jeui hauh yāt go jih móuh	zeoi3 hau6 yat1 zi6 mou5	choi hauh yat ko chih mouh
omen	n	前兆	chìhn siuh	cin4 siu6	chhihn siuh
omission	n	遺漏	wàih làuh	wai4 lau6	waih lauh
omit /to miss	v	遺漏	wàih làuh	wai4 lau6	waih lauh
on /top/on top	prep/n	上	séuhng	soeng5	seuhng
on day duty		值日	jihk yaht	zik6 jat6	chehk yaht
on duty		執勤	jàp kàhn	zap4 kan4	chap khahn
on every occasion		每逢	múih fùhng	mui5 fung4	muih fuhng
on hand		手上	sáu séuhng	sau2 soeng5	sau seuhng
on infront	adv	喺前便	hái chìhn bihn	hai2 cin4 bin6	hai chhihn pihn
on line towards		網上行	móhng séuhng hàahng	mong5 soeng5 haang4	mohng seuhng haahng
on night duty		值夜	jihk yé	zik6 je6	chehk ye
on one hand /one sided /onehand/unilateral	n	單方面	dàan fòng mihn	daan4 fong4 min6	taan fong mihn
on probation[1] /trial /probationary/test	n	試用	si yuhng	si3 jung6	si yuhng
on probation[2]		在試用期	joih si yuhng kèih	zoi6 si3 jung6 kei4	choih si yuhng kheih
on sale		廉售中	lìhm sauh jùng	lim4 sau6 zung4	lihm sauh chung
on the body		身上	sàn seuhng	san4 soeng6	san seuhng
on the crowd		於眾	yū jung	jyu1 zung3	yu chung
on the left /left side /left hand side		左便	jó bihn	zo2 bin6	cho pihn
on the other hand /another aspect/other hand		另一方面	lihng yāt fòng mihn	ling6 jat1 fong4 min6	lehng yat fong mihn
on the public area		於眾	yū jung	jyu1 zung3	yu chung
on the road /on the way		路上	louh sèuhng	lou6 soeng6	louh seuhng
on the sly	adj	暗中	am /ngam jùng	am3 /ngam3 zung4	am /ngam chung
on the top[1] /top/on top of	n	上便	séuhng bihn	soeng6 bin6	seuhng pihn
on the top[2]		喺便	hái bihn	hai2 bin6	hai pihn
on the way (...ing)		返緊	fáan gán	faan2 gan2	faan kan
on top of /upper/upstairs	n	上面	séuhng mìhn	soeng5 min4	seuhng mihn

English		Chinese	Yale	Jyutping	Pinyin-style
on tow		被拖	bèih tò	bei6 to4	peih tho
on vacation		度假	douh ga	dou6 ga3	touh ka
once /once times/one times	adv	一次	yāt chi	jat1 ci3	yat chhi
once again[1] /one more time	n	再次	joi chi	zoi3 ci3	choi chi
once again[2] /again /oncemore/one more time		再一次	joi yāt chi	zoi3 jat1 ci3	choi yat chhi
once or twice		幾次	géi chi	gei2 chi	kei chhi
oncoming		迎面而來	ying mìhn yi loi	jing3 min6 ji4 loi3	yeng mihn yi loi
one after another		一個一個噉	yāt go yāt go gám	jat1 go3 jat1 go3 gam2	yat ko yat ko kam
one by one[1]		逐個	juhk go	zuk6 go3	chuhk ko
one by one[2]		一個個	yāt go go	jat1 go3 go3	yat ko ko
one family /housemate	n	同屋	tùhng ùk /ngùk	tung4 uk4 /nguk4	thuhng uk /nguk
one hour[1]	n	一個鐘	yāt gó jùng	jat1 go2 zung4	yat ko chung
one hour[2]	n	一小時	yāt sīu si	jat1 siu1 si3	yat siu si
one hundred forty eight	n	一百四十八	yāt báak séi sahp báat	jat1 baak2 sei2 sap6 baat2	yat paak sei sahp paat
one minute	n	一分鐘	yāt fàn jùng	jat1 fan4 zung4	yat fan chung
one o'clock[1]	n	一點鐘	yāt dím jùng	jat1 dim2 zung4	yat tim chung
one o'clock[2]	n	一時正	yāt si jéng	jat1 si3 zeng2	yat si cheng
one room	n	一間	yāt gaan	jat1 gaan3	yat kaan
one's own /oneself	pron	自身嘅	jih sàn ge	zi6 san4 ge3	chih san ke
one set meal		餐會着	chāan wuih jeuk	chaan1 wooi6 jeuk3	chaan wuih cheuk
one side[1] /side	n	側	jāk	zak1	chak
one side[2]	n	一邊	yāt bīn	jat1 bin1	yat pin
one side[3]	n	單方	dāan fong	daan1 fong3	taan fong
one sided	n	片面	pin mihn	pin3 min6	phin mihn
one tenth	n	十分之一	saap fahn jì yāt	sap3 fan6 zip4 jat1	saap fahn chi yat
one type /a kind	n	一種	yāt júng	jat1 zung2	yat chung
one way		單向	dàan heung	daan4 hoeng3	taan heung
one way ticket	n	單程	dāan chìhng	daan1 cing4	taan chhehng
one way or another		以某種方法	yíh máuh júng fōng faat	ji5 mau5 zung2 fong1 faat3	yih mauh chung fong faat
onehand /one-sided	n	片面	pin mihn	pin3 min6	phin mihn
oneself[1] /self	n/pron	己	géi	gei2	kei
oneself[2] /self	n/pron	自己	jih géi	zi6 gei2	chih kei
oneself[3] /personally	pron	親身	chàn sàn	can4 san4	chhan san
onion[1]	n	洋蔥	yèuhng chūng	joeng4 cung1	yeuhng chhung
onion[2] (red colored)	n	紅蔥	hùhng chūng	hung4 cung1	huhng chhung
onion[3] (orange colored)	n	洋蔥	yèuhng chūng	joeng4 cung1	yeuhng chhung
online[4] (by computer)	adj	網上	móhng séuhng	mong5 soeng5	mohng seuhng
only[1] /final particle/that's all	interj	啫	jē	ze1	che
only[2] /only have	adv	只有	jí yáuh	zi2 jau5	chi yauh
only just /right now	adv	暗暗	āam āam, ngāam ngāam	aam1 aam1, ngaam1 ngaam1	aam aam, ngaam ngaam

English		Chinese	Yale	Jyutping	Other
only one /so long as /if only	adv	只要	jí yiu	zi2 jiu3	chi yiu
only that	adv	要不是	yiu bāt sih	jiu3 bat3 si6	yiu pat sih
only three persons		三幾個	sàam géi go	saam1 gei2 goh3	saam kei koh
onto /on above/on the	prep	到...之上	dou... jī séuhng	dou3... zi1 soeng5	tou... chi seuhng
oolong tea	n	烏龍茶	wù lùhng chàh	wu4 lung4 caa4	wu luhng chhah
ooze[1] /soft mud	n	軟泥	yúhn làih /nàih	jyun5 lai4 /nai4	yuhn laih /naih
ooze[2] /seep/leak water	v	滲出	sam chēut	sam3 ceot1	sam chhot
opal	n	蛋白石	dāan baahk sehk	daan1 baak6 sek6	dāan paahk sehk
open[1] /unlock/switch on /turn on	adj	開	hòi	hoi4	hoi
open[2] /switch on/turn on /unbutton/undo/unfold/ unpack/unwrap	adj	打開	dá hòi	daa2 hoi4	ta hoi
open[3] /rip/split/tear open	adj	拆	chaak	caak3	chhaak
open[4] /unwrap/unpack	adj	拆開	chaak hòi	caak6 hoi4	chhaak hoi
open an account		開戶口	hòi wuh háu	hoi4 wu6 hau2	hoi wuh hau
open business[1] first day	adj	開業	hòi yihp	hoi4 jip6	hoi yihp
open business[2] first day		開幕	hòi mohk	hoi4 mok6	hoi mohk
open door[1]	adj	開門	hòi mùhn	hoi4 mun4	hoi muhn
open door[2] /pull open	adj	拉開	làai hòi	laai4 hoi4	laai hoi
open door[3]	adj	門戶開放	mùhn wuh hòi fong	mun4 wu6 hoi4 fong3	muhn wuh hoi fong
open eye	adj	開眼	hòi ngáahn	hoi4 ngaan5	hoi ngaahn
open fire[1] /shoot by gun	v	開槍	hòi chēung	hoi4 coeng1	hoi chēung
open fire[2]		開火	hòi fó	hoi4 fo2	hoi fo
open hearted /generous/charitable	adj	闊佬	fut lóu	fut3 lou2	fut lou
open hrs /run/operate	v	營	yìhng	jing4	yehng
open letter		公開信	gùng hòi seun	gung4 hoi4 seon3	kung hoi swon
open market	n	自由市場	jih yàuh síh chèuhng	zi6 jau4 si5 coeng4	chih yauh sih chheuhng
open on public /disclose/make public	adj	公開	gùng hòi	gung4 hoi4	kung hoi
open shop	n	開放工廠	hòi fong gùng chóng	hoi4 fong3 gung4 cong2	hoi fong kung chhong
opener	n	開啟者	hòi kái jé	hoi4 kai2 ze2	hoi khai che
opening (job)/vacancy	adj	空缺	hùng kyut	hung4 kyut3	hung khyut
openly[1]	adv	公開地	gùng hòi deih	gung4 hoi4 dei6	kung hoi teih
openly[2]	adv	直率	jihk sēut	zik6 soet1	chehk swut
opera	n	歌劇	gō kehk	go1 kek6	ko khehk
operate	v	運作	wàhn jók	wan6 zok2	wahn chok
operating sequence /work sequence		操作程序	chòu jok chìhng jeuih	cou4 zok3 cing4 zeoi6	chhou chok chehng cheuih
operation room	n	手術室	sáu seuht sāt	sau2 seot6 sat1	sau swoht sat
operative /in using	adj	運行	wahn hàhng	wan6 hang4	wahn hahng
operator[1]	n	操作員	chòu jok yùhn	cou4 zok3 jyun4	chhou chok yuhn
operator[2] /worker	n	工作者	gùng jok jé	gung4 zok3 ze2	kung chok che
opinion[1] /point of view	n	立場	lahp chèuhng	lap6 coeng4	lahp chheuhng

English	POS	Chinese	Romanization 1	Jyutping	Romanization 2
opinion[2]	n	見解	gin gáai	gin3 gaai2	kin kaai
opinion on /criticize	v	批評	pài pìhng	pai4 ping4	phai phehng
opinioned in my opinion	n	照我嘅意見	jiu ngóh ge yi gin	ziu3 ngo5 ge3 ji3 gin3	chiu ngoh ke yi kin
opium[1]	n	白粉	baahk fán	baak6 fan2	paahk fan
opium[2]	n	鴉片	āa pin, ngā pin	aa1 pin3, ngaa1pin3	aa /nga phin
opposing	adj	相對	sèung déui	soeng4 deoi2	seung toei
opposite	adj	相反的	seung fáan dīk	soeng3 faan2 dik1	seung faan tik
opposite side[1]	n	對面	deui mihn	deoi3 min6	toei mihn
opposite side[2]	n	相反方向	seung fáan fōng heung	soeng3 faan2 fong1 hoeng3	seung faan fong heung
optic /optical/vision /visual/eyesight	adj	視力	sih lihk	si6 lik6	sih lehk
optimism	n	樂觀	lohk gùn	lok6 gun4	lohk kun
optimistic /hopeful	adj	樂觀嘅	lohk gùn ge	lok6 gun4 ge3	lohk kun ke
option[1]	n	選項	syūn hòhng	syun1 hong6	syun hohng
option[2]	n	替代	tái dòih	tai3 doi6	thai toih
or[1]	conj	或	waahk	waak6	waahk
or[2]	conj	或者	waahk jé	waak6 ze2	waahk che
or?[3] (question)	conj	抑或?	yīk waahk?	jik1 waak6?	yek waahk?
or[4] /still/had better	conj	還是	wàahn sih	waan4 si6	waahn sih
or else[1]		約唔係	yeuk m̀ haih	joek3 m4 hai6	yeuk mh haih
or else[2]/if not/otherwise	conj	否則	fáu jāk	fau2 zak1	fau chak
or else[3]		不然	bāt yìhn	bat1 jin4	pat yihn
oral[1] /verbal/spoken	adj	口頭	háu tàuh	hau2 tau4	hau thauh
oral[2] /verbal	adj	口頭上	háu tàuh seuhng	hau2 tau4 soeng6	hau thauh seuhng
oral evidence	n	口頭證據	háu tàuh jing geui	hau2 tau4 zing3 geoi3	hau thauh cheng kwoi
oral test /oral exam	n	口試	háu síh	hau2 si5	hau sih
oral sex[1] (sl)(vdw) blow job	v/xy	口交	háu gàau	hau2 gaau4	hau kaau
oral sex[2] (sl) (dw) blow job	v	口淫	háu yàhm	hau2 jam4	hau yahm
orally	adv	口頭嘅	háu tàuh ge	hau2 tau4 ge3	hau thauh ke
orange	n	橙	cháang	caang2	chhaang
orange colour	n	橙色	cháang sīk	caang2 sik1	chhaang sek
orange juice	n	橙汁	cháang jāp	caang2 zap1	chhaang chap
orbit[1]	n	軌道	gwái douh	gwai2 dou6	kwai touh
orbit[2]	n	運行軌道	wahn hàahng gwái douh	wan6 haang4 gwai2 dou6	wahn haahng kwai touh
orchestra	n	管弦樂隊	gún yìhn ngohk déui	gun2 jin4 ngok6 deui2	kun yihn ngohk toei
order[1]	n	叫	giu	giu3	kiu
order[2]	n	訓令	fan lihng	fan3 ling4	fan lehng
order[3] /command	n	旨意	jí yi	zi2 ji3	chi yi
order[4] /sequence	adj	次序	chi jeuih	ci3 zeoi6	chhi choih
order booking	n	定貨簿	dehng fo bouh	deng6 fo3 bou6	tehng fo pouh
order goods[1]	n	定貨	dehng fo	deng6 fo3	tehng fo
order goods[2]	n	叫貨	giu fo	giu3 fo3	kiu fo

English	Type	Chinese	Yale	Jyutping	Other
order goods[3]	n	定購	dehng /dihng gau	deng6 /ding6 gau3	tehng kau
order merchandise		辦貨	baahn fo	baan6 fo3	paahn fo
orderly /tidy/neat exactly	adj	整	jíng	zing2	cheng
ordinance	n	法令	faat lihng	faat3 ling4	faat lehng
ordinarily time /normal time	adv	平時	pèhng sìh	peng4 si4	phehng sih
ordinary day	n	平日	pèhng yaht	peng4 jat6	phehng yaht
ordinary mail[1]	n	平郵	pèhng yàuh	peng4 jau4	phehng yauh
ordinary mail[2]	n	平信	pèhng seun	peng4 seon3	phehng swon
ordinary meal	n	便飯	bihn faahn	bin6 faan6	pihn faahn
common people /ordinary people/general people/simple people/all the people	n	世人	sai yàhn	sai3 jan4	sai yahn
ordination	n	聖職之任命	sing jīk jì yam mehng /mihng	sing3 zik1 zi4 yam3 meng6 /ming6	seng chek chi yam mehng
organ[1] /body part	n	器官	hei gùn	hei3 gun4	hei kun
organ[2] music instrument	n	風琴	fūng kàhm	fung1 kam4	fung khahm
organic	adj	有機物	yáuh gèi maht	jau5 gei4 mat6	yauh kei maht
organic matter /organic substance	adj	有機物嘅	yáuh gèi maht ge	jau5 gei4 mat6 ge3	yauh kei maht ke
organised	adj	有組織的	yáuh jóu jīk dìk	jau5 zou2 zik1 dik4	yauh chou chek tek
organized & managed /conduct style	n	經營方式	gìng yìhng fòng sīk	ging4 jing4 fong4 sik1	keng yehng fong sek
organiser	n	組織者	jóu jīk jé	zou2 zik1 ze	chou chek che
organization	adj	團體	tyùhn tái	tyun4 tai2	thyuhn thai
orgasm of sex	n	性交高潮	sing gáau gòu chìuh	sing3 gaau2 gou4 ciu4	seng kaau kou chhiuh
orgasmic	adj	似性高潮	chíh sing gòu chìuh	ci5 sing3 gou4 ciu4	chhih seng kou chhiuh
original	adj	原版	yùhn báan	jyun4 baan2	yuhn paan
originally /former	adv	原來	yùhn lòih	jyun4 loi4	yuhn loih
ornament[1] /decorate	n/v	飾	sīk	sik1	sek
ornament[2]	v	裝飾	jòng sīk	zong4 sik1	chong sek
ornament[3]	n	飾物	sīk maht	sik1 mat6	sek maht
ornament[4] /decoration goods	n	裝飾品	jōng sīk bán	zong4 sik1 ban2	chong sek pan
orphan	n	孤兒	gù yìh	gu4 ji4	ku yih
osmosis[1]	n	滲透	sam tau	sam3 tau3	sam thau
osmosis[2]	n	滲透作用	sam tau jok yuhng	sam3 tau3 zok3 jung6	sam thau chok yuhng
other[1] /else	adj	別	biht	bit6	piht
other[2] /separate/another	adj	另	lihng	ling6	lehng
other[3]	adj	另外	lihng oih /ngoih	ling6 oi6 /ngoi6	lehng oih /ngoih
other bad things (sl)		一雨傾盆	yāt yúh kīng pùhn	jat1 jyu5 king1 pun4	yat yuh kheng phuhn
other hand		另外還有	lihng oih /ngoih wàahn yáuh	ling6 oi6 /ngoi6 waan4 jau5	lehng oih /ngoih waahn yauh
other name		其他姓名	kèih tà seng méng	kei4 taa4 seng3 meng2	kheih tha seng meng
other people[1]	n	其他人	kèih tà yàhn	kei4 taa4 jan4	kheih tha yahn

other people[2]	n	別人	biht yàhn	bit6 jan4	piht yahn
other people[3]	n	人哋	yàhn deih	jan4 dei6	yahn teih
other side		對方	deui fòng	deoi3 fong4	toei fong
other than[1](IDM) /except /other		除了	cheuih líuh	ceoi4 liu5	chheuih liuh
other then[2]		除咗	chèuih jó	ceoi4 zo2	chheuih cho
otherwise[1]	adv	唔係	m̀ haih	m4 hai6	mh haih
otherwise[2]	adv	如果唔係	yùh gwó m̀ haih	jyu4 gwo2 m4 hai6	yuh kwo mh haih
otherwise[3]	adv	或者相反	waahk jé sèung fáan	waak6 ze2 soeng4 faan2	waahk che seung faan
otherwise[4]	adv	或用其他方式	waahk yuhng kèih tà fòng sīk	waak6 jung6 kei4 taa4 fong4 sik1	waahk yuhng kheih tha fong sek
ought[1] /respond	v/aux	應	yíng	jing2	yeng
ought[2] /must/should	v/aux	應該	yìng gòi	jing4 goi4	yeng koi
ounce (de) 1/16 a pound	n	盎司	ōn /ngòn sī	on1 /ngon4 si1	on /ngon si
our	pron	我們	ngóh mùhn	ngo5 mun4	ngoh muhn
ourself /ourselves	pron	我們自己	ngóh mùhn jih géi	ngo5 mun4 zi6 gei2	ngoh muhn chih kei
out	adv	出外	chēut oih /ngoih	ceot1 oi6 /ngoi6	chhot oih /ngoih
out _in records		出_入記錄	chēut_yahp gei luhk	ceot1_jap6 gei3 luk6	chhot_yahp kei luhk
out of context		脫離上下文	tyut lèih seuhng hah màhn	tyut3 lei4 soeng6 haa6 man4	thyut leih seuhng hah mahn
out of control		失控	sāt hung	sat1 hung3	sat hung
out of fashion		唔流行	m̀ làuh hàhng	m4 lau4 hang4	mh lauh hahng
out of order /doesn't works		失靈	sāt lèhng /lìhng	sat1 leng4 /ling4	sat lehng
out of season		唔合時	m̀ hahp sìh	m4 hap6 si4	mh hahp sih
out of town	adj	郊野	gàau yéh	gaau1 je5	kaau yeh
out patient	n	門診病人	mùhn chān behng yàhn	mun4 can1 beng6 jan4	muhn chhan pehng yahn
out space	n	太空	taaih hùng	taai6 hung4	thaaih hung
outdoor[1]	adj	室外	sāt oih /ngoih	sat1 oi6 /ngoi6	sat oih /ngoih
outdoor[2]	adj	戶外	wuh oih /ngoih	wu6 oi6 /ngoi6	wuh oih /ngoih
outdoor[3]	adj	在戶外	joih wuh oih /ngoih	zoi6 wu6 oi6 /ngoi6	choih wuh oih /ngoih
outer[1] /external/foreign	adj	外	oih /ngoih	oi6 /ngoi6	oih /ngoih
outer[2]	adj	外邊	oih /ngoih bīn	oi6 /ngoi6 bin1	oih /ngoih pin
outer space	n	外太空	oih /ngoih taai hùng	oi6 /ngoi6 taai3 hung4	oih /ngoih thaai hung
outing /field trip	n	郊遊	gàau yàuh	gaau1 jau4	kaau yauh
outline[1] /sketch/paint	n	劃畫	waahk wá	waak6 waa2	waahk wa
outline[2]	n	輪廓	lèuhn kwok	leon4 kwok3	leuhn khwok
outlive /long-lived	v	活得長	wuht dāk chèuhng	wut6 dak1 coeng4	wuht tak chheuhng
opinion /outlook	n	看法	hōn faat	hon1 faat3	hon faat
outlying	adj	邊遠	bīn yúhn	bin1 jyun5	pin yuhn
output (computing)	n	輸出量	syù chēut lèuhng	syu4 ceot1 loeng4	syu chhot leuhng
outside[1] /out	n	外	oih /ngoih	oi6 /ngoi6	oih /ngoih
outside[2]		出面	chēut mihn	ceot1 min6	chhot mihn

outside[3]	n	出便	chēut bihn	ceot1 bin6	chhot pihn
outside[4] /outer	n	外便	oih /ngoih bihn	oi6 /ngoi6 bin6	oih /ngoih pihn
outside body	n	體外	tái oih	tai2 oi6	thai oih
outside door	n	門外	mùhn oih /ngoih	mun4 oi6 /ngoi6	muhn oih /ngoih
outside hall		廳外面	tèng oih /ngoih mihn	teng4 oi6 /ngoi6 min6	theng oih /ngoih mihn
outside lamp	n	燈外	dāng oih /ngoih	dang1 oi6 /ngoi6	tang oih /ngoih
outside of the city /out of the town /away from the town	adj	城外	sèhng oih /ngoih	seng4 oi6 /ngoi6	sehng oih /ngoih
outside the room		房外面	fóng oih /ngoih mihn	fong2 oi6 /ngoi6 min6	fong oih /ngoih mihn
outspoken[1]	adj	率直	sēut jihk	seot1 zik6	swot chehk
outspoken[2]	adj	直腸直肚	jihk chèuhng jihk tóuh	zik6 coeng4 zik6 tou5	chehk chheuhng chehk thouh
outspoken[3]	adj	直言不諱	jihk yìhn bāt wáih	zik6 jin4 bat1 wai5	chehk yihn pat waih
outstanding[1] performance	adj	傑出	giht chēut	git6 ceot1	kiht chhot
outstanding[2] payment /not settled payment	adj	未解決	meih gáai kyut	mei6 gaai2 kyut3	meih gaai khyut
oval	adj	卵形嘅	léun yìhng ge	leon2 jing4 ge3	leun yehng ke
ovary	n	卵巢	léun chàauh	leon2 caau4	leun chhaauh
oven /cooker/stove	n	烤爐	hàau lòuh	haau4 lou4	haau louh
over[1] /too much	adv	過於	gwo yù	gwo3 jyu4	kwo yu
over[2] (too much)	adv	以上	yíh seuhng	ji5 soeng6	yih seuhng
over[3] /above	adv	之上	jī seuhng	zi1 soeng6	chi seuhng
over head		喺頭頂上便	hái tàuh déng seuhng bihn	hai2 tau4 deng2 soeng6 bin6	hai thauh teng seuhng pihn
over here[1]		喺嗰度	hái gó douh	hai2 go2 dou6	hai ko touh
over here[2]		喺呢喥	hái lī /nī douh	hai2 li1 /ni1 dou6	hai li /ni touh
over shouting		無理鬧	mòuh léih laauh /naauh	mou4 lei5 laau6 /naau6	mouh leih laauh /naauh
over there[1]		前面	chin mìhn	cin4 min6	chhin mihn
over there[2]		那邊	là bīn	laa6 bin1	la pin
overage	adj	超齡	chìu lìhng	ciu4 ling4	chhiu lìhng
overate /overeat /overeaten/overeating	v	食得太飽	sihk dāk taai báau	sik6 dak1 taai3 baau2	sehk tak thaai paau
overbridge /over-pass /flyover/over-pass/bridge/ overhead walkway	n	天橋	tìn kìuh	tin4 kiu4	thin khiuh
overcast	n	陰天	yàm tìn	jam4 tin4	yam thin
overcharge	v	索價過高	sok ga gwo gòu	sok3 ga3 gwo3 gou4	sok ka kwo kou
overcloud	v	使陰暗	sai yām am/ngam	sai3 jam1 am3 / ngam3	sai yam am /ngam
overcoat	n	大衣等	daaih yī dáng	daai6 ji1 dang2	taaih yi tang
overcome[1]	v&i	贏	yèhng	jeng4	yehng
overcome[2] /subdued	v&i	克	hāak	haak1	haak
overcome[3] /won /victorious	v&i	贏咗	yèhng jó	jeng4 zo2 ?	yehng cho
overcome[4]	v&i	克服	hāak fuhk	haak1 fuk6	haak fuhk
overcover	n	遮蔽	jē bai	ze1 bai3	che pai

overcrowd /crowded	adj	擁擠	yúng jāi	jung2 zai1	yung chai
overdo /excess	v	做得過分	jouh dāk gwo fàn	zou6 dak1 gwo3 fan4	chouh tak kwo fan
overdone /overdid (things/work)	v	工作過度	gùng jok gwò douh	gung4 zok3 gwo4 dou6	kung chok kwo touh
overdose[1] try hard	v	過量努力	gwo leuhng lóuh /nóuh lìhk	gwo3 loeng6 lou5 /nou5 lik6	kwo leuhng louh /nouh lehk
overdose[2] /try excess	v	過量	gwo leuhng	gwo3 loeng6	kwo leuhng
overdose[3] (medicine)	n	藥劑過量	yeuhk jāi gwo leuhng	joek6 zai1 gwo3 loeng6	yeuhk chai kwo leuhng
overdraft	n	透支	tau jī	tau3 zi1	thau chih
overdue / date expired	adj	過期嘅	gwo kèih ge	gwo3 kei4 ge3	kwo kheih ke
overdue /unpaid	adj	未錢嘅	meih chín ge	mei6 cin2 ge3	meih chhin ke
overeat[1]	v	食得過量	sihk dāk gwo leuhng	sik6 dak1 gwo3 loeng6	sehk tak kwo leuhng
overeat[2]	v	吃得過飽	hek dāk gwo báau	hek3 dak1 gwo3 baau2	hek tak kwo paau
overeating	n	大量進食	daaih leuhng jeun sihk	daai6 loeng6 zeon3 sik6	taaih leuhng cheun sehk
overestimate /overprize	v	估計過高	gú gai gwo gòu	gu2 gai3 gwo3 gou4	ku kai kwo kou
overexcited /too excited	adj	過度興奮	gwo douh hìng fáhn	gwo3 dou6 hing4 fan5	kwo touh heng fahn
overfill	v/i	滿溢	múhn yaht	mun5 jat6	muhn yaht
overflow[1]	v	溢	yaht	jat6	yaht
overflow[2]	v	溢出	yaht chēut	jat6 ceot1	yaht chhot
overgrow	v	生長過快	sàng jéung gwo faai	sang4 zoeng2 gwo3	sang cheung kwo faai
overgrown[1]	adj	繁茂	fàahn mauh	faan4 mau6	faahn mauh
overgrown[2]	adj	生長過度	sàng jéung gwo douh	sang4 zoeng2 gwo3 dou6	sang cheung kwo touh
overhang[1]	v	突出	dàht chēut	dat6 ceot1	taht chhot
overhang[2]	v	吊喺...上	diu hai...seuhng bihn	diu3 hai2 soeng6 bin6	tiu hai...seuhng pihn
overhappy	adv	過分快樂	gwo fàn faai lohk	gwo3 fan4 faai3 lok6	kwo fan faai lohk
overhead	ad	在頭頂上	joih tàuh déng seuhng	zoi6 tau4 deng2 soeng6	choih thauh teng seuhng
overhear	v	偷聽	tàu tèng	tau4 teng4	thau theng
overheat[1]	v	過熱	gwo yiht	gwo3 jit6	kwo yiht
overheat[2]	v	變得過熱	bin dāk gwo yiht	bin3 dak1 gwo3 jit6	pin tak kwo yiht
overjoy	v	使狂喜	sai kòhng héi	sai3 kong4 hei2	sai khohng hei
overjoyed	adj	開心到極	hòi sàm dou gihk	hoi4 sam4 dou3 gik6	hoi sam tou kehk
overkind	adj	過於友善	gwo yù yáuh sihn	gwo3 jyu4 jau5 sin6	kwo yu yauh sihn
overlabor	v	操勞過度	chòu lòuh gwo douh	cou4 lou4 gwo3 dou6	chhou louh kwo touh
overlap	n	重疊	chùhng dihp	cung4 dip6	chhuhng tihp
overlapping	n	部分重疊	bòuh fàn chung dìhp	bou6 fan4 cung4 dip6	pouh fan chhung tihp
overlay /layering/overlie	v	叠加於	dihp gā yù	dip6 ga1 jyu4	tihp ka yu
overleaf /next page	adv	在次頁	joih chi yihp	zoi6 ci3 jip6	choih chhi yihp
overlived	v	活得久	wuht dāk gáu	wut6 dak1 gau2	wuht tak kau
overload	n	超負荷	chìu fuh hòh	ciu4 fu6 ho6	chhiu fuh hoh
overlong /very long	adj	太長	taai chèuhng	taai3 coeng4	thaai chheuhng
overmuch /so much	adv	過多	gwo dò	gwo3 do4	kwo to
overnight[1]	adv	過夜	gwo yeh	gwo3 je6	kwo yeh

overnight[2]	adj	通宵	tùng sīu	tung4 siu1	thung siu
overnight[3]	adj	一夜間	yāt yeh gaan	jat1 je6 gaan3	yat yeh kaan
overpay	v	多付	dò fuh	do4 fu6	to fuh
overpower	v	壓倒	áat dóu	aat2 dou2	aat tou
overseas	adj	國外	gwok oih /ngoih	gwok3 oi6 /ngoi6	kwok oih /ngoih
overseas /aboard	adj	海外	hói oih /ngoih	hou2 oi6 /ngoi6	hoi oih /ngoih
overseas Chinese[1]	n	華僑	wàh kìuh	waa4 kiu4	wah khiuh
overseas Chinese[2]	n	國外中國人	gwok oih /ngoih jùng gwok yàhn	gwok3 oi6 /ngoi6 zung4 gwok3 jan4	kwok oih /ngoih chung kwok yahn
overseas Nepalese	n	國外尼泊爾	gwok oih /ngoih nèih bòhk yíh	gwok3 oi6 /ngoi6 nei4 bok6 ji5	kwok oih /ngoih neih pohk yih
oversee	v	監管	gàam gún	gaam4 gun2	kaam kun
oversight	n	失察	sāt chaat	sat caat3	sat chhaat
overslept[1]	v	瞓過龍	fan gwo lùhng	fan3 gwo3 lung4	fan gwo luhng
overslept[2]	v	睡過頭	seuih gwo tàuh	seoi6 gwo3 tau4	swoih kwo thauh
overstay	v	逾期	yuh kèih	jyu6 kei4	yuh kheih
overtake[1] by vehicle	v	抽頭	chāu tàuh	cau1 tau4	chhau thauh
overtake[2]	v	追上	jèui séuhng	zeoi4 soeng5	cheui seuhng
overtake[3]	v	趕上	gón séuhng	gon2 soeng5	kon seuhng
overtake[4]	v	超越	chìu yuht	ciu4 jyut6	chhiu yuht
overtax	v	課稅過重	fo seui gwo chúhng	fo3 seoi3 gwo3 cung5	fo swoi kwo chhuhng
overthrow /remove by force/overturn	v	推翻	tèui fàan	teoi4 faan4	thoi faan
overtime	n	過鐘	gwo jūng	gwo3 zung1	kwo chung
overtired /very tired	adj	勞累過度	lòuh lèuih gwo douh	lou4 leoi6 gwo3 dou6	louh lowih kwo touh
overtone music	n	翻音	faan yām	faan3 jam1	faan yam
overturn	v	超過反轉	chìu gwo fáan jyun	ciu4 gwo3 faan2 zyun3	chhiu kwo faan jyun
overturned /pour/pouring	v	傾倒	kìng dóu	king4 dou2	khing tou
overused /too much used	v	便用過度	sai yuhng gwo douh	sai3 jung6 gwo3 dou6	sai yuhng kwo touh
overvalue[1]	v	高估	gòu gú	gou4 gu2	kou ku
overvalue[2]	v	過於重視	gwo yù juhng sih	gwo3 jyu4 zung6 si6	kwo yu chuhng sih
overviolent /violence	v	暴力	bouh lihk	bou6 lik6	pouh lehk
overweight[1]	adj	過重	gwo chúhng	gwo3 cung5	kwo chhuhng
overweight[2]	adj	超重	chìu chúhng	ciu4 cung5	chhiu chohng
overwrite	v	寫得過多	sé dāk gwo dò	se2 dak1 gwo3 do4	se tak kwo toh
overzeal[1]	n	熱衷	yiht chùng	jit6 cung4	yiht chhung
overzeal[2]	n	過分熱心	gwo fahn yiht sàm	gwo3 fan4 jit6 sam4	kwo fahn yiht sam
ovum[1]	n	卵	léun	leon2	leun
ovum[2]	n	卵細胞	léun sai bāau	leon2 sai3 baau1	leun sai paau
owe /lack/be deficient	v	欠	**him** (if combined two) 'jàang'	**him3** (if combined two) 'zaang4'	**him** (if combined two) 'chaang'
owing to	prep	由於	yàuh yù	jau4 jyu3	yauh yu
owl	n	貓頭鷹	māau tàuh yìng	maau1 tau4 jing4	maau thauh yeng

English		Chinese	Yale	Jyutping	Other
own pays /pays yourself /self pays/oneself pays	n	食自己	sihk jih géi	sik6 zi6 gei2	sehk chih kei
own property /individual property/private property/self property	n	個人財產	go yàhn chòih cháan	go3 jan4 coi4 caan2	ko yahn chhoih chhaan
owner[1] /possessor /lord/host	n	主人	jyú yán, jyú yàhn	zyu2 jan2, zyu2 jan4	chyu yan, chyu yahn
owner[2] /ownership	n	物主	maht jyú	mat6 zyu2	maht chyu
owner of house /landlord	n	屋主	ūk /ngūk jyú	uk1 /nguk1 zyu2	uk /nguk chyu
ownership[1]	n	所有權	só yáuh kyùhn	so2 jau5 kyun4	so yauh khyuhn
ownership[2]	n	業權	yihp kyùhn	jip6 kyun4	yihp khyuhn
owning	n	擁有	yúng yáuh	jung2 jau5	yung yauh
ox /bull	n	公牛	gùng ngàuh	gung4 ngau4	kung ngauh
ox offal /ox's entrails	n	牛雜	ngàuh jaahp	ngau4 zaap6	ngauh chaahp
ox tail	n	牛尾	ngàuh méih	ngau4 mei5	ngauh meih
oxide	n	氧化物	yéuhng fa maht	joeng5 fa3 mat6	yeuhng fa maht
oxygen[1] 'o'	n	氧	yéuhng	joeng5	yeuhng
oxygen[2]	n	氧氣	yéuhng hei	joeng5 hei3	yeuhng hei
oxygen mask	n	氧氣面罩	yéuhng hei mihn jaau	joeng5 hei3 min6 zaau3	yeuhng hei mihn chaau
oyster	n	蠔	hòuh	hou4	houh
ozone layer	n	臭氧層	chau yéuhng chàhng	cau6 joeng5 cang4	chhau yeuhng chhahng

English		Chinese	Romanization 1	Jyutping	Romanization 2
p.m. /P.M. Afternoon /post meridiem/noon time	n	下晝	hah jau	haa6 zau3	hah chau
pace /wolking	v	運行	wahn hahng	wan6 hang4	wahn hahng
pacific (sea)	n	和平	wòh pèhng /pihng	wo4 peng4 /ping4	woh phehng
pacific ocean	n	太平洋	taai pèhng /pìhng yèuhng	taai3 peng4 /ping4 joeng4	thaai phehng yeuhng
pack[1]	n	包裝	bāau jōng	baau1 zong1	paau chong
pack[2]	n	一包	yāt bāau	jat1 baau1	yat paau
packet /pack	n	小包	síu bāau	siu2 baau1	siu paau
pack ice	n	浮冰	fàuh bìng	fou4 bing4	fauh beng
pack luggage	v	執行李	jāp hàhng léih	zap1 hang4 lei5	chap haang leih
pack up	v	整理行裝	jing léih hàhng jōng	zing3 lei5 hang4 zong1	cheng leih hahng chong
package[1]	n	包裝	bāau jōng	baau1 zong1	paau chong
package[2] /parcel	n	包裹	bāau gwó	baau1 gwo2	paau kwo
packaging	n	外包裝	òih /ngòih bàau jòng	oi4 /ngoi6 baau4 zong4	oih /ngoih paau chong
packer	n	包裝工	bāau jòng gùng	baau1 zong4 gung4	paau chong kung
paddy	n	水稻	séui douh	seoi2 dou6	swoi touh
paddy field	n	稻田	douh tìhn	dou6 tin4	touh thihn
padlock	n	鎖	só	so2	so
pagoda[1] /tower/tall building	n	塔	taap	taap3	thaap
pagoda[2]	n	寺院塔	jí yún taap	zi2 jyun2 taap	chi yun thaap
paid[1]	adj	俾咗喇	béi jó lā	bei3 zo2 laa1	pei cho la
paid[2]	adj	付	fu	fu3	fu
pain /sore	n	疼	dūng	dung1	tung
pain relief drug	n	安美露強力	òn /ngòn méih louh kèuhng lihk	on4 /ngon4 mei5 lou6 koeng4 lik6	on /ngon meih louh kheuhng lehk
painkiller drug	n	止痛藥	jí tung yeuhk	zi2 tung3 joek6	chi thung yeuhk
paint /painting	n	油漆	yàuh chāt	jau4 cat1	yauh chhat
paint brush	n	油漆刷	yàuh chāt cháat	jau4 cat1 caat2	yauh chhat chhaat
painting /drawing /paint picture/sketch paint	n	繪畫	kúi wá	kui2 wa2	khui wa
painter[1]	n	漆工	chāat gùng	caat1 gung4	chhaat kung
painter[2]	n	畫家	wá gā	waa2 gaa1	wa ka
painter[3]	n	油漆佬	yàuh chāt lóu	jau4 cat1 lou2	yauh chhat lou
painter[4]	n	油漆師傅	yàuh chāt sī fuh	jau4 cat1 si1 fu6	yauh chhat si fuh
painting	n	油油	yàuh yáu	jau4 jau2	yauh yau
pair (de)	n	啤	pē	pe1	phe
pair number /even	n	双數	sèung sou	soeng4 sou3	seung sou
pair of hands	n	雙手	sèung sáu	soeng4 sau2	seung sau
Pakistan	n	巴基斯坦	bā gēi sī táan	ba1 gei1 si1 taan2	pa kei si thaan
palace[1] /palace hall /temple	n	殿	din	din3	tin
palace[2]	n	皇宮	wòhng gùng	wong4 gung4	wohng kung
palace[3]	n	豪華住宅	hòuh wah jyuh jáak	hou4 waa6 zyu6 zaak2	houh wah chyuh chaak

palace worker-man /royal servant	n	自宮	jih gūng	zi6 gung1	chih kung
pale /wan/pallid	adj	蒼白	chōng baahk	cong1 baak6	chhong paahk
pall (cloth /shelter)	n	遮蓋物	jē koi maht	ze1 koi3 mat6	che khoi maht
pallet[1]	n	卡板	ká báan	kaa2 baan2	kha paan
pallet[2]	n	集裝架	jaahp jòng gá	zaap6 zong1 ga2	chaahp chong ka
palm[1] /paw /foot or hand of animal and bird	n	掌	jéung	zoeng2	cheung
palm[2] (of hand)	n	手掌	sáu jēung	sau2 zoeng1	sau cheuhng
palm read (hand reading)	n	掌紋	jéung màhn	zoeng2 man4	cheung mahn
pan /sauce pan/griddle		平底鍋	pèhng dāi wò	peng4 dai1 wo4	phehng tai wo
pan cake[(de)]	n	班戟	bāan gēk	baan1 gek1	paan kek
pancreas	n	胰腺	yìh sin	ji4 sin3	yih sin
panda	n	熊貓	hùhng māau	hung4 maau1	huhng maau
pandemic	n	流行嘅	làuh hàhng ge	lau4 haang4 ge3	lauh hahng ke
panel[1] /board	n	操縱盤	chòu jung pún	cou4 zung3 pun2	chhou chung phun
panel[2] /group of people	n	專門小組	jyūn mún/mùhn síu jóu	zyun1 mun2 /mun4 siu2 zou2	chyun mun /muhn siu chou
panelists	n	參加者	chàam gà jé	caam4 gaa4 ze2	chhaam ka che
panic /sudden fear	v	驚慌	gèng fòng	geng4 fong4	keng fong
panorama view	n	全景	chyùhn gíng	cyun4 ging2	chhyuhn keng
pant /short breaths /breathe quickly	adj/v	氣促	hei chūk	hei3 cuk1	hei chhuk
panties[1] /knickers	n	三角褲	sàam gók fú	saam4 gok2 fu2	saam kok fu
panties[2] /knickers	n	短內褲	dyún lòih /nòih fu	dyun2 loi6 /noi6 fu3	tyun loih /noih fu
pants[1]	n	長褲	chèuhng fu	coeng4 fu3	chheuhng fu
pants[2]	n	西褲	sài fu	sai4 fu3	sai fu
pantyhose	n	襪褲	maht fu	mat6 fu3	maht fu
pap /nipple/teat	n	奶頭	láaih /náaih tàuh	laai5 /naai5 tau4	laaih /naaih thauh
papaya[1] /pawpaw	n	木瓜	muhk gwà	muk6 gwaa4	muhk kwa
papaya[2]	n	番木瓜	fàan muhk gwā	faan4 muk6 gwaa1	faan muhk kwa
paper[1]	n	紙	jí /zí	zi2	chi
paper[2]	n	紙張	jí jèung	zi2 zoeng4	chi cheung
paper[3]	n	紙類	jí leuih	zi2 leoi6	chi leuih
paper bag	n	紙袋	jí dói	zi2 doi2	chi toi
paper boy	n	男報童	làahm bóu tùhng	laam4 bou2 tung6	laahm pou thuhng
paper clip[1]	n	萬字夾	maahn jih gíp	maan6 zi6 gip3	maahn chih kip
paper clip[2]	n	迴形針	wùih yìhng jām	wui4 jing4 zam1	wuih yehng cham
paper clip[3] /folder/clip	n	紙夾	jí gip	zi2 gip3	chi kep
paper cutter	n	裁紙刀	chòih jí dōu	coi4 zi2 dou1	chhoih chi tou
paper fire /wood fire		木材火災	mùhk choi fō jòi	muk6 coi3 fo1 joi4	muhk chhoi fo choi
paper girl	n	女報童	léuih bóu tùhng	leui5 bou2 tung6	lowih pou thuhng
paper mill	n	造紙廠	jouh jí chóng	zou6 zi2 cong2	chouh chi chhong
paper-weight		書鎮	syù jan	syu4 zan3	syu chan
parachute	n	降落傘	gong lohk saan	gong3 lik6 saan3	kong lohk saan

parachute jumping	v	跳傘	tiu saan	tiu3 saan3	thiu saan
parade	n	列隊遊行	liht déui yàuh hàhng	lit6 deoi2 jau4 hang4	liht toei yauh hahng
paragraph[1] /passage /section	n	段	dyuhn	dyun6	tyuhn
paragraph[2] /passage	n	節	jit	zit3	chit
parallel[1]	adj	平行	pèhng hàhng	peng4 hang4	phehng hahng
parallel[2]	adj	平行嘅	pèhng hàhng ge	peng4 hang4 ge3	phehng hahng ke
parallel parking		平行停放	pèhng hàhng tìng fóng	peng4 hang4 ting4 fong2	phehng hahng theng fong
paralysis[1]	n	癱	táan	taan2	thaan
paralysis[2]	n	癱瘓	táan wuhn	taan2 wun6	thaan wuhn
paralysis[3]	n	麻痹	màh bei	maa4 bei3	mah pei
parameter /boundary	n	界限	béi haahn	bei2 haan6	pei haahn
paramour /lover passion man	n	情夫	chìhng fù	cing4 fu4	chhehng fu
parasite	n	寄生生物	gei sāng sāng maht	gei3 sang1 sang1 mat6	kei sang sang maht
parch	v	使乾渴	sái gòn hot	sai2 gon4 hot3	sai kon hot
pardon /excuse/forgiven	n/v	原諒	yun lèuhng	jyun3 loeng6	yun leuhng
pare	v	被削	beih séuk	bei6 soek2	peih seuk
park (de)	n	泊	paak	paak	phaak
parking[1] /car park	n	泊車	paak chè	paak3 ce4	phaak chhe
parking[2]	n	停車處	tìhng chè syu	ting4 ce4 syu3	thehng chhe syu
parking keeper	n	公園管理員	gùng yún gùn léih yùhn	gung4 jyun2 gun2 lei5 jyun4	kung yun kun leih yuhn
parking light	n	泊車信號燈	paak chè seun houh dāng	paak3 ce4 seon3 hou6 dang1	phaak chhe swon houh tang
parking meter	n	停車收費器	tìhng chè sàu fai hei	ting4 ce4 sau4 fai3 hei3	thehng chhe sau fai hei
parking space[1] /parking spot	n	車位	chè wái	ce4 wai2	chhe wai
parking space[2]	n	停車位	tìhng chè wàih	ting4 ce4 wai4	thehng chhe waih
parking ticket (to violate rules) fine for parking	n	違規停車罰款單	wai kwāi tìhng chè faht fún dāan	wai3 kwai1 ting4 ce4 fat6 fun2 daan1	wai khwai thehng chhe faht fun taan
parkland	n	公共用地	gùng guhng yuhng deih	gung4 gung6 jung6 dei6	kung guhng yuhng teih
park'n shop (Hong Kong)	n	百佳	baak gàai	baak3 gaai4	paak kaai
parrot	n	鸚鵡	yìng móuh	jing4 mou5	yeng mouh
part /share	n	份/分	fahn	fan6	fahn
part of speech /word class	n	詞類	chìh leuih	ci4 leoi6	chhih lowih
part time[1]	adv	散工	tái gùng	tai2 gung4	thai kung
part time[2]	adv	散工	sáan gùng	saan2 gung4	saan kung
part time[3]	adv	兼職	gīm jīk	gim1 zik1	kim chek
part timer	n	兼職工作者	gīm jīk gùng jok jé	gim1 zik1 gung4 zok3 ze2	kim chek kung chok che
partiality /bias/one side support/ prejudice/unfair supporting/unreasonable dislike	n	偏見	pīn gin	pin1 gin3	phin kin

English		Chinese	Yale	Jyutping	Romanization
participant person	n	參與者	chàam yúh jé	caam4 jyu5 ze2	chhaam yuh che
participate[1] /participant /involvement	v	參與	chàam yúh	caam4 jyu5	chhaam yuh
participate[2] (in campaign)	v	參加運動	chàam gà wahn duhng	caam4 gaa4 wan6 dung6	chhaam ka wahn dohng
participle (grammar)	n	分詞	fàn chìh	fan4 ci4	fan chhih
particular[1] /special /unusual	adj	特殊	dahk syùh	dak6 syu4	tahk syuh
particular[2]	adj	講究	góng gau	gong2 gau3	kong kau
particular person	n	專	jyūn	zyun1	chyun
particularly[1] /specially	adv	專登	jyūn dāng	zyun1 dang1	chyun tang
particularly[2] /specially	adv	特登	dahk dāng	dak6 dang1	tahk tang
partition[1]	n	隔	gaak	gaak3	kaak
partition[2]	v	分割	fahn got	fan6 got3	fahn kot
partner[1] (de)	n	拍檔	pāat nàh	paat1 naa4	phaat nah
partner[2] (for activity)	n	伙伴	fó buhn	fo2 bun6	fo puhn
partner[3] (for activity)	n	合夥人	hahp fó yàhn	hap6 fo2 jan4	hahp fo yahn
partnership	n	合夥	hahp fó	hap6 fo2	hahp fo
party /club	n	党	dóng	dong2	tong
party leader	n	政党主席	jing dóng jyú jihk	zing3 dong2 zyu2 zik6	cheng tong chyu chehk
party line (of political)	n	政党嘅路線	jing dóng ge louh sin	zing3 dong2 ge3 lou6 sin3	cheng tong ke louh sin
party member[1]	n	党員	dóng yùhn	dong2 jyun4	tong yuhn
party member[2]	n	當事人	dóng sih yàhn	dong2 si6 jan4	tong sih yahn
party spirit	n	社交情結	séh gāau chìhng liht	se5 gaau1 cing4 lit6	seh kaau chhehng liht
pass[1] surpass/go through	v	經過	gìng gwo	ging4 gwo3	keng gwo
pass[2] of time	v	逝去	saih heui	sai6 heoi3	saih hoi
pass[3] of time/take wings	v	流逝	làuh saih	lau4 sai6	lauh saih
pass[4] in exam	v	及格	gahp gaak	gap6 gaak3	kahp kaak
pass[5] in exam	v	合格	hahp gaak	hap6 gaak3	hahp kaak
pass away	v	圓寂	yùhn jihk	jyun4 zik6	yuhn chehk
pass down /next rotation		傳下來	chyùhn hah làih	cyun4 ha6 lai4	chhyuhn hah laih
pass on exam (de)	v	趴士	pā sìh	paa1 si6	pha sih
pass through[1] /via	v	經	gìng	ging4	keng
pass through[2]	n	通	tōng	tong1	thong
pass through[3]	v	通去	tùng heui	tung4 heoi3	thung hoi
pass through[4] /experience	v	經歷	gìng lihk	ging4 lik6	keng lehk
passable[1]	adj	過得去	gwo dāk heui	gwo3 dak1 heoi3	kwo tak hoi
passable[2] /via crossable	adj	可通行	hó tùng hàhng	ho2 tung4 hang4	ho thung hahng
passage[1] /via	n	通過	tùng gwo	tung4 gwo3	thung kwo
passage[2]	n	段落	dyuhn laaih	dyun6 laai6	tyuhn laaih
passbook	n	存摺	chyùhn jip	cyun4 zip3	chhyuhn chip
passed[1] bill or inspection etc	n	通過	tùng gwo	tung4 gwo3	thung kwo

passed[2] /confirmation /sanction	n	批准	pài jéun	pai4 zeon2	phai cheun
passenger[1]	n	乘客	sing haak	sing3 haak3	seng haak
passenger[2]	n	搭客	daap haak	daap3 haak3	taap haak
passer /walker/traveller /pedestrian	n	路人	louh yàhn	lou6 jan4	louh yahn
passing go through	n	經過嘅	gìng gwo ge	ging4 gwo3 ge3	keng gwo ke
passing place	n	避車處	bèih chè chyú	bei6 ce4 cyu2	peih chhe chhyu
passion /strong feeling	n	酷愛	huhk oi /ngoi	huk6 oi3 /ngoi3	huhk oi /ngoi
passionate[1] /exciting	adj	激動	gīk duhng	gik1 dung6	kek tohng
passionate[2]	adj	好容易	hóu yùhng yih	hou2 jung4 ji6	hou yuhng yih
passive[1] grammatical	n	被動	bèih dùhng	bei6 dung6	peih tuhng
passive[2] inactive	adj	被動嘅	bèih dùhng ge	bei6 dung6 ge3	peih tuhng ke
passive voice	n	被動語態	bèih dùhng yùh taai	bei6 dung6 jyu6 taai3	peih tuhng yuh thaai
passover /Jewish's festival	n	聖經 (踰越節)	sing gìng (yùh yuht jit)	sing3 ging4 (jyu4 jyut6 zit3)	seng keng (yuh yuht chit)
passport[1] (de)	n	趴士卜(護照)	pā sih pòt (wuh jiu)	paa1 si6 pot4 (wu6 ziu3)	pha sih phot (wuh jiu)
passport[2]	n	護照	wuh jiu	wu6 ziu3	wuh chiu
passport no	n	護照號碼	wuh jiu houh máh	wu6 ziu3 hou6 maa5	wuh chiu houh mah
password	n	口令	háu lihng	hau2 ling6	hau lehng
past[1] /done	adj	過咗	gwo jó	gwo3 zo2	kwo cho
past[2] /previous	adj	往	wóhng	wong5	wohng
past[3] /in the past	adj	以往	yíh wóhng	ji5 wong5	yih wohng
past participle of English	n	過去分詞	gwo heui fàn chìh	gwo3 heoi3 fan4 ci4	kwo hoi fan chhih
past tense[1]	n	過去式	gwo heui sīk	gwo3 heoi3 sik1	kwo hoi sek
past tense[2]	n	過去時	gwo heui sìh	gwo3 heoi3 si4	kwo hoi sih
past tense[3] used befor verb	n	曾經	chàhng gīng	cang4 ging1	chhahng keng
paste[1] /thick sauce	n	醬	jeung	zoeng3	cheung
paste[2]	n	膏	góu	gou2	kou
paste[3] /cream	n	糊	wùh	wu4	wuh
paste[4]	n	糊狀物	wùh johng maht	wu4 zong6 mat6	wuh chohng maht
paste[5] for teeth /toothpaste	n	牙膏	ngàh góu	ngaa4 gou2	ngah kou
pasteurization	n	巴氏滅菌 作用	bà sìh mìht kwān jók yùhng	baa1 si6 mit6 kwan1 zok2 jung6	pa sih miht khwan chok yuhng
pastime[1] /amusement /recreation/kill time/enjoy in free-time/pleasure	n	消遣	sìu hín	siu4 hin2	siu hin
pastime[2] /recreation /entertainment/enjoy in free-time	n	娛樂	yuh lohk	jyu6 lik6	yuh lohk
pastor /priest/churchman /Church in charge	n	牧師	muhk sī	muk6 si1	muhk si
pastry[1]	n	糕餅	gōu béng	gou1 beng2	kou peng
pastry[2]	n	麵糰	mihn tyùhn	min6 tyun4	mihn thyuhn
pastry dessert	n	點心	dím sām	dim2 sam1	tim sam
pasture[1]	n	牧場	muhk chèuhng	muk6 coeng4	muhk chheuhng

pasture[2]	n	牧草地	muhk chóu deih	muk6 cou2 dei6	muhk chhou teih
pasty pie /samosa /containing meat and vegetables	n	餡餅	haahm béng	haam6 beng2	haahm peng
pat[1] slowly hit on the back	n	表揚	bíu dìk	biu2 dik4	piu tek
pat[2] gentle touch/give pat on /tap/to slap	v	輕拍	hehng /hìhng paak	heng6 /hing6 paak3	hehng phaak
pat[3] an answer	adj	妥貼	tóh tip	to5 tip3	thoh thip
patch	v	補丁	bóu dīng	bou2 ding1	pou deng
patch a worn	v	補	bóu	bou2	pou
patch cloth	v	補衫	bóu sáam	bou2 saam2	pou saam
patch shoe	v	補鞋	bóu hàaih	bou2 haai4	pou haaih
patent right /monopoly	n	專利權	jyùn leih kyùhn	zyun4 lei6 kyun4	chyun leih khyuhn
paternal father side	adj	遺傳嘅	wàih jyuhn ge	wai4 zyung6 ge3	waih chyuhn ke
paternal aunt	n	大姑郎	daaih gù lai	daai6 gu4 lai3	taaih ku lai
path[1] /road/route/way	n	路	louh	lou6	louh
path[2] /track/lane/small way	n	小路	síu louh	siu2 lou6	siu louh
patience[1] /bear	adj	有耐心	yáuh loih /noih sàm	jau5 loi6 /noi6 sam4	yauh loih /noih sam
patience[2] /will/desire /willpower/perseverance	n	毅力	ngaih lihk	ngai6 lik6	ngaih lehk
patient[1] /sick person /sufferer	n	患者	waahn jé	waan6 ze2	waahn che
patient[2] /bear	adj	忍耐	yán loih /noih	jan2 loi6 /noi6	yan loih /noih
patient's condition[1] /sick person situation/ patient's force/power	n	病情	behng /bihng chìhng	beng6 /bing6 cing4	pehng chehng
patient's condition[2] /patient's force/power	n	病勢	behng /bihng sai	beng6 /bing6 sai3	pehng sai
patient's history sheet	n	病歷表	behng /bihng lihk bíu	beng6 /bing6 lik6 biu2	pehng lehk piu
patiently	adv	堅毅	gīn ngaih	gin1 ngai6	kin ngaih
patriot[1] loves country	n	愛國	oi /ngoi gwok	oi3 /ngoi3 gwok3	oi /ngoi kwok
patriot[2] loves country	n	愛國者	oi /ngoi gwok jé	oi3 /ngoi3 gwok3 ze2	oi /ngoi kwok che
patrol go on circuit by security	v/n	巡邏	chèuhn lòh	ceon4 lo4	chheuhn loh
patrol officer (coll) /checker/ runner checker	n	勒更	láhk gang	lak5 kang3	lahk kang
patronize[1]	v	幫襯	bòng chan	bong4 can3	pong chhan
patronize[2]	v	資助	jì joh	zi4 zo6	chi choh
pattern[1] /model	n	欵樣	fún yéung	fun2 joeng2	fun yeung
pattern[2] /style/type	n	樣式	yèuhng sìk	joeng6 sik4	yeuhng sek
pattern[3] /model	n	典範	dín faahn	din2 faan6	tin faahn
pattern[4] /style	n	款式	fún sīk	fun2 sik1	fun sek
pauper /very poor	n	貧民	pàhn màhn	pan4 man4	phahn mahn
pause /suspend/to halt	v	停頓	tìhng deuhn	ting4 deon6	thehng teuhn
pave[1] cover road	v	鋪	pou	pou3	phou
pave[2] cover road	v	鋪路	pòu louh	pou4 lou6	phou louh
pave[3] cover road	v	鋪設	pòu chit	pou4 cit3	phou chhit

English		Chinese	Yale	Jyutping	Romanization
pavement[1] /side road /side walk	n	行人路	hàhng yàhn louh	hang4 jan4 lou6	hahng yahn louh
pavement[2]	n	路面	louh mihn	lou6 min6	louh mihn
pavilion	n	亭	tìhng	ting4	thehng
paw	n	腳爪	geuk jáau	goek3 zaau2	keuk chaau
pawn[1]	v	押	aat /ngaat	aat2 /ngaat3	aat /ngaat
pawn[2] /mortgage	v	抵押	dái aat /ngaat	dai2 aat3 /ngaat3	tai aat /ngaat
pawn shop	n	當鋪	dong póu	dong3 pou2	tong phou
pay[1] cash	v	俾錢	béi chin	bei2 cin3	pei chhin
pay[2] hand over	v	繳付	giu fuh	giu3 fu6	kiu fuh
pay[3] /payment	v	付款	fu fún	fu3 fun2	fu fun
pay[4] the rent	v	交租	gàau jòu	gaau4 zou4	kaau chou
pay[5] tuition fee	v	交學費	gaau hohk fai	gaau3 hok6 fai3	kaau hohk fai
pay[6] water bill	v	交水費	gàau séui bei	gaau4 seoi2 bei3	kaau swoi pei
pay[7] /salary	n	薪	sān	san1	san
pay[8] /salary	n	薪俸	sān fúng	san1 fung2	san fung
pay attention /mind		理	léih	lei5	leih
pay back[1]	n	還有	wàahn yáuh	waan4 jau5	waahn yauh
pay back[2] /return back	n	仲有	juhng yáuh	zung6 jau5	chuhng yauh
pay by me!	n	我請啦!	ngóh chéng lā!	ngo5 ceng2 laa1!	ngoh chheng la!
pay debt of gratitude		報恩	bou yān	bou3 jan1	pou yan
pay electricity bill	v	交電費	gàau dihn fai	gaau4 din6 fai3	kaau tihm fai
pay in advance[1] /prepayment/advance money	adv	預支	yuh jì	jyu6 zi4	yuh chi
pay in advance[2] /prepaid	adj	預付	yuh fuh	jyu6 fu6	yuh fuh
payable[1]	adj	可付	hó fuh	ho2 fu6	ho fuh
payable[2]	adj	應支付	yíng jì fuh	jing2 zi4 fu6	yeng chi fuh
payback[1] /return back	n	還	wàahn	waan4	waahn
payback[2] /returns	n	回報	wùih bou	wui4 bou3	wuih pou
payee /remittee	n	收款人	sàu fún yàhn	sau4 fun2 jan4	sau fun yahn
payer[1]	n	交款人	gàau fún yàhn	gaau4 fun2 jan4	kaau fun yahn
payer[2]	n	付款人	fu fún yàhn	fu3 fun2 jan4	fu fun yahn
PC /personal computer	n	個人電腦	go yàhn dihn lóuh /nóuh	go3 jan4 din6 louh5 /nou5	ko yahn tihn louh /nouh
PDA Personal Digital Assistant	n	個人電子	go yàhn dìhn jī	go3 jan4 din6 zi1	ko yahn tihn chi
peace[1] /calm/peaceful	n	平	pèhng /pìhng	peng4 /ping4	phehng
peace[2] /peaceful	adj	和平	wòh pèhng /pìhng	wo4 peng4 /ping4	woh phehng
peace & security	n	太平	táai pèhng /pìhng	taai2 peng4 /ping4	thaai phehng
peace offering (Jew)	n	猶太人的 謝恩祭	yàuh taai yàhn ge jeh yān jai	jau4 taai3 jan4 ge3 ze6 jan1 zai3	yauh thaai yahn ke cheh yan chai
peaceful[1] /safe & sound	adj	平安	pèhng òn, pìhng ngòn	peng4 on4, ping4 ngon4	phehng on /ngon
peaceful[2]	adj	安寧	òn lìhng, ngòn nìhng	on4 ling4, ngon4 ning4	on lehng, ngon nehng

English		Chinese	Romanization	Jyutping	Yale
peach	n	桃	tòuh	tou4	thouh
peacock	n	孔雀	húng jéuk	hung2 zoek2	hung cheuk
peak /hilltop/summit /topof hill/top of mountain /highest point	n	山頂	sàan déng	saan4 deng2	saan teng
peak season /busy season	n	旺季	wohng gwai	wong6 gwai3	wohng kwai
peak tram /cable car	n	纜車	laahm chè	laam6 ce4	laahm chhe
peal of thunder	v	霆	tìhng	ting4	thehng
peanut	n	花生	fā sāng	faa1 sang1	fa sang
pear[1] furit	n	梨	lèih	lei4	leih
pear[2] furit of Sydney	n	雪梨	syut lèih	syut3 lei4	syut leih
pear[3] /australian pear	n	啤梨	bē léi	be1 lei2	pe lei
pearl	n	珍珠	jàn jyù	zan4 zyu4	chan chyu
Pearl river (of Guangdong)	n	珠江	jyū gōng	zyu1 gong1	chyu kong
peas /bean	n	青豆	chèng dáu	ceng4 dau2	chheng tau
peasant /farmer /cultivator	n	農夫	lùhng /nùhng fù	lung4 /nung4 fu4	luhng /nuhng fu
pebble	n	小卵石	síu léun sehk	siu2 leon2 sek6	siu leun sehk
pebbles /small stone /gravel	n	礫	līk	lik1	lek
peck /sting/bite	v	啄	deuk	doek3	tok
peck eats	v	啄食	dèuk sihk	doek4 sik6	tok sehk
pecker[2]	n	雞巴	gài bā	gai4 ba1	kai pa
pecker[1] (sl) penis	n	陰莖	yàm gíng	jam4 ging2	yam keng
peddle /step on	v	踩	cháai	caai2	chhaai
peddler vender /hawker/vender	n	小販	síu fáan	siu2 faan2	siu faan
pedestrian[1]	n	行人	hàhng yàhn	hang4 jan4	hahng yahn
pedestrian[2]	n	步行者	bòuh hàahng jé	bou6 haang4 ze2	pouh haahng che
pedestrian[3] /crossing /zebra-crossing	n	斑馬線	bàan máh sín	baan4 maa5 sin2	paan mah sin
pedestrian crossing /zebra-crossing	n	人行橫道	yàhn hàhng wàahng douh	jan4 hang4 waang4 dou6	yahn hahng waahng touh
pedestrian subway	n	行人隧道	hàhng yàhn seuih douh	hang4 jan4 seoi6 dou6	hahng yahn swoih touh
pediatrics (sl)	n	小兒科	síu yìh fò	siu2 ji4 fo4	siu yih fo
pedicab /tricycles /rickshaw	n	三輪車	sàam lèuhn chè	saam4 leun4 ce4	saam leuhn chhe
peel[1] /remove layer	v	剝	mōk	mok1	mok
peel[2]	v	削或剝	séuk waahk mōk	soek2 waak6 mok1	swok waahk mok
peel skin	v	剝皮	mōk pèih	mok1 pei4	mok pheih
peel up	v	剝落	mōk lohk	mok1 lok6	mok lohk
peeler[1]	n	削皮器	seuk pèih hei	soek3 pei4 hei3	swok pheih hei
peeler[2]	n	脫皮機	tyut pèih gèi	tyut3 pei4 gei4	thyut pheih kei
peeler[3]	n	脫殼機	tyut hok gèi	tyut3 hok3 gei4	thyut hok kei
peeler[4]	n	脫皮刀	tyut pèih dōu	tyut3 pei4 dou1	thyut pheih tou

peep[1] /investigate/secret /reconnoiter/pry/secret look	v	偵察	jìng chàh	zing4 caa4	cheng chah
peep[2] /secret look	v	窺視	kwāi sih	kwai1 si6	khwai sih
peep peep sound	n	哼哼聲	hāng hāng sēng	hang1 hang1 seng1	hang hang seng
peer /same level/same class/counterpart/similar category	n	同輩	tùhng búi	tung4 bui2	thuhng pui
peg /wedge/short piece of wood/chock/stopper	n	楔子	sit jí	sit3 zi2	sit chi
pen	n	筆	bāt	bat1	pat
pen friend	n	筆友	bāt yáuh	bat1 jau5	pat yauh
pen-pal	n	筆友	bāt yáuh	bat1 jau5	pat yauh
penalty /punish /punishable	n	處罰	chyú faht	cyu2 fat6	chhyu faht
pencil	n	鉛筆	yùhn bāt	jyun4 bat1	yuhn pat
pencil sharpener	n	鉛筆刨	yùhn bāt páau	jyun4 bat1 paau2	yuhn pat phaau
pendant[1] /hang ornament	n	垂飾	sèuih sīk	seoi4 sik1	swoih sek
pendent[2] /dangle	n	吊著	diu jeuk	diu3 zoek3	tiu cheuk
pending	adj	懸而未決	yùhn yìh meih kyut	jyun4 ji4 mei6 kyut3	yuhn yih meih khyut
pendulum (a hang rod)	n	鐘擺	jùng bāai	zung4 baai1	chung paai
penetrate[1]	v	穿透	chyùn tau	cyun4 tau3	chhyun thau
penetrate[2] /see through	v	識破	sīk po	sik1 po3	sek pho
penetration /inserting /thrusting	n	滲透	sam tau	sam3 tau3	sam thau
peninsula	n	半島	bun dóu	bun3 dou2	pun dou
penis[1] (sl)	n	鳩	gàu	gau4	kau
penis[2] (coll) (dw)	n/xy	屌	díu	diu2	tiu
penis[3] (sl)(dw)	n/xy	唶	jèk	zek4	chek
penis[4]	n	陽具	yèuhng geuih	joeng4 geoi6	yeuhng kwoih
penis[5] (sl)	n	香蕉	hèung jìu	hoeng4 ziu4	heung chiu
penis[6] (coll) (dw)	n/ xy	雞巴	gài bā	gai4 ba1	kai pa
penis cut servant /eunuch servant ancient royal place's workers in China		太監	taai gaam	taai3 gaam3	thaai kaam
penis erection(sl)	v/xy	扯旗	ché kèih	ce2 kei4	chhe kheih
penis fondly touch (sl)	v/xy	揸碌鳩	já lùk gáu	zaa2 luk4 gau2	cha luk kau
penis itchy (sl) (vdw)	v /xy	唶痕	jèk hàhn	zek4 han4	chek hahn
penis's head (sl)	n	龜頭	gwāi tàuh	gwai1 tau4	kwai thauh
pension[1]	n	養老金	yéuhng lóuh gàm	joeng5 lou5 gam4	yeuhng louh kam
pension[1] /retire pay /retirement pay	n	退休金	teui yàu gām	teoi3 jau4 gam1	thoi yau kam
pentagon	n	五邊形	ńgh bìn yìhng	ng5 bin4 jing4	ngh pin yehng
peony /flower	n	牡丹	máuh dāan	maau5 daan1	mauh taan
people[1]	n	人物	yàhn maht	jan4 mat6	yahn maht
people[2]	n	人們	yàhn mùhn	jan4 mun4	yahn muhn
people[3]	n	人民嘅	yàhn màhn ge	jan4 man4 ge	yahn mahn ke

pepper mill	n	胡椒碾磨器	wùh jìu líhn mòh hei	wu4 ziu4 lin5 mo4 hei3	wuh chiu lihn moh hei
pepsi	n	百事可樂	báak sìh hō lòhk	baak2 si6 ho1 lok6	paak sih ho lohk
per day 24-hour	n	全日24小時	chyùhn yaht 24 síu si	cyun4 jat6 24 siu2 si3	chhyuhn yaht 24 siu si
percent[1]	n	百分之一	baak fahn jì yāt	baak3 fan6 zi4 jat1	paak fahn chi yat
percent[2]	n	百分比	baak fahn béi	baak3 fan6 bei2	paak fahn pei
percentage	n	百分率	baak fahn léut	baak3 fan6 leot2	paak fahn lowt
perception	n	悟性	ngh síng	ng6 sing2	ngh seng
perfect[1]	adj	完美	yùhn méih	jyun4 mei5	yuhn meih
perfect[2]	adj	十全十美	sahp chyùhn sahp méih	sap6 cyun4 sap6 mei5	sahp chhyuhn sahp meih
perfection	n	完成	yùhn sèhng	jyun4 seng4	yuhn sehng
perfectly /wholly/whole/quite	adv	完全	yùhn chyun	jyun4 cyun4	yuhn chhyun
perforate[1]	v	打窿	dá lūng	daa2 lung1	ta lung
perforate[2] /bore a hole	v	穿孔	chyùn húng	cyun4 hung2	chhyun hung
performance[1] /perform show	v	表演	bīu yíhn	biu1 jin5	piu yihn
performance[2] /show in a play	n	演出	yíhn chēut	jin5 ceot1	yihn chhot
performance[3] /skill	n	技能	geih làhng /nàhng	gei6 lang4 /nang4	keih lahng /nahng
performer[1] /actor/actress	n	演員	yín yùhn	jin2 jyun4	yin yuhn
performer[2]	n	表演者	bíu yín jé	biu2 jin2 ze2	piu yin che
perfume[1] /fragrant	n	芬	fān	fan1	fan
perfume[2]	n	香水	hèung séui	hoeng4 seoi2	heung swoi
perfume[3] /scent/aroma	n	香味	hèung meih	hoeng4 mei6	heung meih
perhaps[1] /possibly/may /may be/possible	adv	或者	waahk jé	waak6 ze2	waahk che
perhaps[2]	adv	或許	waahk héui	waak6 heoi2	waahk hoi
perineum	n	會陰	wúi yām	wui2 jam1	wui yam
period[1] /time	n	時	sìh	si4	sih
period[2]	n	期	kèih	kei4	kheih
period[3]	n	期間	keih gaan	kei4 gaan3	kheih kaan
period of 3 months /quarter of a year/quarter	n	季度	gwai douh	gwai3 dou6	kwai touh
periodical /regularly	n	定期	dehng /dihng kèih	deng6 /ding6 kei4	tehng kheih
periscope[1]	n	潛望鏡	chìhm mohng geng	cim4 mong6 geng3	chhihm mohng keng
periscope[2]	n	展望鏡	jín mohng geng	zim2 mong6 geng3	chin mohng keng
perish /very cold	adj	極冷	gihk láahng	gik6 laang5	kehk laahng
perm[1] /hair create curls	n	電髮	dihn faat	din6 faat3	tihn faat
perm[2] hairstyle	n	燙髮	tong faat	tong3 faat3	thong faat
permanent[1]	adj	恒	hàhng	hang4	hahng
permanent[2] /lasting /eternal	adj	永久	wíhng gáu	wing5 gau2	wehng kau
permanent[3]	adj	永久嘅	wíhng gáu ge	wing5 gau2 ge3	wehng kau ke
permanent[4]	adj	永恆嘅	wíhng hàhng ge	wing5 hang4 ge3	wehng hahng ke

permanent[5]	adj	唔變嘅	m̀ bin ge	m4 bin3 ge3	mh pin ke
permanent[6]	adj	恆	hàhng	hang4	hahng
permanent address	n	固定地址	gu dehng deih jí	gu3 deng6 deii6 zi2	ku tehng teih chi
permanent resident	n	永久性居民	wíhng gáu sing gèui màhn	wing5 gau2 sing3 geoi4 man4	wehng kau seng kwoi mahn
permit document /licence	n	許可證	héui hó jing	heoi2 ho2 zing3	hoi ho cheng
perpetrator[1] /criminal person	n	犯罪者	fáan jeuih jé	faan2 zeoi6 ze2	faan choih che
perpetrator[2] /culprit	n	罪犯	jeuih fáan	zeoi6 faan2	cheuih faahn
perpetuity	n	永久使用權	wíhng gáu sāi yùhng kyùhn	wing5 gau2 sai1 jung6 kyun4	wehng kau sai yuhng khyuhn
persecute	v	殘害	chāan hoih	caan1 hoi6	chhaan hoih
persecutor[1]	n	迫害者	bīk hoih jé	bik1 hoi6 ze2	pek hoih che
persecutor[2]	n	殘害者	chāan hoih jé	caan1 hoi6 ze2	chhaan hoih che
persimmon fruit	n	柿子	chíh jí	ci5 zi2	chhih chi
person[1]	n	人士	yàhn sih	jan4 si6	yahn sih
person[2] who does somethings	n	者	jé	ze2	che
person's death		人死	yàhn séi	jan4 sei2	yahn sei
personage	n	容貌	yùhng maauh	jung4 maau6	yuhng maauh
personal[1] /private	adj	己	géi	gei2	kei
personal[2]	adj	自己	jih géi	zi6 gei2	chih kei
personal[3]	adj	人事	yàhn sih	jan4 si6	yahn sih
personal data	n	個人資料	go yàhn jì líu	go3 jan4 zi4 liu2	ko yahn chi liu
personal distance[1] /proxemics/personal space 1.5 to 4 ft, personal distance for interactions among …	n	人際距離學	yàhn jai kéuih lèih hohk	jan4 zai3 keoi5 lei4 hok6	yahn chai khoih leih hohk
personal distance[2] /proxemics/personal space 1.5 to 4 ft, personal distance for interactions among …	n	個人空間	go yàhn hùng gàan	go3 jan4 hung4 gaan4	ko yahn hung kaan
personal permit	n	個人許可證	go yàhn héui hó jing	go3 jan4 heoi2 ho2 zing3	ko yahn hoi ho cheng
personal pronoun[1]	n	人稱代詞	yàhn chīng doih chìh	jan4 cing1 doi6 ci4	yahn chheng toih chhih
personal pronoun[2]	n	備忘記事	beih mòhng gei sih	bei6 mong4 gei3 si6	peih mohng kei sih
personality[1] /individuality	n	個性	go sing	go3 sing3	ko seng
personality[2]	n	品格	bán gaak	ban2 gaak3	pan kaak
perspiration /sweat	n	汗	hohn	hon6	hohn
perspire /sweat	v	出汗	chēut hohn	ceot1 hon6	chhot hohn
persuade /cajole	v	安撫	òn /ngòn fú	on4 /ngon4 fu2	on /ngon fu
persuade boy	v	探男仔	tam làahm jāi	taam3 laam4 zai1	tham laahm chai
pertain[1] be part of …	v	屬於	suhk yù	suk6 jyu4	suhk yu
pertain[2] /regarding /concerning	v	關於	gwàan yù	gwaan1 jyu4	kwaan yu
pertaining	v	附屬	fuh sùhk	fu6 suk6	fuh suhk
pessimist	n	悲觀論者	bēi gùn leuhn jé	bei1 gun4 leon6 ze2	pei kun lowhn che

English		Chinese	Yale	Jyutping	Other
pessimistic /unhappy	adj	悲觀	bēi gùn	bei1 gun4	pei kun
pest /injurious insects	n	害蟲	hoih chùhng	hoi6 cung4	hoih chhuhng
pestilence	n	瘟疫	wān yihk	wan1 jik6	wan yehk
pet domestic birds/animals	n	寵物	chúng maht	cung2 mat6	chhung maht
petition	v	請願	chéng /chíng yuhn	ceng2 /cing2 jyun6	chheng yuhn
petroleum	n	石油	sehk yàuh	sel6 jau4	sehk yauh
pharmaceutical	adj	製藥嘅	jai yeuhk ge	zai3 joek6 ge3	chai yeuhk ke
pharmacist	n	製藥者	jai yeuhk jé	zai3 joek6 ze2	chai yeuhk che
pharmacy[1] /dispensary /drug store/pharmacist/ chemist/medicine shop	n	藥房	yeuhk fōng	joek6 fong1	yeuhk fong
pharmacy[2]	n	化學家	fa hohk gà	faa3 hok6 gaa4	fa hohk ka
phase /stage	n	階段	gàai dyuhn	gaai4 dyun6	kaai tyuhn
Philippine	n	菲律賓	fēi leuht bān	fei1 leot6 ban1	fei leuht pan
philosopher[1]	n	哲學家	jit hohk gā	zit3 hok6 gaa1	chit hohk ka
philosopher[2] /sir	n	爵士大寫	jeuk sih daaih sé	zoek3 si6 daai6 se2	cheuk sih taaih se
philosophy	n	哲學	jit hohk	zit3 hok6	chit hohk
philosophy of life	n	人生觀	yàhn sāng gùn	jan4 sang1 gun4	yahn sang kun
phoenix[1]	n	鳳	fuhng	fung6	fuhng
phoenix[2] eastern	n	鳳凰	fuhng wòng	fung6 wong4	fuhng wong
phoenix[3]	n	永生鳥	wíhng sàang líuh /níuh	wing5 sang4 liu5 /niu5	wehng sang liuh /niuh
phoenix[4] western	n	不死鳥	bāt sēi líuh /níuh	bat1 sei1 liu5 /niu5	pat sei liuh /niuh
phone book /telephone directory	n	電話簿	dihn wá bóu	din6 waa2 bou2	tihn wa pou
phone booth	n	電話亭	dihn wá ting	din6 waa2 ting3	tihn wa teng
phone card	n	電話卡	dihn wá ká	din6 waa2 kaa2	tihn wa kha
phone incidents[1]		電話打擾	dihn wá dā yīu	din6 waa2 daa1 jiu1	tihn wa ta yiu
phone incidents[2]		電話騷擾	dihn wá sòu yíuh	din6 waa2 sou4 jiu5	tihn wa sou yiuh
phonetic symbol	n	音標	yàm bīu	jam4 biu1	yam piu
phonograph rec[1]		唱碟	cheung díp	cong3 dip2	chheung tip
phonograph rec[2]	n	唱片	cheung pín	coeng3 pin2	chheung phin
phosphate[1]	n	磷肥	leuhn fèih	leon4 fei4	leuhn feih
phosphate[2]	n	磷酸鹽	leuhn syūn yìhm	leon6 syun1 jim4	leuhn syun yihm
photo[1] /picture/portrait /drawing	n	相	séung	soeng2	seung
photo[2]	n	拍照	paak jiu	paak3 ziu3	phaak chiu
photo[3]	n	攝影	síp yéng /yíng	sip2 jeng2 /jing2	sip yeng
photograph[1]	n	照片	jiu pin	ziu3 pin3	chiu phin
photograph[2]	n	影相	yéng séung	jeng2 soeng2	yeng seung
photographer	n	攝影師	síp yéng /yíng sì	sip2 jeng2 /jing2 si4	sip yeng si
photography	n	照相術	jiu séung seuht	ziu3 soeng2 seut6	chiu seung swoht
phrase[1] /part	n	片語	pin yúh	pin3 jyu5	phin yuh
phrase[2] grammar		短語	dyún yúh	dyun2 jyu5	tyun yuh
phrase[3] grammar		詞組	chìh jóu	ci4 zou2	chhih chou
phrase words[1] /word	n	詞	chìh	ci4	chhih

phrase words[2]	n	短詞	dyún chìh	dyun2 ci4	tyun chyu
phrase words[3] /grammar	n	語法	yúh faat	jyu5 faat3	yuh faat
physical[1] /physics	adj	物理	maht léih	mat6 lei5	maht leih
physical[2]	adj	身體	sàn tái	san4 tai2	san thai
physical & personnel		物理同人員	maht léih tùhng yàhn yùhn	mat6 lei5 tung4 jan4 jyun4	maht leih thuhng yahn yuhn
physical education	n	體育課	tái yùhk fo	tai2 juk6 fo3	thai yuhk fo
physical exercise /athletic	adj	運動	wahn duhng	wan6 dung6	wahn tohng
physician /western medicine	n	西醫	sài yì	sai4 ji4	sai yi
physics	n	物理學	maht léih hohk	mat6 lei5 hok6	maht leih hohk
physiological /physiology	a	生理學	sàng léih hohk	sang4 lei5 hok6	sang leih hohk
physique /bodily	n	體格	tái gaak	tai2 gaak3	thai kaak
piano	n	鋼琴	gong kàhm	gong3 kam4	kong khahm
piano store	n	鋼琴商店	gong kàhm sèung dim	gong3 kam4 soeng4 dim3	kong khahm seung tim
pick[1] /pluck / fruit or flower	v	摘	jaahk	zaak6	chaahk
pick[2] fruit / flower	v	採摘	chói jaahk	coi2 zaak6	chhoi chaahk
pick[3] /select/choose	n	挑選	téuh syún	tiu5 syun2	thiuh syun
pick pocket[1]	n	扒手	pàh sáu	paa4 sau2	phah sau
pick pocket[2]	n	扒竊	pàh sit	paa4 sit3	phah sit
pick up[1] /grasp	v	執起	jāp héi	zap1 hei2	chap hei
pick up[2] /grasp	v	拾起	sahp héi	sap6 hei2	sahp hei
pick up[3] /grasp	v	執番	jāp fàan	zap1 faan4	chap faan
pick up[4] /grasp	v	取伄	chéui ńgh	ceoi2 ng5	chheui ngh
pick up[5] to improvement		好轉	hóu jyun	hou2 zyun3	hou chyun
pick up[6] self-learn		自己學會	jih géi hohk wúih	zi6 gei2 hok6 wui5	chih kei hohk wuih
pick up[7] self-learn		自然學會	jih yìhn hohk wúih	zi6 jin4 hok6 wui5	chih yihn hohk wuih
pickaxe	n	鶴嘴鋤	hohk jéui chòh	hok6 zeoi2 co4	hohk choi chhoh
picker	n	採摘者	chói jaahk jé	coi2 zaak6 ze2	chhoi chaahk che
picket fence	n	尖椿柵欄	jīm chèun sáan làahn	zim1 ceon4 saan2 laan4	chim chheun saan laahn
pickle	n	鹽滷	yìhm lóuh	jim4 lou5	yihm louh
pickup truck /van	n	輕型貨車	hèng yīhng fo chè	heng4 jing4 fo3ce4	heng yehng fo chhe
picnicker[1]	n	野餐人	yéh chàan yàhn	je5 caan4 jan4	yeh chhaan yahn
Picnicker[2]	n	野餐者	yéh chàan jé	je5 caan4 ze2	yeh chhaan che
pictographs /hieroglyph	n	象形字	jeuhng yìhng jih	zoeng6 jing4 zi6	cheuhng yehng chih
picture drawing /drawing	n	圖畫	tòuh wá	tou4 waa2	thouh wa
pie dish [(de)]	n	批	pāi	pai1	phai
piece	n	一塊	yāt faai	jat1 faai3	yat faai
piece a paper /a sheet of paper	n	一張	yāt jèung	jat1 zoeng1	yat cheung

piece of story[1]/rumour	n	謠言	yìuh yìhn	jiu4 jin4	yiuh yihn
piece of story[2] /hearsay/rumor/rumour	n	謠傳	yìu chyùhn	jiu4 cyun4	yiu chhyuhn
piece of writing	n	篇	pīn	pin3	phin
pier area /quayside	n	碼頭區	máh tàuh kèui	maa5 tau4 keoi4	mah thauh khoi
pierce[1]	v	拮穿	gāt chyùn	gat1 cyun4	kat chhyun
pierce[2] /to poke	v	刺穿	chi chyùn	ci3 cyun4	chhi chhyun
pig back leg	n	豬腳	jyù geuk	zyu4 goek3	chyu keuk
pig brain	n	豬腦	jyù lóuh /nóuh	zyu4 lou5 /nou5	chyu louh /nouh
pig feed	n	豬飼料	jyù jih líu	zyu4 zi6 liu2	chyu chih liu
pig fore leg	n	豬手	jyù sáu	zyu4 sau2	chyu sau
pig heart	n	豬心	jyù sām	zyu4 sam1	chyu sam
pig intestine	n	豬腸	jyù chéung	zyu4 coeng2	chyu chheung
pig kidney	n	豬腰	jyù yìu	zyu4 jiu4	chyu yiu
pig liver	n	豬潤	jyù yéun	zyu4 jeon2	chyu yeun
pig lung	n	豬肺	jyù fai	zyu4 fai3	chyu fai
pig skin	n	豬皮	jyù pèih	zyu4 pei4	chyu pheih
pig stomach	n	豬肚	jyù tóuh	zyu4 tou5	chyu thouh
pig tripe	n	豬肚	jyù tóuh	zyu4 tou5	chyu thouh
pigeon /homing dove	n	信鴿	seun gáap	seon3 gaap2	swon kaap
pile	n	一堆	yāt dèui	jat1 deoi4	yat toei
pilgrim person	n	朝聖者	chìuh sing jé	ciu4 sing3 ze2	chhiuh seng che
pilgrimage /to holy journey	n	朝聖的人	chìuh sing dìk yàhn	ciu4 sing3 dik4 jan4	chhiuh seng tek yahn
pill[1] small flat round piece	n	丸	yún	jyun2	yun
pill[2] /tablet	n	藥丸	yeuhk yún	joek6 jyun2	yeuhk yun
pillory	n	頸手枷	géng sáu gá	geng2 sau2 gaa2	keng sau ka
pillow	n	枕頭	jám tàuh	zam2 tau4	cham thauh
pillowcase	n	枕頭袋	jám tàuh dói	zam2 tau4 doi2	cham thauh toi
pilot[1]	n	飛行員	fèi hàahng yun	fei4 haang4 jyun3	fei haahng yun
pilot[2]	n	駕駛員	ga sái yùhn	gaa3 sai2 jyun4	ka saai yuhn
pilot[3] of the plane	n	機長	gēi jéung	gei1 zoeng2	kei cheung
pimple[1]	n	暗瘡	ám /ngam chòng	am3 /ngam3 cong4	am /ngam chhong
pimple[2]	n	丘疹	yàu chān	jau4 can1	yau chhan
pin[1] /bamboo needle	n	籤	chīm	cim1	chhim
pin[2]	n	大頭針	daaih tàuh jām	daai6 tau4 zam1	taaih thauh cham
pinch[1]/wring/twist/wrench	v	扭	láu /náu	lau2 /nau2	lau /nau
pinch[2] /steal/thieve	v	偷竊	tàu sít	tau4 sit2	thau sit
pincushion	n	針墊	jām jín	jam1 zin2	cham chin
pine /a tree	n	松	chùhng	cung4	chhuhng
pineapple	n	菠蘿	bō lo	bo1 lo3	po lo
pineapple-juice	n	菠蘿汁	bō lo jāp	bo1 lo3 zap1	po lo chap
ping pong (de)	n	乒乓波	bīng bām bò	bing1 bam1 bo4	peng pam po
pink	n	粉紅色	fán hùhng sīk	fan2 hung4 sik1	fan huhng sek

pins	v	麻	màh	maa4	mah
pint approx 0.47 liter	n	品脫	bán tyút	ban2 tyut2	pan thyut
pipe[1] /tube	n	管	gùn	gun4	kun
pipe[2] /tube	v	管子	gùn jí	gun4 zi2	kun chi
smoke pipe	n	烟/煙斗	yīn dáu	jin1 dau2	yin tau
pipeline	n	導管	douh gùn	dou6 gun4	touh kun
piper /music	n	風笛手	fūng dehk sáu	fung1 dek6 sau2	fung tehk sau
piping sound	n	尖聲	jīm sèng	zim1 seng4	chim seng
pirate /robber of sea	n	海盜	hói douh	hou2 dou6	hoi touh
piss[1] /urine	n	疴尿	ō liuh /niuh	o1 liu6 /niu6	o liuh /niuh
piss[2] /pee (sl) urine	n/v	撒尿	saat liuh /niuh	saat3 liu6 /niu6	saat liuh /niuh
piss[3] make fun	v	拿⋯開心	lāh /nāh hòi sām	laa1 /naa1 hoi4 sam1	lah /nah hoi sam
pistol	n	手槍	sáu chēung	sau2 coeng1	sau chheung
piston /valve	n	活塞	wuht sāk	wut6 sak1	wuht sak
pit[1]	n	坑	hāang	haang1	haang
pit[2]	n	窪坑	wā hāang	wa1 haang1	wa haang
pit[3]	n	窖	gaau	gaau3	kaau
pit[4] /sprout/shoot	n	核	waht	wat6	what
pit of water[1]	n	氹	táhm	tam5	thahm
pit of water[2] /waterhole	n	水坑	séui hāang	seoi2 haang1	swoi haang
pitch tone	n	講嘢好高音	góng yéh hóu gòu yàm	gong2 je5 hou2 gou4 jam4	kong yeh hou kou yam
pitch[1] /speak well	n	講好話	góng hóu wá	gong2 hou2 waa2	kong hou wa
pitch[2] /speak well	n	替⋯說好	tái⋯sùht hōu wā	tai2⋯syut4 hou1 waa1	thai⋯suht hou wa
pitch[3] /asphalt road	v	瀝青	lāp chēng	laap1 ceng1	laap chheng
pitch dark[1]	adj	漆黑	chāat hāak	caat1 haak1	chhaat haak
pitch drak[2] /very drak	adj	黑麻麻	hāak mā mā	haak1 maa1 maa1	haak ma ma
pitched battle	n	攻擊	gùng gìk	gung4 gik4	kung kek
pitfall[1]	n	阱	jihng	zing6	chehng
pitfall[2]	n	陷	hahm	ham6	hahm
pith[1] of fruits	n	精髓	jèng séuih	zeng4 seoi5	cheng swoih
pith[2] (of the matter)	n	事情嘅實質	sih chihng ge saht jāt	si6 cing4 ge3 sat6 zat1	sih chhihng ke saht chat
pitiable condition /distressed	adj	無依無靠	móuh yi móuh kaau	mou5 ji3 mou5 kaau3	mouh yi mouh khaau
pity[1]	n	憐	lèuhn	leon4	leuhn
pity[2]	n	可憐	hó lìhn	ho2 lin6	ho lihn
pity[3]	n	憐憫	lèuhn máhn	leon4 man5	leuhn mahn
pixels /dot	n	像素	jeuhng sou	zoeng6 sou3	cheuhng sou
placard[1] /poster	n	海報	hói bou	hoi2 bou3	hoi pou
placard[2]	n	標語牌	bīu yùh pàaih	biu1 jyu6 paai4	piu yuh phaaih
place[1] /set/put/keep	v	放	fong	fong3	fong
place[2] /put/install	v	置	ji	zi3	chi
place[3] /put	v	擠	jài	zai4	chai
place[4] /spot	n	點	dím	dim2	tim

English		Chinese	Romanization 1	Romanization 2	Romanization 3
place[5] just at /right place	n	當	dòng	dong4	tong
place[6] /abode/small hous	n	所	só	so2	so
place[7] /local place	n	場所	chèuhng só	coeng4 so2	chheuhng so
place[8] /area	n	處所	syu só	syu2 so2	syu so
place aside /set aside	v	置	ji	zi3	chi
place in	v	放在	fong joih	fong3 zoi6	fong choih
place of birth	n	出生地址	chēut sāng deih jí	ceot1 sang1 dei6 zi2	chhot sang teih chi
plain & simple	adj	樸	pok	pok3	phok
plain congee	n	白粥	baahk jūk	baak6 zuk1	paahk chuk
plan[1] /scheme	n	謀	màuh	mau4	mauh
plan[2] /project/scheme /program	n	計劃	gai waahk	gai3 waak6	kai waahk
plan[3] /program	n	概略感	koi leuhk gám	koi3 loek6 gam2	khoi leuhk kam
plan to intend	n	打劃	dá waahk	daa2 waak6	ta waahk
plane[1] /surface	n	面	mín	min2	min
plane[2] /surface	n	平面	pèhng mín	peng4 min2	phehng min
plane[3] level /water level	n	水平	séui pèhng /pìhng	seoi2 peng4 /ping4	swoi phehng
plane[4] /airplane/airbus	n	飛機	fèi gèi	fei4 gei4	fei kei
plane[5] for wood	n	刨子	pàauh jí	paau4 zi2	phaauh chi
plane ticket	n	機票	gèi biu	gei4 biu3	kei piu
planet	n	行星	hàhng sēng /sīng	hang4 seng1 /sing1	hahng seng
planets & stars	n	太陽系的行星	taai yèuhng haih dìk hàhng sēng	taai3 joeng4 hai6 dik4 hang4 seng1	thaai yeuhng haih tek hahng seng
plank /board/wood board	n	木板	muhk báan	muk6 baan2	muhk paan
plant[1]	n	植	jihk	zik6	chehk
plant[2] /farm	n	農作物	lùhng /nùhng jok maht	lung4 /nung4 zok3 mat6	luhng /nuhng chok maht
plantation	n	大農場	daaih lùhng /nùhng chèuhng	daai6 lung4 /nung4 coeng4	taaih luhng /nuhng chheuhng
planter[1]	n	種植嘅人	jung jihk ge yàhn	zung3 zik6 ge3 jan4	chung chehk ke yahn
planter[2]	n	種植園主	jung jihk yún jyú	zung3 zik6 jyun2 zyu2	chung chehk yun chyu
planter[3] /farmer	n	農主	lùhng /nùhng jyú	lung4 /nung4 zyu2	luhng /nuhng chyu
planting /cultivating	n	種植	jung jihk	zung3 zik6	chung chehk
plash /sprinkle	n	潑水	put séui	put3 seoi2	phut swoi
plaster[1] by cement	n	灰泥	fùi làih /nàih	fui4 lai4 /nai4	fui laih /naih
plaster[2] by cement	v	用灰泥抹	yuhng fùi làih /nàih maat	jung6 fui4 lai4 /nai4 maat3	yuhng fui laih /naih maat
plastic	adj	塑膠	sou gàau	sou3 gaau4	sou kaau
plastic bag	n	膠袋	gàau dói	gaau4 doi2	kaau toi
plasticine clay/soil	n	黏土	lìhm tóu	lim4 tou2	lihm thou
plastics	n	塑料	sou līu	sou3 liu1	sou liu
plastics fire	n	塑料火災	sou līu fō jòi	sou3 liu1 fo1 zoi4	sou liu fo choi
plate[1] /dish	n	碟	díp /dihp	dip2 /dip6	tip /tihp
plate[2] /dish	n	盤子	pun jī	pun3 zi1	phun chi
plate rack	n	盤碟架	pùhn dihp gá	pun4 dip6 gaa2	phuhn tihp ka

platelet blood	n	血小板	hyut síu báan	hyut3 siu2 baan2	hyut siu paan
platform¹ of the train	n	月台	yuht tòih	jyut6 toi4	yuht thoih
platform²	n	月臺	yuht tòih	jyut6 toi4	yuht thoih
platform³ /stage	n	臺	tòih	toi4	thoih
platinum⁴	n	鉑	bohk	bok6	pohk
platinum⁵	n	鉑白金	bohk baahk gām	bok6 baak6 gam1	pohk paahk kam
platoon of army	n	軍排	gwàn pàaih	gwan4 paai4	kwan phaaih
play¹ game	v	遊戲	yàuh hei	jau4 hei3	yauh hei
play² of children	v	玩耍	wáan sá	waan2 saa2	waan sa
play again /replay	v	重再	chùhng joi	cung4 zoi3	chhuhng choi
play basketball		打籃球	dá làahm kàuh	da2 laam4 kau6	ta laahm khauh
play chess	v	捉棋	jūk kéi	zuk1 kei2	chuk khei
play electric game	v	玩電子遊戲	wáan dihn ji yàuh hei	waan2 din6 zi3 jau4 hei3	waan tihn chi yauh hei
play foot ball	v	打球	dá káuh	daa2 kau5	ta khauh
play ground	n	操場	chòu chèuhng	cou4 coeng4	chhou cheuhng
play hide & seek	v	捉迷藏	jūk màih chòhng	zuk1 mai4 cong4	chuk maih chhohng
play majong	v	打麻雀	dá màh jeuk	daa2 maa4 zoek3	ta mah cheuk
play piano	v	彈琴	tàahn kàhm	taan4 kam4	thaahn khahm
play prank	v	撚化	nán fa	nan2 faa3	nan fa
play string	v	彈	tàahn	taan4	thaahn
play tennis		打網球	dá móhng káuh	da2 mong5 kau6	ta mohng khauh
player	n	遊戲嘅人	yau héi ge yàhn	jau3 hei2 ge3 jan4	yau hei ke yahn
playground	n	遊樂場	yàuh lohk chèuhng	jau4 lok6 coeng4	yauh lohk chheuhng
playing ball	v	打波	dā bò	daa1 bo4	ta po
playschool /school game	n	學校遊戲	hohk haauh yàuh hei	hok6 haau6 jau4 hei3	hohk haauh yauh hei
plaza /small shopping centre	n	廣場	gwóng chèuhng	gwong2 coeng4	kwong chheuhng
please¹ (coll) excuse me!	v	唔該	m̀ gòi	m4 goi4	mh koi
please² /petition/invite /hire (a person)	v	請	chéng /chíng	ceng2 /cing2	chheng
please³ /ask	v	請問	chéng /chíng mahn	ceng2 /cing2 man6	chheng mahn
please⁴	v	請你	chéng léih /néih	ceng2 lei6 /nei6	chheng leih /neih
please⁵	v	使高興	sái gou hīng	sai2 gou3 hing1	sai kou heng
please⁶ /pretty voice	v	悅	yuht	jyut6	yuht
please⁷ final particle /auxiliary grammar		啦	lā	laa1	la
please attach		請附	chéng /chíng fuh	ceng2 /cing2 fu6	chheng fuh
please contract bank		請與本行聯絡	chéng yùh bún hòhng lyùhn lohk	ceng2 jyu4 bun2 hong4 lyun6 lok6	chheng yuh pun hohng lyuhn lohk
please see	v	請閱	chéng /chíng yuht	ceng2 /cing2 jyut6	chheng yuht
please sit-down	v	請坐	chéng /chíng chóh	ceng2 /cing2 co5	chheng chhoh
please specify	v	請說明	chéng /chíng syut mìhng	ceng2 /cing2 syut3 ming4	chheng syut mehng
please tell		請講啦	chéng /chíng góng lā	ceng2 /cing2 gong2 laa1	chheng kong la

English	POS	漢字	Yale	Jyutping	Romanization
pleasurable	adj	心情舒暢	sàm chìhng syù cheung	sam4 cing4 syu4 coeng3	sam chhehng syu cheung
pleated	adj	起褶	héi jaahp	hei2 zaap6	hei chaahp
pleated skirt	adj	百褶裙	baak jip kwàhn	baak3 zip3 kwan4	paak chip khwahn
pledgee	n	典當人	dín dong yàhn	din2 dong3 jan4	tin tong yahn
plentiful	adj	豐富嘅	fùng fu ge	fung4 fu3 ge3	fung fu ke
plenty /plenty of	adv	許多	héui dò	heoi2 do4	hoi toh
plenty of /rich	adv	大把	daaih bá	daai6 baa2	taaih pa
pleura[1]	n	胸膜	hùng mók	hung4 mok2	hung mok
pleura[2]	n	肋膜	lahk mók	lak6 mok2	lahk mok
pliers /tongs/pinch /pincers/forceps	n	鉗	kím	kim2	khim
plot[1] of land	n	小塊土地	síu fáai tóu deih	siu2 faai2 tou2 dei6	siu faai thou teih
plot[2] secret plan	n	密謀	maht màuh	mat6 mau4	maht mauh
plotter /conspirator	n	共謀者	guhng màuh jé	gung6 mau4 ze2	kuhng mauh che
plough[1] /plow	n	犁	làih /nàih	lai4 /nai4	laih /naih
plough[2]	v	犁地	làih deih	lai4 dei6	laih teih
ploughman	n	扶犁者	fùh làih /nàih jé	fu4 lai4 /nai4 ze2	fuh laih /naih che
pluck /pull	v	搣	māng	mang1	mang
plug[1] /cork/stopper	n	塞	sāk	sak1	sak
plug[2]	n	插頭	chaap tàuh	caap3 tau4	chhaap thauh
plum[1] /apricot	n	梅	mùih	mui4	muih
plum[2]	n	李	léih	lei5	leih
plumber[1]	n	水喉師傅	séui hàuh sī fuh	seoi2 hau4 si1 fu6	swoi hauh si fuh
plumber[2]	n	水喉佬	séui hàuh lóu	seoi2 hau4 lou2	swoi hauh lou
plunder /raven/robbing	n	掠奪	leuhk dyuht	loek6 dyut6	leuhk dyuht
plural[1] (coll)	pron	哋	déi	dei2	tei
plural[2] (wr)	pron	們	mùhn	mun4	muhn
plural[3]	adj	複數	fūk sou	fuk1 sou3	fuk sou
plurally	adj	複數地	fūk sou	fuk1 sou3	fuk sou
plus /add/addition	prep	加	gā	gaa1	ka
pneumatic tire	n	輪胎	lèuhn tói	leon4 toi2	leuhn thoi
pocket	n	口袋	háu dói /doih	hau2 doi2 /doi6	hau toi /toih
podium /small platform	n	講臺	góng tòih	gong2	kong thoih
poem /poetry/verse	n	詩	sì	si4	si
poet writes poems	n	詩人	sì yàhn	si4 jan4	si yahn
poetess women poems	n	女詩人	léuih sì yàhn	leui5 si4 jan4	lowih si yahn
poetry	n	詩歌	sì gō	si4 go1	si ko
point[1] /indicate	v	點	dím	dim2	tim
point[2] /one dot	n	一點	yāt dím	jat1 dim2	yat tim
point[3] main idea	n	要點	yìu dím	jiu4 dim2	yiu tim
point[4] stop point/fullstop	n	給...加標	kāp gā biu dím	kap1 ga1 biu3 dim2	khap ka piu tim
point at	v	指	jí	zi2	chi
point finger at	v	指著...	jí jeuhk	zi2 zoek3	chi cheuhk

point of order	n	議事程序	yíh sih chìhng jeuih	ji5 si6 cing4 zeoi6	yih sih chhehng choih
point out	v	指出	jí chēut	zi2 ceot1	chi chhot
pointed[1]	adj	針銳	jìm yeuih	zim4 jeoi6	chim yeuih
pointed[2]	adj	尖的	jīm dīk	zim1 dik1	chim tik
poison[1]	n	毒	duhk	duk6	tuhk
poison[2] /toxicant	n	毒藥	duhk yeuhk	duk6 joek6	tuhk yeuhk
poison[3]	n	毒害	duhk hoih	duk6 hoi6	tuhk hoih
poisoner	n	投毒者	tàuh duhk jé	tau4 duk6 ze2	thauh tuhk che
poisoning /be poisoned /chemical substance	n	中毒	jung duhk	zung3 duk6	chung tuhk
poisonous	adj	中毒嘅	jung duhk ge	zung3 duk6 ge3	chung tuhk ke
poke (by knife) /to stab /poke through	v	捅	tóng	tong2	thong
pole[1] /stick/rod/lever	n	桿	gòn	gon4	kon
pole[2] /pillar	n	柱子	chyúh jai	cyu5 zai3	chhyuh chai
pole[3] of geography	n	極	gihk	gik6	kehk
pole[4] of magnetic	n	磁極	chih gihk	ci4 gik6	chhih gehk
pole[5] of geography	n	南轅北轍	làahm yùhn bāk chit	laam4 jyun4 bak1 cit3	laahm yuhn pak chhit
police[1]	n	警察	gíng chaat	ging2 caat3	keng chhaat
police[2]	n	差人	chāai yàhn	caai1 jan4	chhaai yahn
police[3]	n	察員	chàai yùhn	caat3 jyun4	chhaai yuhn
police[4]	n	警方	gíng fōng	ging2 fong1	keng fong
police action	n	警察行動	gíng chaat hàhng duhng	ging2 caat hang4 dung6	keng chhaat hahng tohng
police car	n	警車	gíng chè	ging2 ce4	keng chhe
police dept /police force	n	警務處	gíng mouh chyú	ging2 mou6 cyu2	keng mouh chhyu
police inspector	n	幫辦	bòng báan	bong4 baan2	pong paan
police man	n	差佬	chāai lóu	caai1 lou2	chhaai lou
police officer[1]	n	警司	gíng sì	ji5 si4	keng si
police officer[2]	n	警官	gíng gùn	ging2 gun4	keng kun
police station[1]	n	差館	chāai gún	caai1 gun2	chhaai kun
police station[2]	n	警察局	gíng chaat gúk	ging2 caat3 guk2	keng chhaat kuk
police station[3]	n	警署	gíng chyúh	ging2 cyu5	keng chhyuh
police station[4]	n	警局	gíng gúk	ging2 guk2	keng kuk
police-cap[1] /police-hat	n	警帽	gíng mouh	ging2 mou6	keng mouh
police-cap[2]	n	帽章	mouh jēung	mou6 zoeng1	mouh cheung
police-force	n	警隊	gíng déui	ging2 deoi2	keng toei
police-woman[1]	n	女警	leuih gíng	leui5 ging2	lowih keng
police-woman[2]	n	差婆	chāai pòh	caai1 po4	chhaai phoh
policy	n	政策	jing chaak	zing3 caak3	cheng chaak
policymaker	n	決策人	kyut chaak yàhn	kyut3 caak3 jan4	khyut chhaak yahn
polish[1] of shoe	n	鞋油	hàaih yàuh	haai4 jau4	haaih yauh
polish[2]	n	磨光	mòh gwòng	mo4 gwong4	moh kwong
polisher	n	磨光器	mòh gwòng hei	mo4 gwong4 hei3	moh kwong hei

politburo /of communist party	n	共產黨政治局	guhng cháan dóng jing chìh guhk	gung4 caan2 dong2 zing3 ci4 guk6	kuhng chhaan tong cheng chhih kuhk
polite[1] /respectful	adj	恭	gùng	gung4	kung
polite[2] /politeness	adj	禮貌	láih maauh	lai5 maau6	laih maauh
polite[3]	adj	有禮	yáuh láih	jau5 lai5	yauh laih
polite[4] /well behaved	adj	斯文	sì màhn	si4 man4	si mahn
political[1]	adj	政	jing	zing3	cheng
political[2]	adj	政治	jing jih	zing3 zi6	cheng chih
political[3]	adj	事務	sih mouh	si6 mou6	sih mouh
political party	n	政黨	jing dóng	zing3 dong2	cheng tong
political power		政權	jing kyùhn	zing3 kyun4	cheng khyuhn
political prisoner	n	政治反	jing jih fáan	zing3 zi6 faan2	cheng chih faan
political situation		政局	jing guhk	zing3 guk6	cheng kuhk
politically	adj	政治上	jing jih séuhng	zing3 zi6 soeng5	cheng chih seuhng
politician	n	政治家	jing jih gā	zing3 zi6 gaa1	cheng chih ka
polling station	n	投票站	tàuh piu jaahm	tau4 piu3 zaam6	thauh phiu chaahm
pollster	n	民意測驗專家	màhn yi chàak yihm jyūn gā	man4 ji3 caak4 jim6 zyun1 gaa1	mahn yi chhaak yihm chyun ka
polonium	n	一種放射性元素	yāt júng fong seh sing yùhn sou	jat1 zung2 fong3 se6 sing3 jyun4 sou3	yat chung fong seh seng yuhn sou
polyandry /polygamy /more than one wife	n	一夫多妻制	yāt fùh dò chài jai	jat1 fu4 do4 cai4 zai3	yat fuh to chhai chai
polyester fiber[1] (coll)	n	聚酯纖維	leuih jí chīm wàih	leoi6 zi2 cim1 wai4	lowih chi chhim waih
polyester fiber[2] (wr)	n	多元酯	dò yùhn jí	do4 jyun4 zi2	to yuhn chi
polytechnic	n	綜合技術	jung hahp geih seuht	zung3 hap6 gei6 seot6	chung hahp keih swoht
polythene	n	聚乙烯	leuih yut hēi	leoi6 jyut3 hei1	lowih yut hei
pomelo /grape fruit Chinese grape-fruit	n	椂柚	lūk yáu	luk1 jau2	luk yau
pomology	n	果樹栽培學	gwó syuh jòi pùih hohk	gwo2 syu6 zoi4 pui4 hok6	kwo syuh choi phuih hohk
pond[1] /pool	n	池	chìh	ci4	chhih
pond[2]	n	池塘	chìh tòhng	ci4 tong4	chhih thohng
ponder[1] /think over in difficulty	v	諗	lám /nám	lam2 /nam2	lam /nam
ponder[2] /contemplate (in difficulty)	v	仔細考慮	jí sai háau leuih	zi2 sai3 haau2 leoi6	chi sai haau leuih
pony /small horse	n	細種馬	sai júng máh	sai3 zung2 ma5	sai chung mah
pool (small) /small sump	n	小水坑	síu séui hāang	siu2 seoi2 haang1	siu swoi haang
pool-car	n	营销汽車	ying sìu héi chè	jing4 siu4 hei2 ce4	yeng siu hei chhe
pool of blood	n	血泊	hyut paak	hyut3 paak3	hyut phaak
poor[1]	adj	無錢	móuh chín	mou5 cin2	mouh chhin
poor[2] /poverty	adj	貧苦	pàhn fú	pan4 fu2	phahn fu
poor[3] /poverty	adj	窮	kùhng	kung4	khuhng
poor[4] /poverty	adj	貧窮	pàhn kùhng	pan4 kung4	phahn khuhng
poor[5] /poverty	adj	貧窮嘅	pàhn kùhng ge	pan4 kung4 ge3	phahn khuhng ke
poor work	n	劣	lyut	lyut3	lyut

poor good /mediocre /rather poor/not so good	adj	較差	gaau chá	gaau3 ca2	kaau chha
poor people	n	窮人	kùhng yàhn	kung4 jan4	khuhng yahn
poor quality	adj	曳	yáih	jai5	yaih
poor relation	n	同類中較差者	tùhng leuih jùng gaau chá jé	tung4 leoi6 zung4 gaau3 ca2 ze2	thuhng lowih chung kaau chha che
poorhouse	n	救濟院	gau jai yún	gau3 jai3 jyun2	kau chai yun
pop (coll) soft drink/soda	n	汽水	hei séui /séoi	hei3 seoi2	hei swoi
pop music[1]	adj	發出砰嘅響聲	faat chēut pīng ge héung sèng	faat3 ceot1 ping1 ge3 hoeng2 seng4	faat chhot pheng ke heung seng
pop music[2]/remix music	adj	通俗嘅流行	tung jùhk ge làuh hàhng	tung3 zuk6 ge3 lau4 hang4	thung chuhk ke lauh hahng
pop concert	n	流行音樂會	làuh hàhng yàm lohk wúi	lau4 hang4 jam4 lok6 wui2	lauh hahng yam lohk wui
pop group	n	流行樂隊	làuh hàhng lohk deuih	lau4 hang4 lok6 deoi6	lauh hahng lohk twoih
pop remix concert	n	通俗音樂會	tung jùhk yàm lohk wúi	tung3 zuk6 jam4 lok6 wui2	thung chuhk yam lohk wui
pop singer	n	流行歌手	làuh hàhng gō sáu	lau4 hang4 go1 sau2	lauh hahng ko sau
pop song	n	流行曲	làuh hàhng kūk	lau4 hang4 kuk1	lauh hahng khuk
pope	n	教皇	gaau wòhng	gaau3 wong4	kaau wohng
popular[1]	adj	民間人	màhn gaan yàhn	man4 gaan3 jan4	mahn kaan yahn
popular[2]	adj	人民	yàhn màhn	jan4 man4	yahn mahn
popular[3]	adj	民眾嘅	màhn jung ge	man4 zung3 ge3	mahn chung ke
popular[4]	adj	流行人	làuh hàhng yàhn	lau4 hang4 jan4	lauh hahng yahn
popular[5]	adj	得人心	dāk yàhn sàm	dak1 jan4 sam4	tak yahn sam
popular star	n	受歡迎	sauh fùn yìhng	sau6 fun4 jing4	sauh fun yehng
popularity	n	流行	làuh hàhng	lau4 hang4	lauh hahng
popularize	v	宣傳	syùn chùhn	syun4 cun4	syun chhuhn
population	n	人口	yàhn háu	jan4 hau2	yahn hau
porcelain	n	陶瓷古玩	tòuh chìh gú wuhn	tou4 ci4 gu2 wun6	thouh chhih ku wuhn
porch[1] /veranda/raised platform	n	廊	lòhng	long4	lohng
porch[2] of house	n	偏廳	pīn tēng	pin1 teng1	phin theng
porch[3] of house/veranda	n	遊廊	yau long	jau3 long3	yau long
porcupine (animal)	n	箭豬	jin jyū	zin3 zyu1	chin chyu
pore[1] (skin's small hole)	n	毛孔	mòuh húng	mou4 hung2	mouh hung
pore[2]/deep think/to look carefully	v	使專心	sai jyūn sàm	sai3 zyun1 sam1	sai chyun sam
pork[1] /meat from pig	n	豬肉	jyù yuhk	zyu4 juk6	chyu yuhk
pork[2] plain boiled	n	白肉	baahk yuhk	baak6 juk6	paahk yuhk
pork-belly preserved	n	臘肉	laahp yuhk	laap6 juk6	laahp yuhk
pork-bone	n	豬骨	jyù gwāt	zyu4 gwat1	chyu kwat
pork-chop	n	豬扒	jyù pah	zyu4 paa1	chyu phah
pork-chop rice	n	豬扒飯	jyù pah faahn	zyu4 paa1 faan6	chyu phah faahn

pork-lean	n	瘦肉	sau yuhk	sau3 juk6	sau yuhk
pork-ribs	n	排骨	pàaih gwāt	paai4 gwat1	phaaih kwat
pornographic[1]/erotic	adj/xy	咸濕	hàahm sāp	haam4 sap1	haahm sap
pornographic[2] (sl)/naked	adj	黃色	wòhng sīk	wong4 sik1	wohng sek
pornographic[3] /thesis on sex	n	色情文學	sīk chìhng màhn hohk	sik1 cing4 man4 hok6	sek chhehng mahn hohk
porridge	n	稀飯	hei faahn	hei3 faan6	hei faahn
port[1]	n	埠	fauh	fau6	fauh
port[2]	n	海口	hói háu	hoi2 hau2	hoi hau
port[3]	n	港口	góng háu	gong2 hau2	kong hau
port wine (de)	n	砵酒	būt jáu	but1 zau2	put chau
portable[1]	adj	手提式	sáu tàih sīk	sau2 tai4 sik1	sau thaih sek
portable[2]	adj	攜提	kwàih dàih	kwai4 dai4	khwaih taih
portable[3]	adj	可搬運	hó bùn wahn	ho2 bun4 wan6	ho pun wahn
portable[4]	adj	輕便	hèng bihn	heng4 bin6	heng pihn
portage	n	搬運	bùn wahn	bun4 wan6	pun wahn
portfolio	n	投資組合	tàuh jī jóu hahp	tau4 zi1 zou2 hap6	thauh chi chou hahp
porter[1] /remover	n	搬運工	bùn wahn gùng	bun4 wan6 gung4	pun wahn kung
porter[2] (sl)	n	苦力	fú lihk	fu2 lik6	fu lehk
portrait /half photo	n	半身像	bun sàn jeuhng	bun3 san4 zoeng6	pun san cheuhng
portrait man /resemble man	n	人像	yàhn jeuhng	jan4 zoeng6	yahn cheuhng
portraitist	n	肖像畫家	chiu jeuhng wá gà	ciu3 zoeng6 wa2 ga4	chhiu cheuhng wa ka
portray	v	描畫	mìuh waahk	miu4 waak6	miuh waahk
Portugal	n	葡國	pou gwók	pou3 gwok3	phou kwok
pose position	n	姿勢	wái tok	wai2 tok3	wai thok
position[1] job's label	n	職位	jīk waih	zik1 wai6	chek waih
position[2](of the situation)	n	方位	fōng waih	fong1 wai6	fong waih
position title /job title	n	職位名稱	jīk waih mèhng /mihng chìng	zik1 wai6 meng4 /ming4 cing4	chek waih mehng chheng
positive[1]	adj	積極	jīk gihk	zik1 gik6	chek kehk
positive[2]	adj	原級	yùhn kāp	jyun4 kap1	yuhn khap
positive[3] battery	adj	正極	jeng gihk	zeng3 gik6	cheng kehk
positive[4] of electric	adj	陽性	yèuhng sing	joeng4 sing3	yeuhng seng
positive number	adj	正數	jeng sou	zeng3 sou3	cheng sou
possible	adj	可能	hó làhng /nàhng	ho2 lang4 /nang4	ho lahng /nahng
post[1] /rank	n	梯級	tài kāp	tai4 kap1	thai khap
post[2] /booth	n	崗位	gōng waih	gong1 wai6	kong waih
post of the social /caste/social class/social rank	n	階級	gàai kāp	gaai4 kap1	kaai khap
posting /mailing	n	郵寄	yàuh gei	jau4 gei3	yauh kei
post free	adj	唔使俾郵費	m̀ sái béi yàuh fai	m4 sai2 bei2 jau4 fai3	mh sai pei yauh fai
post man	n	快信佬	paai seun lóu	faai3 seon3 lou2	phaai swon lou
post no bills	v	禁止招貼	gam jí jìu tip	gam3 zi2 ziu4 tip3	kam chi chiu thip

English		Chinese	Yale	Jyutping	Reading
post office[1]	n	郵局	yàuh guhk	jau4 guk6	yauh kuhk
post office[2]	n	郵政局	yàuh jing guhk	jau4 zing3 guk6	yauh cheng kuhk
post office[3]	n	郵政署	yàuh jing chyúh	jau4 zing3 cyu5	yauh cheng chhyuh
post office box no	n	郵政信箱	yàuh jing seun sèung	jau4 zing3 seon3 soeng4	yauh cheng swon seung
post paid	adj	郵費已經俾咗	yàuh fai yíh gìng béi jó	jau4 fai3 ji5 ging4 bei2 zo2	yauh fai yih keng pei cho
postage	n	郵費	yàuh fai	jau4 fai3	yauh fai
postage stamp /stamp	n	郵票	yàuh piu	jau4 piu3	yauh phiu
postcard[1]	n	明信片	mìhng seun pín	ming4 seon3 pin2	mehng swon phin
postcard[2] (de)	n	甫士咭	pòu sìh kāat	pou4 si6 kaat1	phou sih khaat
postcard picture	n	美術明信片	méih seuht mìhng seun pín	mei5 seot6 ming4 seon3 pin2	méih seuht mehng swon phin
posted /stick on	v	貼	tip	tip3	thip
poster /placard	n	招貼	jìu tip	ziu4 tip3	chiu thip
postpone[1]	v	延期	yìhn kèih	jin2 kei4	yihn kheih
postpone[2]	v	展期	jín kèih	zin2 kei4	chin kheih
postpone[3]	v	延緩	yìhn wun	jin4 wun3	yihn wun
postponement	n	推遲	tèui chìh	teoi4 ci4	thoi chhih
posture	n	姿勢	jì sai	zi4 sai3	chi sai
pot[1] for cooking	n	煲	bōu	bou1	pou
pot[2] /basin/bowl	n	盆	pùhn	pun4	phuhn
potassium	n	鉀	gaap	gaap3	kaap
potassiun cyanide (de)	n	山埃	sàan (ng) āai	saan4 (ng3) aai1	saan (ng) aai
potato	n	薯仔	syùh jái	syu6 jai2	syuh chai
potential[1]	n	潛在	chìhm jòih	cim4 zoi6	chhihm choih
potential[2]	n	潛力	chìhm lihk	cim4 lik6	chhihm lehk
potential[3]	adj	潛在的	chìhm jòih dìk	cim4 zoi6 dik4	chhihm choih tik
potential[4]	adj	可能嘅	hó làng /nàng ge	ho2 lang4 /nang4 ge3	ho lang /nang ke
pottery /clayware	n	陶器	tòuh hei	tou4 hei3	thouh hei
pouch /small bag	n	腰袋	yìu dòih	jiu4 doi6	yiu toih
pound[1] (de) scales/weight	n	磅	bōng	bong1	pong
pound[2] /ram down /uppress	v	椿	jùng	zong4	chung
pound[3] /smash/pieces	v	搗碎	dóu seui	dou2 seui3	tou swoi
pound sterling	n	英鎊	yìng bóhng	jing4 bong5	yeng pohng
pour /pour out	v	倒	dóu	dou2	tou
pour down	v	淋水	làahm séui	laam4 seoi2	laahm swoi
pour into /put into	v	注	jyu	zyu3	chyu
pouring[1]	v	斟	jàm	zam4	cham
pouring[2]	v	倒水	dóu séui	dou2 seoi2	tou swoi
poverty[1] /poor	n	貧困	pàhn kwan	pan4 kwan3	phahn khwan
poverty[2]	n	窮富	kùhng fú	kung4 fu2	khuhng fu

poverty[3] /shortage /scarcity/short of	n	缺乏	kyut faht	kyut3 fat6	khyut faht
poverty[4]	n	唔足够	m̀ jūk gau	m4 zuk1 gau3	mh chuk kau
powder[1] /rice noodle	n	粉	fán	fan2	fan
powder[2]	n	粉末	fán muht	fan2 mut6	fan muht
powder cleaner	n	去污粉	heui wū fán	heoi3 wu1 fan2	hoi wu fan
powder soap[1] of cloths	n	梘粉	gáan fán	gaan2 fan2	kaan fan
powder soap[2] of cloths /washing powder/laundry detergent	n	洗衣粉	sái yī fán	sai2 ji1 fan2	sai yi fan
powdered	adj	變成粉末	bin sèhng fán muht	bin3 seng4 fan2 mut6	pin sehng fan muht
powdered sugar	n	糖粉	tòhng fán	tong4 fan2	thohng fan
power[1]	n	權力	kyùhn lihk	kyun4 lik6	khyuhn lehk
power[2]	n	權	kyùhn	kyun4	khyuhn
power[3]	n	勢	sai	sai3	sai
power base in political	n	權力基礎	kyuhn lihk gèi chó	kyun4 lik6 gei4 co2	khyuhn lehk kei chho
power cut	n	停電	tìhng dihn	ting4 din6	thehng tihn
power lens	n	透鏡	tau géng	tau3 geng2	thau keng
power sharing	n	權力分掌	kyuhn lihk fahn jéung	kyun4 lik6 fan6 zoeng2	khyuhn lehk fahn cheung
power switch	n	開關	hòi gwàan	hoi4 gwaan4	hoi kwaan
powerful[1]	adj	有力	yáuh lihk	jau5 lik6	yauh lehk
powerful[2]	adj	猛烈	máahng liht	maang5 lik6	maahng liht
power politics /powerful man	adj	權力	kyuhn lihk	kyun4 lik6	khyuhn lehk
powerful	adj	強力	kèuhng lihk	koeng4 lik6	kheuhng lehk
powerful man	adj	够力	gau lihk	gau3 lik6	kau lehk
powerless[1]	adj	無權	mòuh kyuhn	mou4 kyun4	mouh khyuhn
powerless[2]/impotence /sexless/ impotent	adj	性無能	sing mòuh làhng /nàhng	sing3 mou4 lang4 / nang4	seng mouh lahng /nahng
powerless person	n	無能者	móuh làhng /nàhng jé	mou2 lang4 /nang4 ze2	mouh lahng /nahng che
practical[1] /utility	adj	實用	saht yuhng	sat6 jung6	saht yuhng
practical[2] /actual	adj	實際	saht jai	sat6 zai3	saht chai
practical[3]	adj	實際的	sàht jái dìk	sat6 zai2 dik4	saht chai tek
practice[1] /study	n	習	jaahp	zaap6	chaahp
practice[2]	n	實習	saht jaahp	sat6 zaap6	saht chaahp
practice[3]	n	實踐	saht chín	sat6 cin2	saht chhin
practice[4]/act/act as play	n/v	演	yín	jin2	yin
practice makes perfect[1]	n	做得多就熟	jouh dāk dò jauh suhk	zou6 dak1 do4 zau6 suk6	chouh tak to chauh suhk
practice makes perfect[2]	n	熟能生巧	suhk nàhng sàng háau	suk6 nang6 sang4 haau2	suhk nahng sang haau
practitioner	n	執業者	jāp yihp jé	zap1 jip6 ze2	chap yihp che
praise[1] /say good	n	稱	chìng	cing4	chheng
praise[2] /extolment	n	讚	jaan	zaan3	chaan

praise[3]	n	讚美	jaan méih	zaan3 mei5	chaan meih
praise[4] /congratulations	n	讚詞	jaan chìh	zaan3 ci4	chaan chhih
praise[5]	n	誇	kwā	kwaa1	khwa
praise[6]	n	讚揚	jaan yèuhng	zaan3 joeng4	chaan yeuhng
prate /senseless talk	n	無聊話	mòuh lìuh wá	mou4 liu4 wa2	mouh liuh wa
pray[1]	n	禱	tóu	tou2	thou
pray[2] for god	v	祈禱	kèih tóu	kei4 tou2	kheih thou
pray[3] for god	v	禱告	tóu gou	tou2 gou3	thou kou
pray for	v	懇求	hán kàuh	han2 kau4	han khauh
prayer[1]	n	請求嘅人	chéng /chíng kàuh ge yàhn	ceng2 /cing2 kau4 ge3 jan4	chheng khauh Ke yahn
prayer[2]	n	要求人	yìu kàuh yàhn	jiu4 kau4 jan4	yiu khauh yahn
prayer[3]	n	祈禱者	kèih tóu jé	kei4 tou2 ze2	kheih thou che
pre-exist /exist from previously	v	早已存在	jóu yíh chyùhn joih	zou2 ji5 cyun4 zoi6	chou yih chhyuhn choih
preach[1] /to lecture /sermon	v	傳道	chyùhn douh	cyun4 dou6	chhyuhn touh
preach[2]	v	佈道	bou douh	bou3 dou6	pou touh
preacher	n	傳道者	chyùhn douh jé	cyun4 dou6 ze2	chhyuhn touh che
precaution	n	防備措施	fòhng bèih chóu yìh	fong4 bei6 cou2 ji6	fohng peih chhou yih
precautionary	n	防備	fòhng bèih	fong4 bei6	fohng peih
precedence[1]	n	佔先	jim sin	zim3 sin3	chim sin
precedence[2] /precedent	n	前例	chìhn laih	cin4 lai6	chhihn laih
precedence[3]	n	優先次序	yàu sín chí jèuih	jau4 sin2 ci2 zeoi6	yau sin chhi cheuih
precedent	n	前辯	chìhn bihn	cin4 bin6	chhihn pihn
precinct	n	轄區	haht kèui	hat6 keoi4	haht khoi
precious[1]	adj	寶貴	bóu gwai	bou2 gwai3	pou kwai
precious[2]	adj	珍貴	jàn gwai	zan4 gwai3	chan kwai
precious stone	n	寶石	bóu sehk	bou2 sek6	pou sehk
precipitous /steep	adj	陡峭	dáu chiu	dau2 ciu3	tau chhiu
predecessor[1]	n	前人	chìhn yàhn	cin4 jan4	chhihn yahn
predecessor[2]	n	前任	chìhn yahm	cin4 jam6	chhihn yahm
predict[1]	v	捉摸	jūk mō	zuk1 mo1	chuk mo
predict[2] /say future	v	預料	yùh līu	jyu6 liu1	yuh liu
predict[3] /say future	v	預報	yuh bou	jyu6 bou3	yuh pou
predictable	adj	可預測	hó yuh chāk	ho2 jyu6 cak1	ho yuh chhak
preface of a book /front matter	n	序言	jeuih yìhn	zeoi6 jin4	cheuih yihn
prefect	n	級長	kāp jéung	kap1 zoeng2	khap cheung
prefer /prefered	v	更喜歡	gàng héi fùn	gang4 hei2 fun4	kang hei fun
preferable	adj	較適合	gaau sīk hahp	gaau3 sik1 hap6	kaau sek hahp
preference	n	使用偏好	sāi yùhng pìn hōu	sai1 jung6 pin4 hou1	sai yuhng phin hou
preferment	n	晉升	jeun sìng	zeon3 sing4	cheun seng
prefix[1]	n	前綴	chìhn jeui	cin4 zeoi3	chhihn choi
prefix[2]	n	字首	jih sáu	zi6 sau2	chih sau

prefix[3]	n	前加成份	chìhn gà sèhng fahn	cin4 gaa4 seng4 fan6	chhìhn ka sehng fahn
preform /pre-shape	vt	預先形成	yuh sìn yìhng sīk	jyu6 sin4 jing4 sik1	yuh sin yehng sek
preformation	n	預先定形	yuh sìn dehng yìhng	jyu6 sin4 deng6 jing4	yuh sin tehng yehng
pregnant[1]	adj	有身紀	yáuh sàn géi	jau5 san4 gei2	yauh sam kei
pregnant[2] /gestation /become pregnant/embryo period about **266** days	adj	懷孕	wàaih yahn	waai4 jan6	waaih yahn
prehistory /previous history	n	遠古時期	yúhn gú sìh kèih	jyun5 gu2 si4 kei4	yuhn ku sih kheih
prejudge	v	預先判斷	yuh sìn pun dyun	jyu6 sin4 pun3 dyun3	yuh sin phun tyun
premature	adj	預早	yùh jōu	jyu6 zou1	yuh chouu
premature-death /short life		短命	dyún mehng	dyun2 meng6	tyun mehng
premise /premiss	n	前提	chìhn tàih	cin4 tai4	chhìhn thaih
premises[1]	n	佔有面積	jim yáuh mihn jīk	zim3 jau5 min6 zik1	chim yauh mihn chek
premises[2]	n	房屋連地基	fóng ūk /ngūk lìhn deih gēi	fong2 uk1 /nguk1 lin4 dei6 gei1	fong uk /nguk lihn teih kei
premises[3]	n	經營場址	gìng yìhng chèuhng jí	ging4 jing4 coeng4 zi2	keng yehng chheuhng chi
premium	n	優惠	yàu waih	jau4 wai6	yau waih
prepaid	adj	預先付嘅	yuh sìn fuh ge	jyu6 sin4 fu6 ge3	yuh sin fuh ke
prepare /make ready	v	預備	yuh beih	jyu6 bei6	yuh peih
prepared /ready made /ready	adj	預製	yuh jai	jyu6 zai3	yuh chai
prepay /prepayment	n	預付	yuh fuh	jyu6 fu6	yuh fuh
preposition[1]	n	介詞	gaai chìh	gaai3 ci4	kaai chhih
preposition[2]	n	介系詞	gaai haih chìh	gaai3 hai6 ci4	kaai haih chhih
preready for rainy day[(coll)] /rainy day/ready for really need it		好未揾埋落雨柴	hóu tīn wán màaih lohk yúh chàaih	hou2 tin1 wan2 maai4 lok6 jyu5 caai4	hou thin wan maaih lohk yuh chhaaih
prerequisite	n	必要條件	bìt yìu tìuh gihn	bit4 jiu4 tiu4 gin6	pit yiu thiuh kihn
prescription[1]	n	藥方	yeuhk fōng	joek6 fong1	yeuhk fong
prescription[2] /recipe	n	處方	chyu fòng	cyu3 fong4	chhyu fong
present[1] /give	v	有提	yáuh daih	jau5 dai6	yauh taih
present[2] /give	n	送	súng	sung2	sung
present[3] /give	n	禮品	láih bán	lai5 ban2	laih pan
present condition	n	而家嘅情形	yìh gā ge chìhng yìhng	ji4 gaa1 ge3 cing4 jing4	yih ka ke chhehng yehng
present participle	n	現在分詞	yihn joih fàn chìh	jin6 zoi6 fan4 ci4	yihn choih fan chhih
present-report	n	情報	chìhng bou	cing4 bou3	chhehng pou
present tense[1]	n	現在時	yihn joih sìh	jin6 zoi6 si4	yihn choih sih
present tense[2]	n	現在式	yihn joih sīk	jin6 zoi6 sik1	yihn choih sek
presentation[1] /gift	n	贈送	jahng sung	zang6 sung	chahng sung
presentation[2] award	n	授予	sauh yùh	sau6 jyu4	sauh yuh
presentation[3] award to the court	n	呈獻	gou hin	gou3 hin3	kou hin

English		Chinese	Yale	Jyutping	Pronunciation
presentation[4] /submiting/demonstration	n	提交	tàih gāau	tai4 gaau1	thaih kaau
presentation[5] show	n	演出	yín chēut	jin2 ceot1	yin chhot
presenter for /TV & radio	n	節目主持人	jit muhk jyú chìh yàhn	zit3 muk6 zyu2 ci4 jan4	chit muhk chyu chhih yahn
preserver /protector	v	保護人	bóu wùh yàhn	bou2 wu6 jan4	pou wuh yahn
president[1] of federal system	n	總統	júng túng	zung2 tung2	chung thung
president[2] of republic /chairman	n	主席	jyú jihk	zyu2 zik6	chyu chehk
president[3] of a committee /chairman	n	會長	wuih jéung	wui6 zoeng2	wuìh cheung
press[1] /push	v	按	òn /ngòn	on3 /ngon4	on /ngon
press[2] /push	v	搾	ja	zaa3	cha
press button	n	按下	on /ngon hah	on3 /ngon3 haa6	on /ngon hah
press by (finger or hand)	n	撳	gahm	gam6	kahm
press by law	n	出版法	chēut báan faat	ceot1 baan2 faat3	chhot paan faat
press cloth	n	熨平	tong pèhng /pìhng	tong3 peng4 /ping4	thong phehng
press door bell /ring at the door	n/v	按門鐘	on mùhn jùng	on3 mun4 zung4	on /ngon muhn chung
press feeling /emotion /feeling	n	感情	gám chìhng	gam2 cing4	kam chhehng
press media	n	新聞輿論	sàn màhn yùh leuhn	san4 man4 jyu4 leon6	san mahn yuh leuhn
press on	n	強加給	kéuhng ga kāp	koeng5 gaa3 kap1	kheuhng ka khap
press stud /push button	v	摁扣	on /ngòn kau	on3 /ngon4 kau3	on /ngon khau
press to stop	n	按停	on /ngòn tìhng	on3 /ngon4 ting4	on /ngon thehng
press to turn	n	按扭	on láu, ngòn náu	on3 lau2, ngon4 nau2	on lau, ngon nau
press-up /push up /physical exercise	n/v	俯臥撐	fú ngoh chāang	fu2 ngo6 caang1	fu ngoh chhaang
pressure	n	壓力	áat lihk	aat2 lik6	aat lehk
pressure plate	n	壓力盤	áat lìhk pun	aat2 lik6 pun3	aat lehk phun
prestige	n	名望	mèhng /mìhng mohng	meng4 /ming4 mong6	mehng mohng
prestigious /famous family	adj	名門	mèhng /mìhng mùhn	meng4 /ming4 mun4	mehng muhn
presuade[1] /sex into a trap /sexually attract/intended to attract/come-on of sex	n/xy	引誘	yáhn yáuh	jan5 jau5	yahn yauh
presuade[2]	n	勸誘	hyun yáuh	hyun3 jau5	hyun yauh
presume /suspect	v	思疑	sì yìh	si4 ji4	si yih
pretence[1] /pretense /pretend	n	自以為是	jih yíh waih sih	zi6 ji5 wai6 si6	chih yih waih sih
pretence[2] /pretense /pretend	n	詐諦	ja dai	zaa3 dai3	cha tai
pretest /advance check	n	預檢	yùh gīm	jyu6 gim1	yuh kim
pretext /false show	n	詐假而	ja gà yī	zaa3 gaa4 ji1	cha ka yi
pretty /beautiful	adj	秀麗	sau laih	sau3 lai6	sau laih
pretty good	adv	非常如	fei sèuhng yùh	fei3 soeng4 jyu4	fei seuhng yuh

English	Part	Chinese	Romanization 1	Jyutping	Romanization 2
pretty-lady	adv	靚女!	leng léuih /néuih	leng3 leoi5 /neoi5	leng lowih /nowih
pretty voice	adv	悅耳	yuht yíh	jyut6 ji5	yuht yih
prevail	v	戰勝	jin sing	zin3 sing3	chin seng
prevailing	adj	普遍嘅	póu pin	pou2 pin3	phou phin
prevent[1] /protect	v	預防	yuh fòhng	jyu6 fong4	yuh fohng
prevent[2]	v	防止	fòhng jí	fong4 zi2	fohng chi
preventive innoculative /immunization injection	n	預防針	yuh fòhng jām	jyu6 fong4 zam1	yuh fohng cham
preview	n	預先審查	yuh sìn sám chàh	jyu6 sin4 saam2 caa4	yuh sin sam chhah
previously	adv	早前	jóu chìhn	zou2 cin4	chou chhihn
previously renew		往年更新	wóhng lìhn gāng sàn	wong5 lin4 gang2 san1	wohng lihn kang san
prevision	n	預知	yùh jī /ji	jyu6 zi1 /zi	yuh chih /chi
price[1] /value	n	價	ga	gaa3	ka
price[2]	n	價錢	ga chìhn	gaa3 cin4	ka chihn
price rise /price up	adj	漲加	jeung gā	zoeng3 gaa1	cheung ka
price tag	n	價格標籤	ga gaak bīu chīm	gaa3 gaak3 biu1 cim1	ka kaak piu chhim
priceless	adj	貴重	gwai chúhng	gwai3 cung5	kwai chhuhng
prick[1] /stab/thorn	v&i	刺	chi	ci3	chhi
prick[2] /stab/pierce/poke	v&i	拮	gāt	gat1	kat
prickle	v	抽根	chàu gān	cau4 gan1	chhau gan
prickteaser	n	媚態	mouh taai	mou6 taai3	mouh thaai
pride /proud of …	n	驕傲	gìu ngouh	giu4 ngou6	kiu ngouh
prideless[1]	adj	唔驕傲	m̀ gìu ngouh	m4 giu4 ngou6	mh kiu ngouh
prideless[2]	adj	不驕傲	bāt gìu ngouh	bat1 giu4 ngou6	pat kiu ngouh
priest (Catholic) /spiritual father	n	神父	sàhn fuh	san4 fu6	sahn fuh
primary /basic	adj	根本	gān bún	gan1 bun2	kan pun
primary cause	adj	主要嘅	jyú yiu ge	zyu2 jiu3 ge3	chyu yiu ke
primary school[1]	n	小學	síu hohk	siu2 hok6	siu hohk
primary school[2]	n	小學校	síu hòhk hàauh	siu2 hok haau6	siu hohk haauh
prime	v	作準備	jok jéun beih	zok jéun bei6	chok cheun peih
prime life	n	壯年	jong lìhn /nìhn	zong3 lin4 /nin4	chong lihn /nihn
prime minister[1] republics	n	總理	júng léih	zung2 lei5	chung leih
prime minister[2] UK/Japan	n	首相	sáu seung	sau2 soeng3	sau seung
primitive	adj	原始嘅	yùhn chí ge	jyun4 ge3	yuhn chhi ke
princess	n	王族女性成員	wòhng juhk léuih /néoih sing sèhng yùhn	wong4 juk6 leui5 /neui5 sing3 seng4 jyun4	wohng chuhk lowih /nowih seng sehng yuhn
principal[1] /important	adj	資本	jì bún	zi4 bun2	chi pun
principal[2] /most important	adj	首要	sáu yiu	sau2 jiu3	sau yiu
principal[3] chief of the college/headmaster	n	校長	haauh jéung	haau6 zoeng2	haauh cheung
principle[4] /doctrineism /ideology	n	主義	jyú yih	zyu2 ji6	chyu yih

English	Part	Chinese	Romanization	Jyutping	Yale-style
print[1]	v	印	yan	jan3	yan
print[2] /printout	n	打印	dā yan	daa1 jan3	ta yan
print[3]	v	印刷	yan chaat	jan3 caat3	yan chhaat
print[4] /mark/scratch	n	印刷	yan chaat	jan3 caat3	yan chhaat
print in memory	v	銘記	mìhng gei	ming4 gei3	mehng kei
print machine	n	印機	yan gèi	jan3 gei4	yan kei
print of finge /mark of finger	n	紋 (指)	màhn (jí)	man4 (zi2)	mahn (chi)
printed	adj	發行	faat hòhng	faat3 hong4	faat hohng
printed matter	n	印刷品	yan chaat bán	jan3 caat3 ban2	yan chhaat pan
printer[1]	n	印刷者	yan chaat jé	jan3 caat3 ze2	yan chhaat che
printer[2]	n	打印機	dā yan gèi	daa1 jan3 gei4	ta yan kei
printer[3]	n	印刷機	yan chaat gèi	jan3 caat3 gei4	yan chahat kei
printing shop	n	印刷廠	yan chaat bán	jan3 caat3 ban2	yan chhaat pan
printing-press[1]	n	印刷業	yan chaat yihp	jan3 caat3 jip6	yan chhaat yihp
printing-press[2]	n	印刷術	yan chaat seuht	jan3 caat3 seot6	yan chhaat swoht
printouts	n	打印輸出	dā yan syū chēut	daa1 jan3 syu1 ceot1	ta yan syu chhot
prior[1]	adj	在先	joih sin	zoi6 sin3	choih sin
prior[2]	adj	優先	yàu sìn	jau4 sin4	yau sin
prior[3]	adj	居先	gèui sìn	geoi4 sin4	kwoi sin
prioritise	v	給予優先	kāp yùh yāu sìn	kap1 jyu4 jau1 sin4	khap yuh yau sin
priority[1]	n	優先	yàu sìn	jau4 sin4	yau sin
priority[2]	n	優先權	yàu sìn kyùhn	jau4 sin4 kyun4	yau sin khyuhn
priority-power /ridgt of way	adj	優先權	yàu sìn kyùhn	jau4 sin4 kyun4	yau sin khyuhn
prism	n	折光物體	jit gwòng maht tái	zit3 gwong4 mat6 tai2	chit kwong maht thai
prisoner[1] /detention	n	拘留	kèui làuh	keoi4 lau4	khoi lauh
prisoner[2]	n	囚犯	chàuh fáan	cau4 faan2	chhauh faan
prisoner[3]	n	監犯	gàam fáan	gaam4 faan2	kaam faan
prisoner[4] by persons /hostage man	n	人質	yàhn ji	jan4 zi3	yahn chi
privacy	n	私隱	sī tùng	si1 tung4	si thung
privacy right	n	隱私權	yán sì kyun	jan2 si4 kyun3	yan si khyun
private[1] /personal	adj	私人	sī yàhn	si1 jan1	si yahn
private[2] /personal	adj	個人	go yàhn	go3 jan4	ko yahn
private[3] /privately established	adj	私立	sì lahp /laahp	si4 lap6 /laap6	si lahp /laahp
private[4]	adj	私家	sī gā	si1 gaa1	si ka
private[5]	adj	私營	sī yìhng	si1 jing4	si yehng
private & confidential /secret letter	n	密函	maht hàahm	mat6 haam6	maht haahm
private area	n	私家地方	sī gā deih fòng	si1 gaa1 dei6 fong4	si ka teih fong
private company	n	私人公司	sī yàhn gūng sī	si1 jan4 gung1 si1	si yahn kung si
private road	n	私家路	sī gā louh	si1 gaa1 lou6	si ka louh
private sectore	n	私營部分	sī yìhng bouh fahn	si1 jing4 bou6 fan6	si yehng pouh fahn

privately	adv	不公開地	bāt gūng hòi deih	bat1 gung1 hoi4 dei6	pat kung hoi teih
privilege /special rights	v	特權	dahk kyùhn	dak6 kyun4	tahk khyuhn
privileged[1] /respected	adj	榮幸	wìhng hàhng	wing4 hang6	wehng hahng
privileged[2]	adj	榮幸嘅	wìhng hàhng ge	wing4 hang6 ge3	wehng hahng ke
prize /award	n	獎品	jéung bán	zoeng2 ban2	cheung pan
probability	n	可能性	hó làhng /nàhng sing	ho2 lang4 /nang4 sing3	ho lahng /nahng seng
probably[1] /may be	adv	可能	hó làhng /nàhng	ho2 lang4 /nang4	ho lahng /nahng
probably[2] /probable	adv	很可能	hān hó làhng /nàhng	han1 ho2 lang4 /nang4	han ho lahng /nahng
probation[1]	n	見習	gin jaahp	gin3 zaap6	kin chaahp
probation[2]	n	見習嘅	gìn jaahp ge	gin3 zaap6 ge3	kin chaahp ke
probe /examine/test	v	探針	taam jām	taam3 zam1	thaam cham
procedure /order/rule /process /regulations/ sequence/command	n	程	chìhng	cing4	chhehng
proceed /continue /go on/go forward/catty on	v	繼續進行	gai juhk jeun hàhng	gai3 zuk6 zeon3 hang4	kai chuhk cheun haang
proceed-forward of vehicle	v	開車前進	hòi chè chìhn jeun	hoi4 ce4 cin4 zeon3	hoi chhe chhihn cheun
proceed to drive ship or vehicle	v	駛	sái	sai2	sai
proceeding	n	繼續進行	gai jùhk jéun haang	gai3 zuk6 zeon2 hang4	kai chuhk cheun haang
proceedings[1] /meeting report	n	會議記錄	wuih yíh géi luhk	wui6 ji5 gei2 luk6	wuih yíh géi luhk
proceedings[2] lawsuit	n	訴訟程序	sou juhng chìhng jeuih	sou3 zung6 cing4 zeoi6	sou chuhng chhihng choih
proceedings[3] of law action	n	法律程序	faat leuht chìhng jeuih	faat3 leot6 cing4 zeoi6	faat lwoht chhehng choih
procelain /Chinaware	n	瓷器	chìh hei	ci4 hei3	chhih hei
process	n	進程	jeun chìhng	zeon3 cing4	cheun chhehng
process work		工序	gùng jeuih	gung4 zeoi6	kung choih
procession[1] /line up	n	列隊	liht déui	lit6 deoi2	liht toei
procession[2]/queuing /range/series	n	行列	hòhng liht	hong4 lit6	hohng liht
procession[3]	n	隊伍	deuih ńgh	deoi6 ng5	toeih ngh
processor[1] by machine	n	加工機	gā gùng gèi	gaa1 gung4 gei4	ka kung kei
processor[2] by man	n	加工者	gā gùng jé	gaa1 gung4 ze2	ka kung che
proclamation[1]	n	公佈	gūng bou	gung1 bou3	kung pou
proclamation[2]	n	宣佈	syùn bou	syun4 bou3	syun pou
produce[1]	v	成果	sèhng gwó	seng4 gwo2	sehng kwo
produce[2] /production	v	生產	sàng cháan	sang4 caan2	sang chhaan
product	n	出產	chēut cháan	ceot1 caan2	chhot chhaan
production dept	n	生產部	sàng cháan bouh	sang4 caan2 bou6	sang chhaan pouh
productive	adj	收益	sàu yīk	sau4 jik1	sau yek
productivity power	n	生產力	sàng cháan lihk	sang4 caan2 lik6	sang chhaan lehk
profane[1] /nasty	v	世俗	sai juhk	sai3 zuk6	sai chohk
profane[2] /nasty	v	褻瀆	sit duhk	sit3 duk6	sit tuhk

profane talk /abuse speak	n	褻瀆神性嘅說話	sit duhk sàhn sing ge syut wá	sit3 duk6 san4 sing3 ge3 syut3 waa2	sit tuhk sahn seng ke syut wa
profile /brief introduction	n	簡介	gáan gaai	gaan2 gaai3	kaan kaai
profit[1] interest of loan /by interest	n	利錢	leih chìhn	lei6 cin4	leih chhihn
profit[2] by selling	n	利潤	leih yuhn	lei6 jeon	leih yuhn
profit[3] /gain	n	盈利	yìhng leih	jing4 lei6	yehng leih
profit[4] /benefits	n	獲利	wohk leih	wok6 lei6	wohk leih
profit[5] /surplus	n	盈餘	yìhng yùh	jing4 jyu4	yehng yuh
profit[6] /useful	v	有益於	yáuh yīk yū /yùh	jau5 jik1 jyu1 /jyu4	yauh yek yu /yuh
profitable	adj	有利	yáuh lèih	jau5 lei6	yauh leih
profitless	adj	蝕本	siht bún	sit6 bun2	siht pun
profound	adj	深刻	sàm hàak	sam4 haak4	sam haak
program[1]	n	節目	jit muhk	zit3 muk6	chit muhk
program[2]	n	程式	chìhng sīk	cing4 sik1	chhehng sek
programme note	n	劇情	kehk chìhng	kek6 cing4	khehk chhehng
programs operating computer/software of computer	n	軟件	yúhn gihn	jyun5 gin6	yuhn kihn
progress	n	進展	jeun jin	zeon3 zin3	cheun jin
progressive	adj	進步嘅	jeun bouh ge	zeon3 bou6 ge3	cheun pouh ke
progressively	adv	日益增加	yaht yìk jàng gà	jat6 jik4 zang4 gaa4	yaht yek chang ka
prohibit /not allowed /ban/forbid/not to do	v	禁止	gam jí	gam3 zi2	kam chi
prohibition	n	禁錮	gām gu	gam1 gu3	kam ku
prohibitory	adj	禁止嘅	gam jí ge	gam3 zi2 ge3	kam chi ke
project /reflect light	n	映	yíng	jing2	yeng
projector[1] machine	n	放映機	fong yíng gèi	fong3 jing2 gei4	fong ying kei
projector[2] man/schemer	n	計劃者	gai waahk jé	gai3 waak6 ze2	kai waahk che
proletariat[1]	n	無産階級	mòuh cháan gàai kāp	mou4 caan2 gaai4 kap1	mouh chhaan kaai khap
proletariat[2] /no one's property	n	農工階級	lùhng /nùhng gùng gàai kāp	lung4 /nung4 gung4 gaai kap1	luhng /nuhng kung kaai khap
proliferation	n	激增	gīk jāng	gik1 zang1	kek chang
promise[1]	v	承諾	sìhng nohk	sing4 nok6	sehng nohk
promise[2]	v	應承	yìng sìhng	jing4 sing4	yeng sehng
promise[3]	v	實詞	saht chí	sat6 ci2	saht chhi
promise[4]	v	諾言	lohk yìhn	lok6 jin4	lohk yihn
promise to marry	n	訂婚	dehng /dihng fān	deng6 /ding6 fan1	tehng fan
promiser[1]	n	約束者	yeuk chūk jé	joek3 cuk1 ze2	yeuk chhuk che
promiser[2]	n	許諾者	héui nohk jé	heoi2 nok6 ze2	hoi nohk che
promote[1]	v	晉升	jeun sìng	zeon3 sing4	cheun seng
promote[2]	v	提升	tàih sìng	tai4 sing4	thaih seng
promoter	n	促進者	chūk jeun jé	cuk4 zeon3 ze2	chhuk cheun che
promotion[1]	n	推廣	tèui gwóng	teoi4 gwong2	thoi kwong
promotion[2]	n	晉級	jeun kāp	zeon3 kap1	cheun khap

promotion[3] /sales promotion	n	促銷	chūk sīu	cuk1 siu1	chhuk siu
prompt[1]	v	提示	tai sìh	tai4 si6	thai sih
prompt[2]	v	迅促/迅速	seun chùk	seon3 cuk4	swon chhuk
prompting	n	敦促	dèun chūk	deon4 cuk1	ton chhuk
promptly	adv	立即地	lahp jīk deih	lap6 zik1 dei6	lahp chek teih
promulgated[1]	v	頒佈	bàan bou	baan4 bou3	paan pou
promulgated[2]	v	公報消息	gùng bou sìu sīk	gung4 bou3 siu3 sik1	kung pou siu sek
prone[1]	adj	趴係道	pā haih douh	paa1 hai6	pha haih touh
prone[2] /face downward	adv	面向下	mihn heung hah	min6 hoeng3 ha6	mihn heung hah
prone[3] /to suffer	adv	易於遭受	yih yù jòu sauh	ji6 jyu4 zou4 sau6	yih chou sauh
pronoun[1] grammar	n	代詞	doih chìh	doi6 ci4	toih chhih
pronoun[2] grammar	n	代名詞	doih mèhng chìh	doi6 meng4 ci4	toih mehng chhih
pronunciation	n	讀音	duhk yām	duk6 jam1	tuhk yam
proof	n	證	jing	zing3	cheng
proof of identity		身分證明 文件	sàn fán jing mìhng màhn gín	san4 fan2 zing3 ming4 man4 gin2	san fan cheng mehng mahn kin
proofreader[1]	n	校對者	gaau deui	gaau3 deoi3	kaau deui
proofreader[2] /editor	n	校對員	gaau deui yùhn	gaau3 deoi3 jyun4	kaau twoi yuhn
propel /push forward	v	推動	tèui dùhng	teoi4 dung6	thoi tohng
propeller device	n	螺旋槳	lòh syun jéung	lo4 syun3 zoeng2	loh syun cheung
proper[1] /appropriate	adj	妥善	tóh sìhn	to5 sin6	thoh sihn
proper[2]	adj	合適嘅	hahp sīk ge	hap6 sik1 ge3	hahp sek ke
proper[3] /suitable	adj	恰當	hāp dong	hap1 dong3	hap tong
proper lock		鎖好	só hóu	so2 hou2	so hou
proper time		及恰時	kahp hāp sìh	kap6 hap1 si4	khahp hap sih
properly[1]	adv	適當咁	sīk dong gám	sik1 dong3 gam2	sek tong kam
properly[2]	adv	理所當然地	léih só dòng yìhn deih	lei5 so2 dong4 jin4 dei6	leih so tong yihn teih
property[3]	n	物業	maht yihp	mat6 jip6	maht yihp
property[4] /real estate	n	產業	cháan yihp	caan2 jip6	chhaan yihp
prophecy	n	預言	yuh yìhn	jyu6 jin4	yuh yihn
prophylactic	n	預防藥	yuh fòhng yeuhk	jyu6 fong4 joek6	yuh fohng yeuhk
proportionate	adj	相稱	sèung chán	soeng4 can2	seung chhaahn
propose	v	建議	gin yi	gin3 ji3	kin yi
proprietor /owner	n	業主	yihp jyú	jip6 zyu2	yihp chyu
propriety[1]	n	適當	sīk dong	sik1 dong3	sek tong
propriety[2]	n	規矩	kwài géui	kwai4 geoi2	khwai kwoi
propriety[3] /moral /behaviour	n	行為正當	hàhng wàih jeng /jing dong	hang4 wai4 zeng3 /zing3 dong3	hahng waih cheng tong
prosecute	v	起訴	héi sou	hei2 sou3	hei sou
prosecution /sue	v	起訴	héi sou	hei2 sou3	hei sou
prosecutor[1] court case	n	公訴人	gùng sou yàhn	gung4 sou3 jan4	kung sou yahn
prosecutor[2] court case	n	檢察官	gím chaat gùn	gim2 caat3 gun4	kim chhaat kun
prospect /hope for	n	盼望	paan mohng	paan3 mong6	phaan mohng

prospectus	n	內容說明書	loih /noih yung séui ming syù	loi6 /noi6 jung3 seoi3 mung3 syu4	loih /noih yung swoi meng syu
prosperity	n	興旺	hìng wohng	hing4 wong6	hing wohng
prostate gland	n	前列腺	chìhn liht sin	cin4 lit6 sin3	chhihn liht sin
prostitute[1] (coll)	n	雞	gài	gai4	kai
prostitute[2]	n	娼	chēung	coeng1	chheung
prostitute[3]	n	妓	geih	gei6	keih
prostitute[4]	n	娼妓	chēung geih	coeng1 gei6	chheung keih
prostitute[5]	n	賣身	maaih sàn	maai6 san4	maaih san
prostitute[6]	n	濫用	laahm yuhng	laam6 jung6	laahm yuhng
prostitute-girl	n	嫖妓	pìuh geih	piu4 gei6	phiuh geih
prostitution	n	賣淫	maaih yàhm	maai6 jam4	maaih yahm
prostrate	v	爬下地下	pā hah deih hah	paa4 haa6 dei6 haa6	pha hah teih hah
protect	v	護	wuh	wu6	wuh
protein	n	蛋白質	dāan baahk jāt	daan1 baak6 zat1	taan paahk chat
protest	v	抗議	kong yíh	kong3 ji5	khong yih
protestant[1]	n	基督教	gēi dūk gaau	gei1 duk1 gaau3	kei tuk kaau
protestant[2]	adj	提出異議	tàih chēut yih yi	tai4 ceot1 ji6 ji3	thaih chhot yih yi
protestantism	n	基督教	gēi dūk gaau	gei1 duk1 gaau3	kei tuk kaau
protocol[1] /treaty/draft of a plan/rules of conduct	n	草案	chou on /ngon	cou3 on3 /ngon3	chhou on /ngon
protocol[2]	n	議定書	yíh dehng /dihng syù	ji5 deng6 /ding syu4	yih tehng syu
proud[1]	adj	驕	gìu	giu4	kiu
proud[2] /self important /proud of something	adj	驕傲	gìu ngouh	giu4 ngou6	kiu ngouh
proud[3]	adj	自大	jih daaih	zi6 daai6	chih taaih
proud[4](sl) /pride/arrogance	adj	沙塵	sà chàhn	sa4 can4	sa chhahn
proud[5] /boast proud way	adj	自豪	jih hòuh	zi6 hou4	chih houh
proudly[1]	adv	自豪地	jih hòuh deih	zi6 hou4 dei6	chih houh teih
proudly[2]	adv	自高自大	jih gōu jih daaih	zi6 gou1 daai6	chih kou chih taaih
proverb	n	諺	yihn	jin6	yihn
provide /supply	v	提供	tàih gùng	tai4 gung4	thaih kung
provident[1] /needy	adj	儉	gihm	gim6	kihm
provident[2]	adj	節儉	jit gihm	zit3 gim1	chit kihm
provident[3]	adj	深謀遠慮	sàm màuh yúhn leuih	sam4 mau4 jyun5 leoi6	sam mauh yuhn lowih
provider	n	提供者	tàih gùng jé	tai4 gung4 ze2	thaih kung che
province	n	省	sáang	saang2	saang
provision /prepare	n/v	準備	jéun beih	zeon2 bei6	cheun peih
provisional /interim /temporary/short time	adj	臨時	làhm sih	lam4 si4	lahm sih
provoke[1] /infuriate	v	激怒	gīk louh /nouh	gik1 lou6 /nou6	kek louh /nouh
provoke[2] /inflame anger	v	使憤怒	sái fahn louh /nouh	sai2 fan5 lou6 /nou6	sai fahn louh /nouh
provoking[1]	n	叫人冒火	gìu yàhn mouh fó	giu3 jan4 mou6 fo2	kiu yahn mouh fo
provoking[2] /make disturb	n	令人嬲	ling yàhn làu /nàu	ling3 jan4 lau4 /nau4	leng yahn lau /nau

proxemics[1] /personal distance/personal space 1.5 to 4 ft, personal distance for interactions among …	n	人際距離學	yàhn jai kéuih lèih hohk	jan4 zai3 keoi5 lei4 hok6	yahn chai khoih leih hohk
proxemics[2] /personal distance/personal space 1.5 to 4 ft, personal distance for interactions among …	n	個人空間	go yàhn hùng gàan	go3 jan4 hung4 gaan4	ko yahn hung kaan
proxy	n	代理權	doih léih kyùhn	doi6 lei5 kyun4	toih leih khyuhn
pry with secret	v	刺探	chi tāam	ci3 taam1	chhi thaam
pseudo	adj	偽似	ngàih chíh	ngai6 ci5	ngaih chhih
pseudopodium	n	偽足	ngàih jūk	ngai6 zuk1	ngaih chuk
psychological[1] /state of mind	adj	心理	sàm léih	sam4 lei5	sam leih
psychological[2]	adj	心理學	sàm léih hohk	sam4 lei5 hok6	sam leih hohk
pub /bar	n	酒吧	jáu bà	zau2 baa4	chau pa
pubic bone	n	陰部骨	yàm bouh gwāt	jam4 bou6 gwat1	yam pouh kwat
pubic hair[1]	n	陰毛	yàm mòuh	jam4 mou4	yam mouh
pubic hair[2]	n	阴毛	yàm mòuh	jam4 mou4	yam mouh
public[1]	n	公	gùng	gung4	kung
public[2]	n	公眾	gùng jung	gung4 zung3	kung chung
public access	n	向公眾開放	heung gùng jung hòi fong	hoeng gung4 zung3 hoi4 fong3	heung kung chung hoi fong
public charges legal	n	公訴	gùng sou	gung4 sou3	kung sou
public company	n	公開招股公司	gùng hòi jīu gú gūng sī	gung4 hoi4 ziu1 gu2 gung1 si1	kung hoi chiu ku kung si
public figure	n	公眾人士	gùng jung yàhn sih	gung4 zung3 jan4 si6	kung chung yahn sih
public footpath	n	公用道路	gùng yuhng douh louh	gung4 jung6 dou6 lou6	kung yuhng touh louh
public holiday	n	公眾假期	gùng jung ga kèih	gung4 zung3 gaa3 kei4	kung chung ka kheih
public house	n	公屋	gùng ùk	gung4 uk4	kung uk
public housing	n	公共房屋	gùng guhng fóng ùk /ngūk	gung4 gung6 fong2 uk1 /nguk1	kung guhng fong uk /nguk
public library	n	公共圖書館	gung guhng tòuh syù gún	gung3 gung6 tou4 syu4 gun2	kung guhng thouh syu kun
public opinion /consensus	n	輿論	yùh leuhn	jyu4 leon6	yuh leuhn
public park /park/ garden/public garden	n	公園	gùng yún	gung4 jyun2	kung yun
public relation	n	公共關係	gùng guhnggwàan haih	gung4 gung6 gwaan4 hai6	kung guhng kwaan haih
public school	n	公立學校	gùng lahp hohk haauh	gung4 lap6 hok6 haau6	kung lahp hohk haauh
public security bureau	n	公安機關	gùng ōn /ngōn gèi gwāan	gung4 on1 /ngon1 gei4 gwaan1	kung on /ngon kei kwaan
public service	n	公共服務	gùng guhng fuhk mouh	gung4 gung6 fuk6 mou6	kung guhng fuhk mouh
public toilet	n	公共廁所	gùng guhng chi só	gung4 gung6 ci3 so2	kung guhng chhi so
public utility	n	公用事業	gùng yuhng sih yihp	gung4 jung6 si6 jip6	kung yuhng sih yihp

English		Chinese	Yale	Jyutping	Romanization
publish /publication	n	出版	chēut báan	ceot1 baan2	chhot paan
publisher[1] (a person)	n	出版人	chēut báan yàhn	ceot1 baan2 jan4	chhot paan yahn
publisher[2] (a person)	n	出版者	chēut báan jé	ceot1 baan2 ze2	chhot paan che
publisher[3]	n	出版商	chēut báan sēung	ceot1 baan2 soeng1	chhot paan seung
pudding (de)	n	布甸	bou dīn	bou3 din1	pou den
pudenda vagina/vulva	n	女陰	léuih yàm	leui5 jam4	lowih yam
puff /spurt/spray/spray by mouth	v	噴	pan	pan3	phan
pull /trail	v	拖拉	tò làai	to4 laai4	thoh laai
pull drag /pull or draw	n	扳	pāan	paan1	phaan
pull open	n	趟開	tong hòi	tong3 hoi4	thong hoi
pull out	n	抽	chàu	cau4	chhau
pull out widely	n	拉長	làai chèuhng	laai4 coeng4	laai chheuhng
pull skin	n	拉皮	làai pèih	laai4 pei4	laai pheih
pull stop	n	拉住	lāai jyuh	laai1 zyu6	laai chyuh
pull up[1]	n	停下來	tìhng háh làih	ting4 haa5 lai4	thehng hah laih
pull up[2]	n	向上拉	heung séuhng làai	hoeng3 soeng5 lai4	heung seuhng laai
pulley	n	滑輪	waaht lèuhn	waat6 leon4	waaht leuhn
pulp	n	肉質部	yuhk jāt bouh	juk6 zat1 bou6	yuhk chat pouh
pulse	n	脈搏	mahk bok	mak6 bok3	mahk pok
pump (de)	n	泵	bàm /pām	bam4 /bam1	pam
pump[1]	n	唧	jēk	zek1	chek
pump[2]	v	唧筒	jēk tùhng	zek1 tung4	chek thuhng
pump water	v	抽水	chāu séui	cau1 seoi2	chhau swoi
punch /hit by boxing	v	拳打	kyùhn dá	kyun4 daa2	khyuhn ta
puncher	n	打孔器	dá húng hei	daa2 hung2 hei3	ta hung hei
punctual	adj	守時	sáu sìh	sau2 si4	sau sih
punctually	adj	準時地	jéun sìh deih	zeon2 si4 dei6	cheun sih teih
punctuation	n	標點法	bīu dím faat	biu1 dim2 faat3	piu tim faat
punctuation mark	n	標點符號	bīu dím fùh houh	biu1 dim2 fu4 hou6	piu tim fuh houh
puncture	v	損傷	syún sèung	syun2 soeng4	syun seung
pungent[1] /spicy taste /biting	adj	辛辣	sàn laaht	san4 laat6	san laaht
pungent[2]	adj	味道	meih douh	mei6 dou6	meih touh
pungent[3] /irritate taste	adj	刺鼻	chi bèih	ci3 bei6	chhi beih
punish[1] /punishment /penalty/sentence	v	刑	yìhng	jing4	yehng
punish[2]	v	處分	chyū fàn	cyu1 fan4	chhyu fan
punisher	n	懲罰者	chìhng faht jé	cing4 fat6 ze2	chhehng faht che
punk[1] /rude way boys	n	前衛	chìhn waih	cin4 wai6	chhihn waih
punk[1] /violent way boys	n	潮流	chìuh làuh	ciu4 lau4	chhiuh lauh
punk[2] /violent way boys	n	小流氓	síu làuh màhn	siu2 lau4 man4	siu lauh mahn
punk music /rock music rock music popular in the late 1970 &1980s	n	龐客搖滾樂	pàhng haak yìuh gwán lohk	faan4 haak3 jiu4 gwan2 lok6	phahng haak yiuh kwan lohk
pupa /larva	n	蛹	yúng	jung2	yung

English		Chinese	Cantonese	Jyutping	Romanization
pupil[1] (of eye)	n	睛	jìng /zìng	zing4	cheng
pupil[2] /student	n	學生	hohk sāang	hok6 saang1	hohk saang
puppy /dog's baby/pup	n	小狗	síu gáu	siu2 gau2	siu kau
purchase /buy/bought	v	購買	kau máaih	kau3 mai5	khau maaih
purchasing[1] /to buy	n	購	kau	kau3	khau
purchasing[2]	n	採購	chòih káu	coi4 kau2	chhoih khau
pure[1] /unmixed	adj	純淨	sèuhn jehng /jihng	seon4 jeng6 /jing6	swohn chehng
pure[2] /sheer/not mixed	adj	純粹	sèuhn seuih	seon4 seoi6	swohn swoih
purely	adv	純粹地	sèuhn seuih deih	seon4 seoi6 dei6	swohn swoih teih
purge[1] /to settle accounts	v	清算	chìng /chèng syun	cing4 /ceng4 syun3	chheng syun
purge[2]	v	清洗	chèng /chìng sái	ceng4 /cing4 sai2	chheng sai
purify for gold or oil /refine	v	提煉	tàih lihn	tai4 lin6	thaih lihn
purpose	n	宗旨	jung jí	zung3 zi2	chung chi
purpose of visit	n	造訪目	jouh fóng muhk	zou6 fong2 muk6	chouh fong muhk
purr	v	嗚嗚叫	wù wù giu	wu4 wu4 giu3	wu wu kiu
purse[1] /wallet/money bag	n	銀包	ngàhn bāau	ngan4 baau1	ngahn paau
purse[2] /wallet	n	錢包	chín bāau	cin2 baau1	chhin paau
purse[3] lips small round shape	n	嚓起	kyut héi	kyut3 hei2	khyut hei
pursue	v	追趕	jèui gón	zeoi4 gon2	cheui kon
pursuit /to chsase	n	追求	jèui kàuh	zeoi4 kau4	cheui khauh
push button /press stud	v	按鈕	on láu, ngòn náu	on3 lau2, ngon4 nau2	on lau, ngon nau
push strong /strong push	n	猛推	máahng tèui	maang5 teoi4	maahng thoi
pusher	n	推者	tèui jé	teoi4 ze2	thoi che
pushes away /repel /expel	v	擊退	gīk teui	gik1 teoi3	kek thoi
put /place/keep	v	擺	bāai	baai1	paai
put aside		放在一邊	fong joih yāt bīn	fong3 zoi6 jat1 bin1	fong choih yat pin
put down[1]		擠低	jài dài	zai4 dai4	chai tai
put down[2]		放低	fong dài	fong3 dai4	fong tai
put down as		視作	sih jok	si6 jok3	sih chok
put in[1] /insert		插挖	chaap wah	caap3 wa6	chhaap wah
put in[2] entering harbor		入港口	yahp góng háu	jap6 gong2 hau2	yahp kong hau
put in order /things in a place	adj	佈置	bou jí	bou3 zi3	pou chi
put into[1] /insert	v	探入	tám yahp	taam2 jap6	tham yahp
put into[2] /insert	v	放入	fong yahp	fong3 jap6	fong yahp
put off cloths/take out cloth	v	除衫	chèuih sàam	ceoi4 saam4	chheuih saam
put on[1] to wear hat or watch		戴	daai	daai3	taai
put on[2] to wear cloth		穿上	chyùn seuhng	cyun4 soeng6	chhyun seuhng
put out /take out/ unfasten/untie		伸出	sàn chēut	san4 ceot1	san chhot
put right	v	擺正	báai jeng /jing	baai2 zeng3 /jing3	paai cheng
put up	v	吊上面	diu seuhng mihn	diu3 soeng6 min6	tiu seuhng mihn

puzzle[1]	v	謎	màih	mai4	maih
puzzle[2] /crossword	v	縱橫字謎	jùng waahng jih màih	zung4 waang6 zi6 mai4	chung waahng chih maih
pyramid	n	金字塔	gàm jih taap	gam4 zi6 taap3	kam chih thaap
pyre	n	火葬用嘅柴堆	fó jong yuhng ge chàaih dèui	fo2 zong3 jung6 ge3 caai4deoi4	fo chong yuhng ke chhaaih toei
pyrolatry	n	拜火教	baai fó gaau	baai3 fo2 gaa3	paai fo kaau

English		漢字	拼音	Jyutping	Yale
quack[1] /cheater Dr	n	黃綠醫生	wòhng luhk yī sāng	wong4 luk6 ji1 sang1	wohng luhk yi sang
quack[2] duck sound	v	鴨叫聲	áap /ngáap giu sèng	aap2 /ngaap2 giu3 seng4	aap /ngaap kiu seng
quadruped animal /four-footed animal	n	四腳動物	sei geuk duhng maht	sei3 goek3 dung6 mat6	sei keuk tohng maht
quail	n	鵪鶉	ām chēun	am1 ceon1	am chheun
quaint[1]	adj	老式	lóuh sīk	lou5 sik1	louh sek
quaint[2] /odd	adj	古怪	gú gwaai	gu2 gwaai3	ku kwaai
qualification	n	資格	jì gaak	zi4 gaak3	chi kaak
qualified[1]	adj	合格	hahp gaak	hap6 gaak3	hahp kaak
qualified[2]	adj	夠資格	gau jì gaak	gau3 zi4 gaak3	kau chi kaak
qualified[3]	adj	使具有資格	sái geuih yáuh jī gaak	sai2 geoi6 jau5 zi1 gaak3	sai kwoih yauh chi kaak
quality	n	品質	bán jāt	ban2 zat1	pan chat
quantifier/triage /classification	n	分類	fàn lèuih	fan4 leoi6	fan lowih
quantify	v	量化	leuhng fa	loeng6 faa3	leuhng fa
quantum /fixed amount	n	定量	dehng /dihng leuhng	deng6 /ding6 loeng6	tehng leuhng
quarantine	v	進行檢疫	jeun hàhng gím yihk	zeon3 hang4 gim2 jik3	cheun hahng kim yehk
quarantine period /to separate time	n	隔離期	gaak lèih kèih	gaak3 lei4 kei4	kaak leih kheih
quarrel[1] of mouth	n	鬧咬	laauh /naauh gáauh	laau6 /naau6 gaau5	laauh /naauh kaauh
quarrel[2] between wifes's	n	爭寵	jàng chúng	zang4 cung2	chang chhung
quarrel[3] /dispute	n	爭吵	jàang cháau	zang4 caau2	chaang chhaau
quarrel with	n	不同意	bāt tùhng yi	bat1 tung4 ji	pat thuhng yi
quarrelling	n	嗌咬	aai /ngaai gàau	aai3 /ngaai3 gaau4	aai /ngaai kaau
quarry[1]	n	採石場	chói sehk chèuhng	coi2 sek6 coeng4	chhoi sehk cheuhng
quarry[2]	n	獵物	lihp maht	lip6 mat6	lihp maht
quarry[3]	n	採石工人	chói sehk gùng yàhn	coi2 sek6 gung4 jan4	chhoi sehk gung yahn
quarter[1] (de)	n	骨	gwāt	gwat1	kwat
quarter[2] (de)	n	一個骨	yāt go gwāt	jat1 go3 gwat1	yat ko kwat
quarter[3]	n	四分之一	sei fahn jì yāt	sei3 fan1 zi4 jat1	sei fahn chi yat
quartz	n	石英	sehk yīng	sek6 jing1	sehk ying
queen[1]	n	女王	léuih wòhng	leui5 wong4	lowih wohng
queen[2] of cards	n	王后	wohng hauh	wong6 hau6	wohng hauh
quench /quench thirsty	v	解渴	gáai hot	gaai2 hot3	kaai hot
quench thirsty	v	止渴	jí hot	zi2 hot3	chi hot
question?[1] if placed end of the sentence turn it into a question (?)	pron	嗎?	ma?	ma3?	ma?
question[2] (ask question)	v	問你	mahn léih	man6 lei5	mahn leih
question[3] /problem	v	問題	mahn tàih	man6 tai4	mahn thaih
question[4] (polite way)	v	我請問你	ngóh chéng mahn léih	ngo5 ceng2 man6 lei5	ngoh chheng mahn leih
question[5] (polite way)	v	一點問你?	yāt dím mahn léih /néih?	jat1 dim2 man6 lei5 /nei5?	yat tim mahn leih /neih?

English		Chinese	Yale	Jyutping	Romanization
question[6] (polite way)	v	我想問你	ngóh séung mahn léih	ngo5 soeng2 man6 lei5	ngoh seung mahn leih
question[7]/interrogate (no polite way)	v	審問	sám mahn	sam2 man6	sam mahn
question answer	n	問答	mahn daap	man6 daap	mahn taap
question mark	n	問號	mahn houh	man6 hou6	mahn houh
question tag	n	嗎	mā	maa1	ma
questionable /suspicious	adj	可疑	hó yìh	ho2 ji4	ho yih
questioner /asker	n	發問者	faat mahn jé	faat3 man6 ze2	faat mahn che
queue up /line up /stand in line	n/v	排隊	pàaih déui	paai4 deoi2	phaaih toei
quick /swift/quick action	adj	敏捷	máhn jit	man5 zit3	mahn chit
quick angry	n	暴躁脾氣	bouh chou pèih hei	bou6 cou3 pei4 hei3	pouh chhou pheih hei
quick as possible /asap	adv	儘快	jéun faai	zeon2 faai3	cheun faai
quick eyed	adj	眼睛銳利	ngáahn jìng yeuih leih	ngaan5 zing4 jeoi6 lei6	ngaahn cheng yeuih leih
quick run /gallop	n	奔馳	bàn chìh	ban4 ci4	pan chih
quick runner	n	奔馳者	bàn chìh jé	ban4 ci4 ze2	pan chih che
quick shout	n	呼叫等	fù giu dáng	fu4 giu3 dang2	fu kiu tang
quicker way[1]	n	捷徑	jit gíng	zit3 ging2	chit keng
quicker way[2]	n	近路	káhn louh	kan5 lou6	khahn louh
quickly	adv	很快	hān faai	han1 faai3	han faai
quickness	n	敏捷	máhn jit	man5 zit3	mahn chit
quiet /secluded/isolated	adj	幽靜	yàu jehng /jihng	jau4 zeng6 /zing6	yau chehng
quiet & private /secluded	adj	僻靜	pīk jehng /jihng	pik1 zeng6 /zing6	phik chehng
quietly[1] /softly/slowly/very slowly/stealthily /without sound	adv	靜靜地	jèhng jèhng déi, jìhng jìhng déi	zeng6 zeng6 dei2, zing6 zing6 dei2	chehng chehng tei
quietly[2]	adv	輕聲地	hèng sèng deih	heng4 seng4 dei6	heng seng teih
quilt[1] /cover	n	被	péih	pei5	pheih
quilt[2] /comforter	n	棉被	mìhn péih	min4 pei5	mihn pheih
quilt[3]	n	被子	péih jai	pei5 zai3	pheih chai
quintal 100 kg = 220p (unit of weight)	n	重量單位	chúhng leuhng dāan wāi	cung5 loeng6 daan1 wai1	chhuhng lowhng taan wai
quit /remove/unload	v	解除	gaai chèuih	gaai3 ceoi4	kaai chheuih
quite long time	adv	幾耐	geih hóu	gei6 hou2	keih hou
quite well[1]	adv	幾好	geih hóu	gei6 hou2	keih hou
quite well![2]	adv	幾好吖!	gei hóu ā!	gei6 hou2 aa1!	kei hou a!
quits	adj	互不相欠	wuh bāt sèung him	wu6 bat1 soeng4 him3	wuh pat seung him
quiz /test	v	測驗	chàak yihm	caak4 jim6	chhaak yihm
quizzer	n	測驗節目	chàak yihm jit muhk	caak4 jim6 zit3 muk6	chhaak yihm chit muhk
quota[1]	n	額	áak /ngáak	aak2 /ngaak2	aak /ngaak
quota[2]	n	限額	haahn ngáak	haan6 ngaak2	haahn ngaak
quota[3]	n	定額	dehng ngáak	deng6 ngaak2	tehng ngaak

quotation[1] /cost /quoted price	n	報價	bou ga	bou3 gaa3	pou ka
quotation[2] /assessment (for cost)	n	估價	gú ga	gu2 gaa3	ku ka
quotation[3] (marked)	n	引文	yáhn màhn	jan5 man4	yahn mahn
quotation[4] /quote /cite/ marked	n/v	引用	yáhn yuhng	jan5 jung6	yahn yuhng
quotation cost[1]	n	引証	yáhn jeng	jan5 zeng3	yahn cheng
quotation cost[2]	n	報價單	bou ga dāan	bou3 gaa3 daan1	pou ka taan
quotation marks[1] (‚ ‚ ⁄ " ")	n	引號	yáhn houh	jan5 hou6	yahn houh
quotation marks[2]	n	引語	yáhn yúh	jan5 jyu5	yahn yuh

rabbit[1]	n	兔	tóu	tou2	thou
rabbit[2]	n	兔仔	tóu jāi	tou2 zai1	thou chai
race[1] /run/running	v	跑	fáau	faau2	faau
race[2] /run quick/running	n	賽跑	choi pāau	coi3 paau1	chhoi phaau
race[3] /caste/tribe/ethnic/ ethnicity	n	種族	júng juhk	zung2 zuk6	chung chuhk
race boat	n	扒龍船	pàh lùhng syùhn	paa4 lung4 syun4	phah luhng syuhn
race car[1] /sports car	n	跑車	pāau chè	paau1 ce4	phaau chhe
race car[2]	n	賽車	choi chè	coi3 ce4	chhoi chhe
racer[1]	n	賽車人	choi chè yàhn	coi3 ce4 jan4	chhoi chhe yahn
racer[2]	n	賽跑者	choi pāau jé	coi3 paau1 ze2	chhoi phaau che
rack[1]	n	架	gá	gaa2	ka
rack[2]	n	台	tòih	toi4	thoih
rack[3]	n	刑台	yìhng tòih	jing4 toi4	yehng thoih
rack[4] /shelf	n	架子	gá jí	gaa2 zi2	ka chi
racket /to shout	n	喧嚷	hyùn yéuhng	hyun4 joeng5	hyun yeuhng
radar[1] (de)	n	雷達	lèuih daaht	leoi4 daat6	lowih taaht
radar[2] /radio	n	無線電話	mòuh sin dihn wá	mou4 sin3 din6 waa2	mouh sin tihn wa
radiation /radiate	n/v	輻射	fūk seh	fuk1 se6	fuk seh
radical[1] /basic	adj	根生	gàn sàang	gan4 saang4	kan saang
radical[2] /basic	adj	徹底	chit dái	cit3 dai2	chhit tai
radical[3] /basic	adj	根本嘅	gáan būn ge	gaan2 bun1 ge3	kaan pun ke
radical[4] (to sexes/bisexual)	adj	兩性	léuhng sing	loeng5 sing3	leuhng seng
radical[5] /sexes	adj	過激	gwo gīk	gwo3 gik1	kwo kek
radical stroke[1]	n	激烈分子	gīk liht fahn ji	gik1 lit6 fan6 zi2	kek liht fahn chi
radical stroke[2]	n	激進分子	gik jeun fahn ji	gik1 zeon3 fan6 zi2	kek cheun fahn chi
radicals traditional Chinese basic character	adj	部首	bou sáu	bou3 sau2	pou sau
radicate	v	生根	sāng gān	sang1 gan1	sang kan
radio[1]	n	收音機	sàu yàm gèi	sau4 jam4 gei4	sau yam kei
radio[2] /wireless	n	無線電	mòuh sín dihn	mou4 sin2 din6	mouh sin tihn
radio band (SW/MW/AM/FM)	n	波段	bō dyuhn	po1 dyun6	po tyuhn
radio hk	n	港台	góng tòih	gong2 toi4	kong thoih
radio station	n	電台	dihn tòih	din6 toi4	tihn thoih
radioactive element	n	放射性元素	fong seh sing yùhn sou	fong3 se6 sing3 jyun4 sou3	fong seh seng yuhn sou
radios /walkie-talkie	n	帶講機	daai góng gèi	daai3 gong2 gei4	taai kong kei
radish	n	蘿蔔仔	lòh baahk jái	lo4 baak6 zai2	loh paahk chai
radium	n	鐳	lèuih	leoi6	lowih
raffle[1]	v	抽簽	chàu chìm	cau4 cim4	chhau chìm
raffle[2]	v	抽簽買嘢嘅方法	chàu chìm maaih yéh ge fòng faat	cau4 cim4 maai6 je5 ge3 fong4 faat3	chhau chìm maaih yéh ge fòng faat
raft[1] /swimmer	n	浮台	fàuh tòih	fou4 toi4	fauh thoih
raft[2]	n	橡皮筏	jeuhng pèih faht	zoeng6 pei4 fat6	cheuhng pheih faht
rage	n	盛怒	sihng louh	sing6 lou6	sehng louh

English		Chinese	Romanization	Jyutping	Yale
ragged[1] /torn cloth /old torn cloth/damaged cloth	adj	破爛	po laahn	po3 laan6	pho laahn
ragged[2] /worn clothes /torn cloth/worn out cloth/ old torn cloth	adj	破衣爛衫	po yī laahn sàam	po3 ji1 laan6 saam4	pho yi laahn saam
ragged[3] /torn cloth /worn out cloth	adj	衫衣艦褸	sàam yī laahm láuh	saam4 ji1 laam6 lau5	saam yi laahm lauh
raging	adj	強烈	keuhng liht	koeng4 lit6	kheuhng liht
raid /surprise attacker	v	突然襲擊	daht yìhn jaahp gīk	dat6 jim4 zaap6 gik1	taht yihn chaahp gek
raider (by person)	n	襲擊者	jaahp gīk jé	zaap6 gik1 ze2	chaahp kek che
raider person /surprise attacker	n	突襲者	daht jaahp jé	dat6 zaap6 ze2	taht chaahp che
rail[1] /train	n	火車	fó chè	fo2 ce4	fo chhe
rail[2]	n	扶欄	fùh làahn	fu4 laan4	fuh laahn
rail[3] /train station	n	火車站	fó chè jaahm	fo2 ce4 zaam6	fo chhe chaahm
rail road /railway	n	鐵路	tit louh	tit3 lou6	thit louh
railing	n	鐵欄杆	tit làahn gōn	tit3 laan4 gon1	thit laahn kon
rain[1]	n	雨	yúh	jyu5	yuh
rain[2] /rainfall	v	落雨	lohk yúh	lok6 jyu5	lohk yuh
rain[3]	v	下雨	hah yúh	haa6 jyu5	hah yuh
rain[4]	n	雨水	yúh séui	jyu5 seoi2	yuh swoi
rain check /cancel reason by rain	n	因雨取消	yàn yúh chéui sìu	jan4 jyu5 ceoi2 siu4	yan yuh chhoi siu
rain down	n	大量降下	daaih leuhng gong hah	daai6 loeng6 gong3 ha6	taaih leuhng kong hah
rainbow	n	彩虹	chói hùhng	coi2 hung4	chhoi huhng
raincoats	n	雨衣	yúh yí	jyu5 ji2	yuh yi
raincoats	n	雨褸	yúh lāu	jyu5 lau1	yuh lau
raindrop	n	雨點	yúh dím	jyu5 dim2	yuh tim
rainfall	n	降雨	gong yúh	gong3 jyu5	kong yuh
raingauge	n	雨量計	yúh lèuhng gai	jyu5 loeng4 gai3	yuh leuhng kai
rainiest place	n	多雨的地	dò yúh dìk deih	do4 jyu5 dik4 dei6	to yuh tek teih
raining[1]	n	落緊雨	lohk gán yúh	lok6 gan2 jyu5	lohk kan yuh
raining[2]	n	有排落	yáuh pàaih lohk	jau5 paai4 lok6	yauh phaaih lohk
rainless	adj	缺少雨	kyut síu yúh	kyut3 siu2 jyu5	khyut siu yuh
rainproof /waterproof	adj	防水	fòhng séui	fong4 seoi2	fohng swoi
rainstorm[1]	n	雨暴	yúh bouh	jyu5 bou6	yuh pouh
rainstorm[2]	n	暴雨	bòuh yúh	bou4 jyu5	pouh yuh
rainy	adj	陰雨的	yām yúh dìk	jam1 jyu5 dik4	yam yuh tik
rainy day[1] (coll) prepared before rains	adj	未雨綢繆	meih yúh chàuh màuh	mei6 jyu5 cau4 mau4	meih yuh chhauh mauh
rainy day[2] (coll) just in case for	adj	有備無患	yáuh beih mòuh waahn	jau5 bei6 mou4 waan6	yauh peih mouh waahn
rainy season	n	多雨季節	dò yúh gwai jit	do4 jyu5 gwai3 zit3	to yuh kwai chit
rainy day /rainy weather	n	陰雨天	yām yúh tīn	jam1 jyu5 tin1	yam yuh thin
raise hand[1]	v	舉手	géui sáu	geoi2 sau2	kwoi sau
raise hand[2] /threaten	v	威脅	wāi hip	wai1 hip3	wai hip

English		Chinese	Romanization	Jyutping	Reading
raise price	v	起加	héi ga	hei2 gaa3	hei ka
raise salary	v	加薪	gà sàn	gaa4 san4	ka san
raise up[1]	v	舉高	géui gòu	geoi2 gou4	kwoi kou
raise up[2] /easy lift /to pick up easy /light weight	v	拎起	ling /ning héi	ling3 /ning3 hei2	leng /neng hei
raise up[3] 'heavy' /heavy lift	v	舉起	géui héi	geoi2 hei2	kwoi hei
raised educate	v	受過教育	sauh gwo gaau yuhk	sau6 gwo3 gaau3 juk6	sauh kwo kaau yuhk
raised platform	v	階段	gàai dyuhn	gaai4 dyun6	kaai tyuhn
raised room[1] of open space with scaffold	v	帳逢	jeung fùhng	zoeng3 fung4	cheung fuhng
raised room[2] of scaffold	v	閣數	gok sóu	gok3 sou2	kok sou
rambutan fruit	n	紅毛丹	hùhng mòuh dāan	hung4 mou4 daan1	huhng mouh taan
ran (run p.t.) /gone /leaved/left/departed	n	走咗	jáu jó	zau2 zo2	chau cho
random[1] /accidentally	adj	偶然	ngáuh yìhn	ngau5 jin4	ngauh yihn
random[2]	adj	任意	yahm yi	jam6 ji3	yahm yi
random[3]	adj	任意咁	yahm yi gám	jam6 ji3 gam2	yahm yi kam
rang /ring p.t.	v	鈴響	lìhng héung	ling4 hoeng2	lehng heung
rang bell /bell ringing	v	鬧鐘	laauh /naauh jùng	laau6 /naau6 zung4	laauh /naauh chung
range[1] /nearest/scope /extent	n	範圍	faahn wàih	faan6 wai4	faahn waih
range[2] (of mountain)	n	山脈	sāan mahk	saan1 mak6	saan mahk
range[3] (of mountain)	n	排列	pàaih liht	paai4 lit6	phaaih liht
ransom /released from kidnap	n	贖金	suhk gām	suk6 gam1	suhk kam
rape[1] /violently sex	v	強姦	kèuhng gàan	koeng4 gaan4	kheuhng kaan
rape[2] /violently sex	n	強姦罪	kèuhng gàan jeuih	koeng4 gaan4 zeoi6	kheuhng kaan choih
rape[3] (of the wine)	n	葡萄渣	pòuh tòuh jà	pou4 tou4 zaa4	phouh thouh cha
raper[1]	n	強姦者	kèuhng gàan jé	koeng4 gaan4 ze2	kheuhng kaan che
raper[2] (coll) /rapist	n	強姦犯	kèuhng gàan faahn	koeng4 gaan4 faan6	kheuhng kaan faahn
rapid /hurried	adj	急	gāp	gap1	kap
rare /few/small numbers	adj	稀有	hèi yáuh	hei4 jau5	hei yauh
rash[1]	adj	急躁	gāp chou	gap1 cou3	kap chhou
rash[2]	adj	魯莽	lóuh móhng	lou5 mong5	louh mohng
rash[3]	adj	性急	sing gāp	sing3 gap1	seng kap
rash[4]	adj	輕率莽撞	hèng seut móhng johng	heng4 seot3 mong5 zong6	heng swut mohng chohng
raspberry[1]	n	山莓	sàan mùih	saan4 mui4	saan muih
raspberry[2]	n	紅莓	hùhng mùih	hung4 mui4	huhng muih
raspberry[3]	n	覆盆子	fùk pùhn jí	fuk4 pun4 zi2	fuk phuhn chi
ratch /ratchet	n	棘輪	gīk lèuhn	gik1 leon4	kek lowhn
rate[1]	n	率	léut	leot2	leut
rate[2] /ratio	n	比率	béi léut	bei2 leot2	pei lowt
price rate	n	價格	ga gaak	gaa3 gaak3	ka kaak
rather[1] /little	adj	幾多	géi dō	gei2 do1	kei toh

rather[2] /than/compare	adj	較	gaau	gaau3	kaau
rating	n	評分	pìhng fàn	ping4 fan4	phehng fan
ratio /rate	n	比	béi	bei2	pei
rattan /cane/vine creeper plant	n	藤	tàhng	tang4	thahng
rattan basket	n	藤籃	tàhng láam	tang4 laam2	thahng laam
raven /crow	n	烏鴉	wū āa /ngā	wu1 aa1 /ngaa1	wu aa /nga
ravine[1] /ditch	v	溝壑	kàu kok	kau4 kok3	khau khok
ravine[2] /deep valley	v	峽谷	haahp gūk	haap6 guk1	haahp kuk
ravine[3] /deep valley	v	深谷	sàm gūk	sam4 guk1	sam kuk
raw[1] /uncooked/unriped	adj	生	sàang	saang4	saang
raw[2]	adj	原料	yùhn líu	jyun4 liu2	yuhn liu
raw[3]	adj	未煮過	meih jyú gwo	mei6 zyu2 gwo3	meih chyu kwo
raw milk	n	未加工牛奶	meih gā gūng ngàuh láaih /náaih	mei6 gaa1 gung1 ngau4 laai5 /naai5	meih ka kung ngauh laaih /naaih
razor	n	剃刀	tai dōu	tai3 dou1	thai tou
re-echo	v	再反響	joi fáan héung	zoi3 faan2 hoeng2	choi faan heung
re-entry	n	再進入	joi jeun yahp	zoi3 zeon3 yap3	choi cheun yahp
re-export[1]	v	再出口	joi chēut háu	zoi3 ceot1 hau2	choi chhot hau
re-export[2]	v	再輸出	joi syù chēut	zoi3 syu4 ceot1	choi syu chhot
reach	v	抵	dái	dai2	tai
reachable	adj	可達到	hó daaht dou	ho2 daat6 dou3	ho taaht tou
react[1]	v	反應	fáan ying	faan2 jing3	faan yeng
react[2]	v	起反應	héi fáan ying	hei2 faan2 jing3	hei faan yeng
reaction	n	反應	fáan ying	faan2 jing3	faan yeng
reactionary	n	反動份子	fáan duhng bàn jī	faan2 dung6 ban4 zi1	faan dohng pan chi
read /study	v	讀	duhk	duk6	tuhk
reader	n	讀者	duhk jé	duk6 ze2	tuhk che
reading	n	閱讀	yuht duhk	jyut6 duk6	yuht tuhk
reading book	n	睇書	tái syù	tai2 zyu4	thai syu
readmit /readmission	n	重新接納	chùhng sàn jip laahp	cung4 san4 zip3 laap6	chhuhng san chip laahp
reads /studies/studying	n	讀緊	duhk gán	duk6 gan2	tuhk kan
ready[1]	adj	將	jéung	zoeng2	cheung
ready[2]	adj	預備好	yuh beih hou	jyu6 bei6 hou3	yuh peih hou
ready[3]	adj	準備好	jéun beih hóu	zeon2 bei6 hou2	cheun peih hou
ready meal	n	預製食物	yuh jai sihk maht	jyu6 zai3 sik6 mat6	yuh chai sehk maht
ready to use again /reset/set up	v	再設	joi chit	zoi3 cit3	choi chit
reaffirm /reiteration /reiterate	v	重申	chùhng sàn	cung4 san4	chhuhng san
real[1] /true	adj	眞/真	jàn	zan4	chan
real[2] /true/honest/really	adj	實	saht	sat6	saht
real[3] /true/truly/substantial	adj	真實	jàn saht	zan4 sat6	chan saht
real estate	n	地產	deih cháan	dei6 caan2	teih chhaan
real very talkative /talks a lot/talkative	adj	眞好氣	jān hóu hei	jan1 hou2 hei3	chan hou hei

realism	n	現實主義	yihn saht jyú yih	jin6 sat6 zyu2 ji6	yihn saht chyu yih
reality	n	現實	yihn saht	jin6 sat6	yihn saht
realize	v	實現	saht yihn	sat6 jin6	saht yihn
realized	v	明白嘞	mìhng baahk la	ming4 baak6 lak3	mehng paahk lak
really /real/true	adj	眞/真嘅	jàn ge	zan4 ge3	chan ke
ream 500 sheets of paper	n	令	lihng	ling4	lehng
reap /harvest	v	收割	sàu got	sau4 got3	sau kot
reaper	n	收割者	sàu got jé	sau4 got3 ze2	sau kot che
reapplying	v	再應用	joi yīng yuhng	zoi3 jing1 jung6	choi yeng yuhng
rear[1] back side	n	後	hauh	hau6	hauh
rear[2] back side	n	後面	hauh mìhn	hau6 min6	hauh mihn
rear[3] /bring up/rise up	v	培養	púih yéuhng	pui5 joeng5	phuih yeuhng
rear[4] erect/tower/humped	v	高聳	gòu súng	gou4 sung2	kou sung
reason /cause	n	緣因	yùhn yān	jyun4 jan1	yuhn yan
reason for being	n	存在嘅理由	chyuhn joih ge léih yàuh	cyun4 zoi6 ge3 lei5 jau4	chhyuhn choih ke leih yauh
reason for living /reason for alive	n	活著嘅理由	wuht jeuk ge léih yàuh	wut6 zoek3 ge3 lei5 jau4	wuht cheuk ke leih yauh
reasonably[1]	adv	合乎邏輯地	hahp fù lòh chāp deih	hap6 fu4 lo4 cap1 dei6	hahp fu loh chhap teih
reasonably[2]	adv	過得去	gwo dāk heui	gwo3 dak1 heoi3	kwo tak hoi
reasoning /speculative	n	推理	tèui léih	teoi4 lei5	thoi leih
reassure[1]	v	使放心	sī fóng sàm	si1 fong2 sam4	si fong sam
reassure[2]	v	再保證	joi bóu jing	zoi3 bou2 zing3	choi pou cheng
reassure[3]	v	再安慰	joi ōn /ngōn wai	zoi3 on1 /ngon1 wai3	choi on /ngon wai
reaumur 0-80°R /thermometer (1683-1757 French)	n	列氏嘅	liht sih ge	laat6 si6 ge3	liht sih ke
rebate	n	退還	tèui wàahn	teoi4 waan4	thoi waahn
rebel /rise against	v	反抗	fáan kong	faan2 kong3	faan khong
rebellion/violent protest	n	暴動	bouh duhng	bou6 dung6	pouh tohng
rebuke[1] reprove with punish	v	責罰	jaak faht	zaak3 fat6	chaak faht
rebuke[2] with punish	v	懲戒	chìhng gaai	cing4 gaai3	chhehng kaai
recall[1] /think of	v	想起	séung héi	soeng2 hei2	seung hei
recall[2] /think back/think back	v	回想	wùih séung	wui6 soeng2	wuih seung
receipt[1] /voucher	n	收據	sāu geui	sau1 geoi3	sau kwoi
receipt[2]	n	收條	sāu tìuh	sau1 tiu4	sau thiuh
receive[1] /accept/take over	v	收受	sàu sauh	sau4 sau6	sau sauh
receive[2] /recept/accept	v	接收	jip sàu	zip3 sau4	chip sau
received education		受教育	sàuh gaau yuhk	sau4 gaau3 juk6	sauh kaau yuhk
receive goods		收貨	sàu fo	sau4 fo3	sau fo
received	adj	收訖	sàu gāt	sau4 gat1	sau kat
received by /buyer	n	收貨人	sāu fo yàhn	sau1 fo3 jan4	sau fo yahn

receiver /recipient /addressee/consignee of mail or cargo	n	收件人	sàu gihn yàhn	sau4 gin6 jan4	sau kihn yahn
receiving baptism[1]		受洗	sàuh sái	sau6 sai2	sauh sai
receiving baptism[2]		領洗	léhng /líhng sái	leng5 /ling5 sai2	lehng sai
receiving message	n	接收訊	jip sàu sèun	zip3 sau4 seon4	chip sau swon
reception desk /reception at office	v	接待處	jip doih chyu	zip3 doi6 cyu3	chip toih chhyu
reception[1] /service	n	接待	jip doih	zip3 dou6	chip toih
reception[2] /to take over	n	接收	jip sàu	zip3 sau4	chip sau
reception centre	n	接待中心	jip doih jùng sàm	zip3 doi6 zung4 sam4	chip toih chung sam
reception room[1] /waiting room/visitor	n	會客室	wuih haak sāt	wui6 haak3 sat1	wuih haak sat
reception room[2]	n	接待室	jip doih sāt	zip3 doi6 sat1	chip toih sat
receptionist (at office)	n	接待員	jip doih yùhn	zip3 doi6 jyun4	chip toih yuhn
recharge[1]	n	再充電	joi chùng dihn	zoi3 cung4 din6	choi chhung tihn
recharge[2]	n	再襲擊	joi jaahp gīk	zoi3 zaap6 gik1	choi chaahp kek
rechoose	v	再挑選	joi tìu syún	zoi3 tiu4 syun2	choi thiu syun
recipient	n	接受者	jip sauh jé	zip3 sau6 ze2	chip sauh che
reciprocate	v	往復運動	wóhng fuhk wahn duhng	wong5 fuk6 wan6 dung6	wohng fuhk wahn tohng
recite[1] /listen learned	v	背	buih	bui6	puih
recite[2] /listen learned	v	朗誦	lóhng juhng	long5 zung6	lohng chuhng
reckless	adj	不顧一切	bāt gu yāt chai	bat1 gu3 jat1 cai3	pat ku yat chhai
remiss /recklessly	adv	唔小心	m̀ síu sàm	m4 siu2 sam4	mh siu sam
recklessly	adv	魯莽	lóuh móhng	lou5 mong5	louh mohng
reclaim[1] /reclamation	v	回收利用	wui sàu leih yuhng	wui3 sau4 lei6 jung6	wui sau leih yuhng
reclaim[2]	v	要求取回	yìu kàuh chéui wúih	jiu4 kau4 ceoi2 wui5	yiu khauh chheui wuih
recognise	v	認可	yihng hó	jing6 ho2	yehng ho
recognize[1]	v	認識	yihng sīk	jing6 sik1	yehng sek
recognize[2]	v	認得	yihng dāk	jing6 dak1	yehng tak
recognize[3] by listening	v	聽得出	tèng dāk chēut	teng4 dak1 ceot1	theng tak chhot
recognize[4] by looking	v	認得出	yihng dāk chēut	jing6 dak1 ceot1	yehng tak chhot
recollect /to look back	v	追憶	jèui yīk	zeoi4 jik1	cheui yek
recommend[1]	v	推薦	tèui jin	teoi4 zin3	thoi chin
recommend[2] by letter	v	介紹信	gaai siuh seun	gaai3 siu6 seon3	kaai siuh swon
recommend letter[1]	n	推薦信	tèui jin seun	teoi4 zin3 seon3	thoi chin swon
recommend letter[2]	n	理曆	léih līk	lei5 lik1	leih lek
recommendable	adj	可推薦	hó tèui jin	ho2 teoi4 jin3	ho thoi chin
recomposition /recompose/reset	v	重排	chùhng pàaih	cung4 paai4	chhuhng phaaih
recondition[1]	v	重建	chùhng gin	cung4 gin3	chhuhng kin
recondition[2]	v	修整	sàu jíng	sau4 zing2	sau cheng
reconfirm	v	再證實	joi jing saht	zoi3 zing sat6	choi cheng saht
reconsider	v	重新考慮	chùhng sàn háau leuih	cung4 san4 haau2 leoi6	chhuhng san haau lowih

reconsideration	n	再考慮	joi háau leuih	zoi3 haau2 leoi6	choi haau lowih
reconstitute	v	重新構成	chùhng sàn kau sèhng	cung4 san4 kau3 seng4	chhuhng san khau sehng
reconstruction	n	復原	fuhk yùhn	fuk6 jyun4	fuhk yuhn
registration /record in written	n	記錄	gei luhk	gei3 luk6	kei luhk
record (of case)	n	案	on /ngon	on3 /ngon3	on /ngon
record book	n	記錄冊	gei luhk chaak	gei3 luk6 caak3	kei luhk chhaak
record image /video	n	錄影	luhk yíng	luk6 jing2	luhk yeng
record sound[1]	n	錄音	luhk yām	luk6 jam1	luhk yam
record sound[2]	n	電唱機	dihn cheung gèi	din6 coeng3 gei4	tihn chheung kei
recount	v	再數	joi sou	zoi3 sou3	choi joi sou
recover[1] /repeat/resume /return/begins again/go and return	adv	復	fuhk	fuk6	fuhk
recover[2] from sick/get well	v	癒	yuh	jyu6	yuh
recover[3] from sick	v	修復	sàu fuhk	sau4 fuk6	sau fuhk
recover[4] from sick	v	好返	hóu fàan	hou2 faan4	hou faan
recover[5] /recuperate /regain/restart/redtoration/ resume	v	恢復	fùi fuhk	fui4 fuk6	fui fuhk
recover[6]	v	回復	wùih fuhk	wui4 fuk6	wuih fuhk
recover[7]	v	搵返	wán fàan	wan2 faan4	wan faan
recover[8]	v	重新獲得	chùhng sàn wohk dāk	cung4 san4 wok6 dak1	chhuhng san wohk dak
recover[9] /win case	v	勝訴	sing sou	sing3 sou3	seng sou
recovered!?	v	好返呀?	hóu fàan àa!?	hou2 faan4 aa4!?	hou faan aa!?
recreation	n	休養	yàu yéuhng	jau4 joeng5	yau yeuhng
recross	v	再橫渡	joi waahng douh	zoi3 waang6 dou6	choi waahng touh
recruit[1]	v	徵聘	jìng ping	zing4 ping3	cheng pheng
recruit[2]	v	新兵	sàn bīng	san4 bing1	san peng
recruit[3]	v	吸收	kāp sàu	kap1 sau4	khap sau
recruitment /refill	n	補充	bóu chùng	bou2 cung4	pou chhung
rectangular	adj	長方形	chèuhng fòng yìhng	coeng4 fong4 jing4	chheuhng fong yihng
rectify /amend	v	改正	gói jeng /jing	goi2 zeng3 /jing3	koi cheng
rectum	n	直腸	jihk chèuhng	zik6 coeng4	chehk chheuhng
recuperate	v	休養	yàu yéuhng	jau4 joeng5	yau yeuhng
recycle	v	再循環	joi chèuhn wàahn	zoi3 ceon4 waan4	choi chheuhn waahn
recycling	n	回收	wui sàu	wui3 sau4	wui sau
red	n	紅	hùhng	hung4	huhng
red blood cell	n	紅血球	hùhng hyut kàuh	hung4 hyut3 kau4	huhng hyut khauh
red-handed /on the spot	adj	當場	dòng chèuhng	dong4 coeng4	tong chheuhng
red tea	n	紅茶	hùhng chàh	hung4 caa4	huhng chhah
red wine	n	紅酒	hùhng jāu /zāu	hung4 zau1	huhng chau
redaction /new version /new release	n	新版本	sàn báan bún	san4 baan2 pun2	san paan pun
redeem	v	挽回	wáahn wùih	waan5 wui4	waahn wuih

redemption	n	挽回	wáahn wùih	waan5 wui4	waahn wuih
rediscover /to find again	v	再發現	joi faat yihn	zoi3 faat3 jin6	choi faat yihn
redraw	v	重畫	chùhng wá	cung4 wa2	chhuhng wa
reduce[1] /slash	v	減低	gáam dāi	gaam2 dai1	kaam tai
reduce[2]	v	縮小	sūk síu	suk1 siu2	suk siu
reef /shoal rock	n	礁	jīu	ziu1	chiu
reel[1]	n	卷盤	gyun pùhn	gyun3 pun4	kyun phuhn
reel[2]	n	捲軸	gyún juhk	gyun2 zuk6	kyun chohk
refer report /submit report	v	提交	tàih gāau	tai4 gaau1	thaih kaau
reference[1]	n	備考	beih háau	bei6 haau2	peih haau
reference[2]	n	供參考	gùng chàam háau	gung4 caam4 haau2	kung chhaam haau
reference[3]	n	涉及	sip kahp	sip3 kap6	sip khahp
referral	n	提及	tàih kahp	tai4 kap6	thaih khahp
refill	v	再裝滿	joi jòng douh	zoi3 zong4 dou6	choi chong touh
refine	v	精製	jèng jai	zeng4 jai3	cheng chai
refiner	n	精製者	jèng jai jé	zeng4 zai3 ze2	cheng chai che
reflect light of clothes	n	反光衣	fáan gwòng yī	faan2 gwong4 ji1	faan kwong yi
reflected light /reflection light	n	反光	fáan gwòng	faan2 gwong4	faan kwong
reflection in water /reverse image	n	倒影	dóu yéng /yíng	dou2 jeng2 /jing2	tou yeng
reflector	n	反射器	fáan seh hei	faan2 se6 hei3	faan seh hei
refloat	v	再浮起	joi fàuh héi	zoi3 fau4 hei2	choi fauh hei
reflow	v	流回	làuh wùih	lau4 wui4	lauh wuih
reforest	v	重新造林	chùhng sàn chóu làhm	cung4 san4 cou4 lam4	chhuhng san chhou lahm
reform	v	改革	gói gaak	goi2 gaak3	koi kaak
reformatory	n	少年感化院	siu lìhn /nìhn gámfa yún	siu3 lin4 /nin4 gam2 fa3 jyun2	siu lihn /nihn kam fa yun
reformer	n	改革者	gói gaak jé	goi2 gaak3 ze2	koi kaak che
refound	v	再建立	joi gin lahp	zoi3 gin3 lap6	choi kin lahp
refresh	v	恢復精神	fùi fuhk jēng sàn	fui4 fuk6 zeng1 san4	fui fuhk cheng san
refrigerate	v	冷凍	láahng dung	laang5 dung3	laahng tung
refrigerator	n	冰箱	bìng sèung	bing4 soeng4	peng seung
refuge	v	避難	beih laahn/naahn	bei6 laan6 /naan6	peih laahn /naahn
refugee[1]	n	避難人	beih laahn /naahn yàhn	bei6 laan6 /naan6 jan4	peih laahn /naahn yahn
refugee[2]	n	流亡者	làuh mòhng jé	lau4 mong4 ze2	lauh mohng che
refugee[3]	n	難民	làhn /nàhn màhn	laan4 /naan6 man4	lahn /nahn mahn
refund /send back	v	退還	tèui wàahn	teoi4 waan4	thoi waahn
refusal /rejection	n	拒絕	kéuih jyuht	keoi5 zyut6	khoih chyuht
refuse	v	渣	jā	zaa1	cha
refused to visit	v	謝絕探訪	jeh jyut tāam fóng	je6 zyut3 taam1 fong2	cheh chyut thaam fong
regain[1]	v	返倒	fàan dou	faan4 dou3	faan dou
regain[2]	v	得返	dak fàan	dak3 faan4	tak faan

regain³	v	取回	chēui wui	ceoi1 wui3	chheui wui
regard	n	注重	jyu juhng	zyu3 zung6	chyu chuhng
regarding¹ /respecting /about	prep	至於	ji yù	zi3 jyu4	chi yu
regarding² /about	prep	對於	deui yù	deoi3 jyu4	toei yu
regiment	n	軍團	gwàn tyùhn	gwan4 tyun4	kwan thyuhn
regimental	adj	團嘅	tyùhn ge	tyun4 ge3	thyuhn ke
regional	adj	地區嘅	deih kèui ge	dei6 keoi4 ge3	teih khoi ke
register¹ /record/to enter	v	登	dàng	dang4	tang
register²	v	簿	bouh	bou6	pouh
register first¹	v	先登記	sin dàng gei	sing3 dang4 gei3	sin tang kei
register first²	v	登記先	dàng gei sin	dang4 gei3 sin3	tang kei sin
register office	n	登記處	dàng gei chyúh	dang4 gei3 cyu5	tang kei chhyuh
registered	adj	登記過嘅	dàng gei gwò ge	dang4 gei3 gwo4 ge3	tang kei kwo ke
registered letter	n	掛號信	gwa houh seun	gwaa3 hou6 seon3	kwa houh swon
registration	n	註冊	jyu chaak	zyu3 caak3	chyu chhaak
registration form	n	登記表格	dàng gei bíu gaak	dang4 gei3 biu2 gaak3	tang kei piu kaak
registration hotline	n	登記熱線	dàng gei yiht sin	dang4 gei3 jit6 sin3	tang kei yiht sin
regret¹ /repent/feel sad	v	懺	cháam	caam2	chhaam
regret² /repent	v	後悔	hauh fui	hau6 fui3	hauh fui
regretful	adj	遺憾嘅	wàih hahm ge	wai4 ham6 ge3	waih hahm ke
regular	adj	有規律	yáuh kwài leuht	jau5 kwai4 leot6	yauh khwai lwoht
regularly¹	adv	正規	jeng kwài	zeng3 kwai4	cheng khwai
regularly²	adv	規則感	kwài jāk gám	kwai4 zak1 gam2	khwai chak kam
regularly³	adv	規律地	kwài lèuht dèih	kwai4 leot6 dei6	khwai lwoht teih
regularly service	v	不斷做	bāt dyuhn jouh	bat1 dyun6 zou6	pat yyuhn chouh
regulation¹	n	守則	sáu jāk	sau2 zak1	sau chak
regulation² /rules	n	規例	kwài laih	kwai4 lai6	khwai laih
regulation³ /rules	n	規則	kwài jāk	kwai4 zak1	khwai chak
regulation⁴	n	規限	kwài haahn	kwai4 haan6	khwai haahn
regulation⁵	n	章程	jèung chìhng	zoeng4 cing4	cheung chhehng
regulation⁶ /rules	n	規矩	kwài géui	kwai4 geoi2	khwai kwoi
rehabation	n	康復	hōng fuhk	hong1 fuk6	hong fuhk
rehabilitation	n	修復	sàu fàuh	sau4 fau6	sau fauh
rehearsal¹ exercise of activity	n	排練	pàaih lihn	paai4 lin6	phaaih lihn
rehearsal² /recite say from memory	v	背誦	bui juhng	bui3 zung6	pui chohng
reign	n	統治	túng jih	tung3 zi6	thung chih
reimbursement /return back money	n	退款	tèui fún	teoi4 fun2	thoi fun
reimport	v	再輸入	joi jyun yahp	zoi3 zyun3 jap6	choi chyun yahp
reinstall	v	重新裝配	chùhng sàn jōng pui	cung4 san4 zong1 pui3	chhuhng san chong phui
reiteration	n	反覆	fáan fūk	faan2 fuk1	faan fuk
reject¹	v	不予	bāt yúh	bat1 jyu5	pat yuh

English	POS	中文	Yale	Jyutping	Other
reject[2] /refuse/decline /turn down	v	拒絕	kéuih jyuht	keui5 zyut6	khoih chyuht
reject to accept		拒絕接受	kéuih jyuht jip sauh	keui5 zyut6 zip3 sau6	khoih chyuht chip sauh
reject to give[1]		唔使考慮	m̀ sái háau leuih	m4 sai2 haau2 leoi6	mh sai haau lowih
reject to give[2]		唔使惗	m̀ sái lám	m4 sai2 lam2	mh sai lam
reject to give[3]		唔需要考慮	m̀ sèui yiu háau leuih	m4 seoi4 jiu3 haau2 leoi6	mh swoi yiu haau lowih
reject to give[4]		不予考慮	bāt yúh háau leuih	bat1 jyu5 haau2 leoi6	pat yuh haau lowih
rejecter	n	拒絕者	kéuih jyuht jé	keoi5 zyut6 ze2	khoih chyuht che
related[1] /relative /one's own	adj	親	chàn	can4	chhan
related[2] /about	adj	至於	ji yù	zi3 jyu4	chi yu
related[3] /relation	n	有親戚關係	yáuh chàn chīk gwàan haih	jau5 can4 cik1 gwaan4 hai6	yauh chhan chek kwaan haih
relation /relative	n	關	gwàan	gwaan4	kwaan
relationship /relation /relevance	n	關係	gwàan haih	gwaan4 hai6	kwaan haih
relationless	n	小關係	síu gwàan haih	siu2 gwaan4 hai6	siu kwaan haih
relationship[1] father side	n	世伯	sai baak	sai3 baak3	sai baak
relationship[2] mother side	n	令壽堂	lihng sauh tòhng	ling4 sau6 tong4	lehng sauh thohng
relationship[3] mother side	n	表	bíu	biu2	piu
relative[1]	n	相對	sèung déui	soeng4 deoi2	seung toei
relative[2]	n	有關係	yáuh gwàan haih	jau5 gwaan4 hai6	yauh kwaan haih
relatively	adv	相對地	sèung déui dèih	soeng4 deoi2 dei6	seung toei teih
relax[1]	v	舒	syù	syu4	syu
relax[2]	v	舒服	syù fùhk	syu4 fuk4	syu fuhk
relax[3]	v	鬆弛	sùng chìh	sung4 ci4	sung chhih
relax[4]	v	鬆的	sùng dìk	sung4 dik4	sung tek
relax muscles /unhitch relax /loosened/relaxation	v	放鬆	fong sùng	fong3 sung4	fong sung
relax way[1] /easy method	adj/v	簡單方法	gáan dàan fòng faat	gaan2 daan4 fong4 faat3	kaan taan fong faat
relax way[2] (sl)	v	唔使用腦	m̀ sái yuhng lóuh /nóuh	m4 sai2 jung6 lou5 /nou5	mh sai yuhng louh /nouh
relaxation	n	休閒	yàu hàahn	jau4 haan4	yau haahn
relaxation place /pleasure place	n	休閒	yāu hàahn	jau1 haan6	yau haahn
relaxed posture	adj	輕鬆姿勢	hèng sùng jì sai	heng4 sung4 zi4 sai3	heng sung chi sai
release[1] /let out	v	放開	fong hòi	fong3 hoi4	fong hoi
release[2] /discharge	v	放咗	fong jó	fong3 zo2	fong cho
release[3] /loose/discharge	v	釋放	sīk fong	sik1 fong3	sek fong
release[4] /publish	n	發行	faat hòhng	faat3 hong4	faat hohng
release[5] /let go	v	鬆開	sùng hòi	sung4 hoi4	sung hoi
release[6] /shoot/eject /inject/hit/strike	v	射	seh	se6	seh
release[7] /issue/send	v	發佈	faat bou	faat3 bou3	faat pou

release on the mouth	v	口爆	háu baau	hau2 baau3	hau paau
relet	v	再出租	joi chēut jòu	zoi3 ceot1 zou4	choi chhot chou
relevant[1]	adj	有關的	yáuh gwàan dìk	jau5 gwaan4 dik4	yauh kwaan tek
relevant[2]	adj	相關	séung gwāan	soeng2 gwaan1	seung kwaan
reliable[1] /positive /ture/real/tangible	adj	確實	kok saht	kok3 sat6	khok saht
reliable[2]	adj	可靠	hó kaau	ho2 kaau3	ho khaau
reliant /have confidence	adj	信賴	seun làaih	seon3 laai6	swon laaih
relief[1]	n	解除	gaai chèuih	gaai3 ceoi4	kaai chheuih
relief[2]	n	痛苦解除	tung fú gaai chèuih	tung3 fu2 gaai3 ceoi4	thung fu kaai chhoih
relief[3] /relieve	n/v	救濟	gau jai	gau3 zai3	kau chai
relieve[1] /stop pain	v	止	jí	zi2	chi
relieve[2] /rescue	v	解救	gáai gau	gaai2 gau3	kaai kau
relieve from itching /itching relieve	v	止痕	jí hàhn	zi2 han4	chi hahn
relieve pain /stop pain	v	止痛	jí tung	zi2 tung3	chi thung
reliever[1]	n	救濟人	gau jai yàhn	gau3 zai3 jan4	kau chai yahn
reliever[2] (for aid) /rescuer/saver	n	救助者	gau joh jé	gau3 zo6 ze2	kau choh che
religion[1] /religionism	n	教	gaau	gaau3	kaau
religion[2]	n	宗教	jùng gaau	zung4 gaau3	chung kaau
religious[1]	adj	宗教	jùng gaau	zung4 gaau3	chung kaau
religious[2]	adj	道士	dou sih	dou3 si6	tou sih
religious[3]	adj	修女	sau leui /neui	sau3 leoi3 /neoi3	sau lowi /nowi
religious beilef /believe in religion	adj	信仰	seun yéuhng	seon3 joeng5	swon yeuhng
reload	v	再裝	joi jōng	zoi3 zong1	choi chong
relocate /evacuate	v	轉移安置	jyun yih òn /ngòn ji	zyun3 ji4 on4 /ngon4 zi3	chyun yih on /ngon chi
reluctant	adj	不情願	bāt chìhng yuhn	bat1 cing4 jyun6	pat chehng yuhn
rely /depend	v	依賴	yí laaih	ji2 laai6	yi laaih
rely on[1] /to trust/depend	v	信賴	seun laaih	seon3 laai6	swon laaih
rely on[2] /trust to/depend on/rely upon	v	任	yahm	jam4	yahm
rely on[3] /trust	v	信任	seun yahm	seon3 jam4	swon yahm
rely on[4]	v	可靠	hó kaau	ho2 kaau3	ho khaau
rely upon	v	指意	jí yi	zi2 ji3	chi yi
remain[1] /to keep	v	留	làuh	lau4	lauh
remain[2]	v	剩餘	sihng yùh	sing6 jyu6	sehng yuh
remain[3] /unfinished	v	餘留	yùh làuh	jyu4 lau4	yuh lauh
remain[4]	v	仍舊	yìhng gauh	jing4 gau6	yehng kauh
remainder	n	其餘	kèih yùh	kei4 jyu6	kheih yuh
remaining	n	剩餘	sihng yùh	sing6 jyu6	sehng yuh
remains[1] /be left over	n	用剩	yuhng jihng	jung6 zing6	yuhng chehng
remains[2] /debris after damaged	n	殘骸	chàahn hàaih	caan4 haai4	chhaahn haaih

English	POS	Chinese	Romanization	Jyutping	Yale
remains of dead body	n	遺體	wàih tāi	wai4 tai1	waih thai
remains meal	n	食剩嘅	sihk jihng ge	sik6 zing6 ge3	sehk chehng ke
remake	v	再製	joi jai	zoi3 zai3	choi chai
remand /re-investigate	v	重審	chùhng sám	cung4 sam2	chhuhng sam
remarks[1]	v	備註	bèih jyú	bei6 zyu2	peih chyu
remarks[2] /note/notice	v	注意	jyu yi	zyu3 ji3	chyu yi
remarks[3] /comment	v	評論	pìhng leuhn	ping4 leon6	phehng leuhn
remarks[4]	v	註	jyu	zyu3	chyu
remarriage	n	再婚	joi fān	zoi3 fan1	choi fan
remedy	n	藥物	yeuhk maht	joek6 mat6	yeuhk maht
remember[1]	v	記	gei	gei3	kei
remember[2]	v	應切記	yíng chit gei	jing2 cit3 gei3	yeng chhit kei
remember[3] /think back /remembrance	n	記得	gei dāk	gei3 dak1	kei tak
remember me	n	記得我	gei dāk ngóh	gei3 dak1 ngo5	kei tak ngoh
remind	v	令到想起	lihng dou séung héi	ling6 dou3 soeng2 hei2	lehng tou seung hei
reminder	n	提醒者	tàih séng jé	tai4 seng2 ze2	thaih seng che
reminiscent	adj	回憶往事	wùih yīk wóhng sih	wui4 jik1 wong5 si6	wuih yek wohng sih
remiss on the duty /negligent	adj	疏忽	sò fāt	so4 fat1	so fat
remiss	adj	怠慢	tóih màahn	toi5 maan6	thoih maahn
remit money[1]	v	錢款	chín fún	cin2 fun2	chhin fun
remit money[2]	v	匯寄	wuih gei	wui6 gei3	wuih kei
remit /forgive/pardon	v	赦免	se míhn	se3 min5	se mihn
remittance[1]	n	匯寄	wùih géi	wui6 gei2	wuih kei
remittance[2] /to remit	n	匯款	wùih fūn	wui6 fun1	wuih fun
remix music	v	再混合	joi wahn gap	zoi3 wan6 gap3	choi wahn kap
remodel[1]	v	改裝	gói jòng	goi2 zong4	koi chong
remodel[2]	v	改建	gói gin	goi2 gin3	koi kin
remote	adj	遙遠嘅	yìuh yúhn ge	jiu4 jyun5 ge3	yiuh yuhn ke
remote control	n	遙控	yìuh hung	jiu4 hung3	yiuh hung
remote controller	n	遙控制	yìuh hung jai	jiu4 hung3 zai3	yiuh hung chai
removal	n	移動	yìh dúhng	ji4 dung5	yih tuhng
remove[1]	v	去	hói	heoi2	hoi
remove[2] /put off/take off (take out cloth from body)	v	脫去	tyut hói	tyut3 heoi2	thyut hoi
remove layer /strip /take off	v	剝去	mōk heui	mok1 heoi3	mok hoi
removed from	v	遠離	yúhn lèih	jyun5 lei4	yuhn leih
remuneration /reward	n	報酬	bóu chau	bou2 cau3	pou chhau
render /translate	v	譯文	yihk màhn	jik6 man4	yehk mahn
renew	v	使更新	sái gāng sàn	sai2 gang1 san4	sai kang san
renewable	adj	可以更新	hó yíh gàng sàn	ho2 ji5 gang4 san4	ho yih kang san
renovate	v	修整過	sàu jíng gwo	sau4 zing2 gwo3	sau cheng kwo
renovation /repair/refit /rebuild	n	整修	jíng sàu	zing3 sau4	cheng sau

rent[1] /hire/fare/remuneration	n	租	jòu	zou4	chou
rent[2] /tear/rip/split torn place /clothing	n	裂縫	liht fuhng	lit6 fung6	liht fuhng
rent amount /rental	n	租金	jòu gàm	zou4 gam4	chou kam
rent collector	n	收租人	sàu jòu yàhn	sau4 zou4 jan4	sau chou yahn
rent free[1]	adj	唔收租金	m̀ sàu jòu gām	m4 sau4 zou4 gam1	mh sau chou kam
rent free[2]	adj	免租金嘅地	míhn jòu gām ge deih	min5 zou4 gam1 ge3 dei6	mihn chou kam ke teih
rentable	adj	可以出租	hó yíh chēut jòu	ho2 ji5 ceot1 zou4	ho yih chhot chou
rental	n	租金屋	jòu gām ùk	zou4 gam1 uk1	chou kam uk
renter[1]	n	出租人	chēut jòu yàhn	ceot1 zou4 jan4	chhot chho yahn
renter[2]	n	住客	jyuh haak	zyu6 haak3	chyuh haak
renter[3] /tenant	n	租戶	jòu wuh	zou4 wu6	chou wuh
reoccupy	v	再佔領	joi jim léhng /líhng	zoi3 zim3 leng5 /ling5	choi chim lehng
reopen	v	重開	chùhng hòi	cung4 hoi4	chhuhng hoi
reopening	n	再開	joi hòi	zoi3 hoi4	choi hoi
reorder	v	再訂購	joi dehng gau	zoi3 deng gau3	choi tehng kau
repair[1] /work	n	整	jíng	zing2	cheng
repair[2]	n	修	sàu	sau4	sau
repair[3]	n	補	bóu	bou2	pou
repair[4] /fix/mend	n	修理	sau leih	sau3 lei6	sau leih
repair[5]	n	修正	sàu jing	sau4 zing3	sau cheng
repairable	adj	可修理	hó sau leih	ho2 sau3 lei6	ho sau leih
repay[1] /requite/repayment	v	報答	bou daap	bou3 daap3	pou taap
repay[2] /repayment	v	償還	sèuhng wàahn	soeng4 waan4	seuhng waahn
repay money /repaid	v	還錢	wàahn chín	waan4 cin2	waahn chhin
repayment	n	賠償	pùih sèuhng	piu4 soeng4	phuih seuhng
repeat[1]	v	重述	chùhng shēut	cung4 seot6	chhung shwut
repeat[2]	v	再做	joi jouh	zoi3 zou6	choi chouh
repeat[3] /repeat & repeat /repetition/same thing again& again	v	重複	chùhng fūk	cung4 fuk1	chhuhng fuk
repeat & repeat[1] /saying many time	adj	重複乏味	chùhng fūk faht meih	cung4 fuk1 fat6 mei6	chhuhng fuk faht meih
repeat & repeat[2] /reoccurrence/repeat performance	v	重演	chùhng yín	cung4 jin2	chhuhng yin
repeat speak[1] /say again	v	再講	joi góng	zoi3 gong2	choi kong
repeat speak[2] /say again	v	跟住講	gàn jyuh góng	gan4 zyu6 gong2	kan chyuh kong
repeatedly /again and again and again	adv	一再	yāt jói	jat1 zoi2	yat choi
repent /regret	v	悔過	fui gwo	fui3 gwo3	fui gwo
replace[1]	v	替換	tai wuhn	tai3 wun6	thai wuhn
replace[2]	v	換新	wuh sàn	wun6 san4	wuhn san
replace[3]	v	歸還	gwài wàahn	gwai4 waan4	kwai waahn

English		Chinese	Yale	Jyutping	Romanization
replace[4] /change/put back	v	更換	gáng wuhn	gang2 wun6	kang wuhn
replace[5] /renew/renewal /update	n/v	更新	gáng sān	gang2 san1	kang sahn
replace[6] /instead	adv	替	tai	tai3	thai
replace holiday	v	補假	bóu ga	bou2 gaa3	pou ka
replaceable	adj	可以替換	hó yíh tai wuhn	ho2 ji5 tai3 wun6	ho yih thai wuhn
replacement /replace	n/v	接替	jip tai	zip3 tai3	chip thai
replay (in sports)	v	再賽	joi choi	zoi3 coi3	choi choi
reply[1] /answer	v	回	wùih	wui4	wuih
reply[2] /revenge	v	復	fuhk	fuk6	fuhk
reply[3]	v	回覆	wùih fūk	wui4 fuk1	wuih fuk
reply[4]	v	答覆	daap fūk	daap3 fuk1	taap fuk
reply[5] (by letter)	v	回信	wùih seun	wui4 seon3	wuih swon
repolish	v	再磨光	joi mò gwòng	zoi3 mo4 gwong4	choi mo kwong
report[1] /to inform /to report	v	報告	bou gou	bou3 gou3	pou kou
report[2]	v	報道	bou douh	bou3 dou6	pou touh
report[3]	v	報導	bou douh	bou3 dou6	pou touh
report & record	v	報告及記錄	bou gou gahp gei luhk	bou3 gou3 gap6 gei3 luk6	pou kou kahp kei luhk
report form	n	報更表	bou gāng bíu	bou3 gang1 biu2	pou kang piu
report normal condition	v	報正常	bou jeng /jing sèuhng	bou3 zeng3 /jing3 soeng4	pou cheng seuhng
report not correct /misinform	v	誤報	ngh bou	ng6 bou3	ngh pou
report to the police!	v	報警!	bou gíng!	bou3 ging2!	pou keng!
reported /noticed	adj/v	講咗啦	góng jó lā	gong2 zo2 laa1	kong cho la
reporter	n	報告人	bou gou yàhn	bou3 gou3 jan4	pou kou yahn
reporting of news	n	新聞報道	sàn màhn /mán pou douh	san4 man4 /man2 bou3 dou6	san mahn /man pou touh
represent[1] /signify /denote/expression	v	表示	biu sih	biu3 si6	piu sih
represent[2]	v	描繪	mìuh kūi	miu4 kui1	miuh khui
representation /represent	v	象徵	jeuhng jìng	zoeng6 zing4	cheuhng cheng
representative	adj	代表性	doih bíu sing	doi6 biu2 sing3	toih piu seng
repress /suppress	v	鎮壓	jan aat /ngaat	zan3 att3 /ngaat3	chan aat /ngaat
reprint	v	重印	chúhng yan	cung5 jan3	chhuhng yan
reproduce[1]	v	轉載	jyún joi	zyun2 zoi3	chyun choi
reproduce[2] /be reborn	v	再生	joi sàang	zoi3 saang4	choi saang
reproduce[3]	v	繁殖	fàan jihk	faan4 zik6	faan chehk
reproduce[4]	v	殖	jihk	zik6	chehk
reptile[1]	n	爬行	pàh hàhng	paa4 hang4	phah hahng
reptile[2]	n	爬行動物	pàh hàhng duhng maht	paa4 hang4 dung6 mat6	phah hahng tohng maht

republic	n	共和國	guhng wòh gwok	gung6 wo4 gwok3	kuhng wòh gwok
repulsive[1] /to hates	adj	厭惡	yim wu	jim3 wu3	yim wu
repulsive[2]	adj	令人反感	lihng yàhn fáan gám	ling6 jan4 faan2 gam2	lehng yahn faan kam
repulsive forces	adj	斥力	chīk lihk	cik1 lik6	chhek lehk
reputation[1] /smell /famous	n	聞	màhn	man4	mahn
reputation[2] /well known /good name/renown	adj/n	名聲	méng /míng sèng	meng2 /ming2 seng4	meng seng
reputation[3]	n	名譽	mèhng /mìhng yuh	meng4 /ming4 jyu6	mehng yuh
reputation[4]	n	信譽	seun yuh	seon3 jyu6	swon yuh
reputation[5] /prestige	n	聲望	sèng mohng	seng4 mong6	seng mohng
request[1]	n	請	chéng /chíng	ceng2 /cing2	chheng
request[2] /require/need /entail	v	需要	sèui yiu	seoi4 jiu3	swoi yiu
request-help	v	求助	kàuh joh	kau4 zo6	khauh choh
require[1]	v	使	sái	sai2	sai
require[2] /request/petition /desire/requirement	v	要求	yìu kàuh	jiu4 kau4	yiu khauh
require[3]	v	需向	sèui heung	seoi4 hoeng3	swoi heung
required	v	所需	só sēui	so2 seoi1	so swoi
requisite /needs	adj	需要	sèui yiu	seoi4 jiu3	swoi yiu
requisition form	n	申請表	sàn chéng bīu	san4 ceng2 biu1	san chheng piu
resale	n	轉賣	jyún maaih	zyun2 maai6	chyun maaih
rescue[1]	v	救助	gau joh	gau3 zo6	kau choh
rescue[2]	v	搶救	chéung gau	coeng2 gau3	chheung kau
rescue[3] first-aid	n	救護	gau wuh	gau3 wu6	kau wuh
rescue[4] with medical treatment	n	救治	gau jih	gau3 zi6	kau chih
rescue by hand		幫手救	bòng sáu gau	bong1 sau2 gau3	pong sau kau
rescue worker	n	救護人員	gau wuh yàhn yùhn	gau3 wu6 jan4 jyun4	kau wuh yahn yuhn
rescuer[1]	n	救星	gau sèng /sìng	gau3 seng3 /sing3	kau seng
rescuer[2]	n	救援者	gau wùhn jé	gau3 wun4 ze2	kau wuhn che
research[1]	v	考察	haau chaat	haau3 caat3	haau chhaat
research[2] /investigate	v	調查	tìuh chàh	tiu4 caa4	thiuh chhah
research[3]	v	探究	taam gau	taam3 gau3	thaam kau
research and development	n	研究和開發	yìhn gau wòh hòi faat	jin4 gau3 wo4 hoi4 faat3	yihn kau woh hoi faat
resell[1]	v	轉手	jyun sáu	zyun3 sau2	chyun sau
resell[2]	v	再賣	joi maaih	zoi3 maai6	choi maaih
resemble[1] /similarity /seem	v	好相似	hou seung chíh	hou3 soeng3 ci5	hou seung chhih
resemble[2]	v	相似	seung chíh	soeng3 ci5	seung chhih
resemble[3]	v	像似	jeuhng chíh	zoeng6 ci5	cheuhng chhih
resentful /bitter	adj	忿恨	fāt hahn	fat1 han6	fat hahn
reservation	n	預約	yuh yeuk	jyu6 joek3	yuh yeuk
reserve	v	儲備	chyúh bèih	cyu5 bei6	chhyuh peih

reserve seat /book seat	v	預訂	yuh dehng	jyu6 deng6	yuh tehng
reserve time set	v	預約	yuh yeuk	jyu6 joek3	yuh yeuk
reserve arm-force	n	後備軍人	hauh beih gwàn yàhn	hau6 bei6 gwan4 jan4	hauh peih kwan yahn
reserve price[1] /low price	adj	低價	dài ga	dai4 ga3	tai ka
reserve price[2]	n	最低價格	jeui dài ga gaak	zeoi3 dai4 ga3 gaak3	cheui tai ka kaak
reserved already (seat)	n	訂咗	dehng /dihng jó	deng6 /ding6 zo2	tehng cho
reserved table /book a table	v	訂枱	dehng tói	deng6 toi2	tehng thoi
reservoir water /water tank	n	蓄水庫	chūk séui fu	cuk1 seoi2 fu3	chhuk swoi fu
reset[1] machine	v	重組	chùhng jóu	cung4 zou2	chhuhng chou
reset[2]	v	重裝	chùhng jòng	cung4 zong4	chhuhng chong
reset[3]	v	重排	chùhng pàaih	cung4 paai4	chhuhng phaaih
reside	v	居	gèui	geoi4	kwoi
residence[1]	v	住宅	jyuh jáak	zyu6 zaak2	chyuh chaahk
residence[2]	v	居留	gèui làuh	geoi4 lau4	kwoi lauh
residency	n	官邸	gùn dái	gun4 dai2	kun tai
resident at	v	住喺	jyuh hái	zyu6 hai2	chyuh hai
resident foreign	n	外國定居者	oih /ngoih gwok dehng gēui jé	oi6 /ngoi6 gwok3 deng6 geoi1 ze2	oih /ngoih kwok tehng kwoi che
residential	adj	住宅	jyuh jáak	zyu6 zaak2	chyuh chaahk
residential address	adj	住宅地址	jyuh jáak deih jí	zyu6 zaak2 dei6 zi2	chyuh chaahk teih chi
residents association	n	居民委員會	gèui màhn wái yùhn wúi	geoi4 man4 wai2 jyun4 wui2	kwoi mahn wai yuhn wui
resign[1]	v	辭工	chih gùng	ci4 gung4	chhih kung
resign[2]	v	辭去	chih heui	ci4 heoi3	chhih hoi
resign[3]	v	推工	tēui gùng	teoi1 gung4	thoi kung
resignation	n	辭職	chih jīk	ci4 zik1	chhih chek
resigned	adj	已辭職	yíh chìh jīk	ji5 ci4 zik1	yih chhih chek
resistance	n	阻力	jó lihk	zo2 lik6	cho lehk
resistant	adj	抵抗	dái kong	dai2 kong3	tai khap
resolution	n	決心	kyut sàm	kyut sam4	khyut sam
resolve	v	決心	kyut sàm	kyut3 sam4	khyut sam
resort	n	度假勝地	douh ga sing deih	dou6 ga3 sing3 dei6	touh ka seng teih
resort place /holiday resort	n	常去的休閒度假之處	sèuhng heui ge yāu hàahn douh ga jí chyú	soeng4 heoi3 ge3 jau1 haan6 dou6 ga3 zi1 cyu2	seuhng hoi ke yau haahn touh ka chi chhyu
resource	n	資源	jī yùhn	zi1 jyun4	chi yuhn
resourceful	adj	資源豐富	jī yùhn fùng fu	zi1 jyun4 fung4 fu3	chi yuuhn fung fu
resources /source of anythings	n	來源	lòih yùhn	loi4 jyun4	loih yuhn
respect[1]	n	方面	fòng mihn	fong4 min6	fong mihn
respect[2]	n	奉	fuhng	fung6	fuhng
respect greetings /comply/salute/bow	v	順從	seuhn chùhng	seon6 cung4	swohn chhuhng
respectable	adj	得體	dāk tái	dak1 tai2	tak thai

respected sir	n	老爺	lóuh yèh	lou5 je4	louh yeh
respectful[1]	adj	敬	ging	ging3	keng
respectful[2]	adj	恭敬	gùng ging	gung4 ging3	kung geng
respectful salute /salutes/salutations	n	敬禮	ging láih	ging3 lai5	keng laih
respecting	prep	關於	gwàan yù	gwaan4 jyu4	kwaan yu
respective	adj	各個	gok go	gok3 go3	kok ko
respective person	adj	個別	go biht	go3 bit6	ko piht
respectively[1]	adv	各自地	gok jih dèih	gok3 zi6 dei6	kok chih teih
respectively[2] /individually	adv	分別咁	fan biht gam	fan3 bit6 gam3	fan piht kam
respond[1]	v	回應	wùih yíng	wui4 jing2	wuih yeng
respond[2]	v	作答	jók dáap	zok3 daap2	chok taap
response /answer	n	回答	wùih daap	wui4 daap3	wuih taap
responsibility	n	負擔	fuh dàam	fu6 daam4	fuh taam
responsible[1]	adj	責任	jaak yahm	zaak3 jam6	chaak yahm
responsible[2]	adj	有責任	yáuh jaak yahm	zau5 zaak3 jam6	yauh chaak yahm
rest[1]	n	休	yàu	jau4	yau
rest[2] /stop	n	息	sīk	sik1	sek
rest[3] (coll) /to rest	n/v	唞	táu	tau2	thau
rest room[1]	n	休息室	yàu sīk sāt	jau4 sik1 sat1	yau sek sat
rest room[2] (US) toilet /water closet/WC/loo (BT) toilet (washroom/lavatory)	n	洗手間	sái sáu gàan	sai2 sau2 gaan4	sai sau kaan
restate[1] /say again /to speak again	v	重述	chùhng sèuht	cung4 seot6	chhuhng swoht
restate[2] /to speak again	v	重講	chùhng gong	cung4 gong3	chhuhng kong
restaurant[1]	n	茶餐廳	chàh chāan tēng	caa4 caan1 teng1	chhah chaan theng
restaurant[2]	n	飯店	faahn dim	faan6 dim3	faahn tim
restaurant[3]	n	大排檔	daaih pàaih dong	daai6 paai4 dong3	taaih phaaih tong
restaurant[4]	n	餐館	chāan gún	caa4 gun2	chhaan kun
restaurant small[1]	n	酒樓	jáu làuh	zau2 lau4	chau lauh
restaurant small[2]	n	小食店	síu sihk dim	siu2 sek6 dim3	siu sehk tim
restaurant small[3]	n	酒家	jáu gā	zau2 gaa1	chau ka
restfully	adj	安靜地	òn /ngòn jìhng deih	on4 /ngon4 zing6 dei6	on /ngon chehng teih
restless	adj	唔安定	m̀ òn dehng, m̀ ngòn dihng	m4 on4 deng6, m4 ngon4 ding6	mh on tehng, mh ngòn tehng
restock	v	再儲備	joi chyúh beih	zoi3 cyu5 pei6	choi chhyuh peih
restraint[1] /repress /refrain/self control	v	抑制	yìk jái	jik4 zai2	yek chai
restraint[2] /self control	v	約束自己	yeuk chūk jih gei	joek3 cuk1 zi6 gei3	yeuk chhuk chih kei
restrainted	adj	約束力	yéuk chùk lihk	joek2 cuk4 lik6	yéuk chhuk lehk
restrict[1]	v	謝絕	jè jyuht	ze4 zyut6	che chyuht
restrict[2]	v	約束	yéuk chùk	joek2 cuk4	yéuk chhuk
restrict[3]	v	限制	haahn jai	haan6 zai3	haahn chai
restrict[4] /set a limit	v	限定	haahn dehng	haan6 deng6	haahn dehng

English	PoS	Chinese			
restricted	adj	受限制	sàuh hàahn jái	sau6 haan6 zai2	sauh haahn chai
result[1]	n	功	gùng	gung4	kung
result[2] /achievement /performance records (of exam)	n	成績	sèhng jìk	seng4 zik4	sehng chek
resume /restart/begins again	v	重新開始	chùhng sàn hòi chí	cung4 san4 hoi4 ci2	chhuhng san hoi chhi
resurvey	v	再研究	joi yìhn gau	zoi3 jin4 gau3	choi yihn gau
retail	v	零售	lìhng sauh	ling4 sau6	lehng sahn
retailer[1]	n	零售商	lìhng sauh sèung	ling4 sau6 soeng4	lehng sauh seung
retailer[2]	n	零售店	lìhng sauh dim	ling4 sau6 dim3	lehng sauh tim
retell[1] /story again	v	複述	fūk seuht	fuk1 seot6	fuk swoht
retell[2]	v	再講	joi góng	zoi3 gong2	choi kong
retention[1] obstruct	n	閉止	bai ji	bai3 zi3	pai chi
retention[2] clog up	n	阻滯	jó jaih	zo2 zai6	cho chaih
retention[3] keeping	n	留滯	lauh jaih	lau4 zai6	lauh chaih
retention[4] /keeping power	n	保持力	bóu chìh lihk	bou2 ci4 lik6	pou chhih lehk
retention /remember power	n	記憶力	gei yīk lihk	gei3 jik1 lik6	kei yek lehk
retire (from job)	v	退職	teui jīk	teoi3 zik4	thoi chek
retirement /retire from job		退休	teui yāu	teoi3 jau1	thoi yau
retired[1] (from job)	v	使退休	sai teui yāu	sai3 teoi3 jau1	sai teoi yāu
retired[2] (coll) from job	adj	遲左職	chìh jó jīk	ci4 zo2 zik1	chhih cho chek
retired[3] (wr) from job	adj	已退職	yíh teui jīk	ji5 teoi3 zik4	yih thoi chek
retiree	n	退休人員	teui yàu yàhn yùhn	teoi3 jau4 jan4 jyun4	thoi yau yahn yuhn
retouch /to touch up a photo	v	修整	sàu jíng	sau4 zing2	sau cheng
retouch photo	v	執相	jāp séung	zap1 soeng2	chap seung
retrial[1]/new trial of law	n	再審	joi sám	zoi3 sam2	choi sam
retrial[2]/new trial of law	n	復審	fuhk sám	fuk6 sam2	fuhk sam
return[1] /be back/re...	v	返	fàan	faan4	faan
return[2] /turn back	v	返轉	fàan jyun	faan4 zyun3	faan chyun
return back	v	番來	fàan loìh	faan4 loi4	faan loih
return[1] (goods)	v	退回	tèui wui	teoi4 wui3	thoi wui
return?[2] (question)		番嚟呀?	fàan làih àa?	faan4 lai4 aa4	faan laih aa?
return back[1]	v	還有	wàahn yáuh	waan4 jau5	waahn yauh
return back[2] (in cash) /turnover	n	周轉	jàu jyún	zau4 zyun2	chau chyun
return back[3] (come back)	n	歸來	gwài loìh	gwai4 loi4	kwai loih
return back[4] (come back)	n	轉頭先	jyun tàuh sīn	zyun3 tau4 sin1	chyun thauh sin
return back[5] (come back)	n	翻轉嘅	fàan jyūn ge	faan4 zyun1 ge3	faan chyun ke
return ticket[1] (coll)	n	來回飛	lòih wùih fèi	loi4 wui4 fei4	loih wuih fei
return ticket[2] (wr)	n	來回票	lòih wùih piu	loi4 wui4 piu3	loih wuih phiu
return trip /go & back	vt/vi	往復	wóhng fuhk	wong5 fuk6	wohng fuhk
returnable[1]	n	可退還	hó teui wàahn	ho2 teoi3 waan4	ho thoi waahn

English	Part	Chinese	Pronunciation	Jyutping	Yale
returnable[2]	n	應歸還	yíng gwài wàahn	jing2 gwai4 waan4	yeng kwai waahn
returns own country[1] /returnee to the country	n	歸國者	gwāi gwok jé	gwai1 gwok3 ze2	kwai kwok che
returns own country[2] /returnee to the country	n	回國嘅人	wùih gwok ge yàhn	wui4 wui4 ge3 jan4	wuih kwok ke yahn
returner for job after long time	n	再就業者	joi jauh yihp jé	zoi3 zau6 jip6 ze2	choi chauh yihp che
reunion /have a reunion /family gathering	n	團圓	tyùhn yùhn	tyun4 jyun4	thyuhn yuhn
reunite	v	再結合	joi git hahp	zoi3 git3 hap6	choi kit hahp
reusable	adj	可用次使用	hó yuhng chī sái yuhng	ho2 jung6 ci1 sai2 jung6	ho yuhng chhi sai yuhng
reuse	v	用次使用	yuhng chi sái yuhng	jung6 ci6 sai2 jung6	yuhng chi sai yuhng
reveal[1]	v	顯出	hín chēut	hin2 ceot1	hin chhot
reveal[2]	v	顯露出	hín louh chēut	hin2 lou6 ceot1	hin louh chhot
revenge[1]	v	報仇	bou sàuh	bou3 sau4	pou sauh
revenge[2] /reprisal	v	報服	bou fuhk	bou3 fuk6	pou fuhk
revenue	n	稅收	seui sàu	seoi3 sau4	swoi sau
reversal /upside down /turned inside	adv/n	反轉	fàan jyun	faan4 zyun3	faan chyun
reverse[1] /upside-down	adj	顛倒	dìn dóu	din4 dou2	tin tou
reverse[2] /opposite	n	相反	seung fáan	soeng3 faan2	seung faan
reversing light (of vehicle) /back light /white light	n	倒車燈	dóu chè dāng	dou2 ce4 dang1	tou chhe tang
review /look back	v	回顧	wui gú	wui3 gu2	wui ku
reviewer[1]	n	評論員	pìhng leuhn yùhn	ping4 leon6 jyun4	phehng leuhn yuhn
reviewer[2]	n	評論家	pìhng leuhn gà	ping4 leon6 ga4	phehng leuhn ka
reviser	n	修訂者	sau dehng jé	sau3 deng6 ze2	sau tehng che
revisit[1] /visit again	v	重遊	chùhng yàuh	cung4 jau4	chhuhng yauh
revisit[2] /visit again	v	再訪	joi fóng	zoi3 fong2	choi fong
revoke[1] /suspend	v	吊銷	diu sīu	diu3 siu1	tiu siu
revoke[2] /repeal/undo	v	撤消	chit siù	cit3 siu4	chhit siu
revolt[1]	v	叛亂	buhn lyuhn	bun6 lyun6	puhn lyuhn
revolt[2]	v	做反	jouh fáan	zou6 faan2	chouh faan
revolutionary	adj	革命	mihn haap	min6 haap3	mihn haap
revolutions[1] (of political)	n	革命	gaak mehng mihng	gaak3 meng6 /ming6	kaak mehng
revolutions[2] (of political)	n	革命活動	gaak mehng/mihng wuht duhng	gaak3 meng6 /ming6 wut6 dung6	kaak mehng wuht tuhng
revolve /rotate	v	旋轉	syun jyún	syun3 zyun2	syun chyun
revolver[1]	n	左輪手槍	jó lèuhn sáu chēung	zo2 leon4 sau2 coeng1	cho lowhn sau chheung
revolver[2]	n	左輪	jó léun	zo2 leon2	cho leon
revs /accelerate	v	快速運轉	faai chùk wahn jyún	faai3 cuk4 wan6 zyun2	faai chhuk wahn chyun
revving /revs/expedite /accelerate	v	加速	gá chùk	gaa2 cuk4	ka chhuk
reward[1]	n	賞	séung	soeng2	seung
reward[2]	n	懸賞	yùhn séung	jyun4 soeng2	yuhn seung
reward[3]	n	獎賞	jéung séung	zoeng2 soeng2	cheung seung

English		Chinese	Yale	Jyutping	Romanization
rewin	v	再贏	joi yèhng	zoi3 jeng4	choi yehng
rewire	v	換新電線	wuhn sàn dihn sin	wun6 san4 din6 sin3	wuhn san tihn sin
rewrite	v	改寫	gói sé	goi2 se2	koi se
rhetoric[1]	n	修辭	sāu chìh	sau1 ci4	sau chhih
rhetoric[2]	n	華麗虛飾嘅語言	wàh laih hēui sīk ge yúh yìhn	wa4 lai6 heoi1 sik1 ge3 jyu5 jin4	wah laih hoi sek ke yuh yihn
rhino	n	白犀	baahk sāi	baak6 sai1	paahk sai
rhyme	v	押韻	aat wáhn	aat3 wan5	aat wahn
rhythm	n	韻律	wahn leuht	wan6 leot6	wahn lwoht
rib	n	肋骨	lahk gwāt	lak6 gwat1	lahk kwat
ribbon[1]	n	色絲帶	sīk sī dáai	sik1 si1 daai2	sek si taai
ribbon[2] /sash/scarf	n	飾帶	sīk daai	sik1 daai3	sek taai
rice[1]	n	米	máih	mai5	maih
rice[2] /paddy plant	n	稻	douh	dou6	touh
rice[3]	n	穀	gūk	guk1	kuk
rice container	n	米缸	máih gōng	mai5 gong1	maih kong
rice cooker	n	電飯煲	dihn faahn bōu	din6 faan6 bou1	dihn faahn pou
rice ladle /spatula for rice	n	飯殼	faahn hok	faan6 hok3	faahn hok
rice roll	n	腸粉	chèuhng fán	coeng4 fan2	chheuhng fan
rice wine /wine	n	米酒	máih jáu	mai5 zau2	maih chau
rice with barbecued pork & salty egg	n	鹹蛋叉燒飯	hàahm dáan chā sīu faahn	haam4 daan2 caa1 siu1 faan6	haahm taan chha siu faahn
rich[1] /wealthy/abundant /ample	adj	富	fu	fu	fu
rich[2] /wealthy/well off /well to-do	adj	有錢	yáuh chín	jau5 cin2	yauh chhin
rich[3] /wealthy/plentiful /enrichment/abundant/ richness	n/adj	豐富	fùng fu	fung4 fu3	fung fu
rich[4] /wealthy/well off	adj	富有	fù yáuh	fu4 jau5	fu yauh
richter scale[1]	n	里氏	léih sih	lei5 si6	leih sih
richter scale[2]	n	里氏震級	léih sih jan kāp	lei5 si6 zan3 kap1	leih sih chan khap
richter scale[3]	n	里克特震級	léih hāk dahk jan kāp	lei5 hak1 dak6 zan3 kap1	leih hak tahk chan khap
rickshaw	n	人力車	yàhn lihk chè	jan4 lik6 ce4	yahn lehk chhe
riddle[1] /difficult question	n	謎	màih	mai4	maih
riddle[2] /puzzle/difficult question	n	謎語	màih yuh	mai4 jyu6	maih yuh
riddle[3] (funny answer)	n	好難捉摸嘅人	hóu làahn /nàahn jūk mó ge yàhn	hou2 laan4 /naan4 zuk1 mo2 ge3 jan4	hou laahn /naahn chuk mo ke yahn
riddle[4] /clever answer	n	謎一般的人物	màih yāt būn dìk yàhn maht	mai4 jat1 bun1 dik4 jan4 mat6	maih yat pun tek yahn maht
ride /steed (bike/horse)	v	坐騎	chóh kèh	co5 ke4	chhoh kheh
ride bicycle[1]	v	踏單車	daahp dāan chè	daap6 daan1 ce4	taahp taan chhe
ride bicycle[2]	v	踩單車	cháai dāan chè	caai2 daan1 ce4	chhaai daan chhe
ride vehicle[3]	v	乘車	sìhng chè	sing4 ce4	sehng chhe
rider	n	搭乘嘅人	daap sìhng ge yàhn	daap3 sing4 ge3 jan4	taap sehng ke yahn

rides (present tense of ride)		遊樂設施	yàuh lohk chit sì	jau4 lok6 cit3 si4	yauh lohk chhit si
ridge[1] (top of mountain)	n	山脊	sàan jek	saan4 zek3	saan chek
ridge[2] (peak of nose)	n	鼻梁	beih lèuhng	bei6 loeng4	peih lowhng
ridge of field	n	種在壟上	júng joih lúhng seuhng	zung2 zoi6 lung5 soeng6	chung choih luhng seuhng
ridge of roof	n	屋脊	ūk /ngūk jek	uk1 /nguk1 zek3	uk /nguk chek
ridicule	n	蹊落	hàih lohk	hai4 lok6	haih lohk
ridiculous /funny	adj	可笑嘅	hó siu ge	ho2 siu3 ge3	ho siu ke
riding	n	騎乘	kèh sìhng	ke4 sing4	kheh sehng
rifle[1]	n	步槍	bouh chēung	bou6 coeng1	pouh chheung
rifle[2]	n	來福槍	lòih fūk chēung	loi4 fuk1 coeng1	loih fuk chheung
rifle-range	n	靶場	bá cheuhng	ba2 coeng6	pa cheuhng
rift	n	裂痕	liht hàhn	lit6 han4	liht hahn
right[1] (right hand side)	n	右	yauh	jau6	yauh
right[2] (authority)	adj	權	kyùhn	kyun4	khyuhn
right and wrong	adj	黑白	hāk baahk	hak1 baak6	hak paahk
right angle angle of 90°	n	直角	jihk gok	zik6 gok3	chehk kok
right face side		右便面	yauh bihn mihn	jau6 bin6 min6	yauh pihn mihn
right hand man /helper	n	得力助手	dāk lihk joh sáu	dak1 lik6 zo6 sau2	tak lehk choh sau
right hand side		右手面	yauh sáu mihn	jau6 sau2 min6	yauh sau mihn
right now	n	就是現在	jauh sih yihn joih	zau6 si6 jin6 zoi6	chauh sih yihn choih
right of abode	n	居留權	gèui làuh kyùhn	geoi4 lau4 kyun4	kwoi lauh khyuhn
right of way /transit road	n	先行權	sìn hàhng kyùhn	sin4 hang4 kyun4	sin hahng khyuhn
right side[1] /right hand	adj	右邊	yauh bìn	jau6 bin4	yauh pin
right side[2]	adj	右面	yauh mìhn	jau6 min6	yauh mìhn
right side[3] /on the right		右便	yauh bihn	jau6 bin6	yauh pihn
right side[4]	adj	右方	yauh fòng	jau6 fong4	yauh fong
righteous[1]	adj	公正	gùng jeng /jing	gung4 zeng3 /jing3	kung jeng
righteous[2] /honest /integrity	adj	正直	jeng jihk	zeng3 zik6	cheng chehk
rim (edge of circular) /tyre/pneumatic tire	n	輪胎	lèuhn tói	leon4 foi2	leuhn thoi
rind /husk/outer skin /outer thick skin	n	外皮	oih /ngoih pèih	oi6 /ngoi6 pei4	oih /ngoih pheih
ring[1] of finger	n	戒指	gaai jí	gaai3 zi2	kaai chi
ring[2] press button	v	撳門鐘	gahm mùhn jùng	gam6 mun4 zung4	kahm muhn chung
ring[3] circle	n	圈	hyūn	hyun1	hyun
ring[4] bracelet /not for finger	n	環	wàahn	waan4	waahn
ring[5] bell /jangle/noise	n	鈴聲	lìhng sèng	ling4 seng4	lehng seng
ring[6] /iron ring	n	鐵環	tit wàahn	tit3 waan4	thit waahn
ring back	v	回電話	wùih dihn wá	wui4 din6 waa2	wuih tihn wa
ring bell	v	打鐘	dá jùng	daa2 zung4	ta chung
ring off telephone	v	掛斷電話	gwa dúhn dihn wá	gwaa3 dun5 din6 waa2	kwa tuhn tihn wa
ring road	n	環形公路	wàahn yìhng gùng louh	waan4 jing4 gung4 lou6	waahn yehng kung louh

English		Chinese	Romanization	Jyutping	Yale
ring-shaped /round-shaped/circle-shaped	adj	環形	wàahn yìhng	waan4 jing4	waahn yehng
ringer (bell ringer)	n	投環者	tàuh wàahn jé	tau4 waan4 ze2	thauh waahn che
ringing	n	響聲	héung sèng	hoeng2 seng4	heung seng
rings /ring bell rings	v	鐘	jùng	zung4	chung
rinse¹ (clothes) /wash cloths	v	沖洗	chùng sái	cung4 sai2	chhung sai
rinse² /gargle	v	涑口水	chūk háu séui	cuk4 hau2 seoi2	chhuk háu seoi
rinse³ /gargle	v	漂洗	piu sái	piu3 sai2	phiu sai
rinse⁴ /wash/washing	v	洗滌	sái dihk	sai2 dik6	sai tehk
rip¹	v	裂口	liht háu	lit6 hau2	liht hau
rip² /to tear	v	撕	sì	si4	si
rip up /tear open	v	劈開	pek hòi	pek3 hoi4	phek hoi
rip up to open	v	扯開	ché hòi	ce2 hoi4	chhe hoi
ripe	adj	成熟	sèhng suhk	seng4 suk6	sehng suhk
ripped	adj	果皮	gwó pèih	gwo2 pei4	kwo pheih
ripple /small wave	n	波紋	bō màhn	bo1 man4	po mahn
rised value	v	升值	sìng jihk	sing4 zik6	seng chehk
riser man	n	起床的人	héi chòhng dìk yàhn	hei2 cong4 dik4 jan4	hei chhohng tek yahn
riser person	n	起床者	héi chòhng jé	hei2 cong4 ze2	hei chhohng che
rising	n	起高	héi gòu	hei2 gou4	hei kou
rising & falling tones		高音同低音	gòu yàm tùhng dài yām	gou4 jam4 tung4 dai4 jam1	kou yam thuhng tai yam
rising & lowering /up and down	adv	升降	sìng gong	sing4 gong3	seng kong
risk /hazard/take a risks	n	冒險	mouh hím	mou6 him2	mouh him
risk analysis	n	風險分析	fùng hím fàn sīk	fung4 him2 fan6 sik1	fung him fan sek
risker	n	冒險者	mouh hím jé	mou6 him2 ze2	mouh him che
riskful	adj	危險重重	ngàih hīm chùhng chùhng	ngai4 him1 cung4 cung4	ngaih him chhuhng chhuhng
rite	n	儀式	yìh sīk	ji4 sik1	yih sek
rites¹	n	禮	láih	lai5	laih
rites²	n	慣例	gwaan láih	gwaan3 lai5	kwaan laih
river	n	江	gōng	gong1	kong
road¹ /street	n	馬路	máh louh	maa5 lou6	mah louh
road²	n	道路	douh louh	dou6 lou6	touh louh
roadshow¹	n	路迅通	louh seun tōng	lou6 seon3 tong1	louh swon thong
roadshow²	n	巡迴出演	chèuhn wùih chēut yín	ceon4 wui4 ceot1 jin2	chheuhn wuih chhot yin
roam¹	v	遊	yàu	jau4	yau
roam²	v	漫步	maahn bouh	maan6 bou6	maahn pouh
roamer	n	漫遊者	maahn yàuh jé	maan6 jau4 ze2	maahn yauh che
roaming boat /yacht	n	遊艇	yàuh téhng	jau4 teng5/ting5	yauh thehng
roaming card	n	漫遊卡	maahn yàuh kāat	maan6 jau4 kaat1	maahn yauh khaat
roar¹	adj	哮	hāau	haau1	haau
roar² /to snore/noise of breathe	v	呴	paau	paau4	phaau

roar noise[1] /snore	v	咆聲	paau sèng	paau4 seng4/sing4	phaau seng
roar noise[2] /loudly sound	v	大聲咁嘯	daaih sèng gám siu	daai6 seng4 gam2 siu3	taaih seng kam siu
roaring /snoring	adj	咆哮	paau hāau	paau4 haau1	phaau haau
roast[1]	adj	燒	sìu	siu4	siu
roast[2] /bake/grill/parch	v	烤	hàau	haau4	haau
roast duck	n	燒鴨	sìu áap /ngáap	siu4 aap3 /ngaap3	siu aap /ngaap
roast goose	n	燒鵝	sìu ngó	siu4 ngo5	siu ngo
roast meat	n	燒肉	sìu yuhk	siu4 juk6	siu yuhk
roast pig	n	燒豬	sìu jyū	siu4 zyu1	siu chyu
roasted-suckling pig	n	燒乳豬	sìu yúh jyū	siu4 jyu5 zyu1	siu yuh chyu
roaster	n	炙烤嘅人	jek háau ge yàhn	zek haau2 ge3 jan4	chek haau ke yahn
roaster	n	烘烤器	hong hàau hei	hong3 haau4 hei	hong haau hei
roasting	adj	用於烤炙	yuhng yù hàau jek	jung6 jyu4 haau4 zek3	yuhng yuh haau chek
rob /loot/seize by force	v	洗劫	sái gip	sai2 gip3	sai kip
robber	n	盜賊	douh chaahk	dou6 caak6	touh chhaahk
robot man[1]	n	電腦人	dihn nóuh yàhn	din6 nou5 jan4	tihn nouh yahn
robot man[2]	n	機器人	gèi hei yàhn	gei4 hei3 jan4	kei hei yahn
rock[1] /stone	n	石	sehk	sek6	sehk
rock[2] /stone	n	石頭	sehk tàuh	sek6 tau4	sehk thauh
rock[3] /shake/sway	v	搖動	yíu duhng	jiu2 dung6	yiu tohng
rock[4] /shake	v	搖	yìuh	jiu4	yiuh
rock[5] /shake	v	猛烈晃動	máahng liht fóng duhng	maang5 lit6 fong2 dung6	maahng liht fong tohng
rock band	n	搖滾樂團	yìuh gwán ngohk tyùhn	jiu4 gwan2 ngok6 tyun4	yiuh kwan ngohk thyuhn
rock music	n	搖滾樂	yìuh gwán lohk	jiu4 gwan2 lok6	yiuh kwan lohk
rocking /vibrates/jolt	v	振動	jan duhng	zan3 dung6	chan tohng
rocking chair[1]	n	搖椅	yìuh yí	jiu4 ji2	yiuh yi
rocking chair[2] /armchair	n	安樂椅	òn /ngòn lohk yí	on4 /ngon4 lok6 ji2	on /ngon lohk yi
rocks	n	岩石	ngaam sèhk	ngaam3 sek6	ngaam sehk
rodent	n	齧齒目動物	ngaaht chí muhk duhng maht	ngaat6 ci2 muk6 dung6 mat6	ngaaht chhi muhk tohng maht
roiling	v	使焦急	sai jiu gāp	sai3 ziu3 gap3	sai chiu kap
role	n	角色	gok sīk	gok3 sik1	kok sek
roll[1]	v	卷	gyun	gyun3	kyun
roll[2] /turn round/to spin	v	滾	gwán	gwan2	kwan
roll call	n	點名	dím méng	dim2 meng2	tim meng
roll film	n	軟片	yúhn pin	jyun5 pin3	yuhn phin
rolled oats /oatmeal	n	麥片	mahk pín	mak6 pin2	mahk phin
roller	n	滾軸	gwán juhk	gwan2 zuk6	kwan chuhk
roller skates[1]	n	雪屐	syut kehk	syut3 kek6	syut khehk
roller skates[2] /roller shoes	n	溜冰鞋	làuh bīng hàaih	lau4 bing1 haai4	lauh peng haaih

English		Chinese	Yale	Jyutping	
roller skates[3]	n	輪式溜冰鞋	lèuhn sīk làuh bīng hàaih	leon4 sik1 lau4 bing1 haai4	leuhn sek lauh peng haaih
rolling	adj	旋轉	syun jyún	syun3 zyun2	syun chyun
rolling pin	n	擀麵杖	gon mihn jeuhng	gon3 min6 zoeng6	kon mihn cheuhng
roman alphabet	n	羅馬字母	lòh máh jih móuh	lo4 maa5 zi6 mou5	loh mah chih mouh
Roman Catholic Church	n	天主教教堂	Tìn jyú gaau gaau tòhng	tin1 zyu2 gaau3 gaau3 tong4	Thin chyu kaau kaau thohng
romance	n	羅曼語	lòh maahn yúh	lo4 maan6 jyu5	loh maahn yuh
romanization[1]	n	羅馬拼音	lòh máh pìng yām	lo4 man5 ping4 jam1	loh mah pheng yam
romanization[2]	n	羅馬化	lòh máh fa	lo4 maa5 faa3	loh mah fa
romanization[3]	n	古羅馬化	gú lòh máh fa	gu2 lo4 ma5 fa	ku loh mah fa
rome	n	羅馬	lòh máh	lo4 maa5	loh mah
roof	n	屋頂	ùk /ngùk déng	uk4 /nguk4 ding2	uk /nguk teng
roof	n	天棚	tìn páang	tin4 paang2	thin phaang
room[1]	n	宇	yúh	jyu5	yuh
room[2]	n	房間	fóng gàan	fong2 gaan4	fong kaan
room[3] /space/place	n	空間	hùng gàan	hung4 gaan4	hung kaan
room of bridal /bridal room/secret room	n	洞房	duhng fóng	dung6 fong2	tuhng fong
room temperature	n	室溫	sāt wān	sat1 wan1	sat wan
roommate /cohabit	n	同房	tùhng fong	tung4 fong3	thuhng fong
rooms/stores/space /buildings	n	間	gàan	gaan4	kaan
root[1]	n	根	gàn	gan4	kan
root[2] /basis	n	根莖	gàn gìng	gan4 gin3	kan keng
root of cause /main problem	n	根源	gàn yùhn	gan4 jyun4	kan yuhn
root square[1]	n	方根	fōng gàn	fong1 gan4	fong kan
root square[2]	n	根一	gàn yāt	gan4 jat1	kan yat
root square[3]	n	根數	gān sou	gan1 sou3	kan sou
rope[1] /string	n	繩	síng	sing2	seng
rope[2]	n	絞索	gáau sok	gaau2 sok3	kaau sok
rope[3] (of siren)	n	警笛連繩	gíng dehk lìhn sìhng	ging2 dek6 lin4 sing4	keng tehk lihn sehng
rose[1]	n	玫瑰	mùih gwai	mui4 gwai3	muih kwai
rose[2]	n	玫瑰花	mùih gwai fā	mui4 gwai3 fa1	muih kwai fa
rota /work shift	n	值班	jihk baan	zik6 baan1	chehk paan
rotary	adj	轉動的	jyun duhng dī	zyun3 dung6 di1	chyun tohng ti
rotate[1]	v	輪	lèuhn	leon4	leuhn
rotate[2] /turn/twist/wind	v	轉動	jyun duhng	zyun3 dung6	chyun tohng
rotate force[1] /torque	n	轉矩	jyún géui	zyun2 geoi2	chyun kwoi
rotate force[2] /torque	n	扭矩	lāu gēui	lau1 geoi1	lau kwoi
rotate force[3] /torque	n	扭轉力	lāu jyūn lìhk	lau11 zyun1 lik6	lau chyun lehk
rotation[1] /spin/spinning /revolutions	n	旋轉	syun jyún	syun3 zyun2	syun chyun
rotation[2]	n	自轉	jih jyún	zi6 zyun2	chih chyun

rote[1] /repeating	n	死記	séi gei	sei2 gei3	sei kei
rote[2] /repeating /learn by rote	n	死記硬背	séi gei ngaahng bui	sei2 gei3 ngaang6 bui3	sei kei ngaahng pui
rotor	n	旋轉輪	syun jyún leun	syun3 zyun2 leon3	syun chyun leun
rotten[1] /decay/broken	adj	爛	laahn	laan6	laahn
rotten[2] /decay	adj	朽	láu /náu	lau2 /nau2	lau /nau
rotten[3] /abominable	adj	惡劣	ok /ngok lyut	ok3 /ngok3 lyut3	ok /ngok lyut
rotter[1]	n	粗暴者	chòu bouh jé	cou4 bou6 ze2	chhou pouh che
rotter[2] /villain	n	惡棍	ngok gwan	ngok3 gwan3	ngok kwan
rouge /red face powder	n	胭脂	yīn jì	jin1 zi4	yin chi
rough[1]	adj	蠻	màahn	maan4	maahn
rough[2] /bad	adj	粗糙	chòu chou	cou4 cou3	chhou chhou
rough[3] /not flat	adj	唔平滑	m̀ pèhng waaht	m4 peng4 waat6	mh phehng waaht
rough[4] /foul	adj	粗暴咁	chòu bouh gám	cou4 bou6 gam2	chhou pouh kam
rough[5] /not accurate	adj	粗略	chòu leuhk	cou4 loek6	chhou leuhk
rough & ready	adj	將就	jéung jauh	zoeng2 zau6	cheung chauh
rough paper	n	草稿紙	chóu góu jí	cou2 gou2 zi2	chhou kou chi
rough script /in rough /draft/rough writing/make a draft	n/v	起稿	héi góu	hei2 gou2	hei kou
round[1] /circular	n	團	tyùhn	tyun4	thyuhn
round[2] /circle/spherical	adj	圓	yùhn	jyun4	yuhn
round[3] /circle	adj	圓嘅	yùhn ge	jyun4 ge3	yuhn ke
round[4] /ball-shaped	adj	球形	kàuh yìhng	kau4 jing4	khauh yehng
round[5] /surround	adj	環繞地	wàahn yuh deih	waan4 jiu3 dei6	waahn yuh teih
round[6] /all around /surround	prep/v	圍	wàih	wai4	waih
round dance	n	圓舞	yùhn móuh	jyun4 mou5	yuhn mouh
round table	n	圓桌	yùhn cheuk	jyun4 coek3	yuhn chheuk
round trip[1] /two way /return journey/shuttle/go and back/to and from	n	來回	lòih wùih	loi4 wui4	loih wuih
round trip[2]	n	來回旅行	lòih wùih léuih hàahng	loi4 wui4 leoi5 haang4	loih wuih lowih haahng
round trip[3]	n	來回旅程	lòih wùih léuih chìhng	loi4 wui4 leoi5 cing4	loih wuih lowih chhehng
roundabout[1] /traffic circle/traffic rotary	n	繞行路線	yíuh hàhng lòuh sín	jiu5 hang4 lou6 sin2	yiuh hahng louh sin
roundabout[2]	n	繞道	yíuh douh	jiu5 dou6	yiuh touh
rouse /wake up	v	弄醒	luhng /nuhng séng	lung6 /nung6 seng2	luhng /nuhng seng
route /road/way	n	途	tòuh	tou4	thouh
routine[1] /schedule /timetable	n	時間表	sìh gaan bíu	si4 gaan3 biu2	sih kaan piu
routine[2]	n	例行	laih hàng	lai6 hang4	laih hang
routine[3]	n	例行公事	laih hàhng gùng sih	lai6 hang4 gung4 si6	laih hahng kung sih
row[1] /a line	n	一排	yāt tèui	jat1 teoi4	yat thoi
row[2] /to join	n	相連	sèung lìhn	soeng4 lin4	seung lihn

row boat[1]	n	划船	wàh syùhn	waa4 syun4	wah syuhn
row boat[2]	n	划艇	wàh téhng	waa4 teng5	wah thehng
row boat[3] /boat/vessel /sailing	n	扒艇	pàh téhng	paa4 teng5	phah thehng
row house /terraced house	n	牆壁相連 嘅房屋	chèuhng bek sèung lìhn ge fóng ngūk /ùk	coeng4 bek3 soeng4 lin4 ge3 fong2 nguk1 /uk1	chheuhng pek seung lihn ke fong nguk /uk
royal family	n	皇家	wong gà	wong3 gaa4	wong ka
royal highness	n	皇族嘅稱 呼	wòhng juhk ge chìng fù	wong4 zuk6 ge3 cing4 fu4	wohng chuhk ke chhingfu
royal member	n	皇族或王 族成員	wòhng juhk waahk wòhng juhk seng yùhn	wong4 zuk6 waak6 wong4 zuk6 seng3 jyun4	wohng chuhk waahk wohng chuhk seng yùhn
royalty[1] /king's power	n	皇權	wòhng kyùhn	wong4 kyun4	wohng khyuhn
royalty[2] /king (title)	n	皇位	wòhng waih	wong4 wai6	wohng waih
royalty[3] (for books)	n	版稅	báan seui	baan2 seoi3	paan swoi
royalty[4] (taxes)	n	權稅	kyùhn seui	kyun4 seoi3	khyuhn swoi
royalty[5] /copyright cost	n	版權費	báan kyùhn fai	baan2 kyun4 fai3	paan khyuhn fai
rub[1] /wipe	v	擦	cháat	caat2	chhaat
rub[2] /to polish	v	磨	mò	mo4	mo
rubber[1]	n	橡膠	jeuhng gàau	zoeng6 gaau4	cheuhng kaau
rubber[2]	n	橡皮	jeuhng pèih	zoeng6 pei4	cheuhng pheih
rubber band	n	橡皮圈	jeuhng pèih hyùn	zoeng6 pei4 hyun4	cheuhng pheih hyun
rubber pipe	n	膠管	gàau gún	gaau4 gun2	kaau kun
rubber stamp	n	橡皮圖章	jeuhng pèih tòuh jēung	zoeng6 pei4 tou4 zoeng1	cheuhng pheih thouh cheung
rubber synthetic	n	合成橡膠	hahp sehng jeuhng gàau	hap6 seng4 zoeng6 gaau4	hahp sehng cheuhng kaau
rubbing	n	摩擦	mò chaat	mo4 caat3	mo chhaat
rubbish bag	n	垃圾袋	laahp saap doih	laap6 saap3 doi6	laahp saap toih
ruby	n	紅寶石	hùhng bóu sehk	hung4 bou2 sek6	huhng pou sehk
rucksack[1] /backpack	n	背包	buih bāau	bui6 baau1	puih paau
rucksack[2]	n	帆布背包	fàahn bou bui bāau	faan4 bou2 bui3 baau1	faahn pou pui paau
rudely answer	v	駁	bok	bok3	pok
ruffian[1] /violent man	n	暴徒	bouh tòuh	bou6 tou4	pouh thouh
ruffian[2] /violent man	n	無賴	mòuh láaih	mou4 laai5	mouh laaih
rug	n	小地毯	síu deih táan	siu2 dei6 taan2	siu teih thaan
ruin[1] /violently damage	v	殘	chàahn	caan4	chhaahn
ruin[2] /destroy/violently damage	v	毀滅	wái miht	wai2 mit6	wai miht
rule /law/regulation	n	規定	kwài dehng /dihng	kwai4 deng6 /ding6	khwai tehng
rule book /law book	n	規則手冊	kwài jāk sáu chaak	kwai4 zak1 sau2 caak3	khwai chak sau chhaak
ruler[1] /measure	n	間尺	gaan chék	gaan3 cek2	kaan chhek
ruler[2]	n	直尺	jihk chék	zik6 cek2	chehk chjek
ruler[3] /governor/governs /a person who rules	n	統治者	túng jih jé	tung3 zi6 ze2	thung chih che

English	Part	Chinese			
rules[1]	n	則	jāk	zak1	chak
rules[2]	n	條例	tìuh laih	tiu4 lai6	thiuh laih
rules[3]	n	規則嘅	kwài jāk ge	kwai4 zak1 ge3	khwai chak ke
ruling	n	裁決	chòih kyut	coi4 kyut3	chhoih khyut
rumoured	adj	謠言	yìuh yìhn	jiu4 jin4	yiuh yihn
run[1]	v	奔	bàn	ban4	pan
run[2] (as a mad man)	v	狂跑	kòhng pàauh	kong4 paau4	khohng phaauh
run across	v	偶然遇到	ngáuh yìhn yuh dóu	ngau5 jin4 jyu6 dou2	ngauh yihn yuh tou
run ahead	v	向前跑	heung chìhn pāau	hoeng3 cin4 paau1	heung chhihn phaau
run away[1]	v	逃跑	tòuh pāau	tou4 paau1	thouh phaau
run away[2] (by force)	v	走難	jáu laahn /naahn	zau2 laan6 /naan6	chau laahn /naahn
run into trouble	v	撞板	johng báan	zong6 baan2	chohng paan
runner	n	跑步者	páau bouh jé	paau2 bou6 ze2	phaau pouh che
running opposite direction	v	對開	deui hòi	deoi3 hoi4	toei hoi
running vehicle	n	行車	hàahng chè	haang4 ce4	haahng chhe
running water	n	流水	làuh séui	lau4 seoi2	lauh swoi
ruption	n	破裂	po liht	po3 lit6	pho liht
rural[1]	adj	田園嘅農業	tìhn yùhn ge lùhng /nùhng yihp	tin4 jyun4 ge3 lung4 /nung4 jip6	thihn yuhn ke luhng /nuhng yihp
rural[2]	adj	鄉下	hèung háh	hoeng4 haa5	heung hah
rural[3]	adj	田園嘅	tìhn yùhn ge	tin4 jyun4 ge3	thihn yuhn ke
rural-area	n	鄉村區鄉下	hèung chyùn kēui hèung háh	hoeng4 cyun4 keui1 hoeng4 haa5	heung chhyun khoi heung hah
rural-life	adj	鄉村生活	hèung chyùn sàng wuht	hoeng4 cyun4 sang4 wut6	heung chhyun sang wuht
ruse /trick/crafty scheme /mischievous act	n/adj	詭計	gwái gai	gwai2 gai3	kwai kai
rush[1] /towards/go staight ahead	n	衝	chùng	cung4	chhung
rush[2]	n	催	chèui	ceoi4	chheui
rush[3]	n	衝擊	chùng gīk	cung4 gik1	chhung kek
rush[4] /cane (plant)	n	燈芯草	dāng sām chóu	dang1 sam1 cou2	tang sam chhou
rush buying		搶購	chéung kau	coeng2 kau3	chheung khau
rush hour (of traffic)		擠塞時間	jài sāk sìh gaan	zai4 sak1 si4 gaan3	chai sak sih kaan
rush out		衝出	chùng chēut	cung4 ceot1	chhung chhot
rush running		奔走	bàn jáu	ban4 zau2	pan chau
rush to go	n	快走	faai jáu	faai3 zau2	faai chau
Russia	n	俄羅斯	ngóh lo sì	ngo5 lo3 si4	ngoh lo si
Russian language	n	俄文	óh màhn	o5 man4	oh màhn
rust[1] /rusty	n	銹	sau	sau3	sau
rust[2]	n	鏽	sau	sau3	sau
rusticate[1]	v	勒令退學	laahk lihng teui hohk	laak6 ling6 teoi3 hok6	laahk lehng thoi hohk
rusticate[2]	v	擇居鄉村	jaahk gèui hēung chyùn	zaak6 geoi4 hoeng1 cyun4	chaahk kwoi heung chhyun
rusty	adj	生銹/生鏽	sàang sau	saang4 sau3	saang sau

English		Chinese	Pronunciation 1	Pronunciation 2	Pronunciation 3
sack /bag	n	囊	lòhng /nòhng	long4 /nong4	lohng /nohng
sacred	adj	嚴肅	yìhm sūk	jim4 suk1	yihm suk
sacred place /sacred spot	n	聖地	sing deih	sing3 dei6	seng teih
sacred temple	n	聖殿	sing dìn	sing3 din3	seng tin
sacrifice[1]	v	犧牲	hèi sāng	hei4 sang1	hei sang
sacrifice[2]	v	犧牲自己	hèi sāng jih géi	hei4 sang1 zi6 gei2	hei sang chih kei
sad[1] /sorry/pitiful	adj	唔安樂	m̀ on lohk	m4 on3 lok6	mh on lohk
sad![2] /sorry!	adj	難過	làahn gwò	laan4 gwo4	laahn kwo
sad[3] /unhappy/unpleasant	adj	不愉快	bāt yu fáai	bat1 jyu3 faai2	pat yu faai
sad[4] /sadness/sorrow	adj	悲	bèi	bei4	pei
sad[5] /sorrow	adj	悲傷	bèi sèung	bei4 soeng4	pei seung
sad & lonely /sorrowful /unhappy/miserable	adj	凄涼	chài lèuhng	cai4 loeng4	chhai leuhng
sad face /worry face /have a sad look	adj	愁容滿面	sàuh yuhng múhn mihn	sau4 jung4 mun5 min6	sauh yuhng muhn mihn
sad to say	v	不幸嘅事	bāt hahng ge sih	bat1 hang6 ge3 si6	pat hahng ke sih
sadder /saddest/unhappy	n	人滿患	yàhn múhn waahn	yan4 moon5 waan6	yahn muhn waahn
Sadhu Hinduism religion	n	印度教聖人	yan dòuh gaau sing yàhn	jan3 dou6 gaau3 sing3 jan4	yan touh kaau seng yahn
safe	adj	安	òn /ngòn	on4 / ngon4	on /ngon
safe & healthy	adj	康泰	hōng taai	hong1 taai3	hong thaai
safe area	n	安全區	òn /ngòn chyùhn kèui	on4 /ngon4 cyun4 keoi4	on /ngon chhyuhn khoi
safe box /vault	n	夾萬	gaap maahn	gaap3 maan6	kaap maahn
safe conduct	n	安全通行權	òn /ngòn chyùhn tùng hahng kyùhn	on4 /ngon4 cyun4 tung4 hang4 kyun4	on /ngon chhyuhn thung hahng khyuhn
safe deposit	n	保險箱	bóu hím sèung	bou2 him2 soeng4	pou him seung
safe sex	n	安全性行為	òn /ngon chyun sing hàhng wàih	on4 /ngon3 cyun4 sing3 hang6 wai6	on /ngon chhyun seng hahng waih
safely /securely	adv	安全地	òn /ngòn chyùhn deih	on4 /ngon4 cyun4 dei6	on /ngon chhyuhn teih
safely arrived		平安到咗	pèhng òn /ngòn dou jó	peng4 on4 /ngon4 dou3 zo2	phehng on tou cho
safety belt /seat belt	n	安全帶	òn /ngòn chyùhn daai	on4 /ngon4 cyun4 daai3	on /ngon chhyuhn taai
safety card	n	平安咭	pèhng òn /ngòn kāat	peng4 on4 /ngon4 kaat1	phehng on /ngon khaat
safety first	n	安全第一	òn /ngòn chyùhn daih yāt	on4 /ngon4 cyun4 dai6 jat1	on /ngon chhyuhn taai yat
safety helmet /helmet /hard hat	n	安全帽	òn /ngòn chyun mòuh	on4 /ngon4 cyun4 mou6	on /ngon chhyun mouh
safety net	n	安全網	òn /ngòn chyùhn móhng	on4 /ngon4 cyun4 mong5	on /ngon chhyuhn mohng
safety pin[1]	n	扣針	kau jām	kau3 zam1	khau cham
safety pin[2]	n	別針	bìht jām	bit6 zam1	piht cham
safety pin[3]	n	安全別針	òn /ngòn chyùhn bìht jām	on4 /ngon4 cyun4 bit6 zam1	on /ngon chhyuhn piht cham
safety shoe	n	安全鞋	òn /ngòn chyùhn hàaih	on4 /ngon4 cyun4 haai4	on /ngon chhyuhn haaih

English		Chinese	Yale	Jyutping	Romanization
Sagarmatha /Everest[1] the world highest mountain 8.848 m /29.028 ft (in Nepal)	n	珠穆瑯瑪	jyú muhk lòhng máh	zyu2 muk6 long4 maa5	chyu muhk lohng mah
Sagarmatha /Everest[2] the world highest peak 8.848 m /29.028 ft (in Nepal)	n	額菲爾士峰	aahk /ngaahk féi yíh sih fùng	aak6 /ngaak6 fei2 ji5 si6 fung4	aahk /ngaahk fei yih sih fhung
saggy	adj	下垂	hah sèuih	haa6 seoi4	hah swoih
said	adj	講	góng	gong2	kong
sail[1]	n	篷	pùhng	pung4	phuhng
sail[2]	n	帆	fàahn	faan4	faahn
sailing	n	坐船	chóh syùhn	co5 syun4	chhoh syuhn
sailing boat	n	風帆	fùng fàahn	fung4 faan4	fung faahn
sailor	n	水手	séui sáu	seoi2 sau2	swoi sau
salad [(de)]	n	沙律	sà lèuht	saa4 leot6	sa lwoht
sale /sales event/sold	n	賣	maaih	maai6	maaih
sale price	n	成交價	seng gàau ga	seng3 gaau4 gaa3	seng kaau ka
sales	n	行街員	hahng gāai yùhn	hang4 gaai1 jyun4	hahng kaai yuhn
sales-lady /saleswoman	n	女售貨員	léuih sauh fo yùhn	leui5 sau6 fo3 jyun4	lowih sauh fo yuhn
salesman /sales	n	售貨員	sauh fo yùhn	sau6 fo3 jyun4	sauh fo yuhn
salesperson	n	店員	dim yùhn	dim3 jyun4	tim yuhn
sallow	adj	灰黃色	fùi wòhng sīk	fui4 wong4 sik1	fui wohng sek
salmon [(de)]	n	三文魚	sàam man yū	saam4 man3 jyu1	saam man yu
salon[1] hair shop/beauty parlour	n	飛髮店	fèi faat dim	fei4 faat3 dim3	fei faat tim
salon[2]	n	髮廊	faat lòhng	faat3 long4	faat lohng
saloon[1] /hall/living	n	人廳	yàhn tèng	jan4 teng4	yahn theng
saloon[2] /barroom/pub /bar	n	交誼室	gàau yìh sat	gaau4 ji4 sat3	kaau yih sat
saloon bar	n	高級酒店	gòu kāp jáu dim	gou4 kap1 zau2 dim3	kou khap chau tim
saloon car	n	小轎車	síu gíu chè	siu2 giu2 ce4	siu kiu chhe
salt	n	盐/鹽	yìhm	jim4	yihm
salt water	n	咸水	hàahm séui	haam4 seoi2	haahm swoi
salter	n	製鹽者	jai yìhm jé	zai3 jim4 ze2	chai yihm che
saltless	adj	少盐	síu yìhm	siu2 jim4	siu yihm
salty[1]	adj	鹹	hàahm	haam4	haahm
salty[2]	adj	有鹽分	yáuh yìhm fán	jau5 jim4 fan2	yauh yihm fan
salty & wet [(sl)] sexual desire/dirty minded/obscene/ wanton	xy	咸濕	hàahm sāp	haam4 sap1	haahm sap
salute[1] /army greetings	n	行敬禮	hàahng ging láih	haang4 ging3 lai5	haahng keng laih
salute[2] (to bow)	n	躹躬	gūk gūng	guk1 gung1	kuk kung
salute[3]	n	敬	ging	ging3	keng
same[1] /identical	adj	相同	seung tùhng	soeng3 tung4	seung thuhng
same[2] /together with	adj	同	tùhng	tung4	thuhng
same[3]	adj	同一	tùhng yāt	tung4 jat1	thuhng yat
same[4] /same way /likewise	adj	照樣咁	jiu yéung gám	ziu3 joeng2 gam2	chiu yeung kam

English		漢字	Yale	Jyutping	Romanization
same as usual		都係咁	dōu haih gam	dou1 hai6 gam3	tou haih kam
same big size	n	一樣咁大	yāt yeuhng gam daaih	jat1 joeng6 gam3 daai6	yat yeuhng kam taaih
same day	n	即日	jīk yaht	zik1 jat6	chek yaht
same idea /same opinion /same view/by coincidence	n	啱啱	ngāam ngāam	ngaam1 ngaam1	ngaam ngaam
same meaning /having the same/synonymous	adj	同義詞	tùhng yih chì	tung4 ji6 ci4	thuhng yih chhi
same place	n	同地方	tùhng deih fòng	tung4 dei6 fong4	thuhng teih fong
same problems /same sufferers/in the same boat each other	n	同病相憐	tùhng behng sèung lìhn	tung4 beng6 soeng4 lin4	thuhng pehng seung lihn
same room	n	同方	tùhng fóng	tung4 fong2	thuhng fong
same sex	n	同性	tùhng sing	tung4 sing3	thuhng seng
same size	n	一樣咁	yāt yeuhng gam	jat1 joeng6 gam3	yat yeuhng kam
same small size	n	一樣咁細	yāt yeuhng gam sai	jat1 joeng6 gam3 sai3	yat yeuhng kam sai
same type	n	同類	tùhng leuih	tung4 leoi6	thuhng lowih
same villager /same town	n	同鄉	tùhng hēung	tung4 hoeng1	thuhng heung
same way[1]	n	一樣咁	yāt yeuhng gam	jat1 joeng6 gam3	yat yeuhng kam
same way[2] /same /likewise	n	而且	yìh ché	ji4 ce4	yih chhe
same year	n	同年	tùhng lìhn /nìhn	tung4 lin4 /nin4	thuhng lihn /nihn
samosa[1] /singadaa	n	印度三角火餃	yan douh sàam gok fó gáau	jan3 dou6 saam4 gok3 fo2 gaau2	yan touh saam kok fo kaau
samosa[2] /singadaa	n	印度咖喱角	yan douh gā lēi gok	jan3 dou6 gaa1 lei1 gok3	yan touh ka lei kok
sample[1] /swatch	n	樣品	yeuhng bán	joeng6 ban2	yeuhng pan
sample[2] /specimen	n	樣本	yeuhng bún	joeng6 bun2	yeuhng pun
sampling	n	抽樣	chāu yeuhng	cau1 joeng6	chhau yeuhng
san-miguel beer	n	生力	sàng lìhk	sang4 lik4	sang lehk
sand /small grains of rock	n	沙	sà	saa4	sa
sandal	n	涼鞋	lèung hàaih	loeng4 haai4	leung haaih
sandbank	n	沙洲	sà jāu	saa4 zau1	sa chau
sandpaper	n	砂紙	sà jí /zí	saa4 zi2	sa chi
sandwiches (Taiwan dish)	n	三明治	sàam ming jih	saam4 ming3 zi6	saam meng chhih
sandwiches food (HK)	n	三文治	sàam màhn jih	saam4 man4 zi6	saam mahn chih
sanitarian /health-worker	n	公共衛生官員	gùng guhng waih sàng gùn yùhn	gung4 gung6 wai6 sang4 gun4 jyun4	kung guhng waih sang kun yuhn
sanitary[1]	adj	合衞生	hahp waih sāng	hap6 wai6 sang1	hahp waih sang
sanitary[2]	adj	公共衛生	gùng guhng waih sàng	gung4 gung6 wai6 sang4	kung guhng waih sang
sanitizer	n	消毒殺菌劑	sìu duhk saat kwánjāi	siu4 duk6 saat3 kwan2 jai1	siu tuhk saat khwan chai
sink /sank	v	下沈	hah chàhm	haa6 cam4	hah chhahm
sapodilla (fruit /tamarine)	n	人心果	yàhn sàm gwó	jan4 sam4 gwo2	yahn sam kwo
sapphire	n	藍寶石	laahm bóu sehk	laam4 bou2 sek6	laahm pou sehk
sarcasm /satire	n	諷刺	fung chi	fung3 ci3	fung chhi
sardine (a kind of fish)	n	沙甸魚	sà dīn yú	saa4 din1 jyu2	sa tin yu

sari[1] (Nepali women's cloths)	n	卷布	gyun bou	gyun3 bou3	kyun pou
sari[2] (Nepali women's cloths)	n	紗麗	sā laih	sa1 lai6	sa laih
sash /scarf	n	領巾	léhng /líhng gān	leng5 /ling5 gan1	lehng kan
satellite[1]	n	衛星	waih sèng	wai6 seng4	waih seng
satellite[2]	n	人造衛星	yàhn jouh waih sèng	jan4 zou6 wai6 seng4	yahn chouh waih seng
satin /woven fabric	n	緞子	dyuhn jí	dyun6 ji2	tyuhn chi
satirise person[1]	n	慣方諷刺人	gwaan fong fung chi yàhn	gwaan3 fong3 fung3 ci3 jan4	kwaan fong fung chhi yahn
satirise person[2]	n	寫的野諷刺人	sé dì yéh fung chi yàhn	se2 di4 je5 fung3 ci3 jan4	se di yeh fung chhi yahn
satirize[1] (poem)	n	諷刺詩	fung chi sī	fung3 ci3 si1	fung chhi si
satirize[2] (writing)	n	諷刺文	fung chi mahn	fung3 ci3 man6	fung chhi mahn
satisfaction	n	滿意	múhn yi	mun5 ji3	muhn yi
satisfactory[1]	adj	令人滿意	lihng yàhn múhn yi	ling4 jan4 mun5 ji3	lehng yahn muhn yi
satisfactory[2]	adj	滿意嘅	múhn yi ge	mun5 ji3 ge3	muhn yi ke
satisfied[1]	adj	好滿意	hóu múhn yi	hou2 mun5 ji3	hou muhn yi
satisfied[2]	adj	覺得滿意	gok dāk múhn yi	gok3 dak1 mun5 ji3	kok tak muhn yi
satisfy	v	使滿意	sai múhn yi	sai3 mun5 ji3	sai muhn yi
Saturday[1]	n	禮拜六	láih baai luhk	lai5 baai3 luk6	laih paai luhk
Saturday[2]	n	星期六	sìng kèih luhk	seng4 kei4 luk6	seng kheih luhk
sauna[1] (bathing hot air or steam with massage)	n	桑拿	sōng nàh	song1 naa4	song nah
sauna[2] (bathing hot air or steam with massage)	n	三温暖	sàam wān lyúhn /nyúhn	saam4 wan1 lyun5 /nyun5	saam wan lyuhn /nyuhn
sausage	n	香腸	hèung chéung	hoeng4 coeng2	heung chheung
sausage chicken	n	雞肉腸	gài yuhk chéung	gai4 juk6 coeng2	kai yuhk chheung
sausage of veal /beef	n	牛仔肉腸	ngàuh jái yuhk chéung	ngau4 zai2 juk6 coeng2	ngauh chai yuhk chheung
sausage pork	n	臘腸	laahp chéung	laap6 coeng2	laahp chheung
sausage pork liver	n	潤腸	yeuhn chéung	jeon6 coeng2	yeuhn chheung
save[1] /stock/store	v	貯	chyúh	cyu5	chhyuh
save[2] /saving/stock/store	v	儲	chyúh	cyu5	chhyuh
save[3] /preserve/save up	v	維護	wàih wuh	wai4 wu6	waih wuh
save for you		留俾你	láuh béi léih /néih	lau5 bei2 lei5 /nei5	lauh pei leih /neih
save life[1] /relieve	v	救	gau	gau3	kau
save life[2] /rescue	v	救援	gau wùhn	gau3 wun4	kau wuhn
save life[3]	v	挽救	wáahn gau	waan5 gau3	waahn kau
save money[1]	v	積蓄	jīk chūk	zik1 cuk1	chek chhuk
save money[2]	v	儲蓄	chyúh chūk	cyu5 cuk1	chhyuh chhuk
saver	n	存戶	chyùhn wuh	chyun4 wu6	chhyuhn wuh
savings bank	n	存款銀行	chyùhn fún ngàhn hòhng	cyun4 fun2 ngan4 hong4	chhyuhn fun ngahn hohng
savings gold	n	儲金	chyúh gām	cyu5 gam1	chhyuh kam
savior	n	救世主	gau sai jyú	gau3 sai3 zyu2	kau sai chyu
saw[1] /seen (see pt)	v	見到	gin dou	gin3 dou3	kin tou

English	Part	Chinese	Romanization	Jyutping	Romanization 2
saw[2] /seen	v	看見	hōn gin	hon1 gin3	hon kin
saw[3] /proverb/adage	n	諺語	yihn yúh	jin6 jyu5	yihn yuh
saw[4] /cutter	n	鋸	geui	geoi3	kwoi
say /speak	v	言	yìhn	jin4	yihn
say again /retell/repeat again/speak again	v	再講	joi góng	zoi3 gong2	choi kong
say hello![1] /greet! /greetings!	v	打招呼	dā jiu fù	daa1 ziu3 fu4	ta chiu fu
say hello![2]	v	問好	mahn hóu	man6 hou2	mahn hou
say once more[1]	v	講多一次	góng dò yāt chi	gong2 do4 jat1 ci3	kong to yat chhi
say once more[2]	v	再講一次	joi góng yāt chi	zoi3 gong2 jat1 ci3	choi kong yat chi
say one word	v	一言	yāt yìhn	jat1 jing4	yat yihn
say reason	v	表示原因	bíu sih yùhn yàn	biu2 si6 jyun4 jan1	píu sih yùhn yàn
say something[1]	v	出聲	chāut sēng	ceot1 seng1	chhaut seng
say something[2]	v	講嘢	góng yéh	gong2 je5	kong yeh
saying[1] /proverb /aphorism/common	n	古語有云	gú yuh yauh wàhn	gu2 jyu6 jau6 wan4	ku yuh yauh wahn
saying[2] (sl)	n	格言	gaak yìhn	gaak3 jin4	kaak yihn
scabbard /sheath /cover for knife	n	鞘	chiu	ciu3	chhiu
scaffolding	n	腳手架	geuk sáu gá	goek3 sau2 ga2	keuk sau ka
scald[1]	v	渌親	luhk chàn	luk6 can4	luhk chhan
scald[2]	v	燙傷	tong sèung	tong3 soeng4	thong seung
scalding /piping hot	n	滾燙	gwán tong	gwan2 tong3	kwan thong
scale[1] /proportion/ratio	n	比例	béi laih	bei2 lai6	pei laih
scale[2]	n	鱗片	lèuhn pin	leon4 pin3	leuhn phin
scale[3]	n	刻度	hāak douh	haak1 dou6	haak touh
scales of fish	n	魚鱗	yùh lèuhn	jyu4 leon4	yuh leuhn
scallop /fish	n	帶子	daai jí	daai3 zi2	taai chi
scallop dried	n	乾瑤柱	gòn yiuh chyùh	gon4 jiu4 cyu4	kon yiuh chhyuh
scaly	adj	有鱗	yáuh lèuhn	jau5 leon4	yauh leuhn
scan /carefully look	v	審視	sām sìh	sam1 si6	sam sih
scandal	n	醜聞	cháu màhn	cau2 man6	chhau mahn
scapegoat /bad blamed	n	替罪羊	tái jèuih yeung	tai2 zeoi6 joeng3	thai choih yeung
scar[1] /scratch on the skin	n	啦	là /nà	la4 /na4	la /na
scar[2] /mark on the skin	n	疤痕	bā hàhn	baa1 han4	pa hahn
scar[3] /mark on the skin	n	結痕	git hàhn	git3 han4	kit hahn
scarcity	n	稀少	hèi síu	hei4 siu2	hei siu
scare	v	吓	àh?	aa4	ah?
scared /horrify/fright /feeling fear	adj/v	驚嚇	gèng hàak	geng4 haak4	keng haak
scared to death	adj	嚇死	háak séi	haak2 sei2	haak sei
scatter[1]	v	披	pēi	pei1	phei
scatter[2] /let go/let loose	v	撒	saat	saat3	saat
scatter[3]	v	分散	fahn sáan	fan6 saau2	fahn saan

scatter[4]	v	消散	sìu sáan	siu4 saan2	siu saan
scene[1]	n	場面	chèuhng mìhn	coeng4 min6	chheuhng mihn
scene[2] /scenery/vista /panorama/view	n	有景	yáuh gíng	jau5 ging2	yauh keng
scene[3] /take picture	n	現場	yihn chèuhng	jin6 coeng4	yihn chheuhng
scenery	n	景	gíng	ging2	geng
scenic /natural beautiful /beautiful view	n/adj	景色秀麗	gíng sīk sau laih	ging2 sik1 sau3 lai6	keng sek sau laih
scent /odor/aroma /fragrance	n	氣味	hei meih	hei3 mei6	hei meih
scent shop	n	香水當	hèung séui dong	heung1 sui2 dong3	heung swoi tong
schedule	n	日程表	yaht chìhng bíu	jat6 cing4 biu2	yaht chhehng piu
scheme	n	方案	fòng on /ngon	fong4 on3 /ngon3	fong on /ngon
scholar[1] /soldier/warrior	n	士	sih	si6	sih
scholar[2]	n	文人	màhn yàhn	man4 jan4	mahn yahn
scholar[3]	n	學者	hohk jé	hok6 ze2	hohk che
scholarship	n	獎學金	jéung hohk gām	zong2 hok6 gam1	cheung hohk kam
school[1] /study/learn	n/v	學	hohk	hok6	hohk
school[2]	n	校	haauh	haau6	haauh
school[3] /institution	n	院	yún	jyun2	yun
school[4]	n	學校	hohk haauh	hok6 haau6	hohk haauh
school age	n	學齡	hohk lìhng /nìhng	hok6 ling4 /ning4	hohk lehng
school association	n	校友會	haauh yáuh wúi	haau6 jau5 wui2	haauh yauh wui
school bus	n	校車	haauh chè	haau6 ce4	haauh chhe
school kids	n	學童	hohk tùhng	hok6 tung4	hohk tùhng
school physician	n	校醫	haauh yī	haau6 ji1	haauh yi
school uniform	n	校服	haauh fuhk	haau6 fuk6	haauh fuhk
science /scientific	n	科學	fò hohk	fo4 hok6	fo hohk
science college	n	理學院	léih hohk yún	lei5 hok6 jyun2	leih hohk yun
scientific	adj	關於科學	gwàan yù fò hohk	gwaan1 jyu4 fo4 hok6	kwaan yu fo hohk
scientist	n	科學家	fò hohk gà	fo4 hok6 ga4	fo hohk ka
scissors[1]	n	剪	jín	zin2	chin
scissors[2]	n	剪刀	jín dōu	zin2 dou1	chin tou
scissors[3]	n	較剪	gaau jín	gaau3 zin2	kaau chin
scold /speak angrily	v	斥	chīk	cik1	chhek
scoop /large spoon	n	殼 / 勺	hok / cheuk	hok3 / coek3	hok / cheuk
scorched	v	燒焦	sìu jīu	siu4 ziu1	siu chiu
score	n	積分	jīk fahn	zik1 fan6	chek fahn
scorn	n	睇唔起	tái m̀ héi	tai2 m4 hei2	thai mh hei
Scotland	n	蘇格蘭	sòu gáak laan	sou4 gaak2 laan3	sou kaak laan
scout	n	童子軍	tùhng jí gwān	tung4 zi2 gwan1	thuhng chi kwan
scowl /angry look	n	怒容	louh yùhng	lou6 jung4	louh yuhng
scrap[1] /small piece	n	小塊	síu fáai	siu2 faai2	siu faai
scrap[2] /pieces of object	n	塊物	faai maht	faai3 mat6	faai maht
scrap iron	n	爛鐵	laahn tit	laan6 tit3	laahn thit

scrape[1]	v	刮	gwaat	gwaat3	kwaat
scrape[2]	v	刮損	gwaat syún	gwaat3 syun2	kwaat syun
scrape[3] /to scrape	v	刮去	gwaat hói	gwaat3 hoi2	kwaat hoi
scratch[1] /scar/itch	v	抓	jáau	zaau2	chaau
scratch[2]	v	抓傷	jàau sèhung	zaau4 soeng4	chaau sehung
scratch[3]	v	拗痕	àau /ngàau hàhn	aau4 /ngaau4 han4	aau /ngaau hahn
scratch[4]	v	挖痕	wá hàhn	waa2 han4	wa hahn
screen	n	銀幕	ngàhn mohk	ngan4 mok6	ngahn mohk
screen cinema	v	放映	fong yíng	fong3 jing2	fong ying
screen cloth	n	簾	lím	lim2	lim
screen door	n	紗門	sā mùhn	sa1 mun4	sa muhn
screening[1]	n	審查	sām chàh	sam1 caa4	sam chhah
screening[2] /trial /measure & test	n	測試	chàak si /síh	caak4 si3 /si5	chhaak si /sih
screw	n	螺絲釘	lòh sī dēng	lo4 si1 deng1	loh si teng
screw nut	n	螺絲母	lòh sì móuh	lo4 si4 mou5	loh si mouh
screwdriver	n	螺絲批	lòh sī pāi	lo4 si1 pai1	loh si phai
scribble[1]	v	潦草書寫	líu chóu syù sé	liu2 cou2 syu4 se2	liu chhou syu se
scribble[2]	v	寫得好潦草嘅字	sé dāk hóu líu chóu ge jih	se2 dak1 hou2 liu2 cou2 ge3 zi6	se tak hou liu chhou ke chih
scribble[3]	v	雜文	jaahp màhn	zaap6 man4	chaahp mahn
scribe	v	做抄寫	jouh chàau sé	zou6 caau4 se2	chouh chhaau se
scrimp	v	節省	jit sáang	zit3 saang2	chit saang
script /handwriting	v	手稿	sáu góu	sau2 gou2	sau kou
scrotum	n	陰囊	yàm lòhng /nòhng	jam4 long4 /nong4	yam lohng
scrub	v	擦洗	cháat sai	caat3 sai3	chhaat sai
scruple /might be wrong	v	有顧忌	yáuh gu geih	jau5 gu3 gei6	yauh ku keih
scrupulous[1]	adj	細緻	sai ji	sai3 zi3	sai chi
scrupulous[2]	adj	仔細	jí sai	zi2 sai3	chi sai
scrupulous[3]	adj	謹慎	gán sahn	gan2 san6	kan sahn
scrupulous[4]	adj	一絲不苟	yāt sī bāt gáu	jat1 si1 bat1 gau2	yat si pat kau
scrupulous[5]	adj	小心謹慎	síu sàm gán sahn	siu2 sam4 gan2 san6	siu sam kan sahn
scrutiny	n	詳細檢查	chèuhng sai gím chàh	coeng4 sai3 gim2 caa4	chheuhng sai kim chhah
sea	n	海	hói	hou2	hoi
sea animal	n	海動物	hói duhng maht	hou2 dung6 mat6	hoi tohng maht
sea cucumber	n	海參	hói sām	hoi2 sam1	hoi sam
sea food[1] (fresh)	n	海鮮	hói sīn	hoi2 sin1	hoi sin
sea food[2] (dried)	n	海味	hói méi	hoi2 mei2	hoi mei
sea gull	n	海鷗	hói ngāu	hoi2 ngau1	hoi ngau
sea horse	n	海馬	hói máh	hoi2 maa5	hoi mah
sea level	n	海平面	hói pìhng mín	hoi2 peng4 min2	hoi pehng min
sea product	n	海產	hói cháan	hoi2 caan2	hoi chhaan
seal[1] /close envelope	v	封	fùng	fung4	fung
seal[2] /with chop	n	印章	yan jēung	jan3 zoeng1	yan cheung

seal[3] /sea animal	n	海豹	hói paau	hou2 paau3	hoi phaau
seal stamp	v	蓋章	koi jēung	koi3 zoeng1	khoi cheung
sealed	adj	密封咗	maht fùng jó	mat6 fung4 zo2	maht fung cho
sealed letter	n	埋口信	màaih háu seun	maai4 hau2 seon3	maaih hau swon
search[1] /clue/to ask of crime		索	sok	sok3	sok
search[2] /lookup/explore /hunting	n	搜	sáu	sau2	sau
search[3]	n	抄	chaau	caau3	chhaau
search[4]	v	查察	chàh chaat	caa4 caat3	chhah chaat
search[5]	v	搜查	sáu chàh	sau2 caa4	sau chhah
search body	v	搜身	sáu sàn	sau2 san4	sau san
search warrant	n	搜查證	sáu chàh jing	sau2 caa4 zing3	sau chhah cheng
searching	n	搜索	sáu sok	sau2 sok3	sau sok
searching by touch		撳嘢	chaau yéh	caau3 je5	chhaau yeh
seashell	n	蜆殼	hín hok	hin2 hok3	hin hok
seashore /seaside	n	海濱	hói bān	hou2 ban1	hoi pan
seasick[1] /motion sick	adj	暈浪	wàhn lohng	wan4 long6	wahn lohng
seasick[2] /on the ship	adj	暈船	wàhn syùhn	wan4 syun4	wahn syuhn
season	n	季節	gwai jit	gwai3 zit3	kwai chit
season of fruit[1]	n	當造	dòng jouh	dong4 zou6	tong chouh
season of fruit[2]	n	合時	hahp sìh	hap6 si4	hahp sih
seasonal	adj	季節性	gwai jit sing	gwai3 zit3 sing3	kwai chit seng
seat[1] /sit	n	座	chóh	co5	chhoh
seat[2]	n	座位	chóh wái	co5 wai2	chhoh wai
seated		坐嗰處	chóh go syu	co5 go3 syu3	chhoh ko syu
seating toilet /toilet ring	n	坐廁	chóh chi	co5 ci3	chhoh chhi
seawater[1]	n	海水	hói séui	hoi2 seoi2	hoi swoi
seawater[2]	n	鹹水	hàahm séui	haam4 seoi2	haahm swoi
secession[1]	n	退出	teui chēut	teoi3 ceot1	thoi chhot
secession[2]	n	脫離	tyut lèih	tyut3 lei4	thyut leih
secessionist	n	脫離派嘅人	tyut lèih pàai ge yàhn	tyut3 lei4 paai4 ge3 jan4	thyut leih phaai ke yahn
second[1]	n	秒	míuh	miu5	miuh
second[2]	adj	第二	daih yih	dai6 ji6	taih yih
second best[1]	v	第二好	daih yih hóu	dai6 ji6 hou2	taih yih hou
second best[2]	v	第二位	daih yih wàih	dai6 ji6 wai4	taih yih waih
second chance	v	第二次機會	daih yih chi gèi wuih	dai6 ji6 ci6 gei4 wui6	taih yih chhi kei wuih
second class	n	二等	daih yih	dai6 ji6	taih yih
second floor	n	二樓	yíh làuh	ji5 lau4	yih lauh
second hand	n	二手	yih sáu	ji6 sau2	yih sau
second home	n	第二故鄉	daih yih gu hèung	dai6 ji6 gu3 hoeng4	taih yih ku heung
second language	n	第二語言	daih yih yuh yìhn	dai6 ji6 jyu6 jin4	taih yih yuh yihn
second opinion		其他嘅意見	kèih tà ge yi gin	kei4 taa4 ge3 ji3 gin3	kheih tha ke yi kin
second part	n	乙部	yut bouh	jyut3 bou6	yut bouh

second person	n	第二人	daih yih yàhn	dai6 ji6 jan4	taih yih yahn
second position	ad	居第二位	gèui daih yih wàih	geoi4 dai6 ji6 wai4	kwoi taih yih waih
second teeth	n	恒齒	hàhng chí	hang4 ci2	hahng chhi
secondary school	n	中學	jùng hohk	zung4 hok6	chung hohk
secondly /next	adv	其次	kèih chi	kei4 ci3	kheih chhi
secret[1]	n	祕	bei	bei3	pei
secret[2] /dense/confidential	n	密	maht	mat6	maht
secret[3] /secretly/private	n	秘密	bei maht	bei3 mat6	pei maht
secret[4] (trick)	n	祕訣	bei kyút	bei3 kyut2	pei khyut
secret[5]	n	私隱	sī yán	si1 jan2	si yan
secret illegal plan /conspiracy	n	陰謀	yàm màuh	jam4 mau4	yam mauh
secretary /secy	n	秘書	bei syù	bei3 syu4	pei syu
sect /group of people	n	教派	gaau paai	gaau3 paai3	kaau phaai
sectarian /religious views	adj	教派	gaau paai	gaau3 paai3	kaau phaai
sectarianism	n	宗派主義	jùng paai jyú yih	zung4 paai3 zyu2 ji6	chung paai chyu yih
section	n	分組	fàn jóu	fan6 zou2	fàn chou
secure[1]	adj	安	òn /ngòn	on4 /ngon4	on /ngon
secure[2]	adj	安全嘅	òn /ngòn chyùhn ge	on4 /ngon4 cyun4 ge3	on /ngon chhyuhn ke
security[1]	n	警衛	gíng waih	ging2 wai6	keng waih
security[2]	n	保安	bóu on	bou2 on4	pou on
security personal permit	n	保安人員 許可證	bóu òn yàhn yùhn héui hó jing	bou2 on4 jan4 jyun4 heoi2 ho2 zing3	pou on yahn yuhn hoi ho cheng
security post /guard post	n	警崗	gíng gòng	ging2 gong4	keng kong
sedan car /saloon	n	轎車	gíu chè	giu2 ce4	kiu chhe
see /meet/interview	v	見	gin	gin3	kin
see a doctor[1]	n	睇醫生	tái yì sāng	tai2 ji4 sang1	thai yi sang
see a doctor[2] (wr)	n	看醫生	hōn yì sāng	hon1 ji4 sang1	hon yi sang
see through	v	看破	hōn po	hon1 po3	hon pho
see whether /see if /glances/look/look at	v	睇吓	tái háh	tai2 haa5	thai hah
see you later![1]		遲啲見!	chìh dì gin!	ci4 di1 gin3!	chhih ti kin!
see you later![2] /bye bye!/ goodbye!/tata	v/int	再見！	joi gin！	zoi3 gin3!	choi kin！
see you later![3]	v	到時見	dou sìh gin	dou3 si4 gin3	tou sih kin
see you later![4]	v	會見到	wuih gin dou	wui6 gin3 dou3	wuih kin tou
seed[1] (of plant) /sort/kind /type/race/ species	n	種	júng	zung2	chung
seed[2] (of plant)	n	種子	júng jí	zung2 zi2	chung chi
seeding[1]	n	苗	mìuh	miu4	miuh
seeding[2] /seeds/spread	n	播	bo	bo3	po
seeding[3] /sowing /sow seeds	v	播種	bo júng	bo3 zung2	po chung
seeing off	n	歡送	fùn sung	fun4 sung3	fun sung
seeing that	n	因為	yàn waih	jan4 wai6	yan waih

seeker	n	尋找者	cham jáau jé	cam3 zaau2 ze	chham chaau che
seem[1] /resemble	v	好似	hóu chíh	hou2 ci5	hou chhih
seem[2] /appear/look	v	好像	hóu jeuhng	hou2 zoeng6	hou cheuhng
seemingly /not be true /superficially	adv	表面上	bíu mìhn seuhng	biu2 min4 soeng6	piu mihn seuhng
seen mistaked	v	睇錯咗	tái cho jó	tai2 co3 zo2	thai chho cho
seep[1]	v	滲	sam	sam3	sam
seep[2] /seepage	v	滲漏	sam lauh	sam3 lau6	sam lauh
seepage /water leak	v	漏水	lauh séui	lau6 seoi2	lauh swoi
seesaw (playing by childrens)	n	搖搖板	yìuh yìuh báan	jiu4 jiu4 baan2	yiuh yiuh paan
seize[1]	v	抓住	jàu jyuh	zau4 zyu6	chau chyuh
seize[2]	v	拿住	lá jyuh	laa2 zyu6	la chyuh
seize[3] /catch	v	捉住	juk jyuh	zuk3 zyu6	chuk chyuh
seize[4] /take by force	v	奪	dyuht	dyut6	tyuht
seize by force /rob	n/v	劫	gip	gip3	kip
seize-catch	n	攬着	láam jeuk	laam2 zoek3	laam cheuk
seize-up	n	機器故障	gèi hei gu jeung	gei4 hei3 gu3 zoeng3	kei hei ku cheung
seizer /grab hold of	n	扣押者	kau aat jé	kau3 aat3 ze2	khau aat che
seizure[1]	n	佔	jim	zim3	chim
seizure[2]	n	把佔	ba jim	baa3 zim3	pa chim
seizure[3]	n	攻克	gói hāak	goi2 haak1	koi haak
seizure[4] /confiscation	n	佔領	jim léhng /líhng	zim3 leng5 /ling5	chim lehng
select /elect	v	選	syún	syun2	syun
self abuse	adj	自暴自棄	jih bouh jih hei	zi6 bou6 zi6 hei3	chih pouh chih hei
self access	n	自行選擇學習資料	jih hàhng syún jaahk hohk jaahp jì líu	zi6 hang4 syun2 zaak6 hok6 zaap6 zi4 liu2	chih hahng syun chaahk hohk chaahp chi liu
self adjusting	adj	自動調節	jih duhng tìuh jit	zi6 dung6 tiu3 zit3	chih tuhng thiuh chit
self choose /self pick up	adj	自己揀	jih géi gáan	zi6 gei2 gaan2	chih kei kaan
self confidence	adj	自信心	jih seun sàm	zi6 seon3 san4	chih swon sam
self defense	n	自衛	jih waih	zi6 wai6	chih waih
self educated	adj	自學	jih hohk	zi6 hok6	chih hohk
self employed	adj	自由職業	jih yàuh jīk yihp	zi6 jau4 zik1 jip6	chih yauh chek yihp
self evident	adj	明擺着	mìhng báai jeuk	ming4 baai2 zoek3	mehng paai cheuk
self help /not needing /not depending/self support	adj	自立	jih lahp	zi6 lap6	chih lahp
self immolation	adj	自焚	jih fàhn	zi6 fan4	chih fahn
self made	adj	自造	jih chóu	zi6 cou2	chih chhou
self payment /everyone pays	adj	自己俾自己	jih géi béi jih géi	zi6 gei2 bei2 zi6 gei2	chih kei pei chih kei
self pity	n	自憐	jih lìhn	zi6 lin4	chih lehn
self reading (metre)	adj	報錶	bou bīu	bou3 biu1	pou piu
self regarding	adj	利己主義	leih géi jyú yih	lei6 gei2 zyu2 ji6	leih kei chyu yih
self respecting	n	有自尊心嘅	yáuh jih jyùn sàm ge	jau5 zi6 zyun4 sam4 ge3	yauh chih chyun sam ke

English	part	漢字	Yale	Jyutping	Romanization
self righteous	adj	自以為正直嘅	jih yíh waih jeng /jing jihk ge	zi6 ji5 wai6 zeng3 /jing3 zik6 ge3	chih yih waih cheng chehk ke
self sacrifice	n	自我犧牲	jih ngóh hèi sāng	zi6 ngo5 hei4 sang1	chih ngoh hei sang
self same	adj	同一的	tùhng yāt dīk	tung4 jat1dik4	thuhng yat tik
self satisfaction	n	自滿	jih múhn	zi6 mun5	chih muhn
self study room	n	自修室	jih sāu sāt	zi6 sau1 sat1	chih sau sat
self sufficiency	adv	自給自足	jih kāp jih jeui	zi6 kap1 jih zeoi3	chih khap chih choi
self sufficient	adj	自足	jih jeui	zi6 zeoi3	chih choi
self supporting	n	自立嘅	jih lahp ge	zi6 lap6 ge3	chih lahp ke
selfish[1]	adj	私	sì	si4	si
selfish[2] /selfishness	adj	自私	jih sì	zi6 si4	chih si
selfishly	adv	自私地	jih sì deih	zi6 si4 dei6	chih si teih
selfless /unselfish	adj	唔自私	m̀ jih sì	m4 zi6 si4	mh chih si
sell[1] /trade/sell off/deal	v	售	sauh	sau6	sauh
sell[2]	v	銷	sīu	siu1	siu
sell[3] /sale	v	出售	chēut sauh	ceot1 sau6	chhot sauh
sell agent	n	代銷人	doih sīu yàhn	doi6 siu1 jan4	toih siu yahn
sell to you		賣俾你	maaih béi léih /néih	maai6 bei2 lei5 /nei5	maaih pei leih /neih
sell well[1]	v	好賣	hóu maaih dāk	hou2 maai6 dak1	hou maaih tak
sell well[2]	v	好多人買	hóu dò yàhn máaih	hou2 do4 jan4 maai5	hou toh yahn maaih
seller[1]	n	賣嘢嘅人	maaih yéh ge yàhn	maai6 je5 ge3 jan4	maaih yeh ke yahn
seller[2]	n	銷售者	sīu sauh jé	siu1 sau6 ze2	siu sauh che
selling googs[1]	n	賣嘢	maaih yéh	maai6 je5	maaih yeh
selling googs[2]	n	賣物	maaih maht	maai6 mat6	maaih maht
selling	n	銷售	sīu sauh	siu1 sau6	siu sauh
selling machine /vending machine	n	自動售貨機	jih duhng sauh fo gèi	zi6 dung6 sau6 fo3 gei4	chih tuhng sauh fo kei
semen /seminal fluid /cum/come/seed/ejaculate /sperm/spermatozoon	n	精子	jēng jí	zeng1 zi2	cheng chi
semen discharged	v	出精	chēut jēng	ceot1 zeng1	chhot cheng
semen drip	v	漏精	lauh jēng	lau6 zeng1	lauh cheng
semen release on the face [(vdw)]	v xy	顏射	aan /ngaan seh	aan3 /ngaan3 se6	aan /ngaan seh
semester	n	半學年	bun hohk lihn /nihn	bun3 hok6 lin4 /nin4	pun hohk lihn /nihn
semi colon /mark	n	分號	fàn houh	fan4 hou6	fan houh
semi final	n	準決賽	jeun kyut choi	zeon3 kyut3 coi3	cheun khyut chhoi
semi tropical	n	亞熱帶	aa yiht daai	aa3 jit6 daai3	aa yiht taai
semi vowel[1]	n	半母音字	bun móuh yām jih	bun3 mou5 jam1 zi6	pun mouh yam chih
semi vowel[2]	n	半元音	bun yùhn yām	bun3 jyun4 jam1	pun yuhn yam
semicircle	n	半圓	bun yùhn	bun3 jyun4	pun yuhn
semifluid	n	液體的	yihk tái dìk	jik6 tai2 dik4	yehk thai tik
seminar[1]	n	研討會	yìhn tóu wúi	jin4 tou2 wui2	yihn thou wui
seminar[2]	n	研究班	yìhn gau bāan	jin4 gau3 baan1	yihn kau paan
seminude	adj	半裸	bun ló	bun3 lo2	pun lo
senate /upper house	n	參議院	chàam yíh yùhn	caam4 ji5 jyun6	chhaam yih yuhn

senator	n	參議員	chàam yíh yùhn	caam4 ji5 jyun4	chhaam yih yuhn
send (to mail)	v	寄	gei	gei3	kei
send back (in cash /personnel)	v	周轉	jàu jyún	zau4 zyun2	chau chyun
send by	n	發件人	faat ńgh yàhn	faat3 ng5 jan4	faat ngh yahn
send by post	v	郵寄	yàuh gei	jau4 gei3	yauh kei
sender[1] (letter sender)	n	寄信	gei seun	gei3 seon3	kei swon
sender[2]	n	寄件人	gei gihn yàhn	gei3 gin6 jan4	kei kihn yahn
senior[1] /chief/head/elder	n	長	jéung	zoeng2	cheung
senior[2]	n	長者	jéung jé	zoeng2 ze2	cheung che
senior[3] (of age)	adj	年長	lihn jéung	lin4 zoeng2	lihn cheung
seniority	n	年資	lihn jī	lin4 zi1	lihn chi
sense[1]	n	知覺	jì gok	zi4 gok3	chi kok
sense[2]	n	感官	gám gùn	gam2 gun4	kam kun
sense of hearing /hearing	n	聽覺	tèng gok	teng4 gok3	theng kok
sense of smell	adj	嗅覺	chau gok	cau3 gok3	chhau kok
senseless	adj	無咗知覺	móuh jó ji gok	mou5 zo2 zi3 gok3	mouh cho chi kok
senses of touch /touch	v	觸覺	jūk gok	zuk1 gok3	chuk kok
sensible	adj	明智的	mìhng ji dìk	ming4 zi3 dik4	mehng chi tik
sensibly	adj	明智地	mìhng ji deih	ming4 zi3 dei6	mehng chi teih
sensitive[1]	adj	敏感	máhn gám	man5 gam2	mahn kam
sensitive[2]	adj	敏感的	máhn gám dìk	man5 gam2 dik4	mahn kam tik
sensitive paper	n	感光紙	gám gwòng jí	gam2 gwong4 zi2	kam kwong chi
sensor	n	感應器	gám yīng hei	gam2 jing1 hei3	kam yeng hei
sentence[1]	n	句	geui	geoi3	kwoi
sentence[2]	n	句子	geui jí	geoi3 zi2	kwoi chi
sentence[3] /to judge/ judgement	n	判	pun	pun3	phun
sentence[4] /punish	n	判處	pun chyúh	pun3 cyu5	phun chhyu
sentence to death /execution/death penalty	n	死刑	séi yìhng	sei2 jing4	sei yehng
sentence to death	n	被判死刑	beih pun séi yihng	bei6 pun3 sei2 jing4	peih phun sei yehng
sentiment	n	情	chìhng	cing4	chhehng
sentimental[1]	adj	情感	chìhng gám	cing4 gam2	chhehng kam
sentimental[2]	adj	多愁善感	dò sàuh sihn gám	do4 sau4 sin6 gam2	to sauh sihn kam
sentimental[3]	adj	情感上	chìhng gám sèung	cing4 gam2 soeng4	chhehng kam seung
sentry duty	n	站崗	jaahm gōng	zaam6 gong1	chaahm kong
sentry post	n	崗位	gōng waih	gong1 wai6	kong waih
sepal /part of a flower	n	萼片	ngohk pin	ngok6 pin3	ngohk phin
separate[1] /additional /other/different/else	adj	另外	lìhng oih /ngoih	ling6 oi6 /ngoi6	lehng oih /ngoih
separate[2] /good bye	v	分手	fàn sáu	fan4 sau2	fan sau
separate[3] /apart /detachment/severance	adj/n	分離	fàn lèih	fan4 lei4	fan leih
separate[4] /to apart	v	脫離	tyut lèih	tyut3 lei4	thyut leih

English		Chinese	Yale	Jyutping	
separated (married couple)	adj	分居	fàn gēui	fan4 geoi1	fan kwoi
separately	adv	分離地	fàn lèih dèih	fan4 lei4 dei6	fan leih deih
separation	n	分開	fàn hòi	fan4 hoi4	fan hoi
separator	n	分離器	fàn lèih	fan4 lei4	fan leih
September	n	九月	gáu yùht	gau2 jyut6	kau yuht
septic[1]	adj	含膿	hahm lùhng /nùhng	ham4 lung4 /nung4	hahm luhng /nuhng
septic[2] /to be infected	adj	化膿	fa lùhng /nùhng	faa3 lung4 /nung4	fa luhng /nuhng
septic[3] /infected/to be pus	adj	有膿	yáuh lùhng /nùhng	jau5 lung4 /nung4	yauh luhng /nuhng
septic[4]	adj	敗血症	baaih hyut jīng	baai6 hyut3 zing1	paaih hyut cheng
sequence[1]	n	順序	seuhn jeuih	seon6 zeoi6	swohn choih
sequence[2]	n	一連串	yāt lìhn chyun	jat1 lin4 cyun3	yat lihn chhyun
sequential	adj	連續	lìhn juhk	lin4 zuk6	lihn chuhk
sergeant /soldier	n	軍士	gwàn sih	gwan4 si6	kwan sih
sergeant major	n	軍士長	gwàn sih jéung	gwan4 si6 zoeng2	kwan sih cheung
serial[1] /in series/series	n	一連	yāt lìhn	jat1 lin4	yat lihn
serial[2] /ordered	adj	順序	seuhn jeuih	seon6 zeoi6	swohn choih
serial no /sequent/in series/orderly numbers	n	號碼	houh máh	hou6 maa5	houh mah
serialise	v	使連載	sai lìhn joi	sai3 lin4 zoi	sai lihn choi
serially	adv	連續地	lìhn juhk deih	lin4 zuk6 dei6	lihn chuhk teih
series[1]	n	系列	haih liht	hai6 lit6	haih liht
series[2]	n	連起	lìhn hei	lin4 hei3	lìhn hei
series[3] /sequence	n	連續	lìhn juhk	lin4 zuk6	lihn chuhk
series of /string of		一系列	yāt haih liht	jat1 hai6 lit6	yat haih liht
serious /severe	adj	嚴重的	yìhm juhng dìk	jim4 zung6 dik4	yihm chuhng tek
serious & difficult		嚴峻	yìhm jeun	jim4 zeon3	yihm cheun
serious-injured		重傷	chùhng sèung	cung4 soeng4	chhuhng seung
seriously[1]	adv	認真	yihng jàn	jing6 zan4	yehng chan
seriously[2]	adv	嚴重地	yìhm juhng deih	jim4 zung6 dei6	yihm chuhng teih
seriousness	n	嚴肅性	yìhm sūk sing	jim4 suk1 sing3	yihm suk seng
sermon /preach/talk on religious	n/v	講道	góng douh	gong2 dou6	kong touh
servant (man)	n	男工人	làahm gùng yàhn	laam6 gung4 jan4	laahm kung yahn
server	n	侍者	sih jé	si6 ze2	sih che
server of computer	n	伺服器	jih fuhk hei	zi6 fuk6 hei3	chih fuhk hei
service[1]	n	服務	fuhk mouh	fuk6 mou6	fuhk mouh
service[2]	n	上菜	seuhng choi	soeng6 coi3	seuhng chhoi
service[3]	n	招侍	jìu sih	ziu4 si6	chiu sih
service[4]	n	供職	gùng jīk	gung4 zik1	kung chek
service charge[1]	n	小賬	siu jeung	siu3 zoeng3	siu cheung
service charge[2] /service fee	n	服務費	fuhk mouh fai	fuk6 mou6 fai3	fuhk mouh fai
servitude /slave labour	n	做苦工	jouh fú gùng	zou6 fu2 gung4	chouh fu kung
sesame	n	芝麻	jì màh	zi4 maa4	chi mah

session /meeting of parliament	n	開會	hòi wúi	hoi4 wui2	hoi wui
session court	n	開庭	hòi tìhng	hoi4 ting4	hoi thehng
session of school /semester /term academic	n	學期	hohk kèih	hok6 kei4	hohk kheih
set[1]	v	制	jài	zai4	chai
set[2]	v	放置	fong ji	fong3 zi3	fong chi
set foot on	v	踏上	daahp seuhng	daap6 soeng6	taahp seuhng
set lunch[1]	n	客飯	haak faahn	haak3 faan6	haak faahn
set lunch[2]	n	套餐	tou chāan	tou3 caan1	thou chhaan
set off /departure/start out/go out	n	出發	chēut faat	ceot1 faat3	chhot faat
set on fire[1] /set fire /arson	v	放火	fong fó	fong3 fo2	fong fo
set on fire[2] /set fire	v	焚燒	fàhn sìu	fan4 siu4	fahn siu
set time	v	校表	gaau biu	gaau3 biu3	kaau piu
set up[1] /stand	v	立	lahp	lap6	lahp
set up[2] /arrange	v	安排	òn /ngòn pàaih	on4 /ngon4 paai4	on /ngon paai
set up[3]	v	組織	jóu jīk	zou2 zik1	chou chek
setter /installer/installater	n	安裝工人	òn /ngòn jòng gùng yàhn	on4 /ngon4 zong4 gung4 jan4	on /ngon chong kung yahn
settle[1]	v	結賬	git jan	git3 zan3	kit chan
settle[2]	v	安頓	òn /ngòn deuhn	on4 /ngon4 deon6	on /ngon tohn
settle[3] /settlement	v	定居	dehng /dihng gèui	deng6 /ding6 geoi4	tehng kwoi
settle account	v	結算	git syun	git3 syun3	kit syun
settle bill	v	付清	fuh chèng	fu6 ceng4	fuh chheng
settled	adj	穩定	wān dehng /dihng	wan1 deng6 /ding6	wan tehng
settlement[1]	n	開拓	hòi tok	hoi4 tok3	hoi thok
settlement[2]	n	住定	jyuh dehng	zyu6 deng6	chyuh tehng
settlement[3]	n	住落	jyuh lohk	zyu6 lok6	chyuh lohk
settlement[4] /payment /pay money	v	支付	jì fuh	zi4 fu6	chi fuh
settlement[5] (payment)	n	清算	cheng /chìng syun	ceng4 /cing4 syun3	chheng syun
settler	n	開拓者	hòi tok jé	hoi4 tok3 ze2	hoi thok che
seven	n	七	chāt /càt	cat1	chhat
seven eleven (24 hrs shop in Hong Kong)	n	七_十一	chāt_sahp yāt	cat1_sap6 jat1	chhat _sahp yat
seven up /7 up (drink)	n	七喜	chāt /tsat héi	cat1 hei2	chhat hei
sever	v	割斷	got dyún	got3 dyun2	kot tyun
several /few	adj	幾個	géi go	gei2 go3	kei ko
several hundred	n	幾百	géi baak	gei2 baak3	kei paak
severity	n	嚴厲	yim làih	jim3 lai6	yim laih
sew[1] (by needle)	n	聯	lyùhn	lyun4	lyuhn
sew[2] (sewing)	v	縫製	fuhng jai	fung6 zai3	fuhng chai
sewer[1]	n	縫紉工	fuhng yahn gùng	fung6 jan6 gung4	fuhng yahn kung
sewer[2]	n	下水道	hah séui dóu	haa6 seoi2 dou2	hah swoi tou

sewing /stitch/on the body	n	聯針	lyùhn jām	lyun4 zam1	lyuhn cham
sewing machine[1]	n	衣車	yī chè	ji1 ce4	yi chhe
sewing machine[2]	n	縫紉機	fuhng yahn gèi	fung6 jan6 gei4	fuhng yahn kei
sex[1] /gender	n	性	sing	sing3	seng
sex[2] /gender	n	性別	sing biht	sing3 bit6	seng piht
sex[3] /love making	n xy	性愛	sìng oi /ngoi	sing3 oi3 /ngoi3	seng oi /ngoi
sex[4 (coll)] pay money for sex	n/xy	雞竇	gài dau	gai4 dau3	kai tau
sex appeal /sex emotion/sex strong desire	n	性感	sing gám	sing3 gam2	seng kam
sex discrimination /sexism	n	性別歧視	sing biht kèih sih	sing3 bit6 kei4 si6	seng piht kheih sih
sex discriminatist /sexist	n	性別歧視者	sing biht kèih sih jé	sing3 bit6 kei4 ze2	seng piht kheih sih che
sex dog style[(sl) (vdw)]	n/xy	老漢推車	lóuh hon tèui chè	lou5 hon3 teoi4 ce4	louh hon thoi chhe
sex involvement /love-making	v xy	性愛	sìng oi /ngoi	sing3 oi3 /ngoi3	seng oi /ngoi
sex job [(sl)]	n	做鴨	jouh áap, jouh ngáap	zou6 aap2, zou6 ngaap2	chouh aap, chouh ngaap
sex scandal	n	緋聞	fèi màhn	fei4 man4	fei mahn
sexless	adj xy	無男女之分別	móuh làahm/nàahm léoih /néoih jī fān biht	mou5 laam4 /naam4 leoi5 /neoi5 zi1 fan1 bit1	mouh laahm /naahm lowih /nowih chi fan piht
sexual assault	v	妨害風化罪	fòhng hoih fùhng fa jeuih	fong4 hoi6 fung4 fa3 zeoi6	fohng hoih fung fa choih
sexual contact[1 (sl)]	n/xy	召妓	jiuh geih	ziu6 gei6	chiuh keih
sexual contact[2 (sl)]	n/xy	叫雞	giu gài	giu3 gai4	kiu kai
sexual desire /erotic /pornographic/make sexualdesire	adj	色情	sīk chìhng	sik1 cing4	sek chhehng
sexual excitement[1]	xy	性衝動	sing chùng duhng	sing3 cung4 dung6	seng chhung tohng
sexual excitement[2]	xy	因性而興奮	yān sing yìh hīng fáhn	jan1 sing3 ji4 hing1 fan5	yan seng yih heng fahn
sexual highest point /for sex pleasured	adj xy	性高潮	sìng gòu chìuh	sing3 gou4 ciu4	seng kou chhiuh
sexual intercourse[1] /make love/sexually excited	v/xy	做愛	jouh oi /ngoi	zou6 oi3 /ngoi3	chouh oi /ngoi
sexual intercourse[2] /lecher (unwilled sex)	n	色魔	sīk mó	sik1 mo2	sek mo
sexual intercourse[3 (sl)] against one's will	n	色狼	sīk lòhng	sik1 long4	sek lohng
sexual intercourse[4(sl)] sexual behavior	adj xy	性行為	sing hàhng wàih	sing3 hang4 wai4	seng hahng waih
sexual interrupt /coitus interrupt	n xy	體外射精	tái oih sèh jēng	tai2 oi6 se6 zeng1	thai oih seh cheng
sexually	adv	按性別地	on /ngòn sing biht	on3 /ngon4 sing3 bit6	on /ngon seng piht teih
sexually active animal &bird (time of pregnant/rut/ oestrogen /estrogen)	n	發情	faat chìhng	faat3 cing4	faat chehng

sexually promiscuous person/swinger	n	性開放者	sing hòi fong jé	sing3 hoi4 fong3 ze2	seng hoi fong che
sexy /sensual/aphrodisiac	adj	性感	sing gám	sing3 gam2	seng kam
shade /shelter	n	遮住	jē jyuh	ze1 zyu6	che chyuh
shadow[1] /shade/shelter	n	蔭	yam	jam	yam
shadow[2] /image	n	影	yéng /yíng	jeng2 /jing2	yeng
shadow[3] /reflection	n	影子	yéng jí	jeng2 zi2	yeng chi
shadow[4]	n	幽暗	yàu am /ngam	jau4 am3 /ngam3	yau am /ngam
shaft	n	手柄	sáu beng	sau2 beng3	sau peng
shake /shiver/tremble	v	顫抖	jin dáu	zin3 dau2	chin tau
shake before drinking	v	飲用前請先搖勻	yám yuhng chìhn chéng sin yìuh wàhn	jam2 jung6 cin4 ceng2 sin3 jiu4 wan4	yam yuhng chhihn cheng sin yiuh wahn
shall[1] /will (future time)	v/aux	會	wúih	wui5	wuih
shall[2]	v/aux	表示將會	bíu sih jèung wuih	biu2 si6 zoeng4 wui6	piu sih cheung wuih
shall?[3]	v/aux	好嗎？	hóu ma?	hou2 ma3?	hou ma?
shallow /light deep water	adj	淺的	chín dìk	cin2 dik4	chhin tek
shaman /wizard	n	巫師	mou sì	mou3 si4	mou sih
shame	n	恥辱	chi yuhk	ci3 juk6	chhi yuhk
shamefaced	adj	面帶愧色	mihn dáai kwai sīk	min6 daai2 kwai3 sik1	mihn taai khwai sek
shameless	adj	無恥	mòuh chi	mou4 ci3	mouh chhi
shamelessness	n	不要臉	bāt yiu líhm	bat1 jiu3 lim5	pat yiu lihm
shampoo[1]	v	洗頭水	sái tàuh séui	sai2 tau4 seoi2	sai thauh swoi
shampoo[2]	n	洗髮液	sái faat yihk	sai2 faat3 jik6	sai faat yehk
Shanghai	n	上海	séuhng hói	soeng5 hoi2	seuhng hoi
shanghai dialect	n	上海話	séuhng hói wá	soeng5 hoi2 waa2	seuhng hoi wa
shanghainese	n	上海人	séuhng hói yàhn	soeng5 hoi2 jan4	seuhng hoi yahn
shanty /simple hut /simple cottage/shed	n	簡陋小屋	gáan lauh síu ùk /ngùk	gaan2 lau6 siu2 uk4 /nguk4	kaan lauh siu uk /nguk
shape[1] /appearance	n	樣	yeuhng	joeng6	yeuhng
shape[2] (external form/figure)	n	外形	oih /ngoih yìhng	oi6 /ngoi6 jing4	oih /ngoih yehng
shape[3] (circumstance)	n	形式	yìhng sīk	jing4 sik1	yehng sek
shapeless	adj	無形狀	móuh yìhng johng	mou5 jing4 zong6	mouh yehng chohng
share[1]	n	股	gú	gu2	ku
share[2] /stock	n	股份	gú fán	gu2 fan2	ku fan
share a table	v	搭枱	daap tói	daap3 toi2	taap thoi
share joy	v	分享	fahn héung	fan6 hoeng2	fahn heung
shareholding	n	股權	gú kyùhn	gu2 kyun4	ku khyuhn
sharing[1]	n	分攤	fahn tàan	fan6 taan4	fahn thaan
sharing[2]	n	分配	fàn pui	fan4 pui3	fan phui
sharing[3] (power)	n	分掌	fahn jéung	fan6 zoeng2	fahn cheung
shark[1] (fish)	n	鯊魚	sà yù	saa4 jyu4	sa yu
shark[2] (sl) blackmailer/ defrauder/blackmail person	n	詐騙者	ja pin jé	zaa3 pin3 ze2	cha phin che
shark's fin	n	魚翅	yú chí	jyu2 ci2	yu chhi
sharp[1] /sharpen	n	利	leih	lei6	leih

sharp[2] /pointed	n	尖	jìm	zim4	chim
sharp[3] /pointed	n	尖嘅	jìm ge	zim4 ge3	chim ke
sharp[4] /rapid	n	急劇地	gāp kehk dèih	gap1 kek6 dei6	kap khehk teih
sharp eyed	adj	眼光銳利	ngáahn gwòng yeuih leih	ngaan5 gwong4 jeoi6 lei6	ngaahn kwong yeuih leih
sharpen[1]	v	磨利	mòh leih	mo4 lei6	moh leih
sharpen[2]	v	刨尖	pàauh jìm	paau4 zim4	phaauh chim
sharpen[3]	v	快	pài	faai4	phai
sharpen[4]	v	磨刀	mòh dōu	mou4 dou1	moh tou
sharpen[5]	v	刨鉛筆	pàauh yùhn bāt	paau4 jyun4 bat1	phaauh yuhn pat
sharpener (for pencil)	n	捲筆刀	gyún bāt dōu	gyun2 bat1 dou1	kyun pat tou
sharply	adv	明確地	mìhng kok dèih	ming4 kok3 dei6	mehng khok teih
sharpsighted[1]	adj	眼尖	ngáahn jìm	ngaan5 jim4	ngaahn chim
sharpsighted[2]	adj	目光敏銳	muhk gwōng máhn yeuih	muk6 gwong1 man5 jeoi6	muhk kwong mahn yeuih
sharpturn		鋒利轉動	fùng leih jyun duhng	fung4 lei6 zyun3 dung6	fung leih chyun tuhng
shatter /to smash	v	碎裂	seui liht	seoi3 lit6	swoi liht
shave[1]	v	剃	tai	tai3	thai
shave[2]	v	刮臉	gwaat líhm	gwaat3 lim5	kwaat lihm
shave beard	v	剃鬚	tai sōu	tai3 sou1	thai sou
shave blade	n	修面	sau mihn	sau3 min6	sau mihn
sheared /shorn of sheep	v	剪羊毛	jín yèuhng mòuh	zin2 joeng4 mou4	chin yeuhng mouh
shed[1] (slough/cast off/ skin fallen)	n	脫	tyut	tyut3	thyut
shed[2] (slough/skin fallen/ skin throw)	n	使脫落	sai tyut lohk	sai3 tyut3 lok6	sai thyut lohk
shed[3] /spread/flow out	v	流	làuh	lau4	lauh
shed[4] /yard	n	棚	paang	paang3	phaang
shed[5] /little house/small house	n	屋子	ūk /ngūk jái	uk1 /nguk1 zai2	uk /nguk chai
shedding [IDM]	n	照亮	jiu leuhng	ziu3 loeng6	chiu leuhng
sheep[1] (for woo)	n	綿羊	mìhn yèuhng	min4 joeng4	mihn yeuhng
sheep[2] (for meat)	n	黑草羊	haak chóu yèuhng	haak3 cou2 joeng4	haak chhou yeuhng
sheepskin	n	羊皮	yèuhng pèih	joeng4 pei4	yeuhng pheih
sheeting /bed sheet	n	一張	yāt jèung	jat1 zoeng1	yat cheung
shelterless	adj	無所依靠	móuh só yì kaau	mou5 so2 ji4 kaau3	mouh so yi khaau
shepherd	n	牧羊人	muhk yèuhng yàhn	muk6 joeng4 jan4	muhk yeuhng yahn
shield	n	盾	téuhn	teon5	thohn
shift[1] /change/exchange	n	接	jip	zip3	chip
shift[2] /move	v	班	bāan	baan1	paan
shift[3] /move/twist	v	扭轉	láu jyun	lau2 zyun3	lau chyun
shift[4] /move/change shift/take over job/reliver	v	換班	wuhn bāan	wun6 baan1	wuhn paan
shift[5] /move/divert/transfer	v	轉移	jyun yih	zyun3 ji6	chyun yih
shift[6] /move	v	換擋	wuhn dong	wun6 dong3	wuhn tong
shift[7] /move	v	變換	bin wuhn	bin3 wun6	pin wuhn

shiftless	adj	無思上進	móuh sī seuhng jeun	mou5 si1 soeng6 zeon3	mouh si seuhng jeun
shin of pork	n	豬展	jyù jín	zyu4 zin2	chyu chin
shine /radiate/glow/burn	v	發光	faat gwòng	faat3 gwong4	faat kwong
shining	adj	光亮的	gwòng lèuhng dìk	gwong4 loeng6 dik4	kwong leuhng tik
ship[1] /a small ferry/boat /vessel	n	船	syùhn	syun4	syuhn
ship[2] /vessel/small boat	n	艇	téhng	teng5	thehng
shirt[1] (de) t-shirt/blouse	n	裇衫	sèut sàam	seot4 saam4	swot saam
shirt[2] (short sleeves)	n	短袖衫	dyún jauh sāam	dyun2 zau6 saam1	tyun chauh saam
shirt[3] (blue color)	n	藍裇衫	làahm sēut sāam	laam4 seot1 saam1	laahm swot saam
shit[1] /stool/excrement	n	疴屎	ō sí	o1 si2	o si
shit[2] /stool	n	糞	fan	fan3	fan
shit hole /anus/asshole /buttocks	n	屎眼	sí áahn /ngáahn	si2 aan5 /ngaan5	si aahn /ngaahn
shiver[1]	v	發抖	faat dáu	faat3 dau2	faat tau
shiver[2] /shatter/to crush	v	粉碎	fán seui	fan2 seoi3	fan swoi
shoal /flock of fish /group of fish	n	魚群	yú kwàhn	jyu2 kwan4	yu khwahn
shock[1]	n	震動	jan duhng	zan3 dung6	chan tohng
shock[2] (by bad news)	v	打擊	dá gīk	daa2 gik1	ta kek
shock[3] /fear	v	震驚	jan gèng	zan3 geng4	chan keng
shock absorber	n	避震器	bèih ján héi	bei6 zan2 hei2	peih chan hei
shock as by bad news	v	冷淡	láahng daahm	laang5 daam6	laahng taahm
shoe polish	n	鞋油	hàaih yáu	haai4 jau2	haaih yau
shoes	n	鞋	hàaih	haai4	haaih
shoot[1] (basket ball)	v	射籃	seh làahm	se6 laam4	seh laahm
shoot[2] (foot ball)	v	射球	seh kàuh	se6 kau4	seh khauh
shoot[3] (take photo/picture)	v	影相	yéng séung	jeng2 soeng2	yeng seung
shoot dead[1]	adv	擊斃	gīk baih	gik1 bai6	kek paih
shoot dead[2]	adv	槍殺	chèung saat	coeng4 seat3	chheung saat
shoot film /snap	v	拍攝	paak sip	paak3 sip3	phaak sip
shoot hunt	v	打獵	dá lihp	daa2 lip6	ta lihp
shoots /new tip of branch (edible)	n	新梢	sān sāau	san1 saau1	san saau
shop[1]	n	鋪	pou	pou3	phou
shop[2]	n	舍	sé	se2	se
shop[3]	n	門市賣	mùhn síh maaih	moon4 si5 maai6	muhn sih maaih
shop[4] /store	n	鋪頭	pou táu	pou3 tau2	phou thau
shop[5]	n	士多	sih dō	si6 do1	sih toh
shop[6] /store	n	商店	sèung dim	soeng4 dim3	seung tim
shop[7]	n	門市	mùhn síh	mun4 si5	muhn sih
shop front /faces to the street	n	店面	dim mihn	dim3 min6	tim mihn
shop girl	n	女店員	léuih dim yùhn	leui5 dim3 jyun4	lowih tim yuhn
shop name	n	商店名稱	sèung dim méng chìng	soeng4 dim3 meng2 cing4	seung tim meng chheng

shop opened		開咗舖	hòi jó pou	hoi1 joh2 po3	hoi cho phou
shopkeeper[1]	n	事頭	sih tàuh	si6 tau4	sih thauh
shopkeeper[2] /shop assistant	n	店務員	dim mouh yùhn	dim3 mou6 jyun4	tim mouh yuhn
shore /support	v	支撐	jì chāang	zi4 caang1	chi chhaang
short /in length	n	矮	áai /ngái	aai2 /ngai2	aai /ngai
short cut (by scissors)		剪短啲	jín dyún dī	zin2 dyun2 di1	chin tyun ti
short cut road	n	近路	káhn louh	kan5 lou6	khahn louh
short cut way	n	捷徑	jit gíng	zit3 ging2	chit keng
short hair		短頭髮	dyún tàuh faat	dyun2 tau4 faat3	tyun thauh faat
short life		不多時	bāt dò sìh	bat1 do4 si4	pat to sih
short lived	adv	短暫地	dyún jàahm dèih	dyun2 zaam4 dei6	tyun chaahm teih
shorter way[1]	n	捷徑	jit gíng	zit3 ging2	chit keng
shorter way[2]	n	近路	káhn louh	kan5 lou6	khahn louh
short piece of cigarette /stub of cigarette/cigarette's butt	n	煙蒂	yīn dai	jin1 dai3	yin tai
short-stay	adj	臨時停留	làhm sìh tíhng làuh	lam6 si4 ting5 lau4	lahm sih thihng lauh
shortage /lack	n/v	缺少	kyut síu	kyut3 siu2	khyut siu
shortcut (computer)	n	快捷	faai jit	faai3 zit3	faai chit
shot (fire by gun)	n	射擊	sèh gīk	se6 gik1	seh kek
shotdead	n	射死了	sèh séi líuh	se6 sei2 liu5	seh sei liuh
shotgun	n	獵槍	lihp chēung	lip6 coeng1	lihp chheung
should[1]	v/aux	必定要	bīt dehng /dihng yiu	bit1 deng6 /ding6 jiu3	pit dehng yiu
should[2]	v/aux	應當	ying dòng	jing4 dong4	ying tong
should not[1] (coll) /can't		唔可	m̀ hó	m4 ho2	mh ho
should not[2] (wr) /can't		不可	bāt hó	bat1 ho2	pat ho
should not[3] (wr) /can't		不該	bāt gòi	bat1 goi4	pat koi
shoulder[1]	n	膊頭	bok tàuh	bok3 tau4	pok thauh
shoulder[2]	n	肩	gìn	gin4	kin
shoulder[3]	n	肩膀	gīn pòhng	gin1 pong4	kin phohng
shoulder-check		向後望	heung hauh mohng	hoeng3 hau6 mong6	heung hauh mohng
shoulder pad	n	墊肩	jín gìn	zin2 gin4	chin kin
shout[1] /cry/loudly shout	v	呼叫	fù giu	fu4 giu3	fu kiu
shout[2]	v	喊叫	haam giu	haam3 giu3	haam kiu
shout[3]	v	誇口	kwā háu	kwaa1 hau2	khwa hau
shout[4] (as a mad man)	v	狂叫	kòhng giu	kwong4 giu3	khohng kiu
shout down	v	高聲喝采	gòu sèng hot chói	gou4 seng4 hot3 coi2	kou seng hot chhoi
shout loudly	v	喝	hot	hot3	hot
shovel /digging spade		鐵鍬	tít chìu	tit2 ciu4	thit chhiu
show[1] /demo/show up	n	示	sih	si6	sih
show[2] (play/drama/opera)	n	劇	kehk	kek6	khehk
show[3] /let see/display	v	出示	chēut sih	ceot1 si6	chhot sih
show behaviour	v	表示	bíu sih	biu2 si6	piu sih
show entertainment	n	開演	hòi yín	hoi4 jin2	hoi yin

show respect /give respect (for aged parents)	v	孝順	haau seuhn	haau3 seon6	haau seuhn
shower[1] /sprinkler	n	花灑	fā sá	fa1 sa2	fa phuhn
shower[2]	n	陣雨	jahn yúh	zan6 jyu5	chahn yuh
shower gel	n	皂液	jouh yihk	zou6 jik6	chouh yehk
shower head	v	花灑	fā sá	fa1 sa2	fa sa
showers /take a bath /take a shower	v	沖涼	chùng lèung	cung4 loeng4	chhung leong
showman (for things)	n	演出主持人	yíhn chēut jyú chìh yāhn	jin5 ceot1 zyu2 ci4 jan4	yihn chhot chyu chhih yahn
shown	v	表示出來	bíu sih chēut lòih	biu2 si6 ceot loi4	piu sih chhot loih
showroom	n	陳列室	chàhn liht sāt	can4 lit6 sat1	chhahn liht sat
showtime	n	開演時間	hòi yín sìh gaan	hoi4 jin2 si4 gaan3	hoi yin sih kaan
showy fashion	n	架勢	ga sai	gaa3 sai3	ka sai
shrewd[1]	adj	精	jēng /jīng	zeng1 /zing1	cheng
shrewd[2]	adj	精神	jēng sàn	zeng1 san4	cheng san
shrewd[3]	adj	精明	jēng mìhng	zeng1ming4	cheng mehng
shrewish /vixen woman	v	好似潑婦咁	hóu chíh put fúh gám	hou2 ci5 put3 fu5 gam2	hou chhih phut fuh kam
shrimp (fish/prawn)	n	蝦	hā	haa1	ha
shrimp dried	n	蝦米	hā máih	haa1 mai5	ha maih
shrimp dumpling	n	蝦餃	hā gáau	haa1 gaau2	ha kaau
shrimp rice roll	n	蝦腸	hā chèuhng	haa1 coeng4	ha chheuhng
shrink[1] (become smaller)	v	縮	sūk	suk1	suk
shrink[2] (become smaller)	v	收縮	sàu sūk	sau4 suk1	sau suk
shrink back /to cower /shrinkby fear/recoil	v	退縮	tèui sūk	teoi4 suk1	thoi suk
shrinking (of cloth)	v	縮水	sūk séui	suk1 seoi2	suk swoi
shroff /pay fee	n/v	繳費	gíu fai	giu2 fai3	kiu fai
shroud /wrapper cloth /wrapper cloth for dead body	n	裹屍布	gwó si bou	gwo2 si3 bou3	kwo si pou
shrub /bush/many smaller plants	n	灌木	gun muhk	gun3 muk6	kun muhk
shut[1(coll)] /off/close/turn off	v	閂	sàan	saan4	saan
shut door[1] /close door	v	閂門	sàan mùhn	saan4 mun4	saan muhn
shut door[2]	v	閂埋	sàan màaih	saan4 maai4	saan maaih
shut off /unplug/power off/switch off/turn off	v	關掉	gwāan deuh	gwaan4 deu6	kwaan teuh
shut up!	v	咪嘈	máih chòuh	mai5 cou4	maih chhouh
shut your mouth /stop talking	v	住口	jyuh háu	zyu6 hau2	chyuh hau
shutter[1] /latch	n	門閂	mùhn sàan	mun4 saan4	muhn saan
shutter[2] /blind/curtain	n	百葉窗	baak yihp chēung	baak3 jip6 cong1	paak yihp cheung
shutter man /closer	n	關閉者	gwàan bai jé	gwaan4 bai3 ze2	kwaan pai che
shuttle /back and forth	n	梭	sō	so1	so
shuttle cock /badminton's	n	羽毛球	yúh mou kau	jyu5 mou3 kau3	yuh mou khau
shy[1]	adj	怕醜	pa cháu	paa3 cau2	pha chhau

English	Part	Chinese	Romanization 1	Romanization 2	Romanization 3
shy[2] /polite/be polite /nervous/embarrassed	adj	客氣	haak hei	haak3 hei3	haak hei
shy[3]	adj	怕羞	pa sāu	paa3 sau1	pha sau
shyness /bashful	adj	羞怯	sàu hip	sau4 hip3	sau hip
siblings /brothers or sisters	n	兄弟姐妹	hìng daih jí muih	hing4 dai6 zi2 mui6	hing taih chi muih
sick[1] /sufferer/patient	adj/n	患	waahn	waan6	waahn
sick[2] /suffer	adj/v	患病	waahn behng /bihng	waan6 beng6 /bing6	waahn pehng
sick[3] /ill/unwell	adj	唔舒服	m̀ syù fùhk	m4 syu4 fuk6	mh syu fuhk
sick leave[1]	n	攞病假	ló behng gá	lo2 beng6 gaa2	lo pehng ka
sick leave[2]	n	病假	behng /bihng ga	beng6 /bing6 gaa3	pehng ka
sick leave letter	n	病假字	behng /bihng ga jih	beng6 /bing6 gaa3 zi6	pehng ka chih
sick or injured person	n	有人病發 或受傷	yauh yàhn beng faat waahk sauh sèung	jau6 jan4 beng3 faat3 waak6 sau6 soeng4	yauh yahn peng faat waahk sauh seung
sick person[1]	v	病人	behng /bihng yàhn	beng6 /bing6 jan4	pehng yahn
sick person[2]	n	病者	behng /bihng jé	beng6 /bing6 ze2	pehng che
sicken /become ill	v	生病	sàang behng	saan4 beng6	saang pehng
sickle	n	鐮刀	lìhm dōu	lim4 dou1	lihm tou
sickroom /ward of hospital/room of hospital	n	病房	behng /bihng fóng	beng6 /bing6 fong2	pehng fong
side	n	邊	bīn	bin1	pin
side effect	n	副作用	fu jok yuhng	fu3 zok3 jung6	fu chok yuhng
side road	n	路邊	louh bīn	lou6 bin1	louh pin
side step	n	迴避	wùih bèih	wui4 bei6	wuih peih
side walk	n	人行道	yàhn hàhng douh	jan4 hang4 dou6	yahn hahng touh
sideshow /small show	n	小節目	síu jit muhk	siu2 zit3 muk6	siu chit muhk
sideways	adv	旁邊	pòhng bīn	pong4 bin1	phohng pin
sieve /sift/sifter/filter	v	篩	sài	sai4	sai
sifter	v	篩子	sài jí	sai4 zi2	sai chi
sight[1] /vision/senses of vision	n	視覺	sih gók	si6 gok2	sih kok
sight[2]	n	視力	sih lihk	si6 lik6	sih lehk
sight shot	n	視野	sih yéh	si6 je5	sih yeh
sign[1] /trace	n	跡象	jīk jeuhng	zik1 zoeng6	chek cheuhng
sign[2] /mark	n	標牌	bīu pàaih	biu1 paai4	piu phaaih
sign away	n	簽字放棄	chìm jih fong hei	cim4 zi6 fong3 hei3	chhim chih fong hei
sign contract /treaty	n	簽約	chìm yeuk	cim4 joek3	chhim yeuk
sign for	n	簽收	chìm sāu	cim4 sau1	chhim sau
signal	n	信號/訊號	seun hou	seon3 hou3	swon hou
signatory	n	簽約者	chìm yeuk jé	cim4 joek3 ze2	chhim yeuk che
signature[1] /sign/initial	v	簽	chìm	cim4	chhim
signature[2]	n	簽署	chìm chyúh	cim4 cyu5	chhim chyuh
signboard[1]	n	招牌	jīu pàaih	ziu1 paai4	chiu phaaih
signboard[2]	n	顯示牌	hín sih pàaih	hin2 si6 paai4	hin sih phaaih
signer	n	簽名者	chìm méng jé	cim4 meng2 ze2	chhim meng che

significance	n	重要意思	juhng yiu yi sī /si	zung6 jiu3 ji3 si1 /si3	chuhng yiu yi si
significant	adj	有意義	yáuh yi yih	jau5 ji3 ji6	yauh yi yih
signing	n	合同簽署	hahp tùhng chìm chyúh	hap6 tung4 cim4 cyu5	hahp thuhng chhim chhyuh
signs (by tube light box) /neon lamp/light signs	n	霓虹燈	ngàih hùhng dāng	ngai4 hung4 dang1	ngaih huhng tang
silence	n	唔出聲咁	m̀ chēut sèng gám	m4 ceot1 seng4 gam2	mh chhot seng kam
silent[1]	adj	無講多	móuh góng dò	mou5 gong2 do4	mouh kong toh
silent[2] /quiet	adj	靜	jèhng /jìhng	zeng6 /zing6	chehng
silent[3] /secretly	adj	靜靜	jèhng jèhng, jìhng jìhng	zeng6 zeng6, zing6 zing6	chehng chehng
silent[4]	adj	無提及	móuh tàih kahp	mou5 tai4 kap6	mouh thaih khahp
silent[5]	adj	寂靜	jihk jihng	zik6 zing6	chehk chehng
silicon	n	矽膠	jihk gàau	zik6 gaau4	chehk kaau
silk[1]	n	絲	sī	si1	si
silk[2]	n	真絲	jàn sī	zan4 si1	chan si
silk cloth	n	絲綢	sī chàuh	si1 cau4	si chhauh
silky	adj	柔軟光潔	yàuh yúhn gwòng git	jau4 jyun5 gwong4 git3	yauh yuhn kwong kit
sill[1] (of the door)	n	門杉	mùhn cháahm	mun4 caam5	muhn chhaahm
sill[2] (of the window)	n	窗台	chēung toih	coeng1 toi6	chhaung thoih
sill[3] (of the door)	n	基木	gèi muhk	gei4 muk6	kei muhk
sill[4] (of the door)	n	門檻	mùhn laahm	mun4 laam6	muhn laahm
silo[1] /tower tank	n	筒庫	tùhng fu	tung4 fu3	thuhng fu
silo[2]	n	青貯窖	chèng chyúh gaau	ceng4 cyu5 gaau3	chheng chhyuh gaau
silt /mud	n	淤泥	yu làih /nàih	jyu3 lai4 /nai4	yu laih /naih
silver[1]	n	銀	ngàhn	ngan4	ngahn
silver[2] /silverware	n	銀器	ngàhn hei	ngan4 hei3	ngahn hei
silver color	n	銀色	ngàhn sīk	ngan4 sik1	ngahn sek
silver jubilee[1] /annual /anniversary	n/v	週年	jāu lìhn /nìhn	zau1 lin4 /nin4	chau lihn /nihn
silver jubilee[2]	n	二十五週年紀念	yih sahp ńgh jàu lìhn géi lihm	ji6 sap6 ng5 zau4 lin4 gei2 lim6	yih sahp ngh chau lihn kei lihm
similar	adj	同類	tùhng leuih	tung4 leoi6	thuhng lowih
similarity	n	相似	seung chíh	soeng3 ci5	seung chhih
simple	adj	淺白	chín bàahk	cin2 baak6	chhin paahk
simple fraction	n	單分數	dāan fān sou	daan1 fan1 sou3	taan fan sou
simple interest	n	單利	dāan leih	daan1 lei4	taan leih
simple minded	adj	頭腦簡單	tàuh nóuh gáan dàan	tau4 nou5 gaan2 daan4	thauh nouh kaan taan
simplified (Chinese)	n	簡體	gáan tái	gaan2 tai2	kaan thai
simplified Chinese character	n	簡體字	gáan tái jih	gaan2 tai2 zi6	kaan thai chih
simultaneous	adj	同步的	tùhng bouh dīk	tung4 bou6 dik1	thuhng pouh tik
sin /crime	n	罪孽	jeuih yihp	zeoi6 jip6	cheuih yihp
sin wa /news agency	n	新華社	sàn wàh séh	san4 waa4 se5	san wah seh

English	Part	中文	Romanization	Jyutping	Alt
since[1] /since then /from/by then	conj	自	jih	zi6	chih
since[2]	conj	自從	jih chùhng	zi6 cung4	chih chhohng
since[3]	conj	既然	gei yìhn	gei3 jin4	kei yìhn
since[4] /since then	prep	自...以來	jih yíh loìh	zi6 ji5 loi4	chih yih loih
since childhood		自細	jih sai	zi6 sai3	chih sai
sincere[1]	adj	真心	jàn sàm	zan4 sam4	chan sam
sincere[2]	adj	誠	sìhng	sing4	sehng
sincere[3]	adj	誠懇	sìhng háh	sing4 haa5	sehng hah
sincerely yours	adv	你真摯的	léih jàn ji dīk	lei5 zan1 zi3 dik1	leih chan chi tek
sinful[1]	adj	罪	jeuih	zeoi6	cheuih
sinful[2]	adj	罪惡	jeuih ok /ngok	zeoi6 ok3 /ngok3	cheuih ok /ngok
sinful[3]	adj	反罪	faahn jeuih	faan4 zeoi6	faahn cheuih
sing	v	唱	cheung	coeng3	chheung
singer[1]	n	唱歌嘅人	cheung gō ge yàhn	coeng3 go1 ge3 jan4	chheung ko ke yahn
singer[2]	n	歌手	gō sāu	go1 sau1	ko sau
singer[3] /songster	n	歌唱家	gō cheung gā	go1 coeng3 ga1	ko chheung ka
singing[1]	n	唱歌	cheung gò	coeng3 go4	chheung ko
singing[2]	n	歌聲	gō sèng	go1 seng4	ko seng
single /whole/all/as soon as	adj	一	yāt	jat1	yat
single parent	n	單親	dāan chan	daan1 can3	taan chhan
single room	n	單人房	dāan yàhn fóng	daan1 jan4 fong2	taan yahn fong
sinister /dangerous	adj	險惡	hím ok /ngok	him2 ok3 /ngok3	him ok /ngok
sinister person /vicious persin/dangerous person	n	險惡嘅人	hím ok /ngok ge yàhn	him2 ok3 /ngok3 ge3 jan4	him ok /ngok ke yahn
sink[1] /submerge	v	沉	chàhm	cam4	chhahm
sink[2]	v	沉沒	chàhm muht	cam4 mut6	chhahm muht
sink drown /submerge	v	淹	jam	zam3	cham
sink in	v	滲入	sam yahp	sam3 jap6	sam yahp
sinologist	n	中國通	jùng gwok tùng	zung4 gwok3 tung4	chung kwok thung
sir[1] /teacher	n	老師	lóuh sì	lou5 si4	louh si
sir[2] (de)	n	啊蛇	āa sèh	aa1 se4	aa seh
siren[1] /whistle/horn	n	汽笛	hei dehk	hei3 dek6	hei tehk
siren[2] /instrument (bell)	n	警報器	gíng bou hei	ging2 bou3 hei3	keng pou hei
sister[1]	n	姐妹	jé /jí muih	ze2 /zi2 mui6	che /chi muih
sister[2] (elder)	n	家姐	gā jé	gaa1 ze2	ka che
sister[3] (elder)	n	姐姐	jé jé	ze2 ze2	che che
sit down /sit here!	v	坐低	chóh dài	co5 dai4	chhoh tai
sit full	v	無位	móuh wàih	mou5 wai6	mouh waih
sit fulled	v	坐滿	chóh múhn	co5 mun5	chhoh muhn
sit here!	v	坐呢度!	chóh lì /nì dòuh	co5 li4 /ni4 dou6	chhoh li /ni touh
sit down! (coll) /sit here!	v	坐呢度囉	chóh lì /nì dòuh ló	co5 li4 /ni4 dou6 lo2!	chhoh li /ni touh lo!
sit on eggs /hatch	v	孵	fù	fu4	fu

English	POS	Chinese	Romanization 1	Jyutping	Romanization 2
sit up[1] (physical exercise)	n	仰臥起坐	yéuhng ngoh héi joh	joeng5 ngo6 hei2 zo6	yeuhng ngoh hei choh
sit up[2] /stay up to late	adj	熬夜	yiht yeh	jit6 je6	yiht yeh
site	n	場地	chèuhng deih	coeng4 dei6	chheuhng teih
sitting	n	坐在	chóh joih	co5 zoi6	chhoh choih
sitting room	n	起居廳室	héi gèui tèng sāt	hei2 geoi4 teng4 sat1	hei kwoi theng sat
situate	v	喺	hái	hai2	hai
situated[1] /placed	v	使位於	sái wàih yù	sai2 wai6 jyu4	sai waih yu
situated[2]	adj	位於	wái yù	wai2 jyu4	wai yu
situation[1]	n	情	chìhng	cing4	chhehng
situation[2]	n	處境	chyú gíng	cyu2 ging2	chhyu king
situation[3] /position of seated	n	位置	waih ji	wai6 zi3	waih chi
six	n	六	luhk / look /lok	luk6	luhk /look
six forty five[1]	n	六點九	luhk dím gáu	luk6 dim2 gau2	luhk tim kau
six forty five[2]	n	六點四十五分	luhk dím sei sahp m̀ fān	luk6 dim2 sei3 sap6 m4 fan1	luhk tim sei sahp mh fahn
sixfold	adj	六倍	luhk púih	luk6 pui5	luhk phuih
size[1] (de)	n	哂士	sāai sí	saai1 si2	saai si
size[2]	n	尺碼	chek máh	cek3 maa5	chhek mah
size[3]	n	大小	daaih síu	daai6 siu2	taaih siu
size[4]	n	大細	daaih sai	daai6 sai3	taaih sai
size unfit	adj	尺碼不合	chek máh bàt hàhp	cek3 maa5 bat4 hap6	chhek mah pat hahp
skateboard	n	滑板	waaht báan	waat6 baan2	waaht paan
skating rink	n	溜冰場	làuh bīng chèuhng	lau4 bing1 coeng4	lauh peng chheuhng
skeptical /unbeliever /suspecter/skeptic/distrusful/ incredulous	n	懷疑者	wàaih yìh jé	waai4 ji4 ze2	waaih yih che
sketcher	n	草繪器	chóu kūi hei	cou2 kui1 hei3	chhou khui hei
ski-board	n	滑雪板	wàaht syut báan	waat6 syut3 baan2	waaht syut paan
skidding /sliding	n	滑行	wàaht hàhng	waat6 hang4	waaht hahng
skiing (sport on snow)	n	滑雪運動	wàaht syut wahn duhng	waat6 syut3 wan6 dung6	waaht syut wahn tuhng
skill[1]	adj	技	geih	gei6	keih
skill[2]	n	巧	háau	haau2	haau
skill[3] /technic/technique /technology	n	技術	geih seuht	gei6 seot6	keih swoht
skill[4]	n	手藝	sáu ngaih	sau2 ngai6	sau ngaih
skill[5] /technique/kung fu	n	功夫	gùng fù	gung4 fu4	kung fu
skill labor[1]	n	熟手工人	suhk sáu gùng yàhn	suk6 sau2 gung4 jan4	suhk sau kung yahn
skill labor[2]	n	熟練工人	suhk lihn gùng yàhn	suk6 lin6 gung4 jan4	suhk lihn kung yahn
skilled worker	n	熟練功人	suhk lihn gùng yàhn	suk6 lin6 gung4 jan4	suhk lihn kung yahn
skim	v	撇去	pit heui	pit3 heoi3	phit hoi
skin[1]	n	膚	fū	fu1	fu
skin[2] /complexion	n	皮膚	pèih fù	pei4 fu4	pheih fu
skin and bone	n	極瘦	gìhk sau	gik6 sau3	kehk sau
skincare	adj	護膚	wuh fū	wu6 fu1	wuh fu

skinnier /thin body/fit body	n	瘦的	sau dì	sau3 di4	sau ti
skinny person(coll)	n	馬騮	máh lāu	maa5 lau1	mah lau
skip[1]	v	跳升	tiu sìng	tiu3 sing4	thiu seng
skip[2]	v	蹦蹦跳跳	baahng baahng tiu tiu	baang6 baang6 tiu3 tiu3	paahng paahng thiu thiu
skip[3]	v	跳繩	tiu síng	tiu3 sing2	thiu seng
skirt[1]	n	裙	kwàhn	kwan4	khwahn
skirt[2] (long)	n	長裙	chèuhng kwàhn	coeng4 kwan4	chheuhng khwahn
skirt[3] (short)	n	短裙	dyún kwàhn	dyun2 kwan4	tyun khwahn
skirt[4] (half style)	n	半截裙	bun jìht kwàhn	bun3 zit6 kwan4	pun chiht khwahn
skirt[5] (be folded)	n	裙子	kwàhn jí	kwan4 zi2	khwahn chi
skirt[6] (be folded)	n	起褶	héi jaahp	hei2 zaap6	hei chaahp
skull	n	頭顱骨	tàuh lòuh gwàt	tau4 lou4 gwat4	thauh louh kwat
sky	n	天	tìn	tin4	thin
slam	v	猛地撞擊	máahng deih johng gīk	maang5 dei6 zong6 gik1	maahng teih chohng kek
slander	v	口頭誹謗	háu tàuh féi pong	hau2 tau4 fei2 pong3	hau thauh fei phong
slang (informal) /common saying	n	俗語	juhk yúh	zuk6 jyu5	chuhk yuh
slant /tilt/slope	n/v	使傾斜	sái /si kìng chèh	sai2 /si3 king3 ce4	sai /si khing chheh
slavery /toil/work hard	n/v	苦幹	fú gon	fu2 gon3	fu kon
slay /kill in a war/fight	v	殺害	saat hoih	saat3 hoi6	saat hoih
sledge[1]	n	橇	chèuih	ceoi4	chheuih
sledge[2]	n	雪車	syut chè	syut3 ce4	syut chhe
sleekly	adv	光滑地	gwòng wàaht deih	gwong4 waat6 dei6	kwong waaht teih
sleep[1]	n	瞓	fan	fan3	fan
sleep[2]	n	睡	seuih	seoi6	swoih
sleep[3]	n	眠	mìhn	min4	mihn
sleep-rest in afternoon	v	瞓晏覺	fan aan /ngaan gaau	fan3 aan3 /ngaan3 gaau3	fan aan /ngaan kaau
sleeper	n	睡眠者	seuih mìhn jé	seoi6 min4 ze2	swoih mihn che
sleeping	n	睡眠	seuih mìhn	seoi6 min4	swoih mihn
sleeping bag	n	睡袋	seuih doih	seoi6 doi6	swoih toih
sleeping pill	n	安眠藥片	òn /ngòn mìhn yeuhk pin	on4 /ngon4 min4 joek6 pin3	on /ngon mihn yeuhk phin
sleeping tablet	n	安眠藥	òn /ngòn mìhn yeuhk	on4 /ngon4 min4 joek6	on /ngon mihn yeuhk
sleepless	adj	不眠	bāt mìhn	bat1 min4	pat mihn
sleepy[1]	adj	眼瞓	ngáahn fan	ngaan5 fan3	ngaahn fan
sleepy[2] /tired/weary /feel tired/very tired	adj	疲倦	pèih gyùhn	pei4 gyun6	pheih kyuhn
sleepy[3] /tired	adj	困乏	yàn faht	jan4 fat6	yan faht
sleeve[1]	n	袖	jauh	zau6	chauh
sleeve[2]	n	袖子	jauh jí	zau6 zi2	chauh chi
slender[1] /slim/thin	n	修長	sau chèuhng	sau3 coeng4	sau chheuhng

slender[2]	n	幼長	yau chèuhng	jau3 coeng4	yau chheuhng
sliced /thin piece	n	片	pin	pin3	phin
sliced fish	n	魚片	yú pín	jyu2 pin2	yu phin
sliced meat	n	肉片	yuhk pín	juk6 pin2	yuhk phin
slicker person	n	圓滑者	yùhn wàaht jé	jyun4 waat6 ze2	yuhn waaht che
slickest	n	圓滑人	yùhn wàaht yàhn	jyun4 waat6 jan4	yuhn waaht yahn
slide[1] /collapse	n	崩	bāng	bang1	pang
slide[2] /slip/slippery	v	滑	wàaht	waat6	waaht
slide[3] /film	n	幻燈片	waahn dāng pín	waan6 dang1 pin2	waahn tang phin
slide[4] /of microscope	n	載物玻璃片	joi maht bō lèih pin	zoi3 mat6 bo1 lei4 pin3	choi maht po leih phin
sliding[1]	n	跌倒	sin dóu	sin3 dou2	sin tou
sliding[2]	n	滑動	wàaht dùhng	waat6 dung6	waaht tohng
slight[1] /slender/slim/thin	adj	瘦小	sau síu	sau3 siu2	sau siu
slight[2] /slightest/slightly /very	adj	好少	hóu síu	hou2 siu2	hou siu
slightly[1]	adv	梢爲	sáau wàih	saau2 wai6	saau waih
slightly[2] /slight	adv	輕微	hèng mei	heng4 mei3	heng mei
slightly[3]	adv	稍微地	sáau mèih deih	saau2 mei6 dei6	saau meih teih
slim /slender	adj/n	苗條	mìuh tíuh	miu4 tiu5	miuh thiuh
slim reduce	v	減肥	gáam fèih	gaan2 fei4	kaam feih
sling[1]	n	投	tàuh	tau4	thauh
sling[2] /catapult	n	彈弓	tàahn gúng	taan4 gung2	thaahn kung
slip[1] /fall/drop	v	跌	dit	dit3	tit
slip[2] /underskirt/short skirt	v	底裙	dái kwàhn	dai2 kwan4	tai khwahn
slip[3] /slippy	v	滑跤	wàaht gāau	waat6 gaau1	waaht kaau
slip away	v	溜走	làuh jáu	lau4 zau2	lauh chau
slip of paper	n	紙條	jí tìuh	zi2 tiu4	chi thiuh
slippery	adj	滑倒	wàaht dóu	waat6 dou2	waaht tou
slippery surface /floor slippery/wet floor	n	地滑	deih wàaht	dei6 waat6	teih waaht
slippy	adj	滑的	wàaht dīk	waat6 dik1	waaht tik
slogan	n	口號	háu houh	hau2 hou6	hau houh
slogan poster	n	標語	bīu yùh	biu1 jyu6	piu yuh
slope[1]	n	坡	bō	bo1	po
slope[2]	n	斜坡	chèh bō	ce4 bo1	chheh po
sloppy	adj	水皮	séui pèih	seoi2 pei4	swoi pheih
slough[1] (of snake) /molt	v	甩皮	lāt pèih	lat1 pei4	lat pheih
slough[2] (of snake) /molt	v	脫皮	tyut pèih	tyut3 pei4	thyut pheih
slow[1]	adj	慢	maahn	maan6	maahn
slow[2]	adj	緩慢	wun màahn	wun3 maan2	wun maahn
slow[3]	adj	慢的	maahn dì	maan6 di4	maahn ti
slow heat /simmer	n	慢火煮	maahn fó jyú	maan6 fo2 zyu2	maahn fo chyu
slow works /slowly act /tortoise style/very slow work	n	行動遲緩	hàhng duhng chìh wun	hang4 dung6 ci4 wun3	hahng tohng chhih wun

slowly[1]	adv	緩慢地	wun màahn dèih	maan6 maan2 dei6	wun maahn teih
slowly[2] /stealthily/very slowly	adv	悄悄地	chíuh chíuh deih	ciu5 ciu5 dei6	chhiuh chhiuh teih
slug[1] /small soft creature	n	蜓	tìhng	ting4	thehng
slug[2] /small soft creature	n	蛞蝓	kut yùh	kut3 jyu4	khut yuh
slum /dirty & bad houses	n	貧民窟	pàhn màhn fāt	pan4 man4 fat1	phahn mahn fat
small /tiny/minute	adj	細小	sai síu	sai3 siu2	sai siu
small bag /pouch	n	小袋子	síu dói jí, seew doih jí	siu2 doi2 zi2, siu2 doi6 zi2	siu toi chi, siu toih chi
small figure /small size	n	細粒	sái làp	sai2 lap4	sai lap
small fire	n	小火	síu fó	siu2 fo2	siu fo
small island	n	小島	síu dóu	siu2 dou2	siu tou
small meeting		小組討論	síu jóu tóu leuhn	siu2 zou2 tou2 leon6	siu chou thou leuhn
small minded /petty /narrow minded		小氣	síu hei	siu2 hei3	siu hei
small pox	n	天花	tīn fā	tin1 faa1	thin fah
small ship /boat/canoe	n	艇	tíhng	ting5	thehng
small size[1] /dwarf /small/ little/tiny	n	侏	jyù	zyu4	chyu
small size[2] (s)	n	細碼	sai máh	sai3 maa5	sai mah
small station	n	小站	síu jaahm	siu2 zaam6	siu chaahm
small table	n	几	gèi	gei4	kei
small town	adj	小鎮	síu jan	siu2 zan3	siu chan
smaller	n	更小	gáng síu	gang2 siu2	kang siu
smart[1]	adj	叻	lēk	lek1	lek
smart[2] /acute/intelligent /sharp eyed/sharp knowledge /skilful	adj	犀利	sāi leih	sai1 lei6	sai leih
smart[3] /intelligence /intelligent/brainpower	adj	智能	ji làhng /nàhng	zi3 lang4 /nang4	chi lahng /nahng
smart girl	n	醒目女	seng mùhk lèuih, sing mùhk nèuih	seng3 muk6 leoi6, sing3 muk6 neoi6	seng muhk lowih /nowih
smartly	adv	瀟灑地	sīu sá deih	siu1 sa2 dei6	siu sa teih
smash /break/crash	v	打破	dá po	daa2 po3	ta pho
smear[1] (of dirty)	n	污迹	wù jīk	wu4 zik1	wu chek
smear[2] (of blood)	n	血漬	hyut jīk	hyut3 zik1	hyut chek
smell	adj	香	hèung	hoeng4	heung
smell flowers	v	聞花	màhn fā	man4 faa1	mahn fa
smell-less[1]	adj	沒有香	muht yáuh hèung	mut6 jau5 hoeng4	muht yauh heung
smell-less[2]	adj	沒有嗅覺	muht yáuh chau gok	mut6 jau5 cau3 gok3	muht yauh chhau kok
smell taste /sense of smell	v	味覺	meih gok	mei6 gok3	meih kok
smelling[1]	adj	聞到	màhn dóu	man4 dou2	mahn tou
smelling[2] (bad)	adj	嗅到	chau dóu	cau3 dou2	chhau tou
smelly armpit	adj	腋窩有異味	yiht wò yáuh yih meih	jit6 wo4 jau5 ji6 mei6	yiht wo yauh yih meih
smelly breath	adj	口臭	hāu chau	hau1 cau3	hau chhau

English	Part	Chinese	Yale	Jyutping	Romanization
smelly vulva (vdw)	adj	嗅閪	chau hài	cau3 hai4	chhau hai
smile /laugh	v	微笑	mèih siu	mei4 siu3	meih siu
smile face	n	笑容	siu yùhng	siu3 jung4	siu yuhng
smiling express /very happy look	v	好笑容	hóu siu yuhng	hou2 siu3 jung4	hou siu yuhng
smilingly	adv	微笑地	mèih siu deih	mei4 siu3 dei6	meih siu teih
smog	n	烟霧	yīn mouh	jin1 mou6	yin mouh
smoke[1]	n	煙	yīn	jin1	yin
smoke[2]	v	食煙	sihk yīn	sik6 jin1	sehk yin
smoke[3] /smoking	v	吸煙	kāp yīn	kap1 jin1	khap yin
smoke alarm	n	煙霧警報器	yīn mouh gíng bou hei	jin1 mou6 ging2 bou3 hei3	yin mouh keng pou hei
smoke detector	n	煙霧探測器	yīn mouh tàam chàak hei	jin1 mou6 taam4 caak4 hei3	yin mouh thaam chhaak hei
smoke door	n	煙門	yīn mùhn	jin1 mun4	yin muhn
smoke out	v	出煙	chēut yīn	ceot1 jin1	chhot yin
smoke pipe /tobacco pipe	n	食煙斗	sihk yīn dáu	sik6 jin1 dau2	sehk yin tau
smoke signal	n	煙霧信號	yīn mouh seun houh	jin1 mou6 seon3 hou6	yin mouh swon houh
smoker[1]	n	食煙人	sihk yīn yàhn	sik6 jin1 jan4	sehk yin yahn
smoker[2]	n	吸煙者	kāp yīn jé	kap1 jin1 ze2	khap yin che
smoking area[1]	n	吸煙區	kāp yìn kèui	kap1 jin4 keoi4	khap yin khoi
smoking area[2]	n	吸烟区	kāp yìn kèui	kap1 jin4 keoi4	khap yin khoi
smoking prohibited		禁止食煙	gam jí sihk yīn	gam3 zi2 sik6 jin1	kam chi sehk yin
smooth[1] /to slip	adj	滑	wàaht	waat6	waaht
smooth[2]	adj	光滑的	gwòng wàaht dik	gwong4 waat6 dik1	kwong waaht tik
smoothly[1] /unhitch	adj	順利	seuhn leih	seon6 lei6	swohn leih
smoothly[2] /even flat	adj	平滑地	pèhng wàaht dèih	peng4 waat6 dei6	phehng waaht teih
smoothly[3] /peaceful	ad	平穩地	pèhng wān deih	peng4 wan1 dei6	phehng wan teih
smother[1] /suppress	n	抑制	yìk jái	jik4 zai2	yek chai
smother[2] (to cover fire)	n	冚熄的火	kám sīk dī fó	kam2 sik1 di1 fo2	kham sek ti fo
smother[3] /choked die	abbr	悶死	mùhn séi	mun6 sei2	muhn sei
smuggle	v	偷運	tàu wahn	tau4 wan6	thau wahn
smuggling	v	走私	jáu sì	zau2 si4	chau si
smuggled goods	n	走私貨	jáu sì fo	zau2 si4 fo3	chau si fo
smuggler	n	做⋯的走私生意	jouh dìk jáu si sàang yi	zou6 dik4 zau2 si4 saang4 ji3	chouh tik chau si saang yi
smuggler	n	走私者	jáu sì jé	zau2 si4 ze2	chau si che
snack[1]	n	小食	síu sìhk	siu2 sik6	siu sehk
snack[2] (sl)	n	口垃圾	háu lahp sāp	hau2 lap6 saap3	hau lahp sap
snack[3] /refreshments	n	小吃	síu hek	siu2 hek3	siu hek
snack counter /tuck shop/retail department	n	小賣部	siu maaih bouh	siu3 maai6 bou6	siu maaih pouh
snail	n	蝸牛	wò ngàuh	wo4 ngau4	wo ngauh
snake[1]	n	蛇	sèh	se4	seh

English	POS	Chinese	Romanization 1	Jyutping	Romanization 2
snake² (sl) a bad person	n	陰險嘅人	yàm hím ge yàhn	jam4 him2 ge3 jan4	yam him ke yahn
snatch	v	奪走	dyuht jáu	dyut6 zau2	tyuht chau
sneak /sneakily walk	v	偷偷地走	tàu tàu déi jáu	tau4 tau4 dei2 zau2	thau thai tei chau
sneak away		鬆人	sùng yàhn	sung4 jan4	sung yahn
sneaked¹ (coll) avoid being seen	v	鬼鬼鼠鼠人	gwái gwái syú syú yàhn	gwai2 gwai2 syu2 syu2 jan4	kwai kwai syu syu tik yahn
sneaked² (wr) avoid being seen	v	鬼鬼祟祟人	gwái gwái seuih seuih yàhn	gwai2 gwai2 seoi6 seoi6 jan4	kwai kwai swoih swoih yahn
sneaked³ /run away (like steal) /escape as a thief /secretly walk/stalking	v	偷偷地	tàu tàu déi	tau4 tau4 dei2	thau thai tei
sneaked⁴ secretly walker	v	靜靜地鬆人	jèhng jèhng déi sùng yàhn	zeng6 zeng6 dei2 sung4 jan4	chehng chehng tei sung yahn
sneer	v	笑	sìu	siu4	siu
sneerer	n	嘲笑人	jàau sìu yàhn	zaau4 siu4 jan4	chaau siu yahn
sneeze¹	n	乞嚏	hāt chì	hat1 ci4	hat chhi
sneeze²	n	打乞嚏	dá hāt chì	daa2 hat1 ci4	ta hat chhi
sneeze³	n	打噴嚏	dá fáhn tai	daa2 fan5 tai3	ta fahn thai
snore¹	v	鼻鼾聲	beih hòhn sēng /sīng	bei6 hon4 seng1 /sing1	peih hohn seng
snore²	v	扯鼻鼾	ché beih hòhn	ce2 bei6 hon4	chhe peih hohn
snore³	v	打鼾	dá hòhn	daa2 hon4	ta hohn
snorer	n	打鼾者	dá hòhn jé	daa2 hon4 ze2	ta hohn che
snort	v	噴鼻息	pan bèih sīk	pan3 bei6 sik1	phan peih sek
snout	n	豬嘴	jyū jéui	zyu1 zeoi2	chyu choi
snow	n	雪	syut	syut3	syut
snow line	v	雪線	syut sin	syut3 sin3	syut sin
snow wall	v	避雪牆	beih syut chèuhng	bei6 syut3 coeng4	peih syut cheuhng
snow white	adj	雪白	syut baahk	syut3 baak6	syut paahk
snowing¹	v	落雪	lòhk syut	lok6 syut3	lohk syut
snowing²	v	下雪	hah syut	haa6 syut3	hah syut
so¹ /such/then/hence	adj	噉 / 咁	gam	gam3	kam
so² /therefore	adv	咁	gam	gam3	kam
so³	adv	爾	yíh	ji5	yih
so⁴ /therefore	adv	所以	só yíh	so2 ji5	so yih
so as to¹		用以	yuhng yíh	jung6 ji5	yuhng yih
so as to² /so that		以便	yíh bihn	ji5 bin6	yih pihn
so-called /what is called	adv	所謂	só waih	so2 wai6	so waih
so early¹ /early	adj	咁早	gam jóu	gam3 zou2	kam chou
so early?²		咁早啊?	gam jóu a?	gam3 zou2 a3?	kam chou a?
so far away?		咁遠啊?	gam yúhn a?	gam3 jyun5 a3?	kam yuhn a?
so fast?	adj	咁快啊?	gam faai a?	gam3 faai3 a3?	kam faai a?
so hasty?	adj	咁急啊?	gam gāp a?	gam3 gap1 a3?	kam kap a?
so hurry!		快啲呀!	faai dì àa! /āa!	faai3 di4 aa4 /aa1	faai ti aa!
so late¹		咁遲	gam chìh	gam3 ci4	kam chhih
so late?²		咁遲啊?	gam chìh a?	gam3 ci6 a3?	kam chhih a?

English		Chinese	Yale	Jyutping	Romanization
so long time?		咁耐啊?	gam loih /noih a?	gam3 loi6 /noih a3?	kam loih /noih a?
so much as	n	甚至於	sahm ji yū /yùh	sam6 zi3 jyu1 /jyu4	sahm chi yu /yuh
so so[1] /tolerable/not bad /not very good/ not very well	adj	麻麻地	màh má déi	maa4 ma2 dei2	mah ma tei
so so[2]	adj	不好也不壞	bāt hóu yáh bāt waaih	bat1 hou2 jaa5 bat1 waai6	pat hou yah bat waaih
so soon?	adj	咁快啊?	gam faai a?	gam3 faai3 a3?	kam faai a?
so such? /like this?	adj	這麼	jéh mō	ze5 mo1	cheh mo
so then /or so		那麼	là mò	laa6 mo4	la mo
so ugly		咁核突	gam haht daht	gam3 hat6 dat6	kam haht taht
soap[1]	n	番梘	fàan gáan	faan4 gaan2	faan kaan
soap[2]	n	肥皂	fèih jouh	fei4 zou6	feih chouh
soar	v	暴漲	bouh jeung	bou6 zoeng3	pouh cheung
sob	n	啜	jyut	zyut3	chyut
sobbing[1]	n	抽噎	chàu yit	cau4 jit	chhau yit
sobbing[2]	n	啜泣	jyut yāp	zyut3 jap1	chyut yahp
soccer /football	n	足球	jéui kàuh	zeoi2 kau4	cheui khauh
sociable	adj	好交際	hóu gàau jai	hou2 gaau4 jai3	hou kaau chai
social[1] /society	adj	社會	séh wúi	se5 wui2	seh wui
social[2]	adj	社會性	séh wúi sing	se5 wui2 sing3	seh wui seng
social democracy	n	社會民主主義	séh wúi màhn jyú jyú yih	ce5 wui2 man4 zyu2 zyu2 ji6	seh wui mahn chyu chyu yih
social engineering	n	社會工程	séh wúi gùng chìhng	ce5 wui2 gung4 cing4	seh wui kung chhehng
social intercourse	n	交際	gàau jai	gaau4 jai3	kaau chai
social security[1]	n	社會保障	séh wúih bou jeung	se5 wui5 bou3 zoeng3	seh wuih pou cheung
social security[2]	n	社會保險	séh wúih bou hīm	se5 wui5 bou3 him1	seh wuih pou him
social welfare	n	社會福利	séh wúi fūk leih	ce5 wui2 fuk1 lei6	seh wui fuk leih
social welfare depart	n	社署	séh chyúh	se5 cyu5	seh chhyuh
social worker[1]	n	社工	séh gùng	se5 gung4	seh kung
social worker[2]	n	社会工作者	séh wúi gùng jok jé	se5 wui2 gung4 zok3 ze2	seh wui kung chok che
social worker[3]	n	社會福利工作者	séh wúi fūk leih gùng jok jé	ce5 wui2 fuk1 lei6 gung4 zok3 ze2	seh wui fuk leih kung chok che
socialism /socialist	n	社會主義	séh wúi jyú yih	se5 wui2 zyu2 ji6	seh wui chyu yih
sociological	adj	社會學	séh wúih hohk	se5 wui2 hok6	seh wuih hohk
sociologist	n	社會學家	séh wúih hohk gā	se5 wui2 hok6 gaa1	seh wuih hohk ka
sociology	n	社會學	séh wúih hohk	se5 wui5 hok6	seh wuih hohk
sock /hit/slap/punch	v	猛擊	máahng gīk	maang5 gik1	maahng kek
socket of electrics	n	插座	chaap joh	caap3 zo6	chhaap choh
socks /stocking	n	襪	maht	mat6	maht
sodium /sodium chloride	n	鈉	laahp /naahp	laap6 /naap6	laahp /naahp
sodomy[1] /anus sex	n	肛交	gòng gāau	gong4 gaau1	kong kaau
sodomy[2] /anus sex	n	獸姦	sau gāan	sau3 gaan1	sau kaan
sofa (de)	n	梳化	sò fá	so4 faa2	so fa
soft[1]	adj	軟	yúhn	jyun5	yuhn

English	POS	Chinese	Romanization 1	Romanization 2	Romanization 3
soft² /weak/feeble	adj	弱	yeuhk	joek6	yeuhk
soft /not hard/flexible /tender	adj	軟臉臉	yúhn làhm làhm, yúhn nàhm nàhm	jyun5 lam4 lam4, ivun5 nam4 nam4	yuhn lahm lahm, yuhn nahm nahm
soft drink	n	清涼飲料	chèng /chìng lèuhng yám liuh	ceng4 /cing4 loeng4 jam2 liu6	chheng leuhng yam liuh
soft hearted¹	adj	心腸軟	sàm chèuhng yúhn	sam4 coeng4 jyun5	sam chheuhng yuhn
soft hearted²	adj	心地好	sàm deih hóu	sam4 dei6 hou2	sam teih hou
soft touch /touch	adj	接觸	jip chūk	zip3 cuk1	chip chhuk
soft voice	adj	溫柔	wàn yàuh	wan4 jau4	wan yauh
soften¹ /melt	v	軟化	yúhn fa	jyun5 faa3	yuhn fa
soften²	v	偏軟	pīn yúhn	pin1 jyun5	phin yuhn
soften habit /gentle nature	v	使變柔和	sái bin yàuh wòh	sai2 bin3 jau4 wo4	sai pin yauh woh
softener /emollient	n	柔軟劑	yàuh yúhn jāi	jau4 jyun5 zai1	yauh yuhn chai
softly¹	adv	悄悄地	chíuh chíuh deih	ciu5 ciu5 dei6	chhiuh chhiuh teih
softly²	adv	柔和地	yàuh wòh deih	jau4 wo4 dei6	yauh woh teih
softy	n	柔弱	yàuh yeuhk	jau4 joek6	yauh yeuhk
soil ground	n	土壤	tóu yeuhng	tou2 joeng6	thou yeuhng
solar	adj	太陽	taai yèuhng	taai3 joeng4	thaai yeuhng
solar battery	n	太陽能電池	taai yèuhng nàhng dihn chìh	taai3 joeng4 nang4 din6 ci4	thaai yeuhng nahng tihn chhih
solar energy	n	太陽能	taai yèuhng nàhng	taai3 joeng4 nang4	thaai yeuhng nahng
solar month	n	陽曆	yeuhng lihk	joeng4 lik6	yeuhng lehk
solar panel	n	太陽能電池板	taai yèuhng nàhng dihn chìh báan	taai3 joeng4 nang4 din6 ci4 baan2	thaai yeuhng nahng tihn chhih paan
solar system	n	太陽系	taai yèuhng haih	taai3 joeng4 hai6	thaai yeuhng haih
solar year (365¼ days)	n	太陽年	taai yèuhng lìhn /nìhn	taai3 joeng4 lin4 /nin4	thaai yeuhng lihn /nihn
solarism /sun's stories	n	太陽神話論	taai yèuhng sàhn wá leuhn	taai3 joeng4 san4 waa2 leon4	thaai yeuhng sahn wa leuhn
sold	v	售出	sauh chēut	sau6 ceot1	sauh chhot
solder	n	焊料	hón líu	hon2 liu2	hon liu
soldering iron	vt	焊接	hón jip	hon2 zip3	hon chip
soldier	n	軍人	gwàn yàhn	gwan4 jan4	kwan yahn
sole¹ (of feet/bottom/base)	n	底	dái	dai2	tai
sole² (of shoe)	n	腳底	geuk dái	goek3 dai2	keuk tai
sole³ (of shoe)	n	鞋底	hàaih dái	haai4 dai2	haaih tai
sole⁴ /only/single/strange	adj	唯一	wāi yàt	wai1 jat4	wai yat
solicit	v	徵求	jìng kàuh	zing4 kau4	cheng khauh
solid¹	adj	固體	gu tái	gu3 tai2	ku thai
solid² /substantial /compact	adj	結實	git saht	git3 sat6	kit saht
solid³ /shape	n	立體	lahp tái	lap6 tai2	lahp thai
solidarity /worker's union	n	團結工會	tyùhn git gùng wúi	tyun4 git3 gung4 wui2	thyuhn kit kung wui
solo¹ (music /flying)	adj	獨奏	duhk jau	duk6 zau3	tuhk chau
solo² /only one person	adj	單獨的	dāan dùhk dìk	daan1 duk6 dik4	taan tohk tek

solo flight		單飛	dāan fèi	daan1 fei4	taan fei
solo music /solo singing	adj	獨唱	duhk cheung	duk6 coeng3	tuhk chheung
solution[1]	n	解	gáai	gaai2	kaai
solution[2]	n	解決辦法	gáai kyut baahn faat	gaai2 kyut3 baan6 faat3	kaai khyut paahn faat
solved problem[(sl)]	v	補鑊	bóu wohk	bou2 wok6	pou wohk
some	adv	某	máuh	mau5	mauh
some how	ad	不知怎樣	bāt jì jám yeuhng	bat1 zi4 zam2 joeng6	pat chi cham yeuhng
some mistake	adv	搞錯	gáau cho	gaau2 co3	kaau chho
somebody[1] /any body	pron	有人	yauh yàhn	jau6 jan4	yauh yahn
somebody[2] /someone	pron	某人	máuh yàhn	mau5 jan4	mauh yahn
somebody leaved		送行	sung hàhng	sung3 hang4	sung hahng
someone	pron	某個	máuh go	mau5 go3	mauh ko
something[1] /object /things	n/pron	嘢	yéh	je5	yeh
something[2]	pron	有的嘢	yáuh dī yéh	jau5 di1 je5	yauh ti yeh
something[3]	pron	的嘢	dī yéh	di1 je5	ti yeh
something[4]	pron	某人某事	máuh daaih máuh sih	mau5 daai6 mau5 si6	mauh taaih mauh sih
something else	pron	第二的嘢	daih yih dìk yéh	dai6 ji6 dik4 je5	taih yih tek yeh
sometimes /time to time	adv	有時	yáuh sìh	jau5 si4	yauh sih
somewhat /little	adv	有點	yáuh dím	jau5 dim2	yauh tim
somewhere	adv	在某處	joih máuh syu	zoi6 maau5 syu3	choih mauh syu
son[1] /fellow	n	仔	jái /zái	zai2	chai
son[2]	n	兒子	yi jí	ji3 zi1	yi chi
son daughters	n	子女	jí léuih /néuih	zi2 leoi5 /neoi5	chi leuih /neuih
son in law	n	女婿	léuih sai	leui5 sai3	lowih sai
song[1]	n	歌	gō	go1	ko
song[2]	n	副歌	fu go .	fu3 go3	fu ko
song[3] /lay	n	歌曲	gō kūk	go1 kuk1	ko khuk
sonless	adj	無仔	mòuh jái	mou4 zai2	mouh chai
soon[1] /quickly/as quickly /as possible/with all speed	adv	盡快	jeuhn faai	zeon6 faai3	cheuhn faai
soon[2]	adv	很快地	hān faai deih	han1 faai3 dei6	han faai teih
soon after /then /subsequently		隨後	cheui hàuh	ceoi4 hau6	chheui hauh
sooner of schedule	n	提早	tàih jóu	tai4 zou2	thaih chou
sooner or later	n	遲早	chìh jóu	ci4 zou2	chhih chou
soprano[1] (high tone) /female's high tone	n	女高音	léuih gōu yām	leui5 gou1 jam1	lowih kou yam
soprano[2] /high tone /rising tone	n	高音	gòu yàm	gou4 jam4	kou yam
sorcerer /wizard	n	鬼才	gwái chòih	gwai2 coi4	kwai chhoih
sore /sorrow/pain from wound	adj	傷痛	seung tung	soeng4 tung3	seung tung
sorrow[1]	n	傷心	sèung sàm	soeng4 sam4	seung sam
sorrow[2]	n	難過	làahn gwò	laan4 gwo4	laahn kwo

English	POS	Chinese	Jyutping (tone marks)	Jyutping	Romanization
sorrowful[1]	adj	凄慘	chài cháam	cai4 caam2	chhai chaam
sorrowful[2]	adj	傷心的	sèung sàm dīk	soeng4 sam4 dik1	seung sam tik
sorry![1] (for mistake) /i'm sorry!/excuse me!	adj	對唔住！	deui m̀ jyuh	deoi3 m4 zyu6	toei mh chyuh
sorry![2] /excuse me! /embarrassing/ashamed to	adj/v	唔好意思！	m̀ hóu yi si!	m4 hou2 ji3 si3!	mh hou yi si!
sorry![3] /if you please	adj	對不起	deui bāt héi	deoi3 bat1 hei2	toei pat hei
sorry for that	ph	為感到可惜	waih gám dou hó sīk	wai6 gam2 dou3 ho2 sik1	waih kam tou ho sek
sorry we missed you!		到訪不遇	dou fóng bāt yuh	dou3 fong2 bat1 jyu6	tou fong pat yuh
sort /manner	n	樣子	yeuhng jí	joeng6 zi2	yeuhng chi
soul[1] /mind/spirit	n	靈魂	lèhng /lìhng wàhn	leng4 /ling4 wan4	lehng wahn
soul[2] /spirit/mind	n	魂魄	wàhn paak	wan4 paak3	wahn phaak
sound[1] /voice/noise	n	聲	sèng /sìng	seng4 /sing4	seng
sound[2]	n	喧鬧	hyùn naauh	hyun4 naau6	hyun naauh
sound archive	n	音響資料館	yàm héung jì líu gún	jam4 hoeng2 zi4 liu2 gun2	yam heung chi liu gun
sound card	n	聲卡	sèing /sìng ká	seng4 /sing4 kaa2	seing kha
sound movement		聲運動	sèng wahn duhng	seng1 wan6 dung6	seng wahn tohng
sound of birds		鳥叫	líuh /níuh giu	liu5 /niu5 giu3	liuh /niuh kiu
sound of water pump /sex sounds	n/xy	噗唧噗唧	pok jēk bok jēk	pok3 zek1 pok3 zek1	phok chek phok chek
sound to call	n	咪	máih	mai5	maih
sound waves[1]		音波	yàm bō	jam4 bo1	yam po
sound waves[2]		聲浪	sèing /sìng lohng	seng4 /sing4 long6	seing lohng
sound waves[3]		聲波	sèng bo	seng4 bo1	seng po
soundless /lonely place	adj	無聲音	móuh sèing /sìng yàm	mou5 seng4 /sing4 jam4	mouh seing yam
sounds /tones	n	聲音	sèng yàm	seng4 jam4	seng yam
soup[1]	n	湯	tòng	tong4	thong
soup[2]	n	羹	gāng	gang1	kang
soup ladle	n	湯殼	tōng hok	tong1 hok3	thong hok
soupspoon[1]	n	湯羹	tōng gàng	tong1 gang4	thong kang
soupspoon[2]	n	匙羹	chìh gàng	ci4 gang4	chhih kang
source[1] /spring/origin	n	源	yùhn	jyun4	yuhn
source[2] /fountainhead	n	源頭	yùhn tàuh	jyun4 tau4	yuhn thauh
South	n	南	làahm /nàahm	laam4 /naam4	laahm /naahm
Southeast[1]	n	東南	dùng làahm /nàahm	dung4 laam4 /naam4	tung laahm /naahm
Southeast[2]	n	東南邊	dùng làahm/nàahm bihn	dung4 laam4 /naam4 bin6	tung laahm /naahm pihn
Southeast Asia	n	東南亞	dùng làahm/nàahm àa	dung4 laam4 /naam4 aa3	tung laahm /naahm aa
Southeastern	n	東南部	dùng làahm/nàahm bouh	dung4 laam4 /naam4 bou6	tung laahm /naahm pouh
Southern Asian	n	南亞人	làahm áa yàhn	laam4 aa2 jan4	laahm aa yahn
Southwest	n	西南	sài nàahm /làahm	sai4 laam4 /naam4	sai naahm /laahm
souvenir	n	紀念品	géi lihm /nihm bán	gei2 lim6 /nim6 ban2	kei lihm /nihm pan

soy milk	n	豆漿	dauh jèung /dzœng	dau6 zoeng4	tauh jeung
soya sauce[1] /sauce	n	豉油	sih yàuh	si6 jau4	sih yauh
soya sauce[2]	n	醬油	jèung yàuh	zoeng4 jau4	cheung yauh
soya sauce chicken[1]	n	油雞	yàuh gāi	jau4 gai1	yauh kai
soya sauce chicken[2]	n	豉油雞	sih yàuh gāi	si6 jau4 gai1	sih yauh kai
soya sauce chicken with rice	n	油雞飯	yàuh gāi faahn	jau4 gai1 faan6	yauh kai faahn
space[1] /sky	n	太空	taai hùng	taai3 hung4	thaai hung
space[2] /distance	v	距離	kéuih lèih	keoi5 lei4	khoih leih
space[3] /room	n	房地	fòng deih	fong4 dei6	fong teih
space shuttle[1] /space craft	n	太空梭	taai hùng sō	taai3 hung4 so1	thaai hung so
space shuttle[2]	n	太空穿梭機	taai hùng chyūn sōgēi	taai3 hung4 cyun1 so1 gei1	thaai hung chhyun so kei
space station	n	太空站	taai hùng jaahm	taai3 hung4 zaam6	thaai hung chaahm
spaceship	n	太空船	taai hùng syùhn	taai3 hung4 syun4	thaai hung syuhn
spade	n	鏟	cháan	caan2	chhaan
Spain	n	西班牙	sài bàan áa	sai4 baan4 aa2	sai paan aa
Spanish language	n	西班牙語	sài bàan áa yúh	sai4 baan4 aa2 jyu5	sai paan aa yuh
spare	n	騰出	tàhng chēut	tang4 ceot1	thahng chhot
spare part[1] (de)	n	士啤	sih bē	si6 be1	sih pe
spare part[2]	n	配件	pui gihn	pui3 gin6	phui kihn
spare part[3]	n	備用零件	beih yuhng lìhng gihn	bei6 jung6 ling6 gin6	peih yuhng lehng kihn
spare room	n	備用房間	beih yuhng fóng gàan	bei6 jung6 fong2 gaan4	peih yuhng fong kaan
spare time	n	空閑時	hùng hàahn sìh	hung4 haan4 si4	hung haahn sih
spare tire	n	備用胎	beih yuhng tōi	bei6 jung6 toi1	peih yuhng thoi
spark	n	火花	fó fā	fo2 faa1	fo fa
sparking /lightning	n	閃	sím	sim2	sim
sparrow	n	麻雀	màh jéuk	maa4 zoek2	mah cheuk
spasms /tightening of muscle	n	痙攣	gihng lyùhn	ging6 lyun4	kehng lyuhn
spatula[1]	n	壓舌板	áat sìht báan	aat2 sit6 baan2	aat siht paan
spatula[2] /cooking ladle	n	鑊鏟	wohk cháan	wok6 caan2	wohk chhaan
spawn[1]	n	魚子	yùh jí	jyu4 zi2	yuh chi
spawn[2]	n	魚春	yùh chēun	jyu4 ceon1	yuh chhon
speak[1] /spoken/to say	v	話	wá	waa2	wa
speak[2]	v	說話	syut wah	syut3 waa2	syut wah
speak angrily /scold	v	罵	mah	ma6	mah
speak fix		一言爲定	yāt yìhn wàih dehng /dihng	jat1 jing4 wai4 deng6 /ding6	yat yihn waih tehng
speak joke /talk banter	n	講笑	góng síu	gong2 siu2	kong siu
speak low voice /whisper/secret	n	細細聲講嘢	sai sai sèng góng yéh	sai3 sa3 seng4 gong2 je5	sai sai seng kong yeh

speak out		說出	syut chēut	syut3 ceot1	syut chhot
speak slow		講慢啲	góng maahn dì	gong2 maan6 di4	kong maahn ti
speaker[1]	n	喇叭	lā bā	laa1 baa1	la paa
speaker[2]	n	揚聲器	yèuhng sèng hei	joeng4 seng4 hei3	yeuhng seng hei
speaker[3]	n	演講嘅人	yín góng ge yàhn	jin2 gong2 ge3 jan4	yin kong ke yahn
speaker[4]/spokesperson /private orator	n	發言人	faat yìhn yàhn	faat3 jin4 jan4	faat yihn yahn
speaker[5] of legislative	n	議長	yíh jéung	ji5 zoeng2	yih cheung
speaking	n	講說話	góng syut wah	gong2 syut3 waa6	kong syut wah
special[1] /unique	n	特	dahk	dak6	tahk
special[2]/strange/unusual	adj	特別	dahk biht	dak6 bit6	tahk piht
special[3]	adj	專用	jyūn yuhng	zyun1 jung6	chyun yuhng
special offer	n	特價商品	dahk ga sèung bán	dak6 ga3 seung4 ban2	tahk ka seung pan
special price	n	特價	dahk gaa	dak6 gaa3	tahk kaa
specialist /specialized	n	專門	jyūn mún /mùhn	zyun1 mun2 /mun4	chyun mun /muhn
specialized	n	專業	jyùn yihp	zyun4 jip6	chyun yihp
specially /particular	adv	特別地	dahk biht deih	dak6 bit6 dei6	tahk piht teih
species /race	n	物種	maht júng	mat6 zung2	maht chung
specific	adj	特定	dahk dehng	dak6 deng6	tahk tehng
specify	v	具體說明	geuih tái syút mìhng	geoi6 tai2 syut2 ming4	kwoih thai syut mehng
speciology	n	物種學	maht júng hohk	mat6 zung2 hok6	maht chung hohk
spectator	n	旁觀	pòhng gùn	pong4 gun4	phohng kun
spectrum[1]	n	譜	póu	pou2	phou
spectrum[2]	n	光譜	gwòng póu	gwong4 pou2	kwong phou
speculate /would /wish/will/desire/want/plan /think/want to/would like to	aux/v	想	séung	soeng2	seung
speculative /risky investment/high risk investments/risk on financial markets	adj	投機	tàuh gèi	tau4 gei4	thauh kei
speech[1] /address	n	演說	yín syut	jin2 syut3	yin syut
speech[2]	n	言論	yìhn leun	jin4 leon3	yihn leun
speech[3]	n	致詞	ji chìn	zi3 cin4	chi chhin
speech marks ( )	n	一對引號	yāt deui yáhn houh	jat1 deoi3 jan5 hou6	yat toei yahn houh
speed[1] /quick	n	使速	sìh chūk	si4 cuk1	sih chhuk
speed[2] /rete	n	速率	chūk leuht	cuk1 leot6	chhuk lwoht
speed boat[1] /yacht	n	快艇	faai téhng	faai3 teng5	faai tehng
speed boat[2] /hovercraft /speed ship/air cushion	n	氣墊船	hei jin syùhn	hei3 zin3 syun4	hei chin syuhn
speed run	v	快行	faai hahng	faai3 hang6	faai hahng
speeding	n	開快車	hòi faai chè	hoi4 faai3 ce4	hoi faai chhe
speedometer	n	速度計	chūk dòuh gái	cuk4 dou6 gai2	chhuk touh kai
speedy	adj	好快	hóu faai	hou2 faai3	hou faai
spell period	n	工作時間	gùng jok sìh gaan	gung4 zik3 si4 gaan3	kung chok sih kaan
spell writing	v	拼寫	ping sé	ping3 se2	pheng se

speller	n	拼字嘅人	ping jih ge yàhn	ping3 zi6 ge3 jan4	pheng chih ke yahn
spelling	n	拼字	ping jih	ping3 zi6	pheng chih
spend money[1] /to use	v	使	sái	sai2	sai
spend money[2]	v	花錢	fā chín	faa1 cin2	fa chhin
spend time		花時間	fā sìh gaan	faa1 si4 gaan3	fa sih kaan
sphere[1] /ball-shaped	n	球形	kàuh yìhng	kau4 jing4	khauh yehng
sphere[2]	n	球體	kàuh tái	kau4 tai2	khauh thai
spices /flavoring/perfume	n	香料	hèung líu	hoeng4 liu2	heung liu
spider	n	蜘蛛	jì jyū	zi4 zyu1	chi chyu
spill[1] /fall/run out	v	瀉	sé	se2	se
spill[2]	v	倒瀉	dou sé	dou3 se2	tou se
spill[3]	v	使溢出	sai yaht chēut	sai3 jat6 ceot1	sai yaht chhot
spinal cord	n	脊髓	jek seúih	zek3 seoi5	chek swoih
spine[1] /vertebra	n	脊柱	jek chyúh	zek3 cyu5	chek chhyuh
spine[2] /vertebra	n	脊椎	jek jèui	zek3 zeoi4	chek cheui
spiral	n	盤旋	pun syùhn	pun3 syun4	phun syuhn
spire /top	n	尖頂	jīm déng	zim1 deng2	chim teng
spirit[1] /mind/thought	n	精神	jèng sàhn	zeng4 san4	cheng sahn
spirit[2] /sprite/elf	n	精靈	jèng lèhng, jìng lìhng	zeng4 leng4, zing4 ling4	cheng lehng
spirits /wine	n	燒酒	sìu jāu	siu4 zau1	siu chau
spiritual	adj	唯靈論	wàih lèhng leuhn	wai4 leng4/ling4	waih lehng leuhn
spiritual leader	n	唯靈論父	wàih lèhng leuhn fuh	wai4 leng4 leong6 fu6	waih lehng leuhn fu
spiritualism	n	唯靈論	wàih lèhng leuhn	wai4 leng4 leong6	waih lehng leuhn
spit[1] /to vomit/throw up	v	吐	tou	tou3	thou
spit[2]	v	吐痰	tou tàahm	tou3 taam4	thou thaahm
spitter[1]	n	吐口水嘅人	tou háu séui ge yàhn	tou3 hau2 seoi2 ge3 jan4	thou hau swoi ke yahn
spitter[2]	n	吐唾沫嘅人	tou teu mut ge yàhn	tou3 toe3 mut3 ge3 jan4	thou thea mut ke yahn
spitting image	n	一模一樣	yāt mòuh yāt yeuhng	jat1 mou4 jat1 joeng6	yat mouh yat yeuhng
spit /spittle/saliva	n	唾沫	teu mut	toe3 mut3	thea mut
spray /splash/sprinkle	n/v	濺	jīn	jin1	chin
splash /irrigation/watering	n/v	潑	put	put3	phut
spleen[1]	n	脾	pèih	pei4	pheih
spleen[2]	n	怒氣	louh /nouh héi	lou6 /nou6 hei2	louh /nouh hei
splendid clothes /toilette	n	盛裝	sìhng jòng	sing4 zong4	sehng chong
split[1] /tear open	v	裂開	lit hòi	lit3 hoi4	lit hoi
split[2] /tear	v	撕裂	si lit	si3 lit3	si lit
spoiled	v	壞	waaih	waai6	waaih
spoke[1] /speak	v	發言	faat yìhn	faat3 jin4	faat yihn
spoke[2] /thin bars	n	輪輻	lèuhn fūk	leon4 fuk1	leuhn fuhk
spoken[1]	adj	講話	góng wá	gong2 waa2	kong wa
spoken[2]	adj	語言	yúh yin	jyu5 jin3	yuh yin
spoken rude /cheeky /shameless/notorious	adj	厚臉皮	háuh líhm pèih	hau5 lim5 pei4	hauh lihm pheih

spokesman	n	代言人	doih yin yàhn	doi6 jin3 jan4	toih yin yahn
sponge[1] /rubbing	n	海綿	hói mìhn	hou2 min4	hoi mihn
sponge[2]	n	海綿塊	hói mìhn pài	hoi2 min4 pai4	hoi mihn phai
sponge[3] /sea animal	n	海綿動物	hói mìhn duhng maht	hoi2 min6 dung6 mat6	hoi mihn tohng maht
sponge cake	n	蛋糕	daahn gōu	daan6 gou1	taahn kou
sponsor /patron /supporter	n	贊助人	jaan joh yàhn	zaan3 zo6 jan4	chaan choh yahn
spontaneous /self motivated	adj	自發	jih fáat	zi6 faat2	chih faat
spool of thread /bobbin	n	線軸	sin juhk	sin3 zuk6	sin chuhk
spoon[1] (plastic's)	n	膠羹	gāau gāng	gaau1 gang1	kaau kang
spoon[2] (wooden's) /ladle	n	杓	cheuk	coek3	chheuk
spoon[3] (large) /scoop	n	拂	fāt	fat1	fat
spoonful	n	滿滿一匙	múhn múhn yāt chìh	mun5 mun5 jat1 ci4	muhn muhn yat chhih
sport	n	遊戲	yau héi	jau3 hei2	yau hei
sports	n	體育	tái yùhk	tai2 juk6	thai yuhk
sports shoes[1]	n	波鞋	bō hàaih	bo1 haai4	po haaih
sports shoes[2]	n	運動鞋	wahn duhng hàaih	wan6 dung6 haai4	wahn tohng haaih
spot[1] /trace/stain	n	蹟	jīk	sik1	chek
spot[2] /stain	v	沾污	jīm wù	zim1 wu4	chim wu
spot[3] /trace/stain	n	斑點	bàan dím	baan4 dim2	paan tim
spot check	n	抽查	chàu chàh	cau4 caa4	chhau chàh
spot light	n	聚光燈	jeuih gwòng dāng	zeoi6 gwong4 dang1	cheuih kwong tang
spot on	adj	完全正確	yùhn chyùhn jeng kok	jyun4 cyun4 zeng3 kok3	yuhn chhyuhn cheng khok
spouse /better-half /husband or wife	n	配偶	pui áuh	pui3 au5	phui auh
spout[1] /spray	n	噴	pan	pan3	phan
spout[2] /spray/puff out /spray by pipe	v	噴出	pan chèut	pan3 ceot4	phan chhot
spout[1] (of teapot)	n	茶壺嘴	chàh wùh jéui	caa4 wu6 zeoi2	chhah wuh choi
sprain	v	屈親	wāt chàn	wat1 can4	wat chhan
spray[1]	v	灑	sá	saa2	sa
spray[2]	v	噴霧	pan mouh	pan3 mou6	phan mouh
spray[3]	v	噴灑	pan sá	pan3 sa2	phan sa
sprayer /spray gun	n	噴霧器	pan mòuh hei	pan4 mou6 hei3	phan mouh hei
spread[1] /creeper	v	蔓	màahn	maan4	maahn
spread[2] /extend	v	蔓延	màahn yìhn	maan4 jin4	maahn yihn
spread[3] /transmitting disease	n	傳播	chyùhn bo	cyun4 bo3	chhyuhn po
spread disease /infect disease/infection/infective	n	傳染	chyùhn yihm	cyun4 jim5	chhyuhn yihm
spring[1] by metals /rubbers	n	彈簧	dáan wòhng	daan2 wong4	taan wohng
spring[2] jump	n	跳	tiu	tiu3	thiu
spring[3] fountain	n	泉	chyùhn	cyun4	chhyuhn

English		Chinese	Yale	Jyutping	Romanization
spring[4] source	n	源	yùhn	jyun4	yuhn
spring[5] fountain	n	噴泉	pan chyùhn	pan3 cyun4	phan chhyuhn
spring[6] seasons	n	春天	chēun tīn	ceon1 tin1	chhon thin
spring onion	n	蔥	chūng	cung1	chhung
spring roll	n	春卷	chēung gún	coeng1 gun2	chheung kun
spring up	v	湧出上	yúng chēut séuhng	jung2 ceot1 soeng5	yung chhot seuhng
springboard	n	跳板	tiu báan	tiu3 baan2	thiu paan
springide	n	潮漲	chìuh jeung	ciu4 zoeng3	chhiuh cheung
sprinkle	v	灑水	sá séui	saa2 seoi2	sa swoi
sprinkle inlet	n	花灑入水口	fā sá yahp séui háu	faa1 saa2 jap6 seoi2 hau2	fa sa yahp swoi hau
sprinkler can /watering can	n	噴水壺	pan séui wú	pan3 seoi2 wu2	phan swoi wu
sprite (drink)	n	雪碧	syut bīk, süt bik	syut3 bik1	syut pek
sprocket (of wheel)	n	扣鏈齒	kau lihn chí	kau3 lin6 ci2	khau lihn chhi
sprout[1] /new buds	v	發芽	faat ngàh	faat3 ngaa4	faat ngàh
sprout[2] /new buds	v	萌芽	màhng ngàh	mang4 ngaa4	mahng ngah
sprout child	n	年幼者	lìhn yau jé	lin4 jau3 ze2	lihn yau che
spy[1] /CID	n	間諜	gaan dihp	gaan3 dip6	kaan tihp
spy[2] /CID	n	奸細	gàan sai	gaan4 sai3	kaan sai
spying	n	密探	maht tāam	mat6 taam1	maht thaam
square[1]	n	方	fōng	fong1	fong
square[2]	n	四方	sei fōng	sei3 fong1	sei fong
square[3]	n	正方形	jeng fōng yìhng	zeng3 fong1 jing4	cheng fong yehng
square[4] /plaza	n	廣場	gwóng chèuhng	gwong2 coeng4	kwong chheuhng
square kilometer	n	平方公里	pèhng fōng gùng léih	peng4 fong1 gung4 lei5	phehng fong kung leih
square measure	n	平方積	pèhng fōng jīk	peng4 fong1 zik1	phehng fong chek
square obstacle	v	老古板	lóuh gú báan	lou5 gu2 baan2	louh ku paan
square root	n	平方根	pèhng fōng gān	peng4 fong1 gan1	phehng fong kan
squash[1]	v	把...壓扁	bāa aat /ngaat bín	baa1 aat3 /ngaat3 bin2	paa aat /ngaat pin
squash[2]	v	壓碎	aat seui	aat3 seui3	aat swoi
squash[3] (sport game)	v	壁球	bék kau	bek2 kau4	pek khau
squatting /to crouch	v	蹲	gyuhn	gyun6	kyuhn
squatting position /stoop down & squat	v	踎低	màu dài	mau4 dai4	mau tai
squeeze[1] /push against /crowded	v	擠	jài	zai4	chai
squeeze[2]	v	擠壓	jāi aat /ngaat	zai1 aat3 /ngaat3	chai aat /ngaat
squeeze[3]	v	擠出汁液	jài chēut jāp yihk	zai4 ceot1 zap1 jik6	chai chhot chap yehk
squeezer[1]	n	擠壓人	jāi aat yàhn	zai1 aat3 jan4	chai aat yahn
squeezer[2]	n	壓榨者	áat ja jé	aat2 za3 ze2	aat cha che
squeezer[3]	n	擠壓機器	jāi aat gèi hei	zai1 aat3 gei4 hei3	chai aat kei hei
squid dried	n	魷魚	yàuh yú	jau4 jyu2	yauh yu
squint[1] /look askance /cross eyed	v	斜眼	chèh ngáahn	ce4 ngaan5	chheh ngaahn

squint[2] /look in anger	v	斜著眼看	chèh jeuk ngáahn hòn	ce4 zoek3 ngaan5 hon4	chheh cheuk ngaahn hon
squint eyed	n	斜視	chèh sih	ce4 si6	chheh sih
squirrel /aquirrel	n	松鼠	chùhng syú	cung4 syu2	chhuhng syu
stabber[1]	n	刺人	chi yàhn	ci3 jan4	chhi yahn
stabber[2]	n	暗殺者	am /ngam saat jé	am3 /ngam3 saat3 ze2	am /ngam saat che
stabilizer	n	穩定者	wān dèhng jé	wan1 deng6 ze2	wan tehng che
stable[1] /immovable /stability	adj	穩定	wān dèhng	wan1 deng6	wan tehng
stable[2] /horse's shed	n	馬棚	máh pàahng	maa5 paang4	mah phaahng
stack /pile	n	疊成堆	dihp sèhng dēui	dip6 seng4 deoi1	tihp sehng toei
stadium[1] /sports ground	n	大球場	daaih kàuh chèuhng	daai6 kau4 coeng4	taaih khauh chheuhng
stadium[2]	n	運動場	wahn duhng chèuhng	wan6 dung6 coeng4	wahn tohng chheuhng
stadium[3]	n	體育場	tái yùhk chèuhng	tai2 juk6 coeng4	thai yuhk chheuhng
staff[1]	n	人員	yàhn yùhn	jan4 jyun4	yahn yuhn
staff[2] (personnel)	n	工作人員	gùng jok yàhn yùhn	gung4 zik3 jan4 jyun4	kung chok yahn yuhn
staff name	n	職員姓名	jīk yùhn sing méng /míng	zik1 jyun4 sing3 meng4 /ming4	chek yuhn seng meng
staff number	n	職員編號	jīk yùhn pīn houh	zik1 jyun4 pin1 hou6	chek yuhn phin houh
staff signature	n	職員簽名	jīk yùhn chìm méng	zik1 jyun4 cim4 meng2	chek yuhn chhim meng
stage[1] /platform	n	舞臺	móuh tòih	mou5 toi4	mouh thoih
stage[2] (of theatre)	n	舞臺劇	móuh tòih kehk	mou5 tou4 kek6	mouh thoih khehk
stage[3] (period of time)	n	階段	gàai dyuhn	paai4 dyun6	kaai tyuhn
stage of time[1] /period	n	期段	keih dyuhn	kei4 dyun6	kheih tyuhn
stage of time[2] /period /has been/period of time /limit of time	n	時期	sìh kèih	si4 kei4	sih kheih
stagger /lotter /steps unsteady/walk with unsteady	n	行路想跌咁	hàahng louh séung dit gám	haang4 lou6 soeng2 dit3 gam2	haahng louh seung tit kam
stumbling /walk unsteady	v	蹣跚	mùhn sāan	mun4 saan1	muhn saan
staggered /doubtful	adj	難以相信	làahn yíh séung séun	laan4 zi5 soeng2 seun2	laahn yih seung swon
stainless steel	n	不銹鋼	bāt sau gong	bat1 sau3 gong3	pat sau kong
stair[1] /step	n	梯級	tài kāp	tai4 kak1	thai khap
stair[2] /staircase/stairstep	n	樓梯	làuh tài	lau4 tai4	lauh thai
stake /betting	n	賭注	dóu jyu	dou2 zyu3	tou chyu
stake pillar	n	樁	jùng	zong4	chung
stalk[1] /stem	n	梗	gáng	gang2	kang
stalk[2] /hiding walk /secretly to go near	v	偷偷靠近	tàu tàu kaau gahn	tau4 tau4 kaau3 gan6	thau thau khaau kahn
stalk of grain	n	稭	haaih	haai6	haaih
stall[1] /sales counter	n	檔口	dong háu	dong3 hau2	tong hau
stall[2] /vendor's table	n	貨攤	fo tāan	fo3 taan1	fo thaan
stall[3] /shed/livestock	n	牲畜	sàang sàng	saang4 sang4	saang sang
stalling /stop engine	v	熄火	sìk fō	sik4 fo1	sek fo
stamina /endurance	n	耐力	loih /noih lihk	loi6 /noi6 lik6	loih /noih lehk

stamp[1] (de) /postage	n	士担	sih dāam	si6 daam1	sih taam
stamp[2] (of steel)	n	印鑑	yan gaam	jan3 gaam3	yan kaam
stamp[3] (of inked)	n	原子印	yùhn ji yan	jyun4 zi3 jan3	yuhn chi yan
stamp[4] (old stamp)	n	玉璽	yuhk sae	juk6 sae1	yuhk sae
stamp chop	n	郵政印	yàuh jing yan	jau4 zing3 jan3	yauh cheng yan
stamper	n	打印嘅人	dā yan ge yàhn	daa1 jan3 ge3 jan4	ta yan ke yahn
stand[1] /standing	adj/v	企	kéih	kei5	kheih
stand[2]	v	站	jaahm	zaam6	chaahm
stand[3]	v	企立	kéih lahp	kei5 lap6	kheih lahp
stand[4]	vi	座	joh	zo6	choh
stand by	v	準備待命	jéun beih doih mehng	zeon2 bei6 doi6 meng4	cheun peih toih mehng
stand in a long line	v	排長龍	pàaih chèuhng lùhng	paai4 coeng4 lung4	phaaih chheuhng luhng
stand still	v	站著不動	jaahm jeuk bāt duhng	zaam6 zoek3 bat1 dung6	chaahm cheuk pat tohng
stand up[1]	v	企起身	kéih héi sàn	kei5 hei2 san4	kheih hei san
stand up[2]	v	站立	jaahm lahp	zaam6 lap6	chaahm lahp
stand up[3]	v	起立	héi lahp	hei2 lap6	hei lahp
standard[1]	n	準	jéun	zeon2	cheun
standard[2] /class	n	水準	séui jéun	seoi2 zeon2	swoi cheon
standard[3] /level of achievement	n	水平	séui pìhng	seoi2 ping4	swoi phehng
standard[4]	n	平合規格	pèhng hahp kwāi gaak	peng4 hap6 kwai1 gaak3	phehng hahp khwai kaak
standard model	n	指定型號	jí dehng /dihng yìhng houh	zi2 deng6 /ding6 jing4 hou6	chi tehng yehng houh
standard time	n	標準時間	bīu jéun sìh gaan	biu1 zeon2 si4 gaan3	piu cheun sih kaan
standardization	n	標準化	bīu jéun fa	biu1 zeon2 fa3	piu cheun fa
Stander Chartered bank	n	渣打銀行	jā dá ngàhn hòhng	zaa1 daa2 ngan4 hong4	cha ta ngahn hohng
standing[1] (on the bus)	adj	企位	kéih wàih	kei5 wai4	kheih waih
standing[2]	adj	企喺	kéih hái	kei5 hai2	kheih hai
standing[3]	adj	常務	sèuhng mouh	soeng4 mou6	seuhng mouh
standing committee	n	常務委員會	sèuhng mouh wái yùhn wúi	soeng4 mou6 wai2 jyun4 wui2	seuhng mouh wai yuhn wui
staple /pin (to stitch)	n	訂書針	dehng syù jām	deng6 syu4 jam1	tehng syu cham
stapler	n	釘書機	dēng syù gèi	deng1 syu4 gei4	teng syu kei
star[1]	n	星	sèng	seng4	seng
star[2]	n	星球	sèng kàuh	seng4 kau4	seng khauh
star[3] /player star	n	明星	mìhng séng /sìng	ming4 seng4 /sing4	mehng seng
stare[1] /staring/gaze	v	凝視	yìhng sìh	jing4 si6	yehng sih
stare[2] /to gaze	v	注視	jyu sìh	zyu3 si6	chyu sih
stare[3]	v	望實	mohng saht	mong6 sat6	mohng saht
stare at	v	望住	mohng jyuh	mong6 zyu6	mohng chyuh
starfruit[1]	n	五斂子	ńgh lìhm jí	ng5 lim6 zi2	ngh lihm chi

starfruit[2]	n	楊桃	yèuhng tòuh	joeng4 tou4	yeuhng thouh
stark /stiff	adj	僵硬	gèung ngaahng	goeng4 ngaang6	keung ngaahng
start[1] /begin/commence /opening/initiation/initiate /getting start	adj/v	開始	hòi chí	hoi4 ci2	hoi chhi
start[2]	v	首先	sáu sìn	sau2 sin4	sau sin
start journey		起程	héi chìhng	hei2 cing4	hei chhehng
starter	n	開端	hòi dyùn	hoi4 dyun4	hoi tyun
starve	v	挨餓	àai /ngàai ngoh	aai4 /ngai4 ngo6	aai /ngaai ngoh
state[1] /explain	v	解釋	gáai sīk	gaai2 sik1	kaai sek
state[2] /situation	n	狀態	johng taai	zong6 taai3	chohng thaai
state[3] /province (USA)	n	州	jāu	zau1	chau
state[4] /territory/country's territory	n	國土	gwok tóu	gwok3 tou2	kwok thou
state of affairs /condition/situation	n	局勢	guhk sai	guk6 sai3	kuhk sai
state of emergency /emergency		緊急狀態	gán gāp johng taai	gan2 gap1 zong6 taai3	kan kap chohng thaai
state the reasons of detention		有罪入獄 即時嘅解 釋	yáuh jeuih yahp yuhk jīk sih ge gáai sìk	jau5 zeoi6 jap6 juk6 zik1 si4 ge3 gaai2 sik1	yauh cheuih yahp yuhk chek sih ke kaai sek
statement[1]	n	結單	git dāan	git3 daan1	kit taan
statement[2] /statement of witnesses	n	明確	mìhng kok	ming4 kok3	mehng khok
station /stop for buses	n	站	jaahm	zaam6	chaahm
stationery	n	文具	màhn geuih	man4 geoi6	mahn kwoi
stationery shop	n	文具店	màhn geuih dim	man4 geoi6 dim3	mahn kwoi tim
statistical	adj	統計	tūng gái	tung1 gai2	thung kai
statistician	n	統計學	tūng gái hòhk	tung1 gai2 hok6	thung kai hohk
statistics /data	n	統計資料	tūng gái jì líu	tung1 gai2 zi4 liu2	thung kai chi liu
statue /sculpture	n	雕像	dīu jeuhng	diu1 zoeng6	tiu cheuhng
statued /idol	n	以雕像表現	yíh dīu jeuhng bīu yìhn	ji5 diu1 zoeng6 biu1 jin6	yih tiu cheuhng piu yihn
statuette	n	小雕像	síu dīu jeuhng	siu2 diu1 zoeng6	siu tiu cheuhng
stature /figure	n	身材	sàn chòih	san4 coi4	san chhoih
status[1] /position	n	身份	sàn fán	san4 fan2	san fan
status[2] (of marital) /legal husband & wife/marriage	n	婚姻	fàn yàn	fan4 jan4	fan yan
statutory /fixed by law/legal	adj	法定	faat dehng	faat3 deng6	faat tehng
statutory holiday	adj	法定假	faat dehng /dìhng ga	faat3 deng6 /ding6 gaa3	faat tehng ka
stay	v	停留	tíhng làuh	ting5 lau4	thehng lauh
stay behind	v	仍留在原地	yìhng làuh joih yùhn deih	jing4 jyun4 lau4 zoi6 dei6	yehng lauh choih yuhn teih
stay hospital	n	留醫	làuh yì	lau4 ji3	lauh yi
stay late at night	v	熬夜	yiht yeh	jit6 je6	yiht yeh
stay weather	adj	持續天氣	chìh juhk tìn héi	ci4 zuk6 tin4 hei2	chhih chohk thin hei

stay with		同...住在一起	tùhng jyuh joih yāt héi	tung4 zyu6 zoi6 jat1 hei2	thuhng chyuh choih yat hei
steady[1]	adv	平穩	pèhng wān	peng4 wan1	phehng wan
steady[2]	adv	穩固的	wān gú dìk	wan1 gu2 dik4	wan ku tek
steak /beef steak	n	牛扒	ngàuh pá	ngau4 paa2	ngauh pha
steal	v	盜竊	dou sit	dou3 sit3	tou sit
steam[1]	n	蒸	jìng	zing4	cheng
steam[2]	v	蒸氣	jìng héi	zing4 hei2	cheng hei
steam water	n	水蒸汽	séui jīng hei	seoi2 zing1 hei3	swoi cheng hei
steamed-BBQ (pork bun)	n	叉燒包	chà sìu bàau	caa4 siu4 baau4	chha siu paau
steamed chicken[1]	n	白切雞	baahk chit gāi	baak6 cit3 gai1	paahk chit kai
steamed chicken[2] with rice	n	切雞飯	chit gāi faahn	cit3 gai1 faan6	chhit kai faahn
steamed fried rice	n	荷葉飯	ho yìhp fàahn	ho3 jip6 fan6	ho yihp faahn
steamed pork ball	n	燒賣	sìu màaih	siu4 maai6	siu maaih
steamer	n	蒸汽機	jìng hei gèi	zing4 hei3 gei4	cheng hei kei
steaming /stew	v	燉	dahn	dan6	tahn
steel	n	鋼	gong	gong3	kong
steel bar	n	鋼筋	gong gān	gong3 gan1	kong kan
steel wire	n	鋼線	gong sín	gong3 si2	kong sin
steep /soak /to steep	n	浸泡	jam póuh	zam3 pou5	cham phuh
steer[1] (of vehicle)	n	駕駛	ga sái	gaa3 sai2	ka sai
steer[2] (of vehicle)	n	操舵	chou tòh	cou3 to4	chhou thoh
steering lock		駕駛盤鎖	ga sái pun só	gaa3 sai2 pun3 so2	ka sai phun so
steering-wheel[1]	n	舦	táaih	taai5	thaaih
steering-wheel[2]	n	駕駛盤	ga sái pun	gaa3 sai2 pun3	ka sai phun
stem /stalk	n	莖	ging	ging3	keng
stems	n	橫枝	wàahng jī	waang4 zi1	waahng chi
stencil	n	印刷模板	yan chaat mòuh báan	jan3 caat3 mou4 baan2	yan chhaat mouh paan
step[1] /stroll/walk/pace	n	步	bòuh	bou6	pouh
step[2] /footstep	n	腳步	geuk bouh	goek3 bou6	keuk pouh
step[3]	n	階段	gàai dyuhn	gaai4 dyun6	kaai tyuhn
step aside		唔該借借	m̀ gòi je je	m4 goi4 ze3 ze3	mh koi che che
step by step[1]	n	速啲速啲	chūk dī chūk dī	cuk1 di1 cuk1 di1	chhuk ti chhuk ti
step by step[2]	n	一步步	yāt bouh bouh	jat1 bou6 bou6	yat pouh pouh
step by step[3]	n	一步一步	yāt bouh yāt bouh	jat1 bou6 jat1 bou6	yat pouh yat pouh
step by step[4]	n	分期	fàn kèih	fan4 kei4	fan kheih
step by step[5]	n	逐步地	juhk bouh dèih	zuk6 bou6 dei6	chuhk pouh teih
step by step expand	n	逐步擴大	juhk bouh kwong daaih	zuk6 bou6 kwong3 daai6	chuhk pouh khwong taaih
step down	v	傾倒	kìng dóu	king4 dou2	khing tou
step father[1] (coll)	n	後父	hauh fuh	hau6 fu6	hauh fuh
step father[2]	n	繼父	gai fuh	gai3 fu6	kai fuh
step mother[1] (coll)	n	後母	hauh móuh	hau6 mou5	hauh mouh
step mother[2]	n	繼母	gai móuh	gai3 mou5	kai mouh

English	POS	中文	Yale	Jyutping	Romanization
step's sound	n	腳步聲	geuk bouh sèng	goek3 bou6 seng4	keuk pouh seng
stepmother /second mother	n	細媽	sái mā	sai2 ma1	sai ma
stereo[1]	n	立體聲	lahp tái sèng /sìng	lap6 tai2 seng4 /sing4	lahp thai seng
stereo[2]	n	新力聲	sàn lihk sìng	san4 lik6 sing4	san lehk seng
stereo system	n	立體音響系統	lahp tái yām héung haih túng	lap6 tai2 jam1 hoeng2 hai6 tung2	lahp thai yam heung haih thung
sterilisation /stop of childbirth	n	絕育	jyuht yuhk	zyut3 juk6	chyuht yuhk
sterilization[1] /killing germs	n	殺菌	saat kwán	saat3 kwan2	saat khwan
sterilization[2] /sanitize /sterilize/killing germs	n/v	消毒	sìu duhk	siu4 duk6	siu tuhk
sterling	adj	優秀	yàu sau	jau4 sau3	yàu sau
stern[1] /solemn	adj	嚴肅	yìhm sūk	jim4 suk1	yihm suk
stern[2] /severe	adj	嚴厲	yìhm làih	jim4 lai6	yihm laih
sternly	adv	嚴厲地	yìhm làih deih	jim4 lai6 dei6	yihm laih teih
stew[1] /to evaporate	v	蒸	jìng	zing4	cheng
stew[2] /steaming	v	炆	mān	man1	man
stew[3] (coll) very anxious /anxious/anxiety	v	焦急	jìu gāp	ziu4 gap1	chiu kap
stewed	adj	燉嘅	dahn ge	dan6 ge3	than ke
walking stick /stick /rod	n	杖	jeuhng	zoeng6	cheuhng
stick[1] /walking stick	n	手杖	sáu jeuhng	sau2 zoeng6	sau cheuhng
stick[2] (of sports)	n	球棍	kàuh gwan	kau4 gwan3	khauh kwan
stick[3] /glue	v	黏貼	lim /nim típ	lim3 /nim3 tip2	lim /nim thip
stick by man /loyal to	adj	忠於	jùng yū	zung4 jyu1	chung yu
stick on	v	黏	lim /nim	lim3 /nim3	lim /nim
sticker	n	貼紙	tip jí	tip3 zi2	thip chi
sticker cloth on the body		貼身	tip sàn	tip3 san4	thip san
sticker glue	n	粘黏劑	lìhm lìhm jāi	lim4 lim4 zai1	lihm lihm chai
sticky	adj	黏糊的	lim /nim wùh dìk	lim3 /nim3 wu4 dik4	lim /nim wuh tik
sticky rice /dumplings	n	元宵	yùhn sīu	jyun4 siu1	yuhn siu
still[1] /yet	adv	仍	yìhng	jing4	yehng
still[2] /yet	adv	仍然	yìhng yìhn	jing4 jin4	yehng yihn
still[3] /yet	conj	但是	daahn sih	daan6 si6	taahn sih
still[4] /yet	adv	仍舊	yìhng gauh	jing4 gau6	yehng kauh
still not /not yet		尚未	seuhng meih	soeng6 mei6	seuhng meih
still not yet		仍未	yìhng meih	jing4 mei6	yehng meih
still remain		仍留	yìhng làuh	jing4 lau4	yehng lauh
still remaining	adj	仍舊	yìhng gauh	jing4 gau6	yehng kauh
still wet		重濕	chùhng sāp	cung4 sap1	chhuhng sap
sting /stung	v	螫	yìhng	jing4	yehng
sting irritation	v	使疼痛	sāi tung tung	sai1 tung3 tung3	sai thung thung
stingy	adj	小氣嘅	síu hei ge	siu2 hei3 ge3	siu hei ke

English		Chinese	Romanization	Jyutping	Yale
stink	v	有臭味	yáuh chau meih	jau5 cau3 mei6	yauh chhau meih
stir /to mix	v	攪嘢	gáau yéh	gaau2 je5	kaau yeh
stitch /sew/to sew	n	縫	fuhng	fung6	fuhng
stitch by needle	n	一針	yāt jām	jat1 jam1	yat cham
stitch cloths /sewing /tailoring	n	縫紉	fuhng yahn	fung4 jan6	fuhng yahn
stock[1] (of government)	n	存貨	chyùhn fo	cyun4 fo3	chhyuhn fo
stock[2] (of government)	n	政府債券	fong fú jaai gyun	fong3 fu2 zaai3 gyun3	fong fu chaai kyun
stock account	n	股帳	gú jeung	gu2 zoeng3	ku cheung
stock co /stock broker	n	股份公司	gú fán gūng sī	gu2 fan2 gung1 si1	ku fan kuhng si
stock certificate	n	股證券	gú jing gyun	gu2 zing3 gyun3	ku cheng kyun
stock market[1]	n	股市	gú síh	gu2 si5	ku sih
stock market[2]	n	股票市場	gú piu síh chèuhng	gu2 piu3 si5 coeng4	ku phiu sih cheuhng
stock market[3] /stock exchange	n	證券交易	jing gyun gàau yihk	zing3 gyun3 gaau4 jik6	cheng kyun kaau yehk
stockholder /partner	n	股東	gú dùng	gu2 dung4	ku tong
stocking	n	長襪	chèuhng maht	coeng4 mat6	chheuhng maht
stocks & shares	n	股份和股票	gú fán wòh gú piu	gu2 fan2 wo4 gu2 piu3	ku fan woh ku phiu
stole	n	偷咗	tàu jó	tau4 zo2	thau cho
stolen	v	擒咗	kàhm jó	kam4 zo2	khahm cho
stolen purse	v	擒咗銀包	kàhm jó ngán bàau	kam4 zo2 ngan2 baau4	khahm cho ngan paau
stomach[1] /tummy /inside stomach	n	胃	wàih	wai6	waih
stomach[2] /belly /abdomen lower part	n	腹	fùk	fuk4	fuk
stomach pain /colic/ belly-ache	n	腹痛	fùk tung	fuk4 tung3	fuk thung
stomach upset	n	反胃	fáan wàih	faan2 wai6	faan waih
stomachache[1]	n	肚痛	tóuh tung	tou5 tung3	thouh tung
stomachache[2] (inside)	n	胃痛	wàih tung	wai6 tung3	waih thung
stool[1] /small bench	n	櫈/凳仔	dang jái	dang3 zai2	tang chai
stool[2] /feces/shit /excrement	n	糞便	fan bihn	fan3 bin6	fan pihn
stoop /bend body	v	彎低身	wàan dài sàn	waan4 dai4 san4	waan tai san
stoop head /bend head	v	嗒低頭	dāp dài tàuh	dap1 dai4 tau4	tap tai thauh
stooped	adj	彎腰	wàan yīu	waan4 yiu1	waan yiu
stop[1] /halt/park (a car)	n	停	tíhng	ting5	thehng
stop[2] /then	n	已	yíh	ji5	yih
stop[3] (fire)	n	停低!	tìhng dāi	ting5 dai1	thehng tai
stop[4] /halt/cease/desist /close (business)	v	停止	tíhng jí	ting5 zi2	thehng chi
stop[5] (to talk)	v	住	jyuh	zyu6	chyuh
stop after		過在	gwo joih	gwo3 zoi6	kwo choih
stop by hand	adj	住手	jyuh sáu	jyu6 sau2	chyuh sau
stop job	adj	停職	tíhng jīk	ting5 zik1	thehng chek
stop payment		停止支付	tíhng jí jì fuh	ting5 zi2 zi4 fu6	thehng chi chi fuh

stop sleeping /wake up	v	醒來	séng làih	seng2 lai6	seng laih
stop suddenly		忽然停止	fāt yìhn tíhng jí	fat1 jin4 ting5 zi2	fat yihn tehng chi
stop talking		收聲	sàu sèng	sau4 seng4	sau seng
stoped /blocked	v	塞咗	sāk jó	sak1 zo2	sak cho
stoped urine		排尿阻滯	baaih liuh /niuh jó jaih	paai4 liu6 /niu6 zo2 zai6	paaih liuh /niuh cho chaih
storage[1]	n	收埋	sàu màaih	sau4 maai4	sau maaih
storage[2]	n	儲存	chyúh chyùhn	cyu5 cyun4	chhyuh chhyuhun
storage[3]	n	貯物	chyúh maht	cyu5 mat6	chhyuh maht
storage[4]	n	貯藏	chyúh chòhng	cyu5 cong4	chhyuh chhohng
store[1] /keep	v	蓄	chūk	cuk1	chhuk
store[2] /deposit/storage	v	貯存	chyúh chyhùn	cyu5 cyun4	chhyuh chhyuhun
store-room /warehouse	n	庫	fu	fu3	fu
store-keeper	n	倉庫管理員	chōng fu gùn léih yùhn	cong1 fu3 gun2 lei5 jyun4	chhong fu kun leih yuhn
store-place	n	儲藏	chyúh chòhng	cyu5 cong4	chhyuh chhohng
store-room[1]	n	藏室	chòhng sāt	cong4 sat1	chhohng sat
store-room[2]	n	士多房	sih dō fóng	si6 do1 fong2	sih to fong
store-room[3]	n	儲物室	chyúh maht sāt	cyu5 mat6 sat1	chhyuh maht sat
store-room[4]	n	儲藏室	chyúh chòhng sāt	cyu5 cong4 sat1	chhyuh chhohng sat
storm[1] /hurricane	n	大風雨	daaih fùng yúh	daai6 fung4 jyu5	taaih fung yuh
storm[2]	n	暴風雨	bouh fùng yúh	bou6 fung4 jyu5	pouh fung yuh
story[1] /storey/storeys /stories/floor	n	樓	láu	lau2	lau
story[2] / floor (US)	n	層樓	chàhng láu	cang4 lau2	chhahng lau
story[3] /tale	n	故事	gu sih	gu3 si6	ku sih
story[4] /tale	n	古仔	gú jái	gu2 zai2	ku chai
story again	v	再講	joi góng	zoi3 gong2	choi kong
stout	adj	結實嘅	git saht ge	git3 sat6 ge3	kit saht ke
stove	n	火爐	fó lòuh	fo2 lou4	fo louh
stove pipe	n	火爐嘅煙囱	fó lòuh ge yīn chēung	fo2 lou4 ge3 jin1 coeng1	fo louh ke yin chheung
stowage	n	裝貨處	jòng fo syu	zong4 fo3 syu3	chong fo syu
straddle[1]	v	跨立	kwa laahp	kwaa3 laap6	khwa laahp
straddle[2]	v	跨坐	kwa chóh	kwaa3 co5	khwa chhoh
straight[1] /direct/frank /upright/vertical/erect	adj	直	jihk	zik6	chehk
straight[2] /upright	adj	正	jeng	zeng3	cheng
straight[3] /ahead	adj	一直	yāt jihk	jat1 zik6	yat chehk
straight[4]	adj	筆直	bāt jìhk	bat1 zik6	pat chehk
straight[5] /direct/directly /first hand	adj	直接	jihk jip	zik6 zip3	chehk chip
straight[6]	adj	挺直嘅	tīng jìhk ge	ting1 zik6 ge3	thing chehk ke
straight hair		直髮	jihk faat	zik6 faat3	chehk faat
straight road[1]	n	捷徑	jit gíng	zit3 ging2	chit keng
straight road[2]	n	近路	káhn louh	kan5 lou6	khahn louh

straightening		使挺直	saī tīng jìhk	sai1 ting1 zik6	sai theng chehk
straightforward	adj	爽直	sóng jihk	song2 zik6	song chehk
strain[1] /pull	v	拉緊	làai gán	laai4 gan2	laai kan
strain[2]	v	竭力	kit lihk	kit3 lik6	khit lehk
strain[3]	v	竭力使用	kit lihk sí yuhng	kit3 lik6 si2 jung6	khit lehk si yuhng
strained	v	盡力	jeuhn lihk	zeon6 lik6	cheuhn lehk
strainer[1]	n	過濾	gwo louih	gwo3 leoi6	kwo lowih
strainer[2] (made by bamboo or plastic)	n	筲箕	sāau gei	saau1 gei3	saau kei
strainer[3] (of metal)	n	炸籬	ja lēi	zaa3 lei1	cha lei
strainer[4] /tea filter	n	茶隔	chàh gaak	caa4 gaak3	chhah kaak
strainer[5]	n	拉緊者	làai gán jé	laai4 gan2 ze2	laai kan che
strand[1]	n	子線	jí sin	zi2 sin3	chi sin
strand[2]	n	一股繩	yāt gú síng	jat1 gu2 sing2	yat ku seng
strange[1]	adj	陌生	mahk sàang	mak6 saang4	mahk saang
strange[2] /odd	adj	奇怪	kèih gwaai	kei4 gwaai3	kheih kwaai
strange[3]	adj	出奇	chēut kèih	ceot1 kei4	chhot kheih
strange[4]	adj	奇怪嘅	kèih gwaai ge	kei4 gwaai3 ge3	kheih kwaai ke
stranger[1] (coll)	n	生普人	sàang bóu yàhn	saang4 bou2 jan4	saang pou yahn
stranger[2]	n	陌生人	mahk sàng yàhn	mak6 sang4 jan4	mahk sang yahn
stranger[3]	n	門外漢	mùhn oih /ngoih hon	mun4 oi6 /ngoi6 hon3	muhn oih /ngoih hon
strap[1] /tape/ribbon	n	帶子	daai jí	daai3 zi2	taai chi
strap[2]	n	綁	bóng	bong2	pong
strategic[1] /strategy	adj	戰略	jin leuhk	zin3 loek6	chin leuhk
strategic[2] (in a war)	adj	戰略上	jin leuhk seuhng	zin3 loek6 soeng6	chin leuhk seuhng
straw[1] /grass	n	草	chóu	cou2	chhou
straw[2]	n	稻草	douh chóu	dou6 cou2	touh chhou
strawberry[1] (de)	n	士多啤梨	sìh dò bè lei	si6 do4 be4 lei3	sih toh pe lei
strawberry[2] (de)	n	士多啤厘	sìh dò bè lei	si6 do4 be4 lei3	sih toh pe lei
stream[1] /river	n	河	hòh	ho4	hoh
stream[2]	n	川流	chyùn làuh	cyun4 lau4	chhyun lauh
stream[3]	n	小河	síu hòh	siu2 ho4	siu hoh
stream[4]	n	峽谷	haahp gūk	haap6 guk1	haahp kuk
street[1]	n	街	gāai	gaai1	kaai
street[2]	n	街道	gāai douh	gaai1 dou6	kaai touh
street[3] /walk road	n	行路	hàahng louh	haang4 lou6	haahng louh
streetlight	n	路燈	louh dāng	lou6 dang1	louh tang
strength	n	力氣	lihk hei	lik6 hei3	lehk hei
strengthen	v	增強	jāng kèuhng	zang1 koeng4	chang kheuhng
stressed /worn out soul	adj	心力交瘁	sàm lihk gàau seuih	sam4 lik6 gaau4 seoi6	sam lehk kaau swoih
stretch	v	拉長	làai chèuhng	laai4 coeng4	laai chheuhng
stretcher	n	延伸器	yìhn sàn hei	jin2 san4 hei3	yihn san hei
strict[1]	adj	嚴	yìhm	jim4	yihm
strict[2]	adj	嚴密	yìhm maht	jim4 mat6	yihm maht

strict[3]	adj	嚴格	yìhm gaak	jim4 gaak3	yihm kaak
strictly	adv	嚴格地	yìhm gaak deih	jim4 gaak3 dei6	yihm kaak teih
strictly prohibit		嚴禁	yìhm gām	jim4 gam1	yihm kam
strike[1] /hit/shot	n	擊	gīk	gik1	kek
strike[2] /attack	v	攻擊	gùng gìk	gung4 gik4	kung kek
strike down	v	擊倒	gīk dóu	gik1 dau2	kek tou
striker	n	罷工者	bah gùng jé	baa6 gung4 ze2	pah kung che
string or thread (insert on the hole of needle)	v	紉	yahn	jan6	yahn
strip /take off/unload	v	拆卸	cháak sé	caak2 se2	chhaak se
stripe long narrow line	n	條紋	tíuh man	tiu5 man3	thiuh man
strive[1] /effort/attempt /exert	v	努	lóuh /nóuh	lou5 /nou5	louh /nouh
strive[2] /struggle	v	奮鬥	fáhn dau	fan5 dau3	fahn tau
stroke[1] /draw (line or character)	n	劃	waahk	waak6	waahk
stroke[2] /beat	n	敲打	hàau dá	haau4 daa2	haau ta
stroke[3] /all at once	n	一下子	yāt hah jí	jat4 haa6 zi2	yat hah chi
stroke[4] (clock sound)	n	鐘的	jùng dìk	zung4 dik4	chung tek
stroke gently[1] /touch gently/rub with gently/ handle fondly	v	摸摸	mó mō	mo2 mo2	mo mo
stroke gently[2]	v	輕撫	hèng fú	heng4 fu2	heng fu
stroke gently[3]	v	撫摸	fú mò	fu2 mo4	fu mo
stroke painting	n	繪畫嘅	kúi wá ge	kui2 wa2 ge3	khui wa ke
strokes of characters[1]	n	刷子	chaat jí	caat3 zi2	chhaat chi
strokes of characters[2]	n	筆劃	bāt waahk	bat1 waak6	pat waahk
stroking	n	一擊	yāt gīk	jat1 gik1	yat kek
stroking dick[(sl)] have sexual intercourse /sexual intercourse	v/xy	持續性交	chìh juhk sing gaau	ci4 zuk6 sing3 gaau3	chhih chohk seng kaau
strong[1] /powerful	adj	強	kèuhng	koeng4	kheuhng
strong[2] /powerful	adj	強壯	kèuhng jong	koeng4 zong3	kheuhng chong
strong[3] /powerful	adj	強健	kèuhng gihn	koeng4 gin6	kheuhng kihn
strong[4] (as of wine)	adj	酷	huhk	huk6	huhk
strong & healthy /hale	adj	健壯	gihn jong	gin6 zong3	kihn chong
strong box	n	保險櫃箱	bóu hím gwaih sèung	bou2 him2 gwai6 soeng4	pou him kwaih seung
strong desire (as a violently)	n	強烈	keuhng liht	koeng4 lit6	kheuhng liht
strong-hold[1] /strong built castle (political)	n	勢勢	sai sai	sai3 sai3	sai sai
strong-hold[2] /fortress	n	要塞	yìu sāk	jiu4 sak1	yiu sak
strong of emotions /impulse	v	衝動	chùng duhng	cung4 dung6	chhung tohng
strongly	adv	強有力地	keuhng yáuh lihk deih	koeng4 jau5 lik6 dei6	kheuhng yauh lehk teih

structure[1] /organization /institution	n	機構	gèi kau	gei4 kau3	kei khau
structure[2] /composition	n	結構	git kau	git3 kau3	kit khau
struggle[1]	v	掙扎	jàng jaat	zaang4 zaat3	chang chaat
struggle[2]	v	鬥爭	dau jàang	dau3 zaang4	tau chaang
struggler	n	奮鬥者	fáhn dau jé	fan5 dau3 ze2	fahn tau che
stubborn[1] /obstinate	adj	難對付	làahn deuifuh	laan4 deoi3 fu6	laahn toei fuh
stubborn[2](sl) /obstinate	adj	好難攪	hóu làahn /nàahn gáau	hou2 laan4 /naan4 gaau2	hou laahn /naahn kaau
stubborn[3]	adj	不聽話	bāt tèng wá	bat1 teng4 wa2	pat theng wa
stuck[1]	adj	黏貼	lim /nim típ	lim3 /nim3 tip2	lim /nim thip
stuck[2]	adj	陷住	hahm jyuh	ham6 zyu6	hahm chyuh
stud (head of nail)	n	大頭釘	daaih tàuh dèng	daai6 tau4 deng4	taaih thauh teng
student	n	學生	hohk sāang	hok6 saang1	hohk saang
student foreign country	n	留學生	làuh hohk sāang	lau4 hok6 saang1	lauh hohk saang
studio /workshop	n	工作室	gùng jok sāt	gung4 zik3 sat1	kung chok sat
study[1]	n	念	lìhm /nìhm	lim6 /nim6	lihm /nihm
study[2]	v	學習	hohk jaahp	hok6 zaap6	hohk jaahp
study[3] /attend school /to study/to read a book	v	讀書	duhk syù	duk6 syu4	tuhk syu
study hall	n	自修教室	jih sāu gaau sāt	zi6 sau1 gaau3 sat1	chih sau kaau sat
study room	n	書房	syù fóng	syu4 fong2	syu fong
stuff /thing	n	東西	dùng sāi	dung4 sai1	tung sai
stuffy[1] /sultry/hot & stuffy	adj	悶熱	mùhn yiht	mun6 jit6	muhn yiht
stuffy[2] /sultry	adj	翳焗	ai /ngai guhk	ai3 /ngai3 guk6	ai /ngai kuhk
stuffy[3] /old fashioned	adj	古板	gú báan	gu2 baan2	ku paan
stumble[1]	v	綑低	kwaan dài	kwan2 dai4	khwaan tai
stumble[2]	v	絆倒	buhn dóu	bun6 dou2	puhn tou
stumbled	v	絆腳	buhn geuk	bun6 goek3	puhn keuk
stumbled leg	v	俾絆腳	bei buhn geuk	bei2 bun6 goek3	pei puhn keuk
stupid[1] /foolish	adj	笨	bàhn	ban4	pahn
stupid[2]	adj	拙	jyuht	zyut6	chyuht
stupid[3] /unwise	adj	愚笨	yu bàhn	jyu3 ban6	yu pahn
stupid[4]	adj	傻瓜	sòh gwā	so4 gwaa1	soh kwa
stupid[5] /silly/slow-mind /inactive mind	adj	糊塗	wùh tòuh	wu4 tou4	wuh thouh
stupid man	n	麻甩佬	màh lāt lóu	ma4 lat1 lou2	mah lat lou
stupid person	n	蠢人	chéun yàhn	ceon2 jan4	chhon yahn
stupid woman	n	八婆	baat pòh	baat3 pon4	paat pòh
style[1] /character	n	格	gaak	gaak3	kaak
style[2]	n	格式	gaak sīk	gaak3 sik1	kaak sek
style[3]	n	作風	jok fùng	zok3 fung4	chok fung
style bearing	n	風度	fùng douh	fung3 dou6	fung touh

style fashion	n	風格時尚	fùng gaak sìh seuhng	fung4 gaak3 si4 soeng6	fung kaak sih seuhng
style writing	n	文體	màhn tái	man4 tai2	mahn thai
stylish /in style/modern /fashionable	adj	時髦	sìh mōu	si4 mou1	sih mou
stylish[1]	adj	時款	sìh fún	si4 fun2	sih sìh fún
stylish[2]	adj	時興	sìh hìng	si4 hing4	sih heng
subdivision of the city /urban subdivision	n	坊	fòng	fong4	fong
subdue	v	征服	jìng fuhk	zing4 fuk6	cheng fuhk
subscribe	v	捐贈	gyùn jahng	gyun4 zang6	kyun chahng
subject[1] /target/aim /purpose	n	目的	muhk dìk	muk6 dik4	muhk tek
subject[2] /of study	n	科	fò	fo4	fo
subject[3] /topic of talk	n	話題	wah tàih	waa6 tai4	wah thaih
subject[4] /theme	n	主題	jyú tàih	zyu2 tai4	chyu thaih
subject matter	n	題材	tai chòih	tai3 coi4	thai chhoih
subjected to /that is /with regard to		就	jauh	zau6	chauh
submarine	n	潛艇	chìhm téhng	cim4 teng5	chhihm thehng
submerge	v	潛入水中	chìhm yahp séui jùng	cim4 jap6 seoi2 zung4	chhihm yahp swoi chung
submission /obey	v	服從	fuhk chùhng	fuk6 cung4	fuhk chhuhng
subordinate	adj	使隸屬	sai daih suhk	sai3 dai6 suk6	sai taih suhk
subscribe[1]	v	認捐	yihng gyùn	jing6 gyun4	yehng kyun
subscribe[2] /contribute /donate	n	捐獻	gyún hin	gyun2 hin3	kyun hin
subscribe offer /contribute	v	捐助	gyūn joh	gyun1 zo6	kyun choh
subscriber[1]	n	捐助者	gyun joh jé	gyun1 zo6 ze2	kyun choh che
subscriber[2]	n	訂購者	dehng /dihng kau jé	deng6 /ding6 kau3 ze2	tehng khau che
subscriber[3]	n	簽名人	chìm méng yàhn	cim4 meng2 jan4	chhim meng yahn
subscriber[4]	n	訂閱人	dehng /dihng yuht yàhn	deng6 /ding6 jyut6 jan4	tehng yuht yahn
subsequence[1]	n	子序列	ji jeuih liht	zi3 zeoi6 lit6	chi cheuih liht
subsequence[2]		後來發生的事	hauh lòih faat sàng ge sih	hau6 loi4 faat3 sang4 ge3 si6	hauh lòih faat sàng ge sih
subsequent[1]	adj	後來	hauh lòih	hau6 loi4	hauh loih
subsequent[2]	adj	後來嘅	hàuh lái ge	hau6 lai2 ge3	hauh lai ke
subsequently[1] /then	adv	之後	jì hàuh	zi4 hau6	chi hauh
subsequently[2] /then	adv	後來	hàuh lòih	hau6 loi4	hauh loih
subsequently[3] /then	adv	跟住嚟	gàn jyuh lái	gan4 zyu6 lai2	kan chyuh lai
subsides[1]	v	平息	pèhng sìk	peng5 sik4	phehng sek
subsides[2]	v	消退	sìu téui	siu4 teoi2	siu thoi
substation /transformer station	n	變電站	bin dìhn jaahm	bin3 din6 zaam6	pin tihn chaahm
substitute person	n	代替人	doih tai yàhn	doi6 tai3 jan4	toih thai yahn

subtilty	n	狡詐	gáau gai	gaau2 gai3	kaau kai
subtraction	v	減法	gáam faat	gaan2 faat3	kaam faat
suburb /suburbia	n	近郊	gàhn gàau	gan6 gaau1	kahn kaau
suburban district	n	郊區	gàau kèui	gaau1 keoi1	kaau khoi
subversion	n	覆滅	fùk miht	fuk4 mit6	fuk miht
subway[1]	n	地鐵	dèih tit	dei6 tit3	teih thit
subway[2]	n	地下鐵道	deih há tit douh	dei6 haa5 tit3 dou6	teih ha thit touh
success /succeed	v	成功	sèhng gùng	seng4 gung4	sehng kung
successfully	adv	成功地	sèhng gùng deih	seng4 gung4 dei6	sehng kung teih
successively[1] /in turn	adv	一連	yāt lìhn	jat1 lin4	yat lihn
successively[2]	adv	連氣	lìhn hei	lin4 hei3	lihn hei
successor	n	繼任者	gai yahm jé	gai3 jam6 ze2	kai yahm che
succinct /concise	adj	簡潔	gáan git	gaan2 git3	kaan kit
such[1] /than/well!	pron	咁 / 噉	gam	gam3	kam
such[2]	pron	此類的	chí leuih dìk	ci2 leoi6 dik4	chhi lowih tek
such as[1] /such action	pron	這樣	je yeuhng	ze3 joeng6	che yeuhng
such as[2]	pron	好似	hóu chíh	hou2 ci5	hou chhih
such as[3]	pron	譬如	pei yùh	pei3 jyu4	phei yuh
suck[1] (by mouth)	v	啜入	jyut yahp	zyut3 jap6	chyut yahp
suck[2] (milk)	v	啜奶	jyut láaih /náaih	zyut3 laai5 /naai5	chyut laaih /naaih
suck[3]	n	吸吮	kāp syúhn	kap1 syun5	khap syuhn
sucker[1] /baby	n	食奶	sihk láaih /náaih	sik6 laai5 /naai5	sehk laaih /naaih
sucker[2] /baby	n	食奶嘅嬰兒	sihk láaih/náaih ge yīng yìh	sik6 laai5 /naai5 ge3 jing4 ji4	sehk laaih /naaih ke ying yih
sucker[3] /baby	n	食奶嘅啤啤	sihk láaih/náaih ge bìh bī	sik6 laai5 /naai5 ge3 be4 bi1	sehk laaih /naaih ke pih pi
sucker[4] (sl)	n	老襯	louh chan	lou6 can6	louh chhan
sucker person	n	吮吸者	syúhn kāp jé	syun5 kap1 ze2	syuhn khap che
sucker pipe	n	吸管	kāp gún	kap1 gun2	khap kun
sucking[1]	n	吸吮	kāp syúhn	kap1 syun5	khap syuhn
sucking[2] /breast-feeding	n	授乳	sauh yúh	sau6 jyu5	sauh yuh
sudden /suddenly	adj	忽然	fāt yìhn	fat1 jin4	fat yihn
sudden anger	n	突然發怒者	daht yìhn faat louh /nouh jé	dat6 jin4 faat3 lou6 /nou6 ze2	taht yihn faat louh /nouh che
sudden fall down	n	突然發作	daht yìhn faat jok	dat6 jin4 faat3 zok3	taht yihn faat chok
sudden push	n	一推	yāt tèui	jat1 teoi4	yat thoi
sudden speak out		突然說出	daht yìhn syut chēut	dat6 jin4 syut3 ceot1	taht yihn syut chhot
suddenly[1]	adv	突	daht	dat6	taht
suddenly[2] /unexpected /all at once	adv	突然	daht yìhn	dat6 jin4	taht yihn
suddenly[3]	adv	乍	ja	zaa3	cha
suddenly[4]	adv	忽然間	fāt yìhn gāan	fat jin4 gaan1	fat yihn kaan
suddenly die /abruptly die/unexpected die	adj	猝死	shyut séi	syut6 sei2	shyut sei
suddenly threaten		突然發惡	daht yìhn faat ngok	dat6 jin4 faat3 ngok3	taht yihn faat ngok

suffer[1]	v	遭受	jōu sauh	zou1 sau6	chou sauh
suffer[2] (by hardship)	v	受苦	sauh fú	sau6 fu2	sauh fu
sufferer	n	受害者	sauh hoih jé	sau6 hoi6 ze2	sauh hoih che
suffering[1]	n	難受	làhn /nàhn sáu	laan4 /naan6 sau2	lahn /nahn sau
suffering[2] /pitiable /tribulation	n/adj	苦難	fú laahn /naahn	fu2 laan6 /naan6	fu laahn /naahn
sufficiency	n	充分	chùng fàn	cung4 fan4	chhung fan
suffix of noun for "...ist/...er/...ary/...ian" specialist /professionalist	n	家	gā	gaa1	ka
sugar cane[1]	n	蔗	je	ze3	che
sugar cane[2]	n	甘蔗	gām je	gam1 ze3	kam che
sugar is converted into alcohol (fermentation)		發酵	faat hàau	faat3 haau4	faat haau
suggestion /proposal	n	提議	tàih yíh	tai4 ji5	thaih yih
suit[1] /western suit	n	西裝	sài jòhng	sai4 zong4	sai chohng
suit[2] (lawsuit)	n	起訴	héi sou	hei2 sou3	hei sou
suit agree	v	適合	sīk hahp	sik1 hap6	sek hahp
suitable	adj	啱	āam /ngāam	aam1 /ngaam1	aam /ngaam
suitcase[1]	n	皮喼	pèih gīp	pei4 gep1/gip1	pheih kip
suitcase[2]	n	手提箱	sáu tàih sèung	sau2 tai4 soeng4	sau thaih seung
sulphur	n	硫磺	làuh wòhng	lau4 wong4	lauh wohng
summary[1]	adj	摘要	jaahk yiu	zaak6 jiu3	chaahk yiu
summary[2]	adj	扼要	āk yiu	ak1 yiu3	ak yiu
summer season[1]	n	夏天	hah tìn	haa6 tin4	hah thin
summer season[2]	n	熱天	yiht tìn	jit6 tin4	yiht tin
summer shoes	n	涼鞋	lèung hàaih	loeng4 haai4	lèung hàaih
summit	n	頂峰	déng fùng	deng2 fung2	teng fung
summon (to appear in a court)	v	傳喚	chyùhn wuhn	cyun4 wun6	chhyuhn wuhn
sump (waste oil collects pot)	n	機油箱	gèi yàhu sèung	gei4 jau4 soeng4	kei yahu seung
sun	n	太陽	taai yèuhng	taai3 joeng4	thaai yeuhng
sun bathing[1]	v	曬太陽	saai taai yèuhng	saai3 taai3 joeng4	saai thaai yeuhng
sun bathing[2]	v	日光浴	yaht gwōng yuhk	jat6 gwong1 juk6	yaht kwong yuhk
sun block	n	防曬乳	fòhng saai yúh	fong4 saai3 jyu5	fohng saai yuh
sun glasses	n	太陽眼鏡	taai yèuhng ngáahn géng	taai3 joeng4 ngaan5 geng2	thaai yeuhng ngaahn keng
sun protection	n	防曬	fòhng saai	fong4 saai3	fohng saai
sunburn	n	曬紅皮膚	saai hùhng pèih fū	saai3 hung4 pei4 fu1	saai huhng pheih fu
Sunday[1]	n	禮拜日	láih baai yaht	lai5 baai3 jat6	laih paai yaht
Sunday[2]	n	星期日	sèing /sìng kèih yaht	seng4 /sing4 kei4 jat6	seng kheih yaht
sunday school[1]	n	主日學	jyú yaht hohk	zyu2 jat6 hok6	chyu yaht hohk
sunday school[2]	n	主日學校	jyú yaht hohk háau	zyu2 jat6 hok6 haau2	chyu yaht hohk haau
sundown	n	日落	yaht lohk	jat6 lok6	yaht lohk
sunflower	n	向日葵	heung yàht kwaih	hoeng3 jat6 kwai4	heung yaht khwaih

sunkist [de]	n	新奇士	sān kēi sih	san1 kei1 si6	san khei sih
sunny	adj	陽光充足	yeung gwòng chùng jūk	joeng3 gwong4 cung4 zuk1	yeung kwong chhung chuk
sunproof		不透日光	bāt tau yaht gwong	bat1 tau3 jat6 gwong1	pat thau yaht kwong
sunrise	n	日出	yaht chēut	jat6 ceot1	yaht chhot
sunset	n	日落西山	yaht lohk sài sàan	jat6 lok6 sai4 saan4	yaht lohk sai saan
sunshine[1]	n	陽光	yèuhng gwòng	joeng4 gwong4	yeuhng kwong
sunshine[2] (fine of weather)		晴天	chìhng tìn	ceng4/cing4 tin4	chhehng thin
sunny & cloudless /sunshine/fine day of weather	n	晴朗	chèhng /chìhng lóhng	ceng4 /cing4 long5	chhehng lohng
super great & mighty		超偉大	chīu wáih daaih	ciu1 wai5 daai6	chhiu waih taaih
supermarket /super store	n	超級市場	chìu kāp síh chèuhng	ciu4 kap1 si5 coeng4	chhiu khap sih cheuhng
supercharged	adj	提高功率	tàih gòu gùng leuht	tai4 gou4 gung4 leot6	thaih kou kung leuht
superficially	adv	淺薄地	chín bohk deih	cin2 bok6 dei6	chhin pohk teih
superfluous[1] /more then is needed or wanted	adj	多餘	dò yùh	do4 jyu4	to yuh
superfluous[2]	adj	多餘嘅	dò yùh ge	do4 jyu4 ge3	to yuh ke
superintendent of government	n	機關主管	gēi gwāan jyú gún	gei1 gwaan1 zyu2 gun2	kei kwaan chyu kun
superior /excellent /very good	adj	優	yàu	jau4	yau
superior head /boss	n	上司	séuhng sī	soeng5 si1	seuhng si
superior post	n	上級的	seuhng kāp dīk	soeng6 kap1 dik1	seuhng khap tik
superlative	adj	最好嘅	jeui hóu ge	zeoi3 hou2 ge3	cheui hou ke
superman	n	超人	chīu yàhn	ciu1 jan4	chhiu yàhn
supervise /supervision	v	管理	gún léih	gun2 lei5	kun leih
supervision /inspect /superintend	v	監督	gàam dūk	gaam4 duk1	kaam tuk
supervisor[1] /oversight /watch over	n	監督	gàam dūk	gaam4 duk1	kaam tuk
supervisor[2] (de) (sl)	n	掃把	sou bá	sou3 baa2	sou pa
supplementary reading	n	補充讀物	bóu chūng duhk maht	bou2 cung1 duk6 mat6	pou chhung tuhk maht
supplication	n	祈求	kèih kàuh	kei4 kau4	kheih khauh
supplier	n	供應商	gùng ying sèung	gung4 jing3 soeng4	kung ying seung
supply	v	供應	gùng ying	gung4 jing3	kung ying
support[1] /lean on/trust	v	靠	kaau	kaau3	khaau
support[2] (by pole)	v	撐	chāang	caang1	chhaang
support[3] (by hands)	v	扶	fùh	fu4	fuh
support[4] (by raise)	v	支	jì	zi4	chi
support[5] /assist	v	支援	jì wùhn	zi4 wun4	chi wuhn
support[6] /help	n	依靠	yì kaau	ji4 kaau3	yi khaau
support[7] /help	v	證實	jing saht	zing3 sat6	cheng saht
support[8] /look after /to help living	n	關照	gwāan jiu	gwaan1 ziu3	kwaan chiu

support[9] /bring up	n	扶養	fùh yéuhng	fu4 joeng5	fuh yeuhng
raised by hand	v	支托	jì tok	zi4 tok3	chi thok
support group	n	互相小組	wuh sèung síu jóu	wu6 soeng4 siu2 zou2	wuh seung siu chou
supportable	adj	可支持	hó jī chìh	ho2 zi1 ci4	ho chi chhih
suppose[1] /think	v	以為	yíh wàih	ji5 wai6	yih waih
suppose[2]	v	猜想	chàai séung	caai4 soeng2	chhaai seung
suppress /vice by rule	v	鉗制	kìm jai	kim4 zai3	khim chai
supreme	adj	最高	jeui gou	zeoi3 gou3	cheui kou
surcharge[1]	n	罰款	faht fún	fat6 fun2	faht fun
surcharge[2] /to overload	n	超載	chìu joi	ciu4 zoi3	chhiu choi
surcharge[3]	n	額外附加費	aahk /ngaahk òih fuh gā fai	aak6 /ngaak6 oi6 fu6 gaa1 fai3	aahk /ngaahk oih fuh ka fai
sure	adj	把握	bá āak /ngāak	baa2 aak1 /ngaak1	pa aak /ngaak
surely /guarantee	adv	保證	bóu jing	bou2 zing3	pou cheng
surely great & mighty		梗偉大	gáng wáih daaih	gang2 wai5 daai6	kang waih taaih
surf[1] /sea wave	n	海浪	hói lohng	hoi2 long6	hoi lohng
surf[2] (run on the sea wave by plank)	n	衝浪	chùng lòhng	cung4 long4	chhung lòhng
surface[1] /flat/top	n	面	mihn	min6	mihn
surface[2] /top level	n	表面	bíu mín	bi2 min2	piu min
surgeon (operation out part of the body)	n	外科醫生	oih /ngoih fō yī sāng	oi6 /ngoi6 fo1 ji1 sang1	oih /ngoih fo yi sang
surgery[1] /surgical operation	n	手術	sáu seuht	sau2 seot6	sau swoht
surgery[2] /surgical dept	n	外科	oih /ngoih fō	oi6 /ngoi6 fo1	oih /ngoih fo
surgical instruments	n	手術器具	sáu seuht hei geuih	sau2 seot6 hei3 geoi6	sau swoht hei kwoih
surgical operation		外科嘅	oih /ngoih fō ge	oi6 /ngoi6 fo1 ge3	oih /ngoih fo ke
surgical patient	n	外科病人	oih /ngoih fò bèhng yan	oi6 /ngoi6 fo4 beng6 jan3	oih /ngoih fo pehng yan
surprise[1] /wow	exlm	哇	wā	wa1	wa
surprise[2]	exlm	呀	àa	aa4	aa
surprise[3] /scared	v	使吃驚	sái hek gèng	sai2 hek3 geng1	sai hek keng
surprise suddenly /startle	v	使到驚嚇	sí dou geng haak	si2 dou3 geng3 haak3	si tou keng haak
surprised	adj	出人意外	chēut yàhn yi òih /ngoih	ceot1 jan4 ji3 oi6 /ngoi6	chhot yahn yi oih /ngoih
surpriser	n	令人	ling yàhn	ling3 jan4	ling yàhn
surprising	adj	驚人	gèng yàhn	geng4 jan4	keng yahn
surrender (with police)	v	自首	jih sáu	zi6 sau2	chih sau
surrender (with enemy)	v	投降	tàuh hòhng	tau4 hong4	thauh hohng
surround	v	圍繞	wàih yuh	wai4 jiu3	waih yuh
surrounded by land	adj	內陸	loih /noih luhk	loi6 /noi6 luk6	loih /noih luhk
surrounding /around	adj	周圍	jàu wàih	zau4 wai4	chau waih
surroundings[1]	adj	環境	wàahn gíng	waan4 ging2	waahn keng
surroundings[2]	n	四周圍	sei jāu wàih	sei3 zau1 wai4	sei chau waih
survey[1]	v	俯視	fú sih	fu2 si6	fu sih

survey[2]	v	分析問卷	fàn sīk mahn gyun	fan4 sik1 man6 gyun3	fan sek mahn kyun
surveyor	n	測量員	chàak lèuhng yùhn	caak4 loeng4 jyun4	chhaak leuhng yuhn
survive	v	生還	sàng wàahn	sang4 waan4	sang waahn
survived	v	仍然生存	yìhng yìhn sàng chyùhn	jing4 jin4 sang4 cyun4	yehng yihn sang chhyuhn
survivor	n	倖存者	hahng chyùhn jé	hang6 cyun4 ze2	hahng chhyuhn che
susceptible /impressible	adj	易受影響	yìh sàuh yēng héung	ji6 sau6 jeng1 hoeng2	yih sauh yeng heung
suspect[1]	v	嫌疑犯	yim yi fàahn	jim4 ji3 faan6	yim yi faahn
suspect[2]	v	嫌疑	yìhm yìh	jim4 ji4	yihm yih
suspect man	n	疑人	yìh yàhn	ji4 jan4	yih yahn
suspect person	n	嫌疑人	yìhm yìh yàhn	jim4 ji4 jan4	yihm yih yahn
suspender thing	n	懸掛物	yùhn kwa maht	jyun4 kwaa3 mat6	yuhn khwa maht
suspension[1] /terminate	n/v	中止	jūng jí	zung1 zi2	chung chi
suspension[2]	n	懸掛	yùhn kwa	jyun4 kwaa3	yuhn khwa
suspension[3] (from job)	n	停職	tíhng jīk	ting5 zik1	thehng chek
suspension[4] (from school)	n	停學	tíhng hohk	ting5 hok6	thehng hohk
suspicious	adj	猜疑	chàai yìh	caai4 ji4	chhaai yih
suspicious persons	n	可疑人物	hó yi yan màht	ho2 ji3 jan3 mat6	ho yi yan maht
swallow[1]	v	吞	tàn	tan4	than
swallow[2]	v	嚥	yin	jin3	yin
swallow[3]	v	吞下	tàn hah	tan4 haa6	than hah
swallow[4] /small bird	n	燕子	yin jí	jin3 zi2	yin chi
swamp	n	倖水浸咗	béi séui jam jó	bei2 seoi2 zam3 zo2	pei swoi cham cho
swear (an oath)	v	誓願	saih yuhn	sai6 jyun6	saih yuhn
sweat	n	汗水	hohn séui	hon6 seoi2	hohn swoi
sweater[1]	n	冷衫	lāang sāam	laang1 saam1	laang saam
sweater[2] (of wool)	n	毛衣	mòuh yī	mou4 ji1	mouh yi
Sweden	n	瑞典	sèoih dīn	seoi6 din1	swoih tin
sweep /brush	v	掃	sou	sou3	sou
sweep card	v	打咔啦	dā ka la	daa1 kaa3 laa3	ta kha la
sweep floor	v	掃地	sou deih	sou3 dei6	sou teih
sweeper (de)	n	掃把	sou bá	sou3 baa2	sou pa
sweet[1]	adj	甜	tìhm	tim4	thihm
sweet[2]	adj	甜的	tìhm dìk	tim4 dik4	thihm tek
sweet herb tea	n	五花茶	ńgh fa chàh	ng5 faa3 caa4	ngh fa chhah
sweet speaking[1]	n	口材好	háu chòih hóu	hau2 coi4 hou2	hau chhoih hou
sweet speaking[2]	n	口甜舌滑	háu tìhm sit waaht	hau2 tim4 sit3 waat6	hau thihm sit waaht
sweetly	adv	甜蜜地	tìhm maht deih	tim4 dei6 mat6	thihm maht teih
sweetmeat[1]	n	糖果	tòhng gwó	tong4 gwo2	thohng kwo
sweetmeat[2]	n	蜜餞	maht jin	mat6 jin3	maht chin
sweetshop	n	番荔枝	fàan laih jī	faan4 lai6 zi1	faan laih chi
swell /increase	v	增大	jāng daaih	zang1 daai6	chang taaih
swelling[1]	n	腫	júng	zung2	chung
swelling[2]	n	腫塊	júng faai	zung2 faai3	chung faai
swept	v	清掃	chèng /chìng sóu	ceng4 /cing4 sou2	chheng sou

English		Chinese	Yale	Jyutping	Romanization
swerve /sudden change direction	v	突然轉向	daht yihn jyún heung	dat6 jin4 zyun2 hoeng3	taht yihn chyun heung
swift[1] /rapid	adj	快捷	faai jit	faai3 zit3	faai chit
swift[2] /high-speed	adj	快速嘅	faai chùk ge	faai3 cuk4 ge3	faai chhuk ke
swiftly flow out[1]	adv	好快流出	hóu faai làuh chēut	hou2 faai3 lau4 ceot1	hou faai lauh chhot
swiftly flow out[2]	adv	很快流出	hán faai làuh chēut	han2 faai3 lau4 ceot1	han faai lauh chhot
swiftness	n	迅速	seun chùk	seon3 cuk4	swon chhuk
swim	n	游	yauh	jau4	yauh
swimmer[1]	n	游泳人	yauh wing yàhn	jau4 wing3 jan4	yauh wing yahn
swimmer[2]	n	游泳者	yauh wing jé	jau4 wing3 ze2	yauh wing che
swimming[1]	n	游水	yau séui	jau3 seoi2	yau swoi
swimming[2]	n	游泳	yau wìhng	jau3 wing6	yau wihng
swimming cap[1]	n	泳帽	wìhng móu	wing6 mou2	wehng mou
swimming cap[2]	n	游泳帽	yauh wing móu	jau4 wing3 mou2	yauh wing mou
swimming suit /swimming costume	n	游泳衣	yàuh wìhng yī	jau4 wing6 ji1	yauh wihng yi
swimming pool[1]	n	泳池	wìhng chìh	wing6 ci4	wehng chhih
swimming pool[2]	n	游泳池	yauh wing chìh	jau4 wing3 ci4	yauh wing chhih
swimsuit /bathing suit	n	泳衣	wìhng yī	wing6 ji1	wehng yi
swindler /cheater in gambling	n	老千	lóuh chìn	lou5 cin4	louh chhin
swine /pig	n	豬	jyù /dzeu	zyu4	chyu
swing[1]	n	韆鞦	chìn chāu	cin4 cau1	chhin chhau
swing[2] (for kids)	n	鞦韆	chāu chìn	cau1 cin4	chhau chhin
swing[3]	n	擺動	bāai dùhng	baai1 dung6	paai tohng
swinger /fashionist /fashionable man	n	濫交者	laahm gāau jé	laam6 gaau1 ze2	laahm kaau che
swipe	v	揮擊	fài gīk	fai1 gik1	fai kik
switch[1]	n	掣	jai	zai3	chai
switch[2] (for electric)	n	電掣	dihn jai	din6 zai3	tihn chai
swivel chair	n	轉椅	jyún yí	zyun2 ji2	chyun yi
sword (double edged)	adj	劍	gim	gim3	kim
swung /to hang	v	搖擺	yíu bāai	jiu2 baai1	yiu paai
syllable[1]	n	音節	yàm jit	jam4 zit3	yam chit
syllable[2]	n	分成音節	fàn sèhng yàm jit	fan4 seng4 jam4 zit3	fan sehng yam chit
syllabus	n	要目	yìu muhk	jiu4 muk6	yiu muhk
symbol /token	n	象徵	jeuhng jìng	zoeng6 zing4	cheuhng cheng
symbolic	adj	作為象徵	jok wàih jeuhng jing	zok3 wai4 zoeng6 zing3	chok waih cheuhng cheng
sympathize[1]	v	憫	máhn	man5	mahn
sympathize[2]	v	同情	tùhng chìhng	tung4 cing4	thuhng chhehng
sympathy[1]	n	恤	sēut	seot1	swot
sympathy[2] /consolation	n	同情心	tùhng chìhng sàm	tung4 cing4 sam4	thuhng chhehng sam
symphony	n	交響樂	gāau héung ngohk	gaau1 hoeng2 ngok6	kaau heung ngohk
symptom[1]	n	病症	behng /bìhng jìng	beng6 /bing6 zing4	pehng cheng

symptom[2]	n	症狀	jing johng	zing3 zong6	cheng chohng
synopsis[1] /book summary	n	簡介(著作)	gáan gaai (jyu jok)	gaan2 gaai3 (zyu3 zok3)	kaan kaai (chyu chok)
synopsis[2] /book summary	n	提要(著作)	tàih yiu (jyu jok)	tai4 jiu3 (zyu3 zok3)	thaih yiu (chyu chok)
synopsis[3] /book summary	n	大綱(著作)	daaih gòng (jyu jok)	daai6 gong4 (zyu3 zok3)	taaih kong (chyu chok)
syringe[1]	n	注射器	jyu sèh hei	zyu3 se4 hei3	chyu seh hei
syringe[2]	v	注射	jyu seh	zyu3 se6	chyu seh
syrup	n	糖漿	tòhng jēung	tong4 zeung1	thohng cheung
system[1]	n	系統	haih túng	hai6 tung2	haih thung
system[2] (of political)	n	方式	fòng sīk	fong4 sik1	fong sek
system[3] /rules	n	體系	tái haih	tai2 hai6	thai haih
system[4]	n	體制	tái jai	tai2 zai3	thai chai
systematically	adv	有系統地	yáuh hàih tūng dèih	jau5 hai6 tung2 dei6	yauh haih thung teih

table[1] /desk	n	枱	tói	tou2	thoi
table[2] /desk	n	檯	tòih	toi4	thoih
table[3]	n	桌	cheuk	coek	chheuk
table[4]	n	桌子	cheuk jí	coek zi2	chheuk chi
table[5] /list	n	表	bíu	biu2	piu
table[6] /schedule/list	n	表格	bíu gaak	biu2 gaak3	piu kaak
table cloth[1]	n	枱布	tói bou	toi2 bou3	thoi pou
table cloth[2]	n	桌布	cheuk bou	coek bou3	chheuk pou
table knife /kitchen knife	n	餐刀	chāan dōu	caan1 dou1	chhaan tou
table mat	n	盆墊	pùhn jín	pun4 zin2	phuhn chin
table stove[1] (sl) table curry boiler	n	打邊爐	dá bīn lòuh	daa2 bin1 lou4	ta pin louh
table stove[2] (sl) table's curry boiler	n	十吓十吓	sahp há sahp há	sap6 haa2 sap6 haa2	sahp ha sahp ha
table tennis	n	乒乓波	bìng bòng bò	bing4 bong4 bo4	peng pong po
tablespoon	n	湯匙	tōng chìh	tong1 ci4	thong chhih
tablet	n	藥片	yeuhk pin	joek6 pin3	yeuhk phin
tache /to hook	n	鉤	ngāu	ngau1	ngau
tactician	n	有策略嘅人	yáuh chaak leuhk ge yàhn	jau5 caak3 loek6 ge3 jan4	yauh chhaak leuhk ke yahn
tactics /tactfully	adv	戰術	jin seuht	zin3 seot6	chin swoht
tactless[1]	n	唔機智	m̀ gèi ji	m4 gei4 zi3	mh kei chi
tactless[2]	n	唔圓滑	m̀ yùhn waaht	m4 jyun4 waat6	mh yuhn waaht
taekwondo	n	跆拳道	toi kyun dòuh	toi3 kyun4 dou6	thoi khyun touh
tag /label	n	籤	chīm	chum1	chhim
tag no	n	籌號	chàuh houh	cau4 hou6	chhauh houh
tail[1] /end/last/finish/final	n	尾	méih	mei5	meih
tail[2]	n	尾巴	méih bā	mei5 ba1	meih pa
tail[3]	n	末尾	muht méih	mut6 mei5	muht meih
tail[4]	n	髮辮	faat bīn	faat3 bin1	faat pin
tail light (on vehicle)	n	尾燈	méih dāng	mei5 dang1	meih tang
tailor[1] /seamster/sartor	n	裁剪	chòih jín	coi4 zin2	chhoih chin
tailor[2] /dressmaker /seamster/dress-master	n	裁縫	chòih fung	coi4 fung3	chhoih fung
tailor[3]	n	剪裁	jín chòih	zin2 coi4	chin chhoih
tailor[4]	n	裁縫師	chòih fung sì	coi4 fung3 si4	chhoih fung si
tailor's shop	n	裁縫店	chòih fúng dím	coi4 fung2 dim2	chhoih fung tim
tailoring	n	裁縫技術	chòih fung geih seuht	coi4 fung3 gei6 seot6	chhoih fung keih swoht
Taiwan	n	台灣	tòih wāan	toi4 waan1	thoih waan
take[1] /carry/get/receive /fetch	v	攞	ló	lo2	lo
take[2] /hold/catch	v	搦	nīk	nik1	nek
take a chance	n	搏	bok	bok3	pok
take a rest	n	唞吓	táu háh	tau2 haa2	thau hah
take a risk or chance	n	準備冒險	jéun beih mouh hím	zeon2 bei6 mou6 him2	cheun peih mouh him
take a seat!	v	隨便坐啦	chèuih bín chóh lā!	ceoi4 bin2 co5 laa1	chheuih pin choh la!

take a shower	n	淋浴	làahm yuhk	lam4 juk5	laahm yuhk
take a walk /walking	n	散步	saan bouh	saan3 bou6	saan pouh
take action		採取行動	chói chéui hàhng duhng	coi2 ceoi2 hang4 dung6	chhoi cheui hahng tuhng
take an opportunity[1]		利用機會	leih yuhng gèi wúi	lei6 jung6 gei4 wui2	leih yuhng kei wui
take an opportunity[2]		藉此機會	jihk chí gèi wúi	zik6 ci2 gei4 wui2	chehk chhi kei wui
take away[1]	n	攞	ló	lo2	lo
take away[2]	n	外賣	oih /ngoih maaih	oi6 /ngoi6 maaih	oih /ngoih maaih
take back /retake	n	收回	sàu wùih	sau4 wui4	sau wuih
take care[1] /look after /to control/manage	n	管	gún	gun2	kun
take care[2] /manage	n	打理	dá léih	daa2 lei5	ta leih
take care[3]	n	留意	làuh yi	lau4 ji3	lauh yi
take care[4]	n	保重	bóu juhng	bou2 zung6	pou chuhng
take care of	v	照料	jiu liuh	ziu3 liu6	chiu liuh
take down	v	記下	gei hah	gei3 ha6	kei hah
take drugs /dose	v	服	fuhk	fuk6	fuhk
take it easy!	adv	沉住氣	chàhn jyuh hei	cam4 zyu6 hei3	chhahn chyuh hei
take later	v	晏啲攞	aan dì ló	aan3 di4 lo2	aan ti lo
take medicine	v	服藥	fuhk yeuhk	fuk6 joek6	fuhk yeuhk
take money		財款拿	chòih fún làh /nàh	coi4 fun2 laa4 /naa4	chhoih fun lah /nah
take now	v	而家攞	yìh gà ló	ji4 gaa4 lo2	yih ka lo
take off[1] (an airplane)	v	起飛	héi fèi	hei2 fei4	hei fei
take off[2] /move away	v	移去	yi heui	ji3 heoi3	yi hoi
take on	v	具有	geuih yáuh	geui6 jau5	kwoih yauh
take one's turn on duty		接更	jip gàng	zip3 gang4	chip kang
take order in business		接生意	jip sāang yi	zip saang1 ji3	chip saang yi
take out		取出	cheui chēut	ceoi3 ceot1	chheui chhot
take out cloth		剝衫	mōk sāam	mok1 saam1	mok saam
take photo[1]	v	拍	paak	paak3	phaak
take photo[2] /take in	v	攝	sip	sip3	sip
take respond		應採取	yìng chói chéui	jing4 coi2 ceoi2	yeng chhoi chheui
take sample		好似...咁	hóu chíh...gám	hou2 ci5 … gam2	hou chhih...kam
take turns		輪流	lèuhn láu	leon4 lau2	leuhn lau
take up /do start		開始從事	hòi chí chùhng sih	hoi2 ci2 cung4 si6	hoi chhi chhuhng sih
take up with		開始交往	hòi chí gaau wohng	hoi2 ci2 gáau1 wóng5	hoi chhi kaau wohng
take vacation /take holiday/take leave	v	休假	yàu ga	jau4 gaa3	yau ka
take x-ray		照x光	jiu x-gwòng	ziu3 x-gwong4	chiu x-gwong
taker	n	收取者	sàu chéui jé	sau4 ceoi2 ze2	sau chhoi che
taking bus	n	搭巴士	daap bà sìh	daap3 baa4 si6	taap pa sih
talcum powder	n	滑石粉	wàaht sehk fán	waat6 sek6 fan2	waaht sehk fan
tale tell /tattle tell /tell tales	n	散佈流言	sáan bou làuh yìhn	saan2 bou3 lau4 jin4	saan pou lauh yihn

talent person	n	人才	yàhn chòih	jan4 coi4	yahn chhoih
talented	adj	有天才	yáuh tīn chòih	jau5 tin1 coi4	yauh thin chhoih
talk[1]	v	談話	tàahm wah	taam4 waa6	thaahm wah
talk[2]	n	談	tàahm	taam4	thaahm
talk dirty	v	説下流話	syut hah làuh wá	syut3 ha6 lau4 wa2	syut hah lauh wa
talk over	v	漫談	maahn tàahm	maan6 taam6	maahn thaahm
talkative[1] (vexing)	adj	囉嗦	lō sò	lo1 so4	lo so
talkative[2] (positive)	adj	健談	gihn tàahm	gin6 taam4	kihn thaahm
talkative[3] (be fond of)	adj	喜歡説話	héi fūn syut wáh	hei2 fun1 syut3 waa2	hei fun syut wah
talkative[4] (negative meaning)	adj	多嘴	dò jéui	do4 zeoi2	to choi
talkee-talkee	n	喋喋不休	dihp dihp bāt yāu	dip6 dip6 bat1 jau1	tihp tihp pat yau
talker	n	談話者	tàahm wá jé	taam4 wa2 ze2	thaahm wa che
talking[1]	adj	敘述	jeuih seuht	zeoi6 seot6	cheuih swoht
talking[2]	adj	傾吐	kìng tóu	king4 tou2	khing thou
talking[3]	adj	説話的	syut wah dìk	syut3 waa2 dik4	syut wah tik
talkless	adj	多事幹	dò sih gon	do4 si6 gon3	to sih kon
tall	adj	高嘅	gòu ge	gou4 ge3	kou ke
talon	n	爪	geuk jáau	goek3 zaau2	keuk chaau
tame	adj	馴	sèuhn	seon4	swohn
tangerine[1]	n	橘子	gwàt jí	gwat4 zi2	kwat chi
tangerine[2] (small size orange)	n	桔	gāt	gat1	kat
tangible	adj	可觸知嘅	hó chūk jì ge	ho2 cuk1 zi4 ge3	ho chhuk chi ke
tank /big trunk	n	大箱	daaih sèung	daai6 soeng4	taaih seung
tank of milk	n	奶桶	làaih /náaih túng	laai5 /naai5 tung2	laaih /naaih thung
tank of oil[1]	n	油桶	yàuh túng	jau4 tung2	yauh thung
tank of oil[2]	n	貯油	chyúh yàuh	cyu5 jau4	chhyuh yauh
tank of water[1]	n	水櫃	séui gwaih	seoi2 gwai6	swoi kwaih
tank of water[2]	n	貯水	chyúh séui	cyu5 seoi2	chhyuh swoi
tank of wood /feed-box for cattle or birds /wooden feedbox/trough bamboo feedbox	n	槽	chòuh	cou4	chhouh
tanker of oil[1]	n	油車	yàuh chè	jau4 ce4	yauh chhe
tanker of oil[2]	n	油輪	yàuh lèuhn	jau4 leon4	yauh leuhn
tanker plane	n	空中加油飛機	hùng jùng gā yàuh fèi gèi	hung4 zung4 gaa1 jau4 fei4 gei4	hung chung ka yauh fei kei
Taoist	n	道教徒	dou gaau tòuh	dou3 gaau3 tou4	tou kaau thouh
tap /watertap/flow of water/ running water	n	自來水	jih lòih séui	zi6 loih4 seoi2	chih loih swoi
tap faucet /water tap	n	龍頭	lùhng tàuh	lung4 tau4	luhng tàuh
tap key (for water)	n	閥門	faht mùhn	fat6 mun4	faht muhn
tape[1] (measure)	n	捲尺	gyún chék	gyun2 cek2	kyun chhek
tape[2] (bandage)	n	繃帶	bàng dáai	bang4 daai2	pang taai
tape[3] /lace	n	膠帶	gāau dáai	gaau1 daai2	kaau taai

tape dispenser	n	膠帶機	gàau dáai gèi	gaau4 daai2 gei4	kaau taai kei
tape record	v	錄音	luhk yām	luk6 jam1	luhk yam
tardy /be late	adj	遲延	chìh yìhn	ci4 jin4	chhih yihn
target[1] /aim	n/vt	瞄準	mìuh jéun	miu4 zeon2	miuh cheun
target[2]	n	靶子	bá jí	ba2 zi2	pa chi
taro	n	香芋	hèung wuh	hoeng4 wu6	heung wuh
tart (de)	n	蛋撻	daahn tāat	daan6 taat1	taahn taat
tassel[1]	n	纓	yīng	jing1	yeng
tassel[2]	n	流蘇	làuh sòu	lau4 sou4	lauh sou
taste[1]	n	品味	bán meih	ban2 mei6	pan meih
taste[2]	n	試味道	si meih douh	si3 mei6 dou6	si meih touh
taste[3]	n	味覺	meih gok	mei6 gok3	meih kok
taste[4]	n	滋味	jì meih	zi4 mei6	chi meih
tasteless /no taste	adj	冇味	móuh meih	mou5 mei6	mouh meih
taster	n	試味人	si meih yàhn	si3 mei6 jan4	si meih yahn
tasty	adj	好味	hóu meih	hou2 mei6	hou meih
tattoo	v/n	紋身	màhn sàn	man4 san4	mahn san
taught	v	教咗	gaau jó	gaau3 zo2	kaau cho
tax	n	稅務	seui mouh	seoi3 mou6	swoi mouh
tax collector	n	稅務員	seui mouh yùhn	seoi3 mou6 jyun4	swoi mouh yuhn
tax free	adj	免稅的	míhn seui dìk	min5 seoi3 dik4	mihn swoi tek
tax statement		稅單	seui dāan	seoi3 daan1	swoi taan
taxable	adj	納稅	laahp seui	laap6 seoi3	laahp swoi
taxes	n	課稅	fo seui	fo3 seoi3	fo swoi
taxi[1] (coll) /cab	n	的士	dìk sí	dik4 si2	tik si
taxi[2] (wr) /cab	n	出租車	chēut jòu chè	ceot1 zou4 ce4	chhot chho chhe
taxi stand[1]	n	的士站	dìk sí jaahm	dik4 si2 zaam6	tik si chaahm
taxi stand[2]	n	出租汽車總站	chēut jòu hei chè júng jaahm	ceot1 zou4 hei3 ce4 zung2 zaam6	chhot chho hei chhe chung chaahm
taxing /tired/exhausting /hardly/fatiguing/hard	adj/n	辛苦	sàn fú	san4 fu2	san fu
tea[1]	n	茶	chàh /tsa	caa4	chhah /tsa
tea[2] (of chrysanthemum)	n	菊普	gùk póu	guk4 pou2	kuk phou
tea[3] (of Yunnan)	n	普洱茶	póu lei chàh /tsa	pou2 lei3 caa4	phou lei chhah
tea[4] of almond	n	杏仁茶	hàhng yàhn chà	hang6 jan4 caa4	hahng yahn chha
tea[5] (of lap sang sou chong)	n	正山小種	jeng sàan síu jung (lap sang sou chong)	zeng3 saan4 siu2 zung3 (lap3 sang3 sou3 cong3)	cheng saan siu jung (lap sang sou chong)
tea break	n	茶點休息時間	chàh dím yāu sīk sìh gaan	caa4 dim2 jau1 sik1 si4 gaan3	chhàh dím yāu sīk sìh gaan
tea cup	n	茶杯	chàh bùi	caa4 bui4	chhah pui
tea house	n	茶室	chàh sāt	caa4 sat1	chhah sat
tea leaves	n	茶葉	chàh yihp	caa4 jip6	chhah yihp
tea party	n	茶會	chàh wúi	caa4 wui2	chhah wui
tea table	n	茶幾	chàh géi	caa4 gei2	chhah kei
tea towel	n	抹布	maat bou	maat3 bou3	maat pou

teach (at class)	v	教書	gaau syù	gaau3 syu4	kaau syu
teach polite	v	有教養	yáuh gaau yéuhng	jau5 gaau3 joeng5	yauh kaau yeuhng
teaching	n	教學	gaau hohk	gaau3 hok6	kaau hohk
teakwood	n	柚木	yáu muhk	jau2 muk6	yau muhk
team member	n	隊員	deuih yùhn	deoi6 jyun4	toeih yuhn
teamwork	n	配合	pui hahp	pui3 hap6	phui hahp
tear[1] /crying	n	淚	leuih	leoi6	lowih
tear[2] /rend/pull	v	扯	ché	ce2	chhe
tear[3] /crying	n	淚花	leuih fā	leoi6 faa1	lowih fa
tear[4] /crying	n	流淚	làuh leuih	lau4 leoi6	lauh lowih
tear[5] /rip up /to peel	v	搣爛	miht laahn	mit6 laan6	miht laahn
tear[6] /break/rip up /to tear/ tearing	v	撕爛	sì laahn	si4 laan6	si laahn
tear[7] /rip up	v	扯破	ché po	ce2 po3	chhe pho
tear[8] /rip up	v	撕下	sì hah	si4 ha6	si hah
tear down	v	拆除	cháak chyù	caak2 cyu4	chhaak chhyu
tear gas	n	催淚瓦斯	chèui leuih ngáh sī	ceoi4 leoi6 ngaa5 si1	chheui lowih ngah si
tearful[1]	adj	含淚	hàhm leuih	ham4 leoi6	hahm lowih
tearful[2]	adj	流淚	làuh leuih	lau4 leoi6	lauh lowih
tearfully	adj	流淚地	làuh leuih deih	lau4 leoi6 dei6	lauh lowih teih
tease /to offend	v	惹惱	yéh lóuh /nóuh	je5 lou5 /nou5	yeh louh /nouh
teaspoon[1]	n	茶匙	chàh chìh	caa4 ci4	chhah chhih
teaspoon[2]	n	茶羹	chàh gāng	caa4 gang1	chhah kang
technical[1] /industrial /industry	n	工業	gùng yihp	gung4 jip6	kung yihp
technical[1]	adj	技術嘅	geih seuht ge	gei6 seot6 ge3	keih swoht ke
technical exchange	v	技術交流	geih seuht gàau làuh	gei6 seot6 gaau4 lau4	keih swoht kaau lauh
technical support	v	技術支援	geih seuht jī wùhn	gei6 seot6 zi1 wun4	keih swoht chi wuhn
technician	n	技師	geih sì	gei6 si4	keih si
technics	n	術語	seuht wá	seot6 waa2	swoht wa
technique /skill	n	技巧	geih háau	gei6 haau2	keih haau
technological	adj	技術學	geih seuht hohk	gei6 seot6 hok6	keih swoht hohk
technology centre	n	科技中心	fò geih jùng sàm	fo4 gei6 zung4 sam4	fo keih chung sam
tedious	adj	冗長乏味	yúng chèuhngfaht meih	jung2 coeng4 fat6 mei6	yung chheuhng faht meih
teenager[1]	n	青少年	chèng siu lìhn/nìhn	ceng4 siu3 lin4 /nin4	chheng siu lihn /nihn
teenager[2]	n	少年人	siu lìhn /nìhn yàhn	siu3 lin4 /nin4 jan4	siu lihn /nihn yahn
teeth[1] /tooth	n	牙	ngàh	ngaa4	ngah
teeth[2]	n	牙齒	ngàh chī	ngaa4 ci1	ngah chhi
teething	n	出乳牙	chēut yúh ngàh	ceot1 jyu5 ngaa4	chhot yuh ngah
tele office	n	電信局	dihn seun guhk	din6 seon3 guk6	tihn swon kuhk
tele set /telephone receiver	n	聽筒	tèng túng	teng4 tung2	theng tung
telecoms depart	n	電訊管理局	dihn seun gún léih guhk	din6 seon3 gun2 lei5 guk6	tihn swon kun leih kuhk

English		Chinese	Yale	Jyutping	Hakka
telegram	n	電報	dihn bou	din6 bou3	tihn pou
telegraph	n	電信	dihn seun	din6 seon3	tihn swon
telegraph office	n	電報局	dihn bou guhk	din6 bou3 guk6	tihn pou kuhk
telegraphic	adj	電報機	dihn bou gèi	din6 bou3 gei4	tihn pou kei
telephone[1] /phone	n	電話	dihn wá	din6 waa2	tihn wa
telephone[2]	n	電話機	dihn wá gèi	din6 waa2 gei4	tihn wa kei
telephone co	n	電訊公司	dihn seun gūng sī	din6 seon3 gung1 si1	tihn seun kung si
telephone exchange	n	電信局	dihn seun guhk	din6 seon3 guk6	tihn swon guhk
telephone extension		電話分機	dihn wá fān gēi	din6 waa2 fan1 gei1	tihn wa fan kei
telephone number	n	電話號碼	dihn wá houh máh	din6 waa2 hou6 maa5	tihn wa houh mah
telephone outside line	n	街線	gāai sin	gaai1 sin3	kaai sin
telephonist /telephone operator	n	接線生	jip sin sāng	zip3 sin3 sang1	chip sin sang
telephoto	n	傳真照片	chyùhn jàn jiu pín	cyun4 zan4 ziu3 pin2	chhyuhn chan chiu phin
telescope	n	望遠鏡	mohng yúhn geng	mong6 jyun5 geng3	mohng yuhn keng
teletex	n	圖文電視	touh màhn dihn sih	tou6 man4 din6 si6	thouh mahn tihn sih
television /TV	n	電視	dihn sih	din6 si6	tihn sih
television set /TV set	n	電視機	dihn sih gèi	din6 si6 gei4	tihn sih kei
telex	n	電傳	dihn chyùhn	din6 cyun4	tihn chhyuhn
tell[1] /express/state	v	述	seuht	seot6	swoht
tell[2] /say/speak	v	說	syút	syut2	syut
tell[3]	v	講述	góng seuht	gong2 seot6	kong swoht
tell[4] /told	v	告訴	gou sou	gou3 sou3	kou sou
tell lie[1]	v	講大話	góng daaih wá	gong2 daai6 waa2	kong taaih wa
tell lie[2]	v	講大詀	góng daaih jip	gong2 daai6 zip3	kong taaih chip
tell lie[3] /lying	v	說謊	syút fóng	syut2 fong2	syut fong
tellable	adj	可述說	hó seuht syút	ho2 seot6 syut2	ho seuht syut
teller	n	敘述者	jeuih seuht jé	zeoi6 seot6 ze2	cheuih swoht che
temper[1] /angry/tempered	n	脾氣	pèih hei	pei4 hei3	pheih hei
temper[2] (feeling)	n	情緒	chìhng séuih	cing4 seoi5	chhehng swoih
temperature[1]	n	溫	wān	wan1	wan
temperature[2]	n	溫度	wān douh	wan1 dou6	wan touh
temperature air	n	氣溫	hei wān	hei3 wan1	hei wan
temperature of the human body 35.8°c /98°f	n	體溫	tái wān	tai2 wan1	thai wan
temperature of the water	n	水溫	séui wān	seoi2 wan1	swoi wan
temple[1]	n	廟	míu	miu2	miu
temple[2] (Buddhist)	n	寺	jí	zi2	chi
temple[3]	n	宮	gùng	gung4	kung
temple[4] /shrine	n	神殿	sàhn din	san4 din3	sahn tin
Temple Buddhist	n	寺廟	jí miuh	zi2 miu6	chi miuh
Temple monastery	n	寺院	jí yún	zi2 jyun2	chi yun
Temple street	n	廟街	míu gāai	miu2 gaai1	miu kaai

temporarily	adv	暫時地	jaahm sìh deih	zaam6 si4 dei6	chaahm sih teih
temporary /provisional	adj	暫時	jaahm sìh	zaam6 si4	chaahm sih
tempt /lure attract	v	誘惑	yáuh waahk	jau5 waak6	yauh waahk
ten	n	十	sahp	sap6	sahp
ten past one[1]	n	一點二	yāt dīm yìh	jat1 dim1 ji6	yat tim yih
ten past one[2]	n	一點十分	yāt dím sahp fàn	jat1 dim2 sap6 fan4	yat tim sahp fan
ten thousand	n	萬	maahn	maan6	maahn
tenancy /tenant farmer	n	租期	jòu keih	zou4 kei6	chou kheih
tenant[1] /pays rent	n	住客	jyuh haak	zyu6 haak3	chyuh haak
tenant[2] /renters	n	租務	jòu mouh	zou4 mou6	chou mouh
tenant[3] /renters	n	租客	jòu haak	zou4 haak3	chou haak
tenant[4] /renters	n	承租人	sìhng jòu yàhn	sing4 zou4 jan4	sehng chou yahn
tenant[5] /lodger/pays rent	n	房客	fóng haak	fong2 haak3	fong haak
tenant[6] /tenant farmer	n	佃戶	tìhn wuh	tin4 wu6	thihn wuh
tend	v	趨向	chèui héung	ceoi4 hoeng2	chheui heung
tendency[1] /trend	n	趨勢	chèui sai	ceoi4 sai3	chheui sai
tendency[2]	n	傾向	kìng heung	king4 hoeng3	khing heung
tender age	n	年幼	lìhn yau	lin4 jau3	lihn yau
tenement	n	廉價公寓	lìhm ga gūng yuh	lim4 ga3 gung1 ju6	lihm ka kung yuh
tenfold	adj	十倍	sahp púih	sap6 pui5	sahp phuih
tennis	n	網球	móhng kàuh	mong5 kau4	mohng khauh
tenor[1] /main idea	n	大意	daaih yi	daai6 ji	taaih yi
tenor[2] /man's high tone	n	男高音	làahm gòuyàm	laam4 gou4 jam4	laahm kou yam
tense	v	時態	sìh taai	si6 taai3	sih thaai
tension /tensioning	n	拉緊	làai gán	laai4 gan2	laai kan
tensity /nervous situation	n	緊張局勢	gán jèung guhk sai	gan2 zoeng4 guk6 sai3	kan cheung kuhk sai
tent	n	帳	jeung	zoeng3	cheung
tenure	n	佔有權	jim yáuh kyùhn	zim3 jau5 kyun4	chim yauh khyuhn
term conditions	n	條件	tìuh gihn	tiu4 gin6	thiuh kihn
term of time	n	期限	kèih haahn	kei4 haan6	kheih haahn
term period	n	任期	yam kèih	jam3 kei4	yam kheih
terminal[1] /passengers arrival & departure place at the airport	n	航空終點站	hòhng hùng jūng dím jaahm	hong4 hung4 jung1 dim2 zaam6	hohng hung chung tim chaahm
terminal[2] /will lead to death	adj	晚期	máahn máahn	maan5 maan5	maahn maahn
terminator	n	終止者	jūng jí jé	jung1 zi2 je2	chung chi che
termite /insect	n	白蟻	baahk ngáih	baak6 ngai5	paahk ngaih
terrace /porch	n	陽臺	yèuhng tòih	joeng4 toi4	yeuhng thoih
terrible![1] /unhappy /unpleasant/very unpleasant	adj	非常討厭	fèi sèuhng tóu yim	fei4 soeng4 tou2 jim3	fei seuhng thou yim
terrible![2]	adj	好慘	hou cháam	hou3 caam2	hou chhaam
terrible![3]	adj	好慘呀!	hóu cháam ā	hou2 caam2 aa1	hou chhaam a
terrify	v	使害怕	sī hoih pa	si1 hoi6 pa3	si hoih pa

terrifyingly	adv	令人害怕地	ling yàhn hoih pa deih	ling3 jan4 hoi6 paa3 dei6	leng yahn hoih pha teih
terror	n	驚駭	gèng háaih	geng4 haai5	keng haaih
terrorism	n	恐怖主義	húng bou jyú yih	hung2 bou3 zyu2 ji6	hung pou chyu yih
terrorist[1]	n	恐怖分子	húng bou fahn jí	hung2 bou3 fan6 zi2	hung pou fahn chi
terrorist[2]	n	恐怖主義者	húng bou jyú yih jé	hung2 bou3 zyu2 ji6 ze2	hung pou chyu yih che
terrorize	v	使恐怖	sī húng bou	si1 hung2 bou3	si hung pou
test /quiz/exam	n	試驗	si yihm	si3 jim6	si yihm
test driver	n	試驗駕駛	si yihm ga sái	si3 jim6 gaa3 sai2	si yihm ka sai
test engine	n	試機	si gèi	si3 gei4	si kei
test tube	n	試管	si gùn	si3 gun4	si gùn
testament /will/desire	n	遺囑	wàih jūk	wai4 zuk1	waih chuk
tester[1]	n	測試器	chàak si hei	caak4 si3 hei3	chhaak si hei
tester[2]	n	試驗員	si yihm yùhn	si3 jim6 jyun4	si yihm yùhn
testicles[1] /bag of skin	n	春袋	chèun doih	ceon4 doi6	chhon toih
testicles[2] /testis of males	n	睪丸	gòu yún	gou4 jyun2	kou yun
testicles[3] (sl)	n	荔枝	laih jī	lai6 zi1	laih chi
tetanus (disease)	n	破傷風	po sèung fùng	po3 soeng4 fung4	pho seung fung
text[1]	n	正文	jeng màhn	zeng3 man4	cheng mahn
text[2]	n	課文	fo màhn	fo3 man4	fo mahn
text book /school book	n	教科書	gaau fō syù	gaau3 fo1 syu4	kaau fo syu
text message /SMS	n	訊息	sèun sīk	seon4 sik1	swon sek
textile[1]	adj	紡織的	fóng jīk dìk	fong2 zik1 dik4	fong chek tik
textile[2]	adj	紡織品	fóng jīk bán	fong2 zik1 ban2	fong chek pan
textile factory	n	織造廠	jīk jouh chóng	zik1 zou6 long2	chek chouh chhong
textual	adj	原文	yùhn mahn	jyun4 man6	yuhn mahn
thank you[1] (for service)	n	唔該	m̀ gòi	m4 goi4	mh koi
thank you[2] (for service)	n	唔該晒	m̀ gòi saai	m4 goi4 saai3	mh koi saai
thank you[3]	n	感謝您	gám jeh léih /néih	gam2 ze6 lei5 /nei5	kam cheh leih /neih
thank you[4]	n	謝謝你	jèh jèh léih /néih	ze6 ze6 lei5 /nei5	cheh cheh leih /neih
thankfully	adv	感謝地	gám jeh deih	gam2 ze6 dei6	kam cheh teih
thanks a lot![1] /thanks for gift / payment	v	多謝	dò jeh	do4 ze6	to cheh
thanks a lot![2] /many thanks!/thank you (for service)	n	多謝晒	dò jeh saai	do4 ze6 saai3	to cheh saai
thanks for help		辛苦晒	sān fú saai	san1 foo2 saai3	san fu saai
thanks for your inquiry	n	感謝您嘅查詢	gám jeh léih /néih ge chàh sèun	gam2 ze6 lei5 /nei5 ge3 caa4 seon4	kam cheh leih /neih ke chhah swon
thanksgiving day (US) for god	n	感恩節	gám yàn jit	gam2 jan4 zit3	kam yan chit
that[1] (coll) /this	adj	呢	lī /nī	li1 /ni1	li /ni
that[2] (wr)	pron	那	là /láh/ nà/ náh	laa6/ laa5/ naa6/ naa5	la /lah /na /nah
that[3]	pron	嗰個	gó go	go2 go3	ko ko
that[4]	pron	嗰啲	gó dī	go2 di1	ko ti

English	POS	Chinese	Romanization	Jyutping	Romanization
that is		那就是	là jauh sih	laa6 zau6 si6	la chauh sih
that one	n	那個	là gó	laa6 go2	la ko
that person[1]	n	嗰個人	gó go yàhn	go2 go3 jan4	ko ko yahn
that person[2]	n	那個人	là gó yàhn	laa6 go3 jan4	la ko yahn
that's all[1]		係咁多啦	haih gam dò la	hai6 gam3 do4 laa3	haih kam to la
that's all[2] /no more		冇啦	móuh la	mou5 laa3	mouh la
that's also okey		這也是有什麼	jéh yáh sih yáuh sahm mò	ze5 jaa5 si6 jau5 sam6 mo4	cheh yah sih yauh sahm mo
that's it	n	就係啦	jauh hai lā	zau6 hai3 laa1	chauh hai la
that's way	adj	因此	yàn chí	jan4 ci2	yan chhi
that time	n	那時	là sìh	laa6 si6	la sih
thatch	n	茅草	màau chóu	maau4 cou2	maau chhou
theater	n	劇場	kehk chèuhng	kek6 coeng4	khehk chheuhng
theatre /auditorium /ballroom/assembly hall	n	禮堂	láih tòhng	lai5 tong4	laih thohng
them[1] (coll)	n	偷	tàu	tau4	thau
them[2] (coll)	n	偷竊	tàu sít	tau4 sit2	thau sit
them[3] (coll)	pron	佢哋	kuéih deih	keoi5 dei6	khoih teih
them[4] (wr)	pron	他們	tā mùhn	ta1 mun4	tha muhn
thematic	adj	主題嘅	jyú tàih ge	zu2 tai4 ge3	chyu thaih ke
thematic vocabulary		專題詞彙	jyūn tàih chìh waih	zyun1 tai4 ci4 wai6	chyun thaih chhih waih
themselves	pron	它們自己	tà mùhn jih géi	taa4 mun4 zi6 gei2	tha muhn chih kei
then[1] /because	adv	於	yù	jyu4	yu
then[2] /after/later/following /afterwards/subsequently	adv	之後	jì háu	zi4 hau2	chi hau
then[3]	adv	跟住	gān jyuh	gan1 zyu6	kan chyuh
then[4]	adv	那時	là sìh	laa6 si6	la sih
then?[5] (question)	adv	之後呢?	jì háu lé /né?	zi4 hau2 le2 /ne2?	chi hau le /ne?
then elder	adv	較大	gaau daaih	ling4 gaau3 daai6	kaau taaih
then turn left		跟住轉左	gàn jyuh jyún jó	gan4 zyu6 jyun2 zo2	kan chyuh chyun cho
then what?		下一步怎麼辦?	hah yāt bouh ján mò baahn?	haa6 jat1 bou6 zan2 mo4 baan6?	hah yat pouh chan mo paahn?
theorist	n	理論家	léih leuhn gà	lei5 leon6 ga4	léih lowhn ka
theory[1]	n	論	leuhn	leon4	leuhn
theory[2]	n	原理	yùhn léih	jyun4 lei5	yuhn leih
therapeutic	adj	治療學	jih lìuh hohk	zi6 liu4 hok6	chih liuh hohk
therapist	n	治療專家	jih lìuh jyūn gā	zi6 liu4 zyun1 gaa1	chih liuh chyun ka
therapy /medicate /treatment	v	治療	jih lìuh	zi6 liu4	chih liuh
therapy	n	療法	lìuh faat	liu4 faat3	liuh faat
there[1] /here	adv	嗰度	gó dòuh	go2 dou6	ko touh
there[2] (coll)	adv	嗰處	gó syu	go2 syu3	ko syu
there[3] (wr)	adv	那裏	là léuih	laa6 leoi5	la leoih
there[4] (wr)	adv	那兒	là yìh	laa6 ji4	la yih
there[5] (wr)	adv	在那裡	joih lah /nah léuih	zoi6 laa6 /naa6 leoi5	choih lah /nah lowi

there of	adv	由此	yàuh chí	jau4 ci2	yauh chhi
there to fore	adv	直到那時	jihk dou nà /náh sí	zik6 dou3 naa6 /naa5 si2	chehk tou na /nah si
there upon	adv	隨即	cheui jīk	ceoi4 zik1	chheui chek
there you are!		你係嗰度	léih haih gó dòuh	lei5 hai6 go2 dou6	leih haih ko touh
thereby /thus	adv	從而	chùhng yìh	cung4 ji4	chhuhng yìh
therefore[1]/thereby/thus /thereon/hence/there upon/ on it/on that	adv	因此	yàn chí	jan4 ci2	yan chhi
therefore[2]	adv	故此	gu chí	gu3 ci2	ku chhi
thermal	adj	熱的	yiht dìk	jit6 dik4	yiht tik
thermometer[1]	n	寒暑表	hòhn syú bíu	hon4 syu2 biu2	hohn syu piu
thermometer[2]	n	探熱針	taam yiht jām	taam3 jit6 zam1	thaam yiht cham
thermometer[3]	n	溫度計	wān douh gai	wan1 dou6 gai3	wan touh kai
thermos[1]	n	暖水壺	lyúhn séui wú	lyun5 seoi2 wu2	lyuhn swoi wu
thermos[2]	n	保溫瓶	bōu wān pèhng	bou1 wan1 peng4	pou wan phehng
these[1]	pron	這些	jé sè	ze2 se4	che se
these[2] /this one	pron	呢啲	lī /nī dī	li1 /ni1 di1	li /ni ti
thesis[1]	n	論文	leuhn màhn	leon4 man6	leuhn mahn
thesis[2]	n	論題	leuhn tàih	leon4 tai4	leuhn thaih
they /their (coll)	pron	佢哋	kéuih deih	keoi5 dei6	khoih teih
they did	pron	佢地做咗	kéuih deih jouh jó	keoi5 dei6 zou6 zo2	khoih teih chouh cho
thick[1] (liquid/fluid)	adj	杰	giht	git6	kiht
thick[2] /flat things /viscid	adj	厚	háuh	hau5	hauh
thick[3]	adj	密	maht	mat6	maht
thick[4]	adj	厚嘅	háuh ge	hau5 ge3	hauh ke
thief[1]	n	偷	tàu	tau4	thau
thief[2]	n	賊	chaahk	caak6	chhaahk
thief[3]	n	小偷	síu tàu	siu2 tau4	siu thau
thief man[1] /bandit	n	偷	tàu yàhn	tau4 jan4	thau yahn
thief man[2] /bandit	n	賊人	chaahk yàhn	caak6 jan4	chhaahk yahn
thieved run /theft ran /stolen and run away	v	扒咗去	pàh jó heui	paa4 zo2 heoi3	phah cho hoi
thigh[1]	n	大髀	daaih béi	daai6 bei2	taaih pei
thigh[2]	n	大腿	daaih téui	daai6 teoi2	taaih thoi
thin air	adj	稀薄	hèi bohk	hei4 bok6	hei pohk
thin few	adj	稀少	hèi síu	hei4 siu2	hei siu
thin slight	adj	薄	bohk	bok6	pohk
think about /feel about	n	想	séung	soeng2	seung
think better of	n	對...有更高嘅評價	deui yáuh gáng gòu ge pìhng gá	deoi3 jau5 gang2 gou4 ge3 ping4 ga2	toei yauh kang kou ke pehng ka
think deeply	v	思索	sì sok	si3 sok3	si sok
think over[1]	n	諗諗	lám lám	lam2 lam2	lam lam
think over[2]	n	恁恁	láhm láhm	lam5 lam5	laahm laahm
think that	n	感到	gám dou	gam2 dou3	kam tou
thinker[1]	n	思想嘅人	sì sèung ge yàhn	si4 soeng4 ge3 jan4	si seung ke yahn

thinker[2]	n	思想家	sì sèung gā	si4 soeng4 ga1	si seung ka
thinker[3]	n	思考者	sì háau jé	si3 haau2 ze2	si haau che
thinking[1]	adj	機 / 机	gèi	gei4	kei
thinking[2] /thoughtful /considerate	adj	有心机/機	yáuh sàm gèi	jau5 sam4 gei4	yauh sam kei
thinner	n	稀釋劑	hèi sīk jāi	hei4 sik1 zai1	hei sek chai
third	adj	第三	daih sàam	dai6 saam4	taih saam
third person	n	第三者	daih sàam jé	dai6 saam4 ze2	taih saam che
thirsty[1] /thirst	adj	渴	hot	hot3	hot
thirsty[2]	adj	頸渴	géng hot	geng2 hot3	keng hot
thirsty[3]	adj	口渴	háu hot	hau2 hot3	hau hot
thirsty[4]	adj	口乾	háu gòn	hau2 gon4	hau kon
thirty /thirtieth		卅	sā	sa1	sa
this[1] (coll)		呢	lī /nī	li1 /ni1	li /ni
this[2] (wr)	adj	這	jéh /zhè	ze5	cheh
this[3] (thing)	adj	這項	je hohng	ze3 hong6	che hohng
this evening /tonight	n	今晚	gàm máahn	gam4 maan5	kam maahn
this Friday		本周五	bún jāu ńgh	bun2 zau1 ng5	pun chau ngh
this is /it's		呢個喺	lī /nī gó hái	li1 /ni1 go2 hai2	li /ni ko hai
this kind of		這類	jéh léui	ze5 leoi2	cheh lowi
this Monday[1]		本周一	bún jāu yāt	bun2 zau1 jat1	pun chau yat
this Monday[2]		今個禮拜一	gàm go láih baai yāt	gam4 go3 lai5 baai3 jat1	kam ko laih paai yat
this Monday[3]		今個星期一	gàm go sìng kèih yāt	gam4 go3 sing4 kei4 jat1	kam ko seng kheih yat
this morning[1]		今朝	gàm jìu	gam4 ziu4	kam chiu
this morning[2]		今朝早	gàm jìu jóu	gam4 ziu4 zou2	kam chiu chou
this newspaper	n	本報	bún bou	bun2 bou3	pun bou
this one[1] /alternative		伊個	yì gó	ji4 go2	yi ko
this one[2]		呢個	lī /nī gó	li1 /ni1 go2	li /ni ko
this one[3] (people)		嗰位	gó wái	go2 wai2	ko wai
this one[4]		這個	jéh gó	ze5 go2	cheh ko
this one room		呢一間	lì /nì yāt gaan	li4 /ni4 jat4 gaan3	li /ni yat kaan
this pencil		呢枝鉛筆	lì /nì jì yun bàt	li4 /ni4 zi4 jyun3 bat4	li /ni chi yun pat
this side		呢邊呀	lì /nì bīn àa	li4 /ni4 bin1 aa4	li /ni pin aa
this time	n	此次	chí chi	ci2 ci3	chhi chhi
this year		今年	gàm lìhn /nìhn	gam4 lin4 /nin4	kam lihn /nihn
thorough	adj	徹底	chit dái	cit3 dai2	chhit tai
thoroughly	adv	仔細	jí sai	zi2 sai3	chi sai
those	adj	嗰的	gó dī	go2 di1	ko ti
those days		嗰排	gó páai	go2 paai2	ko phaai
those three books		嗰三本書	gó sàam bún syù	go2 saam4 bun2 syu4	ko saam pun syu
though	conj	雖然	sèui yihn	seoi4 jin4	swoi yihn
thousand[1]	n	千	chìn	cin4	chhin
thousand[2]	n	一千	yāt chìn	jat1 cin4	yat chhin
thousands /countless /too many/ uncounted	n	無數	mòuh sou	mou4 sou3	mouh sou

thrash	v	摔打	sèui dá	seoi4 daa2	swoi ta
thrash board	n	浮板	fàuh báan	fau4 baan2	fauh paan
threaten[1]	n	恐嚇	húng haak	hung2 haak3	hung haak
threaten[2]	n	發惡	faat ngok	faat3 ngok3	faat ngok
threatened	v	受到威脅	sauh chi wāi hip	sau6 ci3 wai1 hip3	sauh chhi wai hip
three	n	三	sàam	saam4	saam
three books	n	三本書	sàam būn syù	saam4 bun1 syu4	saam pun syu
three fifteen[1]	n	三點十五分	sàam dīm sàhp ngh fàn	saam4 dim1 sap6 ng5 fan4	saam tim sahp ngh fan
three fifteen[2]	n	三點三	sàam dīm sàam	saam4 dim1 saam4	saam tim saam
three inch	n	三吋	sàam chyun	saam4 cyun3	saam chhyun
three parties	n	三黨	sàam dóng	saam4 dong2	saam tong
threefold	adj	三重地	sàam chùhng deih	saam4 cung4 dei6	saam chhohng teih
threw /throw	v	投	tàuh	tau4	thauh
thrice /treble/triple	adv	三倍	sàam púih	saam4 pui5	saam phuih
thrive /prosperous	v	興旺	hìng wohng	hing4 wong6	hing wohng
throat[1]	n	喉頭	hàuh tàuh	hau4 tau4	hauh thauh
throat[2] /voice	n	嗓	sōng	song1	song
throb[1]	v	悸動	gwai duhng	gwai3 dung6	kwai tuhng
throb[2] /to pulse/acute pain	v	跳動	tiu duhng	tiu3 dung3	thiu tiu tohng
throes[1] /pain of childbirth	n	劇痛	kehk tung	kek6 tung3	khehk thung
throes[2] /pain of childbirth	n	陣痛	jahn tung	zan6 tung3	chahn thung
throne[1] /king's chair	n	王位	wòhng waih	wong4 wai6	wohng waih
throne[2]	n	皇家王位	wong gà wong wāi	wong3 gaa4 wong3 wai1	wong ka wong wai
throttle[1] /strangle/kill by squeezing throat	v	掐死	haap séi	haap3 sei2	haap sei
throttle[2]	v	掐住脖子	haap jyuh buht jí	haap3 zyu6 but6 zi2	haap chyuh puht chi
through[1] /via/go through	adj	通過	tùng gwo	tung4 gwo3	thung kwo
through[2]	adj	行過	hàahng gwo	haang4 gwo3	haahng kwo
through[3]	adj	境過	gìng gwo	ging4 gwo3	keng gwo
throughout	adj	遍佈	pín bóu	pin2 bou2	phin pou
throw[1]	v	摒棄	bíng hei	bing2 hei3	peng hei
throw[2]	v	拋棄	pāau hei	paau1 hei3	phaau hei
throw away /abandon	v	棄	hei	hei3	hei
throw down[1]	v	擲	jaahk	zaak6	chaahk
throw down[2] /wrestle	v	摔角	sēut gok	seot1 gok3	swot kok
thrower	n	投擲者	tàuh jaahk jé	tau4 zaak6 ze2	thauh chaahk che
thumb[1]	n	姆指	móuh jí	mou5 zi2	mouh chi
thumb[2]	n	手指公	sáu jí gùng	sau2 zi2 gung4	sau chi kung
thumb print[1]	n	姆指模	móuh jí móu	mou5 zi2 mou2	mouh chi mou
thumb print[2]	n	拇指嘅指紋	móuh jí ge jí màhn	mou5 zi2 ge3 zi2 man4	mouh chi ke chi mahn
thunder[1]	n	雷	lèuih	leoi4	lowih
thunder[2]	n	雷公	lèuih gùng	leoi4 gung4	lowih kung

thunder[3] /thundering	n	雷聲	lèuih sèng	leoi4 seng4	lowih seng
thunderbolt	n	霹靂	pīk līk /lihk	pik1 lik1 /lik6	phik lek /lehk
thundering[1]	n	行雷	hàahng lèuih	haang4 leoi4	haahng lowih
thundering[2]	a	大發雷霆嘅	daaih faat lèuih tìhng	daai6 faat3 leoi4 thing4	taaih faat leuih thehng
thunderstorm[1]	n	大雷雨	daaih lèuih yúh	daai6 leoi4 jyu5	taaih lowih yuh
thunderstorm[2]	n	雷暴	lèuih bouh	leoi4 bou6	lowih pouh
Thursday[1]	n	禮拜四	láih baai sei	lai5 baai3 sei3	laih paai sei
Thursday[2]	n	星期四	sèng kèih sei	seng4 kei4 sei3	seng kheih sei
thyroid gland	n	甲狀腺	gaap johng sin	gaap3 zong6 sin3	kaap chohng sin
Tiananmen Square	n	天安門廣場	tīn ōn mùhn gwóng chèuhng	tin1 on1 mun4 gwong2 coeng4	thin on muhn kwong chheuhng
tick[1] /drop/drip	n	滴	dihk	dik6	tehk
tick[2] /mark	n	記號	gei houh	gei3 hou6	kei houh
tick tock sound	v	滴答聲	dihk daap sèng	dik6 daap3 seng4	tehk taap seng
ticket[1] (sl)	n	飛	fèi	fei4	fei
ticket[2]	n	票	piu	piu3	phiu
ticket[3] (for vehicle)	n	車票	chè piu	ce4 piu	chhe phiu
ticket[4] (for admission)		入場券	yahp chèung gyun	jap6 coeng4 gyun3	yahp chheung kyun
tickle	v	呵折	hó jit	ho2 zit3	ho chit
tide /time	n	歲月	seui yuht	seoi3 jyut6	swoi yuht
tidily	adv	整齊地	jíng chàih deih	zing2 cai4 dei6	cheng chaih teih
tidy & in orderly	adj	整潔嘅	jíng git ge	zing2 git3 ge3	cheng kit ke
tidy up[1]	n	執拾	jāp sahp	zap1 sap6	chap sahp
tidy up[2] (a room or bedroom)	n	執房	jāp fóng	zap1 fong2	chap fong
tidy up[3]	n	執拾好	jāp sahp hóu	zap1 sap6 hou2	chap sahp hou
tidy up[4]	n	收拾	sàu sahp	sau4 sap6	sau sahp
tie[1] (de)	n	呔	tāai	taai1	thaai
tie[2] /fasten	v	繫	haih	hai6	haih
tie[3] (of neck)	n	領帶	léhng /líhng dāai	leng5 /ling5 daai1	lehng taai
tiffin	n	中飯	jùng fahn	zung4 faan6	chung fahn
tiger[1]	n	虎	fú /foo	fu2	fu /foo
tiger[2]	n	老虎	lóuh fú /foo	lou5 fu2	louh fu
tight[1] /tighten	v	緊	gán	gan2	kan
tight[2]	adj	緊緊	gán gán	gan2 gan2	kan kan
tight[3]	adj	緊的	gán dīk	gan2 dik1	kan tik
tighten /fasten	v	使繃緊	sai bāng gán	sai2 bang1 gan2	sai pang kan
tightly	adv	緊緊地	gán gán deih	gan2 gan2 dei6	kan kan teih
tights	n	緊身衣	gán sàn yī	gan2 san4 ji1	kan san yih
tile[1] /tiles (for the roof)	n	瓦	ngáh	ngaa5	ngah
tile[2]	n	瓦片	ngáh pin	ngaa5 pin3	ngah phin
tiler	n	磚瓦者	jyūn ngáh jé	zyun1 ngaa5 ze3	chyun ngah che
tiles (for the floor)	n	階磚	gāai jyūn	gaai1 zyun1	kaai chyun
till[1] /up to/until	conj	到	dou	dou3	tou

till[2] /until/until then	conj	直到	jihk dou	zik6 dou3	chehk tou
till[3] /until	conj	為止	waih jí	wai6 zi2	waih chi
till[4] /for sales/counter table /sales counter	n	櫃檯	gwaih tói	gwai6 toi2	kwaih thoi
till[5] (money box)	n	錢櫃	chín gwaih	cin2 gwai6	chhin kwaih
till[6] (cultivate)	v	耕種	gàang jung	gaang4 zung3	kaang chung
till death /hunger strike	adv	絕食	jyuht sihk	zyut6 sik6	chyuht sehk
timber /wood	n	木材	mùhk choi	muk6 coi3	muhk chhoi
time[1] /period	n	時間	sìh gaan	si4 gaan3	sih kaan
time[2] /period of age/length of time	n	時候	sìh hauh	si4 hau6	sih hauh
time after time	n	多次	dò chi	do4 ci6	to chhi
time & motion	n	時間與動作	sìh gaan yùh duhng jok	si4 gaan3 jyu4 dung6 zok3	sih kaan yuh tohng chok
time bomb	n	定時炸彈	dehng /dihng sìh ja táan	deng6 /ding6 si4 zaa3 taan2	tehng sih cha thaan
time card	n	考勤卡	háau kàhn kāat	haau2 kan4 kaat1	haau khahn khaat
time clock	n	打卡鐘	dā kāat jūng	daa1 kaat1 zung1	ta khaat chung
time signal	n	報時信號	bou sìh seun houh	bou3 si4 seon3 hou6	pou sih swon houh
time signature (of music)	n	拍子記號	paak màaih jí gei houh	paak3 maai6 zi2 gei3 hou6	phaak maaih chi kei houh
timely[1] /well timed	adj	適時	sīk sìh	sik1 si4	sek sih
timely[2]	adj	及時	kahp sìh	kap6 si4	khahp sih
timer[1]	n	計時器	gai sìh hei	gai3 si4 hei3	kai sih hei
timer[2]	n	計時員	gai sìh yùhn	gai3 si4 jyun4	kai sih yuhn
times[1] /multiply (x)	prep	乘	sìhng	sing4	sehng
times[2] /multiplication /multiply (x)	prep	乘以	sìhng yíh	sing4 ji5	sehng yih
timescale[1]	n	時間尺度	sìh gaan chek douh	si4 gaan3 cek3 dou6	sih kaan chhek touh
timescale[2]	n	時表	sìh bíu	si4 biu2	sih piu
timid[1] /chicken-hearted /cowardly	adj	細膽	sai dáam	sai3 daam2	sai taam
timid[2]	adj	唔夠膽	m̀ gau dáam	m4 gou3 daam2	mh kau taam
timid[3] /say & nervous	adj	膽小嘅	dáam síu ge	daam2 siu2 ge3	taam siu ke
tin /matal	n	錫	sek	sek3	sek
tingle (of body)	v	刺痛感	chi tung gám	cik3 tung3 gam2	chhi thung kam
tingling	n	刺痛	chi tung	ci3 tung3	chhi thung
tiny[1]	adj	啲咁多	dì gam dō	di4 gam3 do1	ti gam toh
tiny[2]	adj	極小的	gihk síu dìk	gik6 siu2 dik4	kehk siu tik
tip[1] /peak/point	n	尖端	jīm dyūn	zim1 dyun1	chim tyun
tip[2] /gift/gratuity/present	v	小費	síu fai	siu2 fai3	siu fai
tip-top[1] /top class	adj	第一流	daih yāt làuh	dai6 jat1 lau4	taih yat lauh
tip-top[2] /foremost /superlative	adj	最好地	jeui hóu deih	zeoi3 hou2 dei6	cheui hou teih
tipcart	n	傾卸車	kìng se chè	king4 se3 ce4	khing se chhe

English	POS	Chinese			
tips ^(de) /gratuity	v	貼士	tìp sí	tip4 si2	thip si
tired¹	adj	好劫 /瘝	hóu guih	hou2 gui6	hou kuih
tired²	adj	厭	yim	jim3	yim
tired³ /very tired	adj	勞累	lòuh lèuih	lou4 leoi6	louh lowih
tireless	adj	唔劫/唔瘝	m̀ guih	m4 gui6	mh kuih
tissue¹ /paper napkin /kleenex/paper kerchief/ facial	n	紙巾	jí gàn	zi2 gan4	chi kan
tissue² (body muscle)	n	組織(肌肉)	jóu jīk (gēi yuhk)	zou2 zik1 (gei1 juk6)	chou chek (kei yuhk)
tissue³ (of fabric)	n	絲織物	si jik maht	si3 zik3 mat6	si chek maht
tissue⁴ (of fabric)	n	薄絹	bohk gyun	bok6 gyun3	pohk kyun
tissue⁵ (of textiles)	n	薄織物	bòhk jīk maht	bok6 zik1 mat6	pohk chek maht
tit for tat	n	針鋒相對	jàm fùng sèung deui	zam4 fung4 soeng4 deoi3	cham fung seung toei
title	n	有爵位	yáuh jeuk waih	jau5 zoek3 wai6	yauh cheuk waih
titled	adj	有稱號	yáuh ching houh	jau5 cing3 hou6	yauh chheng houh
to¹	prep	達	daaht	daat6	taaht
to² /until	adv	直到	jihk dou	zik6 dou3	chehk tou
to act /play	n	演	yíhn	jin5	yihn
to allow /to let	n	任	yahm	jam4	yahm
to arrive	v	至	jí	ji2	chi
to be¹ /to do	v	為	waih	wai6	waih
to be²	v	在	joih	zoi6	choih
to carry		搬走	bùn jáu	bun4 zau2	pun chau
to check on a list		點	dīm	dim1	tim
to climb over /step across	n	跨	kwà	kwaa4	khwa
to climb up /hiking hill	n	爬手	pàh sáu	paa4 sau2	phah sau
to come /coming	adj	未來	meih lòih	mei6 loi4	meih loih
to deceive ^(coll)/to cheat	v	呃	āk / àak/ ngàak	ak1 /aak1/ ngak4	ak /aak /ngaak
to do list		由我辦	yàuh ngóh baahn	yau4 ngoh5 baan6	yauh ngoh paahn
to drive vehicle ^(coll)	v	揸車	jà chè	zaa4 ce4	cha chhe
to ending	n	至尾	ji méih	zi3 mei5	chi meih
to go by /travel by		搭	daap	daap3	taap
to go to	prep	去	heui	heoi3	hoi
to keep /collect/pile /compile	v	收藏	sau chòhng	sau3 cong4	sau chhohng
to learn	n	初學	chò hohk	co4 hok6	chho hohk
to meet	v	會面	wuih mihn	wui6 min6	wuih mihn
to move /unsteady	n	擺下擺下	bāai hah bāai hah	baai1 haa6 baai1 haa6	paai hah baai hah
to offer	v	獻	gyún hin	gyun2 hin3	kyun hin
to regard as	v	當	dong	dong3	tong
to rest ^(wr) rest/recess /off day/interval/break time /cosey	n/v	休息	yàu sīk	jau4 sik1	yau sek
to say /to speak	n	說	syut	syut3	syut

to serve	n	伺候	sih hauh	si6 hau6	sih hauh
to set /to fix	n	規定	kwài dehng /dihng	kwai4 deng6 /ding6	khwai tehng
to sign	n	署	chyúh	cyu5	chhyuh
to travel	v	旅	léuih	leoi5	lowih
to Z /until end/to end	adj	至尾	ji méih	zi3 mei5	chi meih
toast[1] (de)	n	多士	dò sí	do4 si2	to si
toast[2]	n	炕麵包	hong mihn bāau	hong3 min6 baau1	hong mihn paau
toast[3] (de)	n	土司	tóu sī	tou2 si1	thou si
toaster	n	多士爐	dō sí lòuh	do1 si2 lou4	to si louh
tobacco[1]	n	煙草	yìn chóu	jin4 cou2	yin chhou
tobacco[2]	n	抽煙	chàu yīn	cau4 jin1	chhau yin
today[1]	n	今日	gàm yaht	gam4 jat6	kam yaht
today[2]	n	今天	gàm tìn	gam4 tin4	kam thin
today[3] /nowadays	adv	現今	yihn gām	jin6 gam1	yihn kam
today is	n	今日係	gàm yaht haih	gam4 jat6 hai6	kam yaht haih
toenails	n	脚趾甲	geuk jí gaap	goek3 zi2 gaap3	keuk chi kaap
toes	n	脚趾	geuk jí	goek3 zi2	keuk chi
toffee (de)	n	拖肥糖	tò féi tóng	to4 fei2 tong2	thoh fei thong
tofu sweet dessert	n	豆腐花	dáu fū fā	dau2 fu1 faa1	tau fu fa
together[1]	adv	和	wòh	wo4	woh
together[2] /all together	adv	一齊	yāt chái /chàih	zat1 cai2 /cai4	yat chhai /chhaih
together[3]	adv	一起	yāt héi	jat1 hei2	yat hei
together with[1]	adv	與	yùh	jyu4	yuh
together with[2]	adv	同埋	tùhng màaih	tung4 maai4	thuhng maaih
toil	v	勞	lòuh	lou4	louh
toilet cleaner[1] (liquid)	n	潔厠液	git chi yihk	git3 ci3 jik6	kit chhi yehk
toilet cleaner[2] (powder)	n	潔厠粉	git chi fán	git3 ci3 fan2	kit chhi fan
toilet paper /toilet tissue	n	厠紙	chi jí	ci3 zi2	chhi chi
toilet soap	n	香皂	hèung jouh	hoeng4 zou6	heung chouh
toilet tissue	n	衛生紙	waih sàng jí	wai6 sang4 zi2	waih sang chi
token /for counting	n	籌	chàuh	cau4	chhauh
Toki pona language	n	道本文	dou bun màhn	dou3 bun3 man4	tou pun mahn
Tokyo	n	東京	dùng gìng	dung4 ging4	tung geng
tolerable	adj	可容忍	hó yùhng yán	ho2 jung4 jan2	ho yuhng yan
tolerance[1]	n	寬容	fùn yung	fun4 jung3	fun yung
tolerance[2] /endure	n/v	忍耐	yán loih /noih	jan2 loi6 /noi6	yan loih /noih
tolerant	adj	容忍嘅	yùhng yán ge	jung4 jan2 ge3	yuhng yan ke
toll /tariff /cost/expense /charge	n	費用	fai yuhng	fai3 jung6	fai yuhng
tomahawk	n	戰斧	jin fú	zin3 fu2	chin fu
tomato	n	番茄	fàan ké	faan4 ke2	faan khe
tomato juice	n	番茄汁	fàan ké jàp	faan4 ke2 zap4	faan khe chap
tomb /grave	n	墳墓	fàhn mouh	fan4 mou6	fahn mouh
tomorrow morning[1]	n	聽朝	tèng jìu	teng4 ziu4	theng chiu

English	POS	Chinese	Romanization 1	Jyutping	Romanization 2
tomorrow morning[2]	n	聽朝早	tèng jìu jóu	teng4 ziu4 zou2	theng chiu chou
tomorrow never comes[1]		切莫依賴 聽日	chit mohk yī laaih tèng yàht	cit6 mok6 ji1 laai6 teng4 jat6	chhit mohk yi laaih theng yaht
tomorrow never comes[2]		切莫依賴 明天	chit mohk yī laaih mìhng tīn	cit6 mok6 ji1 laai6 ming4 tin1	chhit mohk yī laaih mihng thin
tomorrow night	n	聽晚	tèng máahn	teng4 maan5	theng maahn
ton (de) weight of BT 2240 & US 2000 pounds	n	噸	dèun	deon4	ton
tone[1] /sound/pitch /pronunciation/syllable	n	音	yām	jam1	yam
tone[2]	n	併音	peng yàm	peng3 jam4	pheng yam
tone[3]	n	音質	yàm jāt	jam4 zat1	yam chat
tone[4]	n	音調	yàm diuh	jam4 diu6	yam tiuh
tone[5]	n	語氣	yúh hei	jyu5 hei3	yuh hei
toner ink[1]	n	碳粉	taan fán	taan3 fan2	thaan fan
toner ink[2]	n	調色劑	tìuh sīk jāi	tiu4 sik1 zai1	thiuh sek chai
tones	n	聲調	sèing /sìng diuh	seng4 /sing4 diu6	seing tiuh
tongs[1]	n	火鉗	fó kím	fo2 kim2	fo khim
tongs[2]	n	鉗子	kím jái	kim2 zai2	khim chai
tongs[3]	n	夾具	gip geuih	gip geoi6	kep kwoih
tongue[1]	n	舌	sìht	sit6	siht
tongue[2]	n	舌頭	sìht tau	sit6 tau3	siht thau
tongue[3] (sl)	n	脷	leih	lei6	leih
tonic	n	補藥	bóu yeuhk	bou2 joek6	pou yeuhk
tonsils[1]	n	扁桃腺	bín tòuh sin	bin2 tou4 sin3	pin thouh sin
tonsils[2] /uvula (of the mouth)	n	喉核	hàuh wát	hau4 wat2	hauh wat
tony	adj	時髦	sìh mōu	si4 mou1	sih mou
too[1] /much/extremely /over/excessively	prep	過	gwo	gwo3	kwo
too[2] /as well as	adv	以及	yíh kahp	ji5 kap6	yih khahp
too[3] /and/also/as well	conj	亦都	yihk dōu	jik6 dou1	yehk tou
too bad[1] (sl)	n	弊嘞	baih laa!	bai6 laa3	paih laa!
too bad[2] (sl)	n	真係弊嘞	jan haih baih laak!	zan3 hai6 bai6 laak3	chan haih paih laak!
too big	adj	太	taai	taai3	thaai
too close /very close	adv	太近	taai káhn	taai3 kan5	thaai khahn
too few	adj	太少	táai sīu, ty seew	taai2 siu1	thaai siu
too late		都來不及	dōu làih bāt kahp	dou1 lai4 bat kap6	tou laih pat khahp
too long /overlong /very long	adj	過長	gwo chèuhng	gwo3 coeng4	kwo chheuhng
too much	adj	太多	táai dò	taai2 do4	thaai toh
too much for		力所不能 及	lihk só bāt làhng /nàhng kahp	lik6 so2 bat1 lang4 /nang4 kap6	lehk so pat lahng/ nahng khahp
too noisy		好嘈呀	hóu chòuh āa /ah	hou2 cou4 aa1 /aa6	hou chhouh aa /ah
took & escaped		攞咗去	ló jó heui	lo2 zo2 heoi3	lo cho hoi

tool /utensil/device /equipment	n	器	hei	hei3	hei
tools	n	械	haaih	haai6	haaih
tooth pick[1]	n	牙簽	ngàh chìm	ngaa4 cim4	ngah chhim
tooth pick[2]	n	牙籤	ngàh chīm	ngaa4 cim1	ngah chhim
toothache	n	牙痛	ngàh tung	ngaa4 tung3	ngah thung
toothbrush	n	牙刷	ngàh cháat	ngaa4 caat2	ngah chhaat
toothpick holder	n	牙簽桶	ngàh chìm túng	ngaa4 cim4 tung2	ngah chhim thung
top	n	極	gihk	gik6	kehk
top class[1] /first class	adj	頭等	tàuh dàng	tau4 dang4	thauh tang
top class[2]	adj	頂級	déng kāp	deng2 kap1	teng khap
top leader /highest post	n	最高領導	jeui gōu léhng douh	zeoi3 gou1 leng5 dou6	cheui kou lehng touh
top quality	adj	一流	yāt làuh	jat1 lau4	yat lauh
top to bottom	adj	頂至底	déng ji dái	deng2 zi3 dai2	teng chi tai
top-up money /add sum of money	n	收入補貼	sāu yahp bóu tip	sau1 jap6 bou2 tip3	sau yahp pou thip
topic of a lecture	n	講題	góng tàih	gong2 tai4	kong thaih
topical	adj	話題嘅	wah tàih ge	waa6 tai4 ge3	wah thaih ke
torque /torsion	n	頸鏈	géng lín	geng2 lin2	keng lin
total[1]	n	一共	yāt guhng	jat1 gung6	yat kuhng
total[2] /sum/gross /grand total	n	總數	júng sou	zung2 sou3	chung sou
totally	adv	冚唪唥	kám fúng laahng	kam2 fung2 laang6	kham fung laahng
touch[1]	v	觸摸	jùk mō	zuk4 mo1	chuk mo
touch[2] /get in touch /contact/get in touch with	v	聯絡	lyùhn lok	lyun4 lok3	lyuhn lok
touch by person	n	摸某人	mó máuh yàhn	mo2 mau5 jan4	mo mauh yahn
touch with mouth /rub with mouth	v	用口緊挨	yùhng háu gán āai	jung6 hau2 gan2 aai1	yuhng hau kan aai
touch with nose /rub with nose	v	用鼻緊挨	yùhng bèih gán āai	jung6 bei6 gan2 aai1	yuhng peih kan aai
touchable	adj	可觸	hó chūk	ho2 cuk1	ho chhuk
tour[1] /walk	n	遊	yàuh	jau4	yauh
tour[2] /tourism	n	旅遊	léuih yàuh	leoi5 jau4	lowih yauh
tour group	n	旅行團	léuih hàhng tyùhn	leoi5 hang4 tyun4	lowih hahng thyuhn
tour of service	n	任期	yam kèih	jam3 kei4	yam kheih
tourism[1]	n	觀光業	gùn gwòng yihp	gun4 gwong4 jip6	kun kwong yihp
tourism[2]	n	旅遊業	léuih yàuh yihp	leoi5 jau4 jip6	lowih yauh yihp
tourism coach	n	旅遊巴士	léuih yàuh bā sí	leoi5 jau4 baa1 si2	lowih yauh pah si
tourist[1] /traveller	n	旅客	léuih haak	leoi5 haak3	lowih haak
tourist[2]	n	旅遊者	léuih yàuh jé	leoi5 jau4 ze2	lowih yauh che
tourist office	n	遊客諮詢處	yàu haak jì sèun chyu	jau4 haak3 zi4 seon4 cyu3	yau haak chi swon chhyu
tournament	n	聯賽	lyùhn choi	lyun4 coi3	lyuhn chhoi
tow truck /trailer /traction engine	n	拖車	tō chè	to1 ce4	thoh chhe

English	Part	Chinese	Romanization 1	Jyutping	Romanization 2
toward /front face /forward	prep	向	heung	hoeng3	heung
towards[1] /going ahead /to forward/to go ahead/ towards (direction)	prep	往	wóhng	wong5	wohng
towards[2] (of time)	prep	將近	jèung gahn	zoeng4 gan6	cheung kahn
towel /bath towel	n	毛巾	mòuh gàn	mou4 gan4	mouh kan
towelette	n	濕餐紙巾	sāp chāan jí gān	sap1 caan1 zi2 gan1	sap chhaan chi kan
tower	n	高樓	gòu láu	gou4 lau2	kou lau
town[1] /market/city	n	市	síh	si5	sih
town[2] /city	n	城	sèhng	seng4	sehng
town[3]	n	鎮	jan	zan3	chan
town[4]	n	市鎮	síh jan	si5 zan3	sih chan
town centre /city center/ downtown	n	市中心	síh jùng sàm	si5 zung4 sam4	sih chung sam
town house	n	城市住宅	sèhng síh jyuh jaahk	seng4 si5 zyu6 zaak6	sehng sih chyuh chaahk
town planner	n	規劃者	kwāi waahk jé	kwai1 waak6 ze2	khwai waahk che
town planning	n	城鎮規劃	sèhng jan kwāi waahk	seng4 zan3 kwai1 waak6	sehng chan khwai waahk
towngas /coal gas/gas	n	煤氣	mùih hei	mui4 hei3	muih hei
towngas co	n	煤氣公司	mùih hei gūng sī	mui4 hei3 gung1 si1	muih hei kung si
townspeople[1]	n	市民	síh màhn	si5 man4	sih mahn
townspeople[2]	n	城裏人	sèhng léuih yàhn	seng4 leoi5 jan4	sehng lowih yahn
townspeople[3]	n	鎮民	jan màhn	zan3 man4	chan mahn
toxic[1] /poisonous	adj	有毒	yauh duhk	jau6 duk6	yauh tuhk
toxic[2]	adj	毒性	duhk sing	duk6 sing3	tuhk seng
toxin	n	毒素	duhk sou	duk6 sou3	tuhk sou
toy /doll	adj	玩具	wáan geuih	waan2 geoi6	waan kwoih
trachea /windpipe /airpipe	n	氣管	hei gún	hei3 gun2	hei kun
track[1] /footprint	n	足跡	jūk jek	zuk1 zek3	chuk chek
track[2]	n	軌跡	gwái jīk	gwai2 zik1	kwai chek
track light	n	活動式投射燈	wuht dùhng sīk tàuh seh dāng	wut6 dung6 sik1 tau6 se6 dang1	wuht tuhng sek thauh seh tang
traction	n	牽引	hìn yáhn	hin4 jan5	hin yahn
tractor	n	拖拉機	tō lāai gēi	to1 laai1 gei1	thoh laai kei
trade	n	貿易	mauh yihk	mau6 jik6	mauh yehk
trade fair	n	商品展銷會	sèung bán jín sīu wúih	soeng4 ban2 zin2 siu1 wui5	seung pan chin siu wuih
trade union / labour union/association	n	工會	gùng wúi	gung4 wui2	kung wui
tradition /traditional	n	傳統	chyùhn tung	cyun4 tung3	chhyuhn thung
traditional Chinese character	n	繁體	fàahn tái	faan4 tai2	faahn thai
traditional dress	n	傳統服裝	chyùhn tung fuhk jòng	cyun4 tung3 fuk6 zong4	chhyuhn thung fuhk chong

English	POS	Chinese	Yale	Jyutping	Other
traffic /transport /transportation	n	交通	gāau tùng	gaau1 tung4	kaau thung
traffic accident		車禍	chè woh	ce4 wo6	chhe woh
traffic jam[1]	n	塞車	sàk chè	sak4 ce4	sak chhe
traffic jam[2]	n	交通擁擠	gāau tùng yúng /úng jāi	gaau1 tung4 jung2 /ung2 zai1	kaau thung yung /ung chai
traffic light[1]	n	交通燈	gāau tùng dāng	gaau1 tung4 dang1	kaau thung tang
traffic light[2]	n	燈位	dàng wàih	dang4 wai6	tang waih
traffic sign	n	交通標誌	gāau tùng bīu ji	gaau1 tung4 biu1 zi3	kaau thung piu chi
tragedy[1]	n	慘劇	cháam kehk	caam2 kek6	chhaam khehk
tragedy[2]	n	悲劇	bèi kehk	bei4 kek6	pei khehk
tragic	adj	悲劇嘅	bèi kehk ge	bei4 kek6 ge3	pei khehk ke
tragic comedy	n	悲喜劇	bèi héi kehk	bei4 hei2 kek6	pei hei khehk
tragically	adv	悲劇地	bèi kehk deih	bei4 kek6 dei6	pei khehk teih
trail /trace/mark	n	痕跡	hàhn /hán jīk	han4 /han2 zek3	hahn /han chek
train /to teach	v	訓	fan	fan3	fan
trainee[1] /apprentice	n	學徒	hohk touh	hok6 tou4	hohk thouh
trainee[2]	n	徒弟	tou dàih	tou3 dai6	thou taih
trainer	n	訓練人	fan lihn yàhn	fan3 lin6 jan4	fan lihn yahn
training school	n	訓練所	fan lihn só	fan3 lin6 so2	fan lihn so
trample[1] /step on /press a pedal	v	踏	daahp	daap6	taahp
trample[2] /tread	v	踐踏	chíhn daahp	cin5 daap6	chhihn taahp
tram	n	電車	dihn chè	din6 ce4	tihn chhe
transfer[1] /moving	v	調動	diuh duhng	diu6 dung6	tiuh tohng
transfer[2] (patient)	v	轉院	jyun yuhn	zyun3 jyun6	chyun yuhn
transfer money[1]	v	轉帳	jyún jeung	zyun2 zoeng3	chyun cheung
transfer money[2]	v	過戶	gwo wuh	gwo3 wu3	kwo wuh
transfer to another A/C (money)	v	轉入戶口號碼	jyún yahp wuh háu houh máh	zyun2 jap6 wu6 hau2 hou6 maa5	chyun yahp wuh hau houh mah
transferable	adj	可調動	hó diuh duhng	ho2 diu6 dung6	ho tiuh tohng
transference	n	調動	diuh duhng	diu6 dung6	tiuh tohng
transform	v	改成	gói sèhng	goi2 seng4	koi sehng
transformation	n	變化	bin fa	bin3 faa3	pin fa
transformer	n	變壓器	bin aat /ngaat hei	bin3 aat3 /ngaat3 hei3	pin aat /ngaat hei
transit /transportation	n	運輸	wahn syù	wan6 syu4	wahn syu
transit visa	n	過境簽証	gwo gíng chīm jing	gwo3 ging2 cim6 zing3	kwo keng chhm cheng
transition	n	變遷	bin chìn	bin3 cin4	pin chhin
translate /to turn over	v	翻	fān	faan1	fan
translate into	v	譯成	yihk sèhng /sìhng	jik6 seng4 /sing4	yehk sehng
translator	n	譯者	yihk jé	jik6 ze2	yehk che
transparency	n	透明	tau mìhng	tau3 ming4	thau mehng
transparent	adj	透明嘅	tau mìhng ge	tau3 ming4 ge3	thau mehng ke
transport[1] /move	n	運	wahn	wan6	wahn
transport[2]	v	之交通	jī gāau tùng	zi1 gaau1 tung4	chi kaau thung

transport[3]	v	運輸	wahn syù	wan6 syu4	wahn syu
transport[4]	n	交通工具	gāau tùng gùng geuih	gaau1 tung4 gung4 geoi6	kaau thung kung kwoih
transport dept[1]	n	運輸署	wahn syù chyúh	wan6 syu4 cyu5	wahn syu chhyuh
transport dept[2]	n	交通部	gāau tùng bouh	gaau1 tung4 bou6	kaau thung pouh
transport ship	n	運輸船	wahn syù syùhn	wan6 syu4 syun4	wahn syu syuhn
transportable	a	可運輸	hó wahn syù	ho2 wan6 syu4	ho wahn syu
transporter	n	輸送者	syù sung jé	syu4 sung3 ze2	syu sung che
transpose	v	調換	deuh wuhn	deu6 wun6	teuh wuhn
transsexual[1]	n	易性癖者	yihk sing pīk jé	jik6 sing3 pik1 ze2	yehk seng phik che
transsexual[2]	n	變性人	bìn sing yàhn	bin4 sing3 jan4	pin seng yahn
transverse /perpendicular	adj	橫向	wàahng héung	waang4 hoeng2	waahng heung
travel[1]	v	旅	léuih	leoi5	lowih
travel[2]	v	遊歷	yàuh lihk	jau4 lik6	yauh lehk
travel aboard	v	出外旅行	chēut oih /ngoih léuih hàhng	ceot1 oi6 /ngoi6 leoi5 hang4	chhot oih/ngoih lowih hahng
travel agency /tour operator	n	旅行社	léuih hàhng séh	leoi5 hang4 se5	lowih hahng seh
traveller /visitor	n	遊客	yàu haak	jau4 haak3	yau haak
travelling	n	旅行嘅	léuih hàhng ge	leoi5 hang4 ge3	lowih hahng ke
travelling expenses[1]	n	旅費	léuih fai	leoi5 fai3	lowih fai
travelling expenses[2]	n	水脚	séui geuk	seoi2 goek3	swoi keuk
tray[1]	n	盤仔	pun jái	pun3 zai2	phun chai
tray[2]	n	托盤	tok pún	tok3 pun2	thok phun
treasure[1]	v	珍藏	jàn chòhng	zan4 cong4	chan chhohng
treasure[2]	n	重視	juhng sih	zung6 si6	chuhng sih
treasure[3]	n	珍重	jàn juhng	zan4 zung6	chan chuhng
treasure[4]	n	金銀財寶	gām ngàhn chòih bóu	gam1 ngan4 coi4 bou2	kam ngahn chhoih pou
treasure[5]	v	珍愛	jàn ói /ngoi	zan4 oi2 /ngoi3	chan oi /ngoi
treasury /treasure house	v	寶庫	bóu fu	bou2 fu3	pou fu
treasurer[1]	n	財務員	chòih mouh yùhn	coi4 mou6 jyun4	chhoih mouh yuhn
treasurer[2]	n	司庫者	sì fu jé	si4 fu3 ze2	si fu che
treasurer[3] /treasurership	n	財政者	chòih jing jé	coi4 zing3 ze2	chhoih jeng che
treat[1] /act toward	v	對	deui	deoi3	toei
treat[2] /probe	n	探討	tàam tōu	taam4 tou1	thaam thou
treat[3] /invite for party	n	款待	fūn dòih	fun1 doi6	fun toih
treatable	a	能治療	làhng /nàhng jih lìuh	lang4 /nang4 zi6 liu4	lahng /nahng chih liuh
treating /cure/treatment	v	對待	deui doih	deoi3 doi6	toei toih
treatise	n	論述	leuhn seuht	leon4 seot6	leuhn seuht
treatment[1] /cure	n	治	jih	zi6	chih
treatment[2]	n	待遇	doih yuh	doi6 jyu6	toih yuh
treatment[3]	v	醫診	yī chán	ji1 can2	yi chhan
treatment place		送院治理	sung yún jih leih	sung3 jyun2 zi6 lei5	sung yun chih leih
treaty[1]	n	條約	tìuh yeuk	tiu4 joek3	thiuh yeuk

treaty[2] /negotiation/talks	n	談判	taahm pun	tàam4 pun3	taahm phun
tree	n	樹	syuh	syu6	syuh
leaf (of tree)	n	樹葉	syuh yihp	syu6 jip6	syuh yihp
treeless[1]	adj	無樹木	móuh syuh muhk	mou5 syu6 muk6	mouh syuh muhk
trespass[2]	v	非法侵入	fèi faat chām yahp	fei4 faat3 cam1 jap6	fei faat chham yahp
trespasser[1]	n	擅進	sihn jeun	sin6 zeon3	sihn cheun
trespasser[2]	n	擅闖	sihn chóng	sin6 cong2	sihn chhong
trespasser[3]	n	侵入者	chàm yahp jē	cam4 jap6 ze1	chham yahp che
triage	n	患者鑑別分類	waahn jé gaam bìht fàn lèuih	waan6 ze2 gaam3 bit6 fan4 leoi6	waahn che kaam piht fan lowih
triage station	n	分流處	fàn làuh chyú	fan6 lau4 cyu2	fan lauh chyu
triangle /triangular	adj/n	三角形	sàam gók yeng /ying	saam4 gok2 jeng3 /jing3	saam kok yeng
tribe	n	部落	bouh lohk	bou6 lok6	pouh lohk
tributes[1]	n	拜祭	baai jai	baai3 zai3	paai chai
tributes[2]	n	葬禮獻花	jong láih hin fāa	zong3 lai5 hin3 faa1	chong laih hin faa
trick[1] /cheat	v	招	jīu	ziu1	chiu
trick[2] /ruse/sly	n	花招	fā jīu	faa1 ziu1	fa chiu
trick question	n	偏題	pīn tòih	pin1 toi4	phin thoih
tricky meeting (sl)		蛇鼠一鍋	sèh syu yāt wō	se4 syu3 jat1 wo1	seh syu yat woh
tricky skill	n	狡猾的技巧	gáau waaht dìk gèih hāau	gaau2 waat6 dik4 gei6 haau1	kaau waaht tek geih haau
tried	adj	試咗	si jó	si3 zo2	si cho
trigger	n	槍砲嘅扳機	chèung paau ge pāan gèi	coeng4 paau3 ge3 paan1 gei4	chheung phaau ke phaan kei
triglycerides	n	三酸甘油脂	sàam syūn gām yàuh jī	saam4 syun1 gam1 jau4 zi1	saam syun kam yauh chi
trip[1]	v	旅	léuih	leoi5	lowih
trip[2] /travel/tour/journey	v	旅行	léuih hàhng	leoi5 hang4	lowih hahng
trip[3] /travel	v	旅遊	léuih yàuh	leoi5 jau4	lowih yauh
trip[4]	v	遠足	yúhn jūk	jyun5 zuk1	yuhn chuk
trip[5] /travel/journey /itinerary/to travel	n	旅程	léuih chìhng	leoi5 cing4	lowih chihehng
trolley	n	車仔	chè jai	ce4 zai3	chhe chai
troop	n	群隊	kwàhn déui	kwan4 deoi2	khwahn toei
tropical[1]	adj	熱帶	yiht daai	jit6 daai3	yiht taai
tropical[2]	adj	酷熱	huhk yiht	huk6 jit6	huhk yiht
trouble[1] /annoy	v	使煩惱	si fàahn lóuh /nóuh	si3 faan4 lou5 /nou5	si faahn louh /nouh
trouble[2] /troublesome /worrisome/untoward	adj	麻煩	màh fàahn	maa4 faan4	mah faahn
troubleshooting	n	疑難排解	yih làahn /nàahn pàaih gáai	ji6 laan4 /naan4 paai4 gaai2	yih laahn /naahn phaaih kaai
trouser	n	褲	fu	fu3	fu
truck[1]	n	卡車	kā chè	kaa1 ce4	kha chhe
truck[2]	n	六個轆	luhk go lūk	luk6 go3 luk1	luhk ko luk

516

English	POS	Chinese	Cantonese	Jyutping	Romanization
true case	n	實情	saht chìhng	sat6 cing4	saht chhehng
true-life[1]	adj	寫實	sé saht	se2 sat6	se saht
true-life[2]	adj	真人真事	jàn yàhn jàn sih	zan4 jan4 zan4 si6	chan yahn chan sih
true to form /as usual	adj	和往常一樣	wo wóhng seung yàt yèuhng	wo3 wong5 soeng3 jat4 joeng6	wo wohng seung yat yeuhng
trunk[1] /stem	n	軀幹	kéui gon	keoi2 gon3	khoi kon
trunk[2] (of tree)	n	樹幹	syùh gón	syu6 gon3	syuh kon
trunk[3] safe box/money box	n	大保險箱	daaih bóu hím sèung	daai6 bou2 him2 soeng4	taaih pou him seung
trustee	n	受託管理人	sauh tok gún léih yàhn	sau6 tok3 gun2 lei5 jan4	sauh thok kun leih yahn
trustworthy[1]	adj	信得過	seun dāk gwo	seon3 dak1 gwo3	swon tak kwo
trustworthy[2]	adj	可信賴	hó seun laaih	ho2 seon3 laai6	ho swon laaih
truth[1] /verity truth	n	真理	jàn léih	zan4 lei5	chan leih
truth[2]	n	實話	saht wá	sat6 wa2	saht wa
truthfully	adv	信任地	seun yahm deih	seon3 jam4 dei6	swon yahm teih
try again	v	再試	joi si	zoi3 si3	choi si
try best	v	盡力以為	jeuhn lihk yìh wàih	zeon6 lik6 ji4 wai6	cheuhn lehk yih waih
trying[1]	adj	令人痛苦	lihng yàhn tung fú	ling6 jan4 tung3 fu2	lehng yahn thung fu
trying[2]	adj	難受	làhn /nàhn sáu	laan4 /naan6 sau2	lahn /nahn sau
tsunami[1]	n	海嘯	hói siu	hoi2 siu3	hoi siu
tsunami[2]	n	地震海嘯	deih jan hói siu	dei6 zan3 hoi2 siu3	teih chan hoi siu
tuber (of plants)	n	塊莖	fai ging	faai3 ging3	fai king
tuberculosis	n	肺病	fai behng	fai3 beng6	fai behng
tubule /fistula	n	細管	sai gùn	sai3 gun4	sai kun
tucker /bib	n	圍兜	wàih dāu	wai4 dau1	waih tau
Tuesday[1]	n	禮拜二	láih baai yih	lai5 baai3 ji6	laih paai yih
Tuesday[2]	n	星期二	sèng kèih yih	seng4 kei4 ji6	seng kheih yih
tug /pull by force	v	用力拉	yuhng lihk làai	jung6 lik6 laai4	yuhng lehk laai
tuition	n	交授	gaau sauh	gaau3 sau6	kaau sauh
tuition fee	n	學費	hohk fai	hok6 fai3	hohk fai
tuition learn	n	教學	gaau hohk	gaau3 hok6	kaau hohk
tumble	n	倒塌	dóu taap	dou2 taap3	tou thaap
tumor /tumour /a mass of cell	n	瘤	láu	lau2	lau
tune	n	曲調	kùk diuh	kuk4 diu6	khuk tiuh
tuner[1]	n	調音師	tìuh yàm sī	tiu4 jam4 si1	thiuh yam si
tuner[2]	n	調諧器	tìuh hàaih hei	tiu4 haai4 hei3	thiuh haaih hei
tuning	n	調音	tìuh yām	tiu4 jam1	thiuh yam
tunnel /causeway	n	地道	deih douh	dei6 dou6	teih touh
turbine	n	渦輪	wò leun	wo4 leon3	wo leon
turbocharger /supercharger of exhaust	n	增壓器	jàng aat /ngaat hei	zang4 aat3 /ngaat3 hei3	chang aat /ngaat hei
turkey (bird)	n	火雞	fó gāi	fo2 gai1	fo kai
turmeric	n	薑黃根粉	gèung wòhng gáan fán	goeng4 wong4 gaan2 fan2	keung wohng kaan fan

English		Chinese	Yale	Jyutping	
turmoil	n	動盪	duhng dohng	dung6 dong6	tuhng tohng
turn[1] /change/transition	n	轉變	jyún bin	zyun2 bin3	chyun pin
turn[2] /revolve	v	旋動	syun duhng	syun3 dung6	syun tohng
turn[3] /rotate	v	使轉動	sai jyūn duhng	sai3 zyun1 dung6	sai chyun tuhng
turn around	v	回	wùih	wui4	wuih
turn back	v	折返	jit fàan	zit3 faan4	chit faan
turn back again	v	反轉頭	fàan jyun tàuh	faan4 zyun3 tau4	faan chyun thauh
turn direction /move /shift/make a turn	v	轉	jyun	zyun3	chyun
turn face	v	擰轉面	lehng /nihng jyun mihn	leng4 /ning4 zyun3 min6	lehng chyun mihn
turn head	v	擰轉頭	lehng /nihng jyun tàuh	leng4 /ning4 zyun3 tau4	lehng chyun thauh
turn into1[1]	v	成	sèhng	seng4	sehng
turn into[2]	v	成為	sèhng wàih	seng4 wai6	sehng waih
turn into disaster	v	成災	sèhng jōi	seng4 zoi1	sehng choi
turn it into a question? /if placed end of the sentence		呀?	a? /a!	a3? /a3!	a? /a!
turn left	v	轉左	jyún jó	zyun2 zo2	chyun cho
turn off light		熄燈	sīk dāng	sik1 dang1	sek tang
turn over[1] /to turn	v	掉	diuh	diu6	tiuh
turn over[2] /to turn	v	掉轉	diuh jyun	diu6 zyun3	tiuh chyun
turn over[3]	v	嘞	la	laa3	la
turn over[4]	v	翻倒	fáan dou	faan2 dou3	faan dou
turn right	v	轉右	jyun yauh	zyun3 jau6	chyun yauh
turn right & then?	v	轉右之後呢?	jyun yauh jì hauh le?	zyun3 jau6 zi4 haa6 le3?	chyun yauh chi hauh le?
turnover	n	倒轉	dou jyún	dou3 zyun1	tou chyun
turns of exchange	n	輪流轉	lèuhn láu jyun	leon4 lau4 zyun3	leuhn lau chyun
turns opposite	n	調番轉	diuh fàan jyun	diu6 faan4 zyun3	tiuh faan chyun
turnstyle gate	n	旋轉柵門	syùhn jyún sāan mùhn	syun4 jyun2 saan1 mun4	syuhn chyun saan muhn
turtle	n	烏龜	wù gwài	wu4 gwai4	wu kwai
turtle neck	n	樽領	jēun léhng	zeon1 leng5	cheun lehng
tusk /long tooth	n	長牙	chèuhng ngàh	coeng4 ngaa4	chheuhng ngah
tutor /private teacher	n	私人教師	sī yàhn gaau sì	si1 jan4 gaau3 si4	si yahn kaau si
tutorial /to coach	adj	輔導	fuh dòuh	fu6 dou6	fuh touh
TV movie	n	電視劇	dihn sih kehk	din6 si6 kek6	tihn sih khehk
TV game	n	電視遊戲	dihn sih yàuh hei	dun6 si6 jau4 hei3	tihn sih yauh hei
TV home shopping	n	電視購物	dihn sih kau maht	dun6 si6 kau3 mat6	tihn sih khau maht
TV service	n	電視服務	dihn sih fuhk mouh	dun6 si6 fuk6 mou6	tihn sih fuhk mouh
TV station	n	電視台	dihn sih tòih	dun6 si6 toi4	tihn sih thoih
tweezers /pliers/nippers	n	鑷子	lihp /nihp jí	lip6 /nip6 zi2	lihp /nihp chi
twenty	n	二十	yih sahp	ji6 sap6	yih sahp
twenty four hours	n	二十四個鐘	yih sahp sei go jùng	ji6 sap6 sei3 go3 zung4	yih sahp sei ko chung

twenty four hours shop /convenient shop	n	便利店	bihn leih dim	bin6 lei6 dim3	pihn leih tim
twenty nine	n	二十九	yih sahp gáu	ji6 sap6 gau2	yih sahp kau
twice	adv	兩次	léuhng chi	loeng5 ci3	leuhng chhi
twig /thin branch /very thin branches	n	樹枝	syuh jī	syu6 zi1	syuh chi
twin bed	n	對床	deui chòhng	deoi3 cong4	toei chòhng
twinkle	v	閃爍	sím līk	sim2 lik1	sim lek
twins[1] /two children /pair childs	n	孖	mā	maa1	ma
twins[2]	n	雙胞	sèung bāau	soeng4 baau1	seung paau
twins born	a	雙胞胎	sèung bāau tòi	soeng4 baau1 toi4	seung paau thoi
twins brothers	n	孖仔	mā jái	maa1 zai2	ma chai
twins sisters	n	孖女	mā léui /néui	maa1 leoi5 /neoi5	ma lowi /nowi
twist (threads)	v	搓	chò	cp4	chho
twist ankle /sprain	v	扭親	láu chàn	lau2 can4	lau chhan
twisted[1]	adj	拉柴	lāai chàaih	laai1 caai4	laai chhaaih
twisted[2] /braids	adj	編織	pīn jīk	pin1 zik1	phin chehk
twisting thread[1] /spin /spun	v	紡紗(手藝)	fóng sā (sáu ngaih)	fong2 sa1 (sau2 ngai6)	fong sa (sau ngaih)
twisting thread[2]	n	紡線(手藝)	fóng sin (sáu ngaih)	fong2 sin3 (sau2 ngai6)	fong sin (sau ngaih)
two[1]	n	二	yih /yee	ji6	yih
two[2] /pair/both/dual /double	adj/n	雙	sèung	soeng4	seung
two inches	n	兩吋	léuhng chyun	loeng5 cyun3	leuhng chhyun
two o'clock[1]	n	兩點鐘	léuhng dím jūng	loeng5 dim2 zung1	leuhng tim chung
two o'clock[2]	n	二時正	yìh si jíng	ji6 si3 zing2	yih si cheng
two persons	n	兩個人	léuhng go yàhn	loeng5 go3 yan4	leuhng ko yahn
two vehicle	n	兩架車	léuhng gá chè	loeng5 ga2 ce4	leuhng ka chhe
type[1] /model	n	型	yìhng	jing4	yehng
type[2] /form/features/shape /appearance/pattern/model /mold	n	樣	yéung	joeng2	yeung
type[3] /style/form/pattern	n	式	sīk	sik1	sek
type[4] /style/sort	n	類型	leuih yìhng	leoi6 jing4	lowih yehng
typecast	n	鑄模	jyu mòuh	zyu3 mou4	chyu mouh
typeface	n	字體	jih tái	zi6 tai2	chih thai
typewritter[1]	v	打字	dá jih	daa2 zi6	ta chih
typewritter[2]	n	打字機	dá jih gèi	daa2 zi6 gei4	ta chih kei
typhoon[1]	n	打風	dā fùng	daa1 fung4	ta fung
typhoon[2]	n	颱風	tòih fùng	toi4 fung4	thoih fung
typhoon shelter	n	避風塘	beih fùng tòhng	bei6 fung4 fong4	peih fung thohng
typhoon signal	n	風球	fùng kàuh	fung4 kau4	fung khauh
typhoon-damaged		颱風造成損壞	tòih fùng chóu seng syūn wàaih	toi4 fung4 cou2 seng3 syun3 waai6	thoih fung chhou seng syun waaih
typical[1]	adj	典型	dín yìhng	din2 jing4	tin yehng

typical²	adj	典型嘅	dín yìhng ge	din2 jing4 ge3	tin yehng ke
typical³	n	有代表性	yáuh doih bíu sing	jau5 doi6 biu2 sing3	yauh toih piu seng
typically¹	adj	典型地	dín yìhng dèih	din2 jing4 dei6	tin yehng teih
typically²	adj	象徵嘅	jeuhng jìng ge	zoeng6 zing4 ge3	cheuhng cheng ke
typically³	adj	象徵性	jeuhng jìng sing	zoeng6 zing4 sing3	cheuhng cheng seng
typist	n	打字員	dá jih yùhn	daa2 zi6 jyun4	ta chih yuhn
tyrannical⁽ᶜᵒˡˡ⁾/oppress	adj	虐	fú /foo	fu2	fu /foo
tyranny¹/brutal	n	暴虐	bouh yeuhk	bou6 joek6	pouh yeuhk
tyranny²	n	專橫	jyūn wàahng	zyun1 waang4	chyun waahng
tyranny³	n	苛政	hō jing	ho1 zing3	ho cheng
tyranny⁴	n	專政	jyūn jing	zyun1 zing3	chyun cheng
tyre⁽ᵈᵉ⁾	n	呔	tāai	taai1	thaai

English			Chinese	Yale	Jyutping	Romanization
udder /breast of woman	n		乳房	yúh fòhng	jyu5 fong4	yuh fohng
ugly[1] /not beautiful/bad	adj		壞	waaih	waai6	waaih
ugly[2] /not good	adj		難	làhn /nàhn	laan4 /naan6	lahn /nahn
ugly[3] /unpleasant to look	adj		難睇	làhn /nàhn tái	laan4 /naan6 tai2	lahn /nahn thai
ugly[4] /shameful	adj		醜樣	cháau yéung	caau2 joeng2	chhaau yeung
ugly[5]	adj		核突	haht daht	hat6 dat6	haht taht
ulcer (of stomach)	n		胃潰瘍	waih kwúi yèuhng	wai6 kui2 joeng4	waih khwui yeuhng
ultimate	adj		最終	jeui jūng	zeoi3 jung1	cheui chong
ultimatum	n		最後通牒	jeui hauh tùng dihp	zeoi3 hau6 tung4 dip6	cheui hauh thung tihp
ultra /excessive/overdue	adj		過度	gwo douh	gwo3 dou6	kwo touh
ultra violet ray	adj		紫外	jí oih	zi2 oi6 /ngoi6	chi oih
umbrella[1] /cover up	n		遮	jē	ze1	che
umbrella[2]	n		傘	saan	saan3	saan
umbrella[3]	n		把遮	bāa jè	baa1 ze4	paa che
umbrella[4]	n		雨傘	yúh saan	jyu5 saan3	yuh saan
umbrella[5] (folding style)	n		縮骨遮	sūk gwàt jē	suk1 gwat4 ze1	suk kwat che
umbrella big	n		保護傘	bóu wuh saan	bou2 wu6 saan3	pou wuh saan
umpire (of game)	n		裁判員	chòih pun yùhn	coi4 pun3 jyun4	chhoih phun yuhn
un...[1]	pref		唔 / 不	m̀ / bāt	m4 / bat1	mh / pat
un...[2]	pref		非	fèi	fei4	fei
un...[3]	pref		相反	seung fáan	soeng3 faan2	seung faan
unabated	adj		不減弱	bāt gáam yeuhk	bat1 gaam2 joek6	pat kaam yeuhk
unable[1] /ineffective	adj		唔能夠	m̀ làhng /nàhng gau	m4 lang4 /nang4 gau3	mh lahng /nahng kau
unable[2]	adj		唔會	m̀ wúih	m4 wui5	mh wuih
unable to bear /unbearable	adj		無法接受	mòuh faat jip sauh	mou4 faat3 zip3 sau6	mouh faat chip sauh
unable to get /unavailable	adj		無法得到	mòuh faat dāk dóu	mou4 faat3 dak1 dou2	mouh faat tak tou
unable to use	adj		無法子應用	mòuh faat jí ying yuhng	mou4 faat3 zi2 jing3 jung6	mouh faat chi yeng yuhng
unable to walk	adj		跛腳	bài geuk	bai4 goek3	pai keuk
unaccepted	adj		不受任何	bāt sàuh yam hòh	bat1 sau6 jam3 ho4	pat sauh yam hoh
unaccountable	adj		無法解釋	mòuh faat gáai sīk	mou4 faat3 gaai2 sik1	mouh faat kaai sek
unafraid	adj		無畏	móuh wai	mou5 wai3	mouh wai
unaided	adj		無外援	móuh oih /ngoih wùhn	mou5 oi6 /ngoi6 wun4	mouh oih /ngoih wuhn
unanimous	adj		一致	yāt ji	jat1 zi3	yat chi
unanimously /undivided	ad		一致嘅	yāt ji ge	jat1 zi3 ge3	yat chi ke
unanswered /unanswerable	adj		無反應	mouh faan ying	mou4 faan3 jing3	mouh faan yeng
unanswered	adj		未答復	meih daap fūk	mei6 daap3 fuk1	meih taap fuk
unashamed	adj		唔覺羞恥	m̀ gok sàu chí	m4 gok4 sau4 ci2	mh kok sau chhi
unasked	adj		未出口	meih chēut háu	mei6 ceot1 hau2	meih chhot hau
unattached[1] /single /not married/unmarried	adj		未婚	meih fān	mei6 fan1	meih fan
unattached[2] /unmarried	adj		未戀愛	meih lyún ói	mei6 lyun2 oi2	meih lyun oi

unattractive[1]	adj	唔靚	m̀ leuhng	m4 loeng6	mh leuhng
unattractive[2]	adj	不漂亮	bāt pīu leuhng	bat1 piu1 loeng6	pat phiu leuhng
unattractive[3]	adj	不悦目	bāt yuht muhk	bat1 jyut6 muk6	pat yuht muhk
unauthorized[1]	adj	擅自	sihn jih	sin6 zi6	sihn chih
unauthorized[2]	adj	未授權	meih sauh kyùhn	mei6 sau6 kyun4	meih sauh khyuhn
unavoidable	adj	不可避免	bāt hó beih míhn	bat1 ho2 bei6 min5	pat ho peih mihn
unbelief[1] /disbelief	n	唔信	m̀ seun	m4 seon3	mh swon
unbelief[2] /disbelief	n	好難相信	hóu làahn /nàahn sēung seun	hou2 laan4 /naan4 soeng1 soen3	hou laahn /naahn seung swon
unbelief[3]	n	不信	bāt seun	bat1 seon3	pat swon
unbelievable	adj	非常好	fèi sèuhng hou	fei4 soeng4 hou3	fei seuhng hou
unbeliever	n	無信仰的人	mòuh seun yéuhng dìk yàhn	mou4 soen3 joeng5 dik4 jan4	mouh swon yeuhng tik yahn
unbelted[1]	adj	解下腰帶	gàai hàh yìu dáai	gaai4 haa6 jiu4 daai2	kaai hah yiu taai
unbound[2] /not limit /unlimited	adj	無限	mòuh haahn	mou4 haan6	mouh haahn
unbutton	v	解鈕	gáai náu	gaai2 nau2	kaai nau
unceasingly	adv	繼續地	gai juhk deih	gai3 zuk6 dei6	kai chuhk teih
uncertainty /indefinite	n	不確定	bāt kok dehng	bat1 kok3 deng6	pat khok tehng
uncivilized[1]	adj	野蠻	yéh màahn	je5 maan4	yeh maahn
uncivilized[2]	adj	不合社會	bāt hahp séh wùih	bat1 hap6 se5 wui4	pat hahp seh wuih
unclaimed	adj	未要求	mèih yìu kàhu	mei6 jiu4 kau4	meih yiu khahu
uncle[1] /father's elder brother and others	n	伯伯	baa baa	baa3 baa3	paa paa
uncle[2] /father's elder brother	n	伯父	baa fuh	baa3 fu6	paa fuh
uncle[3] /father's younger brother	n	呀叔	àa sūk /aa sūk	aa4 suk1, aa3 suk1	aa suk
uncle[4] /mother's brother	n	舅父	káuh fú	kau5 fu2	khauh fu
uncle[5] /mother's brother	n	叔叔	sūk sūk	suk1 suk1	suk suk
uncle[6] /mother's brother	n	呀伯	àa baa, aa baa	aa4 baa3, aa3 baa3	aa paa
uncomfortable	adj	不自在	bāt jih joih	bat1 zi6 zoi6	pat chi choih
uncommon	adj	不常有	bāt sèuhng yáuh	bat1 soeng4 jau5	pat seuhng yauh
uncompleted	adj	未完成	meih yùhn sèhng/ sìhng	mei6 jyun4 seng4 /sing4	meih yuhn sehng
uncompromising	adj	唔妥協	m̀ toh hip	m4 to6 hip3	mh thoh hip
unconceivable	adj	無/冇可想像	móuh hó séung jèuhng	mou5 ho2 soeng2 zoeng6	mouh ho seung cheuhng
unconcerned[1]	adj	唔關心	m̀ gwàan sàm	m4 gwaan4 sam4	mh kwaan sam
unconcerned[2]	adj	沒興趣	muht hing cheui	mut6 hing3 ceoi3	muht hing chhoi
unconcerned[3]	adj	漫不經心	maahn bāt gīng sàm	maan6 bat1 ging1 sam4	maahn pat keng sam
unconditional /absolute	adj	絕對	jyuht deui	zyut6 deoi3	chyuht toei
unknowingly /unconsciously	adj	不知不覺	bāt jì bāt gok	bat1 zi4 bat1 gok3	pat chi pat kok
unconsciously	adj	不知道地	bāt jì dou deih	bat1 zi4 dou3 dei6	pat chi tou teih
unconstitutional	adj	違反憲法	wai fāan hin faat	wai3 faan1 hin3 faat3	wai faan hin faat

uncontested[1]	adj	無人反對	mòuh yàhn fáan deui	mou4 jan4 faan2 deui3	mouh yahn faan toei
uncontested[2]	adj	沒有人爭	muht yáuh yàhn jàng	mut6 jau5 jan4 zang4	muht yauh yahn chang
uncontested[3]	adj	無競爭	mòuh ging jàng	mou4 ging3 zang4	mouh keng chang
uncontrollable	adj	無法子控制	móuh faat jí hung jai	mou5 faat3 zi2 hung3 zai3	mouh faat chi hung chai
uncooked[1]	adj	生嘅	sàang ge	saang4 ge3	saang ke
uncooked[2]	adj	未煮得熟	meih jyú dāk suhk	mei6 zyu2 dak1 suk6	meih chyu tak suhk
uncountable	adj	數唔到	sóu m̀ dóu	sou2 m4 dou2	sou mh tou
uncover[1] /unveil	v	揭開	kit hòi	kit3 hoi4	khit hoi
uncover[2]	v	揭開蓋子	kit hòi goi jí	kit3 hoi4 goi3 zi2	khit hoi koi chi
uncultivated	adj	未開墾	meih hòi hán	mei6 hoi4 han2	meih hoi han
undated	adj	冇定期	móuh dehng/dihng kèih	mou5 deng6 /ding6 kei4	mouh tehng keih
undecided /pending /indefinite	adj	未決定	meih kyut dihng	mei6 kyut3 deng6	meih khyut tehng
undemocratic	adj	唔民主	m̀ màhn jyú	m4 man4 zyu2	mh mahn chyu
under[1]	prep	在下	joih hah	zoi6 haa6	choih hah
under[2]	prep	喺...下便	hái ...hah bihn	hai2 ···haa6 bin6	hai ...hah pihn
under circumstances		情況下	chìhng fong hah	cing4 fong3 haa6	chhehng fong hah
under control	n	受控制	sauh hung jai	sau6 hung3 zai3	sauh hung chai
under repair		修理中	sau leih jùng	sau3 lei6 zung4	sau leih chung
under the bed		床下面	chòhng hah mihn	cong4 haa6 min6	chhohng hah mihn
under the chair		櫈下面	dang hah mihn	dang3 haa6 min6	tang hah mihn
underground	adj	樓下	lauh hah	lau6 haa6	lauh hah
underground passage /tunnel/subway	n	隧道	seuih douh	seoi6 dou6	swoih touh
underline[1]	v	劃線	waahk sín	waak6 sin2	waahk sin
underline[2]	v	下面劃線	hah mihn waahk sín	haa6 min6 waak6 sin2	hah mihn waahk sin
underline[3]	v	喺字下便劃線	hái jih hah bihn waahk sin	hei2 zi6 haa6 bin6 waak6 sin3	hai chih hah pihn waahk sin
underpants	n	底褲	dái fu	dai2 fu3	tai fu
underscore	v	底線	dái sín	dai2 sin2	tai sin
undershirt	n	底衫	dái sāam	dai2 saam1	tai saam
understand[1]	v	明	mìhng	ming4	mehng
understand[2] /realize /grasp	v	明白	mìhng baahk	ming4 baak6	mehng paahk
understand[3]	v	識聽	sīk tèng	sik1 teng4	sek theng
understand[4]	v	懂了	dung líuh	dung3 liu5	tung liuh
understand[5]	v	領悟	léhng /líhng ngh	leng5 /ling5 ng6	lehng ngh
understanding /understand	v	理解	leih gaai	lei5 gaai3	leih kaai
understood	adj	明白嘞	mìhng baahk la	ming4 baak6 lak3	mehng paahk lak
undertake	v	承擔	sing dáam	sing3 daam2	seng taam
underwear	n	內衣	loih /noih yī	loi6 /noi6 ji1	loih /noih yi
undeveloped[1]	adj	唔發達	m̀ faat daaht	m4 faat3 daat6	mh faat taaht

undeveloped[2]	adj	未開懇	meih hòi hán	mei6 hoi4 han2	meih hoi han
undid[1]	v	打敗	dá baaih	daa2 baai6	ta paaih
undid[2]	v	挫敗	cho baaih	co3 baai6	chho paaih
undisciplined	adj	放縱	fong jùng	fong3 zung4	fong chung
undisputed	adj	不反對	bāt fáan deui	bat1 faan2 deoi3	pat faan twoi
undisturbed[1]/peaceful	adj	平靜	pèhng jèhng, pìhng jìhng	peng4 zeng4, ping4 zing4	phehng chehng
undisturbed[2]	adj	無受干擾	móuh sauh gòn yíu	mou5 sau6 gon4 jiu2	mouh sauh kon yiu
undisturbed[3]/tranquil	adj	寧靜	lìhng /nìhng jihng	ling4 /ning4 zing6	lehng /nehng chehng
undivided[1]	adj	無分開	móuh fàn hòi	mou5 fan4 hoi4	mouh fan hoi
undivided[2]	adj	一致嘅	yāt ji ge	jat1 zi3 ge3	yat chi ke
undoubtful /unthinkable	adj	無/冇可想像	móuh hó séung jèuhng	mou5 ho2 soeng2 zoeng6	mouh ho seung cheuhng
undress[1]	v	除使衫	chèuih saai sāam	ceoi4 saai3 saam1	chheuih saai saam
undress[2]	v	脫衣服	tyut yī fuhk	tyut3 ji1 fuk6	thyut yi fuhk
undue	adj	不由於	bāt yàuh yù	bat1 jau4 jyu4	pat yauh yu
uneasy state /say difficulty	adj	解釋不安	gáai sīk bāt ngòn	gaai2 sik1 bat1 ngon4	kaai sek pat ngon
uneatable	adj	不宜食用	bāt yìh sihk yuhng	bat1 ji4 sik6 jung6	pat yih sehk yuhng
uneducated[1]/unknowing	adj	無知	mòuh jì	mou4 zi4	mouh chi
uneducated[2]	adj	未受教育	meih sauh gaau yuhk	mei6 sau6 gaau3 juk6	meih sauh kaau yuhk
unemployed[1]	adj	空閒	hùng hàan	hung4 haan4	hung haan
unemployed[2]	adj	未利用	meih leih yuhng	mei6 lei6 jung6	meih leih yuhng
unemployment	adj	失業人數	sāt yihp yàhn sou	sat1 jip6 jan4 sou3	sat yihp yahn sou
uneven[1]	adj	唔平	m̀ pìhng	m4 peng4/ping4	mh phehng
uneven[2]	adj	不平坦	bāt peng tāan	bat1 peng3 taan1	pat pheng thaan
uneven[3]	adj	凹凸不平	lāp /nāp daht bāt pèhng	lap1 /nap1 dat6 bat1 peng4	lap /nap taht pat phehng
uneven rule	adj	唔規則	m̀ kwài jāk	m4 kwai4 zak1	mh khwai chak
unexpected[1]	adj	意外	yi òih /ngoih	ji3 oi6 /ngoi6	yi oih /ngoih
unexpected[2]	adj	出乎意料	chēut fù yi líu	ceot1 fu4 ji3 liu2	chhot fu yi liu
unexpectedly[1]	adj	想唔到	séung m̀ dou	soeng2 m4 dou3	seung mh tou
unexpectedly[2]	adj	居然	gēui yín	geoi1 jin2	kwoi yin
unfair[1] /injustice	adj	不公平	bāt gūng pèhng/ pìhng	bat1 gung1 peng4 /ping4	pat kung phehng
unfair[2] /not fair/not equally treat	adj	無理極	móuh léih gihk	mo4 lei5 gik6	mouh leih kehk
unfair treat (coll)	v	虐	fú /foo	fu2	fu /foo
unfaithful	adj	騙子	pin jí	pin3 zi2	phin chi
unfasten /untie/unhitch /loosened/undo	v	解開	gáai hòi	gaai2 hoi4	kaai hoi
unfold	v	逐漸展現	juhk jīm jí yihn	zuk6 zim1 zi2 jin6	chuhk chim chi yihn
unforeseen	adj	未預見到	meih yuh gin dou	mei6 jyu6 gin3 dou3	meih yuh kin tou
unforeseen loss	adj	意外損失	yi òih /ngoih syún sāt	ji3 oi6 /ngoi6 syun2 sat1	yi oih /ngoih syun sat
unforgettable	adj	難忘記	làahn mòhng gei	laan6 mong4 gei3	laahn mohng kei

English		Chinese	Romanization	Jyutping	Yale
unforgettable cause	adj	令人難忘	lehng yàhn làahn /nàahn mòhng	leng jan4 laan6 /naan6 mong4	lehng yahn laahn mohng
unfortunate /bad luck	adj	厄運	āk /àak wahn	ak1 /aak1wan6	ak /aak wahn
unfounded	adj	沒有事實根據	muht yáuh sih saht gàn geui	mut6 jau5 si6 sat6 gan4 geoi3	muht yauh sih saht kan kwoi
unfriendly[1]	adj	唔友好	m̀ yáuh hóu	m4 jau5 hou2	mh yauh hou
unfriendly[2]	adj	不友好	bāt yáuh hóu	bat1 jau5 hou2	pat yauh hou
ungrateful	adj	不領情	bāt léhng /líhng chèhng	bat1 leng5 /ling5 ceng4	pat lehng chehng
unhappy[1]	adj	呷醋	haap chou	haap3 cou3	haap chhou
unhappy[2] (coll)	adj	唔開心	m̀ hòi sàm	m4 hoi4 sam4	mh hoi sam
unhappy[3] (coll) depression /sad/unpleasant	adj	唔快樂	m̀ faai lohk	m4 faai3 lok6	mh faai lohk
unhappy[4] (coll) depression /sad/unpleasant	adj	唔愉快	m̀ yu fáai	m4 jyu3 faai2	mh yu faai
unhappy[5] (coll) unsatisfied /discontented/dissatisfaction/not satisfied	adj/v	唔滿意	m̀ múhn yi	m4 mun5 ji3	mh muhn yi
unhappy[6]		成晚怒	sìhng máahn louh	sing4 maan5 lou6	sehng maahn louh
unhealthy	adj	不健康	bāt gihn hòng	bat1 gin6 hong4	pat kihn hong
unheard of	adj	前所未聞	chìhn só meih màhn	cin4 so2 mei6 man4	chhihn so meih mahn
unhitch[1] /discharge /take off / unload	v	卸	sé	se2	se
unhitch[2] /unload	v	卸掉	se diuh	se3 diu6	se tiuh
unicorn[1] (story horse)	n	廌	jàaih /zàaih	zaai6	chaaih
unicorn[2] (chinese story horse)	n	麒麟	kèih lèuhn	kei4 leon4	kheih lowhn
unicorn[3] (western story horse)	n	獨角獸	duhk gok sau	duk6 gok3 sau3	tuhk kok sau
unified /join forces	adj	團結	tyùhn git	tyun4 git3	thyuhn kit
uniform (of army/school /employees)	n	制服	jai fuhk	zai3 fuk6	chai fuhk
uniformly	ad	一致地	yāt ji deih	jat1 zi3 dei6	yat chi teih
unify	v	統一	túng yāt	tung2 jat1	thung yat
unilateral	adj	片面嘅	pin mihn ge	pin3 min6 ge3	phin mihn ke
unintentionally	adj	唔覺意	m̀ gok yi	m4 kok3 ji3	mh kok yi
uninvited	adj	未經請求	meih gīng chéng kàuh	mei6 ging1 ceng2 kau4	meih keng chheng khauh
union	adj	社團	séh tyùhn	se5 tyun4	seh thyuhn
unique[1] /unusual/distinct /no other than/namely	adj	獨特	duhk dahk	duk4 dak6	tuhk tahk
unique[2]	adj	唯一	wàih yāt	wai4 zat1	waih yAt
unique[3] /extraordinary	adj	獨一無二	duhk yāt móuh yih	duk6 zat1 mou5 ji6	tuhk yat mouh yih
unisex /commongender	adj	男女皆宜	làahm léoih gāai yìh	laam4 leoi5 gaai1 ji4	laahm lowih kaai yih
unit	n	單元	dāan yùhn	daan1 jyun4	taan yuhn
unit price[1]	n	單位價格	dāan wāi gá gáak	daan1 wai1 gaak2 gaak2	taan wai ka kaak
unit price[2]	n	單價	dāan ga	daan1 ga3	taan ka
unite[1] /together	v	統	túng	tung2	thung

unite[2] /make join	v	使團結	sái tyùhn git	sai2 tyun4 git3	sai thyuhn kit
united	adj	聯合	lyùhn hahp	lyun4 hap6	lyuhn hahp
United Nations /U.N.	n	聯合國	lyuhn hahp gwok	lyun6 hap6 gwok3	lyuhn hahp kwok
unity[1]	n	團一	tyùhn yāt	tyun4 jat1	thyuhn yat
unity[2]	n	統一性	túng yāt sing	tung2 jat1 sing3	thung yat seng
universe[1] /infinite time	n	宙	jauh /zauh	zau6	chauh
universe[2]	n	宇宙	yúh jauh	jyu5 zau6	yuh chauh
university student	n	大學生	daaih hohk sāang	daai6 hok6 saang1	taaih hohk saang
unkind /vile	adj	卑鄙	bèi pēi	bei4 pei1	pei phei
unkindly heart /merciless mind	adj	孤寒鬼	gū hòhn gwái	gu1 hon4 gwai2	ku hohn kwai
unknown[1] (coll) (before)	adj	唔知	m̀ jì	m4 zi4	mh chi
unknown[2] (wr) (before)	adj	不知	bāt jì	bat1 zi4	pat chi
unknown[3] (from now)	adj	未知	meih jì	mei6 zi4	meih chi
unknown[4] (any time)	adj	唔熟識	m̀ suhk sīk	m4 suk6 sik1	mh suhk sek
unless	conj	除非	chèuih fèi	ceoi4 fei4	chheuih fei
unlicensed	adj	沒有執照	muht yáuh jāp jiu	mut6 jau5 zap1 ziu3	muht yauh chap chiu
unlike /different/unusual	adj	相異	sèung yih	soeng4 ji6	seung yih
unlimited	adj	無限嘅	mouh haahn ge	mou4 haan6 ge3	mouh haahn ke
unload	v	卸下	sé hah	se2 ha6	se hah
unloader	n	解除人	gaai chèuih yàhn	gaai3 ceoi4 jan4	kaai chheuih yahn
unloading /discharge /discharge cargo	n	卸貨	sé fó	se2 fo2	se fo
unlock[1]	v	開鎖	hòi só	hoi4 so2	hoi so
unlock[2]	v	未鎖	meih só	mei6 so2	meih so
unlocked	adj	沒有鎖	muht yáuh só	mut6 jau5 so2	muht yauh so
unmanageable[1]	adj	搞唔掂	gáau m̀ dihm	gaau2 m4 dim6	kaau mh tihm
unmanageable[2] /difficult to control	adj	難管理	làhn /nàhn gún léih	laan4 /naan6 gun2 lei5	lahn /nahn kun leih
unmarried	adj	單身	dāan sàn	daan1 san4	taan san
unmarried woman /Miss/young lady	n	小姐	síu jé /zē	siu2 ze1	siu che
unmatchable	adj	無得避	móuh dāk béi	mou5 dak1 bei2	mouh tak pei
unmatched	adj	不相配	bāt séung pui	bat1 soeng2 pui3	pat seung phui
unmeaning[1] /aimless	adj	無目的	móuh muhk dīk	mou5 muk6 dik1	mouh muhk tek
unmeaning[2] /nonsense	adj	無意思	móuh yi sì	mou5 ji3 si4	mouh yi si
unmeaning[3] /nonsense	adj	無意義	móuh yi yih	mou5 ji3 ji6	mouh yi yih
unmistaken	adj	無誤	móuh ngh	mou5 ng6	mouh ngh
unnamed	adj	未命名	meih mehng mèhng	mei6 meng6 meng4	meih mehng mehng
unnecessarily /not necessarily	adv	未必	meih bīt	mei6 bit1	meih pit
unnecessary[1]	adj	唔需要	m̀ sèui yiu	m4 seoi4 jiu3	mh soi yiu
unnecessary[2]	adj	無必要	móuh bīt yiu	mou5 bit1 jiu3	mouh pit yiu
unnecessary[3]	adj	不需要的	bāt sèui yiu dìk	bat1 seoi4 jiu3 dik4	pat swoi yiu tek
unofficial /informal	adj	非正式	fèi jeng /jing sīk	fei4 zeng3 /zing3 sik1	fei cheng sek

English		Chinese	Yale	Jyutping	Romanization
unopened with the seal		把...封閉在...裏	bá fūng bai joih léih	ba2 fung1 bai3 zoi6 leih5	pa fung pai choih leih
unopposed	adj	無對手	mòuh deui sáu	mou4 deoi3 sau2	mouh toei sau
unpaid	adj	未畀錢	meih béi chín	mei6 bei2 cin2	meih pei chhin
unpleasant	adj	討厭	tóu yim	tou2 jim3	thou yim
unpopular[1] /not satisfactory/unsatisfactory	adj	唔得人心	m̀ dak yàhn sàm	m4 dak3 jan4 sam4	mh tak yahn sam
unpopular[2]/unwelcome	adj	唔受歡迎	m̀ sauh fùn yìhng	m4 sau6 fun4 jing4	mh sauh fun yehng
unpopular[3]	adj	不得人心	bāt dāk yàhn sàm	bat1 dak1 jan4 sam4	pat tak yahn sam
unprepared	adj	無預備	móuh yuh beih	mou5 jyu6 bei6	mouh yuh peih
unpresentable	adj	拿不出去	lāh /nāh bāt chēut heui	laa1 /naa1 bat1 ceot1 heoi3	lah /nah pat chhot hoi
unpretentious	adj	不思張揚	bāt sī jèung yèuhng	bat1 si1 zong4 joeng4	pat si cheung yeuhng
unproductive[1]	adj	無生產	móuh sàng cháan	mou5 sang4 caan2	mouh sang chhaan
unproductive[2]	adj	無收益	móuh sàu yīk	mou5 sau4 jik1	mouh sau yek
unprofessional	adj	唔合行規	m̀ hahp hòhng kwài	m4 hap6 hong4 kwai4	mh hahp hohng khwai
unpunctual /not on time	adj	唔準時	m̀ jéun sìh	m4 zeon2 si4	mh cheun sih
unpunished	adj	未受處罰	meih sauh chyū faht	mei6 sau6 cyu1 faat3	meih sauh chhyu faht
unpurchasable /unable to buy	adj	無法買到	mòuh faat máaih dou	mou4 faat3 maai5 dou3	mouh faat maaih tou
unqualified[1]	adj	唔合格	m̀ hahp gaak	m4 hap6 gaak3	mh hahp kaak
unqualified[2]	adj	唔搞資格	m̀ gau jì gaak	m4 gau3 zi4 gaak3	mh kau chi kaak
unready	adv	未準備好	meih jéun beih hóu	mei6 zeon2 bei6 hou2	meih cheun peih hou
unreal	adj	唔真	m̀ jàn	m4 zan4	mh chan
unreasonable[1]	adj	冇道理	móuh dou léih	mou5 dou3 lei5	mouh tou leih
unreasonable[2]	adj	無譜	móuh póu	mou5 pou2	mouh phou
unreasonable[3]	adj	不合理	bāt hahp léih	bat1 hap6 lei5	pat hahp leih
unrecorded[1]	adj	無記錄	mòuh gei luhk	mou4 gei3 luk6	mouh kei luhk
unrecorded[2]	adj	沒有記錄	muht yáuh gei luhk	mut6 jau5 gei3 luk6	muht yauh kei luhk
unrefined	adj	登大雅之堂	dāng daaih ngáh ji tòhng	dang1 daai6 nga5 zi3 tong4	tang taaih ngah chi thohng
unrelated[1]	adj	唔相關	m̀ sèung gwàan	m4 soeng4 gwaan4	mh seung kwaan
unrelated[2]	adj	不相關	bāt sèung gwàan	bat1 soeng4 gwaan4	pat seung kwaan
unreliable[1]	adj	唔可靠	m̀ hó kaau	m4 ho2 kaau3	mh ho khaau
unreliable[2]	adj	靠唔住	kaau m̀ jyuh	kaau3 m4 zyu6	khaau mh chyuh
unrest[1] /worried/uneasy /unpeaceful	n	不安	bat òn /ngòn	bat1 on4 /ngon4	pat on /ngon
unrest[2]	n	動亂	duhng lyuhn	dung6 lyun6	tuhng lyuhn
unrest[3]	n	不平靜	bāt peng jihng	bat1 peng3 zing6	pāt pheng chehng
unripe	adj	未熟	meih suhk	mei6 suk6	meih suhk
unroll /roll open	v	卷開	gyún hòi	gyun2 hoi4	kyun hoi
unruls[1]	adj	難控制	làahn hung jai	laan4 hung3 zai3	laahn hung chai
unruls[2]	adj	難駕馭	làahn gá yùh	laan4 gaa2 jyu6	laahn ka yuh
unruly[1] /obstinate /stubborn/stiff-necked	adj	頑固	wàahn gu	waan4 gu3	waahn ku

unruly[2] /wanton/wilful	adj	唔守規矩	m̀ sáu kwài géui	m4 sai2 kwai4 geoi2	mh sau khwai kwoi
unsafe[1]	adj	唔安全	m̀ òn chyùhn	m4 on4 cyun4	mh on chhyuhn
unsafe[2]	adj	唔穩陣	m̀ wám jahn	m4 wan2 zan6	mh wam chahn
unsaid	adj	未說出口	meih syut chēut háu	mei6 syut3 ceot1 hau2	meih syut chhot hau
unsatisfactory	adj	唔令人滿意	m̀ lehng /lihng yàhn múhn yi	m4 leng4 /ling4 jan4 mun5 ji3	mh lehng yahn muhn yi
unsatisfied	adj	未滿足	meih múhn júk	mei6 mun5 zuk2	meih muhn chuk
unscrew[1] /open screw	v	擰鬆	léhng /níhng sùng	leng5 /ning5 sung4	lehng sung
unscrew[2]	v	鬆開螺絲	sùng hòi lòh sī	sung4 hoi4 lo4 si1	sung hoi loh si
unsealed	adj	未封口	meih fùng háu	mei6 fung4 hau2	meih fung hau
unsealed letter	adj	開口信	hòi háu seun	hoi4 hau2 seon3	hoi hau swon
unseam /unsew cloths	a/v	改衣	gói yī	goi2 ji1	koi yi
unseen[1]	adj	睇唔見	tái m̀ gin	tai2 m4 gin3	thai mh kin
unseen[2]	adj	未看見	meih hòn gin	mei6 hon4 gin3	meih hon kin
unsettle[1] /shaked disorder	v	搖亂	yíu lyuhn	jiu2 lyun6	yiu lyuhn
unsettle[2]	v	攪亂	gáau lyuhn	gaau2 lyun6	kaau lyuhn
unsettle[3]	v	不穩定	bāt wān dèhng	bat1 wan1 deng6	pat wan dehng
unsightly	adj	不悅目	bāt yuhk muhk	bat1 juk6 muk6	pat yuhk muhk
unsold	adj	未售出	meih sauh chēut	mei6 sau6 ceot1	meih sauh chhot
unsolvable /problem	adj	能解決	làhng /nàhng gáai kyut	lang4 /nang4 gaai2 kyut3	lahng /nahng kaai khyut
unsound	adj	唔健全	m̀ gihn chyùhn	m4 gin6 cyun4	mh kihn chhyuhn
unstable	adj	唔穩陣	m̀ wán jahn	m4 wan2 zan6	mh wan chahn
unsteady[1]	adj	唔穩定	m̀ wán dehng /dihng	m4 wan2 deng6 /ding6	mh wan tehng
unsteady[2]	n	擺下擺下	bāai hah bāai hah	baai1 haa6 baai1 haa6	paai hah baai hah
unsteady[3]	adj	易變	yih bin	ji6 bin3	yih pin
unsuccessful[1]	adj	唔成功	m̀ sèhng gùng	m4 seng4 gung4	mh sehng kung
unsuccessful[2]	adj	不成功	bāt sèhng gùng	bat1 seng4 gung4	pat sehng kung
unsuitable	adj	唔啱啱	m̀ ngāam ngāam	m4 ngaam1 ngaam1	mh ngaam ngaam
untidy	adj	凌亂	lìhng lyuhn	ling4 lyun6	lehng lyuhn
untie /to open	v	解	gáai	gaai2	kaai
until[1]	prep	至	ji	zi3	chi
until[2]	v	為止	waih jí	wai6 zi2	waih chi
until now[1]	prep	至今	ji gàm	zi3 gam4	chi kam
until now[2]	prep	一向都	yāt heung dōu	jat1 hoeng3 dou1	yat heung tou
until now[3]	prep	直到現在	jihk dou yihn joih	zik6 dou3 jin6 zoi6	chehk tou yihn choih
untimely	adj	唔合時宜	m̀ hahp sìh yìh	m4 hap6 si4 ji4	mh hahp sih yih
untired	adj	不疲倦	bāt pèih gyùhn	bat1 pei4 gyun6	pat pheih kyuhn
unto	prep	於	yu	jyu3	yu
untold[1] /did not say	adj	未講過	meih góng gwo	mei6 gong2 gwo3	meih kong kwo
untold[2] /did not say	adj	未說過	meih syut gwo	mei6 syut3 gwo3	meih syut kwo
untoward	adj	困難	kwan làahn /nàahn	kwan3 laan4 /naan4	khwan laahn /naahn
untrue /untruthful /unreal/false	adj	唔真實	m̀ jàn saht	m4 zan4 sat6	mh chan saht

English	POS	中文	Romanization 1	Jyutping	Romanization 2
untrusty	adj	不可靠	bāt hó kaau	bat1 ho2 kaau3	pat ho khaau
untruth	n	虛假	hèui gá	heoi4 gaa2	hoi ka
unturned	adj	未顛倒	meih dìn dóu	mei6 din4 dou2	meih tin tou
unused /not used	adj	唔習慣	m̀ jaahp gwaan	m4 zaap6 gwaan3	mh chaahp kwaan
unused[1]	adj	未用過	meih yuhng gwo	mei6 jung6 gwo3	meih yuhng kwo
unused[2]	adj	未使用	meih sái yuhng	mei6 sai2 jung6	meih sai yuhng
unusual[1] /strange	adj	唔平常	m̀ pèhng sèuhng	m4 peng4 soeng4	mh phehng seuhng
unusual[2]	adj	不平常	bāt peng sèuhng	bat1 peng3 soeng4	pat pheng seuhng
unusual[3]	adj	不尋常	bāt chàhm sèuhng	bat1 cam4 soeng4	pat chhahm seuhng
unveil[1] /disclose	v	揭露	kit louh	kit3 lou6	khit louh
unveil[2] /visible	v	顯露	hín louh	hin2 lou6	hin louh
unveil[3] /open veil	v	除面紗	chèuih mihn sā	ceoi4 min6 saa1	chheuih mihn sa
unveil[4] /public announce	v	公佈於眾	gūng bou yū jung	gung1 bou3 jyu1 zung3	kung pou yu chung
unwatchful	adj	不機警	bāt gèi gíng	bat1 gei4 ging2	pat kei keng
unwelcome	adj	唔歡迎	m̀ fùn yìhng	m4 fun4 jing4	mh fun yehng
unwell	adj	不舒服	bāt syù fùhk	bat1 syu4 fuk6	pat syu fuhk
unwept	adj	無人哀悼	móuh yàhn òi /ngòi douh	mou5 jan4 oi4 /ngoi4 dou6	mouh yahn oi /ngoi touh
unwilling[1]	adj	唔願意	m̀ yuhn yi	m4 jyun6 ji3	mh yuhn yi
unwilling[2]	adj	冇情願	móuh chìhng yuhn	mou5 cing4 jyun6	mouh chhehng yuhn
unwilling[3]	adj	不願	bāt yuhn	bat1 jyun6	pat yuhn
unworthy	adj	唔值得	m̀ jihk dāk	m4 zik6 dak1	mh chehk tak
unwrap[1]	v	析開	jìhk hòi	zik4 hoi4	chehk hoi
unwrap[2] /spread/unfold	v	展開	jin hòi	zin3 hoi4	chin hoi
unwritten /oral	adj	未成文	meih sèhng /sìhng	mei6 seng4 /sing4	meih sehng mahn
up to now[1]	n	一向	yāt heung	jat1 hoeng3	yat heung
up to now[2]	n	到目前為止	dou muhk chìhn waih jí	dou3 muk6 cin4 wai6 zi2	tou muhk chhihn waih chi
upcoming	adj	即將來臨	jīk jèung lòih làhm	zik1 zoeng4 loi4 lam4	chek cheung loih lahm
update	v	最新資料	jeui sàn jì líu	zeoi3 san4 zi4 liu2	cheui san chi liu
uphill[1]	n	上山	séuhng sàan	soeng5 saan4	seuhng saan
uphill[2]	n	向上	heung seuhng	hoeng3 soeng6	heung seuhng
uphill road	n	上斜路	séuhng che louh	soeng5 ce3 lou6	seuhng chhe louh
upon[1]	prep	上面	séuhng mìhn	soeng5 min6	seuhng mihn
upon[2]	prep	上便	séuhng bihn	soeng5 bin6	seuhng pihn
upon[3]	prep	依靠	yi kaau	ji3 kaau3	yi khaau
upon[4]	prep	之上	jī seuhng	zi1 soeng6	chi seuhng
upon arrival		到咗至	dou jó ji	dou3 zo2 zi3	tou cho chi
upon receipt		收咗至	sàu jó ji	sau4 zo2 zi3	sau cho chi
upper arm	n	上臂	séuhng béi	soeng5 bei2	seuhng pei
upright[1]	adj	正直	jeng jihk	zeng3 zik6	cheng chehk
upright[2]	adj	挺直	tīng jìhk	ting1 zik6	thing chehk
upright[3]	adj	挺直地	tīng jìhk deih	ting1 zik6 dei6	thing chehk teih
uprise /raise/to ascend	n	升高	sìng gòu	sing4 gou4	seng kou

upset	v	打亂	dá lyuhn	daa2 lyun6	ta lyuhn
upside	n	上部	seuhng bouh	soeng bou6	seuhng bouh
upstairs[1]	n	樓上	làuh séuhng	lau4 soeng5	lauh seuhng
upstairs[2]	n	往樓上	wóhng làuh séuhng	wong5 lau4 soeng5	wohng lauh seuhng
upwards	adv	向上	heung seuhng	hoeng3 soeng6	heung seuhng
uranium (atomic no 92u)	n	鈾	yáu	jau2	yau
urban /civic	adj	城市	sèhng síh	seng4 si5	sehng sih
urbanity	n	都市風格	dōu síh fùng gaak	dou1 si5 fung4 gaak3	tou sih fung kaak
urea (NH2)2CO)	n	尿素	liuh /niuh sou	liu6 /niu6 sou3	liuh /niuh sou
ureter /urine pipe	n	輸尿管	syù liuh /niuh gún	syu4 liu6 /niu6 gun2	syu liuh /niuh kun
urethra /urethral /urinary tract	n	尿道	liuh /niuh douh	liu6 /niu6 dou6	liuh /niuh touh
urge[1]	v	力勸	lihk hyun	lik6 hyun	lehk hyun
urge[2]	v	力陳	lihk chàhn	lik6 can4	lehk chhahn
urge[3]	v	推進	tèui jeun	teoi4 zeon3	thoi cheun
urgent[1]	adj	迫	bīk	bik1	pek
urgent[2] /hot/emergency	adj/n	緊急	gán gāp	gan2 gap1	kan kap
urgent[3]	adj	急件	gāp gihn	gap1 gin6	kap kihn
urgent go to toilet[1]	v	肚瀉	tóuh sé	tou5 se2	thouh se
urgent go to toilet[2]		腹瀉	fūk sé	fuk6 se2	fuk se
urgent hotline	n	緊急熱線	gán gāp yiht sin	gan2 gap1 jit6 sin3	kan kap yiht sin
urgent remember	n	緊記	gán gei	gan2 gei3	kan kei
urgent repairs	n	搶修	chéung sàu	coeng2 sau4	chheung sau
urgent rescue /emergency rescue	n	緊急求救	gán gāp kàuh gau	gan2 gap1 kau4 gau3	kan kap khauh kau
urgent sexual intercourse (sl)	v xy	急色鬼	gāp sīk gwái	gap1 sik1 gwai2	kap sek kwai
urgently	adv	緊急地	gán gāp deih	gan2 gap1 dei6	kan kap teih
uric acid	n	尿酸	liuh /niuh syūn	liu6 /niu6 syun1	liuh /niuh syun
urinal	n	小便池	síu bihn chìh	siu2 bin6 ci4	siu pihn chhih
urine[1] /urinate/pissing	v	小便	síu bihn	siu2 bin6	siu pihn
urine[2] /pee/piss	n	尿	liuh /niuh	liu6 /niu6	liuh /niuh
urine[3]	n	小便	síu bìhn	siu2 bin4	siu pihn
urine[4] /piss	n	尿液	liuh /niuh yihk	liu6 /niu6 jik6	liuh /niuh yehk
urine protein	n	尿蛋白	liuh /niuh dáan baahk	liu6 /niu6 daan2 baak6	liuh /niuh taan paahk
urine sugar	n	尿糖	liuh /niuh tòhng	liu6 /niu6 tong4	liuh /niuh thohng
us /we/our	pron	我哋	ngóh dèih	ngo5 dei6	ngoh teih
US dollar /US $	n	美元	méih yùhn	mei5 jyun4	meih yuhn
usable	adj	可用	hó yuhng	ho2 jung6	ho yuhng
usage	n	用法	yuhng faat	jung6 faat3	yuhng faat
use[1] /usage	n	利用	leih yuhng	lei6 jung6	leih yuhng
use[2]	n	應用	yìng yùhng	jing4 jung6	yeng yuhng
use leather belt	n	用皮帶	yuhng pèih dáai	jung6 pei4 daai2	yuhng pheih taai
used[1]	adj	慣咗	gwaan jó	gwaan3 zo2	kwaan cho

used[2] /old	adj	舊	gauh	gau6	kauh
used to[1] /accustomed to	v	慣	gwaan	gwaan3	kwaan
used to[2]	v	做	jouh	zou6	chouh
used up[1] /already used	v	用曬	yuhng saai	jung6 saai3	yuhng saai
used up[2] /very tired	n	筋疲力盡	gān pèih lihk jeuhn	gan1 pei4 lik6 zeon6	kan pheih lehk cheuhn
useful	adj	有用嘅	yáuh yuhng ge	yau5 jung6 ge3	yauh yuhng ke
usefulness /utility	n	效用	haauh yuhng	haau6 jung6	haauh yuhng
useless[1]	adj	壞咗	waaih jó	wai6 zo2	waaih cho
useless[2] /vain/worthless	adj	徒勞	tòuh lòuh	tou4 lou4	thouh louh
user /consumer	n	用戶	yuhng wuh	jung6 wu6	yuhng wuh
user's manual		用戶手冊	yuhng wuh sáu chaak	jung6 wu6 sau2 caak3	yuhng wuh sau chhaak
users	n	使用者	sāi yùhng jé	sai1 jung6 ze2	sai yuhng che
usher	n	招呼	jiu fù	ziu3 fu4	chiu fu
using amount	n	用量	yuhng leuhng	jung6 loeng6	yuhng leuhng
USSR (old name of the Soviet Union 1922-1991)	n	蘇聯	sòu lyun	sou4 lyun3	sou lyun
usual /usually/regular/as a	adj	通常	tùng sèuhng	tung4 soeng4	thung seuhng
usually /commonly /ordinarily/ordinary	adv	通常地	tùng seung dèih	tung4 soeng3 dei6	thung seung teih
usurp[1] /seize by force	v	霸佔	ba jim	baa3 zim3	pa chim
usurp[2]	v	侵奪	chàm dyuht	cam4 dyut6	chham tyuht
utensil /appliances /tools	n	用具	yuhng geuih	jung6 geoi6	yuhng kwoih
uterus /womb	n	子宮	jí gùng	zi2 gung4	chi kung
utmost /as far as possible	adj	精心	jēng sàm	zeng1 sam4	cheng sam
utter /tell	v	出聲	chēut sēng	ceot1 seng1	chhot seng
utterance /speech	n	講話	góng wá	gong2 waa2	kong wa

V neck /V shape	n	V領	V léhng	V leng5	V lehng
vacancy	n	清閒	cheng /chìng hàahn	ceng4 /cing4 haan4	chheng haahn
vacant	adj	空隙	hùng kwīk	hung4 kwik1	hung khwik
vacate /move out	v	搬出	bùn chēut	but4 ceot1	pun chhot
vacation /day off /furlough	n	休假	yàu ga	jau4 gaa3	yau ka
vaccinate	v	注射疫苗	jyu seh yihk mìuh	zyu3 se6 jik6 miu6	chyu seh yehk miuh
vaccination	n	種痘	júng dauh	zung2 dau6	chung tauh
vaccinator	n	疫苗接種員	yihk mìuh jip júng yùhn	jik6 miu4 zip3 zung2 jyun4	yehk miuh chip chung yuhn
vaccine	adj	疫苗	yihk mìuh	jik6 miu4	yehk miuh
vacillate	v	躊躇	chàuh chyùh	cau4 cyu4	chhauh chhyuh
vacuum	n	真空	jàn hùng	zan4 hung4	chan hung
vacuum cleaner[1]	n	吸塵機	kàp chàhn gèi	kap4 can4 gei1	khap chhahn kei
vacuum cleaner[2]	n	吸塵器	kàp chàhn hei	kap4 can4 hei3	khap chhahn hei
vagina	n	陰道	yàm douh	jam4 dou6	yam touh
vagina itchy	adj	閪痕	hài hàhn	hai4 han4	hai hahn
vague /blur/less clear	adj	模糊不清	mou wu bāt chèng /chìng	mou3 wu3 bat1 ceng4 /cing4	mou wu pat chheng
vain /futile/bootless	adj	徒然	tòuh yìhn	tou4 jin4	thouh yihn
valentine /paramour /lover	n	情人	chìhng yàhn	cing4 jan4	chhehng yahn
Valentine's day (14 Feb)	n	情人節	chìhng yàhn jit	cing4 jan4 zit3	chhehng yahn chit
valid[1]	adj	效	hàauh	haau6	haauh
valid[2]	adj	有效	yauh hàauh	jau6 haau6	yauh haauh
validity	n	正確	jeng kok	zeng3 kok3	cheng khok
valley	n	凹頭	āau tàuh	aau1 tau4	aau thauh
valuable /costly /very expensive!	adj	貴重	gwai juhng	gwai3 zung6	kwai chuhng
valuated	adj	評價咗	pìhng gá jó	ping4 ga2 zo2	phehng ka cho
value[1] /worth	n	值	jihk	zik6	chehk
valve[2] /oneway door	n	活門	wuht mun	wut6 mun3	wuht mun
vampire[1] (eastern ghost)	n	殭屍	gèung sì	gong4 si4	keung gèung sì
vampire[2] (ghost)	n	吸血鬼	kāp hyut gwái	kap1 hyut3 gwai2	khap hyut kwai
vampire[3] (ghost)	n	吸血殭屍	kāp hyut gèung sì	kap1 hyut3 goeng4 si4	khap hyut keung si
van[1] /good's small vehicle	n	van仔	wēng jái	weng1 zai2	weng chai
van[2] /good's small vehicle	n	客貨車	haak fo chè	haak3 fo3 ce4	haak fo chhe
van[3] /to expel/to chsase /to pursue	n	前驅	chìhn kèui	cin4 keoi4	chhihn kheui
vandalic	adj	汪達爾人	wōng daaht yíh yàhn	wong1 daat6 ji5 jan4	wong taaht yih yahn
vantage	n	優越	yàu yuht	jau4 jyut6	yau yuht
vapour	n	水汽	séui hei	seoi2 hei3	swoi hei
varied	adj	多變的	dò bín dìk	do4 bin2 dik4	to pin tek
variegate	adj	雜色	jaahp sīk	zaap6 sik1	chaahp sek
various /miscellaneous /varied/all kinds of/all kinds and sorts	n/adj	各式各樣	gok sīk gok yeuhng	gok3 sik1 gok3 joeng6	kok sek kok yeuhng

vase /pitcher	n	瓶	pèhng /pìhng	peng4 /ping4	phehng
vaseline	n	凡士林	fàahn sih làhm	faan4 si6 lam4	faahn sih lahm
vassal	n	奴僕	lòuh /nòuh buhk	lou4 /nou4 buk6	louh /nouh puhk
vast	adj	廣大	gwōng dàaih	gwong1 daai6	kwong taaih
underground store[1] /vault	n	地下儲藏室	deih há chyúh chòhng sāt	dei6 haa2 cyu5 cong4 sat1	teih ha chhyuh chhohng sat
underground store[2] /vault	n	地下儲物室	deih há chyúh maht sāt	dei6 haa2 cyu5 mat6 sat1	teih ha chhyuh maht sat
vaunted /proudly	adj	自吹自播	jih cheui jih lèuih	zi6 ceoi3 zi6 leoi4	chih chheui chih lowih
vegetable	n	蔬菜	sò chói	so4 coi2	so chhoi
vegetable rack	n	菜架	choi gá	coi3 gaa2	chhoi ka
vegetable dumpling	n	菜餃子	chòih gāau jī	coi4 gaau1 zi1	chhoih kaau chi
vegetarian[1]	n	素食	sou sihk	sou3 sik6	sou sihk
vegetarian[2]	n	素菜	sou chói	sou3 coi2	sou chhoi
vegetarian[3]	n	食齋	sihk jàai	sik6 zaai4	sehk chaai
vegetarian rice roll	n	齋腸	jāai chéung	zaai1 coeng2	chaai chheung
vegetarianism	n	素食主義	sou sihk jyú yih	sou3 sik6 zyu2 ji6	sou sehk chyu yih
vehicle stop /parking	n	停車	tìhng chè	ting4 ce4	thehng chhe
veil[1] /cotton yarn	n	紗	sā	saa1	sa
veil[2]	n	面紗	mihn sā	min6 saa1	mihn sa
vein[1] /blood vessel	n	血管	hyut gún	hyut3 gun2	hyut kun
vein[2]	n	靜脈	jehng mahk	zeng6 mak6	chehng mahk
vein botany	n	葉脈	yìhp mahk	jip6 mak6	yihp mahk
vein mineral	n	礦脈	kwong mahk	kwong3 mak6	khwong mahk
vendor's booth /booth	n	攤位	tàan waih	taan4 wai6	thaan waih
ventilation	n	通風	tùng fùng	tung4 fung4	thung fung
ventilator	n	通風機	tùng fùng gèi	tung4 fung4 gei4	thung fung kei
venue	n	犯罪地點	faahn jeuih deih dím	faan6 zeoi6 dei6 dim2	faahn cheuih teih tim
venus	n	維納斯女神	waìh laahp sī léuih sàhn	wai4 laap6 si1 leoi5 san4	waih laahp si lowih sahn
venus star /gold star	n	金星	gàm sèng /sìng	gam4 seng4 /sing4	kam seng
verb[1] (intransitive)	n	不及物動詞	bāt kahp maht duhng chìh	bat1 kap6 mat6 dung6 ci4	pat khahp maht tuhng chih
verb[2] (transitive)	n	及物動詞	kahp maht duhng chìh	kap6 mat6 dung6 ci4	khahp maht tohng chhih
verbal	adj	言辭上	yìhn chìh seuhng	jin4 ci4 soeng6	yihn chhih seuhng
verbs[1]	n	動	duhng	dung6	tuhng
verbs[2] (grammar)	n	動詞	duhng chìh	dung6 ci4	tuhng chhih
verified[1]	v	無誤	móuh m̀ /ngh	mou5 m4 /ng4	mouh mh /ngh
verified[2]	v	已證實	yíh jing saht	ji5 zing3 sat6	yih cheng saht
verifier	n	核實者	haht saht jé	hat6 sat6 ze2	haht saht che
verify[1]	v	核實	haht saht	hat6 sat6	haht saht
verify[2] /check/exam	v	核對	haht deui	hat6 deoi3	haht toei
vermiform	a	蠕蟲狀	yùh chùhng johng	jyu4 cung4 zong6	yuh chhuhng chohng
version	n	譯本	yihk bún	jik6 bun2	yehk pun
vertebrate	n	脊椎動物	jek jèui duhng maht	zek3 zeoi4 dung6 mat6	chek cheui dohng maht

vertical	adj	垂直	seui jìhk	seoi4 zik6	swoi chehk
vertically	adj	垂直地	seui jìhk deih	seoi4 zik6 dei6	swoi chehk teih
very[1]	n	好	hóu	hou2	hou
very[2]	adv	甚	sahm	sam6	sahm
very[3]	adv	蠻	màahn	maan4	maahn
very[4]	adv	非常	fèi sèuhng	fei4 soeng4	fei seuhng
very afraid[1]	n	好驚	hóu gèng /gīng	hou2 geng4 /ging4	hou keng
very afraid[2]	n	好驚呀	hóu gèng /gīng ā	hou2 geng4 /ging1 a1	hou keng a
very afraid[3] /great fear /uncontroled fear/panic/too much afraid	n	恐慌	húng fòng	hung2 fong4	hung fong
very angry /infuriated	adj/v	火滾	fó gwán	fo2 gwan2	fo kwan
very bad morally	adj	可憎	hó jāng	ho2 zang1	ho chang
very cheap!	adj	咁平呀!	gam pèhng àh!	gam3 peng4 aa6	kam pehng ah!
very early	adj	好早	hóu jóu	hou2 zou2	hou chou
very expensive! /so expensive!	adj	咁貴呀!	gàm gwai àh!	gam3 gwai3 aa6	kam kwai ah!
very famous	adj	好有名	hóu yáuh mèhng /mìhng	hou2 jau5 meng4 /ming4	hou yauh mehng
very fat[1]	adj	好肥	hóu fèih	hou2 fei4	hou feih
very fat[2]	adj	暴肥	bouh fèih	bou6 fei4	pouh feih
very true	adj	實	saht	sat6	saht
very first	adj	咁快	gam faai	gam3 faai3	kam faai
very good	adj	美德	méih dāk	mei5 dak1	meih tak
very good singing		眞好唱	jān hóu cheung	jan1 hou2 cheung3	chan hou chheung
very great	adj	好大	hóu daaih	hou2 daai6	hou taaih
very great person /ambassador	n	大使	daaih si	daai6 si3	taaih si
very happy	adj	好開心	hóu hòi sām	hou2 hoi4 sam1	hou hoi sam
very lean	adj	暴瘦	bouh sao	bou6 sao3	pouh sao
very lights	n	照明彈	jiu mìhng dáan	ziu3 ming4 daan2	chiu mehng taan
very little	adj	咁鬼少	gam gwái síu	gam3 gwai2 siu2	kam kwai siu
very long	adj	很長	hán chèuhng	han2 coeng4	han chheuhng
very loud	adj	巨響	geuih héung	geoi6 hoeng2	kwoih heung
very low	adj	好低	hóu dài	hou2 dai4	hou tai
very low density	adj	超低密度	chìu dāi maht douh	ciu4 dai1 mat6 dou6	chhiu tai maht touh
very noisy	adv	好嘈	hóu chòuh	hou2 cou4	hou chhouh
very old time /ancient times	adj	古代	gú doih	gu2 doi6	ku toih
very pleased with oneself		好得意	hóu dāk yi	hou2 dak1 ji3	hou tak yi
very realism /very romanticism	n	超現實主義	chìu yihn saht jyú yih	ciu4 jin6 sat6 zyu2 ji6	chhiu yihn saht chyu yih
very respect	adj	非常尊敬	fèi sèuhng jyūn ging	fei4 soeng4 zyun1 ging3	fei seuhng chyun keng
very skinny /very thin		好瘦	hóu sau	hou2 sau3	hou sau
very slender[1]	n	好細	hóu sái	hou2 sai2	hou sai
very slender[2]	n	身體弱	sàn tái yeuhk	san4 tai2 joek6	san thai yeuhk

English		Chinese	Yale	Jyutping	Hakka
very small /minimal	adj	最小的	jeui síu dìk	zeoi3 siu2 dik4	cheui siu tik
very suffering /distressed/miserable/ painful/unhappy	adj	痛苦	tung fú	tung3 fu2	thung fu
very tall	n	好高	hóu gōu	hou2 gou1	hou kou
very tasty	n	好滋味	hóu jì meih	hou2 zi4 mei6	hou chi meih
very tired	adj	好累	hóu lèuih	hou2 leoi6	hou lowih
very well!		好好呀!	hóu hóu àa /aa!	hou2 hou2 aa4 /aa3	hou hou aa!
very worn out		好爛呀	hóu laahn àa	hou2 laan6 aa4	hou laahn aa
vestibule[1] (sl) hellow of the vulva	n	前庭	chìhn tìhng	cin4 ting4	chhihn tiehng
vestibule[2] porch of the house	n	前庭	chìhn tìhng	cin4 ting4	chhihn tiehng
veto	v	否決	fáu kyut	fau2 kyut3	fau khyut
veto power	n	否決權	fáu kyut kyùhn	fau2 kyut3 kyun4	fau khyut khyuhn
vex[1] /agony/annoying /trouble	v	煩惱	fàahn lóuh /nóuh	faan4 lou5 /nou5	faahn louh /nouh
vex[2] /annoyed	v	懊惱	óu lóuh /nóuh	ou2 lou5 /nou5	ou louh /nouh
vex[3] /make annoy	v	使苦惱	sìh fú lóuh /nóuh	si6 fu2 lou5 /nou5	sih fu louh /nouh
via[1] /through	prep	透過	tau gwo	tau3 gwo3	thau kwo
via[2] /by/through	prep	經由	gìng yàuh	ging4 jau4	keng yauh
via HK Macau /through HK Macau		通港澳	tùng góng ou	tung1 gong2 o3	thung kong ou
vibrant	adj	振動	jan duhng	zan3 dung6	chan tohng
vibrate /vibration	v	顫動	jin duhng	zin3 dung6	chin duhng
vice[1] /pinch	n	軋鉗	jaat kìhm	zaat3 kim4	chaat khihm
vice[2] /pinch	n	枱鉗	tói kìhm	toi2 kim6	thoi khihm
vice chancellor[1]	n	大學副校長	daaih hohk fu haauh jéung	daai6 hok6 fu3 haau6 zoeng2	taaih hohk fu haauh cheung
vice chancellor[2]	n	大學副教授	daaih hohk fu gaau sauh	daai6 hok6 fu3 gaau3 sau6	taaih hohk fu kaau sauh
vice president	n	副總裁	fu júng choi	fu3 zung2 coi4	fu chung chhoi
vicinity[1] /neighboring	n	附近	fuh gahn	fu6 gan6	fuh kahn
vicinity[2]	n	附近地區	fuh gahn deih kèui	fu6 gan6 dei6 keoi4	fuh kahn teih khoi
victim[1] (casualty/injured person/wounded person)	n	傷者	seung jé	soeng3 ze2	seung che
victim[2] (victim person /fatality)	n	遇難者	yuh làahn /nàahn jé	jyu6 laan6 /naan6 ze2	yuh laahn /naahn che
victim[3] (by accident or murder)	n	受害人	sauh hoih yàhn	sau6 hoi6 jan4	sauh hoih yahn
victim[4] (of disaster)	n	災民	jòi màhn	zoi4 man4	choi mahn
victim family	n	苦主	fú jyú	fu2 zyu2	fu chyu
victimize	v	使受害	saí sauh hoih	sai2 sau6 hoi6	sai sauh hoih
victor[1] /winner	n	勝利者	sing leih jé	sing3 lei6 ze2	seng leih che
victor[2]	n	戰勝者	jin sing jé	zin3 sing3 ze2	chin seng che
victoria cross		維多利亞十字勳章	wàih dò leih aa sahp jih fān jèung	wai4 do4 lei6 aa3 sap6 zi6 fan1 zoeng4	waih to leih aa sahp chih fahn cheung
victory[1] /beat/win	v	贏	yèhng	jeng4	yehng

victory[2]	n	勝利	sing leih	sing3 lei6	seng leih
video camera	n	攝影機	síp yéng /yíng gēi	sip2 jeng2 /jing2 gei1	sip yeng kei
video cassette[1]	n	卡式錄影帶	ká sīk luhk yíng dáai	kaa2 sik1 luk6 jing2 daai2	kha sek luhk yeng taai
video cassette[2] recorder	n	卡式錄放影機	ká sīk luhk fong yéng /yíng gēi	kaa2 sik1 luk6 fong3 jeng2 /jing2 gei1	kha sek luhk fong yeng kei
video conferencing	n	電視會議	dihn sih wuih yíh	dun6 si6 wui6 ji5	tihn sih wuih yih
video recorder	n	錄影機	luhk yíng gēi	luk6 jing2 gei1	luhk yeng kei
video tape	n	錄影帶	luhk yíng dáai	luk6 jing2 daai2	luhk yeng taai
vie /compete/cope/ competition	v	競爭	gihng jāang	ging6 zaang1	kehng chaang
view /watch	v	觀看	gùn hòn	gun4 hon4	kun hon
view of think /aspect /point of view	n	觀點	gùn dím	gun4 dim2	kun tim
viewpoint	n	見解點	gin gáai dím	gin3 gaai2 dim2	kin kaai tim
viewy /daydream	adj	空想	hùng séung	hung4 soeng2	hung seung
vigilante[1]	n	治安會會員	jih òn wùih wùih yùhn	zi6 on4 wui4 wui4 jyun4	chih on wuih wuih yuhn
vigilante[2]	n	義務警員	yih mouh gíng yùhn	ji6 mou6 ging2 jyun4	yih mouh keng yuhn
villa	n	別墅	biht seuih	bit6 seoi6	piht swoih
village[1]	n	邨	chyùn	cyun4	chhyun
village[2]/rural-farming	n	農村	lùhng /nùhng chyūn	lung4 /nung4 cyun4	luhng /nuhng chhyun
villager	n	村民	chyùn màhn	cyun4 man4	chhyun mahn
vine	n	藤蔓	tàhng màhng	tang4 mang6	thahng mahng
vinegar[1] /red color	n	醋	chou	cou3	chhou
vinegar[2] (white color)	n	白醋	baahk chou	baak6 cou3	paahk chou
vinegar[3] (black color)	n	鎮江醋	jan gong chou	zan3 gong3 cou3	chan kong chhou
violate (for law/disobey)	v	違反	wai fāan	wai3 faan1	wai faan
violation law	n	違反	wai fāan	wai3 faan1	wai faan
violator[1]	n	暴民	bouh màhn	bou6 man4	pouh mahn
violator[2]	n	違背者	wai buih jé	wai3 bui6 ze2	wai puih che
violator[3] (sl) (young man)	n	無賴	móuh laaih	mou5 laai6	mouh laaih
violator young man[1](sl) /punk/gangster boy/hoodlum /hooligan	n	小流氓	síu làuh màhn	siu2 lau4 man4	siu lauh mahn
violator young man[2](sl) /punk/gangster boy/hoodlum /hooligan/rude way boys	n	小阿飛	síu á fèi	siu2 a2 fei4	siu a fei
violent attack /attack /onslaught	n	猛攻	máahng gùng	maang5 gung4	maahng kung
violently way /acute way	adv	激烈地	gìk lìht dèih	gik4 lit6 dei6	kek liht teih
violet /purple colour	n	紫	jí	zi2	chi
violet colour	n	紫羅蘭	jí lòh làahn	zi2 lo4 laan4	chi loh laahn
violin /fiddle /musical instrument	n	小提琴	síu tàih kàhm	siu2 tai4 kam4	siu thaih khahm
viral /virus	adj	病毒	behng /bihng duhk	beng6 /bing6 duk6	pehng duhk
virgin /pure	adj	潔白	git baahk	git3 baak6	kit paahk

English	Part	Chinese	Yale	Jyutping	Other
virgin male /bachelor /never had sex	n	處男	chyúh làahm /nàahm	cyu5 laam4 /naam4	chhyuh laaahm /naaahm
virginity /chaste (of women)	adj	殉節	sèuhn jit	seon4 zit3	swohn chit
virtue	n	道德	douh dāk	dou6 dak1	touh tak
visa	n	簽證	chīm jing	cim3 zing3	chhim cheng
viscid /sticky	adj	黏的	lìm /nìm dìk	lim3 /nim3 dik4	lim /nim tik
visibility	n	能見度	làhng /nàhng gín dòuh	lang4 /nang4 gin2 dou6	lahng /nahng kin touh
visible[1]	adj	能見的	làhng /nàhng gín dìk	lang4 /nang4 gin2 dik4	lahng /nahng kin tek
visible[2]	adj	可看見	hó hōn gin	ho2 hon1 gin3	ho hon kin
visibly	adv	明顯地	mìhng hín dèih	ming4 hin2 dei6	mehng hin teih
visit[1]	v	探	taam	taam3	thaam
visit[2]	v	訪客	fóng haak	fong2 haak3	fong haak
visit[3] (hope for see)	n	探望	taam mohng	taam3 mong6	thaam mohng
visit[4] /look over/tour	n	遊覽	yàuh láahm	jau4 laam5	yauh laahm
visit[5] (to see patient)	n	探病	taam behng	taam3 beng6	thaam pehng
visit world /world travel	v	環遊世界	wàahn yàuh sai gaai	waan4 jau4 sai3 gaai3	waahn yauh sai kaai
visitable	adj	適於參觀	sīk yū /yùh chàam gùn	sik1 jyu1 /jyu6 caam4 gun4	sek yu /yuh chhaam kun
visitation punish /punishable	n	懲罰	chìhng faht	cing4 fat6	chhehng faht
visiting (place or area)	v	參觀	chàam gùn	caam4 gun4	chhaam kun
visiting card	ph	名片	kāat pín	kaat1 pin2	khaat phin
visitor /guest/visit /interview/reporter	n	訪問	fóng mahn	fong2 man6	fong mahn
visitor's pass	n	訪客證	fóng haak jing	fong2 haak3 zing3	fong haak cheng
visor[1] (tongue of the cap)	n	帽舌	mouh sìt	mou6 sit4	mouh sit
visor[2] (top of the cap)	n	頭盔上面罩	tàuh kwài séuhng mihn jaau	tau4 kwai4 soeng5 min6 zaau3	thauh khwai seuhng mihn chaau
vista[1]	n	景色	gíng sīk	ging2 sik1	keng sek
VISTA[2]	abbr	志願服務隊	ji yuhn fuhk mouh deuih	zi3 jyun6 fuk6 mou6 deoi6	chi yuhn fuhk mouh twoih
visual	adj	視覺	sih gók	si6 gok2	sih kok
visual acuity	adj	眼力	ngáahn lihk	ngaan5 lik6	ngaahn lehk
vital[1] /essential	adj	好緊要	hóu gán yiu	hou2 gan2 jiu3	hou kan yiu
vital[2] /necessary	adj	極重要	gìhk chung yìu	gik6 cung4 jiu4	kehk chhung yiu
vital of life	adj	生命	sàng mehng /mihng	sang4 meng6 /ming6	sang mehng
vitamin (de)	n	維他命	wàih tà mèhng /mìhng	wai4 taa4 meng6 /ming6	waih tha mehng
vitriol	n	硫酸	làuh syùn	lau4 syun4	lauh syun
vixen woman(sl) bed tempered woman /shrew	n	潑婦	put fùh	put3 fu6	phut fuh
vocabulary[1]	n	詞語	chìh yúh	ci4 jyu5	chhih yuh
vocabulary[2]	n	詞滙	chìh wuih	ci4 wui6	chhih wuih
vocabulary[3]	n	語彙	yùh wuih	jyu6 wui6	yuh wuih

vocal	adj	聲嘅	sèing /sìng ge	seng4 /sing4 ge3	seing ke
vocalist	n	歌唱者	gō cheung jé	go1 coeng3 ze2	ko chheung che
vocational /career/job /occupation/professional	adj	職業	jīk yihp	zik1 jip6	chek yihp
vodka (de)	n	伏特加	fuhk dahk ga	fuk6 dak6 ga3	fuhk tahk ka
voice[1]	n	音	yàm	jam4	yam
voice[2] /throat	n	嗓音	sōng yàm	song1 jam4	song yam
voice[3] (grammatical)	n	語態	yùh taai	jyu6 taai3	yuh thaai
volant	a	能飛的	làhng /nàhng fèi dīk	lang4 /nang4 fei4 dik1	lahng /nahng fei tik
volcano	n	火山	fó sàan	fo2 saan4	fo saan
volley ball	n	排球	pàaih kàuh	paai4 kau4	phaaih khauh
volt[1]	n	伏特	fuhk dahk	fuk6 dak6	fuhk tahk
volt[2]	n	電壓單位	dihn aat dāan wái	din6 aat3 daan1 wai2	tihn aat taan wai
voltage	n	電壓	dihn aat	din6 aat3	tihn aat
volume[1] /cube	n	卷	gyun	gyun3	kyun
volume[2] /density	n	容積	yung jīk	jung3 zik1	yung chek
volume of sound	n	音量	yàm leuhng	jam4 leung6	yam leuhng
voluntary[1]	adj	志願	ji yuhn	zi3 jyun6	chi yuhn
voluntary[2]	adj	自願	jih yuhn	zi6 jyun6	chih yuhn
voluntary[3]	adj	自願的	jih yuhn dīk	zi6 jyun6 dik1	chih yuhn tik
voluntary[4]	adj	自行	jih hàhng	zi6 hang4	chih hahng
volunteer[5]	n	志願	ji yuhn	zi3 jyun6	chi yuhn
volunteer[6]	n	志願者	ji yuhn jé	zi3 jyun6 ze2	chi yuhn che
volunteer[7]	n	義工	yih gùng	ji6 gung4	yih kung
vomit	v	嘔吐	àu /ngau tou	au4 /ngau2 tou3	au /ngau thou
vortex /spiral/whirlpool	n	旋渦	syun wō	syun3 wo1	syun wo
vote[1] /ballot	n	投票	tàuh piu	tau4 piu3	thauh phiu
vote[2]	n	選票	syún piu	syun2 piu3	syun phiu
voter /selector/chooser	n	選舉人	syún géui yàhn	syun2 geoi2 jan4	syun kwoi yahn
vowel /speech sound	n	母音	móuh yām	mou5 jam1	mouh yam
vowel sound	adj	長音	chèuhng yām	coeng4 jam1	chheuhng yam
voyage /sea journey	n	航行	hòhng hàhng	hong4 hang4	hohng hahng
vulgar[1] /filthy	adj	粗俗	chòu juhk	cou4 zuk6	chhou chuhk
vulgar[2] /filthy	adj	庸俗嘅	yùhng juhk ge	jung4 zuk6 ge3	yuhng chuhk ke
vulgar man[1]	n	粗魯嘅人	chòu lóuh ge yan	cou4 lou5 ge3 jan3	chhou louh ke yan
vulgar man[2]	n	粗俗嘅男人	chòu juhk ge làahm yan	cou4 zuk6 ge3 laam4 jan3	chhou chuhk ke laahm yan
vulgar man[3]	n	庸俗嘅男人	yùhng juhk ge làahm yan	jung4 zuk6 ge3 laam4 jan3	yuhng chuhk ke laahm yan
vulgar woman[1]	n	粗魯嘅女	chòu lóuh ge léuih /néuih	cou4 lou5 ge3 leui5 /neui5	chhou louh ke lowih /nowih
vulgar woman[2]	n	粗俗嘅女人	chòu juhk ge léuih /néuih yan	cou4 zuk6 ge3 leui5 /neui5 jan3	chhou chuhk ke leuih /neuih yan
vulgar woman[3]	n	庸俗嘅女人	yùhng juhk ge léuih /néuih yan	jung4 zuk6 ge3 leui5 /neui5 jan3	yuhng chuhk ke lowih /nowih yan

vulgar word	n	多能事	dò nàhng sih	do4 nang4 si6	to nahng sih
vulture[1]	n	禿鷲	tūk jauh	tuk1 zau6	thuk chauh
vulture[2]	n	兀鷲	ngaht jauh	ngat6 zau6	ngaht chauh
vulva (outer of vagina)	n	外陰	oih /ngoih yàm	oi6 /ngoi6 jam4	oih /ngoih yam

wade (swim in the water)	v	涉水	sip séui	sip3 seoi2	sip swoi
wader bird /water bird	n	涉水鳥	síp séui níuh	sip2 seoi2 niu5	sip swoi niuh
waffle(de) flat cake	n	威化餅	wāi fa béng	wai1 faa3 beng2	wai fa peng
wages[1] (coll) /salary	n	人工	yàhn gùng	jan4 gung4	yahn kung
wages[2] (coll) /pay/wage	n	工資	gùng jī	gung4 zi1	kung chi
wages[3] /salary	n	薪水	sān séui	san1 seoi2	san swoi
wages[4] (total salary)	n	工資總額	gùng jī júng aahk /ngaahk	gung4 zi1 zung2 aak6 /ngaak6	kung chi chung aahk /ngaahk
waggle /to waver	v	搖擺	yíu báai	jiu2 baai2	yiu paai
wagon	n	貨車車廂	fo chè chè sèung	fo3 ce4 ce4 soeng4	fo chhe chhe seung
wait a moment[1]		等一陣	dáng yāt jahn	dang2 jat1 zan6	tang yat chahn
wait a moment[2]	v	等陣	dáng jahn	dang2 zan6	tang chahn
wait a minute! /hold on! /wait for/etcetera/and so on	v	等等	dáng dáng	dang2 dang2	tang tang
wait and see		觀望	gun mohng	gun3 mong6	kun mohng
wait behind		留下	làuh hah	lau4 ha6	lauh hah
wait for	v	等	dáng	dang2	tang
wait for me!		等我吓!	dáng ngóh háh!	dang2 ngo5 haa5!	tang ngoh hah!
waiter[1]	n	侍應	sih yīng	si6 jing3	sih yeng
waiter[2] /hotal staff	n	伙記	fó gei	fo2 gei3	fo kei
waiting	n	等候	dáng hauh	dang2 hau6	tang hauh
waiting for		現正等候	yíhn jing dang háuh	jin5 zeng3 dang3 hau6	yihn cheng tang hauh
waiting list	n	等候名單	dáng hauh mèhng dāan	dang2 hau6 meng4 daan1	tang hauh mehng taan
waiting room[1]	n	等候室	dáng hauh sāt	dang2 hau6 sat1	tang hauh sat
waiting room[2] (at airport)	n	候機室	hauh gēi sāt	hau6 gei1 sat1	hauh kei sat
waiting room[3] (at hospital)	n	候診室	hauh chán sāt	hau6 can2 sat1	hauh chhan sat
wake	n	醒	séng	seng2	seng
wake up[1]	n	使醒來	sai séng loìh	sai3 seng2 loi4	sai seng loih
wake up[2] (from dream)	n	白日夢	baahk yaht muhng	baak6 jat6 mung6	paahk yaht muhng
wake up[3] (from dream)	n	發醒夢	faat séng muhng	faat3 seng2 mung6	faat seng muhng
wakeful[1]	adj	醒著的狀態	séng jeuk dìk johng taai	seng2 zoek3 dik4 zong6 taai3	seng cheuk tek chohng thaai
wakeful[2]	adj	失眠	sāt mìhn	sat1 min4	sat mihn
walk[1] /to walk/go	v	行	hàahng	haang4	haahng
walk[2]	n	行走	hàahng jáu/záu	haang4 zau2	haahng chau
walk[3]	v	行路	hàahng louh	haang4 lou6	haahng louh
walk[4]	v	行街	hàahng gāai	haang4 gaai1	haahng kaai
walk along	v	往沿...向前行	wóhng yùhn...heung chìhn hàhng	wong5 jyun4...hoeng3 cin4 hang4	wohng yuhn ... heung chhihn hahng
walk by	v	行過	hàahng gwo	haang4 gwo3	haahng kwo
walk by foot	n	打赤腳	dá chek geuk	daa2 cek3 goek3	ta chhek keuk
walk of life	n	行業	hàahng yihp	haang4 jip6	haahng yihp
walk over	v	輕易地勝過	hèng yih deih sīng gwo	heng4 ji6 dei6 sing1 gwo3	heng yih teih seng kwo

walker /footer	n	步行者	bòuh hàahng jé	bou6 haang4 ze2	pouh haahng che
walkie-talkie /intercom	n	對講機	deui góng gèi	deoi3 gong2 gei4	toei kong kei
walking	n	走在	jáu joih	zau2 zoi6	chau choih
walking stick	n	卜杖	būk jeuhng	buk1 zoeng6	puk cheuhng
wall[1]	n	牆	chèuhng	coeng4	chheuhng
wall[2]	n	牆壁	chèuhng bek	coeng4 bek3	chheuhng pek
wall[3] /castle	n	城	sèhng	seng4	sehng
wall of stone	n	壁	bek	bek3	pek
wall painting	n	壁畫	bék waahk	bek2 waak4	pek waahk
wall street	n	美國金融中心	méih gwók gàm yùhng jùng sàm	mei5 gwok3 gam4 jung4 zung4 sam4	meih kwok kam yuhng chung sam
wallpaper	n	牆紙	chèuhng jí	coeng4 zi2	chheuhng chi
waltz [(de)]	n	華爾滋	wàh yíh jì	waa4 ji5 zi4	wah yih chi
wand /stick/rod/thin stick	n	棍	gwan	gwan3	kwan
wander[1] /roam	v	遊	yàuh	jau4	yauh
wander[2] /roam	v	漫遊	maahn yàuh	maan6 jau4	maahn yauh
wander[3] /on the road	n	路亂	louh lyuhn	lou6 lyun6	louh lyuhn
wanderer	n	流浪者	làuh lohng jé	lau4 long6 ze2	lauh lohng che
wandering	n	錯亂的	cho lyùhn dìk	co3 lyun6 dik4	chho lyuhn tek
want /wanna/want to	v	想要	séung yìu	soeng2 jiu4	seung yiu
want message	v	信想	seun séung	seon3 soeng2	swon seung
want sex	v	好色嘅	hou sīk ge	hou3 sik1 ge3	hou sek ke
want to have	v	想要	séung yìu	soeng2 jiu4	seung yiu
want to stay	v	想住	séung jyuh	soeng2 zyu6	seung chyuh
wanted (searched for arrest /list of wanted)	adj	受通緝	sauh tùng chap	sau6 tung4 cap1	sauh thung chhap
wanted these /i like these	v	要嗰的	yiu gó dī	jiu3 go2 di1	yiu ko ti
wantless	adj	無所需求	móuh só sēui kàuh	mou5 so2 seoi1 kau4	mouh so swoi khauh
wantonly[1]	adv	頑皮	wàahn pèih	waan4 pei4	waahn pheih
wantonly[2]	adv	蕩婦	dohng fúh	dong6 fu5	tohng fuh
war[1] /battle/wage/fight	n	戰	jin	zin3	chin
war[2] /battle/wage	n	戰爭	jin jàang	zin3 zaang4	chin chaang
war time	n	戰時	jin sìh	zin3 si4	chin sih
wardrobe[1]	n	衣柜	yì gwài	ji4 gwai4	yi kwaih
wardrobe[2] [(coll)]	n	衫柜	sàam gwàih	saam4 gwai4	saam kwaih
wardrobe[3]	n	衣櫥	yī chyùh	ji1 cyu4	yi chhyuh
warehouse[1] /storehouse	n	倉	chōng	cong1	chhong
warehouse[2] /goods store /store-house	n	貨倉	fo chōng	fo3 cong1	fo chhong
warehouse[3] /treasury /store-house	n	倉庫	chōng fu	cong1 fu3	chhong fu
warm[1]	adj	溫	wān	wan1	wan
warm[2]	adj	暖	lyúhn /nyúhn	lyun5 /nyun5	lyuhn /nyuhn
warm[3]	adj	溫暖	wān lyúhn /nyúhn	wan1 lyun5 /nyun5	wan lyuhn /nyuhn

warm hearted	adj	溫情	wān chìhng	wan1 cing4	wan chhehng
warm welcome /intense	adj	熱烈	yiht liht	jit6 lit6	yiht liht
warmer	n	取暖器	cheui lyúhn/nyúhn hei	ceoi3 lyun5 /nyun5 hei3	chheui lyuhn/nyuhn hei
warming	n	溫加	wān gā	wan1 gaa1	wan ka
warn /remind	v	提醒	tàih séng	tai4 seng2	thaih seng
warning[1]	n	誡	gaai	gaai3	kaai
warning[2]	n	告誡	gou gaai	gou3 gaai3	kou kaai
warning card /yellow card (for player)	n	黃卡	wòhng ká	wong4 kaa2	wohng kha
warp[1] /twist	v	扭歪	láu mé	lau2 me2	lau me
warp[2] /curly	v	使捲曲	sai gyun kūk	sai3 gyun3 kuk1	sai kyun khuk
warrant[1] /enforcement /duty	n	執行	jāp hàhng	zap1 hang6	chap haang
warrant[2] /arrest (by police)	n	拘捕	kèui bouh	keoi4 bou6	khoi pouh
warrant[3]	n	搜查令	sáu chàh lihng	sau2 caa4 ling6	sau chhah lehng
warrant[4]	n	執行令	jāp hàhng lihng	zap1 hang6 ling4	chap haang lehng
warship[1] (of war)	n	戰艦	jin laahm	zin3 laam6	chin laahm
warship[2]	n	軍艦	gwàn haahm	gwan4 haam6	kwan haahm
was	v	過去式	gwo heui sīk	gwo3 heoi3 sik1	kwo hoi sek
was that successful?		是成功的嗎？	sih sèhng gùng dī mā?	si6 seng4 gung4 di1 maa1?	sih sehng kung tī ma?
wash	v	蕩	dohng	dong6	tohng
wash basin[1]	n	面盤	mihn pún	min6 pun2	mihn phun
wash basin[2] /washbowl	n	洗臉盆	sái líhm pùhn	sai2 lim5 pun4	sai lihm phuhn
wash hand	n	洗手	sái sáu	sai2 sau2	sai sau
washable[1]	adj	可水洗	hó séui sái	ho2 seoi2 sai2	ho swoi sai
washable[2]	adj	耐洗	loih sái	loih sai2	loih sai
washer /for cloths /washing machine	n	洗衣機	sái yì gèi	sai2 ji4 gei4	sai yi kei
washerman	n	男洗衣工人	làahm sái yī gùng yàhn	laam4 sai2 ji gung4 jan4	laahm sai yi kung yahn
wasp[1]	n	黃蜂	wòhng fùng	wong4 fung4	wohng fung
wasp2 /hornet	n	胡蜂	wùh fùng	wu4 fung4	wuh fung
waste paper	n	廢紙	fai jí	fai3 zi2	fai chi
wastebasket	n	廢紙簍	fai jí láuh	fai3 zi2 lau5	fai chi lauh
watch[1] /visit/look at /observe/watching	v	觀	gùn	gun4	kun
watch[2] (of wrist)	n	錶	bīu	biu1	piu
watch[3] (of wrist)	n	手錶	sáu bìu	sau2 biu4	sau piu
watch carefully	v	看透	hon tau	hon3 tau3	hon thau
watch case	n	錶殼	bīu hok	biu1 hok3	piu hok
watch dog[1]	n	警犬	gíng hyún	ging2 hyun2	keng hyun
watch dog[2]	n	看門狗	hon mùhn gáu	hon3 mun4 gau2	hon muhn kau

watch man	n	忠實嘅看守人	jùng saht ge hōn sáu yàhn	zung4 sat6 ge3 hon1 sau2 jan4	chung saht ke hon sau yahn
watch movies	v	看電影	hon dihn yéng	hon3 din6 jeng2	hon tihn yeng
watch over	v	照管	jiu gún	ziu3 gun2	chiu kun
watched /already saw /be seen/be looked	v	睇咗	tái jó	tai2 zo2	thai cho
watchful	adj	機警	gèi gíng	gei4 ging2	kei keng
watching /gaze/looking	n	睇住	tái jyuh	tai2 zyu6	thai chyuh
watching movies[1] /see movie	v	睇戲	tái hei	tai2 hei3	thai hei
watching movies[2]		睇電影	tái dìhn yēng /yīng	tai2 dim6 jeng1 /jing1	thai tihn yeng
watching TV		睇電視	tái dìhn sìh	tai2 din6 si6	thai tihn sih
watchmaker	n	鐘錶匠	jùng bīu jeuhng	zung4 biu1 zoeng6	chung piu cheuhng
water	n	水	séui	seoi2	swoi
water appear out	v	出水	chēut séui	ceot1 seoi2	chhot swoi
water bill	n	水費	séui fai	seoi2 fai3	swoi fai
water cannon	n	水炮	séui pāau	seoi2 paau1	swoi phaau
water color	n	水彩畫	séui chói wá	seoi2 coi2 wa2	swoi chhoi wa
water colour	n	水彩	séui chói	seoi2 coi2	swoi chhoi
water form ice	n	水結成冰	séui git sèhng /sìhng bìng	seoi2 git3 seng4 /sing4 bing4	swoi kit sehng peng
water gun	n	玩具水槍	wáan geuih séui chèung	waan2 seoi2 geoi6 coeng4	waan kwoih swoi chheung
water leak /water seep	n	滲水	sam séui	sam3 seoi2	sam swoi
water meter	n	水錶	séui bìu	seoi2 biu4	swoi piu
water pipe	n	食水管	sihk séui gùn	sik6 seoi2 gun4	sehk swoi kun
water provided /water supply	n	供水	gùng séui	gung4 seoi2	kung swoi
water skateboard	n	滑浪板	waaht lohng báan	waat long6 baan2	waaht lohng paan
water skating	v	滑冰	wàaht séui	waat6 seoi2	waaht swoi
water ski	v	用滑水橇滑行	yùhng wàaht séui chèuih wàaht hàahng	jung6 waat6 seoi2 ceoi4 waat6 haang4	yuhng waaht swoi chhoih waaht haahng
water skiing	n	滑水運動	wàaht séui wahn duhng	waat6 seoi2 wan6 dung6	waaht swoi wahn tohng
water supply dept[1]	n	水務局	séui mouh gúk	seoi2 mou6 guk2	swoi mouh kuk
water supply dept[2]	n	水務署	séui mouh chyúh	seoi2 mou6 cyu5	swoi mouh chhyuh
water tank	n	水箱	séui sēung	seoi2 soeng1	swoi seung
waterfall	n	瀑布	buhk bou	buk6 bou3	puhk pou
watering	n	淋水	làahm séui	lam4 seoi2	laahm swoi
watering can	n	灑水壺	sá séui wú /wùh	saa2 seoi2 wu2 /wu4	sa swoi wu /wùh
waterless	adj	不用水	bāt yuhng séui	bat1 jung6 seoi2	pat yuhng swoi
watermelon	n	西瓜	sài gwà	sai4 gwaa4	sai kwa
watermill	n	水磨	séui mòh	seoi2 mo6	swoi moh
waterpot /kettle	n	水壺	séui wú /wùh	seoi2 wu2 /wu4	swoi wu /wuh
waterway	n	水路	séui louh	seoi2 lou6	swoi louh
watery[1] /thin	adj	稀	hèi	hei4	hei

watery[2]	adj	淡的	táahm dìk	taam5 dik4	thaahm tek
watt	n	瓦特	ngáh dahk	ngaa5 dak6	ngah tahk
wave[1] (of water)	n	浪	lohng	long6	lohng
wave[2] (of water)	n	波浪	bò lohng	bo4 long6	po lohng
wave hand[1]	v	揮手	fāi sáu	fai1 sau2	fai sau
wave hand[2]	v	揩手	hàaih sáu	haai4 sau2	haaih sau
waveless /undisturbed /peaceful	adj	平靜	pèhng jèhng, pìhng jìhng	peng4 zeng4, ping4 zing4	phehng chehng
waverer	n	猶豫不決嘅人	yàuh yuh bāt kyut ge yàhn	jau4 jyu6 bat1 kyut3 ge jan4	yauh yuh pat khyut ke yahn
wax[1] /beeswax	n	蠟	laahp	laap6	laahp
wax[2] /polish	v	打臘	dá laahp	daa2 laap6	ta laahp
wax[3] /gradually bigger	v	漸盈	jihm yìhng	zim1 jing4	chihm yehng
waxed paper	n	蠟紙	laahp jí	laap6 zi2	laahp chi
way[1] /route/lane route /routeline	n	路線	louh sin	lou6 sim3	louh sin
way[2] /method	n	法子	faat jí	faat3 zi2	faat chi
way of thinking	n	我認為	ngóh yihng wàih	ngo5 jing6 wai6	ngoh yehng waih
wayless /no way	adj	無路	móuh louh	mou5 lou6	mouh louh
we ate already	v	我哋食咗喇	ngóh dèih sihk jó la	ngo5 dei6 sik6 zo2 la3	ngoh teih sehk cho la
we don't[1]		我哋唔用	ngóh dèih m̀ yùhng	ngo5 dei6 m4 jung6	mh ngoh teih yuhng
we don't[2]		我哋唔做	ngóh dèih m̀ jouh	ngo5 dei6 m4 zou6	mh ngoh teih chouh
we have found!		我哋搵到	ngóh dèih wán dóu	ngo5 dei6 wan2 dou2	ngoh teih wan tou
we haven't found!		我哋搵唔到	ngóh dèih wán m̀ dóu	ngo5 dei6 wan2 m4 dou2	ngoh teih wan mh tou
weak[1] /impotent /powerless/effeminate	adj	無力/冇力	móuh lihk	mou5 lik6	mouh lehk
weak[2]	adj	軟弱	yúhn yeuhk	jyun5 joek6	yuhn yeuhk
weaken	v	變弱	bín yèuhk	bin2 joek6	pin yeuhk
weakly	adv	虛弱地	hèui yeuhk deih	heoi4 joek6 dei6	hoi yeuhk teih
wealth /riches/assets	n	財富	chòih fu	coi4 fu	chhoih fu
weapon[1] (atomic)	n	原子武器	yùhn jí móuh hei	jyun4 zi2 mou5 hei3	yuhn chi mouh hei
weapon[2] (nuclear)	n	核子武器	haht jí móuh hei	hat6 zi2 mou5 hei3	haht chi mouh hei
wear[1] /put on/apply/use (clothes/powder/ointment)	v	著/着	jeuk	zoek3	cheuk
wear[2] /put on (hat/watch/gloves/glasses)	v	戴	daai	daai3	taai
wear[3] (accessories)	v	佩帶	pui daai	pui3 daai3	phui taai
wear ascarf	v	攬頸巾	laahm géng gàn	laam6 geng2 gan4	laahm keng kan
wear necktie	v	打吠	dá tāai	daa2 taai1	ta thaai
wearer (a person)	n	佩帶人	pui daai yàhn	pui3 daai3 jan4	phui taai yahn
wearing[1] /clothing /dressing	adj	穿戴	chyùn daai	cyun4 daai3	chhyun taai
wearing[2]	adj	令人發倦	lihng yàhn faat gyuhn	ling6 jan4 faat3 gyun6	lehng yahn faat kyuhn
weasel	n	鼬鼠	yau syū	jau3 syu2	yau syu

weather	n	天氣	tìn héi	tin4 hei2	thin hei
weather center	n	氣象中心	tìn héi jùng sàm	tin4 hei2 zung4 sam4	thin hei chung sam
weather forecast	n	天氣預測	tìn héi yuh chāk	tin4 hei2 jyu6 caak1	thin hei yuh chhak
weather forecaster	n	氣象報告員	hei jeuhng bo gou yùhn	hei zoeng6 bou3 gou3 jyun4	hei cheuhng po kou yuhn
weave cloth	n	織布	jīk bou	zik1 bou3	chek pou
weaving	n	迂迴前進	yù wui chin jéun	jyu4 wui3 cin3 zeon3	yu wui chhin cheun
website /network station	n	網站	móhng jaahm	mong5 zaam6	mohng chaahm
wed /marry/to take a wife	v	娶老婆	chéui lóuh pòh	ceoi2 lou5 po4	chheui louh phoh
wedding	n	結婚典禮	git fàn dín láih	git3 fan4 din2 lai5	kit fan tin laih
wedding breakfast	n	喜宴	héi yin	hei2 jin3	hei yin
wedding cake[1]	n	禮餅	láih béng	lai5 beng2	laih peng
wedding cake[2]	n	結婚蛋糕	git fàn daahn gōu	git3 fan4 daan6 gou1	kit fan taahn kou
wedding ceremony	n	婚禮	fàn láih	fan4 lai5	fan laih
wedding dress /wedding gown		結婚禮服	git fàn láih fuhk	git3 fan4 lai5 fuk6	kit fan laih fuhk
wedding ring	n	結婚戒指	git fàn gaai jí	git3 fan4 gaai3 zi2	kit fan kaai chi
wedge insert	v	楔入	sit yahp	sit3 jap6	sit yahp
Wednesday[1]	n	禮拜三	láih baai sàam	lai5 baai3 saam4	laih paai saam
Wednesday[2]	n	星期三	sèng kèih sàam	seng4 kei4 saam4	seng kheih saam
weed	n	除草	chèuih chóu	ceoi4 cou2	chheuih chou
weeds[1]	n	野草	yéh chóu	je5 cou2	yeh chhou
weeds[2]	n	雜草	jaahp chóu	zaap6 cou2	chaahp chhou
week[1]	n	禮拜	láih baai	lai5 baai3	laih paai
week[2] /weekday	n	星期	sèng kèih	seng4 kei4	seng kheih
week[3] /weekly	n	週	jāu	zau1	chau
week by week		逐個禮拜	juhk go láih baai	zuk6 go3 lai5 baai3	chuhk ko laih paai
weekday	n	工作日	gùng jok yaht	gung4 zik3 jat6	kung chok yaht
weekend	n	周末	jàu muht	zau4 mut6	chau muht
weekly	adj	每週	múih jāu	mui5 zau1	muih chau
weep[1] /cry/crying (loudly weep)	n/v	喊	haam	haam3	haam
weep[2]	v	悲嘆	bèi taan	bei4 taan3	pei thaan
weep[3]	v	哭泣	hūk yāp	huk1 jap1	huk yap
weeper[1]	n	喊人	haam yàhn	haam3 jan4	haam yahn
weeper[2]	n	哭泣者	hūk yāp jé	huk1 jap1 ze2	huk yap che
weeping		流眼淚	làuh ngáahn leuih	lau4 ngaan5 lui6	lauh ngaahn lowih
weft line/parallel line	n	緯線	wáih sin	wai5 sin3	waih sin
weigh (Chinese scale)	n	稱	chìng	cing4	chheng
weighbridge	n	地秤	deih chīng	dei6 cing1	teih chheng
weigher	n	秤物機	chīng maht gèi	cing1 mat6 gei4	chheng maht kei
weight[1]	n	磅	bohng	bong6	pohng
weight[2]	v	重量	chúhng leuhng	cung5 loeng6	chhuhng lowhng
weightless	adj	失重	sāt chúhng	sat1 cung5	sat chhuhng
welcome	n	歡迎	fùn yìhng	fun4 jing4	fun yehng

welcome to	n	歡迎使用	fùn yìhng sái yuhng	fun4 jing4 sai2 jung6	fun yehng sai yuhng
welding	v	焊接	hohn jip	hon6 zip	hohn chip
welder	n	焊工	hohn gùng	hon6 gung4	hohn kung
welfare	n	福利	fūk leih	fuk1 lei6	fuk leih
well[1] /good/that'll be fine	adj	很好	hān hóu	han1 hou2	han hou
well[2] /good	adj	良好地	lèuhng hou deih	loeng4 hou3 dei6	leuhng hou teih
well[3] (of water)	n	井	jéng	zeng2	cheng
well[4] (of water)	n	水井	séui jēng	seoi2 zeng1	swoi cheng
well born	adj	出身名門	chēut mèhng mùhn	ceot1 meng4 mun4	chhot mehng muhn
well cultured	adj	文化良好	màhn fa lèuhng hóu	man4 faa3 long4 hou2	mahn fa leuhng hou
well documented	adj	有大量文件證	yáuh daaih lèuhng màhn gihn jing	jau5 daai6 loeng4 man4 gin6 zing3	yauh taaih leuhng mahn kehn cheng
well done![1]	adj	幹得好!	gon dāk hóu!	gon3 dak1 hou2	kon tak hou!
well done![2]	adj	做得好!	jouh dāk hóu!	zou6 dak1 hou2!	chouh tak hou!
well educated	adj	受過良好教育	sauh gwo lèuhng hóu gaau yuhk	sau6 gwo3 loeng4 hou2 gaau3 juk6	sauh kwo leuhng hou kaau yuhk
well handled	adj	處理得當	chyú léih dāk dòng	cyu2 lei5 dak1 dong4	chhyu leih tak tong
well informed[1]	adj	見問講駁	gin màhn góng bok	gin3 man6 gong2 bok6	kin mahn kong pok
well informed[2]	adj	見多識廣	gin dō sīk gwóng	gin3 do1 sik1 gwong2	kin to sek kwong
well intentioned	adj	好心好意	hou sàm hou yi	hou sam4 hou ji3	hou sam hou yi
well kept	adj	保持整齊	bóu chìh jíng chàih	bou2 ci4 zing2 cai4	bou chhih jeng chhaih
well known /famous	adj	有名	yáuh mèhng	jau5 meng4	yauh yáuh mèhng
well known brand	n	名牌	mèhng /mìhng pàaih	meng4 /ming4 paai4	mehng phaaih
well managed /well run	adj	經營得好	gīng yìhng dāk hóu	ging1 jing4 dak1 hou2	keng yehng tak hou
well organized	adj	運轉良好	wahn jyún lèuhng hóu	wan6 zyun2 long4 hou2	wahn chyun leuhng hou
well situated	adj	好位置	hóu waih ji	hou2 wai6 zi3	hou waih chi
well spoken	adj	善於辭令	sihn yū chih lihng	sin6 jyu1 ci4 ling4	sihn yu chhih lehng
well spring	n	水源	séui yùhn	seoi2 jyun4	swoi yuhn
well suited	adj	相配嘅	sèung pui ge	soeng4 pui3 ge3	seung phui ke
well to-do /rich	adj	富裕	fu yuh	fu3 jyu6	fu yuh
well wisher	n	表示祝願者	bíu sih jùk yuhn jé	biu2 si6 zuk4 jyun6 ze2	piu sih chuk yuhn che
well-wishers	n	祝福	jūk fūk	zuk1 fuk1	chuk fuk
wellcome (super market HK)	n	惠康	waih hòng	wai6 hang4	waih hong
went to the shopping		去咗買嘢	heui jó máaih yéh	heoi3 zo2 maai5 je5	hoi cho maaih yeh
west	n	西	sài	sai4	sai
West Rail (HK)	n	西鐵 (港)	sài tit (góng)	sai4 tit3 (gong2)	sai thit (kong)
West Rail Line (HK)	n	西鐵線 (港)	sài tit sin (góng)	sai4 tit3 sin3 (gong2)	sai thit sin (kong)
western	n	西方	sài fòng	sai3 fong4	sai fong
Western cuisine /western food		西餐	sài chàan	sai4 caan4	sai chhaan
western style	n	西式	sài sīk	sai4 sik1	sai sek
westerner[1]	n	洋人	yèuhng yàhn	joeng4 jan4	yeuhng yahn
westerner[2]	n	西方人	sài fòng yàhn	sai4 fong4 jan4	sai fong yahn
westerner[3]	n	西歐人	sài àu yàhn	sai4 au4 jan4	sai au yahn

westwards	adv	向西	heung sài	hoeng3 sai4	heung sai
wet[1] /humid/humidity /moist	n/adv	濕	sāp	sap1	sap
wet[2]	adj	濕氣	sāp hei	sap1 hei3	sap hei
wet[3]	adj	濕嘅	sāp ge	sap1 ge3	sap ke
wet[4] /moisture	adj	水分	séui fahn	seoi2 fan6	swoi fahn
wet bar	n	小酒吧	síu jáu bā	siu2 zau2 ba1	siu chau pa
wet blanket[sl] feel disappointed	v	掃興嘅人	sou hìng ge yàhn	sou3 hing4 ge3 jan4	sou heng ke yahn
wet floor	adj	濕濕地	sāp sāp deih	sap1 sap1 dei6	sap sap teih
wet slippery		濕滑	sāp wàaht	sap1 waat6	sap waaht
wetlands	n	濕地	sāp deih	sap1 dei6	sap teih
whale fish	n	鯨魚	kìhng yùh	king4 jyu4	khihng yuh
wharf /pier/ferry pier /dock (for ship port)	n	碼頭	máh tàuh	maa5 tau4	mah thauh
wharfage	n	碼頭費	máh tàuh fai	maa5 tau4 fai3	mah thauh fai
what?[1 (coll)]	pron	乜?	màt ?	mat4 ?	mat?
what?[2]	pron	甚?	sahm?	sam6?	sahm?
what?[3 (wr)]	pron	麼?	mò?	mo4?	mo?
what?[4] /which?	pron	何?	hòh?	ho4?	hoh?
what?[5(coll)] /what kind of?	pron	乜嘢?	màt yéh?	mat4 je5?	mat yeh?
what?[6 (wr)]	pron	什麼?	sahm mò?	sam6 mo4?	sahm mo?
what?[7] /question?	pron	咩嘢?	mè yéh?	me4 je2?	me yeh?
what?[8] /why?	pron	怎麼?	ján mò?	zan2 mo4?	chan mo?
what about?		點呀?	dím àa /aa?	dim2 aa4 /aa3?	tim aa?
what are you doing		做乜呢?	jouh màt aa?	zou6 mat4 aa3?	chouh mat aa?
what can i do?		點算呢?	dím syun lē /nē?	dim2 syun3 le1 /ne1?	tim syun le /ne?
what do you do?		做咩呀?	jouh mè aa?	zou6 me4 aa3?	chouh me aa?
what for?		點解?	dím gáai?	dim2 gaai2?	tim kaai?
what if?		如果...就點呢?	yuh gwo… jauh dim lē /nē?	jyu3 gwo3 …zau6 dim3 le1 /ne1?	yuh kwo... chauh tim le /ne?
what is? /what?	pron	乜嘢呀?	màt yéh a?, mat ye aa?	mat4 je2 aa3?	mat yeh a?
what is this?		這是甚麼?	jéh sih sahm mò?	ze5 si6 sam6 mo4?	cheh sih sahm mo?
what kind of?		點樣嘅?	dim yéung ge?	dim3 joeng2 ge3?	tim yeung ke?
what time?		幾點?	géi dīm?	gei2 dim1?	kei tim?
what's buy?[1]		買乜嘢?	máaih màt yéh?	maai5 mat4 je5?	maaih mat yeh?
what's buy?[2]		買嘢呀?	máaih yéh àa?	maai5 je5 aa4/aa3?	maaih yeh aa?
what's matter?[1]		有乜嘢事呀?	yáuh màt yéh sih aa?	jau5 mat1 je5 si6 aa3?	yauh mat yeh sih aa?
what's matter?[2] /how?		點樣?	dím yéung?	dim3 joeng2?	tim yeung?
what's number?		幾多號	geih dò houh aa?	gei6 do4 hou6 aa3?	keih toh houh aa?
what's that?		乜嘢嚟?	màt yéh làih? mt ye làih?	mat4 je5 lai4?	mat yeh laih?
what's you say?		你講乜嘢話吖?	léih góng māt yéh wá aa?	lei5 gong2 mat1 je5 waa2 aa3?	leih kong mat yeh wa aa?

what's your name?		你叫咩名?	léih giu mè méng?	lei5 giu3 me4 meng2?	leih kiu me meng?
when?[1] /what time?		幾時?	géi sìh?	gei2 si4?	kei sih?
when?[2] /what time?	adv/ conj	幾時候?	géi sìh hauh?	gei2 si4 hau6?	kei sih hauh?
what time arrived?		幾點到㗎?	géi dīm dou gá?	gei2 dim1 dou3 ga2?	kei tim tou ka?
whatever	pron	不管什麼事	bāt gún sahm mō sih	bat1 gun2 sam6 mo1 si6	pat kun sahm mo sih
wheel[1]	n	車輪	chè lèuhn	ce4 leon4	chhe lowhn
wheel[2]	n	車轆	chè lūk	ce4 luk1	chhe lowk
wheel[3]	n	輪子	lèuhn jí	leon4 zi2	leuhn chi
wheel[4]	n	方向盤	fòng heung pun	fong4 hoeng3 pun3	fong heung phun
wheelchair	n	輪椅	lèuhn yí	leon4 ji2	leuhn yi
when?[1]	adv/ conj	幾時呀?	géi sìh àa /aa?	gei2 si4 aa4 /aa3?	kei sìh aa?
when?[2]	adv/ conj	嗰陣時?	gó jahn sí?	go2 zan6 si2?	ko chahn si?
when you reach		當你去到	dong léih /néih heui dou	dong3 lei5 /nei5 heoi3 dou3	tong leih/neih hoi tou
whenever[1] /when?	adv/ conj	幾時	géi sí, géi sìh?	gei2 si2, gei2 si6?	kei si, kei sih?
whenever[2]	adv	什麼時候	sahm mò sìh hauh	sam6 mo4 si4 hau6	sahm mo sih hauh
where?[1] (coll)	adv/ conj	邊度?	bīn dou?	bin1 dou3?	pin tou?
where?[2] (wr)	adv/ conj	哪兒?	là yìh?	laa1 ji4?	la yih?
where?[3]	adv/ conj	邊處?	bīn syu?	bin1 syu3?	pin syu?
where?[4] /whence?	adv/ conj	何處?	hòh syu?	ho4 syu3?	hoh syu?
where are you from?		你係邊度嚟?	léih hái bīn dou làih?	lei5 hai2 bin1 dou3 lai4?	leih hai pin tou laih?
where do you live?		你住喺邊度?	léih jyuh haih bīn dou?	lei5 zyu6 hai6 bin1 dou6?	leih chyuh haih pin tou?
where does go? bus		去邊度?	heui bīn dou ?	heoi3 bin1 dou3?	hoi pin tou ?
where from?	v	邊度嚟㗎?	bīn dou lái gá?	bin1 dou3 lai2 gaa2?	pin tou lai ka?
where he gone?		佢去咗邊度呀?	kéuih heui jó pīn douh aa?	keoi5 heoi3 zo2 bin4 dou6 aa3?	khoih hoi cho phin touh aa?
where is?		係邊呀?	hai bīn aa?	hai3 bin1 aa3	hai pin aa?
where's?		喺邊度呀?	hái bīn dou aa?	hai2 bin1 dou3 aa3?	hai pin tou aa?
where you are?[1]		你係邊呀?	léih hai bīn aa3?	lei5 hai3 bin1 aa3?	leih hai pin aa?
where you are?[2]		你係邊度?	léih haih bīn dou?	lei5 hai6 bin1 dou3?	leih haih pin tou?
where you are?[3]		你係邊度呀?	léih hai bīn dou aa?	lei5 hai3 bin1 dou3 aa3?	leih hai pin tou aa?
whereabouts (lose road/track)	n	行蹤	hahng jùng	hang4 zung4	hahng chung
whereas	conj	鑑於	gaam yū	gaam3 jyu1	kaam yu
whereas /but	conj	卻	keuk	koek3	kheuk
wherever[1]	conj	無論邊處	mòuh leuhn bīn chyu	mou4 leon6 bin1 cyu3	mouh leuhn pin chhyu
wherever[2]	conj	無論在何處	móuh leuhn joih hòh syu	mou5 leon6 zoi6 ho4 syu	mouh leuhn choih hoh syu
whether? /which?	conj	哪一個?	là yàt gó?	laa4 jat4 go2?	la yat ko?
whether or not	conj	是不是	sih bāt sih	si6 bat1 si6	sih pat sih
whey[1]	n	乳水	yúh séui	jyu5 seoi2	yuh swoi
whey[2]	n	似乳清	chíh yúh chēng	ci5 jyu2 ceng1	chhih yuh cheng
which?[1]	pron	邊?	bīn?	bin1?	pin?

which?[2]	pron	邊呀?	bīn àa /aa3?	bin1 aa4 /aa3?	pin aa
which bus?	n	邊架車?	bīn gá chè?	bin1 gaa2 ce4	pin ka chhe?
which country?	n	邊國嘅?	bīn gwok ge?	bin1 gwok3 ge3?	pin kwok ke?
which floor?	n	幾樓呀?	géi láu àa /aa?	gei2 lau2 aa4 /aa3	kei lau aa?
which one	pron	邊個?	bīn go?	bin1 go3?	pin ko?
whig	n	英國維新黨員	yìng gwók wàih sān dóng yùhn	jing4 gwok2 wai4 sam1 dong2 jyun4	yeng kwok waih san tong yuhn
while[1]/between that time	n	際	jai	zai3	chai
while[1] /right time	conj	當...的時候	dong dìk sìh hauh	dong3 dik4 si4 hau6	tong tek sih hauh
while spend time	v	消磨時光	sìu mòh si gwòng	siu4 mo4 si3 gwong4	siu moh si kwong
whine	v	哀鳴	òi /ngòi mìhng	oi4 /ngoi4 ming4	oi /ngoi mehng
whip[1] (of leather)	n	鞭	bìn	bin4	pin
whip[2] /leather's whip	n	皮鞭	pèih bìn	pei4 bin4	pheih pin
whip[3] (of leather)	n	鞭子	bīn jí	bin1 zi2	pin chi
whip[4] /hit by whip	v	鞭打	bīn da	bin1 da2	pin tá
whirlpool[1]/swirl/eddy /whirl (of water)	n	渦	wō	wo1	wo
whirlpool[2]/whirl/eddy (of water)	n	漩	syùhn	syun4	syuhn
whirlpool[3]	n	漩渦	syùhn wō	syun4 wo1	syuhn wo
whisk /mixer aggs	n	打蛋器	dá dáan hei	daa2 daan2 hei3	ta taan hei
whisker	n	鬍子	wu jí	wu3 zi2	wu chi
whistle[1]	n	哨子	saau jí	saau3 zi2	saau chi
whistle[2] (by lips)	v	吹口哨	chèui háu saau	ceoi4 hau2 saau3	chheui hau saau
whistle[3]	v	銀雞	ngán gài	ngan2 gai4	ngan kai
whistler	n	吹口哨嘅人	chèui háu saau ge yàhn	ceoi4 hau2 saau3 ge3 jan4	chheui hau saau ke yahn
white[1]	n	白	baahk	baak6	paahk
white[2]	n	白色	baahk sīk	baak6 sik1	paahk sek
white blood cells	n	白血球	baahk hyut kàuh	baak6 hyut3 kau4	paahk hyut khauh
white coffee	n	牛奶咖啡	ngàuh láaih/náaih gáa fèi	ngau4 laai5 /naai5 gaa2 fei4	ngauh laaih /naaih kaa fei
White house (USA)	n	白宮 (USA)	baahk gùng	baak6 gung4	paahk kung
white wine	n	白酒	baahk jáu /záu	baak6 zau2	paahk chau
white with red		紅與白	hùhng yùh baahk	hung4 yue5 baak6	hung yuh paahk
whitewash[1]	n	灰水	fùi séui	fui4 seoi2	fui swoi
whitewash[2]	n	石灰水	sehk fùi séui	sek6 fui4 seoi2	sehk fui swoi
who?[1(coll)] /whom?	pron	邊個?	bīn go?	bin1 go3?	pin ko?
who?[2 (wr)] /any body?	pron	誰?	sèuih?	seoi4?	swoih?
who am i?		我係邊個?	ngóh haih bīn go?	ngo5 hai6 bin1 go3?	ngoh haih pin ko?
who are you?[1]		你係邊個?	léih haih bīn go?	lei5 hai6 bin1 go3?	leih haih pin ko?
who are you?[2]		你是誰?	léih sih sèuih?	lei5 si5 seoi4?	leih sih swoih?
who cares?		邊個負責?	bīn go fuh jaak?	bin1 go3 fu6 zaak3?	pin ko fuh chaak?
who is?[1] (polite way)	v	邊位?	bīn wàih?	bin1 wai6?	pin waih?
who is?[2]	v	邊位呢?	bīn wàih lē /nē?	bin1 wai6 le1 /ne1?	pin waih le /ne?

who is?[3]		邊個呀?	bīn go àa /aa?	bin1 go3 aa4 /aa3?	pin ko aa?
who is?[4]		邊鬼個?	bīn gwái go?	bin1 gwai2 goh3?	pin kwai koh?
who looking you? /whom do you want?		你搵邊個呀?	leih wan bin go aa?	lei5 wan3 bin3 go3 aa3?	leih wan bin ko aa?
who won?[1]	aux v	邊個贏咗?	bīn go yèhng jó ?	bin1 go3 jeng4 zo2 ?	pin ko yehng cho?
who won?[2]	aux v	誰贏咗	sèuih yèhng jó ?	seoi4 jeng4 zo2 ?	swoih yehng cho?
whole /full/complete	adj	整	jing	zing3	cheng
whole body	n	全部	chyùhn bouh	cyun4 bou6	chhyuhn pouh
whole story	n	始末	chí muht	ci2 mut6	chhi muht
wholeheartedly	adv	全心全意地	chyùhn sàm chyùhn yi deih	cyun4 sam4 cyun4 ji3 dei6	chhyuhn sam chyuhn yi teih
wholesale /bulk trade	adj	批發	pài faat	pai4 faat3	phai faat
whooping cough	n	百日咳	baak yaht kat	baak3 jat6 kat3	paak yaht khat
why?[1] (coll)	pron	點解?	dím gáai?	dim2 gaai2?	tim kaai?
why?[2] (coll)	pron	為什麼?	wàih sahm mo?	wai4 sam6 mo3?	waih sahm mo?
why?[3]	pron	做乜嘢?	jouh māt yéh?	zo6 mat1 je5?	chouh mat yeh?
why?[4]	pron	為乜嘢?	waih māt yéh?	wai6 mat1 je5?	waih mat yeh?
why?[5] /which reason	n	憑什麼?	pàhng sahm mō?	pang4 sam6 mo1?	phahng sahm mo?
why?[6]	pron	何	hòh	ho4	hoh
why not?	n	何不?	hòh bāt	ho4 bat1?	hoh pat
why should?[1]		駛乜?	sái māt?	sai2 mat1?	sai mat?
why should?[2]		何必?	hòh bīt?	ho4 bit1?	hoh pit?
wick /core/kernel	n	芯	sām	sam1	sam
wicked /morally bad/bad people/malicious/malevolent	adj	黑心	hāk sām	hak1 sam1	hak sam
wicket	n	邊門	bīn mún	bin1 mun2	pin mun
wide[1]	adj	闊	fut	fut3	fut
wide[2]	adj	廣闊	gwóng fut	gwong2 fut3	kwong fut
widen	v	撑闊	chāang fut	caang1 fut3	chhaang fut
widow	n	寡婦	gwá fúh	gwaa2 fu5	kwa fuh
widowed	v	喪偶	sòng áuh /ngáuh	song4 au5 /ngau5	song auh /ngauh
widower	n	鰥夫	gwàan fù /fùh	gwaan4 fu4 /fu4	kwaan fu /fuh
width	n	寬度	fùn dòuh	fun4 dou6	fun touh
wield /handle/manage	v	使用	sái yuhng	sai2 jung6	sai yuhng
wife's father	n	岳丈	ngohk jeuhng	ngok6 zoeng6	ngohk cheuhng
wife's mother[1]	n	岳母	ngohk móuh	ngok6 mou5	ngohk nouh
wife's mother[2]	n	外母	oih /ngoih móuh	oi6 /ngoi6 mou5	oih /ngoih nouh
wifeless	n	無妻	mòuh chai	mou4 caai3	mouh chhai
WiFi /wireless	n	無線	mòuh sín	mou4 sin2	mouh sin
wig	n	假髮	gá faat	gaa2 faat3	ka faat
wild /rude/uncivilized	adj	野	yéh	je5	yeh
wild dog	n	野狗	yéh gáu	je5 gau2	yeh kau
wild man /yahoo	n	野蠻人	yéh màahn yàhn	je5 maan4 jan4	yeh maahn yahn
wild plants	n	野生	yéh sàang	je5 saang4	yeh saang
wildfire	n	野火	yéh fó	je5 fo2	yeh fo

wildfowl	n	野禽	yéh kàm	je5 kam3	yeh kham
will[1] /future	v/aux	就嚟	jauh làih	jau6 lai4	chauh laih
will[2] /wish/desire/to want	n	要	yìu	jiu4	yiu
will be sure punish		實會罰	saht wúih faht	sat6 wui5 fat6	saht wuih faht
will do (in future)	v/aux	會做	wuih jouh	wui6 zou6	wuih chouh
will evaluate		會評估	wúih pìhng gū	wui5 ping4 gu1	wuih phehng ku
will go		會走	wuih jáu	wui6 zau2	wuih chau
will not[1] (act/happen)		不會	bāt wuih	bat1 wui6	pat wuih
will not[2] coming		唔嚟	m̀ lái	m4lai2	mh lai
will valuate		會評價	wúih pìhng gá	wui5 ping4 ga2	wuih phehng ka
willable	adj	可求	hó kàuh	ho2 kau4	ho khaau
willful /obstinate /stubborn/persistent/stiff-necked	adj	固執	gu jāp	gu3 zap1	ku chap
willfully[1]	adv	倔強的	gwaht kéuhng dìk	gwat6 koeng5 dik4	kwaat kheuhng tik
willfully[2]	adv	固執地	gu jāp deih	gu3 zap1 dei6	ku chap teih
willing[1] /to wish/want /hope for	adj/v	願	yuhn	jyun6	yuhn
willing[2] /to wish	adj	願意	yuhn yi	jyun6 ji3	yuhn yi
willing[3] (agree to X than Y /desired/prefer/would rather)	adj	情願	chìhng yuhn	cing4 jyun6	chhehng yuhn
willing[4] (perfectly happy to do/most willing to do)	adj	心甘情願	sàm gàm chìhng yuhn	sam4 gam4 cing4 jyun6	sam kam chhehng yuhn
willing to	n	願意	yuhn yi	jyun6 ji3	yuhn yi
win[1] /succeed	v	成	sèhng	seng4	sehng
win[2] /victorious	v	獲勝	wohk sing	wok6 sing3	wohk seng
win back	v	重獲	chùhng wohk	cung4 wok6	chhuhng wohk
win or loss /succeed or loss/success or fail/success or failure/sink or swim	v	成敗	sèhng baaih	seng4 baai6	sehng paaih
win over /persuade	v	說服	syút fuhk	syut2 fuk6	syut fuhk
win prize	v	得獎	dāk jéung	dak1 zoeng2	tak cheung
wind /air	n	風	fùng	fung4	fung
wind blow	n	風吹	fùng cheui	fung4 ceoi3	fung chhoi
wind round	v	捲	gyún	gyun2	kyun
wind screen wiper	n	水撥	séui buht	seoi2 but6	swoi puht
windbreak	n	防風林	fòhng fùng làhm	fong4 fung4 lam4	fohng fung lahm
winding /wriggle/as zigzag/ zigzag	adj/v	蜿蜒	yūn tìhng	jyun1 ting4	yun theng
windmill /wind fan /pindmill	n	風車	fùng chè	fung4 ce4	fung chhe
window[1]	n	窗	chēung	coeng1	chheung
window[2]	n	窗門	chēung mún	coeng1 mun2	chheung mun
window cleaner	n	門窗清潔工	mùhn chēung chēng /chīng gìt gùng	mun4 coeng1 cing1 /ceng1 git3 gung4	muhn chheung chheng kit kung
window screen		窗簾布	chēung lím bou	cheung1 lim4 bo3	cheung lim pou
window side seat	n	窗口位	chēung háu wái	coeng1 hau2 wai2	chheung hau wai

window shopping[1]	n	行街	hahng gāai	hang4 gaai1	hahng kaai
window shopping[2]	n	觀望	gun mohng	gun3 mong6	kun mohng
window shopping[3]	n	逛商店	kwaang seung dim	kwaang3 soeng3 dim3	khwaang seung tim
windscreen	n	擋風玻璃	dong fùng bō lēi	dong3 fung4 bo1 lei1	tong fung po lei
windy[1]	adj	大風	daaih fùng	daai6 fung4	taaih fung
windy[2]	adj	多風	dò fùng	do4 fung4	to fung
wine	n	葡萄酒	pòuh tòuh jáu	pou4 tou4 zau2	phouh thouh chau
wine bottle[1]	n	酒樽	jáu jèun /zèun	zau2 zeon4	chau cheon
wine bottle[2]	n	葡萄酒瓶	pòuh tòuh jáu pèhng	pou4 tou4 zau2 peng4	phouh thouh chau phehng
wine glass	n	酒杯	jáu bùi	zau2 bui4	chau pui
wine list	n	個酒單	go jáu dāan	go3 zau2 daan1	ko chau taan
wine rack	n	酒瓶架	jáu pèhng gá	zau2 peng4 gaa2	chau pehng ka
wine shop /wines house	n	酒舍	jáu sé	zau2 se2	chau se
wing[1] (of the bird /plane)	n	翼	yihk	jik6	yehk
wing[2] (bird's)	n	翅膀	chi pòhng	ci3 pong4	chhi phohng
wing[3] (of plane)	n	飛行	fèi hàhng	fei4 hang4	fei hahng
wing[4] (part of building)	n	側翼	jāk yihk	zak1 jik6	chak yehk
wing nut	n	蝶形螺母	wu yìhng lòh móuh	wu3 jing4 lo4 mou5	wu yehng loh mouh
wingless	adj	無翅	móuh chi	mou5 ci3	mouh chhi
wink[1] /eye blink	n	眨眼	jáam ngáahn	zaam2 ngaan5	chaam ngaahn
wink[2] (sl) blink (by female)	n	放電	fong dihn	fong3 din6	fong tihn
wink[3] /eye to blink /eye signal to	n	一眨眼	yāt jáam ngáahn	jat1 zaam2 ngaan5	yat chaam ngaahn
wink[4] (for short time)	n	一時間	yāt sìh gāan	jat1 si4 gaan1	yat sih kaan
wink[5] /eye blink /flash light	v	眨眨	jáam jáam	zaam2 zaam2	chaam chaam
wink[6] (of star)	v	閃閃吓	sím sím háh	sim2 sim2 haa5	sim sim hah
winner[1]	n	得將者	dak jéung jé	dāk1 zoeng2 ze2	tak cheung che
winner[2]	n	優勝者	yàu sing jé	jau4 sing3 ze2	yau seng che
winner for lottery(sl) (three years two babies)	n	三年抱倆	sàam lìhn /nìhn póuh léuhng	saam4 lin4 /nin4 pou5 loeng5	saam lihn /nihn phouh leuhng
winning[1] /wins/won	adj	勝利	sing leih	sing3 lei6	seng leih
winning[2] /attractive	adj	迷人	màih yàhn	mai4 jan4	maih yahn
winnow /winnowing /sifting	v	分出好壞	fàn chēut hou waaih	fan4 ceot1 hou3 waai6	fan chhot hou waaih
winter[1]	n	冬天	dūng tīn	dung1 tin1	tung thin
winter[2] (sl)	n	冷天	láahng tīn	laang5 tin1	laahng thin
winter season	n	冬季	dūng gwai	dung1 gwai3	tung kwai
winter sports	n	冬季運動	dūng gwai wahn duhng	dung1 gwai3 wan6 dung6	tung kwai wahn tuhng
wipe	v	抹	maat	maat3	maat
wiper	n	雨刷	yúh cháat	jyu5 caat2	yuh chhaat
wire[1]	v	電線	dihn sin	din6 sin3	tihn sin
wire[2]	n	金屬線	gàm suhk sin	gam4 suk6 sin3	kam suhk sin

wisdom[1]	n	智慧	ji wai	zi3 wai3	chi wai
wisdom[2]/sense /understanding	n	才智	choih ji	coi6 zi3	chhoih chi
wisdom tooth	n	智慧牙	ji wai ngàh	zi3 wai3 ngaa4	chi wai ngah
wise /realize	adj	明白	mìhng baahk	ming4 baak6	mehng paahk
wish[1] /to pray	n	祝	jūk	zuk1	chuk
wish[2] /wanna/willing /hoped-	n/v	願	yún	jyun2	yun
wish[3] /want/well/like	v	但願	daahn yuhn	daan6 jyun6	taahn yuhn
wish[4] /pray	v	祝願	jūk yuhn	zuk1 jyun6	chuk yuhn
wishing /willing to	n	捨得	sé dāk	se2 dak1	se tak
witch	n	巫婆	mòuh pòh	mou6 po4	mouh phoh
witchcraft /wizard	n	巫術	mòuh seuht	mou4 seot6	mouh seuht
with[1]	prep	同	tùhng	tung4	thuhng
with[2]	prep	與	yùh	jyu4	yuh
with[3]	prep	同咪	tùhng màaih	tung4 maai4	thuhng maaih
with[4]	prep	一起	yāt héi	jat1 hei2	yat hei
with an eye to /aware	adj	注意到	jyu yi dou	zyu3 yi3 dou3	chyu yi tou
with confidence		有把握咁	yáuh bá ngāak gám	jau5 baa2 aak1 gam2	yauh pa ngaak kam
with one's own hands		親手	chān sáu	can1 sau2	chhan sau
with respect to		對於	deui yù	deoi3 jyu4	toei yu
with speaking		同佢講	tùhng kéuih góng	tung4 keoi5 gong2	thuhng khoih kong
withcare /maneuver /carefully/cautiously	n	小心地	síu sàm deih	siu2 sam4 dei6	siu sam teih
withdraw[1] /return/get back	v	退	teui	teoi3	thoi
withdraw[2] (coll) (take money from ATM machine or counter)		攞錢	ló chín	lo2 cin2	lo chhin
withdraw[2] (wr) (take money from ATM machine or counter)	n	提款	tàih fún	tai4 fun2	thaih fun
withdraw[3] /idea take out	v	提出	tàih chēut	tai4 ceot1	thaih chhot
withdraw[4] / to go out/ to appear	v	撤回	chit wùih	cit3 wui4	chhit wuih
withdraw[5] /take out	n	撤退	chit teui	cit3 teoi3	chhit thoi
withdraw[6] /take out	n	收返	sàu fàan	sau4 faan4	sau faan
within[1]	prep	喺依...內	hái yíh loih /noih	hai2 ji5 loi6 /noi6	hai yih loih /noih
within[2]	prep	喺...之內	hái...jì loih /noih	hai2···zi4 loi6 /noi6	hai...jì loih /noih
within[3]	prep	不超過	bāt chìu gwo	bat1 ciu4 gwo3	pat chhiu kwo
without	prep	外便	oih /ngoih bihn	oi6 /ngoi6 bin6	oih /ngoih pihn
without accident		安然無恙地	òn /ngòn yìhn mòuh yeuhng deih	on4 /ngon4 jing4 mou4 joeng3 dei6	on /ngon yihn mouh yeuhng teih
without authorization		私自	sì jih	si4 zi6	si chih
without example	adj	無先例	mouh sin laih	mou6 sin3 lai6	mouh sin laih

English	Part	Chinese	Yale	Jyutping	Romanization
without exception /entirely	adj	俱	kèui	keoi4	khoi
without reason	adj	無故	móuh gu	mou5 gu3	mouh ku
witness[1]	n	證人	jing yàhn	zing3 jan4	cheng yahn
witness[2] (by eye)	n	親眼睇見	chàn ngáahn tái gin	can4 ngaan5 tai2 gin3	chhan ngaahn thai kin
witness testimony	v	作見證	jok gin jing	zok3 gin3 zing3	chok kin cheng
wives	n	妻子	chai jí	caai3 zi2	chhai chi
wizard[1]	n	奇才	kèih chòih	kei4 coi4	kheih chhoih
wizard[2] /magician	n	術師	seuht sih	seot6 si4	swoht sih
wolf	n	狼	lòhng	long4	lohng
woman	n	女人	léuih yan	leui5 jan3	lowih yan
woman & child	n	婦孺	fúh yùh	fu5 jyu4	fuh yuh
women's volleyball	n	女排	léuih pàaih	leui5 paai4	lowih phaaih
wonder[1]	n	奇蹟	kèih jīk	kei4 zik1	kheih chek
wonder[2]	v	驚奇	gèng kèih	geng4 kei4	keng kheih
wonder[3]	v	奇觀	kèih gùn	kei4 gun4	kheih kun
wonder[4]	v	意想不到	yí sēung bàt dóu	ji2 soeng1 bat4 dou2	yi seung pat tou
wonder[5]	v	覺得奇怪	gok dāk kèih gwaai	gok3 dak1 kei4 gwaai3	kok tak kheih kwaai
wonderful	adj	精彩	jēng chói	zeng1 coi2	cheng chhoi
woo	n	求愛	kàuh oi /ngoi	kau4 oi3 /ngoi3	khauh oi /ngoi
wood	n	木	muhk	muk6	muhk
wood plate	n	卡板	kāat báan	kaat1 baan2	khaat paan
wooden	adj	木嘅	muhk ge	muk6 ge3	muhk ke
wooden house	n	木屋	muhk ūk /ngūk	muk6 uk1 /nguk1	muhk uk /nguk
wooden spoon	n	木勺	muhk seuk	muk6 soek3	muhk swok
woodpecker	n	啄木鳥	deuk muhk líuh /níuh	doek3 muk6 liu5 /niu5	tok muhk liuh /niuh
woodwork	n	木製品	muhk jai bán	muk6 zai3 ban2	muhk chai pan
woody	adj	木質嘅	muhk jāt ge	muk6 zat1 ge3	muhk chat ke
woof /parallel line	v	緯線	wáih sin	wai5 sin3	waih sin
wooing /to seek	n	追求	jèui kàuh	zeoi4 kau4	cheui khauh
wool[1]	n	羊毛	yèuhng mòuh	joeng4 mou4	yeuhng mouh
wool[2] /like wool	n	似羊毛嘅嘢	chíh yèuhng mòuh ge yéh	ci5 joeng4 mou4 ge3 je5	chhih yeuhng mouh ke yeh
wool[3] (sl)	n	冷	lāang	laang1	laang
woolen[1]	adj	羊毛製	yèuhng mòuh jai	joeng4 mou4 jai3	yeuhng mouh chai
woolen[2]	adj	羊毛嘅	yèuhng mòuh ge	joeng4 mou4 ge3	yeuhng mouh ke
woolen meterial	n	絨	yúng /úng	jung2 /ung2	yung /ung
wording	n	用語	yùhng yùh	jung6 jyu6	yuhng yuh
wordless[1]	adj	唔用言辭	m̀ yuhng yìhng chìh	m4 jung6 jing4 ci4	mh yuhng yihng chhih
wordless[2]	adj	不用言辭	bāt yuhng yìhng chìh	bat1 jung6 jing4 ci4	pat yuhng yihng chhih
words	n	字句	jih geui	zi6 geoi3	chih kwoi
work[1]	n	工	gùng	gung4	kung
work[2] /operation	n	操作	chou jok	cou3 zok3	chhou chok
work daring with careful		膽大心細	dáam daaih sàm sai	daam2 daai6 sam4 sai3	taam taaih sam sai

work evidence[1]		工作証明	gùng jok jing mèhng /mìhng	gung4 zok3 zing3 meng4 /ming4	kung chok cheng mehng
work evidence[2]		工作証件	gùng jok jing gihn	gung4 zok3 zing3 gin6	kung chok cheng kihn
work farm (youngster for punishment)	n	少年感化工場	siu lìhn /nìhn gám fa gùng chèuhng	siu3 lin4 /nin4 gam2 fa3 gung4 coeng4	siu lihn /nihn kam fa fa kung chheuhng
work force	n	勞動力	lòuh duhng lihk	lou4 dung6 lik6	louh tohng lehk
work hard[1]	v	操勞	chòu lòuh	cou4 lou4	chhou louh
work hard[2] /try hard /strive	v	努力	lóuh /nóuh lìhk	lou5 /nou5 lik6	louh /nouh lehk
work load		工作量	gùng jok lèuhng	gung4 zok3 loeng4	kung chok lowhng
work one's shift		當班	dong bāan	dong3 baan1	tong paan
work procedure		工作程序	gùng jok chìhng jeuih	gung4 zok3 cing4 zeoi6	kung chok chhehng choih
work schedule	n	進度	jeun douh	zeon3 dou6	cheun touh
work shop[1] /work house	n	工場	gùng chèuhng	gung4 coeng4	kung chheuhng
work shop[2]	n	工作坊	gùng jok fòng	gung4 zik3 fong4	kung chok fong
work together[1] /cooperative/harmonious	adj	合作	hahp jok	hap6 zok3	hahp chok
work together[2]	adj	一起工作	yāt héi gùng jok	jat1 hei2 gung4 zok3	yat hei kung chok
work together[3]		同我做	tùhng ngóh jouh	tung4 ngoh5 jou6	thuhng ngoh chouh
work with		與...共事	yùh...gúng sih	jyu4...gung2 si6	yuh...kung sih
worker[1] /poter	n	雜工佬	jaahp gūng lóu	zaap6 gung1 lou2	chaahp kung lou
worker[2] /manpower	n	人手	yàhn sáu	jan4 sau2	yahn sau
worker[3] /slave/vassal /forced to work	n	奴隸	lòuh /nòuh daih	lou4 /nou4 dai6	louh /nouh taih
workman	n	工匠	gùng jeuhng	gung4 zoeng6	kung cheuhng
workplace /unit	n	單位	dāan wái	daan1 wai2	taan wai
world[1]	n	世	sai	sai3	sai
world[2]	n	世界	sai gaai	sai3 gaai3	sai kaai
world-famous[1]	adj	舉世聞名	géui sai màhn mèhng /mìhng	geoi2 sai3 man4 meng4 /ming4	kwoi sai mahn mehng
world-famous[2]	adj	世界著名	sai gaai jyu mèhng	sai3 gaai3 jyu3 meng4	sai kaai chyu mehng
worldwide	adj	遍及全球	pín gahp chyùhn kàuh	pin2 gap6 cyun4 kau4	phin kahp chhyuhn khauh
wormwood	n	苦艾	fú ngaaih	fu2 ngaai6	fu ngaaih
worn[1]	adj	好癐	hóu guih	hou2 gui6	hou kuih
worn[2]	adj	舊嘅	gauh ge	gau6 ge3	kauh ke
worn[3]	adj	用舊	yuhng gauh	jung6 gau6	yuhng kauh
worn out /tired	adj	疲乏	pèih fàht	pei4 fat6	pheih faht
worrier	n	煩惱者	fàahn lóuh/nóuh jé	faan4 lou5 /nou5 ze2	faahn louh /nouh che
worries /distress	n	煩惱	fàahn lóuh /nóuh	faan4 lou5 /nou5	faahn louh /nouh
worry[1] (coll) anxiety	v	擔/担心	dàam sàm	daam4 sam4	taam sam
worry[2]	v	掛著	gwa jyuh	gwa3 zyu3	kwa chyuh
worse[1]	adj	更壞嘅事	gang waaih ge sih	gang3 waai6 ge3 si6	kang waaih ke sih
worse[2]	adj	每況愈下	múih fong yuh hah	mui5 fong3 jyu6 haa6	muih fong yuh hah

worse[3]	adj	更壞	gang waaih	gang3 waai6	kang waaih
worship[1] /sacred weekly	v	禮拜	láih baai	lai5 baai3	laih paai
worship[2]	v	崇拜	suhng baai	sung4 baai3	suhng paai
worship	v	宗教	jùng gaau	zung4 gaau3	chung kaau
worshipful /venerable	adj	可敬	hó ging	ho2 ging3	ho king
worst[1]	adv	最壞	jeui waaih	zeoi3 waai6	cheui waaih
worst[2]	adv	打敗	dá baaih	daa2 baai6	ta paaih
worst[3]	adv	擊敗	gīk baaih	gik1 baai6	kek paaih
worthless /useless	adj	無價值	móuh ga jihk	mou5 gaa3 zik6	mouh ka chehk
worthwhile[1]	adj	值得做	jihk dāk jouh	zik6 dak1 zou6	chehk tak chouh
worthwhile[2] /worthy	adj	值得	jihk dāk	zik6 dak1	chehk tak
would[1] /want/wanna	v/aux	願意	yuhn yi	jyun6 ji3	yuhn yi
would[2] (for request)	n	唔該	m̀ gòi	m4 goi4	mh koi
would[3] /want	n	想要	séung yìu	soeng2 jiu4	seung yiu
would be		想要成為	séung yìu sèhng wàih	soeng2 jiu4 seng4 wai6	seung yiu sehng waih
would rather /prefer /favour	adj	寧願	lìhng /nìhng yún	ling4 /ning4 jyun2	lehng /nehng yun
wound	n	創	sèung	soeng4	seung
wound worm	n	蛔蟲	wùih chùhng	wui4 cung4	wuih chhuhng
wounded[1]	adj	創傷	chong sèung	cong3 soeng4	chhong seung
wounded[2] /wounding /physically injured/hurts	adj	受傷	sauh sèung	sau6 soeng4	sauh seung
wrap /cover/parcel/pack	v	包	bàau	baau4	paau
wreckage /destroy	n	破滅	pó mìht	po2 mit6	pho miht
wrench[1] /twister /spanner	n	扳手	pàan sāu	paan4 sau1	phaan sau
wrench[2] /twister	n	板鉗	báan kim	baan2 kim3	paan khim
wrench[3] /twister	n	士巴拿	sih bā ná	si6 baa1 naa2	sih pa na
wrestle	v	搏鬥	bok dau	bok3 dau3	pok tau
wring (to action)	v	扭動	láu duhng	lau2 dung6	lau tong
wrinkle /to crease	n	皺	jau	zau3	chau
wrinkled[1]	v	皺起	jau héi	zau3 hei2	chau hei
wrinkled[2]	n	整縐	jíng jau	zing2 zau3	cheng chau
wrist	n	手腕	sáu wūn	sau2 wun1	sau wun
write[1] (a letter)	v	寫信	sé seun	se2 seon3	se swon
write[2] (a book/written)	adj/v	書寫	syù sē	syu4 se1	syu se
write characters	v	寫字	sé jih	se2 zi6	se chih
write data	v	填寫	tìhn sé	tin4 se2	thihn se
write down[1]	v	寫低	sé dài	se2 dai4	se tai
write down[2]	v	寫落	sé lohk	se2 lok6	se lohk
write down[3]	v	寫下	sé hah	se2 ha6	se hah
write down cost	v	資產值降低	jì cháan jihk gong dāi	zi4 caan2 zik6 gong3 dai1	chi chhaan chehk kong tai
writer[1] /author	n	作家	jok gā	zok3 gaa1	chok ka
writer[2] (for newspaper)	n	撰	syún	syun2	syun

writer³ (for newspaper)	n	撰稿人	syún góu yàhn	syun2 gou2 jan4	syun kou yahn
writing¹	n	書寫	syù sē	syu4 se1	syu se
writing²	n	著作	jyu jok	zyu3 zok3	chyu chok
writing of art	n	作品	jok bán	zok3 ban2	chok pan
writing paper /letter paper	n	信紙	seun jí	seon3 zi2	swon chi
written¹	adj	成文	sèhng màhn	seng4 man6	sehng màhn
written²	adj	書寫嘅	syù sē ge	syu4 se1 ge3	syu se ke
written language	n	文字	màhn jih	man4 zi6	mahn chih
written record	n	書面記錄	syu mín gei luhk	syu3 min2 gei3 luk6	syu min kei luhk
written word	n	書面語	syu mín yúh	syu3 min2 jyu5	syu min yuh
wrong¹	adj	有問題	yáuh mahn tàih	jau5 man6 tai4	yauh mahn thaih
wrong²	adj	錯誤的	cho ngh dìk	co3 ng6 dik4	chho ngh tek
wrongly	adv	錯誤地	cho ngh deih	co3 ng6 dei6	chho ngh teih
wrote	v	寫出	sé chēut	se2 ceot1	se chhot

x-mas (festival)	n	聖誕節	síng dáan jít /zít	sing2 daan2 zit2	seng taan chit
x-ray[1]	n	x光	x-gwòng	x-gwong4	x-kwong
x-ray[2] (take x-ray photo)	v	x光線	x-gwòng sin	x-gwong4 sin3	x-kwong sin
x-ray[3] therapy	n	x光治療法	x-gwòng jih lìuh faat	x-gwong4 zi6 liu4 faat3	x-kwong chih liuh faat
xerox[1] copy	v	影印	yéng /yíng yan	jeng2 /jing2 jan3	yeng yan
xerox[2] machine	n	靜電複印機	jèhng /jìhng dihn fūk yan gèi	zeng6 /zing6 din6 fuk1 jan3 gei4	chehng tihn fuk yan kei
xperience	n	經驗	gìng yihm	ging4 jim6	keng yihm

y'know /you know	v	你知道	léih jì douh	lei5 zi4 dou6	leih chi touh
yachter	n	乘快艇者	sìhng faai téhng jé	sing4 faai3 teng5 ze2	sehng faai thehng che
Yale (American based Chinese Phonetic Romanized)	n	耶魯	yèh lóuh	je4 lou5	yeh louh
yam /sweet potato	n	蕃薯	fàan syú	faan4 syu2	faan syuh
yamen (government office in feudal China)	n	衙門	ngàh mùhn	ngaa4 mun4	ngah muhn
yang (sound of the birds or insect)	n	雁鳴聲	ngaahn mìhng sèng /sìng	ngaan3 ming4 seng4 /sing4	ngaahn mehng seng
yankee /American people	n	美國人	méih gwók yàhn	mei5 gwok3 jan4	meih kwok yahn
yard[1] (3 feets)	n	碼	máh	maa5	mah
yard[2] /back garden /rear of the house	n	後院	hauh yuhn	hau6 jyun6	hauh yuhn
yard[3] (courtyard of the house)	n	院子	yún jí	jyun2 zi2	yun chi
yarn[1] /yarning	n	打喊露	dá haam lòuh	daa2 haam3 lou6	ta haam louh
yarn[2] /wool's thread	n	毛綫	mòuh sin	mou4 sin3	mouh sin
yarn[3]	n	紗線	sā sin	sa1 sin3	sa sin
yawn[1]	n	打呵欠	dā hō him	daa1 ho1 him3	ta ho him
yawn[2]	n	呵欠	hò him	ho2 him3	ho him
yea	adv	是	sih	si6	sih
yeah! /yes! (agree)	n/adv	係呀!	haih àa!	hai6 aa3	haih aa!
year	n	年	lihn /nihn	lin4 /nin4	lihn /nihn
year after year /yearly/every year	adj/n	每年	múih lihn /nihn	mui5 lin4 /nin4	muih lihn /nihn
year by year /every year	n	每一年	múih yāt lihn /nihn	mui5 jat1 lin4 /nin4	muih yat lihn /nihn
year of the end	n	年終	lihn jūng	lin4 zung1	lihn chung
year of birth	n	出生年分	chēut sāng lihn /nihn fàn	ceot1 sang1 lin4 /nin4 fan4	chhot sang lihn /nihn fan
yellow	n	黃	wòhng	wong4	wohng
yellow color	n	黃色	wòhng sīk	wong4 sik1	wohng sek
yellowish /yellow fairly	n	帶黃色	daai wòhng sīk	daai3 wong4 sik1	taai wohng sek
yellow line (road side)	n	黃色標線	wòhng sīk bīu sin	wong4 sik1 biu1 sin3	wohng sek piu sin
yen (Japanese money)	n	日圓	yaht yùhn	jat6 jyun4	yaht yuhn
yes[1]	exlm	係	haih	hai6	haih
yes[2]	exlm	啱	ngāam	ngaam1	ngaam
yes[3] /well	exlm	是	sih	si6	sih
yes[4] /agree/ok/sure	n	好呀	hóu aa	hou2 aa4 /aa3	hou aa
yes[5] /it is/ agree	n	是的	sih dīk	si6 dik1	sih tik
yes! i ate already[1]	v	係,我食飽喇	haih, ngóh sihk báau la	hai6, ngo5 sik6 baau2 la3	haih, ngoh sehk paau la
yes! i ate already[2]	v	係,我食咗喇	haih, ngóh sihk jó la	hai6, ngo5 sik6 zo2 la3	haih, ngoh sehk cho la
yesterday[1] (coll)	n	琴日	kàhm yaht	kam4 jat6	khahm yaht
yesterday[2] (text)	n	尋日	chàhm yaht	cam4 jat6	chhahm yaht
yesterday[3]	n	昨天	jok tīn	zok3 tin1	chok thin

English		Chinese	Yale	Jyutping	
yet /still/even/also/else	adv	還	wàahn	waan4	waahn
yo-yo /toy	n	搖搖	yíu yíu	jiu2 jiu2	yiu yiu
yoga[1]	n	瑜珈	yùh gā	jyu4 ga1	yuh ka
yoga[2]	n	瑜珈術	yùh gā seuht	jyu4 ga1 seot6	yuh ka swoht
yoke /oxen fastened necks /join two animals together	n	結合	git hahp	git3 hap6	kit hahp
you[1]	pron	你	léih /néih	lei5 /nei5	leih /neih
you[2] (plural)	pron	你哋/地	léih dèih	lei5 dei6	leih teih
you[3] (plural)	pron	你們	léih mùhn	lei5 mun4	leih muhn
you animal! (vdw) /son of a bitch	n	畜牲	chūk sàng	cuk1 sang4	chhuk sang
you are		你係	léih haih	lei5 hai6	leih haih
you are beautiful		你好靚	léih hóu leng	lei5 hou2 leng3	leih hou leng
you can get me on		你找找可以潑	léih jáau jáau hó yíh put	lei5 zaau2 zaau2 ho2 ji5 put3	leih chaau chaau ho yih phut
you can sit		你可以坐	léih hó yíh chóh	lei5 ho2 ji5 co5	leih ho yih chhoh
you did it!		你做左未呀!	léih jouh jó meih a!	lei5 zou6 zo2 mei6 a3!	leih chouh cho meih a!
you have it		你攞咗未	léih ló jó meih	lei5 lo2 zo2 mei6	leih lo cho meih
you leaving		見你走	gin léih /néih jáu	gin3 lei5 /nei5 zau2	kin leih /neih chau
you'll see		你會睇	léih wúih tái	lei5 wui5 tai2	leih wuih thai
you play		你玩	léih waan	lei5 waan3	leih waan
you're very kind!		你真和氣	léih jān wòh hei!	lei5 zan1 wo4 hei3!	leih chan woh hei!
you're welcome[1] /welcome		唔使客氣	m̀ sái haak hei	m4 sai2 haak3 hei3	mh sai haak hei
you're welcome[2]		唔使唔該	m̀ sái m̀ gòi	m4 sai2 m4 goi4	mh sai mh koi
you said[1]	v	你講咗	léih góng jó	lei5 gong2 zo2	leih kong cho
you said[2]	v	你叫咗	léih giu jó	lei5 giu3 zo2	leih kiu cho
you speak /you tell /speaking	n	你講	léih góng	lei5 gong2	leih kong
you too	adv	你都	léih dōu	lei5 dou1	leih tou
you wanna		你想	léih séung	lei5 soeng2	leih seung
you wanna see /you wanting		你想見	léih séung gin	lei5 soeng2 gin3	leih seung kin
young[1] /infantile	adj	稚	jih	zi6	chih
young[2]	n	幼	yau	jau3	yau
young[3] /youthful /teenager	adj/n	後生	hauh sàang	hau6 saang4	hauh saang
young[4] /youthful	adj	年輕	lìhn hèng	lin4 heng4	lihn heng
young age	n	後生時	hauh sàang sìh	hou6 saang4 si6	hauh saang sih
young man /youthful	n	青年	chèng lìhn, chìng nìhn	ceng4 lin4, cing4 nin4	chheng lihn, chheng nihn
younger	n	較年少者	gaau lihn /nihn síujé	gaau3 lin4 /nin4 siu2 ze2	kaau lihn /nihn siu che
younger brother[1]	n	細佬	sai lóu	sai3 lou2	sai lou
younger brother[2]	n	弟弟	taih táih	tai6 tai5	thaih thaih
younger sister[1]	n	妹妹	muih muih	mui6 mui6	muih muih

younger sister[2]	n	細妹	sái muih	sai2 mui6	sai muih
youngster /youth	n	年輕人	lìhn hèng yàhn	lin4 heng4 jan4	lihn heng yahn
your	pron	您	léih /néih	lei5 /nei5	leih /neih
your address	n	你個地址	léih go deih jí	lei5 go3 dei6 zi2	leih ko teih chi
your daughter	n	你嘅女	léih ge léoi /néoi	lei5 ge3 leoi5 /neoi5	leih ke loyi /noyi
your name	n	你叫做	léih giu jouh	lei5 giu3 zou6	leih kiu chouh
your sincerely	n	謹啓	gán kái	gan2 kai2	kan khai
your son	n	你嘅子	léih ge jái	lei5 ge3 zai2	leih ke chai
yours[1] /your	pron	您嘅	léih ge	lei5 ge3	leih ke
yours[2]	pron	你個	léih go	lei5 go3	leih ko
yours[3]	pron	您啲	léih dìk	lei5 dik4	leih tek
yourself	pron	你自己	léih jih géi	lei5 zi6 gei2	leih chih kei
youth[1]	n	青年人	chèng lìhn /nìhn yàhn	ceng4 lin4 /nin4 jan4	chheng lihn /nihn yahn
youth[2]	n	青少年時期	chèng siu lìhn/nìhn sìh kèih	ceng4 siu3 lin4 /nin4 si4 kei4	chheng siu lihn /nihn sih kheih
youth centre	n	青年中心	chèng lìhn /nìhn	ceng4 lin4 /nin4 zung3	chheng lihn /nihn
youthful (sl) /adult	adj	四仔	sei jái	sei3 zai2	sei chai
youthfully	adv	精神飽滿地	jèng sàhn báau múhn deih	zeng4 baau2 mun5 dei6	cheng sahn paau muhn teih

zeal /enthusiasm /feel strongly	n	熱心	yiht sām	jit6 sam1	yiht sam
zebra	n	斑馬	bàan máh	baan4 maa5	paan mah
zero[1] /nought/nil	n	零	lìhng	ling4	lehng
zero[2]	n	零號	lìhng houh	ling4 hou6	lehng houh
zigzag	n	曲折	kūk jit	kuk1 zit3	khuk chit
zinc	n	鋅	sān	san1	san
zip[1]	n	尖嘯聲	jīm siu sèng	zim1 siu3 seng4	chim siu seng
zip[2]	n	拉鍊	làai lín	laai4 lin2	laai lin
zip code	n	郵遞區號	yàuh daih kèui hòuh	jau4 dai6 keoi4 hou6	yauh taih khoi houh
zipped	n	用拉鍊扣上	yuhng làai lihn kau séuhng	jung6 laai4 lin6 kau3 soeng5	yuhng laai lihn khau seuhng
zipper	n	拉鏈	làai lín	laai4 lin2	laai lin
zircon	n	鋯石	gou sehk	gou3 sek6	kou sehk
zirconium	n	鋯	gou	gou3	kou
zodiac[1]	n	生肖	sàang chiu	saang4 ciu3	saang chhiu
zodiac[2]	n	黃道帶	wòhng dou daai	wong4 dou3 taai3	wohng tou taai
zone	n	地帶	deih daai	dei6 daai3	teih taai
zoneless	n	沒有分區	muht yáuh fàn kèui	mut6 jau5 fan4 keoi4	muht yauh fan khoi
zoo	n	動物園	duhng maht yùhn	dung6 mat6 jyun4	tuhng maht yuhn
zoology /zoological	adj/n	動物學	duhng maht hohk	dung6 mat6 hok6	tuhng maht hohk
zoom	v/n	變焦鏡頭	bin jīu géng tàuh	bin3 ziu1 geng2 tau4	pin chiu keng thauh
zoometry	n	動物測定	duhng maht chāak dehng	dung6 mat6 caak1 deng6	tuhng maht chhaak dehng
zoon	n	發育完全的個體	faat yuhk yùhn chyùhn dīk go tái	faat3 juk6 jyun4 cyun4 dik1 go3 tai2	faat yuhk yuhn chhyuhn tik ko thai

THE END